The Oxford Handbook of
Affective Computing

OXFORD LIBRARY OF PSYCHOLOGY

Editor in Chief PETER E. NATHAN

The Oxford Handbook of Affective Computing

Edited by

Rafael A. Calvo

Sidney K. D'Mello

Jonathan Gratch

Arvid Kappas

OXFORD

UNIVERSITY PRESS

OXFORD
UNIVERSITY PRESS

Oxford University Press is a department of the University of Oxford.
It furthers the University's objective of excellence in research,
scholarship, and education by publishing worldwide.

Oxford   New York
Auckland   Cape Town   Dar es Salaam   Hong Kong   Karachi
Kuala Lumpur   Madrid   Melbourne   Mexico City   Nairobi
New Delhi   Shanghai   Taipei   Toronto

With offices in
Argentina   Austria   Brazil   Chile   Czech Republic   France   Greece
Guatemala   Hungary   Italy   Japan   Poland   Portugal   Singapore
South Korea   Switzerland   Thailand   Turkey   Ukraine   Vietnam

Oxford is a registered trademark of Oxford University Press
in the UK and certain other countries.

Published in the United States of America by
Oxford University Press
198 Madison Avenue, New York, NY 10016

Library of Congress Cataloging-in-Publication Data
The Oxford handbook of affective computing / edited by Rafael A. Calvo, Sidney D'Mello, Jonathan Gratch, Arvid Kappas.
    pages cm
Includes bibliographical references and index.
ISBN 978–0–19–994223–7
1. Human-computer interaction.   2. User-centered system design.   I. Calvo, Rafael A., editor.
II. D'Mello, Sidney., editor.   III. Gratch, Jonathan (Jonathan Matthew), 1963- editor.   IV. Kappas, Arvid, editor.
QA76.9.H85O93 2015
004.2'1—dc23   2014031719

SHORT CONTENTS

The *Oxford Library of Psychology*, a landmark series of handbooks, is published by Oxford University Press, one of the world's oldest and most highly respected publishers, with a tradition of publishing significant books in psychology. The ambitious goal of the *Oxford Library of Psychology* is nothing less than to span a vibrant, wide-ranging field and, in so doing, to fill a clear market need.

Encompassing a comprehensive set of handbooks, organized hierarchically, the *Library* incorporates volumes at different levels, each designed to meet a distinct need. At one level are a set of handbooks designed broadly to survey the major subfields of psychology; at another are numerous handbooks that cover important current focal research and scholarly areas of psychology in depth and detail. Planned as a reflection of the dynamism of psychology, the *Library* will grow and expand as psychology itself develops, thereby highlighting significant new research that will impact on the field. Adding to its accessibility and ease of use, the *Library* will be published in print and, later on, electronically.

The *Library* surveys psychology's principal subfields with a set of handbooks that capture the current status and future prospects of those major subdisciplines. This initial set includes handbooks of social and personality psychology, clinical psychology, counseling psychology, school psychology, educational psychology, industrial and organizational psychology, cognitive psychology, cognitive neuroscience, methods and measurements, history, neuropsychology, personality assessment, developmental psychology, and more. Each handbook undertakes to review one of psychology's major subdisciplines with breadth, comprehensiveness, and exemplary scholarship. In addition to these broadly conceived volumes, the *Library* also includes a large number of handbooks designed to explore in depth more specialized areas of scholarship and research, such as stress, health and coping, anxiety and related disorders, cognitive development, or child and adolescent assessment. In contrast to the broad coverage of the subfield handbooks, each of these latter volumes focuses on an especially productive, more highly focused line of scholarship and research. Whether at the broadest or most specific level, however, all of the *Library* handbooks offer synthetic coverage that reviews and evaluates the relevant past and present research and anticipates research in the future. Each handbook in the *Library* includes introductory and concluding chapters written by its editor to provide a roadmap to the handbook's table of contents and to offer informed anticipations of significant future developments in that field.

An undertaking of this scope calls for handbook editors and chapter authors who are established scholars in the areas about which they write. Many of the nation's and world's most productive and best-respected psychologists have agreed to edit *Library* handbooks or write authoritative chapters in their areas of expertise.

For whom has the *Oxford Library of Psychology* been written? Because of its breadth, depth, and accessibility, the *Library* serves a diverse audience, including graduate students in psychology and their faculty mentors, scholars, researchers, and practitioners in psychology and related fields. Each will find in the *Library* the information they seek on the subfield or focal area of psychology in which they work or are interested.

Befitting its commitment to accessibility, each handbook includes a comprehensive index, as well as extensive references to help guide research. And because the *Library* was designed from its inception as an online as well as a print resource, its structure and contents will be readily and rationally searchable online. Further, once the *Library* is released online, the handbooks will be regularly and thoroughly updated.

In summary, the *Oxford Library of Psychology* will grow organically to provide a thoroughly informed perspective on the field of psychology, one that reflects both psychology's dynamism and its increasing interdisciplinarity. Once published electronically, the *Library* is also destined to become a uniquely valuable interactive tool, with extended search and browsing capabilities. As you begin to consult this handbook, we sincerely hope you will share our enthusiasm for the more than 500-year tradition of Oxford University Press for excellence, innovation, and quality, as exemplified by the *Oxford Library of Psychology*.

Peter E. Nathan
Editor-in-Chief
Oxford Library of Psychology

ABOUT THE EDITORS

Rafael A. Calvo is an associate professor at the University of Sydney and director of the Software Engineering Group, which focuses on the design of systems that support well-being in areas of mental health, medicine, and education. He has a Ph.D. in artificial intelligence applied to automatic document classification and has also worked at Carnegie Mellon University, the Universidad Nacional de Rosario, and as a consultant for projects worldwide. He is the author of over 150 publications in the areas of affective computing, learning systems, and web engineering; the recipient of five teaching awards; and a senior member of the Institute of Electrical and Electronics Engineers (IEEE). Rafael is associate editor of *IEEE Transactions on Affective Computing* and *IEEE Transactions on Learning Technologies*.

Sidney D'Mello is an assistant professor in the Departments of Computer Science and Psychology at the University of Notre Dame. His primary research interests are in the affective, cognitive, and learning sciences. More specific interests include affective computing, artificial intelligence in education, human-computer interaction, natural language understanding, and computational models of human cognition. He has coedited five books and has published over 150 journal papers, book chapters, and conference proceedings in these areas. D'Mello's work on intelligent learning technologies—including Affective AutoTutor, GazeTutor, ConfusionTutor, and GuruTutor—has received seven outstanding paper awards at international conferences and been featured in several media outlets, including the *Wall Street Journal*. D'Mello serves on the executive board of the International Artificial Intelligence in Education Society; he is a senior reviewer for the *Journal of Educational Psychology* and an associate editor for *IEEE Transactions on Affective Computing* and *IEEE Transactions on Learning Technologies*.

Jonathan Gratch is director of virtual human research at the Institute for Creative Technologies, University of Southern California (USC); he is a research full professor of computer science and psychology at USC and codirector of USC's Computational Emotion Group. He completed his Ph.D. in computer science at the University of Illinois, Urbana-Champaign, in 1995. His research focuses on computational models of human cognitive and social processes, especially emotion, and explores these models' roles in shaping human-computer interactions in virtual environments. He is the founding and current editor-in-chief of IEEE's *Transactions on Affective Computing*, associate editor of *Emotion Review* and the *Journal of Autonomous Agents and Multiagent Systems*, former president of the HUMAINE Association—the international society for research on emotion and human-computer interaction—and is member of the IEEE, the Association for the Advancement of Artificial Intelligence (AAAI), and the International Society for Research on Emotion (ISRE). He is the author of over 200 technical articles.

Arvid Kappas is professor of psychology at Jacobs University Bremen in Bremen, Germany, and has conducted experimental research on affective processes for more than twenty-five years. He social psychology at Dartmouth College in 1989 and has since held university positions in Switzerland, Canada, the United Kingdom, Austria, Italy, and Germany. He is currently the president of the International Society for Research on Emotion. Arvid is particularly interested in emotions in interaction and how they influence expressive behavior, physiology, and subjective experience as well as how, in turn, emotions are regulated at intra- and interpersonal levels, including different levels of social organization and cultural context, within their biological constraints. His research is typically highly interdisciplinary, as exemplified by the recent projects CYBEREMOTIONS, eCUTE, and EMOTE.

CONTRIBUTORS

Shazia Afzal
University of Cambridge
Cambridge, United Kingdom

Elisabeth André
Department of Computer Science
Augsburg University
Augsburg, Germany

Ronald Arkin
College of Computing
Georgia Institute of Technology
Atlanta, Georgia

Paolo Baggia
Loquendo
Torino, Italy

Jeremy Bailenson
Department of Communication
Stanford University
Palo Alto, California

Jakki Bailey
Department of Communication
Stanford University
Palo Alto, California

Jason Baker
Center for Autism
California State University, Fullerton
Fullerton, California

Ryan Baker
Department of Human Development
Teachers College
Columbia University
New York, New York

Nadia Bianchi-Berthouze
Interaction Centre
University College
London, United Kingdom

Timothy Bickmore
College of Computer and Information Science
Northeastern University
Boston, Massachusetts

Judee Burgoon
Center for the Management of Information
Center for Identification Technology Research
University of Arizona
Tucson, Arizona

Felix Burkhardt
Telekom Innovation Laboratories
Deutsche Telekom
Berlin, Germany

Carlos Busso
Department of Electrical Engineering
University of Texas
Dallas, Texas

Rafael A. Calvo
Software Engineering Lab
University of Sydney
New South Wales, Australia

Nick Campbell
Speech Communication Lab
Trinity College Dublin, Ireland

Ginevra Castellano
School of Electronic, Electrical, and Computer
   Engineering
University of Birmingham
Birmingham, United Kingdom

Jeff Cohn
Department of Psychology
University of Pittsburgh
Robotics Institute
Carnegie Mellon University
Pittsburgh, Pennsylvania

Roddy Cowie
Department of Psychology
Queen's University
Belfast, Northern Ireland

Fernando De la Torre
Component Analysis Laboratory
Human Sensing Laboratory
Carnegie Mellon University
Pittsburgh, Pennsylvania

Sidney K. D'Mello
Department of Computer Science
Department of Psychology
University of Notre Dame
South Bend, Indiana

Leticia Lobo Duvivier
Department of Psychology
University of Miami
Miami, Florida

Aaron Elkins
Department of Computing
Imperial College London
London, United Kingdom

Art C. Graesser
Department of Psychology
University of Memphis
Memphis, Tennessee

Jonathan Gratch
Departments of Computer Science
and Psychology
University of Southern California
Los Angeles, California

Hatice Gunes
School of Electronic Engineering and
Computer Science
Queen Mary University of London
London, United Kingdom

Eddie Harmon-Jones
Department of Psychology
University of New South Wales
New South Wales, Australia

Jennifer Healey
Interactions and Experiences Research
Laboratory
Intel Labs
San Jose, California

Dirk Heylen
Department of Computer Science
University of Twente
Enschede, The Netherlands

Eva Hudlicka
Psychometrix Associates
New Amherst, Massachusetts

M. Sazzad Hussain
Department of Electrical Engineering
University of Sydney
New South Wales, Australia

Joris H. Janssen
Sense Observation Systems
Rotterdam, The Netherlands

Despina Kakoudaki
Department of Literature
American University
Washington, DC

Ashish Kapoor
Microsoft Research
Redmond, Washington

Arvid Kappas
Department of Psychology
Jacobs University Bremen
Bremen, Germany

Andrew H. Kemp
Department of Psychology
University of São Paulo
São Paulo, Brazil
University of Sydney
New South Wales, Australia

Jangwon Kim
Department of Electrical Engineering
University of Southern California
Los Angeles, California

Andrea Kleinsmith
Department of Computer and Information
Science and Engineering
University of Florida
Gainesville, Florida

Jacqueline M. Kory
Personal Robots Group
MIT Media Lab
Massachusetts Institute of Technology
Cambridge, Massachusetts

Jonathan Krygier
Department of Psychology
University of Sydney
New South Wales, Australia

Chad Lane
Institute for Creative Sciences
University of Southern California
Los Angeles, California

Chi-Chun Lee
Department of Electrical Engineering
National Tsing Hua University
Hsinchu, Taiwan

Sungbok Lee
Department of Electrical Engineering
University of Southern California
Los Angeles, California

Iolanda Leite
Social Robotics Lab
Yale University
New Haven, Connecticut

Christine Lisetti
School of Computing and Information Sciences
Florida International University
Miami, Florida

Mohammad Mahoor
Department of Electrical and Computer Engineering
University of Denver
Denver, Colorado

Stacy Marsella
Institute for Creative Technologies
University of Southern California
Los Angeles, California

Daniel McDuff
MIT Media Lab
Massachusetts Institute of Technology
Cambridge, Massachusetts

Daniel Messinger
Department of Psychology
University of Miami
Miami, Florida

Angeliki Metallinou
Pearson Knowledge Technologies
Menlo Park, California

Rada Mihalcea
Computer Science and Engineering
    Department
University of Michigan
Ann Arbor, Michigan

Robert R. Morris
Affective Computing Lab
Massachusetts Institute of Technology
Cambridge, Massachusetts

Lilia Moshkina
Freelance Consultant
San Francisco, California

Christian Mühl
Institute for Aerospace Medicine
German Aerospace Center
Cologne, Germany

Shrikanth S. Narayanan
Viterbi School of Engineering
University of Southern California
Los Angeles, California

Radoslaw Niewiadomski
InfomusLab
University of Genoa
Genoa, Italy

Anton Nijholt
Department of Computer Science
University of Twente
Enschede, The Netherlands

Magalie Ochs
CNRS LTCI Télécom ParisTech
Paris, France

Jaclyn Ocumpaugh
Teachers College
Columbia University
New York, New York

Ana Paiva
Intelligent Agents and Synthetic Characters
    Group
Instituto Superior Técnico
University of Lisbon
Lisbon, Portugal

Maja Pantic
Department of Computing
Imperial College London, United Kingdom
Department of Computer Science
University of Twente
Enschede, The Netherlands

Brian Parkinson
Experimental Psychology
University of Oxford
Oxford, United Kingdom

Catherine Pelachaud
CNRS LTCI Télécom ParisTech
Paris, France

Christian Peter
Fraunhofer IGD and Ambertree Assistance
    Technologies
Rostock, Germany

Christopher Peters
School of Computer Science and
    Communication
KTH Royal Institute of Technology
Stockholm, Sweden

Rosalind W. Picard
MIT Media Lab
Massachusetts Institute of Technology
Cambridge, Massachusetts

Rainer Reisenzein
Institute of Psychology
University of Greifswald
Greifswald, Germany

Tiago Ribeiro
Instituto Superior Técnico
University of Lisbon
Lisbon, Portugal

Giuseppe Riva
ATN-P Lab
Istituto Auxologico Italiano
ICE-NET Lab
Università Cattolica del Sacro Cuore
Milan, Italy

Peter Robinson
Computer Laboratory
University of Cambridge
Cambridge, United Kingdom

Paul Ruvolo
Computer Science
Olin College of Engineering
Needham, Massachusetts

Marc Schröder
Das Deutsche Forschungszentrum für
    Künstliche Intelligenz GmbH
Kaiserslautern, Germany

Björn Schuller
Department of Computing
Imperial College London, United Kingdom

Carlo Strapparava
Human Language Technologies Unit
Fondazione Bruno Kessler—IRST
Trento, Italy

Egon L. van den Broek
Utrecht University
Utrecht, The Netherlands

Alessandro Vinciarelli
School of Computing Science
Institute of Neuroscience and Psychology
University of Glasgow
Glasgow, Scotland

Anne Warlaumont
Cognitive and Information Sciences
University of California
Merced, California

Zachary Warren
Pediatrics, Psychiatry, and Special
Education
Vanderbilt University
Nashville, Tennessee

Joyce Westerink
Phillips Research
Eindhoven, The Netherlands

Georgios N. Yannakakis
Institute of Digital Games
University of Malta
Msida, Malta

Stefanos Zafeiriou
Department of Computing
Imperial College
London, United Kingdom

Enrico Zovato
Loquendo
Torino, Italy

CONTENTS

Introduction to Affective Computing

Rafael A. Calvo, Sidney K. D'Mello, Jonathan Gratch, *and* Arvid Kappas

Abstract

The Oxford Handbook of Affective Computing aims to be the definite reference for research in the burgeoning field of affective computing—a field that turns 18 at the time of writing. This introductory chapter is intended to convey the motivations of the editors and content of the chapters in order to orient the readers to the handbook. It begins with a very high overview of the field of affective computing along with a bit of reminiscence about its formation, short history, and major accomplishments. The five main sections of the handbook—history and theory, detection, generation, methodologies, and applications—are then discussed, along with a bird's eye view of the 41 chapters covered in the book. This Introduction is devoted to short descriptions of the chapters featured in the handbook. A brief description of the Glossary concludes the Introduction.

Key Words: affective computing history, affective computing theory, emotion theories, affect detection, affect generation, methodologies, applications

As we write, affective computing (AC) is about to turn 18. Though relatively young but entering the age of maturity, AC is a blossoming multidisciplinary field encompassing computer science, engineering, psychology, education, neuroscience, and many other disciplines. AC research is diverse indeed. It ranges from theories on how affective factors influence interactions between humans and technology, how affect sensing and affect generation techniques can inform our understanding of human affect, and the design, implementation, and evaluation of systems that intricately involve affect at their core.

The 2010 launch of the *IEEE Transactions on Affective Computing* (IEEE TAC), the flagship journal of the field, is indicative of the burgeoning research and promise of AC. The recent release of a number of excellent books on AC, each focusing on one or more topics, is further evidence that AC research is gradually maturing. Furthermore, quite

different from being solely an academic endeavor, AC is being manifested in new products, patent applications, start-up companies, university courses, and new funding programs from agencies around the world. Taken together, interest in and excitement about AC continues to flourish since its launch almost two decades ago.

Despite its recent progress and bright future, the field has been missing a comprehensive handbook that can serve as the go-to reference for AC research, teaching, and practice. This handbook aspires to achieve that goal. It was motivated by the realization that both new and veteran researchers needed a comprehensive reference that discusses the basic theoretical underpinnings of AC, its bread-and-butter research topics, methodologies to conduct AC research, and forward-looking applications of AC systems. In line with this, the *Handbook of Affective Computing* aims to help both new and experienced researchers identify trends, concepts, methodologies, and applications in this exciting research field. The handbook aims to be a coherent compendium, with chapters authored by world leaders in each area. In addition to being the definitive reference for AC, the handbook will also be suitable for use as a textbook for an undergraduate or graduate course in AC. In essence, our hope is that the handbook will serve as an invaluable resource for AC students, researchers, and practitioners worldwide.

The handbook features 41 chapters including this one, and is divided into five key main sections: history and theory, detection, generation, methodologies, and applications. Section 1 begins with a look at the makings of AC and a historical review of the science of emotion. This is followed by chapters discussing the *theoretical underpinnings* of AC from an interdisciplinary perspective encompassing the affective, cognitive, social, media, and brain sciences. Section 2 focuses on *affect detection* or affect recognition, which is among the most commonly investigated areas in AC. Chapters in this section discuss affect detection from facial features, speech (paralinguistics), language (linguistics), body language, physiology, posture, contextual features, and multimodal combinations of these. Chapters in Section 3 focus on aspects of *affect generation*, including the synthesis of emotion and its expression via facial features, speech, postures, and gestures. Cultural issues in affect generation are also discussed. Section 4 takes a different turn and features chapters that discuss *methodological issues* in AC research, including data collection techniques, multimodal affect databases, emotion representation formats, crowdsourcing techniques, machine learning approaches, affect elicitation techniques, useful AC tools, and ethical issues in AC. Finally, Section 5 completes the handbook by highlighting existing and future *applications* of AC in domains such as formal and informal learning, games, robotics, virtual reality, autism research, health care, cyberpsychology, music, deception, reflective writing, and cyberpsychology.

Section 1: History and Theory

AC is a scientific and engineering endeavor that is both inspired by and also inspires theories from a number of related areas, such as psychology, neuroscience, computer science, linguistics, and so on. In addition to providing a short history of the field, the aim of Section 1 is to describe the major theoretical foundations of AC and attempt to coherently connect these different perspectives.

This section begins with Chapter 2, by Rosalind Picard, the field's distinguished pioneer, who also coined its name. It is an adaptation of an introductory paper that was published in the inaugural issue of *IEEE Transactions on Affective Computing*. Picard's chapter, "The Promise of Affective Computing," provides an outline of AC's history and its major goals. Picard shares stories, sometimes personal, and offers historical perspectives and reflections on the birth and evolution of the AC community over the past 18 years.

The field's 18th birthday is a celebration of Picard's seminal book, *Affective Computing*, published in 1997, yet the study of emotions as a scientific endeavor dates back to the nineteenth century, with pioneers like Bell, Duchenne, and Darwin. Although it is daunting to provide a meaningful history of such an entrenched topic in a single chapter, Rainer Reisenzein does an excellent job in his contribution: "A Short History of Psychological Perspectives on Emotion" (Chapter 3). The chapter reviews various psychological perspectives on emotions that have emerged over the last century and beyond with respect to the following five key questions: (1) How are emotions generated? (2) How do they influence cognition and behavior? (3) What is the nature of emotions? (4) How has the emotion system evolved? (5) What are the brain structures and processes involved in emotions?

It is clear that neuroscience is strongly influencing the way we think about affective phenomena, a trend that is only likely to increase in the coming years. In Chapter 4, "Neuroscientific Perspectives of Emotion," Andrew Kemp, Jonathan Krygier, and Eddie Harmon-Jones summarize the exponentially growing affective neuroscientific literature in a way that is meaningful to the technically driven AC community. They discuss the neurobiological basis of fear, anger, disgust, happiness, and sadness—"the basic" emotions still used in much of AC research. Their chapter expands on the current debate as to whether these basic emotions are innate or whether more fundamental neuropsychobiological processes interact to produce these emotions. The "embodied cognition" perspective they adopt has received increased attention in cognitive psychology and human-computer interaction (HCI) literatures and might be beneficial to AC research as well.

Informed by all this science, engineers need concrete ways to represent emotions in computer systems, and appraisal theories provide one of the more promising representational structure to advance this goal. These are discussed in Chapter 5, entitled

"Appraisal Models," by Jonathan Gratch and Stacy Marsella. The appraisal theory of emotions has been the most widely adopted theory in AC. It is well suited for computing research because it provides a structured representation of relationships between a person and the environment, the different appraisal variables, and other components of the information processing ensemble, all of which are needed to model emotions.

Interpersonal information (information relevant to social interactions) plays a critical role in affective human-human interactions, but the dynamics of this information might change during human-computer interactions. An understanding of the complexity of pertinent issues, such as how new media can best communicate social cues, is essential in a world where a significant portion of interpersonal communication occurs through "emotionally challenged" media such as email and social networks. The design of such systems will often incur trade-offs, and these should be informed by a careful analysis of the advantages and disadvantages of different forms of mediated communication. These and other related issues are given a detailed treatment in Chapter 6, by Brian Parkinson, "Emotions in Interpersonal Life: Computer Mediation, Modeling, and Simulation."

Maja Pantic and Alessandro Vinciarelli introduce the wider field of social signal processing in Chapter 7. This area is closely related to AC in that it seeks to combine social science research (for understanding and modeling social interactions) with research in computer science and engineering, which is aimed at developing computers with similar abilities.

There are many reasons for building AC systems, some of which involve the basic scientific goal of understanding psychological phenomena while others are more practical, such as building better software systems. These motivations influence the type of architectures used. In Chapter 8, "Why and How to Build Emotion-Based Agent Architecture," Christine Lisetti and Eva Hudlicka review some of the emotion theories and discuss how they are used for creating artificial agents that can adapt to users' affect.

The motivations and the type of questions researchers ask is also, at least partially, linked to society's perceptions of what computers could and should do—perceptions often reflected in the popular media. In line with this, the first section of the handbook concludes with Chapter 9, by Despina Kakoudaki, titled "Affect and Machines in the Media"—that is, how artificial entities (e.g., computers) that have affective qualities have been portrayed in the media across time and how these portrayals have influenced AC research.

Section 2: Affect Detection

The development of an affect-aware system that senses and responds to an individual's affective states generally requires the system to first detect affect. Affect detection is an extremely challenging endeavor owing to the numerous complexities associated with the experience and expression of affect. Chapters in Section 2 describe several ingenious approaches to this problem.

Facial expressions are perhaps the most natural way in which humans express emotions, so it is fitting to begin Section 2 with a description of facial expression–based affect detection. In "Automated Face Analysis for Affective Computing" (Chapter 10), Jeff Cohn and Fernando De la Torre discuss how computer vision techniques can be informed by human approaches to measure and code facial behavior. Recent advances in face detection and tracking, registration, extraction (of geometric, appearance, and motion features), and supervised learning techniques are discussed. The chapter completes its introduction to the topic with a description of applications such as physical pain assessment and management, detection of psychological distress, depression, and deception, and studies on interpersonal coordination.

Technologies that capture both fine- and coarse-grained body movements are becoming ubiquitous owing to their low cost and easy integration in real-world applications. For example, Microsoft's Kinect camera has made it possible for nonexperts in computer vision to include the detection of gait or gestures (e.g., knocking, touching, and dancing) in applications ranging from games to learning technologies. In Chapter 11, "Automatic Recognition of Affective Body Expressions," Nadia Bianchi-Berthouze and Andrea Kleinsmith discuss the state of the art in this field, including devices to capture body movements, factors associated with perception of affect from these movements, automatic affect recognition systems, and current and potential applications of such systems.

Speech is perhaps the hallmark of human-human communication, and it is widely acknowledged that *how* something is said (i.e., paralinguistics) is as important as *what* is being said (linguistics).

The former is discussed by Chi-Chun Lee, Jangwon Kim, Angeliki Metallinou, Carlos Busso, Sungbok Lee, and Shrikanth S. Narayanan in

Chapter 12, "Speech in Affective Computing." This chapter starts with the fundamental issue of understanding how expressive speech is produced by the vocal organs, followed by the process of extracting acoustic-prosodic features from the speech signal, thereby leading to the development of speech-based affect detectors.

Affect detection from language, sometimes called sentiment analysis, is discussed in Chapter 13 by Carlo Strapparava and Rada Mihalcea entitled "Affect Detection in Texts." They begin with a description of lexical resources that can be leveraged in affective natural language processing tasks. Next, they introduce state-of-the-art knowledge-based and corpus-based methods for detecting affect from text. They conclude their chapter with two very intriguing applications: humor recognition and a study on how extralinguistic features (e.g., music) can be used for affect detection.

Since antiquity, eastern and western philosophers have speculated about how emotions are reflected in our bodies. At the end of the nineteenth century, William James and Charles Darwin studied the relationship between the autonomic nervous system and emotions. More recently, with the introduction of accurate small, portable, and low-cost sensors, physiologically based affect detection has dramatically exploded. Physiological researchers usually make a distinction between central and peripheral physiological signals (brain versus body). Affect detection from peripheral physiology is discussed by Jennifer Healey in Chapter 14, "Physiological Sensing of Affect." This chapter provides a brief history of the psychophysiology of affect, followed by a very accessible introduction to physiological sensors, measures, and features that can be exploited for affect detection.

Applications that monitor central physiology are discussed by Christian Mühl, Dirk Heylen, and Anton Nijholt in "Affective Brain-Computer Interfaces: Neuroscientific Approaches to Affect Detection" (Chapter 15). Their chapter reviews the theory underlying neuropyschological approaches for affect detection along with a discussion of some of the technical aspects of these approaches, with an emphasis on electrophysiological (EEG) signals. Major challenges and some imaginative potential applications are also discussed.

It is difficult to introduce sensors in the physical environment in some interaction contexts, such as classrooms. In these situations, researchers can infer affect from the unfolding interaction between the software and the user. In Chapter 16, "Interaction-Based Affect Detection in Educational Software," Ryan Baker and Jaclyn Ocumpaugh describe pioneering research in this field, particularly in the context of intelligent tutoring systems and educational games. In addition to reviewing the state of the art, their discussion on methodological considerations—such as ground truth measures, feature engineering, and detector validation—will be useful to researchers in other application domains as well.

The aforementioned chapters in this section describe research in one of the many modalities that can be used for affect detection. However, human communication is inherently multimodal, so it is informative to consider multimodal approaches to affect detection. A review of this literature with an emphasis on key issues, methods, and case studies is presented in Chapter 17, "Multimodal Affect Detection for Naturalistic Human-Computer and Human-Robot Interactions," by Ginevra Castellano, Hatice Gunes, Christopher Paters, and Björn Schuller.

Section 3: Affect Generation

Section 3 focuses on another important step toward building affect-aware systems—affect generation. More specifically, chapters in this section focus on embodied conversational agents (ECAs) (e.g., animated agents, virtual characters, avatars) that generate synthetic emotions and express them via nonverbal behaviors.

ECAs can have increasingly expressive faces in order to enhance the range of human-computer interaction. In Chapter 18, "Facial Expressions of Emotions for Virtual Characters," Magalie Ochs, Radoslaw Niewiadomski, and Catherine Pelachaud discuss how researchers are developing ECAs capable of generating a gamut of facial expressions that convey emotions. One of the key challenges in this field is the development of a lexicon linking morphological and dynamic facial features to emotions that need to be expressed. The chapter introduces the methodologies used to identify these morphological and dynamic features. It also discusses the methods that can be used measure the relationship between an ECA's emotional expressions and the user's perception of the interaction.

ECAs, just like humans, can be endowed with a complete body that moves and expresses emotions through its gestures. Margaux Lhommet and Stacy Marsella, in "Expressing Emotion Through Posture and Gesture" (Chapter 19), discuss many of the issues in this line of research. The bodily expressions can be produced via static displays or with movement. New techniques for emotional expressions in ECAs need to be represented in ways that can be used more widely. This is done using markup languages, some of which are briefly described in this chapter as well as in Chapter 18 by Ochs and colleagues. Markup languages require a more extensive coverage, so we have included a chapter on this topic in the next section.

Software agents are increasingly common in applications ranging from marketing to education. Possibly the most commonly used agents communicate over the phone with natural language processing capabilities. Consider Siri, Apple's virtual assistant, or the automated response units that preceded it by providing automated voice-based booking for taxis and other services over the phone. The future of these systems will require the agents to replace the current monotone speech synthesis with an emotional version, as described by Felix Burkhardt and Nick Campbell in Chapter 20, "Emotional Speech Synthesis." Here the authors provide a general architecture for emotional speech synthesis; they discuss basic modeling and technical approaches and offer both use cases and potential applications.

ECAs may have virtual faces and bodies, but they are still software instantiations and therefore implement a limited sense of "embodiment." One way of addressing this limitation is through the physicality of robots. Ana Paiva, Iolanda Leite, and Tiago Ribeiro describe this research in Chapter 20, titled "Emotion Modeling for Social Robots." They begin by describing the affective loop (Höök, 2009), where the user first expresses an emotion and then the system responds by expressing an appropriate emotional response. These responses convey the illusion of a robotic life and demonstrate how even simple behaviors can convey emotions.

The final chapter of Section 3, "Preparing Emotional Agents for Intercultural Communication" (Chapter 22), by Elisabeth André, addresses the challenge of how agents and robots can be designed to communicate with humans from different cultural and social backgrounds. It is already difficult to scaffold human-human communication when there are intercultural differences among communicators. The challenge is even more significant for human-computer communication. We need to understand how emotions are expressed across cultures and improve our emotion detection and generation techniques by either fine-tuning them to particular cultures or by generalizing across

cultures (to the extent possible). This chapter provides an overview of some of the research in this area and touches on several critical topics such as culturally aware models of appraisal and coping and culture-specific variations of emotional behaviors.

Section 4: Affective Computing Methodologies

Although AC utilizes existing methods from standing fields including the affective sciences, machine learning, computer vision, psychophysiology, and so on, it adapts these techniques to its unique needs. This section presents many of these "new" methodologies that are being used by AC researchers to develop interfaces and techniques to make affect compute.

The problem of how to best collect and annotate affective data can be structured in a number of stages. Björn Schuller proposes 10 stages in Chapter 23, the opening chapter of this section, titled "Multimodal Affect Databases—Collection, Challenges, and Chances." The chapter discusses the challenges of collecting and annotating affective data, particularly when more than one sensor or modality is used. Schuller's 10 steps highlight the most important considerations and challenges, including (1) ethical issues, (2) recording and reusing, (3) metainformation, (4) synchronizing streams, (5) modeling, (6) labeling, (7) standardizing, (8) partitioning, (9) verifying perception and baseline results, and (10) releasing the data to the wider community. The chapter also provides a selection of representative audiovisual and other multimodal databases. We have covered these considerations with different depth across a number of chapters in the handbook. Some of these steps are encompassed in multiple chapters, while some chapters address multiple steps. For example, approaches to managing metainformation are discussed in Chapter 29, and Schuller himself discusses the challenges related to synchronizing multimodal data streams.

The first of Schuller's steps toward collecting affective data involves addressing ethical issues, a topic where formal training for engineers is sometimes scarce. In his chapter, "Ethical Issues in Affective Computing" (Chapter 24), Roddie Cowie brings together fundamental issues such as the formal and informal codes of ethics that provide the underpinning for ethical decisions. Practical issues have to do with the enforcement of the codes and ethical principles, which falls under the purview of human research ethics committees. This chapter will help clarify issues that these committees are concerned about, such as informed consent, privacy, and many more.

The second step to building an affective database, according to Schuller, is to make decisions about collecting new data or reusing existing affective databases. This involves deciding on the tools to be used, and some of these are discussed in "Research and Development Tools in Affective Computing" (Chapter 25), by Sazzad Md Hussain, Sidney K. D'Mello, and Rafael A. Calvo. The most common tools were identified by surveying current AC researchers, including several authors of this handbook, and therefore are a reflection of what researchers in the field find useful. Readers can find out about available databases in Schuller's chapter and at emotion-research.net.

Other issues to be taken into account include decisions on the affect representation model, or Schuller's fifth step (e.g., continuous or categorical) and temporal unit of analysis. Several chapters in this section briefly discuss issues that need to be considered in making these decisions, but the topic warranted its own chapter. In "Emotion Data Collection and Its Implications for Affective Computing" (Chapter 26), Shazia Afzal and Peter Robinson discuss naturalistic collection of affective data while people interact with technology, proposing new ways of studying affective phenomena in HCI. They emphasize issues that arise when researcher try to formalize their intuitive understanding of emotion into more formal computational models.

In a related chapter, "Affect Elicitation for Affective Computing" (Chapter 27), Jacqueline Kory and Sidney K. D'Mello discuss ways to reliably elicit emotions in the lab or "in the wild" (i.e., real-world situations). Kory and D'Mello discuss both passive methods—such as video clips, music, or other stimuli—and active methods that involve engaging participants in interactions with other people or where they are asked to enact certain behaviors, postures, or facial expressions. Examples of how these methods have been used by AC researchers are also discussed.

One of the most time-consuming and expensive stages of developing an affective database is affect labeling or annotation. Often this task can be outsourced to a large number of loosely coordinated individuals at a much lower cost and with a much faster turnaround time. This process, called crowdsourcing, is discussed in the context of AC by Robert R. Morris and Daniel McDuff in Chapter 28, "Crowdsourcing Techniques for

Affective Computing." Crowdsourcing already has garnered impressive success stories, as when millions of images were labeled by people playing the ESP game while working for free and even having fun. Hence researchers planning to follow this approach will benefit from Morris and McDuff's account of the development and quality assurance processes involved in affective crowdsourcing.

Schuller's seventh consideration, standardizing, is about seeking compatibility in the data and the annotations, so that the data can be used across systems and research groups. In Chapter 29, "Emotion Markup Language," Marc Schröder, Paolo Baggia, Felix Burkhardt, Catherine Pelachaud, Christian Peter, and Enrico Zovato discuss EmotionML, the markup language for AC recommended by the World Wide Web Consortium (W3C). EmotionML is designed to represent and communicate affective representations across a series of use cases that cover several types of applications. It provides a coding language based on different emotion theories, so emotions can be represented by four types of data: categories, dimensions, appraisals, and action tendencies. Using these four types of data, emotion events can be coded as a data structure that can be implemented in software and shared.

Affect detection algorithms generally use supervised machine learning techniques that use annotated data for training. As Ashish Kapoor explains in Chapter 30, "Machine Learning Techniques in Affective Computing," when considered in tandem, labeling and training of algorithms can be optimized using active information acquisition approaches. Other approaches to annotation, feature extraction, and training that take into account how the data will be used in machine learning are also discussed by Kapoor.

Section 5: Affective Computing Applications

One of the key goals of AC is to develop concrete applications that expand the bandwidth of HCI via affective or emotional design. In line with this, this section highlights existing and emerging applications from a range of domains but with an emphasis on affect at their core.

Learning technologies abound in the digital and physical (e.g., school) spaces and have been among the first AC applications. A prolific research community, known as Intelligent Tutoring Systems and Artificial Intelligence in Education, has focused on developing next-generation learning technologies that model affect in addition to cognition, metacognition, and motivation. Sidney K. D'Mello and Art Graesser present a summary of these technologies in "Feeling, Thinking, and Computing with Affect-Aware Learning Technologies" (Chapter 31). They provide examples of two types of affect-aware educational technologies: reactive systems that respond when affective states are detected and proactive systems that promote or reduce the likelihood of occurrence of certain affective states.

The case studies described in D'Mello and Graesser's chapter focus on learning technologies that support school-related formal learning. However, learning is a lifelong endeavor. and much of learning occurs outside of formal educational settings, including museums, science centers, and zoos. These informal learning environments can also benefit from affect-aware technologies. In "Enhancing Informal Learning Experiences with Affect-Aware Technologies" (Chapter 32), Chad Lane describes how these technologies can be used to promote interest and attitudes in addition to knowledge when visitors engage in informal learning contexts.

Writing is perhaps the quintessential twenty-first-century skill, and both academic and professional work involves considerable writing. Changes in our writing environments brought about by the information age alter the writing process itself. On the positive side, we have access to endless resources and collaborative opportunities than ever before. Yet on the other hand, there are new problems and distractions, such as a continual barrage of email, social media, and countless other distractions of the digital age. In Chapter 33, titled "Affect-Aware Reflective Writing Studios," Rafael A. Calvo explores how new technologies can be used to produce tools that writers can use to reflect on the process they adopt, including circumstances in which they are most productive or enjoy writing the most.

Not everything in life can be learning and work. Georgios N. Yannakakis and Ana Paiva discuss how AC can improve gaming experiences (both for entertainment and learning) in "Emotion in Games" (Chapter 34). They review key studies on the intersection between affect, game design, and technology and discuss how to engineer effective affect-based gaming interactions.

Referring to another form of entertainment, music, Egon van den Broek, Joyce Westerink, and Joris Janssen discuss affect-focused music adaptation in Chapter 35, "Autonomous Closed-Loop Biofeedback: An Introduction and a Melodious Application." The chapter starts by considering some of the key issues involved in engineering closed-loop affective biofeedback systems and applies these insights to the development and real-world validation of an affective music player.

The two previous chapters discuss how education and entertainment could be improved with AC techniques. The following chapters focus on applications where the users interact and collaborate with robots or other humans. In "Affect in Human Robot Interaction" (Chapter 36), Ronald Arkin and Lilia Moshkina discuss various issues involved in this endeavor. They also pose some fundamental research questions, such as how affect-aware robotics can add value (or risks) to human-robot interactions. Other questions include whether such robots can become companions or friends, and issues regarding the role of embodiment in affective robotics (i.e., do the robots need to experience emotions to be able to express them, and what theories and methods can inform affective HRI research?).

The next two chapters focus on human-human interactions. First, in "Virtual Reality and Collaboration" (Chapter 37), Jakki Bailey and Jeremy Bailenson discuss how collaborative virtual environments can be built to support participants' expressions of affect via verbal and nonverbal behaviors. They contextualize their discussions within immersive virtual environment technologies (IVET), where people interact through avatars that act as proxies for their own identities. The chapter reviews the history and common architectures for these IVETs and concludes with a discussion of their ethical implications.

Chapter 38, "Unobtrusive Deception Detection," by Aaron Elkins, Stefanos Zafeiriou, Judee Burgoon, and Maja Pantic, focuses on an aspect of human-human communication that is of great importance in an era that is struggling to strike a balance between security and liberty. This chapter explores algorithms and technology that can be used to detect and classify deception using remote measures of behaviors and physiology. The authors provide a comprehensive treatment of the topic, encompassing its psychological foundations, physiological correlates, automated techniques, and potential applications.

As Cowie notes in his chapter "Ethical Issues in Affective Computing" (Chapter 24) on ethics, "its (AC's) most obvious function is to make technology better able to furnish people with positive experiences and/or less likely to impose negative ones." In line with this, the last three chapters explore how AC can support health and well-being. It is widely known that socioemotional intelligence is at the core of autism spectrum disorders (ASDs). In Chapter 39, "Affective Computing, Emotional Development, and Autism," Daniel Messinger, Leticia Lobo Duvivier, Zachary Warren, Mohammad Mahoor, Jason Baker, Anne Warlaumount, and Paul Ruvolo discuss how AC can serve as the basis for new types of tools for helping children with ASDs. The tools can be used to study the dynamics of emotional expression in children developing normally, those with ASDs, and their high-risk siblings.

One approach to health care is to use avatars that simulate face-to-face doctor-patient interventions. In "Relational Agents in Health Applications: Leveraging Affective Computing to Promote Healing and Wellness" (Chapter 40), Timothy Bickmore surveys research on how affect-aware relational agents can build patient-agent rapport, trust, and the therapeutic alliance that is so important in health-care practices.

In principle, any technology that can help people change their mindsets and behavior can be used to improve psychological well-being. In the last chapter of the handbook (Chapter 41), titled "Cyberpsychology and Affective Computing," Giuseppe Riva, Rafael A. Calvo, and Christine Lissetti propose using AC technologies in the wider context of personal development, an area being called positive technology/computing.

The Glossary

One of the biggest challenges in interdisciplinary collaborations, such as those required in AC, is the development of a language that researchers can share. The disparate terminology used in AC can be overwhelming to researchers new to the field. There is additional confusion when researchers redefine terms for which there are more or less agreed upon operational definitions. It is our hope that *The Oxford Handbook of Affective Computing* will help to develop this common understanding. To facilitate the process, we have included a glossary developed collaboratively by the contributors of each chapter. We asked all contributors to identify key terms in their contributions and to define them in a short paragraph. When more than one definition

was provided, we left all versions, acknowledging that researchers from different backgrounds will have different terminologies. Hence, rather than forcing the common definition, the glossary might be a useful tool to minimize what is often "lost in translation."

Concluding Remarks

It is prudent to end our brief tour of *The Oxford Handbook of Affective Computing* by briefly touching on its origin. The handbook emerged from brief conversations among the editors at the 2011 *Affective Computing and Intelligent Interaction (ACII 2011)* conference in Memphis, Tennessee. We subsequently sent a proposal to Oxford University Press, where it was subsequently approved; the rest is history. By touching on the history and theory of affective computing—its two major thrusts of affect detection and generation, methodological considerations, and existing and emerging applications—we hope that the first *Handbook of Affective Computing* will serve as a useful reference to researchers, students, and practitioners everywhere. Happy reading!

Acknowledgments

This handbook would not have been possible without the enthusiasm of the authors, who have volunteered their time to share their best ideas for this volume. We are very much indebted to them for their excellent work. We could not have compiled and prepared the handbook without the support of Oxford University Press, particularly Joan Bossert and Anne Dellinger, as well as Aishwarya Reddy at Newgen Knowledge Works. We are grateful to Jennifer Neale at the University of Notre Dame and Agnieszka Bachfischer at the Sciences and Technologies of Learning Research network at the University of Sydney for administrative and editing support.

References

Höök K. (2009). Affective loop experiences: Designing for interactional embodiment. *Philosophical Transactions of the Royal Society B, 364,* 3585–3595.

Picard, R. W. (1997). *Affective computing* (p. 275). Cambridge, MA: MIT Press.

Theories and Models

The Promise of Affective Computing

Rosalind W. Picard

Abstract

This chapter is adapted from an invited introduction written for the first issue of the *IEEE Transactions on Affective Computing*, telling personal stories and sharing the viewpoints of a pioneer and visionary of the field of affective computing. This is not intended to be a thorough or a historical account of the development of the field because the author is not a historian and cannot begin to properly credit the extraordinary efforts of hundreds of people who helped bring this field into fruition. Instead, this chapter recounts experiences that contribute to this history, with an eye toward eliciting some of the pleasurable affective and cognitive responses that will be a part of the promise of affective computing.

Key Words: affective computing, agents, autism, psychophysiology, wearable computing

Introduction

Jodie is a young woman I am talking with at a fascinating annual retreat organized by autistic people for autistic people and their friends. Like most people on the autism spectrum (and many neurotypicals, a term for people who don't have a diagnosed developmental disorder), she struggles with stress when unpredictable things happen. Tonight, we are looking at what happened to her emotional arousal as measured by a wristband that gathers three signals—skin conductance, motion, and temperature (Figure 2.1).

Jodie was upset to learn that the event she was supposed to speak at was delayed from 8:00 to 8:30 PM. She started pacing until her friend told her "Stop pacing, that doesn't help you." Many people don't have an accurate read on what they are feeling (this is part of a condition known as alexithymia) and, although she thought pacing helped, she wasn't certain. So, she took his advice. She then started to make the repetitive movements often seen in autism called "stimming" and continued these until the event began at 8:30. In Figure 2.1, we see her skin

conductance on the top graph, going down when she was pacing, up when she was stimming, and hitting its highest peaks while she presents. The level also stays high afterward, during other people's presentations, when she stayed up front to handle problems with the audiovisual technology, including loud audio feedback.

Collecting data related to emotional arousal is not new: for example, skin conductance has been studied for more than 100 years. What is new, however, is how technology can measure, communicate, adapt to, be adapted by, and transform emotion and how we think about it. Powerful new insights and changes can be achieved with these abilities. For example, Jodie collected her emotional arousal data wearing a stretchy wristband, clicked to upload it into a mobile viewer, and showed it to her friend (the one who had asked her to stop pacing). The first words spoken after checking the time stamps on the data display were his. He said, "I'm not going to tell you to stop pacing anymore." The next morning, I saw the two of them again. This time, she was pacing and he sat quietly nearby typing on his

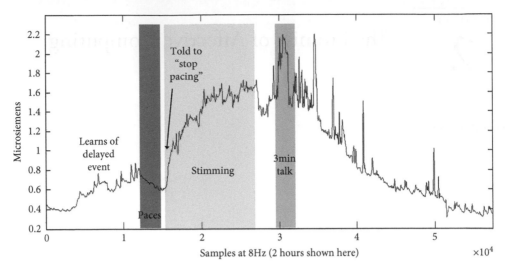

Fig. 2.1 Skin conductance level (top graph). Skin surface temperature (middle graph) and three-axis accelerometer values (lower graph). Skin conductance, which is associated with emotional arousal, was lowered during pacing, while it went up during "stimming," a presentation, and (afterward) while dealing with some audiovisual equipment problems. These data are from a young adult on the autism spectrum.

laptop, letting her pace. The ability to communicate objective data related to her emotional arousal and activity—specifically her sympathetic nervous system activation, of which skin conductance is a sensitive measure—prompted a change in his behavior. Mind you, she had told him in the moment of stress that she thought pacing was helping, but this did not change his behavior. Objective data about emotions carries much more power than self-reported subjective feelings.

The convenience of a new affective computing technology can lead to new self-understanding, as it did for Jodie. Objective data related to emotion is more believable than verbal reports about feelings. Shared affective data can improve communication between people and lead to better understanding and sometimes to beneficial changes in behavior: Jodie's friend could now accept that her pacing might be helpful, and he let Jodie pace.

Researchers inventing future products tend to put in features that marketing people can describe to customers. Features such as more memory, more pixels, and more processing power can all be quantified and designed into explicit goals. The saying "if you can't measure, it you can't manage it" drives progress in many businesses. Measure it, and you can improve it. What if technology enabled you to measure the frustration that a product reduces (or elicits) as easily as you measure processing speed increases (or decreases)? Measuring the frustration caused by a technology when it happens could enable engineers to pinpoint what caused the

frustration and work to prevent or reduce it. With affect measurement, technology can be designed with the explicit goal of giving people significantly better affective experiences.

Technology can also be improved if it has an intelligent ability to respond to emotion. Intelligence about emotion is not easy. For example, you might think it would be intelligent to have a robot smile when it sees its collaborator exhibit the so-called true smile that involves both the lip corner pull and the cheek raise. Shared happiness is usually a positive experience and smart to elicit. However, we recently learned that whereas 90% of participants expressing delight made this facial expression, so too did 90% of participants in a frustration-eliciting scenario who reported feeling significant frustration. Although it might be intelligent to respond to a delighted smile with one of your own, it is probably not intelligent to appear delighted when your collaborator is frustrated if you want him to like you. Although recent progress is making it easier to do things like automatically discriminate smiles of delight and smiles of frustration, the effort to work out the situation, its interaction goals, and the personality differences of the participants is not simple. Affective computing has a lot of problems still to solve before machines will be able to intelligently handle human emotion.

Technology can also be improved by virtue of incorporating principles of emotion learned from biological systems. Emotions guide not only cognition but also other regulatory functions that affect healthy behaviors. Many extraordinarily difficult challenges in the modeling of and understanding of emotion remain to be solved in order to bring about its benefits.

Attitudes toward affective computing, which I defined in 1995 as "computing that relates to, arises from, and deliberately influences emotion," have changed so much in the past decade that it is now hard for some people to believe it used to be a ludicrous idea. In the early '90s, I had never heard of the shorthand "LOL" (Laugh out Loud) but it applied to this research. I beg the reader to let me indulge in some remembrances, starting in 1991, my first year on the MIT faculty.

In the Beginning, Laughter…

One morning, over breakfast cereal and the *Wall Street Journal* (the only nontechnical journal I read regularly), a front-page article about Manfred Clynes caught my eye. He was described as a brilliant inventor who, among better-known inventions that became commercially and scientifically successful, also invented a machine for measuring emotion. His "sentograph" (*sentire* is Latin for "to feel") measured slight changes in directional pressure applied to an immovable button that a person pushed. The finger push showed a characteristic pattern related to joy, sadness, anger, sex, reverence, and more. This is not a list approved by mainstream emotion theorists—who don't include sex or reverence—and Manfred is far from mainstream. Among his many distinctions, Manfred was a child prodigy who later received a fan letter from Einstein for his piano playing and who co-authored the 1960 paper that coined the word "Cyborg." But the *Wall Street Journal* described how he *measured* emotion, with objective physical signals. Later, others replicated the measures. I was amused, although not enough to do anything more than file the article, alongside other crazy ideas I liked such as refrigerators that were powered by the noise of nearby traffic. The article mentioned my friend, Marvin Minsky, who many years later introduced me to Manfred, and we became instant friends.

Manfred never claimed to be the first to build a machine to measure emotional categories. But Manfred may have been the first to get laughed at for his work in making affect computable. He told me about the time when he first tried to present his ideas about measuring emotion to other scientists: the audience laughed and laughed, and it was not the kind of laughter most speakers crave to elicit. He said he was literally laughed off the stage.

Discovering Real Importance for Emotion

When I first started thinking about emotion, it was the last thing I wanted to think about. I was up for tenure at MIT, working hard raising money, and conducting what people later praised as pioneering research in image and video pattern modeling. I liked my work to be rooted solidly in mathematics and machine learning. I was busy working six days and nights a week building the world's first content-based retrieval system, creating and mixing mathematical models from image compression, computer vision, texture modeling, statistical physics, and machine learning with ideas from film makers. I spent all my spare cycles advising students, building and teaching new classes, publishing, reading, reviewing, raising money, and serving on nonstop conference and lab committees. I worked hard to be taken as the serious researcher I was. I had raised more than a million dollars in funding for my group's work. The last thing I wanted was to wreck it all and be associated with emotion. Emotion was associated with being irrational and unreasonable. Heck, I was a *woman* coming from engineering. I did not want to be associated with "emotional," which also was used to stereotype women, typically with a derogatory tone of voice. If anybody needed to start work in this area, it needed to be a man.

However, I kept running into engineering problems that needed…well, something I did not want to address. For example, working on computer vision, I knew that we had a lot to learn from human vision. I collaborated with human vision scientists who focused on the cortex and visual perception. We labored to build computer vision systems that could see like people see, and we learned to build banks of filters, for example, that could detect high-contrast oriented regions and motions in ways that seemed to be similar to stages of the human visual cortex. Much engineering, whether for vision or earlier in my life for computer architectures, was focused on trying to replicate the amazing human cortex. We wanted to figure it out by building it. But nowhere did any of the findings about the human visual cortex address a problem I wanted to answer: How do you find what is *interesting* for a person? How do you find what *matters* to them? How do visual attention systems figure this out and shift automatically when they need to shift? Building a vision system is not just about detecting high-contrast oriented lines or telling a dog from a cat. Vision is affected by attention, and attention is affected by what matters to you. Vision—real seeing—is guided by feelings of importance.

Another problem arose from my years of work at AT&T Bell Labs and at MIT building new kinds of computer architectures for digital signal processing. We came up with many clever ways to parallelize, pipeline, optimize, and otherwise process sounds and sights and other signals humans usually interpret effortlessly. However, never did anyone figure out how to give a computer anything like motivation, drive, and a sense of how to evaluate shifting priorities in a way that acted genuinely intelligent. The machines did not genuinely *care* about anything. We could make it print, "Hello world, I care. Really, . . . " but we weren't fooled by that. We could give it functional programs that approximated some affective motivational components like "drive." Such programs worked under limited conditions that covered all the cases known up front—but always failed pathetically when encountering something new. And it didn't scale—the space of possibilities it needed to consider became intractable.

Today, we know that biological emotion systems operate to help human beings handle complex, unpredictable inputs in real time. Today, we know that emotions signal what matters, what you care about. Today, we know emotion is involved in rational decision making and action selection and that, to behave rationally in real life, you need to have a properly functioning emotion system. But at that time, this was not even on the radar. Emotion was irrational, and if you wanted respect then you didn't want to be associated with emotion.

Most surprising to me was when I learned that emotion interacts deeply in the brain with perception. From human vision research on perception, we all understood perception to be driven by the cortex—the visual cortex for vision, the auditory cortex for audition, and the like. But one Christmas break, while reading Richard Cytowic's "The Man Who Tasted Shapes," I was jolted out of my cortex-centric focus. In synesthesia, in which a person feels shapes in his palms when tasting soup or sees colors with letters involuntarily or experiences other crossed perceptual modalities, the cortex was observed to be showing less activity, not more.

Cytowic argued that multimodal perception was not only happening in the cortex, but also in the limbic structures of the brain, regions physically below the cortex, which were known to be important for three things: attention, memory, and emotion. I was interested in attention and memory. I started to read more neuroscience literature about these limbic regions. I was not interested in emotion. Alas, I found that the third role—emotion—kept coming

up as essential to perception. Emotion biased what we saw and heard. Emotion played major roles not only in perception, but also in many other aspects of intelligence that artificial intelligence (AI) researchers had been trying to solve from a cortical-centric perspective. Emotion was vital in forming memory and attention and in rational decision making. And, of course, emotion communication was vital in human–machine interaction. Emotions influence action selection, language, and whether or not you decide to double-check your mathematical derivations, comment your computer code, initiate a conversation, or read some of the stories below.

Emotion being useful and even necessary was not what I was looking for. I became uneasy. I did not want to work on or be associated with emotion, yet emotion was starting to look vital for solving the difficult engineering problems we needed to solve.

I believe that a scientist has to commit to find what is true, not what is popular. I was becoming quietly convinced that engineers' dreams to build intelligent machines would never succeed without incorporating insights about emotion. I knew somebody had to educate people about the evidence I was collecting and act on it. But I did not want to risk my reputation, and I was too busy. I started looking around, trying to find somebody, ideally male and already tenured, whom I could convince to develop this topic, which clearly needed more attention.

Who Wants to Risk Ruining His Reputation?

I screwed up my courage and invited Jerry Wiesner, former president of MIT and scientific advisor to Presidents Eisenhower, Kennedy and Johnson, to lunch. Jerry was in a suit and always seemed very serious and authoritative. Over fish and bonbons at Legal Sea Foods, I filled him in on some of my work and sought his advice. I asked him what was the most important advice he had for junior faculty at MIT. I strained to hear him over the noise of that too-loud restaurant, but one line came out clear: "You should take risks! This is the time to take risks." As I walked back the one block to the lab, I took a detour and did some thinking about this. I was working in an exciting new research area at the time—content-based retrieval. I liked it and was seen as a pioneer in it. But it was already becoming popular. I didn't think it was really risky.

The Media Lab saw me as one of their more conventional players, as "the electrical engineer." Nicholas Negroponte, architect and founding director, spoke with pride and perfect French pronunciation, of how he formed the Media Lab as a "Sah-lon de ref-oos-say." The original Salon des Refusés was an exhibition by artists of work that was rejected by the authorities in charge. Nicholas was proud of establishing a lab that would do research that others might laugh at and reject. I didn't want to be labeled as a rejected misfit, but I didn't learn he saw our faculty in this way until after I was already a member of the lab. It was freeing to hear that if I were indeed ever viewed as a misfit, it would be valued. If I chose to work on emotion, the misfit title was going to happen. Maybe it would be okay here.

One of the brilliant visionaries Nicholas had recruited to the Media Lab was Seymour Papert, mathematician and leading thinker in education and technology, who told our faculty about researchers long ago who were all focused on trying to build a better wagon. They were making the wheels stronger so they stayed round and so they didn't break or fall off as easily. They worked hard to make wagons last longer, go faster, give smoother rides, and cover more distance. Meanwhile, Seymour said that while all the researchers of that day were improving the wagon wheel, these crazy engineers—the Wright brothers—went off and invented the airplane. He said we faculty in the Media Lab should be the crazies inventing the new way to fly. My maiden name is Wright. This story was inspiring.

Convinced that emotion was important and people should pay attention to it and that maybe my lab wouldn't mind if I detoured a few weeks to address this topic, I spent the holidays and some of the January "Independent Activities Period" writing a thought piece that I titled "Affective Computing" to collect my arguments. I circulated it as a tech note quietly among some open minds in the lab. A student from another group, who was more than a decade older than I, read it and showed up at my door with a stack of six psychology books on emotion. "You should read these," he said. I love how the students at MIT tell the faculty what to do. I needed to hear what he said, and I read the whole stack.

I then read every book on emotion I could get from Harvard, MIT, and the local library network only to learn that psychologists had more than a hundred definitions of emotion, nobody agreed on what emotion was, and almost everyone relied on questionnaires to measure emotion. As an engineer, it bugged me that psychologists and doctors relied on self-reports that they knew were unreliable and inaccurate.

I went to Jerry Kagan at the psychology department in Harvard. His office was high up in the William James building. I wanted to talk to him about my ideas about how to build accurate and systematic ways to measure and characterize affective information. He had been very discouraging to one of my students earlier, and I thought it was important to understand his perspective. He gave me a hard time at first, but after we argued, in the end, he was very nice and almost encouraging: he told me "You're shooting for the moon" when I proposed that my team could build wearable technology to measure and characterize aspects of emotion as it naturally occurred in daily life. I thought psychologists could benefit from the systematic approach engineers bring to difficult problems.

I attended neuroscience talks and read key findings on emotion in the neuroscience literature and found their methods to be more concrete—showing evidence for precise pathways through which aspects of emotional perception and learning appeared to be happening. Neuroscience studies were compelling, especially findings like Joe LeDoux's that showed perceptual learning (e.g., a rat learning to fear a tone) without involving the usual cortical components (e.g., after the audio cortex had been removed). Antonio Damasio's book *Descarte's Error* was also powerful in arguing for the role of emotion in rational decision making and behavior.

I spruced up my technical note envisioning affective computing as a broad area that I thought engineers, computer scientists, and many others should consider working on and submitted it as a manifesto to a non-Institute of Electrical and Electronics Engineers (IEEE) journal that had traditionally printed bold new ideas. It was rejected. Worse, one of the reviews indicated that the content was better suited to an "in-flight magazine." I could hear the laughter between the lines of rejection. I gave a talk on the ideas to our computer vision research group, and people were unusually silent. This was what I feared.

I gave a copy of the thought piece to Andy Lippman, a tall energetic man who always has bountiful words for sharing his opinions. Usually, we talked about signal processing or video processing. One day he showed up in my doorway, silent, with a peculiar look on his face, holding a document. He stabbed it with his finger, shook his head, pointed at it, shook his head some more and said nothing. This was not like him. Had he lost his voice? "Is something the matter?" I angled my head. Andy was never silent. Finally he blurted, "This is crazy! CRAZY!" He looked upset. I hesitated, "Uh, crazy is, good, in the Media Lab, right?" He nodded and then he smiled like a Bostonian being asked if he'd like free ice cream with mix-ins. Then I saw the document: it was my affective computing paper. He waved it, nodded and shook his head, and left with an odd smile. I never did resubmit that tech report, but it provided the only instance where I ever saw the voluble Lippman tongue-tied.

Visionary Supporters Trump Peer Review

I am a big fan of peer review, and I work hard to maintain the integrity of that process. But there are times in the life of new ideas when peer-reviewed papers don't stand a chance of getting published. Sometimes, years of acclimation are needed before an idea can make it through the process, even if the work is done solidly and with the best science and engineering. I realized the early ideas on affective computing were not going to make it into print until a lot more work had been done to prove them, and I only had a year before I was up for tenure. Emotion was just not an acceptable topic. How could I get a whole set of new ideas out when the average time from submission to publication of my computer vision papers was measured in years?

Nicholas Negroponte invited me to co-author his *Wired* column on affective computing. We published it and got a mix of responses. The most memorable responses were letters from people who said, "You are at MIT, you *can't* know *anything* about emotion." *Wired* was no substitute for peer review, but it started to get my ideas out, and the ideas shook some trees.

David Stork invited me to author the chapter on Hal's emotions for the book *Hal's Legacy*, commemorating the famous computer in Stanley Kubrick and Arthur C. Clarke's film, *2001 A Space Odyssey*. All of the other chapters addressed attributes of Hal, like his chess playing ability, his speech, his vision, and the like, and had "the most famous person in the field" to write them. David and I joked that I was the *only* person at the time who visibly represented the field of computers and emotions, and the word "field" was used with a stretch of a smile. I still enjoyed being in the book with a lot of impressive colleagues—Ray Kurzweil, Don Norman, Daniel Dennett, and others—and it was encouraging to be grouped with so many successful scientists. However, when I had dinner with Ray Kurzweil, his wife asked me if I was the "emotion woman," which

only compounded my worries. But I had started digging deeper into affective computing research, and I knew the work was needed, even if it wrecked my image and my career.

The famous scientist Peter Hart, after coaxing me to ride bicycles with him up the "hill" (it felt more like a mountain) of Old La Honda on a 105 degree July day, told me he thought affective computing was going to become very important. He encouraged me to drop all the research I'd just raised more than a million dollars in funding for (content-based retrieval) and pursue affective computing wholeheartedly. I feverishly wondered how I could ever do that. Peter hosted, in July 1995, at Ricoh Silicon Valley, what was the first presentation outside of MIT on the ideas that would become my book *Affective Computing*. I saw Peter as an established outside authority in pattern recognition, not just a Media Lab crazy type, and his encouragement enabled me to believe that a book and more serious dedicated work on affect might be worthwhile. At least he would be one respected technical researcher who wouldn't write me off.

In August 1995, I emailed the director of the Media Lab that I was changing the name of my research group at MIT to "Affective Computing." He said it was a very nice name, "gets you thinking," and "is nicely confused with *effective*." I liked how easily he supported this new direction. I liked that my crazy new work would be confused with being effective.

I was asked to fax my unpublished tech report to Arthur C. Clarke (who didn't do email). I faxed it, and he mailed me a personal paper letter saying he liked it. Arthur added, "I sent your paper to Stanley—he is working on a movie about AI." I never got to meet "Stanley," but I understand he was the brilliant mind behind giving Hal emotions in the film *2001*. When I read Clarke's original screenplay, it had almost nothing on emotion in it, and Clarke's subsequent book on the story also downplayed emotion. But in the film, Hal showed more emotion than any of the human actors.

Through my Media Lab connections, I started to see that there were many mavericks who had recognized the power and importance of emotion, even though there were many more in engineering and computer science who did not think that emotion mattered. I felt encouraged to push ahead in this area, despite that I heard my technical colleagues at conferences whispering behind my back, "Did you hear what weird stuff she's working on?" and some of them blushed when I looked up at them and they realized I'd overheard. I did feel vindicated 5 years later at the same conference when one of them asked me if I would share my affect data with him because he was starting to do work in the field.

TV producer Graham Chedd for *Scientific American Frontiers* came by with one of my favorite actors, Alan Alda, and got interested in what my team was doing. Graham included our very early affective research in two of their shows. I am told that these episodes still air on very late night television, where you can see Alan Alda's emotional arousal going up as he thinks about hot red peppers and going down while he thinks about saltine crackers. I'm standing next to him, pregnant with my first child, trying to look like a serious scientist while I'm clanging a bell in his ear to elicit a startle response from him. Somehow it now seems fitting for late night television.

Dan Goleman called from the *New York Times* during a very busy week, and I asked him if we could talk at a different time. He said he was going to write about our work that week whether I would make time to speak with him or not. Later, his book on *Emotional Intelligence* sold more than 5 million copies. Putting "emotional" and "intelligence" together was a brilliant combination, originally conceived by Jack Mayer and Peter Salovey in their scholarly work under this name. Although the phrase is widely accepted today, at the time it was an oxymoron. Goleman's popular writing did a lot to interest the general public in the important roles emotions play in many areas of success in life—he argued it was more important than verbal and mathematical intelligences, which of course was what AI researchers had been focused on. The topic of emotion was starting to get more respect, although for some reason it was still very hard to get computer scientists to take it seriously.

Much later, William Shatner came by my office, dragged in by his ghostwriter who was creating a new book about the science of *Star Trek* and the role of emotion in their shows. It was kind of a stretch to find some science, given the booming sounds in the vacuum of outer space and more. But, I did confirm that the character of Spock had emotion. Spock was not emotionally expressive and kept emotion under control, but it was important to claim that he still had emotion, deep inside, in order for his intelligent functioning to be scientifically accurate. If he really didn't have emotion and behaved as intelligently as he behaved, then it would have been bad science in the show. The actor Leonard Nimoy, who had played Spock, later came to MIT and hosted a big event I chaired featuring new technology measuring and communicating emotional signals. He appeared remarkably unemotional, even when he was not playing Spock. I tried to convince him that he could show emotion and still be intelligent. He still showed almost no emotion, but his presence attracted more people to come and learn about why my group was developing affective technologies.

A famous high-priced speaker's bureau invited me to join their list of speakers, offering me lots of money if I would give talks about "more broadly interesting" technology topics than affect and computing. They thought emotion was not going to be of sufficiently broad interest to their well-heeled clients. I knew at this point I was going to spend all my spare cycles trying to get high-quality research done on affective computing and trying to get more engineers and computer scientists to consider working on emotion, so I declined their offer. I started giving more talks than ever on affective computing—dozens every year, mostly with zero or low pay to academic groups, trying to interest them in working on affect.

I remember one talk where the famous speech researcher Larry Rabiner came up to me afterward and asked why I was working on emotion. Larry said, "It's a very hard problem to tackle, and it just doesn't matter. Why are you wasting time on it?" I don't think he had paid much attention to my talk, or perhaps I had done a very bad job of explaining. I had always admired Larry's work, and this was tough to hear, but I tried to explain why I thought it was critical in early development for learning of language. I pointed out that dogs and small infants seem to respond to affect in speech. He seemed to think that was interesting. He did listen, but I never heard from him again.

After another talk, I remember a world-famous MIT computer scientist coming up to me, agitated, looking at my feet the whole time and complaining to me, "Why are you working on emotion? It's irrelevant!" I'm told this is how you tell if a CS professor is extroverted or introverted—if he looks at his feet, he's introverted, if he looks at yours, he's extroverted. He sounded angry that I would take emotion seriously. I tried, probably in vain, to convince him of its value, and he was soon joined by others who looked at each other's feet and changed the subject to help calm him down.

On multiple occasions, colleagues confided in me that they didn't know what emotion really was, other than extreme emotions like anger. Some of them even said, "I don't have feelings, and I don't believe they have a physical component you can measure." I think one of the attractions of computer science to many of them was that it was a world of logic largely devoid of emotional requirements, and they didn't want this threatened. I faced quite an uphill battle trying to convince my computer science colleagues of the value of emotion.

Through my talks to various groups, I became increasingly convinced that affective computing needed to be addressed, even if most computer scientists thought emotion was irrelevant. I wanted to make affective computing interesting and respectable so that progress would be made in advancing its science. I was always encouraged when people would go from looking scared of the topic, as if it was going to be an embarrassing talk to be seen at, to wanting to spend lots of time with me afterward talking deeply about the subject.

Somehow, in the midst of all of this, while up for tenure, trying to build and move into a new house, and getting ready to give birth to my first son, I signed a book contract in 1996, moved into the house, delivered the baby, delivered the book nine months later, and submitted my tenure case to MIT with a freshly minted copy of "Affective Computing." At the time, I had no peer-reviewed journal papers related to affective computing—those would come later. All my peer-reviewed scientific articles were on mathematical models for content-based retrieval or were conference papers on affective signal analysis. I was told that reviewers didn't know what to make of my schizophrenic tenure case: they wondered if the book was authored by somebody different from the person who wrote the papers, as if "Rosalind Picard" was a common name and maybe there were two of her.

Fortunately, I was in the Media Lab, probably the only place on the planet that loved you more the weirder you were. They were willing to take big risks. Jerry Wiesner's influence was huge, and our building was named after him. The director of our lab, Nicholas Negroponte, phoned me one day and said, "Roz, good news. Your tenure case went through like a hot knife through butter." The risk I had taken to start out in a totally new area, one that almost nobody wanted to be associated with, had not hurt my career. But I never did it for my career; I did it because I believed then, and I still believe, that affective computing is an extremely important area of research.

I was also amazed how, over time, the appeal of the topic became very broad—not just to researchers in computer science and human computer interaction, but also in medicine, literature, psychology, philosophy, marketing, and more. Peter Weinstock, a leading physician at Boston Children's Hospital, today calls emotion "the fourth vital sign." I had never known there were so many communities interested in affect, and I started to engage with researchers in a huge number of fields. I have learned a ton doing this, and it has been mind expanding.

I was delighted to see workshops on affective computing springing up around the world, led by visionary colleagues in computer science and psychology who were also bold in taking risks. I did not help much in terms of organizing meetings, and I admire greatly the huge efforts put in by so many talented technical colleagues who truly fostered the growth of this field. I cannot properly name them all here; however, Klaus Scherer, Paolo Petta, Robert Trappl, Lola Canamero, Eva Hudlicka, Jean-Marc Fellous, Christine Lisetti, Fiorella de Rosis, Ana Paiva, Jianhua Tao, Juan Velasquez, and Tienu Tan played especially important and memorable roles in instigating some of the early scientific gatherings. Aaron Sloman, Andrew Ortony, and I were frequent speakers at these gatherings, and I enjoyed their philosophical and cognitive perspectives and challenges.

The HUMAINE initiative became very influential in funding significant European research on emotion and computing, propelling them ahead of research efforts in the United States. The community involved a lot of top researchers under the warm leadership of Roddie Cowie, and, with the expert technical support of Marc Schroeder, was well organized and productive, funding dozens of groundbreaking projects.

The United States did not seem as willing as Europe to take bold risks in this new research area, and I always wondered why we lagged so far behind Europe in recognizing the importance of affect. I was lucky to have Media Lab corporate consortium funding with "no strings attached" or our MIT Affective Computing group would never have been able to get up and running. Meanwhile, a National Cancer Institute grant supported Stacy Marsella at the University of Southern California (USC) in developing a pedagogical system to teach emotion coping strategies to mothers of pediatric cancer patients, and an Army Research Institute grant recognized the importance of putting emotions into the cognitive architecture Soar (work by Paul Rosenbloom, also at USC, which not only included Jonathan Gratch, but also hooked him on emotion).

Much later, the National Science Foundation funded work by Art Graesser at Memphis that included my lab helping develop emotion recognition tools for an intelligent tutor, and then still later, work by Rana el Kaliouby and Matthew Goodwin and me building affective technology for autism. Although I remain very grateful for all sources of funding, I especially am grateful for those who find ways to give scientists the freedom to try things before the ordinary peer-review and proposal-review processes are ready to accept them. Emotion did not start out with respect, and if we had to wait for traditional sources of funding to get it to that point, this chapter would probably not be here.

...to IEEE and Beyond

I have a long history with the IEEE, from joining as a student to decades later being honored as a Fellow. I played a small role in helping found the IEEE International Symposium on Wearable Computing and the wearables special interest group. I have served on dozens of program committees, organized workshops, and served as guest editor and associate editor of *IEEE Transactions on Pattern Analysis and Machine Intelligence*. I've reviewed so many IEEE papers that, if combined into vertical stacks, they could bury a poor innocent bystander if they toppled. I know the high integrity and raise-the-bar standards of the IEEE research community.

However, when I submitted my first carefully written technical emotion recognition paper focusing on physiological pattern analysis to the IEEE conference on "computer vision and pattern analysis (CVPR)" the reviewers wrote "the topic does not fit into CVPR since it doesn't have any computer vision in it." Later, I strategically put "Digital processing of..." and "Signal processing for..." in the titles of papers submitted to the IEEE International Conference on Acoustics, Speech, and Signal Processing, and they got accepted. This same trick worked to get past the "it doesn't fit" excuses for our first *IEEE Transactions Pattern Analysis and Machine Intelligence* paper on affective computing as well: I put "machine intelligence" in the title. Of course, it was not that easy: the editor also insisted that five thorough reviewers iterate with me before approving the paper. Usually three will suffice. I had been an associate editor of PAMI and seen a lot of reviews, but I had never seen any set of such length as required for this first paper on emotion. I addressed every comment, and the paper got published.

By the way, it was not just the IEEE—the Association of Computing Machinery (ACM) also rejected my first affective computing submission as "not matching any of the topics or themes in the human–computer area." I wondered from the review if they had even read the paper or just rejected it when they saw it addressed emotion. Years later, I was delighted when several affective topics were added to their official themes. To this day, I still feel slightly amazed when I see conferences that openly solicit affective topics, even though affective computing has its own international conference now, and many other conferences also openly solicit affective computing work. It wasn't always that way—in the beginning, emotion was really fringe, unwelcome, and the few people working on it had to have an unusually large allocation of self-confidence.

In 2010, Jonathan Gratch led our community in launching its first journal, the *IEEE Transactions on Affective Computing*, which truly presents the field as respectable. Jaws dropped. The presence of an IEEE journal sent a message that serious engineering researchers could work on emotion and be respected.

Whether or not affective computing is an area in which you conduct research, you are using emotion when you choose to read this. You are involving your emotion system when you make a decision where to spend your time—when you act on what matters most to you. Affective computing researchers have a chance to elucidate how emotion works: how to build it, how to measure it, how to help people better communicate and understand it, how to use this knowledge to engineer smarter technology, and how to use it to create experiences that improve lives.

Affective computing is a powerful and deeply important area of research, full of extremely difficult technical, scientific, philosophical, and ethical challenges. I believe it contains the most complex real-time problems to be solved in human–computer interaction and in computer science models of human behavior and intelligence. At the same time, the field is not merely a subset of computer science. The complexity and challenge of giving computers real-time skills for understanding and responding intelligently to complex naturally occurring and naturally expressed human emotion spans many fields, including the human sciences of neuroscience, physiology, affective-cognitive science, and psychology. Affective computing is no longer a topic to be treated lightly, although laughter remains one of my favorite emotional expressions.

Acknowledgments

The author wishes to thank all her graduate and undergraduate student researchers over the years, especially those who helped build a solid base of research in affective computing, and those who politely tolerated and supported the group's transition to this topic back when they thought emotion was embarrassing and wished their advisor would go back to doing normal signal processing and machine learning. She also can not begin to properly credit the remarkable learning environment that MIT and the Media Lab have created supporting people who have different ideas, even laughable ones. MIT and the Media Lab are truly special places full of amazing colleagues. Picard would like to thank Drs. Ted Selker, Rich Fletcher, Rana el Kaliouby, and Matthew Goodwin for their significant collaborations, especially in creating new affective technologies that help people with disabilities and with needs for improved emotion communication.

A Short History of Psychological Perspectives on Emotion

Rainer Reisenzein

Abstract

This chapter presents a short history of psychological theory and research on emotion since the beginnings of psychology as an academic discipline in the last third of the nineteenth century. Using William James's theory of emotion as the starting point and anchor, the history of research on five main questions of emotion psychology is charted. These concern, respectively, (1) the causal generation of emotions, (2) the effects of emotion on subsequent cognition and behavior, (3) the nature of emotion, (4) the evolutionary and learning origins of the emotion system, and (5) the neural structures and processes involved in emotions.

Key Words: emotion theory, history of emotion research, James's theory of emotion, cognitive emotion theories, basic emotions theory, neurophysiological basis of emotion

Psychology as an independent academic discipline emerged during the last third of the nineteenth century (see, e.g., Leahey, 2003). I have therefore chosen this period as the starting point of the present short history of psychological perspectives of emotion. However, readers should be aware that academic emotion psychology did not start from scratch. On the contrary, it build on a rich tradition of theorizing about emotions by philosophers, historians, and literary writers that dates back to the Ancient Greeks (see, e.g., Strongman, 2003) and has remained influential up to the present (e.g., Arnold, 1960; Nussbaum, 2001).

When psychology became an independent discipline, it defined itself initially as the science of consciousness (of conscious mental states; e.g., Brentano, 1873; Wundt, 1896). Given that emotions are salient exemplars of conscious mental states, it is not surprising that the psychologists

of consciousness also had a keen interest in the emotions. In fact, most of the basic types of psychological emotion theory discussed today were already present, at least in the outlines, in the psychology of consciousness. During the subsequent, behaviorist phase of psychology (about 1915–1960), and due in large part to its restrictive research doctrines, research on emotions subsided again (see, e.g., Arnold, 1960), although behaviorists did make some important contributions to emotion psychology (e.g., research on the classical conditioning of fear; see Gray, 1975; LeDoux, 1998; Watson, 1919). Immediately after the so-called cognitive revolution of the early 1960s, when behaviorism was replaced by cognitivism—a modern version of mentalism guided by the metaphor of information processing in computers—emotion research took up speed again, until, in the 1990s, it became a boom that also began to affect other scientific disciplines. Today, emotion is an important topic in nearly every subfield of psychology, as well as in many other disciplines ranging from biology to neurophysiology to computer science, linguistics and literary studies. Some already see the emergence of a new interdisciplinary research field, analogous to cognitive science: *affective science*, the interdisciplinary study of emotions and related phenomena (Scherer, 2009).

One important reason for the recent surge of interest in emotions has been a re-evaluation of the adaptive utility of emotions. Traditionally, emotions have often been regarded as maladaptive (because, it was held, they interfere with rational thinking and decision-making; see, e.g., Roberts, 2013). In contrast, during the past 20 or so years, emotions have increasingly come to be seen as overall adaptive (e.g., Feldman-Barrett & Salovey, 2002; Frijda, 1994). Some theorists even regard emotions as indispensable for adaptive behavior (e.g., Damasio, 1994). This changed view of the usefulness of emotions has also been an important motive for launching of the field of affective computing (Picard, 1997).

Five Questions of Emotion Psychology

The task of emotion psychology can be defined as the reconstruction or "reverse engineering" of the structure and functioning of the human emotion system, including its relations to other subsystems of the mind (Reisenzein & Horstmann, 2006). The central subtasks of this task are to explain (Q1) how emotions are elicited or generated; (Q2) what effects (in particular what adaptive or functional effects) emotions have on subsequent cognitive processes and behavior, and, related to both questions, (Q3) what emotions themselves are—how they are to be theoretically defined, what kinds of mental and computational states they are (Reisenzein, 2012). Answering Q1–Q3 amounts to reconstructing the blueprint of the emotion system. However, as already argued by McDougall (1908/1960; see also, Tooby & Cosmides, 1990), to achieve this goal it is helpful, and even necessary, to address a further question that is also of independent interest, one that concerns the origins of the emotion system; namely (Q4), which parts of the emotion system are inherited and which are acquired through learning? Finally, to help answer questions Q1–Q4, it would be useful to know (Q5) how emotions are biologically realized or implemented (i.e., which neural structures and processes underlie them).

A generally accepted theory of emotions that gives detailed answers to all these questions, or even just to the central questions Q1–Q3, still does not exist. Nevertheless, progress has been made. In what follows, I trace the history of the most important proposed answers to the five main questions of emotion psychology. As the starting point and anchor of my report, I use a classical theory of emotion proposed by one of the founding fathers of psychology, the psychologist and philosopher William James (1884; 1890/1950; 1894). My reason for choosing James's theory of emotion for structuring this chapter is not that the theory has stood the test of time particularly well (see Reisenzein & Stephan, 2014), but that it has been highly influential, is widely known, and is possibly the first emotion theory that tries to give answers—if partly only very sketchy answers—to all of the five main questions of emotion psychology. I first describe James's answers to these questions and then discuss, in separate sections, what has been learned about them since James's time.

James's Theory of Emotion

The starting point of James's theory of emotion is the intuition, which I believe readers will confirm, that emotional experiences—for example experiences of joy, sorrow, anger, fear, pity or joy for another, pride, and guilt (see e.g., Ortony, Clore, & Collins, 1988)—have a special *phenomenal quality*; that is, it "is like" or "feels like" a special way to have them. James expressed this intuition with a metaphor that has since been adopted by many other emotion theorists: emotional experiences have "warmth"; they are "hot" experiences, in contrast to "cold" nonemotional mental states such as intellectual perceptions or thoughts, which James (1890/1950, p. 451) described as "purely cognitive in form, pale, colorless, destitute of emotional warmth." In addition, introspection suggests that the experiential quality of emotions is more or less different for different emotions (e.g., it feels different to be happy, angry, and afraid) and that each emotional quality can occur in different intensities (e.g., one can be a little, moderately, or extremely happy, angry, afraid).

James's main aim with his emotion theory was to explain this set of intuitions about emotional experience (Reisenzein & Döring, 2009). A central idea behind the explanation he offered was to notice that the description of emotions suggested by introspection—emotions are a unique group of related experiential qualities that can occur in different intensities—fitted the definition of *sensations* (e.g., of color, tone, or taste) (e.g., Wundt, 1896). Given the similarities between emotions and sensations, it seems natural to try to explain the phenomenal properties of emotions by assuming that they are a class of mental states analogous to sensations, or even that they are a subgroup of sensations. This is the basic idea of the so-called *feeling theory of emotion*, which until today has remained—at least in a "cognitively diluted" version (see the section on the nature of emotion)—the main approach to explaining the phenomenal character of emotions (Reisenzein, 2012; Reisenzein & Döring, 2009).

Q3: What Is an Emotion?

James himself opted for the radical version of feeling theory: he proposed that emotional feelings are not just *analogous to* sensations, but that they literally *are* a class of sensations on a par with sensations of color, taste, touch, and the like. Specifically, James argued, emotional feelings are the sensations of the bodily reactions that (he maintained) are always elicited by emotion-evoking events (see his answers to Q1 and Q4). Emotion-relevant bodily changes include facial and vocal expressions of emotion, as well as emotional actions (e.g., running away in fear), but most important are physiological reactions, such as heart pounding and sweating. In fact, in a response to critics of his theory, James (1894) argued that only physiological reactions are necessary for emotions.

Q1: How Are Emotions Elicited?

According to how James initially (James, 1884; 1890/1950) described the process of emotion generation, the bodily changes experienced as emotions are elicited by perceptions or ideas of suitable objects in a reflex-like (i.e., direct and involuntary) manner. To use James's most famous example, imagine a wanderer in the wilderness who suddenly sees a bear in front of him and feels terrified. According to James, the wanderer's feeling of fear is generated as follows: the perception of the bear elicits, in a reflex-like manner, a specific pattern of bodily reactions—that characteristic for fear (comprising among others an increase in heart rate, constriction of the peripheral blood vessels, sweating, and trembling; see James, 1890/1950, p. 446). The bodily changes are immediately registered by sense organs located in the viscera, skin, and muscles, and communicated back to the brain, where they are presumably integrated into a holistic bodily feeling (James, 1894). This feeling is the experience of fear.

Q2: What Are the Effects of Emotions on Subsequent Cognition and Behavior?

Given the evolutionary foundation of James's emotion theory (see Q4), it is interesting to learn that James was rather reserved about the adaptiveness of the bodily reactions elicited by emotional stimuli: although he believed that some of them are adaptive, he claimed that this is by no means the case for all. Furthermore, the emotion itself (e.g., the feeling of fear) does not seem to have any function of its own; indeed, the assumption of James's theory that emotions are the effects rather than the causes of emotional behaviors seems at first sight to *preclude* any useful function for emotions. However, as McDougall (1908/1960) has pointed out, feelings of bodily changes could still play a role in the control of ongoing emotional behavior (see also, Laird, 2007). Furthermore, if one assumes that emotional feelings are based on physiological changes only (James, 1884), they could at least in principle motivate emotional actions (e.g., fleeing in the case of fear) (see Reisenzein & Stephan, 2014).

Q4: Where Do the Emotion Mechanisms Come From; to Which Degree Are They Inherited Versus Learned?

According to James, the bodily reactions that constitute the basis of emotional feelings are produced by inherited emotion mechanisms that developed in evolution, although they can be substantially modified by learning. As said, James assumed that at least some of the evolutionary emotion mechanisms came into existence because they helped to solve a recurrent adaptive problem (see Q2). For example, the program that generates the fear pattern of physiological responses could be so explained: it developed because it helped our forebears to prepare for rapid flight or defense in dangerous situations (McDougall, 1908/1960). Furthermore, James assumed that the "instinctive" bodily reactions can be naturally elicited only by a small set of inborn releasers. However, as a result of associative learning experiences—essentially what later came to be known as classical conditioning (LeDoux, 1998; Watson, 1919)— all kinds of initially neutral stimuli can become learned elicitors of the inborn emotional reactions (James, 1884; see also McDougall, 1908/1860). Likewise, the reaction patterns can themselves become modified, within limits, as the result of learning (James, 1890/1950; see Reisenzein & Stephan, 2014).

Q5: What Are the Neural Structures and Processes Underlying Emotions?

To show that his psychological emotion theory was compatible with the then available neurophysiological knowledge, James (1884; 1890/1950) supplemented this theory with a sketch of the neural processes underlying the generation of emotions, resulting in what was perhaps the first neurophysiological model of emotion. According to James, at the neurophysiological level, the process of emotion generation can be described as follows: an object or event (e.g., an approaching bear) incites a sense organ (e.g., the eye). From there, afferent neural impulses travel to the sensory cortex, where they elicit a specific neural activation pattern that is the neurophysiological correlate of the perception of the object. Due to inherited or acquired neural connections, some sensory activation patterns (e.g., the pattern corresponding to the perception of a bear) activate one of several evolutionary bodily reaction programs located in the motor cortex (e.g., the "fear" reaction program). As a consequence, efferent impulses are sent to the inner organs and muscles of the body where they produce a complex, emotion-specific pattern of bodily changes (e.g., the fear pattern). These bodily changes are in turn registered by interoceptors in the viscera, skin, and muscles, whose signals are transmitted back to the sensory cortex, where they produce another neural activation pattern that is the neurophysiological correlate of an emotional feeling (e.g., fear). Hence, neurophysiologically speaking, emotions are simply special patterns of excitation in the sensory cortex caused by feedback from the bodily changes reflexively elicited by emotional stimuli.

Let us now look at what has been learned since James's times about the five questions of emotion psychology.

The Process of Emotion Generation
Worcester's Critique

Shortly after it had been proposed, James's theory of emotion came under heavy attack (see Gardiner, 1896). One of the objections raised concerned James's suggestion that emotions are elicited by sense perceptions in a reflex-like manner. Critics such as Worcester (1893) and Irons (1894) argued that this proposal conflicts with several well-known facts. Specifically, referring to James's example of a wanderer who feels fear upon encountering a bear, Worcester pointed out that a well-armed hunter might feel joy rather than fear when sighting a bear and that even an ordinary person might only feel curiosity if the bear were chained or caged. Worcester concluded from these cases that fear is not directly caused by sense perceptions but by certain thoughts to which these perceptions may give rise. Specifically, the wanderer feels afraid of the bear only if he believes that the bear may cause him bodily harm (Worcester, 1893, p. 287). In his response to Worcester's objection, James (1894) in effect conceded the point. Thereby, however, James accepted that, at least in the typical case, emotions are caused by cognitive processes, specifically by appraisals of objects as relevant to one's well-being (Arnold, 1960; see the next section). However, neither James nor Worcester clarified the cognitive processes involved in the generation of different emotions in more detail.

In fact, though, this issue had already been investigated in considerable detail in the cognitive tradition of emotion theorizing dating back to Aristotle (350 BC). In nineteenth-century introspective psychology, this tradition was represented by, among others, the cognitive emotion theories proposed by Alexius Meinong (1894) and Carl Stumpf (1899) (see Reisenzein, 2006; Reisenzein & Schönpflug, 1992). Unfortunately, however, these early cognitive emotion theories[1] became buried under the "behaviorist avalanche" (Leahey, 2003). It was only during the cognitive revolution of the early 1960s that the cognitive tradition of emotion theorizing was rediscovered (and partly reinvented) in psychology. The two theorists most responsible for this development were Magda B. Arnold (1960) and Richard S. Lazarus (1966), the pioneers of cognitive emotion theory in post-behaviorist psychology.

The Arnold-Lazarus Theory

Whereas James regarded the *phenomenal character* of emotions—the fact that it feels a particular way to have emotions—as their most salient feature and that most in need of explanation, Arnold (1960) focused on another property of emotions that had already been emphasized by James's contemporaries Meinong (1894) and Stumpf (1899; see also Irons, 1894): the *object-directedness of emotions* (the technical philosophical term is *intentionality*). Like some other mental states—the paradigmatic examples in this case are beliefs and desires—emotions are directed at objects: if one is happy, sad, or afraid, one is at least in the typical case (according to Arnold, even always) happy about something, sad about something, or afraid of something— or so emotions present themselves to the subject.

This *something* (which may not actually exist) is the intentional object of the emotion. For example, the object of fear of James's wanderer's—what he fears—is *that the bear might cause him bodily harm* (Worcester, 1893). As is the case for fear, the objects of most emotions are *states of affairs* (e.g., states, events, actions).

The object-directedness of emotions rather directly suggests that emotions presuppose cognitions of their objects (Arnold, 1960; Meinong, 1894). Arnold (1960) elaborated this idea by proposing that the cognitions required for an emotion directed at a state of affairs *p* are of two kinds: (a) *factual cognitions* about *p* (paradigmatically, these are beliefs concerning the existence and properties of *p*) and (b) an *evaluation* or *appraisal* of *p* as being good or bad for oneself. Paradigmatically, this appraisal is also a belief, namely, an evaluative belief, the belief that *p* is good or bad for oneself (in fact, appraisals were originally called "value judgments" by Arnold and Gasson, 1954).[2] Hence, for example, to feel joy about *p* (e.g., that Smith was elected as president), Mary must (at minimum) believe that *p* is the case (or, as Arnold [1960, p. 193] says, "is present") and evaluate *p* as good for oneself. Analogously, to experience sorrow about *p*, Mary must believe that *p* is the case and evaluate *p* as bad for herself. Furthermore, under normal circumstances (i.e., if Mary is awake, attentive, not under the influence of emotion-dampening drugs, etc.), the described cognitions are also sufficient for joy and sorrow to occur.

Although Arnold (1960) is not fully explicit on this point, it appears that she thought that the evaluation of an event as positive or negative is the outcome of a comparison of the event with one's goals or desires: events are positive if they are goal-congruent (fulfill a desire) and negative if they are goal-incongruent (frustrate a desire). This view of the appraisal process can be found in explicit form in Lazarus (1966) and has been adopted by most subsequent appraisal theorists (Reisenzein, 2006). However, this theory of the appraisal process implies that emotions presuppose not only beliefs (i.e., informational mental states) but also desires (i.e., motivational mental states), even though the latter are only indirect causes of the emotions: they are the standards to which facts are compared to determine whether they are good or bad.[3] The emotion itself, according to Arnold (and in contrast to James), is an experienced action tendency: a felt impulse to approach objects appraised as good or to avoid objects appraised as bad.

So far, I have only described Arnold's analysis of joy and sorrow. However, Arnold proposed that a parallel analysis is possible for all other emotions (at least all emotions having *states of affairs* [also called "propositions" by philosophers] as objects). Like joy and sorrow, these "propositional" emotions presuppose factual and evaluative beliefs about their objects; however, these beliefs differ more or less for the different emotions. Arnold elaborated this idea by proposing that the cognitions underlying the different emotions vary on (at least) three dimensions of appraisal,[4] two of which were already mentioned: *evaluation of the object* as good or bad for oneself (i.e., "appraisal" in the narrow meaning of the word), *presence-absence of the object*, and *the ease or difficulty to attain or avoid the object* or, as one can also say (with Lazarus, 1966), *coping potential*. As used by Arnold, *presence-absence* refers simultaneously to the subjective temporal location of a state of affairs and to the subjective certainty that it obtains: it contrasts subjectively present or past plus certain states of affairs with those that are subjectively future and still uncertain. *Coping potential* concerns the belief that the state of affairs in question (a) if still absent, is easy, difficult, or impossible to attain (positive state) or avoid (negative state); or (b) if already present, is easy, difficult, or impossible to keep (positive state) or to undo or adapt to (negative state). Note that this third appraisal dimension, like the second, refers to a factual belief. Different combinations of the possible values of the three appraisal dimensions give rise to different emotions. For example, according to Arnold (1960), joy is, precisely speaking, experienced if one believes that a positive state of affairs is present and can be easily maintained, whereas fear is experienced if one believes that a negative event might occur that one cannot prevent.

A very similar appraisal theory to that of Arnold was proposed by Lazarus (1966). As detailed in Reisenzein (2006), Lazarus essentially combined Arnold's first two appraisal dimensions into a single process that he called *primary appraisal* and renamed Arnold's third dimension *secondary appraisal*. However, even though Lazarus's (1966) original appraisal theory (for an expanded and revised version, see Lazarus, 1991) therefore did not go much beyond Arnold's, in contrast to Arnold, he supported his theory by a series of laboratory experiments (see Lazarus, 1966). These experimental studies did much to make appraisal theory scientifically respectable in psychology.

More Recent Appraisal Theories

Since the 1960s, the appraisal theory of emotion has become the dominant model of emotion generation in psychology. Over the years, however, the original version of the theory proposed by Arnold and Lazarus has been found wanting in various respects and, accordingly, improved appraisal theories have been proposed (e.g., Frijda, 1986; Ortony et al., 1988; Roseman, 1984; Scherer, 2001; Smith & Lazarus, 1990; for an overview, see Ellsworth & Scherer, 2003; and for a recent discussion, Moors, Ellsworth, Scherer, & Frijda, 2013). These newer appraisal theories share with the Arnold-Lazarus theory the basic assumption that emotions are products of factual and evaluative cognitions. However, unlike Arnold and Lazarus, they typically distinguish between different kinds of evaluations of the eliciting events (e.g., personally desirable/undesirable vs. morally good/bad) and postulate additional, as well as partly different, factual appraisals (e.g., probability of the event, unexpectedness of the event, and responsibility for the event). Perhaps the most elaborated, as well as the most systematic of the newer appraisal theories was proposed by Ortony et al. (1988). Ortony et al. specify the cognitions underlying 11 positive and 11 emotions and argue with some plausibility that other emotions are subspecies of these 22 emotions. The OCC model, as it is often referred to, has become the most widely used psychological template for computational models of emotion generation. Other more recent appraisal theories, such as those proposed by Smith and Lazarus (1990) and Scherer (2001), also seek to describe the computational processes of emotion generation in greater detail than Arnold and Lazarus did. A common assumption of these "process models" of appraisal is that appraisal processes can occur in several different *modes*, in particular as *nonautomatic* and as *automatic* processes. Whereas nonautomatic appraisal processes are akin to conscious inference strategies, automatic appraisals are assumed to be unconscious and to be triggered fairly directly by the perception of eliciting events. Like other cognitive processes, initially nonautomatic, conscious appraisals can become automatized as a result of their repeated execution (e.g., Reisenzein, 2001). Automatic appraisals can explain why emotions often rapidly follow their eliciting events.

Like the foundational appraisal theory of Lazarus (1966), the more recent appraisal theories have generated a sizable body of empirical research (e.g., Ellsworth & Scherer, 2003). Most of this research has been aimed at providing support for the assumption that different emotions are characterized by distinct patterns of appraisal composed from the values of a limited set of dimensions. This assumption has been reasonably well supported (Ellsworth & Scherer, 2003). However, in my view, the main reason for the success of appraisal theory has not been this and other empirical support for the theory but the fact that it agrees well with implicit common-sense psychology and has unmatched explanatory power (Reisenzein, 2006). Concerning the latter issue, it is simply hard to see *how else* than by assuming intervening cognitive processes of the kind assumed in appraisal theories (or in the belief desire theory of emotion; see Footnote 3), one could explain the following, basic facts of human emotions: (a) emotions are highly differentiated (there are many different emotions); (b) different individuals can react with entirely different emotions (e.g., joy vs. sorrow) to the same objective events (e.g., the victory of a soccer team); (c) the same emotion (e.g., joy) can be elicited by events that have objectively nothing in common (e.g., the victory of a soccer team and the arrival of a friend); (d) the same concrete emotional reaction (e.g., joy about the arrival of a friend) can be caused by information acquired in widely different ways (e.g., when seeing the friend approach, when hearing his voice, when being told by others that he has arrived); and (e) if a person's appraisals of an event changes, then in most cases her emotions about that event change as well.

Can Emotions Be "Noncognitively" Elicited?

Whereas the "cognitive path" to emotion described by cognitive emotion theories is generally acknowledged by today's emotion psychologists, the question of the existence or at least the practical importance of alternative "noncognitive" paths to emotion has given rise to a protracted debate (e.g., Lazarus, 1982; Leventhal & Scherer, 1987; Storbeck & Clore, 2007; Zajonc, 1980). This so-called cognition-emotion debate has suffered, among other things, from the failure to distinguish clearly between two different version of the hypothesis of "noncognitive" emotion generation: (a) the hypothesis that *certain kinds of emotion in the broad sense of the term*, such as sensory pleasures and displeasures or aesthetic feelings, are "noncognitively" caused; that is, they do not presuppose beliefs and desires but only nonpropositional and possibly even nonconceptual representations, such as certain visual patterns or sounds; and (b) the hypothesis that even *prototypical emotions* such as fear, anger, or joy can be (and perhaps even often are) noncognitively caused (e.g., that fear can be elicited by the sight of a dark moving form in the woods, without any mediating thoughts, as James [1890/1950] had claimed). Whereas the first hypothesis is plausible (Reisenzein, 2006), the second is more controversial: on closer inspection, the data that have been adduced to support this hypothesis turn out to be less convincing than is often claimed (see, e.g., Reisenzein, 2009*b*). Most of these data concern fear. For example, it has been argued that noncognitive fear elicitation is demonstrated by studies suggesting that physiological reactions can be elicited by subliminally presented emotional stimuli (e.g., Öhman & Mineka, 2001; see Storbeck & Clore, 2007, for a review). However, it is also possible that these physiological reactions are mediated by automatized and unconscious appraisal processes (e.g., Siemer & Reisenzein, 2007).

The Effects of Emotions

In contrast to James, common-sense psychology assumes that emotional feelings can have powerful effects on cognition and behavior. In fact, this belief is a main reason why emotions interest both lay people and scientists. As mentioned in the chapter's opening, psychologists have traditionally emphasized the negative, maladaptive effects of emotions; however, during the past 20 years or so, the view has increasingly gained acceptance that, notwithstanding their occasional negative consequences, emotions are overall (i.e., across all relevant situations) adaptive. The adaptive effects of emotions are their (evolutionary) *functions*—the reasons why the emotion mechanisms came into existence in the first place (e.g., Mitchell, 1995). However, although emotion psychologists today largely agree that emotions are functional, there is still only partial agreement on what the functional effects of emotions consist of (for overviews, see e.g., Frijda, 1994; Hudlicka, 2011). In what follows, I describe three main proposed functions of emotions concerning which there is reasonable consensus as well as empirical support: the attention-directing, informational, and motivational function of emotions.

The Attention-Directing Function of Emotions

According to this functional hypothesis, a primary function of emotions is to shift the focus of attention to their eliciting events; or,

computationally speaking, to allocate central processing resources to the analysis of these events and give them priority in information processing (e.g., Simon, 1967; Sloman, 1992; see also, Reisenzein, Meyer, & Niepel, 2012).

The Informational Function of Emotions

The informational or epistemic function of emotions consists in providing adaptively useful information to other cognitive (sub-)systems, including other agents. This information presumably concerns (a) the results of (unconscious) appraisal processes (e.g., Schwarz & Clore, 2007) or the occurrence of changes in the person's belief-desire system (Reisenzein, 2009*a*) and/or (b) closely related to this, information about the value of objects and events, including actions and their consequences (e.g., Damasio, 1994; Meinong, 1894; Slovic, Peters, Finucane, & MacGregor, 2005). To illustrate, nervousness experienced when meeting a stranger might function to inform the decision-making system about the subconscious appraisal of the encounter as threatening. Similarly, a pleasant feeling experienced when considering a possible course of action could serve to signal the subconscious approval of the action and mark it as a good one to choose. Empirical evidence for these informational effects (and possibly functions) of emotions can be found in Schwarz and Clore (2007) and Slovic et al. (2005). Analogously, the nonverbal and verbal communication of emotions could serve to convey this information to other agents.

The Motivational Function of Emotions

The motivational function of emotions consists of their adaptive effects on action goals. It has been argued that emotions serve both to reprioritize existing goals or intentions and to generate to new ones (e.g., Frijda, 1986; Oatley & Johnson-Laird, 1987). With respect to the generation of new goals, two main mechanisms have been proposed (Reisenzein, 1996). First, it has been proposed that emotions or their anticipation generate hedonistic desires (e.g., Baumeister, Vohs, DeWall, & Zhang, 2007; Mellers, 2000). This path from emotion to motivation is central in *hedonistic theories of motivation* (e.g., Bentham, 1789/1970; Cox & Klinger, 2004), which assume that one ultimate goal or basic motive of humans, if not their only basic motive, is the desire to maximize pleasure and to minimize pain (displeasure). This hedonistic motive can be activated both by currently experienced emotions and by emotions that are merely anticipated: negative feelings generate a desire to reduce them (if they are present) or to avoid them (if they are anticipated); analogously, positive feelings generate a desire to maintain them or to bring them about. It is widely assumed that hedonistic desires can also influence cognitive processes including appraisals. For example, the unpleasant feeling of fear elicited by a threatening event may motivate the person to avoid thinking about the event or to try to reappraise it in more benign terms (e.g., Gross, 1998; Lazarus, 1991).

There can be little doubt that emotions influence motivation partly through the hedonistic route (see, e.g., Baumeister et al., 2007). However, several emotion and motivation theorists have argued that this is not the only path from emotion to motivation. Rather, according to these theorists, at least some emotions evoke adaptive goals or action tendencies (e.g., fear causes the desire to flee, anger to aggress, pity to help) *directly*, that is, without the mediation of hedonistic desires (e.g., Frijda, 1986; Lazarus, 1991; McDougall, 1908/1960; Weiner, 1995; for a discussion, see Reisenzein, 1996). Conceivably, this nonhedonistic effect of emotions on motivation is based on their attention-directing and informational functions. The nonhedonistic theory of the emotion–action link may be better able than the hedonistic theory to explain the motivational effects of some emotions, such as the effect of pity on helping and of anger on aggression (Rudolph, Roesch, Greitemeyer, & Weiner, 2004).

The three described functions of emotions—the attention-directing, informational, and motivational functions—can be seen as contributing, in different ways, to a single overarching function of emotions: to improve the generation of adaptive intentional actions (at least in the evolutionary environment). To achieve this effect, emotions need to influence the motivational machinery that proximately controls actions. According to the standard view of action generation in psychology and other disciplines, actions are proximately caused by a mechanism whose inputs are the agent's desires (goals) and means-ends beliefs, and whose basic decision principle is that *agents attempt to do what they believe will lead to what they desire* (e.g., Bratman, 1987; Pollock, 1989).[5] These considerations suggest that—contrary to the claims of some emotion theorists (e.g., Bentham, 1789/1970; Damasio, 1994; McDougall, 1908/1960)—emotions are *not*

indispensable for the generation of adaptive actions, although "affect-free" actions may well be overall less adaptive than actions that are also informed by emotions.

The Nature of Emotion
Problems of Bodily Feeling Theory

The central assumption of James's theory concerns the nature of emotion: according to James, emotions are a class of sensations—the feelings of the bodily reactions generated by evolutionary emotion mechanisms. This assumption of James, too, immediately met with criticism (see Cannon, 1927; Gardiner, 1896; Stumpf, 1899). Two main objections were raised. The first was that this theory of the nature of emotion fails to account for other salient properties of emotion, in particular their object-directedness. This objection is considered later. The second objection was that James's theory even fails to account for the phenomenon it was primarily meant to explain, the phenomenal quality of emotions. The arguments that were advanced to support this second objection can be summarized in two main objections to James's explanation of emotional experience, one theoretical and the other empirical (see Reisenzein & Stephan, 2014). The *theoretical* objection was that James's theory is unable to explain in a noncircular way (i.e., without referring back to emotions) what distinguishes "emotional" bodily changes from nonemotional ones (e.g., a quickened pulse from running; Irons, 1894; Stumpf, 1899). The *empirical* objection was that, contrary to what James's theory implies, bodily feelings are neither necessary nor sufficient for emotion and do not match the subtle qualitative differences and intensity gradations of emotional experiences. A particularly convincing version of this objection—because it was supported by systematic experimental data—was published by Walter B. Cannon (1927). As a result, for many years, James's theory of emotion was widely regarded as having been refuted by Cannon.

However, in the wake of the renaissance of emotion research after the cognitive revolution of the 1960s, a number of emotion researchers argued that Cannon's criticisms were overdone and that a revised version of James's theory of the nature of emotion might, after all, be tenable. Accordingly, several more or less strongly modified versions of James's theory were proposed (e.g., Damasio, 1994; Laird, 1974; Schachter, 1964). In support of their views, the Neo-Jamesians refer to a variety of more recent empirical findings. The relatively most convincing of these are studies that suggest that experimentally induced physiological and expressive changes can, under certain circumstances, intensify emotional experiences (see Laird, 2007, for a summary). To illustrate, Strack, Martin, and Stepper (1988) found that when participants held a pen between their front teeth in a way that resulted in an expression resembling a smile, they judged cartoons to be funnier than in a no-smile control condition, suggesting that they felt more strongly amused. However, interesting as these findings are, they do not show that emotions are nothing but sensations of bodily (including facial) changes or even that bodily perceptions are necessary for emotions. In fact, other evidence suggests that this is not the case. In particular, studies of the emotional experiences of spinal cord-injured people, who have much reduced bodily feedback, suggest that their emotional life is largely intact (e.g., Cobos, Sánchez, Garcia, Vera, & Vila, 2002; see Reisenzein & Stephan, 2014). Similarly, studies on the effects of beta-adrenergic blocking agents (which specifically inhibit the reactivity of the cardiovascular system) on emotions typically failed to find reduced emotions in healthy subjects (e.g., Erdmann & van Lindern, 1980). Likewise, the experimental or natural reduction of facial feedback typically does not diminish emotional experience (see Reisenzein & Stephan, 2014).

Mental Feeling Theory

Although the available evidence suggests that emotional experiences are not (at very least not *only*) bodily sensations, James's more basic intuition, that the phenomenal quality of emotions is best explained by assuming that they are *sensation-like* mental states, remains forceful (Reisenzein, 2012). This intuition can be saved if one assumes that although emotions are indeed sensation-like feelings (or at least contain such feelings as components; see the next section), the emotional feelings are not created in the body but in the brain (e.g., Buck, 1985; Cannon, 1927; Oatley & Johnson-Laird, 1987; Wundt, 1896). The oldest and most prominent of these "mental" (as opposed to James's "bodily") feeling theories of emotion holds that emotions are feelings of pleasure and displeasure (e.g., Bentham, 1789/1970). Pleasure–displeasure theory was in fact the standard view of the phenomenal quality of emotional feelings in nineteenth-century psychology (e.g., Meinong, 1894; Wundt, 1896). Notwithstanding James's protest that this "hackneyed psychological doctrine... [is] one of the most artificial and scholastic of the untruths that disfigure our science" (James, 1894, p. 525), pleasure–displeasure theory is in fact much better established empirically than James's own theory of emotional experience (see, e.g., Mellers, 2000; Russell, 2003) and is today held, in some form, by many emotion researchers (e.g., Mellers, 2000; Ortony et al., 1998; Reisenzein, 2009b).

However, one must concede to James (1894) that, taken by itself, pleasure–displeasure theory cannot account for the qualitative distinctions among emotional experiences beyond positive–negative. As one attempt to overcome this problem of the theory, several theorists have postulated other mental feelings in addition to (or in place of; see Footnote 6) pleasure and displeasure. For example, Wundt (1896) proposed that (a) the centrally generated emotional feelings comprise not just pleasure–displeasure, but two more pairs of opposed (mutually exclusive) feeling qualities, excitement–quiescence and tension–relaxation, and that (b) emotions are different mixtures of these six "basic feelings" (e.g., anger is an unpleasant feeling also characterized, at least typically, by excitement and tension). In broad agreement with Wundt, contemporary "dimensional" theories of emotional experience (e.g., Russell, 2003; see also Reisenzein, 1994) assume that the feeling core of emotions consists of mixtures of pleasure or displeasure and (cortically produced) activation or deactivation (which corresponds approximately to Wundt's dimension of excitement–quiescence). Supportive evidence for this theory is summarized in Russell (2003).[6]

Cognition Feeling Theory

Although mental feeling theory is able to solve some problems of bodily feeling theory, it does not solve all. Two remaining problems are: (1) even if one assumes the existence of several different mental feeling qualities, this still does not explain the fine-grained distinctions among emotions, and (2), like the bodily feeling theory, the mental feeling theory has difficulties accounting for the object-directedness of emotions. To solve these problems, several feeling theorists proposed bringing in other mental elements into the emotion in addition to feelings. The most frequently proposed additional emotion components have been the cognitions (appraisals) by which the emotional feelings are caused (e.g., Lazarus, 1991; Oatley & Johnson-Laird, 1987; Schachter, 1964). According to the resulting "hybrid" cognition-feeling theory, emotional experiences are complex mental states that consist of feelings plus the appraisals that caused them. Because appraisals are undoubtedly finely differentiated, cognition feeling theory is able to solve the problem of emotion differentiation. It also seems to be able solve, at first sight at least, the problem of accounting for the object-directedness of emotions: According to cognition feeling theory, emotions have objects because they contain object-directed cognitions as components, and their objects are just the objects of these cognitions (but see Reisenzein, 2012, for objections to this idea).[7]

However, the "hybrid" cognition feeling theory is not the only option available to the feeling theorists. To solve the emotion differentiation problem, feeling theorists need not assume that cognitions are *components* of emotion; they can continue to regard them as the causes of emotions construed as sensation-like feelings but assume that emotions are partly distinguished by their causes (Reisenzein, 1994; 2012). For example, joy can be analyzed as a feeling of pleasure caused by the belief that a desire has been fulfilled, whereas pride can be analyzed as a feeling of pleasure caused by the belief that one has made an extraordinary achievement. With respect to the problem of accounting for the object-directedness of emotions, feeling theorists can argue that subjective impressions are misleading and that emotions do not really represent the objects at which they seem to be focused (e.g., Reisenzein, 2009a). For a discussion of these options, see Reisenzein (2012).

The Evolutionary Core of the Emotion System

In my discussion of the effects of emotion, I already referred to their adaptive effects or biological functions. The assumption that such functions exist implies that at least the core of the emotion system has been created by evolutionary processes, specifically through natural selection. This hypothesis is per se not very controversial among today's emotion psychologists; after all, presumably the cores of all mental subsystems (perception, cognition, motivation, emotion, etc.) were created by natural selection. Controversy starts, however, when it comes to specifying exactly what the evolutionary core of the emotion system consists of and, relatedly, to what degree and in which respects the emotion system is molded and moldable by learning. James's proposal was that the evolutionary core of the emotion system is a multimodular system consisting of a set of discrete emotion mechanisms,

each of which generates a distinct, "basic" emotion (see James, 1890/1950). The set of basic emotion mechanisms was not precisely enumerated by James, but he suggested that they comprise at least anger, fear, joy, grief, love, hate, and pride (see Reisenzein & Stephan, 2014). These evolutionary assumptions have turned out to be even more influential than James's views about the nature of emotional experience. However, this part of James's emotion theory, too, remained a sketch. It was left to William McDougall (1908/1860) to explicate it in the first book-length account of the evolutionary theory of discrete basic emotions.

McDougall's Theory of Discrete Basic Emotions

McDougall claimed that the biological core of the emotion system consists of a small set of modular information processing mechanisms—McDougall called them *instincts*—that developed during evolution because each solved a specific, recurrent adaptive problem. McDougall initially proposed seven basic instincts or emotion modules, including the fear module (or flight instinct), the disgust module (or instinct of repulsion), and the anger module (or instinct of pugnacity). Formulated in information processing terminology, each basic emotion module consists of a *detector* that monitors incoming sensory information and a *reaction program*. When the detector receives appropriate input—namely, information that indicates the presence of the adaptive problem that the module was designed by evolution to solve—the associated reaction program is triggered, which causes the occurrence of a coordinated pattern of mental and bodily responses. According to McDougall, this emotional reaction pattern comprises an emotion-specific action impulse, a specific pattern of bodily (in particular peripheral-physiological) reactions, and a specific kind of emotional experience (see Reisenzein, 2006).

McDougall was much more certain than James that the emotional mechanisms are adaptive. The central biological function of the emotion modules, he claimed, is motivational; that is, they serve to generate impulses for adaptive actions—actions that regularly solved the pertinent adaptive problem in the ancestral environment (e.g., avoidance of bodily injury in the case of fear or protection against poisoning in the case of disgust). Accordingly, the central output of the emotion modules is the action impulse (e.g., the impulse to flee in the case of fear or the impulse to reject offensive substances in the case of disgust). The remaining outputs of the emotion modules, including emotional experience, only serve to support, in one way or other, this main biological function.

According to McDougall, the internal configuration of the emotion modules—the connection between the detector and the reaction program—is "hardwired" and cannot be modified by experience and learning. Nevertheless, during individual development, the emotional system as a whole is greatly modified by learning processes that affect the inputs and outputs of the emotion modules: only very few of the elicitors of the emotion modules are innate; most are acquired. Likewise, although the emotional action impulses are innate, whether they are expressed in action or not—and if they are, to which concrete actions they lead—depends mostly on learning.

Modern Theories of Basic Emotions

Post-behaviorist emotion psychology saw not only a renaissance of cognitive and feeling theories of emotion, but also of evolutionary emotion theories. Most of these theories are modern variants of McDougall's (and James's) theory of discrete basic emotions (e.g., Ekman, 1972; Izard, 1971; Plutchik, 1980; Tooby & Cosmides, 1990). The more recent basic emotions theorists differ from McDougall mainly in that they ascribe a more important role to cognitive processes in the elicitation of emotions as well as, in some cases (e.g., Ekman, 1972; Izard, 1971), to the facial expression of emotion. Perhaps the best-known modern basic emotions theory was proposed by Ekman (1972, 1992). According to Ekman, there are at least six (but possibly up to 15; Ekman, 1992) basic emotion modules: joy, sadness, anger, disgust, fear, and surprise. When activated by suitable perceptions or appraisals, these inherited "affect programs" generate emotion-specific feelings, physiological reaction patterns, and an involuntary tendency to show a particular facial expression (e.g., smiling in the case of joy). However, this "instinctive" tendency need not result in a facial expression because it can be, and often is, voluntarily controlled in an attempt to comply with social norms that regulate emotional expression (so-called *display rules*).

Actually, the influence of the James-McDougall theory of discrete, biologically basic emotions extends far beyond the mentioned, contemporary evolutionary emotion theories because central assumptions of this theory have also found their way into some contemporary appraisal theories (e.g., Arnold, 1960; Lazarus, 1991; Roseman, 1984; see Reisenzein, 2006, for a discussion).

Are There Discrete Basic Emotions?

Given the prominence of the basic emotions view, it is important to realize that it is not the only possibly theory of the evolutionary architecture of the emotion system. The main alternative that has been proposed is that, rather than consisting of multiple discrete emotion modules, the emotion system consists of a small number of more basic mechanisms that produce *all* emotions. This idea, which is already implicit in some classic emotion theories (e.g., Wundt, 1896), has been developed in different ways by different contemporary theorists (e.g., Lang, 1995; Reisenzein, 2009a; Russell, 2003). To illustrate, one proposal is that the emotion system consists of but two mechanisms, one of which compares newly acquired beliefs with existing beliefs and another that compares newly acquired beliefs with existing desires; these mechanisms are assumed to generate sensation-like feelings (e.g., of pleasure and displeasure and of surprise) that combine to form different emotions (Reisenzein, 2009a; 2009b).

Since the 1960s, a great deal of empirical research has been devoted to answering the question of whether the emotion system consist of a multimodular system of discrete "basic emotion" modules. A central testable implication of basic emotions theory is that presumed biologically basic emotions are associated with distinct patterns of physiological and expressive responses (see Barrett, 2006). The comparatively best support for this hypothesis stems from cross-cultural studies of facial expression (e.g., Ekman, Friesen et al., 1987; for summaries, see Elfenbein & Ambady, 2002; Nelson & Russell, 2013). In these studies, judges were presented with photographs of prototypical facial expressions of basic emotions (typically Ekman's six) together with a list of the names of the emotions, and they were asked to indicate which emotion is expressed by which facial expression. Using this method, very high "correct" emotion classifications have been obtained (e.g., Ekman et al., 1987). However, Russell (1994) has pointed out that observer agreement on the expressed emotions is artifactually inflated in these studies. Furthermore, observer agreement decreases significantly with increasing distance to Western cultures (Nelson & Russell, 2013). In addition, being studies of emotion recognition, these investigations do not directly speak to the question of the production of emotional facial expressions, which is the more important test case for basic emotions theory. Recent reviews of studies of spontaneous facial expressions of emotions in laboratory experiments (Reisenzein, Studtmann, & Horstmann, 2013) and naturalistic field studies (Fernández-Dols & Crivelli, 2013) suggest that (a) with the exception of amusement, experiences of basic emotions are accompanied by their presumably characteristic facial expressions only in a minority of cases, and (b) low emotion intensity and attempts to control facial expressions are insufficient to explain the observed emotion–face dissociations. Studies of peripheral-physiological changes in emotions have found even less coherence between emotional experience and behavior (e.g., Mauss & Robinson, 2009). However, it can be argued that the best place look for evidence for basic emotion modules is the brain (cf. James, 1884). This issue is addressed in the next section.

The Neurophysiological Basis of Emotions
James versus Cannon
According to James (1884), the neurophysiological processes that underlie emotions are, in their entirety, ordinary sensory and motor processes in the neocortex. This assumption, too, was rejected by Cannon (1927) in his critique of James's theory. Indeed, brain lesion studies in cats by Cannon's coworker Bard (e.g., Bard, 1934; see also, Cannon, 1931) suggested that the programs for bodily reactions are not located in the motor cortex, as James had thought, but in what Cannon called the "thalamic region," a subcortical brain region comprising the thalamus, hypothalamus, and adjoining structures. Based on these and other findings, Cannon and Bard proposed that emotional experience and expression are generated *simultaneously* when an "affect program" in the thalamic region is activated. However, because Cannon's affect programs were, like those of James, programs for bodily reactions, James need not have been too much disconcerted by Cannon's neurophysiological model and could even have welcomed it as an alternative implementation proposal for his own emotion theory, one that accounted for several problematic findings (Cannon, 1927; Reisenzein & Stephan, 2014). However, another assumption of the Cannon-Bard theory—that physiological reactions are essentially emotion-unspecific—is incompatible with James's theory (Cannon, 1927). In fact, the lack of physiological response differentiation speaks against

any theory that assumes multiple discrete emotion mechanisms.

Limbic System Theory
This conclusion was incorporated in the next historically important neurophysiological emotion model, the limbic system theory proposed by Papez (1937) and MacLean (1952; 1973) (see Dalgleish, 2004, for a summary). The central assumption of this theory is that the neurophysiological basis of emotions, rather than consisting of a set of distinct emotion modules (as James and McDougall had assumed), is a single system—the *limbic system*. With this name, MacLean denoted a group of subcortical and cortical structures (including, among others, nuclei of the thalamus and hypothalamus, as well as the amygdala, on the subcortical side and the cingular cortex and hippocampus on the cortical side) that, he claimed, are tightly connected to each other but relatively isolated from the rest of the brain, in particular the neocortex, and hence form a neurophysiological module. In addition, MacLean proposed that the limbic system is a phylogenetically old part of the brain, whereas the neocortex is of comparatively recent origin.

The limbic system theory of emotion became highly influential; in fact, it dominated neurophysiological theorizing on emotions until the 1990s. Since then, however, the theory has been strongly criticized (e.g., Kotter & Meyer, 1992; LeDoux, 1998; 2012). The basic criticism is that, contrary to MacLean's claims, the structures subsumed under the name "limbic system" are neither neuroanatomically nor phylogenetically clearly distinct from the rest of the brain and hence do not really form a separate processing system. Furthermore, although some limbic system structures (e.g., the amygdala) certainly do play a role in emotions, others (e.g., the hippocampus) seem to have primarily cognitive functions (Dalgleish, 2004; LeDoux, 1998).

The demise of the limbic system theory has led some authors to conclude that some version of a multimodular, discrete basic emotions theory might after all be correct (e.g., LeDoux, 1998). But, of course, it is also possible that all emotions are produced by a single neural system that simply was not correctly described by limbic system theory (see also Arnold, 1960).

In Search of the Emotion Modules in the Brain
Since the 1980s, fostered by the development of new and improved methods of investigating brain

structure and brain activity (such as neuroimaging methods like functional magnetic resonance imaging [fMRI] and positron emission tomography [PET]), neurophysiological emotion research has been growing at an exponential rate. Much of this research has been inspired, indirectly or indirectly, by the discrete basic emotions theory proposed by Ekman and others and has sought to provide evidence for or against the emotion modules assumed by this theory. An important boost to the search for emotion modules in the brain was provided by LeDoux (e.g., 1998). Based on research with animals, LeDoux argued that the amygdala—one of the subcortical structures of MacLean's limbic system—is in fact the "hub in the wheel of fear" (LeDoux, 1998, p. 168), that is, the central structure of a neurophysiological fear module of the kind proposed by the basic emotion theorists. LeDoux's neurophysiological model of fear has been supported by studies that suggest that the amygdala is necessary for the acquisition and display of most (but not all) conditioned fear reactions in animals. Parallel findings have been reported for the conditioning of physiological fear reactions in humans (LeDoux, 1998; 2012).

However, more recent brain imaging research has found that the amygdala is not only activated by fear-related stimuli, but can also be activated by unpleasant pictures and odors and the induction of a sad mood (see Murphy, Nimmo-Smith, & Lawrence, 2003). Even some positive stimuli have been found to activate the amygdala (see Murphy et al., 2003). In addition, the amygdala has been found to respond to novel, unexpected stimuli, to which it rapidly habituates when they have no relevant consequences (Armony, 2013). Furthermore, there is so far no firm evidence that the amygdala is necessary for the *experience* of fear or other emotions. On the contrary, a study by Anderson and Phelps (2002) of people with lesions of the amygdala found no evidence for reduced emotional experience. Taken together, these findings suggest that the function of amygdala activation is not primarily the generation of fear, nor of negative emotions, nor of emotions in general. Rather, as suggested by a number of authors, the function of amygdala activation may be to support the focusing of attention on stimuli that are potentially motivationally relevant.

The fear theory of the amygdala is representative for several other recent claims of having detected modules for discrete basic emotions in the brain. For example, it has been claimed that the disgust module is localized in the insula, the sadness module in the subgenual anterior cingulate cortex, and the anger module in the orbitofrontal cortex (see Lindquist, Wager, Kober, Bliss-Moreau, & Barrett, 2012). As in the case of LeDoux's fear theory, subsequent research has found these claims to be premature. A recent comprehensive meta-analysis of brain imaging studies of emotion concludes that there is little evidence that discrete basic emotions can be localized to distinct brain regions (Lindquist et al., 2012). These data reinforce the doubts about discrete basic emotions theory raised by research on the expression of emotions reported earlier. For further discussion of the conclusions that might be drawn from the neurophysiological data, readers are referred to Lindquist et al. (2012) and LeDoux (2012).

Emotion Psychology and Affective Computing

Many of the theories and findings of emotion psychology discussed in this chapter have been taken up by affective computing researchers. In particular, psychological emotion theories have been the main source of inspiration for the development of computational emotion models, that are implemented in artificial agents to make them more socially intelligent and believable (see Lisetti, Amini, & Hudlicka, 2014). As blueprints for modeling the *emotion elicitation process*, psychological appraisal theories have so far been used nearly exclusively (see Gratch & Marsella, 2014), most often the theory of Ortony et al. (1988) (e.g., Becker & Wachsmuth, 2008). However, other appraisal theories have also been computationally implemented: Gratch and Marsella (2004) used Lazarus's (1991) appraisal theory as the psychological basis of their computational emotion model; and Marinier, Laird, and Lewis (2009) used the appraisal theory proposed by Scherer (2001). In these models, the computed appraisal of a situation are either treated as causes of the emotion, which is for example conceptualized as a mixture of pleasure-displeasure and activation-deactivation (e.g., Becker-Asano & Wachsmuth 2008); or the appraisal pattern is implicitly identified with the emotion (e. g., Gratch and Marsella 2004).

Psychological emotion theories and empirical findings about emotions have also been a decisive source of information for modelling of the *effects of emotions* in artificial agents (see also, Lisetti et al., 2014). Most existing emotional software- and hardware agents model the effect of emotions on expressive behavior such as facial expressions (see Section 3 of this handbook). Here, Ekman's (1992) theory of basic emotions has had a particularly strong influence. However, the effects of emotions on actions proposed in some psychological emotion theories have been modeled as well. For example, Gratch and Marsella (2004)'s EMA model implements a hedonic regulation mechanism: Negative emotions initiate coping actions aimed at changing the environment in such a way that the negative emotions are reduced or mitigated. In addition, the effects of emotions on subsequent cognitions (appraisals) are modeled in EMA and some other emotional agents: They influence both the content of information processing and the way, or strategies of information processing (e g. the depth of future projection in the planning of actions), as well as on the cognitive content (e.g, wishful thinking and resignation).

Although the transfer of concepts has so far mainly been from emotion psychology to affective computing, a reverse influence is becoming increasingly apparent. Indeed, affective computing has much to offer to emotion psychology, both to theory and research methods. Regarding theory, computational emotion models constructed by affective computing researchers can help to clarify and concretize psychological emotion models. Regarding research methods, social simulations populated by artificial agents have the potential of becoming an important method for inducing emotions and studying their effects in social interactions; and automatic methods of affect detection from expression, speech and action (see Section 2 of this Handbook) are likely to become important tools of measuring emotions

Notes

1. In contemporary psychology, the term "cognitive emotion theory" is typically used to denote any emotion theory that assumes that cognitions—paradigmatically, beliefs, in particular evaluative beliefs—are necessary conditions for emotions, even if they are only regarded as causally rather than constitutionally necessary for emotions. In contrast, in contemporary philosophy, the term "cognitive emotion theory" is typically used in a narrower sense to denote emotion theories that claim that emotions *are* cognitions (of a certain kind; typically evaluative beliefs) or *contain* such cognitions as components, thus implying not only that emotions are intentional (object-directed, or representational) mental states, but also, that they are more specifically cognitive (information-providing) mental states (see Reisenzein & Döring, 2009).

2. However, Arnold (1960) subsequently argued that appraisals are a *special kind* of value judgments; in particular, she claimed that they are similar to sense-judgments in being "direct, immediate, nonreflexive, nonintellectual, instinctive, and intuitive"(p. 175). See also Kappas (2006).

3. An alternative version of cognitive emotion theory, the belief-desire theory of emotion, holds that emotions are directly caused by factual beliefs and desires, without intervening appraisals (evaluative beliefs). For example, according to this theory, Mary's joy about Smith's election as president is directly caused by the belief that Smith was elected and the desire that he should be elected. Arguments for the belief-desire theory are summarized in Reisenzein (2009*a*, 2009*b*; see also Castelfranchi & Miceli, 2009; Green, 1992). In this chapter, I follow the mainstream of cognitive emotion theory in psychology, i.e., appraisal theory. Those who find the belief-desire account more plausible should note that it is possible to reformulate (although with a corresponding change of meaning) most of appraisal theory in the belief-desire framework (see, e.g., Adam, Herzig, & Longin, 2009; Reisenzein, Hudlicka et al., 2013; Steunebrink, Dastani, & Meyer, 2012).

4. Note that "appraisal" is here used in a broad sense that includes all emotion-relevant factual and evaluative cognitions. In a narrow meaning, "appraisal" refers to evaluations only.

5. Psychological decision theories (e.g., Ajzen. 1991; Kahneman & Tversky, 1979) can be regarded as quantitatively refined versions of this qualitative belief-desire theory of action (see Reisenzein, 1996).

6. Another version of mental feeling theory postulates several distinct, unanalyzable mental feelings corresponding to presumed biologically basic emotions, such as joy, sadness, fear, anger, and disgust (e.g., Oatley & Johnson-Laird, 1987; see also Buck, 1985). On a broad understanding of "mental feelings," one can also subsume in the category of mental feeling theories the proposal that emotions are felt action tendencies (e.g., Arnold, 1960; Frijda, 1986). However, both of these versions of mental feeling theory have to cope with a number of problems (Reisenzein, 1995; 1996).

7. Impressed by the apparent ability of cognitions (appraisals) to explain the differentiation and object-directedness of emotions, several emotion theorists—mostly in philosophy—have proposed that emotional experiences are simply conscious evaluations (e.g., Nussbaum, 2001; Solomon, 1976). However, this "radically cognitive" theory of the nature of emotions has its own serious problems. In particular, it fails to provide a plausible explanation of the phenomenal quality of emotional experiences (see Reisenzein, 2012).

References

Adam, C., Herzig, A., & Longin, D. (2009). A logical formalization of the OCC theory of emotions. *Synthese, 168*, 201–248.

Ajzen, I. (1991). The theory of planned behavior. *Organizational Behavior and Human Decision Processes, 50*, 179–211.

Anderson, A. K., & Phelps, E. A. (2002). Is the human amygdala critical for the subjective experience of emotion? Evidence of intact dispositional affect in patients with amygdala lesions. *Journal of Cognitive Neuroscience, 14*, 709–720.

Aristotle. (350 bc /1980). *Rhetorik [Rhetoric]*. München: Fink.

Armony, J. L. (2013). Current emotion research in behavioral neuroscience: The role of the amygdala. *Emotion Review, 5*, 104–115.

Arnold, M. B. (1960). *Emotion and personality* (Vols. 1 & 2). New York: Columbia University Press.

Arnold, M. B., & Gasson, S. J. (1954). Feelings and emotions as dynamic factors in personality integration. In M. B. Arnold

(Ed.), *The human person: An approach to an integral theory of personality* (pp. 294–313). New York: Ronald Press.

Bard, P. (1934). On emotional expression after decortication with some remarks on certain theoretical views. *Psychological Review, 41,* 309–329 (Part I), 424–449 (Part II).

Barrett, L. F. (2006). Are emotions natural kinds? *Perspectives on Psychological Science, 1,* 28–58.

Baumeister, R. F., Vohs, K. D., DeWall, C. N., & Zhang, L. (2007). How emotion shapes behavior: Feedback, anticipation, and reflection, rather than direct causation. *Personality and Social Psychology Review, 11,* 167–203.

Becker-Asano, C., & Wachsmuth, I. (2008): Affect simulation with primary and secondary emotions. *Intelligent Virtual Agents, 8,* 15–28.

Bentham, J. (1789/1970). *An introduction to the principles of morals and legislation.* London: Athlone Press. (Original work published 1789).

Bratman, M. E. (1987). *Intentions, plans, and practical reason.* Cambridge, MA: Harvard University Press.

Brentano, F. (1973). *Psychologie vom empirischen Standpunkt [Psychology from the empirical standpoint].* O. Kraus (Ed.). Hamburg: Meiner. (Original work published 1874).

Buck, R. (1985). Prime theory: An integrated view of motivation and emotion. *Psychological Review, 92,* 389–413.

Cannon, W. B. (1927). The James-Lange theory of emotion: A critical examination and an alternative theory. *American Journal of Psychology, 39,* 106–124.

Cannon, W. B. (1931). Again the James-Lange and the thalamic theories of emotion. *Psychological Review, 38,* 281–295.

Castelfranchi, C., & Miceli, M. (2009). The cognitive-motivational compound of emotional experience. *Emotion Review, 1,* 223–231.

Cobos, P., Sánchez, M., Garcia, C., Vera, M., & Vila, J. (2002). Revisiting the James versus Cannon debate on emotion: startle and autonomic modulation in patients with spinal cord injuries. *Biological Psychology, 61,* 251–269.

Cox, W. M., & Klinger, E. (2004). *Handbook of motivational counseling.* Chichester, UK: Wiley.

Dalgleish, T. (2004). The emotional brain. *Nature Reviews Neuroscience, 5,* 582–585.

Damasio, A. R. (1994). *Descartes' error.* New York: Avon.

Ekman, P. (1972). Universals and cultural differences in facial expressions of emotion. In J. K. Cole (Ed.), *Nebraska symposium on motivation* (Vol. *19,* pp. 207–283). Lincoln, NE: University of Nebraska Press.

Ekman, P. (1992). An argument for basic emotions. *Cognition and Emotion, 6,* 169–200.

Ekman, P., Friesen, W. V., et al. (1987). Universals and cultural differences in the judgments of facial expressions of emotions. *Journal of Personality and Social Psychology, 53,* 712–717.

Elfenbein, H. A., & Ambady, N. (2002). On the universality and cultural specificity of emotion recognition: A meta-analysis. *Psychological Bulletin, 128,* 203–235.

Ellsworth, P. C., & Scherer, K. R. (2003). Appraisal processes in emotion. In R. J. Davidson, K. R. Scherer, & H. H. Goldsmith (Eds.), *Handbook of affective sciences* (pp. 572–595). Oxford: Oxford University Press.

Erdmann, G., & van Lindern, B. (1980). The effects of beta-adrenergic stimulation and beta-adrenergic blockade on emotional reactions. *Psychophysiology, 17,* 332–338.

Feldman Barrett, L., & Salovey, P. (2002). *The wisdom in feeling. Psychological processes in emotional intelligence.* New York: Guilford Press.

Fernández-Dols, J. M., & Crivelli, C. (2013). Emotion and Expression: Naturalistic studies. *Emotion Review, 5,* 24–29.

Frijda, N. H. (1986). *The emotions.* Cambridge, UK: Cambridge University Press.

Frijda, N. H. (1994). Emotions are functional, most of the time. In P. Ekman & R. J. Davidson (Eds.), *The nature of emotion* (pp. 112–136). New York: Oxford University Press.

Gardiner, H. N. (1896). Recent discussion of emotion. *Philosophical Review, 5,* 102–112.

Gratch, J., & Marsella, S. (2004). A domain independent framework for modeling emotion. *Journal of Cognitive Systems Research, 5,* 269–306.

Gratch, J., & Marsella, S. (2014). Appraisal models. In Calvo, R. A., D'Mello, S. K., Gratch, J., & Kappas, A. (Eds.) Handbook of Affective Computing. Oxford: Oxford University press.

Gray, J. A. (1975). *Elements of a two-process theory of learning.* London: Academic Press.

Green, O. H. (1992). *The emotions. A philosophical theory.* Dordrecht: Kluwer.

Gross, J. J. (1998). The emerging field of emotion regulation: An integrative review. *Review of General Psychology, 2,* 271–299.

Hudlicka, E. (2011). Guidelines for developing computational models of emotions. *International Journal of Synthetic Emotions, 2,* 26–79.

Irons, D. (1894). Professor James' theory of emotion. *Mind, 3,* 77–97.

Izard, C. E. (1971). *The face of emotion.* New York: Appleton-Century Crofts.

James, W. (1884). What is an emotion? *Mind, 9,* 188–205.

James, W. (1894). The physical basis of emotion. *Psychological Review, 1,* 516–529.

James, W. (1890/1950). *Principles of psychology* (vols. 1 & 2). New York: Dover. (Original work published 1890).

Kahneman, D., & Tversky, A. (1979). Prospect theory: An analysis of decision under risk. *Econometrica, 47,* 263–291.

Kappas, A. (2006). Appraisals are direct, immediate, intuitive, and unwitting…and some are reflective. *Cognition and Emotion, 20,* 952–975.

Kotter, R., & Meyer, N. (1992). The limbic system: a review of its empirical foundation. *Behavioral Brain Research, 52,* 105–127.

Laird, J. D. (1974). Self-attribution of emotion. *Journal of Personality and Social Psychology, 29,* 475–486.

Laird, J. D. (2007). *Feelings: The perception of self.* New York: Oxford University Press.

Lang, P. J. (1995). The emotion probe: Studies of motivation and attention. *American Psychologist, 50,* 372–385.

Lazarus, R. S. (1966). *Psychological stress and the coping process.* New York: McGraw-Hill.

Lazarus, R. S. (1982). Thoughts on the relations between emotion and cognition. *American Psychologist, 37,* 1019–1024.

Lazarus, R. S. (1991). *Emotion and adaptation.* New York: Oxford University Press.

Leahey, T. H. (2003). *A history of psychology: Main currents in psychological thought* (2nd ed.). Englewood Cliffs, NJ: Prentice-Hall.

LeDoux, J. E. (1998). *The emotional brain: The mysterious underpinnings of emotional life.* New York: Simon & Schuster.

LeDoux, J. E. (2012). Rethinking the emotional brain. *Neuron, 73,* 653–676.

Leventhal, H., & Scherer, K. R. (1987). The relationship of emotion and cognition: A functional approach to a semantic controversy. *Cognition and Emotion, 1*, 3–28.

Lindquist, K. A., Wager, T. D., Kober, H., Bliss-Moreau, E., & Barrett, L. F. (2012). The brain basis of emotion: A meta-analytic review. *Behavioral and Brain Sciences, 35*, 121–143.

Lisetti, C., Amini, R., & Hudlicka, E. (2014). Emotion-based agent architectures. In Calvo, R. A., D'Mello, S. K., Gratch, J., & Kappas, A. (Eds.) Handbook of Affective Computing. Oxford: Oxford University press.

MacLean, P. D. (1952). Some psychiatric implications of physiological studies on frontotemporal portion of limbic system (visceral brain). *Electroencephalography and Clinical Neurophysiology, 4*, 407–418.

MacLean, P. D. (1973). *A triune concept of the brain and behavior.* Toronto: University of Toronto Press.

Marinier, R., Laird, J., & Lewis, R. (2009). A computational unification of cognitive behavior and emotion. *Journal of Cognitive Systems Research, 10*, 48–69.

Mauss, I. B., & Robinson, M. D. (2009). Measures of emotion: A review. *Cognition and Emotion, 23*, 209–237.

McDougall, W. (1908/1960). *An introduction to social psychology.* London: Methuen.

Meinong, A. (1894). *Psychologisch-ethische Untersuchungen zur Werttheorie* [Psychological-ethical investigations concerning the theory of value]. Graz: Leuschner & Lubensky. Reprinted in R. Haller & R. Kindinger (Hg.) (1968), *Alexius Meinong Gesamtausgabe Band III* (S. 3–244). Graz: Akademische Druck—und Verlagsanstalt.

Mellers, B. A. (2000). Choice and the relative pleasure of consequences. *Psychological Bulletin, 126*, 910–924.

Mitchell, S. (1995). Function, fitness and disposition. *Biology and Philosophy, 10*, 39–54.

Moors, A., Ellsworth, P. C., Scherer, K. R., & Frijda, N. H. (2013). Appraisal theories of emotion: State of the art and future development. *Emotion Review, 5*, 119–124.

Murphy, F. C., & Nimmo-Smith, I., & Lawrence, A. D. (2003). Functional neuroanatomy of emotions: A meta-analysis. *Cognitive, Affective, & Behavioral Neurosciences, 3*, 207–233.

Nelson, N. L., & Russell, J. A. (2013). Universality revisited. *Emotion Review, 5*, 8–15.

Nussbaum, M. C. (2001). *Upheavals of thought: The intelligence of emotions.* Cambridge, UK: Cambridge University Press.

Oatley, K., & Johnson-Laird, P. N. (1987). Towards a cognitive theory of emotions. *Cognition and Emotion, 1*, 29–50.

Öhman, A., & Mineka, S. (2001). Fears, phobias, and preparedness: Toward an evolved module of fear and fear learning. *Psychological Review, 108*, 483–522.

Ortony, A., Clore, G. L., & Collins, A. (1988). *The cognitive structure of emotions.* Cambridge, UK: Cambridge University Press.

Papez, J. W. (1937). A proposed mechanism of emotion. *Archives of Neurological Psychiatry, 38*, 725–743.

Picard, R. W. (1997). *Affective computing.* Cambridge, MA: MIT Press.

Plutchik, R. (1980). *Emotion. A psychoevolutionary synthesis.* New York: Harper & Row.

Pollock, J. L. (1989). OSCAR: A general theory of rationality. *Journal of Experimental and Theoretical Artificial Intelligence, 1*, 209–226.

Reisenzein, R. (1994). Pleasure-arousal theory and the intensity of emotions. *Journal of Personality and Social Psychology, 67*, 525–539.

Reisenzein, R. (1995). On Oatley and Johnson-Laird's theory of emotions and hierarchical structures in the affective lexicon. *Cognition and Emotion, 9*, 383–416.

Reisenzein, R. (1996). Emotional action generation. In W. Battmann & S. Dutke (Eds.), *Processes of the molar regulation of behavior* (pp. 151–165). Lengerich, DE: Pabst Science Publishers.

Reisenzein, R. (2001). Appraisal processes conceptualized from a schema-theoretic perspective: Contributions to a process analysis of emotions. In K. R. Scherer, A. Schorr & T. Johnstone (Eds.), *Appraisal processes in emotion: Theory, methods, research* (pp. 3–19). Oxford: Oxford University Press.

Reisenzein, R. (2006). Arnold's theory of emotion in historical perspective. *Cognition and Emotion, 20*, 920–951.

Reisenzein, R. (2009a). Emotions as metarepresentational states of mind: Naturalizing the belief-desire theory of emotion. *Cognitive Systems Research, 10*, 6–20.

Reisenzein, R. (2009b). Emotional experience in the computational belief-desire theory of emotion. *Emotion Review, 1*, 214–222.

Reisenzein, R. (2012). What is an emotion in the belief-desire theory of emotion? In F. Paglieri, L. Tummolini, R. Falcone, & M. Miceli (Eds.), *The goals of cognition: Essays in honor of Cristiano Castelfranchi* (pp. 181–211). London: College Publications.

Reisenzein, R., & Döring, S. (2009). Ten perspectives on emotional experience: Introduction to the special issue. *Emotion Review, 1*, 195–205.

Reisenzein, R., & Horstmann, G. (2006). Emotion [emotion]. In H. Spada (Ed.), *Lehrbuch Allgemeine Psychologie [Textbook of general psychology]* (3rd ed., pp. 435–500). Bern, CH: Huber.

Reisenzein, R., Hudlicka, E., Dastani, M., Gratch, J., Lorini, E., Hindriks, K., & Meyer, J.-J. (2013). Computational modeling of emotion: Towards improving the inter—and intradisciplinary exchange. *IEEE Transactions on Affective Computing, 4*, 246–266. http://doi.ieeecomputersociety.org/10.1109/T-AFFC.2013.14

Reisenzein, R., Meyer, W.-U., & Niepel, M. (2012). Surprise. In V. S. Rachmandran (Hrsg.), *Encyclopedia of human behavior* (2nd ed., pp. 564–570). London.

Reisenzein, R., & Stephan, S. (2014). More on James and the physical basis of emotion. *Emotion Review, 6*, 35–46.

Reisenzein, R., & Schönpflug, W. (1992). Stumpf's cognitive-evaluative theory of emotion. *American Psychologist, 47*, 34–45.

Reisenzein, R., Studtmann, M., & Horstmann, G. (2013). Coherence between emotion and facial expression: Evidence from laboratory experiments. *Emotion Review, 5*, 16–23.

Roberts, R. C. (2013). Emotions in the moral life. Cambridge, UK: Cambridge University Press.

Roseman, I. J. (1984). Cognitive determinants of emotion: A structural theory. In P. Shaver (Ed.), *Review of personality and social psychology* (Vol. 5, pp. 11–36). Beverly Hills, CA: Sage.

Rudolph, U., Roesch, S., Greitemeyer, T., & Weiner, B. (2004). A meta-analytic review of help giving and aggression from an attributional perspective: Contributions to a general theory of motivation. *Cognition and Emotion, 18*, 815–848.

Russell, J. A. (1994). Is there universal recognition of emotion from facial expression? A review of the cross-cultural studies. *Psychological Bulletin, 115*, 102–141.

Russell, J. A. (2003). Core affect and the psychological construction of emotion. *Psychological Review, 110*, 145–172.

Schachter, S. (1964). The interaction of cognitive and physiological determinants of emotional state. In L. Berkowitz (Ed.), *Advances in experimental social psychology* (Vol. *1*, pp. 49–80). New York: Academic Press.

Scherer, K. R. (2001). Appraisal considered as a process of multilevel sequential checking. In Scherer, K. R., Schorr, A., & Johnstone, T. (Eds.), *Appraisal processes in emotion: Theory, methods, research* (pp. 92–129). Oxford: Oxford University Press.

Scherer, K. R. (2009). Affective science. In D. Sander & K. R. Scherer (Eds.), *Oxford companion to emotion and the affective sciences* (pp. 16–17). Oxford: Oxford University Press.

Schwarz, N., & Clore, G. L. (2007). Feelings and phenomenal experiences. In E. T. Higgins & A. W. Kruglanski (Eds.), *Social psychology: Handbook of basic principles* (2nd ed., pp. 385–407). New York: Guilford.

Siemer, M., & Reisenzein, R. (2007). Appraisals and emotions: Can you have one without the other? *Emotion, 7*, 26–29.

Simon, H. A. (1967). Motivational and emotional controls of cognition. *Psychological Review, 74*, 29–39.

Sloman, A. (1992). Prolegomena to a theory of communication and affect. In A. Ortony, J. Slack, & O. Stock (Eds.), *Communication from an artificial intelligence perspective: Theoretical and applied issues* (pp. 229–260). Heidelberg, DE: Springer.

Slovic, P., Peters, E., Finucane, M. L., & MacGregor, D. G. (2005). Affect, risk, and decision making. *Health Psychology, 24*, 35–40.

Smith, C. A., & Lazarus, R. S. (1990). Emotion and adaptation. In L. Pervin (Ed.), *Handbook of personality: Theory and research* (pp. 609–637). New York: Guilford.

Solomon, R. C. (1976). *The passions.* Garden City, NY: Anchor Press/Doubleday.

Steunebrink, B. R., Dastani, M., & Meyer, J.-J. Ch. (2012). A formal model of emotion triggers: An approach for BDI agents. *Synthese, 185*, 83–129.

Storbeck, J., & Clore, G. L. (2007). On the interdependence of cognition and emotion. *Cognition & Emotion, 21*, 1212–1237.

Strack, F., Martin, L. L., & Stepper, S. (1988). Inhibiting and facilitating conditions of the human smile: A nonobtrusive test of the facial feedback hypothesis. *Journal of Personality and Social Psychology, 54*, 768–777.

Strongman, K. T. (2003). *The psychology of emotion: From everyday life to theory* (5th ed.). New York: Wiley.

Stumpf, C. (1899). Über den Begriff der Gemüthsbewegung [On the concept of emotion]. *Zeitschrift für Psychologie und Physiologie der Sinnesorgane, 21*, 47–99.

Tooby, J., & Cosmides, L. (1990). The past explains the present: Emotional adaptations and the structure of ancestral environments. *Ethology and Sociobiology, 11*, 375–424.

Watson, J. B. (1919). *Psychology from the standpoint of a behaviorist.* Philadelphia, PA: Lippincott.

Weiner, B. (1995). *Judgments of responsibility. A foundation for a theory of social conduct.* New York: Guilford.

Worcester, W. L. (1893). Observations on some points in James's psychology. II. Emotion. *Monist, 3*, 285–298.

Wundt, W. (1896). *Grundriss der psychologie [Outlines of psychology].* Leipzig: Engelmann.

Zajonc, R. B. (1980). Feeling and thinking: Preferences need no inferences. *American Psychologist, 35*, 151–175.

Neuroscientific Perspectives of Emotion

Andrew H. Kemp, Jonathan Krygier, *and* Eddie Harmon-Jones

Abstract

Emotion is often defined as a multicomponent response to a significant stimulus characterized by brain and body arousal and a subjective feeling state, eliciting a tendency toward motivated action. This chapter reviews the neuroscience of emotion, and the basis for the 'Great Emotion Debate' between the psychological constructionists and the basic emotion theorists. The authors adopt an embodied cognition perspective, highlighting the importance of the whole body—not just the brain—to better understand the biological basis of emotion and drawing on influential theories, including Polyvagal Theory and the Somatic Marker Hypothesis, which emphasize the importance of bidirectional communication between viscera and brain, and the impact of visceral responses on subjective feeling state and decision making, respectively. Embodied cognition has important implications for understanding emotion as well as the benefits of exercise, yoga, and meditation. The authors emphasise the need for research that draws on affective computing principles and focuses on objective measures of body and brain to further elucidate the specificity of different emotional states.

Key Words: basic emotions, natural kinds, psychological constructionism, emotion specificity, embodied cognition, psychophysiology, neuroimaging

Introduction

Bidirectional projections underpin emotional experience, such that the brain impacts on the body via visceral efferent pathways and the body impacts on the brain through afferent feedback. Take, for example, the case of laughter yoga, an activity that involves groups of people getting together to…laugh! Initially, the experience is awkward and forced, but very soon—with the help of yogic breathing techniques and physical movement—the forced laughter becomes spontaneous and contagious. Laughter is not unique to our species: Jaak Panksepp's work on rodent tickling indicates that 50-kHz chirping (laughter?) may be an evolutionary antecedent of human joy (Panksepp, 2005; Panksepp & Burgdorf, 2000; 2003). This research, along with that of others (Wild, Rodden, Grodd, &

Ruch, 2003), suggests that laughter may depend on two partially independent neuronal pathways: an "involuntary," emotionally driven subcortical system and a cortical network that supports the human capacity for verbal joking. Laughter is an excellent example of the impact of the body on emotion experience, highlighting that laughter is possible without humor or cognitive thought. Although autonomic activation normally colors our subjective experience, in some cases, it is able to actually drive the emotions we experience.

Psychological research indicates that voluntary contraction of facial muscles contributes to emotional experience (Strack, Martin, & Stepper, 1988). Participants who hold a pencil with their lips, forcing their face to prevent or inhibit a smile, rate cartoons as less amusing than participants who hold a pencil in their teeth, mimicking a smile. Similarly, participants trained to produce typical emotional expressions muscle by muscle report subjective emotional experience and display specific physiological changes (Levenson, Ekman, & Friesen, 1990). More recent studies on botulinum toxin (or "botox") have shown that injection to the glabellar region—the space between the eyebrows and above the nose—to inhibit the activity of the corrugator and procerus muscles reduces the experience of fear and sadness in healthy females (Lewis & Bowler, 2009). Another study (Wollmer et al., 2012) on patients with major depressive disorder has even reported that glabellar botulinum toxin treatment is associated with a 47% reduction in depression severity over a 6-week treatment period (relative to only 9.2% in placebo-treated participants). These surprising findings are supported by current influential neuroscientific theories of emotion (Damasio, 1994; Porges, 1995; 2011; Reimann & Bechara, 2010; Thayer & Lane, 2000; 2009) that explicitly incorporate brain–body interactions into formal models.

Here, we emphasize the importance of an "embodied cognition" perspective in order to better understand the biological basis for emotion. Emotion is often defined as a multicomponent response to a significant stimulus characterized by brain and bodily arousal and a subjective feeling state that elicits a tendency toward motivated action. Note however, that there may be instances of emotion in which significant stimulus (cf., emotions without obvious causes), subjective feeling state (cf., unconscious emotions), and motivated action (cf., sadness) are not necessary. In this review, we first describe the role of several key brain regions in regards to emotion processing. These include the prefrontal cortex (PFC; involved in emotional experience and its regulation), amygdala (stimulus salience and motivational significance), anterior cingulate (selection of stimuli for further processing), and insula (feelings and consciousness). We then describe a major intellectual stalemate that has arisen with respect to understanding how different emotions arise. This is the debate over whether the basic emotions are "natural kinds" versus a product of "psychological construction." We suggest that one of the reasons for the difficulty in resolving this debate is the tendency to draw conclusions from different theoretical standpoints and experimental approaches. For example, recent efforts to understand human emotion may be characterized by a neurocentric approach arising from the wide

use of functional magnetic resonance imaging (fMRI). This technique, however, has its limitations in regards to advancing our knowledge of emotion. Critically, it is often not clear whether emotional experiences are being evoked by the weak emotional stimuli that are often used in the scanner. Furthermore, fMRI studies require participants to remain in a supine body position during emotion elicitation, yet research has revealed that such a position reduces emotional responses (e.g., asymmetric frontal cortical activity as well as amygdala activity measured with other techniques) to appetitive emotional stimuli (Harmon-Jones, Gable, & Price, 2011; Price, Dieckman, & Harmon-Jones, 2012). (Readers interested in further details on neuroscientific approaches to affect detection are referred to Chapter 17).

There are many challenges to determining emotional specificity and correctly detecting the specificity of emotions. Interested readers are referred to excellent reviews by Calvo & D'Mello, 2010, and Fairclough, 2009. We conclude this review by highlighting the need for research that produce stronger manipulations of affective experiences, draws on affective computing principles, and employs multiple physiological and behavioral response systems under different conditions. We suggest that a multimodal approach to affective neuroscience may help to resolve the debate over whether the brain and body produce emotions as "natural kinds" or as "psychological constructions."

The Emotional Brain

Specific brain regions including the PFC, amygdala, anterior cingulate, and insula play a major role in the neurobiological basis of emotion. These regions and their interconnectivity are briefly described here.

The Prefrontal Cortex

The PFC is the most anterior part of the frontal lobes and is generally considered to play a primary role in higher order cognitive activity, judgment, and planning. However, contemporary neuroscientific views of emotion highlight a role of the PFC in emotional experience, motivation, and its regulation. The PFC is comprised of a number of discrete regions, including the orbitofrontal, dorsomedial, ventromedial, dorsolateral, and ventrolateral cortices, all of which may play specific roles in the generation of emotional processes. The orbitofrontal cortex integrates exteroceptive and interoceptive sensory information to guide behavior and plays a role in core affect, a psychological primitive that relates to the mental representation of bodily changes experienced as pleasure or displeasure with some degree of arousal (Lindquist, Wager, Kober, Bliss-Moreau, & Barrett, 2012). The dorsomedial and ventromedial prefrontal cortices play a role in realizing instances of emotion perception and experience by drawing on stored representations of prior experiences to make meaning of core affect. The dorsolateral PFC is involved in top-down, goal-directed selection of responses and plays a key role in executive function critical for directing other psychological operations involved in the generation of emotion. The ventrolateral PFC is implicated in selecting among competing response representations, response inhibition, and directing attention to salient stimuli in the environment (Lindquist et al., 2012).

Experimental research conducted in the 1950s and 1960s involving suppression of prefrontal cortical activity by injecting Amytal—a barbiturate derivative—into an internal carotid artery demonstrated a role of hemispheric asymmetry in emotion (Alema, Rosadini, & Rossi, 1961; Perria, Rosadini, & Rossi, 1961; Rossi & Rosadini, 1967; Terzian & Cecotto, 1959). Amytal injections in the left side—releasing the right hemisphere from contralateral inhibitory influences of the left—produced depression, whereas injections in the right side—releasing the left hemisphere—produced euphoria (see Harmon-Jones, Gable, & Peterson, 2010, for review). Research using the electroencephalogram (EEG) is consistent with these findings, demonstrating a role for the left PFC in positive affect and well-being and implicating right PFC in emotional vulnerability and affective disturbance, suggesting that activity in the left hemisphere region may provide a neurobiological marker of resilience (Begley & Davidson, 2012). Findings from normative and clinically depressed and anxious samples indicate that relative left-sided activation is decreased or that right-sided activation is increased in affective disturbance (Kemp, Griffiths et al., 2010a; Mathersul, Williams, Hopkinson, & Kemp, 2008; see also Kemp & Felmingham, 2008). Transcranial magnetic stimulation (TMS)—a technique applied to the scalp to either depolarize or hyperpolarize local neurons of the brain up to a depth of 2 cm—is an alternative nonpharmacological treatment for depression (Slotema, Blom, Hoek, & Sommer, 2010). Low-frequency (inhibitory) right-sided repetitive TMS (rTMS) or high-frequency (excitatory) left-sided rTMS is applied to the dorsolateral

PFC of depressed patients to shift hemispheric asymmetry and ameliorate depressive symptoms. Other work (Harmon-Jones et al., 2010), however, demonstrates a role for left PFC in the emotion of anger—a basic emotion characterized by negative valence and approach-related motivation—highlighting a role for PFC in approach and withdrawal motivation, rather than positive and negative valence per se. Consistent with these electrophysiological findings, a meta-analysis of neuroimaging studies reported that the left ventrolateral PFC displays increased activity when participants perceive or experience instances of anger (Lindquist et al., 2012).

The Amygdala

The amygdala is an almond-shaped cluster of nuclei located in the anterior medial temporal lobe. Animal research has highlighted a central role for the amygdala in negative emotions such as fear and anxiety (Ledoux, 1998), and neuroimaging studies have confirmed its role in these emotions in humans (Murphy, Nimmo-Smith, & Lawrence, 2003; Phan, 2002). Amygdala activation is also observed in response to a variety of emotional states and stimuli including fear, disgust, sadness, anger, happiness, humor, sexually explicit images, and social emotions (Costafreda, Brammer, David, & Fu, 2008; Sergerie, Chochol, & Armony, 2008). A recent meta-analysis (Lindquist et al., 2012) concluded that the amygdala is part of a distributed network involved in core affect rather than fear per se and that it responds preferentially to salient exteroceptive sensations that are motivationally significant. Findings from several published meta-analyses of neuroimaging studies focusing on amygdala function in humans (Costafreda et al., 2008; Lindquist et al., 2012; Murphy et al., 2003; Phan, 2002; Sergerie et al., 2008; Vytal & Hamann, 2010) highlight a general role for the amygdala in processing stimulus salience, motivational significance, and arousal.

Although researchers (Costafreda et al., 2008) have emphasized that amygdala activation is more likely to respond to fear and disgust emotions, this may be due to the often weak evocative stimuli using in neuroimaging studies. Notably, a number of studies have examined amygdala activation during the experience of positive emotion, such as sexual arousal, and have produced findings highlighting an important distinction between motivated versus consummatory behavior. One study involving presentation of sexually explicit stimuli (Hamann,

Herman, Nolan, & Wallen, 2004) reported strong activation in amygdala (and hypothalamus) and that this difference was greater in males than in females. The authors interpreted these gender differences in light of greater motivation in men to seek out and interact with such stimuli. An earlier positron emission tomography (PET) study (Holstege et al., 2003) on the brain activation during human male ejaculation reported decreases in amygdala activation. Together, these findings indicate that increased activity is associated with viewing appetitive sexual stimuli associated with approach-related motivation, whereas consummatory sexual behavior (or quiescence) is associated with decreased activity, reflecting conservation of amygdala function (Hamann et al., 2004).

Anterior Cingulate

The anterior cingulate cortex (ACC) forms a collar around the corpus callosum and is a key substrate for conscious emotion experience. The most ventral portion of this structure—known as the subgenual cingulate (sACC; Broadmann's area or BA 25)—is a localized target in deep brain stimulation studies of patients with "treatment resistant" depression. Acute stimulation of this region (up to 9 V at each of the eight electrode contacts; four per hemisphere) is associated with a variety of psychological experiences including "sudden calmness or lightness," "disappearance of the void," "sense of heightened awareness," "increased interest," and "connectedness." Although the rostral ventral region of ACC—including sACC and pregenual ACC (pACC; BAs 24,32)—was initially singled out as the ACC subregion involved in emotional processing (Bush, Luu, & Posner, 2000), a more recent review of the literature (Etkin, Egner, & Kalisch, 2011) focusing on fear conditioning and extinction in particular has characterized the caudal dorsal region as playing an important role in the appraisal and expression of emotion and the ventral rostral region in the regulation of regions such as the amygdala. It was noted (Etkin et al., 2011) that activity within dorsal ACC (and medial PFC [mPFC]) are observed during classical (Pavlovian) fear conditioning and instructed fear-based tasks and that this activity is positively correlated with sympathetic nervous system activity but negatively with ventral ACC (and mPFC regions). By contrast, recall of extinction 24 hours after conditioning—a process that is less confounded by residual expression of fear responses—yields activity in ventral ACC (and mPFC), thus providing support for the proposal

that these regions are a neural correlate of fear inhibition that occurs during extinction (Etkin et al., 2011). Extending on this, a recent meta-analysis of functional neuroimaging studies (Lindquist et al., 2012) characterizes the sACC and pACC (Bas 24,32) (as well as adjacent posterior medial orbitofrontal cortex) as key sites for visceral regulation that helps to resolve which sensory input is selected for processing. By contrast, the more dorsal anterior midcingulate cortex is implicated in executive attention and motor engagement during response selection through connections to lateral PFC and the supplementary motor area.

Insula

The insula is located at the base of the lateral (Sylvian) fissure and plays a role in the experiential and expressive aspects of internally generated emotion. Early work highlighted a role for the insula cortex in gustatory function. Studies conducted in the 1950s demonstrated that electrically stimulating this region in conscious human patients produced nausea, the experience of smelling or tasting something bad, and unpleasant tastes or sensations (Penfield & Faulk, 1955). Consistent with these findings, one of the first meta-analyses of human neuroimaging studies (Murphy et al., 2003) reported that the insula was the most consistently activated brain region (along with the globus pallidus) for the emotion of disgust. This study reported insula activity in more than 70% of neuroimaging studies on disgust, whereas activity in this region was only observed in 40% of the studies on other discrete emotions. A more recent meta-analysis (Lindquist et al., 2012) indicated that the left anterior insula displays consistent increases in activation during instances of both disgust and anger, whereas the right anterior insula displays more consistent increases in activation during disgust, although activity in this region was not specific to this emotion.

The view of the insula's role in emotion has now expanded to a more general role for the awareness of bodily sensations, affective feeling, and consciousness (see Craig, 2009, for review). Work by Bud Craig and colleagues (Craig, 2002; 2003) indicates that ascending pathways originating from lamina I neurons in the spinal cord carry information about the physiological status of the body to the thalamus via the lateral spinothalamic tract. Thalamic nuclei then project to the mid/posterior dorsal insula, which then projects to the anterior insula. These pathways provide a neurophysiological basis for interoception (the physiological condition of the body) (Craig, 2002). The homeostatic afferent input received from the body is first represented in the dorsal insula—the primary sensory cortex of interoception—and this information is then re-represented in the anterior insula, providing a substrate for conscious awareness of the changes in internal physiological states and emotional feelings (Craig, 2002; 2003; 2009). The emotion of disgust involves a mental representation of how an object will affect the body (Lindquist et al., 2012), thus providing a potential explanation for neuroimaging findings that highlight a role for insula in this emotion.

The Great Emotion Debate

The fierce, ongoing debate over whether the emotions are discrete, innate human mental states has been likened to the Hundred Years' War between England and France (Lindquist, Siegel, Quigley, & Barrett, 2013). On the one hand, emotions may be considered as fundamental processes in the brain that exist across species (and human cultures); a phenomenon that is discovered, not created, by the human mind. In this regard, the basic emotions are characterized as "natural kinds," hardwired into the brain and associated with distinctive patterns of neural activation (Panksepp & Watt, 2011; Vytal & Hamann, 2010). On the other hand, those who favor a psychological constructionist approach (Barrett, 2006; 2012; Lindquist et al., 2012) argue that emotions are themselves constructed from activation relating to more basic building blocks, such as core dimensions like valence (positive vs. negative affect) and arousal (deactivation to activation). Ledoux (2012) recently observed that although neuroscientific research on emotion has increased exponentially over the past decade, "emotion" remains ill-defined and that this situation has led to an intellectual stalemate. One of the problems here is that the terms "emotion" and "feeling" are used interchangeably, and this has led to the use of common language "feeling" words such as fear, anger, love, and sadness to guide the scientific study of emotion, rather than focusing on specific phenomena of interest (such as the detection of and response to significant events) (LeDoux, 2012). Another explanation for different competing theories is that researchers have often tackled the same question from different theoretical standpoints and experimental approaches. In this regard, Panksepp (2011) distinguishes between behavioral neuroscientists who study "instinctual" primary processes that provide the foundation for understanding the biological basis of emotion versus cognitive psychologists who study the higher levels of emotion along with their associated "regulatory nuances."

Research on facial expressions—particularly the universally recognizable expressions of emotion—has been central to the ongoing debate about the nature of emotion. In the 1960s, Paul Ekman traveled to Papua New Guinea and conducted experiments on the isolated Fore tribesman who, at that time, had had little or no contact with the outside world. The ability of these tribesmen to reliably recognize certain facial expressions led to the proposal that there are certain "basic" emotions. These included fear, anger, disgust, surprise, happiness, and sadness; all of which are universally recognized, innate, and not reliant on social construction (Ekman, Sorenson, & Friesen, 1969). This work highlights that negative emotions are easily revealed in facial expressions of emotion. Research on vocalizations, however (Sauter & Scott, 2007), has revealed five putative positive emotions, including achievement/triumph, amusement, contentment, sensual pleasure, and relief. More recently, Ekman has expanded the basic emotions to include amusement, contempt, contentment, embarrassment, excitement, guilt, pride, relief, satisfaction, sensory pleasure, and shame (Ekman, 2012), emotions not associated with specific facial expressions. Ekman's work has led to extensive neuroscientific research on the neurobiology of emotion perception, and this research is being conducted more than 40 years after his findings were first reported.

In contrast to the work by Paul Ekman on human facial expressions, Jaak Panksepp has explored emotions through electrical stimulation of discrete subcortical brain structures in the rat. This approach has important methodological advantages over human neuroimaging in that localized electrical stimulation of the brain provides causal evidence for the role of certain subcortical regions in affective experience. Panksepp has employed a different experimental approach to that of Ekman, and his work has led to the identification of a different set of "basic" emotions (Panksepp, 2011) including seeking, rage, fear, lust, care, panic/grief, and play, which he labels as emotional instinctual behaviors. Panksepp employs special nomenclature—full captializations of common emotional words (e.g., RAGE, FEAR, etc.)—to distinguish these primary-process emotions as identified using electrical stimulation of discrete subcortical neural loci from their vernacular use in language. Although (some of) these behaviors are not typically thought of as emotions (i.e.SEEKING,

CARE, and PLAY), Panksepp argues that these basic emotions provide "tools for living" that make up the "building blocks" for the higher emotions (Panksepp & Watt, 2011). Interestingly, and in contrast to Ekman, he specifically argues that disgust is not a basic emotion; rather, he categorizes disgust, like hunger, as a sensory and homeostatic affect. Panksepp argues that the higher emotional feelings experienced by humans are based on primitive emotional feelings emerging from the "ancient reaches of the mammalian brain, influencing the higher cognitive apparatus" (Panksepp, 2007). On the basis of findings obtained during electrical stimulation, Panksepp (2007) highlights the mesencephalon (or midbrain of the brainstem)—especially the periaqueductal gray—extending through the diencephalon (including the thalamus and hypothalamus) to the orbitofrontal cortex and then to the medial (anterior cingulate, medial frontal cortices) and lateral forebrain areas (including the temporal lobes and insula) as critical regions.

Although different experimental approaches have led to different conclusions over what the specific basic emotions may be, researchers have also drawn entirely different conclusions using the same technique in humans (Lindquist et al., 2012; Vytal & Hamann, 2010). An early meta-analysis of 106 neuroimaging studies using PET or fMRI found evidence for distinctive patterns of activity relating to the basic emotions (Murphy et al., 2003). Fear was associated with activation in the amygdala, disgust with activation in the insula and globus pallidus, and anger with activation in the lateral orbitofrontal cortex. Importantly, these regions are also associated with respective processing deficits when damaged. Extending on these findings, a more recent meta-analysis including 30 new studies also obtained results consistent with basic emotion theory (Vytal & Hamann, 2010). The authors reported that fear, happiness, sadness, anger, and disgust all elicited consistent, characteristic, and discriminable patterns of regional brain activity (Vytal & Hamann, 2010), albeit with somewhat different conclusions to the earlier meta-analysis by Murphy and colleagues. Fear was associated with greater activation in the amygdala and insula, happiness with activation in rostral ACC and right superior temporal gyrus, sadness in middle frontal gyrus and subgenual ACC, anger in inferior frontal gyrus (IFG) and parahippocampal gyrus, and disgust in IFG and anterior insula. It is worth noting here that facial emotion stimuli are the most frequently used stimuli in studies of human emotion

and that it is important to distinguish between emotion perception (as is assessed most often in studies using facial emotion) and emotion experience. However, the authors of this meta-analytic study (Vytal & Hamann, 2010) noted that—although preliminary—their results provided evidence to suggest that findings are not unique to studies of facial emotion stimuli.

In direct contrast to these prior studies (Murphy et al., 2003; Vytal & Hamann, 2010), another meta-analysis (Lindquist et al., 2012) on 234 PET or fMRI studies reported that discrete emotion categories are neither consistently nor specifically localized to distinct brain areas. Instead, these authors concluded that their findings provide support for a psychological constructionist model of emotion in which emotions emerge from a more basic set of psychological operations that are not specific to emotion. This model has a number of features; these include core affect underpinned by processing in a host of regions including the amygdala, insula, medial orbitofrontal cortex (mOFC), lateral orbitofrontal cortex (lOFC), ACC, thalamus, hypothalamus, bed nucleus of the stria terminalis, basal forebrain, and the periaqueductal gray. The authors clearly distinguish core affect from the more general term, *affect*, which is often used to mean anything emotional. Although the authors highlight the dimensional constructs of valence and arousal, other dimensional constructs—such as approach and withdrawal (Davidson & Irwin, 1999)—have been proposed. Approach and withdrawal motivations are considered to be fundamental motivational states on which emotional reactions are based and may actually provide a superior explanation for the way some brain regions process emotional stimuli (Barrett & Wager, 2006; Harmon-Jones, 2003).

Systematic reviews using meta-analytic statistical procedures generally provide a more objective review of the literature, allow for generalizations to be made on a body of literature, and avoid low study power. One of the problems associated with individual neuroimaging studies on emotion in humans is the multiple comparisons problem, making it more likely to identify an effect when there is none (otherwise known as a type 1 error). A case in point is a recent fMRI study using a "social perspective-taking task" in a postmortem Atlantic salmon (Bennett & Miller, 2010; Bennett, Baird, Miller, & Wolford, 2011). When statistical analysis did not correct for multiple comparisons, this study observed evidence of activity in the tiny dead salmon's brain. Although farcical, this study has a serious message: that inadequate control for type 1 error risks drawing conclusions on the basis of random noise, in part highlighting an important role for meta-analysis (Radua & Mataix-Cols, 2012). However, the observation that different meta-analyses have led to contradictory findings and entirely opposite conclusions on a body of literature could leave one feeling rather perplexed. Surely, meta-analyses should aid in resolving the many reported inconsistencies rather than making them more explicit and further contributing to contradictory findings!

There are actually a number of explanations to this conundrum and a number of considerations to bear in mind when reviewing the neuroimaging literature. Hamann (2012) suggests that rather than presenting these different proposals as competing theories, an alternative hybrid view could combine the key advantages of both. A major limitation of the work by Lindquist and colleagues (2012) is the focus on single brain regions rather than on networks of two or more regions. Hamann (2012) argues that once the neural correlates of basic emotions are identified—which could relate to brain connectivity rather than discrete brain regions—these correlates could then be encompassed within the psychological constructionist framework as part of core affect. Indeed, recent preliminary work (Tettamanti et al., 2012) has reported that whereas functional integration of visual cortex and amygdala underpins the processing of all emotions (elicited using video clips), distinct pathways of neural coupling were identified (in females) for the emotions of fear, disgust, and happiness. The authors noted that these emotions were associated with cortical networks involved in the processing of sensorimotor (for fear), somatosensory (for disgust), and cognitive aspects (happiness) of basic emotions. We now review various influential neuroscientific models relating to the neural circuitry of emotion.

The "Emotional" Circuitry

Regional brain interconnectivity, rather than the activity in specific regions per se, is critical to further understanding the brain basis of emotion. An early model of brain connectivity relating to emotion experience and the cortical control of emotion was proposed by Papez in 1937 a specific circuit of neural structures lying on the medial wall of the brain. These structures included the hypothalamus, anterior thalamus, cingulate, and hippocampus. Two emotional pathways were proposed, including the "stream of thinking" (involving the cingulate cortex) and the "stream of feeling" (hypothalamus).

Extending on earlier work by Papez and others, LeDoux (1998) highlighted an important role of the amygdala, proposing two pathways associated with the processing of emotional stimuli, the "low road" (thalamo-amygdala) and "high road" (thalamo-cortico-amygdala). The "low road" or direct pathway reflects a preconscious emotional processing route that is fast acting and allows for rapid responsiveness and survival. This pathway transmits sensory messages from the thalamus to the lateral nucleus of the amygdala, which then elicits the fear response. Information from other areas, including the hippocampus, hypothalamus, and cortex, is integrated in the basal and accessory basal nuclei of the amygdala. The signal is then transmitted to the central nucleus of the amygdala (amygdaloid output nuclei), which projects to anatomical targets that elicit a variety of responses characteristic of the fear response (e.g., tachycardia, increased sweating, panting, startle response, facial expressions of fear, and corticosteroid release). By contrast, the "high road" or indirect pathway facilitates conscious and cognitive "emotional processing" that is slow acting and allows for situational assessment. Overprocessing of stimuli by the subcortical emotional processing pathway and ineffective cortical regulation has provided useful insights to understanding affective disturbance displayed by various psychiatric disorders, including posttraumatic stress and panic disorders. Although this theory has been tremendously influential, it has also been criticized for ignoring the "royal road" (Panksepp & Watt, 2011)—involving the central amygdala, ventrolateral hypothalamus and periaqueductal gray (located around the cerebral aqueduct within the tegmentum of the midbrain)—which governs instinctual actions such as freezing and flight that help animals avoid danger.

This low- versus high-road distinction has also been called into question (Pessoa & Adolphs, 2010) with respect to the processing of affective visual stimuli in humans. The work by LeDoux and others is based on rodent studies that identified the subcortical pathway using auditory fear conditioning paradigms. Fear conditioning is a behavioral paradigm in which the relationship between an environmental stimulus and aversive event is learned (Maren, 2001). The assumption that this same subcortical route exists for visual information processing in humans has been questioned (Pessoa & Adolphs, 2010) on the basis of findings indicating that visual processing of emotional stimuli in the subcortical pathway is no faster than in the cortical pathway.

For instance, visual response latencies in some frontal sites including the frontal eye fields may be as short as 40–70 ms, highlighting that subcortical visual processing is not discernably faster than cortical processing (Pessoa & Adolphs, 2010). These findings led to the proposal of a "multiple-waves" model (Pessoa & Adolphs, 2010) that highlights that the amygdala and the pulvinar nucleus of the thalamus coordinate the function of cortical networks during evaluation of biological significance in humans. According to this view, the amygdala is part of a core brain circuit that aggregates and distributes information, whereas the pulvinar—which does not exist in the brains of rodents or other small mammals—acts as an important control site for attentional mechanisms.

Brain–Body Interaction and Embodied Cognition

Here, we consider emotion as an embodied cognition, the idea that the body plays a crucial role in emotion, motivation, and cognition (see Price, Peterson, & Harmon-Jones, 2011, for review). Although regional brain connectivity is a necessary development in neuroscientific understanding of the emotions (discussed in the preceding section), current influential neuroscientific theories of emotion (Damasio, 1994; Porges, 1995; 2011; Reimann & Bechara, 2010; Thayer & Lane, 2000; 2009) incorporate brain–body interactions into formal models. These include the neurovisceral integration model (Thayer & Lane, 2000; 2009; Thayer, Hansen, Saus-Rose, & Johnsen, 2009), the polyvagal theory (Porges, 1995; 2001; 2003; 2007; 2009; 2011), the somatic marker hypothesis (Damasio, 1994; Reimann & Bechara, 2010), and the homeostatic model for awareness (Craig, 2002; 2003; 2005). These complementary models provide mechanisms for better understanding the impact of interventions such as exercise, yoga, and meditation and how they might impact on emotion and mood.

The neurovisceral integration model (Thayer & Lane, 2000; 2009; Thayer et al., 2009) describes a network of brain structures including the PFC, cingulate cortex, insula, amygdala, and brainstem regions in the control of visceral response to stimuli. This *central autonomic network* (CAN) is responsible for the inhibition of medullary cardio-acceleratory circuits, for controlling psychophysiological resources during emotion, for goal-directed behavior, and for flexibility to environmental change. The primary output of the CAN is heart rate variability (HRV), mediated primarily by parasympathetic nervous system innervation—vagal inhibition—of the heart. Increased HRV—reflecting increased parasympathetic nervous system function—is associated with trait positive emotionality (Geisler, Vennewald, Kubiak, & Weber, 2010; Oveis et al., 2009). By contrast, decreased HRV—reflecting decreased parasympathetic nervous system function—is associated with depression and anxiety (Kemp, Quintana, Felmingham, Matthews, & Jelinek, 2012a; Kemp, Quintana, Gray, Felmingham, Brown, & Gatt, 2010b). Polyvagal theory (Porges, 2011) is consistent with the neurovisceral integration model, but further emphasizes vagal afferent feedback from the viscera and internal milieu to the nucleus of solitary tract (NST) and cortex, allowing for subsequent regulation of initial emotional responses. This theory also distinguishes between the myelinated and unmyelinated vagus nerves (hence "polyvagal"), such that the myelinated vagus underpins changes in HRV and approach-related behaviors including social engagement, whereas the phylogenetically older unmyelinated vagus—in combination with the sympathetic nervous system—supports the organism during dangerous or life-threatening events. According to this model, social engagement is associated with cortical inhibition of amygdala; activation of the vagus nerve—increasing vagal tone—and connected cranial nerves then allow socially engaging facial expressions to be elicited, leading to positive interactions with the environment. The NST receives vagal afferent feedback from the viscera and internal milieu, and this information is then directed to cortical structures responsible for the top-down regulation of emotion. Increased activation of the vagus nerve—indexed by increased HRV—therefore provides a psychophysiological framework compatible for social engagement facilitating positive emotion. By contrast, social withdrawal is associated with perception of threat underpinned by increased amygdala activity and vagal withdrawal—decreasing vagal tone—triggering fight-or-flight responses leading to negative social interactions with the environment. Again, information relating to the status of the viscera and internal milieu are fed back to the nucleus of solitary tract and the cortex, allowing for subsequent regulation of the emotion response. Decreased activation of the vagus nerve—indexed by decreased HRV—therefore provides the framework compatible for fight-or-fight responses facilitating negative emotion.

The vagus nerve, which has been termed the single most important nerve in the body (Tracey, 2007), not only supports the capacity for social engagement (Porges, 2011) and mental well-being (Kemp & Quintana, 2013), but also plays an important role in longer term physical health (Kemp & Quintana, 2013). The vagus nerve plays an important regulatory role over a variety of allostatic systems including inflammatory processes, glucose regulation, and hypothalamic-pituitary-adrenal (HPA) function (Thayer, Yamamoto, & Brosschot, 2010). A proper functioning vagus nerve helps to contain acute inflammation and prevent the spread of inflammation to the bloodstream. Intriguingly, increased HRV is not only associated with various indices of psychological well-being including, cheerfulness and calmness (Geisler et al., 2010), trait positive emotionality (Oveis et al., 2009), motivation for social engagement (Porges, 2011), and psychological flexibility (Kashdan & Rottenberg, 2010), but it also appears to be fundamental for resilience and long-term health (Kashdan & Rottenberg, 2010). These observations are also consistent with research findings on the association between positive psychological well-being and cardiovascular health, highlighting a key role for attributes such as mindfulness, optimism, and gratitude in reducing the risk of cardiovascular disease (Boehm & Kubzansky, 2012; DuBois et al., 2012). By contrast, chronic decreases in vagal inhibition—indexed by reductions in HRV—will lead to premature aging, cardiovascular disease, and mortality (Thayer, Yamamoto, & Brosschot, 2010). The process by which vagal activity regulates these allostatic systems relates to the "inflammatory reflex" (Pavlov & Tracey, 2012; Tracey, 2002; 2007): the afferent (sensory) vagus nerve detects cytokines and pathogen-derived products, whereas the efferent (motor) vagus nerve regulates and controls their release.

In addition to parasympathetic (vagal) afferent feedback, afferents from sympathetic and somatic nerves further contribute to interoception and the homeostatic emotions involving distinct sensations such as pain, temperature and itch in particular (Craig, 2002; 2003; 2005). The functional anatomy of the lamina I spinothalamocortical system has only recently been elucidated. This system conveys signals from small-diameter primary afferents that represent the physiological condition of the entire body (the "material me"). It first projects to the spinal cord and brainstem and then generates a direct thalamocortical representation of the state of the body involving the insula and ACC. Consistent with electrophysiological work highlighting a role for prefrontal cortical structures in approach and withdrawal motivation (Harmon-Jones, Gable, & Peterson, 2010), Craig's homeostatic model for awareness (Craig, 2002; 2005; 2009) links approach (appetitive) behaviors, parasympathetic activity, and affiliative emotions to activity in the left anterior insula and ACC and withdrawal (aversive) behaviors, sympathetic activity, and arousal to activity in the right anterior insula and ACC. Stimulation of left insula cortex produces parasympathetic effects including heart rate slowing and blood pressure suppression, whereas stimulation of right insula produces sympathetic effects including tachycardia and pressor response (increased blood pressure) (Oppenheimer, Gelb, Girvin, & Hachinski, 1992). Research, for example, indicates that although left anterior insula (and ACC) are strongly activated during parasympathetic or enrichment emotions such as romantic love and maternal attachment (Bartels & Zeki, 2004; Leibenluft, Gobbini, Harrison, & Haxby, 2004), right-sided activity is observed during aroused or sympathetic emotions elicited through experimental challenge (see Craig, 2005, for review). We note, however, that directly linking positive emotions to parasympathetic activity and negative emotions to sympathetic activity is somewhat problematic on the basis of findings from psychophysiological research. For instance, emotion images containing threat, violent death, and erotica elicit the strongest emotional arousal and the largest skin conductance responses, thus highlighting a role for sympathetic activation in both defensive and appetitive responses (Bradley, Codispoti, Cuthbert, & Lang, 2001). These findings were argued to reflect a motivational system that is engaged and ready for action.

Finally, the somatic marker hypothesis highlights a key role for the ventromedial PFC in translating the sensory properties of external stimuli into "somatic markers" that reflect their biological relevance and guide subsequent decision-making (Damasio, 1994; Reimann & Bechara, 2010). Based on a body of research inspired by Phineas Gage—a nineteenth-century railroad worker who survived an accident involving serious damage to the prefrontal cortices—patients with damage to the ventromedial PFC display major difficulties in decision making that may have negative consequences, such as poor judgment and financial loss, despite having normal intellect (Reimann & Bechara, 2010). According to this model, the ventromedial PFC indexes changes in heart rate, blood pressure, gut motility, and glandular secretion, which then contribute to decision making and affective experience (Reimann & Bechara, 2010). Visceral responses contribute to the subjective feeling state, which subsequently "marks" potential choices of future behavior as advantageous or disadvantageous.

A simplified model of emotion processing is presented in Figure 4.1, drawing on current state of the literature and major theories described earlier. The model highlights the role of hemispheric effects in emotion experience (Craig, 2005; Davidson & Irwin, 1999; Harmon-Jones, 2003), the regulatory role of the central autonomic network (Thayer & Lane, 2009; Thayer et al., 2009), and vagal nerve inhibition over sympathetic nervous system contribution to the heart (Huston & Tracey, 2010; Pavlov & Tracey, 2012; Thayer et al., 2009). An adequately functioning vagal nerve will serve to facilitate positive emotions and social engagement (Porges, 2011), whereas a poorly functioning vagal nerve will lead to negative emotion and, over the longer term, mood and anxiety disorders (Kemp et al., 2012a; Kemp, Quintana, Gray, Felmingham, Brown, & Gatt, 2010b) and poor physical health (Thayer & Brosschot, 2005; Thayer & Lane, 2007; Thayer et al., 2010). The model further highlights an important role of vagal afferent feedback, which makes an important contribution to emotion

experience and subsequent social behavior (i.e., "embodied cognition"). Also highlighted are the many observable outcome measures needed to help move affective neuroscience beyond the current debate over whether the brain and body respects the "natural kind" versus the "psychological constructionist" view of emotion (see also Lindquist et al., 2013, for recent commentary on this debate).

Specificity of the Emotions

There is significant interest (and debate) over the ability to discriminate the emotions using a variety of affect detection methods. Although the basic emotions are characterized by specific facial expressions (Ekman & Friesen, 1975), a single set of facial actions can become different emotional expressions in different contexts (Barrett, 2012). For example, the same face posing the same facial actions appears to become a different facial expression when paired with the words "surprise," "fear," and "anger" (Barrett, 2012). Despite the many challenges to correctly detecting specific emotions—interested readers are referred to reviews by Calvo and D'Mello (2010) and Fairclough (2009)—we are confident that the reliability and validity of detection will be improved in research that draws on affective computing principles, focuses on multiple objective measures of emotion (see Figure 4.1), and utilizes stronger manipulations of emotion. Studies on emotion specificity have employed a variety of detection measures ranging from facial expressions

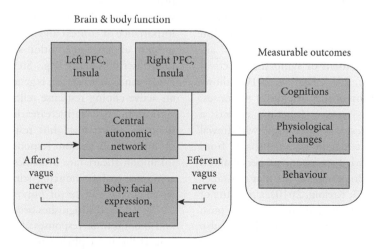

Fig. 4.1 Model of brain and body function with regards to emotion processing highlighting role of hemispheric asymmetry (Davidson, Harmon-Jones), the central autonomic network (Thayer), and inhibition of sympathetic nervous system contribution to the heart (Thayer, Porges, Kemp) via the efferent vagus nerve and afferent feedback. The role of brain and body in emotion is bidirectional, and visceral afferent feedback to the brain makes an important contribution to emotion experience and subsequent social behavior (i.e., "embodied cognition"). Also highlighted are broad categories of measures needed to distinguish between "natural kinds" and "psychological construction" (Lindquist, Barrett).

to psychophysiological measures and neuroimaging. We now provide a brief review of this literature.

Unlike the disagreement over the neural specificity of different emotions (Lindquist et al., 2012; Vytal & Hamann, 2010) discussed earlier, recent reviews of autonomic nervous system (ANS) activity (Harrison, Kreibig, & Critchley, 2013; Kreibig, 2010) highlight considerable specificity in the presentation of emotion. However, it is important to note that these specific patterns are often only revealed by inspection of data from a broad range of autonomic measures, a key point with regards to emotion detection more generally. This specificity of discrete emotions may be understood in the context of the *component model of somatovisceral response organization* (Stemmler, Heldmann, Pauls, & Scherer, 2001). According to this model, state-driven psychophysiological responses are associated with three components. The first relates to demands by processes not in the service of emotions (e.g., ongoing motor activity); the second relates to the effects of organismic, behavioral, and mental demands determined by a certain context (e.g., motivation to approach vs. withdraw); the third relates to the "emotion signature proper," characterized by emotion-specific responses. This model therefore allows for considerable overlap of activity associated with emotion responses but also emotion specificity. Emotion-specific features of fear, anger, disgust, sadness, and happiness detected using a variety of techniques are now briefly reviewed.

The emotion of fear is characterized by eyebrows raised and drawn together, wide-open eyes, tense lowered eyelids, and stretched lips (Ekman & Friesen, 1975). It is associated with activation within frontoparietal brain regions (Tettamanti et al., 2012) and a broad pattern of sympathetic activation (Harrison et al., 2013; Kreibig, 2010), allowing for the preparation of adaptive motor responses. Autonomic nervous system function reflects a general activation response and vagal withdrawal (reduced HRV), but may be distinguishable from anger (associated with harassment or personalized recall) by reduction in peripheral vascular resistance (Harrison et al., 2013; Kreibig, 2010), a measure of resistance to flow that must be overcome to push blood through the circulatory system. Fear is also associated with more numerous skin conductance responses and larger electromyographic corrugator activity than is anger (Stemmler et al., 2001), a finding that was interpreted in line with the adrenaline hypothesis of fear (Funkenstein, 1955). By contrast, the emotion of anger is characterized by lowered eyebrows drawn together, tensed lowered eyelids and pressed lips. A body of literature highlights a role for left frontal PFC in approach-related emotions including positive affect (Begley & Davidson, 2012), as well as the emotion of anger (Harmon-Jones et al., 2010). By contrast, the right PFC is implicated in withdrawal-related behaviors (such as fear), although the EEG literature in this regard has been contradictory (Wacker, Chavanon, Leue, & Stemmler, 2008). Contradictory findings highlight the need for better manipulations of affective experience. It is also important to note that anger may elicit either an anger-mirroring or a reciprocating fear response (Harrison et al., 2013), and that psychophysiological responses will be dependent on the response elicited.

The physiological differentiation between fear and anger in humans has been a topic of great interest for decades (see, e.g., Ax, 1953). Walter Cannon (1929) introduced the concept of the "fight-or-flight" response arguing for similar underlying visceral patterns in the two responses. By contrast, Magda Arnold (1950) highlighted a key role for the sympathetic branch of the ANS in fear and a role for both the sympathetic and parasympathetic branches in anger. Although an interesting proposal in light of an important role of parasympathetic activity in approach-related motivation (Kemp et al., 2012*b*; Porges, 2011)—an important characteristic of anger—research findings have generally reported no change in HRV (e.g., Rainville, Bechara, Naqvi, & Damasio, 2006), a psychophysiological variable primarily driven by the parasympathetic nervous system. Critically, research has highlighted the importance of context and individual differences in order to understand emotion-specific responses and their discriminability (e.g., Stemmler et al., 2001). For instance, whereas fear is generally associated with an active coping response reflected in sympathetic activation, such as increases in heart rate, imminence of threat may shift responses toward more of an immobilization response and sympathetic inhibition (heart rate decreases). These differential responses to fear-inducing stimuli may be understood in the context of polyvagal theory (Porges, 2011), which distinguishes between immobilization and mobilization responses. Although immobilization is the most phylogenetically primitive behavioral response to threat involving the unmyelinated vagus nerve (associated with fear-related bradycardia), mobilization involves the sympathetic nervous system, which prepares the organism for flight or fight.

The emotion of disgust is characterized by a raised upper lip, wrinkled nose bridge and raised cheeks (Ekman & Friesen, 1975). Interestingly, research indicates that gustatory distaste elicited by unpleasant tastes, core disgust elicited by photographs of contaminants, and moral disgust elicited by unfair treatment in an economic game all evoke activation of the levator labii muscle of the face, which raises the upper lip and wrinkles the nose. Disgust is also associated with activity in somatosensory brain regions and reductions in cardiac output reflecting protective responses (Harrison et al., 2013; Tettamanti et al., 2012). Differential skin conductance responses may depend on whether the emotion is elicited by "core-disgust" inducing stimuli (e.g., pictures of dirty toilets, foul smells) or body-boundary violating stimuli (e.g., mutilation scenes, images of injection) (Harrison et al., 2013). For example, whereas "core-disgust" is associated with unchanged or decreased skin conductance (Harrison et al., 2013; Kreibig, 2010), body-boundary violating disgust is associated with increased skin conductance (Bradley et al., 2001).

The emotion of sadness is characterized by raised inner eyebrows and lowered lip corners (Ekman & Friesen, 1975) contributing to facial features like the "omega melancholicum" and Veraguth's folds (Greden, Genero, & Price, 1985). It is associated with increased blood flow in ventral regions, including subgenual cingulate and anterior insula, and decreases in neocortical regions, including dorsolateral prefrontal and inferior parietal cortices (Mayberg et al., 1999). Autonomic nervous system responses may be either activated or deactivated (Harrison et al., 2013), which may depend on whether sadness is associated with crying. Crying-related sadness is associated with increased heart rate—but no change in HRV—and increased skin conductance (Gross, Frederickson, & Levenson, 1994), whereas noncrying sadness is associated with a reduction in heart rate, reduced skin conductance, reduced HRV, and increased respiration (Gross et al., 1994; Rottenberg, Wilhelm, Gross, & Gotlib, 2003). We have observed robust reductions in HRV in patients with major depressive disorder (Kemp et al., 2010b), and these findings have implications for long-term well-being and physical health of patients (see Kemp & Quintana, 2013).

The emotion of happiness is characterized by tensed lowered eyelids, raised cheeks and raised lip corners (Ekman & Friesen, 1975). Reliable expressions of positive emotion—the Duchenne smile—involve contraction of the orbicularis oculi muscles at the corner of the eyes. By contrast, forced smiles only involve contraction of the zygomaticus major, the muscle that raises the corner of the mouth. Interestingly, the intensity of smiling in photographs when a young adult has been found to predict longevity (Abel & Kruger, 2010): longevity ranged from 72.9 years for individuals with no smiles, 75.0 years for those with partial smiles, to 79.9 years for those with Duchenne smiles. With respects to brain function, happiness is associated with activation in medial prefrontal and temporoparietal cortices, which may reflect the cognitive aspects associated with understanding positive social interactions (Tettamanti et al., 2012). A body of work further highlights a role for the left PFC in positive affect (Engels et al., 2007; Urry et al., 2004; see also Begley & Davidson, 2012) consistent with brain-based models of approach related motivation (Harmon-Jones, Gable, & Peterson, 2010).

Like the negative emotions, happiness is associated with cardiac activation secondary to vagal withdrawal (Harrison et al., 2013) but may be distinguishable from the negative emotions by peripheral vasodilation (Harrison et al., 2013; dilation of blood vessels leading to lower blood pressure). Whereas vagal withdrawal during the experience of happiness may be somewhat unexpected, it is important to distinguish between happiness as an emotion—a relatively transient event—and positive mood, a relatively longer lasting emotional state. Unlike the emotion of happiness, positive mood is associated with increased HRV (Geisler et al., 2010; Oveis et al., 2009). It is also important to distinguish among the positive emotions. A review of the studies on ANS function, for example, indicates that whereas happiness is associated with decreased HRV, amusement and joy are associated with increases (Kreibig, 2010).

Conclusion

Here, we reviewed the affective neuroscience of emotion focusing on the basic emotions including fear, anger, disgust, happiness, and sadness and the contrasting approach of psychological constructionism. Although there is considerable debate over whether the brain and body "respect" the basic emotion categories, studies have generally focused on single measures and have reported limited success in discriminating the basic emotions (but see Rainville et al., 2006; Tettamanti et al., 2012). We suggest that this debate may soon be resolved in future research that draws on affective computing principles and focuses on a broad range of objective information from the brain and body (e.g., facial expressions, brain electrical activity, sweat response, heart rate, and respiration), as well as better manipulations of affective experiences. The extent to which consistent and specific changes are observable in various physiological systems for emotion inductions across contexts within and between individuals will help to resolve this "hundred-year emotion war" (Lindquist et al., 2013). With developments in technology, more sophisticated modeling, and increasing knowledge about the neuroanatomical and physiological correlates of emotion, the future is bright for a better understanding of the neuroscientific basis of emotion in humans.

Acknowledgments

The authors A. H. K. and J. K. are supported by an Invited International Visiting Professorship from the University of São Paulo and an Australian Postgraduate Award (APA) from the University of Sydney, respectively.

References

Abel, E. L., & Kruger, M. L. (2010). Smile intensity in photographs predicts longevity. *Psychological Science*, *21*(4), 542–544. doi: 10.1177/0956797610363775

Alema, G., Rosadini, G., & Rossi, G. F. (1961). [Preliminary experiments on the effects of the intracarotid introduction of sodium Amytal in Parkinsonian syndromes]. *Bollettino della Società italiana di biologia sperimentale*, *37*, 1036–1037.

Arnold, M. (1950). An excitatory theory of emotion. In M. L. Reymert (Ed.), *Feelings and emotions*, 11–33. New York: McGraw-Hill.

Ax, A. F. (1953). The physiological differentiation between fear and anger in humans. *Psychosomatic Medicine*, *15*(5), 433–442.

Barrett, L. (2006). Are emotions natural kinds? *Perspectives on Psychological Science*, *1*, 28–58.

Barrett, L. F. (2012). Emotions are real. *Emotion*, *12*(3), 413–429. doi: 10.1037/a0027555

Barrett, L. F., & Wager, T. D. (2006). The structure of emotion. *Current Directions in Psychological Science*, *15*, 79–83.

Bartels, A., & Zeki, S. (2004). The neural correlates of maternal and romantic love. *NeuroImage*, *21*(3), 1155–1166. doi: 10.1016/j.neuroimage.2003.11.003

Begley, S., & Davidson, R. (2012). *The emotional life of your brain*. Hodder.

Bennett, C. M., & Miller, M. B. (2010). How reliable are the results from functional magnetic resonance imaging? *Annals of the New York Academy of Sciences*, *1191*(1), 133–155. doi: 10.1111/j.1749-6632.2010.05446.x

Bennett, C. M., Baird, A. A., Miller, M. B., & Wolford, G. L. (2011). Neural correlates of interspecies perspective taking in the post-mortem Atlantic Salmon: An argument for proper multiple comparisons correction. *Journal of Serendipitous and Unexpected Results*, *1*, 1–5.

Boehm, J. K., & Kubzansky, L. D. (2012). The heart's content: The association between positive psychological well-being and cardiovascular health. *Psychological Bulletin*, *138*(4), 655–691. doi: 10.1037/a0027448

Bradley, M. M., Codispoti, M., Cuthbert, B. N., & Lang, P. J. (2001). Emotion and motivation I: Defensive and appetitive reactions in picture processing. *Emotion*, *1*(3), 276–298. doi: 10.1037//1528-3542.1.3.276

Bush, G., Luu, P., & Posner, M. (2000). Cognitive and emotional influences in anterior cingulate cortex. *Trends in Cognitive Sciences*, *4*(6): 215–222.

Calvo, R. A., & D'Mello, S. (2010). Affect detection: An interdisciplinary review of models, methods, and their applications. *IEEE Transactions on Affective Computing*, *1*(1), 18–37. doi: 10.1109/T-AFFC.2010.1

Cannon, W. B. (1929). *Bodily changes in pain, hunger, fear, and rage* (2nd ed.). New York: Appleton-Century-Crofts.

Costafreda, S. G., Brammer, M. J., David, A. S., & Fu, C. H. Y. (2008). Predictors of amygdala activation during the processing of emotional stimuli: A meta-analysis of 385 PET and fMRI studies. *Brain Research Reviews*, *58*(1), 57–70. doi: 10.1016/j.brainresrev.2007.10.012

Craig, A. D. (2002). How do you feel? Interoception: The sense of the physiological condition of the body. *Nature Reviews Neuroscience*, *3*(8), 655–666. doi: 10.1038/nrn894

Craig, A. D. (2003). Interoception: The sense of the physiological condition of the body. *Current Opinion in Neurobiology*, *13*(4), 500–505.

Craig, A. D. B. (2005). Forebrain emotional asymmetry: A neuroanatomical basis? *Trends in Cognitive Sciences*, *9*(12), 566–571. doi: 10.1016/j.tics.2005.10.005

Craig, A. D. B. (2009). How do you feel—now? The anterior insula and human awareness. *Nature Reviews Neuroscience*, *10*(1), 59–70. doi: 10.1038/nrn2555

Damasio, A. (1994). *Descartes' error: Emotion reason, and the human brain*. New York: Putnam.

Davidson, R., & Irwin, W. (1999). The functional neuroanatomy of emotion and affective style. *Trends in Cognitive Sciences*, *3*(1), 11–21.

DuBois, C. M., Beach, S. R., Kashdan, T. B., Nyer, M. B., Park, E. R., Celano, C. M., & Huffman, J. C. (2012). Positive psychological attributes and cardiac outcomes: Associations, mechanisms, and interventions. *Psychosomatics*, *53*(4), 303–318. doi: 10.1016/j.psym.2012.04.004

Ekman, P. (2012). Basic emotions. In T. Dalgleish & M. Power (Eds.), *Handbook of cognition and emotion*. Sussex, UK: John Wiley & Sons.

Ekman, P., & Friesen, W. V. (1975). *Unmasking the face* (2nd ed.). Prentice Hall.

Ekman, P., Sorenson, E. R., & Friesen, W. V. (1969). Pan-cultural elements in facial displays of emotion. *Science*, *164*(3875), 86–88.

Engels, A. S., Heller, W., Mohanty, A., Herrington, J. D., Banich, M. T., Webb, A. G., & Miller, G. A. (2007). Specificity of regional brain activity in anxiety types during emotion processing. *Psychophysiology*, *44*(3), 352–363. doi: 10.1111/j.1469-8986.2007.00518.x

Etkin, A., Egner, T., & Kalisch, R. (2011). Emotional processing in anterior cingulate and medial prefrontal cortex. *Trends in Cognitive Sciences*, *15*(2), 85–93. doi: 10.1016/j.tics.2010.11.004

Fairclough, S. H. (2009). Fundamentals of physiological computing. Interacting with *Computers*, *21*(1-2), 133–145. doi: 10.1016/j.intcom.2008.10.011

Funkenstein, D. H. (1955). The physiology of fear and anger. *Scientific American*, *192*(5), 74–80.

Geisler, F. C. M., Vennewald, N., Kubiak, T., & Weber, H. (2010). The impact of heart rate variability on subjective well-being is mediated by emotion regulation. *Personality and Individual Differences*, *49*(7), 723–728. doi: 10.1016/j.paid.2010.06.015

Greden, J. F., Genero, N., & Price, H. L. (1985). Agitation-increased electromyogram activity in the corrugator muscle region: A possible explanation of the "Omega sign"? *American Journal of Psychiatry*, *142*(3), 348–351.

Gross, J. J., Frederickson, B. L., & Levenson, R. W. (1994). The psychophysiology of crying. *Psychophysiology*, *31*(5), 460–468.

Hamann S. 2012. What can neuroimaging meta-analyses really tell us about the nature of emotion? *Behav Brain Sci.*, *35*(3):150–152. *doi: 10.1017/S0140525X11001701*

Hamann, S., Herman, R. A., Nolan, C. L., & Wallen, K. (2004). Men and women differ in amygdala response to visual sexual stimuli. *Nature Neuroscience*, *7*(4), 411–416. doi: 10.1038/nn1208

Harmon-Jones, E. (2003). Early career award. Clarifying the emotive functions of asymmetrical frontal cortical activity. *Psychophysiology*, *40*(6), 838–848.

Harmon-Jones, E., Gable, P. A., & Peterson, C. K. (2010). The role of asymmetric frontal cortical activity in emotion-related phenomena: A review and update. *Biological Psychology*, *84*(3), 451–462. doi: 10.1016/j.biopsycho.2009.08.010

Harmon-Jones, E., Gable, P. A., & Price, T. F. (2011). Leaning embodies desire: Evidence that leaning forward increases relative left frontal cortical activation to appetitive stimuli. *Biological Psychology*, *87*(2), 311–313. doi: 10.1016/j.biopsycho.2011.03.009

Harrison, N. A., Kreibig, S. D., & Critchley, H. D. (2013). A two-way road: Efferent and afferent pathways of autonomic activity in emotion. In J. Armony & P. Vuilleumier (Eds.), *The Cambridge handbook of human affective neuroscience* (pp. 82–106). Cambridge: Cambridge University Press.

Holstege, G., Georgiadis, J. R., Paans, A. M. J., Meiners, L. C., van der Graaf, F. H. C. E., & Reinders, A. A. T. S. (2003). Brain activation during human male ejaculation. *Journal of Neuroscience*, *23*(27), 9185–9193.

Huston, J. M., & Tracey, K. J. (2010). The pulse of inflammation: heart rate variability, the cholinergic anti-inflammatory pathway and implications for therapy. *Journal of Internal Medicine*, *269*(1), 45–53. doi: 10.1111/j.1365-2796.2010.02321.x

Kashdan, T. B., & Rottenberg, J. (2010). Psychological flexibility as a fundamental aspect of health. *Clinical Psychology Review*, *30*(7), 865–878. doi: 10.1016/j.cpr.2010.03.001

Kemp, A. H., & Felmingham, K. (2008). The psychology and neuroscience of depression and anxiety: Towards an integrative model of emotion disorders. *Psychology & Neuroscience*, *1*(2), 171–175.

Kemp, A. H., & Quintana, D. S. (2013). The relationship between mental and physical health: insights from the study of heart rate variability. *International Journal of Psychophysiology: Official Journal of the International Organization of Psychophysiology*, *89*(3), 288–296. doi:10.1016/j.ijpsycho.2013.06.018

Kemp, A. H., Griffiths, K., Felmingham, K. L., Shankman, S. A., Drinkenburg, W., Arns, M., et al. (2010a). Disorder specificity despite comorbidity: Resting EEG alpha asymmetry in major depressive disorder and post-traumatic stress disorder. *Biological Psychology*, *85*(2), 350–354. doi: 10.1016/j.biopsycho.2010.08.001

Kemp, A. H., Quintana, D. S., Felmingham, K. L., Matthews, S., & Jelinek, H. F. (2012a). Depression, comorbid anxiety disorders, and heart rate variability in physically healthy, unmedicated patients: Implications for cardiovascular risk. (K. Hashimoto, Ed.). *PLoS ONE*, *7*(2), e30777. doi: 10.1371/journal.pone.0030777.t002

Kemp, A. H., Quintana, D. S., Gray, M. A., Felmingham, K. L., Brown, K., & Gatt, J. M. (2010b). Impact of depression and antidepressant treatment on heart rate variability: A review and meta-analysis. *Biological Psychiatry*, *67*(11), 1067–1074. doi: 10.1016/j.biopsych.2009.12.012

Kemp, A. H., Quintana, D. S., Kuhnert, R.-L., Griffiths, K., Hickie, I. B., & Guastella, A. J. (2012b). Oxytocin increases heart rate variability in humans at rest: Implications for social approach-related motivation and capacity for social engagement. (K. Hashimoto, Ed.). *PLoS ONE*, *7*(8), e44014. doi: 10.1371/journal.pone.0044014.g002

Kreibig, S. D. (2010). Autonomic nervous system activity in emotion: A review. *Biological Psychology*, *84*(3), 14–41. doi: 10.1016/j.biopsycho.2010.03.010

LeDoux, J. (2012). Rethinking the emotional brain. *Neuron*, *73*(4), 653–676. doi: 10.1016/j.neuron.2012.02.004

Ledoux, J. E. (1998). *The emotional brain*. Simon and Schuster, New York.

Leibenluft, E., Gobbini, M. I., Harrison, T., & Haxby, J. V. (2004). Mothers' neural activation in response to pictures of their children and other children. *Biological Psychiatry*, *56*(4), 225–232. doi: 10.1016/j.biopsych.2004.05.017

Levenson, R. W., Ekman, P., & Friesen, W. V. (1990). Voluntary facial action generates emotion-specific autonomic nervous system activity. *Psychophysiology*, *27*(4), 363–384.

Lewis, M. B., & Bowler, P. J. (2009). Botulinum toxin cosmetic therapy correlates with a more positive mood. *Journal of Cosmetic Dermatology*, *8*(1), 24–26. doi: 10.1111/j.1473-2165.2009.00419.x

Lindquist, K. A., Siegel, E. H., Quigley, K. S., & Barrett, L. F. (2013). The hundred-year emotion war: Are emotions natural kinds or psychological constructions? Comment on Lench, Flores, and Bench (2011). *Psychological Bulletin*, *139*(1), 255–263. doi: 10.1037/a0029038

Lindquist, K. A., Wager, T. D., Kober, H., Bliss-Moreau, E., & Barrett, L. F. (2012). The brain basis of emotion: A meta-analytic review. *Behavioral and Brain Sciences*, *35*(03), 121–143. doi: 10.1017/S0140525X11000446

Maren, S. (2001). Neurobiology of Pavlovian fear conditioning. *Annual Review of Neuroscience*, *24*, 897–931. doi: 10.1146/annurev.neuro.24.1.897

Mathersul, D., Williams, L. M., Hopkinson, P. J., & Kemp, A. H. (2008). Investigating models of affect: Relationships among EEG alpha asymmetry, depression, and anxiety. *Emotion*, *8*(4), 560–572. doi: 10.1037/a0012811

Mayberg, H., Liotti, M., Brannan, S., McGinnis, S., Mahurin, R., Jerabek, P., et al. (1999). Reciprocal limbic-cortical function and negative mood: Converging PET findings in depression and normal sadness. *American Journal of Psychiatry*, *156*(5), 675.

Murphy, F. C., Nimmo-Smith, I., & Lawrence, A. D. (2003). Functional neuroanatomy of emotions: A meta-analysis. *Cognitive, Affective, & Behavioral Neuroscience, 3*(3), 207–233.

Oppenheimer, S. M., Gelb, A., Girvin, J. P., & Hachinski, V. C. (1992). Cardiovascular effects of human insular cortex stimulation. *Neurology, 42*(9), 1727–1732.

Oveis, C., Cohen, A. B., Gruber, J., Shiota, M. N., Haidt, J., & Keltner, D. (2009). Resting respiratory sinus arrhythmia is associated with tonic positive emotionality. *Emotion, 9*(2), 265–270. doi: 10.1037/a0015383

Papez, J. W. (1937). A proposed mechanism of emotion. J Neuropsychiatry Clin Neurosci. Winter; *7*(1):103-12. PMID 7711480

Panksepp, J. (2005). Psychology. Beyond a joke: From animal laughter to human joy? *Science, 308*(5718), 62–63. doi: 10.1126/science.1112066

Panksepp, J. (2007). Neurologizing the psychology of affects: How appraisal-based constructivism and basic emotion theory can coexist. *Perspectives on Psychological Science, 2*(3), 281–296.

Panksepp, J. (2011). What is an emotional feeling? Lessons about affective origins from cross-species neuroscience. *Motivation and Emotion, 36*(1), 4–15. doi: 10.1007/s11031-011-9232-y

Panksepp, J., & Burgdorf, J. (2000). 50-kHz chirping (laughter?) in response to conditioned and unconditioned tickle-induced reward in rats: Effects of social housing and genetic variables. *Behavioural Brain Research, 115*(1), 25–38.

Panksepp, J., & Burgdorf, J. (2003). "Laughing" rats and the evolutionary antecedents of human joy? *Physiology & Behavior, 79*(3), 533–547.

Panksepp, J., & Watt, D. (2011). What is basic about basic emotions? Lasting lessons from affective neuroscience. *Emotion Review, 3*(4), 387–396. doi: 10.1177/1754073911410741

Pavlov, V. A., & Tracey, K. J. (2012). The vagus nerve and the inflammatory reflex—linking immunity and metabolism. *Nature Reviews Endocrinology, 8*(12), 743–754. doi: 10.1038/nrendo.2012.189

Penfield, W., & Faulk, M. E. (1955). The insula; further observations on its function. *Brain, 78*(4), 445–470.

Perria, L., Rosadini, G., & Rossi, G. F. (1961). Determination of side of cerebral dominance with amobarbital. *Archives of Neurology, 4*, 173–181.

Pessoa, L., & Adolphs, R. (2010). Emotion processing and the amygdala: From a "low road" to "many roads" of evaluating biological significance. *Nature Reviews Neuroscience, 11*(11), 773–783. doi: 10.1038/nrn2920

Phan, K. (2002). Functional neuroanatomy of emotion: A meta-analysis of emotion activation studies in PET and fMRI. *NeuroImage, 16*(2), 331–348. doi: 10.1006/nimg.2002.1087

Porges, S. W. (1995). Orienting in a defensive world: Mammalian modifications of our evolutionary heritage. A Polyvagal Theory. *Psychophysiology, 32*(4), 301–318.

Porges, S. W. (2001). The polyvagal theory: Phylogenetic substrates of a social nervous system. International journal of psychophysiology. *Official Journal of the International Organization of Psychophysiology, 42*(2), 123–146.

Porges, S. W. (2003). The Polyvagal Theory: phylogenetic contributions to social behavior. *Physiology & Behavior, 79*(3), 503–513.

Porges, S. W. (2007). The polyvagal perspective. *Biological Psychology, 74*(2), 116–143. doi: 10.1016/j.biopsycho.2006.06.009

Porges, S. W. (2009). The Polyvagal Theory: New insights into adaptive reactions of the autonomic nervous system. *Cleveland Clinic Journal of Medicine, 76*(Suppl. 2), S86–90. doi: 10.3949/ccjm.76.s2.17

Porges, S. W. (2011). *The Polyvagal Theory: Neurophysiological foundations of emotions, attachment, communication, and self-regulation* (1st ed.). New York: W. W. Norton & Company.

Price, T. F., Dieckman, L. W., & Harmon-Jones, E. (2012). Embodying approach motivation: body posture influences startle eyeblink and event-related potential responses to appetitive stimuli. *Biological Psychology, 90*(3), 211–217. doi: 10.1016/j.biopsycho.2012.04.001

Price, T. F., Peterson, C. K., & Harmon-Jones, E. (2011). The emotive neuroscience of embodiment. *Motivation and Emotion, 36*(1), 27–37. doi: 10.1007/s11031-011-9258-1

Radua, J., & Mataix-Cols, D. (2012). Meta-analytic methods for neuroimaging data explained. *Biology of Mood & Anxiety Disorders, 2*(1), 6. doi: 10.1186/2045-5380-2-6

Rainville, P., Bechara, A., Naqvi, N., & Damasio, A. R. (2006). Basic emotions are associated with distinct patterns of cardiorespiratory activity. *International Journal of Psychophysiology, 61*(1), 5–18. doi: 10.1016/j.ijpsycho.2005.10.024

Reimann, M., & Bechara, A. (2010). The somatic marker framework as a neurological theory of decision-making: Review, conceptual comparisons, and future neuroeconomics research. *Journal of Economic Psychology, 31*(5), 767–776.

Rossi, G. F., & Rosadini, G. (1967). Experimental analyses of cerebral dominance in man. In D. H. Millikan & F. L. Darley (Eds.), *Brain mechanisms underlying speech and language*. New York: Grune & Stratton.

Rottenberg, J., Wilhelm, F. H., Gross, J. J., & Gotlib, I. H. (2003). Vagal rebound during resolution of tearful crying among depressed and nondepressed individuals. *Psychophysiology, 40*(1), 1–6.

Sauter, D. A., & Scott, S. K. (2007). More than one kind of happiness: Can we recognize vocal expressions of different positive states? *Motivation and Emotion, 31*(3), 192–199. doi: 10.1007/s11031-007-9065-x

Sergerie, K., Chochol, C., & Armony, J. L. (2008). The role of the amygdala in emotional processing: a quantitative meta-analysis of functional neuroimaging studies. *Neuroscience and Biobehavioral Reviews, 32*(4), 811–830. doi: 10.1016/j.neubiorev.2007.12.002

Slotema, C. W., Blom, J. D., Hoek, H. W., & Sommer, I. E. C. (2010). Should we expand the toolbox of psychiatric treatment methods to include repetitive transcranial magnetic stimulation (rTMS)? A meta-analysis of the efficacy of rTMS in psychiatric disorders. *The Journal of Clinical Psychiatry, 71*(7), 873–884. doi: 10.4088/JCP.08m04872gre

Stemmler, G., Heldmann, M., Pauls, C. A., & Scherer, T. (2001). Constraints for emotion specificity in fear and anger: The context counts. *Psychophysiology, 38*(2), 275–291.

Strack, F., Martin, L. L., & Stepper, S. (1988). Inhibiting and facilitating conditions of the human smile: a nonobtrusive test of the facial feedback hypothesis. *Journal of Personality and Social Psychology, 54*(5), 768–777.

Terzian, H., & Cecotto, C. (1959). Determination and study of hemisphere dominance by means of intracarotid sodium Amytal injection in man: II. Electroencephalographic effects. *Bolletino della Societa Italiana Sperimentale, 35*, 1626–1630.

Tettamanti, M., Rognoni, E., Cafiero, R., Costa, T., Galati, D., & Perani, D. (2012). Distinct pathways of neural coupling for different basic emotions. *Human Brain Mapping Journal, 59*(2), 1804–1817. doi: 10.1016/j.neuroimage.2011.08.018

Thayer, J. F., & Brosschot, J. F. (2005). Psychosomatics and psychopathology: Looking up and down from the brain. *Psychoneuroendocrinology, 30*(10), 1050–1058. doi: 10.1016/j.psyneuen.2005.04.014

Thayer, J. F., & Lane, R. D. (2000). A model of neurovisceral integration in emotion regulation and dysregulation. *Journal of Affective Disorders, 61*(3), 201–216.

Thayer, J. F., & Lane, R. D. (2007). The role of vagal function in the risk for cardiovascular disease and mortality. *Biological Psychology, 74*(2), 224–242. doi: 10.1016/j.biopsycho.2005.11.013

Thayer, J. F., & Lane, R. D. (2009). Claude Bernard and the heart–brain connection: Further elaboration of a model of neurovisceral integration. *Neuroscience and Biobehavioral Reviews, 33*(2), 81–88. doi: 10.1016/j.neubiorev.2008.08.004

Thayer, J. F., Hansen, A. L., Saus-Rose, E., & Johnsen, B. H. (2009). Heart rate variability, prefrontal neural function, and cognitive performance: the neurovisceral integration perspective on self-regulation, adaptation, and health. *Annals of Behavioral Medicine, 37*(2), 141–153. doi: 10.1007/s12160-009-9101-z

Thayer, J. F., Yamamoto, S. S., & Brosschot, J. F. (2010). The relationship of autonomic imbalance, heart rate variability and cardiovascular disease risk factors. *International Journal of Cardiology, 141*(2), 122–131. doi: 10.1016/j.ijcard.2009.09.543

Tracey, K. (2002). The inflammatory reflex. *Nature, 420*(6917), 853–859.

Tracey, K. J. (2007). Physiology and immunology of the cholinergic antiinflammatory pathway. *Journal of Clinical Investigation, 117*(2), 289–296. doi: 10.1172/JCI30555

Urry, H. L., Nitschke, J. B., Dolski, I., Jackson, D. C., Dalton, K. M., Mueller, C. J., et al. (2004). Making a life worth living: Neural correlates of well-being. *Psychological science, 15*(6), 367–372. doi: 10.1111/j.0956-7976.2004.00686.x

Vytal, K., & Hamann, S. (2010). Neuroimaging support for discrete neural correlates of basic emotions: A voxel-based meta-analysis. *Journal of Cognitive Neuroscience, 22*(12), 2864–2885. doi: 10.1162/jocn.2009.21366

Wacker, J., Chavanon, M.-L., Leue, A., & Stemmler, G. (2008). Is running away right? The behavioral activation-behavioral inhibition model of anterior asymmetry. *Emotion, 8*(2), 232–249. doi: 10.1037/1528-3542.8.2.232

Wild, B., Rodden, F. A., Grodd, W., & Ruch, W. (2003). Neural correlates of laughter and humour. *Brain: A Journal of Neurology, 126*(Pt 10), 2121–2138. doi: 10.1093/brain/awg226

Wollmer, M. A., de Boer, C., Kalak, N., Beck, J., Götz, T., Schmidt, T., et al. (2012). Facing depression with botulinum toxin: A randomized controlled trial. *Journal of Psychiatric Research, 46*(5), 574–581. doi: 10.1016/j.jpsychires.2012.01.027

Appraisal Models

Jonathan Gratch *and* Stacy Marsella

Abstract

This chapter discusses appraisal theory, the most influential theory of emotion in affective computing today, including how appraisal theory arose, some of its well-known variants, and why appraisal theory plays such a prominent role in computational models of emotion. The authors describe the component model framework, a useful framework for organizing and contrasting alternative computational models of emotion and outline some of the contemporary computational approaches based on appraisal theory and the practical systems they help support. Finally, the authors discuss open challenges and future directions.

Key Words: emotion, appraisal theory, computational models

Introduction

Although psychologists can afford the luxury of describing emotion in broad, abstract terms, computer scientists must get down to brass tacks. For machines to reason about a phenomenon, it must be representable in a formal language and manipulated by well-defined operations. Computer science entrants into the field of emotion are immediately confronted with the challenge of how to represent such imprecise and overlapping concepts as emotion, mood, and temperament. Emotion theory is one useful tool for confronting this imprecision. Psychological theories of emotion are by no means precise, but they posit important constraints on emotion representations and processes. Alternative theories pose quite different and potentially irreconcilable constraints and thus constitute choice points on how one approaches the problem of "implementing" affective computations. This chapter discusses appraisal theory, the most influential theory of emotion in affective computing

today. We discuss how appraisal theory arose and some of its important variants and computational instantiations, but also some of the challenges this theory faces (see Reisenzein's chapter in this volume for a more general overview of emotion theories, including appraisal).

Since the very beginnings of artificial intelligence (AI), theoretical controversies about the nature of the human mind have been reflected in battles over computational techniques. The early years of AI research were dominated by controversies over whether knowledge should be represented as procedures or declarative statements (e.g., Winograd, 1975), reflecting similar debates raging in cognitive science. Within the subdomain of automated planning research, debates erupted over whether intelligent action selection was best conceptualized as processes operating on explicit plan representations or more perceptually driven reactive processes (e.g., Ginsberg, 1989; Suchman, 1987). Even within the sub-subdomain of those who favor explicit plan representations, debates rage as to whether planning is best conceptualized as a search through a space of possible world states or a search through a space of possible plans (e.g., Kambhampati & Srivastava, 1995). These choices are not simply theoretical but have clear implications for the capabilities of the resulting software systems: for example, state-based planners, in that they don't maintain explicit representations of plans, make it exceedingly difficult to compare, identify threats, and de-conflict plans of multiple agents, thus making them (arguably) an ill-suited choice for social or multiagent problem solving.

Emotion theories also have potentially profound implications for computational systems that reason about affective phenomena. As one dramatic example, consider the extremely influential theory of humours that Galen of Pergamum (AD 130–200) used to explain human mood and temperament. According to this view, mood was influenced by specific environmental and physiological processes and life events. Conceptually, mood reflected a mixture of bodily substances: phlegm, black bile, yellow bile, and blood. A predominance of yellow bile led to strong fiery emotions, was promoted by warm and dry weather, and was more common in youth or summer; conversely, phlegm produced a stolidly calm disposition that arose typically in cold and moist environments and in old age or winter. This theory suggests clear ways to represent measure and control mood. For example, the theory of humours implies that mood disorders can be treated by bleeding, blistering, sweating, or vomiting, a process that was common practice well into the eighteenth century (Duffy, 1959).

More contemporary theoretical debates center on the relationship between emotion and cognition. These debates address the following questions: Is emotional reasoning somehow distinct and qualitatively different from unemotional reasoning (Kahneman, 2003; LeDoux, 1996)? Do emotions serve adaptive functions, or do they lead to maladaptive decisions (Frank, 2004; Keltner & Haidt, 1999; Pham, 2007; H. A. Simon, 1967)? Does emotion precede or follow thought (Lazarus, 1984; Zajonc, 1984)? Appraisal theory has played a central role in shaping these debates, although, as we will see in this chapter, appraisal theorists do not always agree on how to answer these questions.

This chapter is structured as follows. We first review appraisal theories, examine why they arose, and discuss some of influential variants. We then discuss why appraisal theories play such a prominent rule in computational models and how some of their properties are particularly well-suited for computational realization. We outline some of the contemporary computational approaches based on appraisal theory and the practical systems they help support. Finally, we discuss open challenges and future directions.

Appraisal Theory

Appraisal theory is currently a predominant force among psychological perspectives on emotion and is arguably the most fruitful source for those interested in the design of AI systems because it emphasizes and explains the connection between emotion and the symbolic reasoning processes that AI favors. Indeed, the large majority of computational models of emotion stem from this tradition. In appraisal theory, emotion arises from patterns of individual judgment concerning the relationship between events and an individual's beliefs, desires, and intentions, sometimes referred to as the *person–environment relationship* (Lazarus, 1991). These judgments are cognitive in nature but not necessarily conscious or controlled. They characterize personally significant events in terms of a fixed set of specific criteria, sometimes referred to as *appraisal variables* or *appraisal dimensions* and include considerations such as whether events are congruent with the individual's goals, expected, or controllable. (Table 5.1 illustrates appraisal variables proposed by some prominent appraisal theorists.) According to appraisal theory, specific emotions are associated with specific patterns of appraisal. For example, a surprising and uncontrollable event might provoke fear. In several versions of appraisal theory, appraisals also trigger cognitive responses, often referred to as *coping strategies*—e.g., planning, procrastination, or resignation—that feed back into a continual cycle of appraisal and reappraisal (Lazarus, 1991, p. 127).

The assumption underlying appraisal theory (i.e., that emotions arise from subjective evaluations) has reoccurred many times in history and can be found in the writings of Aristotle and Hume. The recent usage of the term "appraisal" commences with the writings of Magda Arnold (1960) and was subsequently reinforced by the work of Richard Lazarus (1966). The development of appraisal theory was motivated, in part, by the observation that different individuals might respond quite differently to the same event and

Table 5.1 Appraisal variables proposed by several appraisal theorists.

Scherer	Frijda	Roseman	Smith/Ellsworth
Novelty	Change		Attentional activity
• Suddenness			
• Familiarity	Familiarity		
• Predictability			
Intrinsic pleasantness	Valence		Pleasantness
Goal significance		Appetitive/Aversive	
• Concern relevance	Focality	Motives	importance
Outcome probability	Certainty	Certainty	certainty
• Expectation	Presence		
• Conduciveness	Open/Closed	Motive consistency	Perceived obstacle/Anticipated effort
• Urgency	Urgency		
Coping potential			
• Cause: agent	Intent/Self–other	Agency	Human agency
• Cause: motive			
• Control	Modifiability	Control potential	Situational control
• Power	Controllability		
• Adjustment			
Compatibility Standards			
• External	Value relevance		Legitimacy
• Internal			

Terms that line up horizontally refer to comparable processes, despite the fact that the respective authors use different labels (adapted from Scherer, 2005).

the desire to posit specific mechanisms that could explain these differences. Appraisal theories have been studied for many years, and there is substantial experimental evidence that supports the basic claims underlying this theory (for a more detailed introduction into the different variants of appraisal theory, see Scherer, Schorr, & Johnstone, 2001).

In terms of underlying components of emotion, appraisal theory foregrounds appraisal as a central process. Appraisal theorists typically view appraisal as the cause of emotion, or at least of the physiological, behavioral, and cognitive changes associated with emotion (see Parkinson, 1997, for one critical perspective on this view). Some appraisal theorists emphasize "emotion" as a discrete component within their theories, whereas others treat the term

"emotion" more broadly to refer to some configuration of appraisals, bodily responses, and subjective experience (see Ellsworth & Scherer, 2003, for a discussion). Much of the research has focused on the structural relationship between appraisal variables and specific discrete emotions—that is, which pattern of appraisal variables would elicit hope (see Ortony, Clore, & Collins, 1988), or on the structural relationship between appraisal variables and specific behavioral and cognitive responses— that is, which pattern of appraisal variables would elicit certain facial expressions (Scherer & Ellgring, 2007; Smith & Scott, 1997) or coping tendencies (Lazarus, 1991). Appraisal theorists allow that the same situation may elicit multiple appraisals and, in some cases, that these appraisals can occur at multiple levels of reasoning (Scherer, 2001), but most theorists are relatively silent on how these individual appraisals would combine into an overall emotional state or if this state is best represented by discrete motor programs (corresponding to discrete emotion categories) or more dimensional representations (such as valence and arousal).

Today, most emotion researchers accept that appraisal plays a role in emotion, although they may differ on the centrality of this process. Active research on appraisal theory has moved away from demonstrating the existence of appraisal and has turned to more specific questions about how it impacts individual and social behavior. Some work examines the processing constraints underlying appraisal—to what extent is it parallel or sequential (Moors, De Houwer, Hermans, & Eelen, 2005; Scherer, 2001)? Does it occur at multiple levels (Scherer, 2001; Smith & Kirby, 2000)? Some work seeks to create a better understanding of the cognitive, situational, and dispositional factors that influence appraisal judgments (Kuppens & Van Mechelen, 2007; Smith & Kirby, 2009). Other work focuses more on the consequences of emotion on subsequent appraisal and decision making (Han, Lerner, & Keltner, 2007; Horberg, Oveis, & Keltner, 2011). Finally, a very active area of interest concerns the implications of appraisal theory on social cognition (Gratch & Marsella, 2014; Hareli & Hess, 2009; Manstead & Fischer, 2001).

Although there are many appraisal theorists, work in affective computing has been most influenced by a small set of appraisal theories. The most influential among these has been the so-called *OCC model* (Figure 5.1A) of Ortony, Clore, and Collins (1988)—the name reflects the first initial of each author. OCC is most naturally seen as a structural model (in the sense of structural equation modeling) in that it posits a small set of criteria (appraisal variables) that distinguish between different emotion terms. Thus, it can be seen as an easily implemented decision tree for classifying emotion-evoking situations, which perhaps explains its seduction for computer scientists.

At the top level, the OCC divides emotions into three broad classes. First, objects or events might lead to emotion in that they are intrinsically pleasing/displeasing for a given individual (e.g., "I love chocolate but hate rock concerts"). Second, objects or events might evoke emotion based how they relate to an individual's goals (e.g., "I'm afraid this traffic will make me late for my date"). Finally, from a social perspective, emotions may arise due to how an object (typically a person) or event impact social norms (e.g., "I disapprove of his stealing"). Within these broad categories, emotions are further distinguished by the extent to which they are positive/negative, impact self or other, and so forth. The OCC also posits a large number of criteria that can impact the intensity of emotional reactions.

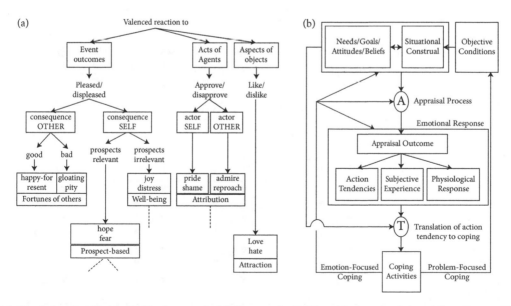

Fig. 5.1 Gratch Appraisal Models. (A) The figure on the left illustrates the OCC model of emotion (adapted from Ortony, Clore, & Collins, 1988). (B) The figure on the right is one visual representation of Lazarus's appraisal theory proposed by Smith and Lazarus (adapted from Smith & Lazarus, 1990).

Whereas the OCC emphasizes the structure of emotion-eliciting events, the work of Richard Lazarus (1991) takes a broader and more process-oriented view that emphasizes both the antecedents and consequences of emotion. Lazarus's work is rich and nuanced, but affective computing researchers have been most influenced by the description of this theory outlined in a joint paper with Craig Smith (Smith & Lazarus, 1990), which recasts the theory in more computational terms (as illustrated in Figure 5.1B). Lazarus's theory follows a similar approach to OCC with regard to emotion antecedents (i.e., emotions arise from patterns of judgments on how objects or event impact beliefs, attitudes, and goals). But inspired by his work with clinical populations, this theory further emphasizes that appraisals shape broader patterns of behavior, which he calls coping strategies, and thus influence subsequent appraisals in a dynamic, cyclical process of appraisal and reappraisal. Coping strategies are roughly grouped into problem-focused strategies (e.g., planning and seeking instrumental social support) that act on the world and emotion-focused strategies (e.g., distancing or avoidance) that act on the self. In either case, coping strategies serve to modify the person–environment relationship to maintain emotional well-being.

Klaus Scherer's *sequential checking theory* (SCT) is the most recent and certainly the most elaborate appraisal theory to significantly impact affective computing researchers (Figure 5.2). As with the OCC and Lazarus's cognitive mediational theory, the SCT posits a set of appraisal dimensions that relate to the assessment of the person–environment relationship. As with Lazarus, the SCT adopts the view of appraisal as a process that unfolds over time, with later stages feeding back and modifying initial appraisals in a cyclical process of appraisal and reappraisal. The SCT goes further than Lazarus in positing a fixed sequential structure to appraisals. First, novel events are appraised as if they are self-relevant. If relevant, they are judged for their implication for the individual's goals. Next, coping potential is assessed, and finally events are appraised with regard to their compatibility with social norms.

Although the SCT is the most elaborate appraisal theory, this doesn't necessarily make it the most suitable starting point for an affective computing researcher. There are many other variants of appraisal theory, and affective computing researchers would benefit by considering multiple theoretical sources and understanding the different processing and representational commitments they might entail. For example, Rainer Reisenzein's belief-desire theory of emotion (Reisenzein, 2009) is a simple and elegant

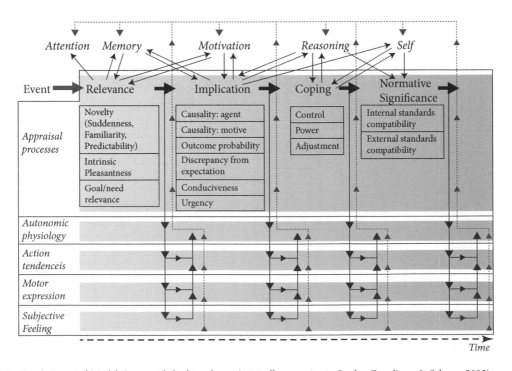

Fig. 5.2 Gratch Appraisal Model. Sequential checking theory (originally appearing in Sander, Grandjean, & Scherer, 2005).

formalization that especially appeals to those interested in formal computational models, and the work of Frijda (1988) emphasizes the connection between emotion and action tendencies and has influenced several computational models (Moffat & Frijda, 1995; Frijda & Swagerman, 1987).

Each of these appraisal theories shares much in common. Each emphasizes that emotions are a relational construct: they represent how an individual is doing vis-à-vis his or her environment. They further share that this relationship is assessed in terms of specific appraisal variables that characterize this relationship. They differ in detail, and this may have implications for affective computing researchers who aim to exploit these theories. For example, appraisals of control and coping potential play a prominent role in SCT and Lazarus's theory (see also Roseman, 2001) but not in the OCC. These differences impact the conceptualization of emotion (e.g., control is a key component of anger for Lazarus but not OCC) as well as the relationship between emotion and behavior (e.g., for Lazarus, appraisals of control dictate the coping strategy an individual will adopt).

Computational Appraisal Theory

Artificial intelligence grew out of cognitive and symbolic approaches to modeling human decision making (e.g., Simon, 1969) so it is hardly surprising that a cognitive theory like appraisal theory should have such affinity for computational scientists of emotion. Unlike some alternative perspectives on emotion (e.g., Russell & Barrett, 1999), appraisal theory aspires to provide a detailed information processing description of the mechanisms underlying emotion production (although perhaps less detailed descriptions of other aspects of emotion processing, such as its bidirectional associations with bodily processes). Further, well-known appraisal theorists (e.g., Andrew Ortony and Craig Smith) were trained in computational methods and tend to describe their theories in ways that resonate with affective computing researchers.

Within affective computing research, models derived from appraisal theories of emotion emphasize appraisal as the central process to be modeled. Computational appraisal models often encode elaborate mechanisms for deriving appraisal variables, such as decision-theoretic plans (Gratch & Marsella, 2004; Marsella & Gratch, 2009), reactive plans (Neal Reilly, 2006; Rank & Petta, 2005; Staller & Petta, 2001), Markov decision processes (El Nasr, Yen, & Ioerger, 2000; Si, Marsella, &

Pynadath, 2008), or detailed cognitive models (Marinier, Laird, & Lewis, 2009). Emotion itself is often less elaborately modeled. It is sometimes treated simply as a label (sometimes with an intensity) to which behavior can be attached (Elliott, 1992). Appraisal is typically modeled as the cause of emotion, with specific emotion labels being derived via *if-then rules* on a set of appraisal variables. Some approaches make a distinction between a specific emotion instance (allowing multiple instances to be derived from the same event) and a more generalized "affective state" or "mood" (see the later discussion of core affect) that summarizes the effect of recent emotion elicitations (Gebhard, 2005; Gratch & Marsella, 2004; Neal Reilly, 1996). Some more recent models attempt to capture the impact of momentary emotion and mood on the appraisal process (Gebhard, 2005; Gratch & Marsella, 2004; Marsella & Gratch, 2009; Paiva, Dias, & Aylett, 2005).

In most computational models, appraisal is not an end of itself, but a means to influence behavior (such as an agent's emotional expressions or decision making). Models make different choices on how behavior is related to appraisal, emotion, and mood. Some systems encode a direct connection between appraisals and behavior. For example, in Gratch and Marsella's (2004) EMA model, coping behaviors are triggered directly from appraisals (although the choice of which appraisal to focus on is moderated by a mood state). Other systems associate behaviors with emotion (Elliott, 1992) or mood (Gebhard, 2005), essentially encoding the theoretical claim that affect mediates behavior. In the former case, the emotional state as a label is not so critical if there are clear rules that determine behavior (including expression) as a function of appraisal patterns.

There are now several computational models based on appraisal theory (for recent overviews, see Hudlicka, 2008; Marsella, Gratch, & Petta, 2010), but modelers often fail to build on each other's work, tending rather to start anew from original psychological sources. This is beginning to change, and there is now a family tree of sorts, illustrated in Figure 5.3. Yet, even when models build on each other, this tends to be at an abstract, conceptual level. Methods may adopt a similar general approach (e.g., cast appraisal as inference over some plan-like data structures) but rarely share identical algorithm or representational choices, as in other fields of computer science.

Steunebrink et al. (2012) used KARO to formalize the cognitive-motivational preconditions

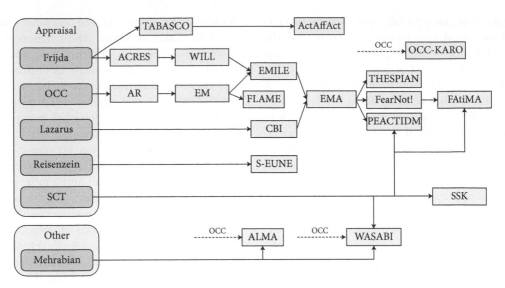

Fig. 5.3 Gratch Appraisal Model. A family history of appraisal models. Blocks on the left correspond to original psychological sources. Blocks on the right correspond to models, and arrows correspond to conceptual links. Models mentioned include ACRES (Frijda & Swagerman, 1987), AR (Elliott, 1992), TABASCO (Staller & Petta, 2001), WILL (Moffat & Frijda, 1995), EM (Neal Reilly, 1996), FLAME (El Nasr et al., 2000), EMILE (Gratch, 2000), CBI (Marsella, Johnson, & LaBore, 2000), S-EUNE (Macedo, Reisenzein, & Cardoso, 2004), ALMA (Gebhard, 2005), ActAffAct (Rank, 2009), EMA (Gratch & Marsella, 2004), THESPIAN (Si et al., 2008), FearNot (Dias & Paiva, 2005), PEACTIDM (Marinier et al., 2009), WASABI (Becker-Asano, 2008), OCC-KARO (Steunebrink, Dastani, & Meyer, 2008), FAtiMA (Dias, Mascarenhas, & Paiva, 2011), and SSK (Broekens, DeGroot, & Kosters, 2008).

of the 22 emotions considered in the OCC theory (Ortony et al., 1988).

When approaching a computational approach to appraisal theory, we encourage affective computing researchers to avoid the temptation to simply "implement" a specific psychological theory. In his 1969 book, *The Sciences of the Artificial*, Herb Simon outlined several ways in which computational scientists bring a unique and complementary perspective to the challenge of understanding human intelligence. First, in contrast to the natural sciences, which seek to describe intelligence as it is found in nature, the "artificial sciences" seek to describe intelligence as it ought to be. This normative emphasis often leads to serviceable abstractions that crisply capture the essence of phenomena while avoiding the messy details of how these functions are implemented in biological organisms. Second, computational scientists approach the problem of achieving function with a mindset emphasizing process, and, from this perspective, apparently complex behavior can often be reduced to simple goal-directed processes interacting over time with a complex environment. Finally, computational scientists produce working artifacts, and these allow theories to be tested in novel and important ways. For example, we might model an artificial ant in terms of a minimal number of theoretically posited

functions, simulate the interaction of this model with complex environments, and thereby empirically work out the implicit consequences of our assumptions. Indeed, Simon's original argument was that psychological theories were sorely in need of rational reinterpretation using the computational tools of function and process. Thus, by faithfully "implementing" a psychological theory, computational scientists are doing a disservice both to computational science and the original theory.

New tools often transform science, opening up new approaches to research and allowing previously unaddressed questions to be explored, as well as revealing new questions. Computational appraisal theory, although still in its infancy, has begun to have an impact in several distinct areas of research, including the design of artificially intelligent entities and research on human–computer interactions. It is even beginning to flow back and shape the psychological research from which it sprang. In terms of AI and robotics, appraisal theory suggests ways to generalize and extend traditional rational models of intelligence (Antos & Pfeffer, 2011; Gmytrasiewicz & Lisetti, 2000). In terms of human–computer interaction, appraisal theory posits that emotions reflect the personal significance of events, thus computers that either generate or recognize emotion may foster a better shared understanding of the beliefs, desires, and intentions of the human–machine system (Conati, 2002; Gratch & Marsella, 2005b). Finally, the exercise of translating psychological appraisal theory into a working artifact allows theory to be tested in novel and important ways.

A Component Model View

Elsewhere, we have argued that research into computational models of emotions could be considerably advanced by a more incremental and compositional approach toward model construction (Marsella et al., 2010), and we summarize these arguments here (see also Hudlicka, 2011; Reisenzein, 2001). This perspective emphasizes that appraisal involves an ensemble of information processing, and, as a consequence, an emotional model is often assembled from individual "submodels" and these smaller components could be (and in some cases, already are) shared. More importantly, these components can be seen as embodying certain content and process assumptions that can be potentially assessed and subsequently abandoned or improved as a result of these assessments, providing insights to all models that share this subapproach. Thus, this chapter summarizes this componential perspective when reviewing computational approaches to appraisal theory.

Figure 5.4 presents an idealized computational appraisal architecture consisting of a set of linked component models. This figure presents what we see as natural joints at which to decompose appraisal systems into coherent and often shared modules, although any given system may fail to implement some of these components or allow

different information paths between components. In this architecture, information flows in a cycle, as argued by several appraisal theorists (Lazarus, 1991; Parkinson, 2009; Scherer, 2001): some representation of the person–environment relationship is appraised, this leads to an affective response of some intensity, the response triggers behavioral and cognitive consequences, these consequences alter the person–environment, this change is appraised, and so on. Each of these stages can be represented by a model that represents or transforms state information relevant to emotion processing. Here, we introduce terminology associated with each of these.

• *Person–environment relationship.* Lazarus (1991) introduced this term to refer to some representation of the agent's relationship with its environment. This representation should allow an agent, in principle, to derive the relationship between external events (real or hypothetical) and the beliefs, desires, and intentions of the agent or other significant entities in the (real or hypothetical) social environment. This representation need not encode these relationships explicitly but must support their derivation. Examples of this include the decision-theoretical planning representations in EMA (Gratch & Marsella, 2004), which combines decision-theoretic planning representation with belief-desire-intention formalisms or the partially observable Markov decision representations in THESPIAN (Si et al., 2008).
• *Appraisal-derivation model.* An appraisal-derivation model transforms some representation of the person–environment relationship into a set of appraisal variables. For example, if an agent's

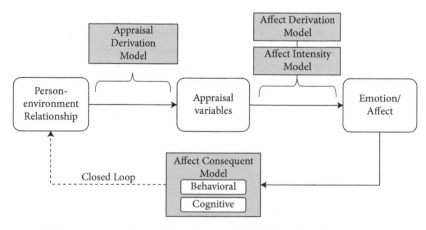

Fig. 5.4 Gratch Appraisal Model. A component model view of computational appraisal models.

goal is potentially thwarted by some external action, an appraisal-derivation model should be able to automatically infer that this circumstance is undesirable, assess its likelihood, and calculate the agent's ability to cope. Several computational appraisal models do not provide an appraisal-derivation model or treat its specification as something lying outside of the system (e.g., Gebhard, 2005), whereas others treat it as a central contribution of their approach (Gratch & Marsella, 2004). Models also differ in the processing constraints that this component should satisfy. For example, models influenced by Scherer's SCT incorporate assumptions about the order in which specific appraisal variables should be derived (Marinier, 2008).

• *Appraisal variables.* Appraisal variables correspond to the set of specific judgments that the agent can use to produce different emotional responses and are generated as a result of an appraisal-derivation model. Different models adopt different sets of appraisal variables or dimensions depending on their favorite appraisal theorist. For example, many approaches utilize the set of variables proposed by the work of Ortony, Collins and Clore (1999), known as the "OCC model," including AR (Elliott, 1992), EM (Neal Reilly, 1996), FLAME (El Nasr et al., 2000), and ALMA (Gebhard, 2005). Others favor the variables proposed by SCT including WASABI (Becker-Asano & Wachsmuth, 2008) and PEACTIDM (Marinier et al., 2009).

• *Affect-derivation model.* An affect-derivation model maps between appraisal variables and an affective state and specifies how an individual will react emotionally once a pattern of appraisals has been determined. There is some diversity in how models define "emotion," and here we consider any mapping from appraisal variables to affective state, where this state could be either a discrete emotion label, a set of discrete emotions, a core affect, or even some combination of these factors. For example, Elliott's AR (1992) maps appraisal variables into discrete emotion labels, Becker-Asano's WASABI (Becker-Asano & Wachsmuth, 2008) maps appraisals into a dimensional (e.g., PAD) representation of emotion, and Gebhard's (2005) ALMA does both simultaneously.

• *Affect-intensity model.* An affect-intensity model specifies the strength of the emotional response resulting from a specific appraisal. There is a close association between the affect-derivation model and intensity model; however, it is useful

to view these separately because they can be independently varied—indeed, computational systems with the same affect-derivation model often have quite different intensity equations (Gratch, Marsella, & Petta, 2009). Intensity models usually utilize a subset of appraisal variables (e.g., most intensity equations involve some notion of desirability and likelihood); however, they may involve several variables unrelated to appraisal (e.g., Elliott & Siegle, 1993).

• *Emotion/Affect.* Affect, in the present context, is a representation of the agent's current emotional state. This could be a discrete emotion label, a set of discrete emotions, a core affect (i.e., a continuous dimensional space), or even some combination of these factors. An important consideration in representing affect, particularly for systems that model the consequences of emotions, is whether the circumstances that provoked the emotion are explicitly represented. Emotions are often viewed as being about something (e.g., I am angry *at Valarie*), and behavioral or coping responses are typically directed at that target. Agents that model affect as some aggregate dimensional space must either preserve the connection between affect and domain objects that initiated changes to the dimensional space, or they must provide some attribution process that post hoc recovers a (possibly incorrect) domain object to apply the emotional response to. For example, EM (Neal Reilly, 1996) has a dimensional representation of core affect (valence and arousal) but also maintains a hierarchal data structure that preserves the linkages through each step of the appraisal process to the multiple instances of discrete emotion that underlie its dimensional calculus. In contrast, WASABI (Becker-Asano & Wachsmuth, 2008) breaks this link.

• *Affect-consequent model.* An affect-consequent model maps affect (or its antecedents) into some behavioral or cognitive change. Consequent models can be usefully described in terms of two dimensions, one distinguishing if the consequence is inner or outer directed (cognitive vs. behavioral), and the other describing whether or not the consequence feeds into a cycle (i.e., is open- or closed-loop). With regard to the inner- versus outer-directed dimension, *behavior consequent models* summarize how affect alters an agent's observable physical behavior (e.g., facial expressions), and *cognitive consequent models* determine how affect alters the nature or content of cognitive processes (e.g., coping strategies).

Most embodied computational systems model the former mapping: for example, WASABI maps regions of core affect into facial expressions (Becker-Asano, 2008, p. 85). Examples of the later include EMA's (Gratch & Marsella, 2004) implementation of *emotion-focused coping strategies* like wishful thinking. The second dimension distinguishes consequences by whether or not they form a cycle by altering the circumstances that triggered the original affective response. For example, a robot that merely expresses fear when its battery is expiring (i.e., an open-loop strategy) does not address the underlying causes of the fear, whereas one that translates this fear into an action tendency to seek power (i.e., a closed-loop strategy) is attempting to address its underlying cause. Open-loop models may be appropriate in multiagent setting where the display is presumed to recruit resources from other agents (e.g., building a robot that expresses fear makes sense if there is a human around who can recognize this display and plug it in). Closed-loop models attempt to realize a direct impact to regulate emotion and suggest ways to enhance the autonomy of intelligent agents and naturally implement a view of emotion as a continuous cycle of appraisal, response, and reappraisal.

Adopting a component model framework can help highlight these similarities and differences and facilitate empirical comparisons that assess the capabilities or validity of alternative algorithms for realizing component models. The FAtiMA modular appraisal framework is a recent important tool that helps these sort of comparisons (Dias, Mascarenhas, & Paiva, 2011). It essentially implements the conceptual framework outlined in Figure 5.4 and allows affective computing researchers to explore the interaction of different modules. Of course, the behavior of a specific component is not necessarily independent of other design choices, so such a strong independence assumption should be treated as a first approximation for assessing how alternative design choices will function in a specific system. However, unless there is a compelling reason to believe choices are correlated, such an analysis should be encouraged. Indeed, a key advantage of the compositional approach is that it forces researchers to explicitly articulate what these dependencies might be, should they wish to argue for a component that is repudiated by an empirical test that adopts a strong assumption of independence.

Challenges and Future Directions

Although influential, appraisal theory is by no means the final word on emotion. Several aspects of the theory are under intense scrutiny from both with the community of appraisal proponents (suggesting novel mechanisms and novel domains within which to explore the implications of the theory) and without (raising sustained criticism of core assumptions and calling the whole enterprise into question). These issues raise interesting challenges and opportunities in the field of affective computing.

Many of the criticisms of appraisal theory attack the core assumption, held by many but not all appraisal theorists, that cognitive processes precede emotional responses. In general, appraisal theory has been criticized for being overly cognitive, and it seemingly fails to capture the apparent reflexive and uncontrolled nature of emotional responses. This conflict was explored in great detail through a series of debates between Richard Lazarus and Robert Zajonc (Lazarus, 1984; Zajonc, 1984), with Zajonc taking the position that affective processes are primary and serve to motivate and recruit subsequent cognitive responses. Appraisal theorists respond with evidence that different emotions arise depending on the content of mental states (e.g., beliefs and goals).

From the perspective of computer science, many of these arguments seem to fall flat and seem to devolve into arguments over definitions: such as, what is cognition, deliberation, and consciousness? For example, AI has helped to highlight how much complexity underlies presumably reactive reasoning, making distinctions between levels less obvious. Nonetheless, this debate extends to more fundamental issues about the sequencing and linkage between cognition and emotion. For example, a strong cognitive perspective on appraisal theory would suggest that my anger is preceded by judgments that another has intentionally caused me harm. However, quite a bit of evidence suggests that the process could act in reverse (at least in some circumstances). According to this view, an initial feeling of anger would motivate cognitive judgments that "rationalize" the feeling: I'm mad, therefore I blame you! (see Parkinson, 1997). Such theorists don't rule out cognitions as a potential source of affective reactions, but take a broader view, arguing that many factors may contribute to a feeling of emotion including symbolic intentional judgments (e.g., appraisal) but also subsymbolic factors such as hormones. Most importantly, this broader perspective argues that the link between any preceding intentional meaning and emotion is not explicitly represented and must be recovered after the fact, sometimes incorrectly (Clore & Plamer, 2009; Clore, Schwarz, & Conway, 1994; Russell, 2003). For example, Russell argues for the following sequence of emotional components: some external event occurs (e.g., a person walks out on a shaky suspension bridge), the event results in a dramatic change in affect (e.g., arousal); this change is attributed to some "object" (which could be the correct object—the potential for falling—or some irrelevant object, such as a person of the opposite sex standing on the bridge); and only then is the object cognitively appraised in terms of its goal relevance, causal antecedents, and future prospects (e.g., get off the bridge following a correct attribution or ask person out for a date for the incorrect one).

The sequencing of emotion and appraisal becomes less relevant if one adopts the view of Lazarus: that is, that emotion involves a continuous cycle of appraisal, response, and reappraisal. In a cycle, deciding if the egg or chicken came first becomes more academic. Nonetheless, misattribution effects—irrelevant factors, such as how the weather may impact decisions about whether to invest in the stock market (Hirshleifer & Shumway, 2003)—present challenges for the current crop of computational models of appraisal processes.

Another challenge to appraisal theory argues that it is not a theory of true emotion, but rather a theory of how people think about emotion (e.g., see Johnson-Laird & Oatley, 1992, for one discussion of this debate). This challenge emphasizes that much of the evidence in support is introspective. For example, people are presented an imaginary situation and decide how they might feel (e.g., see Gratch & Marsella, 2005a). Indeed, the OCC model grew, in part, out of a series of meetings at the University of Illinois where Ortony, Clore, and others tried to sort emotion terms into different categories. Although there is evidence on both sides of this debate, an interesting question for the affective computing researcher is whether it matters. If the goal is to create a robot that effectively communicates emotion or to capture what third-party observers infer from emotional displays, a "folk-theory" of emotion may produce more accurate conclusions.

Even if one accepts the basic tenets of appraisal theory, the approach has been criticized as being too limited in scope for many of the domains of interest in affective computing. One major concern is its relevance for social interaction. Much of appraisal theory has taken the individual as the unit

of analysis: how do emotions arise in the individual, how do they impact individual behavior (e.g., physiology and expressions), and how do they impact subsequent cognitions? As a consequence, "social emotions" such as guilt, shame, and embarrassment are underdeveloped in many appraisal theories, and the impact of emotion displays on the behavior and judgments of others has been explored even less, at from the appraisal perspective (but see de Melo, Gratch, & Carnevale, 2011; Hareli & Hess, 2009; Manstead & Fischer, 2001). This situation is changing, and many of the most exciting developments in appraisal theory deal with its extension to social phenomena (e.g., see Kappas, 2013). For a review of recent developments in the area of social appraisals, see Gratch and Marsella (2014).

Conclusion

Appraisal theory is an influential theory of emotion and an especially useful framework for computational scientists interested in building working models of how emotion influences cognitive and behavioral processes. By postulating that emotions arise from patterns of judgments/information processing, appraisal theory draws fruitful connections with other areas of automated reasoning. Although rarely specified in enough detail to directly inform computational systems (with the consequence that many quite different computer models might be consistent with the same theory), it is specified in sufficient detail to posit clear and falsifiable constraints on information process. Recent research on the social antecedents and consequences of emotion are especially interesting and emphasize the relevance of appraisal theory to those interested in building social systems.

References

Antos, D., & Pfeffer, A. (2011). *Using emotions to enhance decision-making.* Paper presented at the Proceedings of the Twenty-Second international joint conference on Artificial Intelligence-Volume Volume One.

Arnold, M. (1960). *Emotion and personality.* New York: Columbia University Press.

Becker-Asano, C. (2008). *WASABI: Affect simulation for agents with believable interactivity.* PhD dissertation, University of Bielefeld, Germany.

Becker-Asano, C., & Wachsmuth, I. (2008). *Affect simulation with primary and secondary emotions.* Paper presented at the 8th International Conference on Intelligent Virtual Agents, Tokyo.

Broekens, J., DeGroot, D., & Kosters, W. A. (2008). Formal models of appraisal: Theory, specification, and computational model. *Cognitive Systems Research, 9*(3), 173–197.

Clore, G., & Plamer, J. (2009). Affective guidance of intelligent agents: How emotion controls cognition. *Cognitive Systems Research, 10*(1), 21–30.

Clore, G., Schwarz, N., & Conway, M. (1994). Affect as information. In J. P. Forgas (Ed.), *Handbook of affect and social cognition* (pp. 121–144). Mahwah, NJ: Lawrence Erlbaum.

Conati, C. (2002). Probabilistic assessment of user's emotions in educational games. *Journal of Applied Artificial Intelligence (special issue on "Merging Cognition and Affect in HCI")*, *16*(7–8), 555–575.

de Melo, C., Gratch, J., & Carnevale, P. J. (2011). *Reverse appraisal: Inferring from emotion displays who is the cooperator and the competitor in a social dilemma.* Paper presented at the Cognitive Science Conference, Boston.

Dias, J., Mascarenhas, S., & Paiva, A. (2011). *Fatima modular: Towards an agent architecture with a generic appraisal framework.* Paper presented at the Proceedings of the International Workshop on Standards for Emotion Modeling, Leiden, The Netherlands.

Dias, J., & Paiva, A. (2005). *Feeling and Reasoning: A computational model for emotional agents.* Paper presented at the Proceedings of 12th Portuguese Conference on Artificial Intelligence, EPIA 2005, Covilhã, Portugal.

Duffy, J. (1959). Medical practice in the ante bellum South. *The Journal of Southern History, 25*(1), 53–72. doi: 10.2307/2954479

El Nasr, M. S., Yen, J., & Ioerger, T. (2000). FLAME: Fuzzy Logic Adaptive Model of Emotions. *Autonomous Agents and Multi Agent Systems, 3*(3), 219–257.

Elliott, C. (1992). *The affective reasoner: A process model of emotions in a multi-agent system.* Northwestern, IL: Northwestern University Institute for the Learning Sciences.

Elliott, C., & Siegle, G. (1993). *Variables influencing the intensity of simulated affective states.* Paper presented at the AAAI Spring Symposium on Reasoning about Mental States: Formal Theories and Applications, Palo Alto, CA.

Ellsworth, P. C., & Scherer, K. R. (2003). Appraisal processes in emotion. In R. J. Davidson, H. H. Goldsmith, & K. R. Scherer (Eds.), *Handbook of the affective sciences* (pp. 572–595). New York: Oxford University Press.

Frank, R. H. (2004). Introducing moral emotions into models of rational choice. In A. Manstead, N. Frijda, & A. Fischer (Eds.), *Feelings and emotions* (pp. 422–440). Cambridge, UK: Cambridge University Press.

Frijda, N. H. (1988). The laws of emotion. *American Psychologist, 43*, 349–358.

Frijda, N. H., & Swagerman, J. (1987). Can computers feel? Theory and design of an emotional system. *Cognition and Emotion, 1*(3), 235–257.

Gebhard, P. (2005). *ALMA—A Layered Model of Affect.* Paper presented at the Fourth International Joint Conference on Autonomous Agents and Multiagent Systems, Utrecht.

Ginsberg, M. L. (1989). Universal planning: An (almost) universally bad idea. *AI Magazine, 10*(4), 40.

Gmytrasiewicz, P., & Lisetti, C. (2000). *Using decision theory to formalize emotions for multi-agent systems.* Paper presented at the Second ICMAS-2000 Workshop on Game Theoretic and Decision Theoretic Agents, Boston.

Gratch, J. (2000). *Émile: Marshalling passions in training and education.* Paper presented at the Fourth International Conference on Intelligent Agents, Barcelona, Spain.

Gratch, J., & Marsella, S. (2004). A domain independent framework for modeling emotion. *Journal of Cognitive Systems Research, 5*(4), 269–306.

Gratch, J., & Marsella, S. (2005a). Evaluating a computational model of emotion. *Journal of Autonomous Agents and Multiagent Systems, 11*(1), 23–43.

Gratch, J., & Marsella, S. (2005b). Lessons from emotion psychology for the design of lifelike characters. *Applied Artificial Intelligence, 19*(3–4), 215–233.

Gratch, J., & Marsella, S. (Eds.). (2014). *Social emotions in nature and artifact.* Cambridge, MA: Oxford University Press.

Gratch, J., Marsella, S., & Petta, P. (2009). Modeling the antecedents and consequences of emotion. *Journal of Cognitive Systems Research, 10*(1), 1–5.

Han, S., Lerner, J. S., & Keltner, D. (2007). Feelings and consumer decision making: The appraisal-tendency framework. *Journal of Consumer Psychology, 17*(3), 158–168.

Hareli, S., & Hess, U. (2009). What emotional reactions can tell us about the nature of others: An appraisal perspective on person perception. *Cognition and Emotion, 24*(1), 128–140.

Hirshleifer, D., & Shumway, T. (2003). Good day sunshine: Stock returns and the weather. *Journal of Finance, 58*, 1009–1032.

Horberg, E. J., Oveis, C., & Keltner, D. (2011). Emotions as moral amplifiers: An appraisal tendency approach to the influences of distinct emotions upon moral judgment. *Emotion Review, 3*(3), 237–244.

Hudlicka, E. (2008). Review of cognitive-affective architectures. In G. Zacharias, J. McMillan, & S. Van Hemel (Eds.), *Organizational modeling: From individuals to societies.* Washington, DC: National Academies Press.

Hudlicka, E. (2011). Guidelines for designing computational models of emotions. *International Journal of Synthetic Emotions, 2*(1), pp. 26–79.

Johnson-laird, P. N., & Oatley, K. (1992). Basic emotions, rationality, and folk theory. *Cognition & Emotion, 6*(3–4), 201–223. doi: 10.1080/02699939208411069

Kahneman, D. (2003). A perspective on judgment and choice: Mapping bounded rationality. *American Psychologist, 58*(9), 697–720.

Kambhampati, S., & Srivastava, B. (1995). *Universal classical planner: An algorithm for unifying state-space and plan-space planning.* Paper presented at the New Directions in AI Planning, EWSP, Assisi, Italy.

Kappas, A. (2013). Social regulation of emotion: messy layers. *Frontiers in Psychology, 4*, 1–11

Keltner, D., & Haidt, J. (1999). Social functions of emotions at four levels of analysis. *Cognition and Emotion, 13*(5), 505–521.

Kuppens, P., & Van Mechelen, I. (2007). Interactional appraisal models for the anger appraisals of threatened self-esteem, other-blame, and frustration. *Cognition and Emotion, 21*, 56–77.

Lazarus, R. S. (1966). *Psychological stress and the coping process.* New York: McGraw-Hill.

Lazarus, R. S. (1984). On the primacy of cognition. *American Psychologist, 39*(2), 124–129. doi: 10.1037/0003–066X. 39.2.124

Lazarus, R. S. (1991). *Emotion and adaptation.* New York: Oxford University Press.

LeDoux, J. (1996). *The emotional brain: The mysterious underpinnings of emotional life.* New York: Simon & Schuster.

Macedo, L., Reisenzein, R., & Cardoso, A. (2004). *Modeling forms of surprise in artificial agents: Empirical and theoretical study of surprise functions.* Paper presented at the 26th Annual Conference of the Cognitive Science Society, Chicago.

Manstead, A. S. R., & Fischer, A. H. (2001). Social appraisal: The social world as object of and influence on appraisal processes. In K. R. Scherer, A. Schorr, & T. Johnstone (Eds.), *Appraisal processes in emotion: Theory, methods, research* (pp. 221–232)). New York: Oxford University Press.

Marinier, R. P. (2008). *A computational unification of cognitive control, emotion, and learning.* (PhD), University of Michigan, Ann Arbor, MI.

Marinier, R. P., Laird, J. E., & Lewis, R. L. (2009). A computational unification of cognitive behavior and emotion. *Cognitive Systems Research, 10*(1), 48–69.

Marsella, S., & Gratch, J. (2009). EMA: A process model of appraisal dynamics. *Journal of Cognitive Systems Research, 10*(1), 70–90.

Marsella, S., Gratch, J., & Petta, P. (2010). Computational models of emotion. In K. R. Scherer, T. Bänziger & E. Roesch (Eds.), *A blueprint for affective computing: A sourcebook and manual* (pp. 21–46). New York: Oxford University Press.

Marsella, S., Johnson, W. L., & LaBore, C. (2000). *Interactive pedagogical drama.* Paper presented at the Fourth International Conference on Autonomous Agents, Montreal, Canada.

Moffat, D., & Frijda, N. (1995). *Where there's a Will there's an agent.* Paper presented at the Workshop on Agent Theories, Architectures and Languages, Montreal, Canada.

Moors, A., De Houwer, J., Hermans, D., & Eelen, P. (2005). Unintentional processing of motivational valence. *The Quarterly Journal of Experimental Psychology Section A, 58*(6), 1043–1063.

Neal Reilly, W. S. (1996). *Believable social and emotional agents.* Pittsburgh, PA: Carnegie Mellon University.

Neal Reilly, W. S. (2006). *Modeling what happens between emotional antecedents and emotional consequents.* Paper presented at the Eighteenth European Meeting on Cybernetics and Systems Research, Vienna, Austria.

Ortony, A., Clore, G., & Collins, A. (1988). *The cognitive structure of emotions.* Melbourne, AUS: Cambridge University Press.

Paiva, A., Dias, J., & Aylett, R. (2005). Learning by feeling: Evoking empathy with synthetic characters. *Applied Artificial Intelligence (special issue on "Educational Agents—Beyond Virtual Tutors"), 19*(3–4), 235–266.

Parkinson, B. (1997). Untangling the appraisal-emotion connection. *Personality and Social Psychology Review, 1*(1), 62–79.

Parkinson, B. (2009). What holds emotions together? Meaning and response coordination. *Cognitive Systems Research, 10,* 31–47.

Pham, M. T. (2007). Emotion and rationality: A critical review and interpretation of empirical evidence. *Review of General Psychology, 11*(2), 155–178.

Rank, S. (2009). *Behaviour coordination for models of affective behavior.* Ph.D. dissertation, Vienna University of Technology, Vienna, Austria.

Rank, S., & Petta, P. (2005). *Appraisal for a character-based story-world.* Paper presented at the 5th International Working Conference on Intelligent Virtual Agents, Kos, Greece.

Reisenzein, R. (2001). Appraisal processes conceptualized from a schema-theoretic perspective. In K. R. Scherer, A. Schorr, & T. Johnstone (Eds.), *Appraisal processes in emotion: Theory, methods, research* (pp. 187–201). New York: Oxford University Press.

Reisenzein, R. (2009). Emotions as metarepresentational states of mind: Naturalizing the belief-desire theory of emotion. *Journal of Cognitive Systems Research, 10*(1), 6–20

Roseman, I. J. (2001). A model of appraisal in the emotion system: Integrating theory, research, and applications. In K. R. Scherer, A. Schorr, & T. Johnstone (Eds.), *Appraisal processes in emotion: Theory, methods, research.* New York: Oxford University Press.

Russell, J. A. (2003). Core affect and the psychological construction of emotion. *Psychological Review, 110,* 145–172.

Russell, J. A., & Barrett, L. F. (1999). Core affect, prototypical emotional episodes, and other things called emotion: Dissecting the elephant. *Journal of Personality and Social Psychology, 76,* 805–819.

Sander, D., Grandjean, D., & Scherer, K. R. (2005). A systems approach to appraisal mechanisms in emotion. *Neural Networks, 18,* 317–352.

Scherer, K. R. (2001). Appraisal considered as a process of multilevel sequential checking. In K. R. Scherer, A. Schorr, & T. Johnstone (Eds.), *Appraisal processes in emotion: Theory, methods, research* (pp. 92–120). New York: Oxford University Press.

Scherer, K. R. (2005). Appraisal theory. *Handbook of cognition and emotion,* T. Dagleish and M. J. Power (Eds.), John Wiley and Sons, West Sussex, England. 637–663.

Scherer, K. R., & Ellgring, H. (2007). Are facial expressions of emotion produced by categorical affect programs or dynamically driven by appraisal? *Emotion, 7*(1), 113–130. doi: 10.1037/1528-3542.7.1.113

Scherer, K. R., Schorr, A., & Johnstone, T. (Eds.). (2001). *Appraisal processes in emotion.* New York: Oxford University Press.

Si, M., Marsella, S. C., & Pynadath, D. V. (2008). *Modeling appraisal in theory of mind reasoning.* Paper presented at the 8th International Conference on Intelligent Virtual Agents, Tokyo, Japan.

Simon, H. (1969). *The sciences of the artificial.* Cambridge, MA: MIT Press.

Simon, H. A. (1967). Motivational and emotional controls of cognition. *Psychological Review, 74,* 29–39.

Smith, C. A., & Kirby, L. (2000). Consequences require antecedents: Toward a process model of emotion elicitation. In J. P. Forgas (Ed.), *Feeling and thinking: The role of affect in social cognition* (pp. 83–106). New York: Cambridge University Press.

Smith, C. A., & Kirby, L. D. (2009). Putting appraisal in context: Toward a relational model of appraisal and emotion. *Cognition and Emotion, 23*(7), 1352–1372.

Smith, C. A., & Lazarus, R. S. (1990). Emotion and adaptation. In L. A. Pervin (Ed.), *Handbook of personality: Theory & research* (pp. 609–637). New York: Guilford Press.

Smith, C. A., & Scott, H. S. (1997). A componential approach to the meaning of facial expressions. In J. A. Russell & J. M. Fernández-Dols (Eds.), *The psychology of facial expression* (pp. 229–254). Paris: Cambridge University Press.

Staller, A., & Petta, P. (2001). Introducing emotions into the computational study of social norms: A first evaluation. *Journal of Artificial Societies and Social Simulation, 4*(1), 27–60.

Steunebrink, B. R., Dastani, M. M., & Meyer, J.-J. C. (2012). A formal model of emotion triggers: an approach for BDI agents. *Synthese* 185.1, 83–129.

Steunebrink, B. R., Dastani, M. M., & Meyer, J.-J. C. (2008). *A formal model of emotions: Integrating qualitative and quantitative aspects.* Paper presented at the 18th European Conference on Artificial Intelligence, Patras, Greece.

Suchman, L. A. (1987). *Plans and situated actions: The problem of human-machine communication*. New York: Cambridge University Press.

Winograd, T. (1975). Frame representations and the declarative/procedural controversy. *Representation and understanding: Studies in cognitive science,* D. G. Bobrow and A. Collins (Eds.). Academic Press, Inc. Orlando, FL.185–210.

Zajonc, R. B. (1984). On the primacy of affect. *American Psychologist, 39*(2), 117–123. doi: 10.1037/0003–066X. 39.2.117

Emotions in Interpersonal Life: Computer Mediation, Modeling, and Simulation

Brian Parkinson

Abstract

This chapter discusses how emotions operate between people in the social world, how computer mediation might affect emotional communication and coordination, and the challenges that socially situated emotions present for computer simulation and modeling. The first section reviews psychological literature addressing causes, effects, and functions of interpersonally communicated emotions, focusing on both informational and embodied influences, before addressing group and cultural influences on emotions. Relevant findings from the psychological literature concerning social appraisal, emotion contagion, empathy, and mimicry are reviewed. The second section compares computer-mediated emotion communication with face-to-face interaction, exploring their distinctive characteristics and possibilities. The final section discusses challenges in implementing affective computing systems designed to encode and/or decode emotional signals as well as virtual agents and robots intended to interact emotionally with humans in real time.

Key Words: emotional communication, social appraisal, emotion contagion, empathy, mimicry, computer mediation

Emotions in Social Life

How do emotions relate to their social context? They may be caused by social events (someone punching or praising us) and their expression may bring effects on other people (my angry face and clenched fists may lead you either to back off or intensify your own antagonistic stance). For some theorists, a central function of many emotions is precisely to achieve social effects of this kind (Keltner & Haidt, 1999; Parkinson, 1996; Van Kleef, 2009). Whether or not this is true, the interpersonal orientation of emotions clearly needs to be addressed by computer scientists seeking to simulate the operation of realistic emotions or to provide tools for interpreting them or modifying their operation.

This section provides a brief introduction to psychological theory and research concerning the interpersonal causes and effects of emotion, and presents a relation-alignment approach (e.g., Parkinson, 2008). From this perspective, emotions adjust to and operate on other people's orientations to (real or imagined) objects in the shared environment rather than being separable causes or effects of interpersonal events (stimuli or responses, inputs or outputs). However, because most research separates out the different aspects of the relation-alignment process, the early sections of this chapter consider interpersonal causes and effects in turn, before discussing broader social factors relating to group and cultural life.

Interpersonal Causes

What causes emotions? According to some appraisal theorists (e.g., Lazarus, 1991, and see Gratch & Marsella, this volume), the proximal determinant of all emotions is the (implicit or explicit) mental apprehension of the specific personal significance of the current transaction. At some level, we must recognize that what is happening matters to us before we become emotional about it. For example, if I trip over your foot, I will not get angry unless I somehow perceive you as personally accountable for it being in my way. There are issues here about whether my perception of your other-accountability precedes, accompanies, or follows my anger (e.g., Frijda, 1993), but in any case, a social object (your foot) is at one level part of the cause of the emotion, and the appraisal of you as accountable (by whatever process) probably makes some difference to how the emotional reaction unfolds.

Traditional appraisal theory (e.g., Lazarus, 1991) specifies one way in which interpersonal factors may influence emotional outcomes: Information that is processed during appraisal is often interpersonal information. This information may be contained in the object of emotion (e.g., a person behaving in a disgusting manner), but it may also derive from the apparent attitudes of others present on the scene (*social appraisal*, see p. 70). In particular, someone else's apparent disgust may change our appraisal of the object toward which it is directed and may make us see it as more disgusting than otherwise.

Other people may also provide emotional or practical resources that assist in coping with events, thus moderating their emotional impact. For example, if we are threatened with physical violence, the presence of an ally may reduce our trepidation and potentially increase our feelings of aggressiveness. Other people can also help or hinder our attempts to control or modify our current or anticipated emotions (*emotion regulation*, e.g., Gross, 1998). For instance, if we are trying to distract ourselves from worrying about an impending negative event (e.g., a job interview, examination, or medical operation), someone else may either take our mind of things or draw our attention back to our concerns in an attempt at empathy (cf. Parkinson & Simons, 2012; Rose, 2002). Gross (1998) distinguishes between emotion-regulation strategies depending on the stage of the emotional episode that they target. For example, I may cross the road to avoid interacting with someone I find irritating (situation selection), convince myself that the encounter will not be as bad as I was imagining (reappraisal), or try to stop myself from showing my irritation during our conversation (expressive suppression). As this example shows, emotion regulation may be motivated by interpersonal considerations and may bring direct effects on emotion and/or its expression.

Ekman (1972, and see Culture and Emotion Communication, p. 75) argues that socialized cultural display rules dictate when, where, and with whom it is appropriate to express particular emotions. Consequently certain emotional expressions are exaggerated, suppressed, or modified when particular kinds of audiences are present. For example, different societies have different conventions concerning the overt expression of grief in formal funeral ceremonies. A competing account of how social context affects emotion expression is provided by Fridlund's (1994) motive-communication approach (see Parkinson, 2005, for a review), which suggests that facial displays are oriented to specific recipients in the first place and are therefore sensitive to the information needs of those recipients. In either case, facial signals are shaped not only by emotion but also by the interpersonal context in which emotion occurs. Research suggests that a key variable determining the clarity of emotion signals is whether there are other people present and whether those other people are friends or strangers (e.g., Hess, Banse, & Kappas, 1995). For example, people seem to smile more in social settings than when alone, especially when with in-group members or sympathetic others (e.g., Wagner & Smith, 1991). By contrast, sad expressions are sometimes more intense in private (Jakobs, Manstead, & Fischer, 2001). In other words, the interpersonal factors shaping regulation and presentation of emotion expressions vary across contexts and emotions (see Parkinson, 2005).

Other people may directly transform the events causing emotion in addition to changing the way that these causes are appraised or shaping motives for emotion regulation. For instance, another person's financial contribution may lessen the extent of an otherwise worrying debt. Further, other people's movements and postural orientations modulate our own movements and orientations in ways that are not easily captured by existing appraisal models (e.g., Parkinson, 2008; 2013a). As discussed later in this chapter, our adjustments to other people's posture, expression, and gaze direction may lead us to adopt different emotional orientations to environmental events regardless of our perceptions of the emotional meaning of those objects.

Why do the interpersonal causes of emotion and its expression matter for affective computing? First, modelers need to consider the structure and dynamics of the interpersonal environment that sets the context for—and/or constitutes the object of—emotional experiences. Second, models and simulations of appraisal processes should factor in the interpersonal calibration of attention, evaluation, perception, and interpretation that operates during social appraisal. Third, attention should be given to how other people help to regulate emotional events and emotional reactions to, and operations on, those events. Finally, emotion-decoding systems require due sensitivity to the presence of other people and their relationship to the target sender when information is being extracted from faces.

Interpersonal Effects

It is widely acknowledged that emotion can affect perception, attention, judgment, and behavior. However, most early research focused on emotion's intra- rather than interpersonal effects. For example, fear draws the fearful person's attention to potential sources of threat and increases general vigilance. Over the past decade or so, increasing attention has been given to how emotions affect other people and not just ourselves. In this section, I focus on processes of social appraisal, empathy, and contagion to illustrate these interpersonal effects. In all these cases, emotions tend to lead to corresponding emotions in others (*interpersonal emotion transfer*, Parkinson, 2011a). In addition, I consider cases where emotions induce contrasting or complementary emotional reactions and where the effects of emotion on other people are not directly emotional effects.

SOCIAL APPRAISAL

Appraisal theories (e.g., Lazarus, 1991) generally assume that people arrive at evaluations and interpretation of emotional events as a result of individual mental processes, including perception and interpretation (at several levels). According to Manstead and Fischer (2001, see also Parkinson, 1996), appraisals also depend on other people's apparent reactions and orientations to potentially emotional events. In other words, what strikes me as significant, threatening, or challenging partly depends on what seems to strike others as significant, threatening, or challenging as indicated by their emotional reactions or other observable responses. A classic example is social referencing in toddlers (e.g., Sorce et al., 1985). One-year-olds are mostly content to crawl across a plate of glass covering a 30-centimeter drop (the "visual cliff") if their mothers smile at them from the other side, but they stop at the edge if their mothers show a fear face. Their emotional orientation to the emotion object is thus shaped by caregivers' orientations.

In everyday interactions, social appraisal often operates bidirectionally as a nonverbal negotiation about the emotional significance of events. Interactants may arrive at a shared emotional orientation to an unfamiliar object after tentative approaches that encourage approaches from the other. In Latané and Darley's (1968) study of responses to emergencies, participants' responses to smoke entering the room through a vent seemed to depend on their gauging each other's level of calm. When with impassive strangers, participants stayed in the room while it filled with smoke, presumably because they took the other people's impassiveness as a kind of safety signal. Correspondingly, individuals may take greater risks if their friends' faces express less anxiety (Parkinson, Phiri, & Simons, 2012).

Social appraisal need not involve explicit registration of the implications of other people's orientations to events. For example, recent studies show how object evaluations and perceptions depend on the nature of concurrent facial expression stimuli. Bayliss and colleagues (2007) showed that pictures of household objects were evaluated less positively when coupled with disgust faces than with happy faces, but only when those faces appeared to be looking toward rather than away from the objects (see also Mumenthaler & Sander, 2012). Participants were unaware of the contingency between eye gaze and evaluation, suggesting that its influence operated below the level of awareness. Thus the object-directedness of emotion communication seems to moderate affect transfer even without explicit processing (see Parkinson, 2011a).

Modeling of social-appraisal effects requires specification of the relations between people present on the scene and of the objects and events at which their emotions are oriented. Part of the process involves calibration of attention and mutual positioning in relation to what is happening. When environments are complex and contain several people and objects, the task of specifying processes becomes more difficult, especially since emotion objects may be the product of personal perceptions of meaning or private imagination instead of externally available stimulus features. Tracking social appraisal may be more difficult when people discuss emotional topics that do not directly relate to what is happening around them at the time.

EMPATHY

Social appraisal involves interpersonal effects of emotion on appraisals of objects and events and behavior toward those objects and events. However, because of their relational basis (e.g., Frijda, 1986), emotions communicate information about the person who is expressing them as well as the objects toward which they are directed. For example, anger conveys your sense of injustice and fear conveys your uncertainty about coping with events. Reactions to someone else's emotions sometimes depend more on the person-related information that those emotions convey than on their implications for object evaluation. When we are in affiliative rather than competitive or antagonistic situations (e.g., Englis, Vaughan, & Lanzetta, 1982), these effects on appraisals about the person constitute a form of empathic emotion transfer (see Parkinson & Simons, 2012).

Surprisingly little systematic research has focused directly on empathic responses to another person's emotion expression. One reason may be the difficulty in distinguishing many forms of empathy (e.g., Vaughan & Lanzetta, 1980; 1981) from other interpersonal effects of emotion (such as emotion contagion, see p. 72, and Hess & Fischer, 2013; Smith, McHugo, & Kappas, 1996).

One possible means of distinguishing empathy from related processes concerns its underlying motivation. However, the apparent dependence of empathy on affiliative motives, as evidenced by the opposite counterempathic tendencies that may arise in competitive or antagonistic situations (e.g., Englis, Vaughan, & Lanzetta, 1982), similarly characterizes mimicry and contagion (see p. 70 and p. 72), reinforcing the possibility that empathy is a form of contagion or depends on contagion for its operation. Indeed, some authors believe that the process of simulating the embodied basis of another person's emotional state facilitates social connections (e.g., Niedenthal & Brauer, 2012; Niedenthal, Mermillod, Maringer, & Hess, 2010).

MIMICRY

One of the processes that may underlie some forms of empathy is motor mimicry. The basic idea is that adopting the same facial expression and bodily posture as another person helps you to see things from their perspective. Some theorists believe that such processes help to solve the philosophical problem of "other minds": how we can ever get inside a separate human's head (see Reddy, 2008, for a discussion of the inadequacies of this account). Research into the operation of mirror neurons (e.g., Rizzolatti & Craighero, 2004) is often thought to provide evidence that humans are hardwired for

social understanding at some level (e.g., Iacoboni, 2009). From this perspective, seeing someone make a movement automatically triggers a corresponding representation of that movement in the perceiver's brain, which in turn makes it more likely that he or she will make a similar movement. The shared representation and performance of the movement allow calibration of intention and perspective across individuals.

Although it is probably true that the coordination of actions helps to establish shared frames of reference, the specific details of the mirror-mimicry-empathy account do not seem to capture all aspects of this process. For example, so-called mirror neurons are not hardwired to respond to particular movements with corresponding movements but become attuned over time, with learning experiences sometimes leading perceivers to make complementary or contrasting movements to those they observe (e.g., Catmur et al., 2008; Cook et al., in press). Further, there is no direct link between matched movements and empathy (as childhood taunting using ironic or exaggerated copying clearly demonstrates). When someone explicitly does exactly as you do, it is often more irritating than affiliative.

Additional issues arise from the apparent context-dependence of mimicry (e.g., Lakin, Chartrand, & Arkin, 2008; Moody et al., 2007). No one ever copies everything everyone else does, so what determines who is mimicked and when? And if some prior process is responsible for selecting occasions for mimicry, isn't much of the necessary work for empathy already done before any matching of movements comes into play?

At least under some circumstances, mimicry seems to depend on the detected meaning of perceived movements and not simply their physical characteristics. For example, Halberstadt and colleagues (2009) presented participants with morphed faces combining "happy" and "angry" expressions along with verbal cues indicating either of these emotional labels. When they were subsequently presented with the same morphed face, participants mimicked the expression corresponding to the label they had seen when the face was presented originally. Thus cued concepts shape facial interpretations (e.g., Lindquist & Gendron, 2013), and these interpretations shape the response of mimicking. Further supporting the role of meaning in mimicry, Tamietto and colleagues (2009) found that participants showed facial expressions corresponding to the perceived emotional meaning of presented body postures, even when the stimuli were presented to the "blind" visual field of patients suffering from blindsight (Weiskrantz, 2009). In other words, even when participants were unaware of having seen anything, they responded to the apparent emotional meaning of a presented body posture with a corresponding facial expression. Clearly if mimicry already depends on registering emotional meaning, it cannot be a prior condition for recognizing that meaning. Modelers of interactive affective agents need to factor in the selectivity and meaning-dependence of mimicry, with due attention to the observation that reciprocated emotion signals are not necessarily produced in identical form or through identical channels as the original mimicked stimulus.

INTERPERSONAL ATTUNEMENT

Research into social effects of mimicry suggests that there are some circumstances in which other people's liking for the mimicker increases (e.g., Lakin et al., 2003). More generally, studies of ongoing interactions between people show that temporal synchronization of matching or complementary movements is associated with an increased sense of rapport (Bernieri & Rosenthal, 1991). Smooth interactions seem to involve people getting in sync with each other. However, it is unlikely that this depends on mechanical or automatic copying of the other's movements (see p. 70). One possibility is that getting on someone else's wavelength is as much a precondition for calibrating nonverbal patterns as it is a consequence of such calibration. When verbal dialogue is involved, it is unlikely that simple synchrony is sufficient for a sense of interpersonal connection. Communicative meaning also matters.

Appreciation of the context-dependence of attunement and mimicry is important for modeling affective agents. For example, synthesized facial expressions should not simply reflect categorical emotional states but should also adjust dynamically to changing events and to co-present others' responses to those events. These challenges might be avoided by simplifying the simulated environment of affective agents; but when agents need to interact with human users, there is no escaping the impact of the practical and social circumstances surrounding those users' actions and reactions.

CONTAGION

Mimicry is implicated in processes of emotion contagion as well as empathy and rapport. Hatfield

and colleagues (1994) argue that internal sensory feedback from copied movements produces corresponding feelings in perceivers. In effect, mimicked responses make you feel the same thing as the person you are mimicking.

Although few researchers doubt that contagion can be related to motor responses to other people's observed movements, direct evidence for the particular mimicry-feedback-contagion process specified in Hatfield et al.'s model is scant. Indeed, reported effects of facial feedback on emotional experience do not seem large enough to account for the activation from scratch of a full-blown interpersonally matching emotion (e.g., Strack, Martin, & Stepper, 1988). It may be more plausible to argue that ongoing emotional reactions are bolstered by sensory feedback from expressive responses than to suggest that feedback initiates contagion on its own.

Another issue with the contagion account concerns its implicit assumption that specific bodily postures and facial expression are directly associated with categorically distinct emotional experiences regardless of context. By contrast, it seems likely that part of the meaning of movements depends on their relation to objects and events in the environment (including other people) rather than their internal configuration (Parkinson, 2013b). For example, a fixed stare can certainly convey attentiveness, but its affective significance varies depending on whether it is directed at you, at an object in the environment, or at some point in midair. The implications of dynamic shifts in direction and intensity of gaze also depend on what changes in the environment they track, if any. More generally, a range of postural adjustments, gestures, and facial movements may be associated with the same emotion depending on the nature of the object to which it is directed and the specific action tendencies it evokes (cf. Fridlund, 1994). For example, the prototypical anger face showing compressed lips, furrowed brow, and intent stare probably characterizes particular kinds of anger in which disapproval and threatened retaliation is directed at an antagonist who is physically present and squaring up to you. Of course, the association between this facial position and a culturally recognizable prototypic script for anger also permits the use of the face as a communicative device designed to convey anger (see Parkinson, 2013b). However, this does not necessarily imply that the same facial position is spontaneously produced whenever a person is angry under other circumstances (e.g., in a formal meeting, on reading of irritating news at a distance, or when engaged in a complicated mechanical task that repeatedly insists on going wrong). Here, the nature of the muscle movements at least partly depends on ongoing transactions with the unfolding emotional event.

As argued above, mimicry further depends on the perceiver's initial orientation and attitude to the other person and is sensitive to the meaningful nature of perceived movements, not their physical characteristics alone (Hess & Fischer, 2013). As with empathy, these two facts make it likely that part of the reason why we experience corresponding emotions to the person we mimic is that we already share his or her orientation to what is happening and are therefore likely to react in a similar way. In this case, contagion may often reflect a form of social appraisal where orientations toward events are calibrated between people over time. Evidence for pure cases of contagion that cannot be explained by empathy or social appraisal would require establishing that the content of the feelings was transferred interpersonally without also changing feelings about the person or the object of his or her emotion (see Parkinson, 2011a). For example, someone's joy at succeeding in a difficult task might make you joyful even if you do not feel happy *for* them or *about* what they have accomplished. Even if such contingencies are possible in principle, they may be highly difficult to engineer in practice.

The above observations bring obvious implications for the simulation or modeling of affective agents. Preprogrammed emotion displays that fail to factor in object orientation or relationships between senders and receivers are likely to be perceived as unrealistic. However, establishing appropriate relationships between users and agents that permit appropriate coordination of dynamic expressions presents serious challenges.

MEANING-INDEPENDENT EMOTION TRANSFER?

A common distinction between processes underlying interpersonal emotion transfer hinges on the mediating role of emotional meaning (e.g., Parkinson & Simons, 2009). Social appraisal as traditionally conceived assumes that perceivers interpret another person's emotion expression as an indication of their evaluative orientation toward an object or event and use this information to arrive at their own appraisal. In effect, people perform a form of reverse engineering based on their knowledge of the implications of different emotions, working out what appraisals must have provoked the observed reaction (Hareli & Hess, 2010). By contrast, accounts of mimicry-based contagion and empathy often imply that these processes involve more direct embodied processes and do not depend on any form of inference (e.g., Niedenthal et al., 2010).

Van Kleef and colleagues' (2010) emotion as social information (EASI) model similarly distinguishes two routes of interpersonal emotional influence. Someone else's emotion can lead to inferential processes relating to their implications for the perceiver and can more directly activate affective reactions (due to contagion and related processes). According to EASI, inferential effects are more dominant when the perceiver is motivated to process the information conveyed by the other person's emotion expression and when the situation is cooperative rather than competitive.

Although distinctions between meaning-based or inferential effects and embodied or affective effects of emotion are potentially useful, pure cases of either process may be the exception rather than the rule. For example, supposed processes of automatic mimicry do not typically involve direct copying of observed movements (motor resonance) but rather go beyond the information that is given in the stimulus (see also Hess & Fischer, 2013). Correspondingly, social appraisal need not involve explicit registration of an integrated emotional meaning but may operate in a more automatic fashion by responding to low-level cues about gaze direction in conjunction with facial configuration (Parkinson, 2011a). On balance, no all-or-none distinction between embodied and meaning-driven processes seems viable. Instead, different levels and kinds of implicit and explicit meaning are implicated across the board. Similarly, the processing of meaning often depends on bottom-up embodied processes rather than pure inference (e.g., Niedenthal et al., 2010). It is certainly not the case that perceivers need to extract a coherent emotional meaning from a detected expressive movement in order to react to it.

Reciprocal Emotion Transfer in Relation Alignment

The previous sections outline a range of processes that might contribute to the convergent effects of one person's emotion on another's. Each of these processes can also be seen as special cases of *relation alignment*, in which emotions serve to modify actor's orientations to one another and to objects and events happening around them (Parkinson,

2008). Because these processes operate from both sides of any interpersonal encounter, it is important to consider the implications of their mutuality and bidirectionality. In particular, emotions are oriented not only to other people and objects but also to other people's orientations to those objects, including their emotional orientations. Episodes during which interpersonally expressed emotions come to match one another are only one variety of relation alignment. On other occasions, emotions may serve distancing or avoidant interpersonal functions, and contrasting or complementary emotions may emerge (e.g., Englis, Vaughan, & Lanzetta, 1982).

The process of relation alignment has a number of aspects that are not easily accommodated within other accounts of interpersonal emotion processes. A key feature is the coordination of attention between parties. Other things being equal, we tend to check physical locations where other people's gaze is oriented in order to determine what they are attending to. Both gaze direction and bodily orientation toward objects have also acquired communicative functions in actively directing other people's attention. For example, in conversation we may signal the object of our explicit evaluation by directing our gaze to something or pointing at it while commenting nonverbally or verbally ("Ooh, I *hate* that kind of thing!"). Similarly, in social referencing studies (e.g., Sorce et al., 1985), mothers direct their gaze to the object of evaluation (e.g., the visual cliff) while expressing their affective orientation to it and switch between making eye contact with the toddler facing the object and gazing at the object itself in order to shape the toddler's orientation. More usually, the process of coordinating the reference of an evaluative communication operates bidirectionally, with both parties directing their gaze at possible objects.

When an emotion object is imagined or abstract rather than physically present in the shared environment, it is possible that movements that would otherwise be directed at external locations are used to convey similar emotional meanings. However at other times the emotional meaning of expressions about abstract objects either depends on their temporal attunement to changes in current topic or is practically undetectable. However, relationship partners who have experience of one another's presentational style may develop implicit shorthand expressions to convey recurrent emotional meanings of mutual relevance.

Relation alignment involves not only the calibration of interpersonal attention but also mutual adjustment of evaluation, approach/withdrawal, and other action-orientation qualities. Aspects of each of these interpersonal processes may operate at both implicit and explicit levels involving communications about appraisals as well as cuing, mimicry, and countermimicry.

Emotion Within and Between Groups

The previous section has outlined how interpersonal effects of emotion partly depend on the nature of interactants' orientations and relational goals. For instance, your response to anger directed at you in a face-to-face argument is likely to differ from your response to anger directed at someone else (e.g., a common foe). One set of factors clarifying how and why emotions have different interpersonal effects on different targets and audiences concerns group affiliations. Self-categorization theory (e.g., Turner et al., 1987) argues that a range of social identities are available to people, some relating to their personal characteristics and dispositions (e.g., "I am good at math," "I can be clumsy," or "I am 6 feet 1 inch tall"), others to membership of various groups (e.g., "I am male," "I am British," or "I support Manchester United"). Identification in terms of these social categories can shift over time in response to changing circumstances. For example, finding myself the only Manchester United supporter in a pub full of kitted up Manchester City (a rival soccer club) supporters may make this particular soccer-related social identity more salient. As this example also implies, self-categorizing in terms of a particular social identity can also carry consequences for emotion.

According to Smith's (1993) theory of group emotions, appraisals assess the relevance of events for social as well as personal identities. In other words, I can feel emotional about things that affect my group as well as about things that affect me directly as an individual. For example, Cialdini and colleagues (1976) found that students were more likely to wear insignia relating to their college football team and speak of its performance in terms of "we" on days following footballing victories than on days following defeats.

More direct evidence for group-based emotion is provided by studies showing that people report feeling guilty about misdemeanors committed by other in-group members even when they played no personal role and even when these misdemeanors took place in distant history (collective guilt for the sins of our ancestors; see Doosje et al., 1998). Other studies show that fear concerning potential terrorist attacks is greater when victims of a recent attack are categorized as in-group rather than out-group members (Dumont et al., 2003), suggesting that this emotion also depends upon social identifications (see also Yzerbyt et al., 2002, on intergroup anger, and Parkinson, Fischer, & Manstead, 2005 for other examples of group-based emotions).

It is not only our own group that can influence our emotions but also groups that we distinguish ourselves from or directly oppose. A guiding principle of social identity theory is that people accrue self-esteem from identifying with groups that they see as superior to other groups on certain valued dimensions (positive intergroup differentiation). Intergroup life therefore involves selective comparison and competition with out-groups. In this connection, Leach et al. (2003) show how soccer supporters report feelings of Schadenfreude (pleasure taken in someone else's misfortune) when a team that has previously beaten their team subsequently suffers a defeat at the hands of a third team. This is subtly different from gloating when their own team defeats a rival team because the Schadenfreude example does not involve in-group victory, only out-group defeat. In other words, it seems that we care about the fate of our enemies as well as our allies, taking satisfaction in their failures and feeling envy or irritation at their successes.

The phenomenon of intergroup Schadenfreude makes it clear that emotions do not always converge when members of different groups interact: Indeed one group's suffering leads to another group's pleasure in these cases. More generally, our emotional reactions to events experienced by other members of a group with which we identify tend to be similar to theirs (other things being equal), but emotional reactions to out-group emotions depend on factors such as whether they represent a threat to our in-group's status (e.g., supporters of a soccer team who are rivals for the title).

Extending these arguments, it seems unlikely that interpersonal processes of affect transfer—including social appraisal, empathy, and contagion—operate in the same way when we are interacting with a member of a rival out-group and when the relevant social identities are salient. Indeed, Bourgeois and Hess (2008) found that social identifications moderated mimicry of negative facial expressions, with no evidence of mimicry of out-group negative expressions. More generally, processes of relation alignment are likely to take into account the group-based relational orientations of parties to

any intergroup interaction (Parkinson, 2011b). Research into the dynamics of such encounters is sadly underdeveloped, and these conclusions must therefore remain speculative.

Social identities not only affect emotions but are also affected by those emotions. For example, Livingstone, Spears, Manstead, Bruder, and Shepherd (2011) found that participants were more ready to categorize themselves as members of a group if other group members had similar emotional reactions to their own. Further, when the shared emotion was anger, the correspondence between own and group emotions led to increased willingness to participate in collective action on behalf of the group.

Group life clearly adds further complexities to the modeling of realistic affective agents. One implication is that efforts should be made to either make avatars or robots neutral in terms of social categories or to capitalize on users' own social identities. For instance, interactions might be framed using group-relevant cues ensuring that common identifications are made salient. Establishing a common social identity may also be facilitated by modeling convergent emotional reactions to events.

Culture and Emotion Communication

It is widely acknowledged that the encoding and decoding of communicated emotion meaning depends on influences of cultural socialization. The particular objects, events, or transactions that lead to any given emotion differ depending on cultural learning. Further, different societies have different nonverbal styles and symbols and may regulate more universal expressions of emotion or social motive according to different display rules (e.g., Ekman, 1972; and see Interpersonal Causes, p. 68). Jack et al. (2012) showed that participants from Far Eastern cultures categorized facial expressions differently to those from western cultures even when the same six basic emotion categories were supplied.

Elfenbein and Ambady (2002) provide evidence that consistency of emotion attributions to facial expression stimuli is greater when both target and perceiver belong to the same culture. Their conclusion is that members of any society develop expressive dialects and accents that transform the universally provided biological signals. More radically, it may be that the emotional meanings communicated using facial movements themselves may differ to some extent from culture to culture (e.g., Russell, 1994). Supposedly "basic" emotions may not feature or be represented in the same form across the globe.

For all these reasons, computer-based systems that have been developed and fine-tuned using members of a single society may not be as effective in other cultural contexts. Problems of intercultural communication where conventions and display rules differ across interactants may make modeling even more difficult. Such problems may even extend to within-culture differences in communicative style based on idiosyncratic socialization or individual differences relating to temperament or expressivity.

According to some theorists (e.g., Ekman, 2003), it may still be possible to bypass the effects of display rules by capturing fleeting (micromomentary) expressions occurring the instant before attempts at regulation suppress or otherwise disguise them. If so, there might be potential for enhancing the detection of emotion by using appropriately time-sensitive facial expression detection systems. However, evidence about the prevalence, significance, and potential detection of these rapid facial reactions is still underdeveloped, and it is not yet clear whether they always or ever reflect preregulated spontaneous emotions.

Computer-Mediated Emotion Communication

Technologies for mediating interpersonal communication are not new. Indeed, it seems likely that our hominid ancestors were able to indicate their location to conspecifics at a distance by waving long sticks or beating on primitive drums. The advent of written language ultimately allowed messages to be relayed at even greater distances, and telegraphy (Standage, 1998), then telephony (Rutter, 1987), further extended the speed and range of remote communication.

Video technology to supplement long-range spoken interaction has been available for some time but has taken hold more gradually. Even with the wide penetration of Skype, FaceTime, and similarly accessible software applications, video tends to be reserved for prescheduled interactions with close friends, romantic partners, and family members. For many remote interpersonal interactions, people often prefer to use text and email even when richer media are available on the devices that they carry around with them. The following subsections focus on issues relating to effects of computer mediation on the communicative process where emotion is involved and on people's strategic choices about which medium suits their emotional purposes for any given interaction (see also Kappas & Krämer, 2011).

Social Cues and Media Richness

Academic discussions of communication media have historically focused on their richness (Daft & Lengel, 1984) or the level of cues that they can transmit (e.g., Rutter, 1987). According to these accounts, direct face-to-face (FTF)interpersonal communication when lighting is good, background noise is minimal, and other distractions are eradicated provides optimal conditions for cue transmission, consequently maximizing "social presence" (Short et al., 1976). Verbal, vocal, gestural, facial, and even olfactory cues are immediately and readily picked up by communication partners, allowing the full range of everyday modalities to operate. Mediated communication typically involves the removal or degradation of one or more of these channels.

Media richness theory tends to emphasize the quantity of available cues, but it is also important to recognize that different kinds of cue may do different kinds of communicative work. Verbal and text-based communication may be adequate for well-structured interactive tasks with agreed turn-taking conventions, but online nonverbal channels offer more continuous adjustment to another person's communications (cf. Daft & Lengel, 1984). Combining the two to allow back-channeling and signals about floor changes is often but not always helpful. In some cases, selective removal of communication channels may improve performance of particular tasks.

Further, some characteristics of communication media such as recordability and synchrony are not easily captured by generic notions of cues but still make a difference to effectiveness and usability. For example, Hancock and colleagues (2010) found that motivated liars were less easily detected than unmotivated liars in computer-mediated communication (CMC) but more easily detected than unmotivated liars in FTF interaction. The investigators' explanation is that the nonsynchronous nature of offline CMC meant that it allowed time for careful preparation of presentations by motivated liars but the higher desire to deceive became obvious in the "richer" medium of FTF.

Kock (2005) argues that it is not precisely the richness of a medium that is important but rather how closely it matches the characteristics of the "natural" FTF interactions for which human communicative capacities originally evolved. Media richness and naturalness hypotheses yield competing predictions about the effects of possible technological enhancement or supplementation of communicative channels (e.g., subtitling, automated detection of microexpressions, augmented reality techniques for flagging key signals). These developments may bring the potential to take levels of media richness to new heights, but they do not necessarily result in more effective communication in all circumstances (as discussed below). To the extent that enhancement of communication technologies makes them less natural, the prediction of media naturalness theory would be that it worsens outcomes and provokes negative user attitudes *regardless* of the task for which it is used. Media richness theory, by contrast, predicts positive effects of media enhancement for some but not all tasks (see also Chapter Computer-Enhancement of Communication, p. 78).

Advantages and Disadvantages of Mediated Communication

Starting with investigations of communicating by telephone, a number of researchers have addressed questions relating to how well different media suit different communicative tasks. Focusing on emotional communication, Short and colleagues (1976) argue that the lack of cues reduces "social presence" and interferes with the development of interpersonal understanding. Thus the phenomenon of "flaming," where email interactants escalate anger, may reflect senders' failure to factor in the ambiguities of conversational language that lacks nonverbal channels and receivers' misreading of irony or emphasis (Kiesler, Siegel, & McGuire, 1984).

However, cue reduction is not always a bad thing. According to Rutter (1987), the psychological distance encouraged by lower cue levels leads to greater task orientation. For example, addition of an online video channel to remote interaction often fails to improve performance (e.g., Whittaker & O'Connaill, 1997) and enhancement of the quality of video information can even makes things worse (e.g., Matarazzo & Sellen, 2000) by distracting participants from the task at hand.

Further, relatively low-cue situations do not necessarily lead to lower rapport and mutual affection, as the social presence account seems to imply. Walther (e.g., 2011) makes a strong case that high levels of intimacy are sometimes facilitated by restriction rather than enhancement of available cues. Text-based interaction strips away many of the distracting data and permits a kind of hyperpersonal

communication that can get directly to the heart of the matter. Levels of attention and interpretation do not need to track an evanescent unfolding presentation online, making it possible to reread and absorb meaning at whatever pace works best. The effort of "reading between the lines" may pay off with deeper understanding of the other person's underlying intentions and attitudes.

In addition, the editing of self-presentation permitted by restricted modes of communication facilitates interaction between "true selves" rather than the distorted projections people typically present when they are worried about being able to sustain their images. Indeed, McKenna and Bargh (1999) argue that the lack of cues in some forms of remote communication makes it easier for some people, including those suffering from social anxiety, to initiate relationships that they would never have entered in FTF contexts. Further, Bargh and colleagues (2002) show that features of the "true self" become more cognitively accessible in Internet chat rooms than in FTF encounters. An even stronger view of the upsides of mediated interaction was presented by Turkle (1995), who argued that communication technologies facilitate creative experimentation with new online identities.

Rather than seeing any medium as ideal for all purposes, there is growing awareness that different channels carry different advantages and disadvantages in different contexts (see also Daft & Lengel, 1984). Some of the factors that make a difference are salient social identities and cues that activate them, the nature and depth of the relationship between interactants, the presence of multiple audiences and addressees, the nature of transmitted information (e.g., factual, interpretational, opinion-based), and whether communications requires mutual attention to physical objects. More generally, communication effectiveness depends on the particular tasks that users are trying to perform and on agreement between interactants about the nature of this task (Daft & Lengel, 1984). One reason why text-based communication may become hyperpersonal is that both interactants share a goal of getting to know one another over a series of interactions. When strangers with unmeshed intentions and behavioral trajectories meet in cyberspace, clashes and misunderstandings become relatively more likely, especially when nonverbal channels are not available to do their usual work of calibrating common ground (e.g., Clark & Brennan, 1991).

Although technology does not determine the quality of interpersonal interaction, it remains true that certain media characteristics selectively remove certain communicative possibilities. For example, if some kinds of rapport depend on temporal synchronization of gestures in real time, then they cannot be achieved during nonsynchronous interchanges such as email interactions. Even disruptions caused by tiny lags in online video-mediated communication may make it harder to attain a sense of being in tune (see Parkinson, 2008; Parkinson & Lea, 2011).

According to Parkinson (2008), a central function of emotional communication is to align and realign other people's orientations toward objects and events in the shared environment (see also Reciprocal Emotion Transfer in Relation Alignment, p. 73). When those objects or events carry immediate and urgent significance, it becomes important to receive continuous environmental feedback about their status and continuous interpersonal feedback about the communication recipient's orientation both to those objects or events and to the communicator. Text-based messages are unlikely to meet these requirements. Indeed, there may be some specific contexts in which there is no adequate substitute for co-presence in a mutually experienced environment.

Mediated Communication Between Group Members

Many of the emotional effects of mediated emotion communication also depend on group memberships. According to Spears and Lea (1994; see also Spears, Lea, & Postmes, 2007), anonymity may reduce the salience of personal identity, leaving individuals more open to the adoption of relevant social identities. Behavior may then depend on the norms of the salient group rather than on personal motivations. In other words, an absence of social cues does not necessarily lead to unregulated behavior following personal whims but instead may lead to regulation based on different kinds of standard deriving from group memberships. People are not simply disinhibited (as implied by traditional deindividuation accounts, e.g., Zimbardo, 1969) but rather the norms shaping their behavior change when they are online and not personally identifiable to one another. However, anonymity to out-group audiences in mediated settings may also reduce the perceived costs of intergroup hostility and lift some of the usual social constraints against its expression.

Strategic Deployment of Communication Channels

When interactants have the freedom to select media for communication, it is not always advantageous to opt for the maximum levels of cues. In addition to the context-dependent benefits of limiting channels (e.g., Walther, 2011), there may be other motives for removing potential sources of information. In particular, deceptive communication (e.g., in online poker games) may be perceived as easier when the target of deception is unable to pick up "tells" that might otherwise give away hidden intentions.

There are also more prosocial reasons for choosing a medium lower in social cues. A text message may be used for a tentative approach when the pressure of a face-to-face interaction might have made it more difficult for the recipient to say no. Texting also allow us to contact someone without interrupting what they might currently be doing. However, the low social costs associated with email and texts may also lead people to communicate things that would not have been communicated if those media were unavailable. This may help to explain the apparent escalation in the volume of messages that many workers now need to address and a consequent reduction in the attention given to them. For example, students seem less reluctant to contact academic supervisors and tutors by email because of the lower risk of interrupting their busy schedules, but paradoxically their emails may end up making those schedules even busier.

Computer-Enhancement of Communication

As discussed in the previous section, some interpersonal tasks are better suited to low-cue than high-cue communication media. However, under circumstances when greater social presence facilitates interaction, are there additional advantages to raising the level of cues even higher than FTF interaction allows? Similarly, can the addition of supplementary cues that are different from those normally available present advantages for emotion communication? Developments in affective computing raise the possibility of augmenting the level and range of signals transmitted between people, including adding subtitles to spoken communication, incorporating physiological information, morphing facial configurations or movements, detecting fleeting expressive signals, and so on.

There are likely to be downsides as well as upsides to each of these supplementary cues for different tasks and purposes. It is important to recognize that adding information can confuse as well as clarify and that benefits are unlikely to emerge until familiarity with the new forms of interaction reaches a certain level. There is also the associated danger that available technologies will be overused as a consequence of their perceived potential and delimited success in specific settings. Just because something is sometimes helpful does not mean it should be routinely used.

Affective Computing and Interpersonal Emotional Processes

No extant or projected computing system attempts to simulate all aspects of human functioning, and none is likely to implement all processes associated with emotional interactions between people (at least in the foreseeable future). Indeed, many systems are designed not as substitute human emoters but as mechanisms for supplementing or enhancing emotion communication and influence (as discussed above). More commonly, computer scientists focus on particular mechanisms or processes thought to be associated with emotion or its interpersonal transmission, and develop models of those in isolation from other interlocking processes. In principle, these lower-level models might ultimately combine to provide more integrated systems. However, it is also possible that some characteristics of emotion communication cannot be captured piecemeal and may require understanding of relational processes operating between rather than within individual mental systems.

The following sections address issues associated with modeling or simulating subprocesses of emotion communications. For the purposes of exposition, emotion transmission is divided into sequential processes of encoding and decoding. However, subsequent sections suggest how these processes might be interdependent and interpenetrating. Technical details of how systems are implemented are provided elsewhere in this handbook; here, the intention is simply to draw out more general conceptual issues arising from simulation or modeling of interpersonal emotion.

Encoding Emotions

Systems designed to output readable emotional signals are described in this handbook's "Affect Generation" Section. Most focus on facial simulation, but there is also some work on gestures using other parts of the body and on vocal signals. Computer animation is clearly able to generate moving faces and bodies that convincingly convey emotion-relevant information, as evidenced by the success of movies by *Pixar, DreamWorks*, and other companies.

Computer-generated facial stimuli are also widely used in psychological research. The usual aim is to generate specific facial movements that correspond to basic emotion categories or morphs across categories. However, in some cases, researchers sample more widely from facial movements. For example, Jack and colleagues (2012) developed a stimulus set containing a wide range of possible sequences of facial movements in order to show that they were not consistently classified into basic emotion categories by members of different cultures (see Culture and Emotion Communication, p. 75).

Despite their wide sampling of possible facial movements based on Ekman and Friesen's (1978) facial action coding system (FACS), Jack et al. still did not cover the full range of possible nonverbal activity. For one thing, their stimuli were brief in duration. For another, they deployed a delimited range of temporal parameters to specify dynamic change over these brief presentations. In emotion research, the usual tendency is to focus on an even more restricted subset of facial movements and ignore others that serve more explicit communicative purposes (e.g., nodding, shaking one's head) or that do not directly reflect emotion-relevant processes (e.g., sneezing, yawning). Computer scientists and roboticists need to make decisions about which aspects of nonverbal behavior make the most important differences in their application domain before arriving at useful and usable implementations. Given the current state of our knowledge, it would be unrealistic to attempt an all-purpose nonverbal encoding system.

Although generating emotionally communicative static facial positions has so far presented few computational problems, dynamics of moving faces may require more care. For strong and clear nonverbal signals of emotions, moving facial stimuli seem to provide few advantages over nonmoving ones (e.g., Kamachi et al., 2001). However, if emotion cues are more subtle, judgments are more accurate when facial stimuli are presented in their natural dynamic form than as a sequence of still images (Ambadar et al., 2005), convincingly demonstrating that tracking changes over time makes an important difference. Further, changes in dynamics can affect perception of nonverbal communication (Cosker, Krumhuber, & Hilton, 2010; see Krumhuber, Kappas, & Manstead, 2013). It therefore clearly makes a difference whether simulated nonverbal signals conform to ecologically valid (and face valid) dynamics.

Some implementations require not only that animated or robotic faces move in ways that are perceived as realistic but also that their movements meaningfully track the emotional qualities and intensities of ongoing dynamic events. These issues are particularly challenging in applications intended to supplement human-computer interaction with emotion signals from the computer. It seems likely that many of the implicit affects of dynamic attunement cannot operate in the usual way when the avatar's or robot's encoded signals lag behind or otherwise fail to accurately track the human's ongoing communications.

An additional challenge facing this research arises from the fact that decoding tasks are generally used to validate and classify emotion signals from the face as a way of determining how to encode emotions. However, the fact that a face can convey an emotional meaning consistently does not necessarily imply that this face is generated spontaneously when the associated emotion is experienced. For example, a man who was unable to speak English could convey that he was hungry by rubbing his belly and pointing at his mouth, but these movements are more like pantomimes acted out by people playing charades than typical symptoms of being hungry (Russell, 1994). Studies that measure responses to laboratory manipulations of emotion (see Reisenzein, Studtmann, & Horstmann, 2013) or to naturalistic emotional situations (see Fernández-Dols & Crivelli, 2013) typically find relatively low correlations between emotions and supposedly corresponding "expressions." Realism therefore requires that faces often do not reveal emotional qualities of experience regardless of what plausibility might dictate.

Decoding Emotions

There have been several attempts to develop systems that can decode human-generated signals relating to emotion (see this handbook's "Affect Detection" Section). These signals include speech content, voice quality, facial and postural information, autonomic nervous system activity, and sometimes even scanned brain responses. One of the key issues concerns exactly what information needs to be decoded from this available information. It makes a difference whether the system is oriented to discrete basic emotion categories such as happiness, sadness, fear, and anger (e.g., Ekman, 1972); dimensions of pleasure and arousal (e.g., Russell, 1997); social motives (e.g., Fridlund, 1994); action tendencies (e.g., Frijda & Tcherkassof, 1997); or appraisals (e.g., Smith & Scott, 1997). Given that the various available cues may track a range of factors (of which

the above are only a subset) to different degrees in different contexts, problems of arriving at any definitive interpretation are not trivial.

Evidence suggests that the level of coherence of the response syndromes thought to characterize different emotions is too low to allow more than probabilistic identification (e.g., Mauss & Robinson, 2009). Emotion detection when a direct communicative addressee is available or when people are communicating emotion more explicitly tends to be more successful (e.g., Motley & Camden, 1988). It therefore seems important for affective computing systems to incorporate interactive features that encourage their treatment by users as agents to whom emotion communication is appropriate. Whether this necessitates direct simulation of human characteristics and/or close temporal tracking of presented signals remains an open question.

Another set of factors that might increase decoding accuracy concerns the object orientation of emotion communication. As suggested above, dynamic adjustments to ongoing events may give clear information about the target's emotional engagement with what is happening (cf. Michotte, 1950). Indeed, such considerations may contribute to the enhanced readability of dynamic facial expressions even when the perceiver has no visual access to the object to which emotional activity is oriented (e.g., Krumhuber et al., 2013, and see Encoding Emotions, p. 79). In other words, picking up dynamic patterns may provide information about the temporal structure of the emotional event and this, in turn, may clarify subtle emotion cues. One possible implication is that emotion detection and decoding may work best when the parameters of the emotional context are already clear and understood. For example, detecting anger when the nature of a potentially insulting event is already known is likely to be easier than detecting anger without prior information about the context.

Integrating Encoding-Decoding Cycles

The affective computing movement sometimes raises the possibility of arriving at an integrated system capable of decoding emotion signals from humans and responding with encoded emotion signals from an avatar or robot. As discussed above, there are technical issues facing such attempts that relate to appropriate matching of dynamics in real time, especially when two-way communication is required and when responsive signals need to be quickly generated to permit a sense of synchrony and mutual attunement. However, there may also be deeper problems with the assumption that accurate or adequate simulation of emotion communication depends on translating a human's signals into emotion categories or dimensions (decoding), computing the appropriate response to output, and then encoding this into a realistic presentation. What if everyday human-human emotion communication often involves more direct interpersonal adjustments and is not mediated by extraction of represented meaning?

Emotions may consolidate as a consequence of interpersonally distributed processes rather than as individual mental products of private calculations that are transmitted back and forth between interactants (e.g., Fogel, 1993; Parkinson, 2008). In particular, people may arrive at shared or complementary orientations toward events as a consequence of continuous reciprocal adjustments to one another's dynamic movements in relation to objects. To participate in such processes, an affective computing system would need to be responsive to gaze direction and action orientation (among other things) online. Decoding of emotional state would not be of direct importance in this kind of interaction. Similarly, any empathic consequences of dynamic synchrony are not dependent on extracting predefined meaning from diagnostic emotion cues.

In sum, the apparent dynamic complexities of emotional engagement with objects and other people make the project of developing workable affective agents challenging but also deeply interesting. The ultimate hope is that addressing these technical challenges will reveal additional insights about the social and emotional processes that are modeled or simulated.

Acknowledgments

The author would like to thank the Economic and Social Research Council, UK (grant RES-060-25-0044), for financial support while writing this chapter.

References

Ambadar, Z., Schooler, J., & Cohn, J. (2005). Deciphering the enigmatic face: The importance of facial dynamics in interpreting subtle facial expressions. *Psychological Science, 16*, 403–410.

Bargh, J. A., McKenna, K. Y. A., & Fitzsimons, G. M. (2002). Can you see the real me? Activation and expression of the "true self" on the Internet. *Journal of Social Issues, 58*, 33–48.

Bayliss, A. P., Frischen, A., Fenske, M. J., & Tipper, S. P. (2007). Affective evaluations of objects are influenced by observed gaze direction and emotion expression. *Cognition, 104*, 644–653.

Bernieri, F. J., & Rosenthal, R. (1991). Coordinated movement in human interaction. In R. S. Feldman & B. Rimé (Eds.), *Fundamentals of nonverbal behaviour* (pp. 401–431). New York, NY: Cambridge University Press.

Bourgeois, P., & Hess, U. (2008). The impact of social context on mimicry. *Biological Psychology, 77*, 343–352.

Catmur, C., Gillmeister, H., Bird, G., Liepelt, R., Brass, M., & Heyes, C. (2008). Through the looking glass: Counter-mirror activation following incompatible sensorimotor learning. *European Journal of Neuroscience, 28*, 1208–1215.

Cialdini, R. B., Bordon, R. J., Thorne, A., Walker, M. R., Freeman, S., & Sloan, L. R. (1976). Basking in reflected glory: Three field studies. *Journal of Personality and Social Psychology, 34*, 366–375.

Clark, H. H., & Brennan, S. E. (1991). Grounding in communication. In L. B. Resnick, J. Levine, & S. D. Teasley (Eds.). *Perspectives in socially shared cognition* (pp. 127–149). Washington, DC: American Psychological Association.

Cook, R., Bird, G., Catmur, C., Press, C., & Heyes, C. (in press). Mirror neurons: From origin to function. *Behavioral and Brain Sciences*.

Cosker, D., Krumhuber, E., & Hilton, A. (2010). Perception of linear and nonlinear motion properties using a FACS validated 3D facial model. *Proceedings of the Symposium on Applied Perception in Graphics and Visualization (APGV)* (pp. 101–108), New York, NY: Association for Computing Machinery.

Daft, R. L., & Lengel, R. H. (1984). Information richness: A new approach to managerial behavior and organizational design. *Research in Organizational Behavior, 6*, 191–233.

Doosje B., Branscombe, N. R., Spears R., & Manstead, A. S. R. (1998). Guilty by association: When one's group has a negative history. *Journal of Personality and Social Psychology, 75*, 872–886.

Dumont, M., Yzerbyt, V. Y., Wigboldus, D., & Gordijn, E. H. (2003). Social categorization and fear reactions to the September 11th terrorist attacks. *Personality and Social Psychology Bulletin, 29*, 1509–1520.

Ekman, P. (1972). Universals and cultural differences in facial expressions of emotion. *Nebraska Symposium on Motivation, 19*, 207–283.

Ekman, P. (2003). *Emotions revealed: Understanding faces and feeling*. London: Weidenfeld and Nicolson.

Ekman, P., & Friesen, W. (1978). *Facial action coding system: A technique for the measurement of facial movement*. Palo Alto, CA: Consulting Psychologists Press.

Elfenbein, H. A., & Ambady, N. (2002). Is there an in-group advantage in emotion recognition? *Psychological Bulletin, 128*, 243–249.

Englis, B. G., Vaughan, E. B., & Lanzetta, J. T. (1982). Conditioning of counter-empathic emotional responses. *Journal of Experimental Social Psychology, 18*, 375–391.

Fernández-Dols, J.-M., & Crivelli, C. (2013). Emotion and expression: Naturalistic studies. *Emotion Review, 5*, 24–29.

Fogel, A. (1993). *Developing through relationships: Origins of communication, self, and culture*. Chicago, IL: University of Chicago Press.

Fridlund, A. J. (1994). *Human facial expression: An evolutionary view*. San Diego, CA: Academic Press.

Frijda, N. H. (1986). *The emotions*. Cambridge, UK: Cambridge University Press.

Frijda, N. H. (1993). The place of appraisal in emotion. *Cognition and Emotion, 7*, 357–387.

Frijda, N. H., & Tcherkassof, A. (1997). Facial expressions as modes of action readiness. In J. A. Russell & J.-M. Fernández-Dols (Eds.), *The psychology of facial expression* (pp. 78–102). New York, NY: Cambridge University Press.

Gross, J. J. (1998). The emerging field of emotion regulation: An integrative review. *Review of General Psychology, 2*, 271–299.

Halberstadt, J., Winkielmann, P., Niedenthal, P. M., & Dalle, N. (2009). Emotional conception: How embodied emotion concepts guide perception and facial action. *Psychological Science, 20*, 1254–1261

Hancock, J. T., Woodworth, M. T., & Goorha, S. (2010). See no evil: The effect of communication medium and motivation on deception detection. *Group Decision and Negotiation, 19*, 327–343.

Hareli, S., & Hess, U. (2010). What emotional reactions can tell us about the nature of others: An appraisal perspective on person perception. *Cognition and Emotion, 24*, 128–140.

Hatfield, E., Cacioppo, J. T., & Rapson, R. L. (1994). *Emotional contagion*. New York, NY: Cambridge University Press.

Hess, U., Banse, R., & Kappas, A. (1995). The intensity of facial expression is determined by underlying affective state and social situation. *Journal of Personality and Social Psychology, 69*, 280–288.

Hess, U., & Fischer, A. (2013). Emotional mimicry as social regulation. *Personality and Social Psychology Review, 17*, 142–157.

Iacoboni, M. (2009). Imitation, empathy and mirror neurons, *Annual Review of Psychology, 60*, 653–670.

Jack, R. E., Garrod, O. G. B., Yu, H., Caldara, R., & Schyns, P. G. (2012). Facial expressions of emotion are not culturally universal. *Proceedings of the National Academy of Sciences, 109*, 7241–7244.

Jakobs, E., Manstead, A. S. R., & Fischer, A. H. (2001). Social context effects on facial activity in a negative emotional setting. *Emotion, 1*, 51–69.

Kamachi, M., Bruce, V., Mukaida, S., Gyoba, J., Yoshikawa, S., & Akamatsu, S. (2001). Dynamic properties influence the perception of facial expressions. *Perception, 30*, 875–887.

Kappas, A., & Krämer, N. (Eds.) (2011). *Face-to-face communication over the internet: Issues, research, challenges*. Cambridge, UK: Cambridge University Press.

Keltner, D. & Haidt, J. (1999). Social functions of emotions at four levels of analysis. *Cognition and Emotion, 13*, 505–521.

Kiesler, S., Siegel, J., & McGuire, T. W. (1984). Social psychological aspects of computer-mediated communication. *American Psychologist, 39*, 1123–1134.

Kock, N. (2005). Media richness or media naturalness? The evolution of our biological communication apparatus and its influence on our behaviour toward e-communication tools. *IEEE Transactions on Professional Communication, 48*, 117–130.

Krumhuber, E. G., Kappas, A., & Manstead, A. S. R. (2013). Effects of dynamic aspects of facial expressions: A review. *Emotion Review, 5*, 41–46.

Lakin, J. L., Chartrand, T. L., & Arkin, R. M. (2008). I am too just like you: The effects of ostracism on nonconscious mimicry. *Psychological Science, 19*, 816–822.

Lakin, J. L., Jefferis, V. E., Cheng, C. M., & Chartrand, T. L. (2003). The Chameleon effect as social glue: Evidence for the evolutionary significance of nonconscious mimicry. *Journal of Nonverbal Behavior, 27*, 145–162.

Latané, B., & Darley, J. M. (1968). Group inhibition of bystander intervention in emergencies. *Journal of Personality and Social Psychology, 10*, 215–221.

Lazarus, R. S. (1991). *Emotion and adaptation*. New York, NY: Oxford University Press.

Leach, C. W., Spears, R., Branscombe, N. R., & Doosje, B. (2003). Malicious pleasure: Schadenfreude at the suffering of an outgroup. *Journal of Personality and Social Psychology, 84*, 932–943.

Lindquist, K. A., & Gendron, M. (2013). What's in a word? Language constructs emotion perception. *Emotion Review, 5*, 66–71.

Livingstone, A. G., Spears, R., Manstead, A. S. R., Bruder, M., & Shepherd, L. (2011). We feel, therefore we are: Emotion as a basis for self-categorization and social action. *Emotion, 11*, 754–767.

Manstead, A. S. R., & Fischer, A. H. (2001). Social appraisal: The social world as object of and influence on appraisal processes. In K. R. Scherer, A. Schorr, & T. Johnston (Eds.), *Appraisal processes in emotion: Theory, methods, research* (pp. 221–232). New York, NY: Oxford University Press.

Matarazzo, G., & Sellen, A. (2000). The value of video in work at a distance: Addition or distraction? *Behaviour and Information Technology, 19*, 339–348.

Mauss, I. B., & Robinson, M. D. (2009). Measures of emotion: A review. *Cognition and Emotion, 23*, 209–237.

McKenna, K. Y. A., & Bargh, J. A. (1999). Causes and consequences of social interaction on the internet: A conceptual framework. *Media Psychology, 1*, 249–269.

Michotte, A. (1950). The emotions regarded as functional connections. In M. L. Reymert (Ed.), *Feelings and emotions: The Mooseheart symposium* (pp. 114–126). New York, NY: McGraw Hill.

Moody, E., McIntosh, D. N., Mann, L. J., & Weisser, K. R. (2007). More than mere mimicry? The influence of emotion on rapid facial reactions to faces. *Emotion, 7*, 447–457.

Motley, M. T., & Camden, C. T. (1988). Facial expression of emotion: A comparison of posed expressions versus spontaneous expressions in an interpersonal communication setting. *Western Journal of Speech Communication, 52*, 1–22.

Mumenthaler, C., & Sander, D. (2012). Social appraisal influences recognition of emotions. *Journal of Personality and Social Psychology, 102*, 1118–1135.

Niedenthal, P. M., & Brauer, M. (2012). Social functionality of human emotion. *Annual Review of Psychology, 63*, 259–285.

Niedenthal, P. M., Mermillod, M., Maringer, M., & Hess, U. (2010). The simulation of smiles (SIMS) model: Embodied simulation and the meaning of facial expression. *Behavioral and Brain Sciences, 33*, 417–433.

Parkinson, B. (1996). Emotions are social. *British Journal of Psychology, 87*, 663–683.

Parkinson, B. (2001). Putting appraisal in context. In K. R. Scherer, A. Schorr, & T. Johnstone (Eds.), *Appraisal processes in emotion: Theory, research, application* (pp. 173–186). New York, NY: Oxford University Press.

Parkinson, B. (2005). Do facial movements express emotions or communicate motives? *Personality and Social Psychology Review, 9*, 278–311.

Parkinson, B. (2008). Emotions in direct and remote social interaction: Getting through the spaces between us. *Computers in Human Behavior, 24*, 1510–1529.

Parkinson, B. (2011a). Interpersonal emotion transfer: Contagion and social appraisal. *Personality and Social Psychology Compass, 5*, 428–439.

Parkinson, B. (2011b). How social is the social psychology of emotion? *British Journal of Social Psychology, 50*, 405–413.

Parkinson, B. (2013a). Journeys to the center of emotion. *Emotion Review, 5,* 180–184.

Parkinson, B. (2013b). Contextualizing facial activity. *Emotion Review, 5,* 97–103.

Parkinson, B., & Lea, M. (2011). Video linking emotions. In A. Kappas & N. Krämer (Eds.), *Face-to-face communication over the Internet: Issues, research, challenges* (pp. 100–126). Cambridge, UK: Cambridge University Press.

Parkinson, B., Phiri, N., & Simons, G. (2012). Bursting with anxiety: Adult social referencing in an interpersonal balloon analogue risk task (BART). *Emotion, 12,* 817–826.

Parkinson, B., & Simons, G. (2009). Affecting others: Social appraisal and emotion contagion in everyday decision making. *Personality and Social Psychology Bulletin, 35,* 1071–1084.

Parkinson, B., & Simons, G. (2012). Worry spreads: Interpersonal transfer of problem-related anxiety. *Cognition and Emotion, 26,* 462–479.

Reddy, V. (2008). *How infants know minds.* Cambridge, MA: Harvard University Press.

Reisenzein, R., Studtmann, M., & Horstmann, G. (2013). Coherence between emotion and facial expression: Evidence from laboratory experiments. *Emotion Review, 5,* 16–23.

Rizzolatti, G., & Craighero, L. (2004). The mirror-neuron system. *Annual Review of Neuroscience, 27,* 169–192.

Rose, A. J. (2002). Co-rumination in the friendships of girls and boys. *Child Development, 73,* 1830–1843.

Russell, J. A. (1994). Is there universal recognition of emotion from facial expression? A review of the cross-cultural studies. *Psychological Bulletin, 115,* 102–141.

Russell, J. A. (1997). Reading emotions from and into faces: Resurrecting a dimensional-contextual perspective. In J. A. Russell & J.-M. Fernández-Dols (Eds.), *The psychology of facial expression* (pp. 295–320). New York: Cambridge University Press.

Rutter, D. R. (1987). *Communicating by telephone.* Elmsford, NY: Pergamon.

Short, J., Williams, E., & Christie, B. (1976). *The social psychology of telecommunications.* London: Wiley.

Smith, C. A., McHugo, G. J., & Kappas, A. (1996). Epilogue: Overarching themes and enduring contributions of the Lanzetta research. *Motivation and Emotion, 20,* 237–253.

Smith, C. A., & Scott, H. S. (1997). A componential approach to the meaning of facial expressions. In J. A. Russell & J-M. Fernández-Dols (Eds.), *The psychology of facial expression* (pp. 229–254). New York: Cambridge University Press.

Smith, E. R. (1993). Social identity and social emotions: Toward new conceptualizations of prejudice. In D. M. Mackie, D. Hamilton, & D. Lewis (Eds.), *Affect, cognition, and stereotyping: Interactive processes in group perception* (pp. 297–315). San Diego, CA: Academic Press.

Sorce, J. F., Emde, R. N., Campos, J., & Klinnert, M. D. (1985). Maternal emotional signaling: Its effect on the visual cliff behavior of 1 year olds. *Developmental Psychology, 21,* 195–200.

Spears, R., & Lea, M. (1994). Panacea or panopticon? The hidden power in computer-mediated communication. *Communication Research, 21,* 427–459.

Spears, R., Lea, M., & Postmes, T. (2007). Computer-mediated communication and social identity. In A. Joinson, K. McKenna, T. Postmes, & U.-D. Reips (Eds.), *The Oxford handbook of Internet psychology* (pp. 253–269). Oxford, UK: Oxford University Press.

Standage, T. (1998). *The Victorian Internet.* New York: Walker & Co.

Strack, F., Martin, L. L., & Stepper, S. (1988). Inhibiting and facilitating conditions of the human smile: A non-obtrusive test of the facial feedback hypothesis. *Journal of Personality and Social Psychology, 54,* 768–777.

Tamietto, M., Castelli, L., Vighetti, S., Perozzo, P., Geminiani, G., Weiskrantz, L., & de Gelder, B. (2009). Unseen facial and bodily expressions trigger fast emotional reactions. *Proceedings of the National Academy of Sciences of the United States of America, 106,* 17661–17666.

Turkle, S. (1995). *Life on the screen: Identity in the age of the Internet.* London: Weidenfeld & Nicolson.

Turner, J. C., Hogg, M. A., Oakes, P. J., Reicher, S. D., & Wetherell, M. S. (1987). *Rediscovering the social group: A self categorization theory.* Oxford, UK: Blackwell.

Van Kleef, G. A. (2009). How emotions regulate social life: The emotions as social information (EASI) model. *Current Directions in Psychological Science, 18,* 184–188.

Vaughan, K., & Lanzetta, J. T. (1980). Vicarious instigation and conditioning of facial expressive and autonomic responses to a model's expressive display of pain. *Journal of Personality and Social Psychology, 38,* 909–923.

Vaughan, K., & Lanzetta, J. T. (1981). The effect of modification of expressive display on vicarious emotional arousal. *Journal of Experimental Social Psychology, 17,* 16–30.

Wagner, H. L., & Smith, J. (1991). Facial expression in the presence of friends and strangers. *Journal of Nonverbal Behavior, 15,* 201–214.

Walther, J. (2011). Visual cues in computer-mediated communication: Sometimes less is more. In A. Kappas & N. Krämer (Eds.), *Face-to-face communication over the Internet: Issues, research, challenges* (pp. 17–38). Cambridge, UK: Cambridge University Press.

Weiskrantz, L. (2009). *Blindsight: A case study spanning 35 years and new developments.* Oxford, UK; Oxford University Press.

Whittaker, S., O'Connaill, B. (1997). The role of vision in face-to-face and mediated communication. In Finn, K. E., Sellen, A. J., & Wilbur, S. B. (Eds.). *Video-mediated communication* (pp. 23–49). Mahwah, NJ: Erlbaum.

Yzerbyt, V., Dumont, M., Gordijn, E., & Wigboldus, D. (2002). Intergroup emotions and self-categorization: The impact of perspective-taking on reactions to victims of harmful behaviors. In D. M. Mackie & E. R. Smith (Eds.), *From prejudice to intergroup emotions: Differentiated reactions to social groups* (pp. 67–88). Philadelphia, PA: Psychology Press.

Zimbardo, P. G. (1969). The human choice: Individuation, reason, and order vs. deindividuation, impulse, and chaos. In W. J. Arnold & D. Levine (Eds.), *Nebraska Symposium on Motivation* (pp. 237–307). Lincoln: University of Nebraska Press.

Social Signal Processing

Maja Pantic *and* Alessandro Vinciarelli

Abstract

Social signal processing (SSP) is a new cross-disciplinary research domain that aims at understanding and modeling social interactions (research in human sciences) and providing computers with similar abilities (research in computer science). SSP is still in its formative phase, and the journey toward artificial social intelligence and socially aware computing still has a long way to go. This chapter surveys the current state of the art and summarizes issues that the researchers in this field face.

Key Words: social signal processing, artificial social intelligence, socially aware computing

Social Intelligence in Men and Machines

The need to deal effectively with social interactions has driven the evolution of brain structures and cognitive abilities in all species characterized by complex social exchanges, including humans in particular (Gallese, 2006). The relationship between degree of expansion of the neocortex and size of the groups among primates is one of the most conclusive and important pieces of evidence of such a process (Dunbar, 1992). Therefore it is not surprising to observe that the computing community considers the development of socially intelligent machines an important priority (Vinciarelli et al., 2012), especially since computers left their traditional role of enhanced versions of old tools (e.g., word processors replacing typewriters) and became full social actors expected to be integrated seamlessly in our everyday lives (Nass et al., 1994; Vinciarelli, 2009).

Social signal processing (SSP) is one of the domains that contribute to the efforts aimed at endowing machines with social intelligence (see Social Signal Processing: Definition and Context, p. 85); in particular, it focuses on modeling, analysis, and synthesis of nonverbal behavior in social interactions (Vinciarelli

et al., 2009). The key idea of SSP is that computers can participate in social interactions by automatically understanding and/or synthesizing the many nonverbal behavioral cues (facial expressions, vocalizations, gestures, postures, etc.) that people use to express or suggest socially relevant information (attitudes, beliefs, intentions, stances, etc.).

Overall, SSP stems from three major research areas: human behavior, social psychology, and computer science. The first provides methodologies for dealing with nonverbal behavior as a physical (machine-detectable) phenomenon. Social psychology provides quantitative analyses of the relationship between nonverbal behavior and social/psychological phenomena. Computer science provides technologies for the machine detection and synthesis of these relevant phenomena within the contexts of both human-human and human-computer interaction. The result is an interdisciplinary domain where the target is machine modeling and understanding of the social meaning of human behavior in interactive contexts.

Although this field is still in its early stages—the term *social signal processing* was coined only a few years ago (Pentland, 2007)—the areas of SSP research have already seen an impressive development in terms of both knowledge accumulation and increased interest from the research community. The domain has progressed significantly in terms of social phenomena made accessible to technological investigation (roles, personality, conflict, leadership, mimicry, attraction, stances, etc.), methodologies adopted (regression and prediction approaches for dimensional assessments, probabilistic inference for modeling and recognition of multimodal sequences of human behavior, combinations of multiple ratings and crowdsourcing for attaining a more reliable ground truth, etc.), and the benchmarking campaigns that have been carried out (facial expression recognition, automatic personality perception, vocalization detection, etc.). Furthermore, major efforts have been made toward the definition of social signals (Mehu &

Scherer, 2012; Poggi & D'Errico, 2012), the delimitation of the domain's scope (Brunet et al., 2012), and setting a research agenda for further progress in the field (Pantic et al., 2011). Figure 7.1 shows the number of technology-oriented events (workshops, conferences, symposia) and publications revolving around social interactions. The trend speaks for itself and is still growing as this chapter is being written.

The rest of this chapter provides an account of the main results achieved so far as well as an indication of remaining challenges and most promising applications.

Social Signal Processing: Definition and Context

In 2007 Alex Pentland coined the expression *social signal processing* (Pentland, 2007) to describe

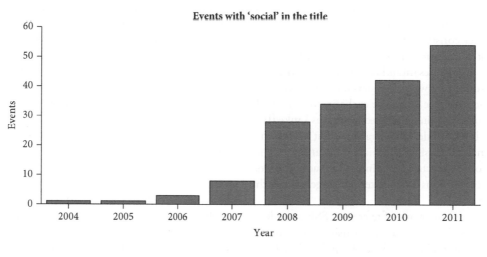

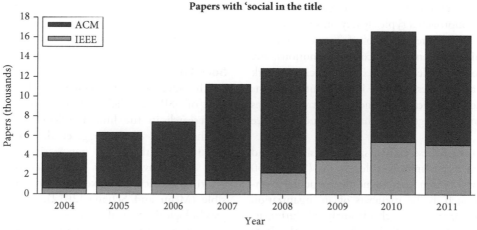

Fig. 7.1 The upper plot shows the number of technology-oriented events (workshops, summer schools, symposia, etc.) with the word *social* in the title, as advertised in the "dbworld" mailing list. The lower plot shows the same information for the papers available via the IEEE-Xplore and the ACM Digital Library.

pioneering efforts at inferring socially relevant information from nonverbal behavioral cues (e.g., predicting the outcome of a salary negotiation based on the way the participants talked but not on what the participants said). Since then, the domain has continued to grow and to address an increasingly wider spectrum of scenarios. The scope of the field, according to a widely accepted definition (Brunet et al., 2012), is to study signals (in a broad everyday sense of the word) that:

• Are produced during social interactions
• Either play a part in the formation and adjustment of relationships and interactions between agents (human and artificial)
• Provide information about the agents
• Can be addressed by technologies of signal processing and synthesis

The relationship between SSP and the other socially aware technologies can be analyzed in terms of two main dimensions: the scale of the interactions under consideration and the processing level. The first dimension ranges between dyads and online communities including millions of individuals, the second between high-level, easily detectable electronic evidence (e.g., the exchange of an email or a "connection" in social media, such as LinkedIn) and low-level, subtle behavioral cues that need complex signal processing and machine learning techniques to be detected (e.g., individual action units in facial expressions or short-term changes in speech prosody).

In such a framework of reference, SSP considers only small-scale scenarios (comprising rarely more than four individuals) where it applies low-level processing techniques, mostly to audio and video data. SSP approaches typically rely on subtle behavioral cues and address social phenomena as complex as role-playing, personality, conflict, emotions, etc. At the opposite side of the spectrum, Social network analysis approaches can take into account millions of people but typically depend on electronic traces left during the usage of web-based technologies (see above).

In between these extremes, it is possible to find areas that target middle-scale groups (50 to 150 individuals), often corresponding to actual communities such as the members of an organization (e.g., a company or a school) analyzed during its operations. One example is *reality mining* (Eagle & Pentland, 2005; Raento et al., 2009), the domain using smartphones as sensors for social and other activities. Interaction evidence used in this case includes both high-level cues (e.g., phone calls or text messages) and low-level behavioral signals such as fidgeting (captured via accelerometers) or proximity to others (captured via Bluetooth). Another example is the design of sociotechnical systems (de Bruijn & Herder, 2009). In this case the goal is to analyze and optimize the impact of technologies on groups of people sharing a particular setting (e.g., the employees of a company or the inhabitants of a building). This area considers high-level evidence such as usage logs, field observations, and questionnaires.

A recent trend is to apply SSP-inspired approaches to data collected in social media such as blogs, YouTube videos, etc. The number of involved subjects is typically high (100 to 500 people), but these tend to be considered individually and not as a community. The main difference with respect to "standard" SSP approaches is the adoption of social network–inspired features (e.g., the number of times a video has been watched, online ratings, etc.) typically available in social media (Biel & Gatica-Perez, 2012; Salvagnini et al., 2012). Last but not least is the research on socially aware approaches aimed at computer-supported communication and collaboration. In this field, the goal is not to understand or synthesize social interactions but to support— and possibly enhance—social contacts between individuals expected to accomplish common tasks or communicate via computer systems (Grudin & Poltrock, 2012). In this case, the focus is typically on building infrastructures (virtual spaces, interfaces, etc.) that facilitate basic social mechanisms such as eye contact, information sharing, turn organization, focus of attention, etc. Such technologies typically address small groups (2 to 10 people) of individuals who are not colocated.

Social Signals

The idea of social signals is the key concept of SSP and their definition is still subject of research in the human sciences community (Mehu et al., 2012; Poggi et al., 2012). In an evolutionary-ethological perspective, social signals are behaviors that have coevolved across multiple subjects to make social interaction possible (Mehu and Scherer, 2012). From a social psychological point of view, social signals include any behavior aimed at engaging others in a joint activity, often communication (Brunet & Cowie, 2012). This work adopts the cognitive perspective proposed by Poggi and D'Errico (2012), where social signals are defined as "communicative or informative signals which... provide information about social facts"—that is, about social actions and interactions, social emotions, social evaluations, social attitudes, and social relations.

Social Interactions

Social interactions are events in which actually or virtually present agents exchange an array of *social actions* (i.e., communicative and informative signals performed by one agent in relation to one or more other agents). Typical communicative signals in social interactions are backchannel signals such as head nods, gaze exchanges, and rapport, which inform the recipient that her interaction partner is following and understanding her (Miles et al., 2009).

Social Emotions

A clear distinction can be made between *individual* and *social* emotions. Happiness and sadness are typical examples of individual emotions—we can be happy or sad on our own; our feelings are not directed toward any other person. On the other hand, admiration, envy, and compassion are typical examples of social emotions—we have these feelings toward another person. Signals revealing individual emotions and those communicating social emotions both include facial expressions, vocal intonations and outbursts, and body gestures and postures (Mayne & Bonanno, 2001).

Social Evaluations

The social evaluation of a person relates to assessing whether and how much his or her characteristics comply with our standards of beauty, intelligence, strength, justice, altruism, etc. We judge other people because, based on our evaluation, we decide whether to engage in a social interaction with them, what types of social actions to perform, and what relations to establish with them (Gladwell, 2005). Typical signals shown in social evaluation are approval and disapproval, at least when it comes to the evaluator. As far as the evaluated person is concerned, typical signals involve those conveying desired characteristics, such as pride, self-confidence, and mental strength, which include raised chin, erect posture, easy and relaxed movements, etc. (Manusov & Patterson, 2006).

Social Attitudes

Social attitude can be defined as the positive or negative evaluation of a person or group of people (Gilbert et al., 1998). Social attitudes include cognitive elements like beliefs, opinions, and social emotions. All these elements determine (and are determined by) preferences and intentions (Fishbein & Ajzen, 1975). Agreement and disagreement can be seen as being related to social attitude. If two persons agree, this usually entails an alliance and a mutually positive attitude. This is in contrast to disagreement, which typically implies conflict and a mutually negative attitude. Typical signals of agreement and disagreement are head nods and head shakes, smiles, crossed arms, etc. (Bousmalis et al., 2012).

Social Relations

A social relation is a relation between two (or more) persons in which these persons have related goals (Kelley & Thibaut, 1978). Hence not every relation is a social relation. Two persons sitting next to each other on a bus have a physical proximity relation, but this is not a social relation, although one can arise from it. We can have many different kinds of social relations with other people: dependency, competition, cooperation, love, exploitation, etc. Typical signals revealing social relations include the manner of greeting (e.g., saying "hello" to signal the wish for a positive social relation, saluting signals belonging to a specific group, like the army), the manner of conversing (e.g., using the word *professor* to signal submission), mirroring (signaling the wish to have a positive social relation), spatial positioning (e.g., making a circle around a certain person to distinguish that person as the leader), etc.

Machine Analysis of Social Signals

The core idea behind the machine analysis of social signals is that these are physical, machine-detectable traces of social and psychological phenomena that may not be observed directly (Vinciarelli et al., 2012). For this reason, typical SSP technologies include two main components (Vinciarelli et al., 2009). The first aims at detecting the morphology (or simple existence) of social signals in data captured with a wide array of sensors, most commonly microphones and cameras. The second aims at interpreting detected social signals in terms of social facts (see above) according to rules/principles proposed in the large body of literature in human sciences.

Social Interactions

In the past decade, significant progress in automatic audio and/or visual recognition of communicative signals such as head nods, smiles, laughter, and hesitation has been reported (De la Torre & Cohn, 2011; Schuller et al., 2013). Reviews of such technologies are included in Section 2 of this volume. However, a multitude of social signals underlying the manifestation of various social facts involve explicit representation of the context, time, and interplay between different modalities. For example, in order to model gaze exchanges or mimicry (Delaherche et al., 2012)—which are crucial for inferring rapport, empathy, and dominance—all interacting parties and their mutual multimodal interplay in time should be modeled. Yet most of the present approaches to the machine analysis of social signals and human behaviors are not multimodal, context-sensitive, or suitable for handling multiple interacting parties and longer time scales (Pantic, 2009; De la Torre & Cohn, 2011; Delaherche et al., 2012). Hence proper machine modeling of social interactions and the related phenomena like rapport and interaction cohesion is yet to be attempted.

Social Emotions

While the state of the art in the machine analysis of basic emotions such as happiness, anger, fear, and disgust is fairly advanced, especially when it comes to the analysis of acted displays recorded in constrained lab settings (Zeng et al., 2009), machine analysis of social emotions such as empathy, envy, admiration, etc., is yet to be attempted. Although some of social emotions could arguably be represented in terms of affect dimensions—valence, arousal, expectation, power, and intensity—and pioneering efforts toward automatic dimensional and continuous emotion recognition have recently been proposed (Gunes & Pantic, 2010; Nicolaou et al., 2012), a number of crucial issues need to be addressed first if these approaches to automatic dimensional and continuous emotion recognition are to be used with freely moving subjects in real-world multiparty scenarios like patient-doctor discussions, talk shows, job interviews, etc. In particular, published techniques revolve around the emotional expressions of a single subject rather than the dynamics of the emotional feedback exchange between two subjects, which is the crux in the analysis of any social emotions. Moreover, the state-of-the-art techniques are still unable to handle natural scenarios such as incomplete information due to occlusions, large and sudden changes in head pose, and other temporal dynamics typical of natural facial expressions (Zeng et al. 2009), which must be expected in real-world scenarios where social emotions occur.

Social Evaluations

Only recently efforts have been reported toward automatic prediction of social evaluations including personality and beauty estimation. Automatic attribution of personality traits, in terms of the "Big Five" personality model, has attracted increasingly more attention in the last years (Mairesse et al., 2012; Olguin-Olguin et al., 2009; Pianesi, 2013; Pianesi et al., 2008; Polzehl et al., 2010; Zen et al., 2010). Most of the works rely on speech, especially after personality perception benchmarking campaigns organized in the speech processing community (Lee et. al. this volume; Schuller et al., 2013). The cues most commonly adopted include prosody (pitch, speaking rate, energy, and their statistics across time), voice quality (statistical spectral measurements), and, whenever the subject is involved in interactions, turn-organization features (see above). Other cues that appear to have an influence, especially from a perception point of view, are facial expressions, focus of attention, fidgeting, interpersonal distances, etc. However, automated approaches using such visual cues are yet to be attempted. The results change depending on the setting, but it is frequently observed that the best-predicted traits are extraversion and conscientiousness, in line with psychology findings showing that such personality dimensions are the most reliably perceived in humans (Judd et al., 2005).

Automatic estimations of facial attractiveness have been attempted based on facial shape (e.g., Gunes & Piccardi, 2006; Schmid et al., 2008; Zhang et al., 2011) as well as on facial appearance information encoded in terms of Gabor filter responses (Whitehill & Movellan, 2008) or eigenfaces (Sutic et al., 2010). A survey of the efforts on the topic is reported by Bottino and Laurentini (2010). However, the research in this domain is still in its very first stage and many basic questions remain unanswered, including exactly which features (and modalities) are the most informative for the target problem.

Social Attitudes

Similarly to social emotions and social evaluations, the automatic assessment of social attitudes has been attempted only recently, and there are just a few studies on the topic. Conflict and disagreement have been detected and measured in both dimensional and categorical terms using prosody, overlapping speech, facial expressions, gestures, and head movements (Bousmalis et al., 2012, 2013; Kim et al., 2012). Dominance has been studied in particular in meetings, where turn-organization features and received visual attention were shown to be the best predictors (Gatica-Perez, 2009; Jayagopi et al, 2009).

Social Relations

One of the most common problems addressed in SSP is the recognition of roles, whether this means identifying people who are fulfilling specific functions in well-defined settings—as, for example, the role of anchorman in a talk show or chairman in a meeting (Barzilay et al., 2000; Gatica-Perez, 2009; Laskowski et al., 2008; Liu, 2006; Salamin & Vinciarelli, 2012)—or addressing the very structure of social interactions in small groups by tackling roles observable in every social situation (e.g., attacker, neutral, supporter, etc.) (Banerjee & Rudnicky, 2004; Dong et al., 2007; Valente & Vinciarelli, 2011). The social signals that appear to be most effective in this problem are those related to turn organization—who talks when, how much and with whom—in line with the indications of conversation analysis, the domain that studies the social meaning behind the way interaction is organized (Sacks et al., 1974). Speaking-time distribution across different interaction participants, adjacency pair statistics between different individuals, average length of turns, number of turns per individual, number of turns between consecutive turns of the same individual, and variants of these measurements lead to high role-recognition performances in almost every setting considered in the literature. The analysis of turn organization is typically performed by applying speaker diarization approaches to audio data (i.e., technologies that segment audio data into time intervals expected to correspond to an individual voice). After such a step, it is possible to measure turn-organization features and apply pattern recognition to assign each person a role. Limited but statistically significant improvements come from a variety of other cues, including lexical choices, fidgeting, focus of attention, prosody, etc. None of these cues taken individually produces satisfactory results. Therefore they appear only in multimodal approaches where they improve the performance achieved with turn-organization cues.

Machine Synthesis of Social Signals

Most of the efforts in the machine synthesis of social signals aim at generating social actions artificially via informative and communicative signals displayed by an artificial agent in relation to another, typically a human (Poggi & D'Errico, 2012). However, the latest efforts target the synthesis of more complex constructs, in particular emotions and attitudes, which typically require the coordinated synthesis of several social actions at the same time (Vinciarelli et al., 2012).

Social Interactions

One of the most challenging goals for an artificial agent is to become involved in conversations with humans. Therefore social actions typical of such a setting are those that have received the most attention. Since an agent is expected to participate actively, the ability to grab and release the floor appropriately is a priority, and it is typically modeled via action-perception loops (Bonaiuto & Thorisson, 2008) or imitation (Prepin & Revel, 2007). However, in order to appear natural, agents must be active not only when they intervene and talk but also when they listen. Such a goal is achieved by simulating back-channel cues like head nodding, laughter, vocalizations (e.g., "yeah," "ah-hah," etc.) and other behaviors people display to show attention. The main issue is to identify the moments when such cues are appropriate. The most common approaches consist of reacting when the speaker shows certain cues (Maatman et al., 2005), using probabilistic models that predict the best back-channel "spots" (Huang et al 2010), or analyzing what the interlocutors say (Kopp et al., 2007). When the agent is a robot or any other machine that can move, listening behavior includes proxemics as well (i.e. the use of space and distances as a social cue). Two approaches are commonly adopted for this purpose, the social force model (Jan & Traum, 2007) and the simulation of human territoriality (Pedica & Vilhjalmsson, 2009).

Social Emotions

In many scenarios, the expression of social emotions like empathy through a virtual human's face (Niewiadomski et al. 2008, Ochs et al. 2010) and voice (Schroeder, 2009) or any other form of nonverbal behavior is very important. Besides expression synthesis, the research community has devoted much energy to defining and implementing computational models of behaviors that underlie the decisions on the choice of emotional expression. For an overview see Marsella et al. (2010).

Social Evaluations

The computational models of emotions based on appraisal models typically contain variables that deal with the evaluation of the human interlocutor and the situation the agent is in. On the other hand, many studies dealing with the evaluation of virtual humans

(Ruttkay & Pelachaud 2004) consider the other side of the coin: the question of how the agent is perceived by the human. This can pertain to any of the behaviors exhibited by the agent and any dimension. For instance, Ter Maat and Heylen (2009) consider how different turn-taking strategies evoke different impressions, while De Melo & Gratch (2009) consider the effect of wrinkles, just to give two extreme examples of behaviors and dimensions of expression that have been related to social evaluation.

Social Attitudes

The synthesis of attitudes requires the artificial generation of several cues in a coordinated fashion as well as coherence in the behavior displayed by the agent. Since artificial agents are used in scenarios where they are expected to provide a service (museum guiding, tutoring, help-desk dialogues, etc.), the attitude most commonly addressed is politeness. In the simplest approaches, politeness does not arise from an analysis of the interlocutor's behavior but from predefined settings that account for power distance (Gupta et al., 2007; Porayska-Pomsta & Mellish, 2004). Such a problem is overcome in de Jong et al. (2008), where the interlocutor's degree of politeness is matched by the agent in a museum guide scenario.

A crucial channel through which any attitude can be conveyed is speech, and major efforts have been made toward the synthesis of "expressive" voices (i.e., voices capable of conveying something more than just the words being uttered) (Schroeder, 2009). Initial approaches were based on the collection of short speech snippets extracted from natural speech expressing different attitudes. The snippets were then played back to reproduce the same attitude. Such an approach has been used to make agents capable of reporting differently on good rather than bad news (Pitrelli et al., 2006), of giving orders (Johnson et al., 2002), or of playing characters (Gebhard et al., 2008). The main drawback of such approaches is that it is necessary to collect examples for each and every attitude to be synthesized. Thus current techniques try to represent expressiveness in terms of parameters that can be manipulated to allow agents to express desired attitudes (Schroeder, 2007; Zovato et al., 2004).

Social Relations

The Laura agent was one of the first to be extensively subjected to a longitudinal study (Bickmore & Picard, 2005). One of the major research interests in developing the agent for this study was modeling the long-term relations that might develop between the agent and the user over the course of repeated interactions. This involved modeling many social psychological theories on relationship formation and friendship. Currently there is a surge of work on companion agents and robots (Leite et al., 2010, Robins et al., 2012).

Conclusions

Social signal processing (SSP) is a new research and technological domain that aims at providing computers with the ability to sense and understand human social signals. SSP is in its initial phase and the researchers in the field face many challenges (Pantic et al., 2011). Given the current state of the art in the automatic analysis of social signals, the focus of future research efforts in the field should be on tackling the problem of context-constrained and multiparty analysis of multimodal behavioral signals shown in temporal intervals of various lengths. As suggested by Pantic (2009), this should be treated as one complex problem rather than a number of distinct problems in human sensing, context sensing, and the elucidation of human behavior. Given the current state of the art in automatic analysis of social signals, it may take decades to fully understand and be able to synthesize various combinations of social signals that are appropriate for different contexts and different conversational agents. Among the many issues involved is the fact that it is not self-evident that synthetic agents should behave in the same way as humans do or that they should exhibit faithful copies of human social behaviors. On the contrary, evidence from the cartoon industry suggests that, in order to be believable, cartoon characters must show strongly exaggerated behavior. This suggests further that a trade-off between the degree of naturalness and the type of (exaggerated) gestural and vocal expression may be necessary for modeling the behavior of believable conversational agents. All in all, the journey towards artificial social intelligence and socially aware computing is long and many of its aspects are yet to be attempted.

Acknowledgments

The research that has led to this work has been supported in part by the European Community's Seventh Framework Programme (FP7/2007–2013) under grant agreement no. 231287 (SSPNet).

References

Albrecht, K. (2005). *Social intelligence: The new science of success.* Hoboken, NJ: Wiley.

Banerjee, S., & Rudnicky, A. (2004). Using simple speech based features to detect the state of a meeting and the roles of the meeting participants. In *Proceedings of the international conference on spoken language processing* (pp. 221–231).

Barzilay, R., Collins, M., Hirschberg, J., & Whittaker, S. (2000). The rules behind the roles: Identifying speaker roles in radio broadcasts. In *Proceedings of the conference on artificial intelligence* (pp. 679–684).

Bickmore, T., & Picard, R. (2005). Establishing and maintaining long-term human-computer relationships. *ACM Transactions on Computer Human Interaction, 59*(1), 21–30.

Biel, J., & Gatica-Perez, D. (2012). The YouTube lens: Crowdsourced personality impressions and audiovisual analysis of Vlogs. In *IEEE Trans. Multimedia*, to appear.

Bonaiuto, J., & Thorisson, K. R. (2008). Towards a neurocognitive model of realtime turntaking in face-to-face dialogue. In G. K. I. Wachsmuth, & M. Lenzen (Eds.), *Embodied communication in humans and machines* (pp. 451–484). New York: Oxford University Press.

Bottino, A., & Laurentini, A. (2010). The analysis of facial beauty: An emerging area of research in pattern analysis. *Lecture Notes in Computer Science, 6111*, 425–435.

Bousmalis, K., Mehu, M., & Pantic, M. (2012). Spotting agreement and disagreement based on nonverbal audiovisual cues: A survey. *Image and Vision Computing Journal*.

Bousmalis, K., Zafeiriou, S., Morencey, L. P., & Pantic, M. (2013). Infinite hidden conditional random fields for human behavior analysis. *IEEE Transactions on Neural Networks and Learning Systems, 24*(1), 170–177.

Brunet, P., & Cowie, R. (2012). Towards a conceptual framework of research on social signal processing. *Journal of Multimodal User Interfaces, 6*(3–4), 101–115.

Brunet, P. M., Cowie, R., Heylen, D., Nijholt, A., & Schroeder, M. (2012). Conceptual frameworks for multimodal social signal processing. *Journal of Multimodal User Interfaces*.

de Bruijn, H., & Herder, P. M. (2009). System and actor perspectives on sociotechnical systems. *IEEE Transactions on Systems, Man and Cybernetics, 39*(5), 981–992.

de Jong, M., Theune, M.,& Hofs, D. (2008). Politeness and alignment in dialogues with a virtual guide. In *Proceedings of the international conference on autonomous agents and multiagent systems* (pp. 207–214).

Delaherche, E., Chetouani, M., Mahdhaoui, A., Saint-Georges, C., Viaux, S., & Cohen, D. (2012). Interpersonal synchrony: A survey of evaluation methods across disciplines. *IEEE Transactions in Affective Computing, 3*(3), 349–365.

De La Torre, F., & Cohn, J. F. (2011). Facial expression analysis. In T. B. Moeslund, A. Hilton, V. Kruger, & L. Sigal (Eds.), *Visual analysis of humans* (pp. 377–409). New York: Springer.

de Melo, C., & Gratch, J. (2009). Expression of emotions using wrinkles, blushing, sweating and tears. In *Proceedings of the international conference on intelligent virtual agents* (pp. 188–200).

Dong, W., Lepri, B., Cappelletti, A., Pentland, A., Pianesi, F., & Zancanaro, M. (2007). Using the influence model to recognize functional roles in meetings. In *Proceedings of the international conference on multimodal interfaces* (pp. 271–278).

Dunbar, R. (1992). Neocortex size as a constraint on group size in primates. *Journal of Human Evolution, 20*, 469–493.

Eagle, N., & Pentland, A. (2005). Reality mining: Sensing complex social systems. *Personal and Ubiquitous Computing, 10*(4), 255–268.

Fishbein, M., & Ajzen, I. (1975). *Belief, attitude, intention, and behavior: An introduction to theory and research.* Addison-Wesley.

Gatica-Perez, D. (2009). Automatic nonverbal analysis of social interaction in small groups: A review. *Image and Vision Computing, 27*(12), 1775–1787.

Gallese, V. (2006). Intentional attunement: A neurophysiological perspective on social cognition and its disruption in autism. *Brain Research, 1079*(1), 15–24.

Gebhard, P., Schröder, M., Charfuelan, M., Endres, C., Kipp, M., Pammi, S., Rumpler, M., & Türk, O. (2008). "IDEAS4Games: building expressive virtual characters for computer games," in *Proceedings of Intelligent Virtual Agents*, vol. LNCS 5208, pp. 426–440.

Gilbert, D. T., Fiske, S. T., & Lindzey, G. (Eds.). (1998). *Handbook of social psychology.* New York: McGraw-Hill.

Gladwell, M. (2005). *Blink: The power of thinking without thinking.* Boston: Little, Brown.

Gunes, H., & Pantic, M. (2010). Automatic, dimensional and continuous emotion recognition (a survey). *International Journal of Synthetic Emotions, 1*(1), 68–99.

Gunes, H., & Piccardi, M. (2006). Assessing facial beauty through proportion analysis by image processing and supervised learning. *International Journal of Human-Computer Studies, 64*, 1184–1199.

Jayagopi, D. B., Hung, H., Yeo, C., & Gatica-Perez, D. (2009). Modeling dominance in group conversations using nonverbal activity cues. *IEEE Transactions in Audio, Speech, and Language Processing, 17*(3), 501–513.

Grudin, J., & Poltrock, S. (2012). Taxonomy and theory in computer supported cooperative work. In S. W. J. Kozlowski (Ed.), *The Oxford handbook of organizational psychology.* New York: Oxford University Press.

Gupta, S., Walker, M. A., & Romano, D. M. (2007). Generating politeness in task based interaction: An evaluation of the effect of linguistic form and culture. In *Proceedings of the European workshop on natural language generation* (pp. 57–64).

Huang, L., Morency, L. P., & Gratch, J. (2010). Learning Backchannel Prediction Model from Parasocial Consensus Sampling: A Subjective Evaluation, Lecture Notes in Computer Science, vol. 6356, pp. 159–172.

Jan, D., & Traum, D. R. (2007). Dynamic movement and positioning of embodied agents in multiparty conversations. In *Proceedings of the joint international conference on autonomous agents and multiagent systems.*

Johnson, W. L., Narayanan, S. S., Whitney, R., Das, R., Bulut, M., & LaBore, C. (2002). Limited domain synthesis of expressive military speech for animated characters, In *Proceedings of the IEEE Workshop on Speech Synthesis*, pp. 163–166.

Judd, C., James-Hawkins, L., Yzerbyt, V., & Kashima, Y. (2005). Fundamental dimensions of social judgment: Understanding the relations between judgments of competence and warmth. *Journal of Personality and Social Psychology, 89*(6), 899–913.

Kelley, H. H. & Thibaut, J. (1978). *Interpersonal relations: A theory of interdependence.* Hoboken, NJ: Wiley.

Kim, S., Filippone, M., Valente, F., & Vinciarelli, A. (2012). Predicting the conflict level in television political debates: An approach based on crowdsourcing, nonverbal communication and Gaussian processes. In *Proceedings of the ACM international conference on multimedia* (pp. 793–796).

Kopp, S., Stocksmeier, T., & Gibbon, D. (2007). Incremental multimodal feedback for conversational agents. In *Proceedings of the international conference on intelligent virtual agents* (pp. 139–146).

Laskowski, K., Ostendorf, M., & Schultz, T. (2008). Modeling vocal interaction for text-independent participant characterization in multi-party conversation. In *Proceedings of the ISCA/ACL SIGdial workshop on discourse and dialogue* (pp. 148–155).

Leite, I., Mascarenhas, S., Pereira, A., Martinho, C., Prada, R., & Paiva, A. (2010). Why can't we be friends?—An empathic game companion for long-term interaction. In *Proceedings of the international conference on intelligent virtual agents* (pp. 315–321).

Liu, Y. (2006). Initial study on automatic identification of speaker role in broadcast news speech. In *Proc. human language technology conf. of the NAACL* (pp. 81–84).

Maatman, R. M., Gratch, J., & Marsella, S. (2005). Natural behavior of a listening agent. In *Proceedings of the international conference on intelligent virtual agents* (pp. 25–36).

Mairesse, F., Poifroni, J., & Di Fabbrizio, G. (2012). Can prosody inform sentiment analysis? Experiments on short spoken reviews. In IEEE Int'l Conf Acoustics, Speech and Signal Processing, pp. 5093–5096.

Manusov, V., & Patterson, M. L. (Eds.). (2006). *The Sage handbook of nonverbal communication*. Palo Alto, CA: Sage.

Marsella, S., Gratch, J., & Petta, P. (2010). Computational models of emotions. In K. R. Scherer, T. Banzinger, & E. Roesch (Eds.), *A blueprint for an affectively competent agent.* New York: Oxford University Press.

Mayne, T. J., & Bonanno, G. A. (2001). *Emotions: Current issues and future directions.* New York: Guilford Press.

Mehu, M., & Scherer, K. (2012). A psycho-ethological approach to social signal processing. *Cognitive Processing, 13*(2), 397–414.

Mehu, M., D'Errico, F., & Heylen, D. (2012). Conceptual analysis of social signals: The importance of clarifying terminology. *Journal on Multimodal User Interfaces, 6*(3–4), 179–189.

Miles, L. K., Nind, L. K., & Macrae, C. N. (2009). The rhythm of rapport: Interpersonal synchrony and social perception. *Journal of Experimental Social Psychology, 45*, 585–589.

Nass, C., Steuer, J., & Tauber, E. R. (1994). Computers are social actors. In *Proceedings of the. SIGCHI conference on factors in computing systems: Celebrating interdependence* (pp. 72–78).

Nicolaou, M., Pavlovic, V., & Pantic, M. (2012). Dynamic probabilistic CCA for analysis of affective behaviour. In *Proceedings of the European conference on computer vision.*

Niewiadomski, R., Ochs, M., & Pelachaud, C. (2008). Expressions of empathy in ECAs. In *Proceedings of the international conference on intelligent virtual agents* (pp. 37–44).

Ochs, M., Niewiadomski, R., & Pelachaud, C. (2010). How a virtual agent should smile? Morphological and dynamic characteristics of virtual agent's smiles. In *Proceedings of the international conference on intelligent virtual agents* (pp. 427–440).

Olguin-Olguin D., Gloor, P. A., & Pentland, A. (2009). Capturing individual and group behavior with wearable sensors. In *Proceedings of the AAAI spring symposium.*

Pantic, M. (2009). Machine analysis of facial Behaviour: Naturalistic and dynamic behaviour. *Philosophical Transactions of the Royal Society B, 364*, 3505–3513.

Pantic, M., Cowie, R., D'Errico, F., Heylen, D., Mehu, M., Pelachaud, C.,...Vinciarelli, A. (2011). Social signal processing: The research agenda. In T. B. Moeslund, A. Hilton, V. Kruger, & L. Sigal (Eds.), *Visual analysis of humans* (pp. 511–538). New York: Springer.

Pedica C., & Vilhjalmsson, H. H. (2009). Spontaneous avatar behavior for human territoriality. In *Proceedings of the international conference on intelligent virtual agents* (pp. 344–357).

Pentland, A. (2005). Socially aware computation and communication. *IEEE Computer, 38*(3), 33–40.

Pentland, A. (2007). Social signal processing. *IEEE Signal Processing Magazine, 24*(4), 108–111.

Pianesi, F. Searching for personality (2013). *IEEE Signal Processing Magazine*, to appear.

Pianesi, F., Mana, N., & Cappelletti, A. (2008). Multimodal recognition of personality traits in social interactions. In *Proceedings of the international conference on multimodal interfaces* (pp. 53–60).

Pitrelli, J. F., Bakis, R., Eide, E. M., Fernandez, R., Hamza, W., & Picheny, M. A. (2006). The IBM expressive Text-to-Speech synthesis system for american english, *IEEE Transactions on Audio, Speech and Language Processing*, vol. 14, no. 4, pp. 1099–1108.

Poggi, I., & D'Errico, F. (2012). Social signals: A framework in terms of goals and beliefs. *Cognitive Processing, 13*(2), 427–445.

Poggi, I., D'Errico, F., & Vinciarelli, A. (2012). Social signals: From theory to application. *Cognitive Processing, 13*(2), 189–196.

Polzehl, T., Moller, S., & Metze, F. (2010). Automatically assessing personality from speech. In *Proceedings of the IEEE international conference on semantic computing* (pp. 134–140).

Porayska-Pomsta, K., & Mellish, C. (2004). Modelling politeness in natural language generation. In *Proceedings of the international conference on natural language generation*, LNAI 3123 (pp. 141–150).

Prepin, K., & Revel, A. (2007). Human-machine interaction as a model of machine-machine interaction: How to make machines interact as humans do. *Advanced Robotics, 21*(15), 1709–1723.

Raento, M., Oulasvirta, A., & Eagle, N. (2009). Smartphones: An emerging tool for social scientists. *Sociological Methods & Research, 37*(3), 426–454.

Robins, B., Dautenhahn, K., Ferrari, E., Kronreif, G., Prazak-Aram, B.,...Laudanna, E. (2012). Scenarios of robot-assisted play for children with cognitive and physical disabilities. *Interaction Studies, 13*(2), 189–234.

Ruttkay, Z., & Pelachaud, C. (Eds.). (2004). *From brows to trust: Evaluating embodied conversational agents.* Kluwer.

Sacks, H., Schegloff, E., & Jefferson, G. (1974). A simplest systematics for the organization of turn-taking for conversation. *Language*, 696–735.

Salamin, H., & Vinciarelli, A. (2012). Automatic role recognition in multiparty conversations: An approach based on turn organization, prosody and conditional random fields. *IEEE Transactions in Multimedia, 14*(2), 338–345.

Salvagnini, P., Salamin, H., Cristani, M., Vinciarelli, A., & Murino, V. (2012). Learning to teach from videolectures: Predicting lecture ratings based on lecturer's nonverbal behaviour. In *Proceedings of the IEEE international conference on cognitive infocommunications* (pp. 415–419).

Schmid, K., Marx, D., & Samal, A. (2008). Computation of face attractiveness index based on neoclassic canons, symmetry and golden ratio. *Pattern Recognition, 41*, 2710–2717.

Schroeder, M. (2007). Interpolating expressions in unit selection. In *Proceedings of the international conference on affective computing and intelligent interaction* (pp. 718–720).

Schroeder, M. (2009). Expressive speech synthesis: Past, present, and possible futures In J. Tao & T. Tan (Eds.), *Affective information processing* (pp. 111–126). New York: Springer.

Schuller, B., Steidl, S., Batliner, A., Burkhardt, F., Devillers, L., Muller, C., & Narayanan, S. (2013). Paralinguistics in speech and language—State of the art and the challenge. *Computer Speech and Language, 27,* 4–39.

Sutic, D., Breskovic, I., Huic, R., & Jukic, I. (2010). Automatic evaluation of facial attractiveness. In *Proceedings of the international MIRO convention* (pp. 1339–1342).

ter Maat, M., & Heylen, D. (2009). Turn management or impressions management? In *Proceedings of the international conference on intelligent virtual agents* (pp. 467–473).

Valente F., & Vinciarelli, A. (2011). Language-independent socio-emotional role recognition in the AMI meetings corpus. In *Proc. interspeech* (pp. 3077–3080).

Vinciarelli, A. (2009). Capturing order in social interactions. *IEEE Signal Processing Magazine, 26*(5), 133–137.

Vinciarelli, A., Pantic, M., & Bourlard, H. (2009). Social signal processing: Survey of an emerging domain. *Image and Vision Computing Journal, 27*(12), 1743–1759.

Vinciarelli, A., Pantic, M., Heylen, D., Pelachaud, C., Poggi, I., D'Errico, F., & Schroeder, M. (2012). Bridging the gap between social animal and unsocial machine: A survey of social signal processing. *IEEE Transactions in Affective Computing, 3*(1), 69–87.

Whitehehill J., & Movellan, J. (2008). Personalized facial attractiveness prediction. In *Proceedings of the IEEE international conference on automatic face and gesture recognition.*

Zen, G., Lepri, B., Ricci, E., & Lanz, O. (2010). Space speaks: Towards socially and personality aware visual surveillance. In *Proceedings of the ACM international workshop on multimodal pervasive video analysis* (pp. 37–42).

Zeng, Z., Pantic, M., Roisman, G. I., & Huang, T. H. (2009). A survey of affect recognition methods: Audio, visual and spontaneous expressions. *IEEE Transactions on Pattern Analysis and Machine Intelligence, 31*(1), 39–58.

Zhang, D., Zhao, Q., & Chen, F. (2011). Quantitative analysis of human facial beauty using geometric features. *Pattern Recognition, 44*(4), 940–950.

Zovato, E., Pacchiotti, A., Quazza, S., & Sandri, S. (2004). Towards emotional speech synthesis: A rule based approach. In *Proceedings of the ISCA speech synthesis workshop* (pp. 219–220).

Why and How to Build Emotion-Based Agent Architectures

Christine Lisetti *and* Eva Hudlicka

Abstract

In this chapter we explain the motivation, goals, and advantages of building artificial systems that simulate aspects of affective phenomena in humans, from architectures for rational agents to the simulation of empathic processes and affective disorders. We briefly review some of the main psychological and neuroscience theories of affect and emotion that inspire such computational modeling of affective processes. We also describe some of the diverse approaches explored to date to implement emotion-based architectures, including appraisal-based architectures, biologically inspired architectures, and hybrid architectures. Successes, challenges, and applications of emotion-based agent architectures and models are also discussed (e.g., modeling virtual patients and affective disorders with virtual humans, designing cybertherapy interventions, and building empathic virtual agents).

Key Words: computational models of emotions, affective architectures, cognitive-affective architectures, emotion-based agent architectures, virtual humans, virtual patients, affective disorder computational modeling, cybertherapy interventions, empathic virtual agents, applications of agent-based architectures

Motivation

There are many reasons for researchers and developers to be interested in creating computational models of, and agent architectures inspired from, affective phenomena. Affective phenomena include core affect, mood, emotion, as well as personality. This chapter discusses useful terminology and specific theories of affective phenomena and introduces some of the main motivations for this topic.

Building computational models of the roles of affective phenomena in human cognition is of interest to the cognitive science community. The main objective of cognitive science is to understand the human mind by developing theories of mind, creating computational models of these theories, and testing whether the input/output and timing behaviors of the resulting systems correspond to human behaviors (Thagard, 2008). Computational models of emerging cognitive and affective science theories

of human emotion and affect will enable us to shed new light on the complexity of human affective phenomena.

Building emotion—or affect-based agent architectures—is also useful in subfields of computer science, such as artificial intelligence (AI), human-computer interaction (HCI), among others. AI, which focuses on developing algorithms to make rational intelligent decisions, can simulate and emulate the functional roles of affect and rational emotions in human decision making (Johnson-Laird & Oatley, 1992; Picard, 1997; Lisetti & Gmytrasiewicz, 2002). HCI on the other hand, is concerned with creating artificial agents that can adapt to users' emotion or personality to enhance adaptive human-computer interaction (Hudlicka, 2003; Picard, 1997).

The interest in building emotion-based agent architectures revolves around the notion that emotions have recently been fully acknowledged as an important part of human rational intelligence (Johnson-Laird & Oatley, 1992). Emotion research only recently emerged from its "dark ages," dated roughly from 1920 to 1960, in contrast with its classical phase, which started at the end of the nineteenth century. While psychologist William James (1984)—offering a very Darwinian view of emotion (Darwin, 1872)—restored affect as a valuable component of the evolutionary process, Cannon (1927) disagreed completely and relegated the roles of emotions to nonspecific, disruptive processes. Cannon's view contributed to the temporary demise of emotion research in the 1920s. The field of artificial intelligence, which formally emerged in 1956, founded most of its models of intelligence on previously established affectless theories of intelligence, originally rooted exclusively in logic (Russell & Norwig, 2011).

However, findings about the evidence of the universality and specificity in affective expressive behavior (Davidson and Cacioppo 1992; Ekman & Freisen, 1978; Ekman et al., 1983; among others), began the emotion research renaissance of the early 1980s. Furthermore, the 1990s benefited from neuroscience discoveries which confirmed the strong interconnections between the mechanisms mediating affective processes and those mediating cognition and reasoning (Damasio, 1994).

Since creating artificial agents that act rationally, in terms of achieving the best expected outcome, has been one of the main objectives of traditional AI (Russell & Norwig, 2011), the newly rediscovered role of emotions in rational human intelligence (de Sousa, 1990; Elster, 1999; Frank, 1988; Johnson-Laird & Oatley, 1992; Muramatsu, 2005) has begun to be modeled in architectures of rational agents in terms of their goal determination and interruption mechanisms (Frijda, 1987, 1995; Frijda & Swagerman, 1987; Jiang, 2008; Lisetti & Gmytrasiewicz, 2002; Murphy, et al., 2001; Ochs et al., 2012; Simon, 1967; Sloman, 1987; Sloman & Croucher, 1981; Sloman et al., 2001; Scheutz, 2011; Scheutz & Schermerhorn, 2009).

The more recent expressive AI endeavor (Mateas, 2011) is concerned with creating virtual agents that are socially intelligent and believable (1) in terms of their communicative expressiveness and behavior (Bates, 1994; Becker-Asano & Wachsmuth, 2009; Brave & Nass, 2002; Breazeal, 2003a, 2003b; Huang, et al., 2011; Lisetti et al., 2013; Loyall & Bates, 1997; Mateas, 2001, Pelachaud, 2009, Pütten et al., 2009) and (2) in terms of their awareness of the user's affective states (Calvo & DMello, 2010;

Hudlicka & McNeese, 2002; Nasoz et al., 2010). For expressive AI, the simulation and recognition of the expressive patterns associated with emotion and personality is therefore essential.

Another reason to simulate and model some of the not-so-perfectly-rational aspects of affective human life, as well as the clearly dysfunctional ones, is emerging in domains such as entertainment, health care, medicine, and training across a variety of domains.

Creating goal-conflicted or even neurotic protagonists enhances the realism and complexity of computer games and interactive narratives in the same manner as in films and literature; complex characters engage audiences more deeply than simpler, happy, and stable characters (Campbell, 2008). Conflicted virtual characters can retain a player's interest in and engagement with the game by being unpredictable (in terms of rational behavior) and by portraying personality traits that make them unique, thereby giving the illusion of life (Bates, 1992, 1994; Johnson & Thomas, 1981; Loyall, 1997; Mateas, 2003; Ochs et al., 2012).

The design of virtual patients or mentally ill individuals has also begun to emerge to meet the recent training needs in health care, medicine, the military, and the police. These specialized personnel need to be trained in recognizing, understanding, and knowing how to deal with individuals with mental disorders (e.g., mood or personality disorders, schizophrenia, paranoia) or to help people with milder behavioral issues such as overeating, drinking, or smoking (Dunn, 2001). Emotions associated with these disorders and problematic mental states require different modeling approaches than the traditional modeling of the rationality of emotions discussed above. This modeling has begun to be addressed by the development of virtual patients (Campbell et al., 2011; Cook & Triola, 2009; Hubal et al., 2003; Rossen & Lok, 2012; Stevens et al., 2006; among others).

In the following pages we provide some background on the main psychological theories of affect and emotion and describe some of the recent progress and advances in (1) computational models of affect and emotion from a cognitive science perspective and (2) in emotion-based agent architectures from an AI and HCI perspective.

Theories of Emotion
Categorical Theories of Discrete Basic Emotions

Beginning with Darwin's evolutionary view of emotions (Darwin, 1872), Darwinian theories propose that emotions are "primary" or "basic" in the sense that they are considered to correspond to distinct and elementary forms of reactions, or action tendencies. Each discrete emotion calls into readiness a small and distinctive suite of action plans— action tendencies—that have been evolutionarily more successful than alternative kinds of reactions for survival and/or well-being and which have a large innate "hard-wired" component. Table 8.1, derived from Frijda (1986, 2008), shows a small set of the quadruples (action tendency, end state, function, emotion) that recur consistently across discrete basic emotion theories.

Although the number and choice of basic emotions vary depending on the different theories, ranging from 2 to 18 (Frijda, 1986, 1987; Izard 1971, 1992; James, 1984; Plutchik, 1980), these discrete theories share a number of features and consider emotions as (1) mental and physiological processes, (2) caused by the perception of phylogenetic categories of events,[1] (3) eliciting internal and external signals, and (4) being associated with a matching suite of innate hard-wired action plans or tendencies.

Perhaps the most well-known categorical theory of emotions to the affective computing community is Ekman's (1999), and we will show later how it has been used as a basis for modeling emotion in agent architectures. Ekman identifies seven characteristics that distinguish basic emotions from one another, and from other affective phenomena: (1) automatic appraisal, (2) distinctive universals in antecedent events, (3) presence in other primates, (4) quick

onset, (5) brief duration (minutes, seconds), (6) unbidden occurrence (involuntary), and (7) distinctive physiology (e.g., autonomic nervous system, facial expressions).

According to Ekman, these seven characteristics are found in the following 17 basic emotions: amusement, anger, awe, contempt, contentment, disgust, embarrassment, excitement, fear, guilt, interest, pride in achievement, relief, sadness, satisfaction, sensory pleasure, and shame.

In addition, whereas Ekman initially thought that every basic emotion was associated with a unique facial expression (Ekman, 1984), he revised his theory in 1993 to account for emotions for which no facial signals exist (such as potentially awe, guilt, and shame) and for emotions that share the same expression (e.g., different categories of positive emotions all sharing a smile). In total, Ekman (1993) identified seven emotions with distinctive universal unique facial expressions: anger, fear, disgust, sadness, happiness, surprise, and (the one added last) contempt.

As described later, although highly popular in affective computing (Picard, 1997), the notion of basic emotions is still controversial among psychologists (Ortony, 1990; Russell & Barrett, 1999).

Dimensional Theories and Models of Core Affect and Mood

One important distinction that has been made by Russell and Barrett (1999), involves the use of the term *prototypical emotional episode* to refer to

Table 8.1 Examples of Action Tendencies

Action Tendency	End State	Function	Emotion
Approach	Access	Permission for consummatory activity	Desire
Avoidance	Own inaccessibility	Protection	Fear
Attendance	Identification	Orientation	Interest
Rejection	Removal of object	Protection	Disgust
Antagonism	Removal of obstruction	Regaining of control	Anger
Interruption	Reorientation	Reorientation	Shock, surprise
Free activation	Action tendency's end state	Generalized readiness	Joy
Inactivity	Action tendency's end state	Recuperation	Contentment
Inhibition/preparation	Absence of response	Caution	Anxiety

Source: Adapted from Frijda, 1986.

what is typically called "emotion," and the use of the term *core affect* to refer to the most elementary affective feelings (and their neurophysiological counterparts).

According to Russell and Barrett (1999), core affect is not necessarily part of a person's consciousness, nor is it consciously directed at anything (e.g., sense of pleasure or displeasure, tension or relaxation, depression or elation). Core affect can be as free-floating as a mood but it can be directed when it becomes part of an emotional episode or emotions. Core affect is always caused, although its causes might be beyond human ability to detect (e.g., from specific events, to weather changes, to diurnal cycles). Core affect is also the underlying, always present feeling one has about whether one is in a positive or negative state, aroused or relaxed (or neutral, since core affect is always present).

Core affect elemental feeling is to be understood as included within a full-blown prototypical emotional episode, if one occurs. A prototypical emotional episode also includes behavior in relation to the object/event, attention toward and appraisal of that object, subjective experience, and physiologic responses.

In making this distinction between core affect and prototypical emotional episodes, Russell and Barrett (1999) establish that since core affect is more basic than a full-blown emotional episode it carries less information than emotions and needs to be studied and measured with fewer dimensions (although if considered as a component of an emotional episode, its low-dimensional structure is still valid).

Typically, two or three dimensions are used to represent core affect. Most frequently these are valence and arousal (Russell, 1980, 2003; Russell & Barrett, 1999; Russell & Mehrabian, 1977). Valence reflects a positive or negative evaluation, and the associated felt state of pleasure (vs. displeasure). Arousal reflects a general degree of intensity or activation of the organism. The degree of arousal reflects a general readiness to act: low arousal is associated with less energy, high arousal with more energy.

Since this two-dimensional space cannot easily differentiate among core affective states that share the same values of arousal and valence (e.g., anger and fear, both characterized by high arousal and negative valence), a third dimension is often added. This is variously termed dominance or stance (versus submissiveness). The resulting three-dimensional space is often referred to as the PAD space, for pleasure (synonymous with valence), arousal, and dominance (Mehrabian, 1995).

It is important to note that according to Russell (1980), the dimensional structure is useful only to characterize core affect (versus full-blown emotions) because full-blown emotions fall into only certain regions of the circumplex structure defined by the core affect dimensions. Qualitatively different events can appear similar or identical when only this dimensional structure is considered. For example, fear, anger, embarrassment, and disgust could share identical core affect and therefore fall in identical points or regions in the circumplex structure.

Note that the pleasure and arousal dimensions and the resulting circumplex structure represent only one component of a prototypical emotional episode, but not all of the components. These other components then differentiate among fear, anger, embarrassment, and disgust. Thus assessment devices based on the dimensional-circumplex approach can capture core affect but miss the (other) components of a prototypical emotional episode. This is an important aspect to consider when aiming to recognize emotion automatically.

Componential and Appraisal-Based Theories of Emotions

The componential perspective or appraisal-based theories emphasize distinct components of emotions (Leventhal & Scherer, 1987). The term *components* refers to both the distinct modalities of emotions (e.g., cognitive, physiologic, behavioral, subjective) but frequently also to the components of the cognitive appraisal process. In the latter case, these are referred to as appraisal dimensions or appraisal variables (Lazarus, 1991) and include novelty, valence, goal relevance, goal congruence, and coping abilities.

A stimulus, whether real or imagined, is analyzed in terms of its meaning and consequences for the agent in order to determine the affective reaction. The analysis involves assigning specific values to the appraisal variables. Once the appraisal variable values are determined by the organism's evaluative processes, the resulting vector is mapped onto a particular emotion, within the n-dimensional space defined by the n appraisal variables.

Appraisal theories of emotions have been modeled most predominantly within the affective computing community, and appraisal models are described in Gratch and Marsella's chapter in this volume. We therefore mention some of their main tenets only briefly in this chapter.

ORTONY'S OCC MODEL

The best-known theory of cognitive appraisal, and one most frequently used by the affective computing community, is a theory developed by Ortony, Collins and Clore (1988), which describes the cognitive structure of emotions. It is frequently referred to as the OCC model. Because it is covered extensively in Gratch & Marsella (this volume), we provide only a brief summary below. The OCC model describes a hierarchy that classifies 22 different types of emotions along three main branches: emotions classified in terms of (1) consequences of events (pleased, displeased), (2) actions of agents (approving or disapproving), and (3) aspects of objects (liking, disliking). Emotions are *valenced* (positive or negative) reactions to one or another of these three aspects of experience. Some subsequent branches combine to form compound emotions.

The popularity of the OCC model in the affective computing community is due in part to its relatively simple taxonomy of classes of emotions, relying on concepts such as agents and actions that are already used to conceptualize and implement agent architectures.

SCHERER'S CPT

Another influential theory of emotions in affective computing is Scherer's component process theory of emotions (CPT) (2001b). Scherer's CPT describes emotions as arising from a process of evaluation of the surrounding events with respect to their significance for the survival and well-being of the organism. The nature of this appraisal is related to a sequential evaluation of each event with regards to a set of parameters called sequential evaluation checks (SECs). SECs are chosen to represent the minimum set of dimensions necessary to differentiate among distinct emotions and are organized into four classes or in terms of four appraisal objectives. These objectives reflect answers to the following questions: How relevant is the event for me? (Relevance SECs.) What are the implications or consequences of this event? (Implications SECs.) How well can I cope with these consequences? (Coping Potential SECs.) What is the significance of this event with respect to social norms and to my self concept? (Normative significance SECs.)

One of the primary reasons for the sequential approach is to provide a mechanism whereby focusing of attention is only employed when needed and information processing (computational loading) is theoretically reduced. The SEC approach also parallels the three-layered hybrid AI architectures when it describes a three-layered emotional processing of events:

1. *Sensorimotor Level*: Checking occurs through innate feature detection and reflex systems based on specific stimulus patterns. Generally it involves genetically determined reflex behaviors and the generation of primary emotions in response to basic stimulus features.

2. *Schematic Level*: Checking is a learned automatic nondeliberative rapid response to specific stimulus patterns largely based on social learning processes.

3. *Conceptual Level*: Checking is based on conscious reflective (deliberative) processing of evaluation criteria provided through propositional memory storage mechanisms. Planning, thinking and anticipating events and reactions are typical conceptual-level actions.

Other appraisal-based theories of emotions have also been developed and, as we mention later, some of them have also influenced the affective computing community (e.g., Smith & Lazarus, 1990; Lazarus, 1991).

Challenges in Modeling Neurophysiologic Theories and Unconscious Appraisal

Neurophysiologic theories of emotions have the potential to enable the affective computing community to develop new emotion-based architectures, ones focused on how neural circuitry can generate emotions. However, these theories typically address processes that take place in the unconscious and which have not yet been widely explored in affective computing.

We briefly mention three researchers whose work is relevant for biologically inspired emotion-based agent architectures: LeDoux, Zajonc, and Damasio, although many others should also be studied.

Until recently, neuroscientists assumed that all sensory information was processed in the thalamus, then sent to the neocortex, and finally to the amygdala, where the information was translated into an emotional response. Research by LeDoux (1992) on fear conditioning and the amygdala showed that information from the thalamus can also go directly to the amygdala, bypassing the neocortex. Fear conditioning has been modeled with anatomically constrained neural networks to show how emotional information and behavior are related to anatomical and physiological observations (Armony et al., 1995).

Zajonc (1980, 1984) suggested that the processing pathways identified by LeDoux—the direct connection between the thalamus and the amygdala—are extremely important, because they indicate that emotional reactions can take place without the participation of cognitive processes. According to Zajonc, these findings would explain, for example, why individuals with phobias do not respond to logic, and the difficulty of bringing these fears or neuroses under control with psychological interventions (Zajonc, 1980, 1984b). Although Zajonc's work has not been greatly influential in affective computing, its focus on core affect may become more relevant when researchers begin to model the unconscious processes of affect (Zajonc, 1984).

It should be noted that most of LeDoux's research, which views emotions as separate from cognition, remains within the scope of one single emotion—namely fear (LeDoux, 1995). However, as LeDoux states, "[F]ear is an interesting emotion to study because many disorders of fear regulation are at the heart of many psychopathologic conditions, including anxiety, panic, phobias, and posttraumatic stress disorders." (see Riva et al., this volume to learn about how cybertherapy has been helping people with such disorders).

The somatic markers hypothesis proposed by Damasio (1994) brings another contribution to the notion that emotional guidance helps rationality. Somatic markers are those emotionally borne physical sensations "telling" those who experience them that an event is likely to lead to pleasure or pain. Somatic markers precede thought and reason. They do not replace inference or calculation, but they enhance decision making by drastically reducing the number of options for consideration.

Agent Architectures and Cognitive Models of Affective Phenomena
Identifying Theoretical Assumptions

Computational models of affect and emotion necessarily make tacit assumptions about the overall cognitive architecture of the agent, specifically, assumptions about how the agent represents the world, chooses actions, and learns over time. Cognitive theories (Ortony et al., 1988; Scherer, 2001; Smith & Kirby, 2001), which ground affect in inferences about the effects of objects, states, and events on the agent's goals, necessarily assume the presence of an inference system to make those inferences, together with a world model capable of supporting those inferences.

Neurophysiological theories by contrast, being generally grounded in human unconscious processes (Bechara et al., 1997; Damasio, 1994; Zajonc, 1980), or animal models (Gray & McNaughton, 2003; LeDoux, 1992, 1995, 2000; Rolls, 2007), are less likely to highlight the role of inference and more likely to highlight other organizations such as competition between quasi-independent behavior systems.

As discussed above, a variety of neurologic and psychologic processes are involved in producing affective phenomena: core affect, emotional episodes or full-blown emotions, moods, attitudes, and, to some extent, personality, as it influences an individual's patterns of behavior, including affective patterns.

The different theories of affect and emotions discussed above—discrete, dimensional, and componential—are applied in the context of the architectures for which they are most natural. Cognitive theories are generally applied to planner/executive architectures or reactive planners. Biological theories are generally applied to behavior-based architectures (Arbib, 2004; Arkin, 1998; Murphy, 2000). At the same time, the different theories often seek to explain different aspects of the overall phenomenon of affect.

Consequently, developing an overall theory for affect/emotion modeling would require reconciling not just the theories themselves, narrowly construed, but also their architectural assumptions. This aim, however, resembles the early dreams of strong AI, and its disillusions (Dreyfus, 1992; Dreyfus & Dreyfus, 1988) and is currently considered out of reach. Building agents and models with some limited aspects of affective phenomena, however, is feasible and desirable, as discussed earlier. It requires choosing a theory in terms of its architectural assumptions or adapting particular theoretical aspects to produce the desired functionality of the agent.

Emotion-Based Agent Architecture
Overview

A typical intelligent agent architecture comprises the sensors that the agent uses to perceive its environment, a decision-making mechanism to decide what most appropriate action(s) to take at any time, and actuators that the agent activates to carry out its actions. At any time, the agent keeps track of its changing environment by using those different knowledge-representation schemas that are most relevant to the nature of its environment.

Emotion-based architectures are developed primarily for interactive intelligent agents capable of adapting to their user's affective states and manifesting affective behavior and empathy. These architectures are also developed to enhance the adaptive functioning of robots (e.g., Scheutz, 2000), and for research purposes, to explore the mechanisms of affective processes (e.g., Hudlicka, 2008). Emotion-based architectures vary in type, but they usually include (a subset of) the following components.

SENSORS

Sensors must be able to sense the user's emotional states (to some degree of accuracy appropriate for a given context) shown via one or more human emotional expressive modalities (sometimes referred to as user-centered modes). Communicative affective signals of human expression include facial expressions (which can be categorized slightly differently depending on which theory is used), gestures, vocal intonation (primarily volume, pitch), sensorimotor cues (e.g., pressure), autonomic nervous system signals associated with valence and arousal, as well natural language (which is used to communicate feelings or the subjective experience of affective states).

The agent can then capture and interpret those multimodal affective signals and translate them in terms of the most probable of the user's affective states. Depending upon the context of interaction, unimodal recognition of affect can be sufficient, whereas other types of interaction might require multimodal recognition and sensor fusion (Calvo & D'Mello, 2010; Paleari & Lisetti, 2006), as well as other nonaffective sensors.

DECISION-MAKING ALGORITHMS

Based on the agent's specific role and goals, the decision-making algorithm varies depending upon (as discussed above) which affect/emotion theory or combination of theories inspires the architecture. These decisions can be designed to have an effect not only on the agent's simulated affective state itself but also on the agent's expression of emotion via a variety of modalities (or agent-centered modes) activated by actuators.

ACTUATORS

The agent actuators can be chosen to control anthropomorphic embodiments endowed with modalities such as facial expressions, verbal, vocal intonation, or body posture. Anthropomorphic agents have the advantage that users innately understand them because they use the same social and emotional cues as those found in human-human communication. Anthropomorphic agents also elicit reciprocal social behaviors in their users (Reeves & Nass, 1996). Such actuators are most often portrayed by embodied conversational agents (Cassell et al., 2000); they can have graphical or robotic platforms (Breazeal, 2003b) or a mix of both (Lisetti et al., 2004). Other approaches to communicate affective expression have been explored in terms of nonfacial and nonverbal channels, such as appropriate social distance (see (Bethel & Murphy, 2008) for a survey), or the use of shape and color (Hook, 2004).

The majority of existing emotion-based architectures emphasize the generation of emotion via cognitive appraisal, and the effects of emotions on expressive behavior and choice of action. These are the focus of the remainder of this chapter. Less frequent are architectures that emphasize the effects of emotions on internal cognitive processing, or the cognitive consequences of emotions. A detailed discussion of these models is beyond the scope of this chapter, but examples include the MAMID architecture, which focuses on modeling affective biases on cognition (Hudlicka, 1998; 2007; 2011) and models developed by Ritter and colleagues in the context of ACT-R (Ritter & Avramides, 2000).

Basic Emotions and Agent Architectures

As mentioned earlier, categorical theories of basic emotions have had a very large influence on the affective computing community. The computational appeal of these theories lies in a clear mapping between a small set of universal antecedents to corresponding emotions along with their associated action tendencies.

Using categorical theories, an artificial agent can be designed to (1) sense a set of triggers (e.g., dangers, appeals) specific to its physicality or embodiment, (2) respond to these with action tendencies (approach, avoid, attend, reject, interrupt) implemented as a reflex-based agent (Russell and Norwig, 2011) using action-reaction rules, and (3) actuate these actions via its actuators (e.g. robot motors, two- or three-dimensional character graphics) in a manner that is psychologically valid. It should be noted however, that the reflex like nature of action tendencies is also present in noncategorical theories such as Scherer's CPT (2001), where action tendencies are activated at the lowest level of processing, namely the sensorimotor level (discussed in the previous section). For example, such an agent architecture has been implemented in two cooperative robots (Murphy et al., 2001) where states such as anger and frustration prompted robots to adjust their collaborative task strategy.

Ekman's theory of basic emotion, in particular, has had an additional appeal to the affective computing research community because (in addition to a small finite set of emotion/action tendency pairs), it provides a detailed description of the muscular activity of facial expressions. Specifically, using the widely known facial action coding system (FACS) (Ekman, 1978, 1983, 2002), Ekman's theory of basic emotions provides encoding for all of the facial movements involved in Ekman's six universal basic expressions of emotions (or EmFACS): anger, fear, disgust, sadness, happiness, and surprise (Friesen & Ekman, 1983).

Understandably, FACS, EmFACS, and the corresponding CMU-Pittsburgh AU-coded face expression image database (Kanade et al, 2000) have been very instrumental to the progress of automatic facial expression recognition and analysis, on the one hand, and of facial expression generation or synthesis on the other. Given a proper facial expression recognition sensing algorithm (Tian, 2001; Wolf et al., 2011), an agent can consistently recognize the user's state associated with the user's facial expressions. If desirable, it can also respond with synthesized facial expressions of its own (robotic head animations or a graphical virtual character's face) (Breazeal, 2003a, 2004; Pelachaud, 2009, Lisetti et al., 2013).

The quasi-exclusive focus on Ekman's six emotions, however, has limited the impact that emotion-based agents can have during human-computer interaction (HCI) in real-life scenarios. For example, users' facial expressions are often more varied than Ekman's six basic expressions (e.g., student's confusion or boredom) (Calvo & D'Mello, 2010).

Alternative approaches have studied how expressions of emotion are associated with fine-grained cognitive (thinking) processes (Scherer, 1992) (discussed earlier), or expressions that display mixed emotions (Ochs et al., 2005). Affective computing researchers need to continue to work toward including fine-grained AU-based facial expressions as a modality of agents' emotional expressions (Amini & Lisetti, 2013).

Appraisal Theories of Emotions, Agent Architectures, and Cognitive Models
COGNITIVE SCIENCE MODELS OF EMOTIONS

One of the first cognitive science modeling attempts was Newell and Simon's general problem solver (1961) which allowed a comparison of the traces of its reasoning steps with traces of human thinking processes on the same task. Other attempts followed, such as the SOAR theory of mind modeling long- and short-term memory (Laird et al., 1987; Lewis, et al., 1990) which continued to evolve (Laird & Rosenbloom, 1996). Another important cognitive science approach can be found in the adaptive control of thought-rational (ACT-R) symbolic theory of human knowledge (in terms of declarative representations of objects with schema like structures or chunks) and procedural representations of transformations in the environment (with production rules) (Anderson, 1993, 1996; Anderson and Lebiere, 1998). ACT has continued to evolve with ACT-R 5.0 (Anderson et al., 2004).

Whereas these cognitive theories of mind did not model emotions (and even considered them as noise) (Posner, 1993), recent cognitive models have begun to include the roles of emotion in cognition. EMA (Gratch, 2004; Marsella & Gratch, 2009), a rule-based domain-independent framework based on SOAR for modeling emotion, models how emotion and cognition influence each other using Lazarus' appraisal theory (1991). EMA models an agent's cognitive evaluation of a situation using a set of appraisal variables to represent the resulting emotion (possibly recalling previous situations from memory), as well as emotion-focused coping strategies that the agent can activate to reappraise the situation.

Another cognitive model of emotions is found in the SOAR-Emote model (Marinier, 2004), which is a simplified version of the basic SOAR-based cognitive appraisal model used in EMA. It uses Damasio's theory of emotions and feelings (Damasio, 1994) to also account for the influences of the body and physiology in determining affect. Furthermore following Damasio's view, the direction of causality for feelings and physiological effects in SOAR-Emote is reversed compared to EMA in which the agent first determines how it feels via cognitive appraisal and then displays appropriate body language to reflect that emotion. In subsequent work, SOAR-Emote (Marinier & Laird, 2007) comes closer to Scherer's theory of emotion generation (2001).

There have also been attempts in the ACT-R community to model emotion and motivation (Fum & Stocco, 2004).

Finally, it is interesting to note that cognitive science models of emotions and affect can also be constructed from the noncognitive nonappraisal theories of emotions (Armony et al., 1995), though much more research is called for in that domain.

APPRAISAL-BASED AGENT ARCHITECTURES

The mapping of the emotion elicitors (also referred to as emotion antecedents or emotion triggers) from the environment onto the resulting emotion (or other affective state) is the core task of the emotion generation process, implemented via cognitive appraisal. It reflects the agent's evaluation of these stimuli, in light of its goals, beliefs and behavioral capabilities and available resources.

This computational task has extensive theoretical support in the cognitive theories of emotion generation (e.g., OCC, CPT). Existing empirical data also provide a rich source of evidence regarding the nature of the trigger-to-emotion mappings (see discussion above). We know that the possibility of bodily harm triggers fear; obstruction of one's goals triggers anger; loss of love objects triggers sadness; achieving an important goal triggers happiness, and so on. When a componential model is used, a series of evaluative criteria or appraisal variables are used to represent the results of the evaluation of the triggers with respect to the agent's goals and beliefs.

As mentioned, the most commonly used set of evaluative criteria are those first identified by the OCC model, and OCC is the most frequently implemented model of emotion generation via cognitive appraisal. It uses concepts such as agents, objects, and events that are very similar to constructs used to implement virtual agents. A few of these OCC-inspired systems are Oz, EM, HAP, Affective Reasoner, FearNot!, EMA, MAMID, Greta (Adam, 2006; Andre et al., 2000; Aylett et al., 2007; Bates, 1992, 1994; De Rosis et al., 2003; Elliott, 1992; Gratch, 2004; Gratch et al., 2007b; Hudlicka, 1998; Loyall, 1997; Reilly, 1997; Marsella, 2000; Marsella & Gratch, 2009; Mateas, 2003; Predinger & Ishizuka, 2004a, Hermann et al., 2007).

The component process theory (CPT) (Scherer, 2001, 2009) has been interesting for emotion-based agents for two main reasons: (1) it considers emotions with their complex three levels (sensorimotor, schematic, and conceptual) nature and (2) it addresses human multimodal expression of emotion. CPT has been used as a guideline for developing both the generation and recognition of emotive expression and has been applied to the generation of virtual character facial expression (Paleari & Lisetti, 2006) and to sensor fusion (Paleari et al., 2007).

Few models have used appraisal variables defined by componential theorists. These include the GENESE (Scherer, 1993) and the GATE model (Wehrle & Scherer, 2001). The GATE model uses appraisal variables defined by Scherer (2001) to implement the second stage of the mapping process and maps the appraisal variable values onto the associated emotions in the multidimensional space defined by the variables.

Increasingly, models of emotion generation via cognitive appraisal are combining both the OCC evaluative criteria and appraisal variables from componential theories—for example, FLAME (El-Nasr, 2000) and EMA (Gratch & Marsella, 2004).

Furthermore, while the majority of existing symbolic agent architectures use cognitive appraisal theory as the basis for emotion generation, several models have emerged that attempt to integrate additional modalities, most often a simulation of the physiologic modality (e.g., Breazeal, 2003a; Canamero, 1997; Hiolle et al., 2012; Scheutz, 2004; Velásquez, 1997).

Dimensional Computational Models of Affective States

When the dimensional perspective is used, affective states are represented in terms of doubles or triples, representing the two dimensions of pleasure and arousal, or the three dimensions of pleasure, arousal, and dominance (see previous section).

Examples of architectures using the dimensional model for emotion generation include the social robot Kismet (Breazeal, 2003a), the WASABI architecture used for synthetic agent Max (Becker, Kopp, & Wachsmuth, 2004; Becker-Asano & Wachsmuth, 2009), and the arousal-based model of dyadic human-robot attachment interactions (Hiolle et al., 2012).

The dimensional theories of emotions have also contributed to progress in emotion recognition from physiological signals; in that respect, they are very relevant to emotion-based agents with abilities to sense the continuous nature of affect (Calvo, 2010; Gunes & Pantic, 2010; Lisetti & Nasoz, 2004; Peter & Herbon, 2006; Predinger & Ishizuka, 2004a).

Emerging Challenges: Modeling Emotional Conflicts and Affective Disorders
Modeling Affective Disorders

We have already discussed how the modeling of rationality has been one of the main motivations of AI until recently. We also want to point out that human quirks and failings can be at least as interesting to study as our intelligence.

This is not a new argument; Colby's (1975) seminal PARRY system, a model of paranoid belief structures implemented as a LISP simulation, is perhaps the earliest example of work in this vein.

Since then, a few psychologists and psychiatrists exploring the relationship between cognitive deficits and disturbances of neuroanatomy and neurophysiology (e.g., schizophrenia, paranoia, Alzheimer's disease), have built computer models of these phenomena to gather further insights into their theories (Cohen and Servan-Schreiber, 1992; Servan-Schreiber, 1986), and to make predictions of the effects of brain disturbance on cognitive function (O'Donnell, 2006). These models use a connectionist approach to represent cognitive or neural processes with artificial neural networks (McClelland & Rumelhart, 1986; Rumelhart & McClelland, 1986).

One of the challenges facing affective computing researchers interested in modeling affective disorders is the identification of the mechanisms underlying psychopathology and affective disorders. Whereas the primary theories of emotions discussed above focus on adaptive affective functioning, modeling of affective disorders will require a more nuanced understanding of the mechanisms underlying psychopathology. In addition, modeling of these mechanisms will also enhance our understanding of normal affective functioning.

Work in this area is in its infancy, and more research in both psychological theories and computational approaches will be required to address these challenges. An example of this effort is a recent attempt to model alternative mechanisms underlying a range of anxiety disorders, within an agent architecture that models the effects of emotions on cognition in terms global parameters influencing multiple cognitive processes (Hudlicka, 2008).

Virtual Counseling and Virtual Humans

Some of the same psychologists at the forefront of computational models of affective disorders (Servan-Schreiber, 1986) also favored early on the notion of computerized psychotherapy.

This concept is not new either: Weizenbaum's ELIZA (1967) was the first program to simulate a psychotherapist and used simple textual pattern matching to imitate the responses of a Rogerian psychotherapist (Rogers, 1959). However, after ELIZA's unsuspected success in terms of its ability to engage users in ongoing "conversations," Weizenbaum (1976) became ambivalent about the possibility of using computers for therapy because computers would always lack essential human qualities such as compassion, empathy, and wisdom.

However, since research results established that people respond socially to computers displaying social cues (Reeves & Nass, 1996), the motivation to build socially intelligent computers as a new mode for HCI grew steadily (and, as we will see, including for therapy). The tremendous recent progress in the design of embodied conversational agents (ECAs) and intelligent virtual agents (IVAs), since their first appearance (Cassell, 2000), have changed our views of human-computer interaction. They have now become so effectively communicative in their anthropomorphic forms that they are often referred to as virtual humans (VHs) (Hill et al., 2003; Swartout et al., 2001; Swartout, 2010.

Virtual human characters now use sophisticated multimodal communication abilities such as facial expressions, gaze, and gestures (Amini & Lisetti, 2013; Bailenson, et al., 2001; De Rosis et al., 2003; Pelachaud, 2002, 2003, 2004, 2009; Poggi, 2005; Predinger and Ishizuka, 2004a, 2004b; Rutter, et al., 1984). They can establish rapport with back-channel cues such as head nods, smiles, shift of gaze or posture, or mimicry of head gestures (Gratch 2006, 2007, 2007a; Huang et al, 2011; Kang, 2008; McQuiggan, 2008; Pelachaud 2009; Prendinger & Ishizuka, 2005; Putten, et al., 2009; Wang 2010, 2009), communicate empathically (Aylett, 2007; Boukricha, 2007, 2009, 2011; McQuiggan & Lester, 2007; Nguyen, 2009; Prendinger & Ishizuka, 2005), and engage in social talk (Bickmore, 2005a, 2005; Bickmore & Giorgino, 2006; Cassell and Bickmore, 2003; Kluwer, 2011; Schulman & Bickmore, 2011).

As a result, virtual human characters open many new domains for HCI that were not feasible earlier and reopen old debates about the potential roles of computers, including the use of computers for augmenting psychotherapy (Hudlicka, 2005; Hudlicka et al., 2008, Lisetti et al., 2013). Virtual humans are making their debut as virtual counselors (Bickmore, 2010; Lisetti, 2012; Lisetti & Wagner, 2008; Rizzo et al., 2012, Lisetti et al., 2013). Robots are also being studied in a therapeutic context (Stiehl & Lieberman, 2005). Riva et al. in this volume survey some of latest progress in cybertherapy, and van den Broeck et al. (this volume) discuss the role of ECAs in health applications in general.

Virtual Patients for Mental Health

One obvious case where the simulation and modeling of human psychological problems is useful is in the treatment of such problems. Virtual patients are currently being designed to model these problems from the cognitive science approach we discussed earlier. Virtual patients are also used to train health-care and medical personnel via role playing with virtual patients exhibiting the symptoms of affective disorders before they begin to work with real patients (Cook & Triola, 2009; Cook et al., 2010; Hoffman, 2011; Hubal, 2003; Magerko, 2011; Stevens et al., 2006; Villaume, 2006).

Another potential use is to model these systems within synthetic characters with whom the patient interacts. The patient could then experiment with the character's behavior, subjecting them to different situations and observing the results, as a way of coming to better understand their own behavior. The system could also display the internal state variables of the character, such as their level of effortful control, so as to help the patient better understand the dynamics of their own behavior. Some systems have taken a similar approach (Aylett, 2007; Wilkinson et al., 2008), and their potential impact on a wide range of interventions for mental issues calls for more work in that direction.

Conflicted Protagonist Characters for Computer Games

Another case for modeling affective disorders is found in entertainment scenarios such as interactive storytelling or computer games. To build interactive games and storytelling, one needs to construct synthetic characters whose reactions are believable in the sense of making a user willing to suspend disbelief (Johnston, 1981) regardless of their overall realism. For these applications, the pauses and hesitations due to the internal inhibition of a conflicted character, or the obvious lack of inhibition of a drunken character, can be important to establishing the believability of a character.

Narrative traditionally involves characters who are presented with conflicts and challenges, often from within (Campbell, 2008). These applications provide a wonderful sandbox in which to experiment with simulations of human psychology, including humans who are not at their best.

More generally, a disproportionate amount of storytelling involves characters who are flawed or simply not at their best, particularly in applications such as interactive drama (Bates, 1992, 1994;

Johnson & Thomas, 1981; Loyall, 1997; Mateas, 2003; Marsella, 2000; Hermann et al., 2007).

With the continuous rise of entertainment applications, this area of research is also very promising, where affective computing researchers can reach out to artists and vice versa.

Conclusions

In this chapter we have explained the various motivations for building emotion-based agents and provided a brief overview of the main emotion theories relevant for such architectures. We then surveyed some of the recent progress in the field, including interactive expressive virtual characters. We also briefly mentioned some less known neurophysiologic theories in the hope that they might give rise to novel approaches for biologically inspired emotion-based architectures. Finally, we discussed some of the latest application domains for emotion-based intelligent agents, such as interactive drama, mental health promotion, and personnel training. We hope to have demonstrated the importance of emotion-based agent architectures and models in current and future digital artifacts.

Note

1. In an attempt to catalogue human phylogenetic sets of affectively loaded events that consistently trigger the same emotion across human subjects, a set of emotional stimuli for experimental investigations of emotion and attention was compiled (Lang et al., 1997)—the International Affective Picture System (IAPS)—with the goal of providing researchers with a large set of standardized emotionally evocative, internationally accessible color photographs with content across a wide range of semantic categories. IAPS has been heavily used for the recognition of emotion across subjects as it attempts to provide an objective baseline for the generation of human emotion.

References

Adam, C., Gaudou, B., Herzig, A., & Longin, D. (2006). OCC's emotions: A formalization in BDI logic. In J. Euzenat & J. Domingue (Eds.), *Proceedings of the international conference on artificial intelligence: Methodology, systems, applications* (pp. 24–32). Berlin: Springer-Verlag, LNAI 4183.

Anderson, J. (1993). *Rules of the mind*. Hillsdale, NJ: Erlbaum.

Anderson, J. (1996). ACT: A simple theory of complex cognition. *American Psychologist, 51*(4), 355–365.

Anderson, J. R., Bothell, D., Byrne, M. D., Douglass, S., Lebiere, C., & Qin, Y.(2004). An integrated theory of the mind. *Psychological Review, 111*(4), 1036–1060.

Anderson, J. R., & Lebiere, C. (1998). *The atomic components of thought*. Mahwah, NJ: Erlbaum.

Andre, E., Klesen, M., Gebhard, P., Allen, S., & Rist, T. (2000). Exploiting models of personality and emotions to control the behavior of animated interactive agents.... on Autonomous Agents, (October).

Amini, R., & Lisetti, C. (2013). HapFACS: An opensource API/software for AU-based generation of facial expressions for embodied conversational agents. In *Proceedings of Affective Computing and Intelligent Interactions.*

Arbib, M., & Fellous, J.-M. (2004). Emotions: From brain to robot. *Trends in Cognitive Sciences, 8*(12), 554–561.

Arkin, R. (1998). *Behavior-based robotics.* Cambridge, MA: MIT Press.

Armony, J., Cohen, J., Servan-Schreiber, D., & Ledoux, J. (1995). An anatomically constrained neural network model of fear conditioning. *Behavioral Neuroscience, 109*(2), 246–257.

Aylett, R., Vala, M., Sequeira, P., & Paiva, A. (2007). *Fearnot! An emergent narrative approach to virtual dramas for anti-bullying education* (Vol. LNCS 4871, pp. 202–205). Berlin: Springer-Verlag.

Bailenson, J., Blascovich, J., Beall, A., & Loomis, J. (2001). Equilibrium revisited: Mutual gaze and personal space in virtual environments. *Presence: Teleoperators and Virtual Environments, 10*(6), 583–598.

Bates, J. (1992). Virtual reality, art, and entertainment. *Presence: Teleoperators and Virtual Environments, 1*(1), 133–138.

Bates, J. (1994). The role of emotion in believable agents. *Communications of the ACM, 37*(7).

Bechara, A., Damasio, H, Tranel, D., & Damasio, A. R. (1997). Deciding advantageously before knowing the advantageous strategy. *Science, 275*(5304), 1293–1295.

Becker-Asano, C., & Wachsmuth, I. (2009). Affective computing with primary and secondary emotions in a virtual human. *Autonomous Agents and Multi-Agent Systems, 20*(1), 32–49.

Bethel, C., & Murphy, R. (2008). Survey of non-facial/non-verbal affective expressions for appearance-constrained robots. *IEEE Transactions on Systems, Man, and Cybernetics, Part C, 38*(1), 83–92.

Bickmore, T., & Giorgino, T. (2006). Methodological review: Health dialog systems for patients and consumers. *Journal of Biomedical Informatics, 39*(5), 65–467.

Bickmore, T., & Gruber, A. (2010). Relational agents in clinical psychiatry. *Harvard Review of Psychiatry, 18*(2), 119–130.

Bickmore, T., Gruber, A., & Picard, R. (2005). Establishing the computer patient working alliance in automated health behavior change interventions. *Patient Education and Counseling, 59,* 21–30.

Bickmore, T. W., & Picard, R. W. (2005). Establishing and maintaining long-term human-computer relationships. *ACM Transactions on Computer-Human Interaction,* 617–638.

Boukricha, H., Becker-Asano, C., & Wachsmuth, I. (2007). Simulating empathy for the virtual human Max. In D. Reichardt & P. Levi (Eds.), *2nd Workshop on Emotion and Computing, In conjunction with 30th German Conf. on Artificial Intelligence (KI 2007)* (pp. 23–28), Osnabrück.

Boukricha, H., & Wachsmuth, I. (2011). Empathy-based emotional alignment for a virtual human: A three-step approach. *KI—Kunstliche Intelligenz, 25*(3), 195–204.

Boukricha, H., Wachsmuth, I., Hofstatter, A., & Grammer, K. (2009). Pleasure-arousal-dominance driven facial expression simulation. In *Affective computing and intelligent interaction and workshops, 2009* (pp. 1–7). ACII 2009. 3rd International Conference on, IEEE.

Brave, S., & Nass, C. (2002). Emotion in human-computer interaction. In J. Jacko & A. Sears (Eds.), *The human-computer interaction handbook: Fundamentals, evolving technologies, and emerging applications* (pp. 81–97). Mahwah, NJ: Erlbaum.

Breazeal, C. (2003a). Emotion and sociable humanoid robots. *International Journal of Human Computer Studies, 59*(1–2), 119–155.

Breazeal, C. (2003b). Towards sociable robots. *Robotics and Autonomous Systems, 42*(3–4), 167–175.

Breazeal, C. (2004). Function meets style: Insights from emotion theory applied to HRI. *IEEE Transactions on Systems, Man and Cybernetics, Part C* (Applications and Reviews), *34*(2), 187–194.

Calvo, R., & D'Mello, S. (2010). Affect detection: An interdisciplinary review of models, methods, and their applications. *IEEE Transactions on Affective Computing, 1*(1), 18–37.

Campbell, J. (2008). *The hero with a thousand faces,* 3rd ed. New World Library.

Campbell, J. C., Hays, M. J., Core, M., Birch, M., Bosack, M., & Clark, R. E. (2011). Interpersonal and leadership skills: Using virtual humans to teach new officers. In *Interservice/Industry Training, Simulation, and Education Conference,* number 11358; 1–11.

Canamero, D. (1997). A hormonal model of emotions for behavior control. VUB. AI-Lab Memo.

Cannon, W. (1927). The James-Lange theory of emotions: A critical examination and an alternative theory. *American Journal of Psychology, 39,* 106–124.

Cassell, J. Sullivan, J., Prevost, S., & Churchill, E. (2000). Embodied conversational agents. *Social Psychology, 40*(1), 26–36.

Cassell, J., & Bickmore, T. (2003). Negotiated Collusion: Modeling Social Language and its Relationship Effects in Intelligent Agents. *User Modeling and User-Adapted Interaction* 13: 89–132.

Cohen, J. D., & Servan-Schreiber, D. (1992). Context, cortex, and dopamine: a connectionist approach to behavior and biology in schizophrenia. *Psychological Review, 99*(1), 45–77.

Colby, K. (1975). *Artificial paranoia.* Pergamon Press.

Cook, D. A., Erwin, P. J., & Triola, M. M. (2010). Computerized virtual patients in health professions education: a systematic review and meta-analysis. *Academic Medicine: Journal of the Association of American Medical Colleges, 85*(10), 1589–602.

Cook, D. A., & Triola, M. M. (2009). Virtual patients: A critical literature review and proposed next steps. *Medical Education, 43*(4), 303–311.

Damasio, A. R. (1994). *Descartes' error: Emotion, reason, and the human brain.* New York: Avon.

Darwin, C. (1872). *The expression of emotions in man and animals.* London: John Murray. (Republished by University of Chicago Press, 1965.)

Davidson, R., & Cacioppo, J. (1992). New developments in the scientific study of emotion: An introduction to the special section. *Psychological Science, 3*(1), 21–22.

De Rosis, F., Pelachaud, C., Poggi, I., Carofiglio, V., & de Carolis, B. (2003). From Greta's mind to her face: Modeling the dynamics of affective states in a conversational embodied agent. *International Journal of Human-Computer Studies, 59*(1–2), 81–118.

de Sousa, R. (1990). *The rationality of emotions.* Cambridge, MA: MIT Press.

Dreyfus, H. (1992). *What computers still can't do.* Cambridge, MA: MIT Press.

Dreyfus, H., & Dreyfus, S. (Winter 1988). Making a mind versus modeling the brain: Artificial intelligence back at a branchpoint. *Dædalus,* 15–43.

Dunn, C., Deroo, L., & Rivara, F. P. (2001). The use of brief interventions adapted from motivational interviewing across behavioral domains: A systematic review. *Addiction 96*(12), 1725–1742.

Ekman, P. (1984). Expression and the nature of emotion. In K. Scherer (Ed.), *Approaches to emotion* (pp. 319–343). Hillsdale, NJ: Erlbaum.

Ekman, P. (1999). Basic emotions. In T. Dalgleish & M. Power (Eds.), *Handbook of cognition and emotion*. Hoboken, NJ: Wiley.

Ekman, P., & Freisen, W. V. (1978). *Facial action coding system: A technique for the measurement of facial movement*. Consulting Psychologists Press.

Ekman, P., Freisen, W. V., & Hager, J. C. (2002). *Facial action coding system*, 2nd ed. (Vol. 160). Salt Lake City: Research Nexus eBook.

Ekman, P., Levenson, R. W., & Freisen, W. V. (1983). Autonomic nervous system activity distinguishes among emotions. *Science, 221*(4616), 1208–1210.

Elliott, C. (1992). Affective reasoner. Ph.D. thesis. The Institute for the Learning Sciences Technical Report #32. Evanston, IL: Northwestern University.

El-Nasr, M., Yen, J., & Ioerger, T. (2000). FLAME: fuzzy logic adaptive model of emotions. autonomous agents and multi-agent systems, *Autonomous Agents and Multi-Agent Systems*, 3(3), 219–257.

Elster, J. (1999). *Alchemies of the mind: Rationality and the emotions*. Cambridge, UK: Cambridge University Press.

Frank, R. (1988). *Passions within reason: The strategic role of the emotions*. New York: Norton.

Friesen, W., & Ekman, P. (1983). *EMFACS-7: Emotional facial action coding system*.

Frijda, N. and Swagerman, J. (1987). Can computers feel? Theory and design of an emotional system. *Cognition and Emotion, 1*(3), 235–257.

Frijda, N. H. (1986). *The Emotions: Studies in Emotion and Social Interaction* (Vol. 1). New York: Cambridge University Press.

Frijda, N. H. (1995). *Emotions in robots*. Cambridge, MA: MIT Press.

Frijda, N. H. (1987). Emotion, cognitive structure, and action tendency. *Cognition and Emotion, 1*(2), 115–143.

Fum, D., & Stocco, A. (2004). Memory, emotion, and rationality: An ACT-R interpretation for gambling task results. In *Proceedings of the Sixth International Conference on Cognitive Modeling*.

Gratch, J., & Marsella, S. (2004). A domain-independent framework for modeling emotion. *Cognitive Systems Research, 5*(4), 269–306.

Gratch, J., Okhmatovskaia, A., & Lamothe, F. (2006). Virtual rapport. *Intelligent Virtual*.

Gratch, J., Wang, N., Gerten, J., & Fast, E. (2007a). Creating rapport with virtual agents. In *Proceedings of the international conference on intelligent virtual agents*.

Gratch, J., Wang, N., & Okhmatovskaia, A. (2007b). Can virtual humans be more engaging than real ones? In *Proceedings of the 12th international conference on human-computer interaction: Intelligent multimodal interaction environments*, HCI'07. Berlin and Heidelberg: Springer-Verlag.

Gunes, H. and Pantic, M. (2010). Automatic, dimensional and continuous emotion recognition. *International Journal of Synthetic Emotions, 1*(1), 68–99.

Hermann, C., Melcher, H., Rank, S., & Trappl, R. (2007). Neuroticism a competitive advantage (also) for IVAs? In *International conference on intelligent virtual agents, intelligence, lecture notes in artificial intelligence* (pp. 64–71).

Hill, R. W., Gratch, J., Marsella, S., Rickel, J., Swartout, W., & Traum, D. (2003). Virtual humans in the mission rehearsal exercise system. *Kunstliche Intelligenz (KI Journal), Special issue on Embodied Conversational Agents, 17*(4), 5–10.

Hiolle, A., Cañamero, L., Davila-Ross, M., and Bard, K. a. (2012). Eliciting caregiving behavior in dyadic human-robot attachment-like interactions. *ACM Transactions on Interactive Intelligent Systems, 2*(1), 1–24.

Hoffman, R. E., Grasemann, U., Gueorguieva, R., Quinlan, D., Lane, D., & Miikkulainen, R. (2011). Using computational patients to evaluate illness mechanisms in schizophrenia. *Biological Psychiatry, 69*(10), 997–1005.

Huang, L., Morency, L.-P., & Gratch, J. (2011). Virtual rapport 2.0. In *International conference on intelligent virtual agents, intelligence: Lecture notes in artificial intelligence* (pp. 68–79). Berlin and Heidelberg: Springer-Verlag.

Hubal, R. C., Frank, G. A., & Guinn, C. I. (2003). Lessons learned in modeling schizophrenic and depressed responsive virtual humans for training. In *Proceedings of the 2003 international conference on intelligent user interfaces* (IUI'03), (pp. 85–92). New York: ACM.

Hudlicka, E., & McNeese, M. (2002). User's affective & belief state: Assessment and GUI adaptation. *International Journal of User Modeling and User Adapted Interaction, 12*(1), 1–47.

Hudlicka, E. (1998). Modeling emotion in symbolic cognitive architectures. *AAAI fall symposium on emotional and intelligent: the tangled knot of cognition. TR FS-98-03*, 92-97. Menlo Park, CA: AAAI Press.

Hudlicka, E. 2002. This time with feeling: Integrated model of trait and state effects on cognition and behavior. *Applied Artificial Intelligence, 16*(7–8), 1–31.

Hudlicka, E. (2003). To feel or not to feel: The role of affect in human-computer interaction. *International Journal of Human-Computer Studies, 59*(1–2).

Hudlicka, E., (2005). Computational models of emotion and personality: Applications to psychotherapy research and practice. In *Proceedings of the 10th annual cybertherapy 2005 conference: A decade of virtual reality*, Basel.

Hudlicka, E. (2007). Reasons for emotions: Modeling emotions in integrated cognitive systems. In W. E. Gray (Ed.), *Integrated models of cognitive systems* (pp. 1–37). New York: Oxford University Press.

Hudlicka, E., (2008). Modeling the mechanisms of emotion effects on cognition. In *Proceedings of the AAAI fall symposium on biologically inspired cognitive architectures*. TR FS-08-04 (pp. 82–86). Menlo Park, CA: AAAI Press.

Hudlicka, E. (2011). Guidelines for Developing Computational Models of Emotions. *International Journal of Synthetic Emotions, 2*(1), 26–79.

Hudlicka, E., Lisetti, C., Hodge, D., Paiva, A., Rizzo, A., & Wagner, E. (2008). Artificial agents for psychotherapy. In *Proceedings of the AAAI spring symposium on emotion, personality and social behavior*, TR SS-08-04, 60–64. Menlo Park, CA: AAAI.

Izard, C. E. (1971). *The face of emotion*. New York: Appleton-Century Crofts.

Izard, C. E. (1992). Basic emotions, relations among emotions, and emotion-cognition relations. *Psychological Review, 99*(3), 561–565.

James, W. (1884). What is an emotion? *Mind, 9*(34), 188–205.

Gray, J., & McNaughton, N. (2003). *The neuropsychology of anxiety: An enquiry into the functions of the septo-hippocampal system*, 2nd ed. Oxford, UK: Oxford University Press.

Jiang, H. (2008). *From rational to emotional agents: A way to design emotional agents*. VDM Verlag Dr. Muller.

Johnson-Laird, P. & Oatley, K. (1992). Basic emotions, rationality, and folk theory. *Cognition and Emotion*, 6(3/4), 201–223.

Johnson, O., & Thomas, F. (1981). *The illusion of life: Disney animation*. Hyperion Press.

Kanade, T., Cohn, J. F., & Tian, Y. (2000). Comprehensive database for facial expression analysis. In *Proceedings fourth IEEE international conference on automatic face and gesture recognition* (Vol. 4, pp. 46–53). Grenoble, France: IEEE Computer Society.

Kang, S.-H., Gratch, J., Wang, N., & Watt, J. (2008). Does the contingency of agents' nonverbal feedback affect users' social anxiety? In *Proceedings of the 7th international joint conference on Autonomous agents and multiagent systems* (Vol. 1 pp. 120–127). International Foundation for Autonomous Agents and Multiagent Systems.

Kluwer, T. (2011). I like your shirt—Dialogue acts for enabling social talk in conversational agents. In Proceedings of Intelligent Virtual Agents 11th International Conference (IVA 2011) Reykjavik, Iceland. *Lecture Notes in Computer Science*, 6895: 14–27.

Laird, J. E., Newell, A., & Rosenbloom, P. S. (1987). SOAR: An architecture for general intelligence. *Artificial Intelligence*, 33(1), 1–64.

Laird, J. E., & Rosenbloom, P. (1996). Evolution of the SOAR architecture. In D. M. Steier. &, T. M. Mitchell (Eds.), *Mind matters: A tribute to Allen Newell* (pp. 1–50). Mahwah, NJ: Erlbaum.

Lang, P. J., Bradley, M. M., & Cuthbert, B. (1997). *International affective picture system (IAPS): Technical manual and affective ratings*. Technical report. Washington, DC: NIMH Center for the Study of Emotion and Attention.

Lazarus, R. S. (1991). Cognition and motivation in emotion. *Journal of the American Psychologist*, 46, 352–367.

Ledoux, J. (1992). Emotion and the amygdala. In *Current Opinion in Neurobiology*, (Vol. 2, pp. 339–351). Hoboken, NJ: Wiley-Liss.

Ledoux, J. (1995). Emotion: Clues from the brain. *Annual Review Psychology*, 46, 209–235.

Ledoux, J. (2000). Emotion circuits in the brain. *Annual Review of Neuroscience*, 23, 155–184.

Leventhal, H., & Scherer, K. R. (1987). The relationship of emotion to cognition: A functional approach to a semantic controversy. *Cognition and Emotion*, 1, 3–28.

Lewis, R. L., Huffman, S. B., John, B. E., Laird, J. E., Lehman, J. F., Newell, A.,…Tessler, S. G. (1990). Soar as a unified theory of cognition: Spring 90. In *Twelfth annual conference of the cognitive science society* (pp. 1035–1042).

Lisetti, C. L. (2008). Embodied conversational agents for psychotherapy. In *Proceedings of the CHI 2008 conference workshop on technology in mental health* (pp. 1–12). New York: ACM.

Lisetti, C. L. & Gmytrasiewicz, P. (2002). *Can a rational agent afford to be affectless? A formal approach. in applied artificial intelligence* (Vol. 16, pp. 577–609). Taylor & Francis.

Lisetti, C. L. & Nasoz, F. (2004). Using noninvasive wearable computers to recognize human emotions from physiological signals. EURASIP. *Journal on Applied Signal Processing*, 11, 1672–1687.

Lisetti, C. L., Amini, R., Yasavur, U., & Rishe, N. (2013). I Can Help You Change! An Empathic Virtual Agent Delivers Behavior Change Health Interventions. *ACM Transactions on Management Information Systems*, Vol. 4, No. 4, Article 19, 2013. Lisetti, C. L, Nasoz, F., Alvarez, K., & Marpaung, A. (2004). A social informatics approach to human-robot interaction with an office service robot. *IEEE Transactions on Systems, Man, and Cybernetics—Special Issue on Human Robot Interaction*, 34(2).

Loyall, B., & Bates, J. (1997). Personality-rich believable agents that use language. In *Proceedings of the first international conference on autonomous agents*.

Magerko, B., Dean, J., Idnani, A., Pantalon, M., & D'Onofrio, G. (2011). Dr. Vicky: A virtual coach for learning brief negotiated interview techniques for treating emergency room patients. In AAAI Spring Symposium.

Marinier, R., & Laird, J. (2004). Toward a comprehensive computational model of emotions and feelings. In *Proceedings of the 6th international conference on cognitive modeling*.

Marinier, R. P., & Laird, J. E. (2007). Computational modeling of mood and feeling from emotion. In *Cognitive science* (pp. 461–466).

Marsella, S. C., & Gratch, J. (2009). EMA: A process model of appraisal dynamics. *Cognitive Systems Research*, 10(2000), 70–90.

Marsella, S. C., Johnson, W. L., & LaBore, C. (2000). Interactive pedagogical drama. In *Proceedings of the fourth international conference on autonomous agents* (pp. 301–308).

Mateas, M. (2001). Expressive AI: A hybrid art and science practice. *Leonardo: Journal of the International Society for Arts, Sciences and Technology*, 34(2), 147–153.

Mateas, M. (2003). Façade, an experiment in building a fully-realized interactive drama. In *Game Developer's Conference: Game Design Track*, San Jose, California, March.

McClelland, J., Rumelhart, D. & the PDP Research Group (1986). *Parallel distributed processing: Explorations in the microstructures of cognition: Vol. 2. Psychological and biological models*. Cambridge, MA: MIT Press.

McQuiggan, S., & Lester, J. (2007). Modeling and evaluating empathy in embodied companion agents. *International Journal of Human-Computer Studies*, 65, 348–360.

McQuiggan, S., Robison, J., & Phillips, R. (2008). Modeling parallel and reactive empathy in virtual agents: An inductive approach. In *Proceedings of the 7th International Joint Conference on Autonomous Agents and Multiagent Systems*, 1: 167–174.

Mehrabian, A. (1995). Framework for a comprehensive description and measurement of emotional states *Genetic, Social, and General Psychology Monographs*. 121, 339–361.

Muramatsu, R., & Hanoch, Y. (2005). Emotions as a mechanism for boundedly rational agents: The fast and frugal way. *Journal of Economic Psychology*, 26(2), 201–221.

Murphy, R., Lisetti, C. L., Irish, L., Tardif, R., & Gage, A. (2001). Emotion-based control of cooperating heterogeneous mobile robots. *IEEE Transactions on Robotics and Automation: Special Issue on Multi-Robots Systems*. 18(5), 744–757.

Murphy, R. R. (2000). *Introduction to AI robotics*. Cambridge, MA: MIT Press.

Nguyen, H., & Masthoff, J. (2009). Designing empathic computers: The effect of multimodal empathic feedback using animated agent. In *Proceedings of the 4th international conference on persuasive technology* (p. 7). New York: ACM.

Ochs, M., & Niewiadomski, R. (2005). Intelligent expressions of emotions. In *Proceedings of the first affective computing and intelligent and intelligent interactions* (pp. 707–714).

Ochs, M., & Sadek, D., and Pelachaud, C. (2012). A formal model of emotions for an empathic rational dialog agent. *Autonomous Agents and Multi-Agent Systems, 24*(3), 410–440.

O'Donnell, B. F., & Wilt, M. A. (2006). *Computational models of mental disorders. Encyclopedia of Cognitive Science.* Wiley Online Library.

Ortony, A., Clore, G. L., & Collins, A. (1988). *The cognitive structure of emotions.* Cambridge, UK: Cambridge University Press.

Ortony, A., & Turner, T. J. (1990). What's basic about basic emotions? *Psychological Review, 97*(3), 315–331.

Paleari, M., Grizard, A., & Lisetti, C. L. (2007). Adapting psychologically grounded facial emotional expressions to different anthropomorphic embodiment platforms. In *Proceedings of the FLAIRS conference.*

Paleari, M., & Lisetti, C. L. (2006). *Toward multimodal fusion of affective cues.*

Pelachaud, C. (2009). Modelling multimodal expression of emotion in a virtual agent. *Philosophical Transactions of the Royal Society of London. Series B, Biological sciences, 364*(1535), 3539–3548.

Pelachaud, C., & Bilvi, M. (2003). Communication in multiagent systems: Background, current trends and future. In *Lecture notes in computer science* (pp. 300–317) Berlin: Springer.

Pelachaud, C., Carofiglio, V., & Poggi, I. (2002). Embodied contextual agent in information delivering application. In *Proceedings of the first international joint conference on autonomous agents & multi-agent systems.*

Pelachaud, C., Maya, V., & Lamolle, M. (2004). Representation of expressivity for embodied conversational agents. Embodied conversational agents: Balanced perception and action. In *Proceedings of the AAMAS, 4.*

Peter, C., & Herbon, A. (2006). Emotion representation and physiology assignments in digital systems. *Interacting with Computers, 18*(2), 139–170.

Picard, R. W. (1997). *Affective computing.* Cambridge, MA: MIT Press.

Plutchik, R. (1980). *Emotion theory, research and experience: Vol. 1. Theories of emotion.* New York: Academic Press.

Poggi, I., Pelachaud, C., de Rosis, F., Carofiglio, V., de Carolis, B., Poggi, I., . . . Carolis, B. D. (2005). *Multimodal intelligent information presentation* (Vol. 27)., New York: Springer.

Posner, M. (1993). *The foundations of cognitive science.* Cambridge, MA: MIT Press.

Predinger, H., & Ishizuka, M. (2004a). *Life-like characters.* New York: Springer.

Predinger, H., & Ishizuka, M. (2004b). What affective computing and life-like character technology can do for tele-home health care. In *Workshop on HCI and homecare: connecting families and clinicians* (pp. 1–3) in conjunction with CHI. Citeseer.

Prendinger, H., & Ishizuka, M. (2005). The empathic companion: A character-based interface that addresses user's affective states. *Applied Artificial Intelligence, 19,* 267–285.

Pütten, A. M. V. D., Krämer, N. C., & Gratch, J. (2009). Who's there? Can a virtual agent really elicit social presence?

Reeves, B., Nass, C., & Reeves, B. (1996). *The media equation: How people treat computers, television, and new media like real people and places.* Chicago: University of Chicago Press.

Reilly, W. S. N. (1997). A methodology for building believable social agents. In W. L. Johnson, and B. Hayes-Roth (Eds.), *Proceedings of the first international conference on autonomous agents agents* (pp. 114–121). New York: ACM.

Ritter, F. E., & Avraamides, M. N. (2000). *Steps towards including behavior moderators in human performance models*: College Station: Penn State University

Rizzo, A., Forbell, E., Lange, B., Galen Buckwalter, J., Williams, J., Sagae, K., & Traum, D. (2012). Simcoach: an online intelligent virtual human agent system for breaking down barriers to care for service members and veterans. In Monsour Scurfield, R., & Platoni, K. (Eds). *Healing War Trauma A Handbook of Creative Approaches.* Taylor & Francis.

Rogers, C. (1959). A theory of therapy, personality and interpersonal relation—Developed in the client-centered framework. In S. Koch (Ed.), *Psychology: The study of a science,* (Vol. 3, pp. 184–256). New York: McGraw-Hill.

Rolls, E. (2007). *Emotion explained.* Oxford Univeristy Press, Oxford, England.

Rossen, B., & Lok, B. (2012). A crowdsourcing method to develop virtual human conversational agents. *International Journal of Human-Computer Studies, 70*(4), 301–319.

Rumelhart, D., McClelland, J., & the PDP Research Group (1986). *Parallel distributed processing: Explorations in the microstructures of cognition: Vol. 1. Explorations in the microstructure of cognition.*

Russell, J. A. (1980). A circumplex model of affect. *Journal of Personality and Social Psychology, 39*(6), 1161–1178.

Russell, J. A. (2003). *Core affect and the psychological construction of emotion. Psychological Review, 110*(1), 145–172.

Russell, J. A., & Barrett, L. F. (1999). Core affect, prototypical emotional episodes, and other things called emotion: dissecting the elephant. *Journal of Personality and Social Psychology, 76*(5), 805–819.

Russell, S., & Norwig, P. (2011). *No artificial intelligence: A modern approach.* Upper Saddle River, NJ: Prentice Hall.

Russell, J., & Mehrabian, A. (1977). Evidence for a three-factor theory of emotions. *Journal of Research in Personality, 11,* 273–294.

Rutter, D., Pennington, D., Dewey, M., & Swain, J. (1984). Eye-contact as a chance product of individual looking: Implications for the intimacy model of argyle and dean. *Journal of Nonverbal Behavior, 8*(4), 250–258.

Scherer, K. R. (1992). What Does Facial Expression Express? In K. Strongman (Ed.), *International review of studies on emotion* (Vol. 2). Hoboken, NY: Wiley.

Scherer, K. R. (2001). *Appraisal processes in emotion: Theory, methods, research* (pp. 92–120). New York: Oxford University Press.

Scherer, K. R. (2009). Emotions are emergent processes: They require a dynamic computational architecture. *Philosophical transactions of the Royal Society of London, Series B, Biological Sciences, 364*(1535), 3459–3474.

Scheutz, M. (2000). Surviving in a hostile multiagent environment: How simple affective states can aid in the competition for resources. Paper presented at the Advances in Artificial Intelligence—13th Biennial Conference of the Canadian Society for Computational Studies of Intelligence, Montreal, Quebec, Canada.

Scheutz, M. (2011). Architectural roles of affect and how to evaluate them in artificial agents. *International Journal of Synthetic Emotions, 2*(2), 48–65.

Scheutz, M., & Schermerhorn, P. (2009). Affective goal and task selection for social robots. In J. Vallverdu &

D. Casacuberta (Eds.), *The handbook of research on synthetic emotions and sociable robotics* (pp. 74–87). Hershey, PA: IGI Publishing.

Schulman, D., Bickmore, T., & Sidner, C. (2011). In 2011 AAAI Spring Symposium Series, *An intelligent conversational agent for promoting long-term health behavior change using motivational interviewing* (pp. 61–64).

Servan-Schreiber, D. (1986). Artificial intelligence and psychiatry. *Journal of Nervous and Mental Disease, 174,* 191–202.

Simon, H. (1967). Motivational and emotional controls of cognition. *Psychological Review, 1,* 29–39.

Sloman, A. (1987). Motives, mechanisms, and emotions. *Emotion and Cognition, 1*(2), 217–234.

Sloman, A., & Croucher, M. (1981). Why robots will have emotions. In *Proceedings of the seventh IJCAI* (pp. 197–202). San Mateo, CA: Morgan-Kaufmann.

Smith, C. A., & Kirby, L. D. (2001). Toward delivering on the promise of appraisal theory. In K. Scherer, A. Schorr, and T. Johnstone (Eds.), *Appraisal processes in emotion: Theory, methods, research* (pp. 121–140). New York: Oxford University Press.

Smith, C., & Lazarus, R. (1990). Emotion and adaptation. In *Handbook of personality: Theory and research* (pp. 609–637). New York: Guilford.

Stevens, A., Hernandez, J., Johnsen, K., Dickerson, R., Raij, A., Harrison, C.,...Lind, D. S. (2006). The use of virtual patients to teach medical students history taking and communication skills. *American Journal of Surgery, 191*(6), 806–811.

Stiehl, W., & Lieberman, J. (2005). Design of a therapeutic robotic companion for relational, affective touch. In *ROMAN 2005 IEEE international workshop on robot and human interactive communication* (Vol. 1). AAAI Press.

Swartout, W. (2010). Lessons learned from virtual humans. *AI Magazine, 31*(1), 9–20.

Swartout, W. Jr., Gratch, R. H., Johnson, R. H., Kyriakakis, W. L., Labore, C., Lindheim, C. M.,...Thiebaux, L. (2001). Towards the holodeck: Integrating graphics, sound, character and story. In J. P. Miller, E. Andre, S. Sen, & C. Frasson (Eds), *Proceedings of the fifth international conference on autonomous agents* (pp. 409–416). ACM.

Thagard, P. (2008). Cognitive science. In *The Stanford encyclopedia of philosophy.* Cambridge, MA: MIT Press.

Tian, Y.-I., Kanade, T., & Cohn, J. (2001). Recognizing action units for facial expression analysis. *IEEE Transactions on Pattern Analysis and Machine Intelligence Analysis, 23*(2), 97–115.

Velásquez, J. (1997). Modeling emotions and other motivations in synthetic agents. Proceedings of the National Conference on Artificial Intellligence.

Villaume, W. A., Berger, B. A., & Barker, B. N. (2006). Learning motivational interviewing: Scripting a virtual patient. *American Journal of Pharmaceutical Education, 70*(2), 33.

Wang, N. (2009). *Rapport and facial expression,* 3rd ed. (pp. 1–6). and Workshops. ACII 2009.

Wang, N., & Gratch, J. (2010). Don't just stare at me! In *28th ACM conference on human factors in computing systems* (pp. 1241–1249). Atlanta: Association for Computing Machinery.

Wehrle, T., & Scherer, K. (2001). Toward Computational Modeling of Appraisal Theories. In Scherer, K., Schorr, A., & Johnstone, T. (Eds.). Appraisal processes in emotion: Theory, Methods, Research (pp. 350–365). New-York: Oxford University Press.

Weizenbaum, J. (1967). Contextual understanding by computers. *Communications of the ACM, 10*(8), 474–480.

Weizenbaum, J. (1976). *Computer power and human reason: From judgment to calculation.* Freeman.

Wilkinson, N., Ang, R. P., and Goh, D. H. (2008). Online video game therapy for mental health concerns: A review. *International Journal of Social Psychiatry, 54*(4), 370–382.

Wolf, L., Hassner, T., & Taigman, Y. (2011). Effective unconstrained face recognition by combining multiple descriptors and learned background statistics. *IEEE Transactions on Pattern Analysis and Machine Intelligence, 33*(10), 1978–1990.

Zajonc, B., & Markus, H. (1984). Affect and cognition: The hard interface. In C. Izard, J. Kagan, & R. Zajonc (Eds.), *Emotion, cognition and behavior* (pp. 73–102). Cambridge, UK: Cambridge University Press.

Zajonc, R. (1980). Feeling and thinking: Preferences need no inferences. *American Psychologist, 35,* 151–175.

Zajonc, R. (1984). On the primacy of affect. *American Psychologist, 39,* 117–124.

Affect and Machines in the Media

Despina Kakoudaki

Abstract

This chapter traces literary and cinematic representations of intelligent machines in order to provide background for the fantasies and implicit assumptions that accompany these figures in contemporary popular culture. Using examples from media depictions of robots, androids, cyborgs, and computers, this analysis offers a historical and theoretical overview of the cultural archive of fictional robots and intelligent machines—an archive that implicitly affects contemporary responses to technological projects.

Key Words: robots, androids, cyborgs, computers, artificial people, intelligent machines, popular culture, literary and cinematic representations, media depictions, fictional robots

Reality and Fiction

Long before they became possible in technological terms, intelligent, responsive, and even emotional machines featured prominently in the popular imagination, as well as in literature, film, drama, art, public discourse, and popular culture. While contemporary research aims to create the basis for better communications and denser interactions between people and advanced applications in robotics or computing, fictional and representational media depict intelligent machines and human-machine interactions through long-standing patterns and stereotypes that remain independent of the current state of scientific knowledge. Despite their unreality, fictional entities such as the robots, androids, cyborgs, computers, and artificial intelligences of science fiction and popular culture channel a range of feelings about technology and partly inform contemporary expectations and assumptions about what robotics applications would look and act like and what they would do.

It is especially important for researchers and scientists working in robotics, automation, computing, and related fields to recognize the potential interaction between fictional intelligent machines and actual research. Our collective cultural literacy about the fictional robot or android may be implicit or unconscious, or it may become visible in everyday fascinations with the figures and images of popular culture as well as beloved characters from science fiction literature and film and their funny or campy bodies and behaviors. Children can define and draw robots long before they are old enough to read a science fiction story or watch a relevant film; collectors of all ages gravitate toward both high-tech and retro robot toys; television advertisements promote innovation or just novelty through images of future robotics; and cinematic characters such as R2-D2 ad C-3PO, the robots of *Star Wars* (George Lucas, 1977), are as familiar as folk figures, their bodies and voice patterns instantly recognizable around the world (Figure 9.1. Researchers who work on designing emotional or intelligent machines share this cultural archive with everyday users of their applications. It is thus essential for them to become conscious of the fictional tradition, both in order to be able to identify how their own cultural assumptions and unconscious expectations may affect their research and to anticipate or interpret the reactions of their prospective users to new technological constructs. Although it may seem that fictional robots have little to do with contemporary scientific and theoretical debates and the high-tech tenor of robotics research, a closer look at this relationship reveals that fiction and reality are intertwined in important ways.

This chapter aims to provide an approach to this cultural archive of assumptions and expectations through a brief overview of the main texts that have contributed to its formation in fiction, film, and popular culture. Precisely because they are so pervasive and familiar, fictional robots function as mental, psychological, and cultural benchmarks for robotic presence—benchmarks that actual robots and robotics projects might strive to reach or evoke, even implicitly. When we discuss robots in the public sphere today, we combine our understanding of actual robotic applications in universities, research teams, and companies around the world, as these are becoming increasingly familiar to a mainstream audience, with our implicit sense of imaginary and fictional robots. Indeed, while contemporary research promises to transform our interactions with machines by allowing the machines themselves to become more responsive, this promise draws part of its emotional and cultural power from literary and cinematic traditions that have little to do with technological possibility. As a result of this paradigm meld, real robots are inseparable from their imaginary counterparts, since it is often the fictions that supply the emotional and intellectual context for much of the robot's cultural presence. As an imaginary entity, the fictional robot is so evocative that it sets the tone of our expectations from future robotics research and technological actuality.

In order to be able to distinguish the cultural influence of the fictional traditions of robotic presence, we first need to identify the ways in which contemporary technoculture criticism and popular writings on technology tend to use elements from this tradition, utilizing our sense of the aims, appearance, and functionality of fictional robots and other intelligent machines in order to explain or popularize actual research (Menzel and D'Alusio, 2001). The rise of technological discourse in the humanities, social sciences, and cultural criticism in the 1980s and 1990s was partly inspired by Donna Haraway's conceptualization of the cyborg as a theoretical entity (1985/1991) and expanded after N. Katherine Hayles (1999) described post-Enlightenment philosophical tendencies through the concept of the posthuman. These approaches brought new interest to the intersections between science and culture but also made

Fig. 9.1 R2-D2 and C-3PO, the expressive robots of Star Wars (George Lucas, 1977).
Credit: Twentieth Century Fox/ Photofest. © Twentieth Century Fox.

important connections between imaginative fiction and contemporary technological and critical contexts (Gray, Figueroa-Sarriera, and Mentor, 1995; Milburn, 2008). Cyborg criticism often resolves the paradoxical connection between real technologies and the imaginary presence of figures such as robots and cyborgs by focusing not on the depiction of such entities in fictional texts and films but on their potential as concepts that represent current modes of technological embodiment. Cyborg criticism tends to avoid the fantasmatic presence of fictional intelligent machines, emphasizing instead the ways in which our technologies are literally transforming us into hybrid technological beings, changing the ways in which we relate to our bodies, experience our environment, and communicate with others.

Popular writing about future technology is also characterized by an ambient and pervasive sense of apocalypticism. Writers such as Ray Kurzweil (2000) propose a "transhuman" future in which advanced technologies help people overcome the limits of the body or the self, while Hans Moravec (2000) offers visions of the evolution of robotic intelligence. While some of this work is based on contemporary technology and research and helps popularize questions of machine intelligence, nanotechnology, and biologically based systems research, it also presents heroic or exaggerated visions of science and traffics in transcendentalist notions. Fantasies of uploading one's consciousness into networks or databases, of memories or selves surviving in virtual space, of discarding the human body, of enhancing or radically altering biology, of eternal life through cryonic preservation of the body, and so on reveal a deep-seated desire for nonembodied presence—for a kind of virtual self that is immune to the conditions of reality.

Such approaches also, in effect, absorb elements of the science fiction tradition, which they transpose into a future reality of robotic evolution, robot-human competition, and an increasingly robotized or instrumental world—a world that they do not necessarily critique or problematize. In science fiction, stories that present the cryonic preservation of the body emerged as early as the end of the nineteenth century, while notions of enhancing the human body through technological means so that it could survive in space and on other planets appear in fiction throughout the twentieth and twenty-first centuries, often presenting accurate visions of cybernetic transformation, as in Frederick Pohl's *Man Plus* (1976/2011). Jacked-in and virtual selves are a staple of science fiction writing and feature prominently in cyberpunk work by writers such as

William Gibson, Bruce Sterling, Pat Cadigan, and Neal Stephenson (McCaffery, 1991). In fact, science fiction literature often offers a more serious exploration of contemporary conditions of technological possibility and future trends than many popular technoculture works presented as nonfiction. Current science fiction explores biotechnology and genetically engineered crops and animal species, as in Paolo Bacigalupi's *The Windup Girl* (2010), with deep awareness of the far-reaching implications of contemporary experiments and debates.

In contrast to the desire for disembodiment implicit in transhumanist research, current research in robotics accentuates the importance of situated and embodied knowledge. Rodney Brooks (2003), for example, alerts us to the potential of designing with an eye to specific and practical robotics applications, learning from the natural world and from biological organizational principles. His ideas about swarms of robots, to name one strand of his work, are based on observation of insect activities (Figure 9.2). Instead of positing that a robot has to have a cognitive mapping of the world or that it must possess some aspects of will and judgment before acting, Brooks offers a profound insight about how simple and specific actions conducted in programmed sequence can become effective on a larger scale.[1] Action and cognition are embodied and interrelated in this approach; in fact, it may be action that predates or inspires cognition rather than the other way around. Both the design of such robots and their functionality avoid apocalyptic tendencies and also avoid anthropomorphic stylizations and grand claims about humans becoming robots or robots becoming human.

In popular media, discussions of robotics tend to mix fiction and reality, to present unchallenged continuities among ancient and premodern inventions; fictional, imaginary, and cinematic robots; and actual contemporary robots. Time lines that trace a prehistory for modern robotics may include a range of older mechanical contraptions, from the ancient pneumatic automata of Hero of Alexandria in the first century CE—which used liquids, pressure, and steam in order to open doors or move objects in secular and religious settings—to the famous eighteenth-century performances of complex human-form clockwork automata that could play musical instruments, draw, and write. In addition to objects with legitimate links to technological processes, some of the artifacts included in such listings may be mythical or apocryphal, their technological properties having been exaggerated or misreported.

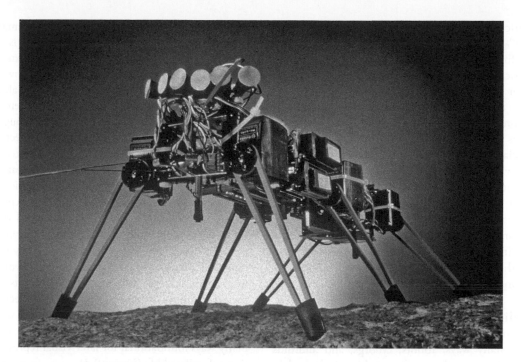

Fig. 9.2 Robot designed by Rodney Brooks, featured in the documentary *Fast, Cheap & Out of Control* (Errol Morris, 1997). Credit: Sony Pictures Classics/Photofest. © Sony Pictures Classics. Photo: Nubuar Alexanian.

Historians of science strive to complicate these approaches by exploring the relationship between premodern and modern approaches to the concept of artificial life (Kang, 2010; Riskin, 2007). Despite extensive contextualizing work in the history and theory of science, popular media insist on grand and often unexamined genealogies. The cumulative effect of this approach is that any number and type of entities may be presented as precursors of modern robots; this creates a problematic teleological tendency in which earlier experiments and historical contexts are either misunderstood or discussed as if they had all clearly led to the current state of robotics. The result is an often anachronistic and ahistorical tendency to describe all kinds of premodern and early modern myths, fictions, allegories, and technological processes as if they were contributing to an eternal dream, the dream of creating artificial life through technological means. Although pervasive and resonant in modernity, such notions of artificial animation are very different from their ritual and mythic counterparts of earlier eras.

In mainstream media we also see the tendency to publicize popular research projects, high-profile robot prototypes and robotic toys, in order to promise the future development of actual work-related robots, all the while mostly ignoring many practical applications as well as the industrial robots in existence today and industrial robotics as a marketplace. Popular publications favor apocalyptic claims and anthropomorphic designs that operate in an implicitly gothic continuum in which robots are designed as imitations of human form and performance. Despite the fact that they get a certain amount of attention from the popular press, some of these projects must be recognized as being artistic and sculptural rather than robotic, closer to long-familiar puppets, animatronic structures, and remote-controlled dolls than to contemporary computing. Many are public relations events in which a specialty robot promotes the research aspirations or capabilities of a particular company without necessarily representing these capabilities in technological terms. Actual industrial applications that do not conform to such anthropomorphic performance tenets also get less public exposure despite their importance and efficacy. Automotive factories have long been radically automated, robots are central to packaging and palletizing industrial processes, while robotics and automation applications in materials handling are changing the way research in biotechnology is conducted.[2] Despite the precision and versatility of these applications and their potential for revolutionizing research and industry, such real robotic innovations are less familiar to the general public.[3] Depictions and performances of symbolic robotics appropriate the popular meanings of "the robot"—as these have been defined over time by fiction, film, and popular culture—in ways that actual robotics usually do not.

For research in affective computing, the tendency to mix fictional and actual research and to interpret ancient and premodern experiments as tokens of an unbroken focus on artificial bodies, artificial life, or robotic futurity confuses the issue of how to distinguish the fictional power of robotics fantasies from the everyday power and potential of human-machine interactions in real-world contexts. Tracing the fictional tradition in a more self-conscious way instead allows us to recognize the ways in which the contemporary vernacular may miss the point of what robots embody, both in fiction and potentially in reality.

Intelligent Machines in Science Fiction

In many ways, robots, cyborgs, and androids are the latest products of a transhistorical trend in human culture, a fascination with imagining the animation of artificial bodies that characterizes both modern and ancient myths and texts. Some ancient origin stories indeed depict the creation of people as such a scene of animation, in which an inanimate body—made of clay, earth, stone, wood, and other natural materials—is animated by gods through their own breath or touch but also through fire, incantations, divine body fluids, or other mysterious powers. Later stories return to the patterns of ancient animations and warn of the dangers of such processes when they are disconnected from ritual settings and spiritual discipline. In golem stories for example, a rabbi or group of initiates may animate a man of clay through incantation and ritual, but they may lose control of this supersized servant if they do not follow precise instructions (Baer, 2012; Idel, 1990; Scholem, 1996).

Modern stories and films depict similar animating scenes, orchestrated by aspiring scientists or mystics, and featuring bodies made of deceased body parts, metals, plastics, complex electronic circuitry, or mysterious "positronic" brains. It is important to note that modern animating scenes usually avoid natural materials such as clay, wood, or stone, instead displaying a preference for human and animal body parts, as in the case of the creature in Mary Shelley's *Frankenstein or The Modern Prometheus* (1818), as well as technological materials and mechanical and electric processes. Victor Frankenstein's monster in the novel is composed of scavenged human and perhaps also animal remains, while his stitched-together supersized body is animated by an undisclosed process that later texts and films translate into electrical spectacles powered by lightning. Partly alchemical or apocryphal, the process by which the monster is animated remains mysterious and invisible in the novel, although it has become increasingly visible, visually spectacular and technological as the book was adapted for visual media, first for the stage and then, repeatedly, for cinema. Early film depictions of animation, as in the expressionist film *The Golem* (Paul Wegener, 1920), may follow a mystical and alchemical visual vocabulary, while the classic film *Frankenstein* (James Whale, 1931) presents a more overtly technological view of the animating process, devoid of magical and kabbalistic symbolism despite its own pseudoscientific bubbling liquids and electrical spectacles. The monster's physicality and the scenes of the monster's animation in *Frankenstein* are in many ways foundational for later visual representations of artificial life (Figure 9.3).

Shelley's novel offers an evocative portrait of an artificial person's experience in the monster's awakening and education, his quest for recognition and acceptance, and his constant rejection by the people around him. Partly because of its fractured and complex point of view, the novel remains pivotal for later narratives of artificial beings and for the kinds of emotions we associate with artificial life. The monster's violence anticipates depictions of violent robots, while his quest for acceptance resonates with existential narratives of artificial people in the twentieth and twenty-first centuries. Contemporary critical approaches to the novel also complicate the popular stereotype of Victor Frankenstein as a hubristic or "overreaching" scientist: despite its currency in popular culture, this depiction of Victor as a man who aims to play God does not occur in the novel's first edition, published in 1818. Mary Shelley added a moralistic thread of commentary to the agnostic tone of the novel when she revised the book for the 1831 edition, and most of the passages that characterize Victor's quest as unholy or sacrilegious stem from these revisions.[4]

It is important to remember that if one aspect of the novel's poignancy revolves around scientific aspirations and unforeseen results, a second aspect, equally important, revolves around the novel's depiction of social exclusion and injustice. In the novel, the monster is an eloquent and forceful critic of the limited ways in which humanity is defined, while in later theatrical and cinematic adaptations

Fig. 9.3 Publicity materials and popular culture stereotypes highlight the iconic physicality of the monster (Boris Karloff) in *Frankenstein* (James Whale, 1931). © Universal Pictures.

the monster is silent, a hulking form of surprising emotional sensitivity. Although the stereotypical treatment of the monster in popular media may begin from people's fear of his radical otherness, he is in fact a very sympathetic character. The affective power of the monster in popular culture hinges on depictions of his silent pathos, which become recognizable as registers of the creature's disenfranchisement and abuse despite the absence of the fiery rhetoric and sustained ideological critique of social injustice we find in the novel. The monster's silence and his embodiment of abjection resonate with long-standing sentimental and lyrical traditions, in which giving voice to inanimate or mute entities occasions powerful emotional responses for readers or viewers. In the 1931 film, scenes of persecution, in which the monster is confused, lost, hurt, or hunted, may be followed by scenes of silent longing, in which the monster responds to music or beauty or seeks understanding with children, whose innocence matches his own (Figure 9.4). Despite his uncanny appearance and his potential for violence, the monster remains a creature of sympathy for most of the film, as the viewer's allegiance shifts

from the human characters to the nonhuman but understandable and even archetypal pathos of the abused and rejected monster.

As an entity in contemporary culture, the mechanical person or robot emerges in a multitude of texts and films in the early twentieth century. In addition to figures we might recognize as precursors, such as the Tin Man from L. Frank Baum's Oz stories originally published in the 1900s, it is in the 1920s that robots become vernacular, emerging in Karel Čapek's 1921 play *R.U.R. (Rossum's Universal Robots)*. The internationally successful play introduced the term *robot*, from the word *robota*—which means "work" in Slovak and "forced labor" in Czech—to describe the androidlike manufactured workers of the Rossum factory. Designed as perfect servants and workers, cheap, efficient, and expendable, the Robots (which Čapek capitalizes) eventually revolt, kill the engineers who designed them, and destroy human civilization. Spectacles of mechanization and modern life also emerge in Fritz Lang's *Metropolis* (1926) and its stirring images of the animation of an artificial person, a

Fig. 9.4 Two kinds of innocence: the monster (Boris Karloff) and Little Maria (Marilyn Harris) in *Frankenstein* (James Whale, 1931). © Universal Pictures.

robotic woman who acts as an agent of disorder but also represents sexual energy and primitive passion (Elsaesser, 2008; Huyssen, 1982). The film engages a visual and narrative vocabulary of revolution: The oppressed workers of Metropolis are depicted as little more than cogs in the giant machinery of the city, figuratively devoured by the machines they operate. Stirred into revolution by the robotic Maria, who acts as a provocateur, the workers unleash incredible violence until the rulers of the city agree to a new balance of power. In the allegorical language of the film, compassion—the heart—brokers a new unity between capital and labor, between the brain and the hands. Both *R.U.R.* and *Metropolis* depict robotic beings that embody our cultural fascination with machines even as they allegorize or bemoan the position of the worker in industrial capitalism.

By the middle of the 1930s, robot figures play the roles of both golemlike protectors and terrifying enemies. Classic robots are often imagined as having metal bodies and electronic (or "positronic") brains, no capacity for emotion, and little social and cultural understanding. The quintessential robots of Isaac Asimov's *I, Robot*, a series of short stories

written between 1940 and 1950, are oversized, metallic, superlogical, unemotional, and generally clearly nonhuman despite their attempts to make a logical claim to human status. Robots are often depicted as supersoldiers, superworkers, or super-slaves, as their exaggerated body stature, association with industrial and military environments, and material connections to machinery and metal surfaces evoke a nineteenth-century "cog and wheel" aesthetic. On more intimate terms, robotic bodies are characterized by an absence of or even an aversion to body fluids, emotional attachments, and sexual experience. In addition, mechanical bodies implicitly propose that compartmentalized functions and replaceable body parts render one invulnerable or provide an antidote to death. The classic robot's usual dependence on logical propositions and explanations extends this desire for compartmentalization to language as well.

Despite the presence of advanced electronics in robot stories, our fascination with classic robots pivots on their mechanical presence—their bodily otherness. Beloved film robots, such as Robby in *Forbidden Planet* (Fred M. Wilcox, 1956), or Gort in *The Day the Earth Stood Still* (Robert Wise, 1951), are recognizable and familiar in their trademarked body presence. The emphasis on exaggerated stature and metal surfaces has been replaced in recent years by smaller robot styles and new materials, but the association with overt technological registers persists. In the recent film *I, Robot* (Alex Proyas, 2004), for example, the robots are depicted through a material vocabulary of translucency, white plastic surfaces, and ethereal blue lights—a vocabulary that directly evokes the design of Apple Computers. Both old and new aesthetic traditions are also present in *WALL-E* (Andrew Stanton, 2008), with one robot, WALL-E, rendered in a dirty and dingy version of the traditional industrial paradigm, while the other, EVE, embodies the ideals and pleasures of contemporary design, its seamless opacity contrasting sharply with the rivets and joints of WALL-E's classic industrial looks.

What is most important to note about the narrative and visual patterns of representing intelligent machines is that they align visual representation with narrative function. What a certain type of artificial person can do or evoke in a text is closely related to how this being looks and is represented visually. The issue is not whether artificial people succeed or fail based on their successful imitation of human appearance but that each type of visual and physical depiction has certain associated fantasies

and capacities. The robot's body type structures the text, in other words. For example, the design of classic robots externalizes an important relationship with industrial technology, and insists on establishing visually the distinction between human and nonhuman status. Even when a text shows a narrative investment in transcending this boundary, the visual and material choices of robot stylization often offer an intuitive solution to the problems of distinction. We see this pattern in *The Bicentennial Man* (Chris Columbus, 1999), the film based on an award-winning novella by Isaac Asimov (1976). Andrew, the robot protagonist, fights for 200 years to acquire a series of rights, such as the right to own his own labor, to wear clothes, to own property and so on. Regardless of the sympathetic tone of the text and despite the consistent focus on rights rather than ontological categories, Andrew's metal exterior offers an easy and intuitive distinction between people and robots for the audience: We cannot help but recognize immediately who is what. Indeed, the robot's visible difference registers everybody around him as more clearly and reliably human (Figure 9.5). It is only after Andrew undertakes to modify his own body to become more humanlike that he is even marginally eligible to acquire full human rights. Both his exterior appearance and his interior organs are gradually transformed, and in

Fig. 9.5 The contrast between human and robot in *The Bicentennial Man* (Chris Columbus, 1999). Even after the robot Andrew (Robin Williams) has acquired the right to wear clothes, he is clearly distinguishable from his human owner, Richard Martin (Sam Neill).

Credit: Buena Vista/ Photofest. © Buena Vista Pictures.

the end he decides to allow his body to decline so that he will fully qualify as human as he dies.

When they are depicted as metallic or oversized, robots cannot "pass for human," and passing for human is a recurring textual element in stories that feature artificial people. While marginally more passable in terms of their humanlike exterior, androids are similarly distinguishable from the human norm. One could argue that robots and androids are "born" together and share similar limitations, since Čapek's *R.U.R.* depicts mechanical beings that are technically androids. Humanlike in their general physicality, the artificial people of *R.U.R.* display verbal rigidity, and stilted, mechanical body language—behaviors that differentiate them from the human norm. Since then, the physical depiction of androids has included a mechanical or electronic interior covered by a layer of latex, artificial skin, or other material that gives them a humanlike exterior. But the androids' often unnatural skin tone, lack of facial expression, rigid body language, and overall demeanor still render them clearly *other* in many texts. Androids are often inept at dealing with humor, emotion, sexuality, and human culture in general and have trouble with ethical dilemmas.

Traditionally, fictional robots and androids are often designed as artificial servants, soldiers, or workers. In the Čapekian vein, such robots are poised to revolt and overturn the social status quo, functioning as figures of a repressed proletariat or slave worker class. In the Asimovian vein, such revolt is thwarted by the design of robots with built-in ethical safeguards, superlogical intellectual styles, and limited initiative. Asimov's "Three Laws of Robotics," now widely but unevenly dispersed in contexts other than science fiction, offset an imagined amplification of robotic action and autonomy with the assurance that such power would not be used against human life. Although aspects of the "Three Laws of Robotics" are mentioned in earlier stories by Asimov and other writers, Asimov articulated their generally accepted form with John W. Campbell, then editor of *Astounding Science Fiction*, and included them for the first time in the 1942 story "Runaround."[5] These laws are as follows:

1. A robot may not injure a human being or, through inaction, allow a human being to come to harm.
2. A robot must obey orders given it by human beings except where such orders would conflict with the First Law.

3. A robot must protect its own existence as long as such protection does not conflict with the First or Second Law.

In his Foundation novels of the 1950s, Asimov eventually also added the "Zeroth Law," which partly allows a robot to harm a human in the service of a more abstract notion of humanity. The law was eventually expressed as: "0. A robot may not injure humanity, or, through inaction, allow humanity to come to harm."

While the two modes of imagining robots, as enemies or as helpers, often complicate each other, they can help to identify dominant styles and preoccupations in different historical periods of the last fifty years. While robots in science fiction often express existential concerns, becoming vehicles for evocative and poignant explorations of what it means to be human or nonhuman (in the Asimovian tradition), the ominous robot or cyborg that is running amuck and is about "to get us," echoing some of Čapek's concerns, has also enjoyed widespread appeal throughout the twentieth and twenty-first centuries (Telotte, 1995). Visual representational styles contribute to such variations. After the 1980s, for example, fictional robots were often depicted as more humanlike, with synthetic skin and eyes and a human demeanor, but they were also more violent. In science fiction films of the 1990s, cybernetic entities that combine computer-related intellectual power with robot-related mechanical and metallic interiors and a humanlike visual presence are depicted as more dangerous and ominous because of their hybridity. They can think and act autonomously, pass for human, and still possess the mechanical qualities of the unfeeling and indestructible imaginary robots of long ago.

Memorable android characters such as Commander Data (Brent Spiner) on *Star Trek: The Next Generation* (aired 1987–1994) embody the combination of anthropomorphic aspirations and subtle visual distancing that characterize android representations in general. Commander Data is portrayed with an unnatural skin tone, yellow eyes, and a special kind of gaze, inquisitive but also impassive and impersonal (Figure 9.6). Despite his success in the Fleet, his long-lasting friendships and insightful cultural interpretations, he always remains somewhat removed from human status. In a sustained narrative strand that recurs throughout the seven seasons of the popular series, Data's poignant quests to understand and attain full humanity reveal the ever more subtle ways in which humanity is defined

Fig. 9.6 Commander Data (Brent Spiner) in *Star Trek: The Next Generation* (Season 2, 1988–1989).

Credit: Paramount/Photofest. © Paramount.

as being beyond his reach. And in contrast to the expressive simplicity and matter-of-factness of most classic robots, Commander Data experiences his difference from humans with some wistfulness. He is aware that it is precisely in terms of emotion and affect that he differs from people, and he often tries to intellectualize, abstract, or just plainly imitate the emotions that he lacks. Humanity in this case is defined in terms of emotional range, with humor, guilt, anger, love, resentment, and other complex emotions and psychological states presented as unavailable to Data. His human and alien friends also find these emotions difficult to explain or describe. Feeling thus emerges as a natural, innate, or embodied aspect of being—an aspect that resists adequate description and cannot be learned or imitated.

In other texts, such as *Alien* (Ridley Scott, 1979) and the *Alien* franchise in general, android characters present different problems precisely because of their closeness to the human form. They may live and work near humans but follow orders and directives from corporations or computer programs

that endanger human life or consider humans as obstacles to corporate goals. Despite their proximity to humans, androids in these stories do not share human goals, acting instead like the proverbial "wolf in sheep's clothing": The very fact of the android's ability to partly pass for human leads to this paranoid scenario, as the android's ill-fitting human form becomes a stand-in for its dubious aims and renders it inauthentic. If the reigning vocabulary for robots revolves around emptiness, being empty of feeling and flesh, the basic android modality revolves around paranoia, with androids being just passable and versatile enough to endanger human values.

Although the representation of computers as characters in such fictions is not standardized, they are also frequently structured by their distinct kind of embodiment or their lack of a body. Especially in the 1970s and 1980s, a computer's lack of embodied specificity and its association with electronic networks tended to create even more paranoid narratives, in which a computer intelligence might control objects and people from afar, as in *Demon Seed* (Donald Cammell, 1977), or could become pervasively powerful and ever present precisely because it was able to travel through electronic networks. By not being specifically embodied and located *somewhere*, computer-based entities inspire the fear that they are instead *everywhere*. The paranoid strand of such narratives often involves questions of surveillance and the loss of privacy and frequently returns to the instabilities of disembodiment, a tendency fueled by a perennial fascination with the parameters of the Turing test, in which the task of distinguishing between human and mechanical operators is complicated by the presumed impersonality of disembodied and mediated communication. In novels such as Richard Powers's *Galatea 2.2* (1995), the lack of physicality in the mode of communication between the human operator and the artificial intelligence he trains facilitates massive processes of projection, in which language itself emerges as a medium.

Finally, the humanlike bodies of fictional cyborgs bring such figures closest to human status, but their capacity for violence, their relative indestructibility, and their resistance to pain still render them clearly nonhuman in other ways. As a theoretical concept, the Cyborg (short for "cybernetic organism") was described in 1960 by Manfred E. Clynes and Nathan S. Kline in a paper outlining the adjustments that might be made to the human body to enable astronauts and other explorers to survive in hostile environments (Gray, 1995). In contrast to this fundamentally human-form Cyborg (a term which the authors capitalize), the cyborgs of science fiction are often depicted as superstrong, exaggeratedly physical beings "clothed" in humanlike forms but supremely resilient, focused, indestructible, and often dangerous or lethal. In films such as *The Terminator* (James Cameron, 1984), the cyborg character's ability to pass for human is a source of anxiety, while its association with machinery is allegorized in behavioral patterns such as repetition, relentlessness, and lack of emotion. Indeed, the cyborg's indifference to the emotions and pain of others registers to viewers as cruelty. By the end of the film the human form has burned away from the metal skeleton of the cyborg, returning the text to the representational parameters of robotic fictions that enact the difference between the metal presence of nonhuman entities and the fleshy vulnerability of human characters. The human form in these cases enables a range of action and emotion that includes aggression, violence, and the use of slang language, in contrast to Asimov's original robots and their superethical directives.

With more lifelike bodies come more humanlike dilemmas and ethical complexities. In the implicit opposition these narratives suggest, the intense focus on rationality that robots embody contrasts sharply with the ostensibly more human qualities of emotional and moral unpredictability. A cyborg's ability to act in emotionally unpredictable and ethically complicated ways crosses a certain implicit threshold that separates human from nonhuman action. In addition, cyborg bodies are more overtly gendered and in exaggerated ways, with male cyborgs appearing as oversized, muscular, and supermasculine and female cyborgs as sexualized and often sexually exploited by the narrative. Tracing the gender implications of these robotic bodies is very important. While robots and androids may be presented as if they were nongendered or gender-neutral, they usually have a gendered demeanor or gendered voice. And while artificial men are often not presented as sexual beings, artificial women are marked by their sexuality, either in terms of a conventional and compliant hyperfemininity, as in Lester del Rey's classic short story "Helen O'Loy" (1938) and the android wives in *The Stepford Wives* (Bryan Forbes, 1975) or, in more recent decades, in terms of a dangerous sexuality and pinup looks. The female cyborg characters of the reimagined *Battlestar Galactica* (Ron Moore and David Eick, 2004–2009), for example, are depicted

as dangerous or even lethal partly because of their sex appeal and are presented as sexually active in ways we don't often find in the depiction of male cyborgs (Figure 9.7).

For robotic and artificial beings, associations between body type and narrative function thus revolve around certain selections for particular materials, linguistic patterns, or professional connections for different types of artificial persons. While each new text partly revises this tradition, there are substantial continuities in such treatments, which allow us to theorize the artificial body as a body that channels certain consistent desires or trends in contemporary popular culture. In broad historical strokes, these representational patterns can be considered as coalescing in a classic mode, roughly evolving in the period from the 1920s to the 1960s and extending to the 1980s, and a more existential, alternative, revised, self-conscious, or postmodern tradition that dominates representations of fictional nonhumans in science fiction literature after the 1960s, especially in the work of Philip K. Dick, for example. This second style becomes a major mode for the depiction of artificial beings in science fiction cinema after the 1980s. Although the two modes interconnect in contemporary texts, theorizing them in this schema can provide a rough outline for the discursive choices that inform the design of new artificial bodies. Precisely because body difference and visual representation function so centrally in the classic tradition, texts that eliminate embodied differentiators open different questions. The existential strand of texts reverses the certainties of the classic paradigm by destabilizing structures of discernment.

Texts that return to the blurry existential terrain popularized by *Blade Runner* (Ridley Scott, 1982), for example, recalibrate the tendency of depictions of artificial people to enable intuitive distinctions between human and nonhuman. The lingering relevance of *Blade Runner* indeed pivots on its treatment of conflicting desires: On the one hand, the text presents the imperative to find and exterminate the Replicants, whose presence on Earth destabilizes the social order. The need to distinguish between real people and Replicants thus becomes urgent and has high stakes, since it makes the difference between living and dying for those identified as Replicants. On the other hand, however, the text removes all simple or intuitive differentiators that would allow viewers to safely allocate the human. Depicted as being virtually indistinguishable from regular people, the Replicants also possess complex memories

Fig. 9.7 Publicity image of two of the humanoid Cylon women of *Battlestar Galactica* (Sci Fi Season 2, Fall 2005). Number 6 (Tricia Helfer) embodies the fantasy of the sexy artificial woman, while in her numerous incarnations Number 8 (Grace Park) has played the role of a fighter, a saboteur, a human defender, and a mother figure in the show.

Credit: Sci Fi Channel/Photofest © Sci Fi Photographer: Justic Stevens.

and desires and experience sexual and emotional ties that cannot be discarded as mere imitations (Neale, 1989). By the end of the story, instead of producing a sense of order, the film further destabilizes the human, especially in the "Director's Cut" version that implies that Deckard (Harrison Ford), the policeman who has been charged with making these life-and-death decisions, may also be a Replicant (Brooker, 2006; Bukatman, 2012).

While the classic science fictional paradigm of the artificial human safeguards some vestiges of the human through implicit textual strategies, the existential strand exemplified in *Blade Runner* undermines the possibility of locating the differences between human and nonhuman. It is no coincidence, of course, that this existential strand deploys artificial people who are thoroughly human-looking and human-acting: Their bodies are clearly marked in terms of gender, race, ethnicity, and age, and they display expert use of human language and a coherent understanding of cultural institutions. Their ability to fully pass for human plays a major role in their existential potential. Films

such as *Ghost in the Shell* (Mamoru Oshii, 1995), *A.I. Artificial Intelligence* (Steven Spielberg, 2001), and television series such as the reimagined *Battlestar Galactica* similarly get much of their emotional power from the fact that they present us with artificial characters that are in many respects equivalent to the real humans of their respective worlds. They also depict the artificial person in urgent and far-reaching identity quests, in which attaining human status is no longer a matter of logic, calculation, or behavior but of emotion and embodied experience. The power of such texts lies precisely in their deployment and understanding of humanity not as a state but as a becoming: While ambiguous and perhaps confusing, the existential terrain that opens up when a text does not safely distinguish between the human and the nonhuman allows us to experience the human as a negotiation rather than as a state of being.

Interface Fantasies

Even this short typology of artificial people and intelligent machines in fiction, film, science fiction, and popular culture reveals the ways in which the body type and physical design of an artificial being, a robot, android, computer, or cyborg structures both its narrative potential and its emotional predisposition. This is not a deterministic schema because, as with everything in popular culture, new texts and films have the potential to revise and alter established paradigms. And while the examples offered here are mostly drawn from western media and literary traditions, many of the basic tendencies of the depiction of robots, cyborgs, and intelligent machines are found in texts from other traditions as well, often translated or transformed as they are adapted for use in different cultural contexts. In Japanese popular culture, for example, the robotic body has become a prime expressive locus for work in literature, cinema, manga, comics, anime, and art. Cultural differences, literary heritage, and historical context transform the tenets of the basic discursive paradigms into forms more aligned with these new contexts (Lunning, 2008).

The longevity of certain tendencies and stereotypes (robots as unemotional, cyborgs as dangerous) also offers important insights about the cultural expectations and fantasies associated with these fictional characters—expectations that may exert a latent influence on cultural assumptions about technologies and mechanisms. The relationship between fiction and reality is again paradoxical even for entities such as computers, which do exist in some form in contemporary contexts. For example, advanced computer systems in fiction and film usually do not exhibit the strict adherence to well-formed commands required in actual programming. Instead, they have often been depicted as able to interpret fuzzy commands or infer implied meanings, and this long before real-language flexibility or intuitive interfaces were technologically possible. In fiction, the computer seems to have absolute versatility and absolute access. Fictional depictions of present and future technology often presume that all aspects of life have been translated into packets of information, into data, and these data have already been digitized, codified, and rendered searchable without the expenditure of human labor for this process, without delay, and without gaps in coverage. Films such as *Minority Report* (Steven Spielberg, 2002) wow us with stunning depictions of interface design, presenting visions of an interface that is absolutely responsive and intuitive, that never resists the formulation or range of a command, never requires clarification, and never fails. In such depictions of future technology, the interface is partly dematerialized, transparent, present as spectacle, but never present as boundary, threshold, or challenge. It both is and is not there. And if the interface is experienced as being there, as a *something* and not just as a facilitating *nothing*, then it is depicted as either superbly subservient or as ominous and dangerous, as another entity or will within the system.

Similarly, depictions of a particular technology in fiction and film tend to ignore the material conditions required for its operation. It is as if a computer could access all information without any restrictions, without any interference that might arise from its design, power demands, or the state of local and global networks and infrastructure. In the disaster film *2012* (Roland Emmerich, 2009), for example, cell phones still work even while the surface of the world is melting into lava and massive earthquakes and tsunamis destroy Earth's land masses. We value and advertise technologies for the mobility they give our lives, but in the process we might forget that the technological objects themselves are bound by their design capabilities and operational needs. The scale of these needs is now so expansive as to be almost unfathomable, extending to the state of power sources, cables, servers, and routers in faraway places, the range of communication satellites floating in space, the actions of governmental structures and regulatory agencies, and the effects of political conditions around the world. In fact, the more dispersed that our networks of interrelated technologies become, the less cognizant we are of their practical limits and material requirements in our daily lives. The human labor required to ensure their operation is especially overlooked, in an implicit extension of the tendency toward dematerialization: Because advanced machines promise and often deliver access from everywhere, we forget that their operations depend on entities that are in fact somewhere and are invented, operated, and maintained by someone. People often describe advanced technology in terms of magic, but the technological dream is in fact partly a dream of dematerialization, in which both the technological object and the laborer disappear. Fictions of robotic and automated worlds feed the desire for action without labor even as they then allegorize and personalize the laborer in the body of the robot or android.

We must understand this affective tendency in the popular imaginary because it can explain why actual technologies are so fundamentally frustrating. If the fantasy of the ideal technology tends toward dematerialization, the ideal technological event would combine desire and action seamlessly, as if action could result from mere thinking, mere wishing. In this schema, *any* expenditure of energy to program or operate a machine may be felt or imagined as being too much, especially compared with the infinite abilities and nonexistent requirements of machines in fiction. The sense of frustration with technology and the dream of dematerialization it implies are familiar in everyday life, an emotional rubric that structures people's responses to mechanical operation and human-machine interactions. Put in a simplified and schematic way, in addition to its other goals, research in affective computing aims to redirect the expenditure of labor by imagining solutions that allow the machine to absorb more or different aspects of the labor involved in interacting with it. The promise of affective computing is that users will have to do less to ensure fluid and satisfying interactions with a technology because—by adapting its operations to match the dynamic pace of the human world and the ever-changing reactions of human users—the technology has the ability to meet them more than halfway.

Emotional Patterns

Given the fact that technological fantasies traffic in the promise of the absolute absence of labor, would we want our machines to have more presence, more personality? This question fuels the sarcastic representation of technology in Douglas Adams's *The Hitchhiker's Guide to the Galaxy*, where everyday machines are designed with "Genuine People Personalities" in the form of perennially and annoyingly cheerful automatic doors as well as Marvin the Paranoid Android, not so much paranoid as severely depressed. What we need to recognize here is the distinction between responsiveness, which might be desirable in a machine because it might enhance its interactions with a human user, and characterization, which is what we respond to with fictional robots but would probably find problematic in a machine we intend to use. Although Marvin is a spoof on the science fictional tradition for robots and androids, intelligent machines are never merely responsive or impersonal in fiction and film and are usually highly individualized. They are characters, memorable because of their personalities rather than their mechanical functions.

Consider, for example, the emotional responsiveness and range of the main *Star Wars* robots R2-D2 and C-3PO. Given the emotional patterns of the classic tradition, which tends to present robots as unemotional, these are highly unusual robots and quite individual. While in the company of human characters, C-3PO seems more stilted and command-driven than when he is with other robots, although his insistence on explanations occasionally makes him annoying to humans, aliens, and robots alike. He is articulate, almost verbose, but also nerdy, slightly neurotic in his insistence on detail, whiny and chatty during hard times, and especially talkative when he is stressed and fearful, which happens often, as dangerous situations render him almost hysterical. Despite this versatility, he often seems unable to understand the human characters' motives, and this serves as a narrative device, as his bewilderment allows people and robots to explain things to him and thus to the viewers. In contrast and despite the presumably utilitarian simplicity of his design, R2-D2 is emotionally perceptive and adept at figuring out what is going on at any given point in the story. Indeed, R2-D2 can register, interpret, and anticipate the emotional needs of the human characters. The little robot's many clicking, whirring, and beeping noises are so perfectly suited to the context that they become their own language, and the robot's ability to understand and react is sometimes more direct and effective than what we see as the emotional range of the human characters. Taken together, the two robots play a central role in the narrative: They often express the emotional content of a situation that the human characters are unable or unwilling to articulate; they explain or externalize aspects of the story that may be confusing for viewers; and they express the sense of danger or fear at a particular moment that the characters disavow or that the action-driven narrative bypasses. In fact, despite their physical depiction as robots, they act out exactly the kinds of questions that a child or young viewer would ask in order to grasp the flow of the story. In addition to being the sidekicks of the main human characters, they anticipate the viewer's emotions and questions.

The humor or poignancy of these depictions of robotic characters stems from the way in which they identify just how limited and specific the emotions one expects from a mechanical entity are, how funny it is to hear C3PO whine about the rough terrain, or how unexpected it is to hear Marvin, designed as a classic android servant, complain about the menial tasks he is asked to perform. These dense characterizations break with the overall tendency to depict intelligent machines as obedient, reliable, and predictable. Some of the other common emotional stereotypes we find in fictional depictions of simpler machines include cheerfulness or mindlessness, relentlessness, the inability to stop or change course, repetitiveness, and lack of contact or connection with the environment. The distinction between action (which can be preprogrammed) and intention (which implies will or choice) is often manipulated in fictional media to create gothic effects, as in the depiction of the dangerous androids of *Westworld* (Michael Crichton, 1973), in which a gunslinger robot pursues and kills people in the high-tech adventure park. The killing spree may just be the result of a malfunction, but the emotional effect follows the classic "robot running amok" theme, which in science fiction literature and film is also related to the fear of racial uprising or class warfare.

Popular media may use the figure of the robot as a stereotype of automation, efficiency, mindlessness, and automatism. This in a way enables a definition of the human as impulsive, poetic, creative, and messy. In fiction, science fiction, and cinema, these fantasies are projective and dynamic, as any figuration of the robot also creates a figuration of what the human would be. Robots, androids, cyborgs, and other fictional intelligent machines open a narrative space for projection and are rather dynamic as characters despite their often stilted body language and limited emotional range. Even figures that are designed not to experience or express emotion can be read in emotional ways, and such characters often inspire rather deep feelings—of fascination, recognition, pity, identification, compassion, or understanding in their audiences. For example, when a character such as Commander Data receives what humans might consider an insult and replies blithely "I am unable to feel that emotion," his emotional immunity inspires both his colleagues and the viewers of the show to feel the insult for him. At that moment we may, as viewers, feel sorry for this character, as he cannot experience an emotion we associate with complex humanity. But on the other hand, perhaps we create these kinds of characters because sometimes we crave emotional immunity and wish that we did not feel that emotion either. Wouldn't it be great if bullying, intimidation, discrimination, and other forms of emotional violence in our everyday lives could be brushed aside with "I am unable to feel that emotion"?

When machines display overt emotion in fiction and film, the effect can be destabilizing for the story and for readers or viewers. In *2001: A Space Odyssey* (Stanley Kubrick, 1968), for example, as the main computer system HAL malfunctions, it begins singing an old-fashioned love song ("Daisy Bell" written in 1892). This entity is responsible for the death of the crew of the spaceship and has been not just indifferent but criminally aggressive toward the human astronauts. And yet the resonance of the song in the empty spaceship and its association with the computer's last minutes of function give this moment human poignancy, especially since much of the rest of the film refrains from romantic, emotional, or sentimental registers. While HAL is a prime example of the worry that depending too much on technology may have unforeseen or deadly effects, the film treats the computer's disassembly as if it were a death, as the song presents a nostalgic or childlike perspective for an entity that never had a childhood. We do not know HAL's motivations or reasons—if there are any—but at this point it is hard to assign to his actions the simple label of "malfunction." In these last moments HAL acquires a kind of emotional humanity, albeit a confusing, murderous, or manipulative one, just through the song. And of course the song is saturated with emotion partly because it is presented through the use of a human voice for HAL, a breathy whisper, instead of a mechanical or computerized voice. We associate voice with emotion, voices are gendered and inflected, and singing is an emotional act.

Fictional media thus treat the representation of machines and emotion on two separate axes: The emotion that is represented as being felt by the machine itself is completely independent and may contrast sharply with the emotion that the representation produces in the audience. A very unemotional entity, an inanimate object, an unfeeling robot, an impersonal voice can become the vehicle for massive modes of emotional projection and trigger intense reactions in a human audience. We supply the emotion, we interpret the inanimate, the inarticulate, the unemotional as figures of pathos, we project ourselves into the emotional void or the silence of a mechanical or artificial entity. In addition to engaging with a fundamental lyrical or poetic premise that art, poetry, or language animate the inanimate, the desire to give voice to the silenced, or to read silence as oppression refers to historical precedents for negotiating important questions of human suffering and injustice, evoking the sentimental traditions and historical contexts of the eighteenth and nineteenth centuries and the legal and political struggles of that era for political representation, enfranchisement, justice, and the abolition of slavery. This tradition has paradoxical effects for the design of affective computing solutions, because such solutions often prioritize responsiveness and relatedness. Yet in fiction, the more inanimate, simple, and static an entity is, the more it can function as a figure of pathos. An independently responsive or active figure will receive a different treatment because it provides less room for the projective processes that work implicitly in these stories. We are more direct and perhaps even more confrontational with something that can talk back, whereas we may be emotionally or even unconsciously invested in silence and inaction because these qualities allow for narcissistic projection into the object.

Indeed, the personalities and emotions commonly associated with intelligent machines in fiction and film would be unnerving in real life because so many of the representations of such figures revolve around a depiction of pathos. They may not be as overtly depressed as Marvin the Paranoid Android, but artificial people such as the Replicants of *Blade Runner* or the cyborgs of *Ghost in the Shell* display a depressive tendency. They appear distant, melancholy, or disaffected and have a noir-ish or countercultural demeanor just by virtue of their complex characterization. Especially after the 1950s and 1960s, science fiction literature and film focus on the existential implications of ontological insecurity. Both paranoia and depression emerge as important emotional registers for human-looking artificial people as the characters experience the problem of knowing or not knowing what one is or whether one is surrounded by people or robots. In giving the artificial person a depressive and wistful affect, many contemporary texts counter the campiness of earlier cheerful robots but also enhance the impression of depth for these characters and add layers of psychological motivation or characterization.

Recognizing the effects of silence, voice, responsiveness, and projection is especially important for designers of affective computing and robotics applications. Designing a mechanical entity with anthropomorphic features and with a voice or with patterns of responsiveness may at first appear as a guarantee for imparting friendliness or openness. But human users are quite complex in their reactions to objects and to machines, and while a responsive design may inspire a sense of play or experimentation, the same design may become cumbersome or annoying when the focus of the user is more specifically utilitarian or when the task is complex. In an affective computing application, a tone that might appear friendly at first may not be trusted to guide or give instructions, or it may be experienced as slow or falsely cheerful as the user becomes more competent in navigating the interface. In human interactions, emotion is reciprocal and reacting to emotion is immediate and intuitive. A human helper can tell that you are in a hurry and may give instructions faster or decide to dispense with parts of the process. A person can tell that a word or term was not understood and may switch the style or tone of directions midsentence without making you feel ignorant. A person lives in the same real-world context as the user and might also feel the emotional weight or emotional content of a particular day or a particular part of the year. The subtlety and variety of human reactions is nothing short of overwhelming when seen in context, and all this is complicated further by cultural and historical factors and by the wide range of human differences and modes of demeanor or performance. Indeed, one important consideration for any affective computing project is that it may not be necessary or even desirable to try to replicate such versatility in machines. On an especially difficult or hurried day, the impersonality of a mechanical system may be reassuring. What may appear as impersonal or cold in one schema may be experienced as efficient or professional in another. And we should not forget that human cultures have a variety of patterns for understated emotion, scripted interaction, respectful distance, and established patterns of formality and social decorum. Such emotive tendencies may be more appropriate for use in the design of affective systems than the fully emotional behaviors we sometimes see robots display in fiction and film.

In addition, as the fictional and cinematic tradition implies, it may not be necessary to implement humanlike capacities for affective systems because capacities that are *not* humanlike can be both eloquent and efficacious: Human users can establish and sustain a wide range of relationships with machines and inanimate objects. Recent texts are more self-conscious about the nexus of projection, narcissism, and interrelatedness that informs our relationship to machines; this is partly because they take into consideration recent developments in robotics research. The short narratives of *Robot Stories* (Greg Pak, 2003), for example, offer thoughtful perspectives about what living with intelligent and emotionally responsive machines might entail, not because of what the machines will do but because of what humans might do. In one story a young couple requests permission to adopt a human child, but they must first learn to care for a robotic "baby" assigned to them by a government agency. Through the process of caring for the robot baby, they realize just how projection and selfishness become involved in the act of caring and are soon shocked to discover that they have subjected the robot to forms of emotional abuse they remember from their own childhoods. Similarly, the human fighter of *Real Steel* (Shawn Levy, 2011) creates a narcissistic bond with the boxing robot that has been repaired and retrained by his son. The human-robot interaction here is truly a form of mirroring, in which the robot is programmed and partly trained to replicate the exact motions of the human boxer. Instead of depicting the robot as a separate entity, an entity whose difference from the human might entail a kind of adaptation or confrontation with otherness, the robot is easily folded into the human boxer's ego, his love of boxing, his skill and craft. This robot functions as an extension of human ego in much the same way as the supersuits of *Iron Man* (Jon Favreau, 2008) facilitate Tony Stark's desires without ever becoming a boundary. These tales identify implicitly just how narcissistic our relationships with tools and machines might be, as they showcase how the human user's desire powers both human and robot.

The idea that human users project their desires onto robots also informs the story of *Robot and Frank* (Jake Schreier, 2012), in which Frank, a retired jewelry thief who is in the early stages of dementia or Alzheimer's disease, becomes friends with the robot that takes care of him (Figure 9.8). Frank teaches the robot to pick locks, and they go out on jewel heists together. This robot is designed according to contemporary projections about medical or household robots that would aid aging or ailing humans in the future, and its stylization,

body design, and functionality follow more or less realistic parameters. And since the robot as a character is portrayed in a more realistic way, the story also affirms how central the human user's desires are for the interaction between human and robot. By the end of the story, the robot suggests that its memory would have to be erased so that the police cannot prove the crimes of the two conspirators. The film creates poignant contrasts between Frank's failing memory and the robot's perfect memory; and between the robot's utilitarian suggestion about erasing the past and Frank's desire to hold on to all the actions and events that transform this robot into an individual, his friend. A fragile reciprocity emerges, as the robot possesses their shared memories in a way that Frank no longer can. As Frank's memories fade, the robot would be in the position of projecting this remembered shared identity back onto Frank.

As robotics applications become more familiar to the general public, the representation of robots and other intelligent machines in fiction and film changes. In some texts, the depiction of robots may tend toward realism, as fictional robots are designed to resemble or approximate what we now know to be possible (Gates, 2007; Goldberg, 2000; Goldberg and Siegwart 2002). Other texts remain free from such requirements and continue to engage and revise the literary and cinematic tradition for the behavior and characterization of robots. For researchers in affective computing and robotics, this evolving cultural archive and its complex depictions and interpretations of human-machine interaction can provide valuable information about the responses and expectations of the scientists designing such applications as well as their users.

Fig. 9.8 The domestic robot and the former jewel thief (Frank Langella) come to an understanding in *Robot and Frank* (Jake Schreier, 2012). © Sony Pictures.

Notes

1. Brooks and his research are featured in the documentary *Fast, Cheap & Out of Control* (Errol Morris, 1997).
2. For general information and market data and trends in the use of industrial robotics, see the Robotics Industries Association, available at: http://www.robotics.org/index.cfm.
3. For example, robots manufactured by the KUKA Robotics Corporation have a wide range of uses, from automotive to materials handling to entertainment. Despite their efficiency and versatility, these robots are often not recognizable by the general public as being at the cutting edge of robotics research.
4. Contemporary editions of the novel, like those by Marilyn Butler (1998) and J. Paul Hunter (2012), for example, mark the differences between the two editions. See also Butler (1993) for a discussion of the scientific context that might have affected Shelley's changes.
5. The first instance of the word *robotics* is in Isaac Asimov's "Liar" (*Astounding Science Fiction*, May 1941). Isaac Asimov, "Runaround" (*Astounding Science Fiction*, March 1942). See Gunn, 1996, 41–65.

References

Adams, D. (1997). *The hitchhiker's guide to the galaxy.* New York: Del Rey.

Asimov, I. (1976). *The bicentennial man and other stories.* New York: Doubleday.

Asimov, I. (2004). *I, robot.* New York: Bantam Spectra. (Originally published 1950.)

Baer, E. (2012). *The golem redux: From Prague to post-Holocaust fiction.* Detroit: Wayne State University.

Baum, L. F. (2006). *The wonderful wizard of Oz.* New York: Signet. (Originally published 1900.)

Brooker, W. (2006). *The blade runner experience: The legacy of a science fiction classic.* London: Wallflower Press.

Brooks, R. (2003). *Flesh and machines: How robots will change us.* New York: Vintage.

Bukatman, S. (2012). *Blade runner.* London: British Film Institute.

Butler, M. (1993, April 4). Frankenstein and radical science. *Times Literary Supplement.* Rpt. in J. P. Hunter (Ed.), *Frankenstein: A Norton Critical Edition.* New York: Norton.

Čapek, K. (2004). *R.U.R. (Rossum's universal Robots).* Claudia Novack, Trans. New York: Penguin.

del Rey, L. (1970). Helen O'Loy. In Robert Silverberg (Ed.), *The science fiction hall of fame* (Vol. 1). New York: Doubleday. (Originally published 1938.)

Elsaesser, T. (2008). *Metropolis.* London: British Film Institute.

Gates, B. (2007, January). Dawn of the age of robots: A robot in every home. *Scientific American, 296*(1), 58–63.

Goldberg, K. (Ed.). (2000). *The robot in the garden: Telerobotics and telepistemology in the age of the Internet.* Cambridge, MA: MIT Press.

Goldberg, K., and Siegwart, R. (Eds.). (2002). *Beyond webcams: An introduction to online robots.* Cambridge, MA: MIT Press.

Gray, C. H. (1995). An interview with Manfred Clynes. In C. H. Gray (Ed.), *The cyborg handbook* (pp. 43–53). New York: Routledge.

Gray, C. H., Figueroa-Sarriera, H., and Mentor, S. (Eds.). (1995). *The cyborg handbook.* New York: Routledge.

Gunn, J. (1996). *Isaac Asimov: The foundations of science fiction.* London: Scarecrow Press.

Haraway, D. (1991). A cyborg manifesto: Science, technology, and socialism-feminism in the late twentieth century. In *Simians, cyborgs and women: The reinvention of nature* (pp. 149–181). New York: Routledge. (Reprinted from *Socialist Review,* 80 [1985], pp. 65–108.)

Hayles, N. K. (1999). *How we became posthuman: Virtual bodies in cybernetics, literature, and informatics.* Chicago: University of Chicago Press.

Hunter, P. J. (Ed.). (1995). *Frankenstein: A Norton critical edition.* New York: Norton.

Huyssen, A. (1982). The vamp and the machine: Technology and sexuality in Fritz Lang's *Metropolis. New German Critique 24/25,* 221–237.

Idel, M. (1990). *Golem: Jewish magical and mystical traditions on the artificial anthropoid.* Albany: State University of New York Press.

Kang, M. (2010). *Sublime dreams of living machines: The automaton in the European imagination.* Cambridge, MA: Harvard University Press.

Kurzweil, R. (2000). *The age of spiritual machines: When computers exceed human intelligence.* New York: Penguin.

Lunning, F. (Ed.). (2008). *Mechademia 3: Limits of the human.* Minneapolis: University of Minnesota Press.

McCaffery, L. (Ed.). (1991). *Storming the reality studio: A casebook of cyberpunk & postmodern science fiction.* Durham, NC: Duke University Press.

Menzel, P., and D'Alusio, F. (2001). *Robo sapiens: Evolution of a new species.* Cambridge, MA: MIT Press.

Milburn, C. (2008). *Nanovision: Engineering the future.* Durham, NC: Duke University Press.

Moravec, H. (2000). *Robot: Mere machine to transcendent mind.* New York: Oxford University Press.

Neale, S. (1989). Issues of difference: *Alien* and *Blade Runner.* In J. Donald (Ed.), *Fantasy and the cinema.* London: British Film Institute.

Riskin, J. (Ed.). (2007). *Genesis redux: Essays in the history and philosophy of artificial life.* Chicago: University of Chicago Press.

Scholem, G. (1996). *On the Kabbalah and its symbolism.* R. Manheim, Trans. New York: Schocken Books.

Shelley, M. Wollstonecraft. (1998). *Frankenstein or the modern Prometheus. The 1818 Text.* Ed. Marilyn Butler. New York: Oxford University Press.

Shelley, M. Wollstonecraft. (2012). *Frankenstein or the modern Prometheus.* Ed. J. Paul Hunter. New York: Norton.

Telotte, J. P. (1995). *Replications: A robotic history of the science fiction film.* Chicago: University of Illinois Press.

Suggested Fiction

Adams, D. (1997). *The hitchhiker's guide to the galaxy.* New York: Del Rey. (Originally aired 1978, BBC Radio 4.)

Asimov, I. (2004). *I, robot.* New York: Bantam Spectra. (Originally published 1950.)

Bacigalupi, P. (2010). *The windup girl.* San Francisco: Nightshade Books.

Cadigan, P. (1987). *Mindplayers.* New York: Bantam Spectra.

Cadigan, P. (1991). *Synners.* New York: Bantam Spectra.

Čapek, K. (2004). *R.U.R. (Rossum's universal Robots).* Trans. Claudia Novack. New York: Penguin.

del Rey, L. (1970). Helen O'Loy. In R. Silverberg (Ed.), *The science fiction hall of fame* (Vol. 1). New York: Doubleday. (Originally published 1938.)

Dick, P. K. (1996). *Do androids dream of electric sheep?* New York: Del Rey. (Originally published 1968.)

Gibson, W. (1997). *Mona Lisa overdrive.* Spectra. (Originally published 1988.)

Gibson, W. (2000). *Neuromancer*. New York: Ace. (Originally published 1984.)

Gibson, W. (2006). *Count zero*. New York: Ace. (Originally published 1986.)

McCaffery, L. (Ed.). (1991). *Storming the reality studio: A casebook of cyberpunk & postmodern science fiction*. Durham, NC: Duke University Press.

Pohl, F. (2011). *Man plus*. New York: Orb Books. (Originally published 1976.)

Powers R. (1995). *Galatea 2.2*. New York: Farrar Straus & Giroux.

Scott, M. (2011). *Trouble and her friends*. New York: Orb Books. (Originally published 1994.)

Shelley, M. Wollstonecraft. (1998). *Frankenstein or the modern Prometheus. The 1818 text*. M. Butler, Ed. New York: Oxford University Press.

Shelley, M. Wollstonecraft. (2012). *Frankenstein or the modern Prometheus*. J. P. Hunter, Ed. New York: Norton.

Stephenson, N. (2000). *Snow crash*. New York: Bantam Spectra. (Originally published 1992.)

Stephenson, N. (2000). *The diamond age: Or, a young lady's illustrated primer*. New York: Bantam Spectra. (Originally published 1996.)

Sterling, B. (Ed.). (1988). *Mirrorshades: The cyberpunk anthology*. New York: Ace. (Originally published 1986.)

Sterling, B. (1989). *Islands in the net*. New York: Ace. (Originally published 1988.)

Sterling, B. (1996). *Schismatrix plus*. New York: Ace.

Suggested Film and Television

The golem (Eg Paul Wegener, 1920)

Metropolis (Fritz Lang, 1927)

Frankenstein (James Whale, 1931)

The day the earth stood still (Robert Wise, 1951)

Forbidden planet (Fred M. Wilcox 1956)

2001: A space odyssey (Stanley Kubrick, 1968)

Westworld (Michael Crichton, 1973)

The Stepford wives (Bryan Forbes, 1975)

Demon seed (Donald Cammell, 1977)

Star Wars (George Lucas, 1977)

Alien (Ridley Scott, 1979)

Blade runner (Ridley Scott, 1982)

The terminator (James Cameron, 1984)

Star trek: The next generation (Gene Roddenberry, 1987–1994)

Ghost in the shell (Mamoru Oshii, 1995)

Fast, cheap & out of control (Erroll Morris, 1997)

The bicentennial man (Chris Columbus, 1999)

A. I. artificial intelligence (Steven Spielberg, 2001)

Minority report (Steven Spielberg, 2002)

Robot stories (Greg Pak, 2003)

I, robot (Alex Proyas, 2004)

Battlestar Galactica (Ron Moore and David Eick, 2004–2009)

WALL-E (Andrew Stanton, 2008)

Iron man (Jon Favreau, 2008)

2012 (Roland Emmerich, 2009)

Real steel (Shawn Levy, 2011)

Robot and Frank (Jake Schreier, 2012)

Affect Detection

Automated Face Analysis for Affective Computing

Jeffrey F. Cohn *and* Fernando De la Torre

Abstract

Facial expression communicates emotion, intention, and physical state; it also regulates interpersonal behavior. Automated face analysis (AFA) for the detection, synthesis, and understanding of facial expression is a vital focus of basic research. While open research questions remain, the field has become sufficiently mature to support initial applications in a variety of areas. We review (1) human observer–based approaches to measurement that inform AFA; (2) advances in face detection and tracking, feature extraction, registration, and supervised learning; and (3) applications in action unit and intensity detection, physical pain, psychological distress and depression, detection of deception, interpersonal coordination, expression transfer, and other applications. We consider "user in the loop" as well as fully automated systems and discuss open questions in basic and applied research.

Key Words: automated face analysis and synthesis, facial action coding system (FACS), continuous measurement, emotion

Introduction

The face conveys information about a person's age, sex, background, and identity as well as what they are feeling or thinking (Bruce & Young, 1998; Darwin, 1872/1998; Ekman & Rosenberg, 2005). Facial expression regulates face-to-face interactions, indicates reciprocity and interpersonal attraction or repulsion, and communicates subjective feelings between members of different cultures (Bråten, 2006; Fridlund, 1994; Tronick, 1989). Facial expression reveals comparative evolution, social and emotional development, neurological and psychiatric functioning, and personality processes (Burrows & Cohn, In press; Campos, Barrett, Lamb, Goldsmith, & Stenberg, 1983; Girard, Cohn, Mahoor, Mavadati, & Rosenwald, In press; Schmidt & Cohn, 2001). Not surprisingly, the face has been of keen interest to behavioral scientists.

Beginning in the 1970s, computer scientists became interested in the face as a potential biometric (Kanade, 1973). Later, in the 1990s, they became interested in use of computer vision and graphics to automatically analyze and synthesize facial expression (Ekman, Huang, & Sejnowski, 1992; Parke & Waters, 1996). This effort was made possible in part by the development in behavioral science of detailed annotation schemes for use in studying human emotion, cognition, and related processes. The most detailed of these systems, the facial action coding system (Ekman & Friesen, 1978; Ekman, Friesen, & Hager, 2002), informed the development of the MPEG-4 facial animation parameters (Pandzic & Forchheimer, 2002) for video transmission and enabled progress toward automated measurement and synthesis of facial actions for research in affective computing, social signal processing, and behavioral science.

Early work focused on expression recognition between mutually exclusive posed facial actions. More recently, investigators have focused on the twin challenges of expression detection in naturalistic settings in which low base rates, partial occlusion, pose variation, rigid head motion, and lip movements associated with speech complicate detection, and, real-time synthesis of photorealistic avatars that are accepted as live video by naïve participants.

With advances, automated face analysis (AFA) is beginning to realize the goal of advancing human understanding (Ekman et al., 1992). AFA is leading to discoveries in areas that include detection of pain, frustration, emotion intensity, depression and psychological distress, and reciprocity. New applications are emerging in instructional technology, marketing, mental health, and entertainment. This chapter reviews methodological advances that have made these developments possible, surveys their scope, and addresses outstanding issues.

Human Observer–Based Approaches to Measurement

Supervised learning of facial expression requires well-coded video. What are the major approaches to manually coding behavior? At least three can be distinguished: message-based, sign-based, and dimensional.

Approaches
MESSAGE-BASED MEASUREMENT

In *message-based* measurment (Cohn & Ekman, 2005), observers make inferences about emotion or affective state. Darwin (1872/1998) described facial expressions for more than 30 emotions. Ekman and others (Ekman & Friesen, 1975; Izard, 1977; Keltner & Ekman, 2000; Plutchik, 1979) narrowed the list to a smaller number that they refer to as "basic" (see Figure 10.1) (Ekman, 1992; Keltner & Ekman, 2000). Ekman's criteria for "basic emotions" include evidence of univeral signals across all human groups, physiologic specificity, homologous expressions in other primates, and unbidden occurrence (Ekman, 1992; Keltner & Ekman, 2000). Baron-Cohen and colleagues proposed a much larger set of cognitive-emotional states that are

less tied to an evolutionary perspective. Examples include concentration, worry, playfulness, and kindness (Baron-Cohen, 2003).

An appealing assumption of message-based approaches is that the face provides a direct "read-out" of emotion (Buck, 1984). This assumption is problematic. The meaning of an expression is context dependent. The same expression can connote anger or triumph depending on where, with what, and how it occurs. The exaltation of winning a hard-fought match and the rage of losing can be difficult to distinguish without knowing context (Feldman Barrett, Mesquita, & Gendron, 2011). Similarly, smiles accompanied by cheek raising convey enjoyment; the same smiles accompanied by head lowering and turning to the side convey embarrassment (Cohn & Schmidt, 2004; Keltner & Buswell, 1997). Smiles of short duration and with a single peak are more likely to be perceived as polite (Ambadar, Cohn, & Reed, 2009). Too, expressions may be posed or faked. In the latter case, there is a dissociation between the assumed and the actual subjective emotion. For these reasons and others, there is reason to be dubious of one-to-one correspondences between expression and emotion (Cacioppo & Tassinary, 1990).

SIGN-BASED MEASUREMENT

An alternative to message-based measurement is to use a purely descriptive, *sign-based* approach and then use experimental or observational methods to discover the relation between such signs and emotion. The most widely used method is the facial action coding system (FACS) (Cohn, Ambadar, & Ekman, 2007; Ekman et al., 2002). FACS describes facial activity in terms of anatomically based action units (AUs) (Figure 10.2). The FACS taxonomy was developed by manually observing gray-level variation between expressions in images, recording the electrical activity of facial muscles, and observing the effects of electrically stimulating facial muscles (Cohn & Ekman, 2005). Depending on the version of FACS, there are 33 to 44 AUs and a large number of additional "action descriptors" and other

Fig. 10.1 Basic emotions. from left to right: amusement, sadness, anger, fear, surprise, disgust, contempt, and embarrassment

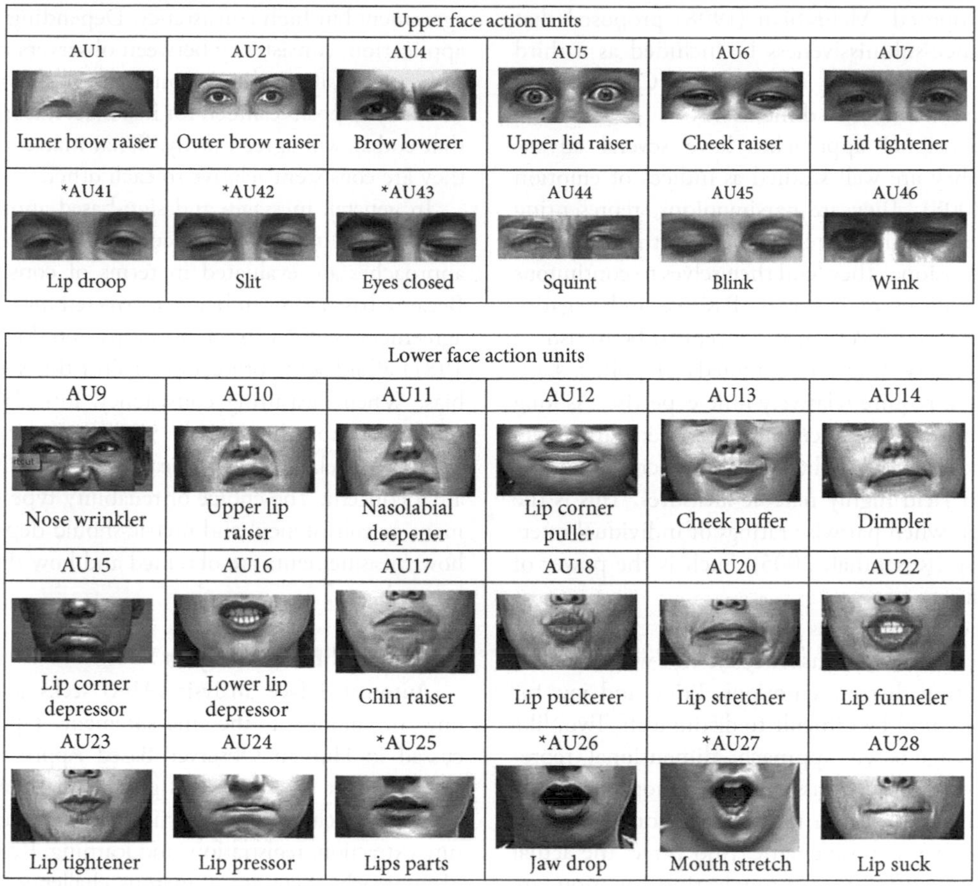

Upper face action units					
AU1	AU2	AU4	AU5	AU6	AU7
Inner brow raiser	Outer brow raiser	Brow lowerer	Upper lid raiser	Cheek raiser	Lid tightener
*AU41	*AU42	*AU43	AU44	AU45	AU46
Lip droop	Slit	Eyes closed	Squint	Blink	Wink

Lower face action units					
AU9	AU10	AU11	AU12	AU13	AU14
Nose wrinkler	Upper lip raiser	Nasolabial deepener	Lip corner puller	Cheek puffer	Dimpler
AU15	AU16	AU17	AU18	AU20	AU22
Lip corner depressor	Lower lip depressor	Chin raiser	Lip puckerer	Lip stretcher	Lip funneler
AU23	AU24	*AU25	*AU26	*AU27	AU28
Lip tightener	Lip pressor	Lips parts	Jaw drop	Mouth stretch	Lip suck

Fig. 10.2 Action units (AUs), facial action coding system.

Sources: Ekman & Friesen (1978); Ekman et al., (2002). Images from C-K database, Kanade et al. (2000).

movements. AUs may be coded using either binary (presence versus absence) or ordinal (intensity) labels. Figures 10.2 and 10.3 show examples of each.

While FACS itself includes no emotion labels, empirically based guidelines for emotion interpretation have been proposed. The FACS investigator's guide and other sources hypothesize mappings between AU and emotion (Ambadar et al., 2009; Ekman & Rosenberg, 2005; Knapp & Hall, 2010). Sign-based approaches in addition to FACS, are reviewed in Cohn and Ekman (2005).

DIMENSIONAL MEASUREMENT

Both message- and sign-based approaches emphasize differences between emotions. An alternative emphasizes their similarities. Schlosberg (1952, 1954) proposed that the range of facial expressions conforms to a circular surface with pleasantness-unpleastness (i.e., valence) and attention-rejection as the principal axes (activity was proposed as a possible third). Russell and Bullock (1985), like Schlosberg, proposed that emotion conforms to a circumplex structure with pleasantness-unpleasantness (valence) as one axis, but they replaced attention-rejection with arousal-sleepiness. Watson and Tellegen (1985) proposed an orthogonal rotation of the axes to yield positive and negative affect (PA and NA, respectively, each ranging in intensity from low to high). More complex structures have

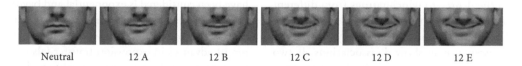

| Neutral | 12 A | 12 B | 12 C | 12 D | 12 E |

Fig. 10.3 Intensity variation in AU 12.

been proposed. Mehrabian (1998) proposed that dominance-submissiveness be included as a third dimension. Tellegen, Watson, and Clark (1999) proposed hierarchical dimensions.

Dimensional approaches have several advantages. They are well studied as indices of emotion (Fox, 2008). They are parsimonious, representing any given emotion in terms of two or three underlying dimensions. They lend themselves to continuous representations of intensity. Positive and negative affect (PA and NA), for instance, can be measured over intensity ranges of hundreds of points. Last, they often require relatively little expertise. As long as multiple independent and unbiased ratings are obtained, scores may be aggregated across multiple raters to yield highly reliable measures. This is the case even when pairwise ratings of individual raters are noisy (Rosenthal, 2005). Such is the power of aggregating.

Some disadvantages may be noted. One, because they are parsiomonious, they are not well suited to representing discrete emotions. Pride and joy, for instance could be difficult to distinguish. Two, like the message-based approach, dimensional representations implicitly assume that emotion may be inferred directly from facial expression, which, as noted above, is problematic. And three, the actual signals involved in communicating emotion are unspecified.

Reliability

Reliabilility concerns the extent to which measurement is repeatable and consistent—that is, free from random error (Martin & Bateson, 2007). Whether facial expression is measured using a message, sign, or dimensional approach, we wish to know to what extent variability in the measurements represents true variation in facial expression rather than error. In general, reliability between observers can be considered in at least two ways (Tinsley & Weiss, 1975). One is whether coders make exactly the same judgments (i.e., Do they agree?). The other is whether their judgments are consistent. When judgments are made on a nomimal scale, *agreement* means that each coder assigns the same score. When judgments are made on an ordinal or interval scale, *consistency* refers to the degree to which ratings from different sources are proportional when expressed as deviations from their means. Accordingly, agreement and consistency may show disassociations. If two coders always differ by *x* points in the same direction on an ordinal or interval scale, they have low

agreement but high consistency. Depending on the application, consistency between observers may be sufficient. Using a dimensional approach to assess intensity of positve affect, for instance, it is unlikely that coders will agree exactly. What matters is that they are consistent relative to each other.

In general, message- and sign-based approaches are evaluated in terms of agreement and dimensional approaches are evaluated in terms of consistency. Because base rates can bias uncorrected measures of agreement, statistics such as kappa and *F1* (Fleiss, 1981) afford some protection against this source of bias. When measuring consistency, intraclass correlation (Shrout & Fleiss, 1979) is preferable to Pearson correlation when mean differences in level are a concern. The choice of reliability type (agreement or consistency) and metric should depend on how measurements are obtained and how they will be used.

Automated Face Analysis

Automated face analysis (AFA) seeks to detect one or more of the measurement types discussed in Human Observer–Based Approaches to Measurement (p. 132). This goal requires multiple steps that include face detection and tracking, feature extraction, registration, and learning. Regardless of approach, there are numerous challenges. These include (1) non-frontal pose and moderate to large head motion make facial image registration difficult; (2) many facial actions are inherently subtle, making them difficult to model; (3) the temporal dynamics of actions can be highly variable; (4) discrete AUs can modify each other's appearance (i.e., nonadditive combinations); (5) individual differences in face shape and appearance undermine generalization across subjects; and (6) classifiers can suffer from overfitting when trained with insufficient examples.

To address these and other issues, a large number of facial expression and AU recognition/detection systems have been proposed. The pipeline depicted in Figure 10.4 is common to many. Key differences among them include types of two- or three-dimensional (2D or 3D) input images, face detection and tracking, types of features, registration, dimensionality reduction, classifiers, and databases. The number of possible combinations that have been considered is exponential and beyond the bounds of what can be considered here. With this in mind, we review essential aspects. We then review recent advances in expression transfer (also referred to as automated face synthesis, or AFS) and applications made possible by advances in AFA.

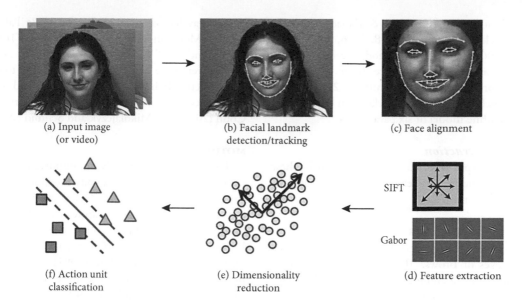

(a) Input image (or video)	(b) Facial landmark detection/tracking	(c) Face alignment
(f) Action unit classification	(e) Dimensionality reduction	(d) Feature extraction

Fig. 10.4 Example of the facial action unit recognition system.

Face and Facial Feature Detection and Tracking

AFA begins with face detection. In the case of relatively frontal pose, the Viola and Jones (2004) face detector may be the most widely used. This and others are reviewed in Zhang and Zhang (2010). Following face detection, either a sparse (e.g., eyes or eye corners) or dense set of facial features (e.g., the contours of the eyes and other permanent facial features) is detected and tracked in the video. An advantage of the latter is that it affords information from which to infer a 3D pose (especially yaw, pitch, and roll) and viewpoint-registered representations (e.g., warp face image to a frontal view).

To track a dense set of facial features, active appearance models (AAMs) (Cootes, Edwards, & Taylor, 2001) are often used. AAMs decouple the shape and appearance of a face image. Given a predefined linear shape model with linear appearance variation, AAMs align the shape model to an unseen image containing the face and facial expression of interest. The shape of an AAM is described by a 2D triangulated mesh. In particular, the coordinates of the mesh vertices define the shape (Ashraf et al., 2009). The vertex locations correspond to a source appearance image, from which the shape is aligned. Since AAMs allow linear shape variation, the shape can be expressed as a base shape s_0 plus a linear combination of m shape vectors s_i. Because AAMs are invertible, they can be used both for analysis and for synthesizing new images and video. Theobald and Matthews (Boker et al., 2011; Theobald, Matthews,

Cohn, & Boker, 2007) used this approach to generate real-time near videorealistic avatars, which we discuss below.

The precision of AAMs comes at a price. Prior to use they must be trained for each person. That is, they are "person-dependent" (as well as camera- and illumination-dependent). To overcome this limitation, Saragih, Lucey, and Cohn (2011a) extended the work of Cristinacce and Cootes (2006) and others to develop what is referred to as a constrained local model (CLM). Compared with AAMs, CLMs generalize well to unseen appearance variation and offer greater invariance to global illumination variation and occlusion (Lucey Wang, Saragih, & Cohn, 2009, 2010). They are sufficiently fast to support real-time tracking and synthesis (Lucey, Wang, Saragih, & Cohn, 2010). A disadvantage of CLMs relative to AAMs is that they detect shape less precisely. For this reason, there has been much effort to identify ways to compensate for their reduced precision (Chew et al., 2012).

Registration

To remove the effects of spatial variation in face position, rotation, and facial proportions, images must be registered to a canonical size and orientation. Three-dimensional rotation is especially challenging because the face looks different from different orientations. Three-dimensional transformations can be estimated from monocular (up to a scale factor) or multiple cameras using structure from motion algorithms (Matthews, Xiao, & Baker,

2007; Xiao, Baker, Matthews, & Kanade, 2004) or head trackers (Morency, 2008; Xiao, Kanade, & Cohn, 2003). For small to moderate out-of-plane rotation a moderate distance from the camera (assume orthographic projection), the 2D projected motion field of a 3D planar surface can be recovered with an affine model of six parameters.

Feature Extraction

Several types of features have been used. These include geometry (also referred to as shape), appearance, and motion.

GEOMETRIC FEATURES

Geometric features refer to facial landmarks such as the eyes or brows. They can be represented as fiducial points, a connected face mesh, active shape model, or face component shape parameterization (Tian, Cohn, & Kanade, 2005). To detect actions such as brow raise (AU 1 + 2); changes in displacement between points around the eyes and those on the brows can be discriminative. While most approaches model shape as 2D features, a more powerful approach is to use structure from motion to model them as 3D features (Saragih et al., 2011a) (Xiao et al., 2004). Jeni (2012) found that this approach improves AU detection.

Shape or geometric features alone are insufficient for some AUs. Both AU 6 and AU 7 narrow the eye aperture. The addition of appearance or texture information aids in discriminating between them. AU 6 but not AU 7, for instance, causes wrinkles lateral to the eye corners. Other AUs, such as AU 11 (nasolabial furrow deepener) and AU 14 (mouth corner dimpler) may be undetectable without reference to appearance because they occasion minimal changes in shape. AU 11 causes a deepening of the middle portion of the nasolabial furrow. AU 14 and AU 15 each cause distinctive pouching around the lip corners.

APPEARANCE FEATURES

Appearance features represent changes in skin texture such as wrinkling and deepening of facial furrows and pouching of the skin. Many techniques for describing local image texture have been proposed. The simplest is a vector of raw pixel-intensity values. However, if an unknown error in registration occurs, there is an inherent variability associated with the true (i.e., correctly registered) local image appearance. Another problem is that lightning conditions affect texture in gray-scale representations. Biologically inspired appearance features, such as

Gabor wavelets or magnitudes (Jones & Palmer, 1987), (Movellan, n.d.), HOG (Dalal & Triggs, 2005), and SIFT (Mikolajczyk & Schmid, 2005) have proven more robust than pixel intensity to registration error (Chew et al., 2012). These and other appearance features are reviewed in De la Torre and Cohn (2011) and Mikolajczyk and Schmid (2005).

MOTION FEATURES

For humans, motion is an important cue to expression recognition, especially for subtle expressions (Ambadar, Schooler, & Cohn, 2005). No less is true for AFA. Motion features include optical flow (Mase, 1991) and dynamic textures or motion history images (MHI) (Chetverikov & Peteri, 2005). In early work, Mase (1991) used optical flow to estimate activity in a subset of the facial muscles. Essa and Pentland (1997) extended this approach, using optic flow to estimate activity in a detailed anatomical and physical model of the face. Yacoob and Davis (1997) bypassed the physical model and constructed a midlevel representation of facial motion directly from the optic flow. Cohen and colleagues (2003) implicitly recovered motion representations by building features such that each feature motion corresponds to a simple deformation on the face. Motion history images (MHIs) were first proposed by Bobick and Davis (2001). MHIs compress into one frame the motion over a number of consecutive ones. Valstar, Pantic, and Patras (2004) encoded face motion into motion history images. Zhao and Pietikainen (2007) used volume local binary patterns (LBPs), a temporal extension of local binary patterns often used in 2D texture analysis. These methods all encode motion in a video sequence.

DATA REDUCTION/SELECTION

Features typically have high dimensionality, especially so for appearance. To reduce dimensionality, several approaches have been proposed. Widely used linear techniques are principal components analysis (PCA) (Hotelling, 1933), Kernel PCA (Schokopf, Smola, & Muller, 1997), and independent components analysis (Comon, 1994). Nonlinear techniques include Laplacian eigenmaps (Belkin & Niyogi, 2001), local linear embedding (LLE) (Roweis & Saul, 2000), and locality preserving projections (LPPs) (Cai, He, Zhou, Han, & Bao, 2007; Chang, Hu, Feris, & Turk, 2006)). Supervised methods include linear discriminant analysis, AdaBoost, kernel LDA, and locally sensitive LDA.

Learning

Most approaches use supervised learning. In supervised learning, event categories (e.g., emotion labels or AU) or dimensions are defined in advance in labeled training data. In unsupervised learning, labeled training data are not used. Here, we consider supervised approaches. For a review of unsupervised approaches, see De la Torre and Cohn (2011).

Two approaches to supervised learning are: (1) static modeling—typically posed as a discriminative classification problem in which each video frame is evaluated independently; (2) temporal modeling—frames are segmented into sequences and typically modeled with a variant of dynamic Bayesian networks (e.g., hidden Markov models, conditional random fields).

In static modeling, early work used neural networks (Tian, Kanade, & Cohn, 2001). More recently, support vector machine classifiers (SVMs) have predominated. Boosting has been used to a lesser extent both for classification as well as for feature selection (Littlewort, Bartlett, Fasel, Susskind, & Movellan, 2006; Y. Zhu, De la Torre, Cohn, & Zhang, 2011). Others have explored rule-based systems (Pantic & Rothkrantz, 2000).

In temporal modeling, recent work has focused on incorporating motion features to improve performance. A popular strategy uses HMMs to temporally segment actions by establishing a correspondence between the action's onset, peak, and offset and an underlying latent state. Valstar and Pantic (Valstar & Pantic, 2007) used a combination of SVM and HMM to temporally segment and recognize AUs. Koelstra and Pantic (Koelstra & Pantic, 2008) used Gentle-Boost classifiers on motion from a nonrigid registration combined with an HMM. Similar approaches include a nonparametric discriminant HMM (Shang & Chan, 2009) and partially observed hidden conditional random fields (Chang, Liu, & Lai, 2009). In related work, Cohen and colleagues (2003) used Bayesian networks to classify the six universal expressions from video. Naive-Bayes classifiers and Gaussian tree-augmented naïve Bayes (TAN) classifiers learned dependencies among different facial motion features. In a series of papers, Qiang and colleagues (Li, Chen, Zhao, & Ji, 2013; Tong, Chen, & Ji, 2010; Tong, Liao, & Ji, 2007) used dynamic Bayesian networks to detect facial action units.

Databases

Data drives research. Development and validation of supervised and unsupervised algorithms requires access to large video databases that span the range of variation expected in target applications. Relevant variation in video includes pose, illumination, resolution, occlusion, facial expression, actions, and their intensity and timing, and individual differences in subjects. An algorithm that performs well for frontal, high-resolution, well-lit video with few occlusions may perform rather differently when such factors vary (Cohn & Sayette, 2010).

Most face expression databases have used directed facial action tasks; subjects are asked to pose discrete facial actions or holistic expressions. Posed expressions, however, often differ in appearance and timing from those that occur spontaneously. Two reliable signals of sadness, AU 15 (lip corners pulled down) and AU 1 + 4 (raising and narrowing the inner corners of the brow) are difficult for most people to perform on command. Even when such actions can be performed deliberately, they may differ markedly in timing from what occurs spontaneously (Cohn & Schmidt, 2004). Differences in the timing of spontaneous and deliberate facial actions are particularly important in that many pattern recognition approaches, such as hidden Markov models (HMMs), are highly dependent on the timing of the appearance change. Unless a database includes both deliberate and spontaneous facial actions, it will likely prove inadequate for developing face expression methods that are robust to these differences.

Variability within and among coders is an important source of error that too often is overlooked by database users. Human performance is inherently variable. An individual coder may assign different AUs to the same segment on different occasions ("test-retest" unreliability); and different coders may assign different AU ("alternate-form" unreliability). Although FACS coders are (or should be) certified in its use, they can vary markedly in their expertise and in how they operationalize FACS criteria. An additional source of error relates to manual data entry. Software for computer-assisted behavioral coding can lessen but not eliminate this error source. All of these types of error in "ground truth" can adversely affect classifier training and performance. Differences in manual coding between databases may and do occur as well and can contribute to impaired generalizability of classifiers from one database to another.

Section 4 of this handbook and earlier reviews (Zeng, Pantic, Roisman, & Huang, 2009) detail relevant databases. Several very recent databases merit mention. DISFA (Mavadati, Mahoor, Bartlett, Trinh, & Cohn, 2013) consists of FACS-coded high-resolution facial behavior in response to emotion-inducing videos. AU are coded on a 6-point intensity scale (0 to 5). The Binghamton-Pittsburgh 4D database (BP4D) is a high-resolution 4D (3D * time) AU-coded database of facial behavior in response to varied emotion inductions (Zhang et al., 2013). Several databases include participants with depression or related disorders (Girard et al., 2014; Scherer et al., 2013; Valstar et al., 2013; Wang et al., 2008). Human use restrictions limit access to some of these. Two other large AU-coded databases not yet publically are the Sayette group formation task (GFT) (Sayette et al., 2012) and the AMFED facial expression database (McDuff, Kaliouby, Senechal et al., 2013). GFT includes manually FACS-coded video of 720 participants in 240 three-person groups (approximately 30 minutes each). AMFED includes manually FACS-coded video of thousands of participants recorded via webcam while viewing commercials for television.

Applications

AU detection and, to a lesser extent, detection of emotion expressions, has been a major focus of research. Action units of interest have been those strongly related to emotion expression and that occur sufficiently often in naturalistic settings. As automated face analysis and synthesis has matured, many additional applications have emerged.

AU Detection

There is a large, vigorous literature on AU detection (De la Torre & Cohn, 2011; Tian et al., 2005; Zeng et al., 2009). Many algorithms and systems have been bench-marked on posed facial databases, such as Cohn-Kanade (Kanade, Cohn, & Tian, 2000; Lucey, Cohn, Kanade, Saragih, Ambadar & Matthews,, 2010), MMI (Pantic, Valstar, Rademaker, & Maat, 2005), and the UNBC Pain Archive (Lucey, Cohn, Prkachin, Solomon, & Matthews, 2011). Benchmarking on spontaneous facial behavior has occurred more recently. The FERA 2011 Facial Expression Recognition Challenge enrolled 20 teams to compete in AU and emotion detection (Valstar, Mehu, Jiang, Pantic, & Scherer, 2012). Of these 20 teams, 15 participated in the challenge and submitted papers. Eleven papers were accepted for publication in a double-blind review. On the AU detection sub-challenge, the winning group achieved an F1 score of 0.63 across 12 AUs at the frame level. On the less difficult

emotion detection sub-challenge, the top alogrithm classified 84% correctly at the sequence level.

The FERA organizers noted that the scores for AU were well above baseline but still far from perfect. Without knowing the F1 score for interobserver agreement (see Reliability, p. 134), it is difficult to know to what extent this score may have been attenuated by measurement error in the ground truth AU. An additional caveat is that results were for a single database of rather modest size (10 trained actors portraying emotions). Further opportunities for comparative testing on spontaneous behavior are planned for the 3rd International Audio/Visual Emotion Challenge (http://sspnet.eu/avec2013/) (and the Emotion Recognition in the Wild Challenge and Workshop (EmotiW 2013) (http://cs.anu.edu.au/few/emotiw.html) (Dhall, Goecke, Joshi, Wagner, & Gedeon, 2013). Because database sizes in these two tests will be larger than in FERA, more informed comparisons between alternative approaches will be possible.

In comparing AU detection results within and between studies, AU base rate is a potential confound. Some AU occur more frequently than others within and between databases. AU 12 is relatively common; AU 11 or AU 16 much less so. With exception of area under the ROC, performance metrics are confounded by such differences (Jeni, Cohn, & De la Torre, 2013). A classifier that appears to perform better for one AU than another may do so because of differences in base rate between them. Skew-normalized metrics have been proposed to address this problem (Jeni et al., 2013). When metrics are skew-normalized, detection metrics are independent of differences in base rate and thus directly comparable.

Intensity

Message-based and dimensional measurement may be performed on both ordinal and continuous scales. Sign-based measurement, such as FACS, conventionally use an ordinal scale (0 to 3 points in the 1978 edition of FACS; 0 to 5 in the 2002 edition). Action unit intensity has been of particular interest. AU unfold over time. Initial efforts focused on estimating their maximum, or "peak," intensity (Bartlett et al., 2006). More recent work has sought to measure intensity for each video frame (Girard, 2013; Mavadati et al., 2013; Messinger, Mahoor, Chow, & Cohn, 2009).

Early work suggested that AU intensity could be estimated by computing distance from the hyperplane of a binary classifier. For posed action units in Cohn-Kanade, distance from the hyperplane and (manually coded) AU intensity were moderately correlated for maximum AU intensity ($r = .60$) (Bartlett et al., 2006b). Theory and some data, however, suggest that distance from the hyperplane may be a poor proxy for intensity in spontaneous facial behavior. In RU-FACS, in which facial expression is unposed (also referred to as spontaneous), the correlation between distance from the hyperplane and AU intensity for maximum intensity was $r = .35$ or less (Bartlett et al., 2006a). Yang, Liu, and Metaxas (2009) proposed that supervised training from intensity-labeled training data is a better option than training from distance from the hyperplane of a binary classifier.

Recent findings in AU-coded spontaneous facial expression support this hypothesis. All estimated intensity on a frame-by-frame basis, which is more challenging than measuring AU intensity only at its maximum. In the DISFA database, intraclass correlation (ICC) between manual and automatic coding of intensity (0 to 5 ordinal scale) was 0.77 for Gabor features (Mavadati et al., 2013). Using support vector regression in the UNBC Pain Archive, Kaltwang and colleagues (Kaltwang, Rudovic, & Pantic, 2012) achieved a correlation of about 0.5. In the BP4D database, a multiclass SVM achieved an ICC of 0.92 for AU 12 intensity (Girard, 2013), far greater than what was achieved using distance from the hyperplane of a binary SVM. These findings suggest that for spontaneous facial expression at the frame level, it is essential to train on intensity-coded AU and a classifier that directly measures intensity (e.g., multiclass SVM or support vector regression).

Physical Pain

Pain assessment and management are important across a wide range of disorders and treatment interventions. Pain measurement is fundamentally subjective and is typically measured by patient self-report, which has notable limitations. Self-report is idiosyncratic; susceptible to suggestion, impression management, and deception; and lacks utility with young children, individuals with certain types of neurological impairment, many patients in postoperative care or transient states of consciousness, and those with severe disorders requiring assisted breathing, among other conditions.

Using behavioral measures, pain researchers have made significant progress toward identifying reliable and valid facial indicators of pain. In these studies pain is widely characterized by brow lowering (AU 4), orbital tightening (AU 6 and 7), eye closure (AU 43), nose wrinkling, and lip raise (AU 9 and 10) (Prkachin & Solomon, 2008). This development led investigators from the affective computing community to ask whether pain and pain intensity could be detected automatically. Several groups working on different datasets have found the answer to be yes. Littlewort and colleagues (Littlewort, Bartlett, & Lee) discriminated between actual and feigned pain. Hammal and Kunz (2012) discriminated pain from the six basic facial expressions and neutral. We and others detected occurrence and intensity of shoulder pain in a clinical sample (Ashraf et al., 2009; Hammal & Cohn, 2012; Kaltwang et al., 2012; Lucey, Cohn, Howlett, Lucey, & Sridharan, 2011).

From these studies, two findings that have more general implications emerged. One, pain could be detected with comparable accuracy whether features were fed directly to a classifier or by a two-step classification in which action units were first detected and AU then were input to a classifier to detect pain. The comparability of results suggests that the AU recognition step may be unnecessary when detecting holistic expressions, such as pain. Two, good results could be achieved even when training and testing on coarse (sequence level) ground truth in place of frame-by-frame behavioral coding (Ashraf et al., 2009). Future research will be needed to test these suggestions.

Depression and Psychological Distress

Diagnosis and assessment of symptom severity in psychopathology are almost entirely informed by what patients, their families, or caregivers report. Standardized procedures for incorporating facial and related nonverbal expression are lacking. This is especially salient for depression, for which there are strong indications that facial expression and other nonverbal communication may be powerful indicators of disorder severity and response to treatment. In comparison with nondepressed individuals, depressed individuals have been observed to look less at conversation partners, gesture less, show fewer Duchenne smiles, more smile suppressor movements, and less facial animation. Human-observer based findings such as these have now been replicated using automated analyses of facial and multimodal expression (Joshi, Dhall, Goecke, Breakspear, & Parker, 2012; Scherer et al., 2013). An exciting implication is that facial expression could prove useful for screening efforts in mental health.

To investigate possible functions of depression, we (Girard et al., 2014) recorded serial interviews over multiple weeks in a clinical sample that was undergoing treatment for major depressive disorder. We found high congruence between automated and manual measurement of facial expression in testing hypotheses about change over time in depression severity.

The results provided theoretical support for the hypothesis that depression functions to reduce social risk. When symptoms were highest, subjects showed fewer displays intended to seek interpersonal engagement (i.e., less smiling as well as fewer sadness displays) and more displays that communicate rejection of others (i.e., disgust and contempt). These findings underscore the importance of accounting for individual differences (All subjects were compared with themselves over the course of depressive disorder); provide further evidence in support of AFA's readiness for hypothesis testing about psychological mechanisms; and suggest that automated measurement may be useful in detecting recovery and relapse as well as in contributing to public health efforts to screen for depression and psychological distress.

Deception Detection

Theory and some data suggest that deception and hostile intent can be inferred in part from facial expression (Ekman, 2009). The RU-FACS database (Bartlett et al., 2006a), which has been extensively used for AU detection, was originally collected for the purpose of learning to detect deception. While no deception results to our knowledge have yet been reported, others using different databases have realized some success in detecting deception from facial expression and other modalities. Metaxas, Burgoon, and their colleagues (Michael, Dilsizian, Metaxas, & Burgoon, 2010; Yu et al., 2013) proposed an automated approach that uses head motion, facial expression, and body motion to detect deception. Tsiamyrtzis (2006) and others achieved close to 90% accuracy using thermal cameras to image the face (Tsiamyrtzis et al.). Further progress in this area will require ecologically valid training and testing data. Too often, laboratory studies of deception have lacked verisimilatude or failed to include the kinds of people most likely to attempt deception or hostile actions. While the need for good data is well recognized, barriers to its use have been difficult to overcome. Recent work in deception detection

was presented at FG 2013: Visions on Deception and Non-cooperation Workshop (http://hmi. ewi.utwente.nl/vdnc-workshop/) (Vinciarelli, Nijholt, & Aghajan. 2013).

Interpersonal Coordination

Facial expression of emotion most often occurs in an interpersonal context. Breakthroughs in automated facial expression analysis make possible to model patterns of interpersonal coordination in this context. With Messinger and colleagues (Hammal, Cohn, & Messinger, 2013; Messinger et al., 2009), we modeled mother and infant synchrony in action unit intensity and head motion. For both action unit intensity and head motion we found strong evidence of synchrony with frequent changes in phase, or direction of influence, between mother and infant. Figure 10.5 shows an example for mother and infant head nod amplitude. A related example for mother-infant action unit intensity is presented in Chapter 42 of this volume.

The pattern of association we observed for head motion and action units between mothers and infants was nonstationary with frequent changes in which partner is leading the other. Hammal and Cohn (2013) found similar nonstationarity in the head pose coordination of distressed intimate adults. Head amplitude and velocity for pitch (nod) and yaw (turn) was strongly correlated between them, with alternating periods of instability (low correlation) followed by brief stability in which one or the other partner led the other. Until recently, most research in affective computing has focused on individuals. Attention to temporal coordination expands the scope of affective computing and has implications for robot-human communication as well. To achieve more human like capabilities and make robot-human interaction feel more natural, designers might broaden their attention to consider the dynamics of communicative behavior.

Expression Transfer

Many approaches to automated face analysis are invertible. That is, their parameters can be used to synthesize images that closely resemble or are nearly identical to the originals. This capability makes possible expression transfer from an image of one person's face to that of another (Theobald & Cohn, 2009). Theobald, Matthews, and their colleagues developed an early prototype for expression transfer using AAM (Theobald, Bangham, Matthews, & Cawley, 2004). This was followed by a real-time system implemented over an

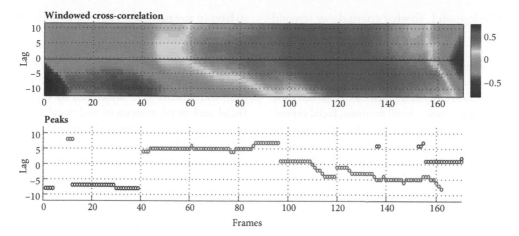

Fig. 10.5 Top panel: Windowed cross-correlation within a 130-frame sliding window between mother and infant head-pitch amplitude. The area above the midline (Lag > 0) represents the relative magnitude of correlations for which the mother's head amplitude predicts her infant's; the corresponding area below the midline (Lag < 0) represents the converse. The midline (Lag = 0) indicates that both partners are changing their head amplitudes at the same time. Positive correlations (red) convey that the head amplitudes of both partners are changing in the same way (i.e., increasing together or decreasing together). Negative correlation (blue) conveys that the head amplitudes of both partners are changing in the opposite way (e.g., head amplitude of one partner increases as that of the other partner decreases). Note that the direction of the correlations changes dynamically over time. Bottom panel: Peaks ($r > .40$) in the windowed cross-correlations as found using an algorithm proposed by Boker (Boker, Rotondo, Xu, & King, 2002).

audiovisual link in which naïve participants interacted with realistic avatars animated by an actual person (Theobald et al., 2009) (Figure 10.6). Similar though less realistic approaches have been developed using CLM (Saragih, Lucey, & Cohn, 2011b). Expression transfer has been applied in computational behavioral science and media arts.

EXPRESSION TRANSFER IN COMPUTATIONAL BEHAVIORAL SCIENCE

In conversation, expectations about another person's identity are closely involved with his or her actions. Even over the telephone, when visual information is unavailable, we make inferences from the sound of the voice about the other person's gender,

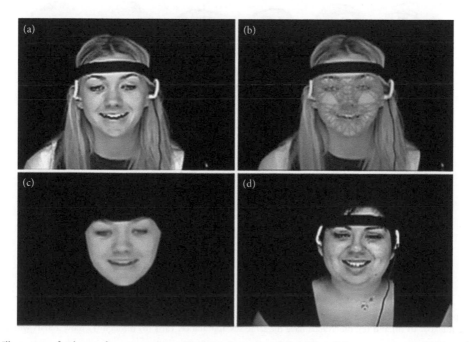

Fig. 10.6 Illustration of video-conference paradigm. Clockwise from upper left: Video of the source person; AAM tracking of the source person; their partner; and the AAM reconstruction that is viewed by the partner.

age, and background. To what extent do we respond to whom we think we are talking rather than to the dynamics of their behavior? This question had been unanswered because it is difficult to separately manipulate expectations about a person's identity from their actions. An individual has a characteristic and unified appearance, head motions, facial expressions, and vocal inflection. For this reason, most studies of person perception and social expectation are naturalistic or manipulations in which behavior is artificially scripted and acted. But scripted and natural conversations have different dynamics. AFA provides a way out of this dilemma. For the first time, static and dynamic cues become separable (Boker et al., 2011).

Pairs of participants had conversations in a video-conference paradigm (Figure 10.6). One was a confederate for whom an AAM had previously been trained. Unbeknownst to the other participant, a resynthetized avatar was substituted for the live video of the confederate (Figure 10.7). The avatar had the face of the confederate or another person of same or opposite sex. All were animated by the actual motion parameters of the confederate.

The apparent identity and gender of a confederate was randomly assigned and the confederate was blind to the identity and gender that they appeared to have in any particular conversation. The manipulation was believable in that, when given an opportunity to guess the manipulation at the end of experiment, none of the naïve participants was able to do so. Significantly, the amplitude and velocity of head movements were influenced by the dynamics (head and facial movement and vocal timing) but not the perceived gender of the partner.

These findings suggest that gender-based social expectations are unlikely to be the source of reported gender differences in head nodding between partners. Although men and women adapt to each other's head movement amplitudes it appears that adaptation may simply be a case of people (independent of gender) adapting to each other's head movement amplitude. A shared equilibrium is formed when two people interact.

EXPRESSION TRANSFER IN MEDIA ARTS

Expression transfer has been widely used in the entertainment industry where there is an increasing synnergy between computer vision and computer graphics. Well-known examples in film include *Avatar* and the *Hobbit* (http://www.iainm.com/iainm/Home.html). Emotion transfer has made significant inroads in gaming and other applications as well. Sony's Everquest II, as but one example,

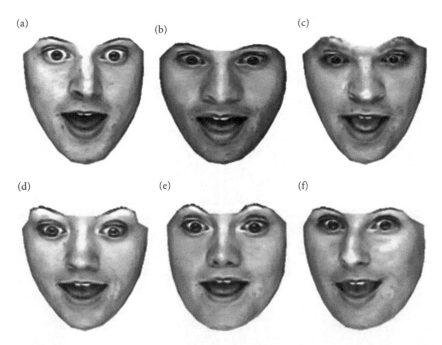

Fig. 10.7 Applying expressions of a male to the appearances of other persons. In (a), the avatar has the appearance of the person whose motions were tracked. In (b) and (c), the avatars have the same-sex appearance. Parts (d) through (f) show avatars with opposite-sex appearances.

Source: Images courtesy of the American Psychological Association.

enables users to animate avatars in multiperson games (Hutchings, 2012).

Other Applications

DISCRIMINATING BETWEEN SUBTLE DIFFERENCES IN RELATED EXPRESSIONS

Most efforts to detect emotion expressions have focused on the basic emotions defined by Ekman. Others have discriminated between posed and unposed smiles (Cohn & Schmidt, 2004; Valstar, Gunes, & Pantic, 2007) and between smiles of delight and actual and feigned frustration (Hoque & Picard, 2011). Ambadar and colleagues (2009) found that smiles perceived as polite, embarrassed, or amused varied in both the occurrence of specific facial actions and in their timing. Whitehill and colleagues (Whitehill, Littlewort, Fasel, Bartlett, & Movellan) developed an automatic smile detector based on appearance features. Gratch (Gratch, 2013) used automated analysis of smiles and smile controls in testing the hypothesis of Hess that smiling is determined by both social context and appraisal. Together, these studies highlight the potential of automated measurement to make fine-grained discrimination among emotion signals.

MARKETING

Until a few years ago, self-report and focus groups were the primary means of gauging reaction to new products. With the advent of AFA, more revealing approaches have become possible. Using web-cam technology, companies are able to record thousands of viewers in dozens of countries and proces their facial expression to infer liking or disliking of commercials and products (McDuff, Kaliouby, & Picard, 2013; Szirtes, Szolgay, Utasi, Takacs, Petras, & Fodor, 2013). The methodology is well suited to the current state of the art. Participants are seated in front of a monitor, which limits out-of-plane head motion and facial expression is detected in part by knowledge of context (i.e., strong priors).

DROWSY-DRIVER DETECTION

Falling asleep while driving contributes to as many as 15% of fatal crashes. A number of systems to detect drowsy driving and take preventive actions have been proposed and are in various stages of development. Using either normal or infrared cameras, some monitor eyeblink patterns (Danisman, Bilasco, Djeraba, & Ihaddadene, 2010), while others incorporate additional behaviors, such as yawning and face touching (Matsuo & Khiat, 2012;

Vural et al., 2010), head movements (Lee, Oh, Heo, & Hahn, 2008), and pupil detection (Deng, Xiong, Zhou, Gan, & Deng, 2010).

INSTRUCTIONAL TECHNOLOGY

Interest, confusion, rapport, frustration, and other emotion and cognitive-emotional states are important process variables in the classroom and in tutoring (Craig, D'Mello, Witherspoon, & Graesser, 2007). Until recently, they could be measured reliably only offline, which limited their usefulness. Recent work by Whitehill and Littlewort (Whitehill et al., 2011) evaluates the feasibility of realtime recognition. Initial results are promising. In the course of demonstrating feasibility, they found that in some contexts smiles are indicative of frustration or embarrassment rather than achievement. This finding suggests that automated methods have sufficient precision to distinguish in realtime between closely related facial actions that signal student cognitive-emotional states.

User in the Loop

While fully automated systems are desirable, significant advantages exist in systems that integrate user and machine input. With respect to tracking, person-specific AAMs and manually initialized head tracking are two examples. Person-specific AAMs that have been trained using manually labeled video achieve higher precision than fully automatic generic AAMs or CLMs. Some head trackers (Jang & Kanade, 2008) achieve higher precision when users first manually initialize them on one or more frames. User-in-the-loop approaches have been applied in several studies to reveal the dynamics of different types smiles. In an early application, (Cohn & Schmidt, 2004; Schmidt, Ambadar, Cohn, & Reed, 2006) and also (Valstar, Pantic, Ambadar, & Cohn, 2006) found that manually coded spontaneous and deliberate smiles systematically differed in their timing as measured using AFA. Extending this approach, (Ambadar et al., 2009) used a combination of manual FACS coding and automated measurement to discover variation between smiles perceived as embarrassed, amused, and polite. FACS coders first detected the onset and offset of smiles (AU 12 along with AU 6 and smile controls, e.g., AU 14). Amplitude and velocity then were measured using AFA. They found that the three types of smiles systematically varied in both shape and timing. These findings would not have been possible with only manual measurement.

Manual FACS coding is highly labor intensive. Several groups have explored the potential of AFA to reduce that burden (Simon, De la Torre, Ambadar, & Cohn, 2011; Zhang, Tong, & Ji, 2008). In one, referred to as Fast-FACS, manual FACS coders first detect AU peaks. An algorithm then automatically detects their onsets and offsets. Simon, De la Torre, & Cohn (2011) found that Fast-FACS achieved more than 50% reduction in the time required for manual FACS coding. Zhang, Tong, and Ji (Zhang et al., 2008) developed an alternative approach that uses active learning. The system performs initial labeling automatically; a FACS coder manualy makes any corrections that are needed; and the result is fed back to the system to further train the classifier. In this way, system performance is iteratively improved with a manual FACS coder in the loop. In other work, Hammal (Hammal, 2011) proposed an automatic method for successive detection of onsets, apexes, and offsets of consecutive facial expressions. All of these efforts combine manual and automated methods with the aim of achieving synergistic increases in efficiency.

Discussion

Automated facial analysis and synthesis is progressing rapidly with numerous initial applications in affective computing. Its vitality is evident in the breadth of approaches (in types of features, dimensionality reduction, and classifiers) and emerging uses (e.g., AU, valence, pain intensity, depression or stress, marketing, and expression transfer). Even as new applications come online, open research questions remain.

Challenges include more robust real-time systems for face acquisition, facial data extraction and representation, and facial expression recognition. Most systems perform within a range of only 15 to 20 degrees of frontal pose. Other challenges include illumination, occlusion, subtle facial expressions, and individual differences in subjects. Current systems are limited to indoors. Systems that would work in outdoor environments or with dynamic changes in illumination would greatly expand the range of possible applications. Occlusion is a problem in any context. Self-occlusion from head turns or face touching and occlusion by other persons passing in front of the camera are common. In a three-person social interaction in which participants have drinks, occlusion occurred about 10% of the time (Cohn & Sayette, 2010). Occlusion can spoil tracking, especially for holistic methods such as AAM and accuracy of AU detection. Approaches

to recovery of tracking following occlusion and estimation of facial actions in presence of occlusion are research topics.

Zhu, Ramanan, and their colleagues (Zhu, Vondrick, Ramanan, & Fowlkes, 2012) in object recognition raised the critical question: Do we need better features and classifiers or more data? The question applies as well to expression detection. Because most datasets to date are relatively small, the answer so far is unknown. The FERA GEMEP corpus (Valstar, Mehu, Jiang, Maja Pantic, & Scherer, 2012) consisted of emotion portrayals from only 10 actors. The widely used Cohn-Kanade (Kanade et al., 2000; Lucey, Wang, Saragih, & Cohn, 2010) and MMI (Pantic et al., 2005) corpuses have more subjects but relatively brief behavioral samples from each. To what extent is classifier performance attenuated by the relative paucity of training data? Humans are pre-adapted to perceive faces and facial expressions (i.e. strong priors) and have thousands of hours or more of experience in that task. To achieve humanlike accuracy, both access to big data and learning approaches that can scale to it may be necessary. Initial evidence from object recognition (Zhu et al., 2012), gesture recognition (Sutton, 2011), and smile detection (Whitehill et al., 2009) suggest that datasets orders of magnitude larger than those available to date will be needed to achieve optimal AFA.

As AFA is increasingly applied to real-world problems, the ability to apply trackers and classifiers across different contexts will become increasingly important. Success will require solutions to multiple sources of database specific biases. For one, approaches that appeal to domain-specific knowledge may transfer poorly to domains in which that knowledge fails to apply. Consider the HMM approach of Li and colleagues (Li et al., 2013). They improved upon detection of AU 12 (oblique lip-corner raise) and AU 15 (lip corners pulled down) by incorporating a constraint that these AU are mutually inhibiting. While this constraint may apply in the posed and enacted portrayals of amusement that they considered, in other contexts this dependency may be troublesome. In situations in which embarrassment (Keltner & Buswell, 1997) or depressed mood (Girard et al., 2014) are likely, AU 12 and AU 15 have been found to be positively correlated. AU 15 is a "smile control," defined as an action that counteracts the upward pull of AU 12. In both embarrassment and depression, occurrence of AU 12 increases the likelihood of AU 15. Use of HMM to encode spatial and temporal dependencies requires thoughtful application. Context (watching amusing videos versus clinical interview with depressed patients) may be especially important for HMM approaches.

Individual differences among persons affect both feature extraction and learning. Facial geometry and appearance change markedly over the course of development (Bruce & Young, 1998). Infants have larger eyes, greater fatty tissue in their cheeks, larger heads relative to their bodies, and smoother skin than adults. In adulthood, permanent lines and wrinkles become more common, and changes in fatty tissue and cartilage alter appearance. Large differences exist both between and within males and females and different ethnic groups. One of the most challenging factors may be skin color. Experience suggests that face tracking more often fails in persons that have very dark skin. Use of depth cameras, such as the Leap (Leap Motion) and Microsoft Kinect (Sutton, 2011), or infrared cameras (Buddharaju et al., 2005), may sidestep this problem. Other individual differences include characteristic patterns of emotion expression. Facial expression encodes person identity (Cohn, Schmidt, Gross, & Ekman, 2002; Peleg et al., 2006).

Individual differences affect learning, as well. Person-specific classifiers perform better than ones that are generic. Recent work by Chu and colleagues (Chu, Torre, & Cohn, 2013) proposed a method to narrow the distance between person-specific and generic classifiers. Their approach, referred to as a selective transfer machine (STM), simultaneously learns the parameters of a classifier and selectively minimizes the mismatch between training and test distributions. By attenuating the influence of inherent biases in appearance, STM achieved results that surpass nonpersonalized generic classifiers and approach the performance of classifiers that have been trained for individual persons (i.e., person-dependent classifiers).

At present taxonomies of facial expression are based on observer-based schemes, such as FACS. Consequently approaches to automatic facial expression recognition are dependent on access to corpuses of well-labeled video. An open question in facial analysis is whether facial actions can be learned directly from video in an unsupervised manner. That is, can the taxonomy be learned directly from video? And unlike FACS and similar systems that were initially developed to label static expressions, can we learn dynamic trajectories of facial actions? In our preliminary findings on unsupervised learning using RU-FACS database (Zhou,

De la Torre, & Cohn, 2010), moderate agreement between facial actions identified by unsupervised analysis of face dynamics and FACS approached the level of agreement that has been found between independent FACS coders. These findings suggest that unsupervised learning of facial expression is a promising alternative to supervised learning of FACS-based actions.

Because unsupervised learning is fully empirical, it potentially can identify regularities in video that have not been anticipated by the top-down approaches such as FACS. New discoveries become possible. Recent efforts by Guerra-Filho and Aloimonos (2007) to develop vocabularies and grammars of human actions suggest that this may be a fruitful approach.

Facial expression is one of several modes of nonverbal communication. The contribution of different modalities may well vary with context. In mother-infant interaction, touch appears to be especially important and tightly integrated with facial expression and head motion (Messinger et al., 2009). In depression, vocal prosody is highly related to severity of symptoms. We found that over 60% of the variance in depression severity could be accounted for by vocal prosody. Multimodal approaches that combine face, body language, and vocal prosody represent upcoming areas of research. Interdisciplinary efforts will be needed to progress in this direction.

While much basic research still is needed, AFA is becoming sufficiently mature to address real-world problems in behavioral science, biomedicine, affective computing, and entertainment. The range and depth of applications is just beginning.

Acknowledgments

Research reported in this chapter was supported in part by the National Institutes of Health (NIH) under Award Number MHR01MH096951 and by the US Army Research Laboratory (ARL) under the Collaborative Technology Alliance Program, Cooperative Agreement W911NF-10-2-0016. We thank Nicole Siverling, Wen-Sheng Chu, and Zakia Hammal for their help. The content is solely the responsibility of the authors and does not necessarily represent the official views of the NIH or ARL.

References

Ambadar, Z., Cohn, J. F., & Reed, L. I. (2009). All smiles are not created equal: Morphology and timing of smiles perceived as amused, polite, and embarrassed/nervous. *Journal of Nonverbal Behavior, 33*(1), 17–34.

Ambadar, Z., Schooler, J., & Cohn, J. F. (2005). Deciphering the Enigmatic Face: The Importance of facial dynamics in interpreting subtle facial expressions. *Psychological Science, 16*, 403-410.

Ashraf, A. B., Lucey, S., Cohn, J. F., Chen, T., Prkachin, K. M., & Solomon, P. E. (2009). The painful face: Pain expression recognition using active appearance models. *Image and Vision Computing, 27*(12), 1788–1796.

Baron-Cohen, S. (2003). *Mind reading: The interactive guide to emotion.*

Bartlett, M. S., Littlewort, G. C., Frank, M. G., Lainscsek, C., Fasel, I. R., & Movellan, J. R. (2006a). Automatic recognition of facial actions in spontaneous expressions. *Journal of Multimedia, 1*(6), 22-35.

Bartlett, M. S., Littlewort, G. C., Frank, M. G., Lainscsek, C., Fasel, I. R., & Movellan, J. R. (2006b). Fully automatic facial action recognition in spontaneous behavior. In *Proceedings of the seventh IEEE international conference on automatic face and gesture recognition* (pp. 223-228). IEEE Computer Society: Washington, DC.

Belkin, M., & Niyogi, P. (2001). Laplacian Eigenmaps and spectral techniques for embedding and clustering. *Advances in Neural Information Processing Systems, 14*, 586–691.

Bobick, A. F., & Davis, J. W. (2001). The recognition of human movement using temporal templates. *IEEE Transactions on Pattern Analysis and Machine Intelligence, 23*(3), 257–267.

Boker, S. M., Cohn, J. F., Theobald, B. J., Matthews, I., Mangini, M., Spies, J. R.,...Brick, T. R. (2011). Something in the way we move: Motion, not perceived sex, influences nods in conversation. *Journal of Experimental Psychology: Human Perception and Performance, 37*(3), 874–891.

Boker, S. M., Rotondo, J. L., Xu, M., & King, K. (2002). Windowed cross–correlation and peak picking for the analysis of variability in the association between behavioral time series. *Psychological Methods, 7*(1), 338–355.

Bråten, S. (2006). *Intersubjective communication and cmotion in early ontogeny* New York: Cambridge University Press.

Bruce, V., & Young, A. (1998). *In the eye of the beholder: The science of face perception.* New York: Oxford University Press.

Buck, R. (1984). *The Communication of emotion.* New York: The Guilford Press.

Buddharaju, P., Dowdall, J., Tsiamyrtzis, P., Shastri, D., Pavlidis, I., & Frank, M. G. (2005, June). Automatic thermal monitoring system (ATHEMOS) for deception detection. In *Proceedings of the IEEE International conference on computer vision and pattern recognition* (pp. 1–6). IEEE Computer Society: New York, NY.

Burrows, A., & Cohn, J. F. (In press). Comparative anatomy of the face. In S. Z. Li (Ed.), *Handbook of biometrics,* 2nd ed. Berlin and Heidelberg: Springer.

Cacioppo, J. T., & Tassinary, L. G. (1990). Inferring psychological significance from physiological signals. *American Psychologist, 45*(1), 16–28.

Cai, D., He, X., Zhou, K., Han, J., & Bao, H. (2007). Locality sensitive discriminant analysis. In *International joint conference on artificial intelligence.* IJCAI: USA.

Campos, J. J., Barrett, K. C., Lamb, M. E., Goldsmith, H. H., & Stenberg, C. (1983). Socioemotional development. In M. M. Haith & J. J. Campos (Eds.), *Handbook of child psychology,* 4th ed. (Vol. II, pp. 783–916). Hoboken, NJ: Wiley.

Chang, K. Y., Liu, T. L., & Lai, S. H. (2009). Learning partially-observed hidden conditional random fields for facial expression recognition. In *Proceedings of the IEEE international conference on computer vision and pattern recognition* (pp. 533–540). IEEE Computer Society: New York, NY.

Chang, Y., Hu, C., Feris, R., & Turk, M. (2006). Manifold based analysis of facial expression. *Image and Vision Computing, 24*, 605–614.

Chetverikov, D., & Peteri, R. (2005). A brief survey of dynamic texture description and recognition *Computer Recognition Systems: Advances in Soft Computing, 30*, 17–26.

Chew, S. W., Lucey, P., Lucey, S., Saragih, J. M., Cohn, J. F., Matthews, I., & Sridharan, S. (2012). In the pursuit of effective affective computing: The relationship between features and registration. *IEEE Transactions on Systems, Man, and Cybernetics—Part B, 42*(4), 1–12.

Chu, W.-S., Torre, F. D. l., & Cohn, J. F. (2013). Selective transfer machine for personalized facial action unit detection. *Proceedings of the IEEE international conference on computer vision and pattern recognition* (pp. 1–8). New York, NY: IEEE Computer Society.

Cohen, I., Sebe, N., Garg, A., Lew, M. S., & Huang, T. S. (2003). Facial expression recognition from video sequences. *Computer Vision and Image Understanding, 91*(1–2), 160–187.

Cohn, J. F., Ambadar, Z., & Ekman, P. (2007). Observer-based measurement of facial expression with the facial action coding system. In J. A. Coan & J. J. B. Allen (Eds.), *The handbook of emotion elicitation and assessment* (pp. 203–221). New York: Oxford University Press.

Cohn, J. F., & Ekman, P. (2005). Measuring facial action by manual coding, facial EMG, and automatic facial image analysis. In J. A. Harrigan, R. Rosenthal, & K. R. Scherer (Eds.), *Handbook of nonverbal behavior research methods in the affective sciences* (pp. 9–64). New York: Oxford University Press.

Cohn, J. F., & Sayette, M. A. (2010). Spontaneous facial expression in a small group can be automatically measured: An initial demonstration. *Behavior Research Methods, 42*(4), 1079–1086.

Cohn, J. F., & Schmidt, K. L. (2004). The timing of facial motion in posed and spontaneous smiles. *International Journal of Wavelets, Multiresolution and Information Processing, 2*, 1–12.

Cohn, J. F., Schmidt, K. L., Gross, R., & Ekman, P. (2002). Individual differences in facial expression: Stability over time, relation to self-reported emotion, and ability to inform person identification. In *Proceedings of the international conference on multimodal user interfaces,* (pp. 491–496). New York, NY: IEEE Computer Society.

Comon, P. (1994). Independent component analysis: A new concept? *Signal Processing, 36*(3), 287–314.

Cootes, T. F., Edwards, G. J., & Taylor, C. J. (2001). Active appearance models. *IEEE Transactions on Pattern Analysis and Machine Intelligence, 23*(6), 681–685.

Craig, S. D., D'Mello, S. K., Witherspoon, A., & Graesser, A. (2007). Emote aloud during learning with AutoTutor: Applying the facial action coding system to cognitive-affective states during learning. *Cognition and Emotion, 22*, 777–788.

Cristinacce, D., & Cootes, T. F. (2006). Feature detection and tracking with constrained local models. In *Proceedings of the British machine vision conference* (pp.929–938). United Kingdom: BMVC.

Dalal, N., & Triggs, B. (2005). Histograms of oriented gradients for human detection. In *Proceedings of the IEEE international conference on computer vision and pattern recognition* (pp. 886-893). Los Alamitos, CA: IEEE Computer Society.

Danisman, T., Bilasco, I. M., Djeraba, C., & Ihaddadene, N. (2010). Drowsy driver detection system using eye blink patterns. In *Proceedings of the international conference on machine and web intelligence (ICMWI)*. Available at: http://ieeexplore.ieee.org/xpl/mostRecentIssue.jsp?punumber=5628557

Darwin, C. (1872/1998). *The expression of the emotions in man and animals*, 3rd ed. New York: Oxford University Press.

De la Torre, F., & Cohn, J. F. (2011). Visual analysis of humans: Facial expression analysis. In T. B. Moeslund, A. Hilton, A. U. Volker Krüger & L. Sigal (Eds.), *Visual analysis of humans: Looking at people* (pp. 377–410). New York, NY: Springer.

Deng, L., Xiong, X., Zhou, J., Gan, P., & Deng, S. (2010). Fatigue detection based on infrared video puillography. In *Proceedings of the bioinformatics and biomedical engineering (iCBBE)*.

Dhall, A., Goecke, R., Joshi, J., Wagner, M., & Gedeon, T. (Eds.). (2013). ICMI 2013 emotion recognition in the wild challenge and workshop. *ACM International Conference on Multimodal Processing*. New York, NY: ACM.

Ekman, P. (1992). An argument for basic emotions. *Cognition and Emotion*, 6(3/4), 169–200.

Ekman, P. (2009). *Telling lies*. New York: Norton.

Ekman, P., & Friesen, W. V. (1975). *Unmasking the face: A guide to emotions from facial cues*. Englewood Cliffs, NJ: Prentice-Hall.

Ekman, P., & Friesen, W. V. (1978). *Facial action coding system*. Palo Alto, CA: Consulting Psychologists Press.

Ekman, P., Friesen, W. V., & Hager, J. C. (2002). *Facial action coding system*. Research Nexus, Network Research Information. Salt Lake City, UT:.

Ekman, P., Huang, T. S., & Sejnowski, T. J. (1992). *Final report to NSF of the planning workshop on facial expression understanding*. Washington, DC: National Science Foundation.

Ekman, P., & Rosenberg, E. (2005). *What the face reveals*, 2nd ed. New York: Oxford University Press.

Essa, I., & Pentland, A. (1997). Coding, analysis, interpretation and recognition of facial expressions. *IEEE Transactions on Pattern Analysis and Machine Intelligence*, 7, 757–763.

Feldman Barrett, L., Mesquita, B., & Gendron, M. (2011). Context in emotion perception. *Current Directions in Psychological Science*, 20(5), 286–290.

Fleiss, J. L. (1981). *Statistical methods for rates and proportions*. Hoboken, NJ: Wiley.

Fox, E. (2008). *Emotion science: Cognitive and neuroscientific approaches to understanding human emotions*. New York: Palgrave Macmillan.

Fridlund, A. J. (1994). *Human facial expression: An evolutionary view*. New York: Academic Press.

Girard, J. M. (2013). *Automatic detection and intensity estimation of spontaneous smiles*. (M.S.), Pittsburgh, PA: University of Pittsburgh.

Girard, J. M., Cohn, J. F., Mahoor, M. H., Mavadati, S. M., & Rosenwald, D. (In press). Social risk and depression: Evidence from manual and automatic facial expression analysis *Image and Vision Computing*

Gratch, J. (2013). Felt emotion and social context determine the intensity of smiles in a competitive video game. In *Proceedings of the IEEE international conference on automatic face and gesture recognition*. (pp. 1–8). Los Alamitos, CA: IEEE Computer Society.

Guerra-Filho, G., & Aloimonos, Y. (2007). A language for human action. *Computer*, 40(5), 42–51.

Hammal, Z. (Ed.). (2011). *Efficient detection of consecutive facial expression apices using biologically based log-normal filters*. Berlin: Springer.

Hammal, Z., & Cohn, J. F. (2012). Automatic detection of pain intensity. In *Proceedings of the international conference on multimodal interaction* (pp. 1–6). New York, NY: ACM.

Hammal, Z., Cohn, J. F., Baiile, T., George, D. T., Saragih, J. M., Nuevo-Chiquero, J., & Lucey, S. (2013). Temporal coordination of head motion in couples with history of interpersonal violence. In *IEEE international conference on automatic face and gesture recognition* (pp. 1–8). Los Alamitos, CA: IEEE Computer Society.

Hammal, Z., Cohn, J. F., & Messinger, D. S. (2013). Head movement dynamics during normal and perturbed parent-infant interaction. In *Proceedings of the international conference on affective computing and intelligent interaction* (pp. 276–282). Los Alamitos, CA: IEEE Computer Society.

Hammal, Z., & Kunz, M. (2012). Pain monitoring: A dynamic and context-sensitive system. *Pattern Recognition*, 45, 1265–1280.

Hoque, M. E., & Picard, R. W. (2011). Acted vs. natural frustration and delight: Many people smile in natural frustration. In *Proceedings of the IEEE international conference on automatic face and gesture recognition* (pp. 354 – 359). Los Alamitos, CA: IEEE Computer Society

Hotelling, H. (1933). Analysis of complex statistical variables into principal components. *Journal of Educational Psychology*, 24(6), 417–441.

Hutchings, E. (2012). Sony technology gives gaming avatars same facial expressions as players. Available at: http://www.psfk.com/2012/08/avatars-human-facial-expressions.html (Retrieved March 24, 2013.)

Izard, C. E. (1977). *Human emotions*. New York, NY: Plenum.

Jang, J.-S., & Kanade, T. (2008, September). Robust 3D head tracking by online feature registration. In *Proceedings of the IEEE international conference on automatic face and gesture recognition*. Los Alamitos, CA: IEEE Computer Society.

Jeni, L. A., Cohn, J. F., & De la Torre, F. (2013). Facing imbalanced data recommendations for the use of performance metrics. In Proceedings of the Affective Computing and Intelligent Interaction (pp. 245-251). Geneva, Switzerland.

Jeni, L. A., Lorincz, A., Nagy, T., Palotai, Z., Sebok, J., Szabo, Z., & Taka, D. (2012). 3D shape estimation in video sequences provides high precision evaluation of facial expressions. *Image and Vision Computing Journal*, 30(10), 785–795.

Jones, J. P., & Palmer, L. A. (1987). An evaluation of the two-dimensional gabor filter model of simple receptive fields in cat striate cortex. *Journal of Neurophysiology*, 58(6), 1233–1258.

Joshi, J., Dhall, A., Goecke, R., Breakspear, M., & Parker, G. (2012). Neural-net classification for spatio-temporal descriptor based depression analysis. In *Proceedings of the IEEE international conference on pattern recognition* (pp. 1–5). Los Alamitos, CA: IEEE Computer Society

Kaltwang, S., Rudovic, O., & Pantic, M. (2012). Continuous pain intensity estimation from facial expressions. *Lecture Notes in Comptuer Science*, 7432, 368–377.

Kanade, T. (1973). *Picture processing system by computer complex and recognition of human faces*. Kyoto:.

Kanade, T., Cohn, J. F., & Tian, Y. (2000). Comprehensive database for facial expression analysis. In *Proceedings of the fourth international conference on automatic face and gesture recognition* (pp. 46–53). Los Alamitos, CA: IEEE Computer Society

Keltner, D., & Buswell, B. N. (1997). Embarrassment: Its distinct form and appeasement functions. *Psychological Bulletin, 122*(3), 250–270.

Keltner, D., & Ekman, P. (2000). Facial expression of emotion. In M. Lewis & J. M. Haviland (Eds.), *Handbook of emotions* (2nd ed., pp. 236–249). New York: Guilford.

Knapp, M. L., & Hall, J. A. (2010). *Nonverbal behavior in human communication,* 7th ed. Boston: Wadsworth/Cengage.

Koelstra, S., & Pantic, M. (2008). Non-rigid registration using free-form deformations for recognition of facial actions and their temporal dynamics. In *Proceedings of the international conference on automatic face and gesture recognition.* (pp. 1–8). Los Alamitos, CA: IEEE Computer Society

Leap Motion. (2013). Leap. Available at: http://thecomputervision.blogspot.com/2012/05/leap-motion-new-reliable-low-cost-depth.html

Lee, D., Oh, S., Heo, S., & Hahn, M.-S. (2008). Drowsy driving detection based on the driver's head movement using infrared sensors. In *Proceedings of the second international symposium on universal communication* (pp. 231–236). New York, NY: IEEE

Li, Y., Chen, J., Zhao, Y., & Ji, Q. (2013). Data-free prior model for facial action unit recognition. *Transactions on Affective Computing, 4*(2), 127–141.

Littlewort, G. C., Bartlett, M. S., Fasel, I. R., Susskind, J., & Movellan, J. R. (2006). Dynamics of facial expression extracted automatically from video. *Journal of Image & Vision Computing, 24*(6), 615–625.

Littlewort, G. C., Bartlett, M. S., & Lee, K. (2009). Automatic coding of facial expressions displayed during posed and genuine pain. *Image and Vision Computing, 27*(12), 1797–1803.

Lucey, P., Cohn, J. F., Howlett, J., Lucey, S., & Sridharan, S. (2011). Recognizing emotion with head pose variation: Identifying pain segments in video. *IEEE Transactions on Systems, Man, and Cybernetics—Part B, 41*(3), 664–674.

Lucey, P., Cohn, J. F., Kanade, T., Saragih, J. M., Ambadar, Z., & Matthews, I. (2010). The extended Cohn-Kade Dataset (CK+): A complete facial expression dataset for action unit and emotion-specified expression. *Third IEEE Workshop on CVPR for Human Communicative Behavior Analysis (CVPR4HB 2010)* (pp. 1–8). Los Alamitos, CA: IEEE Computer Society.

Lucey, P., Cohn, J. F., Prkachin, K. M., Solomon, P. E., & Matthews, I. (2011). Painful data: The UNBC-McMaster shoulder pain expression archive database. *IEEE international conference on automatic face and gesture recognition* (pp. 1–8). New York, NY: IEEE Computer Society.

Lucey, S., Wang, Y., Saragih, J. M., & Cohn, J. F. (2010). Non-rigid face tracking with enforced convexity and local appearance consistency constraint. *Image and Vision Computing, 28*(5), 781–789.

Martin, P., & Bateson, P. (2007). *Measuring behavior: An introductory guide,* 3rd ed. Cambridge, UK: Cambridge University Press.

Mase, K. (1991). Recognition of facial expression from optical flow. *IEICE Transactions on Information and Systems, E74-D*(10), 3474–3483.

Matsuo, H., & Khiat, A. (2012). Prediction of drowsy driving by monitoring driver's behavior. In *Proceedings of the international conference on pattern recognition* (pp. 231–236). New York, NY: IEEE Computer Society.

Matthews, I., Xiao, J., & Baker, S. (2007). 2D vs. 3D deformable face models: Representational power, construction, and real-time fitting. *International Journal of Computer Vision, 75*(1), 93–113.

Mavadati, S. M., Mahoor, M. H., Bartlett, K., Trinh, P., & Cohn, J. F. (2013). DISFA: A non-posed facial expression video database with FACS-AU intensity coding. *IEEE Transactions on Affective Computing. 4*(2), 151–160.

McDuff, D., Kaliouby, R. E., & Picard, R. (2013). Predicting online media effectiveness based on smile responses gathered over the Internet. In *Proceedings of the international conference on automatic face and gesture recognition.*(pp. 1–8).. New York, NY: IEEE Computer Society.

McDuff, D., Kaliouby, R. E., Senechal, T., Amr, M., Cohn, J. F., & Picard, R. (2013). AMFED facial expression dataset: Naturalistic and spontaneous facial expressions collected "in-the-wild." In *Proceedings of the IEEE international workshop on analysis and modeling of faces and gestures* (pp. 1-8). New York, NY: IEEE Computer Society.

Mehrabian, A. (1998). Correlations of the PAD emotion scales with self-reported satisfaction in marriage and work. *Genetic, Social, and General Psychology Monographs 124*(3):311–334 (3), 311–334.

Messinger, D. S., Mahoor, M. H., Chow, S. M., & Cohn, J. F. (2009). Automated measurement of facial expression in infant-mother interaction: A pilot study. *Infancy, 14*(3), 285–305.

Michael, N., Dilsizian, M., Metaxas, D., & Burgoon, J. K. (2010). Motion profiles for deception detection using visual cues. In *Proceedings of the European conference on computer vision* (pp. 1–14). New York, NY: IEEE Computer Society.

Mikolajczyk, K., & Schmid, C. (2005). A performance evaluation of local descriptors. *IEEE Transactions on Pattern Analysis and Machine Intelligence, 27*(10), 1615–1630.

Morency, L.-P. (2008). *Watson user guide* (Version 2.6A).

Movellan, J. R. (n.d.). *Tutorial on Gabor filters.* San Diego: University of California.

Pandzic, I. S., & Forchheimer, R. (Eds.). (2002). *MPEG-4 facial animation: The standard, implementation and applications.* Hoboken, NJ: Wiley.

Pantic, M., & Rothkrantz, L. (2000). Expert system for automatic analysis of facial expression. *Image and Vision Computing, 18,* 881–905.

Pantic, M., Valstar, M. F., Rademaker, R., & Maat, L. (2005). Web-based database for facial expression analysis. In *Proceedings of the IEEE international conference on multimodal interfaces* (pp. 1–4). Los Alamitos, CA: IEEE Computer Society.

Parke, F. I., & Waters, K. (1996). *Computer facial animation.* Wellesley, MA: A. K. Peters.

Peleg, G., Katzir, G., Peleg, O., Kamara, M., Brodsky, L., Hel-Or, H.,…Nevo, E. (2006, October 24, 2006). From the cover: Hereditary family signature of facial expression. Available at: http://www.pnas.org/cgi/content/abstract/103/43/15921

Plutchik, R. (1979). *Emotion: A psychoevolutionary synthesis.* New York: Harper & Row.

Prkachin, K. M., & Solomon, P. E. (2008). The structure, reliability and validity of pain expression: Evidence from patients with shoulder pain. *Pain, 139,* 267–274.

Rosenthal, R. (2005). Conducting judgment studies. In J. A. Harrigan, R. Rosenthal & K. R. Scherer (Eds.), *Handbook of nonverbal behavior research methods in the affective sciences* (pp. 199–236). New York: Oxford University Press.

Roweis, S. T., & Saul, L. K. (2000). Nonlinear dimensionality reduction by locally linear embedding. *Science, 290*(5500), 2323–2326.

Russell, J. A., & Bullock, M. (1985). Multidimensional scaling of emotional facial expressions: Similarity from preschoolers to adults. *Journal of Personality and Social Psychology, 48*(5), 1290–1298.

Saragih, J. M., Lucey, S., & Cohn, J. F. (2011a). Deformable model fitting by regularized landmark mean-shift. *International Journal of Computer Vision, 91*(2), 200–215. doi: 10.1007/s11263-010-0335-9

Saragih, J. M., Lucey, S., & Cohn, J. F. (2011b). Real-time avatar animation from a single image. In *Proceedings of the 9th IEEE international conference on automatic face and gesture recognition.* (pp. 1–8). Los Alamitos, CA: IEEE Computer Society.

Sayette, M. A., Creswell, K. G., Dimoff, J. D., Fairbairn, C. E., Cohn, J. F., Heckman, B. W.,...Moreland, R. L. (2012). Alcohol and group formation: A multimodal investigation of the effects of alcohol on emotion and social bonding. *Psychological Science, 23*(8), 869–878

Scherer, S., Stratou, G., Gratch, J., Boberg, J., Mahmoud, M., Rizzo, A. S., & Morency, L.-P. (2013). Automatic behavior descriptors for psychological disorder analysis. *IEEE International Conference on Automatic Face and Gesture Recognition* (pp. 1–8). Los Alamitos, CA: IEEE Computer Society.

Schlosberg, H. (1952). The description of facial expressions in terms of two dimensions. *Journal of Experimental Psychology, 44*, 229–237.

Schlosberg, H. (1954). Three dimensions of emotion. *Psychological Review, 61*, 81–88.

Schmidt, K. L., Ambadar, Z., Cohn, J. F., & Reed, L. I. (2006). Movement differences between deliberate and spontaneous facial expressions: Zygomaticus major action in smiling. *Journal of Nonverbal Behavior, 30*, 37–52.

Schmidt, K. L., & Cohn, J. F. (2001). Human facial expressions as adaptations: Evolutionary perspectives in facial expression research. *Yearbook of Physical Anthropology, 116*, 8–24.

Schokopf, B., Smola, A., & Muller, K. (1997). Kernel principal component analysis. *Artificial Neural Networks, 583*–588.

Shang, C. F., & Chan, K. P. (2009). Nonparametric discriminant HMM and application to facial expression recognition. In *Proceedings of the IEEE international conference on computer vision and pattern recognition* (pp. 2090–2096). Los Alamitos, CA: IEEE Computer Society.

Shrout, P. E., & Fleiss, J. L. (1979). Intraclass correlations: Uses in assessing rater reliability. *Psychological Bulletin, 86*, 420–428.

Simon, T. K., De la Torre, F., Ambadar, Z., & Cohn, J. F. (2011). Fast-FACS: A computer vision assisted system to increase the speed and reliability of manual FACS coding. In *Proceedings of the HUMAINE association conference on affective computing and intelligent interaction* (pp. 57–66).

Sutton, J. (2011). Body part recognition: Making Kinect robust. *IEEE international conference on automatic face and gesture recognition.* Los Alamitos, CA: IEEE Computer Society.

Tellegen, A., Watson, D., & Clark, L. A. (1999). On the dimensional and hierarchical structure of affect. *Psychological Science, 10*(4), 297–303.

Theobald, B. J., Bangham, J. A., Matthews, I., & Cawley, G. C. (2004). Near-videorealistic synthetic talking faces: Implementation and evaluation. *Speech Communication, 44*, 127–140.

Theobald, B. J., & Cohn, J. F. (2009). Facial image synthesis. In D. Sander & K. R. Scherer (Eds.), *Oxford companion to emotion and the affective sciences* (pp. 176–179). New York: Oxford University Press.

Theobald, B. J., Matthews, I., Cohn, J. F., & Boker, S. M. (2007). *Real-time expression cloning using appearance models.* In *Proceedings of the ACM international conference on multimodal interfaces.*

Theobald, B. J., Matthews, I., Mangini, M., Spies, J. R., Brick, T., Cohn, J. F., & Boker, S. M. (2009). Mapping and manipulating facial expression. *Language and Speech, 52*(2–3), 369–386.

Tian, Y., Cohn, J. F., & Kanade, T. (2005). Facial expression analysis. In S. Z. Li & A. K. Jain (Eds.), *Handbook of face recognition* (pp. 247–276). New York: Springer.

Tian, Y., Kanade, T., & Cohn, J. F. (2001). Recognizing action units for facial expression analysis. *IEEE Transactions on Pattern Analysis and Machine Intelligence, 23*(2), 97–115.

Tinsley, H. E., & Weiss, D. J. (1975). Interrater reliability and agreement of subjective judgements. *Journal of Counseling Psychology, 22*, 358–376.

Tong, Y., Chen, J., & Ji, Q. (2010). A unified probabilistic framework for spontaneous facial action modeling and understanding. *IEEE Transactions on Pattern Analysis and Machine Intelligence, 32*(2), 258–273.

Tong, Y., Liao, W., & Ji, Q. (2007). Facial action unit recognition by exploiting their dynamic and semantic relationships. *IEEE Transactions on Pattern Analysis and Machine Intelligence, 29*(10), 1683–1699.

Tronick, E. Z. (1989). Emotions and emotional communication in infants. *American Psychologist, 44*(2), 112–119.

Tsiamyrtzis, P., J. Dowdall, Shastri, D., Pavlidis, I. T., Frank, M. G., & Ekman, P. (2006). Imaging facial physiology for the detection of deceit. *International Journal of Computer Vision, 71*, 197–214.

Valstar, M. F., Gunes, H., & Pantic, M. (2007). How to distinguish posed from spontaneous smiles using geometric features. *ACM international conference on multimodal interfaces* (pp. 38–45).

Valstar, M. F., Mehu, M., Jiang, B., Pantic, M., & Scherer, K. (2012). Meta-analyis of the first facial expression recognition challenge. *IEEE Transactions of Systems, Man and Cybernetics—Part B, 42*(4), 966–979

Valstar, M. F., & Pantic, M. (2007). Combined support vector machines and hidden Markov models for modeling facial action temporal dynamics. In *Proceedings of the IEEE conference on computer vision (ICCV'07).*(pp. 1–10). Los Alamitos, CA: IEEE Computer Society.

Valstar, M. F., Pantic, M., Ambadar, Z., & Cohn, J. F. (2006). Spontaneous vs. posed facial behavior: Automatic analysis of brow actions. In *Proceedings of the ACM international conference on multimodal interfaces.* (pp. 162–170). New York, NY: ACM.

Valstar, M. F., Pantic, M., & Patras, I. (2004). Motion history for facial action detection in video. In *Proceedings of the IEEE conference on systems, man, and cybernetics* (pp. 635–640). Los Alamitos, CA: IEEE Computer Society.

Valstar, M. F., Schuller, B., Smith, K., Eyben, F., Jiang, B., Bilakhia, S.,...Pantic, M. (2013). AVEC 2013—The continuous audio/visual emotion and depression recognition challenge. *Proceedings of the third international audio/video challenge workshop. International Conference on Multimodal Processing.* New York, NY: ACM.

Viola, P. A., & Jones, M. J. (2004). Robust real-time face detection. *International Journal of Computer Vision, 57*(2), 137–154.

Vinciarelli, A., Valente, F., Bourlard, H., Pantic, M., & Renals, S. et al. (Eds.). *Audiovisual emotion challenge workshop. ACM International Conference on Multimedia.* New York, NY: ACM.

Vinciarelli, A., Nijholt, A., & Aghajan, A. (Eds.). (2013). International workshop on vision(s) of deception and non-cooperation. IEEE International Conference on Automatic Face and Gesture Recognition. Los Alamitos, CA: IEEE Computer Society.

Vural, E., Bartlett, M., Littlewort, G., Cetin, M., Ercil, A., & Movellan, J. (2010). Discrimination of moderate and acute drowsiness based on spontaneous facial expressions. In *Proceedings of the IEEE international conference on machine learning.* (pp. 3874–3877). Los Alamitos, CA: IEEE Computer Society.

Wang, P., Barrett, F., Martin, E., Milonova, M., Gurd, R. E., Gur, R. C.,...Verma, R. (2008). Automated video-based facial expression analysis of neuropsychiatric disorders. *Journal of Neuroscience Methods, 168*, 224–238.

Watson, D., & Tellegen, A. (1985). Toward a consensual structure of mood. *Psychological Bulletin, 98*(2), 219–235.

Whitehill, J., Littlewort, G., Fasel, I., Bartlett, M. S., & Movellan, J. R. (2009). Towards practical smile detection. *IEEE Transactions on Pattern Analysis and Machine Intelligence, 31*(11), 2106–2111.

Whitehill, J., Serpell, Z., Foster, A., Lin, Y.-C., Pearson, B., Bartlett, M., & Movellan, J. (2011). Towards an optimal affect-sensitive instructional system of cognitive skills. In *Proceedings of the IEEE conference on computer vision and pattern recognition workshop on human communicative behavior* (pp. 20–25). Los Alamitos, CA: IEEE Computer Society.

Xiao, J., Baker, S., Matthews, I., & Kanade, T. (2004). Real-time combined 2D+3D active appearance models. *IEEE computer society conference on computer vision and pattern recognition* (pp. 535–542). Los Alamitos, CA: IEEE Computer Society.

Xiao, J., Kanade, T., & Cohn, J. F. (2003). Robust full motion recovery of head by dynamic templates and re-registration techniques. *International Journal of Imaging Systems and Technology, 13*, 85–94.

Yacoob, Y., & Davis, L. (1997). Recognizing human facial expression from long image sequence using optical flow. *IEEE Transactions on Pattern Analysis and Machine Intelligence, 18*, 636–642.

Yang, P., Liu, Q., & Metaxas, D. N. (2009). Boosting encoded dynamic features for facial expression recognition *Pattern Recognition Letters, 30*, 132–139.

Yu, X., Zhang, S., Yan, Z., Yang, F., Huang, J., Dunbar, N.,...Metaxas, D. (2013). Interactional dissynchrony a clue to deception: Insights from automated analysis of nonverbal visual cues. In *Proceedings of the rapid screening technologies, deception detection and credibility assessment symposium.* (pp. 1–7). Tucson, AR: University of Arizona.

Zeng, Z., Pantic, M., Roisman, G. I., & Huang, T. S. (2009). A survey of affect recognition methods: Audio, visual, and spontaneous expressions. *Pattern Analysis and Machine Intelligence, 31*(1), 31–58.

Zhang, C., & Zhang, Z. (2010). *A survey of recent advances in face detection: Microsoft research technical report.* Redmond, WA: Microsoft.

Zhang, L., Tong, Y., & Ji, Q. (2008). Active image labeling and its application to facial action labeling. In D. Forsyth, P. Torr & A. Zisserman (Eds.), *Lecture notes in computer science: 10th European conference on computer vision: Proceedings, Part II* (Vol. 5303/2008, pp. 706–719). Berlin and Heidelberg: Springer.

Zhang, X., Yin, L., Cohn, J. F., Canavan, S., Reale, M., Horowitz, A., & Liu, P. (2013). A 3D spontaneous dynamic facial expression database. In *Proceedings of the international conference on automatic face and gesture recognition.* Los Alamitos, CA: IEEE Computer Society.

Zhao, G., & Pietikainen, M. (2007). Dynamic texture recognition using local binary patterns with an application to facial expressions. In *IEEE transactions on pattern analysis and machine intelligence, 29*(6), 915–928

Zhou, F., De la Torre, F., & Cohn, J. F. (2010). Unsupervised discovery of facial events. In *IEEE international conference on computer vision and pattern recognition* (pp. 1–8). Los Alamitos, CA: IEEE Computer Society.

Zhu, X., Vondrick, C., Ramanan, D., & Fowlkes, C. C. (2012). *Do we need more training data or better models for object detection.* In *Proceedings of the British machine vision conference* (pp. 1–11). United Kingdom: BMVC.

Zhu, Y., De la Torre, F., Cohn, J. F., & Zhang, Y.-J. (2011). Dynamic cascades with bidirectional bootstrapping for action unit detection in spontaneous facial behavior. *IEEE Transactions on Affective Computing, 2*(2), 1–13.

CHAPTER 1

Automatic Recognition of Affective Body Expressions

Nadia Bianchi-Berthouze *and* Andrea Kleinsmith

Abstract

As technology for capturing human body movement is becoming more affordable and ubiquitous, the importance of bodily expressions is increasing as a channel for human-computer interaction. In this chapter we provide an overview of the area of automatic emotion recognition from bodily expressions. In particular, we discuss how affective bodily expressions can be captured and described to build recognition models. We briefly review the literature on affective body movement and body posture detection to identify the factors that can affect this process. We then discuss the recent advances in building systems that can automatically track and categorize affective bodily expressions. We conclude by discussing open issues and challenges as well as new directions that are being tackled in this field. We finally briefly direct the attention to aspects of body behavior that are often overlooked; some of which are dictated by the needs of real-world applications.

Key Words: body movement, automatic emotion recognition, touch behavior

Introduction

Over the last several years, interest in developing technology that has the ability to recognize people's affective states (Fragopanagos & Taylor, 2005) has grown rapidly, and particular attention is being paid to the possibility of recognizing affect from body expressions. The relevance of body expressions and the benefits of developing applications into which affect detection from body expressions can be integrated is evident from the many nondigital applications to security, law enforcement, games and entertainment, education, and health care. For example, teachers are sometimes taught how to read affective aspects of students' body language and how to react appropriately through their own body language and actions (Neill & Caswell, 1993) in an effort to help students maintain motivation. In chronic pain rehabilitation (Haugstad, et al., 2006; Kvåle, Ljunggren, & Johnsen, 2003), specific movements and postural patterns (called protective

behavior) inform about the emotional state experienced by the patients during physical activity (e.g., fear of movement, fear of injury, fear of pain, anxiety, need for psychological support) (Bunkan, Ljunggren, Opjordsmoen, Moen, & Friis, 2001; Vlaeyen & Linton, 2000). Clinical practitioners make use of such information to tailor their support to patients during therapy (Aung et al. 2013; Singh et al., 2014).

However, only recently have affective computing research and related disciplines (e.g., affective sciences) focused on body movement and posture. The majority of research on nonverbal affect recognition has concentrated on facial expressions (Anderson & McOwan, 2006; Pantic & Patras, 2006; Pantic & Rothkrantz, 2000; Zhao, Chellapa & Rosenfeld, 2003) (see Cohn's chapter on facial expression, this volume), voice/speech (Lee & Narayanan, 2005; Morrison, Wang & De Silva, 2007; Yacoub, Simske, Lin, & Burns, 2003) (see the chapter by Lee et al., this volume) and physiology (Kim & André, 2008; Kim, Bang & Kim, 2004; Wagner, Kim & André, 2005) (see Healey's chapter on physiology, this volume). This is evidenced by an article by de Gelder (2009), which states that 95% of the studies on emotion in humans have been conducted using facial expression stimuli, while research using information from voice, music, and environmental sounds make up the majority of the remaining 5%, with research on whole-body expressions comprising the smallest proportion of studies. However, several studies have shown that some affective expressions may be better communicated by the body than the face (Argyle, 1988; Bull, 1987; de Gelder, 2006). For example, De Gelder (2006) postulates that for fear, it is possible to discern not only the cause of a threat but also the action to be carried out (i.e., the action tendency) by evaluating body posture. Instead, the face communicates mainly that there is a threat.

Mehrabian and Friar (1969) found that bodily configuration and orientation are significantly affected by a communicator's attitude toward her or his interaction partner. Ekman and Friesen (1967, 1969) conjecture that postural changes due to affective state aid a person's ability to cope with the experienced affective state. This is also supported by the emerging embodied perspective on emotion discussed in the chapter by Kemp et al. in this volume.

While there is a clear need to create technologies that exploit the body as an affective communication modality, there is a less clear understanding on how these systems should be built, validated, and compared (Gross, Crane, & Fredrickson, 2010; Gunes & Pantic, 2010). This chapter outlines our ideas on these issues and is organized as follows: first, we discuss different types of systems that can be used to capture body motions and expressions. Next we report on factors and features that may affect the way people perceive and categorize affective body expressions. We then discuss issues, challenges, and new directions related to the construction of automatic affect recognition models. We conclude by discussing new aspects of body behavior that are often overlooked and the possibility of measuring body behavior on the move.

Capturing Body Expressions

There are many different methods for collecting body expression data. The most notable are optical and electromechanical/electromagnetic motion capture systems and markerless vision-based systems. Many optical motion capture systems make use of infrared cameras (generally 8 to 12) to track the movement of retroreflective markers placed on the body. Optical systems provide the three dimensional (3D) positions of each marker as output. The more markers used, the more accurate the description of the configuration. Electromechanical or electromagnetic motion capture systems instead require the person to wear active sensors (e.g., inertial sensors, accelerometers, or magnetometers) on various parts of the body. In the case of full body capture, these sensors are generally integrated in a suit for easy wearing. These active sensors detect rotational or acceleration information of the body segments on which the sensors are placed. Markerless vision-based systems use video or web cameras to record movement, after which the data are processed with image-processing techniques to determine the position and orientation of the body.

Each type of system comes with its own advantages and disadvantages for capturing body expressions. An advantage of using optical and electromechanical motion capture systems is accuracy. Using these systems, a precise numeric representation of the body in a 3D space can be easily obtained; either in terms of x, y, z coordinates or Euler rotations. This allows for a person to be represented in varying degrees of detail (e.g., point light display, skeleton, full body) (Ma, Paterson, & Pollick, 2006). According to Thomas, McGinley, Carruth, & Blackledge (2007), the data from optical systems are more accurate than those from electromechanical systems. Another advantage is privacy. Optical and electromechanical motion capture systems allow for complete anonymity because it is only the trajectories of the reflective markers that are recorded, not the person's physical characteristics. Anonymous data are beneficial for many types of potential research and commercial applications, from health care to video games, as the individuals being recorded may wish to remain unidentifiable to others.

A disadvantage of optical motion capture systems is mobility. Typically, once these systems are in place, they are not moved owing to the difficulties of camera transportation and placement as well as issues of calibration. On the other hand, electromechanical and electromagnetic motion capture systems are highly portable, allowing them to be used in almost any setting, indoors or outdoors, making them feasible for use in real applications.

While mobility issues are not as significant a problem for vision-based systems, environmental conditions can pose some challenges. Often, vision-based systems have constraints or difficulties with variations in lighting conditions, skin color, clothing, body part occlusion or touching, etc. Similarly, marker occlusion is an issue with optical motion capture systems when markers are not seen by the cameras (e.g., a hand or an object is between the marker and some of the cameras) or not easily discriminable from other markers because of their close position. In the case of electromagnetic motion capture systems, a drawback is that they are sensitive to magnetic fields.

The cost of most optical systems is also a disadvantage as they are typically more expensive. As reported in Thomas et al. (2007), according to Inition (http://www.inition.co.uk/inition/guide_19.htm), "electromechanical systems cost[ing] a fraction of infrared systems ". However, new vision-based motion capture systems are emerging at a significantly lower cost. One of the cheapest and newest motion capture options is Microsoft's Kinect, a markerless vision-based sensor, which retails for $150. These types of motion capture systems make use of cameras that project infrared patterns for depth recovery of motion. An advantage of this latter type of system together with traditional vision-based systems is that they are not intrusive (i.e., participants are not required to wear suits or sensors), which makes it a more natural experience. Therefore vision-based systems lend themselves well to certain areas of research, such as security and surveillance (Moeslund & Granum, 2001). However, these systems require expertise in computer vision to track and extract body position over time.

A significant disadvantage from which all three types of motion capture systems suffer is the inability to record detailed hand and finger positions. While there are motion tracking gloves that can be worn, they can be more intrusive and/or sometimes cannot be used in conjunction with full body systems. A recent study by Oikonomidis, Kyriazis, & Argyros (2011) solved some of these issues by proposing a model-based approach to 3D hand tracking using a Kinect sensor. Some commercial products are also beginning to appear, such as Leap Motion (https://leapmotion.com/).

These new motion capture technologies make the investigation and modeling of affective body expressions more accessible to a larger number of researchers, as these systems provide direct access to body configuration and kinematic features. This has brought increased attention to this modality and in particular to researchers investigating which factors affect the perception of emotion from the body and which bodily features are diagnostic of different emotional states.

The Perception of Affective Body Expressions
Factors Affecting the Perception of Affect Through the Body

Although there are many factors that determine how affect is expressed and perceived from body expressions, most of the work in this area has investigated cross-cultural differences. The most notable studies examining cross-cultural differences in body expressions have focused on Japanese and Americans, such as those of Matsumoto and Kudoh in the 1980s. They examined cross-cultural differences in judging body posture according to a set of 16 semantic dimensions (e.g., tense-relaxed, dominant-submissive, happy-sad, etc.) (Kudoh & Matsumoto, 1985; Matsumoto & Kudoh, 1987). They argued that differences between these two cultures typically are due to the fact that social status is more important to Japanese than it is to Americans. In each study, a corpus of written descriptions of posture expressions (obtained from the Japanese participants) was evaluated by each culture separately using the same methodology, with Japanese participants in the first study (Kudoh & Matsumoto, 1985) and American participants in the second (Matsumoto & Kudoh, 1987). The methodology called for the participants to rate the posture expression descriptions on a five-point scale according to the 16 semantic dimensions; one posture description and the 16 dimensions appeared per page in a booklet. The participants were told to picture themselves in a conversation with someone who adopted the posture description at some point during the conversation and to judge how that person would be feeling based on the adopted posture. The results showed that the same factors (self-fulfillment, interpersonal positiveness, and interpersonal consciousness) were extracted from the two sets of participants but that the ranking of the factors was different between the two cultures. The authors questioned whether cultural differences would be found with posture *images* instead of verbal descriptions of postures.

More recently, Kleinsmith, De Silva, and Bianchi-Berthouze (2006) included Sri Lankans and examined similarities and differences between all three cultures in perceiving emotion from whole-body postures of a 3D faceless, cultureless, genderless "humanoid" avatar. Similarities were found between the three cultures for sad/depressed postures, as expected according to a study showing that the cultures share similar lexicons for depression-type words (Brandt & Boucher, 1986).

However, differences were found in how the cultures assigned intensity ratings to the emotions. The Japanese consistently assigned higher intensity ratings to more animated postures than did the Sri Lankans or the Americans. The authors asserted that, similar to the findings of Matsumoto et al. (2002) for facial expressions, the Japanese may believe that the emotion being expressed is more intense than what is actually portrayed. Another cross-cultural study is presented in Shibata et al. (2013). They compared Japanese and British observers in how they categorized seated postures. Participants rated each seated posture according to a list of emotion terms and judged the intensity level of each emotion on a 7-point Likert scale (1 = no emotion, 7 = very intense). Principal component analysis (PCA) showed that the perceptual space built for the Japanese observers needed three dimensions (arousal, valence, and dominance) to account for the variance in the categorization, whereas two dimensions (arousal and valence) were sufficient for the British observers. Using sensors placed on the chair and the body, they also identified the body features that account for the similarities and differences between the two spaces.

Another factor affecting the expression and perception of affect is gender. However, the majority of the work examining gender differences has focused on facial expressions (Elfenbein, Marsh, & Ambady, 2002; Hall & Matsumoto, 2004). Kleinsmith, Bianchi-Berthouze, and Berthouze (2006) examined the effect of the decoder's gender on the recognition of affect from whole-body postures of 3D avatars. The results indicated that females tend to be faster in recognizing affect from body posture. This seems to reinforce the results of studies on the recognition of affect from facial expressions.

Recently researchers have started to investigate personality as a factor in perceiving emotion from body expressions. McKeown et al. (2013) investigated people's ability to detect laughter types in full-body stick-figure animations built from naturalistic laughter expressions captured using a motion capture system. Their results showed that people scoring high in positive emotional contagion traits tended to rate stimuli as expressing hilarious laughter or social laughter rather than classifying it as no laughter or fake laughter. They also found that gelotophiles (people who like to be laughed at) were better at recognizing the gender of the person laughing that nongelotophiles.

The recognition of emotions from body expressions may also be affected by idiosyncratic behavior (i.e., behaviors that are characteristic of the person expressing them). Bernhardt and Robinson (2007) and more recently Gong et al. (2010) tested the differences between recognition models built with and without individual idiosyncrasies using the same preexisting motion capture database (Ma et al., 2006). The automatic recognition rates achieved in both studies were considerably higher when individual idiosyncrasies were removed. Furthermore, a comparison of the results with the results on the percentage of agreement between the observers from the original study on the motion capture database (Pollick, Paterson, & Bruderlin, 2001) indicated that the automatic models (Bernhardt & Robinson, 2007; Gong et al., 2010) and the observers' rates (Pollick et al., 2001) were similar. Bernhardt and Robinson (2009) recently extended their system using additional motion capture data from the same database to detect emotion from connected action sequences. Their system achieved higher recognition rates when individual idiosyncrasies were removed, reinforcing individual differences as an important factor to take into account in building affect recognition systems from body expressions. This was recently supported by other studies (Romera-Paredes et al. 2012, 2013; 2014), discussed in Automatic Recognition Systems, (p. 157).

Body Features Affecting the Perception of Emotion

Neuroscience studies have shown that there are two separate pathways in the brain for recognizing biological motion, one for form and another for motion information (Giese & Poggio, 2003; Vania, Lemay, Bienfang, Choi, & Nakayama, 1990). Previous findings from several studies indicate that form information can be instrumental in the recognition of biological motion (Hirai & Hiraki, 2006; McLeod, Dittrich, Driver, Perret, & Zihl, 1996; Peelen, Wiggett & Downing, 2006) and that the temporal information is used to solve inconsistencies when necessary (Lange & Lappe, 2007). Following these findings, the same question was investigated in the recognition of emotion from body expressions. According to Atkinson, Dittrich, Gemmell, and Young (2007), motion signals can be sufficient for recognizing basic emotions from affectively expressed human motion, but that recognition accuracy is significantly impaired when the form information is disrupted by inverting and reversing the motion. Analyzing posture cues aids in discriminating between emotions that are linked with similar dynamic cues or movement activation

(Roether, Omlor, Christensen, & Giese, 2009). Ultimately, dynamic information may be not only complementary to form but also partially redundant to it. These studies indicate that it may be advantageous to focus on developing feature extraction algorithms and fusion models that take into account the role that each feature (or combinations of features) plays in the classification process.

Another important question that has been explored in modeling affective body expressions is the level of feature description that may help to discriminate between affective states. One approach is to investigate the relationship between affective states and a *high-level* description of body expressions. Dahl and Friberg (2007) explored to what extent the emotional intentions and movement cues of a musician could be recognized from her body movements; they found that happiness, sadness, and anger were better recognized than fear. According to the observers' ratings, anger is indicated by large, fairly fast and jerky movements, while sadness is exhibited by fluid, slow movements. It should be noted that the observers in this study were not expert musicians. It is possible that expert musicians may be more sensitive to subtle body cues that are not perceived by naïve observers. Castellano, Mortillaro, Camurri, Volpe, & Scherer (2008) examined the quantity of motion of the upper body and the velocity of head movements of a pianist across performances played with a specific emotional intention and found differences mainly between sad and serene, especially in the velocity of head movements. They also identified a relationship between the temporal aspects of a gesture and the emotional expression it conveys but highlighted the need for more analysis of such features.

Gross et al. (2010) aimed to establish a qualitative description of the movement qualities associated with specific emotions for a single movement task—knocking, and found that motion perception was predicted most strongly for high activation emotions (pride, angry and joyful); however only 15 expressions were analyzed. They also carried out a quantitative assessment of the value of different emotions on different body expressions. For instance, they found that the arm was raised at least 17 degrees higher for angry movements than for other emotions. Their results indicate that it may be necessary to quantify individual features as body expressions may differ according to the presence or absence and quantitative value of each feature. Glowinski et al. (2011) hypothesized that it would be possible to classify a large amount of

affective behavior using only upper-body features. Acted upper-body emotional expressions from the GEMEP corpus (Bänziger & Scherer, 2010) were statistically clustered according to the four quadrants of the valence-arousal plane. The authors concluded that "meaningful groups of emotions"[1] could be clustered in each quadrant and that the results are similar to existing nonverbal behavior research (De Meijer, 1989; Pollick, Paterson, Bruderlin, & Sanford, 2001; Wallbott, 1998).

Another approach is to ground affective body expressions into *low-level* descriptions of body configurations to examine which cues afford humans the ability to distinguish between specific emotions. For instance, Wallbott (1998) constructed a category system which consisted of body movements, postures, and movement quality. Coulson (2004) used computer-generated avatars and a body description comprising six joint rotations (e.g., abdomen twist, head bend, etc.). A high level of agreement between observers was reached for angry, happy, and sad postures. De Meijer's study (1989) considered seven movement dimensions (e.g., arm opening and closing, fast to slow velocity of movement, etc.) and enlisted a group of observers to rate the movements performed by dancers according to their compatibility with nine emotions. Trunk movement was the most predictive for all emotions except anger and was found to distinguish between positive and negative emotions. More recently, Dael, Mortillaro, and Scherer (2012) proposed a body action and posture coding system for the description of body expressions at an anatomical, form, and functional level with the aim to increase intercoder reliability.

De Silva and Bianchi-Berthouze (2004) used 24 features to describe upper-body joint positions and the orientation of the shoulders, head, and feet to analyze affective postures from the UCLIC affective database (Kleinsmith, De Silva & Berthouze, 2006). PCA showed that two to four principal components covered approximately 80% of the variability in form configuration associated with different emotions. Similar results were obtained by clustering the postures according to the average observer labels. Kleinsmith and Bianchi-Berthouze (2005, 2007) extended this analysis by investigating how the features contributed to the discrimination between different levels of four affective dimensions.

Roether et al. (2009) carried out a study to extract and validate the minimum set of spatiotemporal motor primitives that drive the perception of particular emotions in gait. Through validation by creating walking patterns that reflect these primitives, they showed that perception of emotions is based on specific changes of joint-angle amplitudes with respect to the pattern of neutral walking. Kleinsmith, Bianchi-Berthouze, and Steed (2011) used nonacted affective postures of people playing whole-body video games. A statistical analysis of a set of features derived from the Euler rotations recorded by a motion capture system determined that the arms and the upper body were most important for distinguishing between active (triumphant and frustrated) and nonactive (concentrating and defeated) affective states.

This aim of this section is to provide an overview of the literature on how the detection of affect from body expressions is grounded on body features, both configurational and temporal. It also shows that there are certain constants in the way such features are mapped into affective states or levels of affective dimensions. An extended review of the features that have been explored and of their relation to affect is reported in Kleinsmith and Bianchi-Berthouze (2013). This growing body of work provides the foundation for creating a model like the facial action coding system (FACS) (Ekman & Friesen, 1978) for body expressions and creates the basis for building affective body expression recognition systems. It also points to the fact that the design of such systems needs to take into account factors such as culture, individual idiosyncrasies, and context to increase their performances.

Automatic Recognition of Affective Body Expressions
Considerations for Building the Ground Truth

Regardless of modality, an important step when building an emotion recognition system is to define the ground truth. A first question to ask is which emotion framework should be used. Two approaches are typically adopted: the discrete model and the dimensional model. In the discrete model (Izard & Malatesta, 1987), an expression is associated with one or a set of discrete emotion categories. In the continuous model (Fontaine, Scherer, Roesch, & Ellsworth, 2007), each expression is rated over a set of continuous dimensions (e.g., arousal, valence, pain intensity). The continuous approach is considered to provide a more comprehensive description of an emotional state (Fontaine et al., 2007). Although most work on emotion recognition from body expressions has been carried out on discrete emotions, there is an increasing interest in modeling affective expressions over continuous dimensions

and also continuously over time (Gunes & Pantic, 2010; Meng & Bianchi-Berthouze, 2013).

Once the labeling *model* has been defined, the second step is to define the labeling *process*. In the case of facial expressions, the ground truth is often based on the FACS model (Ekman & Friesen, 1978). Using this model, expert FACS coders analyze a facial expression frame by frame to identify groups of active muscles and then apply well defined rules to map these muscle activation patterns into discrete emotion categories. Unfortunately accepted systematic models for mapping body expressions into emotion categories do not yet exist. Until recently, this was not a critical problem, as most studies used acted expressions or elicited emotions with the ground truth predefined by the experimenter. However, as we move toward naturalistic data collection, this has become a critical step in the modeling process. A typical approach is to use the expresser's self-reported affective label. Unfortunately this approach is often not feasible or reliable (Kapoor, Burleson, & Picard, 2007; Kleinsmith et al., 2011). Another approach is to use experts or naïve observers to label the affective state conveyed by a body expression (Kleinsmith et al., 2011). A problem with this approach is the high variability between observers even when expert body language coders are used. This is partially due to the lack of a predefined principled approach (i.e., set of rules) to be applied. It should also be noted that, differently from the face, muscle activation is often not directly visible (e.g., because of clothing); hence less information is provided to the observers.

In order to address this variability, various methods have been used to determine the ground truth. The conventional method is to use the "most frequent label" (e.g., (Kleinsmith et al., 2011) used by the observers in coding a specific body expression. This is a low-cost, easy approach and is very useful when the level of variability between observers is not very high. As for other affective modalities such as facial expressions (McDuff, Kaliouby, & Picard, 2012) or affective media such as images of hotels (Bianchi-Berthouze, 2002; Inder, Bianchi-Berthouze & Kato, 1999) or clothes (Hughes, Atkinson, Bianchi-Berthouze, & Baurley, 2012), crowd sourcing the expression labeling could become a possible low-cost method to address the variability issue and create more reliable estimates of ground truth (Sheng, Provost, & Ipeirotis, 2008). The idea is that noise could be partly cancelled out over a large number of observers.

Other approaches attempt to take into account the cause of variability between observers. For example, rather than simply selecting the most frequent label, each label is weighted against the ability of the observers to read others' emotions. Typical measures of such skills are obtained by using empathy profile questionnaires (Mehrabian & Epstein, 1972)—that is, the expertise of the observers in reading body expressions (e.g., a physiotherapist for a physical rehabilitation context). While these measures capture long-term and stable characteristics of an observer's ability to interpret another person's affective expressions, there are other observer characteristics that may need to be taken into account in evaluating their labeling. Various studies in psychology have found that one's own emotional state affects the way one perceives events and people. Studies (Bianchi-Berthouze, 2013; Chandler & Schwarz, 2009; Niedenthal, Barsalou, Winkielman, Krauth-Gruber, & Ric, 2005) state that such biases may even be triggered by the valence associated with the postural stance of the observer.

Research on embodied cognition (e.g., Barsalou, 1999) has also challenged previous views on conceptual knowledge (i.e., representation of concepts). According to this view, the perception of an affective expression requires a partial reenactment of the sensorimotor events associated with that affective state. Lindquist, Barrett, Bliss-Moreau, and Russell (2006) argue that the fact that overexposing observers to a particular emotion word reduces their ability to recognize prototypical expressions of that emotion may be due to the inhibition of the motor system necessary to enact that emotion. It follows that the emotional state of the observers may also bias the perception of another person's expression as it may inhibit or facilitate access to the sensorimotor information necessary to reenact that expression. Given this evidence, it is critical that observer contextual factors such as mood and even posture be taken into account in determining the ground truth.

While forcing the attribution of one label to a body expression makes the modeling and evaluation processes simpler, it has its own limitations. To address these limitations, multilabeling techniques have been proposed. For example, weighted labeling is used with probabilistic modeling approaches (Raykar et al., 2010) or to evaluate the ranking between multiple outcomes (Meng, Kleinsmith, & Bianchi-Berthouze, 2011). Other more complex approaches have also been proposed. For example, preference learning (Fürnkranz & Häullermeier,

2005; Doyle, 2004; Yannakakis, 2009) is used to construct computational models of affect based on users' preferences. To this aim, observers or expressers are asked to view two stimuli (e.g., two postures) and indicate which stimulus better represents a certain affective state (e.g., happy). This process is repeated for each pair of stimuli. The approach models the order of preferences instead of an absolute match. It can reduce the noise caused by a strict forced-choice approach, in which the observers or expressers are obliged to provide an absolute judgment.

As we move toward real-life applications, we need to be able to model the subtlety and ambiguity of body expressions seen "in the wild" rather than in controlled lab experiments. This section has highlighted some of the challenges posed by the data preparation techniques used to build affective body expression recognition systems for real-life applications. These challenges must be carefully addressed by taking into account the demands that the application's context of use poses and the granularity of recognition required. In the next section we discuss how the mapping between body features and the selected ground truth can be carried out and other issues that need to be taken into account.

Automatic Recognition Systems

Many studies have shown that automatic recognition of affective states from body expressions is possible with results similar to those obtained over other modalities and to performances that reflect the level of agreement between observers. Refer to Kleinsmith and Bianchi-Berthouze (2013) for an extensive review. Table 11.1 provides a summary of the studies discussed throughout the remainder of Automatic Recognition of Affective Body Expressions (p. 156).

Some of the earlier work on affective body expression recognition systems focused on recognizing basic emotions from dance sequences (Camurri, Trocca & Volpe, 2002; Kamisato, Odo, Ishikawa, & Hoshino, 2004; Park, Park, Kim, & Woo, 2004). Camurri and colleagues (Camurri, Lagerlof & Volpe, 2003; Camurri, Mazzarino, Ricchetti, Timmers, & Volpe, 2004) examined cues and features involved in emotion expression in dance for four affective states. Kapur, Kapur, Virji-Babul, Tzanetakis, and Driessen (2005) used acted dance movements from professional and nonprofessional dancers. Observers correctly classified the majority of the movements, and automatic recognition models achieved comparable recognition rates. Using a high-level description of the body movements of

Table 11.1 Automatic Affective Body Expression Recognition Systems—Unimodal and Multimodal, Including the Body as One Modality

Ref	Affective States/ Affective Dimensions	Acted/ Not-Acted	Stimuli	Ground Truth	Method	Accuracy
Camurri et al., 2004	(4) Anger, fear, grief, joy	5 actors	20 videos	actor	decision tree	36%
Pollick et al., 2002	(2) Angry, neutral	26 actors	1,560 movements	actor	MLP	33% efficient
Kapur et al., 2005	(4) Anger, fear, joy, sadness	30 actors	40 point-lights	actor	5 different classifiers	62%–93%
Gong et al., 2010	(4) Angry, happy, sad, neutral	30 actors	1,200 movements	actor	SVM	59% (B) 76% (U)
Savva et al., 2012	(4) High- and low-intensity negative, happiness, concentration	9 nonactors	423 playing windows	obs	Recurrent NN	57%
Bernhardt & Robinson, 2007	(4) Angry, happy, sad neutral	30 actors	1200 movements	n/a	SVM	50% (B) 81% (U)
Bernhardt & Robinson, 2009	(4) Angry, happy, sad, neutral	30 actors	1200 movements	n/a	HMM	81%
Karg et al., 2010	(4) Angry, happy, sad, neutral (3) Valence, arousal, dominance	13 actors	520 strides 780 strides	actor	Naïve Bayes, NN, SVM NN	69% (II) 95% (PD) 88% (V) 97% (A) 96% (D)
Sanghvi et al., 2011	(2) Levels of engagement	5 nonactors	44 videos	obs	ADTree, OneR	82%
Bianchi-Berthouze & Kleinsmith 2003	(3) Angry, happy, sad	13 actors	138 postures	actor	CALM	96%
Kleinsmith & Bianchi-Berthouze 2007	Levels of valence, arousal, potency, avoidance	13 actors	111 postures	actor	BP	79%–81%
Kleinsmith et al., 2011	(4) Concentrating, defeated, frustrated, triumphant (2) valence and arousal	11 nonactors	103 postures	obs	MLP	60% 84% (V) 87% (A)
Gao et al., 2012	(4) Excitement, frustration, boredom, relaxation (2) valence and arousal	15 nonactors	127 game sessions (touch behaviour)	Self-report (naturalistic)	SVM	76% 89% (V) 86% (A)

(continued)

Table 11.1 Continued

Ref	Affective States/ Affective Dimensions	Acted/ Not-Acted	Stimuli	Ground Truth	Method	Accuracy
Griffin et al., 2013	(4) Laughter: hilarious, social, awkward, fake, none	10 nonactors	126 video clips	obs	Random Forest	92%
Aung et al., 2013	(2) Protective (e.g., guarding) or no protective behavior	20 chronic pain patients	– 10 minute motion captured physical exercises	Physio-therapists	RMTL	70%

Multimodal Emotion Recognition Systems Including Body Expressions

Ref	Affective States/ Affective Dimensions	Acted/Not Acted	Stimuli	Ground Truth	Method	Accuracy
Kapoor et al., 2004	(3) Levels of interest	8 actors	262 multimodal	obs	NN	55%*
Kapoor et al., 2007	(2) Pre- or not prefrustration	24 nonactors	24 multimodal	actor	kNN, SVM, GP	79%
Gunes & Piccardi, 2007	(6) Four basic + anxiety, uncertainty	4 actors	27 face videos 27 body videos	actor	BayesNet	91% & 94%
Shan et al., 2007	(7) Anger, anxiety, boredom, disgust, joy, puzzle, surprise	23 actors	262 videos	actor	SVM, 1-NN	82%-89%
Gunes & Piccardi, 2009	(12) Anger, anxiety, boredom, disgust, fear, happy, positive and negative surprise, neutral, uncertainty, puzzlement, sadness	23 actors	539 videos	Observers	Adaboost with Random Forest	83%
Varni et al., 2010	(5) Anger, joy, sadness, Pleasure, deadpan + # (synchronization, leadership)	4 actors (musicians)	54 videos	actor	CPR	45%
Joshi et al. 2013	(2) Depression, no depression	60 depressed patients and 30 healthy people	90 videos	standardized depression test	SVM	76%
Metallinou et al. 2012	Levels of activation, pleasantness & dominance	16 actors	50 voice and motion capture recordings	Observers	GMM-based model	0.59, 0.22, 0.33 (median correlation)

Basic = anger, disgust, fear, happiness, sadness, surprise; SVM = support vector machine; CALM = categorizing and learning module; k-NN = k nearest neighbor; MLP = multilayer perceptron; GP = Gaussian process; GMM = Gaussian mixture model; RMTL = regularized multitask learning; * = recognition rate for posture modality alone; F = frame-level labeling; S = sequence-level labeling; B = biased; U = unbiased; II = interindividual; PD = person-dependent; V = valence; A = arousal; D = dominance; # = recognition of small group behaviors triggered by emotion, not emotion recognition directly; CPR = correlation probability of recurrence.

Source: Adapted and updated from Kleinsmith & Bianchi-Berthouze (2013).

the dancers (e.g., compact versus expanded movements), machine learning algorithms were applied to map these features into basic emotion categories. Subsequent studies explored the possibility of mapping static acted body expressions (postures) into emotion labels. Bianchi-Berthouze and Kleinsmith (2003) used low-level descriptions of body configurations (i.e., distances between joints and angles between body segments such as the distance of the left wrist from the right shoulder on the x, y, and z planes) to build the models with the intent of making these models independent of any a priori knowledge about the type of body configurations expected in the context of application and let the machine learning algorithm determine the mapping.

Studies have also been conducted to investigate the possibility of automatically discriminating between affective dimension levels. Karg, Kuhnlenz, and Buss (2010) examined automatic affect recognition for discrete levels of valence, arousal and dominance in acted, affective gait patterns. Recognition rates were best for arousal and dominance and worst for valence. The results were significantly higher than observer agreement on the same corpus. Slightly different results were obtained by Kleinsmith et al. (2011) on naturalistic static expressions, with recognition rates highest for arousal, slightly lower for valence, and lowest for dominance. While the high recognition rate on arousal confirms previous studies in psychology showing that body expressions are a strong indication of the level of activation of a person's emotional state, the difference in the results for the valence and dominance dimensions may be due to the different contexts of the two studies (i.e., dynamic, acted expressions versus static, nonacted expressions).

As discussed in The Perception of Affective Body Expressions, p. 153, recent studies show that building a person-independent recognition model is often more difficult than building a person-specific model. This is even truer in dealing with naturalistic expressions (Savva & Bianchi-Berthouze, 2012). A typical approach is to normalize the body expression features by subtracting personal characteristics (Bernhardt & Robinson, 2007; Savva & Bianchi-Berthouze, 2012). A different approach is taken by Romera-Paredes, Argyriou, Bianchi-Berthouze, and Pontil (2012). They propose to exploit idiosyncratic information to improve emotion classification. Their approach aims at learning to recognize the identity of the person together with his or her emotional expressions. The rationale is that by learning two tasks together through modeling the knowledge available about

their relationship, the identification of the discriminative features for each of the tasks is optimized. Emotion recognition and identity recognition tasks appear to be grounded on quasiorthogonal features (Calder, Burton, Miller, Young, & Akamatsu, 2001), thus their shared learning process favors the separation of these features and improves the learning on both tasks. This is especially true in the case of small subsets compared with the general person-independent approach. Although their algorithm has only been tested on facial expressions, not body expressions, the underlying principles remain valid, and it would be worth investigating this approach with body expressions.

Finally, while most of these systems make use of supervised learning, a few studies employ either unsupervised or semisupervised learning to investigate the possibility of a specialized affective body language that emerges through continued interaction with the system. De Silva, Kleinsmith, and Bianchi-Berthouze (2005) investigated the possibility of identifying clusters of affective body expressions that represent nuances of the same emotion category (e.g., sad/depressed and angry/upset). The postures were grouped in clusters that highly overlapped with manual classification carried out by human observers on nuances of four basic emotions. A different approach was proposed by Kleinsmith, Fushimi, and Bianchi-Berthouze (2005). Their perspective was that the emotional language (i.e., the vocabulary to describe emotions) is not predefined but that the system learns both the emotion language and the way a person expresses emotions through continued interaction with the system. Using both supervised and unsupervised machine learning algorithms, the system identifies clusters of body expressions of the user and assigns symbolic names to each cluster. Through continued interaction, these clusters are confirmed and reinforced and an emotion name is assigned to them or counterexamples are provided as a negative reinforcement. This approach could be useful in contexts where a prolonged interaction is feasible and acceptable.

This section has provided an overview of some of the affective body expression recognition systems that can be found in the literature and highlights some of the challenges that the modeling process raises and some possible solutions. As motion capture technology becomes cheaper and easier to use, an increasing number of studies attempt to address these issues, making the use of affective body expressions in real life applications easier.

Applications

In terms of real-world applications for affective body expression recognition, many have started to appear; some are unimodal while others investigate the role of body expressions as one modality in a multimodal context.

Unimodal applications include the work of Sanghvi et al. (2011), in which a combination of postures and dynamic information is used to assess the engagement level of children playing chess with the iCat robot from Philips Research (http://www.hitech-projects.com/icat/). A user study indicated that both posture configuration features (e.g., body lean angle) and spatio-temporal features (e.g., quantity of motion) may be important for detecting engagement. The best automatic models achieved recognition rates (82%) that were significantly higher than the average human baseline (56%). Kleinsmith et al. (2011) investigated the possibility of automatically recognizing the emotional expressions of players engaged in whole-body computer games. This information could be used either to evaluate the game or to adapt gameplay at run time. The automatic recognition rates for three discrete categories and four affective dimensions in respective studies were comparable to the level of agreement achieved between observers. Savva, Scarinzi, and Bianchi-Berthouze (2012) proposed a system using dynamic features and removing individual idiosyncrasies to recognize emotional states of people playing Wii tennis. The best results were obtained using angular velocity, angular frequency, and amount of movement. Overall, the system was able to correctly classify a high percentage of both high- and low-intensity negative emotion expressions and happiness expressions but considerably fewer concentrating expressions. An analysis of the results highlighted the high variability between expressions belonging to the same category. The high variability was due to the diversity of the players' playing styles, which is consistent with the results of other studies (Nijhar, Bianchi-Berthouze & Boguslawski, 2012; Pasch, Bianchi-Berthouze, van Dijk, & Nijholt, 2009). Griffin et al. (2013) explore the possibility of detecting and discriminating between different types of laughter (e.g., hilarious laughter, fake laughter, etc.) from body movements captured in a naturalistic game context and video watching. Their system reaches 92% correct recognition compared to 94% agreement between observers.

Systems for clinical applications are also starting to emerge. The study by Joshi, Goecke, Breakspear, and Parker (2013) aims to design a system able to discriminate between people suffering from depression and people not suffering from depression. They investigated the contribution of upper body expressions and head movement over facial dynamics only. The results show that by adding body information, the recognition performance increases significantly with an average accuracy of 76% instead of 71% obtained when using facial expressions only. The "Emo&Pain" project (Aung et al. 2013, Aung et al. 2014) aims to detect emotional states that are related to fear of movement (e.g., anxiety, fear of pain, fear of injury) from body behavior of people with chronic musculoskeletal pain. The system reaches 70% correct recognition. The detection of the emotional state of the person helps run-time personalization of the type of support that the technology can provide to motivate the person to do physical activity despite the pain (Singh et al., 2014; Swann-Stenbergh et al., 2012). In addition to facilitating and making rehabilitation more effective, the aim is also to make the person more aware of her or his affective behavioral patterns to learn to address the causes of such behavior and also to improve her or his social relationships (Martel, Wideman, & Sullivan, 2012).

Multimodal affect recognition systems that explore body expressions as one of the multiple modalities include the work of Gunes and Piccardi (2007). Their system is bimodal, recognizing affect in video sequences of facial expressions and upper-body expressions. They examined the automatic recognition performance of each modality separately before fusing information from the two modalities into a single system. The automatic recognition performance was highest for the upper body sequences, compared to the facial expression sequences. In a more recent implementation of the system using the same database (Gunes & Piccardi, 2009), they exploited temporal dynamics between facial expressions and upper-body gestures to improve the reliability of emotion recognition. The best bimodal classification performances were comparable to the body-only classification performances, and the bimodal system outperformed the unimodal system based on facial expressions.

Kapoor et al. (2007) developed a system to recognize discrete levels of a child's interest and self-reported frustration in an educational context. Their system makes use of facial expressions, task performance and body postures. Body postures were detected through the implementation of a chair embedded with pressure sensors. Of the three types of input examined, the highest recognition accuracy was obtained for posture activity over game status and individual facial action units (Kapoor, Picard & Ivanov, 2004).

In real-life situations, body movement does not occur in isolation; instead, people act in response to other people's body movements. Hence it becomes interesting to study and model the relationship between body expressions. Varni, Volpe, and Camurri (2010) focused on the analysis of real-time multimodal affective nonverbal social interactions. The inputs to the system are posture and movement features as well as physiological signals. Their aim was to detect the synchronization of affective behavior and leadership as triggered by emotions. This work is interesting, as it is one of the first steps toward the use of body movements to track group emotions during social phenomena.

Other interesting studies conducted in this direction are in the context of art performances. Using a motion capture system, Metallinou, Katsamanis, and Narayanan (2013) investigate how affect is expressed through body expressions and speech during theater performances. The aim was to continuously track variation in valence, activation and dominance levels in actor dyads. The work shows interesting results for activation and dominance with correlation predictions of 0.5 with the observers' annotations. Less clear correlations were found for valence, possibly due to the use of mainly dynamic rather than configurational (i.e., form) features. An interesting question raised by this work is how to measure performances, not only over continuous dimensions, but also over time. This is an important, timely and open question, as in real-life applications we cannot expect the data to be pre-segmented before being labeled. The correlation between system performance and observer annotation must be measured over time; the trend of the curve representing the affective levels is what matters. However, it is possible that delays in the rating time may introduce noise. So it is possible that such measures may have to take into account the need for stretching the performance curve to measure the trend.

As these systems highlight the possibilities for real-world applications, one question that should be asked is when is a system valid for deployment? A typical approach is to use the level of agreement demonstrated by naïve observers or experts as the acceptable target rate to be achieved by the system. Kleinsmith et al. (2011) set the bar higher and argue that the target rate should be based on an unseen set of observers; reasoning that training and testing systems on the same set of observers may produce results that do not take into account the high variability that may exist between observers (especially when they are not experts). Hence, their approach is to test recognition systems for their ability to generalize not only to new *postures* but also to new *observers* (i.e., the people judging the emotions). This is an important issue, as failure of the system to correctly recognize the affective state may have critical consequences in certain applications.

Future Directions

The previous sections have highlighted several important issues and challenges being tackled by researchers working on affective body expressions: which features to use, how to address possible biases, building ground truth models, classifiers, and system evaluation. Progress has been made with respect to those issues and real-world applications are appearing and more interest from industry is emerging. However, there are some topics that are severely underexplored. Two of these are discussed in the remainder of this section; these are (1) other potential aspects of body expressions that should be considered and modeled and (2) possibilities for and challenges to be addressed in capturing body expressions on the move.

There Is More to the Body Than Just Its Kinematics

There are two modalities closely related to body expressions that have been underexplored even though evidence shows that they could in fact be a very rich source of information for automatic body expression recognition. These are affective touch behavior and body muscle activation patterns. They are discussed below to highlight their potential and hopefully give rise to an increased interest in them.

TOUCH

Affective touch can be seen as an extension of, or coupled with affective body behavior. One reason is that they share the proprioceptive feedback system. Given numerous touch-based devices, it becomes critical to investigate the possibility that touch behavior offers as a window into the emotional state of a person. Unfortunately this affective modality has been quite unexplored not only in computing but also in psychology (Hertenstein,

Holmes, McCullough, & Keltner, 2009). Initial studies on touch behavior as an affective modality argued that the role of touch was mainly to communicate the valence of an emotion and its intensity (Jones & Yarbrough, 1985; Knapp & Hall, 1997). More recently, research has instead shown that touch communicates much more about emotions as it also enables the recognition of the discrete emotions communicated. Hertenstein et al. (2009) and Hertenstein, Keltner, App, Bulleit, and Jaskolka (2006) investigated 23 different types of tactile behavior (e.g., stroking, squeezing, patting) and achieved human recognition rates comparable to those obtained with other modalities. They showed that in addition to the type of tactile behavior, other features such as location, duration, and pressure were important to discriminate the emotional content of the stroke.

Bailenson, Brave, Merget, and Koslow (2007) investigated whether a two-degrees-of-freedom force-feedback joystick could be used to communicate acted emotions. For each joystick movement, measures of distance, acceleration, jerkiness, and direction were computed and used to identify possible discriminative affective profiles. Distance, speed, and acceleration were shown to be much greater for joy and anger and much less for sadness. The direction measures were also very discriminative for fear and sadness. Following the seminal work of Clynes (1973), Khanna and Sasikumar (2010) found that keyboard typing behavior is affected by the user's emotional state. People reported not only that their emotional states affected the frequency of selection of certain keys (e.g., backspace), but that in a positive mood their typing speed tended to increase. Matsuda et al. (2010) investigated the possibility of using finger behavior to automatically recognize the emotional state of deaf people when communicating through a Braille device. The researchers used duration and acceleration of finger dotting (a tactile communication media utilized by deaf-blind individuals) to discriminate between neutral, joy, sadness and anger. The duration of dotting in the joy condition was significantly shorter than in the other conditions, while it was significantly longer in the sadness condition. The finger load was significantly stronger in the anger condition.

Gao, Bianchi-Berthouze, and Meng (2012) investigated naturalistic touch behavior in touch-based game devices. By measuring the length, pressure, direction, and speed of finger strokes in gameplay, they examined the possibility of automatically recognizing the emotional state of the player.

A visual analysis of the stroke features as well as the results of a discriminant analysis showed that the length and pressure of the stroke were particularly informative in discriminating between two levels of valence (positive versus negative states), whereas the speed and the direction of the stroke were linked to variations in arousal. Pressure also supported such discrimination. The analysis further showed that pressure strongly discriminated frustration from the other three states and length was particularly informative for the identification of the relaxed state. Better performances were obtained for both person-dependent and person-independent models using SVMs. This study shows how touch could be a useful modality, especially when the user is on the move and other modalities are harder to capture and analyze. In (Bianchi-Berthouze & Tajadura Jimenez, 2014; Funfaro, Bianchi-Berthouze, Bevilacqua, Tajadura Jimenez, 2013), the authors also propose touch behavior as a measure of user experience when evaluating interactive technology.

ELECTROMYOGRAPHY

Another modality that is rarely used but particularly important in body expression analysis is muscle activation. Electromyograms (EMGs) have been used for facial expression analysis but rarely for the study of body expressions even though a few medical studies have found evidence of a relationship between patterns of activation in body muscles and emotional states (Geisser, Haig, Wallbom, & Wiggert, 2004; Pluess, Conrad & Wilhelm, 2009; Watson, Booker, Main, & Chen, 1997). For example, fear of movement in people with back pain may cause them to freeze their muscles and produce more guarded movements. Muscle tension has also been examined by De Meijer (1989) and Gross et al. (2010); however, these ratings were based on visual subjective perception from videos. While muscle activation affects the way a movement is performed, unfortunately these effects may not always be easily detected through motion capture systems and/or video cameras. Hence, even if EMG data provides various challenges from a modeling perspective, it could provide valuable information that may help resolve misclassifications between some affective states. Fully wireless EMG systems (e.g., Noraxon and BTS systems) offer less obtrusive ways to measure such information, which can make the recording more natural. The electrodes are small and individually placed on the person's body without requiring cables. While these systems have generally been used for biomechanics, their importance in the field of affective body expressions is becoming clear (Romera-Paredes et al., 2013). Wireless EMG systems also provide a way to measure affect on the move. Romera-Paredes et al. (2013) explore the possibility of using machine learning algorithms to predict EMG activity from body movement during physical activity in people with chronic pain (Aung et al., 2013) in order to limit the types of sensors to be worn.

Capturing Body Expressions on the Move: Opportunities and Challenges

As technology becomes more and more ubiquitous, it is important to consider how it can be used to capture and interpret body behavior on the move. The first question to ask is what sensors are available or acceptable in this context. Other than the use of wireless EMG (the limitations of which are discussed in the previous section (Romera-Paredes et al., 2013), various studies have explored the use of accelerometers contained in smart phones to capture kinematic information about a person. This information, combined with other contextual information (e.g., location through GPS or daily schedule) could be used to interpret the emotional state of the person. Amount of motion and jerkiness are in fact quite related to the level of arousal of a person (Glowinski et al., 2011). Gyroscopic sensors that are integrated in devices and possibly in clothes are also becoming available. The combination of gyroscopes and accelerometers can provide a richer description of a body expression because they are able to capture not only kinematic but also body configuration features. The latter (also called form features) may help in better discriminating between valence levels of person states (e.g., a more open, expansive body versus a more closed body—that is, with the limbs remaining closer together).

The ubiquitous use of gyroscopic sensors and accelerometers raises challenges for emotion recognition systems based on body movement. Given the unconstrained and high variability of possible actions in which the body may be involved, it becomes important to investigate the possibility of an action-independent model of how affect is expressed rather than building a recognition system for each type of action. To add to this, it is also possible that the role of form and dynamic features may depend not only on the emotions expressed but also on the type of action performed. This raises another issue: the separation of the temporal relationship between the movement phases characterizing a body action (either cycled, as in knocking, or not cycled, as in standing up) and the characteristics of its expressive content. Studies have in fact shown that kinematic and form-from-motion features are more relevant to discriminate noninstrumental actions (e.g., locomotory actions) rather than instrumental actions (i.e., goal-directed) or social actions (e.g., emotional expressions) (Atkinson, 2009; Atkinson et al., 2007; Dittrich, 1993). Furthermore, Atkinson's study (2009) on autism spectrum disorders showed that emotion recognition seems to depend more on global and global form features, whereas noninstrumental (e.g., jumping jacks, hopping, and walking on the spot) and instrumental (e.g., digging, kicking, and knocking) actions depend on relatively local motion and form cues (e.g., angles of the particular joints of the body involved in the action). This suggests that affect recognition systems may benefit from the investigation of feature representation spaces that allow for the separation of affect recognition tasks from idiosyncrasy tasks (e.g., recognition of a person's identity or a person's idiosyncratic behavior) as well as noninstrumental action tasks such as the recognition of locomotory actions. In fact, perceptual and neuroscience studies provide evidence for the existence of separate neural structures for the processing of these three tasks (Calder et al., 2001; Gallagher & Frith, 2004; Martens, Leutold, & Schweinberger, 2010).

Another interesting research question raised by the possibility of integrating gyroscopic sensors and accelerometers into devices is whether these devices become an extended part of the body. At the moment the devices considered are mainly smart phones or tablets, and they are either kept within a person's pocket or in his or her hands. Hence they are sensors *attached* to one's own body and hence *measuring* that body. What if, instead, these sensors were attached to walking aids (e.g., walking sticks, umbrella, wheelchairs, etc.), for example? Could they be considered an extension of the body and hence have their own behavioral patterns? Such sensors could be easily integrated into these devices, thereby removing the burden of integrating them into clothes and being able to gather interesting information to support people with body motor difficulties. We can envisage that the emotional cues provided by walking aids could be similar to those observed in touch (for a review, see Gao et al. (2012) with pressure against the floor, length of steps, and speed of movement as some of their affective cues. Wheelchairs may be seen more as an extension of the legs, with possibly similar patterns of emotional behavior. As for touch and body movement, the features will need to be normalized to remove idiosyncrasies and possibly contextual information about the task the person is doing and the type of surface on which the person is moving.

Summary

This chapter has provided an overview of the research on automatic recognition of affective body expressions; an in-depth review can be found in the survey by Kleinsmith & Bianchi-Berthouze (2013). This body of work has created the basis for the new possibilities offered by emerging and low-cost technologies (such as Microsoft's Kinect). We expect that in the coming year, research on the automatic recognition of affective body expressions will see a steady increase and real-life applications will begin to appear. This will increase our understanding of how the body *conveys* emotions, the factors that affect how emotion is *detected* from the body; it may also possibly lead to the creation of FACS-like models for the body.

Note

1. Cluster 1: high arousal-positive valence: elation, amusement, pride; cluster 2: high arousal-negative valence: hot anger, fear, despair; cluster 3: low arousal-positive valence: pleasure, relief, interest; 4: low arousal-negative valence: cold anger, anxiety, sadness.

References

Anderson, K., & McOwan, P. W. (2006). A real-time automated system for the recognition of human facial expressions. *IEEE Transactions on Systems, Man, and Cybernetics: Part B, 36*(1), 96–105.

Argyle, M. (1988). *Bodily communication*. London: Methuen.

Atkinson, A. P. (2009). Impaired recognition of emotions from body movements is associated with elevated motion coherence thresholds in autism spectrum disorders. *Neuropsychologia, 47*(13), 3023–3029.

Atkinson, A. P., Dittrich, W. H., Gemmell, A. J., & Young, A. W. (2007). Evidence for distinct contributions of form and motion information to the recognition of emotions from body gestures. *Cognition, 104*, 59–72.

Aung, M. S. H., Bianchi-Berthouze, N., Watson, P., C de C. Williams, A. (2014). Automatic Recognition of Fear-Avoidance Behaviour in Chronic Pain Physical Rehabilitation, *Pervasive Computing Technologies for Healthcare*.

Aung, M. S. H., Romera-Paredes, B., Singh, A., Lim, S., Kanakam, N., C de C Williams, A., & Bianchi-Berthouze, N. (2013). Getting rid of pain-related behaviour to improve social and self perception: A technology-based perspective. In *The 14th international IEEE workshop on image and audio analysis for multimedia interactive services*, 1–4, IEEE.

Bailenson, N. J., Brave, N. Y. S., Merget, D., & Koslow, D. (2007). Virtual interpersonal touch: expressing and recognizing emotions through haptic devices. *Human-Computer Interaction, 22*, 325–353.

Bänziger, T. & Scherer, K. (2010). Chapter blueprint for affective computing: A sourcebook. *Introducing the Geneva multimodal emotion portrayal corpus* (pp. 271–294). New York: Oxford University Press.

Barsalou, L. W. (1999). Perceptual symbol systems. *Behavioral & Brain Sciences, 22*, 577–660.

Bernhardt, D., & Robinson, P. (2007). Detecting affect from non-stylised body motions. In *Proceedings of the 2nd international conference on affective computing and intelligent interaction, LNCS:4738* (pp. 59–70). Berlin-Heidelberg, Germany: Springer.

Bernhardt, D. & Robinson, P. (2009). Detecting emotions from connected action sequences. In *Visual informatics: bridging research and practice, LNCS: 5857* (pp. 1–11). Berlin-Heidelberg, Germany: Springer.

Bianchi-Berthouze, N. (2002). Mining multimedia subjective feedback. *Journal of Intelligent Information Systems, 19*(1), 43–59.

Bianchi-Berthouze, N. (2013). Understanding the role of body movement in player engagement. *Human-Computer Interaction, 28*(1), 40–75.

Bianchi-Berthouze, N., & Kleinsmith, A. (2003). A categorical approach to affective gesture recognition. *Connection Science, 15*, 259–269.

Bianchi-Berthouze, N., & Tajadura Jimenez, A. It's not just what we touch but also how we touch it. *Workshop on "Touch Me": Tactile User Experience Evaluation Methods, CHI'14*.

Brandt, M., & Boucher, J. (1986). Concepts of depression in emotion lexicons of eight cultures. *International Journal of Intercultural Relations, 10*, 321–346.

Bull, P. E. (1987). *Posture and gesture*. Oxford, UK: Pergamon Press.

Bunkan, B., Ljunggren, A. E., Opjordsmoen, S., Moen, O., & Friis, S. (2001). What are the dimensions of movement? *Nordic Journal of Psychiatry, 55*, 33–40.

Calder, A. J., Burton, A. M., Miller, P., Young, A. W., & Akamatsu, S. (2001). A principal component analysis of facial expressions. *Vision Research, 41*(9), 1179–1208.

Camurri, A., Lagerlof, I., & Volpe, G. (2003). Recognizing emotion from dance movement: Comparison of spectator recognition and automated techniques. *International Journal of Human-Computer Studies, 59*(1–2), 213–225.

Camurri, A., Mazzarino, B., Ricchetti, M., Timmers, R., & Volpe, G. (2004). Multimodal analysis of expressive gesture in music and dance performances. In *Gesture-based communication in human computer interaction, LNCS:2915* (pp. 20–39). Berlin-Heidelberg, Germany: Springer.

Camurri, A., Trocca, R., & Volpe, G. (2002). Interactive systems design: A KANSEI-based approach. In *Proceedings of the conference on new interfaces for musical expression* (pp. 1–8).

Castellano, G., Mortillaro, M., Camurri, A., Volpe, G., & Scherer, K. (2008). Automated analysis of body movement in emotionally expressive piano performances. *Music Perception, 26*(2), 103–120.

Chandler, J., & Schwarz, N. (2009). How extending your middle finger affects your perception of others: Learned movements influence concept accessibility. *Journal of Experimental Social Psychology, 45*(1), 123–128.

Clynes, M. (1973). Sentography: dynamic forms of communication of emotion and qualities. *Computers in Biology and Medicine, 3*, 119–130.

Coulson, M. (2004). Attributing emotion to static body postures: Recognition accuracy, confusions, and viewpoint dependence. *Journal of Nonverbal Behavior, 28*, 117–139.

Dael, N., Mortillaro, M., & Scherer, K. R. (2012). The body action and posture coding system (BAP): Development and reliability. *Journal of Nonverbal Behavior, 36*, 97–121.

Dahl, S., & Friberg, A. (2007). Visual perception of expressiveness in musicians' body movements. *Music Perception, 24*(5), 433–454.

de Gelder, B. (2006). Towards the neurobiology of emotional body language. *Nature Reviews Neuroscience, 7*(3), 242–249.

de Gelder, B. (2009). Why bodies? Twelve reasons for including bodily expressions in affective neuroscience. *Philosophical Transactions of the Royal Society, 364*(3), 3475–3484.

De Meijer, M. (1989). The contribution of general features of body movement to the attribution of emotions. *Journal of Nonverbal Behavior, 13*, 247–268.

De Silva, P. R. & Bianchi-Berthouze, N. (2004). Modeling human affective postures: An information theoretic characterization of posture features. *Journal of Computer Animation and Virtual Worlds, 15*(3–4), 269–276.

De Silva, P. R., Kleinsmith, A., & Bianchi-Berthouze, N. (2005). Towards unsupervised detection of affective body posture nuances. In *Proceedings of the 1st international conference on affective computing and intelligent interaction, LNCS:3784* (pp. 32–39). Berlin-Heidelberg, Germany: Springer.

Dittrich, W. H. (1993). Action categories and the perception of biological motion. *Perception, 22*(1), 15–22.

Doyle, J. (2004). Prospects for preferences. *Computational Intelligence, 20*(2), 111–136.

Ekman, P., & Friesen, W. (1967). Head and body cues in the judgment of emotion: A reformulation. *Perceptual and Motor Skills, 24*, 711–724.

Ekman, P., & Friesen, W. (1969). The repertoire of non-verbal behavioral categories: Origins, usage and coding. *Semiotica, 1*, 49–98.

Ekman, P., & Friesen, W. (1978). *Manual for the facial action coding system*. Palo Alto, CA: Consulting Psychology Press.

Elfenbein, H. A., Marsh, A. A., & Ambady, N. (2002). Emotional intelligence and the recognition of emotion from facial expressions. In L. F. Barrett & P. Salovey (Eds.), *The wisdom in feeling: Psychological processes in emotional intelligence* (pp. 37–59). New York: Guilford Press.

Fontaine, J. R. J., Scherer, K. R., Roesch, E. B., & Ellsworth, P. C. (2007). The world of emotions is not two-dimensional. *Psychological Science, 18*(12), 1050–1057.

Fragopanagos, N., & Taylor, J. G. (2005). Emotion recognition in human-computer interaction. *Neural Networks, 18*(4), 389–405.

Funfaro, E., Berthouze, N., Bevilacqua, F., and Tajadura-Jiménez, A. (2013). Sonification of surface tapping: Influences on behaviour, emotion and surface perception. ISON'13.

Fürnkranz, J., & Häullermeier, E. (2005). Preference learning. *Kunstliche Intelligenz, 19*(1), 60–61.

Gallagher, H. L., & Frith, C. D. (2004). Dissociable neural pathways for the perception and recognition of expressive and instrumental gestures. *Neuropsychologia, 42*(13), 1725–1736.

Gao, Y., Bianchi-Berthouze, N., & Meng, H. (2012). What does touch tell us about emotions in touchscreen-based gameplay? *ACM Transactions on Computer-Human Interaction (TOCHI), 19*(4), 31.

Geisser, M. E., Haig, A. J., Wallbom, A. S., & Wiggert, E. A. (2004). Pain-related fear, lumbar flexion, and dynamic EMG among persons with chronic musculoskeletal low back pain. *Clinical Journal of Pain, 20*(2), 61–9.

Giese, A., & Poggio, T. (2003). Neural mechanisms for the recognition of biological movements. *Neuroscience, 4*, 179–191.

Glowinski, D., Dael, N., Camurri, A., Volpe, G., Mortillaro, M., & Scherer, K. (2011). Towards a minimal representation of affective gestures. *IEEE Transactions on Affective Computing, 2*(2), 106–118.

Gong, L., Wang, T., Wang, C., Liu, F., Zhang, F., & Yu, X. (2010). Recognizing affect from non-stylized body motion using shape of Gaussian descriptors. In *Proceedings of ACM symposium on applied computing*, 1203–1206, New York, USA.

Griffin, H. J., Aung, M. S. H., Romera-Paredes, B., McKeown, G., Curran, W., McLoughlin, C., & Bianchi-Berthouze, N. (2013). Laughter type recognition from whole body motion. In IEEE *Proceedings of the 5th international conference on affective computing and intelligent interaction.*, 349–355, IEEE.

Gross, M. M., Crane, E. A., & Fredrickson, B. L. (2010). Methodology for assessing bodily expression of emotion. *Journal of Nonverbal Behavior, 34*, 223–248.

Gunes, H., & Pantic, M. (2010). Automatic, dimensional and continuous emotion recognition. *International Journal of Synthetic Emotion, 1*(1), 68–99.

Gunes, H., & Piccardi, M. (2007). Bi-modal emotion recognition from expressive face and body gestures. *Journal of Network and Computer Applications, 30*, 1334–1345.

Gunes, H., & Piccardi, M. (2009). Automatic temporal segment detection and affect recognition from face and body display. *IEEE Transactions on Systems, Man, and Cybernetics, Part B, 39*(1), 64–84.

Hall, J. A. & Matsumoto, D. (2004). Gender differences in judgments of multiple emotions from facial expressions, *Emotion, 4*(2), 201–206.

Haugstad, G. K., Haugstad, T. S., Kirste, U. M., Leganger, S., Wojniusz, S., Klemmetsen, I., & Malt, U. F. (2006). Posture, movement patterns, and body awareness in women with chronic pelvic pain. *Journal of Psychosomatic Research, 61*(5), 637–644.

Hertenstein, M. J., Holmes, R., Mccullough, M., & Keltner, D. (2009). The communication of emotion via touch. *Emotion, 9*(4), 566–573.

Hertenstein, M. J., Keltner, D., App, B., Bulleit, B. A., & Jaskolka, A. R. (2006). Touch communicates distinct emotions. *Emotion, 6*, 528–533.

Hirai, M., & Hiraki, K. (2006). The relative importance of spatial versus temporal structure in the perception of biological motion: An event-related potential study. *Cognition, 99*, B15–B29.

Hughes, L., Atkinson, D., Bianchi-Berthouze, N., & Baurley, S. (2012). Crowdsourcing an emotional wardrobe. In *Extended abstracts on human factors in computing systems* (pp. 231–240). New York, USA: ACM.

Inder, R., Bianchi-Berthouze, N., & Kato, T. (1999). K-DIME: A software framework for Kansei filtering of Internet material. In *Proceedings of the IEEE Conference in Systems, Man, and Cybernetics, 6*, 241–246.

Izard, C. E., & Malatesta, C. Z. (1987). Perspectives on emotional development: Differential emotions theory of early emotional development. In J. D. Osofsky (Ed.), *Handbook of infant development*, 2nd ed. (pp. 494–540). Hoboken, NJ: Wiley.

Jones, S. E., & Yarbrough, A. E. (1985). A naturalistic study of the meanings of touch. *Communication Monographs, 52,* 19–56.

Joshi, J., Goecke, R., Breakspear, M., & Parker, G. (2013). Can body expressions contribute to automatic depression analysis? In *Proceedings of the IEEE international conference on automatic face and gesture recognition,* 1–7, IEEE.

Kamisato, S., Odo, S., Ishikawa, Y., & Hoshino, K. (2004). Extraction of motion characteristics corresponding to sensitivity information using dance movement. *Journal of Advanced Computational Intelligence and Intelligent Informatics, 8*(2), 167–178.

Kapoor, A., Burleson, W., & Picard, R. W. (2007). Automatic prediction of frustration. *International Journal of Human Computer Studies, 65*(8), 724–736.

Kapoor, A., Picard, R. W., & Ivanov, Y. (2004). Probabilistic combination of multiple modalities to detect interest. In *Proceedings of the 17th international conference on pattern recognition* Vol. 3, pp. 969–972). Washington, DC, USA: IEEE Computer Society.

Kapur, A., Virji-Babul, N., Tzanetakis, G., & Driessen, P. F. (2005). Gesture-based affective computing on motion capture data. In *Proceedings of the 1st international conference on affective computing and intelligent interaction, LNCS:3784* (pp. 1–7). Berlin-Heidelberg, Germany: Springer.

Karg, M., Kuhnlenz, K., & Buss, M. (2010). Recognition of affect based on gait patterns. *IEEE Transactions on Systems, Man, and Cybernetics, Part B, 40*(4), 1050–1061.

Khanna, P. & Sasikumar, M. (2010). Recognising emotions from keyboard stroke pattern. *International Journal of Computer Applications, 11*(9), 0975–8887.

Kim, J., & André, E. (2008). Emotion recognition based on physiological changes in music listening. *IEEE Transactions on Pattern Analysis and Machine Intelligence, 30*(12), 2067–2083.

Kim, K. H., Bang, S. W., & Kim, S. R. (2004). Emotion recognition system using short-term monitoring of physiological signals. *Medical & Biological Engineering & Computing, 42*(3), 419–427.

Kleinsmith, A., & Bianchi-Berthouze, N. (2013). Affective body expression perception and recognition: A survey. *IEEE Transactions on Affective Computing, 4*(1), 15–33.

Kleinsmith, A. & Bianchi-Berthouze, N. (2007). Recognizing affective dimensions from body posture. In *Proceedings of the 2nd international conference on affective computing and intelligent interaction, LNCS:4738* (pp. 48–58). Berlin-Heidelberg, Germany: Springer.

Kleinsmith, A., Bianchi-Berthouze, N., & Berthouze, L. (2006). An effect of gender in the interpretation of affective cues in avatars. In *Proceedings of workshop on gender and interaction: Real and virtual women in a male world, in conjunction with advanced visual interfaces.*

Kleinsmith, A., Bianchi-Berthouze, N., & Steed, A. (2011). Automatic recognition of non-acted affective postures. *IEEE Transactions on Systems, Man, and Cybernetics: Part B, 41*(4), 1027–1038.

Kleinsmith, A., De Silva, P. R., & Bianchi-Berthouze, N. (2005). Grounding affective dimensions into posture features. Affective Computing and Intelligent Interaction, LNCS: 3784, (pp. 263–270). Berlin-Heidelberg, Germany: Springer.

Kleinsmith, A., De Silva, P. R., & Bianchi-Berthouze, N. (2006). Cross-cultural differences in recognizing affect from body posture. *Interacting with Computers, 18,* 1371–1389.

Kleinsmith, A., Fushimi, T., & Bianchi-Berthouze, N. (2005). An incremental and interactive affective posture recognition system. In *International workshop on adapting the interaction style to affective factors, in conjunction with user modeling.*

Knapp, M. L., & Hall, J. A. (1997). *Nonverbal communication in human interaction,* 4th ed. San Diego, CA: Harcourt Brace.

Kudoh, T., & Matsumoto, D. (1985). Cross-cultural examination of the semantic dimensions of body postures. *Journal of Personality and Social Psychology, 48*(6), 1440–1446.

Kvåle, A, Ljunggren, A. E., & Johnsen, T. B. (2003). Examination of movement in patients with long-lasting musculoskeletal pain: Reliability and validity. *Physiotherapy Research International, 8*(1), 36–52.

Lange, J., & Lappe, M. (2007). The role of spatial and temporal information in biological motion perception. *Advances in Cognitive Psychology, 3*(4), 419–428.

Lee, C. M., & Narayanan, S. S. (2005). Toward detecting emotions in spoken dialogs. *IEEE Transactions on Speech and Audio Processing, 13*(2), 293–303.

Lindquist, K. A., Barrett, L. F., Bliss-Moreau, E., & Russell, J. A. (2006). Language and the perception of emotion. *Emotion, 6,* 125–138.

Ma, Y., Paterson, H. M., & Pollick, F. E. (2006). A motion capture library for the study of identity, gender, and emotion perception from biological motion. *Behavior Research Methods, 38*(1), 134–141.

Martel, M. O., Wideman, T. H., & Sullivan, M. J. L. (2012). Patients who display protective pain behaviors are viewed as less likable, less dependable, and less likely to return to work. *Pain, 153*(4), 843–849.

Martens, U., Leuthold, H., & Schweinberger, S. R. (2010). On the temporal organization of facial identity and expression analysis: Inferences from event-related brain potentials. *Cognitive, Affective, & Behavioral Neuroscience, 10*(4), 505–522.

Matsuda, Y., Sakuma, I., Jimbo, Y., Kobayashi, E., Arafune, T., & Isomura, T. (2010). Emotion recognition of finger Braille. *International Journal of Innovative Computing, Information and Control, 6*(3B), 1363–1377.

Matsumoto, D., Consolacion, T., Yamada, H., Suzuki, R., Franklin, B., Paul, S., Ray, R., & Uchida, H. (2002). American-Japanese cultural differences in judgments of emotional expressions of different intensities. *Cognition and Emotion 16,* 721–747.

Matsumoto, D., & Kudoh, T. (1987). Cultural similarities and differences in the semantic dimensions of body postures. *Journal of Nonverbal Behavior, 11*(3), 166–179.

McDuff, D., Kaliouby, R. E., & Picard, R. W. (2012). Crowdsourcing facial responses to online videos. *IEEE Transactions on Affective Computing, 3*(4), 456, 468.

McKeown, G., Curran, W., Kane, D., McCahon, R., Griffin, H., McLoughlin, C., & Bianchi-Berthouze, N. (2013). Human perception of laughter from context-free whole body motion dynamic stimuli. In IEEE *Proceedings of the 5th international conference on affective computing and intelligent interaction,* 306–311, IEEE.

McLeod, P., Dittrich, W., Driver, J., Perret, D., & Zihl, J. (1996). Preserved and impaired detection of structure from motion by a "motion-blind" patient. *Visual Cognition, 3,* 363–391.

Mehrabian, A. (1996). Pleasure-arousal-dominance: A general framework for describing and measuring individual differences in temperament. *Current Psychology: Developmental, Learning, Personality, Social, 14*(4), 261–292.

Mehrabian, A., & Epstein, N. (1972). A measure of emotional empathy. *Journal of Personality, 40*, 525–543.

Mehrabian, A. & Friar, J. (1969). Encoding of attitude by a seated communicator via posture and position cues. *Journal of Consulting and Clinical Psychology, 33*, 330–336.

Meng, H.,, Bianchi-Berthouze, N., (2013). Affective State Level Recognition in Naturalistic Facial and Vocal Expressions. *IEEE Transactions on Systems, Man and Cybernetics Part B: Cybernetics, 44*(3).

Meng, H., Kleinsmith, A., & Bianchi-Berthouze, N. (2011). Multi-score learning for affect recognition: The case of body postures. In *Proceedings of the 4th international conference on affective computing and intelligent interaction, LNCS:6974* (pp. 225–234). Berlin-Heidelberg, Germany: Springer.

Metallinou, A., Katsamanis, A., & Narayanan, S. (2013). Tracking continuous emotional trends of participants during affective dyadic interactions using body language and speech information. *Image and Vision Computing, 31*(2), 137–152.

Moeslund, T. B., & Granum, E. (2001). A survey of computer vision-based human motion capture. *Computer Vision and Image Understanding 81*, 231–268.

Morrison, D., Wang, R., & De Silva, L. C. (2007). Ensemble methods for spoken emotion recognition in call-centres. *Speech Communication, 49*, 98–112.

Neill, S., & Caswell, C. (1993). *Body language for competent teachers*. New York: Routledge.

Niedenthal, P. M., Barsalou, L. W., Winkielman, P., Krauth-Gruber, S., & Ric, F. (2005). Embodiment in attitudes, social perception, and emotion. *Personality and Social Psychology Review, 9*(3), 184–211.

Nijhar, J., Bianchi-Berthouze, N., & Boguslawski, G. (2012). Does movement recognition precision affect the player experience in exertion games? In *International conference on intelligent technologies for interactive entertainment*, Lecture Notes of the Institute for Computer Sciences, Social Informatics and Telecommunications Engineering, Vol 78, 73–82, Springer, Berlin-Heidelberg, Germany.

Oikonomidis, I., Kyriazis, N., & Argyros, A. (2011). Efficient model-based 3D tracking of hand articulations using Kinect. *Proceedings of the British machine vision conference.*

Pantic, M., & Patras, I. (2006). Dynamics of facial expression: recognition of facial actions and their temporal segments from face profile image sequences. *IEEE Transactions on Systems, Man, and Cybernetics—Part B, 36*(2), 433–449.

Pantic, M., & Rothkrantz, L. J. M. (2000). Automatic analysis of facial expressions: The state of the art. In *IEEE Transactions on pattern analysis and machine intelligence, 22*(12), 1424–1445.

Park, H., Park, J., Kim, U., & Woo, W. (2004). Emotion recognition from dance image sequences using contour approximation. In *Proceedings of the International Workshop on Structural, Syntactic, and Statistical Pattern Recognition* LNCS 3138, (pp. 547–555). Springer, Berlin-heidelberg, Germany.

Pasch, M., Bianchi-Berthouze, N., van Dijk, B., & Nijholt, A. (2009). Movement-based sports video games: Investigating motivation and gaming experience. *Entertainment Computing, 9*(2), 169–180.

Peelen, M. V., Wiggett, A. J., & Downing, P. E. (2006). Patterns of fMRI activity dissociate overlapping functional brain areas that respond to biological motion. *Neuron, 49*, 815–822.

Pluess, M., Conrad, A., & Wilhelm, F. H. (2009). Muscle tension in generalized anxiety disorder: A critical review of the literature. *Journal of Anxiety Disorders, 23*(1), 1–11.

Pollick, F. E., Paterson, H. M., Bruderlin, A., & Sanford, A. J. (2001). Perceiving affect from arm movement. *Cognition, 82*, 51–61.

Raykar, V., Yu, S., Zhao, L., Valadez, G., Florin, C., Bogoni, L., & Moy, L. (2010). Learning from crowds. *Journal of Machine Learning Research, 11*(7), 1297–1322.

Roether, C., Omlor, L., Christensen, A., Giese, M. A. (2009). Critical features for the perception of emotion from gait. *Journal of Vision, 8*(6):15, 1–32.

Romera-Paredes, B., Argyriou, A., Bianchi-Berthouze, N., & Pontil, M. (2012). Exploiting unrelated tasks in multi-task learning. *Journal of Machine Learning Research—Proceedings Track, 22*, 951–959.

Romera-Paredes, B., Aung, S. H. M., Bianchi-Berthouze, N., Watson, P., C de C Williams, A., & Pontil, M. (2013). Transfer learning to account for idiosyncrasy in face and body expressions. In *Proceedings of the 10th international conference on automatic face and gesture recognition.* 1–6, IEEE.

Sanghvi, J., Castellano, G., Leite, I., Pereira, A., McOwan, P. W., & Paiva, A. (2011). Automatic analysis of affective postures and body motion to detect engagement with a game companion. In *Proceedings of the international conference on human-robot interaction*, (pp. 305–312), IEEE.

Savva, N., & Bianchi-Berthouze, N. (2011). Automatic recognition of affective body movement in a video game scenario. *International conference on intelligent technologies for interactive entertainment*, Lecture Notes of the Institute for Computer Sciences, Social Informatics and Telecommunications Engineering, Vol. 78, 149–159, Springer, Berlin-Heidelberg, Germany.

Savva, N., Scarinzi, A., & Bianchi-Berthouze, N. (2012). Continuous recognition of player's affective body expression as dynamic quality of aesthetic experience. *IEEE Transactions on Computational Intelligence and AI in Games, 4*(3), 199–212.

Sheng, V. S., Provost, F., & Ipeirotis, P. G. (2008). Get another label? Improving data quality and data mining using multiple, noisy labellers. In *Proceedings of the 14th ACM SIGKDD international conference on knowledge disc and data mining* (pp. 614–622), ACM, New York, USA.

Shibata, T., Michishita, A., & Bianchi-Berthouze, N. (2013). Analysis and modeling of affective Japanese sitting postures by Japanese and British observers. In IEEE *Proceedings of the 5th international conference on affective computing and intelligent interaction*, 91–96.

Singh, A., Klapper, A., Jia, J., Fidalgo, A., Tajadura Jimenez, A., Kanakam, N., C de C Williams, A., & Bianchi-Berthouze, N. (2014). opportunities for technology in motivating people with chronic pain to do physical activity, CHI'14, ACM, New York, USA.

Swann-Sternberg, T., Singh, A., Bianchi-Berthouze, N., & CdeC Williams, A. (2012). User needs for an interactive technology to support physical activity in chronic pain. In *Extended Abstracts, CHI'12* (pp. 2241–2246), ACM, New York, NY, USA.

Thomas, M., McGinley, J., Carruth, D., & Blackledge, C. (2007). Cross-validation of an infrared motion capture system and an electromechanical motion capture device. In *SAE Technical Paper, Digital Human Modeling Conference*, Seattle, WA.

Vania, L. M., Lemay, M., Bienfang, D. C., Choi, A. Y., & Nakayama, K. (1990). Intact biological motion and structure from motion perception in a patient with impaired motion mechanisms: A case study. *Visual Neuroscience, 5*, 353–369.

Varni, G., Volpe, G., & Camurri, A. (2010). A system for real-time multimodal analysis of nonverbal affective social interaction in user-centric media. *IEEE Transactions on Multimedia, 12*(6), 576–590.

Vlaeyen, J. W. S., & Linton, S. J. (2000). Fear-avoidance and its consequences in muscleskeleton pain: A state of the art. *Pain, 85*(3), 317–332.

Wagner, J., Kim, J., & André, E. (2005). From physiological signals to emotions: Implementing and comparing selected methods for feature extraction and classification. IEEE *Multimedia and Expo. ICME* (pp. 940–943).

Wallbott, H. G. (1998). Bodily expression of emotion. *European Journal of Social Psychology, 28*, 879–896.

Watson, P. J., Booker, C. K., Main, C. J., & Chen, A. C. (1997). Surface electromyography in the identification of chronic low back pain patients: The development of the flexion relaxation ratio. *Clinical Biomechanics, 12*(3), 165–171.

Yacoub, S., Simske, S., Lin, X., & Burns, J. (2003). Recognition of emotions in interactive voice response systems. In *Proceedings of Eurospeech.*

Yannakakis, G. N. (2009). Preference learning for affective modelling. In IEEE *Proceedings of the 3rd International Conference on Affective Computing and Intelligent Interaction* (pp. 126–131).

Zhao, W., Chellappa, R., & Rosenfeld, A. (2003). Face recognition: A literature survey, *ACM Computing Surveys, 35*, 399–458.

Speech in Affective Computing

Chi-Chun Lee, Jangwon Kim, Angeliki Metallinou, Carlos Busso, Sungbok Lee,
and Shrikanth S. Narayanan

Abstract

Speech is a key communication modality for humans to encode emotion. In this chapter, we address three main aspects of speech in affective computing: emotional speech production, acoustic feature extraction for emotion analysis, and the design of a speech-based emotion recognizer. Specifically we discuss the current understanding of the interplay of speech production vocal organs during expressive speech, extracting informative acoustic features from speech recording waveforms, and the engineering design of automatic emotion recognizers using speech acoustic-based features. The latter includes a discussion of emotion labeling for generating ground truth references, acoustic feature normalization for controlling signal variability, and choice of computational frameworks for emotion recognition. Finally, we present some open challenges and applications of a robust emotion recognizer.

Key Words: emotional speech production, acoustic feature extraction for emotion analysis, computational frameworks for emotion recognition, acoustic feature normalization

Introduction

Speech is a natural and rich communication medium for humans to interact with one another. It encodes both linguistic intent and paralinguistic information (e.g., emotion, age, gender, etc.). In this chapter, we focus our discussion on this unique human behavior modality, speech, in the context of affective computing, in order to measure and quantify the internal emotional state of a person by observing external affective and expressive behaviors. The specific focus is on describing the emotional encoding process in speech production—that is, the state-of-the-art computational approaches and future directions and applications of computing affect from speech signals.

The human speech signal is a result of complex and integrative movement of various speech production organs including the vocal chords, larynx, pharynx, tongue, velum, and jaw. With the availability of instrumental technologies—including ultrasound, x-ray microbeam, electromagnetic articulography (EMA), and (real time) magnetic resonance imaging (MRI)—researchers have begun to investigate various scientific questions in order to bring insights into the emotional speech production mechanisms. In this chapter, we start by providing some empirical details of how emotional information is encoded at the speech production level (Affective Speech Production, p. 171).

Research in understanding the production mechanisms of emotional speech is still evolving. However, empirical computational approaches for extracting acoustic signal features that characterize emotional speech have emerged from scientific advances both in emotion perception and speech signal analysis. In Computation of Affective Speech Features (p. 173), we summarize the set of features of vocal cues that have become a de facto standard, often termed as the speech low-level descriptors (LLDs), for automatic emotion recognition.

In Affect Recognition and Modeling Using Speech (p. 175), we describe three essential components of a proper design of an automatic emotion recognition system using speech-acoustic features: definition and implementation of emotion labeling that serve as the basis for computing (Emotion Labels for Computing, p. 175), acoustic feature normalization that helps address issues related to signal variability due to factors other than the core emotions being targeted (Robust Acoustic Feature Normalization, p. 176), and machine learning algorithms that offer the means for achieving the desired modeling goal (Computational Framework for Emotion Recognition, p. 177).

Emotion labeling (or annotation) typically provides a ground truth for training and evaluating emotion recognition systems. The specific choice of representations (descriptors) used for computing depends on the theoretical underpinnings and the application goal. In addition to traditionally used categorical (happy, angry, sad, and neutral) and dimensional labels (of arousal, valence, and dominance), researchers have made advances in computationally integrating behavior descriptors in the characterization of emotion. These advancements can better handle the ambiguity in the definition of emotions compared with traditional labeling schemes (Emotion Labels for Computing, p. 175).

Normalization of acoustic features aims to minimize unwanted variability due to sources other than the construct (i.e., emotion) being modeled. The speech signal is influenced by numerous factors including what is being said (linguistic content), who is saying it (speaker identity, age, gender), how the signal is being captured and transmitted (telephone, cellphone, microphone types), and the context in which the speech signal is generated (room acoustics and environment effects including background noise). In Robust Acoustic Feature Normalization, p. 176, we discuss several techniques for feature normalization that ensure that the features contain more information about emotion and less about other nonemotional confounding variability.

Machine learning algorithms are used to train the recognition system to learn a mapping between the extracted speech features and the given target emotion labels. Many standard pattern recognition techniques used in other engineering applications have shown to be appropriate for emotion recognition system with speech features. We also describe other recent state-of-the-art emotion recognition frameworks that have been proposed to take into account of the various contextual influences in the expression of emotions in speech, including the nature of human interactions for obtaining improved emotion recognition accuracies (Computational Framework for Emotion Recognition, p. 177).

There remain many challenges that require further investigation and future research; however, potential engineering applications, including new generation of human-machine interfaces, have made the development of robust emotion-sensing technology essential. A recent research endeavor of the rapidly growing field of behavior signal processing (BSP) (Narayanan & Georgiou, 2013) has demonstrated that development can provide analytical tools for advancing behavioral analyses desired by domain experts across a wide range of disciplines, especially in fields related to mental health (Speech in Affective Computing: Future Works and Applications, p. 180).

Affective Speech Production

Often, speech production research is conducted under the "source filter" theory (Fant, 1970), which views the speech production system as consisting of two components: source activities, which generate airflow, and vocal tract shaping filtering, which modulates the airflow. Although laryngeal behavior is not fully independent of supralaryngeal elements, the modulation of vocal folds, or vocal cords, in the larynx is the primary control of source activity. This modulation results in the variation of pitch (the frequency of vocal fold vibration), intensity (the pressure of the airflow), and voice quality dynamics (degrees of aperiodicity in the resulting glottal cycle). Note that the filter affects the variation of intensity and voice quality, too. The air stream passed through the vocal fold is modulated by articulatory controls of tongue, velum, lips, and jaw in the vocal tract, resulting in dynamic spectral changes in the speech signal. The interaction and interplay between voice source activities and articulatory controls also contribute to the speech sound modulation.

Most emotional speech studies have focused on the acoustic characteristics of the resulting speech signal level—such as the underlying prosodic variation, spectral shape, and voice quality change—across various time scales rather than considering the underlying production mechanisms directly. In order to understand complex acoustic structure and further the human communication process that involves information encoding and decoding, a deeper understanding of orchestrated articulatory activity is needed. In this section, we describe scientific findings of emotional speech production in terms of articulatory mechanisms, vocal folds actions, and the interplay between voice source and articulatory kinematics.

Articulatory Mechanisms in Emotionally Expressive Speech

The number of studies on articulatory mechanisms of expressive speech is limited compared with studies in the acoustic domain presumably due to the difficulties in obtaining direct articulatory data. Contemporary instrumental methods for collecting articulatory data include ultrasound (Stone, 2005), x-ray microbeam (Fujimura, Kiritani, & Ishida, 1973), electromagnetic articulography (EMA) (Perkell et al., 1992), and (real time) magnetic resonance imaging (MRI) (Narayanan, Alwan, & Haker, 1995; Narayanan, Nayak, Lee, Sethy, & Byrd, 2004). While it is often challenging for subjects to express emotions naturally in these data collection environments, there have been some systematic studies with these data collection technologies showing that articulatory patterns of acted emotional speech are different from neutral (nonemotional) speech.

Lee et al. analyzed the surface articulatory motions by using emotional speech data for four acted emotions (angry, happy, sad, and neutral) collected with EMA (Lee, Yildirim, Kazemzadeh, & Narayanan, 2005). The study showed that that the speech production of emotional speech is associated more with peripheral articulatory motions than that of neutral speech. For example, the tongue tip (TT), jaw, and lip positioning are more advanced (extreme) in emotional speech than in neutral speech (Figure 12.1). Furthermore, the results of multiple simple discriminant analyses treating the four emotion categories as dependent variable showed that the classification recalls of using articulatory features are higher than those of acoustic features. The result implied that the articulatory features carry valuable emotion-dependent information.

Lee et al. also found that there was more prominent usage of the pharyngeal region for anger than neutral, sadness and happiness in emotional speech (Lee, Bresch, Adams, Kazemzadeh, & Narayanan, 2006). It was further observed that happiness is associated with greater laryngeal elevation than anger, neutrality, and sadness. This emotional variation of the larynx was related to wider pitch and second formant (F2) ranges and higher third formant frequencies (F3) in the acoustic signal. It was also reported that the variation of articulatory positions and speed as well as pitch and energy are significantly associated with perceptual strength of emotion in general (Kim, Lee, & Narayanan, 2011).

Most of the emotional speech production studies rely on acted emotion recorded using actors/actresses as subjects. Although acted emotional speech could be different from spontaneous emotional speech in terms of articulatory positions (Erickson, Menezes, & Fujino, 2004), using acted emotional expression remains one of the most effective methods for collecting articulatory data in order to carry out studies in emotional speech production. A certain degree of ecological validity is achieved by following consistent experimental techniques such as those expressed by Busso and Narayanan (Busso & Narayanan, 2008).

Vocal Fold Controls in Emotionally Expressive Speech

Vocal fold controls or, more precisely, the controls of the tension and length of vocal fold muscles, enable major modulations of voice source activities. Voice source is defined as the airflow passing through the glottis in the larynx. The configuration of voice source is determined by the actions of opening and closing of vocal folds

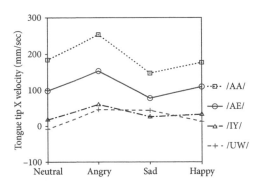 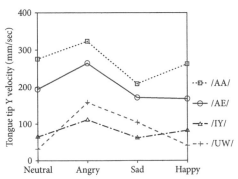

Fig. 12.1 Tongue tip horizontal (left) and vertical (right) movement velocity plots of four peripheral vowels as a function of emotion. *Source*: Lee, Yildirim, Kazemzadeh, and Narayanan (2005).

with different levels of tensions in the laryngeal muscles. During speech production, the voice source is filtered by supralaryngeal vocal organs. Since the speech waveform is the result of complex modulations (filtering) of glottal airflow in the supraglottal structure, it is difficult to recover the glottal airflow information from the speech output acoustics. One of the most popular techniques to recover voice source is through inverse filtering; however, it remains challenging to estimate the voice source information from natural spontaneous speech even with little noise and distortion.

Despite these difficulties, there are interesting studies reporting on paralinguistic aspects of voice source activities in the domain of emotional speech production. For example, for sustained /aa/, Murphy et al. showed that the estimated contacting quotient (i.e., contact time of the vocal folds divided by cycle duration) and speed quotient, or velocity of closure divided by velocity of opening, from the electroglottogram (EGG), are different among five categorical (simulated) emotions (angry, joy, neutrality, sadness, and tenderness) (Murphy & Laukkanen, 2009). Gobl et al. also showed that voice qualities—such as harsh, tense, modal, breathy, whispery, creaky and lax-creaky, and combinations of them—are associated with affective states using synthesized speech (Gobl & Chasaide, 2003).

Interplay Between Voice Source and Articulatory Kinematics

Another essential source of emotional information in speech production is present in the interplay between voice source activities and articulatory kinematics. Kim et al. reported that angry speech introduces the greatest articulatory speed modulations, while pitch modulations were most prominent for happy speech (Kim, Lee, & Narayanan, 2010) (Figure 12.2). This study underscores the complexity and the importance of better understanding the interplay between voice source behavior and articulatory motion in the analysis of emotional speech production.

Open Challenges

One of the biggest challenges and opportunities in studying emotional variation in speech production lies in the inter- and intraspeaker variability. Interspeaker variability includes heterogeneous display of emotion and differences in individual's vocal tract structures (Lammert, Proctor, & Narayanan,

2013). Intraspeaker variability results from the fact that a speaker can express an emotion in a number of ways and is influenced by the context. The invariant nature of controls of speech production components still remains elusive, making comprehensive modeling of emotional speech challenging and largely open.

Computation of Affective Speech Features

As described in Affective Speech Production (p. 171), the analysis of speech production data suggests that a complex interaction between vocal source activities and vocal tract modulations likely underlies how emotional information is encoded in speech waveform. While an understanding of this complex emotional speech production mechanism is emerging only as more research is being carried out, many studies have examined the relationship between the perceptual quality of emotional content and acoustic signal characteristics.

Bachorowski has summarized a wide range of results from various psychological perceptual tests indicating that humans are significantly more accurate at judging emotional content than merely guessing at chance level while listening to speech recordings (Bachorowski, 1999). Furthermore, Scherer described a comprehensive theoretical production-perception model of vocal communication of emotion and provided a detailed review on how each acoustic parameter (e.g., pitch, intensity, speech rate, etc.) covaries with different intensities of emotion perception (Scherer, 2003); this classic study was further expanded upon in the handbook for nonverbal behavior research focusing on the vocal expression of affect (Juslin & Scherer, 2005). These studies of the processing of emotional speech by humans have formed the bases for affective computing using speech owing to its extensive scientific grounding. They have also served as an initial foundation for developing engineering applications of affective computing (e.g., emotion recognition using speech and emotional speech synthesis).

Acoustic Feature Extraction for Emotion Recognition

Computing affect from speech signals has benefited greatly from the perceptual understanding and, to a smaller extent, the production details of vocal expressions and affect. A list of commonly used acoustic low-level descriptors (LLDs), extracted from speech recordings that can be used in emotion recognition tasks is given below.

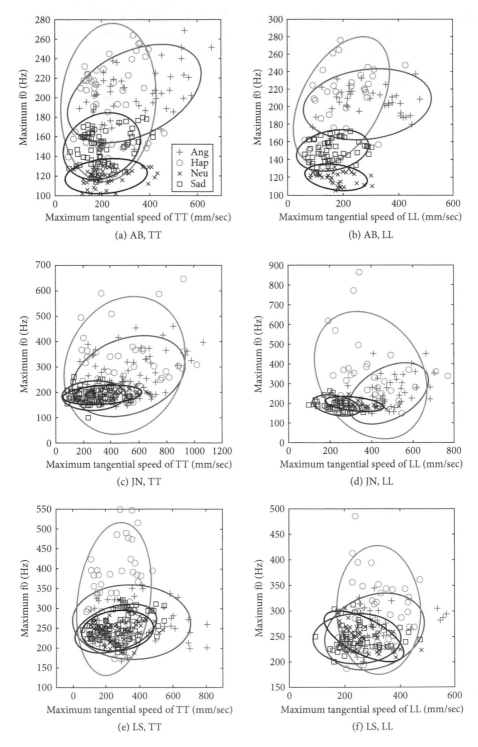

Fig. 12. 2 Example plots of the maximum tangential speed of critical articulators and the maximum pitch. A circle indicates that Gaussian contour with 2 sigma standard deviation for each emotion (red-Ang, green-Hap, black-Neu, blue-Sad). Different emotions show distinctive variation patterns in the articulatory speed dimension and the pitch dimension. *Source*: Kim, Lee, and Narayanan (2010).

Prosody-related signal measures

- Fundamental frequency (f_0)
- Short-term energy
- Speech rate: syllable/phoneme rate

Spectral characteristics measures

- Mel-frequency cepstral coefficients (MFCCs)
- Mel-filter bank energy coefficients (MFBs)

Voice quality–related measures

- Jitter
- Shimmer
- Harmonic-to-noise ratio

Prosody relates to characteristics such as rhythm, stress, and intonation of speech; spectral characteristics are related to the harmonic/resonant structures resulting as the airflow is modulated by dynamic vocal tract configurations; and voice quality measures are related to the characteristics of vocal fold vibrations (e.g., degrees of aperiodicity in the resulting speech waveform).

Many publicly available toolboxes are capable of performing such acoustic feature computation. OpenSmile (Eyben, Wöllmer, & Schuller, 2010) is one such toolbox designed specifically for emotion recognition tasks; other generic audio/speech processing toolboxes—such as Praat (Boersma, 2001), Wavesurfer,[1] and Voicebox[2]—are all capable of extracting relevant acoustic features.

In practice, after extracting these LLDs, researchers frequently further apply a data processing approach, often computed at a time-scale of 10 to 25 milliseconds, in order to capture the rich dynamics. The approach first involves computing various statistical functionals (i.e., mean, standard deviation, range, interquartile range, regression residuals, etc.) on these LLDs at different time scale granularities (e.g., at 0.1, 0.5, 1, and 10 seconds, etc.). Furthermore, in order to measure the dynamics at multilevel time scales, statistical functional operators can also be stacked on top of each other; for example, one can compute the mean of pitch LLDs (i.e., fundamental frequency) for every 0.1 second, then compute the mean of "the mean of pitch (at 0.1s)" for every 0.5 second, and repeat this process with increasing time scales across different statistical functional operators.

This data processing technique has been applied successfully in tasks such as emotion recognition (Lee, Mower, Busso, Lee, & Narayanan, 2011; Schuller, Arsic, Wallhoff, & Rigoll, 2006; Schuller,

Batliner, et al., 2007), paralinguistic prediction (Bone, Li, Black, & Narayanan, 2012; Björn Schuller et al., 2013), and other behavioral modeling (Black et al., 2013; Black, Georgiou, Katsamanis, Baucom, & Narayanan, 2011). This approach can often result in a very high-dimensional feature vector—for example, depending on the length of audio segment, it can range from hundreds of features to thousands or more. Feature selection techniques—stand-alone (e.g., correlation-based) (Hall, 1999) and mutual information based (Peng, Long, & Ding, 2005) or wrapper selection techniques (e.g., sequential forward feature selection, sequential floating forward feature selection) (Jain & Zongker, 1997)—can be carried out to reduce the dimension appropriately for the set of emotion classes of interest.

Open Challenges

While the aforementioned data processing approach has been shown to be effective in various emotion prediction tasks, it remains unclear why the large number of acoustic LLDs work well and what aspects of emotional production-perception mechanisms are captured with this technique. From a computational point of view, since it is an exhaustive and computationally expensive approach, an efficient and reliable real-life emotional recognizer built upon this approach may be impractical. Future works lie in designing better-informed features based on the understanding of emotional speech production-perception mechanisms while maintaining reliable prediction accuracies compared with the current approach.

Affect Recognition and Modeling Using Speech

Recognizing and tracking emotional states in human interactions based on spoken utterances requires a series of appropriate engineering design including the following: specifying an annotation scheme of appropriate emotion labels, implementing a feature normalization technique for robust recognition, and designing context-aware machine learning frameworks to model the temporal and interaction aspect of emotion evolution in dialogs.

Emotion Labels for Computing

Annotating (coding) data with appropriate emotion labels is a crucial first step in providing the basis for implementing and evaluating the computational modeling approaches. Traditionally, behavioral assessment of one's emotional state can be done in two different ways: self-reports or perceived ratings. Self-reported emotion assessment instruments are designed to ask the subjects to recall his or her experience and memory about how he or she has felt during a particular interaction (e.g., the positive and negative affect schedule (PANAS) (Watson, Clark, & Tellegen, 1988). Perceived-ratings are often carried out by asking external (trained) observers to assign labels of emotion as they watch a given audiovideo recording. Tools such as ELAN (Wittenburg, Brugman, Russel, Klassmann, & Sloetjes, 2006) and Anvil (Kipp, 2001) are commonly used software for carrying out such annotations.

Many studies of emotion in behavioral science rely on self-assessment of emotional states to approximate the true underlying emotional states of the subject. This method of emotion labeling is often used to clarify the role of human affective process under different scientific hypotheses. In affective computing, recognizing emotion automatically from recorded behavioral data often adopts annotation based on perceived emotion. The perceived emotional states can be coded either as categorical emotional states (e.g., angry, happy, sad, neutral) or as dimensional representations (e.g., valence, activation, and dominance). This method of labeling emotion is motivated by the premise that automatic emotion recognition systems are often designed with an aim of recognizing emotions through perceiving/sensing other humans' behaviors.

Depending on the applications, one can take an approach of labeling behavioral data with self-reported assessment instrument or perceived emotional states. The design of labeling serves as ground truth for training and testing machine learning algorithms and the choice of different labeling schemes also often comes with a distinct interpretation of whether the model is capturing the underlying human affective production or perception process.

RECENT ADVANCES IN EMOTION LABELING

Many of the traditional emotion labels can be seen as a compact representation of a large emotion space. Individual differences in internalizing what constitutes a specific emotion label often arise from the variation of an integrative process of cognitive evaluation of personal experience and spontaneous behavioral reaction to affective stimuli. There are some recent computational works aimed at advancing representations of emotions by incorporating signal-based behavior descriptors that are more conducive to capture the nonprototypical blended nature in real life (Mower et al., 2009). A recent work demonstrated the representation of emotion as emotion profile (i.e., a mixture of categorical emotional labels based on models built with visual-acoustic descriptors). This approach can model the inherent ambiguity and subtle nature of emotional expressions (Mower, Mataric, & Narayanan, 2011). Another recent representation in exploring computational method to better represent this large emotion space is through the use of natural language (Kazamzadeh, Lee, Georgiou, & Narayanan, 2011). This approach aims at representing any emotion word in terms of humans' natural language either describing a past event, a memorable experience, or simply closely related traditionally used categorical emotional states.

Robust Acoustic Feature Normalization

Speech is a rich communication medium conveying emotional, lexical, cultural, and idiosyncratic information, among others, and it is often affected by the environment (e.g., noise, reverberation) and recording and signal transmission setup (e.g., microphone quality, sampling rate, wireless/VoIP channels, etc.).

Previous studies have indicated the importance of speaker normalization in recognizing paralinguistic information (Bone, Li, et al., 2012; Busso, Lee, & Narayanan, 2009; Rahman & Busso, 2012). For example, the structure and the size of the larynx and the vocal folds determine the values of the fundamental frequency (f_0), which span the range of 50 to 250Hz for men, 120 to 500Hz for women, and even higher for children (Deller, Hansen, & Proakis, 2000). Therefore, although angry speech has a higher f_0 values than neutral speech (Yildirim et al., 2004), the emotional differences can be blurred by interspeaker differences—the difference between the mean values of the fundamental frequency of neutral and anger speech during spontaneous interaction (e.g., the USC IEMOCAP database (Busso et al., 2008) is merely a 68-Hz shift.

A common approach to normalize the data is to estimate global acoustic parameters across speakers and utterances. For example, the z-normalization approach transforms the features by subtracting their mean and dividing by their standard deviation (i.e., each feature will have zero mean and unit variance across all data) (Lee & Narayanan,

2005; Lee et al., 2011; Metallinou, Katsamanis, & Narayanan, 2012; Schuller, Rigoll, & Lang, 2003). The min-max approach scales the feature to a predefined range (Clavel, Vasilescu, Devillers, Richard, & Ehrette, 2008; Pao, Yeh, Chen, Cheng, & Lin, 2007; Wöllmer et al., 2008). Other nonlinear normalization approaches aim to convert the features' distributions into normal distributions (Yan, Li, Cairong, & Yinhua, 2008). Studies have applied these approaches in speaker-dependent conditions in which the normalization parameters are separately estimated for each individual (Bitouk, Verma, & Nenkova, 2010; Le, Quénot, & Castelli, 2004; Schuller, Vlasenko, Minguez, Rigoll, & Wendemuth, 2007; Sethu, Ambikairajah, & Epps, 2007; Vlasenko, Schuller, Wendemuth, & Rigoll, 2007; Wöllmer et al., 2008).

ITERATIVE FEATURE NORMALIZATION (IFN)

Busso et al. demonstrated that global normalization is not always effective in increasing the performance of an emotion recognition system (Busso, Metallinou, & Narayanan, 2011). This is because applying a single normalization scheme across the entire corpus can adversely affect the emotional discrimination of the features (e.g., all features having the same mean and range across sentences). A new transformation is done by normalizing features by estimating the parameters of an affine transformation (e.g., z-normalization) using only neutral (non-emotional) samples.

Multiple studies have consistently observed statistically significant improvements in performance (Busso et al., 2009, 2011; Rahman & Busso, 2012) when this approach is separately applied for each subject. Given that neutral samples may not be available for each of the target individual, Busso et al. proposed the iterative feature normalization (IFN) scheme (Figure 12.3) (Busso et al., 2011). This unsupervised

front-end scheme implements the aforementioned ideas by estimating the neutral subset of the data iteratively and using this partition to estimate the normalization parameters. As the features are better normalized, the emotion detection system provides more reliable estimation, which, in turn, produces better normalization parameters. The IFN approach is also robust against different recording conditions, achieving over 19% improvement in unweighted accuracy (Rahman & Busso, 2012).

Computational Framework for Emotion Recognition

Supervised machine learning algorithms are at the heart of many emotion recognition efforts. These machine learning algorithms map input behavioral descriptions (automatically derived acoustic features, Acoustic Feature Extraction for Emotion Recognition, p. 173) through normalization (Robust Acoustic Feature Normalization, p. 176) to desired emotion representations (emotional labeling, Emotion Labels for Computing, p. 175).

An excellent survey of the various machine learning methodologies of affective modeling can be found in Zeng, Pantic, Roisman, and Huang (2009). If an input signal is given an emotion label using categorical attributes, many state-of-the-art static classifiers (e.g., support vector machine, decision tree, naive Bayes, hidden Markov model, etc.) can be implemented directly as the basic classifier. Furthermore, when an utterance is evaluated based on dimensional representation (i.e., valence, activation, and dominance), various well-established regression techniques such as ordinary/robust least square regression and support vector regression, can be utilized. Publicly available machine learning toolboxes such as WEKA (Hall et al., 2009), LIBSVM (Chang & Lin, 2011), and HTK (Young et al.,

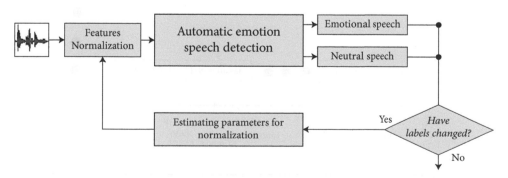

Fig. 12.3 Iterative feature normalization. This unsupervised front end uses an automatic emotional speech detector to identify neutral samples, which are used to estimate the normalization parameters. The process is iteratively repeated until the labels are not modified. *Source*: Busso, Metallinou, and Narayanan (2011).

2006) have implemented the above-mentioned classification/regression techniques and are widely used.

In this section, we discuss three different exemplary, recently developed novel emotion recognition frameworks for automatically recognizing emotional attributes from speech: The first is a *static* emotion attributes classification system based on a binary decision hierarchical tree structure, the second comprises two *context*-sensitive frameworks for emotion recognition in dialogues, and the third is a framework for continuous evaluation of emotion flow in human interactions.

STATIC EMOTION RECOGNITION FOR SINGLE UTTERANCE

In order to map an individual input utterance to a predefined set of categorical emotion classes given acoustic features, an exemplary approach is a hierarchical tree-based approach (Lee et al., 2011). It is a method that is loosely motivated by the appraisal theory of emotion (i.e., emotion is a result of an individual's cognitive assessment), which is theorized to be in stages, of a stimulus. This theory inspires a computational framework of emotion recognition in which the method is based on first processing the clear perceptual differences of emotion information in the acoustic features at the top (root) of the tree, and highly ambiguous emotions are recognized at the leaves of the tree.

The key idea is that the levels in the tree are designed to solve the easiest classification tasks first, allowing us to mitigate error propagation (Figure 12.4). Each node of a tree can be a binary classifier in which the top level is designed to classify between sets of emotion classes that are most easily discriminated through modeling acoustic behaviors (e.g., angry versus sad). The leaves of the tree can be used to identify the most ambiguous emotion class, which often is the class of *neutral*. The framework was evaluated on two different emotional databases using audio-only features, the FAU AIBO database and the USC IEMOCAP database. In the FAU AIBO database, it obtained a balanced recall on each of the individual emotion classes, and the performance measure improves by 3.37% absolute (8.82% relative) over using a standard support vector machine baseline model. In the USC IEMOCAP database, it achieved an absolute

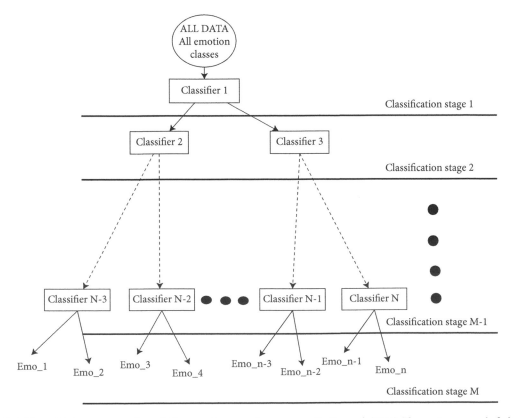

Fig. 12.4 Hierarchical tree structure for multiclass emotion recognition proposed by Lee et al. (2011). The tree is composed of a binary classifier at each node; the design of the tree takes into account of emotionally relevant discrimination given acoustic behavioral cues to optimize prediction accuracy.

improvement of 7.44% (14.58%) also over a base-line support vector machine modeling.

CONTEXT-SENSITIVE EMOTION RECOGNITION IN SPOKEN DIALOGUES

In human-human interaction, the emotion of each interaction participant is temporally smooth and conditioned on the emotion state on the other speaker. Such conditional dependency between the two interacting partners' emotion states and their own temporal dynamics in a dialogue has been explicitly modeled, for example, using a dynamic Bayesian network (Lee, Busso, Lee, & Narayanan, 2009). Lee et al. applied the framework to recognizing emotion attributes described using a valence-activation dimension with speech acoustic features. Results showed improvements in classification accuracy by 3.67% absolute and 7.12% relative over the Gaussian mixture model (GMM) baseline on isolated turn-by-turn (static) emotion classification for the USC IEMOCAP database.

Other studies have examined different modeling techniques in a more general setup of context-sensitive framework (i.e., modeling emotions between interlocutors' emotion in a given dialogue (Mariooryad & Busso, 2013; Metallinou, Katsamanis, et al., 2012; Metallinou, Wöllmer, et al., 2012; Wöllmer et al., 2008; Wöllmer, Kaiser, Eyben, Schuller, & Rigoll, 2012). In particular, Metallinou et al. (Metallinou, Katsamanis, et al., 2012; Metallinou, Wöllmer, et al., 2012) have proposed a context-sensitive emotion recognition framework (see Figure 12.5). The idea was centered on the fact that emotional content of past and future observations can offer additional contextual information benefiting the emotion classification accuracy of the current utterances. Techniques such as bidirectional long short-term memory (BLSTM) neural networks, hierarchical hidden Markov model classifiers (HMMs) and hybrid HMM/BLSTM classifiers were used for modeling emotional flow within an utterance and between utterances over the course of a dialogue. Results from these studies further underscore the importance and usefulness of jointly model interlocutors and incorporating surrounding contexts to improve recognition accuracies.

TRACKING OF CONTINUOUSLY RATED EMOTION ATTRIBUTES

Another line of work that has emerged recently aims at describing emotion as a continuous *flow* instead of a sequence of discrete-states (i.e., a time-continuous profile instead of one decision per speech turn). In real life, many expressive behaviors and emotion manifestations are often subtle and difficult to be assigned into discrete categories. Metallinou et al. have addressed this issue by tracking continuous levels of a participant's activation, valence, and dominance during the entire course of dyadic interactions without restriction on assigning a label just for each speaking turn (Angeliki Metallinou, Katsamanis, & Narayanan, 2012).

The computational technique is based on a Gaussian mixture model–based approach that computes a mapping from a set of observed audiovisual cues to an underlying emotional state—that is, given by annotators rating over time on a continuous scale (values range from –1 to 1) along the axis of valence, activation, and dominance. The continuous emotion annotation tool is based on Feeltrace (Cowie et al., 2000). Promising results were obtained in tracking trends of participant' activation and dominance values with the GMM-based approach

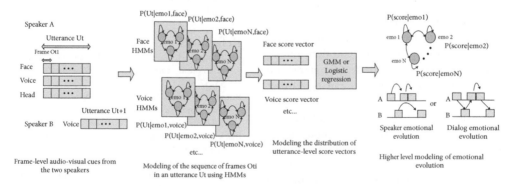

Fig. 12.5 Context sensitive emotion recognition. Metallinou et al. proposed a flexible context-sensitive emotion recognition framework that captures both the utterance-level emotional dynamics and the long-range context dependencies of emotional flow in dialogues. *Sources*: Metallinou, Katsamanis, et al. (2012) and Metallinou, Wöllmer, et al. (2012).

compared to other regression-based approaches in a database of two actors' improvisations (Angeliki Metallinou, Lee, Busso, Carnicke, & Narayanan, 2010). The tracking of continuously rated emotion attributes is an area of research still in its formative stages, and attempts to complement the standard approach of assigning a specific segment of data to predefined discrete categorical emotional attributes.

Open Challenges

Each of the aforementioned three components in the design of a reliable emotion recognizer remains an active research direction. The inherent ambiguity in emotion categorizations, the variability of acoustic features in different conditions, the complex nature of the interplay between the linguistic and paralinguistic aspects manifested in speech as well as the interplay between the speech signal and signals of visual nonbehavior, and the nature of human coupling and interaction in emotional expression and perception are some of the key issues that need deeper investigation and further advance in the related computational frameworks.

Speech in Affective Computing: Future Works and Applications

Future challenges in the area of affective computing with speech lie in both improving our understanding of emotional speech production mechanisms and in designing generalizable cross-domain robust emotion recognition systems. In summary, on the acoustic feature extraction side, while the common data processing approach of feature extraction has been able to provide the state-of-art emotion recognition accuracy, it remains unclear how exactly emotional information is encoded in these acoustic waveforms. Also, the current approaches of feature computation are often difficult to be generalized across and scaled-up to real-life applications. With growing knowledge and insights into articulatory and voice source movements and their interplay in the emotion encoding process, the related acoustic feature extraction procedure in the acoustic domain can be further advanced. This holds promises to a more robust and principled ways for speech emotion processing.

Another hurdle in affective computing is the ability to obtain reliable cross-domain (and cross-corpora) recognition results. Until now, most of the emotion recognition efforts have concentrated on optimizing recognition accuracy for an individual database. Few works have started to examine the

technique to achieve higher accuracy across corpora (Bone, Lee, & Narayanan, 2012; Schuller et al., 2010). It is inherently a much more difficult modeling task on top of the issues that one has to solve related to the subjectivity in the design of the emotional attributes, the lack of solid understanding on which acoustic features are robust across databases, and the issue of modeling the interactive nature of human affective dynamics. All of these remain as open questions to be investigated in paving the way for robust real-life emotion recognition engineering systems of the future.

Having the ability to infer a person's emotional state from speech is of great importance to many scientific domains. This is because emotion is a fundamental attribute governing the generation of human expressive behavior and a key indicator in developing human behavior analytics and in designing novel user interfaces for a wide range of disciplines. Exemplary domains for such applications include commerce (e.g., measuring user frustration and satisfaction), medicine (e.g., diagnosis and treatment), psychotherapy (e.g., tracking in distressed couples research, addiction, autism spectrum disorder, depression, posttraumatic stress disorder), and educational settings (e.g., measuring engagement). Affective computing is indeed an integral component and a key building block in the field of behavioral signal processing.

Acknowledgments

The authors would like to thank National Institute of Health, National Science Foundation, United States Army, and Defense Advanced Research Agency for their funding support.

Notes

1. http://sourceforge.net/projects/wavesurfer
2. http://www.ee.ic.ac.uk/hp/staff/dmb/voicebox/voicebox.html

References

Bachorowski, J.-A. (1999). Vocal expression and perception of emotion. *Current Directions in Psychological Science*, 8, 53–57.

Bitouk, D., Verma, R., & Nenkova, A. (2010). Class-level spectral features for emotion recognition. *Speech Communication*, 52(7–8), 613–625. doi:10.1016/j.specom.2010.02.010

Black, M. P., Georgiou, P. G., Katsamanis, A., Baucom, B. R., & Narayanan, S. (2011). "You made me do it": Classification of blame in married couples' interactions by fusing automatically derived speech and language information. *Proceedings of interspeech* (pp. 89–92).

Black, M. P., Katsamanis, A., Baucom, B. R., Lee, C.-C., Lammert, A. C., Christensen, A., Georgiou, P. G., ... &

Narayanan, S. (2013). Toward automating a human behavioral coding system for married couples' interactions using speech acoustic features. *Speech Communication, 55*, 1–21.

Boersma, P. (2001). Praat, a system for doing phonetics by computer. *Glot International, 5*, 341–345.

Bone, D., Lee, C.-C., & Narayanan, S. (2012). A robust unsupervised arousal rating framework using prosody with cross-corpora evaluation. *Proceedings of Interspeech.*

Bone, D., Li, M., Black, M. P., & Narayanan, S. S. (2014). Intoxicated speech detection: A fusion framework with speaker-normalized hierarchical functionals and GMM supervectors. *Computer Speech & Language, 28*:2, 375–391

Busso, C., Bulut, M., Lee, C.-C., Kazemzadeh, A., Mower, E., Kim, S., Chang, J.,…& Narayanan, S. (2008). IEMOCAP: Interactive emotional dyadic motion capture database. *Journal of Language Resources and Evaluation, 42*, 335–359.

Busso, C., Lee, S., & Narayanan, S. S. (2009). Analysis of emotionally salient aspects of fundamental frequency for emotion detection. *IEEE transactions on audio, speech and language processing, 17*, 582–596. doi:10.1109/TASL.2008.2009578

Busso, C., Metallinou, A., & Narayanan, S. (2011). Iterative feature normalization for emotional speech detection. *international conference on acoustics, speech, and signal processing (ICASSP)* (pp. 5692–5695).

Busso, C., & Narayanan, S. S. (2008). Recording audio-visual emotional databases from actors: a closer look. *Second international workshop on emotion: Corpora for research on emotion and affect, international conference on language resources and evaluation (LREC 2008)* (pp. 17–22), Marrakesh, Morocco.

Chang, C.-C., & Lin, C.-J. (2011). LIBSVM: A library for support vector machines. *ACM Transactions on Intelligent Systems and Technology (TIST), 2, 27*, 1–27.

Clavel, C., Vasilescu, I., Devillers, L., Richard, G., & Ehrette, T. (2008). Fear-type emotion recognition for future audio-based surveillance systems. *Speech Communication, 50*, 487–503.

Cowie, R., Douglas-Cowie, E., Savvidou, S., McMahon, E., Sawey, M., & Schröder, M. (2000). FEELTRACE: An instrument for recording perceived emotion in real time. *ISCA tutorial and research workshop (ITRW) on speech and emotion* (pp. 19–24). Winona, MN: International Society for Computers and Their Applications.

Deller, J. R., Hansen, J. H. L., & Proakis, J. G. (2000). *Discrete-time processing of speech signals.* Piscataway, NJ: IEEE Press.

Erickson, D., Menezes, C., & Fujino, A. (2004). Some articulatory measurements of real sadness. *Proceedings of interspeech* (pp. 1825–1828).

Eyben, F., Wöllmer, M., & Schuller, B. (2010). OpenSMILE: The Munich versatile and fast open-source audio feature extractor. *ACM international conference on multimedia (MM 2010)* (pp. 1459–1462).

Fant, G. (1970). *Acoustic theory of speech production.* The Hague, Netherlands: Walter de Gruyter.

Fujimura, O., Kiritani, S., & Ishida, H. (1973). Computer controlled radiography for observation of movements of articulatory and other human organs. *Computers in Biology and Medicine, 3*, 371–384.

Gobl, C., & Chasaide, A. N. (2003). The role of voice quality in communicating emotion, mood and attitude. *Speech Communication—Special issue on speech and emotion, 40*, 189–212.

Hall, M. A. (1999). *Correlation-based feature selection for machine learning.* Hamilton, New Zealand: The University of Waikato.

Hall, M., Frank, E., Holmes, G., Pfahringer, B., Reutemann, P., & Witten, I. H. (2009). The WEKA data mining software: An update. *ACM SIGKDD Explorations Newsletter, 11*, 10–18. doi:10.1145/1656274.1656278

Jain, A., & Zongker, D. (1997). Feature selection: Evaluation, application, and small sample performance. *IEEE Transactions on Pattern Analysis and Machine Intelligence, 19*, 153–158.

Juslin, P. N., & Scherer, K. R. (2005). Vocal expression of affect. *The new handbook of methods in nonverbal behavior research*, 65–135, New York City, New York: Oxford University Press

Kazamzadeh, A., Lee, S., Georgiou, P., & Narayanan, S. (2011). Emotion twenty question (EMO20Q): Toward a crowd-sourced theory of emotions. *Proceedings of affective computing and intelligent interaction (ACII)* (pp. 1–10), Memphis, Tennessee

Kim, J., Lee, S., & Narayanan, S. (2010). A study of interplay between articulatory movement and prosodic characteristics in emotional speech production. *Proceedings of interspeech* (pp. 1173–1176).

Kim, J., Lee, S., & Narayanan, S. (2011). An exploratory study of the relations between perceived emotion strength and articulatory kinematics. *Proceedings of interspeech* (pp. 2961–2964).

Kipp, M. (2001). ANVIL—A generic annotation tool for multimodal dialogue. *European conference on speech communication and technology (Eurospeech)* (pp. 1367–1370).

Lammert, A., Proctor, M., & Narayanan, S. (2013). Morphological variation in the adult hard palate and posterior pharyngeal wall. *Speech, Language, and Hearing Research, 56*, 521–530.

Le, X., Quénot, G., & Castelli, E. (2004). Recognizing emotions for the audio-visual document indexing. *Ninth international symposium on computers and communications (ISCC)* (Vol. 2, pp. 580–584).

Lee, C. M., & Narayanan, S. S. (2005). Toward detecting emotions in spoken dialogs. *IEEE Transactions on Speech and Audio Processing, 13*, 293–303.

Lee, C.-C., Busso, C., Lee, S., & Narayanan, S. S. (2009). Modeling mutual influence of interlocutor emotion states in dyadic spoken interactions. *Proceedings of interspeech* (pp. 1983–1986).

Lee, C.-C., Mower, E., Busso, C., Lee, S., & Narayanan, S. S. (2011). Emotion recognition using a hierarchical binary decision tree approach. *Speech Communication, 53*, 1162–1171. doi:10.1016/j.specom.2011.06.004

Lee, S., Bresch, E., Adams, J., Kazemzadeh, A., & Narayanan, S. S. (2006). A study of emotional speech articulation using a fast magnetic resonance imaging technique. *International Conference on spoken language (ICSLP)* (pp. 2234–2237).

Lee, S., Yildirim, S., Kazemzadeh, A., & Narayanan, S. S. (2005). An articulatory study of emotional speech production. *Proceedings of Interspeech* (pp. 497–500).

Mariooryad, S., & Busso, C. (2013). Exploring cross-modality affective reactions for audiovisual emotion recognition. *IEEE Transactions on Affective Computing.* In press. doi:10.1109/T-AFFC.2013.11

Metallinou, A., Katsamanis, A., & Narayanan, S. S. (2012). A hierarchical framework for modeling multimodality and emotional evolution in affective dialogs. *International* conference on acoustics, speech, and signal processing (ICASSP) (pp. 2401–2404). doi:10.1109/ICASSP.2012.6288399

Metallinou, A., Wöllmer, M., Katsamanis, A., Eyben, F., Schuller, B., & Narayanan, S. S. (2012). Context-sensitive learning for enhanced audiovisual emotion classification. *IEEE Transactions on Affective Computing*, 3, 184–198. doi:10.1109/T-AFFC.2011.40

Metallinou, A., Katsamanis, A., & Narayanan, S. (2013). Tracking continuous emotional trends of participants during affective dyadic interactions using body language and speech information. *Image and Vision Computing*, 31:2, 137–152

Metallinou, A., Lee, C.-C., Busso, C., Carnicke, S., & Narayanan, S. S. (2010). The USC CreativeIT database: a multimodal database of theatrical improvisation. *Proceedings of the multimodal corpora workshop: advances in capturing, coding and analyzing, multimodality (MMC)* (pp. 64–68), Valetta, Malta

Mower, E., Mataric, M. J., & Narayanan, S. S. (2011). A framework for automatic human emotion classification using emotional profiles. *IEEE Transactions on Audio, Speech and Language Processing*, 19:5, 1057–1070.

Mower, E., Metallinou, A., Lee, C.-C., Kazemzadeh, A., Busso, C., Lee, S., & Narayanan, S. (2009). Interpreting ambiguous emotional expressions. *Proceedings of affective computing and intelligent interaction and workshops (ACII)* (pp. 1–8), Amsterdam, Netherlands

Murphy, P. J., & Laukkanen, A.-M. (2009). Electroglottogram analysis of emotionally styled phonation. *Multimodal signals: Cognitive and algorithmic issues*, 264–270, Vietri sul Mare, Italy

Narayanan, S. S., Alwan, A. A., & Haker, K. (1995). An articulatory study of fricative consonants using magnetic resonance imaging. *The Journal of the Acoustical Society of America*, 98, 1325–1347.

Narayanan, S. S., & Georgiou, P. (2013). Behavioral signal processing: Deriving human behavioral informatics from speech and language. *Proceedings of the IEEE*, 101, 1203–1233. doi:10.1109/JPROC.2012.2236291

Narayanan, S. S., Nayak, K., Lee, S., Sethy, A., & Byrd, D. (2004). An approach to real-time magnetic resonance imaging for speech production. *The Journal of the Acoustical Society of America*, 115, 1771–1776.

Pao, T.-L., Yeh, J.-H., Chen, Y.-T., Cheng, Y.-M., & Lin, Y.-Y. (2007). A comparative study of different weighting schemes on knn-based emotion recognition in Mandarin speech. In D.-S. Huang, L. Heutte, & M. Loog (Eds.), *advanced intelligent computing theories and applications with aspects of theoretical and methodological issues* (pp. 997–1005). Berlin: Springer-Verlag. doi:10.1007/978-3-540-74171-8_101

Peng, H., Long, F., & Ding, C. (2005). Feature selection based on mutual information criteria of max-dependency, max-relevance, and min-redundancy. *IEEE Transactions on Pattern Analysis and Machine Intelligence*, 27, 1226–1238.

Perkell, J. S., Cohen, M. H., Svirsky, M. A., Matthies, M. L., Garabieta, I., & Jackson, M. T. (1992). Electromagnetic midsagittal articulometer systems for transducing speech articulatory movements. *The Journal of the Acoustical Society of America*, 92, 3078–3096.

Rahman, T., & Busso, C. (2012). A personalized emotion recognition system using an unsupervised feature adaptation

scheme. *International conference on acoustics, speech, and signal processing (ICASSP)* (pp. 5117–5120).

Scherer, K. R. (2003). Vocal communication of emotion: A review of research paradigms. *Speech communication*, 40, 227–256.

Schuller, B., Arsic, D., Wallhoff, F., & Rigoll, G. (2006). Emotion recognition in the noise applying large acoustic feature sets. *Speech prosody*, (pp. 276–289), Dresden, Germany.

Schuller, B., Batliner, A., Seppi, D., Steidl, S., Vogt, T., Wagner, J., Devillers, L., . . . & VeredAharonson (2007). The relevance of feature type for the automatic classification of emotional user states: Low level descriptors and functionals. *Proceedings of interspeech* (pp. 2253–2256).

Schuller, B., Rigoll, G., & Lang, M. (2003). Hidden Markov model–based speech emotion recognition. *International conference on acoustics, speech, and signal processing (ICASSP)* (Vol. 2, pp. 1–4).

Schuller, B., Vlasenko, B., Eyben, F., Wöllmer, M., Stuhlsatz, A., Wendemuth, A., & Rigoll, G. (2010). Cross-corpus acoustic emotion recognition: Variances and strategies. *IEEE Transactions on affective computing*, 1(2), 119–131. doi:10.1109/T-AFFC.2010.8

Schuller, B., Vlasenko, B., Minguez, R., Rigoll, G., & Wendemuth, A. (2007). Comparing one and two-stage acoustic modeling in the recognition of emotion in speech. *IEEE workshop on automatic speech recognition & understanding (ASRU)* (pp. 596–600).

Schuller, B., Steidl, S., Batliner, A., Burkhardt, F., Devillers, L., Müller, C., & Narayanan, S. S. (2013). Paralinguistics in speech and language—State-of-the-art and the challenge. *Computer Speech & Language*, 27, 4–39.

Sethu, V., Ambikairajah, E., & Epps, J. (2007). Speaker normalisation for speech based emotion detection. *15th International Conference on Digital Signal Processing (DSP)* (pp. 611–614).

Stone, M. (2005). A guide to analysing tongue motion from ultrasound images. *Clinical Linguistics & Phonetics*, 19, 455–501.

Vlasenko, B., Schuller, B., Wendemuth, A., & Rigoll, G. (2007). Frame vs. turn-level: Emotion recognition from speech considering static and dynamic processing. In A. Paiva, R. Prada, & R. W. Picard (Eds.), *Affective computing and intelligent interaction* (pp. 139–147). Berlin and Heidelberg: Springer. doi:10.1007/978-3-540-74889-2_13

Watson, D., Clark, L. A., & Tellegen, A. (1988). Developement and validation of brief measures of positive and negative affect: The PANAS Scale. *Personality and Social Psychology*, 47, 1063–1070.

Wittenburg, P., Brugman, H., Russel, A., Klassmann, A., & Sloetjes, H. (2006). Elan: A professional framework for multimodality research. *Proceedings of LREC* (Vol. 2006), Genoa, Italy

Wöllmer, M., Eyben, F., Reiter, S., Schuller, B., Cox, C., Douglas-Cowie, E., & Cowie, R. (2008). Abandoning emotion classes—Towards continuous emotion recognition with modelling of long-range dependencies. *Proceedings of Interspeech* (pp. 597–600)..

Wöllmer, M., Kaiser, M., Eyben, F., Schuller, B., & Rigoll, G. (2012). LSTM-Modeling of continuous emotions in an audiovisual affect recognition framework. *Image and Vision Computing*, 31(2), 153–163. doi:10.1016/j.imavis.2012.03.001

Yan, Z., Li, Z., Cairong, Z., & Yinhua, Y. (2008). Speech emotion recognition using modified quadratic discrimination function. *Journal of Electronics (China)*, *25*, 840–844. doi:10.1007/s11767-008-0041-8

Yildirim, S., Bulut, M., Lee, C. M., Kazemzadeh, A., Busso, C., Deng, Z., Lee, S., et al. (2004). An acoustic study of emotions expressed in speech. *International conference on spoken language processing (ICSLP)* (pp. 2193–2196).

Young, S., Evermann, G., Kershaw, D., Moore, G., Odell, J., Ollason, D., . . . & Woodland, P. (2002). The HTK book. Cambridge University Engineering Department, *3*, 175.

Zeng, Z., Pantic, M., Roisman, G. I., & Huang, T. S. (2009). A survey of affect recognition methods: audio, visual, and spontaneous expressions. *IEEE transactions on pattern analysis and machine intelligence*, *31*, 39–58.

Affect Detection in Texts

Carlo Strapparava *and* Rada Mihalcea

Abstract

The field of affective natural language processing (NLP), in particular the recognition of emotion in text, presents many challenges. Nonetheless with current NLP techniques it is possible to approach the problem with interesting results, opening up exciting applicative perspectives for the future. In this chapter we present some explorations in dealing with the automatic recognition of affect in text. We start by describing some available lexical resources, the problem of creating a "gold standard" using emotion annotations, and the affective text task at SemEval-2007, an evaluation contest of computational semantic analysis systems. That task focused on the classification of emotions in news headlines and was meant to explore the connection between emotions and lexical semantics. Then we approach the problem of recognizing emotions in texts, presenting some state-of-the-art knowledge- and corpus-based methods. We conclude by presenting two promising lines of research in the field of affective NLP. The first approaches the related task of humor recognition; the second proposes the exploitation of extralinguistic features (e.g., music) for emotion detection.

Key Words: affective natural language processing, emotion annotation, affect in text

Introduction

Emotions have been widely studied in psychology and behavior sciences, as they are an important element of human nature. For instance, emotions have been studied with respect to facial expressions (Ekman, 1977), action tendencies (Frijda, 1982), physiological activity (Ax, 1953), or subjective experience (Rivera, 1998). They have also attracted the attention of researchers in computer science, especially in the field of human computer interaction, where studies have been carried out on the recognition of emotions through a variety of sensors (e.g., Picard, 1997). In contrast to the considerable work focusing on the nonverbal expression of emotions, surprisingly little research has explored how emotions are reflected verbally (Fussell, 2002; Ortony, Clore, & Foss, 1987b). Important contributions come from social psychologists, studying language

as a way of expressing emotions (Osgood et al., 1975; Pennbaker, 2002). From the perspective of computational linguistics, it is not easy to define emotion. Emotions are not linguistic constructs. However the most convenient access we have to them is *through language*. This is very much true nowadays, in the web age, in which large quantities of texts (and some of them, such as blogs, particularly affectively oriented) are readily available.

In computational linguistics, the automatic detection of emotions in texts is also becoming increasingly important from an applicative point of view. Consider for example the tasks of opinion mining and market analysis, affective computing, or natural language interfaces such as e-learning environments or educational/edutainment games. Possible beneficial effects of emotions on memory and attention of the users and in general on fostering their creativity are also well known in the field of psychology.

For instance, the following represent examples of applicative scenarios in which affective analysis could make valuable and interesting contributions:

• *Sentiment Analysis.* Text categorization according to affective relevance, opinion exploration for market analysis, and so on are examples of applications of these techniques. While positive/negative valence annotation is an active area in sentiment analysis, we believe that a fine-grained emotion annotation could increase the effectiveness of these applications.

• *Computer-Assisted Creativity.* The automated generation of evaluative expressions with a bias on a certain polarity orientation is a key component in automatic personalized advertisement and persuasive communication. Possible applicative contexts can be creative computational environments that help produce what human graphic designers sometimes do completely manually for TV/Web presentations (e.g., advertisements, news titles).

• *Verbal Expressivity in Human-Computer Interaction.* Future human-computer interaction is expected to emphasize naturalness and effectiveness, and hence the integration of models of possibly many human cognitive capabilities, including affective analysis and generation. For example, the expression of emotions by synthetic characters (e.g., embodied conversational agents) is now considered a key element for their believability. Affective word selection and understanding are crucial for realizing appropriate and expressive conversations.

This chapter presents some explorations in dealing with automatic recognition of affect in text. We start describing some available lexical resources, the problem of creating a gold standard using emotion annotations, and the "affective text" task, presented at SemEval 2007. That task focused on the classification of emotions in news headlines and was meant as an exploration of the connection between emotions and lexical semantics. Then we approach the problem of recognizing emotions expressed in texts, presenting some state-of-the-art knowledge- and corpus-based methods. We conclude the chapter by presenting two promising lines of research in the field of affective NLP. The first approaches the related task of humor recognition; the second proposes the exploitation of extralinguistic features (e.g., music) for emotion detection.

Affective Lexical Resources

The starting point of a computational linguistic approach to the study of emotion in text is the use of specific affective lexicons. The work of Ortony, Clore, and Foss (1987a) was among the first to introduce the problem of the referential structure of the affective lexicon. In that work the authors conducted an analysis of about 500 words taken from the literature on emotions. Then they developed a taxonomy that helps isolate terms that explicitly refer to emotions.

In recent years, the research community has developed several interesting resources that can be operatively exploited in natural language processing tasks that deal with affect. We briefly review some of them below.

General Enquirer

The General Inquirer (Stone et al., 1966) is basically a mapping tool, which maps dictionary-supplied categories to lists of words and word senses. The currently distributed version combines the "Harvard IV-4" dictionary content-analysis categories, the "Lasswell" dictionary content-analysis categories, and five categories based on the social cognition work of Semin and Fiedler (1988), making for 182 categories in all. Each category is a list of words and word senses. It uses stemming and disambiguation; for example it distinguishes between *race* as a contest, *race* as moving rapidly, and *race* as a group of people of common descent. A sketch of some categories from the General Inquirer is shown below.

• XI. Emotions (EMOT): anger, fury, distress, happy, etc.
• XII. Frequency (FREQ): occasional, seldom, often, etc.
• XIII. Evaluative Adjective (EVAL): good, bad, beautiful, hard, easy, etc.
• XIV. Dimensionality Adjective (DIM): big, little, short, long, tall, etc.
• XV. Position Adjective (POS): low, lower, upper, high, middle, first, fourth, etc.
• XVI. Degree Adverbs (DEG): very, extremely, too, rather, somewhat...
• ...

SentiWordNet

SentiWordNet (Esuli & Sebastiani, 2006) is a lexical resource that focuses on polarity of subjective terms (i.e., whether a term that is a marker of opinionated content has a *positive* or a *negative* connotation). In practice each synset *s* (i.e. a synonym set) in

WordNet is associated with three numerical scores *Obj(s)*, *Pos(s)* and *Neg(s)*, describing how objective, positive, and negative the terms contained in the synset are. These three scores are derived by combining the results produced by a committee of eight ternary classifiers. These scores are interconnected, in particular the objectivity score can be calculated as: $Obj(s) = 1-[Pos(s) + Neg(s)]$. The rationale behind this formula is that a given text has a factual nature (i.e., describes objectively a given situation or event) if there is no presence of a positive or a negative opinion on it; otherwise it expresses an opinion on its subject matter.

While SentiWordNet does not address emotions directly, it can be exploited whenever detection along the positive versus negative dimension is required.

Affective Norms for English Words

The affective norms for English words (ANEW) provides a set of normative emotional ratings for a large number of words in the English language (Bradley & Lang, 1999). In particular, the goal was to develop a set of verbal materials that have been rated, as perceived by readers[1], in terms of *pleasure, arousal*, and *dominance*. This view is founded on the semantic differential, in which factor analyses conducted on a wide variety of verbal judgments indicated that the variance in emotional assessments was accounted for by those three major dimensions: the two primary dimensions were one of affective valence (from pleasant to unpleasant) and one of arousal (from calm to excited). A third, less strongly related dimension was variously called "dominance" or "control." To assess these three dimensions, an affective rating system (the self-assessment manikin), originally formulated by Lang (1980), was exploited. Bradley and Lang (1994) had determined that this rating system correlates well with factors of pleasure and arousal obtained using the more extended verbal semantic differential scale (Mehrabian & Russell 1974). For an example of how the resource has been exploited computationally, see Calvo and Kim (2012).

There are 1,034 words currently normed in ANEW, with the ratings respectively for pleasure, arousal, and dominance. Each rating scale runs from 1 to 9, with a rating of 1 indicating a low value on each dimension (e.g., low pleasure, low arousal, low dominance) and 9 indicating a high value on each dimension (high pleasure, high arousal, high dominance). An excerpt from the ANEW lexical resource is presented in Table 13.1.

WordNet Affect

The development of WordNet-Affect (Strapparava & Valitutti, 2004; Strapparava, Valitutti, & Stock, 2006) was motivated by the need of a lexical resource with explicit fine-grained emotion annotations.

As claimed by Ortony et al. (1987b), we have to distinguish between words directly referring to emotional states (e.g. *fear, cheerful*) and those having only an indirect reference that depends on the context (e.g., words that indicate possible emotional causes, such as *monster*, or emotional responses, such as *cry*). We call the former *direct* affective words and the latter *indirect* affective words. The rationale behind WordNet-Affect is to provide a resource with fine-grained emotion annotations only for the direct affective lexicon, leaving to other techniques the capabilities to classify the emotional load of the indirect affective words. All words can potentially convey affective meaning. Each of them, even those more apparently neutral, can evoke pleasant or

Table 13.1 Some Entries from ANEW

Word	Valence (Mean)	Valence (SD)	Arousal (Mean)	Arousal (SD)	Dominance (Mean)	Dominance (SD)
abduction	2.76	2.06	5.53	2.43	3.49	2.38
abortion	3.5	2.3	5.39	2.8	4.59	2.54
absurd	4.26	1.82	4.36	2.2	4.73	1.72
abundance	6.59	2.01	5.51	2.63	5.8	2.16
abuse	1.8	1.23	6.83	2.7	3.69	2.94
acceptance	7.98	1.42	5.4	2.7	6.64	1.91
accident	2.05	1.19	6.26	2.87	3.76	2.22

Table 13.2 Number of Elements in the Emotional Hierarchy

	#Synsets	#Words	#Senses
Nouns	280	539	564
Adjectives	342	601	951
Verbs	142	294	430
Adverbs	154	203	270
Total	981	1,637	2,215

painful experiences. While some words have emotional meaning with respect to the individual story, for many others the affective power is part of the collective imagination (e.g., *mum, ghost, war*, etc.). Thus, in principle, it could be incorrect to conduct an a priori annotation on the whole lexicon. Strapparava, Valitutti, and Stock (2006) suggest using corpus-driven annotation (possibly exploiting specific corpora for particular purposes) for inferring the emotional load of generic words. More specifically they propose a semantic similarity function, acquired automatically in an unsupervised way from a large corpus of texts, which allows us to put into relation generic concepts with direct emotional categories. We describe a similar approach in Recognizing Emotions in Texts (p. 190).

WordNet-Affect is an extension of the WordNet database (Fellbaum, 1998), including a subset of synsets suitable to represent affective concepts. Similar to the annotation method for domain labels (Magnini & Cavaglià, 2000), a number of WordNet synsets were assigned to one or more affective labels (*a-labels*). In particular,

the affective concepts representing emotional state are individuated by synsets marked with the a-label EMOTION. There are also other a-labels for those concepts representing moods, situations eliciting emotions, or emotional responses. WordNet-Affect is freely available for research purposes at http://wndomains.fbk.eu. See Strapparava and Valitutti (2004) for a complete description of the resource.

The emotional categories are hierarchically organized, in order to specialize synsets with a-label EMOTION. Regarding emotional valence, four additional a-labels are introduced: POSITIVE, NEGATIVE, AMBIGUOUS, NEUTRAL. The first one corresponds to "positive emotions" related to words expressing positive emotional states. It includes synsets such as joy#1 or enthusiasm#1. Similarly, the NEGATIVE a-label identifies "negative emotions"—for example, labeling synsets such as anger#1 or sadness#1. Synsets representing affective states whose valence depends on semantic context (e.g., surprise#1) were marked with the tag AMBIGUOUS. Finally, synsets referring to mental states that are generally considered affective but are not characterized by valence were marked with the tag NEUTRAL.

Annotating Texts with Emotions

In order to explore the classification of emotions in texts, gold standards are required, consisting of manual emotion annotations. This is a rather difficult task, in particular given its subjectivity, where humans themselves often disagree on the emotions present in a given text. The task can also be very time-consuming, even more so when, for the purpose of reaching higher interannotator agreements, a large number of annotations are sought. Because

Table 13.3 Some of the Emotional Categories in WordNet-Affect and Some Corresponding Word Senses

A-Labels	Valence	Example of Word Senses
Joy	Positive	Noun joy#1, adjective elated#2, verb gladden#2, adverb gleefully#1
Love	Positive	Noun love#1, adjective loving#1, verb love#1, adverb fondly#1
Apprehension	Negative	Noun apprehension#1, adjective apprehensive#3, adverb anxiously#1
Sadness	Negative	Noun sadness#1, adjective unhappy#1, verb sadden#1
Surprise	Ambiguous	Noun surprise#1, adjective surprised#1, verb surprise#1
Apathy	Neutral	Noun apathy#1, adjective apathetic#1, adverb apathetically#1
Negative-fear	Negative	Noun scare#2, adjective afraid#1, verb frighten#1, adverb horryfyingly#1
Positive-fear	Positive	Noun frisson#1

Table 13.4 Valence Distribution of Emotional Categories

Positive	Negative	Ambiguous	Neutral	Total
97	156	20	7	280

of its specificity, the granularity of the task is on short texts (e.g., single sentences, news headlines).

Previous work on emotion annotation of text (Alm, Roth, & Sproat, 2005; Strapparava & Mihalcea, 2007; Aman & Szpakowicz, 2008) has usually relied on the six basic emotions proposed by (Ekman, 1993): ANGER, DISGUST, FEAR, JOY, SADNESS, SURPRISE. We also focus on these six emotions in this chapter and review two annotation efforts: one that targeted the annotation of emotions in lyrics using crowdsourcing and one that aimed at building a gold standard consisting of news headlines annotated for emotion.

Emotion Annotations via Crowdsourcing

In a recent project concerned with the classification of emotions in songs (Strapparava, Mihalcea, & Battocchi, 2012; Mihalcea & Strapparava, 2012), we introduced a novel corpus consisting of 100 songs annotated for emotions. The songs were sampled from among some of the most popular pop, rock, and evergreen songs, such as *Dancing Queen* by ABBA, *Hotel California* by the Eagles, and *Let It Be* by the Beatles.

To collect the annotations, we used the Amazon Mechanical Turk service, which was previously found to produce reliable annotations with a quality comparable to those generated by experts (Snow et al., 2008).

The annotations were collected at line level, with a separate annotation for each of the six emotions. We collected numerical annotations using a scale between 0 and 10, with 0 corresponding to the absence of an emotion, and 10 corresponding to the highest intensity. Each HIT (i.e., annotation session) contains an entire song, with a number of lines ranging from 14 to 110, for an average of 50 lines per song.

Annotation Guidelines

The annotators were instructed to (1) score the emotions from the writer's perspective, not their own perspective; (2) read and interpret each line in context (i.e., they were asked to read and understand the entire song before producing any annotations); and (3) Produce the six emotion annotations

independent of each other, accounting for the fact that a line could contain none, one, or multiple emotions. In addition to the lyrics, the song was also available online, so they could listen to it in case they were not familiar with it. The annotators were also given three different examples to illustrate the annotation.

Controlling for Annotation Errors

While the use of crowdsourcing for data annotation can result in a large number of annotations in a very short time, it also has the drawback of potential spamming, which can interfere with the quality of the annotations. To address this aspect, we used two different techniques to prevent inappropriate annotations. First, in each song we inserted a "checkpoint" at a random position in the song—a fake line that reads "Please enter 7 for each of the six emotions." Those annotators who did not follow this concrete instruction were deemed as spammers who produce annotations without reading the content of the song; they were therefore removed. Second, for each remaining annotator, we calculated the Pearson correlation between her emotion scores and the average emotion scores of all the other annotators. Those annotators with a correlation with the average of the other annotators below 0.4 were also removed, thus leaving only the reliable annotators in the pool.

For each song, we started by asking for 10 annotations. After spam removal, we were left with about two to five annotations per song. The final annotations were produced by averaging the emotions scores produced by the reliable annotators. Figure 13.2 shows an example of the emotion scores produced for two lines. The overall correlation between the remaining reliable annotators was 0.73, which represents a strong correlation.

Emotions in the Corpus of 100 Songs

For each of the six emotions, Table 13.5 shows the number of lines that had that emotion present (i.e., the score of the emotion was different from 0) as well as the average score for that emotion over all 4,976 lines in the corpus. Perhaps not surprisingly, the emotions that are dominant in the corpus are JOY and SADNESS—the emotions often invoked by people as the reason behind a song.

Note that the emotions do not exclude each other—that is, a line labeled as containing joy may also contain a certain amount of SADNESS, which is the reason for the high percentage of songs containing both JOY and SADNESS. The emotional load for

Table 13.5 Emotions in the Corpus of 100 Songs: Number of Lines Including a Certain Emotion, and Average Emotion Score Computed over All the 4,976 lines

Emotion	Number of lines	Average
Anger	2,516	0.95
Disgust	2,461	0.71
Fear	2,719	0.77
Joy	3,890	3.24
Sadness	3,840	2.27
Surprise	2,982	0.83

the overlapping emotions is, however, very different. For instance, the lines that have a joy score of 5 or higher have an average SADNESS score of 0.34. Conversely, the lines with a SADNESS score of 5 or higher have a joy score of 0.22.

SemEval-2007 "Affective Text" Task

In the context of SemEval-2007,[2] we organized a task focused on the classification of emotions and valence (i.e., positive/negative polarity) in news headlines; it was meant as an exploration of the connection between emotions and lexical semantics. In this section, we describe the dataset used in the evaluation.

Task Definition

We proposed to focus on the emotion classification of news headlines extracted from news websites. The news headlines typically consist of a few words and are often written by creative people with the intention of "provoking" emotions and consequently to attract the readers' attention. These characteristics make the news headlines particularly suitable for use in an automatic emotion recognition setting, as the affective/emotional features (if present) are guaranteed to appear in these short sentences.

The structure of the task was as follows:

Corpus: News titles, extracted from news web sites (such as Google news, CNN) and/or newspapers. In the case of websites, a few thousand titles can easily be collected in a short time.

Objective: Provided a set of predefined six emotion labels (i.e., anger, disgust, fear, joy, sadness, surprise), classify the titles with the appropriate emotion label and/or with a valence indication (i.e., positive/negative).

The emotion labeling and valence classifications were seen as independent tasks; thus a team was able to participate in one or both. The task was carried out in an unsupervised setting and no training was provided. This was because we wanted to emphasize the study of emotion lexical semantics and avoid biasing the participants toward simple "text categorization" approaches. Nonetheless, supervised systems were not precluded, and in this case participating teams were allowed to create their own supervised training sets.

Participants were free to use any resources they wished. We provided a set words extracted from WordNet Affect (Strapparava & Valitutti, 2004), relevant to the six emotions of interest. However the use of this list of words was entirely optional.

Dataset

The dataset consists of news headlines drawn from major news sources such as the *New York Times*, CNN, and BBC News as well as from the Google News search engine. We decided to focus on headlines for two main reasons. First, news headlines typically have a high load of emotional content, as they describe major national or worldwide events, and are written in a style meant to attract attention. Second, the structure of headlines was appropriate for our goal of conducting sentence-level annotations of emotions.

Two datasets were made available: a development dataset consisting of 250 annotated headlines, and a test data set with 1,000 annotated headlines.

Data Annotation

To perform the annotations, we developed a Web-based annotation interface that displayed one headline at a time, together with six slide bars for emotions and one slide bar for valence. The interval for the emotion annotations was set to [0, 100], where 0 means the emotion is missing from the given headline and 100 represents maximum emotional load. The interval for the valence annotations was set to [–100, 100], where 0 represents a neutral headline, –100 represents a highly negative headline, and 100 corresponds to a highly positive headline.

Unlike previous annotations of sentiment or subjectivity (Pang & Lee, 2004; Wiebe, Wilson, & Cardie, 2005), which typically relied on binary 0/1 annotations, we decided to use a finer-grained scale, hence allowing the annotators to select different degrees of emotional load.

Table 13.6 Sample Headlines and Manual Annotations of Emotions

		Emotions					
	Anger	Disgust	Fear	Joy	Sadness	Surprise	Valence
Inter Milan set Series A win record	2	0	0	50	0	9	50
After Iraq trip, Clinton proposes war limits	8	0	8	53	13	25	38
7 dead in apartment building fire	14	2	47	0	86	10	–86

Six annotators independently labeled the test dataset. The annotators were instructed to select the appropriate emotions for each headline based on the presence of words or phrases with emotional content as well as the overall feeling evoked by the headline. Annotation examples were also provided, including examples of headlines bearing two or more emotions to illustrate the case where several emotions were jointly applicable. Finally, the annotators were encouraged to follow their "first intuition" and to use the full range of the annotation scale bars.

The final annotation labels were created as the average of the six independent annotations after normalizing the set of annotations provided by each annotator for each emotion to the range of 0 to 100. Table 13.6 shows three sample headlines in the dataset along with their final gold standard annotations.

Interannotator Agreement

We conducted interannotater agreement studies for each of the six emotions and for the valence annotations. The agreement evaluations were carried out using the Pearson correlation measure and are shown in Table 13.7. To measure the agreement among the six annotators, we first measured the agreement between each annotator and the average of the remaining five annotators, followed by an average over the six resulting agreement figures.

Fine- and Coarse-Grained Evaluations

Fine-grained evaluations were conducted using the Pearson measure of correlation between the system scores and the gold standard scores averaged over all the headlines in the dataset.

We have also run a coarse-grained evaluation, where each emotion was mapped to a 0/1 classification (0 = [0,50), 1 = [50,100]), and each valence was mapped to a –1/0/1 classification (–1 = [–100, –50],

0 = (–50, 50), 1 = [50, 100]). For the coarse-grained evaluations, we calculated accuracy, precision, and recall. Note that the accuracy is calculated with respect to all the possible classes and thus can be artificially high in the case of unbalanced datasets (as some of the emotions are, owing to the high number of neutral headlines). Instead, the precision and recall figures exclude the neutral annotations.

Recognizing Emotions in Texts

In this section we present several algorithms for detecting emotion in texts, ranging from simple heuristics (e.g., directly checking specific affective lexicons) to more refined algorithms (e.g., checking similarity in a latent semantic space in which explicit representations of emotions are built and exploiting naïve Bayes classifiers trained on mood-labeled blog posts). It is worth noting that the proposed methodologies are either completely unsupervised or, when supervision is used, the training data can be easily collected from online mood-annotated materials. To give an idea of difficulties of the task, we present the evaluation of the algorithms and a

Table 13.7 Interannotator Agreement

Emotions	
Anger	49.55
Disgust	44.51
Fear	63.81
Joy	59.91
Sadness	68.19
Surprise	36.07
Valence	
Valence	78.01

comparison with the systems that participated in the SemEval-2007 task on affective text. As noted in Annotating Texts with Emotions (p. 187), the focus is on short texts (e.g., news titles, single sentences, lines of lyrics).

Affective Semantic Similarity

As we have seen above, a crucial issue is to have a mechanism for evaluating the emotional load of generic terms. We introduce in this section a possible methodology to deal with the problem, based on the similarity among generic terms and affective lexical concepts. To this aim we estimated term similarity from a large-scale corpus. In particular we implemented a variation of latent semantic analysis (LSA) in order to obtain a vector representation for words, texts, and synsets.

In LSA (Deerwester et al., 1990), term co-occurrences in the documents of the corpus are captured by means of a dimensionality reduction operated by a singular value decomposition (SVD) on the term-by-document matrix. SVD is a well-known operation in linear algebra that can be applied to any rectangular matrix in order to find correlations among its rows and columns. In our case, SVD decomposes the term-by-document matrix T into three matrices $T = U\Sigma_k V^T$ where Σ_k is the diagonal $k{\times}k$ matrix containing the k singular values of T, $\sigma_1 \geq \sigma_2 \geq \ldots \geq \sigma_k$, and U and V are column-orthogonal matrices. When the three matrices are multiplied together the original term-by-document matrix is recomposed. Typically we can choose $k' \ll k$ obtaining the approximation $T = U\Sigma_k V^T$.

LSA can be viewed as a way to overcome some of the drawbacks of the standard vector space model (sparseness and high dimensionality). In fact, the LSA similarity is computed in a lower dimensional space, in which second-order relations among terms and texts are exploited. For the experiments reported in this paper, we ran the SVD operation on the British National Corpus[3] using $k' = 400$ dimensions.

The resulting LSA vectors can be exploited to estimate both term and document similarity. Regarding document similarity, latent semantic indexing (LSI) is a technique that allows us to represent a document by means of a LSA vector. In particular, we used a variation of the *pseudodocument* methodology described in (Berry, 1992). This variation takes into account also a *tf-idf* weighting schema (see Gliozzo & Strapparava, 2005, for more details). Each document can be represented in the LSA space by summing up the normalized LSA vectors of all the terms contained in it. Also a synset in WordNet (and then an emotional category) can be represent in the LSA space, performing the pseudodocument technique on all the words contained in the synset. Thus it is possible to have a vectorial representation of each emotional category in the LSA space (i.e., the *emotional vectors*). With an appropriate metric (e.g., cosine), we can compute a similarity measure among terms and affective categories. We defined the *affective weight* as the similarity value between an emotional vector and an input term vector.

For example, the term *sex* shows high similarity with respect to the positive emotional category AMOROUSNESS, with the negative category MISOGYNY, and with the ambiguous valence tagged category AMBIGUOUS_EXPECTATION. The noun *gift* is highly related to the emotional categories: LOVE (with positive valence), COMPASSION (with negative valence), SURPRISE (with ambiguous valence), and INDIFFERENCE (with neutral valence).

In conclusion, the vectorial representation in the latent semantic space allows us to represent in a uniform way emotional categories, terms, concepts and possibly full documents. The affective weight function can be used in order to select the emotional categories that can best express or evoke valenced emotional states with respect to input term. Moreover, it allows us to individuate a set of terms that are semantically similar to the input term and that share with it the same affective constraints (e.g., emotional categories with the same value of valence).

For example, given the noun *university* as input term, it is possible to check for related terms that have a positive affective valence, possibly focusing only on some specific emotional categories (e.g., *sympathy*). On the other hand, given two terms, it is possible to check whether they are semantically related, and with respect to which emotional category. Table 13.8 shows a portion of the affective lexicon related to *university*, with some emotional categories grouped by valence.

Variations of this technique (i.e., exploiting non-negative matrix factorization [NMF] or probabilistic LSA) are reported in Calvo and Kim (2012).

Knowledge-Based Classification of Emotion

We can also approach the task of emotion recognition by exploiting the use of words in a text, and in particular their co-occurrence with words that have explicit affective meaning.

Table 13.8 Some Terms Related to *University* Through Some Emotional Categories

Related Generic Terms	Positive Emotional Category	Emotional Weight
University	Enthusiasm	0.36
Professor	Sympathy	0.56
Scholarship	Devotion	0.72
Achievement	Encouragement	0.76
	Negative emotional category	
University	Downheartedness	0.33
Professor	Antipathy	0.46
Scholarship	Isolation	0.49
Achievement	Melancholy	0.53

For this method, as far as direct affective words are concerned, we followed the classification found in WordNet-Affect. In particular, we collected six lists of affective words by using the synsets labeled with the six emotions considered in our dataset. Thus, as a baseline, we implemented a simple algorithm that checks the presence of these direct affective words in the headlines, and computes a score that reflects the frequency of the words in this affective lexicon in the text.

A crucial aspect is the availability of a mechanism for evaluating the semantic similarity among "generic" terms and affective lexical concepts. For this purpose, we exploited the affective semantic similarity described in the previous section. We acquired an LSA space from the British National Corpus.[4] As we have seen, LSA yields a vector space model that allows for a *homogeneous* representation (and hence comparison) of words, word sets, sentences, and texts. Then, regardless of how an emotion is represented in the LSA space, we can compute a similarity measure among (generic) terms in an input text and affective categories. In the LSA space, an emotion can be represented at least in three ways: (1) the vector of the specific word denoting the emotion (e.g., anger), (2) the vector representing the synset of the emotion (e.g., anger, choler, ire), and (3) the vector of all the words in the synsets labeled with the emotion. Here we describe experiments with all these representations.

We have implemented four different systems for emotion analysis by using the knowledge-based approaches.

1. WN-AFFECT PRESENCE, which is used as a baseline system and annotates the emotions in a text simply based on the presence of words from the WordNet Affect lexicon.

2. LSA SINGLE WORD, which calculates the LSA similarity between the given text and each emotion, where an emotion is represented as the vector of the specific word denoting the emotion (e.g., joy).

3. LSA EMOTION SYNSET, where in addition to the word denoting an emotion, its synonyms from the WordNet synset are also used.

4. LSA ALL EMOTION WORDS, which augments the previous set by adding the words in all the synsets labeled with a given emotion, as found in WordNet Affect.

The results obtained with each of these methods, on the corpus of news headlines described in Annotation Guidelines, p.188 are presented below in Table 13.11.

Corpus-Based Classification of Emotion

In addition to the experiments based on WordNet-Affect, we also present corpus-based experiments relying on blog entries from LiveJournal.com. We used a collection of blog posts annotated with moods that were mapped to the six emotions used in the classification. While every blog community practices a different genre of writing, LiveJournal.com blogs seem to more closely recount the goings-on of everyday life than any other blog community.

The indication of the mood is optional when posting on LiveJournal, therefore the mood-annotated posts used here are likely to reflect the true mood of the blog authors, since they were explicitly specified without particular coercion from the interface. Our corpus consists of 8,761 blog posts, with the distribution over the six emotions shown in Table 13.9. This corpus is a subset of the corpus used in the experiments reported in Mishne (2005).

In a preprocessing step, all the SGML tags were removed and only the body of the blog posts was kept, which was then passed through a tokenizer. Only blog posts with a length within a range comparable to that of the headlines (i.e., 100 to 400 characters) were kept. The average length of the blog posts in the final corpus was 60 words per entry. Six sample entries are shown in Table 13.10.

Table 13.9 Blogposts and Mood Annotations Extracted from LiveJournal

Emotion	LiveJournal Mood	Number of Blog Posts
Anger	Angry	951
Disgust	Disgusted	72
Fear	Scared	637
Joy	Happy	4,856
Sadness	Sad	1,794
Surprise	Surprised	451

The blog posts were then used to train a naïve Bayes classifier, where for each emotion we used the blogs associated with it as positive examples and the blogs associated with all the other five emotions as negative examples.

Evaluation of the SemEval-2007 task

The five systems (four knowledge-based and one corpus-based) were evaluated on the dataset of 1,000 newspaper headlines. As mentioned earlier, both fine- and coarse-grained evaluations can be conducted. Table 13.11 shows the results obtained by each system for the annotation of the six emotions. The best results obtained according to each individual metric are marked in bold.

As expected, different systems have different strengths. The system based exclusively on the presence of words from the WordNet-Affect lexicon has the highest precision at the cost of low recall. Instead, the LSA system using all the emotion words has by far the largest recall, although the precision is significantly lower. In terms of performance for individual emotions, the system based on blogs gives the best results for joy, which correlates with the size of the training data set (joy had the largest number of blog posts). The blogs also provide the best results for anger (which also had a relatively large number of blog posts). For all the other emotions, the best performance is obtained with the LSA models.

We also compared our results with those obtained by three systems participating in the SemEval emotion annotation task: SWAT, UPAR7, and UA. Table 13.12 shows the results obtained by these systems on the same dataset using the same evaluation metrics. We briefly describe each of these three systems below.

Table 13.10 Sample Blog Posts Labeled with Moods Corresponding to the Six Emotions

ANGER

I am so angry. Nicci can't get work of for the Used's show on the 30th, and we were stuck in traffic for almost 3 hours today, preventing us from seeing them. bastards

DISGUST

It's time to snap out of this. It's time to pull things together. This is ridiculous. I'm going nowhere. I'm doing nothing.

FEAR

He might have lung cancer. It's just a rumor…but it makes sense. is very depressed and that's just the beginning of things

JOY

This week has been the best week I've had since I can't remember when! I have been so hyper all week, it's been awesome!!!

SADNESS

Oh and a girl from my old school got run over and died the other day which is horrible, especially as it was a very small village school so everybody knew her.

SURPRISE

Small note: Frenchmen shake your hand as they say good morning to you. This is a little shocking to us fragile Americans, who are used to waving to each other in greeting.

UPAR7 (Chaumartin, 2007) is a rule-based system using a linguistic approach. A first pass through the data "uncapitalizes" common words in the news title. The system then used the Stanford syntactic parser on the modified titles and identifies what is being said about the main subject by exploiting the dependency graph obtained from the parser. Each word is first rated separately for each emotion and then the main subject rating is boosted. The system uses a combination of SentiWordNet (Esuli & Sebastiani, 2006) and WordNet-Affect (Strapparava & Valitutti, 2004), which were semi-automatically enriched on the basis of the original trial data provided during the SemEval task.

UA (Kozareva et al., 2007) uses statistics gathered from three search engines (MyWay, AlltheWeb, and Yahoo) to determine the kind and the amount of emotion in each headline. Emotion

Table 13.11 Performance of the Proposed Algorithms

	Fine	Coarse		
	r	Prec.	Rec.	F1
ANGER				
WordNet-Affect presence	12.08	**33.33**	3.33	6.06
LSA single word	8.32	6.28	63.33	11.43
LSA emotion synset	17.80	7.29	86.67	13.45
LSA all emotion words	5.77	6.20	**88.33**	11.58
NB trained on blogs	**19.78**	13.68	21.67	**16.77**
DISGUST				
WordNet-Affect presence	−1.59	0	0	−
LSA single word	**13.54**	**2.41**	70.59	**4.68**
LSA emotion synset	7.41	1.53	64.71	3.00
LSA all emotion words	8.25	1.98	**94.12**	3.87
NB trained on blogs	4.77	0	0	−
FEAR				
WordNet-Affect presence	24.86	**100.00**	1.69	3.33
LSA single word	**29.56**	12.93	**96.61**	**22.80**
LSA emotion synset	18.11	12.44	94.92	22.00
LSA all emotion words	10.28	12.55	86.44	21.91
NB trained on blogs	7.41	16.67	3.39	5.63
JOY				
WordNet-Affect presence	10.32	**50.00**	0.56	1.10
LSA single word	4.92	17.81	47.22	25.88
LSA emotion synset	6.34	19.37	72.22	30.55
LSA all emotion words	7.00	18.60	**90.00**	30.83
NB trained on blogs	**13.81**	22.71	59.44	**32.87**
SADNESS				
WordNet-Affect presence	8.56	**33.33**	3.67	6.61
LSA single word	8.13	13.13	55.05	21.20
LSA emotion synset	13.27	14.35	58.71	**23.06**
LSA all emotion words	10.71	11.69	**87.16**	20.61
NB trained on blogs	**16.01**	20.87	22.02	21.43

(*continued*)

Table 13.11 Continued

	Fine	Coarse		
	r	Prec.	Rec.	F1
SURPRISE				
WordNet-Affect presence	3.06	**13.04**	4.68	6.90
LSA single word	9.71	6.73	67.19	12.23
LSA emotion synset	12.07	7.23	89.06	13.38
LSA all emotion words	**12.35**	7.62	**95.31**	**14.10**
NB trained on blogs	3.08	8.33	1.56	2.63

Table 13.12 Results of the Systems Participating in the SemEval-Task for Emotion Annotations

	Fine	Coarse		
	r	Prec.	Rec.	F1
ANGER				
SWAT	24.51	12.00	5.00	7.06
UA	23.20	12.74	**21.6**	16.03
UPAR7	**32.33**	**16.67**	1.66	3.02
DISGUST				
SWAT	**18.55**	0.00	0.00	–
UA	16.21	0.00	0.00	–
UPAR7	12.85	0.00	0.00	–
FEAR				
SWAT	32.52	25.00	14.40	18.27
UA	23.15	16.23	**26.27**	20.06
UPAR7	**44.92**	**33.33**	2.54	4.72
JOY				
SWAT	**26.11**	35.41	**9.44**	14.91
UA	2.35	40.00	2.22	4.21
UPAR7	22.49	**54.54**	6.66	11.87
SADNESS				
SWAT	38.98	32.50	11.92	17.44
UA	12.28	25.00	0.91	1.76
UPAR7	**40.98**	48.97	**22.02**	30.38
SURPRISE				
SWAT	11.82	11.86	10.93	11.78
UA	7.75	**13.70**	**16.56**	15.00
UPAR7	**16.71**	12.12	1.25	2.27

Table 13.13 Overall Average Results Obtained by the Five Proposed Systems and by the Three SemEval Systems

	Fine	Coarse		
	r	Prec.	Rec.	F1
WordNet-Affect presence	9.54	**38.28**	1.54	4.00
LSA single word	12.36	9.88	66.72	16.37
LSA emotion synset	12.50	9.20	77.71	13.38
LSA all emotion words	9.06	9.77	**90.22**	**17.57**
NB trained on blogs	10.81	12.04	18.01	13.22
SWAT	25.41	19.46	8.61	11.57
UA	14.15	17.94	11.26	9.51
UPAR7	**28.38**	27.60	5.68	8.71

scores are obtained by using pointwise mutual information (PMI). First, the number of documents obtained from the three Web search engines using a query that contains all the headline words and an emotion (the words occur in an independent proximity across the Web documents) is divided by the number of documents containing only an emotion and the number of documents containing all the headline words. Second, an associative score between each content word and an emotion is estimated and used to weight the final PMI score. The final results are normalized to the range of 0 to 100.

SWAT (Katz, Singleton, & Wicentowski, 2007) is a supervised system using a unigram model trained to annotate emotional content. Synonym expansion on the emotion label words is also performed, using *Roget's Thesaurus*. In addition to the development data provided by the task organizers, the SWAT team annotated an additional set of 1,000 headlines, which was used for training.

For an overall comparison, the average over all six emotions for each system was calculated. Table 13.13 shows the overall results obtained by the five systems described above and by the three SemEval systems. The best results in terms of fine-grained evaluations are obtained by the UPAR7 system, which is perhaps due to the deep syntactic analysis performed by this system. Our systems give however the best performance in terms of coarse-grained evaluations, with the WordNet-Affect presence providing the best precision, and the LSA all emotion words leading to the highest recall and F-measure.

Future Directions

Affect detection from text only started to be explored quite recently, so several new directions will probably be developed in the future. In the following section we present two promising lines of research. The first one approaches the related task of humor recognition; the second proposes the exploitation of extralinguistic features (e.g., music) for emotion detection.

Humor Recognition

Of all the phenomena that fall under the study of emotions, humor is one of the least explored from a computational point of view. Humor involves both cognitive and emotional processes, and understanding its subtle mechanisms is certainly a challenge. Nonetheless, given the importance of humor in our everyday life and the increasing importance of computers in work and entertainment, we believe that studies related to computational humor will become increasingly important in fields such as human-computer interaction, intelligent interactive entertainment, and computer-assisted education.

Previous work in computational humor has focused mainly on the task of humor generation (Binsted & Ritchie, 1997; Stock & Strapparava, 2003), and very few attempts have been made to develop systems for automatic humor recognition (Taylor & Mazlack, 2004). Mihalcea and Strapparava (2006) explored the applicability of computational approaches to the recognition and use of verbally expressed humor.

Since a deep comprehension of humor in all of its aspects is probably too ambitious and beyond existing computational capabilities, the investigation was restricted to the type of humor found in one-liners. A one-liner is a short sentence with comic effects and an interesting linguistic structure: simple syntax, deliberate use of rhetorical devices (e.g., alliteration, rhyme), and frequent use of creative language constructions meant to attract the reader's attention.

To test the hypothesis that automatic classification techniques represent a viable approach to humor recognition, we needed in the first place a dataset consisting of both humorous (positive) and nonhumorous (negative) examples. Such datasets can be used to learn computational models for humor recognition automatically and also to evaluate the performance of such models.

We tested two different sets of "negative" examples (see Table 13.14):

1. *Reuters* titles, extracted from news articles published in the Reuters newswire over a period of one year (8/20/1996 to 8/19/1997) (Lewis et al., 2004). The titles consist of short sentences with simple syntax and are often phrased to catch the reader's attention (an effect similar to the one rendered by one-liners).

2. *Proverbs* extracted from an online proverb collection. Proverbs are sayings that transmit, usually in one short sentence, important facts or experiences that are considered true by many people. Their property of being condensed but memorable sayings make them very similar to the one-liners. In fact, some one-liners attempt to reproduce proverbs, with a comic effect, as in "Beauty is in the eye of the beer holder," derived from "Beauty is in the eye of the beholder."

The dimension of the datasets is 16,000 one-liners, with the same number respectively for titles and proverbs.

To test the feasibility of automatically differentiating between humorous and nonhumorous texts using *content-based* features, we performed experiments where the humor-recognition task is formulated as a traditional text classification problem. We decided to use two of the most frequently employed text classifiers, naïve Bayes (McCallum & Nigam, 1998; Yang & Liu, 1999) and support vector machines (Joachims, 1998; Vapnik, 1995), selected based on their performance in previously reported work and for their diversity of learning methodologies.

The classification experiments are performed using stratified 10-fold cross-validations for accurate evaluations. The baseline for all the experiments is 50%, which represents the classification accuracy obtained if a label of "humorous" (or "nonhumorous") would be assigned by default to all the examples in the dataset. Table 13.15 shows results obtained using the two datasets, using the naïve Bayes and SVM classifiers. Learning curves are plotted in Figure 13.1.

The results obtained in the automatic classification experiments reveal that computational approaches represent a viable solution for the task of humor recognition, and good performance can be achieved using classification techniques based on stylistic and content features.

Figure 13.1 shows that regardless of the type of negative data or classification methodology, there is significant learning only up to about 60% of the data (i.e., about 10,000 positive examples and the same number of negative examples). The rather steep ascent of the curve, especially in the first

Table 13.14 Examples of One-Liners, Reuters Titles, and Proverbs

One-Liners

Take my advice; I don't use it anyway.

I get enough exercise just pushing my luck.

I just got lost in thought, it was unfamiliar territory.

Beauty is in the eye of the beer holder.

I took an IQ test and the results were negative.

Reuters titles

Trocadero expects tripling of revenues.

Silver fixes at two-month high, but gold lags.

Oil prices slip as refiners shop for bargains.

Japanese prime minister arrives in Mexico.

Chains may raise prices after minimum wage hike.

Proverbs

Creativity is more important than knowledge.

Beauty is in the eye of the beholder.

I believe no tales from an enemy's tongue.

Do not look at the coat, but at what is under the coat.

A man is known by the company he keeps.

Table 13.15 Humor-Recognition Accuracy Using Content-Based Features and Naïve Bayes and SVM Text Classifiers

Classifier	One-Liners Reuters	One-Liners Proverbs
Naïve Bayes	96.67%	84.81%
SVM	96.09%	84.48%

part of the learning, suggests that humorous and nonhumorous texts represent well-distinguishable types of data. The plateau toward the end of the learning also suggests that more data are not likely to help improve the quality of an automatic

humor recognizer; more sophisticated features are probably required. Linguistic theories of humor (Attardo, 1994) have suggested many *stylistic features* that characterize humorous texts. (Mihalcea & Strapparava, 2006) tried to identify a set of features that were both significant and feasible to implement using existing machine-readable resources. Specifically they focused on alliteration, antonymy, and adult slang, which were previously suggested as potentially good indicators of humor (Bucaria, 2004; Ruch, 2002).

Exploiting Extralinguistic Features

Extralinguistic features comprise anything outside of language that is relevant to the meaning and

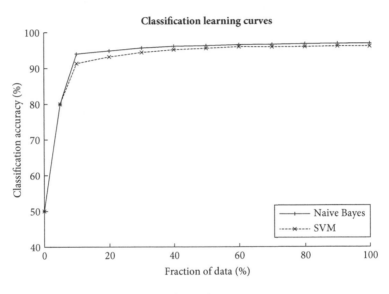

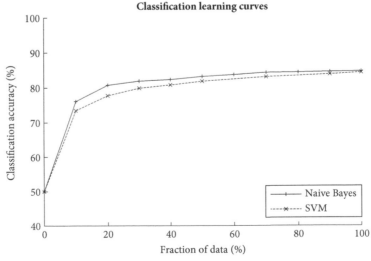

Fig. 13.1 Learning curves for humor recognition using text classification techniques; one-liners/Reuters on the left, and one-liners/proverbs on the right.

the pragmatics of an utterance. The careful use of these features can be exploited to the automatic processing of the language, improving or even making possible some tasks. This issue becomes quite important, especially if we are dealing with any form of emotion classification of language.

As an example, we can mention the CORPS corpus (CORpus of tagged Political Speeches), a resource freely available for research purposes (Guerini, Strapparava, & Stock, 2008), which contains political speeches tagged with *audience reactions* (e.g., applause, standing ovation, booing). The collected texts come from various Web sources (e.g., politicians' official sites, News websites) to create a specific resource useful for the study of *persuasive language*. The corpus was built relying on the hypothesis that tags about public reaction, such as APPLAUSE, are indicators of hot spots where attempts at persuasion succeeded or at least a persuasive attempt had been recognized by the audience. Exploiting that corpus, Strapparava, Guerini, and Stock (2010) explored the possibility of classifying the transcripts of political discourses according to their persuasive power, predicting the sentences that might possibly trigger applause.

MUSIC AND LYRICS: A PARALLEL
CORPUS-BASED PERSPECTIVE

As another example of the usefulness of extra-linguistic features, we can analyze the case of the emotion classification of lyrics. After introducing a parallel corpus of music and lyrics annotated with emotions at line level, we describe some experiments on emotion classification using the music as well as the lyric representations of the songs.

Popular songs exert a lot of power on people, both at an individual level as well as on groups, mainly because of the message and emotions they communicate. Songs can lift our moods, make us dance, or move us to tears. Songs are able to embody deep feelings, usually through a combined effect of both the music and the lyrics. Songwriters know that music and lyrics have to be coherent, and the art of shaping words for music involves precise techniques of creative writing, using elements of grammar, phonetics, metrics, or rhyme, which make this genre a suitable candidate to be investigated by NLP techniques.

The computational treatment of music is a very active research field. The increasing availability of music in digital format (e.g., MIDI) has motivated the development of tools for music accessing, filtering, classification, and retrieval. For instance, the task of music retrieval and music recommendation has received a lot of attention from both the arts and the computer science communities; see, for instance, Orio (2006) for an introduction to this task.

There are several works on MIDI analysis. We report mainly those that are relevant for the purpose of the present work. For example Das, Howard, and Smith (2000) describe an analysis of predominant up-down motion types within music, through extraction of the kinematic variables of music velocity and acceleration from MIDI data streams. Cataltepe, Yaslan, and Sonmez (2007) address music genre classification using MIDI and audio features, while Wang et al. (2004) automatically align acoustic musical signals with their corresponding textual lyrics.

MIDI files are typically organized into one or more parallel "tracks" for independent recording and editing. A reliable system to identify the MIDI track containing the *melody*[5] is very relevant for music information retrieval, and several approaches that have been proposed to address this issue (Rizo et al., 2006; Velusamy, Thoshkahna, & Ramakrishnan, 2007).

Regarding natural language processing techniques applied to lyrics, there have been a few studies that mainly exploit the song lyrics components only while ignoring the musical component. For Instance, Mahedero, Martinez, and Cano (2005) deal with language identification, structure extraction, and thematic categorization for lyrics. Yang and Lee (2009) approach the problem of emotion identification in lyrics.

Despite the interest of the researchers in music and language and despite the long history of the interaction between music and lyrics, there is little scholarly research that explicitly focuses on the connection between music and lyrics. Here we focus on the connection between the musical and linguistic representations in popular songs and their role in the expression of *affect*. Strapparava, Mihalcea, and Battocchi (2012) introduced a corpus of songs with a strict alignment between notes and words, which can be regarded and used as a *parallel* corpus suitable for common parallel corpora techniques previously used in computational linguistics. The corpus consists of 100 popular songs, such as "On Happy Days" or "All the Time in the World," covering famous interpreters such as the Beatles or Sting. For each song, both the music (extracted from MIDI format) and the lyrics (as raw text) were included, along with an alignment between the MIDI features and the words. Moreover, because of the important

Table 13.16 Some Statistics of the Corpus

Songs	100
Songs in "major" key	59
Songs in "minor" key	41
Lines	4,976
Aligned syllables / notes	34,045

role played by emotions in songs, the corpus also embeds manual annotations of six basic emotions collected via crowdsourcing, as described earlier in Annotating Texts with Emotions, p. 187. Table 13.16 shows some statistics collected on the entire corpus.

Figure 13.2 shows an example from the corpus consisting of the first two lines in the Beatles' song "A Hard Day's Night."

We explicitly encode the following features. At the song level, the key of the song (e.g., G major, C minor). At the line level, we represent the *raising*, which is the musical interval (in half steps) between the first note in the line and the most important note (i.e., the note in the line with the longest duration) as well as the manual emotion annotations. Finally, at the note level, we encode the time code

of the note with respect to the beginning of the song, the note aligned with the corresponding syllable, the degree of the note with relation to the key of the song, and the duration of the note.

Mihalcea and Strapparava (2012) have described some experiments that display the usefulness of the joint music/text representation in this corpus of songs. Below we outline an experiment for emotion recognition in songs that relies on both music and text features. A corpus of 100 songs was used, which at this stage had full lyrics, text, and emotion annotations. Using a simple bag-of-words representations fed to a machine learning classifier, two comparative experiments were run: one using only the lyrics and one using both the lyrics and the notes for a joint model of music and lyrics. The task was transformed into a binary classification task by using a threshold empirically set at 3. If the score for an emotion was below 3, it was recorded as absent, whereas if the score is equal to or above 3, it was recorded as present.

For the classification, support vector machines (SVMs) were used—binary classifiers that seek to find the hyperplane that best separates a set of positive examples from a set of negative examples with maximum margin (Vapnik, 1995). Applications of SVM classifiers to text categorization have led to

```
<song filename=AHARDDAY.m2a>
<key time=0>G major</key>
<line pvers=1 raising=3 anger=1.5 disgust=0.7 sadness=2.5 surprise=0.8 >
<token time=5040 orig−note=B degree=3 duration=210>IT</token>
<token time=5050 orig−note=B degree=3 duration=210>'S </token>
<token time=5280 orig−note=C' degree=4 duration=210>BEEN </token>
<token time=5520 orig−note=B degree=3 duration=210>A </token>
<token time=5760 orig−note=D' degree=5 duration=810>HARD </token>
<token time=6720 orig−note=D' degree=5 duration=570>DAY</token>
<token time=6730 orig−note=D' degree=5 duration=570>'S </token>
<token time=7440 orig−note=D' degree=5 duration=690>NIGHT</token>
</line>
<line pvers=2 raising=5 anger=3.5 disgust=2 sadness=1.2 surprise=0.2 >
<token time=8880 orig−note=C' degree=4 duration=212>AND </token>
<token time=9120 orig−note=D' degree=5 duration=210>I</token>
<token time=9130 orig−note=D' degree=5 duration=210>'VE </token>
<token time=9360 orig−note=C' degree=4 duration=210>BEEN </token>
<token time=9600 orig−note=D' degree=5 duration=210>WOR</token>
<token time=9840 orig−note=F' degree=7− duration=930>KING </token>
<token time=10800 orig−note=D' degree=5 duration=210>LI</token>
<token time=11040 orig−note=C' degree=4 duration=210>KE </token>
<token time=11050 orig−note=C' degree=4 duration=210>A </token>
<token time=11280 orig−note=D' degree=5 duration=330>D</token>
<token time=11640 orig−note=C' degree=4 duration=90>O</token>
<token time=11760 orig−note=B degree=3 duration=330>G</token>
</line>
```

Fig. 13.2 Two lines of a song in the corpus: "It's been a hard day's night, and I've been working like a dog."

Table 13.17 Evaluations Using a Coarse-Grained Binary Classification

Emotion	Baseline	Textual	Musical	Textual and Musical
Anger	89.27%	91.14%	89.63%	92.40%
Disgust	93.85%	94.67%	93.85%	94.77%
Fear	93.58%	93.87%	93.58%	93.87%
Joy	50.26%	70.92%	61.95%	75.64%
Sadness	67.40%	75.84%	70.65%	79.42%
Surprise	94.83%	94.83%	94.83%	94.83%
Average	81.53%	86.87%	84.08%	88.49%

some of the best results reported in the literature (Joachims, 1998).

Table 13.17 shows the results obtained for each of the six emotions and for the three major settings that we consider: textual features only, musical features only, and a classifier that jointly uses the textual and the musical features. The classification accuracy for each experiment is reported as the average of the accuracies obtained during a 10-fold cross-validation on the corpus. The table also shows a baseline, computed as the average of the accuracies obtained when using the most frequent class observed on the training data for each fold.

As seen from the table, on average the joint use of textual and musical features is beneficial for the classification of emotions. Perhaps not surprisingly, the effect of the classifier is stronger for those emotions that are dominant in the corpus (i.e., JOY and SADNESS (seeTable 13.5). The improvement obtained with the classifiers is much smaller for the other emotions (or even absent, as for SURPRISE), which is also explained by their high baseline of over 90%.

Conclusions

The field of affective NLP—in particular the recognition of emotions in texts—is a challenging one. Nonetheless, with current NLP techniques it is possible to approach the problem with interesting results, opening up exciting applicative perspectives for the future.

In this chapter we presented some explorations in dealing with automatic recognition of affect in text. We began by describing some available lexical resources, the problem of creating a gold standard using emotion annotations, and the affective text task at SemEval-2007. That task focused on the classification of emotions in news headlines

and was meant as an exploration of the connection between emotions and lexical semantics. Then we approached the problem of recognizing emotions in texts, presenting some state-of-the-art knowledge- and corpus-based methods. We concluded by presenting two promising lines of research in the field of affective NLP. The first approaches the related task of humor recognition and the second proposes the exploitation of extralinguistic features (e.g., music) for emotion detection.

Acknowledgments

Carlo Strapparava was partially supported by the PerTe project (Trento RISE). This material is based in part upon work supported by National Science Foundation award #0917170.

Notes

1. In ANEW the communicative perspective is that the term acts as a stimulus to elicit a particular emotion in the reader.
2. http://nlp.cs.swarthmore.edu/semeval/
3. The British National Corpus is a very large (over 100 million words) corpus of modern English, both spoken and written (BNC Consortium 2000).
4. Other more specific corpora could also be considered, to obtain a more domain-oriented similarity.
5. A melody can be defined as a "cantabile" sequence of notes, usually the sequence that a listener can remember after hearing a song.

References

Alm, C., D. Roth, & R. Sproat (2005). Emotions from text: Machine learning for text-based emotion prediction. In *Proceedings of the conference on empirical methods in natural language processing* (pp. 347–354). Stroudsburg, Pennsylvania: The Association for Computational Linguistics.

Aman, S., & S. Szpakowicz (2008). Using Roget's Thesaurus for fine-grained emotion recognition. In *Proceedings of the international joint conference on natural language processing*. Stroudsburg, Pennsylvania: The Association for Computational Linguistics.

Attardo, S. (1994). *Linguistic theory of humor*. Berlin: Mouton de Gruyter.

Ax, A. F. (1953). The physiological differentiation between fear and anger in humans. In: *Psychosomatic Medicine*, 15, 433–442.

Berry, M. (1992). Large-scale sparse singular value computations. *International Journal of Supercomputer Applications*, 6(1), 13–49.

Binsted, K., & G. Ritchie (1997). *Computational rules for punning riddles*. Humor 10(1).

BNC Consortium (2000). British National Corpus. Humanities Computing Unit of Oxford University. Available at: http://www.hcu.ox.ac.uk/BNC/

Bradley, M. M., & P. J. Lang (1994). Measuring emotion: The self-assessment manikin and the semantic differential. *Journal of Behavioral Therapy and Experimental Psychiatry* 25, 49–59.

Bradley, M. M., & P. J. Lang (1999). Affective norms for English words (ANEW): Instruction manual and affective ratings. Technical report. Gainesville: The Center for Research in Psychophysiology, University of Florida.

Bucaria, C. (2004). Lexical and syntactic ambiguity as a source of humor. *Humor 17*(3).

Calvo R., & M. Kim (2012) Emotions in text: dimensional and categorical models. *Computational Intelligence 29*(3), 527–543

Cataltepe, Z., Y. Yaslan, & A. Sonmez (2007). Music genre classification using MIDI and audio features. *Journal on Advances in Signal Processing. 2007*(1), 1–8.

Chaumartin, F. R. (2007). UPAR7: A knowledge-based system for headline sentiment tagging. In *Proceedings of SemEval 2007*. Stroudsburg, Pennsylvania: The Association for Computational Linguistics.

Das, M., D. Howard, & S. Smith (2000). The kinematic analysis of motion curves through MIDI data analysis. In *Organised sound 5.1* (pp. 137–145).

Deerwester, S., et al. (1990). Indexing by latent semantic analysis. *Journal of the American Society for Information Science*, *41*(6), 391–407.

Ekman, P. (1977). Biological and cultural contributions to body and facial movement. In J. Blacking (Ed.), *Anthropology of the body* (pp. 34–84). London: Academic Press.

Ekman, P. (1993). Facial expression of emotion. *American Psychologist*, 48, 384–392.

Esuli, A., & F. Sebastiani (2006). SentiWordNet: A publicly available lexical resource for opinion mining. In *Proceedings of the 5th conference on language resources and evaluation*. European Language Resources Association.

Fellbaum, C. (1998). *WordNet. An electronic lexical database*. Cambridge, MA: MIT Press.

Frijda, N. (1982). *The emotions (studies in emotion and social interaction)*. New York: Cambridge University Press.

Fussell, S. R. (2002). The verbal communication of emotion. In S. R. Fussell Ed.), *The verbal communication of emotion: Interdisciplinary perspective*. Mahwah, NJ: Erlbaum.

Gliozzo, A., & C. Strapparava (2005). Domains kernels for text categorization. In *Proceedings of the ninth conference on computational natural language learning (CoNLL-2005)*. Stroudsburg, Pennsylvania: The Association for Computational Linguistics.

Guerini, M., C. Strapparava, & O. Stock (2008). CORPS: A corpus of tagged political speeches for persuasive communication processing. *Journal of Information Technology & Politics 5*(1), 19–32.

Joachims, T. (1998). Text categorization with support vector machines: learning with many relevant features. In *Proceedings of the European conference on machine learning*. Berlin: Springer.

Katz, P., M. Singleton, & R. Wicentowski (2007). SWAT-MP: The SemEval-2007 systems for task 5 and task 14. In *Proceedings of SemEval-2007*. Stroudsburg, Pennsylvania: The Association for Computational Linguistics.

Kim, S., & R. A. Calvo. (2011). Sentiment-oriented summarisation of peer reviews. In G. Biswas, S. Bull, J. Kay, & A. Mitrovic (Eds.), *Artificial intelligence in education* (pp. 491–493) LNAI Vol. 6738. Auckland, New Zealand: Springer.

Kozareva, Z., B. Navarro, S. Vazquez & A. Montoyo (2007). UA-ZBSA: A headline emotion classification through web information. In *Proceedings of SemEval-2007*. Stroudsburg, Pennsylvania: The Association for Computational Linguistics.

Lang, P. J. (1980). Behavioral treatment and bio-behavioral assessment: Computer applications. In J. B. Sidowski, J. H. Johnson, & T. A. Williams (Eds.), *Technology in mental health care delivery systems* (pp. 119–137). Ablex.

Lewis, D., Y. Yang, T. Rose & F. Li (2004). RCV1: A new benchmark collection for text categorization research. *The Journal of Machine Learning Research 5*, 361–397.

Magnini, B., & G. Cavaglia` (2000). Integrating subject field codes into WordNet. In *Proceedings of LREC-2000, second international conference on language resources and evaluation* (pp. 1413–1418). European Language Resources Association.

Mahedero, J., A. Martinez, & P. Cano (2005). Natural language processing of lyrics. In *Proceedings of MM'05*.

McCallum, A., & K. Nigam (1998). A comparison of event models for Naive Bayes text classification. In *Proceedings of AAAI-98 workshop on learning for text categorization*.

Mehrabian, A., & J. A. Russell (1974). An approach to environmental psychology. Cambridge, MA: MIT Press.

Mihalcea, R., & C. Strapparava (2006). Learning to laugh (automatically): Computational models for humor recognition. *Journal of Computational Intelligence 22*(2), 126–142.

Mihalcea, R., & C. Strapparava (2012). Lyrics, music, and emotions. In *Proceedings of the 2012 joint conference on empirical methods in natural language processing and computational natural language learning (EMNLP-CoNLL 2012)*. Stroudsburg, Pennsylvania: The Association for Computational Linguistics.

Mishne, G. (2005). Experiments with mood classification in blog posts. In *Proceedings of the 1st workshop on stylistic analysis of text for information access (Style 2005)*. SICS Technical Report T2005:14, Swedish Institute of Computer Science.

Orio, N. (2006). Music retrieval: A tutorial and review. *Foundations and Trends in Information Retrieval*, *1*(1), 1–90.

Ortony, A., G. Clore, & M. Foss (1987a). The referential structure of the affective lexicon. *Cognitive Science*, *11*(3), 341–364.

Ortony, A., G. L. Clore, & M. A. Foss (1987b). The psychological foundations of the affective lexicon. *Journal of Personality and Social Psychology*, 53, 751–766.

Osgood, C. E., W. H. May, & M. S. Miron (1975). *Cross-cultural universals of affective meaning*. Urbana: University of Illinois Press.

Pang, B., & L. Lee (2004). A sentimental education: Sentiment analysis using subjectivity summarization based on minimum cuts. In *Proceedings of the 42nd meeting of the association for computational linguistics*. Stroudsburg, Pennsylvania: The Association for Computational Linguistics.

Pennbaker, J. (2002). *Emotion, disclosure, and health*. Washington, DC: American Psychological Association.

Picard, R. (1997). *Affective computing*. Cambridge, MA: MIT Press.

Rivera, J. de. (1998). *A structural theory of the emotions*. New York: International Universities Press.

Rizo, D., P. Ponce de Leon, C. Perez-Sancho, A. Pertusa & J. Inesta (2006). A pattern recognition approach for melody track selection in MIDI files. In *Proceedings of 7th international symposium on music information retrieval (ISMIR-06)* (pp. 61–66). Victoria, Canada: University of Victoria.

Ruch, W. (2002). Computers with a personality? Lessons to be learned from studies of the psychology of humor. In: Proceedings of the The April Fools Day Workshop on Computational Humour. Enschede, Nederland: University of Twente.

Semin, G. R., & K. Fiedler (1988). The cognitive functions of linguistic categories in describing persons: Social cognition and language. *Journal of Personality and Social Psychology, 54*(4), 558–568.

Snow, R. et al. (2008). Cheap and fast—But is it good? Evaluating non-expert annotations for natural language tasks. In *Proceedings of the conference on empirical methods in natural language processing*. Stroudsburg, Pennsylvania: The Association for Computational Linguistics.

Stock, O., & C. Strapparava (2003). Getting serious about the development of computational humour. In *Proceedings of the 8th international joint conference on artificial intelligence (IJCAI-03)*. International Joint Conferences on Artificial Intelligence Organization.

Stone, P., D. Dunphy, M. Smith & D. Ogilvie (1966). *The general inquirer: A computer approach to content analysis*. Cambridge, MA: MIT Press.

Strapparava, C., M. Guerini, & O. Stock (2010). Predicting persuasiveness in political discourses. In *Proceedings of the seventh conference on international language resources and evaluation (LREC'10)* (pp. 1342–1345). European Language Resources Association.

Strapparava, C., & R. Mihalcea (2007). SemEval-2007 task 14: Affective text. In *Proceedings of the 4th international workshop on the semantic evaluations* (SemEval-2007). Stroudsburg, Pennsylvania: The Association for Computational Linguistics.

Strapparava, C., R. Mihalcea, & A. Battocchi (2012). A parallel corpus of music and lyrics annotated with emotions. In *Proceedings of the 8th international conference on language resources and evaluation (LREC-2012)*. European Language Resources Association.

Strapparava, C., & A. Valitutti (2004). WordNet-Affect: An affective extension of WordNet. In *Proceedings of the 4th international conference on language resources and evaluation*. European Language Resources Association.

Strapparava, C., A. Valitutti, & O. Stock (2006). The affective weight of lexicon. In *Proceedings of the fifth international conference on language resources and evaluation*. European Language Resources Association.

Taylor, J., & L. Mazlack (2004). Computationally recognizing wordplay in jokes. In *Proceedings of CogSci 2004*. Available at: http://www.cogsci.northwestern.edu/cogsci2004/.

Vapnik, V. (1995). *The nature of statistical learning theory*. New York: Springer.

Velusamy, S., B. Thoshkahna, & K. Ramakrishnan (2007). Novel melody line identification algorithm for polyphonic MIDI music. In *Proceedings of 13th international multimedia modeling conference (MMM 2007)*. Berlin: Springer.

Wang, Y., M. Kan, T. Nwe, A. Shenoy & J. Yin (2004). LyricAlly: Automatic synchronization of acoustic musical signals and textual lyrics. In *Proceedings of MM'04*. Association for Computing Machinery Press.

Wiebe, J., T. Wilson, & C. Cardic (2005). Annotating expressions of opinions and emotions in language. *Language Resources and Evaluation, 39*, 2–3.

Yang, D., & W. Lee (2009). Music emotion identification from lyrics. In *Proceedings of 11th IEEE symposium on multimedia*. IEEE Computer Society.

Yang, Y., & X. Liu (1999). A reexamination of text categorization methods. In *Proceedings of the 22nd ACM SIGIR conference on research and development in information retrieval*. Association for Computing Machinery Press.

Physiological Sensing of Emotion

Jennifer Healey

Abstract

Physiological changes have long been associated with emotion. Although the relative role of cognitive versus physiological processes in emotion has been debated, it is acknowledged that in almost all cases, measurable physiological changes co-occur with emotion—for example, changes in heart rate, galvanic skin response, muscle tension, breathing rate, facial expression and electrical activity in the brain. By sensing these changes we can hope to build computer systems that can automatically recognize emotion by recognizing patterns in these sensor signals that capture physiological responses. This chapter provides a detailed introduction to the measurement of physiological signals that reflect affect (emotion), with a focus on measuring cardiac activity and skin conductance. The discussion includes why these signals are important for measuring emotional activity, how they are most commonly measured, which features are most often extracted for use in recognition algorithms, and the trade-offs between signal quality and wearability and convenience for different sensing systems.

Key Words: physiological, emotion, heart rate variability, galvanic skin response, signals, sensing

Emotion and Physiology

Emotion has long been presumed to have a physiological component, although the primacy and extent of that component is often debated. Research on affective computing has primarily focused on detecting changes in variables such as heart rate and skin conductance as well as changes in muscle activity, respiration, skin temperature, and other variables. Various methods can be employed to monitor physiological signals for the purpose of emotion detection. These methods often vary in the degree of invasiveness required and have associated differences in signal fidelity and the kinds of features that can be reliably extracted from the signals. Some methods are more "wearable" and therefore more suited for monitoring "in the wild," whereas other methods are more awkward or sensitive and should be restricted to use in controlled settings. This chapter presents an overview of why we might want to measure physiological signals and gives a detailed description of monitoring heart rate and skin conductance variables.

Since ancient times, it has been speculated that emotion has a physiological component. In ancient China it was believed that emotions resided in the physical body and that excess emotion could cause damage to a person's life energy and affect the function of vital organs. In ancient Greece, the physician Hippocrates theorized that the body comprised four "humors," which were described as: yellow bile, black bile, phlegm, and blood. These humors were thought to be essential to a person's physiology and responsible for health and that emotion and behaviors were caused by humoral action or imbalance. An excess of one of the fluids would result in a temperament that was choleric, melancholic, phlegmatic, or sanguine, respectively. Aristotle also had a physiological view of emotions and viewed them as "passions" that could be compared with physical states like changes in appetite. Many of these ideas still pervade our thinking and directly influence modern emotion theorists; for example, Hans Eysenck cited the idea of temperament as a mixture of humors as a primary inspiration for defining dimensions of personality such as neuroticism and extraversion in his factor analysis method (Eysenck, 1947).

In modern times, the first theorist to put forth a physiological theory of emotion was William James (James, 1893). He viewed the physical response as primary to the feeling of an emotion: We feel happy because we laugh or smile; we feel fear because our hair stands on end and our hands go cold, and we feel grief when we cry uncontrollably. James believed that a stimulus would first trigger activity in the autonomic nervous system (ANS), which would then produce an emotional response in the brain. At about the same time Carl Lange proposed a similar theory, so the view of emotion as a being primarily a physiological reaction became known as the James-Lange theory of emotion. William James was also one of the first researchers to list the specific patterns of response that corresponded to specific emotions; for example, he described anger as "increased blood flow to hands, increased heart rate, snarling and increases involuntary nervous system arousal" and fear as "a high arousal state, in which a person has a decrease in voluntary muscle activity, a greater number of involuntary muscular contractions and a decrease of circulation in the peripheral blood vessels." At about this same time Charles Darwin also began cataloging specific patterns of observable physiological responses in both animals and people. In particular, he studied fear reactions and used different responses to help classify different species. He also speculated on how these repeated, identifiable patterns of physical expressions could aid an organism's survival (Darwin, 1872).

The description of a set of physiological patterns corresponding to unique emotional states as put forth by James and Darwin is the theoretical basis for using physiological pattern recognition to recognize emotion in affective computing. While the descriptions of James and Darwin make sense to human readers, computer algorithms need more mathematically quantifiable metrics to use as features. As a result, affective computing researcher use electronic sensors and digital recording devices to calculate such features as heart-rate acceleration and skin conductivity metrics to classify emotion (Ekman, Levenson, & Friesen, 1983; Levenson, 1992).

It should also be noted that all the nuances of emotion may not be reflected in physiological signals. One of the greatest critics of the James-Lange theory of emotion was the neurologist Walter Cannon, who argued that autonomic patterns were too slow and nonspecific to be unique to each emotion and that emotion therefore had to be primarily a cognitive event (Cannon, 1927). Cannon was famous for coining the term *fight-or-flight reaction*; in his view, the sympathetic nervous system simply prepared the organism to take some sort of action, and which action to take —"fight" or "flight"— was determined by cognitive processes. In Cannon's view, an organism always struggled to maintain physical homeostasis, and emotions such as "distress" were experienced when an organism was thrown off balance and trying to recover. Cannon thought that the physical reactions of the organism as it returned to homeostasis were too gross to be the emotion itself and that any sense of emotional "feeling" associated with these physical changes had to be primarily cognitive; otherwise "anger," "fear," and "excitement" should all "feel" the same (Cannon, 1927).

The psychologist Stanley Schachter proposed a compromise between the two views, saying that emotion is both cognitive and physiological in his "two-factor" theory of emotion (Schachter, 1964). In his experiments, Schachter attempted to create the physical "state" of an emotion artificially in the absence of an actual emotional prime by injecting subjects with epinephrine. He then sought to determine if, from purely physical state changes, the subject would be able to correctly identify or "feel" the emotion as he imagined must be the case in James's theory, where the physical effect "was" the emotion. He found overall that subjects could not clearly identify an emotion from the physical changes he induced. In another experiment, he injected some subjects with epinephrine and then exposed them to situations that would induce either anger or happiness. He found that the subjects given epinephrine reported feeling "more" of both types of induced emotion: the positive and the negative. In conclusion, Schachter determined that physiology was part of the emotional experience, but that emotions were the result of two factors: physiological changes and cognitive interpretation of those changes.

While Schachter's experiments are informative, they do not entirely explain the complex nature of the interactions between cognitive and physiological responses in emotion. One criticism is that the injection of epinephrine is too coarse a physiological prime to elicit particular emotional feelings. In more recent work, for example, psychologist Robert Zajonc showed that when he put subjects' facial muscles in the position of a smile, they reported feeling happy (Zajonc, 1994). In the end, it may be that Cannon's intuition about ANS activation alone being too gross to solely distinguish nuanced emotions might be true and that a wider range of systems, such as facial muscles and neurochemical reactions, need to be considered within the scope of physiological responses and that these must be recorded to distinguish between emotions.

Measuring physiological signals is the first step toward creating a system that can automatically recognize physiological patterns associated with emotion. In the widest view, all bodily changes could be considered physiological signals, including changes in brain activity, facial expression, vocal patterns, and body chemistry; however, the primary focus of this chapter is on measuring continuous physiological signals that can be sensed from the surface of the skin and reflect ANS activity. In particular, this chapter discusses various methods of measuring features of cardiac activity (heart rate, heart-rate variability, and blood volume pulse, features of galvanic skin response (specifically skin conductivity), surface electromyography (EMG), and respiration through expansion of the chest cavity (as opposed to gas exchange). The methods typically used to detect these signals are introduced and the trade-offs of different monitoring methods, such as wearability and signal fidelity, are discussed.

Measuring Cardiac Activity

Cardiac activity has been studied extensively by the medical community. The heart is a major muscle and its activity can easily be measured either by monitoring electrical changes on the surface of the skin or measuring pulse signals at various locations on the body. In affective computing, heart rate and heart-rate variability have been used measures of overall physical activation and effort (Aasman, Mulder, & Mulder, 1987; Itoh, Takeda, & Nakamura, 1995), and changes in heart rate have been used to mediate computer-human interaction (Kamath & Fallen, 1998). They have also been reported as indicators of fear (Levenson, 1992), panic (Hofmann & Barlow, 1996), anger (Levenson, 1992) (Kahneman, 1973), and appreciation (McCraty, Atkinsom, & Tiller, 1995).

The Effects of a Heartbeat

The beating of the heart is not a subtle event. When the heart pumps blood, major physiological changes occur. The process of a heartbeat begins when the two upper, smaller chambers of the heart, the atria, depolarize, pumping blood into the larger ventricles; then the ventricles depolarize, pumping blood into the rest of the body. The heartbeat is controlled by the body's own electrical signal and the polarizations of the heart's chambers result in electrical changes that can be detected on the surface of the skin. The recording of these surface electrical signals is called an electrocardiogram, an example of which can be seen in Figure 14.1. The beating of the heart also causes blood to be pushed out into the peripheral blood vessels, which causes them to swell. The result of this effect is the pulse; an example of a pulse trace can be seen in Figure 14.2.

The Electrocardiogram

An electrocardiogram (ECG) is a trace of electrical activity captured from the surface of the skin. The inflection points of the time-voltage signal indicate the various polarizations of the heart over the beat. The first inflection point is the P wave, indicating atrial depolarization. The next three inflection points are labeled Q, R, and S, and the triangular complex they form is called the QRS complex. This complex represents ventricular depolarization and is dominated by the large R wave. Finally, a T and potentially in some cases a U inflection point indicate ventricular repolarization (Goldberger, 2006). The ECG has many uses in the medical community but is particularly interesting for researchers in affective computing because the most precise noninvasive measurements of heart rate can be found by measuring the distance between successive R waves, as shown in Figure 14.1b.

Challenges with the metric occur if an R wave fails to be correctly recorded or is in fact missing. This causes a gap in the R-R time series that would indicate an erroneous low instantaneous heart rate. Affective computing researchers should be aware that the signal processing algorithms included with many physiological monitoring systems may employ different methods for compensating with "missed" beats and that each of these methods may introduce kinds of errors into her or his calculations. Some algorithms will simply ignore anomalous beats, whereas others will divide the interval in two equal parts to correct for the "missing" beat. Inserting a missing beat will introduce artifacts into heart-rate variability (HRV) metrics however, it may give a

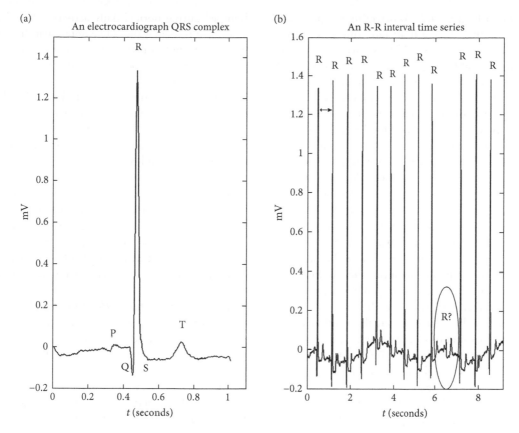

(a)
An electrocardiograph QRS complex

(b)
An R-R interval time series

Fig. 14.1 (a) An example of the P, Q, R, S and T waves in a single heart beat recorded from an ECG. (b) An example of an ambulatory ECG time series. The distance between successive R wave peaks is the "R-R" interval. This recording shows a suspicious gap in the R-R interval time series, perhaps due to a missed or dropped sample by the recording device or some other error, or perhaps a heartbeat was skipped. Such outliers can have a large impact on short-term heart rate and heart-rate variability metrics.

more robust estimate of average heart rate. Before calculating precision metrics, researchers should aware of any signal processing that is being done by the monitoring equipment, which may be include in the product literature or that can be found out by contacting the manufacturer in most cases.

One drawback to using an ECG to measure heart rate is that the measurement requires contact of the electrode with the skin, which can be uncomfortable. In fact for the best-quality signal, as is used for medical diagnosis, the person wearing the device must have excess hair removed from the adhesion sites and also have his or her skin cleaned with alcohol and abraded. In most ECGs, gel is applied to the electrodes and the electrodes are embedded in an adhesive patch that keeps the electrode-skin contact secure. These adhesive patches need to be changed daily and are often irritating to the skin. An alternative to using gel is to rely on the body's natural sweat to act as a conductive layer between the skin and the electrode; however, this is less reliable than gel and produces a poorer-quality signal. Pressure can also be used instead of adhesives to keep the electrodes in place, but this is also less reliable and in some cases even more uncomfortable for the wearer.

The Photoplethysmograph

A photoplethysmograph (PPG) sensor can be used to measure blood volume pulse in peripheral vessels as an alternative to the ECG; for example, a pulse oximeter is a PPG sensor that also measure blood oxygenation. With every heartbeat, blood is pumped through the blood vessels, which produces an engorgement of the vessels. This change is most pronounced in peripheral vessels, such as those in the fingers and earlobe. With the use of a PPG sensor, a device that emits light is placed near one of these peripheral vessels; then the amount of blood in the vessel can be monitored by looking at the amount of light reflected by the vessel over time. As blood fills the vessel, more light is reflected back to the sensor. The more blood present in the vessel, the higher the reflectance reading. A series of heartbeats will result in a light reflectance pattern similar to the one in Figure 14.2. By detecting the peaks and valleys of this signal, a heart-rate time series can be extracted. In some cases, if the subject is stationary, it is also possible to get a measure of the vasoconstriction (vessel constriction) of peripheral blood vessels by looking at the envelope of the signal. Vasoconstriction is a defensive reaction (Kahneman, 1973) in which peripheral blood vessels constrict. This phenomena increases in response to pain, hunger, fear, and rage and decreases in response to quiet relaxation; it may also be a valuable signal indicating affect (Frija, 1986). Figure 14.2 shows an example of a reflectance PPG reading of a blood volume pulse signal with increasing vasoconstriction.

The PPG sensor can be placed anywhere on the body where the capillaries are close to the surface of the skin, but peripheral locations such as the fingers are recommended for studying emotional responses (Thought Technology, 1994). PPG sensors require no gels or adhesives; however, the reading is very sensitive to variations in placement and to motion artifacts. For example, if the light sensor is moved with respect to the blood vessel, the envelope of the signal will change or the signal might be lost entirely. This can happen if the sensor slips from an ear clip or, using a finger placement, if the sensor is

bumped during normal daily activities. If a finger placement is used, it should be noted that the signal will also strongly attenuate if the wearer lifts his or her hand up, since blood flow to the extremity will thus be diminished.

Recently new noncontact technologies have been developed to measure the photoplethysmographic effect using a webcam and visible light sources (red, green, and blue color sensors) in conjunction with blind source-separation techniques (Poh, McDuff, & Picard, 2010). These techniques have been shown to correlate PPG and visible sensor results, particularly from the green sensor, and have been shown to accurately estimate mean heart rate for many users; however, this signal does not exactly replicate the details of standard PPG signals and requires the user to remain facing the camera.

Heart Rate and Heart-Rate Variability

Two of features most commonly used in affective computing research are heart rate and heart-rate variability. Heart rate gives an excellent view of ANS activity because it is controlled by both the sympathetic and parasympathetic nervous systems. The sympathetic nervous system accelerates heart rate and can be viewed as the part of the ANS that

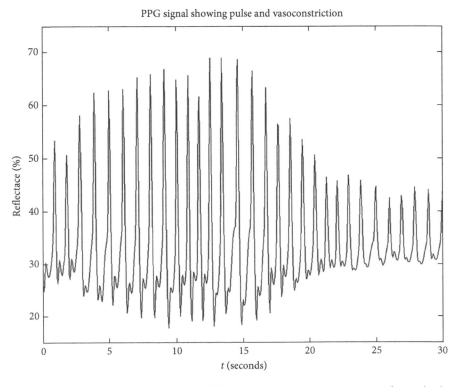

Fig. 14.2 An example of blood volume pulse recorded by a PPG sensor showing vasoconstriction as can be seen by the narrowing of the envelope of the signal.

is related to "stress," or activation. The parasympathetic nervous system is responsible for recovering heart rate from sympathetic activation (decelerating heart rate) and can be viewed as the system responsible for "relaxation," or rest and healing.

An increase in heart rate indicates an overall increase in sympathetic nervous system activity; a decrease in heart rate indicates that the parasympathetic nervous system is moving toward a relaxation state. Many different features can be extracted from periods of acceleration and deceleration—for example, the mean difference over baseline, the amount of time spent in acceleration versus deceleration and the magnitude or slope of the acceleration or deceleration.

Heart-rate variability (HRV) has also been used as a measure of affect. The term *heart rate variability* is used to describe a number of metrics, some of which are calculated in the time domain and others in the frequency domain. An HRV metric can be as simple as the measure of the standard deviation of the length of time between successive heartbeats within a certain time window (also called "the recording epoch") (Berntson, et al., 1997). Simple robust metrics like this are often best for use with short time windows, since the amount of information available in the window is limited (van Ravenswaaij-Arts, Kollee, Hopman, Stoelinga, & van Geijn, 1993). Other metrics of HRV include calculating the difference between the maximum and the minimum normal R-R interval lengths within the window (van Ravenswaaij-Arts, Kollee, Hopman, Stoelinga, & van Geijn, 1993), the percent differences between successive normal R-R intervals that exceed 50 milliseconds (pNN50), and the root mean square successive difference,also referred to by its acronym RMSSD (Kamath & Fallen, 1998).

As digital recording devices and signal processing algorithms have come into more common usage, short-term power spectral density analysis of the heart rate has become more popular as a method for assessing heart- rate variability. Since it is known that the parasympathetic nervous system is able to modulate heart rate effectively at all frequencies between 0.04 and 0.5 Hz, whereas the sympathetic system modulates heart rate with significant gain only below 0.1Hz (Akselrod, Gordon, Ubel, Shannon, & Cohen, 1981; Berntson, et al., 1997), the relative strengths of the sympathetic and parasympathetic influence on HRV can be discriminated in the spectral domain. This ratio is often referred to as the sympathovagal balance. There are many different ways to calculate this balance, each with its own merits. More specific metrics—for example, narrower and lower-frequency bands—usually require longer time windows of heartbeats to obtain the detailed information necessary to fill specific bands with enough data points to be meaningful.

One simple sympathovagal ratio calculation is to take the energy in the low frequency band (0.04 and 0.1Hz) and divide by the total energy in the (0.04 to 0.5Hz) band which gives the ratio of sympathetic to all heart rate activity. Other researchers suggest comparing low frequency energy to different combinations of low, medium and high frequency energy (Aasman, Mulder, & Mulder, 1987; Akselrod, Gordon, Ubel, Shannon, & Cohen, 1981; Itoh, Takeda, & Nakamura, 1995; Kamath & Fallen, 1998; van Ravenswaaij-Arts, Kollee, Hopman, Stoelinga, & van Geijn, 1993). Another spectral feature that is of interest to affective computing researchers is the 0.1-Hz peak of the heart-rate spectrum, which has been associated with sympathetic tone and mental stress (Nickel, Nachreiner, & von Ossietzky, 2003), although other researchers have found that an increase in the 0.1-Hz spectrum can occur with practiced relaxed breathing (McCraty, Atkinsom, & Tiller, 1995).

Each HRV metric is differently robust to noise, outliers, irregular beats, and the precision with which it can distinguish sympathetic versus parasympathetic activity. In addition to choosing the appropriate metric, researchers must also choose the appropriate time window for the heart-rate series over which she or he wishes to calculate the metric. The choice of metric will largely be determined by which variables are of interest and the quality of the heart-rate time series that can be derived from the cardiac signal. In general, a time window of 5 minutes or more is recommended; assuming a resting heart rate of 60 beats per minute, this generates a sample size of 300 beats from which to estimate variability statistics. As with all statistics, the more samples you have, the better your estimate. In particular with heart-rate variability, it should be considered that heart rate varies naturally over the breath cycle, accelerating after inhalation and decelerating after exhalation. Taking a longer time window allows multiple heart-rate samples from all parts of the breath cycle to be incorporated into the estimate.

Other Factors

Emotion is not the only factor that affects heart rate and heart-rate variability, and these other factors also need to be taken into account in interpreting heart-rate features. These factors include age, posture, level of physical conditioning, breathing frequency (van Ravenswaaij-Arts et al., 1993), and circadian cycle (Berntson et al., 1997). As age increases, heart-rate variability decreases. For example, infants have a high level of sympathetic activity, but this decreases quickly between ages 5 and 10 (van Ravenswaaij-Arts et al., 1993). In the case of certain diseases, such as congestive heart failure, heart-rate variability goes to near zero and the heart beats like a metronome. In pooling data between subjects, especially subjects of different ages and physical conditions, these differences need to be considered, in addition to potentially excluding participants who have pacemakers or are taking medication to control heart rate. Physical activity, talking, and posture (sitting versus standing versus lying down) also all affect heart rate and HRV (Picard & Healey, 1997; van Ravenswaaij-Arts et al., 1993). This should be considered in monitoring HRV "in the wild," as it can confound affective signals and the planning of experiments that may involve different activities, postures, or posture transitions.

A nonphysiological factor that must also be considered is the quality of the heart-rate signal. Many factors can affect how well the measured heart rate actually reflects the true heart rate. One factor is the measurement method. The ECG can give a much more accurate instantaneous heart rate and is the preferred signal for calculating heart rate variability; this is mainly because the sharp R waves of the ECG give a much clearer picture of when the heart beats than do the more gentle slopes of the PPG signal. However, no beat detection is perfect, and if the underlying signal was not sampled at the appropriate rate, R waves can be entirely missed by some digital recordings. Alternatively, there may be irregular "ectopic" heartbeats that can confound some algorithms. As mentioned previously, when a beat is perceived to be "missed," some signal processing algorithms may employ corrective measures such as dividing the long intervals in half, which can introduce artifacts into the HRV metric (the evenly split interval would indicate less variability than was actually present).

Finally, researchers should be aware that HRV metrics assume that the statistics of the heart-rate time series are stationary(relatively unchanging circumstances) over the time window of interest. This assumption is more likely to be true for supine, resting subjects in hospitals than it is for active subjects going about the activities of daily living. It is generally assumed that longer time windows will give more accurate HRV estimates because there will be more data points in each spectral bin; however, this is true only if the stationarity assumption is not violated. Windows as short as 30 seconds have been used on ECGs that are free of missed beats and motion artifacts (Kamath & Fallen, 1998; van Ravenswaaij-Arts et al., 1993).

Skin Conductance

Skin conductance, also commonly referred to as the galvanic skin response (GSR) or electrodermal activity, is another commonly used measure of affect. Skin conductance is used to indirectly measure the amount of sweat in a person's sweat glands, since the skin is normally an insulator and its conductivity primarily changes in response to ionic sweat filling the sweat glands. Sweat-gland activity is an indicator of sympathetic activation and GSR is a robust noninvasive way to measure this activation (Caccioppo, Berntson, Larsen, Poehlmann, & Ito, 2000). GSR was first famously used by Carl Jung to identify "negative complexes" in word-association tests (Jung & Montague, 1969) and is a key component in lie detector tests—tests that actually measure the emotional stress associated with lying rather than untrue facts (Marston, 1938). In laboratory studies to measure affect (Ekman, Levenson, & Friesen, 1983; Levenson, 1992; Winton, Putnam, & Krauss, 1984), skin conductivity response has been found to vary linearly with the emotional aspect of arousal (Lang, 1995), and skin conductance measurements have been used to differentiate between states such as anger and fear (Ax, 1953) and conflict and no conflict (Kahneman, 1973). Skin conductance has also been used as a measure of stress in studies on anticipatory anxiety and stress during task performance (Boucsein, 1992).

Skin conductance can be measured anywhere on the body; however, the most emotionally reactive sweat glands are concentrated on the palms of the hands and the soles of the feet (Boucsein, 1992). In laboratory studies, the most common placement for electrodes is on the lower segment of the middle and index finger of the dominant hand. A low-conductivity gel is usually used between the skin and the electrodes to ensure good contact and better signal quality. To measure conductance, a small current is injected into the skin and the resulting change of voltage is measured (Dawson, Schell, & Fillon, 1990, Boucsein 1992). Using the standard placement, the electrical path of the current passes through the palm as it travels from the base of one finger to the other. By constantly measuring the change in voltage across the electrodes, the continuously changing conductance of the skin can be measured.

For ambulatory studies, alternative placements are sometimes used, since hand placement is often found to be inconvenient by participants and signal quality from hand placements can be compromised by hand motion and activities that deposit or remove residue from the surface of the palms, such as handwashing or eating. Additionally, since hands are frequently in use, the electrodes can become dislodged during daily life. Therefore many ambulatory skin conductivity sensors measure conductivity on the wrist, arm, or leg (BodyMedia, Q Sensor, Basis). Some research systems have also included measuring skin conductivity through clothing or jewelry (Healey, 2011a; Picard & Healey, 1997).

An example of the time-varying skin conductance response is shown in Figure 14.3. Here an audio stimulus (a 20-millisecond white noise burst) was played as a prime to elicit "orienting responses" (also known as startle responses). We recorded ground truth for the audio prime using a microphone trace, which was overlaid on the figure at the mean value of 3 as a reference for interpreting the signal. Examples of seven orienting responses are labeled in the figure. The first major response, 1, occurred at the beginning of the experiment and was not stimulated by an audio burst. It was likely caused by the computer making a small "click" at the beginning of the audio program, but because this ground truth was not recorded we would say that this response was "unstimulated," meaning simply that we did not intentionally stimulate it. The second reaction, 2, is stimulated by the first sound burst, and responses 3, 5, and 7 are stimulated by the successive sound bursts. A second "unstimulated" response occurs between 5 and 7.

The amplitude of an orienting response is usually measured as the height difference between the minimum at the upward inflection point and the next local maximum and the following downwards inflection point. This amplitude is indicated in Figure 14.3 by the dotted lines just preceding (to the left of) each labeled peak. Responses 3, 4, and 5 show successively decreased magnitudes, indicating habituation to the stimulus. Response 7 shows recovery from habituation.

In affective computing, commonly extracted features from skin conductance include mean

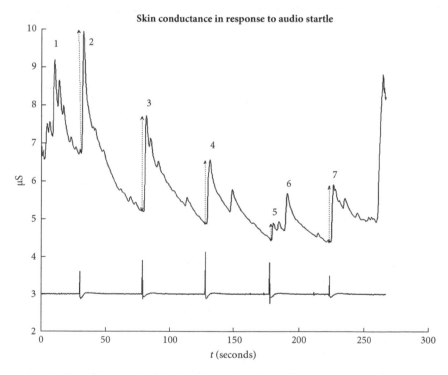

Fig. 14.3 An example of a skin conductance signal showing characteristic orienting in response to an audio stimulus. The microphone signal used to record ground truth for the stimulus is superimposed (at 3 micro Siemens) to show the relationship between stimulus and response.

conductivity level, variance, slope, and maximum and minimum levels from this signal as well as features of the orienting response described in the previous paragraph. Commonly used features of the orienting response include the amplitude (the distance from the inflection point of the slope at the beginning of the rise to the point of zero slope at the peak), the latency (the time between the prime and the inflection point), the rise time (the time between the inflection point and the peak), and the half-recovery time (the time between the zero slope at peak until the conductivity has dropped to the value at the inflection point plus half of the amplitude) (Boucsein, 1992; Damasio, 1994). Figure 14.3 also shows habituation (Groves & Thompson, 1970), or a decrease in response after repeated stimuli. Most engineering analytics make the assumption that responses to stimuli are both linear and time-invariant (meaning that the system will give the same response at different times, regardless of history). This example shows that skin conductance response is neither linear nor time invariant. The violation of these assumptionsand other factors, such as baseline drift and conductance changes due increased or decreased contact between the electrodes and the skin, introduce confounding factors into interpreting GSR and into pooling features from different time periods (for example, morning vs. evening)(Healey, 2011b).

Additional Physiological Signals

Although most of this chapter focuses on a detailed presentation of the measurement of cardiac activity and skin conductance, there many other physiological signals have been considered in affective computing research, including those derived from electroencephalography, electromyography, the measurement of blood pressure (sphygmomanometry) and respiration, and others. This section gives a brief overview of these measures and how they are used by affective computing researchers.

Electroencephalography

The electroencephalogram (EEG) measures electrical activity of the brain by the placement of electrodes on the surface of the head. The topic of electroencephalography is vast and has been extensively studied in the field of neuroscience (see Muhl et al., this volume); however, the electrical signals from the brain that an EEG reads are also physiological signals and should be mentioned here in that context. Recently there has been a widening body of literature (Coan & Allen, 2004; Davidson,

2004) indicating that asymmetries in the prefrontal cortex (PFC) seem to correspond to how different emotions, such as anger, are processed and how the PFC may be acting as a moderator or mediator between physiological responses and cognitive processing. For the first time we may begin to see and model how the "mind" and "body" work together in processing emotion and thus gain greater insights into the duality that James and Cannon debated.

From the perspective of the physiological processing of affective signals, most researchers tend to gravitate toward EEG because it is one of the most noninvasive and accessible tools for getting some sense of brain activity, even if other metrics such as functional magnetic resonance imaging are far more accurate. A full EEG incorporates over 128 electrodes; however, simpler metrics using two or four channels are used in biofeedback practice (Thought Technology, 1994). In laboratory experiments, full EEG has been shown to distinguish between positive and negative emotional valence (Davidson, 1994) and different arousal levels (Leventhal, 1990). EEG can also be used to detect the orienting response by detecting "alpha blocking." In this phenomenon, alpha waves (8 to 13 Hz) become extinguished and beta waves (14 to 26 Hz) become dominant when the person experiences a startling event (Leventhal, 1990). In the past, EEG has been less favored as a measure of emotion detection because the full EEG was challenging to both apply and interpret and the reduced electrode sets were considered unreliable. The EEG also reacts to changes in light and sound and is sensitive to both motion and muscle activity, so it is sometimes difficult to interpret outside of controlled laboratory conditions. During normal waking activity, it has been hypothesized that EEG could only be used as a crude measure of arousal (Leventhal, 1990), but perhaps new discoveries such as the asymmetry properties may change this view.

Electromyography

The electromyogram (EMG) measures muscle activity by detecting surface voltages that occur when a muscle is contracted. In affective computing, the EMG is used to measure muscle activation. For example, the EMG has been used on facial muscles to study facial expression (Levenson, Ekman, & Friesen, 1990), on the body to study affective gestures (Marrin & Picard, 1998), and as both an indicator of emotional valence (Lang, 1995) and emotional arousal (Caccioppo et al., 2000; Cacioppo & Tassinary, 1990). EMG can be used as a wearable substitute for affective changes that are usually detected by computer vision from a camera looking at a subject. The main difficulty is that EMG electrodes need both adhesives and gels under normal use and, when placed on the face, they can be seen, which may attract unwanted attention.

Like both the ECG and the EEG, the EMG works by detecting electrical signals on the surface of the skin. In a typical configuration, three electrodes are used, two placed along the axis of the muscle of interest and a third off axis to act as a ground. The EMG signal is actually a very high frequency signal, but in most common usages the signal is low-pass filtered to reflect the aggregate muscle activity and is sampled at 10 to 20 Hz.

Blood Pressure (Sphygmomanometry)

Blood pressure is used as a metric for overall health and general emotional stress. In affective computing research, blood pressure has been found to correlate with increases in emotional stress (Selye, 1956) and with the repression of emotional responses (Gross, 2002; Harris, 2001; Innes, Millar, & Valentine, 1959). The main challenges with blood pressure as a metric in affective computing are that it is difficult to measure continuously and the measurement itself requires constricting a blood vessel to measure pressure, which can be noticeable and might cause discomfort. Continuous ambulatory blood pressure monitoring systems have been used in medical practice (Pickering, Shimbo, & Haas, 2006), but these can be perceived as cumbersome. Smaller, more portable systems that measure blood pressure from peripheral blood vessels exist (Finapres, 2013), but with long-term use they may cause damage to these smaller vessels.

Respiration

Owing to the strong influence of respiration on heart rate, respiration is an interesting physiological signal to consider for affective computing both as a signal in its own right and to consider in conjunction with other measures such as cardiac activity. Respiration is most accurately recorded by measuring the gas exchange of the lungs; however, this method is excessively cumbersome and inhibits natural activities. Because of this, an approximate measure of respiratory activity, such as chest cavity expansion, is often recorded instead. Chest cavity expansion can be measured by a strap sensor that incorporates a strain gauge, a Hall effect sensor, or a capacitance sensor.

Both physical activity and emotional arousal are reported to cause faster and deeper respiration, while peaceful rest and relaxation are reported to lead to slower and shallower respiration (Frija, 1986). Sudden, intense, or startling stimuli can cause a momentary cessation of respiration, and negative emotions have been reported to cause irregularity in respiration patterns (Frija, 1986). The respiration signal can also be used to assess physical activities such as talking, laughing, sneezing, and coughing (Picard & Healey, 1997).

Conclusions

Physiological sensing is an important tool for affective computing researchers. While the extent to which emotion is a cognitive versus physiological processes is still unresolved, there is wide agreement that physiological responses at least in some way reflect emotional state. Physiological monitoring offers a continuous, discreet method for computer systems to get information about a person's emotional state. Physiological signals have been used successfully to distinguish among different levels of stress (86% to 97%) (Healey & Picard, 2005; van den Broek, Janssen, Westerink, & Healey, 2009), different categories of emotion in the laboratory (70% to 91%) (van den Broek et al., 2009) and in the wild (Healey, 2011b; Healey, Nachman, Subramanian, Shahabdeen, & Morris, 2010; van den Broek et al., 2009).

There are many challenges to recognizing emotion from physiology. One of the most basic challenges pervades all of affective computing: that of correctly labeling the data with an emotion descriptor. In a laboratory, emotions can be acted or primed (e.g., the subject can be scared, frustrated, rewarded, be made to laugh, etc.); while acting may not result in a purely authentic response and primes might not always be successful, at least the start time of the attempted emotion is known. This greatly facilitates windowing the continuous physiological data for analysis. In the wild, the onset of an emotion is often unclear, especially because the subject may be unaware of the occurrence of the natural "prime" because he or she is caught up in the emotion itself. And not only does the participant have to notice the onset, he or she must record the time precisely. Often, in end-of-day interviews, participants can remember being upset "during a meeting," but the exact onset is often imprecise, which makes the data difficult to window (Healey, Nachman, Subramanian, Shahabdeen, & Morris, 2010). This causes noise in the windowing of the data. Another challenge is subject self-perception of emotion. Everyone has his or her own personal experience of emotion, and while emotion theorists have worked hard to try to identify universal commonalities of emotion, subject often self-describe emotions in colloquial terms that are hard to classify; for example, a participant might say that he or she felt "happy to be out of that meeting," and if given a forced choice of basic emotions (e.g., anger, sadness, fear, joy, surprise, or disgust), the participant might describe this emotion as "joy" when actually it might more accurately be described as "relief." In emotion theory this would be considered a negative value for "fear," but it is not likely that ordinary people would describe it this way. People also tend to report as emotion feelings such as "boredom, anxiety, fatigue, loneliness, and hunger," which fall outside of what is traditionally studied in emotion research. In dealing with subject self-reports, the best solution is either to educate the participants about the particular emotion types you, as the researcher, are interested in studying (Healey, 2011b) or consider building algorithms for these nonemotion categories that seem to be of interest for people to record.

A different type of challenge is the many-to-one mapping between nonemotional and emotional influences on physiology (Cacioppo & Tassinary, 1990). If a physiological change occurs, there is no guarantee that an emotion generated the change; conversely, nonemotional changes can occur during emotional episodes and add their effect to the physiological response. For example, a person who is quite calm and relaxed could suddenly sneeze, which would cause a dramatic rise in instantaneous heart rate, blood pressure, and galvanic skin response. Physiologically the person is startled by the experience, but to what extent is this an affective change? A sneeze does not likely impact mood as dramatically as it does physiology. Similarly, if a person gets up from a desk and walks down a hallway, he or she will have a physiological activation but not necessarily a change of emotion. An accelerometer can be used to capture the occurrence of motion, so that these episodes can be excluded from affective analysis, but is very difficult to extract affective signals in the presence of motion. The main reasons for this are that humans are not identical, nor are they linear, time-invariant systems. Heart rate does not increase linearly with effort or emotion even for an individual person, and it increases differently in response to both effort and emotion across individuals. There is currently no method for accurately predicting an individual's physiological response to motion, so it is

even more difficult to attempt to "subtract it off" from the emotional signal. There is also no known method for doing source separation between emotional and nonemotional responses.

A less fundamental challenge is that of recording sufficient physiological data for analysis. Currently high-quality recording devices are both expensive and inconvenient to wear. This often limits the number of subjects that can be run in a study and the length of time the subjects are willing to wear the sensors. As a result, affective physiological datasets tend to be small and are often not shared, which makes collecting large sample sizes for collective and individual models difficult (Healey, 2012).

This chapter has presented different ways of measuring some of the most commonly used physiological metrics in affective computing as well as the advantages of using different methods to record these signals. The goal has been to impart a basic understanding of physiological mechanisms behind some of the most popular features reported in the literature and to introduce different sensing methods so that researchers can make informed decisions as to which method is best for a particular experiment or application. With the materials presented in this chapter, a practitioner in affective computing research can be better equipped to incorporate physiological sensing methods into her or his research methods. As sensing methods improve in popularity and wearability and our access to contextual information grows, affective physiological signal processing may soon start to move into the realm of big data, which could lead to a breakthrough in the field. If enough participants were able to own and wear sensors at all times and were willing to allow contextual data to be collected from their phones, we might finally be able have a large collection of physiological signals with high-confidence affect labels (Healey, 2012). Data could be labeled with both subject self-report and contextual information such as time of day, weather, activity, and who the subject was with so as to make an assessment of affective state. Even friends could contribute labels for each other's data. With sufficiently large ground truth datasets, we will likely be able to develop better contextually aware algorithms for individuals and like groups even if the sensor data are noisier. These algorithms will enable affective computing in a private, personal, and continuous way and allow our devices to both know us better and be able to communicate more effectively on our behalf with the world around us.

References

Aasman, J., Mulder, G., & Mulder, L. (1987). Operator effort and the measurement of heart rate variability. *Human Factors, 29*(2), 161–170.

Akselrod, S., Gordon, D., Ubel, F. A., Shannon, D. C., & Cohen, R. J. (Jul 10, 1981). Power spectrum analysis of heart rate fluctuation: A quantitative probe of beat-to-beat cardiovascular control. *Science, 213*(4504), 220–222.

Ax, A. F. (September 1, 1953). The physiological differentiation between fear and anger in humans. *Psychosomatic Medicine, 15*(5), 433–442.

Berntson, G. C., Bigger, J. T., Eckberg, D. L., Grossman, P., Kaufmann, P. G., Malik, M.,…van der Molen, M. W. (November, 1997). Heart rate variability: origins, methods, and interpretive caveats. *Psychophysiology, 34*(6), 623–648.

Boucsein, W. (1992). *Electrodermal activity.* New York: Plenum Press.

Caccioppo, J. T., Berntson, G. G., Larsen, J. T., Poehlmann, K. M., & Ito, T. A. (2000). The psychophysiology of emotion. In M. Lewis & J. M. Haviland (Eds.),, *Handbook of emotions* (pp. 173–191). New York: Guilford Press.

Cacioppo, J. T., & Tassinary, L. G. (1990). *Principles of psychophysiology: Physical, social, and inferential elements.* New York: Cambridge University Press.

Cannon, W. B. (1927). The James-Lange theory of emotion: A critical examination and an alternative theory. *American Journal of Psychology, 39*, 10–124.

Coan, J. A., & Allen, J. B. (October 2004). Frontal EEG as a moderator and mediator of emotion. *Biological Psychology, 67*(1–2), 7–50.

Damasio, A. R. (1994). *Descartes' error: Emotion, reason and the human brain.* New York: Gosset Putnam Press.

Darwin, C. (1872). *The expression of emotion in man and animals.* London: John Murray.

Davidson, R. J. (1994). Asymmetric brain function, affective style and psychopathology: The role of early experience and plasticity. *Development and Psychopathology, 6*, 741–758.

Davidson, R. J. (2004). What does the prefrontal cortex "do" in affect: Perspectives on frontal EEG asymmetry research. *Biological Psychology, 67*, 219–233.

Dawson, M., Schell, A., & Fillon, D. (1990). The electrodermal system. In J. T. Cacioppo, & L. G. Tassinary (Eds.), *Principles of psychophysiology* (pp. 295–324). New York: Cambridge University Press.

Ekman, P., Levenson, R. W., & Friesen, W. V. (September 16, 1983). autonomic nervous system activity distinguishes among emotions. *Science, 221*(4616), 1208–1210.

Eysenck, H. J. (1947). *Dimensions of personality.* London: Routledge and Kegan Paul.

Finapres. (August 1, 2013). Portapres product page. Available at: http://www.finapres.com/site/page/2/9/Portapres/

Frija, N. (1986). *The emotions.* Cambridge, UK: Cambridge University Press.

Goldberger, A. (2006). *Clinical electrocardiography: A simplified approach.* Philadelphia,: Mosby Elsevier.

Gross, J. J. (2002). Emotion regulation: Affective, cognitive, and social consequences. *Psychophysiology, 39*, 281–291.

Groves, P. M., & Thompson, R. F. (September 1970). Habituation: A dual process theory. *Psychological Review, 77*(5), 419–450.

Harris, C. R. (2001). Cardiovascular responses of embarrassment and effects of emotional suppression in a social setting. *Journal of Personality and Social Psychology, 81*, 886–897.

Healey, J. (2011a). GSR sock: A new e-Textile sensor prototype. *Fifteenth annual international symposium on wearable computers* (pp. 113–114). Washington, DC: IEEE.

Healey, J. (2011b). Recording affect in the field: Towards methods and metrics for improving ground truth labels. *Affective computing and intelligent interaction* (pp. 107–116). New York: Springer.

Healey, J. (December 8, 2012). Towards creating a standardized data set for mobile emotion context awareness. *NIPS 2012 workshop—Machine learning approaches to mobile context awareness.* Available at: goo.gl/VQl29x

Healey, J., & Picard, R. W. (2005). Detecting stress during real-world driving tasks using physiological sensors. *Transactions on intelligent transportation systems, 6*(2), 156–166.

Healey, J., Nachman, L., Subramanian, S., Shahabdeen, J., & Morris, M. (2010). Out of the lab and into the fray: Towards modeling emotion in everyday life. In Floréen, P., Krüger, A. and Spasojevic, M. (Ed.), Lecture Notes in Computer Science: Pervasive Computing (pp. 156–173). Berlin: Springer.

Hofmann, S. G., & Barlow, D. H. (1996). Ambulatory psychophysiological monitoring: A potentially useful tool when treating panic relapse. *Cognitive and Behavioral Practice, 3*, 53–61.

Innes, G., Millar, W. M., & Valentine, M. (1959). Emotion and blood pressure. *The British Journal of Psychiatry, 105*, 840–851.

Itoh, H., Takeda, K., & Nakamura, K. (August 4, 1995). Young borderline hypertensives and hyperreactive to mental arithmetic stress: Spectral analysis of r-r intervals. *Journal of the Autonomic Nervous System, 54*(2), 155–162.

James, W. (1893). *The principles of psychology.* Cambridge, MA: Harvard University Press.

Jung, C. G., & Montague, D. E. (1969). *Studies in word association: Experiments in the diagnosis of psychopathological conditions carried out at the Psychiatric Clinic of the University of Zurich under the direction of C. G. Jung.* New York: Routledge and Kegan Paul.

Kahneman, D. (1973). Arousal and attention. In D. Kahneman (Ed.), *Attention and effort* (pp. 28–49). Englewood Cliffs, NJ: Prentice-Hall.

Kamath, M. V., & Fallen, E. L. (1998). Heart rate variability: Indicators of user state as an aid to human computer interaction. *SIGCHI conference on human factors in computing systems* (pp. 480–487). Los Angeles: Association for Computing Machinery.

Lang, P. J. (1995). The emotion probe: Studies of motivation and attention. *American Psychologist, 50*(5), 372–385.

Levenson, R. W. (1992). Autonomic nervous system differences among emotions. *Psychological Science, 3*(1), 23–27.

Levenson, R. W., Ekman, P., & Friesen, W. V. (1990). Voluntary facial action generates emotion-specific autonomic nervous system activity. *Psychophysiology, 27*(4), 363–384.

Leventhal, C. F. (1990). *Introduction to physiological psychology.* Englewood Cliffs, NJ: Prentice Hall.

Marrin, T., & Picard, R. W. (1998). Analysis of affective musical expression with the conductor's jacket. Paper presented at the *XII colloquium for musical informatics*, September 24-26, 1998, Gorizia, Italy. Retrieved from http://vismod.media.mit.edu/pub/tech-reports/TR-475.pdf.

Marston, W. M. (1938). *The lie detector test.* New York: R. R. Smith.

McCraty, R., Atkinsom, M., & Tiller, W. (1995). The effects of emotions on short term power spectrum spectrum analysis of heart rate variability. *American Journal of Cardiology, 76,* 1089–1093.

Nickel, P., Nachreiner, F., & von Ossietzky, C. (2003). Sensitivity and diagnosticity of the 0.1-Hz component of heart rate variability as an indicator of mental workload. *Human Factors, 45*(4), 575–590.

Picard, R. W., & Healey, J. (1997). Affective wearables. *1st international symposium on wearable computers.* Washington, DC: IEEE.

Pickering, T. G., Shimbo, D., & Haas, D. (2006). Ambulatory blood-pressure monitoring. *New England Journal of Medicine, 354,* 2368–2374.

Poh, M.-Z., McDuff, D. J., & Picard, R. W. (2010). Noncontact, automated cardiac pulse measurements using video imaging and blind source separation. *Optics Express, 18*(10), 10762–10774.

Schachter, S. (1964). The interaction of cognitive and physiological determinants of emotional state. In L. Berkowitz (Ed.), *Advances in experimental social psychology* (pp. 49–79). New York: Academic Press.

Selye, H. (1956). *The stress of life.* New York: McGraw-Hill.

Thought Technology. (1994). ProComp user's manual software version 1.41. Quebec: Author.

van den Broek, E., Janssen, J. H., Westerink, J., & Healey, J. A. (2009). Prerequsites for affective signal processing (ASP). *International conference on bio-inspired systems and signal processing* (pp. 426–433). New York: Springer.

van Ravenswaaij-Arts, C., Kollee, L. A., Hopman, J. C., Stoelinga, G. B., & van Geijn, H. P. (1993). Heart rate variability. *Annals of Internal Medicine,* 118 (6), 436–447.

Winton, W. M., Putnam, L. E., & Krauss, R. M. (1984). Facial and autonomic manifestations of the dimensional structure of emotion. *Journal of Experimental Social Psychology,* 20, 195–216.

Zajonc, R. B. (1994). Evidence for non-conscious emotions. In P. Ekman, & R. J. Davidson (Eds.), *The nature of emotion: Fundamental questions* (pp. 293–297). New York: Oxford University Press.

Affective Brain-Computer Interfaces: Neuroscientific Approaches to Affect Detection

Christian Mühl, Dirk Heylen, *and* Anton Nijholt

Abstract

The brain is involved in the registration, evaluation, and representation of emotional events and in the subsequent planning and execution of appropriate actions. Novel interface technologies—so-called affective brain-computer interfaces (aBCI)—can use this rich neural information, occurring in response to affective stimulation, for the detection of the user's affective state. This chapter gives an overview of the promises and challenges that arise from the possibility of neurophysiology-based affect detection, with a special focus on electrophysiological signals. After outlining the potential of aBCI relative to other sensing modalities, the reader is introduced to the neurophysiological and neurotechnological background of this interface technology. Potential application scenarios are situated in a general framework of brain-computer interfaces. Finally, the main scientific and technological challenges that have yet to be solved on the way toward reliable affective brain-computer interfaces are discussed.

Key Words: brain-computer interfaces, emotion, neurophysiology, affective state

Introduction

Affect-sensitive human-computer interaction (HCI), in order to provide the choice of adequate responses to adapt the computer to the affective states of its user, requires a reliable detection of these states—that is, of the user's emotions. A number of behavioral cues, such as facial expression, posture, and voice, can be informative about these states. Other sources, less open to conscious control and therefore more reliable in situations where behavioral cues are concealed, can be assessed in the form of physiological responses to emotional events; for example, changes in heart rate and skin conductance. A special set of physiological responses comprises those originating from the most complex organ of the human body, the brain. These neurophysiological responses to emotionally significant events can, alone or in combination with other sources of affective information, be used to detect affective states continuously, clarify the context in which they occur, and help to guide affect-sensitive HCI. In this chapter, we elucidate the motivation and background of affective brain-computer interfaces (aBCIs), the devices that enable the transformation of neural activity into affect-sensitive HCI; outline their working principles and their applications in a general framework of BCI; and discuss main challenges of this novel affect-sensing technology.

The Motivation Behind Affective Brain-Computer Interfaces

The brain is an interesting organ for the detection of cues about the affective state. Numerous lesion studies, neuroimaging evidence, and theoretical arguments have strengthened the notion that the brain is not only the seat of our rational thought but also heavily involved in emotional responses that often are perceived as disruptive to our rational behavior (Damasio, 2000). Scherer's component process model (Scherer, 2005) postulates the existence of several components of affective responses that reside in the central nervous system, including processes of emotional event perception and evaluation, self-monitoring, and action planning and execution.[1]

Therefore the brain seems to possess great potential to differentiate affective states in terms of their neurophysiological characteristics, mostly of the neural responses that occur after encountering an emotionally salient stimulus event. Such emotional responses occur within tens of milliseconds; they are not under the volitional control of a person and hence are reliable in terms of their true nature. Such fast and automatic neurophysiological responses are contrasted by slower physiological responses in the range of seconds after the event and with behavioral cues that are more amenable to conscious influence.

In addition to the promises for a fast and reliable differentiation of affective states, the complexity of the brain also holds the potential to reveal *details* about an ongoing emotional response elicited by emotional stimulus events. Visual or auditory cortices reflect the modality-specific processing resources allocated to emotionally salient events (Mühl et al., 2011), allowing for conscious identification of the object that elicited the emotional response. Similarly, motor regions might reveal behavioral dispositions—that is, planned and prepared motor responses—to an emotional stimulus event.

Finally, certain patient populations that lose the ability to communicate with the outside world owing to the loss of musculature or its control; they need alternative communication channels—using the information available from unimpaired physiological and neurophysiological processes—that are able to reflect their emotions to loved ones as well as to caretakers.

However, the realization of all this potential, including the advantages of neurophysiological signals over other sources of information on affect, is dependent on the advancement of research within several disciplines: psychology, affective neuroscience, and machine learning. We begin with the introduction of relevant sensor technologies and then go on to discuss the neurophysiological basis and the technological principles and applications of aBCIs.

Sensor Modalities Assessing Neurophysiological Activity

Several sensor technologies enable the assessment of neurophysiological activity. Two types of methods can be distinguished by the way they function: one measures cortical electric or magnetic fields directly resulting from the nerve impulses of groups of pyramidal neurons while the other measures metabolic activity within cortical structures—for example, blood oxygenation resulting from the increased activity of these structures.

The first type of electrophysiological method, including sensor modalities such as electroencephalography (EEG) and magnetoencephalography (MEG), has a high temporal resolution of neural activity recordings (instantaneous signals with millisecond resolution) but lacks high spatial resolution owing to the smearing of the signals on their way through multiple layers of cerebrospinal fluid, bone, and skin. Most of the methods of the second type, including sensor modalities such as functional magnetic resonance imaging (fMRI) or positron emission tomography (PET), have a high spatial resolution (in the range of millimeters), but are slow because of their dependence on metabolic changes (resulting in a lag of several seconds) and their working principle (resulting in measurement rhythms of seconds rather than milliseconds).

Each of the neuroimaging methods mentioned above has its advantages, and their use depends on researchers' goals. Regarding affective computing scenarios, EEG seems to be the most practicable method: EEG has the advantage of being relatively unobtrusive and can be recorded using wearable devices, thus increasing the mobility and options for locations in which data are collected. Furthermore, the technology is affordable for private households and relatively easy to set up, especially the cheaper commercial versions for the general public, although these have limitations for research. Comparable wearable sensor modalities that are based on the brain metabolism, such as functional near-infrared spectroscopy (fNIRS), are currently not affordable nor do they feature a high spatial resolution.

To focus on the technologies relevant for aBCIs in the normal, healthy population, we briefly review below the affect-related neural structures of the central nervous system and then introduce the neurophysiological correlates of affect that are the basis for aBCI systems using EEG technology as their sensor modality.

Neurophysiological Measurements of Affect
The Neural Structures of Affect

The brain comprises a number of structures that have been associated with affective responses by different types of evidence. Much of the early evidence of the function of certain brain regions comes from observations of the detrimental effects of lesions in animals and humans. More recently, functional imaging approaches, such as PET and fMRI, have yielded insights into the processes occurring during affective responses in normal functioning (for reviews, see Barrett, Mesquita, Ochsner, & Gross, 2007; Lindquist, Wager, Kober, Bliss-moreau, & Barrett, 2011). Here we only briefly discuss the most prominent structures that have been identified as central during the evaluation of the emotional significance of stimulus events and the processes that lead to the emergence of the emotional experience. The interested reader can refer to Barrett et al. (2007) for a detailed description of the structures and processes involved.

The core of the system involved in the translation of external and internal events to the affective state is a set of neural structures in the ventral portion of the brain: the medial temporal lobe (including the amygdala, insula, and striatum), orbitofrontal cortex (OFC), and ventromedial prefrontal cortex (VMPFC). These structures compose two related functional circuits that represent the sensory information about the stimulus event and its somatovisceral impact as remembered or predicted from previous experience.

The first circuit—comprising the basolateral complex of the amygdala, the ventral and lateral aspects of the OFC, and the anterior insula—is involved in the gathering and binding of information from external and internal sensory sources. Both the amygdala and the OFC structures possess connections to the sensory cortices, enabling information exchange about perceived events and objects. While the amygdala is coding the original value of the stimulus, the OFC creates a flexible experience and context-dependent representation of the object's value. The insula represents interoceptive information from the inner organs and skin, playing a role in forming awareness about the state of the body. By the integration of sensory information and information about the body's state, a value-based representation of the event or object is created.

The second circuit, composed of the VMPFC (including the anterior cingulate cortex [ACC]) and the amygdala, is involved in the modulation of parts of the value-based representation via its control over autonomous, chemical, and behavioral visceromotor responses. Specifically, the VMPFC links the sensory information about the event, as integrated by the first circuit, to its visceromotor outcomes. It can be considered as an affective working memory that informs judgments and choices and is active during decisions based on intuitions and feelings.

Both circuits project directly and indirectly to the hypothalamus and brainstem, which are involved in a fast and efficient computation of object values and influence autonomous chemical and behavioral responses. The outcome of the complex interplay of ventral cortical structures, amygdala, hypothalamus, and brainstem establishes the "core affective" state that the event induced: an event-specific perturbation of the internal milieu of the body that directs the body to prepare for the responses necessary to deal with the event. These responses include the attentional orienting to the source of the stimulation, the enhancement of sensory processes, and the preparation of motor behavior. Perturbation of the visceromotor state is also the basis of the conscious experience of the pleasantness and physical and cortical arousal that accompany affective responses. However, as stated by Barrett et al. (2007), the emotional experience is unlikely to be the outcome of one of the structures involved in establishing the "core affect" but rather emerges on the system level as the result of the activity of many or all of the involved structures.[2]

Correlates of Affect in Electroencephalography

Before reviewing the electrophysiological correlates of affect, we must note that because of the working principles and the resulting limited spatial resolution of the EEG, a simple measurement of the activation of affect-related structures, as obtainable by fMRI, is not possible. Furthermore, most of the core-affective structures are located in the ventral part of the brain (but see Davidson, 1992; Harmon-Jones, 2003), making a direct assessment of their activity by EEG, focusing on signals from superficial neocortical regions, difficult. Hence we concentrate on electrophysiological signals that have been associated with affect and on their cognitive functions but also mention their neural origins if available.

TIME-DOMAIN CORRELATES

A significant body of research has focused on the time domain and explores the consequences of emotional stimulation on event-related potentials. Event-related potentials (ERPs) are prototypical deflections of the recorded EEG trace in response to a specific stimulus event—for example, a picture stimulus.

ERPs are computed by (samplewise) averaging of the traces following multiple stimulation events of the same condition, which reduces sporadic parts of the EEG trace not associated with the functional processes involved in response to the stimulus but originating from artifacts or background EEG.

Examples of ERPs responsive to affective manipulations include early and late potentials. Early potentials, for example P1 or N1, indicate processes involved in the initial perception and automatic evaluation of the presented stimuli. They are affected by the emotional value of a stimulus; differential ERPs are observed in response to negative and positive valence as well as low and high arousal stimuli (Olofsson, Nordin, Sequeira, & Polich, 2008). However, the evidence is far from parsimonious, as the variety of the findings shows.

Late event-related potentials are supposed to reflect higher-level processes, which are already more amenable to the conscious evaluation of the stimulus. The two most prominent potentials that have been found susceptible to affective manipulation are the P300 and the late positive potential (LPPs). The P300 has been associated with attentional mechanisms involved in the orientation toward an especially salient stimulus—for example, very rare (deviant) or expected stimuli (Polich, 2007). Coherently, P300 components show a greater amplitude in response to highly salient emotional stimuli, especially aversive ones (Briggs & Martin, 2009). The LPP has been observed after emotionally arousing visual stimuli (Schupp et al., 2000), and was associated with a stronger perceptive evaluation of emotionally salient stimuli as evidenced by increased activity of posterior visual cortices (Sabatinelli, Lang, Keil, & Bradley, 2006).

As in real-world applications, the averaging of several epochs of EEG traces with respect to the onset of a repeatedly presented stimulus is not feasible; the use of such time-domain analysis techniques is limited for affective BCIs. An alternative to ERPs—more feasible in a context without known stimulus onsets or repetitive stimulation—are effects on brain rhythms observed in the frequency domain.

FREQUENCY-DOMAIN CORRELATES

The frequency domain can be investigated with two simple but fundamentally different power extraction methods, yielding evoked and induced oscillatory responses to a stimulus event (Tallon-Baudry, Bertrand, Baudry, & Bertrand, 1999). Evoked frequency responses are computed by a frequency transformation applied to the averaged EEG trace, yielding a frequency-domain representation of the ERP components. Induced frequency responses, on the other hand, are computed by applying the frequency transform on the single EEG traces before then averaging the frequency responses. Induced responses therefore capture oscillatory characteristics of the EEG traces that are not phase-locked to the stimulus onset and averaged out in the evoked oscillatory response. In an everyday context, where the mental states or processes of interest are not elicited by repetitive stimulation with a known stimulus onset and short stimulus duration, the use of evoked oscillatory responses is just as limited as the use of ERPs. Therefore the induced oscillatory responses are of specific interest in attempting to detect affect based on a single and unique emotional event or period.

The analysis of oscillatory activity in the EEG has a tradition that reaches back over almost 90 years, to the twenties of the last century, when Hans Berger reported the existence of certain oscillatory characteristics in the EEG, now referred to as alpha and beta rhythms (Berger, 1929). The decades of research since then have led to the discovery of a multitude of cognitive and affective functions that influence the oscillatory activity in different frequency ranges. Below, we briefly review the frequency ranges of the conventional broad frequency bands—namely delta, theta, alpha, beta, and gamma, their cognitive functions, and their association with affect.

The *delta frequency band* comprises the frequencies between 0.5 and 4 Hz. Delta oscillations are especially prominent during the late stages of sleep (Steriade, McCormick, & Sejnowski, 1993). However, during waking they have been associated with motivational states such as hunger and drug craving (see Knyazev, 2012). In such states, they are supposed to reflect the workings of the brain reward system, some of the structures of which are believed to be generators of delta oscillations (Knyazev, 2012). Delta activity has also been identified as a correlate of the P300 potential, which is seen in response to salient stimuli. This has led to the belief that delta oscillations play a role in the detection of emotionally salient stimuli. Congruously, increases of delta band power have been reported in response to more arousing stimuli (Aftanas, Varlamov, Pavlov, Makhnev, & Reva, 2002; Balconi & Lucchiari, 2006; Klados et al., 2009).

The *theta rhythm* comprises the frequencies between 4 and 8 Hz. Theta activity has been observed in a number of cognitive processes; its most prominent form, frontomedial theta, is believed to originate from limbic and associated structures (i.e., ACCs) (Başar, Schürmann, & Sakowitz, 2001). It is a hallmark of working memory processes and has been found to increase with higher memory demands in various experimental paradigms (see Klimesch, Freunberger, Sauseng, & Gruber, 2008). Specifically, theta oscillations subserve central executive function, integrating different sources of information, as necessary in working memory tasks (Kawasaki, Kitajo, & Yamaguchi, 2010).

Concerning affect, early reports mention a "hedonic theta" that was reported to occur with the interruption of pleasurable stimulation. However, studies in children between 6 months and 6 years of age showed increases in theta activity upon exposure to pleasurable stimuli (see Niedermeyer, 2005). Recent studies on musically induced feelings of pleasure and displeasure found an increase of frontomedial theta activity with more positive valence (Lin, Duann, Chen, & Jung, 2010; Sammler, Grigutsch, Fritz, & Koelsch, 2007), which originated from ventral structures in the ACC. For emotionally arousing stimuli, increases in theta band power have been reported over frontal (Balconi & Lucchiari, 2006; Balconi & Pozzoli, 2009) and frontal and parietal regions (Aftanas et al., 2002). Congruously, a theta increase was also reported during anxious personal compared to nonanxious object rumination (Andersen, Moore, Venables, Corr, & Venebles, 2009).

The *alpha rhythm* comprises the frequencies between 8 and 13 Hz. It is most prominent over parietal and occipital regions, especially during the closing of the eyelids, and decreases in response to sensory stimulation, especially during visual stimulation but in a weaker manner also during auditory and tactile stimulation or during mental tasks. More anterior alpha rhythms have been specifically associated with sensorimotor activity (central mu-rhythm) (Pfurtscheller, Brunner, Schlögl, & Lopes da Silva, 2006) and with auditory processing (tau-rhythm) (Lehtelä, Salmelin, & Hari, 1997). The observed decrease of the alpha rhythm in response to (visual) stimulation, the event-related desynchronization in the alpha band, is believed to index the increased sensory processing and hence has been associated with an activation of task-relevant (sensory) cortical regions. The opposite phenomenon, an event-related synchronization in the alpha band, has been reported in a variety of studies on mental activities, such as working memory tasks, and is believed to support an active process of cortical inhibition of task-irrelevant regions (see Klimesch, Sauseng, & Hanslmayr, 2007).

The most prominent association between affective states and neurophysiology has been reported in the form of frontal alpha asymmetries (Coan & Allen, 2004), which vary as a function of valence (Silberman, 1986) or motivational direction (Davidson, 1992; Harmon-Jones, 2003). The stronger rightward lateralization of frontal alpha power during positive or approach-related emotions compared with negative or withdrawal-related emotions is believed to originate from the stronger activation of left as compared with right prefrontal structures involved in affective processes. Despite fMRI studies (e.g., Engels et al., 2007) suggesting that such simple models of lateralization underestimate the complexity of the human brain, evidence for alpha asymmetry has been found in response to a variety of different induction procedures using pictures (Balconi & Mazza, 2010; Huster, Stevens, Gerlach, & Rist, 2009), music pieces (Altenmüller, Schürmann, Lim, & Parlitz, 2002; Schmidt & Trainor, 2001; Tsang, Trainor, Santesso, Tasker, & Schmidt, 2006), and film excerpts (Jones & Fox, 1992).

The alpha rhythm has also been associated with a relaxed and wakeful state of mind (Niedermeyer, 2005). Coherently, increases of alpha power are observed during states of relaxation, as indexed by physiological measures (Barry, Clarke, Johnstone, & Brown, 2009; Barry, Clarke, Johnstone, Magee, & Rushby, 2007) and subjective self-report (Nowlis & Kamiya, 1970; Teplan & Krakovska, 2009).

The *beta rhythm* comprises the frequencies between 13 and 30 Hz. Central beta activity has been associated with the sensorimotor system, as it is weak during motor activity, motor imagination or tactile stimulation, but increases afterward (Neuper et al., 2006). That has led to the view that the beta rhythm is a sign of an "idling" motor cortex (Pfurtscheller et al., 1996). A recent proposal for a general theory of the function of the beta rhythm, however, suggests that beta oscillations impose the maintenance of the sensorimotor set for the upcoming time interval (or "signals the status quo") (see Engel & Fries, 2010). Concerning affect, increases of beta band activity have been observed over temporal regions in response to visual and self-induced positive as compared with negative emotions (Cole & Ray, 1985; Onton & Makeig, 2009). A general decrease of beta band power has been reported for stimuli that had an emotional impact on the subjective experience compared with those that were not experienced as emotional (Dan Glauser & Scherer, 2008) (see gamma rhythm for elaboration). A note of caution for the interpretation of high-frequency bands of beta and gamma is in order, as their power increases during the tension of (scalp) muscles (Goncharova et al., 2003), which are also involved in frowning and smiling.

The *gamma rhythm* comprises the frequencies above 30 Hz. Gamma band oscillations are supposed to be a key mechanism in the integration of information represented in different sensory and nonsensory cortical networks (Fries, 2009). Accordingly they have been observed in association with a number of cognitive processes, such as attention (Gruber, Müller, Keil, & Elbert, 1999), multisensory integration (Daniel Senkowski, Schneider, Tandler, & Engel, 2009), memory (Jensen, Kaiser, & Lachaux, 2007), and even consciousness (Ward, 2003).

Concerning valence, temporal gamma rhythms have been found to increase with increasingly positive valence (Müller, Keil, Gruber, & Elbert, 1999; Onton & Makeig, 2009). For arousal, posterior increases of gamma band power have been associated with the processing of high versus low arousing visual stimuli (Aftanas, Reva, Varlamov, Pavlov, & Makhnev, 2004; Balconi & Pozzoli, 2009; Keil et al., 2001). Similarly, increases of gamma activity over somatosensory cortices have also been linked to the awareness to painful stimuli (Gross, Schnitzler, Timmermann, & Ploner, 2007; Senkowski, Kautz, Hauck, Zimmermann, & Engel, 2011). However, Dan Glauser and Scherer (2008) found lower (frontal) gamma power for emotion for stimuli *with* versus those *without* an emotional impact on the subjective experience. They interpreted their findings as a correlate of the *ongoing* emotional processing in those trials that were not (yet) identified as having a specific emotional effect, and hence without impact on subjective experience. In general, increases in gamma power are often interpreted as synonymous with an increase of activity in the associated region.

Taken together, the different frequency bands of the EEG have been associated with changes in the affective state as well as with a multitude of cognitive functions. Consequently it is rather unlikely to find simple one-to-one mappings between any oscillatory activity and a given affective or cognitive function. In Controversies, Challenges, Conclusion (p. 227) we elaborate on the challenge that many-to-one mappings pose for aBCI. Nevertheless, there is an abundance of studies evidencing the association of brain rhythms with affective responses. aBCIs can thus make use of the frequency domain as a source of information about their users' affective states. In the following section, we introduce the concept of aBCIs in more detail.

Affective Brain-Computer Interfaces

The term *affective brain-computer interfaces* (aBCIs) is a direct result of the nomenclature of the field that motivates their existence: *affective computing*. With different means, aBCI research and affective computing aim toward the same end: the detection of the user's emotional state for the enrichment of human-computer interaction. While affective computing tries to integrate all the disciplines involved in this endeavor, from sensing of affect to its effective integration into human-computer interaction processes, aBCI research is mainly concerned with the detection of the affective state from neurophysiological measurements. Information about the successful detection of affective states can then be used in a variety of applications, ranging from unobtrusive mental-state monitoring and the corresponding adaptation of interfaces to neurofeedback-guided relaxation.

Originally, the term *brain-computer interface* was defined as "a communication system in which messages or commands that an individual sends to the external world do not pass through the brain's normal output pathways of peripheral nerves and muscles" (Wolpaw, Birbaumer, McFarland, Pfurtscheller, & Vaughan, 2002). The notion of an individual (volitionally) sending commands directly from the brain to a computer, circumventing standard means of communication, is of great importance considering the original target population of patients with severe neuromuscular disorders. More recently, the human-computer interaction community has developed great interest in the application of BCI approaches for larger groups of users that are not dependent on BCIs as their sole means of communication. This development and the ensuing research projects hold great potential for the further development of devices, algorithms, and approaches for BCI, also necessary for its advancement for patient populations. Along with the development of this broad interest for BCI, parts of the BCI community slowly started to incorporate new BCI approaches, such as aBCI, into its research portfolio, thus easing the confinement of BCI to interfaces serving purely volitional means of control (Nijboer, Clausen, Allison, & Haselager, 2011).

Below, we briefly introduce the parts of the aBCI: signal acquisition, signal processing (feature extraction and translation algorithm), feedback, and protocol. Then we offer an overview of the various existing and possible approaches to aBCI based on a general taxonomy of BCI approaches.

Parts of an Affective Brain-Computer Interface

Being an instance of general BCI systems (Wolpaw et al., 2002), the aBCI is defined by a sequence of procedures that transform neurophysiological signals into control signals. In Figure 15.1, we briefly outline the successive processing steps that a signal has to undergo, starting with the acquisition of the signal from the user and finishing with the application feedback given back to the user.

SIGNAL-ACQUISITION BRAIN-COMPUTER INTERFACES

These can make use of several sensor modalities that measure brain activity. Roughly, we can differentiate between invasive and noninvasive measures. While invasive measures, implanted electrodes or electrode grids, enable a more direct recording of neurophysiological activity from the cortex and therefore have a better signal-to-noise ratio, they are currently reserved for patient populations and hence are less relevant for the current overview. Noninvasive measures, on the other hand, as recorded with EEG, fNIRS, or fMRI, are also available for the healthy population. Furthermore, some of the noninvasive signal acquisition devices, especially EEG, are already available for consumers in the form of easy-to-handle and affordable headsets.[3] The present work focuses on EEG as a neurophysiological measurement tool, for which we detail the following processing steps in the BCI pipeline. A further distinction in terms of the acquired signals can be made, differentiating between those signals that are partially dependent on the standard output pathways of the brain (e.g., moving the eyes to direct the gaze toward a specific stimulus) and those that are independent on these output pathways, merely registering user intention or state. These varieties of BCI are referred to as dependent and independent BCIs, respectively. Affective BCIs, measuring the affective state of the user, are usually a variety of the latter sort of BCIs.

SIGNAL PROCESSING—FEATURE EXTRACTION

From the signals that are captured from the scalp, several signal features can be computed. We can differentiate between features in the time and in the frequency domains. An example of features in the time domain is the amplitude of stimulus-evoked potentials occurring at well-known time points after a stimulus event is observed. One of the event-related potentials used in BCI is the P300, occurring in the interval between 300 to 500 ms after an attended stimulus event. An example for signal features in the frequency domain is the power of a certain frequency band. A well-known frequency band that is used in BCI paradigms is the alpha band, which comprises the frequencies between 8 and 13 Hz. Both the time- and frequency-domain features of the EEG have been found to respond to the manipulation of affective states and are therefore in principle interesting for the detection of affective states (see Neurophysiological Measurements of Affect, p. 218). However, aBCI studies almost exclusively use features from the frequency domain (see Table 1.1 in Mühl, 2012). Conveniently, however, frequency-domain features, such as the power in the lower frequency bands (<13 Hz) are correlated with the amplitude of event-related potentials, especially the P300, and hence partially include information about time-domain features.

Standard BCI approaches focus on very specific features—for example, the mu rhythm over central scalp regions in the case of motor imagery paradigms (Pfurtscheller & Neuper, 2001), or the mean signal amplitude between 200 and 500 ms associated with

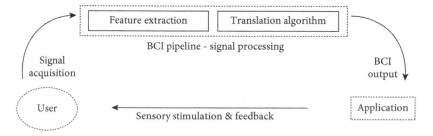

Fig. 15.1 The schematic of a general BCI system as defined by Wolpaw et al. (2002). The neurophysiological signal is recorded from the user, and the relevant features, those that are informative about user intent or state, are extracted. They are then translated into the control parameters that are used by the application to respond adequately to the user's state or intent."

each attended stimulus in P300 spellers (Farwell & Donchin, 1988). To date, however, affective BCI approaches often lack such clear-cut information on affect-related responses. Most of the current aBCI approaches make use of a wide spectrum of frequency bands, as these have been found responsive to affect manipulation (see Correlates of Affect in Electroencephalography, p. 219), resulting in a large number of potential features. However, large numbers of features require a large number of trials to train a classifier (the "curse of dimensionality") (Lotte, Congedo, Lécuyer, Lamarche, & Arnaldi, 2007), which are seldom available owing to the limitations of affect induction (e.g., the habituation of the responses toward affective stimulation with time). Therefore one of the tasks on the road toward affective BCI is the evaluation and identification of reliable signal features that carry information about the affective state, especially in the complexity of real-world environments. Another important task is the development of potent affect-induction procedures—for example, using naturally affect-inducing stimuli that increase the likelihood of inducing affective responses.

SIGNAL PROCESSING—TRANSLATION ALGORITHMS

The core part of the BCI is the translation of the selected signal features into a command for the application or device, such as a cursor movement for active BCIs or the creation of an emotion label for affective BCIs. The simple one-to-one mapping between feature and command requires a feature that conveniently mirrors the state in such manner. Because such ideal features are rare in the neurophysiological signal domain, most BCI studies use machine learning approaches that are trained to find a mapping between a number of signal features and the labels for two or more classes (see Lotte et al., 2007, for an overview of BCI classifiers). These classifiers have to adapt to the signal characteristics of the particular user, adapt to changes over time and changing contexts of interaction, and deal with the changes in brain activity due to the user's efforts in learning and adapting to the system. Classifiers used for affective BCI include linear discriminant analysis (Chanel et al., 2005; Chanel, Kierkels, Soleymani, & Pun, 2009; Chanel, Rebetez, Bétrancourt, Pun, & Bétrancourt, 2011; Makeig et al., 2011; Murugappan, 2010; Winkler, Jäger, Mihajlović, & Tsoneva, 2010) and support vector machines (Frantzidis et al., 2010; Horlings, Datcu, & Rothkrantz, 2008; Koelstra et al., 2010; Li & Lu, 2009; Y. P. Lin, Wang, Wu, Jeng, & Chen, 2009; Petrantonakis & Hadjileontiadis, 2010;

Soleymani, Lichtenauer, Pun, & Pantic, 2011; Takahashi, 2004).

THE OUTPUT DEVICE/FEEDBACK

Depending on the application the affective BCI is serving, the output can assume different forms. For BCI in general, the most prominent output devices are monitors and speakers, providing visual and auditory feedback about the user and BCI performance. In a few cases, robots (a wheelchair or car) have been controlled (Hongtao, Ting, & Zhenfeng, 2010; Leeb et al., 2007). An exceptional example of BCI output, however, is control of one's own hand by the BCI-informed functional electrical stimulation of a paralyzed hand (Pfurtscheller, Müller-Putz, Pfurtscheller, & Rupp, 2005). In the case of standard BCIs, the output has a major function relating to the adaptation of the user to the BCI mentioned above. As BCI control can be considered to be a skill, any learning necessitates the provision of feedback about successful and unsuccessful performance.

In the specific case of aBCI, the same is possible, but the smaller proportion of applications requiring active and volitional mental control, typical for standard BCI systems, and the dominance of passive paradigms (see The Different Approaches to Affective Brain-Computer Interfaces, p. 225), make explicit performance-based feedback optional rather than mandatory. Depending on their function, aBCI systems will vary in the output device and the type of feedback employed. For example, for implicit tagging or affect monitoring (for later evaluation), the feedback is not immediate. It might take hours, days, or weeks until the information is used (e.g., during affect-tagged media replay) and then it might be in a subtle way that escapes the user's attention. Such cases, in which no clear relation between state and feedback is perceivable, make the notion of feedback in these aBCI applications almost obsolete. However, in many other aBCI applications, the feedback is still existent and relevant, since the affective data are used to produce a system response in a reasonably near future. Examples are the applications that reflect the current affective state (e.g., in a game like *Alpha World of Warcraft* (Plass-Oude Bos et al., 2010), any neurofeedback-like application (e.g., warn of unhealthy states or reward healthy states), the active self-induction of affective states (e.g., relaxation), or the adaptation of games or e-learning applications to the state of the user.

THE OPERATING PROTOCOL

The operating protocol guides the operation of the BCI system—for example, switching it on and off (how/when) if the actions are triggered by the system (synchronous) or by the user (asynchronous) and when and in which manner feedback is given to the user. Other characteristics of the interaction that are defined by the protocol are whether the information is actively produced by the user or passively read by the system and whether the information is gathered dependent of a specific stimulus event (stimulus dependent/independent). These two characteristics of BCI, voluntariness and stimulus dependency, are also the basis for the characterization of different BCI approaches in the next section.

Below, we outline the different existing applications and approaches to aBCI and try to locate aBCI within the general landscape of BCI.

The Different Approaches to Affective Brain-Computer Interfaces

There are several possible applications of neurophysiology-informed affect sensing that can be categorized in terms of their dependence on stimuli and user volition. In the following, a two-dimensional classification of some of these BCI paradigms is given. It is derived from the three-category classification for BCI approaches (active, reactive, and passive) suggested by Zander and Kothe (2011).

The dimensions of this classification are defined by (1) the dependence on external stimuli and (2) the dependence on an intention to create a neural activity pattern as illustrated in Figure 15.2.

The horizontal axis stretches from exogenous (or evoked) to endogenous (or induced) input. The former covers all forms of BCI, which necessarily presuppose an external stimulus. Steady-state visually evoked potentials (Farwell & Donchin, 1988) as neural correlates of (target) stimulus frequencies, for instance, may be detected if and only if evoked by a stimulus. They are therefore a clear example of exogenous input. Endogenous input, on the other hand, does not presuppose an external stimulus but is generated by the user either volitionally, as seen in motor imagery–based BCIs (Pfurtscheller & Neuper, 2001) or involuntarily, as during the monitoring of affective or cognitive states. In the case of involuntary endogenous input—for example, during general affect monitoring—the distinction between stimulus-dependent and independent input might not always be possible, as affective responses are often induced by external stimulus events, though these might not always be obvious.

The vertical axis stretches from active to passive input. Active input presupposes an intention to

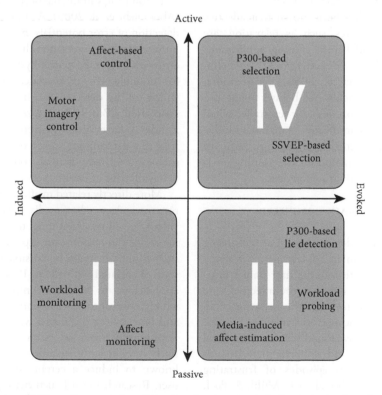

Fig. 15.2 A classification of BCI paradigms spanning voluntariness (passive versus active) and stimulus dependency (user self-induced versus stimulus-evoked).

control brain activity, while passive input does not require any effort on the part of the user. Imagined movements, for instance, can only be detected when users intend to perform these, making the paradigm a prototypical application of aBCI. All methods that probe the user's mental state, on the other hand, can also be measured when he or she does not exhibit an intention to produce it. Affective BCI approaches can be located in several of the four quadrants (categories) spanned by the two dimensions, as quite different approaches to aBCI have been suggested and implemented.

INDUCED-ACTIVE BRAIN-COMPUTER INTERFACES

This category is well known in terms of neurofeedback systems, which encourage the user to attain a certain goal state. While neurofeedback approaches do not necessarily focus on affective states, a long line of this research is concerned with the decrease of anxiety or depression by making the users more aware of their bodily and mental states (Hammond, 2005). Neurophysiological features that have been associated with a certain favorable state (e.g., relaxed wakefulness) are visualized or sonified, enabling the users of such feedback systems to learn to induce them themselves.

More recently it has been shown that affective self-induction techniques, such as relaxation, are a viable control modality in gaming applications (George, Lotte, Abad, & Lecuyer, 2011; Hjelm, 2003; but see Mühl et al., 2010). Furthermore, induced passive approaches (see below) might also turn into active approaches—for example, when players realize that their affective state has an influence on game parameters and therefore begin to self-induce states to manipulate the gaming environment according to their preferences.

INDUCED-PASSIVE BRAIN-COMPUTER INTERFACES

This category includes the typical affect-sensing method for application in HCI scenarios where a response of an application to the user state is critical. Information that identifies the affective state of a user can be used to adapt the behavior of an application to keep the user satisfied or engaged. For example, studies have found neurophysiological responses in the theta and alpha frequency bands to differentiate between episodes of frustrating and normal game play (Reuderink, Mühl, & Poel, 2013). Applications could respond to the frustration of the user with helpful advice or clarifying information. Alternatively, parameters of computer games or e-learning applications could be adjusted to keep users engaged in the interaction—for example, by decreasing or increasing difficulty to counteract the detected episodes of frustration or boredom, respectively (Chanel et al., 2011).

Another approach is the manipulation of the game world in response to the player's affective state, as demonstrated in *Alpha World of Warcraft* (Plass-Oude Bos et al., 2010), where the avatar shifts its shape according to the degree of relaxation the user experiences. Such reactive games could strengthen the players' association with their avatars, leading to a stronger immersion and an increased sense of presence in the game world.

EVOKED-PASSIVE BRAIN-COMPUTER INTERFACES

BCI research suggests that evoked responses can be informative about the state of the user. Allison and Polich (2008) have used evoked responses to simple auditory stimuli to probe the workload of a user during a computer game, a measure that might reflect attentional and affective engagement. Similarly, neurophysiology-based lie detection, assessing neurophysiological orientation responses (P300) to compromising stimuli, has been shown to be feasible (Abootalebi et al. 2009). A similar approach is the detection of error potentials in response to errors in human-machine interaction. It was shown that such errors evoke specific neurophysiological responses— for example, the error-related negativity (ERN), which can be detected and used to trigger system adaptation (Buttfield, Ferrez, & Millán, 2006; Zander & Jatzev, 2009). Given that goal conduciveness is a determining factor of affective responses, such error-related potentials could be understood as being affective in nature (Scherer, 2005).

More directly related to affect, however, are those responses observed to media, such as songs, music videos, or films. Assuming the genuine affective nature of the response to experiences delivered by such stimuli, it might be possible to detect the user states associated with them. Possible uses for such approaches are media recommendation systems, which monitor the user response to media exposure and label or tag the media with the affective state it produced. Later on, such systems could selectively offer or automatically play back media items known to induce a certain affective state in the user. Research toward such neurophysiology-based implicit tagging approaches of multimedia content has suggested its feasibility (Koelstra et al., 2012;

Soleymani et al., 2011). Furthermore, assuming that general indicators of affect can be identified using music excerpts or film clips for affect-induction protocols, such multimodal and natural media seem suited to collect data for the training of aBCIs that detect affective states occurring in rather uncontrolled, real-life environments.

EVOKED-REACTIVE BRAIN-COMPUTER INTERFACES

This category seems less likely to be used for aBCI approaches, as the volitional control of affect in response to presented stimuli is as yet unexplored. However, standard BCI paradigms that use evoked brain activity to enable users to select from several choices were the first approaches to BCI and have been thoroughly explored. A prominent example is the P300 speller, which relies on the enhanced P300 potential observed in response to attended compared to unattended stimuli (Farwell & Donchin, 1988). Similarly, BCI control via steady-state evoked potentials relies on the increase of an EEG frequency response when a stimulus oscillating with the same frequency (e.g., a flicker, vibration, or sound) is attended (Vidal, 1973).

Summarizing, there are a multitude of possible applications for aBCIs that can be categorized according to the axes of induced/evoked and active/passive control. Main applications, however, are those that cover the passive control of applications. The challenges that have to be dealt with in moving beyond proof-of-concept studies and toward aBCIs working reliably in the complexity of the real world are addressed in the final section.

Controversies, Challenges, Conclusion

Although the possibility of neurophysiology-based affect detection has been suggested by theoretical and empirical works (see Neurophysiological Measurements of Affect, p. 218 and Affective Brain-Computer Interfaces, p. 222), several neuroscientific and neurotechnological challenges remain on the way toward reliable aBCIs.

Neuroscientific Challenges

The primary neuroscientific challenge is the lack of reliable signal features that characterize affective states in noninvasive electrophysiological measures, such as EEG. It is often argued that EEG has neither the spatial resolution nor the necessary sensitivity to register core affective neural activity from deep subcortical structures of the limbic system. While this might *partially* be true, especially in comparison

to techniques like fMRI, many studies report electrophysiological correlates of emotion manipulations in terms of amplitude changes of either potentials or oscillations (see Correlates of Affect in Electroencephalography, p. 219). However, it is indeed seldom assessed which parts of these responses to affective stimulation are reflected within these differentiating signal features: *core affective correlates versus cognitive coactivations of affect*. Modern emotion theories—for example, the component process model of Scherer (2005)—acknowledge the complex and interwoven nature of affective and cognitive concepts and processes that are present during emotional responses. Therefore it must be acknowledged as well that different affective states are differentiated not only by the correlates of their core affective features but also by concurrent coactivations of regions and processes that can be observed independently of affect. An example is enhanced sensory processing, which can be observed in response to emotionally arousing stimuli as well as during heightened levels of attention (see Mühl, 2012, for further elaboration).

Consequently, to avoid misclassification of cognitive state changes as affective state changes, a major challenge for aBCI is the identification of the nature of affect correlates and the development of methods that allow focus on reliable indicators of affect while still making use of the indicative power of those correlates that are not of purely affective nature. As noted earlier, richer information about the response to an affective event—for example, its origin or its behavioral consequences—is one of the major promises of aBCIs. To resolve the uncertainties pertaining to the nature of neurophysiological correlates of affect and to develop the next generation of affect-sensitive but context-aware aBCIs, the design of affect-induction approaches needs special care.[4] Beside the need to carefully balance all factors but the induced emotion to avoid confounds, affect-induction designs should vary factors that are co-occurring with affective responses and known to be reflected in brain activity. Examples are visual or auditory attention processes as elicited by the use of stimuli in the respective sensory modalities (Mühl et al., 2011).

However, this requirement for a stringently controlled affect-induction protocol conflicts with another condition for the study of reliable neurophysiological indicators: an *ecologically valid affect induction*. To ensure the generalization of the classifier from training to real-world context, the training samples must be collected in a context as similar as possible to the envisioned application scenario. Unfortunately this often means that the affect-induction approach would be of a complex nature, either using complex (e.g., multimedia) stimuli or complex interactive tasks. The many factors involved in realistic scenarios in which affect detection would be used make the limitation of changes to the factor that is to be manipulated (i.e., emotion) rather difficult, leading to the occurrence of confounding variables (e.g., stimulus features, motor responses). Furthermore, factoring out those variables that potentially reflect cognitive coactivations (see above) underlies practical limitations of experiment design (e.g., time, number of participants).

To satisfy these contradictory demands on affect-induction protocols, researchers must carefully analyze the factors implied in a given application scenario. Knowing these factors, they can devise experimental designs that manipulate the affect-relevant factors with little variation in other factors or that manipulate affective and nonaffective factors in an independent and counterbalanced manner to factor out the most prominent cognitive coactivations.

Related to the search for reliable correlates of core affect is the exploration of *novel signal features* that are informative of the affective state. As mentioned in Neurophysiological Measurements of Affect (p. 218), the neurophysiological features that have been associated with affect manipulations are not uniquely affective in nature. These potentials and oscillations are also implied in cognitive processes. Therefore the discriminatory value of novel signal features—such as cross-regional or cross-frequency coherence (Miskovic & Schmidt, 2010), assessing the interaction between neural regions and mental processes, or the chronology of different neural processes (Grandjean & Scherer, 2008)—must be explored in the context of affect. Researchers can profit from existing neurophysiological databases (Koelstra et al., 2012; Soleymani et al., 2011) in exploring such novel features.

Neurotechnological Challenges

Neurotechnological challenges exist for software as well as for hardware components of aBCIs. Concerning *software*, the development of appropriate signal processing and classification algorithms are key issues. *Signal processing algorithms* need to become able to deconstruct the electrode signals into their components: neural activity originating from within the skull, and so-called artefacts, originating from eyes, facial musculature and other noneural sources. One can differ between informative and destructive artifacts. Muscular activity (EMG), for example, is treated as a potentially confounding influence in conventional EEG studies and hence always removed. However, in an applied context, EMG can, although it is not of neural origin, inform about the user state, especially taking into account how involved the facial musculature is during emotional episodes. On the other hand, artifacts—independent of origin—might conceal much smaller neural signals and therefore have to be removed. Nevertheless, it makes sense to also examine these artifacts for their informativeness. Techniques like independent component analysis (ICA)(Onton & Makeig, 2009) are able to deconstruct the electrophysiological signals into neural, ocular, and muscular components and might allow an independent assessment of the information of these sources.

Classification algorithms have to be able to take the complexity of the neurophysiological signals into account. Assuming a possible differentiation between core affective and associated cognitive correlates, machine learning approaches that are able to deal with these complex signals are needed. They need to be able to ignore or penalize the learning of those features that are only co-varying with affect, thus avoiding misclassifications due to the cognitive parts of the affective response (e.g., falsely recognizing increased visual attention as visually induced emotion). Alternatively, they could learn to use these coactivations to differentiate contextual details of the emotional episode, such as its origin or its intended behavioral consequence.

Another challenge for learning algorithms is the capability to learn from relatively few examples. The induction of affective states is limited by effects of habituation and the requirement of ecological validity, leading to a restricted number of samples for training and testing. A possible alternative is the development of classifiers that learn from a pool of samples of several participants, rendering their results subject-independent and thereby making subject-specific training sessions obsolete.

Concerning *hardware*, the main challenge concerns the wearability and ease of use of aBCI systems. To ensure optimal user experience, the system should have as few sensors as possible, reducing the time for setup and its intrusiveness during use. There are already several commercial devices that enable the recording of an EEG from a small number of sensors (1 to 16 compared with 32 to 256 electrodes in research devices) and that function without conductive gel. The small number of electrodes minimizes the laborious optimization of electrode contacts to improve signal quality and thereby increases usability. Furthermore, the achievable signal quality of dry or contactless electrode systems seems close to that of gel-based systems (Zander et al., 2011). However, signal processing techniques like ICA require a certain number of electrodes to deconstruct neural and nonneural signal components, posing problems for a reliable EEG/EMG differentiation. As alternatives to EEG-only aBCI systems, such systems can be combined with other affect-sensing modalities assessing physiological or behavioral cues. Such hybrid or multimodal BCI systems (Pfurtscheller et al., 2010) have the potential to assess the constellation of different aspects of an affective response—for example, preparatory homeostatic or communicative aspects—but also to enable the use of redundant information from these sources and therefore decrease the susceptibility to artifacts and increase the reliability of the prediction. For information regarding the integration of signals from body and brain, see the chapter by Kemp and colleagues in this volume.

Taken together, the main challenges for reliable aBCIs are affect-induction protocols that allow the identification and differentiation of core affective correlates and cognitive coactivations, preprocessing methods that can differentiate between neural and nonneural signal sources, and classification methods that are able to automatically acquire that information from a limited set of electrodes and samples. Should the development of smaller and cheaper sensor technology continue, wearable and easy-to-use aBCI systems could soon become an effective alternative or addition to behavior- and physiology-based affect detection.

Acknowledgments

The authors gratefully acknowledge the support of the BrainGain Smart Mix Programme of the Netherlands Ministry of Economic Affairs and the Netherlands Ministry of Education, Culture and Science.

Notes

1. See also Kemp and colleagues' chapter in this volume, which highlights the importance of brain and body responses and their integration.
2. This constructivist position, readily compatible with functional appraisal models of emotion and with evidence collected by neuroimaging meta-analyses (Lindquist et al., 2011), is opposed by the localist position, which is defended by the proponents of basic emotion models. For a neuroimaging meta-analysis supporting the localist position, see (Vytal & Hamann, 2010). The interested reader is also

referred to the chapter by Kemp and colleagues in this volume.
3. Examples of such consumer EEG devices are the emotive headset with 14 sensors (http://www.emotiv.com) and the Neurosky headset with 1 sensor (http://www.neurosky.com).
4. In this regard interested readers may wish to refer to the *Handbook of Emotion Elicitation and Its Assessment* by Coan & Allen.

References

Abootalebi, V., Moradi, M. H., & Khalilzadeh, M. A. (2009). A new approach for EEG feature extraction in P300-based lie detection. *Computer Methods and Programs in Biomedicine*, 94(1), 48–57.

Aftanas, L. I., Varlamov, A. A., Pavlov, S. V., Makhnev, V. P., & Reva, N. V. (2002). Time-dependent cortical asymmetries induced by emotional arousal: EEG analysis of event-related synchronization and desynchronization in individually defined frequency bands. *International Journal of Psychophysiology*, 44(1), 67–82.

Aftanas, LI I, Reva, N. V, Varlamov, A. A., Pavlov, S. V, & Makhnev, V. P. (2004). Analysis of evoked EEG synchronization and desynchronization in conditions of emotional activation in humans: temporal and topographic characteristics. *Neuroscience and Behavioral Physiology*, 34(8), 859–867.

Allison, B. Z., & Polich, J. (2008). Workload assessment of computer gaming using a single-stimulus event-related potential paradigm. *Biological Psychology*, 77(3), 277–283.

Altenmüller, E., Schürmann, K., Lim, V. K., & Parlitz, D. (2002). Hits to the left, flops to the right: different emotions during listening to music are reflected in cortical lateralisation patterns. *Neuropsychologia*, 40(13), 2242–2256.

Andersen, S. B., Moore, R. A., Venables, L., Corr, P. J., & Venebles, L. (2009). Electrophysiological correlates of anxious rumination. *International Journal of Psychophysiology*, 71(2), 156–169.

Balconi, M., & Lucchiari, C. (2006). EEG correlates (event-related desynchronization) of emotional face elaboration: a temporal analysis. *Neuroscience Letters*, 392(1–2), 118–23.

Balconi, M., & Mazza, G. (2010). Lateralisation effect in comprehension of emotional facial expression: a comparison between EEG alpha band power and behavioural inhibition (BIS) and activation (BAS) systems. *Laterality*, 15(3), 361–384.

Balconi, M., & Pozzoli, U. (2009). Arousal effect on emotional face comprehension: Frequency band changes in different time intervals. *Physiology & Behavior*, 97(3–4), 455–462.

Barrett, L. F., Mesquita, B., Ochsner, K. N., & Gross, J. J. (2007). The experience of emotion. *Annual Review of Psychology*, 58(1), 373–403.

Barry, R. J., Clarke, A. R., Johnstone, S. J., & Brown, C. R. (2009). EEG differences in children between eyes-closed and eyes-open resting conditions. *Clinical Neurophysiology*, 120(10), 1806–1811.

Barry, R. J., Clarke, A. R., Johnstone, S. J., Magee, C. A., & Rushby, J. A. (2007). EEG differences between eyes-closed and eyes-open resting conditions. *Clinical Neurophysiology*, 118(12), 2765–2773.

Başar, E., Schürmann, M., & Sakowitz, O. (2001). The selectively distributed theta system: functions. *International Journal of Psychophysiology*, 39(2–3), 197–212.

Berger, H. (1929). Über das Elektrenkephalogramm des Menschen. *Archiv für Psychiatrie und Nervenkrankheiten, 87*, 527–570.

Briggs, K. E., & Martin, F. H. (2009). Affective picture processing and motivational relevance: Arousal and valence effects on ERPs in an oddball task. *International Journal of Psychophysiology, 72*(3), 299–306.

Buttfield, A., Ferrez, P. W., & Millán, J. del R. (2006). Towards a robust BCI: error potentials and online learning. *IEEE Transactions on Neural Systems and Rehabilitation Engineering: A publication of the IEEE Engineering in Medicine and Biology Society, 14*(2), 164–168.

Chanel, G., Kierkels, J. J. M., Soleymani, M., & Pun, T. (2009). Short-term emotion assessment in a recall paradigm. *International Journal of Human-Computer Studies, 67*(8), 607–627.

Chanel, G., Rebetez, C., Bétrancourt, M., Pun, T., & Bétrancourt, M. (2011). Emotion assessment from physiological signals for adaptation of game difficulty. *IEEE Transactions on Systems, Man, and Cybernetics, Part A: Systems and Humans, 41*(6), 1052–1063.

Chanel, G., Rebetez, C., Bétrancourt, M., Pun, T., Kronegg, J., & Grandjean, D. (2005). Emotion assessment: Arousal evaluation using EEG's and peripheral physiological signals. In B. Gunsel, A. Jain, A. Tekalp, & B. Sankur (Eds.), *Multimedia content representation, classification and security in lecture notes of computer science* (Vol. 4105, pp. 1052–1063). Berlin and Heidelberg: Springer.

Coan, J. A., & Allen, J. J. B. (2004). Frontal EEG asymmetry as a moderator and mediator of emotion. *Biological Psychology, 67*(1–2), 7–50. doi:10.1016/j.biopsycho.2004.03.002

Cole, H. W., & Ray, W. J. (1985). EEG correlates of emotional tasks related to attentional demands. *International Journal of Psychophysiology, 3*(1), 33–41.

Damasio, A. R. (2000). *The feeling of what happens.* New York: Harcourt Brace. Random House.

Dan Glauser, E. S., & Scherer, K. (2008). Neuronal processes involved in subjective feeling emergence: Oscillatory activity during an emotional monitoring task. *Brain Topography, 20*(4), 224–231.

Davidson, R. R. J. (1992). Anterior cerebral asymmetry and the nature of emotion. *Brain and Cognition, 20*(1), 125–151.

Engel, A. K., & Fries, P. (2010). Beta-band oscillations—signalling the status quo? *Current Opinion in Neurobiology, 20*(2), 156–165.

Engels, A. S., Heller, W., Mohanty, A., Herrington, J. D., Banich, M. T., Webb, A. G., & Miller, G. A. (2007). Specificity of regional brain activity in anxiety types during emotion processing. *Psychophysiology, 44*(3), 352–363.

Farwell, L. A., & Donchin, E. (1988). Talking off the top of your head: Toward a mental prosthesis utilizing event-related brain potentials. *Electroencephalography and Clinical Neurophysiology, 70*(6), 510–523.

Frantzidis, C. A., Bratsas, C., Papadelis, C. L., Konstantinidis, E., Pappas, C., & Bamidis, P. D. (2010). Toward emotion aware computing: an integrated approach using multichannel neurophysiological recordings and affective visual stimuli. *IEEE Transactions on Information Technology in Biomedicine, 14*(3), 589–597.

Fries, P. (2009). Neuronal gamma-band synchronization as a fundamental process in cortical computation. *Annual Review of Neuroscience, 32*, 209–224.

George, L., Lotte, F., Abad, R. V., & Lecuyer, A. (2011). Using scalp electrical biosignals to control an object by concentration and relaxation tasks: design and evaluation. In *Proceedings of the 33th annual international conference of the IEEE engineering in medicine and biology society.* (Vol. 2011, pp. 6299–302). Washington, DC: IEEE Computer Society Press.

Goncharova, I. I., McFarland, D. J., Vaughan, T. M., Wolpaw, J. R. (2003). EMG contamination of EEG: spectral and topographical characteristics. *Clinical Neurophysiology, 114*(9), 1580–1593.

Grandjean, D., & Scherer, K. (2008). Unpacking the cognitive architecture of emotion processes. *Emotion, 8*(3), 341–351.

Gross, J., Schnitzler, A., Timmermann, L., & Ploner, M. (2007). Gamma oscillations in human primary somatosensory cortex reflect pain perception. *PLoS Biology, 5*(5), e133.

Gruber, T., Müller, M. M., Keil, A., & Elbert, T. (1999). Selective visual-spatial attention alters induced gamma band responses in the human EEG. *Clinical Neurophysiology, 110*(12), 2074–2085.

Hammond, D. C. (2005). Neurofeedback treatment of depression and anxiety. *Journal of Adult Development, 12*(2), 131–137.

Harmon-Jones, E. (2003). Clarifying the emotive functions of asymmetrical frontal cortical activity. *Psychophysiology, 40*(6), 838–848. doi:10.1111/1469-8986.00121

Hjelm, S. I. (2003). Research + design: the making of Brainball. *Interactions, 10*(1), 26–34.

Hongtao, W., Ting, L., & Zhenfeng, H. (2010). Remote control of an electrical car with SSVEP-based BCI. In *2010 IEEE international conference on information theory and information security* (pp. 837–840). Washington, DC: IEEE Computer Society Press.

Horlings, R., Datcu, D., & Rothkrantz, L. J. M. (2008). Emotion recognition using brain activity. In *CompSysTech '08 proceedings of the 9th international conference on computer systems and technologies and workshop for PhD students in computing.* New York: Association for Computing Machinery.

Huster, R. J., Stevens, S., Gerlach, A. L., & Rist, F. (2009). A spectralanalytic approach to emotional responses evoked through picture presentation. *International Journal of Psychophysiology, 72*(2), 212–216.

Jensen, O., Kaiser, J., & Lachaux, J. P. (2007). Human gamma-frequency oscillations associated with attention and memory. *Trends in Neurosciences, 30*(7), 317–324.

Jones, N. A., & Fox, N. A. (1992). Electroencephalogram asymmetry during emotionally evocative films and its relation to positive and negative affectivity. *Brain and Cognition, 20*(2), 280–299.

Kawasaki, M., Kitajo, K., & Yamaguchi, Y. (2010). Dynamic links between theta executive functions and alpha storage buffers in auditory and visual working memory. *The European Journal of Neuroscience, 31*(9), 1683–1689.

Keil, A., Müller, M. M., Gruber, T., Wienbruch, C., Stolarova, M., & Elbert, T. (2001). Effects of emotional arousal in the cerebral hemispheres: a study of oscillatory brain activity and event-related potentials. *Clinical Neurophysiology, 112*(11), 2057–2068.

Klados, M. A., Frantzidis, C., Vivas, A. B., Papadelis, C., Lithari, C., Pappas, C., & Bamidis, P. D. (2009). A framework combining delta event-related oscillations (EROs) and synchronisation effects (ERD/ERS) to study emotional processing. *Computational Intelligence and Neuroscience*, Article 12

(January 2009), 16. DOI=10.1155/2009/549419 http://dx.doi.org/10.1155/2009/549419

Klimesch, W., Freunberger, R., Sauseng, P., & Gruber, W. (2008). A short review of slow phase synchronization and memory: evidence for control processes in different memory systems? *Brain Research, 1235*, 31–44.

Klimesch, W., Sauseng, P., & Hanslmayr, S. (2007). EEG alpha oscillations: the inhibition-timing hypothesis. *Brain Research Reviews, 53*(1), 63–88.

Knyazev, G. G. (2012). EEG delta oscillations as a correlate of basic homeostatic and motivational processes. *Neuroscience and Biobehavioral Reviews, 36*(1), 677–695.

Koelstra, S., Mühl, C., Soleymani, M., Lee, J.-S., Yazdani, A., Ebrahimi, T., Pun, T., Nijholt, A., & Patras, I. (2012). DEAP: A database for emotion analysis using physiological signals. *IEEE Transactions on Affective Computing, 3*(1), 18–31.

Koelstra, S., Yazdani, A., Soleymani, M., Mühl, C., Lee, J.-S., Nijholt, A., Pun, T., Ebrahimi, T., & Patras, I. (2010). Single trial classification of EEG and peripheral physiological signals for recognition of emotions induced by music videos. In *Proceedings of the 2010 international conference on brain informatics (BI 2010)* (Vol. 6334, pp. 89–100). New York: Springer.

Leeb, R., Friedman, D., Müller-Putz, G. R., Scherer, R., Slater, M., & Pfurtscheller, G. (2007). Self-paced (asynchronous) BCI control of a wheelchair in virtual environments: A case study with a tetraplegic. *Computational Intelligence and Neuroscience, 2007*, 79642.

Lehtelä, L., Salmelin, R., & Hari, R. (1997). Evidence for reactive magnetic 10-Hz rhythm in the human auditory cortex. *Neuroscience Letters, 222*(2), 111–114.

Li, M., & Lu, B.-L. (2009). Emotion classification based on gamma-band EEG. In *Proceedings of the Annual International Conference of the IEEE engineering in medicine and biology society. ieee engineering in medicine and biology society.* (pp. 1223–1226). Washington, DC: IEEE Computer Society Press.

Lin, Y. P., Wang, C. H., Wu, T. L., Jeng, S. K., & Chen, J. H. (2009). EEG-based emotion recognition in music listening: A comparison of schemes for multiclass support vector machine. In *Proceedings of the IEEE international conference on acoustics, speech, and signal processing* (pp. 489–492). Washington, DC: IEEE Computer Society Press.

Lin, Y.-P., Duann, J.-R., Chen, J.-H., & Jung, T.-P. (2010). Electroencephalographic dynamics of musical emotion perception revealed by independent spectral components. *NeuroReport, 21*(6), 410–415.

Lindquist, K. A., Wager, T. D., Kober, H., Bliss-moreau, E., & Barrett, L. F. (2011). The brain basis of emotion: A meta-analytic review. *Behavioral and Brain Sciences, 173*(4), 1–86.

Lotte, F., Congedo, M., Lécuyer, A., Lamarche, F., & Arnaldi, B. (2007). A review of classification algorithms for EEG-based brain-computer interfaces. *Journal of Neural Engineering, 4*(2), R1–R13.

Makeig, S., Leslie, G., Mullen, T., Sarma, D., Bigdely-Shamlo, N., & Kothe, C. (2011). First demonstration of a musical emotion BCI. In *Proceedings of the 4th international conference on affective computing and intelligent interaction and workshops, 2011 (ACII 2011), 2nd workshop on affective brain-computer interfaces* (Vol. 6975, pp. 487–496). New York: Springer.

Miskovic, V., & Schmidt, L. a. (2010). Cross-regional cortical synchronization during affective image viewing. *Brain Research, 1362*, 102–11.

Mühl, C. (2012). Toward affective brain-computer interfaces. Ph.D. thesis. University of Twente.

Mühl, C., Gürkök, H., Plass-Oude Bos, D., Thurlings, M. E., Scherffig, L., Duvinage, M.,... Heylen, D. (2010). Bacteria hunt—Evaluating multi-paradigm BCI interaction. *Journal on Multimodal User Interfaces, 4*(1), 11–25.

Mühl, C., van den Broek, E., Brouwer, A.-M., Nijboer, F., van Wouwe, N., & Heylen, D. (2011). Multi-modal affect induction for affective brain-computer interfaces. In S. D'Mello, A. Graesser, B. Schuller, & J.-C. Martin (Eds.), *Proceedings of the 4th international conference on affective computing and intelligent interaction and workshops, 2011 (ACII 2011)* (Vol. 6974, pp. 235–245). Berlin and Heidelberg: Springer.

Müller, M. M., Keil, A., Gruber, T., & Elbert, T. (1999). Processing of affective pictures modulates right-hemispheric gamma band EEG activity. *Clinical Neurophysiology, 110*(11), 1913–1920.

Murugappan, M. (2010). Inferring of Human Emotional States using Multichannel EEG. *European Journal of Scientific Research, 48*(2), 281–299.

Neuper, C., Wörtz, M., & Pfurtscheller, G. (2006). ERD/ERS patterns reflecting sensorimotor activation and deactivation. *Progress in Brain Research*, 159, 211–222. doi:10.1016/S0079-6123(06)59014-4.

Niedermeyer, E. (2005). The normal EEG of the waking adult. In E. Niedermeyer & F. Lopes Da Silva (Eds.), *Electroencephalography basic principles clinical applications and related fields* (pp. 167–192). Baltimore, MD: Lippincott Williams & Wilkins.

Nijboer, F., Clausen, J., Allison, B. Z., & Haselager, P. (2011). The Asilomar survey: Stakeholders' opinions on ethical issues related to brain-computer interfacing. *Neuroethics 6*(3), 541–578.

Nowlis, D. P., & Kamiya, J. (1970). The control of electroencephalographic alpha rhythms through auditory feedback and the associated mental activity. *Psychophysiology, 6*(4), 476–484.

Olofsson, J. K., Nordin, S., Sequeira, H., & Polich, J. (2008). Affective picture processing: an integrative review of ERP findings. *Biological Psychology, 77*(3), 247–265.

Onton, J., & Makeig, S. (2009). High-frequency Broadband Modulations of Electroencephalographic Spectra. *Frontiers in Human Neuroscience, 3*, 61. doi: 10.3389/neuro.09.061.2009

Petrantonakis, P. C., & Hadjileontiadis, L. J. (2010). Emotion Recognition from Brain Signals Using Hybrid Adaptive Filtering and Higher Order Crossings Analysis. *IEEE Transactions on Affective Computing, 1*(2), 81–97.

Pfurtscheller, G., Brunner, C., Schlögl, A., & Lopes da Silva, F. H. (2006). Mu rhythm (de)synchronization and EEG single-trial classification of different motor imagery tasks. *NeuroImage, 31*(1), 153–159.

Pfurtscheller, G., & Neuper, C. (2001). Motor imagery and direct brain-computer communication. *Proceedings of the IEEE, 89*(7), 1123–1134. doi:10.1109/5.939829

Pfurtscheller, Gert, Allison, B. Z., Brunner, C., Bauernfeind, G., Solis-Escalante, T., Scherer, R.,... Birbaumer, N. (2010). The hybrid BCI. *Frontiers in Neuroscience, 4*, 30.

Pfurtscheller, Gert, Müller-Putz, G. R., Pfurtscheller, J., & Rupp, R. (2005). EEG-based asynchronous BCI controls functional electrical stimulation in a tetraplegic patient. *EURASIP Journal on Advances in Signal Processing, 2005*(19), 3152–3155.

Pfurtscheller, Gert, Stancák, A., & Neuper, C. (1996). Post-movement beta synchronization. A correlate of an idling motor area? *Electroencephalography and Clinical Neurophysiology*, *98*(4), 281–293.

Plass-Oude Bos, D., Reuderink, B., Laar, B., Gürkök, H., Mühl, C., Poel, M., ... Heylen, D. (2010). Brain-computer interfacing and games. In D. S. Tan & A. Nijholt (Eds.), *Brain-computer interfaces: Applying our minds to human-computer interaction* (pp. 149–178). London: Springer.

Polich, J. (2007). Updating P300: an integrative theory of P3a and P3b. *Clinical Neurophysiology*, *118*(10), 2128–2148.

Reuderink, B., Mühl, C., & Poel, M. (2013). Valence, arousal and dominance in the EEG during game play. *International Journal of Autonomous and Adaptive Communication Systems*, *6*(1).

Sabatinelli, D., Lang, P. J. J., Keil, A., & Bradley, M. M. M. (2006). Emotional perception: Correlation of functional MRI and event-related potentials. *Cerebral Cortex*, *17*(5), 1085–1091.

Sammler, D., Grigutsch, M., Fritz, T., & Koelsch, S. (2007). Music and emotion: Electrophysiological correlates of the processing of pleasant and unpleasant music. *Psychophysiology*, *44*(2), 293–304.

Scherer, K. R. (2005). What are emotions? And how can they be measured? *Social Science Information*, *44*(4), 695–729.

Schmidt, L. A., & Trainor, L. J. (2001). Frontal brain electrical activity (EEG) distinguishes valence and intensity of musical emotions. *Cognition and Emotion*, *15*(4), 487–500.

Schupp, H. T., Cuthbert, B. N., Bradley, M. M., Cacioppo, J. T., Ito, T., & Lang, P. J. (2000). Affective picture processing: the late positive potential is modulated by motivational relevance. *Psychophysiology*, *37*(2), 257–261.

Senkowski, D., Kautz, J., Hauck, M., Zimmermann, R., & Engel, A. K. (2011). Emotional facial expressions modulate pain-induced beta and gamma oscillations in sensorimotor cortex. *Journal of Neuroscience*, *31*(41), 14542–14550.

Senkowski, Daniel, Schneider, T. R., Tandler, F., & Engel, A. K. (2009). Gamma-band activity reflects multisensory matching in working memory. *Experimental Brain Research*, *198*(2–3), 363–372.

Silberman, E. (1986). Hemispheric lateralization of functions related to emotion. *Brain and Cognition*, *5*(3), 322–353.

Soleymani, M., Lichtenauer, J., Pun, T., & Pantic, M. (2011). A multimodal database for affect recognition and implicit tagging. *IEEE Transactions on Affective Computing*, *3*(1), 42–55.

Steriade, M., McCormick, D. A., & Sejnowski, T. J. (1993). Thalamocortical oscillations in the sleeping and aroused brain. *Science*, *262*(5134), 679–685.

Takahashi, K. (2004). Remarks on emotion recognition from biopotential signals. In S. C. Mukhopadhyay & S. G. Gupta (Eds.), *Proceedings of the 2nd international conference on autonomous robots and agents* (pp. 186–191). Palmerston North, New Zealand: Massey University.

Tallon-Baudry, C., Bertrand, O., Baudry, T., & Bertrand. (1999). Oscillatory gamma activity in humans and its role in object representation. *Trends in Cognitive Sciences*, *3*(4), 151–162.

Teplan, M., & Krakovska, A. (2009). EEG features of psycho-physiological relaxation. In *proceedings of the 2nd international symposium on applied sciences in biomedical and communication technologies (ISABEL 2009)*. Washington, DC: The IEEE Computer Society Press.

Tsang, C. D., Trainor, L. J., Santesso, D. L., Tasker, S. L., & Schmidt, L. A. (2006). Frontal EEG responses as a function of affective musical features. *Annals of the New York Academy of Sciences*, *930*(1), 439–442.

Vidal, J. J. (1973). Toward direct brain-computer communication. *Annual Review of Biophysics and Bioengineering*, *2*, 157–180.

Vytal, K., & Hamann, S. (2010). Neuroimaging support for discrete neural correlates of basic emotions: a voxel-based meta-analysis. *Journal of Cognitive Neuroscience*, *22*(12), 2864–2885.

Ward, R. (2004). Affective computing: problems, reactions and intentions. *Interacting with Computers*, *16*(4), 707–713.

Winkler, I., Jäger, M., Mihajlovic, V., & Tsoneva, T. (2010). Frontal EEG asymmetry based classification of emotional valence using common spatial patterns. *World Academy of Science, Engineering and Technology*, *69*, 373–378.

Wolpaw, J. R., Birbaumer, N., McFarland, D. J., Pfurtscheller, G., & Vaughan, T. M. (2002). Brain-computer interfaces for communication and control. *Clinical Neurophysiology*, *113*(6), 767–791.

Zander, T. O., & Kothe, C. (2011). Towards passive brain-computer interfaces: applying brain-computer interface technology to human-machine systems in general. *Journal of neural engineering*, *8*(2), 025005.

Zander, T. O., & Jatzev, S. (2009). Detecting affective covert user states with passive brain-computer interfaces. In J. Cohn, A. Nijholt, & M. Pantic (Eds.), *Proceedings of the 3rd international conference on affective computing and intelligent interaction (ACII2009), Part II*. Washington, DC: IEEE Computer Society Press.

Zander, T. O., Lehne, M., Ihme, K., Jatzev, S., Correia, J., Kothe, C., ... Nijboer, F. (2011). A dry EEG-system for scientific research and brain–computer interfaces. *Frontiers in Neuroscience*, *5*.

16

Interaction-Based Affect Detection in Educational Software

Ryan S. J. D. Baker *and* Jaclyn Ocumpaugh

Abstract

In recent years, the essential role that affect plays during learning has received greater attention. Accordingly, there has been increasing interest in developing affect-sensitive learning systems that can infer student affect and respond appropriately to it. In many domains, researchers have leveraged physical sensors to make substantial progress in affect detection, but this approach can be challenging in educational settings, where physical sensors can be infeasible. As such, there has been increasing interest in developing detectors of student affect that operate solely on data from the interaction (within the user interface) between the student and the computer. This chapter reviews recent research in this area, discussing approaches used both for collecting training labels of affect and approaches for predicting those affect labels from features of the student interaction. The authors also discuss some of the methodological insights that are emerging from this area of research.

Key Words: affect detector, educational data mining, features, interaction log, intelligent tutoring system, overfitting

Over the past two decades, researchers have increasingly realized the importance of recognizing the emotional components of human–computer interaction (HCI) in building the field of affective computing. Scholarship in this area reflects a wide range of approaches, both in terms of the psychological theories of emotion that it incorporates and in terms of the multimodal methods of detection and study of affective constructs that it uses.

Several scholars have already provided important reviews of this literature. The review in Picard (1997) has heavily influenced the field for more than a decade, whereas Calvo and D'Mello's (2010) more recent review has provided an important guidepost for researchers and developers who are trying to implement affect-sensitive interfaces that rely on effective detection of user affect. They comprehensively review methods using sensor-based detection of facial, auditory, and biometric features

(e.g., Alzoubi, Calvo, & Stevens, 2009; Pantic & Rothkrantz, 2003; Sebe, Cohen, Gevers, & Huang, 2005; Zeng, Pantic, Roisman, & Huang, 2009), methods that have shown considerable promise. This work is also reviewed in Calvo and D'Mello (2011).

In recent years, an alternate approach to affect detection has emerged: inferring affect solely from the interaction between the user and the software. Researchers in this area have restricted themselves to the data available from any modern computer (e.g., no physical or biometric sensors) and to interactions that do not involve the type of rich and extensive text used in the research on sentiment analysis. Instead, they focus on detecting affect from semantically meaningful user interactions with the software being used. For example, in an intelligent tutoring system for mathematics, this might consist of the answers entered by the student, their uses of help systems, and their responses to feedback about their misconceptions (as well as details and timing of these actions). In a narrative-centered learning environment, this might consist of students' interactions with nonplayer characters, the information students collect within the environment, and the fashion in which they interact with objects in the environment.

Much of this research can be seen as fitting within the information processing approach to affective computing (see in, Calvo, Peters, & Peters 2009). In this tradition, affect is treated as discrete, internally processed information that can be communicated between individuals but that is individually experienced. This approach contrasts with the interactionist approach (Boehner, DePaula, Dourish, & Sengers, 2005), which emphasizes that affect is a dynamically co-constructed product of an individual and his or her cultural environment. Note that the interactionist approach is distinct from the interaction-based methods for inferring affect, as we discuss later.

In this chapter, we discuss the emergence of interaction-based methods for inferring affect within educational software. These methods are particularly relevant in public school systems where physical sensors often meet political resistance and financial limitations. Adopting these restrictions enables scalable, low-cost alternatives when sensors are not feasible and can potentially provide a complement to other detection methods. In the past few years, the nascent field of educational data mining (EDM) has provided researchers with new techniques for modeling such data. In this survey, we discuss progress made toward sensor-free affect detection in these contexts.

Research on Interaction-Based Affect Detection in Educational Software

To date, only a limited number of studies have been published in which affect detectors were developed solely from interactions with educational software. In this section, we review some of the pioneering research in this area in approximate chronological order, organizing publications according to the learning systems they investigate: Why-2Atlas, AutoTutor, Prime Climb, Wayang Outpost, BlueJ, Crystal Island, and Cognitive Tutor Algebra. Interfaces for AutoTutor and Cognitive Tutor are shown in Figures 16.1–16.3.

Why-2Atlas

The first sensor-free detectors of affect meeting the criteria we have outlined emerged in 2006. In that year, three publications presented detectors based on natural language dialogue, including Ai, Litman, Forbes-Riley, Rotaru, Tetreault, Amruta, and Purandare (2006), who modeled the affective state of confusion in the text-based physics tutor, Why-2Atlas (VanLehn et al., 2002).

This detector was developed from data drawn from student interactions, which were facilitated by the ITSPOKE audio dialogue system (Litman & Silliman 2004). Data were collected for 100 dialogues composed of a total of 2,252 student turns, drawn from 20 students. Ground truth for confusion was obtained by having external coders label each student turn as "certain," "uncertain," "mixed," or "neutral," with "mixed" and "uncertain" combined into a single category for detector development. Interrater reliability was only reported for a different combination of categories, in which "certain"

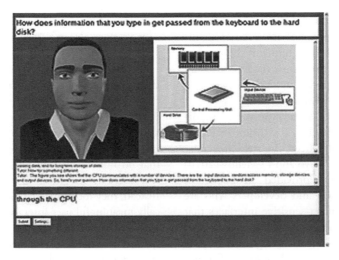

Fig. 16.1 Interfaces for AutoTutor (see in, D'Mello et al., 2008; D'Mello & Graesser, 2010).

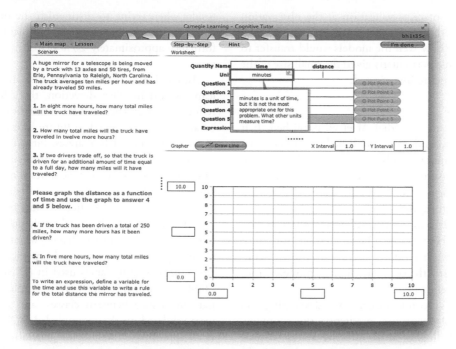

Fig. 16.2 Cognitive Tutor Algebra (see in, Baker et al., 2012).

and "neutral" were combined and "uncertain" and "mixed" were combined, but the κ (agreement after correcting for chance) was at an acceptable 0.68.

Ai et al.'s (2006) detector building system was additive: multiple types of features were used in turn, with interaction-based features (termed "lexical features") used first. The AdaBoost algorithm (based on J48 decision trees) was used to build detectors to predict confusion. Detectors were cross-validated at the level of specific observations. A detector based on interaction features achieved a κ of 0.24. One limitation to this pioneering research

Fig. 16.3 Prime Climb (see in, Conati & Maclaren, 2009a).

was the use of cross-validation at the observation level rather than at the student level, raising questions about how well the models would transfer to new students, particularly given the small size of the population being investigated.

AutoTutor

In the same year that Ai et al. published their research, a second group published two articles that integrated interaction-based detectors of affect into AutoTutor. AutoTutor is an intelligent tutoring system that engages in natural language dialog with students, prompting students with questions to explore their conceptual understanding (Graesser, Chipman, Haynes, & Olney, 2005). AutoTutor modules have been developed for a variety of content, including the computer literacy modules studied by D'Mello's team.

D'Mello's team began by developing an emote-aloud procedure, predicting the spontaneous self-labeling of three affective states (eureka, confusion, and frustration) exclusively through the use of dialogue clues (D'Mello, Craig, Sullins, & Graesser, 2006). The success of this study, which included data from only seven students, was followed by a second article (D'Mello & Graesser, 2006) that modeled confusion, flow, frustration, and the neutral state among a slightly large sample of 28 students. In addition to the emote-aloud method employed in the first article, this study also employed labels from students' peers and from two judges who had been trained in Eckman's facial action coding system (Ekman & Frisen, 1978). They then distilled a range of interaction and contextual features from the logs, including features based on temporal information and features based on AutoTutor's assessments of the quality of student answers. Finally, they built a model predicting each affective state from the interaction features using six machine learning algorithms.

The interaction-based models in D'Mello and Graesser (2006) were further refined in D'Mello, Craig, Witherspoon, McDaniel, and Graesser (2008). As in D'Mello and Graesser (2006), they obtained a ground truth definition of affect from a combination of self-report measures and affect coding data collected by a peer and two trained judges. Their best detectors were based either on logistic regression (frustration or flow) or the AdaBoost algorithm (boredom or confusion). Their approach was most successful for frustration, distinguishing it from students' neutral states approximately 40% better than the base rate. It achieved more modest results when trying to distinguish the other three emotions from the neutral state, only achieving performance approximately 20% better than the base rate.

Although this research represents an important leap forward in affect detection, three limitations reduce the confidence that the resultant models can be appropriately applied in future interventions or discovery with models analyses. First, comparing a specific affective state to the neutral state and discarding data on other affective states is not a natural comparison. In real-world usage of a model, it is necessary to discern one affective state from all others. The detectors achieved relatively poorer performance (16.3% better than chance) when attempting to distinguish affective states from each other for the unified training labels used in (D'Mello et al., 2008). Second, the data were resampled to eliminate imbalance between classes, and the models were validated on the resampled data. Resampling is an appropriate method for generating unbiased classifiers, but the resultant models should ideally be tested on a non-resampled dataset to verify detector effectiveness for future application of the models to data with natural class distribution. Third, their models were cross-validated at the observation level rather than at the student level, as with Ai et al. (2006), thus providing less information on detector generalizability to new students.

Prime Climb

The next publication of interaction-based affect detection was produced by Conati and Maclaren (2009a) who developed their models for Prime Climb, a game-based learning system for mathematics, with an affective agent. In Prime Climb, sixth- and seventh-grade students learn prime factorization from an interface in which mathematics tutoring is embedded into a mountain climbing game. The player is rewarded or penalized based on his or her success with mathematics. For example, giving an incorrect answer can cause the student to fall down the mountain. Prime Climb is significantly different from Why2Atlas and AutoTutor in terms of the kind of input students provide (numerical answers vs. dialogue). In Conati and Maclaren's research, more than 60 sixth- and seventh-grade students (in three different schools) used Prime Climb for approximately 10 minutes apiece.

To obtain ground truth estimates of affect, students were given pop-up survey items during tutor usage. Students could choose when to respond but were automatically queried after a certain time interval elapsed without a response. Within these items, students identified their affect using scales between two opposite emotions (e.g., joy vs. distress). This reporting method allowed a natural comparison of contrasting affective states. A dynamic decision network was then created using features based on a combination of data from students' self-report responses and from semantically meaningful interactions (such as the student falling multiple times due to incorrect responses).

Conati and Maclaren cross-validated their detectors at the student level, permitting an evaluation of model applicability to new students, but resampled the data to facilitate model development. Within their resampled data, their models were successful at distinguishing joy from distress (32% better than chance), and were somewhat successful at distinguishing admiration from reproach (6% better than chance). However, when their models were revalidated using the original data distribution, the models achieved accuracy below the base rate. They achieved accuracy of 69% when distinguishing joy from distress, compared to a base rate of 91%. Likewise, accuracy in distinguishing admiration from reproach was 61% compared to a base rate of 77%. Such results indicate that, in their present versions, these models might not be usable for data with a natural class distribution.

Wayang Outpost

Also in 2009, Arroyo et al. (2009) published affect detectors for a mathematics intelligent tutor, Wayang Outpost. Wayang Outpost (Woolf et al., 2009) provides dynamic instruction on mathematics topics that are commonly covered in the Scholastic Aptitude Tests (SATs). Students are supported in problem solving by embodied learning companions who present practical problems embedded into fantasy-like narratives.

In Arroyo et al. (2009), Wayang Outpost was used in classroom settings by 38 high school students and 29 undergraduate education majors, for 4–5 days apiece. During this study, pop-up menus queried students on their affect every 5 minutes and after finishing each mathematics problem in the system. In each pop-up item, data on one of four affective continua (confident vs. anxious, frustrated vs. not frustrated, excited vs. not excited, and interested vs. bored) were elicited using a 1–5-point Likert scale. Varying numbers of reports of each affective state were obtained, with between 62 and 94 data points available. Features were distilled from recent interactions (including the number of

incorrect attempts in the most recent problem and the number of seconds needed to solve that problem). Linear regression models were built to predict each affective variable. No cross-validation was used; instead, models were tested on the same dataset for which they were developed. Excellent correlations were obtained using only interaction data (r between 0.37 and 0.53), but the small dataset and lack of cross-validation raise some concerns about overfitting.

BlueJ Interactive Development Environment

That same year (2009), affect detection was also being developed for the BlueJ Interactive Development Environment (Kölling, Quig, Patterson, & Rosenberg, 2003), which teaches undergraduates to program in Java. Models to infer frustration solely from student interactions were developed for this environment by Rodrigo and Baker (2009). In this work, data was obtained from 40 students using BlueJ during the lab sessions of their undergraduate computer science classes. (Note that "lab session" in this context refers to a scheduled classroom activity in a campus computer lab, rather than a study conducted in a researcher's laboratory.) Data included interactions from log files synchronized with field observations of the students. (Field observations were conducted using the BROMP field observation protocol, discussed in detail later). Features of student compiled behaviors were distilled from log files, including characterizations of the changes between successive compilations and the time between compilations. Then linear regression was used to detect student frustration from these features. In this paper, frustration was detected at a coarse-grained level, at the level of the overall degree of frustration across lab sessions rather than at a specific time. Cross-validated correlation was 0.32, significantly better than chance according to the Bayesian information criterion (–7.86, where –6 or lower indicates a model that is significantly better than chance).

In addition to providing a platform for detecting frustration (Rodrigo & Baker 2009), BlueJ has also provided a platform for detecting confusion (Lee, Rodrigo, Baker, Sugay, & Coronel, 2011). In this work, sequences of eight student compilations of a computer program were displayed to expert coders using text replays (see in, Baker, Corbett, & Wagner, 2006) and evaluated in terms of whether the student appeared to be confused. Features of student compilation behaviors were distilled, as in Rodrigo and

Baker (2009), and detectors were built using the J48 decision tree algorithm. The resultant detectors were cross-validated at the student level, using the original data distributions, and were found to achieve a κ of 0.86 to the text replay assessments of student confusion. One limitation to this work is in the original training labels of confusion: coders identified which students were struggling (those who appeared not to understand how to create a correct program). This simplification of the operational definition does not map exactly to the affective state of confusion as it is generally understood, and it may have artificially increased the model's eventual goodness.

Crystal Island

A sixth program of research on interaction-based detection of student affect was conducted in Crystal Island, a narrative-centered learning environment where middle-school students develop science inquiry skills. Sabourin, Mott, and Lester (2011) collected data on students' affect by asking students to identify when they were anxious, bored, confused, curious, excited, focused, and frustrated within a pop-up survey item presented every 7 minutes. As in Rodrigo and Baker (2009), this research was conducted on data from a classroom setting, and interaction features (such as the number of tests run by the student and the number of books read by the student) were distilled from the data. Affect was modeled using a dynamic Bayesian network, which also incorporated data from an initial questionnaire on student goals. Cross-validation was conducted at the student level, on the original data distribution, comparing each affective state to all other affective states.

This approach was successful at identifying curious students (24% better than baseline) and focused students (38% better than baseline), but their model was less successful at identifying students who were confused (19% better than baseline), frustrated (14% better than baseline), bored (10% better than baseline), excited (6% better than baseline), or anxious (3% worse than baseline). Cross-validation was conducted at the student level and for the original data distribution, eliminating some of the potential concerns raised for previous research. However, the use of questionnaires remains somewhat of a limitation because it requires new students to complete a task outside of regular interaction with the learning task before the detector can be applied.

Cognitive Tutor Algebra

A seventh program of research is work to detect student affect in Cognitive Tutor Algebra (Koedinger & Corbett, 2006), a program that provides scaffolded tutoring for a first-year algebra course. In Baker et al. (2012), 89 students were observed as they used Cognitive Tutor Algebra as part of their regular classroom activities. Using the BROMP method (discussed later), trained field observers coded for whether each student was demonstrating boredom, frustration, confusion, engaged concentration, or "other" affect.

Once these ground truth observations were obtained by the field observers, features based on student interactions with the Cognitive Tutors were distilled, including features related to the student's current action (such as whether the student requested help on the current action and how long the student paused after requesting help) and features related to the student's past behavior (such as the student's history of errors on the current skill). Next, a set of algorithms were investigated, including K* (best for engaged concentration), JRip (best for confusion), REPTree (best for frustration), and Naïve Bayes (best for boredom). Student-level cross-validation and the original data distributions were used to validate these interaction-only detectors. Their detectors were able to detect engaged concentration (κ = .31), confusion (κ = 0.40), frustration (κ = 0.23), and boredom (κ = .30).

Integration with Other Detection Paradigms

As a whole, the studies of these learning systems show the general potential of sensor-free affect detection. Over the course of the 7 years since Ai et al. (2006), our understanding of feature engineering has improved substantially, and detector validation has become steadily more stringent. Currently, the best sensor-free detectors of student affect achieve κ at about half of what expert coders in field settings can achieve; this shows that there is considerable room for improvement, while also indicating that substantial progress has been made. By studying the features and validation methods of these pioneering publications, we should be able to learn from their successes (and failures), allowing continued improvement in detectors that infer affect solely from student interactions with log files.

As discussed in other chapters within this volume, there has been considerable work to detect affect from physical sensors. There is also some evidence that integrating interaction-based detectors with sensor-based detection can produce more effective assessment of affect than is possible with either method alone. Not surprisingly, many of the studies along these lines have been conducted by the same research groups who produced interaction-only detectors.

The first example of a multimodal detector using both sensors and interaction data is found in one of the first papers reporting an interaction-only detector of affect in educational software data (Ai et al., 2006). In this paper, the interaction-only (e.g., lexical feature) detector was followed with a detector that also used prosodic features. This detector, under observation-level cross-validation, achieved a κ of 0.31, moderately better than the interaction-only detector, which achieved a κ of 0.24.

A second detector that integrates sensor and interaction data is found in Conati and Maclaren's (2009*b*) analysis of Prime Climb, discussed earlier. In a comparison between causal and diagnostic models, they employed an electromyography (EMG) sensor in a dynamic decision network framework. Specifically, they analyzed the movement of facial muscles that have been shown to be associated with negative affect, adding that data to detectors that used survey items and interaction log data (as in their 2009*a* publication, discussed earlier). Accuracy generally improved when models were tested only on data points with clear valence (e.g., strongly positive or negative for at least one affective dimension), but the combined (sensor and interaction) models were less successful when applied to data with more ambiguous valence. Also, when models were tested on data with the original distribution, model performance remained below the baseline, as in Conati and Maclaren (2009*a*).

A third study using both sensor and interaction data is found in Arroyo et al. (2009), also discussed earlier. By adding data from a webcam, a chair posture sensor, a wrist sensor, and a mouse sensor, they were able to improve correlation for their models to between 0.54 and 0.82. However, the sample size for all sensors was substantially smaller (between 15 and 37 data points), and cross-validation was again not used, raising some concerns about potential model overfit.

Finally, the fourth example of the integration of interaction and sensor data is found in D'Mello and Graesser (2010), which analyzes data from 32 minutes of use of AutoTutor by 28 students. In this paper, they demonstrate the effectiveness of models that use multiple channels of information, particularly when the models are constructed using the most diagnostic features from each channel. Specifically, they incorporated dialogue features from interaction logs with gross body language cues (e.g., current seat pressure and temporal changes in

posture) and facial action units (e.g., eye, eyebrow, lip, and jaw movements). By constructing and comparing models using different combinations of information, they demonstrate that using a multimodal approach improved model performance. They found that adding either facial or posture information to interaction data led to better κs than did a detector based on interaction data alone and that using all three data sources led to the best detector of all. This held true whether affect detection was based on codes at fixed time intervals or spontaneous coding in which only codes volunteered by coders without prompting were used. Within this analysis, all affective states were compared to all others, and twofold student-level cross-validation was conducted. Their models achieved κs of 0.323 for fixed-interval, mandatory affect codes and 0.353 for those that were spontaneously offered.

Research that combines sensor and interaction-log data yields important results because these detectors generally show improved performance over those which use only one form of data. In addition, these approaches may eventually provide better training labels that can be used to build better sensor-free models. At present, multimodal approaches using sensors do not scale easily in existing classrooms, but, going forward, these multimodal approaches may become more relevant to classroom settings. For example, as tablet computers that have built-in webcams become used in more schools, it may be more feasible to use facial data in the detection of affect in classroom settings. However, since these sensors are unlikely to become ubiquitous in classrooms in the near future (particularly in classrooms in poorer areas), it will be important to continue developing models that can infer affect solely from student interaction, at least in the medium term.

Methodological Considerations

A number of methodological considerations apply to the development of automated detectors of affect in educational software using only student interaction data. Within this section, we discuss considerations that can be grouped, broadly, into three categories: (1) the ground truth measures of affect used to build detectors, (2) the engineering of appropriate features for detector development, and (3) the validation of detectors.

Ground Truth Measures of Affect

Within the machine learning/data mining paradigm, the caliber of a prediction model is intrinsically linked to the quality of the ground truth labels used to define that construct during model fitting. This issue is particularly relevant when considering the study by Lee et al. (2011), which achieved excellent prediction of confusion, but was modeled on a questionable definition of that construct.

Broadly, three types of methods are typically used to obtain ground truth measures of affect: observational methods (see in, Baker et al., 2012; D'Mello et al., 2008; Rodrigo & Baker, 2009), self-report methods (see in, Conati & Maclaren, 2009a; D'Mello et al., 2008; Sabourin et al., 2011), and log-file annotation methods (Ai et al., 2006; Lee et al., 2011). An overview of these methods is provided here, but readers may also be interested in the review provided in (Porayska-Pomsta et al., 2013).

Within the techniques classified as observation methods, substantial variation exists. Observation can be carried out live, for example in the BROMP protocol for quantitative field observation used by Baker and Rodrigo (Baker, D'Mello, Rodrigo, & Graesser, 2010; Ocumpaugh, Baker, & Rodrigo, 2012) or in Dragon et al. (2008). It can also be conducted using video data. Video data is often considered to be more definitive, but typically achieves lower interrater reliability for affect coding than field observation methods. Whereas field coding of affect has been reported to obtain interrater reliabilities of around 0.6 (see., Baker et al., 2010; 2011), video coding of affect has typically been reported to achieve lower interrater reliability (see in, Graesser et al., 2006; Sayette, Cohn, Wertz, Perrott, & Parrott, 2001) for comparable coding approaches. It is possible that this difference may be due to the greater feasibility of shifting positions and seeing the full context of student behavior in field settings. Modifying video coding techniques to only code affect spontaneously (e.g., when the coder clearly recognizes an affective state, rather than coding at regular intervals) substantially increases interrater agreement to $\kappa = 0.71$ in Graesser et al. (2006). This methodological modification, however, may decrease the number of observations that it is possible to gather in a given session and biases in favor of clearer examples of affect, thus potentially reducing the frequency of more subtle forms of affect. Coding of affect has also been conducted solely from replays of learners' screens (Porayska-Pomsta, Mavrikis, & Pain, 2008), but this provides relatively less information than video coding as conducted by D'Mello and colleagues.

To be used effectively, field observations require training and careful methodological consideration.

Our group's BROMP protocol (see training manual by Ocumpaugh et al., 2012) has been refined over the course of several years. In this paradigm, trained field observers repeatedly observe students in a predetermined order, using this procedure to avoid biases toward more interesting activities in the classroom and thus ensuring that data collection is not weighted toward more conspicuous affective states. The field observer observes one student at a time, usually standing diagonally behind that student so that it is not clear which student is being observed (although positions might differ based on classroom layout). Observations are conducted via side glances in order to reduce observer effects. (Peripheral vision can also be used for coding behavior, but is typically insufficient for affect.) The student is observed for up to 20 seconds, and the observer records the first affect that the student displays. Data recording is conducted via an Android app that both enforces the observation protocol and synchronizes observations to software log files.

Within this approach, observers are trained to look holistically for a range of physical and verbal evidence rather than any single factor. That is, an observer is not simply categorizing from a list of potential behaviors. Instead, he or she will consider the cumulative representation of affect based on evidence from posture, eye movement, facial expressions, verbal expressions, and other cues. It is important not to base the field observations on a single piece of evidence. Instead, field observers are trained to code affect in line with evidence collected by Planalp and colleagues (Planalp, 1998; Planalp, DeFrancisco, & Rutherford, 1996) that people identify emotion "not on an array of cues that might be added up or averaged, or even of one important cue that might dominate others, but rather of a complex combination of cues that often unfold over a period of time."

In our group's experience in training more than 40 coders, attempting to identify specific behaviors (such as irregular fidgeting) typically leads to lower interrater reliability than this more holistic approach, in line with theory from Planalp (1998). In general, it is easiest to conduct this type of holistic coding effectively if field observers are drawn from approximately the same cultural background as the students they are observing. However, in unusual cases, highly sensitive individuals who have high familiarity with a specific culture have been able to achieve acceptable interrater reliability compared to observers from that culture.

An alternate approach to obtaining ground truth is to use self-report methods, such as emote-aloud methods (both in real-time and retrospective), as in D'Mello et al. (2006) and questionnaire-based approaches like those seen in Conati and Maclaren (2009*a*).

In D'Mello et al.'s emote-aloud method, students are presented with a defined list of emotions relevant to learning (anger, boredom, confusion, contempt, curious, disgust, eureka, and frustration). They are then asked to volunteer their emotions (without prompting), either as they complete the educational task in real time or retrospectively as they watch a video of their interactions with the learning system. Audio recordings of these reports are collected for later analysis. The emote-aloud method has the benefit of synchronizing students' own descriptions with their interactions with minimal effort, but it might be difficult to implement in a normal classroom environment where a student's verbalizations could distract those seated nearby.

Questionnaire methods can be conducted in multiple fashions. One approach is to use pop-up windows that prompt students for responses at predetermined intervals. In Arroyo et al. (2009), for example, students were queried every 5 minutes and between problems, and in Sabourin et al. (2011), students were queried every 7 minutes. Other researchers have developed methods that allow for more spontaneous reporting. In Conati and Maclaren (2009*a*), for example, students are given the opportunity to enter affect information at any time in a permanently displayed dialogue window, but the system mandates self-reports after a certain threshold of time expires or if the system predicts that a change in the student's affective state has occurred, thus allowing the automated detector to refine itself.

Self-report methods have the advantage of coming directly from the individual being studied; as such, they are less prone to errors of interpretation so long as the subjects' understanding of the affective labels are consistent. However, they have some implementational challenges. First, they are prone to demand effects and self-presentation effects, which may vary by culture.

A second challenge for self-reports is the impact on what is being measured. Students must be surveyed at semiregular intervals to ensure that self-report data connects to actual affect at a specific moment (as opposed to representing a student's general perception of their affect), but overusing self-reports can be problematic. If a student's workflow is interrupted regularly with self-report items,

these interruptions may change the student's affect (potentially inducing frustration or boredom). Interrupting student interactions may also cause student responses to the survey items to be driven by the survey items rather than by the learning task. It may also change the overall affective patterns that the student experiences, potentially reducing detector appropriateness for a population not being prompted regularly about their affect. Allowing students to decide when they report on their affect (as in Conati & Maclaren, 2009*a*) can address this challenge but may reduce the frequency of report of affective states with lower valence. Similarly, only surveying affect between problems or at other interruptible points can lead to nonrepresentative measures of affect.

Other challenges are specific to particular types of self-report measures. For example, the emote-aloud method could be difficult to implement in a normal classroom setting where a student who is emoting aloud could distract other students, but it may elicit more natural self-reporting among young students than designs that rely on typed reports. Retrospective emote-aloud reports are less likely to disrupt the natural flow of students work patterns than pop-up questions, which may increase their cognitive load and remind them that their affect is being measured. However, students may offer different labels in the moment than they do after the learning task has ended, due either to lack of memory or to being influenced by the outcome of the learning task or by the experience of watching themselves on video.

Finally, human log file annotation methods, which are considerably more rare for affect research than observational or self-report methods, have been used in some cases (see in, Ai et al., 2006; Lee et al., 2011). This method, which can be conducted through labeling "text replays" of data (see Figure 16.4) when analyzing log files, is more commonly used for identifying behaviors (see in, Baker, Corbett, & Wagner, 2006; Sao Pedro, Baker, Montalvo, Nakama, & Gobert, 2010) than affect. Although there are cases in which a student's affect is very clearly indicated by their behavior (e.g., Figure 16.4), in many cases, affect can be ambiguous for a human coder from this indicator alone. For most cases, we recommend obtaining other ground truth measures of affect whenever possible. These methods (e.g., video or field observations) may then be used to develop machine-learned annotations of log files, rather than annotating log files with affect by hand.

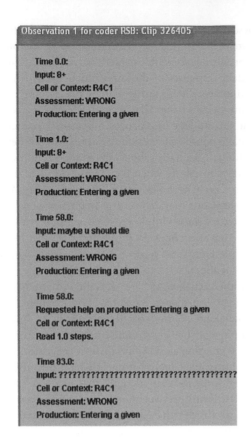

Observation 1 for coder RSB: Clip 326405

Time 0.0:
Input: 8+
Cell or Context: R4C1
Assessment: WRONG
Production: Entering a given

Time 1.0:
Input: 8+
Cell or Context: R4C1
Assessment: WRONG
Production: Entering a given

Time 58.0:
Input: maybe u should die
Cell or Context: R4C1
Assessment: WRONG
Production: Entering a given

Time 58.0:
Requested help on production: Entering a given
Cell or Context: R4C1
Read 1.0 steps.

Time 83.0:
Input: ??
Cell or Context: R4C1
Assessment: WRONG
Production: Entering a given

Fig. 16.4 An example of frustration in a text replay (data from student use of Cognitive Tutor Algebra).

Feature Engineering

Feature engineering, the process of distilling aspects of student interactions into numerical or categorical predictor variables that can be used within the data mining process, is one of the most challenging parts of developing models of student affect (or indeed, of any construct). Selecting, designing, and implementing the distillation of appropriate data features is a time-consuming step, and the quality of the features developed will have a major impact on the performance of the eventual detector.

There is sometimes a perception that feature engineering is like "throwing spaghetti at a wall and seeing what sticks"—that a vast number of arbitrary features are created and then tested to see which work. Indeed, it is often desirable to engineer more features than are needed, utilizing the data to determine which features are most useful. However, using too many features often leads to overfitting.

Setting a goal of testing model generalization to new datasets rather than testing model fit within the current dataset reduces the risks incurred by generating large numbers of features because spurious features are unlikely to be effective both in the original dataset and in held-out or new datasets, particularly if the new datasets represent different populations or contexts.

As the field develops, some consideration to feature quality and appropriateness is also warranted. One approach to selecting appropriate features is to cull from those used in previous research (as in the papers discussed in this chapter), both those which have been used to predict similar constructs and those which have effectively predicted other constructs in related learning systems. For example, researchers building detectors of affect in a science microworld might find it helpful to study the features used to detect other constructs in that microworld. Previously developed models may also prove useful; for example, models that contextually estimate the probability that a correct response is a guess have proven useful in detectors of both confusion and boredom in an intelligent tutoring system for mathematics (Baker et al., 2012).

Expert domain knowledge can also be leveraged to improve the feature engineering process, explicitly considering the appropriateness of each feature for predicting a given construct. This is often done informally, in selecting which features to engineer first. However, it can also be done more formally, when an overly large feature set has already been developed. In the domain of knowledge modeling, Sao Pedro et al. (2012) have found that weighting expert theoretical perspectives on construct validity along with evidence on goodness of fit results in better performance on held-out test set data than solely considering evidence on goodness of fit.

Detector Validation

To obtain a comprehensive picture of an affect detector's quality, it is useful to validate it in a number of fashions. There are also some considerations (discussed earlier to some degree) that can make for improved validity of a detector for a specific use.

One method for establishing validity is to examine models in terms of multiple performance metrics. For example, accuracy, which was once frequently employed in the validation process, is now less common this metric ignores the base rates of the affective states being modeled. One method for establishing validity is to examine models in terms of multiple performance metrics. This reduces the chance of using a metric that is misleading or otherwise difficult to interpret. For example, accuracy, which was once frequently employed in the validation process, has become less common as researchers observed that models which achieved high statistical accuracy often performed worse than chance. That is, because accuracy ignores the base rates of the affective states being modeled, a model may appear accurate but still perform worse than a model that always predicts the majority class. (See discussion of this issue in Sayette et al., 2001.) For this reason, it is now common to use alternative metrics. One alternative that address this issue is Cohen's κ, which indicates the degree to which a detector is better than the base rate. However, κ also has some limitations. It treats false positives and false negatives as equivalent when they have different costs in many applications. It does not have an easily computable standard error, making statistical calculations involving κ difficult. Most seriously, it ignores model confidence, treating detector confidences of 0.51 the same as detector confidences of 1, and confidences of 0.49 the same as confidences of 0. This implies that confidences of 0.51 and 0.99 are more similar than confidences of 0.51 and 0.49. As such, κ can underestimate the quality of models that appropriately indicate their confidence and do well at classifying unambiguous cases.

For that reason, researchers should also validate using metrics that account for the differences in meaning between obtaining false positives and false negatives. Among these metrics, precision and recall are preferred by many researchers (Davis & Goadrich, 2006). These metrics provide indicators of a detector's ability to identify those cases where an intervention is needed and to exclude those cases where intervention is not needed. Both precision and recall are scaled between 0 and 1. Like κ, neither of these metrics take model confidence into account.

One metric that takes model confidence into better account is A', which very closely approximates AUC, the area under the ROC curve (Hanley & McNeil, 1982). A' is the probability that a model can distinguish between an example where a construct is present and an example where that construct is not present—for example, comparing between a 20-second clip of behavior where a student is bored and a 20-second clip of behavior where the student is not bored. In making this comparison, A' explicitly considers model confidence rather than just overall predictions, giving credit to a case in which the bored clip receives a confidence of 0.47 and the not bored clip receives a confidence of 0.46. It is also feasible to conduct statistical significance testing with A', even in cases in which data is distributed across many students (see discussion in Baker, Corbett, Roll, & Koedinger, 2008).

When validating affect detectors, researchers are also beginning to pay more attention to the contexts in which the model will be used. As discussed earlier, it is now common to cross-validate at the student level, which increases confidence that a model will be appropriate when applied to data from new students drawn from the same population as the original sample. Depending on how a model will be used, it can also be valuable to explicitly consider model generalizability at the population level (increasing confidence that a model will transfer to new populations) (see in, San Pedro, Rodrigo, & Baker, 2011) or at the content level (see in, Baker, Corbett, Roll, & Koedinger, 2008). Another important factor to consider is cultural differences, both in terms of detector validation and the original ground truth training labels. It can be difficult for field observers to successfully identify affect in students of other cultures. Although some automated detectors of related constructs have been shown to transfer between specific cultures (e.g., San Pedro et al., 2011), there are sufficient differences in educational software usage between different countries (see in, Nicaud, Bitta, Chaachoua, Inamdar, & Maffei, 2006; Ogan et al., 2012) to warrant concern about detector appropriateness when detectors are transferred between cultures. These concerns may also apply for differences among urban, rural, and suburban schools.

In general, it is important to make sure that the validation of a model is representative of expected conditions of use. As discussed earlier, there were some limits on validation in early work on sensor-free affect detection. For example, validating on only a single affective state versus the neutral state does not indicate if the desired affective state can be distinguished from other affective states. Similarly, Conati and Maclaren (2009a) have shown that validating on a resampled distribution can bias in favor of better results than would be obtained on the original distribution, an important methodological contribution. By taking the steps detailed earlier to validate in a comprehensive fashion, we increase the chances that our models will be valid, appropriate, and useful in all of the contexts where they are applied, be it for intervention or discovery with models analyses.

Conclusion

At the time of this writing, interaction-based sensor-free affect detection is getting steadily better every year. Model validation is becoming more stringent, yet, at the same time, model performance is also improving. It is not clear what the asymptotic performance of stringently validated interaction-based detectors will be, but detector performance is steadily improving. Even at the point when D'Mello et al. (2008) was published, computer agreement was comparable to agreement between novice judges making continual ratings of affect from video. Over time, we may be able to develop detectors with the same level of performance as expert human judges under more favorable conditions.

One key trend enabling the field to mature is the continued improvement in feature engineering. The data mining algorithms used vary by research groups, but progress in feature engineering appears to transfer between groups. As multiple groups model these constructs, share their approaches with each other, and refine their understanding of these constructs (see in, Sao Pedro et al., 2012), we are able to capitalize on each other's successes.

As these detectors continue to improve, they will support two types of use: discovery about the nature and context of these constructs' emergence and the development of interventions. In turn, these developments will enhance the science of affect and support the development of affectively adaptive systems that can improve student affect and affective regulation skills.

References

Ai, H., Litman, D., Forbes-Riley, K., Rotaru, M., Tetreault, J., & Purandare, A. (2006). Using system and user performance features to improve emotion detection in spoken tutoring dialogs. *Proceedings of Interspeech*, 797–800.

AlZoubi, O., Calvo, R. A., & Stevens, R. H. (2009). Classification of EEG for emotion recognition: An adaptive approach. *Proceedings of the 22nd Australasian Joint Conference on Artificial Intelligence*, 52–61.

Arroyo, I., Cooper, D. G., Burleson, W., Woolf, B. P., Muldner, K., & Christopherson, R. (2009, July). Emotion sensors go to school. In *Proceeding of the 2009 conference on Artificial Intelligence in Education* (pp. 17–24). July 6–10, Brighton, UK: IOS Press.

Baker, R. S., Corbett, A. T. & Koedinger, K. R. (2007). The difficulty factors approach to the design of lessons in intelligent tutor curricula. *International Journal of Artificial Intelligence in Education*, *17*(4), 341–369.

Baker, R. S. J. d., Corbett, A. T., Roll, I., Koedinger, K. R. (2008). Developing a Generalizable Detector of When Students Game the System. *User Modeling and User-Adapted Interaction*, *18*(3) 287–314.

Baker, R. S. J. d., Corbett, A. T., & Wagner, A. Z. (2006). Human classification of low-fidelity replays of student actions. *Proceedings of the Educational DataMining Workshop at the 8th International Conference on Intelligent Tutoring Systems* (pp. 29–36).

Baker, R. S. J. d., D'Mello, S. K., Rodrigo, M. M. T., & Graesser, A. C. (2010). Better to be frustrated than bored: The incidence, persistence, and impact of learners' cognitive-affective states during interactions with three different computer-based learning environments. *International Journal of Human-Computer Studies*, *68*(4), 223–241.

Baker, R. S. J. d., Gowda, S. M., Wixon, M., Kalka, J., Wagner, A. Z., Salvi, A., Aleven, V., Kusbit, G., Ocumpaugh, J., & Rossi, L. (2012). Sensor-free automated detection of affect in a cognitive tutor for algebra. *Proceedings of the 5th International Conference on Educational Data Mining*, 126–133.

Baker, R. S. J. d., Moore, G., Wagner, A., Kalka, J., Karabinos, M., Ashe, C., & Yaron, D. (2011). The dynamics between student affect and behavior occurring outside of educational software. *Proceedings of the 4th Bi-annual International Conference on Affective Computing and Intelligent Interaction*.

Boehner, K., DePaula, R., Dourish, P., & Sengers. P. (2005). Affect: From information to interaction. In *Proceedings of the 4th decennial conference on Critical computing: Between sense and sensibility* (pp. 59–68). New York: ACM Press.

Calvo, R., & D'Mello, S. K. (2010). Affect detection: An interdisciplinary review of models, methods, and their applications. *IEEE Transactions on Affective Computing*, *1*(1), 18–37.

Calvo, R., & D'Mello, S. K. (2011). Introduction to affect-sensitive learning technologies. In R. A. Calvo & S. D'Mello (Eds.), *New perspectives on affect and learning technologies*. New York: Springer.

Calvo, R., Peters D., & Peters L. (2009). Two approaches for the design of affective computing environments for education. In *Proceedings of the Workshop Closing the Affective Loop in Intelligent Learning Environments*. AIED Brighton, UK, July 2009.

Conati, C., & Maclaren, H. (2009a). Empirically building and evaluating a probabilistic model of user affect. *User Modeling and User-Adapted Interaction*, *19*(3), 267–303.

Conati C., & Maclaren H. (2009b). Modeling user affect from causes and effects. *Proceedings of UMAP 2009, First International Conference on User Modeling, Adaptation and Personalization* (pp. 4–15). Springer.

Davis, J., & Goadrich, M. (2006). The relationship between Precision-Recall and ROC curves. In *Proceedings of the 23rd International Conference on Machine Learning* (pp. 233–240). ACM.

D'Mello, S., Craig, S., Sullins, J., & Graesser, A. (2006). Predicting affective states expressed through an emote-aloud procedure from AutoTutor's mixed-initiative dialogue. *International Journal of Artificial Intelligence in Education*, *16*(1), 3–28.

D'Mello, S., & Graesser, A. C. (2006). Affect detection from human-computer dialogue with an intelligent tutoring system. In J. Gratch et al. (Eds.), *IVA 2006, LNAI 4133* (pp. 54–67). Springer-Verlag Berlin Heidelberg.

D'Mello, S. K., Craig, S. D., Witherspoon, A. W., McDaniel, B. T., & Graesser, A. C. (2008). Automatic detection of learner's affect from conversational cues. *User Modeling and User-Adapted Interaction*, *18*(1–2), 45–80.

D'Mello, S. K., & Graesser, A. (2010). Multimodal semi-automated affect detection from conversational cues, gross body language, and facial features. *User Modeling and User-Adapted Interaction*, *20*(2), 147–187.

Dragon, T., Arroyo, I., Woolf, B. P., Burleson, W., Kaliouby, R. E., & Eydgahi, H. (2008). Viewing student affect and learning through classroom observation and physical sensors. In *Proceedings of the International Conference on Intelligent Tutoring Systems* (pp. 29–39).

Ekman, P. & Friesen, W. V. (1978). *The facial action coding system: A technique for the measurement of facial movement.* Palo Alto, CA: Consulting Psychologists Press.

Fogarty, J., Baker, R., & Hudson, S. (2005). Case studies in the use of ROC curve analysis for sensor-based estimates in human computer interaction. *Proceedings of Graphics Interface (GI 2005),* 129–136.

Hanley, J. A., & McNeil, B. J. (1982). The meaning and use of the area under a receiver operating characteristic (ROC) curve. *Radiology, 143,* 29–36.

Graesser, A. C., Chipman, P., Haynes, B. C., & Olney, A. (2005). AutoTutor: An intelligent tutoring system with mixed-initiative dialogue. *IEEE Transactions on Education, 48*(4), 612–618.

Graesser, A. C., McDaniel, B., Chipman, P., Witherspoon, A., D'Mello, S., & Gholson, B. (2006). Detection of emotions during learning with AutoTutor. In *Proceedings of the 28th Annual Meetings of the Cognitive Science Society* (pp. 285–290).

Koedinger, K. R., & Corbett, A. T. (2006). Cognitive tutors: Technology bringing learning sciences to the classroom. In R. K. Sawyer (Ed.), *The Cambridge handbook of the learning sciences.* New York: Cambridge University Press.

Kölling, M., Quig, B., Patterson, A., & Rosenberg, J. (2003). The BlueJ system and its pedagogy. *Computer Science Education, 13*(4), 249–268.

Lee, D., Rodrigo, M., Baker, R., Sugay, J., & Coronel, A. (2011). Exploring the relationship between novice programmer confusion and achievement. *Affective Computing and Intelligent Interaction,* 175–184.

Litman, D. J., & Silliman, S. (2004, May). ITSPOKE: An intelligent tutoring spoken dialogue system. In *Demonstration Papers at Human Language Technologies—North American Association Computational Linguistics 2004* (pp. 5–8). Association for Computational Linguistics.

Muldner, K., & Conati, C. (2007). Evaluating a Decision-Theoretic Approach to Tailored Example Selection. In Veloso, M. (Ed.), *Proceedings of the 20th International Joint Conference on Artificial Intelligence* (pp. 483–489). Menlo Park: AAAI Press.

Nicaud, J. F., Bitta, M., Chaachoua, H., Inamdar, P., & Maffei, L. (2006). Experiments with Aplusix in Four Countries. *International Journal for Technology in Mathematics Education, 13*(2), 79–88.

Ocumpaugh, J., Baker, R. S. J. d., Rodrigo, M. M. T. (2012). *Baker-Rodrigo Observation Method Protocol (BROMP) 1.0. Training Manual version 1.0.* Technical Report. New York: EdLab/Manila, Philippines: Ateneo Laboratory for the Learning Sciences.

Ogan, A., Walker, E., Baker, R. S., Rebolledo Mendez, G., Jimenez Castro, M., Laurentino, T., & de Carvalho, A. (2012, May). Collaboration in cognitive tutor use in Latin America: Field study and design recommendations. In *Proceedings of the 2012 ACM annual conference on Human Factors in Computing Systems* (pp. 1381–1390). ACM.

Pantic, M., & Rothkrantz, L. J. (2003). Toward an affect-sensitive multimodal human—computer interaction. *Proceedings of the IEEE, 91*(9), 1370–1390.

Picard, R. (1997). *Affective computing.* Cambridge, MA: MIT Press.

Planalp, S. (1998). Communicating emotion in everyday life: Cues, channels and processes. In P. Andersen & L. Guerrero (Eds.), *Handbook of communication and emotion.* New York: Academic Press.

Planalp, S., DeFrancisco, V. L., & Rutherford, D. (1996). Varieties of cues to emotion in naturally occurring settings. *Cognition and Emotion, 10*(2), 137–153.

Porayska-Pomsta, K., Mavrikis, M., D'Mello, S. K., Conati, C., and Baker. I. J, (2013). *Artificial Intelligence in Education, 22*(3):107–140.

Porayska-Pomsta, K., Mavrikis, M., & Pain, H. (2008). Diagnosing and acting on student affect: The tutor's perspective. *User Modeling and User-Adapted Interaction, 18*(1–2), 125–173.

Rodrigo, M. M. T., & Baker, R. S. J. d. (2009). Coarse-grained detection of student frustration in an introductory programming course. In *Proceedings of ICER 2009: The International Computing Education Workshop.*

Sabourin, J., Mott, B., & Lester, J. (2011). Modeling learner affect with theoretically grounded dynamic Bayesian networks. *Affective Computing and Intelligent Interaction,* 286–295.

San Pedro, M. O. C., Rodrigo, M. M., & Baker, R. S. J. d. (2011). The relationship between carelessness and affect in a cognitive tutor. In *Proceedings of the 4th Bi-annual International Conference on Affective Computing and Intelligent Interaction.*

Sao Pedro, M., Baker, R. S. J. d., & Gobert, J. (2012). Improving construct validity yields better models of systematic inquiry, even with less information. In *Proceedings of the 20th International Conference on User Modeling, Adaptation and Personalization (UMAP 2012)* (pp. 249–260).

Sao Pedro, M. A., Baker, R. S. J. d., Montalvo, O., Nakama, A., & Gobert, J. D. (2010). Using text replay tagging to produce detectors of systematic experimentation behavior patterns. In Proceedings of the 3rd International Conference on Educational Data Mining (pp. 181–190).

Sayette, M. A., Cohn, J. F., Wertz, J. M., Perrott, M. A., & Parrott, D. J. (2001). A psychometric evaluation of the facial action coding system for assessing spontaneous expression. *Journal of Nonverbal Behavior, 25*(3), 167–185.

Sebe, N., Cohen, I., Gevers, T., & Huang, T. S. (2005, January). Multimodal approaches for emotion recognition: A survey. In *Proceedings of SPIE—the International Society for Optical Engineering* (vol. 5670, pp. 56–67).

VanLehn, K., Jordan, P., Rosé, C., Bhembe, D., Böttner, M., Gaydos, A., Maxim, M., Pappuswamy, U., Riggenberg, M. Roque, A., Siler, S. & Srivastava, R. (2002). The architecture of Why2-Atlas: A coach for qualitative physics essay writing. In *Intelligent tutoring systems* (pp. 158–167). Berlin/Heidelberg: Springer.

Woolf, B., Burleson, W., Arroyo, I., Dragon, T., Cooper, D., & Picard, R. (2009). Affect—aware tutors: Recognising and responding to student affect. *International Journal of Learning Technology, 4*(3), 129–164.

Zeng, Z., Pantic, M., Roisman, G. I., & Huang, T. S. (2009). A survey of affect recognition methods: Audio, visual, and spontaneous expressions. *Pattern Analysis and Machine Intelligence, IEEE Transactions, 31*(1), 39–58.

Multimodal Affect Recognition for Naturalistic Human-Computer and Human-Robot Interactions

Ginevra Castellano, Hatice Gunes, Christopher Peters, *and* Björn Schuller

Abstract

This chapter provides a synthesis of research on multimodal affect recognition and discusses methodological considerations and challenges arising from the design of a multimodal affect recognition system for naturalistic human-computer and human-robot interactions. Identified challenges include the collection and annotation of spontaneous affective expressions, the choice of appropriate methods for feature representation and selection in a multimodal context, and the need for context sensitivity and for classification schemes that take into account the dynamic nature of affect and the relationship between different modalities. Finally, two examples of multimodal affect recognition systems used in (soft) real-time naturalistic human-computer and human-robot interaction frameworks are presented.

Key Words: multimodal affect recognition, feature representation and selection, context sensitivity, human-computer interaction, human-robot interaction

Introduction

Recent work in human-computer interaction (HCI) and human-robot interaction (HRI) has shown that embodied agents and robots are increasingly being studied as partners that collaborate and do things with people (Breazeal, 2009; Schroeder et al., 2012). For example, the use of embodied agents and robots is being investigated in many HCI and HRI applications, such as providing assistance for the elderly at home, serving as tutors for children by enriching their learning experiences, and acting as therapeutic tools or as game buddies for entertainment purposes.

These applications require embodied agents and robots to be endowed with social skills. Social perception abilities include affect sensitivity—that is, the ability to recognise people's affective expressions and states, understand their social signals—and account for the context in which the interaction takes place (Castellano et al., 2010a). Affect sensitive embodied agents and robots are more likely to be able to engage with human users over extended periods of time as compared with their nonaffective counterparts (Bickmore & Picard, 2005).

Research on automatic affect recognition has contributed several studies on the design of systems capable of perceiving multimodal social, cognitive, and affective cues (e.g., facial expressions, eye gaze, body movement, physiological data, etc.) and using them to infer a user's affective and cognitive state (Calvo & D'Mello, 2010; Zeng et al., 2009).

Recently there has been a shift toward real-world HCI and HRI, which has led to the emergence of new trends in multimodal affect recognition. These include, among others, an increased focus on the automatic recognition of spontaneous and nonprototypical affective states, the development of techniques for continuous affect prediction— which allows for the dynamics of affective states to be taken into consideration, and the design of context-sensitive affect recognition systems.

Compared with systems based on a single modality, multimodal affect recognition has the potential to achieve increased recognition performances. It is still an open question, however, why improvements of multimodal affect recognition systems over their unimodal counterparts are still relatively modest, especially when natural data is used, as shown by D'Mello and Kory (2012) in a recent meta-analysis of thirty affect recognition studies.

This chapter provides an overview of the state of the art on multimodal affect recognition, the challenges that underlie the design of a multimodal affect recognition system, and two examples of successful integration of multimodal affect recognition systems for real-time HCI and HRI.

Multimodal Affect Recognition: State of the Art and Challenges

While affect recognition systems based on one modality have been extensively investigated, studies taking into account the multimodal nature of affective states have been gaining ground only recently (Zeng et al., 2009). D'Mello and Kory (2012) showed that multimodal affect recognition systems are consistently better than their unimodal counterparts, supporting the general tendency in the literature to move toward systems that combine multiple modalities for the purpose of predicting a user's affect. Nevertheless, evidence shows that improvements over unimodal systems are still modest, suggesting the need for classifiers and fusion methods that better capture the relationships between different modalities, and for affective corpora that contain adequate samples of synchronized expressions (D'Mello & Kory, 2012).

The latest shift toward real-world HCI and HRI is driving research on multimodal affect recognition in new directions. This, in turn, has brought new challenges that need to be considered as opportunities that open up new avenues for research.

For example, of late there has been an increased interest in the automatic recognition of spontaneous, nonprototypical affective states (Castellano et al., 2012; Kleinsmith et al., 2011; Lucey et al., 2011), rather than of prototypical or basic emotions (such as anger, disgust, fear, happiness, sadness, and surprise) and a shift toward dimensional affect recognition (Gunes & Schuller, 2013; Gunes et al., 2011), which is based on a description of human affect in terms of a set of dimensions, such as valence (i.e., positive or negative affect) and arousal (i.e., affect characterized by low or high activation).

Another aspect that is receiving a lot of attention is the development of novel methods for multimodal fusion (Metallinou et al., 2013; Nicolaou et al., 2012), which should take into consideration the underlying relationships and correlation between feature sets in different modalities and affect dimensions, how different affective expressions influence each other, and how much information each of them provides about the expressed affect.

An emerging trend that addresses the need for the dynamics of affective states to be accounted for is continuous affect prediction, based on a user's input that is continuously available and analyzed over time, which aims to produce continuous values for the target affect or affect dimensions (Meng & Bianchi-Berthouze, 2011; Nicolaou et al., 2012). This is especially important for the integration of affect recognition systems in real-time HCI and HRI frameworks.

Finally, some studies have started to address the issue of context-sensitive affect recognition, which takes into account the context in which the interaction takes place (e.g., task, user preferences, presence of other people, behavior of the interactant, etc.) in order to improve affect recognition performances (Castellano et al., 2012; Kapoor & Picard, 2005; Martinez & Yannakakis, 2011).

The following sections discuss in detail how the current challenges in affect recognition research are being addressed in the literature, with a specific focus on multimodal affect recognition systems.

Data Collection
BEYOND PROTOTYPICAL EMOTIONS AND ACTED AFFECTIVE EXPRESSIONS

Research on multimodal affect recognition is moving from the lab to the real world; hence the need for corpora and databases that contain spontaneous and subtle, rather than acted, prototypical and exaggerated affective expressions. While examples of naturalistic databases are gradually increasing in the literature (e.g., Lucey et al., 2011; McKeown et al., 2012, 2013), currently most affect recognition systems have been trained on databases of acted affective expressions. These often reflect stereotypes and exaggerated expressions, and they are often decontextualized. Moreover, most of the available databases contain expressions of prototypical emotions that seldom represent affective states emerging in HCI and HRI applications. This has been the case, so far, for most unimodal and multimodal affect recognition systems.

Real-world HCI and HRI require affect recognition systems trained with databases containing contextual descriptions synchronized with other modalities (Castellano et al., 2010b), a research direction that is still underexplored. Moreover, most of the available acted databases contain expressions recorded in contexts that are not specific to a particular application. While the availability of affect databases that can be used for training affect recognition systems applicable to several interaction scenarios is a pressing need, real-world HCI and HRI scenarios require contextualized affective expressions (i.e., expressions that emerge in the same scenario of the final application) for system training and validation.

ANNOTATION

The training and testing of affect recognition systems requires ground truth data, which are usually obtained via observational assessment. While ideally one would ask the participants of an HCI or HRI experiment to rate the affective states they experienced, this is seldom a viable solution. First of all, ratings are usually collected at the end of the experiment via questionnaires, but this does not allow for affective states emerging at specific instants of the interaction to be captured. On the other hand, continuous self-annotation of affect during the experiment is not practical. Another option is to ask participants to watch videos of their experiment and label the affective states they feel they experienced; however, this may be problematic—for example, when children are involved. Alternatively, affect annotation can be performed with the help of external coders. These are usually assigned presegmented videos and asked to label each one (Castellano et al., 2010). Another approach is continuous annotation of affect dimensions from videos using tools such as Feeltrace (McKeown et al., 2012).

Affect annotation still presents open issues—for example, the difficulty of achieving good intercoder agreement and the time-consuming nature of the annotation process, which often requires enormous efforts in recruiting and training coders. Another open question concerns whether affective stimuli should be labeled by simultaneously taking into account all the modalities available to the coder rather than considering the single modalities separately. The first approach has the advantage of providing the coder with an overall perspective of the emergence of an affective state, including the context in which the affective cues are displayed.

Feature Extraction
FEATURE REPRESENTATION—FRAME- VERSUS WINDOW-BASED

Different modalities tend to operate on different time scales. In addition, the feature sampling frequency can be variable: For example, for video processing (e.g., facial expression analysis or body gestures by motion capture, depth cameras or similar), often a constant frame rate, such as 25 frames per second (fps), is chosen as a basis to calculate features such as tracked facial points, global motions, local (Gabor) binary patterns, or transformed image information, etc., for the analysis of shape- or appearance-based characteristics. This is often similar for physiological feature information. In acoustic speech analysis, suprasegmental features are calculated per word, turn, or similar entity with differing length over frame-level features typically extracted at around 100 fps. This usually includes prosodic (intonation, intensity, duration, etc.), cepstral, spectral (Mel frequency cepstral coefficients, formant information, etc.), and voice quality description (harmonicity, perturbations, etc.). Frame-level features are often referred to as *low-level descriptors* (LLDs), and the suprasegmental features are *functionals*—that is, the time series of unknown length of frame-level LLD features is projected onto a single scalar value per LLD. Such functionals comprise extremes, means, higher moments, peaks, percentiles, regression coefficients, segments, or spectral and temporal characteristics; one can also apply these in a hierarchical manner such as the extremes of means and vice versa. For linguistic feature information, it seems obvious that the sampling interval cannot be fixed, as it depends on the speech rate, and one usually has to wait until the end of linguistic entities such as words. Based on individual entities or sequences of these, one can apply knowledge from resources such as affective word lists, execute deeper linguistic analyses, or extract functional-type feature information such as bags of words, etc.

At some point, however, some form of synchronization will be needed—either to unite the feature information or to come to a decision at a certain moment in time informed by the diverse modalities (see Stream Fusion, p. 251). One option to reach this goal is the application of functionals to the diverse LLDs from different modalities and also to the processing of video, physiological, or other multimodal information on a suprasegmental level. Decisive in this case is the unit of analysis of interest, which can be linguistic entities if linguistic analysis is involved. This allows a recognition system to directly attach affective information to these units—such as words, turns or similar—which may be well suited from an application point of view. In case of absence of speech, or a multimodal fusion without availability of such linguistically motivated information, fixed intervals at a larger "macro" window size can be a good choice. Again, the application scenario will have an influence on the choice of the window length as a compromise between reasonably fast update, sufficient LLD feature information, and "stationary emotion" (i.e., the emotion can be assumed not to change over the unit of analysis) within this macro window. A typical value can be around 1 second, as was used in the SEMAINE project (see Multimodal Affect Detection for a Sensitive Artificial Listener, p. 252); however, more research will be needed to identify an optimal value.

FEATURE SELECTION IN A MULTIMODAL CONTEXT

Obviously one can optimize the feature space individually per information stream, such as acoustic or video features. However, the multimodal context allows for a combined feature selection, in particular in the case of a feature-level fusion (see Early Feature-Level Fusion, p. 251). This can lead to improved performance (Schuller et al., 2008). In fact, an individual optimisation per stream followed by a combined selection process can be an interesting choice: At first, the often highly correlated information should be reduced individually per modality. Then, a secondary optimisation process can lead to further improvements reducing cross-modal redundancy (Schuller et al., 2008). As unimodal data are usually available in larger amounts than multimodal data, the optimization per single modality can partly benefit from more available data. Likewise, if the number of considered modalities or feature streams is greater than two, selection of subgroupings of modalities could be considered.

Context Sensitivity

To correctly understand a phenomenon—an affective display for example—it is often necessary to move beyond the phenomenon in isolation to consider broader circumstances and aspects. These can be thought of as surrounding the phenomenon in both space (a smile interpreted in the context of the movements of the rest of the face) and time (dialogue preceding the smile), and can potentially include many factors relating to the interactants (personality, gender, culture, preferences, moods, goals), their impressions of each other and even themselves (how others perceive them, their goals, and so on), and the state of the interaction (commencing, maintained, closing). For example, ratings of the behavior of individuals may vary depending on their accompanying background (Ennis et al.,

2011). Context is therefore of great importance in attempting to improve the performance and robustness of affect recognition systems, especially when other modalities are not sufficient or lead to nonmeaningful interpretations. Context is typically difficult to account for, however, as it necessarily involves the identification of those features, from among a large number of potential candidates, that are most relevant to understanding and interpreting an unfolding situation.

While some efforts have been reported in the literature, only a limited number of studies have addressed the problem of context-sensitive affect recognition. Kapoor and Picard (Kapoor & Picard, 2005), for example, proposed an approach for the recognition of interest in a learning environment by combining nonverbal cues and information about the learner's task (e.g., level of difficulty and state of the game). Peters and colleagues (Peters et al., 2010) used eye gaze and head direction to model user engagement with a virtual agent. Interpretation of the quality of user engagement with the interaction is contextualized by accounting for gaze toward relevant objects at appropriate times in the interaction. In this case, participant gaze toward an object when it has not been part of the recent discussion is deemed to signal less engagement than participant gaze toward an object that has just been described by the system. Context sensitivity is also a vital basis for determining the novelty of events and objects (Grandjean & Peters, 2011), which is fundamental to social attention, recollection, and learning capabilities in artificial social entities.

A key challenge is contextual feature representation—that is, how to model and encode relationships between different types of context and between context and other modalities. Morency et al. (2008) proposed a context-based recognition framework that integrates information from human participants engaged in a conversation to improve visual gesture recognition. They proposed the idea of an encoding dictionary, a technique for contextual feature representation that models different relationships between a contextual feature and visual gestures. Martinez and Yannakakis (2011) proposed a method for the fusion of physiological signals and game-related information for automatic affect recognition in a game scenario. Their approach uses frequent sequence mining to extract sequential features that combine events across different user input modalities. Castellano and colleagues (2012) investigated contextual feature representation in a game-based HRI scenario and explored how to encode task and game context and their relationships in a timely manner for automatic engagement prediction. They investigated the use of overall features, which capture game and social context in an independent way at the interaction level, and turn-based features, which encode the interdependencies of game and social context at each turn of the game. They found that the integration of game- and social context–based features with features encoding their interdependencies leads to higher recognition performances.

Classification Schemes

Classification methods for affect recognition can be viewed under two schemes: static versus dynamic classification and discrete versus continuous recognition.

STATIC VERSUS DYNAMIC MODELING

Analysis of automatic human nonverbal behavior can be performed either by using the features from one frame at a time or by considering the sequential nature of the frame sequence, as in a time series. These two approaches are referred to as *static or frame-based* and *dynamic or sequence-based* classification, respectively (Petridis et al., 2009). Commonly used static classifiers are support vector machines, neural networks, and decision trees. Dynamic Bayesian networks, hidden Markov models, and their variations (e.g., coupled hidden Markov models) constitute the well-known dynamic classifiers.

Researchers claim that in the static classification case, dynamic properties of human affective behavior should be captured by the features, while in dynamic classification, they are dealt with by the classifier. Vogt et al. (2008) argue that in speech-based emotion recognition, most works use different feature representation for static and dynamic classification; therefore, it is not possible to clearly attribute the higher recognition accuracy to either classification technique (dynamic versus static). A number of researchers reported that dynamic classifiers are better suited for person-dependent facial expression recognition (e.g., Cohen et al., 2003), which is likely to be the case for affect recognition from other modalities. This was attributed to the fact that dynamic classifiers are more sensitive to both differences in terms of appearance change and differences in temporal patterns among individuals. Static classifiers were reported as being more reliable when the frames represent the apex of an expression (Cohen et al., 2003). Other researchers reported that the frame-based classification outperforms the sequence-based classification in the task of temporal segment detection from face and body displays (e.g., Gunes & Piccardi, 2009). Overall, the usefulness of static versus dynamic classification depends on the feature representation (frame- versus window-based feature representation) and the task at hand (Petridis et al., 2009).

DISCRETE VERSUS CONTINUOUS RECOGNITION

Traditionally, research in the field of automatic affect recognition has focused on recognizing discrete, basic emotional states from posed data acquired in laboratory settings. However, these models are deemed unrealistic, as they are unable to capture the nonbasic and subtle affective states exhibited by humans in everyday interactions. Therefore researchers have started adopting a dimensional description of human emotion, where an emotional state is characterized in terms of a number of latent dimensions (Gunes & Schuller, 2013; Gunes et al., 2011, Kleinsmith et al., 2011). Two dimensions are deemed sufficient for capturing most of the affective variability: valence and arousal, signifying respectively how negative/positive and active/inactive an emotional state is. Other dimensions have also been proposed (Fontaine et al., 2007).

Dimensional quantized (discrete) classification of affect is usually done by reducing the prediction problem to a two/three/four-class classification problem (e.g., positive versus negative or active versus passive classification (Nicolaou et al., 2010, 2011a). The choice of classifier depends on the context and the application. Classification methods used for discrete affect detection and recognition include, among others, support vector machines (SVMs), multilayer perceptron networks, k-nearest neighbor classifiers, naïve Bayes classifiers, radial basis function networks, linear discriminant analysis, conditional random fields, hidden Markov models (HMMs), and variations of these (e.g., coupled HMMs or asynchronous HMMs) (Nicolaou et al., 2010). Various frameworks that combine the benefits of multiple classifiers have also been proposed (e.g., a multilayer hybrid framework for classification (Nicolaou et al., 2011b; Meng et al., 2013).

Continuous affect measurements should be able to produce continuous values for the target dimensions. Some of the classification schemes that have been explored for this task are support vector regression, relevance vector machines, and long short-term recurrent neural networks (e.g., Nicolaou et al., 2011a, 2012). Overall, for automatic affect analysis of continuous input, there is no agreement on how to model dimensional affect space (continuous versus quantized) and which classifier is better suited for automatic multimodal analysis of continuous affective input.

The two emerging trends in continuous affect prediction are the so-called output-associative prediction (e.g., Nicolaou et al., 2012) and the design of emotion-specific classification schemes (e.g., Nicolaou et al., 2011b). Output-associative prediction exploits the correlations between the dimensions and learns dependencies among the predicted values. Creating emotion-specific schemes for continuous prediction of emotions is relatively new and needs to be investigated further.

Stream Fusion

EARLY FEATURE-LEVEL FUSION

In automatic affect prediction, feature-level fusion is obtained by concatenating all the features from multiple cues into one feature vector, which is then fed into a machine learning model (e.g., Nicolaou et al., 2011a). If the frame rate of the audio stream differs from that of the video stream (e.g., 50 Hz versus 25 fps), some form of adaptation is needed during feature-level fusion (e.g., Nicolaou et al., 2011a; Petridis et al., 2009). Feature-level fusion becomes more challenging as the number of features increases and when the features are of very different nature. Synchronization then becomes of utmost importance.

LATE SEMANTIC FUSION

The most straightforward approach whereby to tackle modality fusion is at the decision level, since feature and time dependence are abstracted. Each classifier processes its own data stream and the multiple sets of outputs are combined at a later stage to produce the final hypothesis. Decision-level fusion can be obtained at the *soft level* (a measure of confidence is associated with the decision) or at the *hard level* (the combining mechanism operates on single hypothesis decisions). There has been some work on combining classifiers and providing theoretical justification for using simple operators such as majority vote, sum, product, maximum/minimum/median, and adaptation of weights.

Explicit fusion of multimodal data refers to first automatically detecting behavioral cues that are known to convey important affective information (e.g., head nods, smiles, pauses) and then fusing explicitly only these higher-level cues. A representative example of explicit fusion is the work of Eyben et al. (2011), who proposed a string-based approach for fusing the behavioral events from visual and audio modalities (i.e., facial action units, head nods and shakes, and verbal and nonverbal vocal cues) to predict human affect in a continuous dimensional space in terms of arousal, expectation, intensity, power, and valence dimensions. A number of approaches have also been reported for explicit synchronization purposes of multiple streams. For instance, Gunes et al. (2009) identified the neutral-onset-apex-offset-neutral phases of face and body expressions recorded via separate cameras and synchronized the information from face and body streams at the phase level (i.e., by detecting the apex phase of face and body expressions stream).

HYBRID FUSION

Since humans display multimodal expressions in a complementary and redundant manner, the assumption of conditional independence between modalities and cues in decision-level fusion can result in loss of information (i.e., loss of mutual correlation between the modalities). *Model-level fusion* has been adopted to mitigate the issues pertinent to feature- and decision-level fusion by exploiting the correlations between the modalities while relaxing the requirement of synchronization. By doing this, model-level fusion has the potential of capturing correlations and structures embedded in the continuous output of the classifiers or regressors from different sets of cues. It may use Bayesian networks, multistream fused HMM, tripled HMM, neural networks, etc. (see Zeng et al., 2009 for details on these).

Overall, finding the best way to fuse the modalities for automatic emotion prediction remains an open issue in the field. An emerging trend in affective data fusion is called output-associative fusion (e.g., Nicolaou et al., 2011a). This fusion method capitalizes on the fact that the emotion dimensions (valence and arousal) are correlated. In order to exploit these correlations and patterns, the output-associative fusion framework aims to learn the dependencies that exist among the predicted dimensional values.

Multimodal Affect Detection for (Soft) Real-Time HCI and HRI: Methodological Considerations and Case Studies

The timely analysis and interpretation of a user's affective state is of primary importance for HCI and HRI in real-world settings. For example, it is vital for embodied agents and robots to establish an affective loop with the user through the generation of a response that is appropriate to the way the user is feeling. Despite the large body of existing literature on affect recognition, examples of automatic affect recognition systems for integration in HCI and HRI frameworks are still not numerous. Further, not many system prototypes have been designed which can work in real environments in the long term. The next sections present two case studies where a multimodal affect recognition system has been successfully applied to real-world HCI and HRI scenarios.

Multimodal Affect Detection for a Sensitive Artificial Listener—Results and Lessons Learned from the SEMAINE Project

The SEMAINE system is a pioneering effort in creating dynamic, expressive, and adaptive virtual agents by analyzing the multimodal nonverbal communicative behavior of the human user in soft real-time. The system aims to engage the user in a dialog and create an emotional workout by paying attention to the user's nonverbal expressions, and reacting accordingly. It focuses on the *soft skills* that humans naturally use to keep a conversation alive (e.g., backchannel feedback such as nodding and smiling). The SEMAINE system avoids task-oriented dialogue, instead, it models the type of interaction sometimes found at parties: you listen to someone you want to chat with, and without really understanding much of what the other person is saying, you exhibit all the signs that are needed for him or her to continue talking to you. The SAL characters can speak to engage the user in a simple dialogue as well as show nonverbal listener signals (Figure 17.1). The approach has been test run using various "Wizard of Oz" setups that have allowed the fine tuning of the scripts used by the various characters in order to react to the emotional

state of the user in plausible ways despite the lack of language understanding. The SEMAINE system has been demonstrated at]: International Conference on Affective Computing and Intelligent Interaction (ACII 2009) (Schröder et al., 2009) and IEEE International Conference on Automatic Face and Gesture Recognition FG'11 (Schröder et al., 2011).

AUDIOVISUAL AFFECT RECOGNITION IN A REAL-LIFE SYSTEM

In a real-life system, such as the SEMAINE system, affective data can be thought of as uninterrupted streams originating from a variety of sensors (cameras, microphones, etc.); to achieve optimal affect prediction, prior to recognition, or simultaneously with this, there is a requirement to segment the data and to determine analysis duration (Gunes et al., 2011) or the unit of analysis (Schuller et al., 2011b). Segmenting multimodal data in a meaningful way is directly related to the level at which the detection results should be accurate and that at which the detection results should be analyzed and outputted (frame, millisecond, second, or minute level). The current solution is to employ various window sizes depending on the modality. The achievement of real-time affect prediction requires a small window size to be used for analysis (i.e., a few seconds), but obtaining a reliable prediction accuracy requires longer-term monitoring. Overall, the challenge for future research is to find an appropriate unit of analysis which is sensitive to the context at hand. Another issue is that research on affect analysis and affect generation (synthesis) appear to be detached from each other even in multiparty and multidisciplinary projects such as SEMAINE (Schröder et al., 2011). Investigation of how to interrelate these in earlier stages will provide valuable insight into the realization of affect-sensitive systems that are able to interpret multimodal and continuous input and respond appropriately.

Fig. 17.1 A user conversing with one of the SAL characters (i.e., Poppy).

THE AUDIOVISUAL EMOTION CHALLENGES

The AVEC series of two consecutive public challenges on audiovisual emotion recognition is the first of its kind for multimodal affect detection. It is based on data collected in the SEMAINE project, and offers a test bed for uni- and multimodal emotion recognition including acoustic, linguistic, and video cues. Four affect dimensions are to be assessed: arousal, expectation, power, and valence. While the annotation of the data was done in a continuous manner both in time and values, the first challenge, as held in 2011 (Schuller et al., 2011), required participants to solve a two-class problem with respect to above or below the average value per dimension. In addition, the video stream was chunked in two ways over time: per frame for the video only task and per word for the audio and audiovisual tasks. In the second round held in 2012 (Schuller et al., 2012), this was changed to a continuous regression-type measurement in value either at the frame or word level. The 2011 installation thus used three different test partitions for three subchallenges, providing files containing either audio only (as test partition for the audio subchallenge), or video only (as test partition for the video subchallenge), or both (for the audiovisual subchallenge) to ensure that only this modality was used for result assessment. In the 2012 installation, the same test partition was used no matter which modality was exploited for the best result. Instead, two types of subchallenges focused either on fully continuous (i.e., frame-level emotion assessment) or word-level assessment. This means that emotion needed to be recognized either for every frame or per word (i.e., over a larger frame that lasted as long as each spoken word). Only parts where audio was actually present were used.

Besides the audiovisual data, 1,941 (2011)/1,841 (2012) precomputed audio features brute-forced by functional application to LLDs (see Feature Representation—Frame- Versus Window-Based, p. 248) and 5,908 video features are given for optional usage and baselines. These features and the data are freely available to experiment with; however, the labels of the test partition remain with the organizers and results can be acquired by submission of predictions on these instances.

Various classification methods have been applied to the 2011 audiovisual task of AVEC: support vector machines, extreme learning machine-based feed forward neural networks, AdaBoost, Gaussian mixture models, and a combined system consisting of MLPs and HMMs. At the time of the challenge, latent-dynamic conditional random fields led to the best result of 60.3% weighted accuracy on average over the four dimensions (Ramirez et al., 2011). Later, the best audiovisual result to date was reached by long short-term recurrent neural networks (Wöllmer et al., 2012) with 64.6% weighted accuracy for late fusion. The authors used the baseline acoustic feature set and optical flow video features after rectifying the tracked facial region.

The 2012 event highlights the particular challenge of fully continuous emotion assessment: 0.456 as cross-correlation coefficient was reached by the winning team (Nicolle et al.) as averaged over the four affective dimensions. In the case of the word-level subchallenge, this measure exceeded only 0.28.

Multimodal Affect Recognition for a Robotic Companion—Results and Lessons Learned from the LIREC Project

The EU FP7 LIREC (LIving with Robots and intEractive Companions) project (2008–2012) explored long-term social relationships with socially intelligent robotic companions. Within LIREC, MyFriend is an HRI scenario that showcases an iCat robot acting as a game companion for young children (Figure 17.2). The robot plays chess with children, provides affective feedback based on the moves on an electronic chessboard, interacts with them by displaying facial expressions and verbal utterances, and reacts empathically based on the valence of the affects the children experience throughout the game (Castellano et al., 2013).

CONTEXT-SENSITIVE AFFECT RECOGNITION IN REAL-WORLD HRI SETTINGS

The robotic game companion is built on a novel platform for affect sensitive, adaptive HRI. The platform integrates an array of sensors in a modular client-server architecture that includes a vision module, a game engine, an affect recognition module, an empathic behavior generation engine coupled with an action selection and an appraisal mechanism, and the iCat robot module. After every move made by the user, the user's affective state is inferred by the affect recognition module based on behavioral indicators provided by the vision module (i.e., probability of smile, eye gaze) and contextual indicators (i.e., game-related features) extracted by the game engine (Castellano et al., 2012).

The affect recognition module consists of an SVM-based valence detector. It continuously receives synchronized features from the vision module and the game engine and, as output, provides

Fig. 17.2 A user interacting with iCat in a primary school.

probability values for the valence of the user's affect. At any time during the interaction, the iCat module can send a request to the affect recognition module to evaluate the affective state experienced by the user in the previous N seconds of the game/interaction. Information about the user's affective state is then used by the robot to select and generate an empathic intervention, such as providing encouraging comments or suggesting a good move. The valence detector was trained using the Inter-ACT corpus, an affective and contextually rich multimodal video corpus including spontaneous expressions of children playing chess with the iCat robot in a primary school and a chess club (Castellano et al., 2010b). Nonverbal behaviors (i.e., smiles and eye gaze) and game-based features (i.e., state of the game and game evolution) were automatically extracted and synchronized before being combined in a joint feature space for training the valence detector. An SVM classifier with radial basis function (RBF) kernel achieved a recognition performance of 63% in a three-class valence classification problem (three labels: positive, negative, or neutral) (Castellano et al., 2013).

Results from studies integrating the platform for affect-sensitive, adaptive human-robot interaction in the robotic companion and carried out in a semicontrolled environment in a primary school showed that affect sensing and empathic interventions lead to increased engagement with the robot and an increased perception of friendship from the robot (Leite et al., 2012a) as compared with neutral behavior. Affect sensing and empathic interventions also allowed the establishment of interactions that were more engaging and more successful over extended periods of time, which is an important requirement for companionship (Leite et al., 2012b).

Important challenges for future research in the domain of affect recognition for social robots include the design of systems that can adapt to specific users, successfully encode relationships between contextual features and between context and other modalities, and are highly robust (e.g., they are capable of performing successful continuous affect prediction over extended periods of time).

Conclusions and Future Directions

This chapter provided an introduction to multimodal affect recognition for naturalistic HCI and HRI. We showed how the latest trends in multimodal affect recognition research are opening up new opportunities for real-time interactions with embodied agents and robots in real-world settings. Particularly, we identified key challenges in the design of a multimodal affect recognition system for naturalistic HCI and HRI. These include:

1. *The collection and annotation of data containing spontaneous affective expressions.* Real-world HCI and HRI require affect recognition systems trained with corpora and databases that contain spontaneous and subtle rather than acted and prototypical affective expressions.

2. *The choice of appropriate methods for feature representation and feature selection in a multimodal context.*

Different modalities tend to operate on different time levels and may be dependent one another; additionally, some of them may be more important than others for the purpose of affect prediction in a specific application scenario. Hence there is the need to choose appropriate methods for feature representation and feature selection in a multimodal context.

3. *The design of affect recognition systems sensitive to context.*

Context can be used as an additional modality to improve the performance of an affect recognition system. A key challenge here is how to model and encode relationships between different types of context and between context and other modalities.

4. *The design of classification schemes that take into account the dynamic nature of affect and the relationship between different feature sets.*

Continuous affect prediction has been shown to be successful in addressing the dynamic nature of affective states; novel methods for multimodal fusion need to take into consideration the underlying relationships and correlations between feature sets in different modalities and affect dimensions.

While several issues in multimodal affect recognition require further investigation, we have shown how initial attempts at addressing these challenges can lead to the successful integration of multimodal affect recognition systems in HCI and HRI frameworks.

Acknowledgement

The works of the authors are partially supported by the following grants: G. Castellano by the European Commission (EC) via by the EU FP7 ICT-317923 project EMOTE (EMbOdied-perceptive Tutors for Empathy-based learning), H. Gunes by the EPSRC EP/L00416X/1 Digital Personhood project 'Being There' (Humans and Robots in Public Space). The authors acknowledge that they are solely responsible for the content of this publication. It does not represent the opinion of the EC and/or EPSRC and the EC and/or EPSRC is not responsible for any use that might be made of data appearing therein

References

Bickmore, T., & Picard, R. (2005). Establishing and maintaining long-term human—computer relationships. *ACM Transactions on Computer-Human Interaction* 12(2), 293–327.

Breazeal, C. (2009). Role of expressive behaviour for robots that learn from people. *Philosophical Transactions of the Royal Society D, 364, 3527–3538.*

Calvo, R. A., & D'Mello, S. K. (2010). Affect Detection: An interdisciplinary review of models, methods, and their applications. *IEEE Transactions on Affective Computing*, 1(1), 18–37.

Castellano, G., Leite, I., Pereira, A., Martinho, C., Paiva, A., & McOwan, P. W. (2010a). Affect recognition for interactive companions: Challenges and design in real-world scenarios. *Journal on Multimodal User Interfaces*, 3(1–2), 89–98.

Castellano, G., Leite, I., Pereira, A., Martinho, C., Paiva, A., & McOwan, P. W. (2010b). Inter-ACT: An affective and contextually rich multimodal video corpus for studying interaction with robots. In *Proceedings of the ACM international conference on multimedia 2010* (pp. 1031–1034). New York: Association for Computing Machinery.

Castellano, G., Leite, I., Pereira, A., Martinho, C., Paiva, A., & McOwan, P. W. (2012). Detecting engagement in HRI: An exploration of social and task-based context. In *Proceedings of the IEEE/ASE international conference on social computing (SocialCom'12)* IEEE Press.

Castellano, G., Leite, I., Pereira, A., Martinho, C., Paiva, A., & McOwan, P. W. (2013). Multimodal affect modelling and recognition for empathic robot companions. *International Journal of Humanoid Robotics*, 10(1), 1–23

Cohen, I., Sebe N., Garg, A., Chen, L. S., & Huang, T. S. (2003). Facial expression recognition from video sequences: temporal and static modeling. *Computer Vision and Image Understanding*, 91(1–2), 160–187.

D'Mello, S. K., & Kory, J. (2012). Consistent but Modest: A Meta-Analysis on Unimodal and Multimodal Affect Detection Accuracies from 30 Studies. In L. P. Morency et al. (Eds.), *Proceedings of the 14th ACM international conference on multimodal interaction* (pp. 31–38). New York: Association for Computing Machinery.

Ennis, C., Peters, C., & O' Sullivan, C. (2011). Perceptual effects of scene context and viewpoint for virtual pedestrian crowds, *ACM Transactions on Applied Perception*, 8(2), 10:1–10:22.

Eyben, F., Woellmer, M., Valstar, M. F., Gunes, H., Schuller, B., & Pantic, M. (2011). String-based audiovisual fusion of behavioural events for the assessment of dimensional affect.

Proceedings of IEEE conference on automatic face and gesture recognition (pp. 322–329), IEEE Press

Fontaine, J., Scherer, K., Roesch, E., & Ellsworth, P. (2007). The world of emotions is not two-dimensional. *Psychological Science*, 18(12).

Grandjean, D., & Peters, C. (2011). Novelty processing and emotion: conceptual developments, empirical findings and virtual environments. In P. Petta, C. Pelachaud, & R. Cowie (Eds.), *Emotion-oriented systems: The humaine handbook* (pp. 441–458). New York: Springer.

Gunes, H., & Schuller, B. (2013). Categorical and dimensional affect analysis in continuous input: Current trends and future directions. *Image and Vision Computing*, 31(2), 120–136.

Gunes, H., Schuller, B., Pantic, M., & Cowie, R. (2011). Emotion representation, analysis and synthesis in continuous space: A survey. In *Proceedings of IEEE FG 2011* (pp. 827–834).

Gunes, H., & Piccardi, M. (2009). Automatic temporal segment detection and affect recognition from face and body display. *IEEE Transactions on Systems, Man, and Cybernetics-Part B*, 39(1), 64–84.

Kapoor, A., & Picard, R. W. (2005). Multimodal affect recognition in learning environments. In *Proceedings of the ACM international conference on multimedia 2005* (pp. 677–682).

Kleinsmith, A., Bianchi-Berthouze, N., & Steed, A. (2011). Automatic recognition of non-acted affective postures. *IEEE Transactions on Systems, Man and Cybernetics Part B.*, 41, 1027–1038.

Leite, I., Castellano, G., Pereira, A., Martinho, C. & Paiva, A. (2012a). Modelling empathic behaviour in a robotic game companion for children: an ethnographic study in real-world settings. In *Proceedings of the ACM/IEEE international conference on human-robot interaction (HRI'12)*. ACM Press

Leite, I., Castellano, G., Pereira, A., Martinho, C., & Paiva, A. (2012b). Long-term Interactions with empathic robots: Evaluating perceived support in children. In *Proceedings of the international conference on social robotics*. Springer-Verlag, 298–307.

Lucey, P., Cohn, J. F., Prkachin, K. M., Solomon, P. E., & Matthews, I. (2011). Painful data: The UNBC-McMaster shoulder pain expression archive database. In *IEEE International conference on automatic face and gesture recognition (FG2011)* (pp. 57–64).

Martinez, H. P., & Yannakakis, G. N. (2011). Mining multimodal sequential patterns: A case study on affect recognition. In *Proceedings of the 13th international conference on multimodal interaction (ICMI'11)*. New York: Association for Computing Machinery. (pp. 3–10)

McKeown, G., Valstar, M., Cowie, R., Pantic, M., & Schroeder, M. (2012). The SEMAINE database: Annotated multimodal records of emotionally coloured conversations between a person and a limited agent. *IEEE Transactions on Affective Computing*, 3, 5–17.

McKeown, G., Curran, W., McLoughlin, C., Griffin, H., & Bianchi-Berthouze, N. (2013). Laughter induction techniques suitable for generating motion capture data of laughter associated body movements. In *Proceedings of 2nd international workshop on emotion representation, analysis and synthesis in continuous time and space (EmoSPACE), in conjunction with the IEEE conference on automatic face and gesture recognition*.

Meng, H., & Bianchi-Berthouze, N. (2013). Affective state level recognition in naturalistic facial and vocal expressions, *IEEE Transactions on Systems, Man, and Cybernetics Part B*, in press.

Meng, H., & Bianchi-Berthouze, N. (2011). Naturalistic affective expression classification by a multi-stage approach based on hidden markov models. In *Proceedings of the 4th international conference on affective computing and intelligent interaction* (pp. 378–387). New York: Springer.

Metallinou, A., Katsamanis, A., & Narayanan, S. (2013). Tracking continuous emotional trends of participants during affective dyadic interactions using body language and speech information. *Image and Vision Computing (IMAVIS)* (Special Issue on Affect Analysis in Continuous Input), 31(2), 137–152.

Morency, L.-P., de Kok, I., & Gratch, J. (2008). Context-based recognition during human interactions: Automatic feature selection and encoding dictionary. In *Proceedings of the ACM International Conference on Multimodal Interfaces (ICMI'08)* (pp. 181–188), ACM Press.

Nicolaou, M. A., Gunes, H., & Pantic, M. (2012). Output-associative RVM regression for dimensional and continuous emotion prediction. *Image and Vision Computing Journal*(Invited Paper for the Special Issue on Best of 2011 Automatic Face and Gesture Recognition), 30 (3), 186–196.

Nicolaou, M. A., Gunes, H., & Pantic, M. (2011a). Continuous prediction of spontaneous affect from multiple cues and modalities in valence-arousal space. *IEEE Transactions on Affective Computing* (Special Issue on Affect Based Human Behavior Understanding), 2(2), 92–105.

Nicolaou, M. A., Gunes, H., & Pantic, M. (2011b). A multi-layer hybrid framework for dimensional emotion classification. In *Proceedings of ACM multimedia* (pp. 933–936).

Nicolaou, M. A., Gunes, H., & Pantic, M. (2010). Audio-visual classification and fusion of spontaneous affective data in likelihood space. In *Proceedings of international conference on pattern recognition* (pp. 3695–3699).

Nicolle, J., Rapp, V., Bailly, K., Prevost, L. & Chetouani, M. (2012). Robust continuous prediction of human emotions using multiscale dynamic cues. In *Proceedings of the 14th ACM international conference on multimodal interaction* (pp. 501–508). New York: Association for Computing Machinery.

Peters, C., Asteriadis, S., & Karpouzis, K. (2010). Investigating shared attention with a virtual agent using a gaze-based interface. *Journal on Multimodal User Interfaces*, 3(1–2), 119–130.

Petridis, S., Gunes, H., Kaltwang, S., & Pantic, M. (2009), Static vs. dynamic modeling of human nonverbal behavior from multiple cues and modalities. *Proceedings of ACM international conference on multimodal interfaces* (pp. 23–30).

Ramirez, G., Baltrusaitis, T., & Morency, L. P. (2011). Modeling latent discriminative dynamic of multi-dimensional affective signals. In *Proceedings first international audio/visual emotion challenge and workshop, AVEC 2011* (held in conjunction with the international HUMAINE association conference on affective computing and intelligent interaction 2011, ACII 2011) (Vol. II, pp. 396–406). New York: Springer.

Schuller, B., Wimmer, M., Arsic, D., Moosmayr, T., & Rigoll, G. (2008). Detection of security related affect and behaviour in passenger transport. In *Proceedings INTERSPEECH 2008, 9th annual conference of the international speech communication association* (pp. 265–268), ISCA/ASSTA, ISCA.

Schuller, B., Valstar, M., Eyben, F., McKeown, G., Cowie, R., & Pantic, M. (2011). AVEC 2011—The first international audio/visual emotion challenge. In *Proceedings first international audio/visual emotion challenge and workshop, AVEC 2011* (held in conjunction with the international

HUMAINE association conference on affective computing and intelligent interaction 2011, ACII 2011) (Vol. II, pp. 415–424). New York: Springer.

Schuller, B., Valstar, M., Cowie, R., & Pantic, M. (2012). AVEC 2012—The continuous audio/visual emotion challenge. In *Proceedings of the 14th ACM international conference on multimodal interaction* (pp. 449–456). New York: Association for Computing Machinery.

Schröder, M., Bevacqua, E., Cowie, R., Eyben, F., Gunes, H., Heylen, D.,...Wöllmer, M. (2012). Building autonomous sensitive artificial listeners. *IEEE Transactions on Affective Computing*, 3(2), 165–183.

Schröder, M., Bevacqua, E., Eyben, F., Gunes, H., Heylen, D., ter Maat, M.,...Wöllmer, M. (2009). A demonstration of audiovisual sensitive artificial listeners. In *Proceedings of IEEE conference on affective computing and intelligent interaction* (pp. 263–264).

Schröder, M., Pammi, S., Gunes, H., Pantic, M., Valstar, M., Cowie, R.,...de Sevin, E. (2011). Come and have an emotional workout with sensitive artificial listeners! In *Proceedings of IEEE conference on automatic face and gesture recognition* (pp. 646).

Vogt, T., Andre, E., & Wagner, J. (2008). Automatic recognition of emotions from speech: a review of the literature and recommendations for practical realisation. In *LNCS 4868*, (pp. 75–91).

Wöllmer, M., Kaiser, M., Eyben, F., Schuller, B. & Rigoll, G. (2012). LSTM-modeling of continuous emotions in an audiovisual affect recognition framework. *Image and Vision Computing* (special issue on affect analysis in continuous input), 31(2), 153–163.

Zeng, Z., Pantic, M., Roisman, G. I., & Huang, T. S. (2009). A survey of affect recognition methods: Audio, visual, and spontaneous expressions. *IEEE Transactions on Pattern Analysis and Machine Intelligence*, 31(1), 39–58.

Affect Generation

Facial Expressions of Emotions for Virtual Characters

Magalie Ochs, Radoslaw Niewiadomski, *and* Catherine Pelachaud

Abstract

A virtual character's expressions of emotions may significantly enhance human-machine interaction. To give virtual characters the ability to display emotions, they should be endowed with a lexicon of facial expressions that convey emotional meanings in conversational settings. In this chapter, we explore research works highlighting different methodologies both to identify the morphological and dynamic characteristics of emotional facial expressions and to measure the effects of the emotional expressions on the user's perception during human-machine interaction.

Key Words: embodied conversational agent (ECA), nonverbal behavior, stereotypical expression, lexicon

Introduction

Facial expressions convey information about emotional states, mood, intentions, stances, and so on. Even what seems a very simple signal such as head nod (Heylen, 2006) or smile (Ochs et al., 2011) can convey a large number of meanings. A slight change in their dynamism or morphology can be perceived by human observers and can be interpreted as transmitting different intentions and emotional states.

Embodied conversational agents (ECAs) are dialogue partners to human users endowed with human-like communicative capabilities. As such, they ought to display a large repertoire of communicative and emotional behaviors. Moreover, several researches have shown that such a virtual character expressing emotions enhances human-machine interaction. By creating an *illusion of life,* one well-known effect of the expressions of emotionsis an increase in the agent's believability (Bates, 1994; Thomas & Johnston, 1981) but also an improvement in the user's perception of the virtual character (Maldonado et al., 2004), of the user's satisfaction (Hone, 2006), and of the user's relationship with the virtual agent (Bickmore & Picard, 2005).

In building a repertoire of nonverbal behaviors for virtual agents, one is faced with the need to gather a variety of signals where subtle variation can alter their meaning (within a given discourse context). So one of the difficulties that must be addressed is to find the adequate level of signals description to capture subtle variations while not overfitting the signals description. Another difficulty is to ensure that the agent can display multiple signals to convey any specific high-level communicative function. This is crucial for the agents so that they will not appear to be too repetitive. So this issue concerns creating signals with morphological or dynamic variations without altering their associated meaning. Another related difficulty is to ensure that facial expressions displayed by the agent correlate with the events the agent is facing. Psychological theories, such as the appraisal theory of emotions (Scherer, 2001), highlight how the evaluation of the characteristics of a situation may trigger an emotional response. There is a tight connection between the evaluation process, the arousal of an emotion, and its expression through behavioral changes. It is also important that human users interpret the created expressions as conveying specific messages. While it is necessary to be able to interpret the nonverbal behaviors of a virtual agent in a dialogue context, this does not mean that they should be highly readable. Indeed, highly recognizable expression may look too much like caricatures and may lose in naturalness.

The challenges described above need to be addressed in building a lexicon of multimodal behaviors for ECAs. We review below various attempts, some relying on theoretical models and other on data analysis or even computational models.

Creation of a Lexicon of Virtual Characters' Facial Expressions

A facial expression arises from muscular contraction. To animate the facial expression of a virtual character, both the morphological and dynamic characteristics of the virtual face should be considered. Moreover, the combination of particular muscular activities may be associated to the expressions of emotions (Ekman & Friesen, 1975) and to communicative intentions (Poggi & Pelachaud, 2002). To give a virtual character the ability to express particular emotional states and communicative intentions through its face, the latter should be endowed with a *lexicon, i.e.* a dictionary of facial expressions linking morphological and dynamic characteristics of the face to specific meanings. For the sake of simplicity, this mapping is defined here without considering the conversational settings. However the display of emotions and communicative intentions is influenced by the sociocultural settings (Ekman, 2003).

To create a lexicon of a virtual character's emotional facial expressions, two methods may be distinguished. The first consists in exploiting the empirical and theoretical research in human and social sciences on the characteristics of human's emotional faces (Theoretical-based Lexicon of Facial Expressions, p. 262). The second is based on the study of an annotated corpus containing the expressions of emotions displayed by humans or virtual characters (Corpus-Based Lexicon of Facial Expressions, p. 264).

Theoretical-based Lexicon of Facial Expressions

To create a repertoire of a virtual character's facial expressions, the method that is commonly used consists in exploiting the empirical and theoretical studies in psychology that have highlighted the morphological and dynamic characteristics of human's facial expressions. Different theories lead to different approaches.

CATEGORICAL APPROACH

Most of the computational models of a virtual character's facial expressions are based on the *categorical approach* proposed by Ekman and Friesen (1975). This approach is based on the hypothesis that humans categorize facial expressions of emotions into a number of categories that are similar across cultures: happiness, fear, anger, surprise, disgust, and sadness (also known as the "big six" basic emotions). Moreover, Ekman and colleagues (2002) have developed a system to describe human facial expressions called the *FACS* (facial action coding system). This system is widely used in the domain of virtual characters to simulate emotional facial expressions. The moving pictures experts group MPEG-4 standards support facial animation by providing facial animation parameters (FAPs) as well as a description of the expression of the six basic emotions (Ostermann, 2002).

DIMENSIONAL APPROACH

To allow virtual characters to express a large number of emotions, a *dimensional approach* was proposed (Albrecht et al., 2005; Courgeon et al., 2009; Ruttkay, Noot, & Hagen, 2003; Tsapatsoulis et al., 2002; Zhang et al., 2007). In dimensional models, a new expression is often created by applying some arithmetical operations, such as linear interpolation, on numerical definitions of discrete emotions placed in the multidimensional space. For instance, the model called emotion disc (Ruttkay, Noot, & Hagen, 2003) uses a bilinear interpolation between two basic expressions and the neutral one. In this approach, six expressions are spread evenly around the disc, while the neutral expression is set at its center. The distance from the center of the circle and an expression represents its intensity. The spatial relations in two dimensions (2D) are used to establish the expression corresponding to any point of the emotion disc.

Two models by Tsapatsoulis and colleagues (2002) and by Albrecht and colleagues (2005) use a similar approach to compute new emotional displays. Both models use the expressions of two "neighboring" basic emotions to compute a new facial expression. In Tsapatsoulis et al. (2002), a new expression can be derived from a basic one by "'scaling" it or combining the spatially closest two basic emotions. In the latter case the parameters of these two expressions are weighted by their coordinates. Albrecht et al. (2005) extend this approach by introducing a three-dimensional

(3D) space of emotional states defined by activation, evaluation, and power and an anatomical model of the face based on FACS (Ekman & Friesen, 2002).

Several other models of emotional behavior rely on a 3D space called PAD, defining emotions in terms of pleasure (P), arousal (A) and dominance (D) (Mehrabian, 1980). The model proposed by Zhang and colleagues (Zhang et al., 2007) is based on PAD and a new parameterization of facial expressions: partial expression parameters (PEPs). Each PEP defines a facial movement in a specific area of the face. Compared with other existing parameterizations—for example, MPEG-4 (Ostermann, 2002)—PEPs ensure a similar amount of detail while using fewer parameters. The authors linked PEPs with values of P, A, and D by conducting an experimental study. The validity of the expressions generated from PAD values was further confirmed in an evaluation study, where participants had to attribute the PAD and emotional labels to several generated animations (Zhang et al., 2007).

The same 3D model was also used in a study by Courgeon et al. (2009), where participants navigated in a PAD space with corresponding facial animations using a 3D control device. Eight expressions (fear, admiration, anger, joy, reproach, relief, distress, satisfaction) were attributed to the extreme points of the three dimensions (valence, activation, and dominance), while an interpolation of facial parameters defining an expression allowed for the generation of intermediate expressions (Courgeon, Buisine, & Martin, 2009).

The dimensional approach has the advantage allowing the generation of a large number of emotional facial expressions. However, the dynamic and the temporal characteristics of the expressions are generally not considered. Moreover, the large number of facial expressions pose the problem of evaluating all the generated emotional expressions.

APPRAISAL APPROACH

Other models are based on an *appraisal approach* (Scherer, Schorr, & Johnstone, 2001), such as Scherer's componential process model (Scherer, 2001). This cognitive psychological approach considers that facial expressions of emotions reflect how an individual appraises and deals with his environment. In this approach, values of appraisal variables (e.g., novelty, intrinsic pleasantness, conduciveness, and coping potential) are associated to the activation of action units (the smallest units of perceptible facial activity defined in FACS).

Among others, Paleari and Lisetti (2006) and Malatesta and colleagues (2009) focus on the temporal relations between different facial actions predicted by the sequence of appraisal evaluations of the Scherer's model. In Paleari and Lisetti (2006), the different facial actions are activated at different moments. The final animation generated on the virtual character's face is a sequence of several subexpressions linked to the SEC (Sequential Evaluation Check)'s cognitive evaluations.

In Malatesta et al. (2009), the emotional expressions are created manually from sequences predicted by Scherer's theory. As opposed to Paleari and Lisetti's work, each expression is derived by adding each new AU onto previous ones. What is more, Malatesta et al. (2009) compare their additive approach with a sequential one. Results show an above-chance level of recognition in the case of the additive approach and only marginally above random choice in the case of the sequential approach (Malatesta et al., 2009).

Recently another partial implementation of the Scherer's model was proposed by Courgeon, Clavel, and Martin (2009). In this model, the generation of facial expressions is directly driven by the evaluation of events appraised by the virtual character. For this purpose an appraisal module is implemented for a game-based scenario to associate to an event the values of seven appraisal checks (expectedness, unpleasantness, goal hindrance, external causation, copying potential, immorality, and self-consistence). Four emotions are implemented and described by their appraisal profile: anger, sadness, guilt, and joy. Expressions are generated at two levels. First, a temporary animation corresponding to the currently evaluated appraisal variable is displayed. When the evaluation of the event through all appraisal variables is finished, the system computes which emotion corresponds with the sequence of appraisal values and displays the corresponding full facial expression. The result of this evaluation can be one or more emotions. In the latter case the system displays a blend of emotions.

The appraisal approach offers a detailed control on the single elements of facial expressions as well as on their dynamics (i.e., sequence). However, the appraisal theories are still incomplete regarding the facial action predictions. They are also complex and difficult to implement, since the modeling of cognitive capabilities to infer the values of appraisal variables is required.

Corpus-Based Lexicon of Facial Expressions

To gather more subtle and natural expressions, other approaches are based on the analysis of an annotated corpus of human or virtual faces.

SYNTHESIS OF EMOTIONAL FACIAL EXPRESSIONS FROM ANNOTATED HUMAN FACES

To collect real data of persons expressing emotions, a first method consists in recording videos of actors who have been instructed to express specific emotions. Another method consists in collecting spontaneous expressions by exposing people to situations triggering various emotions. For instance, a common method to generate frustration is to simulate a bug in a computer program with which participants have to interact. The second step is the annotation of the corpus to attribute labels to expressions and to determine the morphological and dynamic characteristics of the emotion to create the lexicon of emotional facial expressions.

Based on an annotated corpus of humans expressing emotions, two approaches to synthesize virtual emotional faces have been explored. The facial expressions can be synthesized at a very low level by retargeting the points tracked on a human face to a virtual mesh or, at the higher level, using a copy-synthesis approach. In the latter, the virtual character's expressions are synthesized from the manual annotation of human facial behavior.

The synthesized facial expressions are labeled and stored in the lexicon using a low-level animation format such as MPEG4 (Ostermann, 2002) or FACS (Ekman & Friesen, 2002).

These two different approaches for building a lexicon of facial expressions were used in (Niewiadomski & Pelachaud, 2012) to build a repository of laughs. The authors built a lexicon of facial expressions using high-level procedural animation synthesis from manual annotation and low-level data-driven animation synthesis based on an optical motion capture system. The first approach consists of manually annotating the facial expressions using FACS coding (Ekman & Friesen, 2002). Then, the FACS-based manual annotation of each episode is converted into behavior markup language (BML) (Vilhjálmsson et al., 2007). BML is an XML-like standard script language used to control the behavior of a virtual character, including the face. The other method uses a machine learning algorithm and motion capture data. The 3D points of 27 markers are captured for each frame of the expression and then retargeted to the virtual mesh using temporal restricted Boltzmann machines (Zeiler et al., 2011). In this approach the model was trained to find a mapping between the 84 dimensional space of input data and the 68 FAPs in MPEG-4. The model, once trained, can be successfully applied to different data sources with only a minimum of manual tuning (Niewiadomski & Pelachaud, 2012).

These two approaches offer different degrees of flexibility and control over the expression and different levels of realism and precision of the movements. Motion capture–based animation is usually richer in movements and consequently may be perceived as more realistic. Also, the motion capture data permit maintaining the temporal and dynamic characteristics of the original expression. At the same time, the optical motion capture system is invasive, as markers must be placed on the actors' faces, which may limit their spontaneous reactions. It is also costly in resources and time.

On the other hand, describing animation by sequences of action units allows one to control an animation and its meaning precisely (e.g., by adding or removing AU6, a marker of the Duchenne smile), but it has all the weaknesses of procedural approaches to facial animation. The animation is poor in details and the dynamics of the movements are not very realistic.

USER-PERCEPTIVE APPROACH FOR EMOTIONAL FACIAL EXPRESSION SYNTHESIS

As highlighted in Grammer and Oberzaucher (2006), most of these corpus-based studies on emotional facial expressions consider a *top-down approach*. An emotion label is attributed to each facial expression. This approach assumes that each emotion corresponds with a facial expression. However, each emotion may be represented by different facial expressions. Some researchers have explored other methods to investigate different facial expressions for each emotion type. For instance, in Snodgrass (1992) and Grammer and Oberzaucher (2006), a *bottom-up approach* is proposed.

In this approach, one to several action units selected randomly are activated on a virtual face. Observers rated the randomly generated facial expressions using two emotional dimensions (pleasure and arousal); in a second step, these two dimensions are mapped onto emotion types. This method has the advantage of not restricting the emotional facial expressions to a limited number of emotion types. Moreover, the lexicon of virtual characters' emotional facial expressions is directly created based on human perception.

More recently, Boukricha and colleagues (2009) ran a perceptive study to investigate the link between randomly generated facial expressions composed of several action units and their perception along the 3D space PAD (Mehrabian, 1980). These PAD ratings resulted from naïve participants' evaluations of bipolar adjectives using a Likert scale (semantic differential measures of emotional state or characteristic [trait] emotions, as proposed by Mehrabian 1980).

The evaluated expressions were placed in the dimensional space, where dominance takes one of two discrete values (high or low dominance) and pleasure and activation values were mapped onto a continuous space. A facial expression control space was constructed from multivariate regressions. It consisted in mapping AUs and the dimensions allowing one to generate a facial expression to any point of the 3D space.

Following a user-perceptive approach, another method to create a repertoire of emotional facial expressions for virtual characters consists in collecting a corpus of virtual characters' expressions

directly created by users. This method breaks with the traditional approach used to create a repertoire of expressions: instead of asking people to label existing expressions, users are at the heart of the creation process of the virtual character's expressions. This method was first used to identify the morphological and dynamic characteristics of different types of smile (amused, polite, and embarrassed smiles) (Ochs et al., 2011). A web application has been developed to enable a user to easily create different smiles on a virtual character's face (Figure 18.1).

Through radio buttons on an interface, the user can generate any smile by choosing a combination of seven parameters (amplitude of smile, duration of smile, mouth opening, symmetry of the lip corner, lip press, and velocity of the onset and offset of the smile). Two or three discrete values were considered for each of these parameters (for instance, small or large for the amplitude of the smile). When the user changes the value of one of the parameters, a virtual character shows the corresponding animation automatically. Considering all the possible combinations of the discrete values of the parameters, there are 192 different ones, each corresponding to a smile. Users were instructed to create one

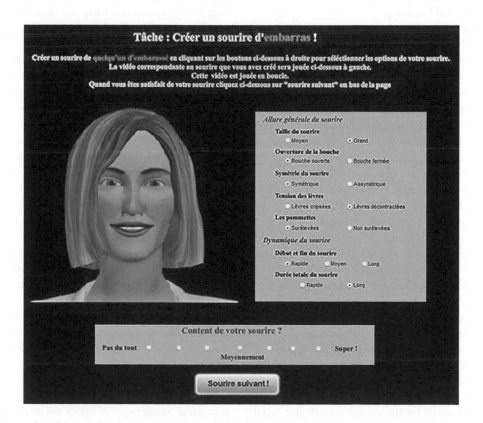

Fig 18.1 Screenshot of the interface to create a virtual character's facial expressions.

animation for each type of smile. The collected corpus contained 348 descriptions for each smile (amused, embarrassed, and polite). Based on this smile corpus and a decision tree classification technique, an algorithm was defined to determine the morphological and dynamic characteristics of the smile types (Ochs et al., 2011). As in the approach proposed by Grammer and Oberzaucher (2006), the advantage of such a method is to consider not only one single expression for each smile type but a variety of facial expressions. That enables one to increase the repertoire of the virtual character's expressions.

Rendering of Facial Expressions

The past 10 years have seen many works on creating photorealistic skin rendering. Remarkable results have been obtained that imitate digital photos of human faces extremely well. Several aspects of rendering need to be addressed. To begin with, the skin is rendered. Skin is a complex material that is translucent and partially reflects light. Wrinkles are also an important feature of realistic faces. Wrinkles can be due to muscular contraction resulting from facial expressions and can be static because of aging. Other communicative features of faces include tears, pallor, and blushing.

The Emily project led by Debevec's group (Alexander et al., 2010) aims to pass the Turing test in facial performance; that is, it aims to reproduce with a very high degree of realism the rendering and animation of faces. To this end a sophisticated scan system called light stage was built; it is made of a dome of hundreds of LEDs that allow the face of an actress to be captured with light coming from all directions. The LEDs can be modified to simulate various lighting conditions. From the captured images of the actress, the subsurface and specular reflections of the actress's face are separated. Moreover, ambient occlusion corresponding to self-shadowing and interreflections along cavities of the nose, eyes, and mouth is taken care of. The final rendering of the face uses a hybrid normal rendering algorithm (Ma et al., 2007). Animation is obtained by capturing the actress enacting various expressions and creating corresponding blend shapes.

Stoiber et al. (2010) developed an algorithm to reproduce facial rendering and animation with high resolution in real time and with a less heavy device than the previous model. A camera mounted on a helmet worn by the actress records her facial expressions. Facial expressions of a participant are recorded and tracked using contours in real time. Using motion models and after some retargeting, the recorded facial expressions are reproduced on synthetic models. The dynamism of the facial expressions is maintained: The motion models are learned using statistical approach applied on motion capture data; they incorporate the non-linearity of facial expression dynamisms (Stoiber, Breton, & Séguier, 2010).

Jimenez et al. (2010) proposed a model that renders perceptually realistic human skin. To ensure their computational model is real-time, their idea was to translate the simulation of subsurface scattering effects from texture to screen space. Later on, the authors added expressive wrinkles to their model (Jimenez et al., 2011). Wrinkles are designed as normal maps that are added to base normal maps and blend shapes in a weighted manner. To validate that their approximation did not introduce a loss of realism, the authors conducted perceptual studies. Participants viewed images of faces rendered with different lighting conditions and had to choose which faces were the closest to real human faces.

Other models of wrinkles have been proposed. They can be gathered into two main approaches: geometry- and texture-based methods. While geometric methods simulate dynamic wrinkles by directly deforming mesh geometry (Courgeon, Buisine, & Martin, 2009), texture-based methods use bump mapping (Blinn, 1978). For instance, Niewiadomski et al. (2012) use the texture-based technique called "screen space bump wrinkle" to model wrinkles. In this approach the surface normal vector is modified before the lighting computation. Using this new surface normal vector in the render process gives a visually satisfying result without changing the surface geometry. Simulation of wrinkle effects is performed by computing the perturbed normal vector in screen space with Pixel Shader. Thus the complexity of the computation depends only on the number of pixels and not on the number of vertices of the facial model. Twelve groups of wrinkles related to different AUs are defined as texture. In runtime, when an action unit is activated on the face mesh, the Graphics Processing Unit - GPU receives its intensity value and computes the corresponding wrinkles. The final result is the composition of all active wrinkles (Figures 18.2 and 18.3).

de Melo and Gratch (2009) integrate not only wrinkles but also blushing, tears, and sweating effects into facial rendering. Wrinkles are modeled using bump mapping and then are synchronized with

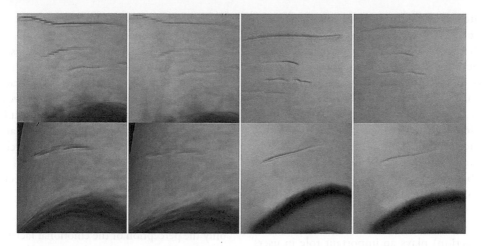

Fig. 18.2 Wrinkles for the raised eyebrows movement (AU1 + AU2).

the muscle-based facial model. Interestingly, the simulated wrinkles are copied from the pictures of a human displaying the respective wrinkle configuration. Photographed wrinkles are then converted to gray scale, blurred, and applied to the virtual human texture. The tearing and sweating animations are also modeled through bump mapping and rely on the modeling of the properties and dynamics of water.

Works by Larboulette and Cani, (2004) and Courgeon, Buisine, and Martin (2009) offer examples of geometry deformation approaches. Mesh editing tools are used to define control points, which are perpendicular to the wrinkles, and to define the influence regions associated to each wrinkling curve. The wrinkling behavior is controlled by a set of parameters that specify the way the mesh deforms.

The Virtual Character's Emotional Facial Expressions in Interaction

The virtual character's emotional facial expressions are generally constructed without considering the context of the interaction. To take advantage of a virtual character displaying emotions, the emotional facial expressions should be seen in appropriate situations during the interaction.

Expressions of Emotions in Context

Several researches have shown that virtual characters expressing emotions enhance human-machine interaction (Bates, 2009; Bickmore & Picard, 2005; Hone, 2006; Maldonado et al., 2004; Thomas & Johnston, 1981). However, some studies (Beale & Creed, 2009; Ochs, Pelachaud, & Sadek, 2008) have

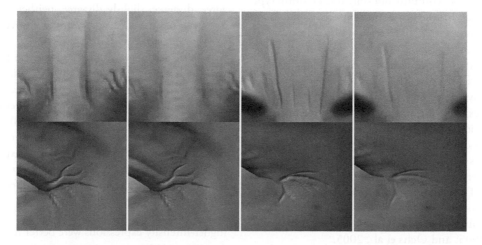

Fig. 18.3 Wrinkles corresponding to action AU4 and AU6.

highlighted the importance of the *social context*. The social context includes the situation in which the user and the virtual characters are (place, actions, etc.), the social roles of the participants in the interaction, the cultural context, and social norms (Riek & Robinson, 2011). For instance, as shown by Beale and Creed (2009), an emotional virtual character may have a different impact on users depending on its social role. For example, an emotional learning companion leads to better effects on users' perception than an emotional tutor (Beale & Creed, 2009). The situation in which the emotions are expressed (i.e., when and which emotions are displayed during the interaction) plays an important role in users' behavior. Some emotional behaviors, such as the expression of empathy, seem to enhance the interaction, whereas expressions of self-emotions may have little impact (Beale & Creed, 2009). Moreover, an emotion expressed in an inappropriate situation may even have negative effects on the interaction—for instance, by degrading users' perceptions of virtual characters (Ochs, Pelachaud, & Sadek, 2008).

To automatically compute the emotions that a virtual character should express, some existing tools can be used. For instance, the open-source computational model FATIMA (FearnotAffecTIve Mind Architecture) (João & Paiva, 2005) computes the emotions of a virtual character elicited by events occurring in the environment, considering the influence of the character's personality, social relations, culture, and empathy. Other computational models of emotion have been developed (for more details, see the chapter by Gratch and Marsella in this volume). Such a model of emotions may compute not only one emotion type but several. Indeed, an event may elicit a sad emotion in the virtual character but also a little bit of surprise; at the same time, the social norms may indicate that in this situation the virtual character should express joy. This kind of situation occurs every day in human life. To create an emotionally reflexive agent and not an impulsive one with an emotional behavior similar to that of a child, a virtual character should convey these emotional subtleties (Ochs et al., 2005). Consequently the expressions of emotions might result in a combination of several emotion types. Several computational models have been proposed for the synthesis or blending of emotions—for instance, Albrecht et al., 2005, and Ochs et al., 2005.

Perceptive Studies of Emotional Virtual Characters

A virtual character's facial expressions of emotions may have significant impacts on the interaction, especially on users' behavior. The same facial expression of emotion may lead to positive or negative effects depending on the social context in which the emotion is displayed. Consequently an important step is the evaluation of the virtual character's expression of emotions.

Perceptive studies of emotional virtual characters may be considered at two levels:

1. A *context-free level* of evaluation, in which only the perception of the emotional facial expressions is evaluated without considering any information about the context

2. An *in-context level* of evaluation, in which the perception of a virtual character expressing emotions is evaluated in a particular context of interaction

CONTEXT-FREE LEVEL OF EVALUATION

In a *context-free level* of evaluation, the objective is to validate that the emotional facial expressions are recognized with the expected intensities and types—or dimensions such as pleasure and dominance, as proposed by Grammer and Oberzaucher (2006). The context of the interaction is not considered. The method generally used to perform such an evaluation is to present videos of virtual characters expressing the emotions and to ask users to indicate the recognized emotion types and intensity through a forced-choice questionnaire.

To capture the uncertainty of the users regarding the recognized emotions, Likert scales (with for instance different levels of agreement: strongly disagree, disagree, slightly disagree, neither agree nor disagree, slightly agree, agree, strongly agree) can be used to collect the users' responses.

Several perceptive studies at a context-free level have highlighted the role of the dynamics, intensity, and rendering of synthesized facial expressions of virtual characters on the user's perception. For instance, Katsyri and Sams (2008) showed that synthetic dynamic expressions were identified better than static ones only for expressions whose static displays were not similar. In a similar study by Noëland et al. (2006), the effect of the dynamics was, however, not observed. Bartneck and Reichenbach's work (2005) shows that the higher-intensity expressions were better recognized.

Courgeon, Buisine, and Martin (2009) showed that the application of wrinkles increases the agent's expressivity but does not improve recognition. Also in de Melo and Gratch (2009), wrinkles, blushing, and sweating added to the expressivity of some stereotypical (basic) expressions such as anger, fear, and sadness.

Keltner (1995) showed that expressions of emotion are more like a sequence of facial actions than full-blown single-shot displays. The later ones occur rarely in real-life interactions. Single facial actions are ambiguous, as they can be the components of different facial expressions. The action unit identification on virtual faces can be more challenging than the identification of stereotypical full-blown expressions. While the latter can be easily identified from a subset of features (i.e., some information is redundant), the identification of atomic facial actions is local and requires that attention be paid to details. Nevertheless, it can be supposed—following, for example, the appraisal theory—that the appearance of each action unit in the sequence is significant and meaningful; thus, if some of these are not properly identified, the meaning of a facial expression can be altered. The work presented by Niewiadomski, Huang, and Pelachaud (2012) offers an example of a perceptive study at a context-free level that focuses on the perception of single facial actions rather than stereotypical expressions. The results show that single facial actions are better identified when they are dynamic and of higher intensity. On the other hand, intense expressions of single facial actions are perceived as less natural and less realistic. Finally, wrinkles did not significantly improve the identification of facial actions (Niewiadomski, Huang, & Pelachaud, 2012).

Even if the evaluation at a context-free level is done out of the context of an interaction, some elements of the social context may impact users' perceptions. The gender of the virtual character as well as the gender of the users rating the expression might lead to different perceptions. For instance, as shown by Krumhuber, Manstead, and Kappas (2007) and Katsikitis, Pilowsky, and Innes (1997), women are more sensitive to nonverbal signs and more able to decode facial cues, even for virtual characters' faces. Moreover, in decoding facial expressions, women make more extreme judgments than do men (Katsikitis, Pilowsky, & Innes, 1997).

IN-CONTEXT LEVEL OF EVALUATION

One main drawback to the evaluation presented above is the lack of interactivity with the user. Indeed, the user remains passive, since she is not involved in the conversation with the virtual character. The *in-context level* of evaluation consists in studying the effects of emotions expressions on the overall interaction. The objective, in this case, is to measure the benefits of the emotional virtual character for the user who is involved in an interaction with the virtual character. More than an evaluation of the facial expressions themselves, it is the emotional behavior of the virtual character (i.e., when and which emotions are displayed during the interaction) at the *in-context level* that is analyzed. As highlighted in the previous section, this kind of evaluation is all the more important, since the effects of emotion expressions may vary from positive to negative depending in the circumstances in which they are expressed.

To measure the effects of a virtual character's emotional behavior, users generally interact with a virtual character in at least two conditions: one in which the virtual character does not express any emotion (control condition) and another in which the virtual character does express emotion. A questionnaire at the end of the interaction is generally used to collect the users' overall perception of the virtual character and/or of the interaction. Objective measures may also be collected to analyze the effects of emotions. For instance, physiological sensors may be used to study the emotional reactions of users (Becker et al., 2005). The analysis of users' performances (i.e., score of test or ability to recall information) may enable one to study the benefits of an emotional character in task achievement (Maldonado et al., 2004). As proposed by Klein, Moon, and Picard (1999), the length of time during which users interact with a virtual character may be an indication of the users' engagement.

Several studies have evaluated the appropriateness of the facial behavior to the context of an interaction. In the experiment by Walker, Sproull, and Subramani (1994), people liked the facial interface that displayed a negative expression less than the one showing a neutral expression. However, in a card game, the agent that displayed only positive expressions irrespectively of the event was evaluated as less like a real human being than the one that also expressed negative emotions (Becker et al., 2005). In Rehm and André (2005), the agent expressing emotions was compared with the agent showing additionally subtle expressions of deception. The agent with deceptive facial expressions was perceived as less credible and less trustworthy. In Lim and Aylett's (2007) study of an interactive guide using appropriate emotional displays, the latter was perceived as being more believable, natural, and interesting than the one without emotional displays. These results suggest that the choice of emotional displays influences the perception of the agent. They also highlight the role of the context in the judgment.

Conclusion

In conclusion, the emotional facial expressions of virtual characters are generally created with the assumption that virtual characters should display emotions as humans do—that is, with the same morphological and dynamic characteristics of the face. Most of the models of emotional facial expressions are based on either empirical or theoretical research in human and social sciences. However, computational models may enable us to go beyond these methodologies by analyzing automatically generated facial expressions that humans may not simulate well on demand (i.e., during corpus generation with actors), and that then may be difficult to study.

During human-machine interaction, the same emotional facial expression of a virtual character may have a different effect, from positive to negative, on the user's perception depending on the situation in which the emotion is expressed. For instance, the expression of joy of a virtual agent in response to the user expressing sadness will certainly have a negative effect on the user's perception of the agent. The display of emotions should be appropriate or plausible in the situation of the interaction. As highlighted in Demeure, Niewiadomski, and Pelachaud (2011), the emotional facial expressions are appropriate if they meet expectations of what one is supposed to feel in a given situation. However, an emotional expression may be inappropriate but plausible when the expression is displayed in a situation even if the expression is not the appropriate one. The recent work of de Melo et al. (2012) shows that the user applies "reverse appraisal" to interpret the virtual character's emotional expression and then deduces information from the virtual character's facial expressions regarding, for instance, its goal-conduciveness. An emotional expression may then be displayed depending on the values of the appraisal variables that the virtual character wants to convey to the user.

Acknowledgment

This research has been partially supported by the European Community Seventh Framework Program (FP7/2007–2013), under grant agreement no. 231287 (SSPNet) and under grant agreement no. 270780 (HILAIRE).

References

Albrecht, I., Schroder, M., Haber, J., & Seidel, H. (2005). Mixed feelings: Expression of non-basic emotions in a muscle-based talking head. *Journal of Virtual Reality on Language, Speech and Gesture (Special Issue)*, 8(4), 201–212.

Alexander, O., Rogers, M., Lambeth, W., Chiang, J. Y., Ma, W. C., Wang, C. C., & Debevec, P. E. (2010). The digital Emily project: Achieving a photorealistic digital actor. *IEEE Computer Graphics and Applications*, 30(4), 20–31.

Ambady, N., & Weisbuch, M. (2010). Nonverbal behavior. In S. T. Fiske, D. T. Gilbert, & G. Lindzey (Eds.), *Handbook of social psychology*. Hoboken, NJ: Wiley.

Bartneck, C., & Reichenbach, J. (2005). Subtle emotional expressions of synthetic characters. *International Journal Human-Computer Studies*, 62(3), 179–192.

Bates, J. (July 1994) The role of emotion in believable agents. *Communications of the ACM*, 37(7):122–125.

Beale, R., & Creed, C. (2009). Affective interaction: How emotional agents affect users. *International Journal of Human-Computer Studies*, 67(9), 755–776.

Becker, C., Wachsmuth, I., Prendinger, H., & Ishizuka, M. (2005). Evaluating affective feedback of the 3D agent max in a competitive cards game. In J. Tao, T. Tan, & R. W. Picard (Eds.), *Proceedings of the international conference on affective computing and intelligent interaction (ACII)*. New York: Springer.

Bickmore, T. W., & Picard, R. W. (2005). Establishing and maintaining long-term human-computer relationships. *ACM Transaction on Computer-Human Interaction (TOCHI)*, 12(2), 293–327.

Blinn, J. F. Simulation of wrinkled surfaces. (1978). In *Proceedings of SIGGRAPH '78* (pp. 286–292). New York: Association for Computing Machinery.

Boukricha, H, Wachsmuth, I., Hofstaetter, A., & Grammer, K. (2009). Pleasure arousal dominance driven facial expression simulation. In *Proceedings of third international conference on affective computing and intelligent interaction (ACII 2009)* (pp. 119–125). New York: Springer.

Courgeon, M., Buisine, S., & Martin, J.-C. (2009). Impact of expressive wrinkles on perception of a virtual character's facial expressions of emotions. In *The 9th international conference on intelligent virtual agents* (pp. 201–214), Springer Berlin Heidelberg.

Courgeon, M., Clavel, C., & Martin, J.-C. (2009). Appraising emotional events during a real-time interactive game. In G. Castellano, J-C. Martin, J. Murray, K. Karpouzis, & C. Peters (Eds.), *Proceedings of the international workshop on affective-aware virtual agents and social robots (AFFINE '09)*. New York: Association for Computing Machinery.

de Melo, C., Carnevale, P., & Gratch, J. (2012). The effect of virtual agent's emotion displays and appraisals on people's decision making in negotiation. In *The 12th international conference on intelligent virtual agents* (pp. 53–66). Springer Berlin Heidelberg

de Melo, C., & Gratch, J. (2009). Expression of emotions using wrinkles, blushing, sweating and tears. In *The 9th international conference on intelligent virtual agents* (pp. 188–200). Springer Berlin Heidelberg

Demeure, V., Niewiadomski, R., & Pelachaud, C. (2011). How is believability of a virtual agent related to warmth, competence, personification and embodiment? *MIT Presence*, 20(5), 431–448.

Ekman, P. (2003). *Emotions revealed*. London: Weidenfeld and Nicolson.

Ekman, P., & Friesen, W. V. (1975). *Unmasking the face. A guide to recognizing emotions from facial clues*. Englewood Cliffs, NJ: Prentice Hall.

Ekman, P., Friesen, W. V., & Hager, J. C. (2002). *The facial action coding system*. London: Weidenfeld and Nicolson.

Grammer, K., & Oberzaucher, E. (2006). *The reconstruction of facial expressions in embodied systems*. ZiF: Mitteilungen, 2.

Heylen, D. (2006). Head gestures, gaze and the principles of conversational structure. *International Journal of Humanoid Robotics*, 3(3), 241–267.

Hone, K. (2006, March). Empathic agents to reduce user frustration: The effects of varying agent characteristics. *Interacting with Computers*, 18(2), 227–245.

Jimenez, J., Echevarria, J. I., Oat, C., & Gutierrez, D. (2011). GPU Pro 2. In *Practical and realistic facial wrinkles animation* (pp. 15–27). AK Peters.

Jimenez, J., Whelan, D., Sundstedt, V., & Gutierrez, D. (2010.). Real-time realistic skin translucency. *Computer Graphics and Applications, IEEE*, 30(4), 32–41.

João, D., & Paiva, A. (2005). Feeling and reasoning: A computational model for emotional characters. In C. Bento, A. Cardoso, &G. Dias (Eds.), *Progress in artificial intelligence: Lecture notes in computer science* (Vol. 3808, pp. 127–140). Berlin and Heidelberg: Springer.

Katsikitis, M., Pilowsky, I., & Innes, J. M. (1997). Encoding and decoding of facial expression. *Journal of General Psychology*, 124, 357–370.

Katsyri, J., & Sams, M. (2008). The effect of dynamics on identifying basic emotions from synthetic and natural faces. *International Journal Human-Computer Studies*, 66(4), 233–242.

Keltner, D. (1995). Signs of appeasement: Evidence for the distinct displays of embarrassment, amusement, and shame. *Journal of Personality and Social Psychology*, 68, 441–454.

Klein, J., Moon, Y., & Picard, R. W. (1999). This computer responds to user frustration. In *Proceedings of the conference on human factors in computing systems* (pp. 242–243). New York: Association for Computing Machinery.

Krumhuber, E., Manstead, A., & Kappas, A. (2007). Temporal aspects of facial displays in person and expression perception. The effects of smile dynamics, head tilt and gender. *Journal of Nonverbal Behavior*, 31, 39–56.

Larboulette, C., & Cani, M.-P. (2004). Real-time dynamic wrinkles. In *Proceedings of CGI'04*. IEEE. p. 522-525.

Lim, M. Y., & Aylett, R. (2007). Feel the difference: A guide with attitude! In *The 7th international conference on intelligent virtual agents* (pp. 17–19).

Ma, W. C., Hawkins, T., Peers, P., Chabert, C. F., Weiss, M., & Debevec, P. (2007). Rapid acquisition of specular and diffuse normal maps from polarized spherical gradient illumination. In *Proceedings of the 18th Eurographics conference on rendering techniques, EGSR'07*. (pp. 183–194).

Malatesta, L., Raouzaiou, A., Karpouzis, K., & Kollias, S. D. (2009). Towards modeling embodied conversational agent character profiles using appraisal theory predictions in expression synthesis. *Applied Intelligence*, 30(1), 58–64.

Maldonado, H., Lee, J. R., Brave, S., Nass, C., Nakajima, H., Yamada, R.,…Morishima, Y. (2004). We learn better together: Enhancing elearning with emotional characters. In T. Koschmann, D. Suthers, & T. W. Chan (Eds.), *Computer supported collaborative learning 2005: The next 10 years!* (pp. 408–417). Mahwah, NJ: Erlbaum.

Mehrabian, A. (1980). Basic dimensions for a general psychological theory: Implications for personality, social, environmental, and developmental studies. Cambridge, MA: Oelgeschlager, Gunn & Hain.

Niewiadomski, R., Huang, J., & Pelachaud, C. (2012). Effect of facial cues on identification. In *Proceedings of the 25th annual conference on computer animation and social agents, CASA 2012* (pp. 37–44).

Niewiadomski, R., & Pelachaud, C. (2012). Towards multimodal expression of laughter. In *The 12th international conference on intelligent virtual agents* (pp. 231–244).

Noëland, S., Dumoulin, SWhalen, T., & Stewart, J. (2006). Recognizing emotions on static and animated avatar faces. In *HAVE 2006 Haptic Audio Visual Environments and their Applications* (pp. 99–104).

Ochs, M., Niewiadomski, R., Brunet, P., & Pelachaud, C. (2011). Smiling virtual agent in social context. *Cognitive Processing, Special Issue on Social Agents*, 1–14.

Ochs, M., Niewiadomski, R., Pelachaud, C., & Sadek, D. (2005). Intelligent expressions of emotions. In *Affective computing and intelligent interaction* (pp. 707–714). New York: Springer.

Ochs, M., Pelachaud, C., & Sadek, D. (2008). An empathic virtual dialog agent to improve human-machine interaction. In *Proceedings of the 7th international joint conference on autonomous agents and multiagent systems* (pp. 89–96).

Ostermann, J. (2002). Face animation in mpeg-4. In I. S. Pandzic & R. Forchheimer (Eds.), *MPEG-4 facial animation—The standard implementation and applications* (pp. 17–55). Hoboken, NJ: Wiley.

Paleari, M., & Lisetti, C. (2006). Psychologically grounded avatar expressions. In *1st workshop on emotion and computing at KI 2006, 29th annual conference on artificial intelligence* (pp. 14–19).

Petta, P., Pelachaud, C., & Cowie, R. (2011). *Emotion-oriented systems: The Humaine handbook*. New York: Springer.

Poggi, I., Pelachaud, C., & de Rosis, F. (2000). Eye communication in a conversational 3D synthetic agent. *AI Communications*, 13(3), 169–182.

Rehm, M., & André, E. (2005). Informing the design of embodied conversational agents by analyzing multimodal politeness behaviors in human-human communication. In *Workshop on conversational informatics for supporting social intelligence and interaction*.

Riek, L. D., & Robinson, P. (2011). Challenges and opportunities in building socially intelligent machines. *IEEE Signal Processing*, 28(3):146–149.

Ruttkay, Z., Noot, H., & Ten Hagen, P. (2003). Emotion disc and emotion squares: Tools to explore the facial expression face. *Computer Graphics Forum*, 22(1), 49–53.

Scherer, K., Schorr, A., & Johnstone, T. (2001). *Appraisal processes in emotion: Theory, methods, research*. New York: Oxford University Press.

Scherer, K. R. (2001). Appraisal considered as a process of multilevel sequential checking. In K. R. Scherer, A. Schorr, & T. Johnstone (Eds.), *Appraisal processes in emotion: Theory, methods, research* (pp. 92–119). New York: Oxford University Press.

Snodgrass, J. (1992). Judgment of feeling states from facial behavior: A bottom-up approach. PhD thesis. Canada: University of British Columbia.

Stoiber, N., Breton, G., & Séguier, R. (2010). Modeling short-term dynamics and variability for realistic interactive facial animation. *IEEE Computer Graphics and Applications*, 30(4), 51–61.

Thomas, F., & Johnston, O. (1981). *Disney animation: The illusion of life*. Abbeville Press.

Tsapatsoulis, N., Raouzaiou, A., Kollias, S., Crowie, R., & Douglas-Cowie, E. (2002). Emotion recognition and synthesis based on MPEG-4 FAPS. In I. S. Pandzic & R. Forchheimer (Eds.), *MPEG-4 facial animation—The standard, implementations, applications* (pp. 141–168). Hoboken, NJ: Wiley.

Vilhjálmsson, H., Cantelmo, N., Cassell, J., Ech-Chafai, N., Kipp, M., Kopp, S.,…van der Werf, R. J. (2007). The behavior markup language: Recent developments and challenges. In C. Pelachaud, J.-C. Martin, E. André, G. Chollet,

K. Karpouzis, & D. Pelé (Eds.), *Lecture notes in computer science, LNAI 4722* (pp. 99–111). New York: Springer.

Janet H. Walker, LeeSproull, and R. Subramani. 1994. Using a human face in an interface. In *Proceedings of the SIGCHI Conference on Human Factors in Computing Systems* (CHI '94), BethAdelson, SusanDumais, and JudithOlson (Eds.). ACM, New York, NY, USA, 85-91. DOI=10.1145/191666.191708 http://doi.acm.org/10.1145/191666.191708

Zeiler, M. D., Taylor, G. W., Sigal, L., Matthews, I., & Fergus, R. (2011). Facial expression transfer with input-output temporal restricted boltzmann machines. In *Proceedings of the conference on neural information processing systems foundation (NIPS)*.

Zhang, S., Wu, Z., Meng, H. M., & Cai, L. (2007). Facial expression synthesis using PAD emotional parameters for a Chinese expressive avatar. In *Proceedings of the second affective computing and intelligent interaction conference (ACII 2007)* (pp. 24–35). New York: Springer.

Expressing Emotion Through Posture and Gesture

Margaux Lhommet *and* Stacy C. Marsella

Abstract

This chapter addresses the bodily expression of emotion, specifically, how people communicate emotion through body posture and gesture and how they make inferences about someone else's emotional state based on perceived posture and gesture. A range of empirical, methodological, and theoretical issues are identified that arise in studying the bodily expression of emotion. Then, an overview of some of the key psychological studies of the expressive elements of posture and gesture is presented. The last section describes computational models of bodily expression that have been designed for embodied conversational agents (ECAs). ECAs are animated virtual humans capable of social interaction with people through dialogue and nonverbal behaviors, using the same modalities such as voice, facial expression, postural shifts, and gestures that people use in face-to-face interaction.

Key Words: emotion, posture, gesture, expressive posture and gesture, embodied conversational agent, virtual human, computational model, nonverbal behaviors

Introduction

Emotion and its physical expression are an integral part of social interaction, informing others about how we are feeling and affecting social outcomes (Vosk, Forehand, & Figueroa, 1983). Modern studies on the physical expression of emotion can be traced back to the nineteenth century with Darwin's seminal book[1] *The Expression of the Emotions in Man and Animals*, which reveals the key role of facial expressions and body movement in communicating status and emotion (Darwin, 1872).

While emotions can be expressed through different modalities, facial expressions have been the most extensively studied. More than 95% of the literature on emotion in humans has used faces as stimuli, at the expense of other modalities (Gelder, 2009). Less studied are the ways our bodies also convey emotional information, such as by adopting a collapsed posture when one is feeling depressed

or leaning forward to show interest. This chapter focuses on this less extensively studied field of *bodily expression of emotion*. Specifically it addresses how people communicate emotion through body posture and gesture and how they make inferences about someone else's emotional state based on perceived posture and gesture.

In addition to furthering our basic understanding of human behavior, work on the bodily expression of emotion has played a key role in research on embodied conversational agents (ECAs) (Cassell, 2000), also known as virtual humans (Rickel et al., 2002). ECAs are animated characters capable of social interaction with people through dialogue and nonverbal behaviors, using the same modalities—such as voice, facial expression, postural shifts, and gestures—that people use in face-to-face interaction.

Given emotion's impact on human social interaction, it is not surprising that research on ECAs has sought to endow them with the ability to employ emotion and emotional expression. A computational model of the relation between emotion and its bodily expression can play several roles in the design of ECAs. For one, it can guide the recognition of the emotional state of the user (see Mühl, this volume). This chapter focuses on another role, the generation of appropriate bodily expression for ECAs.

A range of empirical, methodological, and theoretical issues arise in studying the bodily expression of emotion. One of the fundamental issues concerns how emotion itself is defined. As discussed elsewhere in this volume, there are distinct alternative theories of how emotions arise, what constitutes an emotional state, and what its constituent parts are. These different theories define emotions and emotion processes differently, and the theory to which one subscribes strongly influences one's study of emotional expression. In addition there are methodological issues concerning how one collects data to study the bodily expression of emotion.

This chapter identifies these issues and the solutions that have been proposed. Then an overview is presented of some of the key psychological studies of the expressive elements of posture and gesture. The last section describes the computational models of bodily expression that have been designed to enable virtual humans to perform postures and gestures that convey emotional states.

Theoretical and Methodological Issues

The study of expressive behavior has been guided by a distinction between encoding and decoding. *Encoding* refers to the process and extent to which people provide information about their mental states and traits, such as emotion and personality, through their behavior, in particular their physical, nonverbal behavior. *Decoding* refers to an observer's recovery of such information from observation of another's behavior. The study of the bodily expression of emotion concerns itself with the precise nature of this encoding and decoding, including what aspects of emotion are encoded in what behaviors and similarly what behaviors observers use to decode emotional information. A key question inherent in making an encoding-decoding distinction is whether and how the encoding of emotion in physical behavior differs from how it is decoded by an observer (see Gifford, 1994, for related seminal work on personality and nonverbal behavior).

The encoding-decoding distinction also provides a useful lens on many of the challenges faced in the study of the bodily expression of emotion. To study or model the encoding and decoding of emotion in behavior, data of human behavior is needed. Indeed, one of the major obstacles researchers have encountered is obtaining realistic encoding nonverbal expressions that are valid indicators of various emotional states (Bänziger & Scherer, 2007).

Studies have often used acted performances to create data for analysis or stimuli for experiments. For instance, actors are given a short script that contains a description of the situation as well as a few dialogue lines. Expressive behaviors are improvised during the course of the scene (Wallbott, 1998; Wallbott & Scherer, 1986). However, intentionally portrayed performances can be stereotyped, unnatural, or even exaggerated, or they may have more subtle differences in the dynamics of the motion, timing, and symmetry. Even professional actors, depending on their training and approach to acting, may realize behavior that facilitates how an audience decodes a behavior as opposed to a natural encoding. Exaggerated expressions enhance emotion recognition but produce higher emotional-intensity ratings (Atkinson et al., 2004), leading the observer to judge the performance as inappropriately portraying the emotion (Wallbott, 1998).

Alternatively, emotional states can be induced in people and the resulting behavior assessed. A key challenge here is how to induce the emotional state. The simplest approach, showing the subject emotionally arousing pictures and videos, has been used since the first emotion studies (James, 1932). Another approach is the autobiographical memory paradigm, in which subjects are asked to recall a memory during which they experienced a specific emotion. In a study conducted by Gross, Crane, and Fredrickson (2010), 92% of the participants reported actually feeling the target emotion during their performance by using the autobiographical memory paradigm–inducing strategy. Interestingly, the participants also reported feeling other emotions, close to the target one, at the same time.

Research can also take a more ecologically valid approach of observing other people's emotional expressions in naturally occurring situations, in effect outside the laboratory. This still leaves the issue of determining the emotion that is being encoded. Here, researchers must rely on post hoc reports (Bänziger & Scherer, 2007; Nisbett & Wilson, 1977). Asking observers to focus on emotions may alter the way they describe emotions, leading them to notice more subtle emotional states than they normally would, or, to the contrary, to report only very obvious emotional expressions. Another bias is the interpretation of someone else's (or one's own) emotional state, which may significantly differ from the underlying emotional state.

Further, there is also a fundamental question, raised typically in the context of facial expression, as to whether expressive behavior is truly an encoding of an underlying emotional state (Ekman & Friesen, 1967) as opposed to the view that expressive behaviors serve only as social signals aimed at influencing the behaviors of others (Fridlund 1991, 1997). In other words, the encoding is not of an underlying emotional state but rather an intention to influence the observer. Further, emotion, as well as its expression, can be viewed as an evolving dynamic product of a social interactional context in which the behavior is embedded. This social interactional approach essentially draws into a question the validity of the separation into encoding and decoding whereby emotion is seen as being encoded into behavior and then subsequently decoded by an observer.

These issues also impact designers of virtual humans/ECAs, who must address both whether naturalistic encoding versus ease of decoding is the design goal for a virtual human as well as whether emotion is conveying underlying emotion of the virtual human and/or is being used as an explicit social signal. The designer of a virtual human can choose to use a model based on encoding of behavior—to get a naturalistic performance—or choose to model based on the decoding—to get a performance that an observer can easily decode. Similarly, a choice can be made as to whether expression is conveying underlying emotion of the ECA and/or is being used as explicit social signal. The approach a designer takes depends on the goals of the environment/application in which the virtual human is embedded.

Characterization of Emotions and Behavior

Whether one is designing experiments to explore the bodily expression of emotion in humans or attempting to create an expressive virtual human, an issue to be faced is how to characterize, represent, and measure the objects under study. In other words, what is being encoded, how it is encoded, and what is decoded need to be precisely characterized. This includes characterizing both the emotional properties that are being studied or modeled

as well as the space of behaviors from which an observer decodes emotional information.

Characterizing Emotions

Researchers must determine what emotions will be studied and how they will be represented. However, there is no theoretical consensus on what an emotion is. Discrete emotion theories claim that there are a limited number of basic emotions, including fear, happiness, anger, sadness, surprise, and disgust (Ekman & Friesen, 1969) as well as interest, shame, and guilt (Izard, 1977). Dimensional theories define dimensional spaces that account for the similarities and differences in emotional experience. For example, the PAD model describes an emotional state with values of pleasure, arousal, and dominance (Russell & Mehrabian, 1977) and is used by the virtual human MAX (Becker, Kopp, & Wachsmuth, 2004). Appraisal theory posits that emotions arise from an assessment of a person's relation to the environment. This assessment is in terms of a set of criteria, variously called appraisal variables, checks, or dimensions (e.g., is this event *desirable with respect to one's goals or concerns,* who *caused* it, was it expected, what *power* do I have over its unfolding, etc.). Patterns of appraisal are associated to specific mental states as well as physiological and behavioral reactions, including emotions and action tendencies that are "states of readiness to execute a certain kind of action"—for example, "impulses to approach or avoid, desires to shout and sing or move" (Frijda, 2007, p. 273).

Emotion theory has a central influence on the study of emotionally expressive behavior. The theory impacts how emotion is defined and explored in a study. An approach grounded in a discrete model of emotion would look for the relation between emotion categories like anger or happiness and their behavioral expression, while an approach using a dimensional model would focus on intensity and valence and therefore look for those dimensions in the bodily expression. That is why some studies have looked at this problem from the opposite side, seeking to address whether a discrete or dimensional theory would best explain the observed data.

A key issue here is how emotion and its bodily expression are characterized and measured. Such methodological issues impact basic research questions including whether posture and movement reliably convey emotion categories, such as anger or joy, or more abstract qualities, such as the intensity of the emotion (for a discussion of this point, see Ekman, 1965; Ekman & Friesen, 1967), as well as which features of the bodily movement are relevant to inferences of emotion, the form of the movement or posture, the quantity of movement, or the dynamics of the motion. It has been argued that posture and movement do not convey discrete emotion categories but rather more abstract qualities such as pleasure, arousal, or dominance. This suggests that what is encoded may in fundamental ways differ from what is decoded.

Characterizing Posture, Movement, and Gesture

In addition to the issue of characterizing emotions, a study must also address how to characterize and therefore measure the space of posture, movement, and gesture. Here, research has faced the absence of a standard that codifies the features under study, including what the components of the movement are and how their dynamics are specified. In contrast, the work on facial expressions has relied on an agreed upon standard: the facial action coding system (FACS) (Ekman, Friesen, & Hager, 1978, 2002). Such a standard facilitates the coding of observed behaviors, the design of stimuli for experiments, and the comparison of results. In the absence of an agreed upon standard, researchers must answer the question of how to represent the parts of the body that are involved, the dynamics of the movement, and the form of the movement. The following describes some of the coding approaches that have been used to study the bodily expression of emotion.

POSTURE

Posture refers to the quasistatic configuration of the whole body. Posture is usually defined by the position and orientation of specific body parts. Orientation can be relative. For example, Mehrabian (1972) uses a few global descriptors, such as relative orientation to the partner, closeness or openness, and symmetry of body limb. Harrigan (2005) reports that posture coding systems use the following common descriptors: trunk lean (upright, forward, or backward), trunk orientation (facing, turned), arm and leg positions and configurations (e.g., hands in pockets, legs crossed). Absolute orientation values are described regarding the sagittal, frontal, and transverse axis of the body (e.g., Gross, Crane, & Fredrickson, 2012).

MOVEMENT

The task of describing the movement of the body raises additional challenges. To represent movement, early studies manually detailed the position of each body part over time (Birdwhistell, 1970; Frey & Pool, 1976). Such an approach can be tedious and time-consuming. Modern motion-capture techniques can now provide highly detailed moment-to-moment joint angle descriptions. However, when low-level descriptions are not the goal of the research, the challenge remains of forming more abstract descriptions that support the generalization of findings.

To that end, some research has explored ideas from other disciplines. Specifically, choreographers describe the body movement to preserve and transmit a dance score to dancers. In particular, Laban, his students, and his colleagues have developed several frameworks to represent movement. The Laban movement analysis describes the actions of the body parts over time by using a notation system composed of symbols that represent the quantitative and qualitative features of movements. Symbols are organized into five categories: body (parts of the body involved), space (locale, directions and path of a movement), effort (how the body performs movements) and shape (forms that the body makes in space). The effort-shape analysis (Dell, 1977) derives from Laban and focuses only on the effort and shape dimensions. EMOTE is a three-dimensional graphic engine that proposes a computational realization of the shape-effort analysis and focuses on torso and arm movements (Badler et al., 2000; Chi et al. 2000; Zhao & Badler, 2001).

GESTURE

Broadly defined, gestures are movements that communicate information, intentionally or not (McNeill, 2008). However, most of the literature on gesture concerns hand and arm gestures used in verbal communication.[2] Additionally, the focus of research has been on the relation of gestures to the spoken dialogue, with less of a concern on emotion's role in influencing gesture. Nevertheless this work on gesture is highly relevant to investigations of emotion's impact, so we touch on it here.

Gestures have been distinguished into several categories (Ekman & Friesen, 1969; Kendon, 1983). Emblems are gestures that convey meaning by themselves and are assumed to be deliberately performed by the speaker. They are conventionalized symbols and strongly culture-dependent (Efron, 1941, 1972; Kendon, 1983). For example, a thumb pointing up has well-defined but different meaning across different cultures. Illustrators (or conversational gestures) are gestures that accompany the speech. One particular category of illustrators is the *beats* (i.e., simple, repetitive, rhythmic movements that bear no obvious relation to the semantic content of the accompanying speech). Other categories of conversational gestures have a communicative intent and are semantically linked to the meaning of the speech. They can further be distinguished into deictic, iconic, and metaphorical gestures (McNeill, 1985, 1987). Deictics consist in pointing toward a concrete object or an abstract concept that has been materialized in front of the speaker. Iconics and metaphorics are gestures that represent derived features of an object or an action, such as drawing a square to represent a frame or mimicking writing. Iconics describe concrete objects and actions, while metaphorics represent abstract concepts.

Gesture may also convey additional information, although such information is not, strictly speaking, part of the speaker's intended meaning. Adaptors are not communicatively intended or perceived to be meaningfully related to the speech. Self adaptors (also named self manipulators and body manipulators) involve one part of the body doing something to another part of the body, such as scratching one's head, stroking one's chin, hand-to-hand movement, and licking of the lips or hair. Object manipulation involves handling or using an object for some type of body contact, like playing with a pencil or scratching one's ear with a paper clip (Ekman & Friesen, 1977, p. 47).

A segmentation-and-classification approach has been proposed to integrate dynamics into gesture descriptions (McNeill, 1992, 2008). Segmentation is done by using the concept of three sequential movement phases in a gesture: preparation, stroke, and retraction. The stroke is the meaningful part of the gesture. Before the stroke, the arm moves from the rest position to the position to get ready for the stroke (preparation phase). After the stroke, the arm gets back to a rest position (retraction phase). Classification consists in describing gestures with objective features like handedness, hand shape, palm orientation, or motion direction (e.g., Calbris & Doyle, 1990).

COMBINING POSTURE, MOVEMENT, AND GESTURE

Recently an effort has been made to propose a comprehensive system that could guide the coding of body and body parts positions, movement, and communicative intent of gestures. The body action and posture (BAP) coding system integrates several coding approaches to study emotion expression by using a multilevel (anatomical, form, and functional) coding system (Dael, Mortillaro, & Scherer, 2012b).

The anatomical level specifies which body parts are described. Available articulators are the neck, the trunk (including spine and chest), the upper and lower arms (including shoulders, elbow, wrist, and fingers) and the legs. The form level describes the form of the movement of a set of articulators. Movement is characterized with respect to the sagittal, vertical, and transverse axis of the body. The functional level distinguishes between emblems, illustrators, and manipulators gestures (Ekman & Friesen, 1972). The classification of Calbris and Doyle (1990) is used to describe the meaning conveyed by the gesture.

Overall, BAP includes 141 objective behaviors that can be combined to describe the position and movement of body and body parts as well as, when applicable, the communicative intent of a gesture. Additionally, this system can be used to conduct multimodal behavior analyses by integrating facial and speech features. BAP has been used to code the performance of professional actors encoding emotional states in the GEMEP corpus (Dael, Mortillaro, & Scherer, 2012a).

Individual Differences in Encoding

Individuals differ considerably in the degree to which emotion is encoded in behavior as well as how it is encoded (Gross, Crane, & Fredrickson, 2010). They also have different styles, preferring to use certain gestures instead of others (Kipp & Martin, 2009), as well as preferences regarding the modalities to use (facial expressions, voice, body) and the overall amount of expressive behavior. These differences have a significant impact on the study of expressive behavior and its computational modeling. Using a small number of subjects may fail to illuminate the range of encoded gestures and styles associated to a particular emotion and may also make it difficult to find general trends that underlie the differences. Thus some researchers studying human behavior suggest using a relatively large number of individuals to capture the whole range of expression (Atkinson et al., 2004; Fredrickson, 2010; Gross, Crane, Wallbott 1998; Wallbott, 1998). There is also an impact on the design of virtual humans, with some researchers arguing for crafting virtual human behavior around general trends (e.g., Scherer et al., 2012), while others (e.g., Kopp & Bergmann, 2012) argue that crafting using data from multiple individuals averages over individual differences and consequently has a negative impact on the expressivity of a model learned from such conjoined data.

Isolating the Encoding and Decoding of Emotion in Bodily Expression

The behavior of the body, of course, serves many roles and is not simply a means to convey emotional state. Not surprisingly, therefore, the collection and study of human data on bodily expression faces the methodological challenge of isolating the role of emotion. Other mental states can be encoded in the modalities of posture and gesture. Posture and gestures, for example, often encode intentions or requests (Dittmann, 1987). In particular, the role of gesture in supplementing, replicating, or supplanting what is conveyed in spoken language has been extensively studied, independently of the impact of emotion. Similarly, postures such as folded arms across the chest do not necessarily indicate emotions such as pride but may be used to increase one's body temperature when feeling cold (Harrigan, 2005). The distinction is theoretically and methodologically important but difficult to tease apart empirically (Coulson, 2004).

Conversely, other modalities, such as facial expressions, convey emotions. Since the goal is to study the encoding and decoding of emotion in posture and gesture, this raises the methodological challenge of how to eliminate these other modalities in the encoding and how to mask them so as not to interfere in the decoding of emotion. For the purposes of decoding studies, avoiding interferences from facial expression is comparatively easy. The encoder can be masked while performing, or the facial expression can be blurred afterward (e.g., Gross, Crane, & Fredrickson, 2010; Sprengelmeyer et al., 1999). Avoiding interferences from the voice is more challenging. Researchers have used nonsense sentences (i.e., that do not convey semantic meaning) and flattened the pitch and prosody of the voice (e.g., Banse & Scherer, 1996; Wallbott, 1998). However, using a verbal utterance without meaning may constrain the variety of emotional expressions that are used, leading to performances that lack spontaneity and naturalness.

Studies of the Expressive Elements of Posture and Gesture

Studies on the bodily expression of emotions can be characterized broadly in terms of the types of behaviors in which they are interested. Accordingly we break down our overview in terms of focus: on posture, body movement, hand gestures, as well as the multimodal approaches that investigate the combination of bodily movement with facial expressions and vocal qualities.

Expressing Emotion Through Static Posture

Early studies conducted by Ekman suggested that, while the face is the most effective channel for expressing specific emotion, the posture provides more information about the *gross affect*—that is, dimensional information such as the degree of arousal or tenseness of the emotional state (Ekman, 1965; Ekman & Friesen, 1967). Dance choreographers have known for a long time that body posture can signal an affect-related meaning: An angular posture suggests a threatening character and a round posture a warm character (Aronoff, Woike, & Hyman, 1992). Accordingly some studies have confirmed that dimensional information can be derived from static posture. For example, Schouwstra and Hoogstraten (1995) generated 21 figures by varying three head positions and also seven spinal positions; they reported that a straight posture is judged more positively, whereas the figure with pelvis backward and the shoulder and head forward (leaning posture) was judged the most negatively.

However, contrary to Ekman's view, studies report that some specific emotions can be accurately decoded from a static posture (Coulson, 2004; Walters & Walk, 1986). Coulson (2004) presents an interesting review of these studies and also demonstrates that the observer's point of view also strongly influences the recognition of the encoded emotion. In particular, anger, sadness, and joy obtain the same recognition rate when expressed with a static body posture as through facial expression. Disgust is not recognized, and surprise and joy are often confused. Table 19.1 presents the characteristics of postures used to express specific emotional states and compiles data from various studies (Atkinson et al., 2004; Coulson, 2004; Wallbott, 1998).

Expressing Emotion Through Movement

Beyond the shape of the posture, movements also involve emotional states. Both objective (using motion-capture data) and subjective (decoding) studies showed that velocity, acceleration, and jerk are particularly affected by an emotional state.

Most studies on kinesics have taken a holistic approach by focusing on the dynamics of

Table 19.1 Elements of Posture Expressing Specific Emotions

Emotion	Frequent Posture Features
Anger	Head backward, no chest backward, no abdominal twist, arms raised forward and upward, shoulders lifted
Joy	Head backward, no chest forward, arms raised above shoulder and straight at the elbow, shoulders lifted
Sadness	Head forward, chest forward, no abdominal twist, arms at the side of the trunk, collapsed posture
Surprise	Head backward, chest backward, abdominal twist, arms raised with straight forearms
Pride	Head backward or lightly tilted, expanded posture, hands on the hips or raised above the head
Fear	Head backward, no abdominal twist, arms are raised forward, shoulders forward
Disgust	Shoulders forward, head downward
Boredom	Collapsed posture, head backward, not facing the interlocutor

the whole body. In particular, human walk has received the most attention (Hicheur et al., 2013; Montepare, Goldstein, & Clausen, 1987; Roether et al., 2009; Rossberg-Gempton & Poole, 1993). The general level of movement activity and spatial extent seem to be important features for decoding emotion from body movement. Angry movements tend to be large, fast, and relatively jerky, while fearful and sad movements are smaller, slower, and less energetic.

The body seems to present an asymmetry in its emotional expressivity. More particularly, the left side uses more energy and a greater amplitude in realizing emotional movements than the right (Roether, Omlor, & Giese, 2010; Rossberg-Gempton & Poole, 1993). Kipp and Martin (2009) suggest that the handedness of the performer might play a role in this asymmetry. They observed that two hand-righted actors tend to use their right hands in experiencing anger and their left hands in experiencing relaxed and positive feelings.

Studies focusing on specific body parts, generally involving the arms and the hands, confirm and detail these results, whether by using encoding-decoding methodology only (Hietanen, Leppänen, & Lehtonen, 2004; Patterson, Pollick, & Sanford, 2001; Pollick et al., 2001) or combining the results with data obtained by motion capture (Gross, Crane, & Fredrickson, 2012). The amplitude and speed of body parts involved in the movement, as well as the timing of the different gestural phases (preparation, stroke, relaxation) also seem to be affected. For example, Table 19.2 reports the observations made by Gross, Crane, and Fredrickson (2010) and Wallbott (1998) on which

arm movement features are characteristic of certain emotional categories.

Expressing Emotion Through Specific Gestures

Emotion influences not only the way we move but also the kinds of gestures we choose to use. In particular, *adaptors* comprise gestures that may reveal unconscious thoughts or feelings (Mahl, 1956, 1968) or thoughts and feelings that the speaker is trying to conceal (Ekman & Friesen, 1969, 1974). Several investigators (Argyle, 1975; Dittmann, 1972; Wallbott, 1998; Wolff, 1972) report that object adaptors (e.g., playing with an object) and self adaptors (e.g., scratching or touching oneself) are more frequently displayed when the performer is experiencing negative valence emotions (e.g., anxiety, inhibition, depression, and shame).

Expressing Emotion Through Multimodal Combinations

Emotion is usually simultaneously expressed through the face, voice, posture, and gestures. This raises the question of how these modalities complement, supplement, or contrast with each other.

It has been shown that observers detecting discrepancies between the information conveyed by different modalities tend to attribute pathologies or intents of deception to the performer (Ekman, 2001; Ekman et al., 1991).

Surprisingly, there are rare studies focusing on the simultaneous expressive patterns of these modalities (Bänziger & Scherer, 2007). Scherer and Ellgring (2007) aim at identifying intra- and intermodality clusters in gestures, voice, and face

Table 19.2 Expressive Features of Arm Movement

Emotion	Frequent Features of Arm Movement
Anger	Lateralized hand/arm movement, arms stretched out to the front, largest amplitude of elbow motion, largest elbow extensor velocity, highest rising arm
Joy	High peak flexor and extensor elbow velocities, arms stretched out to the front
Sadness	Longest movement time, smallest amplitude of elbow motion, least elbow extensor velocity
Anxiety	Short movement time, constrained torso range of motion
Interest	Lateralized hand/arm movement, arms stretched out to the front
Fear	Arms stretched sideways

that would be characteristic of emotion dimensions (arousal and valence). For example, one highly expressive gesturing cluster they mention is particularly used in experiencing high arousal: it combines arms stretched out frontally, the use of gestures, hands opening and closing, and shoulders moving up. This cluster is further combined with face and voice clusters into multimodal clusters that are representative of agitation (high-arousal situations) and joyful surprise (positive valence).

Computational Models for Generating Emotionally Expressive Movement

Mirroring the psychological work, computational modeling of the expression of emotion in virtual characters has been more concerned with facial expressions (see Andre, this volume) than with bodily movements.

There has nevertheless been significant work in this area, particularly in the field of ECAs. Most of the systems have built on the psychological studies discussed earlier to generate bodily expressions that are congruent with an emotional state. But given the absence of a comprehensive psychological theory of the relation between emotion and expressive bodily movements, the results are only partial.

Following the psychological work that distinguishes the impact of emotion on the quality of movement and on the types of movement, computational work can similarly be broadly characterized in terms of expressive animation of a motion versus selection among expressive behaviors. Below, the ECA literature is reviewed according to these two specific axes, addressing how the emotional state influences movement realization as well as how it affects behavior and, in particular, gesture selection.

Expressive Realization of Nonverbal Behaviors

Expressive animation systems allow changing the dynamics of a movement by using a set of parameters (e.g., speed, amplitude, trajectory) and a set of constraints to be respected (e.g., body position and balance (Neff & Fiume, 2006). Following this idea, emotionally expressive animations can be procedurally generated by applying transformations on neutral gestures. Different techniques have been proposed to create these emotional transformations involving different degrees of connection to the ECA's mental state (and in particular its emotional state).

INFLUENCE OF THE EMOTIONAL STATE ON THE QUALITY OF MOVEMENT

Some researchers have proposed the use of direct mapping from aspects of emotional state to aspects of movement. A direct relation between dimensions of emotion and dimensions of movement has been made. For example, Ball and Breese (2000) link the arousal of the emotional state to the size and speed of gestures as well as aspects of facial expressions and speed speech, while the valence impacts the facial expression and voice pitch. This approach was integrated into a domain-dependent Bayesian network that recognizes the emotional state of the user and generates appropriate behavior in response to the user's action.

Emotional transforms can also be representative of certain emotional categories. For example, the "emotion from motion" system compares motion-capture data of a movement performed with a specific emotion with the same movement performed with a neutral emotion (Amaya, Bruderlin, & Calvert, 1996). This process generates emotional transformations that represent the difference of speed and spatial amplitude of the movement over time and can be later applied to encode the emotional state in movements. Using this system, sad and angry transforms were created using motion-capture data of drinking (focusing on the arm) and were successfully applied to generate sad and angry knocking and kicking movements.

MARC (Tan et al., 2010) is another example of direct mapping between the emotional movement and the virtual human's emotional state. MARC models emotions as action tendencies (e.g., exuberant or attending), and the mapping consists in selecting an appropriate posture from a manually annotated library.

INFLUENCE OF THE MENTAL STATE ON THE QUALITY OF MOVEMENT

Several virtual human architectures try to capture individual differences by integrating other components, such as personality or cultural differences, into the virtual human's mental states. Indeed, these things have an influence on how the virtual human behaves and on how it expresses its emotions.

The parameterized action representation system (PARSYS) is a component that allows an agent to act, plan, and reason about its actions or actions of others (Badler et al., 2002). It takes into account the mental state of the virtual human, composed of a personality (the OCEAN model) (Wiggins, 1996), to capture individual differences and an emotional state based on appraisal theory—specifically the OCC model developed by Ortony, Clore, and Collins (1988). The mental state influences the action selection as well as its realization, by using a mapping between the mental state's elements and expressivity transform. A mapping from personality to the shape and effort transforms has been implemented (Allbeck & Badler, 2002), and a mapping from the emotional state to expressivity transforms could be integrated. The expressivity transforms are transmitted to the expressive motion engine that realizes them (EMOTE) (Badler et al., 2000; Chi et al., 2000; Zhao & Badler, 2001). EMOTE is a three-dimensional graphic engine that proposes a computational realization of the shape-effort analysis from Laban movement analysis (Dell, 1977) and focuses on torso and arm movements. By applying a set of shape and effort transformations neutral animations, the original performance is altered to represent the mental state of the virtual human.

In GRETA (Mancini & Pelachaud, 2008), ECAs are given a baseline that represents their gesture personality; it contains their default expressivity parameters for gesture and facial expression (e.g., the ECA prefers using gestures with high power, low fluidity, etc.). These expressivity parameters are based on the psychology literature (Gallaher, 1992; Walbot & Scherer, 1986): the *spatial extent* represents how large the gesture is in space, the *temporal extent* indicates how fast it is executed, the *fluidity* shows how two consecutive gestures are coarticulated, the *repetition* refers to how many times it is repeated, the *power* to how strong it is, and the *overall activation* points to the overall quantity of movement in a given modality. This personality baseline is dynamically modified depending on the communicative intentions that represent the information the ECA wants to convey (for example, an emotional state or information about the state of the world). A set of handcrafted rules based on the literature (Wallbott, 1998; Wallbott & Scherer, 1986) eventually generates an expressive multimodal behavior, ensuring that the final overall performance conveys the desired meaning (Hartmann, Mancini, & Pelachaud, 2005; Pelachaud 2009).

INFLUENCE OF THE QUALITY OF MOVEMENT ON THE MEANING OF GESTURE

Modifying the movement of a gesture can alter it globally, regardless of its meaningful parts. For example, transforming a deictic gesture (i.e., pointing hand) can obscure the form of the pointing finger or change the pointed direction. This is particularly problematic for ECAs, since it can override the meaning conveyed by a gesture. GRETA addresses this issue by ensuring that the emotional transformations applied to gestures do not change their meaningful parts. A language specifies for each gesture phase (preparation, stroke, retraction) which elements carry semantic meaning and which ones can be modulated (Björn Hartmann, Mancini, & Pelachaud, 2006).

Expressive Selection of Nonverbal Behaviors

Emotions change not only the movement quality but also the type of movement, such as a raised fist in anger or yawning with boredom. Several ECA architectures have modeled the influence of the emotional state on movement and gesture selection, and they differ in their degree of automation.

Some systems use markup languages to manually annotate the utterance text and represent the influence that individual style must have on the performance. In GESTYLE (Noot & Ruttkay, 2004), each ECA has a unique style that contains specific behavioral repertoires as well as performance characteristics in terms of amplitude, speed, and smoothness. GESTYLE does not have specific tags for emotion, but the approach is generic enough to define new style categories that would implicitly represent emotions.

Similarly to how emotion can be directly mapped to expressivity parameters and influences how a movement is realized, emotion can be mapped to specific gestures. For example, MAX uses a direct mapping between particular emotional states and specific behaviors. MAX's emotions are computed by an appraisal model (WASABI) (Becker, Kopp, & Wachsmuth, 2004) and aggregated over time in a mood (using the PAD dimensional model with the addition of a boredom dimension). MAX's mood determines facial expressions and voice prosody. Moreover, the system uses a direct mapping between the boredom dimension and specific actions (i.e., when the level of boredom reaches a certain threshold, secondary actions such as yawning of stretching are triggered).

The physical focus model uses the emotional state of a virtual human to drive a finite state machine that determines behavior selection (Gratch & Marsella, 2001; Marsella, Johnson, & LaBore, 2000). Four focus modes are defined (*strong body focus*, *body focus*, *transitional*, and *communicative*) and transitions between modes are linked to changes of emotional state. Action tendencies as well as the number and types of nonverbal behaviors depend on the focus mode the virtual human is currently in. For example, the *body focus* mode represents emotional states like depression and guilt. It generates gaze aversion, inhibited verbal activity, and self adaptors (soothing or self-punitive) as well as minimal communicative gestures such as deictic and beats, following the nonverbal observations of Freedman (1972).

Combining Expressive Selection and Expressive Realization

Currently no system explicitly combines selection and realization of expressive nonverbal behavior, but such a combination can be implicitly realized. Nonverbal behavior is tightly linked to the speech, and synchrony occurs at different levels of speech. At the most local level, gesture and words are aligned. The *stroke* (i.e., the most meaningful part of the gesture) occurs with or just before the accentuated syllable of the word. Gestures can also be aggregated into *gesture units* that span on longer parts of speech (Kendon, 1983; McNeill,

1992). Integrating such synchrony in ECAs requires dynamically modifying and coarticulating gesture animations so that they match the speech timings, whether because the gestures are too close in time or need to be stretched out on a longer speech segment. Therefore changing the speed of speech according to the emotional state may also impact the gesture speed. In MAX, for example, a high-arousal emotional state (e.g., happy, angry, excited) increases the speed of the speech, thus leading to faster movements, while a low-arousal emotional state slows down the speech and associated gestures (Becker, Kopp, & Wachsmuth, 2004). The speed of the animation gesture is modified, but some of the other meaningful features, such as the amplitude of the motion, are left unchanged.

Discussion

This chapter has provided an overview of psychological studies on the influence of emotion on posture and gesture and described some of the attempts within the ECA community to develop bodily expressive virtual characters and behaviors. In the absence of a full computational model of this influence, the results obtained so far are only partial. For example, no system integrates both the realization of expressive animation and selection of expressive behaviors.

The main issue in the creation of such a model is the need for a formal methodology to study the expression of emotion. Recently some progress has been made with the BAP coding system, which objectively combines the positions of the body and body parts, movements, and gestures. Additionally, objective measurement of body movement has recently been made possible by modern technologies like motion tracking (Ma, Paterson, & Pollick, 2006) and muscular activity instruments (e.g., accelerometry, electromyography).

Virtual humans have proven to be particularly convenient in conducting studies of human behavior, especially in the field of face-to-face interactions. Their behaviors can be easily manipulated and reproduced and they do not induce individual bias in the experimental process. Actually, some of the psychological studies of bodily expression of emotions reported here used virtual humans to encode expressive stimuli (e.g., Coulson, 2004; Tan et al., 2010).

But research is still restricted by human constraints: inducing a genuine emotional state and distinguishing the influence of emotions from other mental state components—such as social relationships, culture or personality—are challenges to be addressed.

Solving these issues would benefit several fields, especially the psychological research on emotion, since studying the expression of emotions through the body will challenge, improve, and enrich the existing emotion models as well as impact work on the effect of emotional expression on human behavior and social interaction.

A comprehensive computational model of the influence of emotion on posture and gesture would also benefit the ECA community. It would improve the automatic detection of the emotional state of the user (see Mühl, this volume) as well as the generation of bodily expression of emotion, leading to more believable and humanlike ECAs and more effective social interactions with virtual humans.

Notes

1. Of course Darwin was strongly influenced by his contemporaries, including, for example, Pierre Gratiolet, a French anatomist who explored the "body language" shared by men and animals. Gratiolet's work remains largely unknown, since his book (Gratiolet, 1865) has never been translated into English.
2. Head nods and gaze are also nonverbal behaviors that convey meaning, but they are beyond the scope of this chapter.

References

Allbeck, J., & Badler, N. 2002. Toward representing agent behaviors modified by personality and emotion. *Embodied Conversational Agents at AAMAS*, 2, 15–19.

Amaya, K., Bruderlin, A., & Calvert, T. 1996. Emotion from motion. In *Graphics Interface*, 96, 222–229.

Argyle, M. 1975. *Bodily communication*. Oxford, England: International Universities Press.

Aronoff, J., Woike, B. A., & Hyman, L. M. 1992. Which are the stimuli in facial displays of anger and happiness? Configurational bases of emotion recognition. *Journal of Personality and Social Psychology*, 62(6), 1050–1066.

Atkinson, A. P., Dittrich, W. H., Gemmell, A. J., & Young, A. W. 2004. Emotion perception from dynamic and static body expressions in point-light and full-light displays. *Perception-London*, 33, 717–746.

Badler, N., Allbeck, J., Zhao, L., & Byun, M. 2002. Representing and parameterizing agent behaviors. In *Proceedings of computer animation 2002* (pp. 133–143). IEEE Computer Society.

Badler, N., Costa, M., Zhao, L., & Chi, D. 2000. To gesture or not to gesture: What is the question? In *Proceedings of computer graphics international 2000* (pp. 3–9). IEEE Computer Society.

Ball, G., & Breese, J. 2000. Emotion and personality in a conversational agent. In Cassell, J., Sullivan, J., Prevost, S. & Churchill, E. (Eds.), *Embodied conversational agents* (pp. 189–219). Cambridge, MA, USA: MIT Press.

Banse, R., & Scherer, K. R. 1996. Acoustic profiles in vocal emotion expression. *Journal of Personality and Social Psychology*, 70, 614–636.

Bänziger, T., & Scherer, K. R. 2007. Using actor portrayals to systematically study multimodal emotion expression: The GEMEP corpus. In A. C. R. Paiva, R. Prada, & R. W. Picard (Eds.), *Affective computing and intelligent interaction* (pp. 476–487). Lecture Notes in Computer Science 4738. Berlin and Heidelberg: Springer.

Becker, C., Kopp, S., & Wachsmuth, I. 2004. Simulating the emotion dynamics of a multimodal conversational agent. In *Affective dialogue systems* (pp. 154–165). Berlin and Heidelberg: Springer.

Birdwhistell, R. 1970. *Kinesics and context*. Philadelphia, PA, USA: University of Pennsylvania Press.

Calbris, G., & Doyle, O. 1990. *The semiotics of French gestures*. Bloomington: Indiana University Press.

Cassell, J. 2000. *Embodied conversational agents*. Cambridge, MA, USA: MIT Press.

Chi, D., Costa, M., Zhao, L., & Badler, N. 2000. The EMOTE model for effort and shape. In *Proceedings of the 27th annual conference on computer graphics and interactive techniques* (pp. 173–182). New York, NY, USA: ACM Press/Addison-Wesley Publishing Co.

Coulson, M. 2004. Attributing emotion to static body postures: Recognition accuracy, confusions, and viewpoint dependence. *Journal of Nonverbal Behavior*, 28(2), 117–139.

Dael, N., Mortillaro, M., & Scherer, K. R. 2012a. Emotion expression in body action and posture. *Emotion*, 12(5), 1085–1101.

Dael, N., Mortillaro, M., & Scherer, K. R. 2012b. The body action and posture coding system (BAP): Development and reliability. *Journal of Nonverbal Behavior*, 36(2), 97–121.

Darwin, C. 1872. *The expression of the emotions in man and animals*. New York: Oxford University Press.

Dell, C. 1977. *A primer for movement description*. New York: Dance Notation Bureau.

Dittmann, A. T. 1972. The body movement-speech rhythm relationship as a cue to speech encoding. In Siegman, A. W. & Pope, B. (Eds.), *Studies in Dyadic Communication* (pp. 131–151). New York: Pergamon Press.

Dittmann, A. T. 1987. The role of body movement in communication. In Siegman, A. W. & Feldstein, S. (Eds.), *Nonverbal behavior and communication* (2nd ed. pp. 37-63). Hillsdale, NJ, England: Lawrence Erlbaum Associates, Inc.

Efron, D. 1941. *Gesture and environment*. Oxford, England: King's Crown Press.

Efron, D. 1972. *Gesture, race and culture*. The Hague: Mouton.

Ekman, P. 1965. Differential communication of affect by head and body cues. *Journal of Personality and Social Psychology*, 2(5), 726–735.

Ekman, P. 2001. *Telling lies: Clues to deceit in the marketplace, politics, and marriage*. New York: Norton.

Ekman, P., & Friesen, W. V. 1967. Head and body cues in the judgment of emotion: A reformulation. *Perceptual and Motor Skills*, 24(3), 711–724.

Ekman, P., & Friesen, W. V. 1969. Nonverbal leakage and clues to deception. *Psychiatry: Journal for the Study of Interpersonal Processes*, 32(1), 88–106.

Ekman, P., & Friesen, W. V. 1969. The repertoire of nonverbal behavior: categories, origins, usage, and coding. *Semiotica*, 1, 49–98.

Ekman, P., & Friesen, W. V. 1972. Hand movements. *Journal of Communication*, 22(4), 353–374.

Ekman, P., & Friesen, W. V. 1974. Detecting deception from the body or face. *Journal of Personality and Social Psychology*, 29(3), 288–298.

Ekman, P., & Friesen, W. V. 1977. Nonverbal behavior. In P. Ostwald (Ed.), *Communication and human interaction* (pp. 37–46). New York: Grune & Stratton.

Ekman, P., Friesen, W. V., & Hager, J. 1978. *The facial action coding system (FACS): A technique for the measurement of facial action*. Palo Alto. CA: Consulting Psychologists Press.

Ekman, P., Friesen, W. V., & Hager, J. C. 2002. *Facial* action coding system. Salt Lake City, UT: Research Nexus.

Ekman, P., O'Sullivan, M., Friesen, W. V., & Scherer, K. R. 1991. Face, voice, and body in detecting deceit. *Journal of Nonverbal Behavior, 15*(2), 125–135.

Freedman, N. 1972. The analysis of movement behavior during the clinical interview. In Siegman, A. W. & Pope, B. (Eds.), *Studies in Dyadic Communication* (pp. 153–175). New York: Pergamon Press.

Frey, S., & Pool, J. 1976. *A new approach to the analysis of visible behavior*. Bern: University of Bern, Department of Psychology.

Fridlund, A. J. 1991. Evolution and facial action in reflex, social motive, and paralanguage. *Biological Psychology, 32*(1), 3–100.

Fridlund, A. J. 1997. The new ethology of human facial expressions. In Russell, J. A.& Fernández-Dols, J. M. (Eds.), *The Psychology of Facial Expression* (pp. 103–129). Studies in emotion and social interaction, 2nd series. New York, NY, US: Cambridge University Press & Paris, France: Editions de la Maison des Sciences de l'Homme.

Frijda, N. H. 2007. *The laws of emotion*. Mahwah, NJ: Lawrence Erlbaum Associates.

Gallaher, P. E. 1992. Individual differences in nonverbal behavior: Dimensions of style. *Journal of Personality and Social Psychology, 63*(1), 133–145.

Gelder, B. de. 2009. Why bodies? Twelve reasons for including bodily expressions in affective neuroscience. *Philosophical Transactions of the Royal Society B: Biological Sciences, 364*(1535), 3475–3484.

Gifford, R. 1994. A Lens-mapping framework for understanding the encoding and decoding of interpersonal dispositions in nonverbal behavior. *Journal of Personality and Social Psychology, 66*(2), 398–412.

Gratch, J., & Marsella, S. 2001. Tears and fears: Modeling emotions and emotional behaviors in synthetic agents. In *Proceedings of the fifth international conference on autonomous agents* (pp. 278–285). New York, NY, USA: ACM.

Gratiolet, P. 1865. *De la physionomie et des mouvements d'expression*. Paris, France: J. Hetzel.

Gross, M. M., Crane, E. A., & Fredrickson, B. L. 2010. Methodology for assessing bodily expression of emotion. *Journal of Nonverbal Behavior, 34*(4), 223–248.

Gross, M. M., Crane, E. A., & Fredrickson, B. L. 2012. Effort-shape and kinematic assessment of bodily expression of emotion during gait. *Human Movement Science, 31*(1), 202–221.

Hanke, T. 2004. HamNoSys-Representing sign language data in language resources and language processing contexts. In *Fourth International Conference on Language Resources and Evaluation* (pp. 1–6). Paris: European Language Resources Association.

Harrigan, J. A. 2005. Proxemics, kinesics, and gaze. In Harrigan, J., Rosenthal, R. & Scherer K. (Eds.), *The new handbook of methods in nonverbal behavior research* (pp. 137–198). New York: Oxford University Press.

Hartmann, B., Mancini, M. & Pelachaud, C. 2005. Towards affective agent action: Modelling expressive ECA gestures. In *Intelligent user interfaces 2005 workshop on affective interaction*. ACM Press.

Hartmann, B., Mancini, M. & Pelachaud, C. 2006. Implementing expressive gesture synthesis for embodied conversational agents. In Gibet, S., Courty, N. & Kamp, J.-F. (Eds.), *Gesture in human-computer interaction and simulation* (pp. 188–199). Lecture Notes in Artificial Intelligence 3881. New York: Springer.

Hicheur, H., Kadone, H., Grèzes, J., & Berthoz, A. 2013. The combined role of motion-related cues and upper body posture for the expression of emotions during human walking. In Mombaur, K. & Berns, K. (Eds.), *Modeling, simulation and optimization of bipedal walking* (pp. 71–85). Cognitive Systems Monographs 18. Berlin and Heidelberg: Springer.

Hietanen, J. K., Leppänen, J. M., & Lehtonen, U. 2004. Perception of emotions in the hand movement quality of Finnish sign language. *Journal of Nonverbal Behavior, 28*(1), 53–64.

Izard, C. E. 1977. *Human emotions*. New York: Springer.

James, W. T. 1932. A study of the expression of bodily posture. *The Journal of General Psychology, 7*(2), 405–437.

Kendon, A. 1983. Gesture and speech: How they interact. *Nonverbal Interaction, 11*, 13–45.

Kipp, M., & Martin, J.-C. 2009. Gesture and emotion: Can basic gestural form features discriminate emotions? In *3rd international conference on affective computing and intelligent interaction and workshops* (pp. 1–8). IEEE Press.

Kopp, S., & Bergmann, K. 2012. Individualized gesture production in embodied conversational agents. In Zacarias, M., & Oliveira, J. V. (Eds.), *Human-computer interaction: The agency perspective* (pp. 287–301). Studies in Computational Intelligence 396. Springer Berlin Heidelberg.

Ma, Y., Paterson, H. M., & Pollick, F. E. 2006. A motion capture library for the study of identity, gender, and emotion perception from biological motion. *Behavior Research Methods, 38*(1), 134–141.

Mahl, G. F. 1956. Disturbances and silences in the patient's speech in psychotherapy. *Journal of Abnormal Psychology, 53*(1), 1–15.

Mahl, G. F. 1968. Gestures and body movements in interviews. In *3rd conference on research in psychotherapy* (pp. 295–346). Washington, DC, USA: American Psychological Association.

Mancini, M., & Pelachaud, C. 2008. Distinctiveness in multimodal behaviors. In *Proceedings of the conference on autonomous agents and multiagent systems* (pp. 159–166). Richland, SC: International Foundation for Autonomous Agents and Multiagent Systems.

Marsella, S. C., Johnson, W. L., & LaBore, C. 2000. Interactive pedagogical drama. In *Proceedings of the fourth international conference on autonomous agents* (pp. 301–308). New York, NY, USA: ACM.

McNeill, D. 1985. So you think gestures are nonverbal? *Psychological review 92*(3), 350–371.

McNeill, D. 1987. *Psycholinguistics: A new approach*. New York: Harper & Row.

McNeill, D. 1992. *Hand and mind: What gestures reveal about thought*. Chicago: University of Chicago Press.

McNeill, D. 2008. *Gesture and thought*. Chicago: University of Chicago Press.

Mehrabian, A. 1972. *Nonverbal communication*. New Brunswick, NJ: Transaction Publishers.

Montepare, J. M., Goldstein. S. B., & Clausen, A. 1987. The identification of emotions from gait information. *Journal of Nonverbal Behavior 11*(1): 33–42.

Neff, M., & Fiume, E. 2006. Methods for exploring expressive stance. *Graphical Models, 68*(2), 133–157.

Nisbett, R. E., & Wilson, T. D. 1977. Telling more than we can know: Verbal reports on mental processes. *Psychological Review, 84*(3), 231–259.

Noot, H., & Ruttkay, Z. 2004. Gesture in style. In Camurri, A., & Volpe, G. (Eds.), *Gesture-Based Communication in Human-Computer Interaction* (pp. 324–337). Lecture Notes in Computer Science 2915. New York: Springer.

Ortony, A., Clore, G. L., & Collins, A. 1988. *The cognitive structure of emotions.* Cambridge, UK: Cambridge University Press.

Patterson, H. M., Pollick, F. E., & Sanford, A. J. 2001. The role of velocity in affect discrimination. In *Proceedings of the Twenty-Third Annual Conference of the Cognitive Science Society* (pp. 756–761). Lawrence Erlbaum Associates.

Pelachaud, C. 2009. Studies on gesture expressivity for a virtual agent. *Speech Communication 51*(7), 630–639.

Pollick, F. E., Paterson, H. M., Bruderlin, A., & Sanford, A. J. 2001. Perceiving affect from arm movement. *Cognition, 82*(2), B51–B61.

Rickel, J., Marsella, S., Gratch, J., Hill, R., Traum, D., & Swartout, W. 2002. Toward a new generation of virtual humans for interactive experiences. *Intelligent Systems, IEEE, 17*(4), 32–38.

Roether, C. L., Omlor, L., & Giese, M. A. 2009. Critical features for the perception of emotion from gait. *Journal of Vision, 9*(6).

Roether, C. L., Omlor, L., & Giese, M. A. 2010. Features in the recognition of emotions from dynamic bodily expression. In J. Ilg, U. T. & Masson, G. S. (Eds.), *Dynamics of visual motion processing* (pp. 313–340). New York: Springer.

Rossberg-Gempton, I., & Poole G. D. 1993. The effect of open and closed postures on pleasant and unpleasant emotions. *The Arts in Psychotherapy, 20*(1), 75–82.

Russell, J. A., & Mehrabian, A. 1977. Evidence for a three-factor theory of emotions. *Journal of Research in Personality, 11*(3), 273–294.

Scherer, K. R., & Ellgring, H. 2007. Multimodal expression of emotion: Affect programs or componential appraisal patterns? *Emotion, 7*(1), 158–171.

Scherer, S., Glodek, M., Layher, G., Schels, M., Schmidt, M., Brosch, T., Tschechne, S., ... Palm, G. 2012. A generic framework for the inference of user states in human computer interaction: How patterns of low level communicational cues support complex affective states. *Journal on Multimodal User Interfaces, 6*(3), 117–141.

Schouwstra, S. J., & Hoogstraten, J. 1995. Head position and spinal position as determinants of perceived emotional state. *Perceptual and Motor Skills, 81*(2), 673–674.

Sprengelmeyer, R., Young, A. W., Schroeder, U., Grossenbacher, P. G., Federlein, J., Buttner, T., & Przuntek, H. 1999. Knowing no fear. *Proceedings of the Royal Society of London. Series B: Biological Sciences, 266*(1437), 2451–2456. Royal Society Publishing.

Tan, N., Clavel, C., Courgeon, M., & Martin, J.-C. 2010. Postural expressions of action tendencies. In *Proceedings of the 2nd international workshop on social signal processing* (pp. 53–58). New York: ACM.

Vosk, B. N., Forehand, R., & Figueroa, R. 1983. Perception of emotions by accepted and rejected children. *Journal of Behavioral Assessment, 5*(2), 151–160.

Wallbott, H. G. 1998. Bodily expression of emotion. *European Journal of Social Psychology, 28*(6), 879–896.

Wallbott, H. G., & Scherer, K. R. 1986. Cues and channels in emotion recognition. *Journal of Personality and Social Psychology, 51*(4), 690–699.

Walters, K. L., & Walk, R. D. 1986. Perception of emotion from body posture. *Bulletin of the Psychonomic Society, 24*(5), 329–329.

Wiggins, J. S. 1996. *The five-factor model of personality: Theoretical perspectives.* New York: Guilford Press.

Wolff, C. 1972. *A psychology of gesture.* New York: Arno Press.

Zhao, L., & Badler, N. I. 2001. *Synthesis and acquisition of Laban movement analysis qualitative parameters for communicative gestures.* University of Pennsylvania.

Emotional Speech Synthesis

Felix Burkhardt *and* Nick Campbell

Abstract

Emotional speech synthesis is an important part of the puzzle on the long way to humanlike artificial human-machine interaction. On the way, lots of stations like emotional audio messages or believable characters in gaming will be reached. This chapter deals with the expression of emotions with speech synthesizers or articficial talkers. After some introductory remarks, it starts out by discussing potential applications that can be realized with emotional speech synthesis. Emotion models and how they relate to speech synthesis are a further topic as well as a discussion on the acoustic aspects of the expression of emotion in a speech signal. The main part of this chapter deals with the technical aspects of emotional speech synthesis by introducing the most important speech synthesis techniques like articulatory synthesis, formant synthesis, diphone synthesis, non-uniform unit selection based synthesis, HMM based synthesis and voice transformation techniques while discussing the implications on the simulation of emotional expression that each approach has. The chapter closes with some thoughts on the evaluation of emotional speech synthesis and tries to give an outlook on the possible future.

Key Words: speech synthesis, nonuniform unit-selection, hmm synthesis, voice transformation, diphone synthesis, articulatory synthesis, formant synthesis, evaluation

Introduction

No one ever speaks without emotion. Despite this, emotional simulation is not yet a self-evident feature in current speech synthesizers. One reason for this perhaps lies in the complexity of human vocal expression: current state-of-the-art synthesizers still struggle with the challenge of generating understandable (for domain-independent systems) and natural-sounding speech, although the latter requirement in itself already indicates the importance of affective expression.

This chapter gives an overview on the state of art with respect to different aspects of emotional speech synthesis, ranging from use cases and emotion models to technical approaches. For a deeper understanding of the principles of speech synthesis, see Taylor (2009); for a deeper history of emotional

speech synthesis, the reader is referred to Murray & Arnott (1993) and Schröder (2001).

The notion of emotional behavior is most imprecise and difficult to describe. As a psychologist once famously remarked: "everyone except a psychologist knows what an emotion is" (Young, 1973; cited in Kleinginna & Kleinginna, 1981).

Fortunately this problem concerns emotion recognition much more than emotional speech synthesis, because in the former case one needs an accurate model of "the real world" in order to capture the multitude of emotional expressions, while in the latter a simple model based on a few basic emotions might suffice for many applications, even if a "natural" expression is rarely of this form. Simulated emotional expression is typically very well recognized when limited to the display of some exaggerated prototypical emotions (Burkhardt, 2000; Murray & Arnott, 1993; Schröder, 2001).

Generally speaking, speech synthesis can be classified under the following three types (although hybrid forms are possible):

• Voice response systems, as used in recorded announcements of stops in public transport systems.

• Resynthesis or copy synthesis, as used to alter a speech signal in its voice-related features. A special case would be voice transformation—for example, changing, in the case of voice conversion, a speech signal from a source to a target speaker. Voice-transformation techniques can be used to generate an emotional expression.

• Arbitrary speech synthesizers, which, in contrast, can process any kind of input given the limits of a target language. It must be noted, however, that all synthesizers are somewhat domain-restricted. They might be divided into text-to-speech versus concept-to-speech systems, depending on the information given with the text. With respect to the topic at hand, concept-to-speech systems might be able to label text with target emotions automatically.

An overall architecture of an emotional speech synthesis system is shown in Figure 20.1. The text to be synthesized is either given as input or generated by a text-generation system. Although such systems are beyond the scope of this chapter, formalisms to annotate text emotionally are discussed in Annotation Formalisms (p. 288) below as well as in chapter 29.

A text-to-speech synthesizer converts text into speech by first analyzing the text by natural language processing (NLP) and conversion to a phonemic representation aligned with a prosodic structure, which is passed to a digital speech processing (DSP) component in order to generate a speech signal. Both of these submodules might be influenced by the emotion-modeling component.

Approaches to generating emotional speech are be discussed further in Synthesis Approaches (p. 289).

Features of the speech signal are spectral (the "sound" of the voice), prosodic (the "melody" of the speech), phonetic (spoken phones, reductions, and elaborations), ideolectal (choice of words), and semantic (giving the meaning). All of these can be influenced by emotional expression, although, for practical reasons, speech synthesis systems typically take only a subset of these features into account. Aspects of emotional expression affecting speech features are discussed in Perceptual Clues in the Speech Signal (p. 289).

The component responsible for generating the emotional expression must be trained on a database of emotional examples, irrespective of whether rules are derived from the data or statistical algorithms are produced. Databases are often recorded by actors (Burkhardt, 2005), taken from real-life

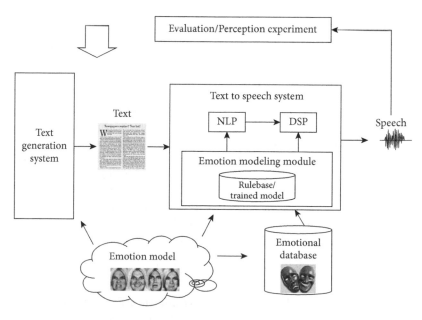

Fig. 20.1 General architecture for an emotional text-to-speech synthesis system.

data (Campbell, 2004), or obtained from TV (Devilliers et al., 2006).

From these, a rule base or model can be generated and used to control the synthesizer. All the components of the emotion processing system must have the same emotion model as a basis.

Different approaches to designating and describing emotions are discussed further in Emotion Modeling (p. 288).

A productive system must be evaluated by some means or other. Performance results and listening-test designs are discussed in Evaluation (p. 293).

Of course the quality of an emotion synthesizer depends primarily on its application, as in the character appearance. A synthesizer giving a cartoon figure a voice meets different demands than one used to make the voice of a speech-disabled person more natural. Applications of emotion in speech synthesis are discussed in the following section.

Applications of Emotion in Speech Synthesis

Batliner et al. (2006) discussed some ways of using emotion speech processing. Speech synthesis can be used to express or transmit emotional states, which is important to a growing variety of use cases. The following are some typical applications:

- Fun, for example emotional greetings
- Prostheses
- Emotional chat avatars
- Gaming, believable characters
- Adapted dialogue design
- Adapted persona design
- Target group–specific advertising
- Believable agents/artificial humans

The list is ordered in an ascending time line, as we believe that these applications will be realized. Because a technology must be used for a long time before it is stable and able to work reliably under pressure, the early applications will include less serious domains of application, like gaming and entertainment, or will be adopted by users having a strong need—for example, when voice synthesis is used as prosthesis.

The applications further down the list are closely related to the development of artificial intelligence. Because emotions and intelligence are closely intermingled (Damasio, 1994), great care is needed when computer systems appear to react emotionally without having the intelligence to meet the user's expectations with respect to dialogue abilities.

Note that many of the use cases require the modeling of subtle speaking styles and addition of natural

extralinguistic sounds to the synthesized speech. Considering the achievements of the past, which mainly synthesized a set of exaggerated so-called basic emotions, there is still a long way to go.

Emotion Modeling

As discussed in Chapter 5, the emotional expression is usually either modeled by a categorical system, distinguishing between a specific set of emotion categories like anger, fear, or boredom, or by the use of emotional dimensions like arousal, valence, or dominance. The categorical model has the advantage of being intuitively easy to understand and being well established in human everyday communication.

With the dimensional model, an emotion is modeled as a point in a multidimensional space describing emotionally relevant dimensions like arousal or activation (describing muscle relaxation and therefore being directly mappable to articulatory speech synthesizer parameters), pleasantness or valence (distinguishing between the subjective positivity of an emotion), and dominance (which indicates the strength of emotion a person feels). Numerous additional dimensions have been suggested, but these three are traditionally the most common (Rubin & Talerico, 2009). With speech synthesis in mind, it is easy to derive appropriate acoustic modification rules for the "arousal" dimension, because this is directly related to muscle tension, but it is very difficult for the other dimensions. Therefore emotional states are usually modeled by a categorical system, although dimensional systems are more flexible and better suited to model the imprecision of the "real world," in which "full blown" emotions rarely occur.

Today, other models that are more closer related to psychology and artificial intelligence, like appraisal theory or the OCC model (Ortony et al., 1988), do not play a big role with respect to emotion in speech synthesis directly, although many appraisal theories posit basic emotions corresponding to a categorical system (Chapter 5). For most of the use cases mentioned in the previous section, the simulation of "emotions" is perhaps not the most pressing requirement, instead, it is the ability of the synthesizer to express different "speaking styles." These either derive from the use case and can be described by some "speaking style to acoustic property" rules or are learned implicitly from data.

Annotation Formalisms

The problem of how to decide with which emotional attitude to speak a given text is beyond the scope of this chapter. Nonetheless, a specific format is needed to determine the display of affect for a synthesizer. For an overview article on this subject, see Schröder et al. (2011).

Current commercial synthesizers—for example, by Loquendo (now acquired by Nuance Inc.) or IBM—simply add emotional paralinguistic events to the unit inventory, as described in an IBM article (Eide et al., 2003). With the Loquendo TTS director, a tool to tune the text-to-speech system, expressive units can be selected from hierarchical drop-down menus.

A more complex approach was followed by the W3C incubator group for an emotional markup language (Schröder et al., 2008; Chapter 29 in this book). This group aimed at the development of a markup language for the expression of emotion that would be usable for annotation, recognition, synthesis, and modeling in human-machine interaction.

Here is an example:

```
<speak version="1.0" xmlns="http://www.
w3.org/2001/10/synthesis"
xml:lang="en-US">
<voice gender="female">
<prosody contour="(0\%,+20Hz)(10\%,+30\%)
(40\%,+10Hz)">
Hi, I am sad now but start getting angry…
</prosody>
</voice>
<emotion>
<category name="sadness set="basic"
intensity="0.6"/>
<timing start="10\%" end="50\%"/>
</emotion>
<emotion>
<category name="anger" set="basic"
intensity="0.4"/>
<timing start="50\%" end="100\%"/>
</emotion>
</speak>
```

Embedded in a speech synthesis markup language (SSML), another standard proposed by the W3C tag, the synthesizer is instructed to change the vocal expression of the output from sadness to anger. The language is still under development but will hopefully provide a common basis for emotion research, enabling easy data and subcomponent exchange as well as a distributed market for emotion processing systems.

Extensibility is possible, but the most frequently used models mentioned in Emotion Modeling (p. 288)—like categories, dimensions or appraisal models—are already supported.

Perceptual Clues in the Speech Signal

Features of the speech signal are spectral (the "sound" of the voice), prosodic (the "melody" of the speech), phonetic (spoken phones, reductions, and elaborations), ideolectal (choice of words), and semantic.

In order to investigate the perceptual clues of emotional speech, Burkhardt et al. (2005) recorded a database with acted speech, generally known as the EmoDB, which is available for free download.

In Figure 20.2, spectrograms of several emotions, spoken by different actors but always in the same sentence (*In sieben Stunden wird es soweit sein*, "in seven hours it will happen"), are displayed. A spectrogram shows the amplitude of frequencies over time. Although the Berlin database was recorded at 48 kHz, the frequency scale of these spectrograms is limited to 8 kHz, which is the normal upper limit of most synthesized speech.

The displayed emotions diverge with respect to prosody, phonetic realization, and voice quality, as can be seen from the different amplitudes of the frequency bands.

The modification of features like semantics and idiolect lies within the scope of the text generation system, whereas the acoustic features are within the control of the speech synthesizer itself.

As shown in the next section, different synthesis approaches currently have a trade-off between naturalness of the speech and flexibility with respect to speech manipulation.

Synthesis Approaches

This section discusses the most common synthesis approaches in the current research landscape. The main difference between them can be characterized by a trade-off with respect to unnatural but flexible parametric synthesis and natura-sounding but inflexible (with respect to out-of-domain utterances) concatenation of audio samples. All of these are working in real time and could thus be used for human-machine interaction. As explained in the following, the approaches differ with regard to the possibility of simulating emotional arousal. General advice on which technology to use for emotional systems cannot be given. The "uncanny valley" effect says that the more natural systems are not necessarily the ones that are accepted as best by users. This

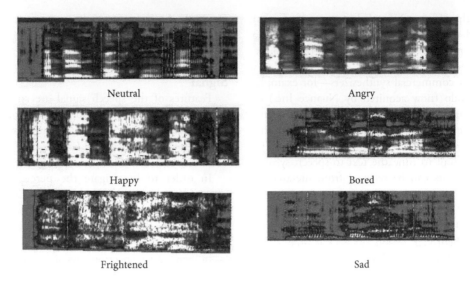

Neutral   Angry

Happy   Bored

Frightened   Sad

Fig. 20.2 Spectrograms from emotionally acted speech, always using the same sentence.

means that more artificial-sounding systems might be preferred in certain conditions.

Rule-Based Approaches

In contrast to purely data-based statistical approaches, production models synthesize human speech by modeling aspects of the human production mechanism to a varying degree. These can be summarized by "system modeling" approaches, in contrast to "signal modeling" ones. Essentially, articulatory models interpolate between target positions of the articulators while kinetic limitations with respect to velocity and degree of freedom are taken into account; the speech signal is then generated based on aerodynamic acoustic models. With the simulation of emotional speech in mind, articulatory synthesis is very attractive because the relation between the influence of emotional arousal on muscles and tissue and the acoustic properties of the body parts involved in the speech production process can be directly modeled. However, it must be noted that articulatory synthesis is still suffering from an insufficiency of data. Very high quality speech has been produced, but the processes are difficult to automate. The correlation between speech and articulator movements is not well researched owing to the lack of efficient data-capture and measurement methods. Also, the connection between laryngeal and articulator positions and variations in the sound wave is highly complex; existing tube models represent only a crude simplification of the human vocal tract. Nevertheless, experiments with the resynthesis of

natural speech and vowel-consonant-vowel logatoms show promising results (Birkholz et al., 2006), and clearly constrained phenomena like coarticulation can be studied in a controlled environment (Perrier et al., 2005). Furthermore, the database is improving because of advanced technology. For example, using new electromagnetic measurement methodologies, Lee et al. (2005) recently investigated the influence of emotional arousal on articulatory movement.

Data-Based Approaches
DIPHONE CONCATENATION

Around 1986, the invention of the new signal processing technique PSOLA (Pitch Synchronous Overlap and Add, a technique that allows to change the pitch contour of a given segment of speech, Moulines & Charpentier, 1990).) marked the birth of diphone synthesis, which proceeds by concatenating small units of recorded speech taken from a minimal set covering a given language. From the 1990s on, diphone concatenation was the primary instrument for a large number of studies in emotional speech synthesis. Owing to the nature of the decoding algorithms, only pitch and durational features could be modified, whereas voice quality was preserved by the natural waveform shaping. In order to control voice quality, there have been experiments with multiple diphone databases from the same speaker. Both formant and diphone synthesis used handcrafted rules to modify the voice acoustics in order to express different emotions (Cahn, 1990; Murray & Arnott, 1993).

NONUNIFORM UNIT SELECTION

With the commercially most successful approach to speech synthesis, nonuniform unit selection, best-fitting chunks of speech from large databases are concatenated, thereby minimizing a double cost function: best fit to neighbor unit and best fit to target prosody.

Because signal manipulation is reduced as much as possible, the resulting speech sounds most natural (similar to the original speaker) as long as the utterance to synthesize is close to the original domain of the database. In order to simulate emotional variation, three approaches are possible.

• Duplicate the database for each emotional style (Iida et al., 2000). This can be seen as the "brute force" method and has been used successfully for prosthesis products, but of course it only allows for the simulation of a very limited number of styles.
• Integrate an emotional target function in the unit selection process (Campbell, 2004). This is a very elegant method explicitly including the possibility to display extralinguistic speech sounds, but it requires the manual annotation of very large databases.
• Apply signal manipulation methods on the speech signal (Agiomyrgiannakis & Rosec, 2009). This requires the units to be coded in a (semi-) parametric way. Voice transformation techniques can than be used to alter the speech style.

Hybrid Approaches

Statistical approaches combine the flexibility of the parametric synthesis with the naturalness of large databases. Currently, hidden Markov model (HMM)–based models are most successful (Yoshimura et al., 1999). The speech is modeled by a source-filter model and parameterized by an excitation signal and either Mel Frequency Cepstrum coefficients, which are related to vocal tract shapes, or line spectrum pairs (LSPs), which are related to formant positions.

This approach inherits many of the tools and processes of automatic speech recognition, which models the speech sounds by means of a sequence of states, each representing part of a phoneme, with statistical probabilities learnt for the transitions between states and the mapping of these transitions onto sequences of words in a text. HMM-based synthesis reverses the process, to predict the sequence of subphonemic states from a given input text. It differs from standard speech recognition in that it includes a representation of phoneme duration and pitch as a characteristic of each state model and thus produces not just an acoustic sequence for synthesis but also an indication of the prosody of the utterance.

The simulation of emotional styles is usually done by shifting the parameters of the source speech signal with respect to a target emotional style. With respect to the excitation signal, different voice qualities may be simulated by varying the parameters of a glottal flow model like the Liljencrants Fant model (Fant et al., 1985). In Figure 20.3, several phonation types were simulated by formant synthesizer based on the Liljencrants Fant model (Burkhardt, 2009).

Synthesis of Nonverbal Vocalizations

Beneath spoken words, human speech consists to a large degree of nonverbal vocalizations, which might be divided into "vegetative sounds," "affect sounds," "interjections," and "feedback and fillers sounds" (Trouvain & Truong, 2012). Since there is no standard to define and to classify (possible) nonspeech sounds, the annotations for these vocalizations differ very much for various corpora of conversational speech.

The analysis of these phenomena is a foundation for introducing nonverbal vocalizations into speech synthesis in order to make the output more natural. There seems to be agreement in that hesitation sounds and feedback vocalizations are considered as words (without a standard orthography), while the most frequent nonverbal vocalization are laughter on the one hand and, if considered a vocal sound, breathing noises on the other (Trouvain & Truong, 2012).

Laughter and other feedback mechanisms are an essential part of normal face-to-face spoken interaction. These sounds are now beginning to be modeled both as part of the communication process and as components of advanced speech synthesis.

To date, except from some studies (Sundaram & Narayanan, 2006), there has not been much effort devoted to reproducing the sounds of laughter in rule-based synthesis, but it is easy to include in concatenative methods if present in the source speech material (Eide et al., 2003).

The classification of laughter remains as an active research field, but for conversational speech synthesis there will be a need for several different types of laughter, including embarrassed nervous laughs, gutsy humorous laughs, polite social laughs, and ice-breaking speech laughs. Ultimately, there may be a need to synthesize laughing speech as well, but that still remains as work for the future.

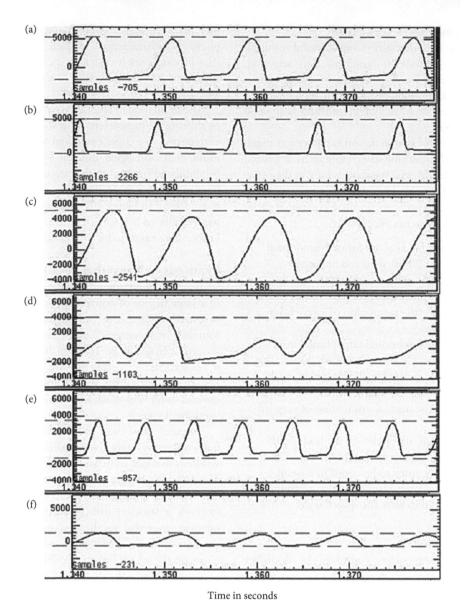

Fig. 20.3 Source signal waveforms for different phonation types: (a) modal, (b) tense, (c) breathy, (d) creaky, (e) falsetto, and (f) whispery.

Feedback is essential in face-to-face communication, allowing the speaker to know that his or her utterance has been heard, processed, and understood, and this presents special challenges for computer speech synthesis. Even the simple word *yes* can be said in many different ways, varying in meaning from a simple "go ahead" through the literal "I agree" and even as far as "I hear you but completely *dis*agree" (when spoken with a slow rise-fall-rise intonation). The simplest sounds present the greatest problems for synthesis because their text does not indicate their meaning, and the intention of "words" such as *um, oh, ah*, etc., is carried largely by their prosody. There

is a need for extension to the markup languages to allow indication of speaker (or usually listener) intention in specifying such sounds for synthesis.

Large Source Corpus–Based Emotional Speech Synthesis

Expressivity varies according to complex interactions of factors, with the speaker's emotional state being just one of many. In daily life, a person's voice and speaking style changes according to politeness, to their health, their various social and personal relationships to the interlocutor, and to the context of the conversation.

Speech synthesis is reliant on good data to model these variations in order to reproduce the necessary tones and intonations required for interactive speech synthesis. Figure 20.3 shows that the voice changes during different speaking styles, and this range of variation is common in everyday speech. The types of recordings made for early speech synthesis used actors and were recorded in a studio, often from textual prompts. More recent recordings capture the speech of ordinary people in a wide range of everyday situations. The recording technology is now cheap and ubiquitous, but the manual effort required for the annotation of such recordings is still very costly. That said, the amount of effort required in producing reliable annotations is finite and can result in a rich source of material for resynthesis. Furthermore, by massively increasing the amounts of recorded speech, we then find multiple tokens of the same phonemic sequence but with subtle differences in intonation, prosody, and voice quality, such that they become ideal for use in rich expressive synthesis without the need for complex signal modifications. The challenge, as said above, is to label them appropriately so that suitable tokens can be retrieved from the corpus to express the target intentions and cognitive states of the speaker.

Technology might come to our aid here, as the dependencies between cognitive state and speech acoustics become known and as the ability to automatically recognize and label different voice qualities and prosodic contours improves. Currently, little use is made of the natural variety in voice characteristics in a large source corpus; but by sophisticated selection and careful concatenation, we may find that recordings of everyday speech provide all the necessary material for complex expression of emotion and interlocutor relationships. Rather than going for larger corpora, it may be wiser to make finer use of the variability we already have.

An alternative to everyday speech corpora is the use of audiobook recordings. Székely et al. describe an approach to automatically cluster audiobook speech into emotion-related categories based on acoustic properties (Székely et al 2011). The clustered speech is then used as the database for a data-driven synthesizer.

Evaluation

Emotional speech is usually evaluated with perception tests, often of the forced-choice variety. Evaluation texts are designed to be emotionally neutral, although some authors criticize the inherent unnaturalness of this approach and prefer to use emotional sentences (Schröder 2004). The task for the judges then is to rate the adequacy of the vocal expression instead of using simple (categorical) identification.

As stated earlier, synthetic emotional expression tends to be exaggerated, and this results in a recognition rates of 80% and higher (of course depending on the number of emotions to identify) compared with emotion recognition. Interestingly, the analysis of the resulting confusion matrices gives insights to the most prominent emotional dimensions in vocal emotional expression. Often, emotion pairs with a similar degree of activation (like anger-joy or boredom-sadness) get confused, whereas differences with respect to pleasantness and dominance seem to be primarily revealed in the facial expression.

As the demands of speech synthesis go beyond cartoon-voice generation and it finds uses in everyday conversational situations, these extreme stereotypical emotions will be less welcome and the need will be to synthesize subtle differences in voice and prosody that signal more complex speaker-hearer interactions. For this work, simple forced-choice evaluations will give way to more sophisticated measures of appropriateness for a given context or situation and more subtle statistical processes to provide diagnostic as well as likeability information.

Outlook

The challenge for the near future in this area is to improve both selection and conversion technology and to make the unit selection approach more robust against missing data. In the very long term, however, model-based approaches, which are inherently more flexible, may supersede unit selection technology if their quality approaches that of unit selection.

The main challenge for the speech synthesis of emotion results from the discrepancy between natural but inflexible versus artificial-sounding but flexible synthesis approaches. The solutions in the short to middle term consist of the following:

• The usage of very large databases for nonuniform unit selection incorporating a cost function for emotional expression, possibly based on voice quality and prosodic characteristics as selection criteria.
• The further development of statistically based hybrid parametric nonuniform unit selection techniques, especially with respect to naturalness.
• Promising are the advances in voice transformation techniques, which can be used

to introduce different speaking styles to speech resulting from a unit selection process.

• The development of a high-quality source filter model–based synthesis, such as a wide-band formant synthesizer or integrated source-filter modification models.

• The ability to automatically categorize voice characteristics and to include these alongside phonemic features in the training or selection of material.

In order to reach the "holy grail" of speech synthesis—to have a synthesizer capable of modeling speaker characteristics from very small data—further achievements in physical modeling techniques like articulatory synthesis are needed. Until then, the manual labor required in the careful annotation of large recordings of natural conversational speech continues to produce high-quality output. Moreover, competitive evaluations like the Blizzard Challenge confirm that the winners typically are those who devote more time to careful annotation of the data and manual cleaning up of the training material before going on to the more technical aspects of synthesizer production.

The two worlds—rule-based physical modeling systems on the one hand and statistical algorithms based on very large datasets on the other—need to be combined to tackle demanding challenges such as the simulation of affect in speech synthesis.

References

Agiomyrgiannakis, Y., & Rosec, O. (2009). Arx-lf-based source-filter methods for voice modification and transformation. In *Proceedings of the international conference on acoustics, speech, and signal processing* (pp. 3589–3592). Institute of Electrical and Electronics Engineers Inc., Washington, DC

Batliner, A., Burkhardt, F., van Ballegooy, M., & Nöth, E. (2006). A taxonomy of applications that utilize emotional awareness. In *Proceedings of the fifth Slovenian and first international language technologies conference* (pp. 246–250). Jožef Stefan Institute, Ljubljana, Slovenia

Birkholz, P., Jackel, D., & Kröger, B. J. (2006). Construction and control of a three-dimensional vocal tract model. *Proceedings of the international conference on acoustics, speech, and signal processing* (pp. 873–876). Institute of Electrical and Electronics Engineers Inc., Washington, DC

Burkhardt, F. (2000). *Simulation emotionaler Sprechweise mit Sprachsynthesesystemen.* Shaker, Aachen, Germany.

Burkhardt, F., Paeschke, A., Rolfes, M., Sendlmeier, W. F., & Weiss, B. (2005). A database of German emotional speech. In *Proceedings of interspeech* (pp. 1517–1520). International Speech Communication Association, Baixas, France.

Burkhardt, F. (2009). Rule-based voice quality variation with formant synthesis. In *Proceedings of interspeech* (pp. 2659–2662). International Speech Communication Association, Baixas, France.

Cahn, J. E. (1990). The generation of affect in synthesized speech. *Journal of the American Voice I/O Society, 8,* 1–19.

Campbell, N. (2004). Databases of expressive speech. In Journal of Chinese Language and Computing, Vol 14, N.4, pp 295–304, Chinese and Oriental Languages Information Processing Society, Singapre.

Damasio, A. R. (1994). *Descartes' error: Emotion, reason, and the human brain.* New York: Avon Books.

Devillers, L., Cowie, R., Martin, J.-C., Douglas-Cowie, E., Abrilian, S., & McRorie, M. (2006). Real life emotions in French and English tv video clips: An integrated annotation protocol combining continuous and discrete approaches. In *Proceedings of the 5th international conference on language resources and evaluation (LREC)* European Language Resources Association, Paris, France

Eide, E., Aaron, A., Bakis, R., Hamza, W., Picheny, M., & Pitrelli, J. (2003). A corpus-based approach to expressive speech synthesis. In *Proceedings of ISCA ITRW on speech synthesis* (pp. 79–84). International Speech Communication Association, Baixas, France.

Fant, G., Liljencrants, J., & Lin, Q. (1985). *A four-parameter model of glottal flow* (Vol. 4, pp. 1–13). Prog.Stat.Rep (STL-QPSR), Royal Institute of Technology, Stockholm

Iida, A., Campbell, N., Iga, S., Higuchi, F., & Yasumura, M. (2000). A speech synthesis system with emotion for assisting communication. In *Proceedings of the ISCA workshop on speech and emotion* (pp. 167–172) International Speech Communication Association, Baixas, France.

Kleinginna P. R., & Kleinginna, A. M. (1981). A categorized list of emotion definitionns, with suggestions for a consensual definition. *Motivation & Emotion,* Vol 5, No. 4 345–379.

Lee, S., Yildirim, S., Kazemzadeh, A., & Narayanan, S. (2005). An articulatory study of emotional speech production. In *Proceedings of interspeech* (pp. 497–500) International Speech Communication Association, Baixas, France.

Moulines, E. & Charpentier, F. (1990). Pitch-Synchronous Waveform Processing Techniques for Text-To-Speech Synthesis using Diphones, Speech Communication, Vol. 9, (pp 453–467), Elsevier, Amsterdam, The Netherlands.

Murray, I. R., & Arnott, J. L.(1993). *Toward the simulation of emotion in synthetic speech: A review of the literature on human vocal emotion* Journal of the Acoustic Society of America (Vol. 2, pp. 1097–1107) Acoustical Society of America, Melville, NY.

Ortony, A., Clore, G. L., & Collins, A. (1988). *The cognitive structure of emotion.* Cambridge, UK: Cambridge University Press.

Perrier, P., Ma, L., & Payan, Y. (2005). Modeling the production of vcv sequences via the inversion of a biomechanical model of the tongue. In *Proceedings of interspeech* (pp. 1041–1044), International Speech Communication Association, Baixas, France

Rubin, D. C., & Talerico, J. M. (2009). A comparison of dimensional models of emotion. *Memory, 17,* 802–808.

Schröder, M. (2001). Emotional speech synthesis—a review. In *Proceedings of Eurospeech* (pp. 561–564)., International Speech Communication Association, Baixas, France

Schröder, M. (2004). *Speech and emotion research: An overview of research frameworks and a dimensional approach to emotional speech synthesis.* PHONUS 7, research report. Saarbrücken, Germany: Institute of Phonetics, Saarland University.

Schröder, M., Zovato, E., Pirker, H., Peter, C., & Burkhardt, F. (2008). W3c emotion incubator group report.

Available at: http://www.w3.org/2005/Incubator/emotion/XGR-emotion/

Schröder, M., Pirker, H., Lamolle, M., Burkhardt, F., Peter, C., & Zovato, E. (2011). Representing emotions and related states in technological systems. In P. Petta, R. Cowie, & C. Pelachaud (Eds.), *Emotion-oriented systems—The Humaine handbook* (pp. 367–386). New York: Springer.

Sundaram, S., & Narayanan, S. (2006). Automatic acoustic synthesis of human-like laughter, JASA (pp. 527–535). Journal of the Acoustical Society of America, Acoustical Society of America, Melville, NY

Székely, E., Cabral, J. P., Cahill, P., & Carson-Berndsen, J. (2011). Clustering expressive speech styles in audiobooks using glottal source parameters. In *Proceedings of Iinterspeech* (pp. 2409–2412)., Florence, Italy, International Speech Communication Association (ISCA)

Taylor, P. (2009). *Text to speech synthesis*. Cambridge, UK: Cambridge University Press.

Trouvain, J., & Truong, K. 2012. Comparing non-verbal vocalisations in conversational speech corpora. In *Proceedings of the 4th international workshop on corpora for research on emotion sentiment & social signals* (pp. 36–39). European Language Resources Association, Paris, France

Yoshimura, T., Tokuda, K., Masuko, T., Kobayashi, T., & Kitamura, T. (1999). Simultaneous modeling of spectrum, pitch and duration in hmm-based speech synthesis. In *Sixth European Conference on Speech Communication and Technology, EUROSPEECH 1999, Budapest, Hungary, International Speech Communication Association, Baixas, France* (pp. 2347–2350).

Young P. T. 1973 Feeling and emotion. In B. B. Wolman (Ed.) / Handbook of general psychology. Englewood Cliffs, New Jersey: Prentice-Hall.

Emotion Modeling for Social Robots

Ana Paiva, Iolanda Leite *and* Tiago Ribeiro

Abstract

This chapter describes current advances in emotion modeling for social robots. It begins by contextualizing the role of emotions in social robots, considering the concept of the affective loop. It describes a number of elements for the synthesis and expression of emotions through robotic embodiments and provides an overview of emotional adaptation and empathy in social robots.

Key Words: emotion modeling, social robots, human-robot interaction, affective loop

Introduction: Robots in the Affective Loop

The concept of a self-operating machine that resembles humans and behaves similarly to humans dates to ancient civilizations. From Homer, Leonardo da Vinci, and Isaac Asimov, robots have captured the imagination of philosophers and writers throughout history, and robots continue to inspire us. Robotics is a technology that is expected to change the world and the way we live. During the early stages of robotics research, much of the development focused on the usefulness of robots in industrial settings. As robots progress from these very controlled settings and laboratory environments and are deployed in homes and social contexts, their ability to interact with humans in ways that resemble human interaction becomes increasingly more relevant (Breazeal, 2009). Emotions are essential for that interaction. To portray emotions in robots, researchers require methods to model and express emotions with different embodiments and distinct manners. Such modeling of emotions allows the placement of robots in the context of the affective loop to foster social interaction. As defined by Höök (2009), the *affective loop* is the

interactive process in which "the user [of the system] first expresses her emotions through some physical interaction involving her body, for example, through gestures or manipulations; and the system then responds by generating affective expression, using for example, colours, animations, and haptics" which "in turn affects the user (mind and body) making the user respond and step by step feel more and more involved with the system."

To establish this affective loop between users and robots (Figure 21.1), robots will require an affect detection system that recognizes, among other states, whether the user is experiencing positive or negative feelings; they will also need a reasoning and action selection mechanism that chooses the optimum emotional response to display at a cognitive level. The method by which robots express the intended affective states should be effective (to be perceived by the users), and the actions of the emotional robot will affect the user (the third step of the affective loop). The robot perceives the user with the goal of personalizing the interaction by analyzing the user's responses to the robot's various affective expressions and adapting its emotional behavior for each particular user.

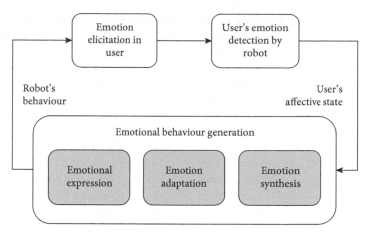

Fig. 21.1 Affective loop of emotional robots.

Affective interactions play different roles and have various purposes in the context of human-robot interaction (HRI). Among others, we can distinguish the following:

1. *Give the illusion of life*—The design of adaptive emotional behavior must take particular care to avoid unexpected or unintelligible behavior. This problem can be solved by following a number of guidelines on the methods for creating expressive behavior in robots, providing the robots with the "illusion of life" (Ribeiro & Paiva, 2012). This illusion will lead to the user's "suspension of disbelief," which increases the perception of social presence, thus making the robot a believable character (Bates, 1994).

2. *Augment engagement*—Emotions contribute to engagement in a social interaction context. Engagement, in this context, is defined as "the process by which two (or more) participants establish, maintain and end their perceived connection" (Sidner et al., 2004); it has received increasing attention from the HRI community (Rich et al., 2010). As previous research has highlighted, appropriate displays of affect have a significant effect on the user's engagement while he or she is interacting with social robots (Leite et al., 2012).

3. *Augment social presence in the long term*—The lack of adaptive emotional behavior decreases the user's perception of social presence, especially during long-term interactions (Leite et al., 2009), which in turn make the robots into nonbelievable characters (Bates, 1994). To be perceived as socially present, social robots must not only convey believable affective expressions but also do so in an intelligent and personalized manner—for example,

by gradually adapting their affective behavior to the particular needs and/or preferences of the users.

This chapter discusses the modeling of emotions in robots, not only through explicit computational mechanisms in which the emotions are captured but also in terms of adaptation, personalization, and expression, leading our emotional robots to become empathic, emotional creatures that can sustain an affective loop with the user.

Creating Synthetic Emotions in Robots

Robots possess the power to convey the illusion of life just by their physical presence and simple movements. When a robot moves toward a door and suddenly backs up, one may interpret its actions as avoidance and fear. Our perception of robots' actions may be biased, or perhaps enriched, by our inclination to suspend our disbelief and see robots as intelligent creatures that act according to their desires, goals, and emotions. However, a robot's behavior can result from computational mechanisms that do not explicitly capture any of those aspects. Significant work on emotional behavior in robots has been driven by the fact that simple behavior may "fool us" by leading us to perceive robots as having "emotions" when, in reality, those "emotions" are not explicitly modeled and just arise as an emergent effect of specific simple patterns of behavior.

When situations are such that a robot may need to interact with users at a higher level, often using natural language and gestures, and their actions need to be rich enough to convey some goal-oriented behavior, emotions may represent a way to model different responses and thus provide the robot with more believable and appropriate responses to the tasks. In those situations, emotions may represent abstract constructs that simplify the generation of robots' behaviors, as described by Leite et al. (2013). In this case, emotion modeling in robots becomes explicit, and specific architectures for that modeling have emerged in recent years. Emotions, modeled explicitly, may affect not only the action selection but also other cognitive processes such as reasoning, planning, and learning. As this area grows, new types of architectures exploring different mental processes (e.g., theory of mind or affect regulation) are also arising, allowing robots to perform better in the world and to interact with humans in a more natural way.

In general, emotional architectures for robots (and virtual agents) seek inspiration from the way humans and other species perceive, reason, learn, and act upon the world. We may distinguish different types of architectures according to their inspiration (from a neurobiological inspiration to more psychological or data-driven models); the affective states they try to model (e.g., emotions, moods, personality); the types of processes captured (e.g., appraisal, coping); their integration with other cognitive capabilities; and the expressive power they possess. Most of the existing types of architectures are built with different processes and levels, thus extending a generic hybrid model. As argued by Sloman (2002), different types of architectures will support distinct collections of states and processes. A number of these types rely on symbolic models to represent the perceptual elements of the world, whereas others take a nonsymbolic approach based on neural modeling.

The neurobiological approaches generally take the view that modeling of emotions can be done through different computational constructs associated with structures from the central nervous system, such as the amygdala and the hypothalamus (Arbib, 2004). One of the earlier types of architectures for emotions in robots was Cathexis (Velazquez, 1998), a computational model of emotions and action selection inspired by neurobiological theories. The architecture integrates drives and emotions in a way that guides the behaviors and decision making of the robot.

Many models capture affective states in an emergent manner, as the resulting pattern of behavior arising from a variety of different processes embedded in the agent. More explicit modeling is accomplished by representing affective states using a symbolic approach. The classic reference model presented by Wooldridge (1995) considers "beliefs, desires and intentions" to be the basic mental attitudes for generating an agent's intelligent behavior. This reference model has been extended to capture other mental states, in particular, emotions (see, for example, Gratch & Marsella, 2004, and Dias & Paiva, 2005). The majority of these types of architectures focus primarily on representing emotional states (e.g., quickly active, short and focused states such as anger or joy), in particular the six basic emotional states (e.g., anger, joy, surprise, sadness, disgust, and fear), as hypothesized by Ekman and Friesen (1975). Other affective states have been considered, such as moods (for example, by Leite et al., 2008, and Álvarez, 2010), dispositions, sentiments, or personality (Tapus et al., 2008; Woods et al., 2005).

The construction of the models mentioned above relies on theories of specific emotion, which are adopted as the basis for a computational system and thus dictate how an emotional state is triggered in a robot. One of the most influential theories, proposed by Magda Arnold in the 1960s, considers that emotions arise from the appraisal of situations and that an emotion is thus a result of the evaluation of the interconnection between the self and the environment and its objects (see Gratch and Marsella's chapter in this volume for more details on appraisal models of emotion). Appraisals result from an attraction to or repulsion from objects, which in turn give a valence to the emotion. In robots, we can imagine the process of emotion generation as resulting from the subjective evaluation of the situation that the robot is facing. If a robot is presented with a situation that favors it (for example, if it is playing a game and is at an advantage), the situation should lead to an internal process that will create specific variables to attain values that lead to the triggering of the emotional status of joy.

The process of appraising the situation has been treated differently in various types of emotion architectures for robots. In the iCat chess player (Leite et al., 2008), a robot that provides affective feedback to the user, emotions result from affective signals that emerge from an anticipatory system containing a predictive model of itself and/or of its environment (Martinho & Paiva, 2006). This anticipatory system generates an affective signal resulting from the mismatch between what is expected and what the robot senses. If the robot expects the user to perform well in the game and the user makes a mistake, it is an unexpected and positive (for the robot) situation, leading to the generation of a positive valence affective signal.

Emotions condition and structure our perceptions, direct our attention, and prepare us for action. The signaling in the nervous system that occurs from the primary appraisal processes is key to emotional priming and thus to our perception of emotion. Robots are situated in and rely strongly on their perceptions from the environment to act upon that environment. In an emotional robot, not only are its perceptual processes affected by its emotional states but a number of emotional states may also arise directly from those "untreated" perceptions. For example, Kismet (Breazeal, 2003) possessed a quite advanced perceptual system and evaluated external stimuli according to the robot's context in terms of its affective state and drives.

Emotions affect behavior. They are associated with different types of actions, such as fight-or-flight responses. In his seminal work, Frijda (2007) argued that our autonomic activity, the core of our emotional states, leads to states of "action readiness." As a response to the environment, emotions prepare the individual for action. Many different types of action tendencies have been studied and can be captured in our agent architectures. As such, one should consider the ways in which the affective states influence the actions of the agents and, considering emotional states, which types of internal mechanisms are considered in the process of action selection.

Emotional Expression in Robots: The Illusion of Robotic Life

It is necessary for a social robot to model and select actions based on affective goals and conditions, and a robot must be able to properly express those actions with an adequate affective display. This expression of emotion can be observed in the affective loop as the connection point between the generation of emotional behavior (resulting from the use of an emotional model) and elicitation of emotion in the user. How should one generate expressive behavior in robots that can be interpreted correctly by humans? How can such expressive behavior be generated in a way that is flexible and, as much as possible, transposed between different embodiments?

In terms of concrete emotions, studies from psychology can inform us about how humans interpret emotions and their expression. Authors such as Ekman and Friesen (1975), Russell (1994), and Elfenbein and Ambady (2002) have studied and published papers about how the human ability to recognize emotions in other humans is universal. If

it were possible to develop robotic characters able to process and express emotions as humans do, then these links to psychology would most likely be the best starting point. The majority of current robots are very limited in terms of expression, and many of them lack a number of expressive features that humans have, such as a mouth or facial muscles. This has led many researchers to turn to the arts in search of inspiration and solutions.

Principles of Animation for Expressing Emotions in Robots

Bates (1994) was one of the first to seek inspiration from the arts, in particular from *The Illusion of Life,* a well-known book by Frank Thomas and Ollie Johnston, that recounts over 60 years of experience in creating characters at the Walt Disney Animation Studios (Thomas & Johnston, 1995). The book intrinsically refers to the affective loop—the way in which Disney characters are brought to (an illusion of) life, by enacting stories that "make people laugh—and even cry." Other authors have followed the identical philosophy, including Reilly (1996), who demonstrated that "it is artists who best know how to create believable characters and how to imbue them with emotions." More recently, van Breemen (2004) has taken this concept into the expressive robotics field by claiming that "user-interface robots have the same problem as the early day of animation: they miss the illusion of life."

These ideas lead the HRI community to look at one key concept for social robotic characters—the concept of the robot as a "believable character." Bates (1994) defines a believable character as "not an honest or reliable character, but one that provides the illusion of life, and thus permits the audience's suspension of disbelief." The core of Thomas and Johnston's *The Illusion of Life* is a description of Disney's 12 principles of animation. These principles are serve as rules for professional animators and guidelines as to how to create believable and expressive characters. The reader can refer to the book to understand each of the 12 principles from the authors, who were Disney animators.

The attempt to apply these principles of animation to robots has continued for almost a decade. Several authors have proposed this method, starting with van Breemen (2004), who defined robot animation as "the process of computing how the robot should act such that it is believable and interactive." His attempt was to look at a number of the principles to understand how to create better expressions for the iCat robot, and he implemented a method that he named "merging logic," which corresponds to the principle of "slow in/slow out."

Wistort (2010) has looked at the Disney principles so as to discuss how a number of them could be applied to robots. He emphasizes the need for robots to have expressive eyes and insists that actuated pupils help to convey life through the eyes. He stresses the need to have silent eyes, because most robots rely on motors to move their eyes, and these are usually quite noisy. This work is interesting because it tries to bend the definition of the principles with a more scientific understanding of how the principles actually work. That is a necessary step, because the traditional principles help explain the methods that animators use to design animation. In considering social robots, we must understand how such principles can be adapted or extended to work under autonomous animation.

Takayama et al. (2011) used anticipation, engagement, confidence and timing to enhance the readability of a robot's actions. They refer to the definition of "thinking characters" by Lasseter (1987), in which "the animator gives life to the character by connecting its actions with a thought process." One especially interesting distinction they demonstrate concerns functional motions versus expressive motions. Because robots are part of our physical world, it is likely that they will perform a blend of these two types of motions. A simple locomotive behavior may carry both types of motion: functional motion to enable the robot to move from one place to another and expressive motion to express how the robot is feeling. Speaking to or requesting something from someone is functional and expressive. In a number of situations, we will want to separate them, as when a robot first looks at a door handle (expressive motion) and then grasps it to open the door (functional motion). By looking at the door handle, the robot first expresses interest in and attention to the handle, so humans can anticipate that it is going to grasp the handle and open the door.

Mead and Mataric (2010) used a number of principles of animation to improve autistic children's understanding of a robot's intentions. For "exaggeration," they were inspired by a process of creating caricatures by exaggerating the difference from the mean. The features that uniquely identify an expression are isolated, and those features are amplified to make them even more relevant, thus producing exaggerated expressions. Gielniak et al. (2012) followed a similar idea but addressed it as a motion signal processing technique. They successfully developed an algorithm that creates exaggerated variants of a motion in real time by contrasting the motion signal, and they demonstrated this idea by applying it to their SIMON robot.

In our recent work, we examined this issue from a holistic point of view by providing insight on how each of the traditional principles of animation could be used in robotics and how they could serve to enhance the readability of Ekman's six basic emotions in the EMYS robot (Ribeiro & Paiva, 2012). The majority of the traditional principles of animation seem to apply to robot animation.

There is much to understand about how the traditional principles of animation can be applied to robots. The major difference that we find is that they are not only robots but also interactive, and Disney's traditional principles were not intended for interactive characters. This difference does not mean that we cannot apply the traditional principles, but it does convert the issue into an engineering problem. Slow-in/slow-out, arcs, and exaggeration may be easily incorporated into an animation system by warping the motion signals. However, what about the other principles? How do we programmatically define the use of correct timing?

Computing Emotional Expressions in Robots

To support the generation of complex expressive behavior in robots, we need a flexible and consistent architecture. The robotics community, influenced by the work on conversational characters, adopts generic frameworks such as the SAIBA (situation, agent, intention, behavior, animation) framework (Kopp et al., 2006). This framework, illustrated in Figure 21.2, is divided into three phases:

Intent planning produces a functional markup language (FML), which contains a definition of that which the character has intended to do.

Behavior planning receives the FML and produces a behavior markup language (BML) (Vilhjalmsson et al., 2007), which contains specific details regarding the manner in which the character is planning to perform the behavior generally specified in the FML.

Behavior realization receives the BML, interprets it regarding the actual character that will perform it, and applies the actual behaviors to the character. In an analogy to film, it can be viewed as the actor performing and following the orders of the director and casting director.

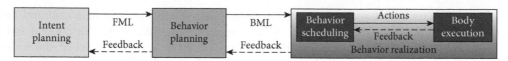

Fig. 21.2 The SAIBA framework.

Although SAIBA was initially intended for virtual characters, a number of authors have applied it to robot animation, because BML is not character-specific (meaning that an identical BML script can be used by different realizers). It has been used to make the GRETA animated agent interact with an AIBO robot (Moubayed et al., 2008) and an NAO robot (Niewiadomski et al., 2011). We developed a system based on BML that allows for continuous interaction with robots by providing mechanisms that can cause external events (perceptions) to interact with predefined BML sequences. Following the trend of Niewiadomski et al. (2011) and Kipp et al. (2010), we divided the behavior realization phase into the behavior scheduling and body execution subphases. The system was demonstrated with an interaction between an EMYS robot and an NAO robot, with external audio, visual, and tangible events (Ribeiro & Paiva, 2012).

A popular middleware developed by Willow Garage[1] is the robot operating system (ROS) (Quigley et al., 2009). Although it actually works as a communication layer, the development of the

robots and the modules that run them has grown. By having an ROS-compliant robot, one can use any of the ROS modules that have been made freely available and can be used especially for navigation, vision, or arm manipulation. Following Holroyd and Rich (2012), who recently developed a BML module for ROS, other authors may develop expressive modules for ROS that could be shared throughout the robotics community.

Beyond Traditional Emotion Expression in Robots: Using Form, Color, and Sound

If we are able to develop a model that can compute an emotion and the intention of its display, we must map that to the expressive features of a robot. With as many diverse embodiments as are illustrated in Figure 21.3, it is very difficult to generalize on how this mapping could be done.

On the left side of Figure 21.3, with mid- to high expressive articulation, we first highlight the work using eMuu (Bartneck, 2002), Lino (Krose et al., 2003), EMYS (Ribeiro & Paiva, 2012),

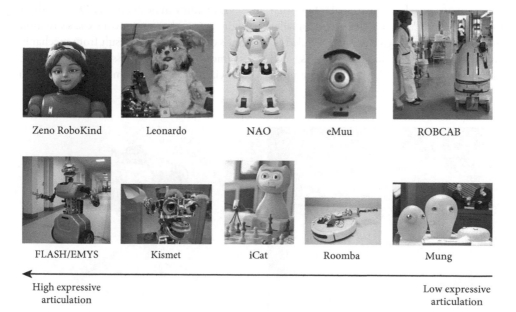

Zeno RoboKind   Leonardo   NAO   eMuu   ROBCAB

FLASH/EMYS   Kismet   iCat   Roomba   Mung

High expressive articulation ← → Low expressive articulation

Fig. 21.3 A multitude of robotic embodiments along a dimension of expressive articulation. Robots on the left contain more degrees of freedom available for expressivity.

Kismet (Breazeal, 2003), the iCat (Breemen, 2004; Leite et al., 2008) and Leonardo (Breazeal et al., 2004). These robots are not humanoids, but they perform emotional expression through the use of many degrees of freedom to try to mimic human expressions (in a simplified and iconic way).

With respect to humanoids, there have been studies of emotional expression, especially with the QRIO robot (Tanaka et al., 2004) and the NAO robot (Beck et al., 2010). The majority of humanoid robots have very simple faces and therefore rely solely on body expression—which is more difficult to model and more ambiguous to read. Hanson Robotics has recently developed the Zeno RoboKind (Hanson et al., 2009), which features a highly articulated body and a highly expressive face based on muscular features. This robot introduces an accessible and flexible platform that contains facial and bodily expression, but there are no studies on its expressivity yet.

Focusing on the right side of Figure 21.3 presents an issue. Although social robots are generally designed to be expressive, there are some types of robots (social or not) that do not display expressive features. As Bethel (2009) notes, search-and-rescue robots are designed to move across disaster zones to find and reach victims. Some socially assistive robots may be designed to help elderly or disabled people get out of bed and move around; therefore their purpose is to be steady and move safely, as does the RobCab robot (Ljungblad et al., 2012). In a domestic environment, we may have functional robots such as Roomba[2] (a robotic vacuum cleaner) or smaller robots with a minimal design that are intended to behave as personal companions and assistants, such as the Mung robot (Kim et al., 2009). These more

simplistic robots may rely on sound and light to augment their expressivity. Using sound and light can actually be considered part of the traditional "staging" principle of animation because it refers to focusing on the elements that are important. One of the ways to achieve that is by properly using sound, music, lights, and shadows. By redefining this principle into "intention," we do not invalidate these practices because it helps focus on the clear meaning of that which the robot is expressing. Recently a number of researchers have augmented the expressivity of a Roomba robot by adding expressive lights (Rea et al., 2012) and an expressive tail (Singh & Young, 2012) (Figure 21.4). Other researchers have added a projector to a telemedicine robot that can project signals on the ground to demonstrate the robot's intention (Shindev et al., 2012).

Emotion Adaptation in Robots: Toward Empathic Robots

An emotional robot should appraise its surrounding environment and react emotionally to it, and it should perceive other robots' and the user's affective states. Such perception and sensitivity of the other's affective states is essential to place the robot in the affective loop. A robot should perceive the user's affective state and act in response to such perceptions. But how can the robot close the loop and empathize with the user by providing more appropriate and adaptive responses during the interaction?

Empathy can be defined as "an affective response more appropriate to someone else's situation than to one's own," which can result from mechanisms such as motor mimicry, classical conditioning, direct association of cues from the person with whom

 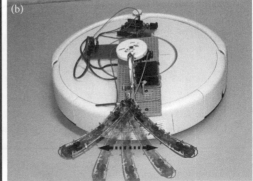

Fig. 21.4 (a) A Roomba robot modified to include expressive lights (Rea et al., 2012). (b) A Roomba robot modified to include an expressive tail (Singh & Young, 2012).

we are empathizing, mediated association of cues through semantic processing, and perspective-taking (Hoffman, 2001). Hoffman considers the first three mechanisms to be automatic and involuntary, whereas the last two are higher-order cognitive modes. The process of empathy can go beyond a merely affective response in tune with the affective state of the person with whom we are empathizing. Empathy has been considered one of the major determinants of prosocial actions (Davis, 1994; Eisenberg & Fabes, 1990; Feshbach, 1978)—that is, "voluntary behavior intended to benefit another such as helping, donating, sharing and comforting" (Eisenberg et al., 1997). In the literature, prosocial behaviors are often designated as socially supportive behaviors (Cutrona et al., 1990). These behaviors are more likely to be triggered in observing someone in pain, danger, or some other type of distress (Hoffman, 2001).

In the virtual agents community, empathy is a research topic that has received much attention in the last decade (Bickmore & Picard, 2005; Brave et al., 2005; McQuiggan & Lester, 2007; Paiva et al., 2004; Prendinger & Ishizuka 2005). In HRI, research addressing empathy has recently appeared. One possible reason for this delay is that robots share our physical space, and recognizing the user's affective state is thus a more challenging task because the interactions tend to be more open-ended. When users interact with virtual agents, they are usually in front of a computer screen, and there is frequently the possibility of selecting predefined dialogues or actions to inform the agent about the user's affective state (Bickmore & Picard, 2005). Recent advances in automatic affect recognition using different modalities—including vision, speech, or physiological signals—contribute significantly to overcoming this obstacle (for a review, see Zeng et al., 2009). Many important questions remain unanswered: Will social robots benefit for being empathic? Will interactions become more natural and enjoyable if robots can adapt their behavior to the user's affective state? What is the state of the art on empathic robots?

A significant segment of the research addressing empathy in social robots has focused on automatic and involuntary processes (as defined by Hoffman), such as mimicking the user's affective state. Hegel et al. (2006) presented a study with an anthropomorphic robot that recognizes the user's emotional state through speech intonation and mirrors the inferred state using a corresponding facial expression. The results suggested that the users who interacted with this version of the robot found the robot's responses to be more adequate in their appropriateness to the social situation and timing than the users who interacted with the robot without affective expressions. In another study (Riek et al., 2010), a robot in the form of a chimpanzee's head mimicked the user's mouth and head movements. After interacting with this robot, most of the subjects considered the interaction to be more satisfactory than participants who interacted with a version of the robot without the mimicking capabilities.

Perspective taking is considered to be one of the most "empathy-arousing" mechanisms in humans. The process of taking the perspective of others and attributing mental states such as thoughts, desires, knowledge, and intentions that are not directly observable is known as theory of mind (Baron-Cohen, 1997; Premack, 1978). This capability has been considered an essential component of empathy by several authors (Baron-Cohen et al., 2009; Feshbach, 1978), especially because of its importance in emotion recognition (Adolphs 2002; Heberlein et al., 2009). Appraising the context of a task can be computationally more reliable than the affect recognition mechanisms based on other modalities used today, and perspective taking has also been used in HRI. Cramer et al. (2010) used perspective taking to drive the behavior of a social robot in a study that was conducted to assess how empathy affects human attitudes toward robots. Using a between-subjects design, two groups of participants saw a 4-minute video with an actor playing a cooperative game with an iCat robot. In one condition, the robot accurately expressed empathic behavior toward the actor, whereas in the other condition, the robot inaccurately expressed empathic behavior toward the actor (i.e., incongruent to the situation). Because the robot varied its empathic behavior according to the performance of the other player in the game, we say that it was taking the perspective of the human in the scenario. In this study, there was a significant negative effect on the participants' trust in the inaccurate empathic behavior condition. Conversely, the participants who observed the robot displaying accurate empathic behaviors perceived their relationship with the robot as closer than did those participants who observed the robot inaccurately expressing empathic behavior.

In our previous work (Leite et al., 2013), we presented an empathic model based on perspective taking. To evaluate this model, we developed a scenario in which an iCat robot acts as a social companion to two players in a chess game. The robot reacted to the moves played on the chessboard by displaying several facial expressions and verbal utterances, showing empathic behavior towards one player and behaving neutrally towards the other. The empathic responses were modulated by the relationship with the players (companion or opponent). The results of this study indicate that the users toward whom the robot behaved empathically perceived the robot as friendlier, suggesting that empathy plays a key role in HRI. There are a number of examples of perspective taking in HRI with the goal of improving a robot's effectiveness in learning simple tasks from ambiguous demonstrations (Breazeal et al., 2006) or facilitating human-robot communication (Torrey et al., 2010).

In cases in which a social robot is able to display empathy by changing its behavior according to the affective state that the user is experiencing, one can consider that adaptation to the user is occurring. There are several types of empathic responses that a person (or, eventually, a social robot) can take, from affective reactions to socially supportive behaviors. A relevant question arises as to how robots should select appropriate empathic responses for a particular user.

The answer to this question poses another opportunity for personalisation. Because the theoretical literature on empathy does not clearly specify which types of empathic responses are more likely to be triggered by certain affective states, the robot can adjust its empathic behavior based on the preferences of particular users. In a recent empirical study, we found that the presence of adaptive empathic behaviors in a social robot resulted in the perception of the robot by children as being socially supportive in a similar extent to the way in which they feel about their peers (Leite et al., 2012). In this study, the robot was able to use a no-regret Reinforcement Learning (RL) algorithm to learn the types of supportive behaviors that were more effective for each child, i.e., the behaviors that were more likely to increase a positive affective state in the child. The reward function of the RL algorithm was based on the non-verbal responses of the child captured a few seconds after the robot employed each supportive strategy. At each time step, no-regret algorithms make the best use of the feedback received so far. A policy that allows the iCat to select the next supportive behavior by considering the previous history of employed behaviors and consequent rewards was implemented to learn the most effective supportive behaviors for a particular user and adapt to the interaction accordingly. The intuition that is the

basis of this policy is simple: the robot selects the supportive behaviors with higher average rewards more often because they have higher probabilities. There is a possibility that other behaviors could be selected because although they had lower rewards in the past, the user may find them more suitable in the future.

Other researchers have explored the user's affective state as a mechanism to adapt the robot's behaviors. Liu et al. (2008) developed a scenario in which the robot learns the most appropriate behaviors by accounting for the physiological signals of the subjects, a group of children. A preliminary study conducted with six autistic children showed that the robot was able to select appropriate behaviors based on the attraction levels, collected through physiological signals, expressed by the children. The question of adaptation has received particular attention in robot-assisted therapy, particularly in interaction with children with autism spectrum disorders, because they require unique capabilities that nonadaptive robots might be unable to fulfil (Dautenhahn et al., 2003). Bekele et al. (2011) developed a head tracker that allows an NAO robot to adapt its postures, thus encouraging cooperative attention between autistic children and the robot.

Gonsior et al. (2012) conducted a study in which a social robot adapts its own mood to the user's mood in an attempt to increase empathy and helpfulness. The robot adjusts its nonverbal and verbal behaviors considering the user's self-assessments of affect. The results show that the subjects who interacted with the adaptive version showed a significantly greater desire to help the robot in further tasks than the participants in the control group, who interacted with a version of the robot with emotional behavior but without adaptive capabilities.

Considering the work presented in this section, we hypothesize that empathy and, in particular, the consequent user adaptation that empathy facilitates will most likely make social robots more flexible and personalized to particular users in the same way as other types of adaptation have been reported to be facilitators of HRI (Koay et al., 2007; Lee et al., 2012). As stated by Dautenhahn (2004), "rather than relying on an inbuilt fixed repertoire of social behaviours, a robot should be able to learn and adapt to the social manners, routines and personal preferences of the people it is living with." These behaviors can play an important role in facilitating the interactions between users and social robots in several application domains and can ultimately lead to personalization, which is a feature that is frequently mentioned to be relevant in social robots or agents that interact with users for extended periods of time (Castellano et al., 2008).

Where to Next?

We are entering an amazing new era for robotics, AI, and affective computing because concrete emotional robots are being developed to a level at which they can be deployed in social settings. As new opportunities for affective robots appear, there will be new challenges and research problems. The affective computing community must embrace the challenges posed by the advancements in robotic platforms.

The community should consider these challenges, which will shape the way in which we build the emotional robots of the future:

• *Studies and more studies in real settings.* The deployment of emotional robots will necessarily indicate that tests should be conducted in valid social settings where emotional robots are placed in authentic situations. Such studies, although informed by "Wizard of Oz" (WOZ) tests, must be realized with autonomous systems as much as possible. This requirement poses a difficult challenge to the community in terms of performance and reliability of the systems and of the validity, believability, and appropriateness of the emotional models adopted and expressions rendered.

• *New bodies for new behaviors and new situations.* Innovative new materials and mechanical engineering developments will facilitate novel embodiments of robotics. As the new embodiments become available to researchers in affective computing, we should combine them with new computational models of emotions, new forms of perceiving emotions. and new means of implementing expressions, and we should conduct studies of the outcomes.

• *Emotions are dynamic states, also for robots.* Emotional robots must be placed in real settings and must be capable of interacting with changing environments in a dynamic manner. We should use the dynamic features of emotions to create new models and, perhaps, more neurobiologically inspired models that can provide additional adaptation to the changing environments.

• *Emotions are embodied.* Although robots have bodies, the majority of the work with emotions in robots treats emotions at a cognitive level. If we consider the embodiment aspects of emotional states, we can consider the various robotic embodiments associated with different emotions. Relying on humanlike emotions is not required. With the development of new bodies, novel affective concepts may emerge as a synergistic endeavor between psychologists, computer scientists, neuroscientists, roboticists, and cognitive scientists. Only in a multidisciplinary way will we be able to design the next theories that will lead to the modeling of emotions in robots.

• *Can robots be our companions?* Companionship, attachment, and long-term interaction with robots is definitely one of the greatest challenges to our community. This challenge involves new developments in learning, adaptation and memory; extensive additional research is needed in this endeavour.

• *Affective symbiosis with robots.* The exploration of new types of links between humans and robots can be increasingly connected to humans and their physiological and affective states. These links range from physiological signals, brain-machine interfaces, and robotics platforms. Novel types of interdependence between robots and humans can be created and explored.

Acknowledgments

This research was supported by European Commission (EC) 7th FP project EMOTE under grant agreement no. 317923 and by national funds through the Fundação para a Ciência e a Tecnologia (FTC) under project Pest—OE/EEI/LA0021/2011 and the PIDDAC Program funds. The authors are solely responsible for the content of this publication. It does not represent the opinion of the EC, and the EC is not responsible for any use that might be made of data appearing therein.

Notes
1. http://www.willowgarage.com/
2. http://www.irobot.com

References

Adolphs, R. A. (2002). Neural systems for recognizing emotions. *Current Opinion in Neurobiology, 12*, 169–177.

Álvarez, M., Galán, R., Matía, F., Rodríguez-Losada, D., & Jiménez, A. (2010). An emotional model for a guide robot. *IEEE Transactions.on Systems, Man and Cybernetics. Part A, 40*(5), 982–992.

Arbib, M. A., & Fellous, J. M. (2004). Emotions: From brain to robot. *Trends in Cognitive Sciences, 8*, 554–561.

Baron-Cohen, S. (1997). *Mindblindness: An essay on autism and theory of mind.* Cambridge, MA: MIT Press.

Baron-Cohen, S., Golan, O., & Ashwin, E. (2009). Can emotion recognition be taught to children with autism spectrum conditions? *Philosophical Transactions of the Royal Society B: Biological Sciences, 364*(1535), 3567–3574.

Bartneck, C. (2002). eMuu—An embodied emotional character for the ambient intelligent home. PhD thesis, Technische Universiteit Eindhoven.

Bates, J. (1994). The role of emotion in believable agents. *Communications of the ACM, 37*, 122–125.

Beck, A., Cañamero, L., & Bard, K. A. (2010). Towards an affect space for robots to display emotional body language. In *IEEE international symposium on robots and human interactive communications* (pp. 491–496). New York, NY: ACM.

Bekele, E., Lahiri, U., Davidson, J., Warren, Z., & Sarkar, N. (2011). Development of a novel robot-mediated adaptive response system for joint attention task for children with autism. In *Proceedings of the IEEE International Symposium on Robots and Human Interactive Communications RO-MAN'11*, (pp. 276–281). Washington, DC: IEEE Computer Society.

Bethel, C. L. (2009). Robots without faces: Non-verbal social human-robot interaction. Ph.D. thesis, University of South Florida.

Bickmore, T., & Picard, R. (2005). Establishing and maintaining long-term human-computer relationships. *ACM Transactions on Computer-Human Interaction (TOCHI), 12*(2), 327.

Brave, S., Nass, C., & Hutchinson, K. (2005). Computers that care: Investigating the effects of orientation of emotion exhibited by an embodied computer agent. *International Journal of Human-Computer Studies, 62* (2), 161–178.

Breazeal, C. (2003). Emotion and sociable humanoid robots. *International Journal of Human-Computer Studies, 59* (1–2) (July), 119–155.

Breazeal, C. (2009). Role of expressive behaviour for robots that learn from people. *Philosophical Transactions of the Royal Society B: Biological Sciences, 364* (1535), 3527.

Breazeal, C., Berlin, M., Brooks, A., Gray, J., & Thomaz, A. L. (2006). Using perspective taking to learn from ambiguous demonstrations. *Robotics and Autonomous Systems, 54* (5), 385–393.

Breazeal, C., Buchsbaum, D., Gray, J., Gatenby, D., & Blumberg, B. (2004). Learning from and about others: Towards using imitation to bootstrap the social understanding of others by robots. *Artificial Life, 11*(1–2), 31–62.

Breemen, A. J. N. van (2004). Bringing robots to life: Applying principles of animation to robots. *CHI'04 workshop on shaping human-robot interaction* (pp. 5–8). New York, NY: ACM.

Castellano, G., Aylett, R., Dautenhahn, K., Paiva, A., McOwan, P. W., & Ho, S. (2008). Long-term affect sensitive and socially interactive companions. In *Proceedings of the 4th international workshop on human-computer conversation*.

Cramer, H., Goddijn, J., Wielinga, B., & Evers, V. (2010). Effects of (in)accurate empathy and situational valence on attitudes towards robots. In *HRI'10: Proceeding of the 5th ACM/IEEE international conference on Human-robot interaction* (pp. 141–142). New York: Association for Computer Mechanics.

Cutrona, C. E., Suhr, J. A., & MacFarlane., R. (1990). Interpersonal transactions and the psychological sense of support. *Personal Relationships and Social Support*, 30–45.

Dautenhahn, K. (2004). Robots we like to live with?!—A developmental perspective on a personalized, life-long robot companion. In *13th IEEE international workshop on robot and human interactive communication*, (pp. 17–22). IEEE Computer Society.

Dautenhahn, K., Werry, I., Salter, T., & Boekhorst, R. (2003). Towards adaptive autonomous robots in autism therapy: Varieties of interactions. *IEEE international symposium on computational intelligence in robotics and automation (CIRA'03)* (pp. 577–582).

Davis, M. H. (1994). *Empathy: A social psychological approach.* Westview Press.

Dias, J., & Paiva, A. (2005). Feeling and reasoning: A computational model for emotional characters. *Progress in artificial intelligence* (pp. 127–140). New York: Springer.

Eisenberg, N., & Fabes, R. A. (1990). Empathy: Conceptualization, measurement, and relation to prosocial behavior. *Motivation and Emotion, 14*, 131–149.

Eisenberg, N., Losoya, S., & Guthrie, I. K. (1997). Social cognition and prosocial development. *The Development of Social Cognition*, 329–363.

Ekman, P., & Friesen, W. V. (1975). *Unmasking the face.* Englewood Cliffs, NJ: Prentice-Hall.

Elfenbein, H., & Ambady, N. (2002). On the universality and cultural specificity of emotion recognition: A meta-analysis. *Psychological Bulletin, 128*(2), 203–235. doi: 10.1037//0 033-2909.128.2.203

Feshbach, N. D. (1978). Studies of empathic behavior in children. *Progress in Experimental Personality Research, 8*, 1–47.

Frijda, N. H. (2007). The Laws of Emotion. L. Erlbaum Associates.

Gielniak, M. J., & Thomaz, A. L. (2012). Enhancing interaction through exaggerated motion synthesis. *Proceedings of the seventh annual ACM/IEEE international conference on human-robot interaction (HRI'12)* (p. 375). New York, NY: ACM.

Gonsior, B., Sosnowski, S., Buß, M., Wollherr, D., & Kühnlenz, K. (2012). An emotional adaption approach to increase helpfulness towards a robot. *Proceedings of Intelligent Robots and Systems (IROS) 2012*, IEEE Computer Society.

Gratch, J., & Marsella, S. (2004). A domain-independent framework for modeling emotion. *Cognitive Systems Research, 5*(4), 269–306.

Hanson, D., Baurmann, S., Riccio, T., Margolin, R., Docking, T., Tavares, M., & Carpenter, K. (2009). Zeno: A cognitive character. *AI Magazine*, 9–11.

Heberlein, A., & Atkinson, A. (2009). Neuroscientific evidence for simulation and shared substrates in emotion recognition: Beyond faces. *Emotion Review, 1*(2), 162–177.

Hegel, F., Spexard, T., Vogt, T., Horstmann, G., & Wrede, B. (2006). Playing a different imitation game: Interaction with an empathic Android robot. In *Proceedings of the 2006 IEEE-RAS international conference on humanoid robots (Humanoids06)* (pp. 56–61).

Hoffman, M. (2001). *Empathy and moral development: Implications for caring and justice.* Cambridge, UK: Cambridge University Press.

Holroyd, A., & Rich, C. (2012). Using the behavior markup language for human-robot interaction. *Proceedings of the seventh annual ACM/IEEE international conference on human-robot interaction (HRI'12)* (pp. 147–148). New York, NY: ACM.

Höök K. (2009). Affective loop experiences: Designing for interactional embodiment. *Philosophical. Transactions of the Royal Society. B, 364*, 3585–3595.(doi:10.1098/rstb.2009.0202)

Kim, E. H., Kwak, S. S., Hyun, K. H., Kim, S. H., & Kwak, Y. K. (2009). Design and development of an emotional interaction robot, Mung. *Advanced Robotics, 23* (6), 767–784.

Kipp, M., Heloir, A., Schröder, M., & Gebhard, P. (2010). Realizing multimodal behavior: Closing the gap between behavior planning and embodied agent presentation. In *Proceedings of the 10th international conference on intelligent virtual agents (IVA'10)* (pp. 57–63). Berlin: Springer.

Koay, K. L., Syrdal, D. S., Walters, M. L., & Dautenhahn, K. (2007). Living with robots: Investigating the habituation effect in participants' preferences during a longitudinal human-robot interaction study. In *16th IEEE international symposium on robot and human interactive communication, 2007. RO-MAN 2007* (pp. 564–569). Washington, DC: IEEE Computer Society.

Kopp, S., Krenn, B., Marsella, S., & Marshall, A. N. (2006). Towards a common framework for multimodal generation: The behavior markup language. In *Proceedings of the 6th international conference on Intelligent Virtual Agents (IVA'06) 205–217.* Springer-Verlag, Berlin, Heidelberg.

Krose, B. J. A., Porta, J. M., Van Breemen, A. J. N., Crucq K., Nuttin, M., & Demester, E. (2003). Lino, the user-interface robot. In *First European symposium on ambient intelligence* (pp. 1–10). Springer Verlag Berlin Heidelberg.

Lasseter, J. (1987). Principles of traditional animation applied to 3D computer animation. *Proceedings of the 14th annual conference on computer graphics and interactive techniques (SIGGRAPH'87)* (pp. 35–44). New York, NY: ACM.

Lee, M. K., Forlizzi, J., Kiesler, S., Rybski, P., Antanitis, J., & Savetsila, S. (2012). Personalization in HRI: A longitudinal field experiment. In *7th ACM/IEEE international conference human-robot interaction (HRI'2012)* (pp. 319–326).

Leite, I., Castellano, C., Pereira, A., Martinho, C., & Paiva, A. (2012). Long-term interactions with empathic robots: evaluating perceived support in children. *Proceedings of the 4th international conference of social robotics.* Berlin: Springer.

Leite, I., Martinho, C., Pereira, A., & Paiva, A. (2008). iCat: An affective game buddy based on anticipatory mechanisms. *Proceedings of the 7th international joint conference on autonomous agents and multiagent systems (AAMAS'2008)* (pp. 1229–1232).

Leite, I., Martinho, C., Pereira, A., & Paiva, A. (2009). As time goes by: Long-term evaluation of social presence in robotic companions. In *IEEE international symposium on robot and human interactive communication, RO-MAN 2009* (pp. 669–674).

Leite, I., Pereira, A., Mascarenhas, S., Martinho, C., Prada, R., & Paiva, A. (2013), The influence of empathy in human-robot relations, *International Journal of Human-Computer Studies, 71*(3), 250–260, ISSN 1071-5819, 10.1016/j.ijhcs.2012.09.005.

Liu, C., Conn, K., Sarkar, N., & Stone, W. (2008). Online affect detection and robot behavior adaptation for intervention of children with autism. *IEEE Transactions on Robotics, 24,* 883–896 doi:10.1109/TRO.2008.2001362

Ljungblad, S., Kotrbova, J., Jacobsson, M., Cramer, H., & Niechwiadowicz, K. (2012). Hospital robot at work: Something alien or an intelligent colleague? In *Proceedings of the ACM 2012 conference on computer supported cooperative work.* New York, NY: ACM.

Martinho, C., & Paiva, A. (2006). Using Anticipation to Create Believable Behaviour. In *Proceedings of The National Conference on Artificial Intelligence* (Vol. *21*, No. 1, p. 175).

Menlo Park, CA; Cambridge, MA; London; AAAI Press; MIT Press.

McQuiggan, S. W., & Lester, J. C. (2007). Modeling and evaluating empathy in embodied companion agents. *International Journal of Human-Computer Studies, 65,* 348–360.

Mead, R., & Mataric, M. J. (2010). Automated caricature of robot expressions in socially assistive human-robot interaction. In *The 5th ACM/IEEE international conference on human-robot interaction (HRI'10) workshop on what do collaborations with the arts have to say about.* New York, NY: ACM.

Moubayed, S. A., Baklouti, M., Chetouani, M., Dutoit T., Mahdhaoui, A., Martin, J. C.,...Yilmaz, M. (2008). Multimodal feedback from robots and agents in a storytelling experiment. *Project 7: Final Project Report, eNTERFACE'08,* Paris, France.

Niewiadomski, R., Obaid, M., Bevacqua, E., Looser, J., Le, Q. A., & Pelachaud, C. (2011). Cross-media agent platform. In *Proceedings of the 16th international conference on 3D web technology* (pp. 11–19). New York, NY: ACM.

Paiva, A., Dias, J., Sobral, D., Aylett, R., Sobreperez, P., Woods, S., Zoll, C., & Hall, L. (2004). Caring for agents and agents that care: Building empathic relations with synthetic agents. In *Proceedings of the third international joint conference on autonomous agents and multiagent systems* (Vol. I, pp. 194–201). Washington, DC: IEEE Computer Society.

Premack, D., & Woodruff, G. (1978). Does the chimpanzee have a theory of mind?. *Behavioral and Brain Sciences, 1*(04), 515–526.

Prendinger, H., & Ishizuka, M. (2005). The empathic companion: A character-based interface that addresses users' affective states. *Applied Artificial Intelligence, 19* (3–4), 267–285.

Quigley, M., & Gerkey, B. (2009). ROS: An open-source robot operating system. Available at: http://pub1.willowgarage.com/~konolige/cs225B/docs/quigley-icra2009-ros.pdf

Rea, D., Young, J. E., & Irani, P. (2012). The Roomba mood ring: An ambient-display robot. In *Proceedings of the 7th annual ACM/IEEE international conference on human-robot interaction (HRI'12)* (pp. 217–218). New York, NY: ACM.

Reilly, W. S. N., (1996). Believable social and emotional agents. *Ph.D. thesis. Carnegie Mellon University.*

Ribeiro, T., & Paiva, A. (2012). The illusion of robotic life: Principles and practices of animation for robots. *In proceedings of the 7th annual ACM/IEEE international conference on human-robot interaction (HRI'12).* New York, NY: ACM.

Rich, C., Ponsler, B., Holroyd, A., & Sidner, C. L. (2010). Recognizing engagement in human-robot interaction. In *Proceedings of the 5th ACM/IEEE international conference on human-robot interaction* (pp. 375–382). New York: Association for Computer Mechanics.

Riek, L. D., Paul, P. C., & Robinson, P. (2010). When my robot smiles at me: Enabling human-robot rapport via real-time head gesture mimicry. *Journal on Multimodal User Interfaces, 3* (1–2), 99–108.

Russell, J. (1994). Is there universal recognition of emotion from facial expression—A review of the cross-cultural studies. *Psychological Bulletin, 115*(1), 102–141.

Shindev, I., Sun, Y., Coovert, M., Pavlova, J., & Lee, T. (2012). Exploration of Intention Expression for Robots. In *Proceedings of the 7th annual ACM/IEEE international conference on human-robot interaction (HRI'12)* (pp. 247–248). New York, NY: ACM.

Sidner, C. L., Kidd, C. D., Lee, C., & Lesh, N. (2004). Where to look: A study of human-robot engagement. *Proceedings of the*

9th International Conference on Intelligent User Interfaces, (pp. 78–84). New York: Association for Computer Mechanics.

Singh, A., & Young, J. E. (2012). Animal-inspired human-robot interaction: A robotic tail for communicating state. In *Proceedings of the 7th annual ACM/IEEE international conference on human-robot interaction (HRI'12)* (pp. 237–238). New York, NY: ACM.

Sloman, A. (2002). How many separately evolved emotional beasties live within us. *Emotions in humans and artifacts*, 35–114.

Takayama, L., Park, M., Dooley, D., & Ju, W. (2011). Expressing thought: Improving robot readability with animation principles. In *Proceedings of the 6th annual ACM/IEEE international conference on human-robot interaction (HRI'11)* (pp. 69–76). ACM, New York, NY.

Tanaka, F., Noda, K., Sawada, T., & Fujita, M. (2004). Associated emotion and its expression in an entertainment robot QRIO. In *International conference on entertainment computing* (pp. 1–6). Springer-Verlag Berlin Heidelberg.

Tapus, A., Țăpuș, C., & Matarić, M. J. (2008). User-robot personality matching and assistive robot behavior adaptation for post-stroke rehabilitation therapy. *Intelligent Service Robotics*, *1*(2), 169–183.

Thomas, F., & Johnston, O. (1995). *The illusion of life: Disney animation.* New York: Hyperion.

Torrey, C., Fussell, S., & Kiesler, S. (2010). What robots could teach us about perspective-taking. In E. Morsella (Ed.), *Expressing oneself/Expressing one's self: A festschrift in honor of Robert M. Krauss* (pp. 93–106). New York: Taylor and Francis.

Velásquez, J. D. (1998). When robots weep: emotional memories and decision-making. In *Proceedings of the fifteenth national/tenth conference on Artificial intelligence/innovative applications of artificial intelligence (AAAI '98/IAAI '98)* (pp. 70–75) American Association for Artificial Intelligence.

Vilhjalmsson, H., Cantelmo, N., Cassell, J., Chafai, N. E., Kipp, M., Kopp, S.,...van der Wert, R. J. (2007). The behavior markup language: Recent developments and challenges. *Artificial Intelligence*, *4722*, 99–111.

Wistort, R. (2010). Only Robots on the Inside. *Interactions.*

Woods, S., Dautenhahn, K., Kaouri, C., Boekhorst, R., & Koay, K. L. (2005). Is this robot like me? Links between human and robot personality traits. In *5th IEEE-RAS International Conference on Humanoid Robots* (pp. 375–380). IEEE. Washington, DC: IEEE Computer Society.

Wooldridge, M., & Jennings, N. R. (1995). Intelligent agents: Theory and practice. *Knowledge Engineering Review*, *10*(2), 115–152.

Zeng, Z., Pantic, M., Roisman, G. I., & Huang, T. S. (2009). A survey of affect recognition methods: Audio, visual and spontaneous expressions. *IEEE Transactions on Pattern Analysis and Machine Intelligence*, *31*(1), 39–58.

Preparing Emotional Agents
for Intercultural Communication

Elisabeth André

Abstract

Although many papers emphasize the need to incorporate cultural values and norms into emotional agent architectures, work that actually follows such an integrative approach is rare. To construct anthropomorphic agents that show culture-specific emotional behaviors, researchers must investigate how emotions are conveyed across cultures and how this knowledge can be used to tune emotion recognizers to a particular culture. Models of appraisal and coping have to be enriched by models of culture to simulate how the agent appraises events and actions and manages its emotions depending on its alleged culture. Finally, mechanisms are required to modulate the expressiveness of emotions by cultural traits to convey emotions with right level of intensity and force. Starting from work done in the agent research community, this paper discusses how existing work on equipping anthropomorphic agents with emotional behaviors can be extended by considering culture-specific variations.

Key Words: modeling emotions, virtual agents, emotional agent architectures, culture, emotion, behavior, appraisal, coping, anthropomorphic agents

Introduction

Many studies indicate that at least basic emotions are conveyed universally in a similar manner across culture (see Ekman, 1994). However, emotions that occur in human–human communication usually do not correspond to one particular basic emotion and are not always expressed in a prototypical manner. Despite many similarities, there are a number of culture-specific differences in emotional expression that may impact communication across cultures (Elfenbein & Ambady, 2003). In addition, emotional behaviors may have social implications that are highly culturally dependent. Cultural norms and values determine which emotions we experience (Scherer, 1997), whether it is appropriate to show them in a particular social setting (Matsumoto, 1990), and how they are interpreted by others (Matsumoto, 1989). As a German, I tend to express emotions in a less intense manner

than a US American. Showing happiness about a friendly offer in a manner that is common in Germany, I am every now and then a bit worried that I appear unappreciative to a US colleague who does me a favor. The example shows that emotional exchanges between people from different cultures may lead to misconceptions even in cases in which emotional displays are correctly analyzed. Similar issues may arise when humans communicate with virtual agents or robots that do not match their culture. If such agents adhere to the emotional display rules of a culture that does not correspond to the user's culture, the user might perceive the agent as funny, weird, or even irritating. Such an unintended effect could even be enhanced if the agent's appearance, but not its behavior, matches the user's culture.

In the agent research community, significant progress has been made in the development of virtual agents and robots that model human emotional behavior (Marsella, Gratch, & Petta, 2010). It is often emphasized by researchers in this community that emotional behaviors are highly variable and are influenced by, among other things, a person's cultural background. However, culture is usually not taken explicitly taken into account as a factor when building computational models of emotion. Rather, the agent's emotional behavior reflects the cultural background of the designer. Although some users might find it inspiring to converse with an agent that represents a different culture, others might get the impression that the developers of the agent are imposing their own values and norms on them. Indeed Rosis, Pelachaud, and Poggi (2004) found that the appearance and animations of most characters on the Microsoft Agents website were based on Western cultural norms. Thus, there is the danger that an application that ignores the user's cultural background violates the basic principles of value-sensitive design (Friedman, 1996).

Allwood and Ahlsén (2009) analyzed the emotional behavior of a female character called Anna that appeared on the IKEA web pages in several countries. They observed that the character showed different emotional behaviors to a rude answer from a customer. Whereas the Australian Anna ignored the impolite behavior of a customer, the Swedish Anna expressed her concern by her voice and facial displays.[1] Allwood and Ahlsén (2009) speculate that the differences in the agent's emotional behavior might result from differences between the Australian and Swedish culture and wonder whether the interface designers followed their intuition or empirically acquired knowledge about culture. Šabanović (2010) describes a number of examples that illustrate how different robotic designs are reflected by the cultural background of the designer. Western researchers aim at the development of robots that convey emotions in a rather explicit manner. The most prominent example includes the Kismet robot by Brezeal (2004) that is able to express emotions through facial expressions, voice, and body movement. Conversely, Japanese researchers tend to build robots that portray emotions more implicitly, similar to actors in a Japanese Noh theater. As an example, Šabanović (2010) mentions the social robot Muu developed at Toyohashi University of Technology.

Starting from work done in the agent research community, this paper investigates how to model culture-specific emotional behaviors within computer-based systems. In particular, we focus on the following questions:

• *Is it possible to build a universal emotion detection engine?* To show emotional sensitivity toward people with a different cultural background, an agent needs to be equipped with a robust mechanism for the recognition of emotions from facial displays, body gestures, and speech. To some extent, it seems possible to detect emotions without understanding a culture's language. Consequently, it might be feasible to use the same mechanism to recognize emotional expressions that have been recorded for different cultures. Here, we discuss first attempts to conduct universal emotion recognition research.

• *How do we model culture-specific appraisal and coping mechanisms in a synthetic agent?* To simulate culture-specific emotional behaviors in embodied agents, we need to enrich models of appraisal and coping with culture-specific norms and values that determine how an agent's emotional behaviors should be adapted based on its assumed cultural background. Here, we present first approaches that combine emotional agent architectures with theories of culture to model culture-specific emotional profiles.

• *How can we generate culture-specific emotional displays in an anthropomorphic agent?* Many studies show that there is a high level of consistency in emotional displays across cultures. For example, joy is typically expressed by pulling up the sides of the mouth and tightening the muscles around the eyes. However, there are also variants in emotional behavior that are modulated by the sociocultural setting. For example, depending on the culture, emotions are shown with different intensity. Here, we investigate how to adapt a given set of expressiveness parameters to an agent's alleged culture, which is typically portrayed by the agent's appearance.

• *Do culture-specific differences in the emotional display of anthropomorphic agents influence the perception and emotional response of human observers?* Here, we present the results of various studies that focus on the reactions of human observers toward anthropomorphic agents that show a culture-specific emotional behavior. We discuss whether culture-specific emotional displays can be universally recognized and how they influence the attitude of human observers toward the agents. Furthermore, we investigate of whether culture-specific differences in emotional human–human interactions can also be found in emotional human–agent interactions.

Linking Emotions to Cultural Models

Studies that look for culture-specific differences in the expression of emotions typically start from a theory of culture to predict how emotions are expressed in a particular cultural context. A common approach to characterizing a culture is to use dichotomies, which are particularly suitable for integration into a computer model. Based on the score of a particular culture according to these dichotomies, different stereotypical behaviors may be derived. In particular, so-called display rules (Ekman & Friesen, 1975) that define which emotions should or should not be expressed in a particular social situation can be directly linked to cultural dichotomies.

Probably the most influential model of culture that relies on dichotomies has been presented by Hofstede (2001). In his model, cultures are defined using five scales from which stereotypical behavior patterns can be derived: Power Distance, Identity, Gender, Uncertainty Avoidance, and Long-Term Orientation.

• The *Power Distance* scale describes the extent to which an unequal distribution of power is accepted by the less powerful members of a culture. Compared to individuals belonging to low power distance cultures, individuals belonging to high power distance cultures tend to show more negative emotions toward people with a lower status and more positive emotions toward people with a higher status (Matsumoto, 1990). Overall, individuals belonging to low power distance cultures feel less restricted in the expression of emotions when interacting with individuals who have a higher status.

• The *Identity* scale distinguishes between individualistic and collectivistic cultures and describes the degree to which the group is valued over the individual. Collectivistic cultures place more emphasis on emotions that keep the group together than do individualistic cultures and tend to suppress emotions that might threaten group cohesion (Matsumoto et al., 2008). In collectivistic cultures, smiling occurs more frequently toward ingroup members than toward outgroup members (Matsumoto, 1990). In individualistic cultures, there is no such difference. In individualistic cultures, it is more accepted to show emotions in public than it is in collectivistic cultures. As a consequence, one would expect a higher amount of emotional expressivity in individualistic than in collectivistic cultures.

• The *Gender* scale describes to what extent a culture emphasizes gender-specific differences. In a masculine culture, men are supposed to be tough and focused on success while women are expected to be tender and focused on harmony of life. In feminine cultures, gender-specific differences are less preeminent. Consequently, one would also expect greater gender-specific differences in emotional behavior in masculine than in feminine cultures. That is, in masculine cultures, men would reinforce emotions that are related to competitive behaviors, such as anger, but avoid emotions, such as sadness, that might indicate weakness. Generally, the display of emotions is more accepted in feminine than in masculine cultures. Indeed, a number of studies indicate that emotional expressiveness is higher in feminine cultures than in masculine cultures (Fernández et al., 2000).

• The *Uncertainty Avoidance* scale explains a society's tolerance for uncertainty and ambiguity. It is reasonable to assume that members of a culture with a high score on the uncertainty avoidance scale experience a high amount of anxiety and stress when confronted with unexpected situations. At the same time, such cultures have a tendency to reduce the amount of uncertainty by enforcing norms that regulate the display of emotions (Matsumoto et al., 2008). Dhillon, Kocielnik, Politis, Swerts, and Szostak (2011) evaluated an error-prone speech interface with Greek users (i.e., participants from a culture with a high score on the Uncertainty Avoidance scale) and Dutch users (i.e., participants from a culture with a low score on the Uncertainty Avoidance scale). As expected, the Greek participants were more expressive in their facial expressions than the Dutch users when encountering errors.

• The *Long-Term Orientation* scale describes to what extent a culture focuses on the future. Cultures that score high on this scale aim to preserve good relationships for the future and follow emotional display rules that support this goal (Matsumoto et al., 2008).

Another cultural scale was introduced by Hall (1976) who distinguished between *low-* and *high-context* cultures. Low-context cultures are more explicit in the communication of messages whereas high-context cultures rely to a large extent on implicitly conveyed information, for example, information that can be inferred from the conversational context. As a consequence, one would expect that high-context cultures convey emotional states in a more indirect manner than do low-context cultures.

A similar approach is presented by Sagiv and Schwartz (2007) who characterize cultures by the prioritization of values within a society. As an example, cultures with a high mastery score value competition, performance, and ambition whereas cultures with a high harmony score place more importance to equality, social relationships, and quality of life. Butler, Lee, and Gross (2007) investigated how such culture-specific values influence the process of emotion regulation. For example, Asian values, such as group harmony, encourage the expression of emotions that are shared by the group, whereas Western values, such as individualist independence, endorse the display of emotions that reflect positive experiences.

A more linguistically motivated model of culture has been presented by Allwood (1985) who gives several examples that show how emotional displays in natural language dialogue are determined by the cultural background of the interlocutors. For example, although members of Mediterranean countries do not hesitate to show intense emotions in public, such behavior is avoided in Sweden and Japan. Allwood does not provide dichotomies along which different cultures may be described. Rather, he presents a structured collection of characteristics, such as ways of thinking or speaking, that may be used to describe a particular culture.

Automated Recognition of Emotions across Cultures

There is strong evidence that a set of basic emotions can be universally recognized across all cultures. Experiments have shown that judges from different cultures are able to determine visual and vocal emotions that are expressed by members of a culture that does not correspond to their own culture at a level that is better than chance (see Ekman, 1994, for a study on the cross-cultural recognition of facial expressions and Scherer, 2000, for a study on the cross-cultural recognition of vocal emotions). Elfenbein and Ambady (2003) conducted a meta-analysis of previous studies on the perception of emotions across cultures. Their study provides evidence for an ingroup advantage. The higher the exposure of two cultures, the higher the accuracy at which emotions are recognized across cultures.

Furthermore, cross-cultural accuracy was higher for acted emotions than for spontaneous emotions. Typically, negative emotions are recognized at a higher level of accuracy across cultural boundaries than are positive emotions, with the exception of self-enhancing emotions, such as postural pride. Scherer (2000) assumes that negative emotions tend to be employed for outgroup communication whereas positive emotions serve to increase cohesion within a group.

Motivated by research that aims to find evidence for the universality of emotions, various attempts have been made in the engineering sciences to build a universal emotion recognition system. Typically, classifiers are trained from corpora with emotional behaviors recorded and annotated in one or several cultures and tested against emotional behaviors from a different culture. Cross-cultural training and testing seems to be possible even in cases where different languages are spoken. Language understanding does not seem to be vital for vocal emotion recognition.

Conducting cross-cultural emotion recognition studies is challenging. First of all, the collection and annotation of data from a variety of cultures is time-consuming and requires a multinational effort. It is reasonable to have the corpora annotated by members of the culture that has been recorded. Nevertheless, using coders from different cultures for the annotation of corpora might provide additional insights on the perception of expressive behaviors. Second, it is hard to factor out other variables, such as gender and personality, that might influence the expression of emotions. For instance, it might be observed that the spatial extent of gestures in a corpus is unusually high. This behavior might be attributed to a particular culture. But what if the data stem from an extremely extraverted person? Third, when relying on existing corpora, the used annotation schemes might not match. As a consequence, emotional labels from different corpora have to be converted into a format that allows for cross-cultural processing. Usually, emotional categories, such as anger or surprise, are mapped onto the values of a dimensional model of emotions. However, since emotions are likely to occur with different frequencies in different corpora, cross-cultural training and testing might not yield satisfying results. Nevertheless, a few researchers have taken up the challenge.

Schuller, Vlasenko, Eyben, Wöllmer, Stuhlsatz, Wendemuth, and Rigoll (2010) conducted a cross-corpus classification of acoustic emotions employing six standard databases with emotional acted or spontaneous speech from native speakers of German, Danish, and English. They started from the same set of acoustic features across all corpora. However, to cope with the high variances of the different corpora, they tested various normalization procedures. Even though the performance of the classifiers dropped significantly when applied to a corpus from a different culture, it was still above chance in most cases. Since Schuller and colleagues relied on existing corpora that were recorded under very different conditions, it is, however, hard to derive any conclusions about the universality of vocal features. Relevant features may differ significantly from one corpus to the other, even if people from the same culture have been recorded. For example, good feature sets for acted and spontaneous emotions were showed to overlap little in study conducted by Vogt and André (2005) for two German corpora. Consequently, it is hard to extract any culture-specific patterns of emotional expression if one corpus included acted data and the other was recorded under naturalistic conditions.

To facilitate the identification of culture-specific emotional patterns, Caridakis, Wagner, Raouzaiou, Lingenfelser, Karpouzis, and André (2012) defined a common corpus construction protocol for the collection of cross-cultural multimodal emotional corpora. In their experimental setting, German, Greek, and Italian speakers had to utter a set of sentences that were supposed to elicit particular emotions in them. Even though multimodal data including speech, facial expressions, and body movements were recorded, the focus of their analyses was on gestural expressivity. Compared North European cultures, Mediterranean cultures are characterized by a higher amount of gestural expressivity (Allwood, 1985). In line with this observation, Caridakis and colleagues found that the overall activity in an Italian and Greek subcorpus was twice as high as in the German subcorpus. Similar results were obtained for the spatial extent of gestures. Spatial extent was generally highest for Greek gestures, which were, however, executed with lower speed than Italian gestures. No significant differences were found in terms of power and fluidity.

Another experiment investigated the feasibility of cross-cultural training and testing as a basis for a universal emotion recognition system. This study was only conducted for the German and the Italian subcorpus. First, classifiers were trained and tested individually for each language. For both languages, the classifiers performed on a nearly equal

level. For the German corpus, the spoken modality performed slightly better than the facial modality. For the Italian corpus, it was the other way round. When applying classifiers across cultures, the performance dropped as expected but was still significantly above chance.

Overall, the experiments conducted by Caridakis et al. (2012) provided results that support the universality of emotions across cultures, but also reveal findings that provide evidence of cross-cultural differences. Italians tend to perform fast gestures while occupying more space than Germans. Since the experimental setting was similar for all corpus recordings, the observed differences can be traced back to cultural differences. That is, we can exclude the possibility that the quality of the Italian gestures was different because of a more engaging social setting. Caridakis et al. (2012) obtained the best cross-cultural results for negative emotions when using vocal features and the best cross-cultural results for positive emotions when using visual features. This result is in line with earlier studies that seem to indicate that joy is hard to recognize when using voice, but the easiest to recognize emotion when using facial displays; for anger, it is the other way round (Ekman, 1994; Scherer, 2000).

Cross-cultural classification yields results that go well beyond chance. Nevertheless, the accuracy rates do not yet allow for an application in realistic scenarios. As studies by D'Mello and Calvo (2013) have shown that most emotions in human–machine interaction are nonbasic emotions. However, evidence for the universality of emotions mainly stems from studies on basic emotions. To improve recognition rates, we need to look at culture-specific variations in the expression of emotions and investigate which features are universally conveyed across culture and which features are characteristic of a particular culture. Furthermore, research that approaches the problem of universal emotion recognition from an engineering point of view has concentrated on the recognition of isolated emotional behaviors. A decisive question, however, is how to interpret emotional behaviors in a particular social situation (Scherer, 1997). Cultures do not only vary in the expression of emotions, but also in their interpretation. What does it mean if a user smiles at the agent? Is the behavior a sign of amusement? Or should it interpreted as a form of politeness? To interpret emotional behaviors, it does not suffice to analyze verbal and nonverbal cues in isolation. Rather, the sociocultural context needs to be taken into account.

Modeling the Cultural Background of Agents with Emotional Behaviors

In the past 20 years, significant advances have been made in enhancing the believability of virtual agents by endowing them not only with multimodal conversational behaviors, but also tailoring their behavior to emotional and/or personality. However, few researchers have taken up the challenge of modeling the influences culture has on behavior. In many cases, culture-specific behaviors are not explicitly modeled, but the designer's culture is implicitly coded in the system. Although this approach might be reasonable in many cases, there are a number of applications that would benefit from an explicit model of culture. Typical examples include learning environments that aim to enhance the user's intercultural sensitivity or competence by role play with virtual characters. For the purpose of learning, the virtual characters reflect a different cultural background than the user. Conversely, globally operating companies that employ virtual agents on their web pages might decide to adapt the alleged cultural background of the agent in such a way that it matches the user's cultural background. One challenge when combining different behavioral components into an agent is consistency. Independent of whether the agent is supposed to match the user's culture or to represent a completely different culture, the integration of an explicit model of culture may help maintain consistency between the agent's alleged culture and the various channels of outward behavior. Nevertheless, research on computational models of culture is rare. Basically, two approaches may be distinguished: data-driven approaches and model-driven approaches.

Data-Driven Computational Models of Culture

In the data-driven approach, computational models of cultural behavior are based on annotated multimodal recordings of existing cultures from which culture-specific behavior profiles are learned.

An example of project that makes use of a data-driven approach is the German-Japanese CUBE-G project (Endraß, André, Rehm, & Nakano, 2013). In this project, a social simulation environment was developed with virtual characters that portray typical Japanese and German behaviors by gestures and dialogue behaviors. The modeling of the behaviors was based on multimodal corpora that included verbal and nonverbal conversational behaviors of German and Japanese speakers in selected dialogue situations. For these corpora, a

statistical analysis was performed to identify differences between German and Japanese speakers in the use of gestures and postures, communication management, choice of topics, and the like.

The focus of the project was not on the analysis of culture-specific emotional behaviors. However, the project partners compared the expressivity of gestures recorded for German and Japanese speakers. In individualistic cultures, it is more accepted to portray emotions more openly than in collectivistic cultures. Since Japan represents a collectivistic culture and German an individualistic culture, one would expect that Germans are more expressive in their gestures than are Japanese. To measure differences in the dynamic variation of gestures, five expressivity parameters were taken into account that were inspired by perceptions studies conducted by Wallbott (1998) and Gallaher (1992): repetition, fluidity, power, speed, and spatial extent. The analysis of the corpus data confirmed the project members' predictions based on Hofstede's model of culture. The recorded Germans were indeed more expressive in their gestures than the recorded Japanese. In particular, the gestures in the German videos were performed significantly faster and with more power. Furthermore, they took up more space and were more fluent. Also, the stroke of a gesture was repeated at a higher rate in the German than in the Japanese videos.

Based on a statistical analysis of the corpora, they created a variety of conversational settings with characters that reflected typical German and Japanese behaviors. For example, gestures accompanying speech acts were selected with a higher probability for agents reflecting the German culture than for agents representing the Japanese culture. Furthermore, animation parameters, such as spatial extent or speed, for the single agents were adapted according to their assumed cultural background.

The advantage of data-driven computational models of cultural behavior lies in their empirical foundation. Data-driven models are typically used to model existing cultures because their simulation requires concrete instantiations of behavior patterns. For example, by analyzing cross-cultural corpora, we may extract typical emotional display patterns, such as a higher amount of gestural activity in one culture compared to another. However, the collection and annotation of cross-cultural corpora is extremely time-consuming and usually requires a multinational effort. Although data-driven models allow for a representation of culture-specific emotional behaviors, they do not explicitly link cultural factors with emotional models. That is, they describe how emotional behaviors are influenced by an agent's alleged culture, but they do not allow for an explicit culture-specific adaptation of emotional appraisal and coping processes.

Computational Models of Culture Based on Agent Mind Architectures

Model-driven approaches start from the assumption that emotional behaviors result from culture-specific norms and values. Typically, they start from existing agent mind architectures and extend them to allow for the culture-specific modulation of goals, beliefs, and plans.

One of the earliest and most well-known systems that models culture-specific behaviors within an agent mind architecture is the Tactical Language System (http://www.tacticallanguage.com/), which has formed the basis of a variety of products for language and culture training by Alelo Inc. Tactical Language is based on architecture for social behavior called Thespian that implements a version of theory of mind (Si, Marsella, & Pynadath, 2006). Thespian supports the creation of virtual characters that understand and follow culture-specific social norms when interacting with each other or with human users. Although the user converses with the characters of a training scenario, Thespian tracks the affinity between the single characters and the human user, which depends on the appropriateness of the user's behavior. For example, a violation of social norms would result in a decreased affinity value.

Taylor and Sims (2009) present a computational model of culture that combines appraisal theory with cultural schema theory to model how an agent responds to events and actions based on its assumed cultural background. The implemented schemata are not based on cultural theories, but on collected anecdotal sources. They include references to an agent's culture-specific expectations and goals that influence the agent's appraisal and coping processes. The main motivation for the simulation of culture-specific behaviors was to increase the agent's believability in a training application for soldiers.

Although these approaches focused on the simulation of a particular existing culture, Mascarenhas, Dias, Prada, and Paiva (2009) aim at the modeling of synthetic cultures that may be obtained by systematically varying particular behavior determinants. To this end, they extend an agent mind architecture called FAtiMA that implements a cognitive model of appraisal by representations of the Hofstede cultural scales. Based on the extended architecture, agents with distinct cultural background were modeled. In their model, an agent's alleged culture determines its decision processes (i.e., the selection of goals) and its appraisal processes (i.e., how an action is evaluated). An action that is of benefit to others is the more praiseworthy, the more collectivistic the culture is. Furthermore, the cultural model determines which agent reaction is triggered as a response to an emotional stimulus. Depending on the assumed culture of the agent, the most adequate coping strategy is selected.

Approaches based on agent mind architectures bear the advantage that interdependencies between cultural scales and verbal and nonverbal behaviors can be modeled in an intuitive manner. They are very well suited for the implementation of synthetic cultures, which are obtained by variations of the cultural scales. Although a more formal approach to cultural models usually ensures a higher level of consistency than the data-driven approach, it is not grounded in real data and thus may not completely realistically simulate existing cultures. Another limitation is that it is difficult to decide which specific gestures and behaviors to choose for externalizing the goals and needs generated in the agent minds.

Culture-Specific Expression of Emotions

Although a number of studies aim at finding evidence for the universality of emotional expression, others focus on culture-specific variations of emotional expression. For example, various studies indicate that motions are expressed with lower intensity in collectivistic cultures than in individualistic cultures.

Although some work has been conducted to manually create emotional expressions for culture-specific agents, for example, by employing human designers with a particular cultural background, hardly any work has been conducted to explicitly model such behaviors based on an explicit representation of an agent's assumed cultural background. An example of such an approach has been presented by Endraß et al. (2013) based on a dimensional characterization of expressivity in human bodily movement.

To model the link between culture and the expressivity of gestures, Endraß et al. (2013) made use of Bayesian networks. Although it is rather tempting to code explicit rules from the literature in a computational model of culture, such an approach would result into monotonous agent behaviors. Furthermore, it would enhance the risk

Fig. 22.1 Virtual agents with different emotional expressivity generated by the Advanced Agent Animation (AAA) Engine Presented in Damian, Endraß, Huber, Bee, and André (2011).

of overstereotyping cultures. Bayesian networks bear the advantage that they allow us to model culture-specific behavior adaptations based on probabilities. For example, we may represent by means of conditional probabilities how likely it is that a member of a collectivistic culture makes use of tight gestures. Furthermore, Bayesian networks enable us to model the relationship between cultural scales and behavioral variables in an intuitive manner. For example, it is rather straightforward how to model within a Bayesian network that a member of a collectivistic culture tends to use emotional expressions of low intensity.

Figure 22.1 shows how an agent's emotional expressivity can be adapted according to cultural traits. Compared to the agents on the left, the agents on the right make use of more powerful gestures with a higher amount of spatial extent.

Endraß et al. (2013) determine the probabilities of their Bayesian network based on typical culture-specific behavior patterns found in the literature. Interestingly, most predictions based on the Bayesian network could be confirmed by their own empirical studies. As an alternative, the probabilities of the Bayesian network could be determined automatically from multimodal corpora collected for human behaviors. Such an approach was presented by Bergmann and Kopp (2010) to model coverbal iconic gestures. To extend it to cross-cultural models of gestures, an immense amount of data would be required depending on the number of cultures to be considered.

Cross-Cultural Perception of Emotions Portrayed by Virtual Agents and Robots

According to the meta-analysis by Elfenbein and Ambady (2003), human emotional expressions are recognized with a higher accuracy within than

between cultures. The question arises of whether this finding also holds for synthetic faces.

Koda (2007) conducted an open web experiment to investigate whether facial expressions of cartoon figures created by a Japanese designer could be recognized equally well across cultures. All together 1,237 participants from 31 countries (675 male and 561 female) took part in the experiment. The responses from the countries with more than 40 participants were analyzed by determining the degree of agreement (i.e., the proportion of adjective pairs of each country that matched the intention of the Japanese designer). It turned out that the agreement of the Japanese with the Japanese designer was the highest, followed by the Koreans. Obviously, the recognition rates are higher the closer the culture of the judging person is to the culture of the designer. Furthermore, the authors were able to confirm earlier findings from psychologists that negative emotions could be identified more easily than positive emotions. Negative emotional expressions had a significantly higher recognition rate independent of the culture of the judging person, whereas positive emotions were more easily confused. The experiment was later refined by recruiting designers from different countries. Basically, the results of the earlier experiment could be confirmed (Koda, Ishida, Rehm, & André, 2009).

Kleinsmith, Silva, and Bianchi-Berthouze (2006) investigated cultural differences in the perception of four emotions (anger, fear, happiness, and sadness) conveyed by full-body postures of a 3D gender-neutral and culture-neutral humanoid avatar. The study was performed with Japanese, Sri Lankans, and Caucasian Americans viewers who had to judge the presented postures according to given emotion labels. The authors found a moderate level of agreement for the judgments, which was highest for sadness. As an explanation, the authors state that the emotion lexicons for words describing depression were very similar for the investigated cultures. The authors also detected some interesting culture-specific differences in the evaluation of postures. For example, the Japanese judges tended to give higher ratings for the intensity of the postures than did judges from the two other cultures. Furthermore, the authors observed that the investigated cultures did not associate postural characteristics with the same emotional states. For example, the Sri Lankans and Caucasian Americans attributed sadness to postures with the hands close to the chest, whereas the Japanese viewers did not consider this feature a relevant indicator of sadness.

The ingroup advantage could also be confirmed by Trovato, Kishi, Endo, Hashimoto, and Takanishi (2012) for emotional expressions of the humanoid social robot KOBIAN. They created different versions of emotional expressions using the robot's head and the neck that were either adapted to the Western or the Japanese culture following the work of illustrators or cartoonists. In line with earlier work on virtual characters, they observed that emotional expressions are easier to recognize if the culture of the judge matches the alleged culture of the robot.

Emotional Responses to Culture-Specific Virtual Characters and Robots

According to sociological studies, our impression of others is shaped by a categorization into ingroup and outgroup membership using simple cues, such as gender or ethnicity. Usually, people show a preference for ingroup members over outgroup members. There is evidence that these findings can be transferred to interactions with virtual characters and robots. Studies have shown that people respond more positively toward virtual characters and robots that reflect their own cultural background than a different one.

Nass and Gong (2000) have shown that computer agents representing a user's ethnic group are perceived as socially more attractive and trustworthy. Similar results were obtained by Baylor and Kim (2004). Eyssel and Kuchenbrandt (2012) found that very small cues referring to an agent's culture, such as the German name "Armin" and the Persian name "Arman," suffice to influence people's rating. They asked German students to evaluate a robot based on photos presented to them. Test persons were divided into two groups. One group was told the robot was called "Armin" and developed by a German university. The other group was told the robot was called "Arman" and developed at a Turkish university. The robot that was supposed to be developed by the German university was evaluated more positively than the robot that was supposed to be developed by the Turkish University.

Endraß et al. (2013) conducted a variety of experiments in Germany and Japan to investigate whether characters that portray behaviors of their own culture find higher acceptance than characters that reflect a different cultural background in their behaviors. To this end, they presented German and Japanese participants with two versions of the same dialogue between two agents. In both versions, the appearance of the agents was adapted to the participants' cultural background. To avoid any bias due to the semantics of the dialogue, the agents communicated in a fantasy language that had the same statistical distribution of syllables as the native language of the participants. In one version, the agents' nonverbal behavior was tuned to the Japanese culture. In the other version, the agents' nonverbal behavior reflected the German culture. The experiments conducted revealed that the German and Japanese participants had in most cases a preference for nonverbal behaviors that reflected their own culture.

Although these studies investigated the attitude of people toward agents and robots that portray a particular cultural background, Mascarenhas et al. (2009) investigated whether it is possible to model agents with distinguishable cultural behavior based on a model of culture. Results of experiments conducted for two synthetic cultures revealed that simulated cultural differences in the agents' behaviors were recognized by viewers and actually attributed to the alleged cultural background of the agent.

Shahid, Krahmer, and Swerts (2008) analyzed the emotional behavior of Pakistani and Dutch children playing card games together, with the Philips iCAT robot or alone. Based on the collected visual data, Dutch adult viewers had to guess from the children's facial expressions whether they had just won or lost the game. Independent of the children's nationality, the classification rate was higher for children playing with the robot than for individually playing children, but lower than for children playing with each other. Furthermore, the classification rate was higher for the Pakistani children than for the Dutch children. The authors conclude from these results that the Pakistani children were more expressive than the Dutch children. The underlying assumption was that higher expressiveness in the children would result into a higher classification rate in the judges.

Conclusion

Although a significant amount of work has been done in the social sciences to investigate the interdependencies between emotional behaviors and cultural traits, the agent research community has made little use of this knowledge so far. Examples of agents whose behavior is guided by culture-specific emotional profiles are still rare. In this paper, we identified two approaches to creating culture-specific variants of emotional behaviors: a data-driven approach that synthesizes agent behaviors based on empirical data acquired for particular cultures and a model-driven approach that generates agent behavior based on rules and scripts that may be derived from cultural theories. Furthermore, we may distinguish approaches that focus on the simulation of culture-specific appraisal and coping mechanisms and approaches that implement mechanisms to generate culture-specific variants of emotional displays.

Although the consideration of cultural traits and values may enhance an agent's believability, they also increase the complexity of existing agent architectures. For a system designer, it may be hard to identify the causes for a particular agent behavior. A great difficulty in the modeling of culture-specific emotional behaviors lies in the fact that emotional behaviors are not only influenced by culture, but also by other factors, such as gender or personality. For example, one would avoid extreme emotional behaviors to simulate emotional behaviors of an agent that represents a collectivistic culture, but increase the intensity of emotional behaviors if the agent is supposed to portray an extravert personality. Furthermore, it is not clear how to handle conflicts resulting from emotional display rules. For example, cultures that score high on power distance are said to encourage self-enhancing emotions, such as pride, for people with a high status. Conversely, cultures that score high on collectivism are supposed to avoid self-enhancing emotions. Thus, the question arises of which behavior would be predicted for cultures that score high on both scales.

Despite the challenges that still need to be solved, first attempts to implement culture-specific emotional profiles in anthropomorphic agents have been successful insofar as the developers were able to show that the agent's alleged culture had an important impact on how it was perceived by the user.

Acknowledgments

This research was partially funded by the EU under grant agreement eCUTE (FP7-ICT-257666). The authors are solely responsible for the content of this publication. It does not represent the opinion of the EC, and the EC is not responsible for any use that might be made of data appearing therein.

Correspondence concerning this article should be addressed to Elisabeth André, Human-Centered Multimedia, Fakultät für Angewandte Informatik, Universität Augsburg, Universitätsstr. 6a, 86159 Augsburg, Germany. E-mail: andre@informatik. uni-augsburg.de

Notes

1. As the author of this paper convinced herself, the German Anna seems to behave rather like the Australian Anna.

References

Allwood, J. (1985). Tvärkulturell kommunikation. In J. Allwood (Ed.), *Tvärkulturell kommunikation*. Papers in Anthropological Linguistics 12, University of Göteborg, Dept. of Linguistics. Also in English: Intercultural Communication.

Allwood, J., Ahlsén, E. (2009). Multimodal intercultural information and communication technology—A framework for designing and evaluating multimodal intercultural communicators. In M. Kipp, J. -C. Martin, & P. Paggio (Eds.), *Multimodal corpora—From models of natural interaction to systems and applications* (vol. 5509, pp. 160–175). Berlin, Heidelberg: Springer.

Baylor, A. L., & Kim, Y. (2004). Pedagogical agent design: The impact of agent realism, gender, ethnicity, and instructional role. In J. C. Lester, R. M. Vicari, & F. Paraguaçu (Eds.), *Intelligent tutoring systems, 7th International Conference, ITS 2004*. Maceió, Alagoas, Brazil, August 30–September 3, 2004, Proceedings (vol. 3220, pp. 592–603). Berlin, Heidelberg: Springer.

Bergmann, K., & Kopp, S. (2010). Modeling the production of coverbal iconic gestures by learning bayesian decision networks. *Applied Artificial Intelligence*, 24(6), 530–551.

Brezeal, C. (2004). *Designing sociable robots*. A Bradford Book. Boston, MA: MIT Press.

Butler, E. A., Lee, T. L., & Gross, J. J. (2007). Emotion regulation and culture: Are the social consequences of emotion suppression culture-specific? *Emotion*, 7(1), 30–48.

Caridakis, G., Wagner, J., Raouzaiou, A., Lingenfelser, F., Karpouzis, K., & André, E. (2012). A cross-cultural, multimodal, affective corpus for gesture expressivity analysis. *Journal on Multimodal User Interfaces*, 7(1-2), 121–134.

Damian, I., Endraß, B., Huber, P., Bee, N., & André, E. (2011). *Individualized agent interactions. Motion in Games* (pp. 15–26). 4th International Conference, MIG 2011, Edinburgh, UK, November 13–15. Berlin, Heidelberg: Springer.

Dhillon, B., Kocielnik, R., Politis, I., Swerts, M., & Szostak, D. (2011). Culture and facial expressions: A case study with a speech interface. In P. Campos, T. C. N. Graham, J. A. Jorge, N. J. Nunes, P. A. Palanque, & M. Winckler (Eds.), *Human-Computer Interaction*. Interact 2011, 13th IFIP TC 13 International Conference, Lisbon, Portugal, September

5–9, 2011, Proceedings (part ii, vol. 6947, pp. 392–404). Berlin, Heidelberg: Springer.

D'Mello, S., & Calvo, R. A. (2013). Beyond the basic emotions: What should affective computing compute? In W. E. Mackay, S. Brewster, S. Bødker (Eds.), CHI '13 Extended *Abstracts on Human Factors in Computing Systems* (pp. 2287–2294). Paris, France, April 27–May 2. New York, NY: ACM.

Ekman, P. (1994). Strong evidence for universals in facial expressions: A reply to Russell's mistaken critique. *Psychological Bulletin*, 115, 268–287.

Ekman, P., & Friesen, W. V. (1975). Unmasking the face. Englewood Cliffs, N.J.: Prentice-Hall.

Elfenbein, H. A., & Ambady, N. (2003). Cultural similarity's consequences a distance perspective on cross-cultural differences in emotion recognition. *Journal of Cross-Cultural Psychology*, 34(1),92–110.

Endraß, B., André, E., Rehm, M., & Nakano, Y. I. (2013). Investigating culture-related aspects of behavior for virtual characters. *Autonomous Agents and Multi-Agent Systems*, 27(2), 277–304.

Eyssel, F., & Kuchenbrandt, D. (2012). Social categorization of social robots: Anthropomorphism as a function of robot group membership. *British Journal of Social Psychology*, 51(4), 724–731.

Fernández, I., Carrera, P., Sánchez, F., Rovira, Páez, D., & Candia, L. (2000). Differences between cultures in emotional verbal and nonverbal reactions. *Psicothema*, 12(1), 83–92.

Friedman, B. (1996). Value-sensitive design. *Interactions*, 3(6), 16–23.

Gallaher, P. E. (1992). Individual differences in nonverbal behavior: Dimensions of style. *Journal of Personality and Social Psychology*, 63(1), 133–145.

Hall, E. T. (1976) Beyond Culture, Anchor Books, New York, USA. Hofstede, G. (2001). *Cultures consequences: Comparing values, behaviors, institutions, and organizations across nations*. Thousand Oaks, CA: Sage Publications.

Kleinsmith, A., De Silva, P. R. & Bianchi-Berthouze, N. (2006). Cross-cultural differences in recognizing affect from body posture. *Interacting with Computers* 18(6): 1371-1389.

Koda, T. (2007). Cross-cultural study of avatars' facial expressions and design considerations within Asian countries. In T. Ishida, S. R. Fussell, & P. T. J. M. Vossen (Eds.), *Intercultural Collaboration*. First International Workshop, IWIC 2007, Kyoto, Japan, January 25–26, 2007. Invited and Selected Papers (vol. 4568, pp. 207–220). Berlin, Heidelberg: Springer.

Koda, T., Ishida, T., Rehm, M., & André, E. (2009). Avatar culture: Cross-cultural evaluations of avatar facial expressions. *AI Society*, 24(3), 237–250.

Marsella, S., Gratch, J., & Petta, P. (2010). Computational models of emotion. In Scherer, K. R., Bänziger, T., & Roesch, E. (Eds.), *A blueprint for affective computing: A sourcebook and manual, cross-fertilization between emotion psychology, affective neuroscience, and affective computing* (pp. 21–46). Oxford: Oxford University Press.

Matsumoto, D. (1989). Cultural influences on the perception of emotion. *Journal of Cross-Cultural Psychology*, 20, 92–105

Matsumoto, D. (1990). Cultural similarities and differences in display rules. *Motivation and Emotion*, 14(3), 195–214.

Matsumoto, D., Yoo, S. H., Nakagawa, S., Alexandre, J., Altarriba, J., Anguas-Wong, A., & Zengeya, A. (2008).

Culture, emotion regulation, and adjustment. *Journal of Personality and Social Psychology*, 94(6), 925–937.

Mascarenhas, S., Dias, J., Prada, R., & Paiva, A. (2009). One for all or one for one? The influence of cultural dimensions in virtual agents' behaviour. In Z. Ruttkay, M. Kipp, A. Nijholt, & H. H. Vilhjálmsson (Eds.), *Intelligent virtual agents*. 9th International Conference, IVA 2009, Amsterdam, The Netherlands, September 14–16, 2009, Proceedings (vol. 5773, pp. 272–286). Berlin, Heidelberg: Springer.

Nass, C., & Gong, L. (2000). Speech interfaces from an evolutionary perspective. *Communication ACM*, 43(9), 36–43.

Rosis, F. de, Pelachaud, C., & Poggi, I. (2004). Transcultural believability in embodied agents: A matter of consistent adaptation. In: S. Payr & R. Trappl (Eds.), *Agent culture: Human agent interaction in a multicultural world* (pp. 75–106). Mahwah, New Jersey: LEA.

Šabanović, S. (2010). Emotion in robot cultures: Cultural models of affect in social robot design. *Proceedings of Design and Emotion 2010 (D&E2010)*. Chicago IL, October 2010.

Sagiv, L., & Schwartz, S. H. (2007). Cultural values in organisations: Insights for Europe. *European Journal of International Management*, 1(3), 176–190.

Scherer, K. R. (1997). The role of culture in emotion-antecedent appraisal. *Journal of Personality and Social Psychology*, 73(5), 902–922.

Scherer, K. R. (2000). A cross-cultural investigation of emotion inferences from voice and speech: Implications for speech technology. In D. Guan, R. Zhang, B. Yua, T. Huang (Eds.), *Sixth International Conference on Spoken Language Processing, ICSLP 2000/Interspeech 2000* (pp. 379–382). Beijing, China, October 16–20, 2000. Baixas, France: ISCA.

Schuller, B., Vlasenko, B., Eyben, F., Wöllmer, M., Stuhlsatz, A., Wendemuth, A., & Rigoll, G. (2010). Cross-corpus acoustic emotion recognition: Variances and strategies. *IEEE Transactions on Affective Computing*, 1(2), 119–131.

Shahid, S., Krahmer, E., & Swerts, M. (2008). Alone or together: Exploring the effect of physical co-presence on the emotional expressions of game playing children across cultures. In P. Markopoulos, B. E. R. de Ruyter, W. IJsselsteijn, & D. Rowland (Eds.), *Fun and games*. Second International Conference, Eindhoven, The Netherlands, October 20–21, 2008. Proceedings (vol. 5294, pp. 94–105). Berlin, Heidelberg: Springer.

Si, M., Marsella, S., & Pynadath, D. V. (2006). Thespian: Modeling socially normative behavior in a decision-theoretic framework. In J. Gratch, M. Young, R. Aylett, D. Ballin, & P. Olivier (Eds.), *Intelligent virtual agent*. 6th International Conference, IVA 2006, Marina del Rey, CA, August 21–23, 2006. Proceedings (vol. 4133, pp. 369–382). Berlin, Heidelberg: Springer.

Taylor, G., & Sims, E. (2009). Developing believable interactive cultural characters for cross-cultural training. In A. A. Ozok & P. Zaphiris (Eds.), *Online Communities and Social Computing*. Third International Conference, OCSC 2009, held as part of HCI International 2009, San Diego, CA, July 19–24, 2009. Proceedings (vol. 5621, pp. 282–291). Berlin, Heidelberg: Springer.

Trovato, G., Kishi, T., Endo, N., Hashimoto, K., & Takanishi, A. (2012). A cross-cultural study on generation of culture dependent facial expressions of humanoid social robot. In S. S. Ge, O. Khatib, J. -J. Cabibihan, R. G. Simmons, & M.-A. Williams (Eds.), *Social robotics—4th International Conference, ICSR 2012*. Chengdu, China, October

29–31, 2012. Proceedings (vol. 7621, pp. 35–44). Berlin, Heidelberg: Springer.

Vogt, T., & André, E. (2005). Comparing feature sets for acted and spontaneous speech in view of automatic emotion recognition. In *Proceedings of the 2005 IEEE International Conference on Multimedia and Expo, ICME 2005* (pp. 474–477). July 6–9, 2005, Amsterdam, The Netherlands. Washington, DC: IEEE.

Wallbott, H. G. (1998). Bodily expression of emotion. *European Journal of Social Psychology*, 28(6), 879–896.

Methodologies and Databases

Multimodal Affect Databases: Collection, Challenges, and Chances

Björn Schuller

Abstract

This chapter focuses on multimodal affect databases. After a short introduction, the collection of affective data is discussed in 10 steps highlighting methodological considerations and challenges of building new resources of multimodal data and affect labels. It then touches upon quality assessment of collected emotion corpora. A section is also dedicated to "saving labor" by sharing annotation between human and machine and reusing data. Then a selection of representative audiovisual and further multimodal databases is introduced. Finally, the chapter concludes with a discussion of controversial issues and future directions.

Key Words: multimodal affect databases, emotion corpora

Introduction

In order to train and test multimodal affect recognition and synthesis systems or analyze human affective behavior, data are needed. In fact, this is often considered to be one of the main bottlenecks, and a common opinion in machine learning is that there are "no data like more data." In this vein, this chapter aims to first, in Introduction (p. 323), give insight into the state of the art in multimodal affect data, then to outline requirements and discuss challenges. It then deals with steps toward preparation of such a multimodal database in Data Collection—Ten Steps Toward a Multimodal Affect Database (p. 324). Quality Assessment—Is This Really Joyful? (p. 327) deals with quality assessment of the annotation and weighting of raters. In Efficiency—How to Save Annotation Labor (p. 328) avenues toward reduction of human annotation efforts are shown, including active, semisupervised, and unsupervised learning. Selected examples of existing multimodal affect resources are shown in Existing Multimodal Resources—What's There? (p. 330), after which

Conclusions and Future Avenues—Wrapping Up (p. 331) wraps up the discussion.

State of the Art

While there are increasingly multimodal recordings of affect displays available, to date these tend to be smaller in size and more often recorded in the lab than their unimodal counterparts (Gunes & Schuller, 2012). Until recently, the larger portion of affective databases comprised bimodal databases—usually of audiovisual nature. In addition, multicultural and multilingual data, the latter being especially important for text-based detection, are still considerably sparse. This is even truer when it comes to data in naturalistic or working system contexts. More "exotic" and richer combinations of data—such as physiological measures or speech alongside depth images—are, however, progressively more available. Further, more and more languages are covered and more natural databases with more complex affect labels are increasingly available to the community. In general, ever more multimodal resources are to be expected (Schuller, Douglas-Cowie, Batliner, 2012).

Requirements

There are several prerequisites apart from the sheer quantity of the data required, and obtaining considerable amounts of data can be difficult and labo-intensive, since data must usually be labeled. The most relevant of these requirements include *quantity*; high diversity with respect to multiple factors such as the age, gender, and culture of subjects and the situational context; and reasonably balanced distribution of instances among classes or even along the range in case of continuous models. Next is the *quality* of the data, in the sense of adequate data, realistic and naturalistic data, and adhering to ideal capture conditions within acceptable parameters for levels of noise, reverberations, occlusions, and so on. A further requirement is *appropriate modeling* in terms of reasonable categorization or choice of appropriate dimensions together with well-defined mappings between potential models. The *labeling* demands *consistency* as well as additional provision of metainformation such as transcripts of spoken text and nonlinguistic vocalizations, context and events, individual labeler tracks, and so forth. There must be a high number of *annotators* (or *coders, labelers,* or *raters*)—ideally again with high demographic diversity, and the provision of a "gold standard" along with its reliability and potential additional emotion perception tests for verification of trustworthiness. Finally, the *release of data* requires additional considerations such as documentation of detailed recording conditions and metainformation on the subjects, provision of baseline recognition results by automatic engines for others to compare with, free release of the data with high accessibility, and suggested partitioning of the data into test, development, and training partitions to avoid arbitrary testing partitions.

Challenges

One of the major challenges in recording multimodal affective data is to obtain naturalistic displays of affect. The complex setups for multimodal recordings often require very careful control of lab conditions. However, when recording is done in the lab, one of the problems is the "observer's paradox": According to Labov (1984) and one's general intuition, the presence of the experimenter and the awareness of being recorded may influence the subject.

Another challenge typical for the recording of multimodal data is the synchronization of the multimodal capture streams, as these are often recorded by individual hardware devices and additionally may operate at different time scales. The sampling interval of these different hardware devices can partly be nonconstant, which makes the challenge of synchronization more demanding.

Then, a major challenge is the labeling of the data by a sufficient number of independent labelers or by the subjects themselves. In some multimodal setups, not all modalities' recorded data may be sufficiently informative for human labelers to make affect judgments. This may require self-assessment, ideally online, which again can be highly disruptive with respect to an awareness of being in an experimental setting. New methods for community or distributed annotation such as crowdsourcing (e. g., by Amazon Mechanical Turk) may be useful to obtain annotations with labels for a data instance with high variability of raters and to potentially reduce the cost of obtaining annotations (see Chapter 30, this volume, on crowdsourcing for affective computing).

Data Collection—Ten Steps Toward a Multimodal Affect Database

This section aims to highlight usual steps in preparing an affect database with a focus on multimodal data (a general introduction to the topic of affect databases is given in Chapter 26, this volume). The 10 aspects considered include ethics, the actual data acquisition by recording or "reusing" data, collection of metainformation, synchronization of the multimodal streams, choice of an appropriate affect modeling for the subsequent labeling while considering standards to be used, partitioning of the data for experimentation, human perception studies and baseline results (e.g., by automatic recognition), and the actual release to the community.

Considering Ethics

Ethical considerations represent one of the major issues with affect data collection. Affect can be very private, and subjects in the real world or in lab studies might not always agree with making genuine and spontaneous affect data available for study, in particular when it comes to video or audio recordings. With a gradual increase in the multimodal collection of data, this may become even more crucial, as the information will be increasingly "complete," potentially containing electroencephalographic (EEG) or physiological data alongside audio and video.

The major questions to ask oneself prior to recording or releasing affect data include, according to (Ragin & Amoroso, 2011) the moral principles that guide the research, how the ethical issues influence the selection of the research problem itself, and the conduct of the research. These further include the responsibility one has toward the subjects as to whether they were sufficiently informed and whether one has obtained their consent. In fact, obtaining consent a priori may be challenging, because this might reduce the spontaneity and naturalness of the data. Ethical issues are also concerned with the question of which parts to release and/or publish. In multimodal data collection, subjects may, for example, agree to different levels of release for different contained modalities. An important question is further whether the research will be beneficial in some way in the near or far future to the subjects themselves. Finally, although it may seem obvious, it is important to point out that participants in studies should not be harmed in any way.

Recording and Reusing

The actual data are either obtained by recording new data or, as an often efficient alternative, by reusing existing material such as videos of political debates (Vinciarelli et al., 2009). The latter is, however, considerably more difficult if physiological measures are involved, as such data are usually only sparsely available—in particular in multimodal combination let alone in sufficiently emotional contexts.

The types of data obtained usually cover acted emotion, induced, for example, by recalling emotional memories or watching movie clips (see Chapter 32, this volume, on emotion elicitation methods for affective computing), and naturalistic emotion. However, in particular, the recording of multimodal data may make it difficult to record highly naturalistic data, as laboratory settings may be needed and may influence the recording. However, with the increasing availability of mobile and wearable ubiquitous devices, this challenge is expected to ease over time.

Collecting Metainformation

It may sound trivial, but in fact only a few databases contain rich metainformation on the subjects involved, the situational context, and so on. Besides obvious demographic aspects such as the age or gender of subjects, information such as cultural background, height, or spoken dialect may be beneficial in some cases. In particular, the personality of the subjects may be of interest in further data analysis. This can be assessed by standardized personality tests such as the 10-item questionnaire by Rammstedt and John (2007). For the different modalities, metainformation may in addition contain the recording equipment used and how it was synchronized.

Synchronizing Streams

One major issue during multimodal recording can be the synchronization of input streams. Even for the synchronization of audio and video, this may become a challenge if several microphones and cameras are involved. In other cases, such as the combination of worn physiological devices alongside video or depth capture, the recording may occur on individual devices that are not routed via the same computer. Aligned time stamps or markers are straightforward practical solutions allowing for later synchronization. Usually these markers may need to be repeated during a take (or trial) to compensate for temporal deviations. Another option, albeit usually involving greater effort and potentially leading to suboptimal solutions, is postrecording machine-based alignment, as by dynamic programming (Gunes, Piccardi & Pantic, 2008). However, this is generally an option only for the alignment of several captures from the same modality. Cross-modal alignment can become considerably more challenging.

Modeling

There are two decisions to be made in finding an appropriate model of emotion before (human) data labeling can start: (1) the emotion model and (2) the temporal unit of analysis. The choice of the most appropriate emotion model (e.g., continuous or categorical) can be influenced by the types of modalities involved in the multimodal setup. In any case, the temporal unit of analysis will usually be trickier to determine. For example, physiological measures and video could be annotated on a per-frame basis, whereas acoustic parameters are usually extracted over larger chunks, such as words or turns, and textual parameters may be most informative over whole phrases or dialogue acts. A recently adopted compromise is to choose a fully continuous annotation (Gunes & Schuller, 2012). *Fully* here means that the annotation should be continuous in its emotion dimension(s), such as arousal and valence, but also in time (i.e., an emotion value is given, for example, every 100 milliseconds). This allows for diverse mappings—for example, by averaging over a certain chunk. Another option is to use multiple models, which enriches the flexibility of the database but requires considerable extra effort. In the case of multimodal data, these different models could be applied for modality-specific annotation.

Labeling

Emotion labeling is probably the major effort besides the actual collection of the data. In a multimodal database, this labeling can be tricky, as not all modalities can be easily annotated by a human rater. For example, physiological signals may be difficult to interpret. In fact, some recorded modalities may even serve as additional information for labeling, such as physiological measures in the case of arousal or video data for the annotation of physiological data.

Self-assessment is not always an option. Thus, usually several external labelers serve to approximate the "expertise of the mass" (e.g., by majority voting or by taking the mean and median in the case of continuous emotion models). The number of labelers should usually be increased with increasing subjectivity or ambiguity of the target labeling task at hand and the complexity of the chosen model.

Interestingly, multimodal recordings can be annotated modality-wise or in combination, which can lead to considerable differences. For example, acoustic and physiological data usually better convey arousal, whereas video or textual data are particularly well suited to convey valence (Karadogan & Larsen, 2012). Note, however, that not all modalities are necessarily present at all times. For example, speech is available only when a subject is talking.

Standardizing

A number of standards exist that may be considered to foster compatibility of the metadata and the annotations (Schröder et al., 2007). Of these, EmotionML (see Chapter 29, this volume) is a particular example of a markup language recommended by the World Wide Web Consortium (W3C). It allows for very high flexibility, including the use of one's own emotion lists. Further, it includes a number of mechanisms to describe multimodal data and to add contextual information. An earlier standard is EARL—the emotion annotation and representation language (Schröder, Pirker & Lamolle, 2006). It was partly suggested by the same researchers as EmotionML and laid the foundations for it.

Partitioning

Partitioning in the sense of dividing the affect data into partitions for different phases in modeling, optimizing, and testing is a crucial factor: If multimodal affect databases are not prepartitioned by their creators, one runs the risk that those working on the data will use diverse partitioning schemes, rendering the comparison of results and findings almost impossible. It is thus strongly recommended that a default or suggested form of partitioning be provided at the time of release.

Because data evaluation should ideally be based on test partitions that have not been "seen" during model creation and system optimization, *development* partitions are needed in addition to *training* and *test partitions*. A solution for using as much data as possible for all partitions is cross-validation, where the overall corpus is partitioned into J sets of equal size. These should be stratified (i.e., each set should show the same distribution of instances among classes or in the continuum in the case of numeric labels). For multimodal data, stratification may also aim at a good balance of presence and diversity in each modality in each partition. The evaluation is repeated J times, changing the roles of the partitions. Further criteria for partitioning include independence of subjects, context, and so on. A particularly frequent example is leaving out a subject or subject group at a time. Next, one wishes to keep good balance of all factors throughout the partitions. Further, partitioning should ideally be transparent and easy to reproduce. Thus random partitioning can be considered as a somewhat suboptimal choice, as one must provide the instance list or random seed and random function in order to allow for others to reproduce the partitions.

Verifying Perception and Baseline Results

An independent perception test with individuals other than the annotators may provide useful insights into the reliability of the annotation. Often, only a partition of the data such as the test set is used in such experiments, albeit with a potentially higher number of participants. This independent perception evaluation is then often used to compare a system's performance.

Again, as with the original labeling, such a study may be conducted individually per modality or for modality combinations. In addition, crowdsourcing (see Chapter 30, this volume) may be appropriate. A positive trend is to further include machine-based baseline recognition results in a data release for the orientation of others working on the data. These could give "just a rough first impression" on how difficult the task is for a machine and should ideally include results for unimodal and (different combinations of) multimodal fusion.

Releasing

The release of the data usually first requires the design of an end-user license agreement. Then, obviously, the highest spread and usage of the data can usually be reached by making the data (almost) freely accessible. Ideally, the data will be accessible directly via the Internet, albeit restricted access must usually be guaranteed owing to the private nature of affect data. Another option is to release the data in the framework of a comparative or competitive evaluation campaign, such as the first two of their kind dealing with multimodal affect data—the Audio/Visual Emotion Challenges held in 2011 (Schuller et al., 2011a) and 2012 (Schuller et al., 2012a) (see also Chapter 18, this volume).

Quality Assessment—Is This Really Joyful?
Ground Truth Versus the "Gold Standard"

In affect computing, the "gold standard" is practically never reliable—that is, the training and testing labels themselves are ambiguous to a certain degree, as the emotion of a subject is usually difficult to assess, even in self-assessment (see Sneddon et al., 2012). Further, emotions are complex and often may not be mapped unambiguously to a single category or point in space (Schuller et al., 2010). The terms *ground truth* and *gold standard* are often used more or less synonymously in the literature; here, we want to define *ground truth* as the actual truth as measured "on the ground"—the term itself in fact originated in the fields of aerial photographs and satellite imagery—as compared with the gold standard that might ideally be identical to the ground truth; however, it might also be the (slightly) error-prone labeling as seen from the "sky above."

In interpreting results, one thus has to bear in mind that the reference is usually the gold standard and not necessarily the ground truth. This has a double impact: On one hand, trained models of computer systems that process affect data are error-prone. On the other hand, the test results have to be taken with a grain of salt, given that a "classification error" might not be so wrong in ambiguous cases. Thus, in order to achieve a reliable gold standard close to the ground truth, usually several annotators are used. This method also offers interesting implications for machine learning, as systems can be trained on individual annotator tracks in addition to an overall gold standard.

Measuring Reliability—From Alpha to Kappa

There are several commonly used measures to assess agreement among the labelers—the *interrater reliability*—in the usual case where not a single rater

but around 4 to 10 or more raters are involved. If the affect is modeled continuously, the (mean) correlation coefficient (CC) or (average) mean linear/absolute error (MLE, MAE), mean square error (MSE), and standard deviation among labelers are frequently used. If only one measure is to be considered, it may be the correlation, as it is usually more informative in the given case of a gold standard without a reliable reference point (Schuller et al., 2012a).

In the case of categorical modeling, a variety of measures can be employed for agreement evaluation, such as Krippendorff's alpha or Cohen's or Fleiss' kappa. As a continuum can be discretized, the latter statistics can also be used in this case—often with a linear or quadratic weighting. Pearson's intraclass correlation coefficient and Spearman's rank correlation coefficient rho are particularly suited for such ranked intervals—albeit only for two raters. Fleiss' Kappa K—a generalization of Scott's pi for more than two raters—is one of the most frequently encountered measures in the field. It requires all raters to rate all data. If labelers agree throughout, K equals 1. If they agree only on the same level as chance would, then K equals 0. Negative values indicate systematic disagreement. According to Landis and Koch (1977), values of .4 to .6 indicate moderate agreement, and values above are considered good to excellent agreement. However, these levels of reliability are difficult to achieve with affecte labeling given the often ambiguous and partially subjective nature of affect data.

Weighting Evaluators—I Don't Trust This Labeler

Further, if some labellers provide a rather different annotation than the majority do, labelers can be weighted individually in order to reach a more consistent gold standard. The justification is that some labelers may lack concentration if they have to label huge amounts of data or do not take labeling seriously at all times. This may become particularly relevant if naïve labelers in large number are involved, as by crowdsourcing via the Internet.

The evaluator-weighted estimator (EWE) as described by Grimm & Kroschel (2005) provides an elegant model to reach a rater-weighted gold standard. EWE's average of the individual evaluators' responses takes into account the fact that each evaluator is subject to an individual amount of disturbance during evaluation. The weights measure the correlation between the individual annotator's estimations and the average ratings of all evaluators.

If the weights are constant among raters, the gold standard is the simple mean of the raters' continuous labels.

An alternative can be to filter outliers; for example, by Peirce's outlier detection (Karadogan & Larsen, 2012). One can also imagine combinations of generally weighting raters and filtering or weighting individual labels.

Efficiency—How to Save Annotation Labor

Apart from the actual collection of data, the annotation usually consumes the most resources. In this section, five strategies that are recently gaining interest in the community are presented. These strategies are used to reduce costs and "feed" machines with partly self-labeled data, to reuse resources by pooling existing databases, or to avoid risking the loss of potentially interesting data by machine-based preselection of the "interesting bits."

Active Learning: "Help me, I'm a machine"

Active learning (Zhang & Schuller, 2012) aims at finding a needle in a haystack when massive amounts of data are available of which only a few items are of interest. In affect data, the haystack is usually the neutral data around the origin in a dimensional model, and the needle is usually "non-neutral" data, such as anger. Rather than having the human look over all recorded data, the machine tries to locate potential cases of interest and then asks the human for help or confirmation. As a supervised learning approach, active learning thus aims to minimize the amount of human supervision required in cases where one can afford to lose samples of emotional data; the goal thus is to identify the "most informative" samples in the unlabelled data—that is, those that we would gain most by if they were manually labeled—and then to present only these sample to human labelers. Several approaches have been investigated for selecting these most informative samples (Settles, 2010). A well-known method is *uncertainty-based* active learning, in which the active learner determines the certainties of the predictions on the unlabeled data based on posterior probabilities. The samples with least certainty are then generally presented to the labelers for annotation. Another common strategy is a *committee-based* method. Predictions for unlabeled data are made by multiple classifiers. The samples considered as most informative are those with the lowest agreement. Other methods include the *expected-error-reduction* method, which aims to measure how much the generalization error is likely to be reduced; the *expected-model-change*–based method, which chooses the instances that impact the current model the most; and the *diversity-density*–related method.

A major drawback of these methods is that they ignore the problem of class unbalance or the issue of scarcity of certain classes, as is mostly the case in affect data. Zhang and Schuller (2012) thus present a tailored sparse-instances–based strategy that selects the samples "likely to be" the fewest to be annotated manually from the candidate data in the pool.

In the case of multimodal data, different modalities may be used to search for different aspects of interest in the data. For example, physiological measurement may indicate moments of high arousal. Then, preferably at these moments, the human may be asked to annotate the data from an audiovisual point of view.

Semisupervised Learning: "Okay, I can label this!"

One step further is, after a supervised initialization, allowing the machine to label data by itself without further supervision—the so-called *semisupervised approach* (Zhang et al., 2011).

Assuming sufficiently robust automatic emotion recognition engines, unlabeled data can be classified and integrated into an iterative retraining process. Two parameters are then of primary interest: the *iteration number* indicating how often the unlabeled data are relabeled by the incremental addition of new data, and the *upsampling factor*, which can be used to weight the original human-labeled data more strongly than the later added machine-labeled data.

As a rule of thumb, roughly ten times the amount of unlabeled data are needed in comparison to labeled data in order to obtain the same gain as when human-labeled data are used exclusively. This makes it clear that this method is particularly suited ton cases where practically infinite amounts of data are available. An example can be the exploitation of audiovisual resources on the web, as on YouTube.

So far, initial studies in semisupervised learning for emotion recognition in speech show promising results (Mahdhaoui & Chetouani, 2009), and it will be interesting to see how far self-learning affect processing can take us for multimodal data. It seems worth mentioning that first successes are reported to entirely synthesize affect data for usage in recognition systems (Schuller et al., 2012b). This renders the labeling need completely obsolete. In multimodal tasks, this may be even more challenging, but with the increasing availability of multimodal affective agents, the possibility of using their synthesized affective behavior exists to train other systems.

Unsupervised Learning: "Trust me—I'm a machine"

Without any human-labeled data, *unsupervised learning* needs to find its own categorization, as by the EM algorithm, k-means, or other techniques (Wöllmer et al., 2009). Unsupervised learning may be of interest, as it omits the need to find an appropriate model. In most clustering approaches, however, the number of target clusters, (i.e., classes) needs to be given as input. This can be used as a design parameter to keep this number either low to aim at a rough yet robust categorization, or to keep it high in case of a need for a fine-grained model. In multimodal data, the clustering can first be carried out individually per modality to better take peculiarities into account, such as the previously mentioned higher correlation of acoustics with arousal and video feed with valence, and so on.

Generally speaking, fully unsupervised learning can be particularly useful in autonomous systems that need to recognize and synthesize affect—they use automatically learned emotional clusters in analysis and the appropriate counterpart for synthesis. It must be ensured, however, that the derived clusters are not too strongly influenced by other factors, such as the gender of the recorded subjects or similar differences. If such an influence gains too strong an effect, the data may first be separated according to these factors.

If human feedback or system context can be exploited during runtime, learning can further be *reinforced* (Hyung-il Ahn, 2010). This may lead to genuine online "lifelong learning" of affective systems that recognize and react to affect and, from the reaction of their users and the environment, improve their future processing abilities. Such systems can then collect data themselves "in the wild." This may become particularly challenging if the *emotional* reaction itself is used as contextual knowledge.

Shared Learning: "Together we're best"

In fact, active learning and semisupervised learning attack the same problem from opposite directions (Settles, 2010): Semisupervised learning exploits the learner's assumptions on the unlabeled data; active learning aims to explore the unknown aspects of the data. This lets one strive to combine the two strategies. Figuratively speaking, it means shared work between the (pretrained) machine and the human during annotation, with the machine having the lead: It labels data by itself if it is confident that it can label correctly. From the remaining unlabeled data, it decides which cases appear to be interesting and should be labeled by humans while disregarding the rest. Again, this may benefit from modality-specific analysis, so that the machine prefers some modalities such as audio and video for human feedback but will be more "aggressive" in labeling other modalities by itself (e.g., when it is labeling physiological data). Further, the machine could ask for human help if it came to different conclusions in looking at different modalities.

Pooling Data: "Let's save the environment"

The reusage of existing labeled data seems to be straightforward in general. However, in the field of affective computing, this is less obvious, as data often come labeled in different models, as in categories or dimensions or chunked in different units of time. Therefore to obtain a larger pool of labeled data by reusing and uniting existing material, a mapping scheme may be needed. The dimensional model offers an elegant solution in this case, as categories can be mapped onto coordinates and corpora with different label sets can thus be united based on the dimensional model. However, this mapping step has to be carried out by experts (Schuller et al., 2011b) or optimized (e.g., by machine learning strategies). In addition, algorithms can then select and weight instances. For example, the joyful data of a particular database may fit less well than the angry data of the same set. Further, some databases may be better suited for a certain target domain, but further data still enriches the pool. In such a case, these instances may be weighted (e.g., by repeated upsampling). It seems particularly interesting to find measures to compare corpus and emotion data similarity a priori—that is, without the need for computationally expensive repeated model training (Brendel et al., 2010).

As for temporal unification, usually the larger unit of time (e.g., word or turn in speech analysis) needs to be taken as basis, since emotion may only be *quasistationary* or not at all stationary along the larger unit; think, for example, of a phrase like *"Thursdays are quite ok, but I hate Mondays!"* The overall phrase may be labeled with negative valence, whereas the first frames are probably not negative

(Batliner et al., 2010). For example, the average over frames can be used to map this shorter unit of annotation onto a longer one, such as the named words or turns.

Existing Multimodal Resources—What's There?

Luckily, a large number of multimodal resources of affect data currently exist. However, only a selection of representative corpora can be presented in this chapter. One can also expect further corpora to be available in the near future.

Exemplary Audiovisual Resources

In the following, some characteristic resources are introduced, of which some are immediately available for download; others may be per request.

Some of the first multimodal databases were of bimodal nature. Most prominent in this group are audiovisual databases, which to the present day form by far the lion's share of multimodal affect databases. As these feature speech, some tend to describe them as more than bimodal, given that acoustic and textual cues can be interpreted with different means. However, in the strict sense of modality, these can be subsumed. In a similar fashion, some consider partly contained motion capture information from video as an additional modality, which can, however, be subsumed under the video modality.

An example of single-person noninteractive data is the freely accessible eNTERFACE corpus (Martin et al., 2006). This corpus targets the Ekman "big six" basic emotions by short story–based induction for around 40 subjects. The stories are basically short texts that are read by the subjects before enacting given target phrases that fit the context of these short texts.

Next, the "mind reading" corpus by Baron-Cohen and Tead (2003) features an extremely high diversity of more than 400 emotional nuances performed by six professional actors.

A particularly early example of human-technology recordings is the SMARTKOM database of Wizard of Oz–type human-machine interactions with an information service in public, home, or mobile environment, including affect annotation. The users are interacting with information services in rather natural ways—the functionality was simulated by human operators. The database features a categorical annotation in nine categories and 224 subjects (Schiel, Steininger, & Türk, 2002).

The freely available SEMAINE database (McKeown, 2012) deals with high-quality audiovisual recordings of 150 participants. In these recordings, humans interact with four different versions of a sensitive artificial listener agent. It includes 959 conversations (approximately 5 minutes each). Six to eight raters labeled the data in five dimensions. A subset of these data was used in the two Audio/Visual Emotion Challenges (Schuller et al, 2012).

Aiming at more naturalistic data, the EmoTV corpus (Abrilian et al., 2005) exploits film clips. Another example of the emerging trend to record multiple-subject dyadic interactions, rather than human-computer or human-technology interaction, is The TUM Audio Visual Interest Corpus (TUM AVIC) (Schuller et al., 2007). It features audiovisual recordings of conversations between a product presenter and 21 participating subjects. Transcriptions including nonverbal outbursts are available as metainformation, and this data set provides a one-dimensional labeling by averaging over four labelers. Its audio track was featured in the INTERSPEECH 2010 Paralinguistic Challenge's Affect Sub-Challenge.

Further, the IEMOCAP database (Busso et al., 2008) contains 12 hours of acted multimodal recordings of multiple subjects. Besides video and speech, text transcriptions and facial motion capture are provided. In the dyadic sessions, actors perform improvisations or scripted scenarios. These were selected to elicit emotional expressions. The database is annotated by multiple annotators and contains categorical labels, such as anger, happiness, sadness, neutrality, and continuous emotion primitives including valence, activation, and dominance.

A more recent example of dyadic interaction is the UCS CreativeIT database. Its purpose is to study affective communication and interaction between humans (Metallinou et al., 2010). The data contained are based on improvisation of pairs of theater actors. These were recorded with cameras; motion capture markers were placed over their full bodies, and close-talking microphones were worn by the actors to capture their speech. The rather long, unsegmented recordings last from 2 to 8 minutes. The annotation was carried out fully continuously in value and time for the dimensions of activation, valence, and dominance.

Finally, a multimodal database particularly designed for mimicry analysis has been introduced by Sun et al. (2011). Eighteen synchronized audio and video sensors were used in the recording setup and two dyadic interaction settings were given.

In these, participants engaged in a discussion on a political topic as well as in a role-playing game. Overall, the database contains 54 recordings from 40 participants and 3 confederates. Metadata such as dialogue acts or turn taking are released together with the recordings.

Exemplary Resources Containing EEG and Physiological Data

More recently, increasingly multimodal data with additional multiple modalities have appeared. Three examples to illustrate the available resources are discussed here.

The QMUL-UT EEG dataset features multimodal affect data of 17 subjects, including EEG and physiological signals such as electrooculography (EOG), galvanic skin response (GSR), heart rate, respiration, and temperature. The subjects were watching seven video sequences for each of seven categories depicting events, followed by either a matching or a nonmatching emotion label (Koelstra, Muehl & Patras, 2009).

The freely available database for emotion analysis using physiological signals (DEAP) (Koelstra et al., 2012) contains spontaneous physiological signal recordings and face videos (not for all participants) of 32 participants watching and rating online their emotional response to 40 music videos along the scales of arousal, dominance, and valence as well as ratings of how much they liked and were familiar with the videos. The authors also provide classification results using various features (from the EEG, peripheral physiological signals, and other modalities) and combinations of features, also performing single-trial (single-participant) classification (for the scales of arousal, valence, and liking). They report that modalities appear to perform in a moderately complementary fashion, where EEG performs best for arousal and peripheral physiological signals for valence.

Next, Ringeval et al. (2013) collected the freely available French RECOLA multimodal corpus of remote collaborative and affective interactions. Its 46 subjects were recorded in dyads during a video conference for collaborative task completion. Modalities comprised audio, video, electrocardiogram (ECG), and electrodermal activity(EDA). Six annotators rated continuous arousal and valence, as well as social behavior labels on five dimensions. Further, self-report measures are included.

Finally, the freely accessible multimodal affect database for affect recognition and implicit tagging (MAHNOB-HCI) (Soleymani et al., 2012) is a collection of various modalities recorded in a synchronized manner. The recorded cues include six camera views of the face and head, sound from both a head-worn microphone and one located in the room, eye gaze, pupil size, and peripheral/central nervous system physiological signals: ECG, EEG, GSR, respiration amplitude, and skin temperature. The authors also provide baseline emotion recognition using three modalities and implicit labeling results for two modalities. The 30 participating subjects watched 20 emotional videos and subsequently self-reported their felt emotions. They also judged videos or images with or without correct or incorrect emotion labels.

As indicated above, with the increasing availability of wireless sensors, more databases with data from outside the lab and with physiological information can be expected to be available in the near future.

Conclusions and Future Avenues—Wrapping Up

The above discussion shows that multimodal affect data are increasingly available. However, more data recorded in real-life situations (Lucey et al., 2011) outside of the lab will be needed and will likely be seen soon. Ideally these will also feature a higher diversity of participants, labeling, contained cultural aspects, languages, and situational context. Luckily, machine intelligence can help to reduce human labor costs during the annotation of data by active learning, identifying the interesting data instances for annotation in large unlabeled collections, or by weakly supervised learning, having the machine label when it is sufficiently confident it "can do the job."

Future initiatives could help foster combined community efforts for merging and common labeling of resources and could also make such desperately needed larger amounts of resources accessible with prepartitioning, human perception results, baselines, and rich metainformation.

References

Abrilian, S., Devillers, L., Buisine, S., & Martin, J. (2005). EmoTV1: Annotation of real-life emotions for the specification of multimodal affective interfaces. In *Proceedings International Conference on Human-Computer Interaction.*, Las Vegas, NV. Hillsdale, NJ: Lawrence Erlbaum Associates, Inc.

Ahn, H. (2010). *Modeling and analysis of affective influences on human experience, prediction, decision making, and behavior.* PhD thesis. Cambridge, MA: Massachusetts Institute of Technology.

Baron-Cohen, S. & Tead, T. (2003). *Mind reading: The interactive guide to emotion.* London: Jessica Kingsley.

Batliner, A., Seppi, D., Steidl, S., & Schuller, B. (2010). Segmenting into adequate units for automatic recognition of emotion-related episodes: A speech-based approach. In *Advances in human computer interaction, special issue on emotion-aware natural interaction*, Article ID 782802. Hindawi.

Brendel, M., Zaccarelli, R., Schuller, B., & Devillers, L. (2010). Towards measuring similarity between emotional corpora. In *Proceedings LREC 2010* (pp. 58–64). Valletta, Malta: ELRA.

Busso, C., Bulut, M., Lee, C.-C., Kazemzadeh, A., Mower, E., Kim, S.,…Narayanan, S. S. (2008). IEMOCAP: Interactive emotional dyadic motion capture database, *Journal of Language Resources and Evaluation, 42* (4), 335–359.

Grimm, M., & Kroschel, K. (2005). Evaluation of natural emotions using self assessment manikins. In *Proceedings of the ASRU 2005* (pp. 381–385). Cancun, Mexico: IEEE.

Gunes, H., Piccardi, M., & Pantic, M. (2008). From the Lab to the real world: Affect recognition using multiple cues and modalities. In *Affective computing: Focus on emotion expression, synthesis, and recognition.*, (pp. 185–218). Vienna, Austria: Tech Education and Publishing.

Gunes, H., & Schuller, B. (2012). Categorical and dimensional affect analysis in continuous input: Current trends and future directions. *Image and Vision Computing, 31* (2), 120–136.

Karadogan, S., & Larsen, J. (2012). Combining semantics and acoustic features for valence and arousal recognition of speech. In *Proceedings of the 3rd International Workshop on Cognitive Information Processing.*, Parador de Baiona, Spain. IEEE.

Koelstra, S., Mühl, C., & Patras, I. (2009). EEG analysis for implicit tagging of video data. In *Proceedings ACII, Affective Brain-Computer Interfaces Workshop* (pp. 27–32), Amsterdam, The Netherlands.

Koelstra, S., Mühl, C., Soleymani, M., Yazdani, A., Lee, J.-S., Ebrahimi, T.,…Patras, I. (2012). DEAP: A database for emotion analysis using physiological signals. *IEEE Transactions on Affective Computing, 3* (1), 18–31.

Labov, W. (1984). Field methods of the project in linguistic change and variation. In *Language in use* (pp. 28–53). Englewood Cliffs, NJ: Prentice-Hall.

Landis, J., & Koch, G. (1977). The measurement of observer agreement for categorical data. *Biometrics, 33*, 159–174.

Lucey, P., Cohn, J. F., Prkachin, K. M., Solomon, P. E., & Matthews, I. (2011). Painful data: The UNBC-McMaster shoulder pain expression archive database. In *Proceedings IEEE International Conference on Automatic Face and Gesture Recognition* (pp. 57–64), Santa Barbara, CA.

Mahdhaoui, A., & Chetouani, M. (2009). A new approach for motherese detection using a semi-supervised algorithm. In *Proceedings IEEE International Workshop on Machine Learning for Signal Processing.* IEEE, pp. 1–6.

Martin, O., Kotsia, I., Macq, B., & Pitas, I. (2006). The enterface'05 audiovisual emotion database. In *Proceedings International Conference on Data Engineering* (pp. 1–8)., Atlanta, GA. IEEE

McKeown, G., Valstar, M., Cowie, R., Pantic, M., & Schroeder, M. (2012). The SEMAINE database: Annotated multimodal records of emotionally coloured conversations between a person and a limited agent. *IEEE Transactions on Affective Computing, 3* (1), 5–17.

Metallinou, A., Lee, C.-C., Busso, C., Carnicke, S., & Narayanan, S. (2010). The USC CreativeIT database: A multimodal database of theatrical improvisation. In *Proceedings LREC Workshop on Multimodal Corpora.*: ELRA.

Ragin, C. C., & Amoroso, L. M. (2011). The ethics of social research. In *Constructing social research*, 2nd ed. (pp. 59–89). Thousand Oaks, CA: Sage.

Rammstedt, B., & John, O. P. (2007). Measuring personality in one minute or less: A 10-item short version of the Big Five Inventory in English and German. *Journal of Research in Personality, 41*, 203–212.

Ringeval, F., Sonderegger, A., Sauer, J., & Lalanne, D. (2013). Introducing the RECOLA multimodal corpus of remote collaborative and affective interactions. In *Proceedings 2nd International Workshop on Emotion Representation, Analysis and Synthesis in Continuous Time and Space (EmoSPACE).* IEEE Face & Gestures 2013, Shanghai, China).

Schiel, F., Steininger, S., & Türk U. (2002). The SmartKom Multimodal Corpus at BAS. In *Proceedings LREC 2002* (pp. 200–206), Las Palmas, Gran Canaria, Spain, ELRA.

Schröder, M., Devillers, L., Karpouzis, K., Martin, J.-C., Pelachaud, C., Peter, C.,…Wilson, I. (2007). What should a generic emotion markup language be able to represent? In *Proceedings ACII 2007* (pp. 440–451). Berlin and Heidelberg: Springer.

Schröder, M., Pirker, H., & Lamolle, M. (2006). First suggestions for an emotion annotation and representation language. In *Proceedings LREC 2006 Workshop on Emotion: Corpora for Research on Emotion and Affect*, Genoa, Italy. ELRA.

Schuller, B., Douglas-Cowie, E., & Batliner, A (2012). Guest editorial: Special section on naturalistic affect resources for system building and evaluation. *IEEE Transactions on Affective Computing, 3* (1), 3–4.

Schuller, B., Müller, R., Hörnler, B., Höthker, A., Konosu, H., & Rigoll, G. (2007). Audiovisual recognition of spontaneous interest within conversations. In *Proceedings of the ICMI 2007* (pp. 30–37), Nagoya, Japan. ACM, ACM.

Schuller, B., Valstar, M., Cowie, R., & Pantic, M. (2012a). AVEC 2012—The continuous audio/visual emotion challenge. In *Proceedings of the ICMI 2012.*, Santa Monica, CA. ACM, ACM.

Schuller, B., Valstar, M., Eyben, F., McKeown, G., Cowie, R., & Pantic, M. (2011a). AVEC 2011—The first international audio/visual emotion challenge. In *Proceedings ACII 2011* (Vol. II, pp. 415–424)., Memphis, TN. Berlin, Heidelberg NY: Springer

Schuller, B., Zaccarelli, R., Rollet, N., & Devillers, L. (2010). CINEMO—A French spoken language resource for complex emotions: Facts and baselines. In *Proceedings of the LREC 2010* (pp. 1643–1647). Valletta, Malta. ELRA.

Schuller, B., Zhang, Z., Weninger, F., & Burkhardt, F. (2012b). synthesized speech for model training in cross-corpus recognition of human emotion. *International Journal of Speech Technology, 15* (3), 32–41.

Schuller, B., Zhang, Z., Weninger, F., & Rigoll, G. (2011b). Using multiple databases for training in emotion recognition: To unite or to vote? In: *Proceedings of INTERSPEECH 2011* (pp. 1553–1556)., Florence, Italy. ISCA.

Settles, B. (2010). Active learning literature survey. In *Computer sciences technical report 1648*. Madison: University of Wisconsin-Madison.

Sneddon, I., McRorie, M., McKeown, G., & Hanratty, J. (2012). The Belfast induced natural emotion database. *IEEE Transactions on Affective Computing, 3* (1), 32–41.

Soleymani, M., Lichtenauer, J., Pun, T., & Pantic, M. (2012). A multimodal database for affect recognition and implicit tagging. *IEEE Transactions on Affective Computing, 3* (1), 42–55.

Sun, X., Lichtenauer, J., Valstar, M., Nijholt, A., & Pantic, M. (2011). A multimodal database for mimicry analysis. In *Proceedings ACII* (pp. 367–376)., Memphis, TN. Berlin, Heidelberg, NY: Springer.

Vinciarelli, A., Dielmann, A., Favre, S., & Salamin, H. (2009). Canal9: A Database of Political Debates for Analysis of Social Interactions. In: *Proceedings ACII*, Amsterdam, The Netherlands, IEEE/Humaine Association.

Wöllmer, M., Eyben, F., Schuller, B., Douglas-Cowie, E., & Cowie, R. (2009). Data-driven clustering in emotional space for affect recognition using discriminatively trained LSTM networks. In *Proceedings INTERSPEECH 2009* (pp. 1595–1598). Brighton, UK. ISCA, ISCA.

Zhang, Z., Weninger, F., Wollmer, M., & Schuller, B. (2011). Unsupervised Learning in cross-corpus acoustic emotion recognition. In *Proceedings of the ASRU 2011* (pp. 523–528). Big Island, HY. IEEE.

Zhang, Z., & Schuller, B. (2012). Active learning by sparse instance tracking and classifier confidence in acoustic emotion recognition. In *Proceedings INTERSPEECH 2012*, Portland, OR. ISCA, ISCA.

Ethical Issues in Affective Computing

Roddy Cowie

Abstract

Affective computing is bound up with ethics at multiple levels, from codes governing studies with human participants to debates about the proper relationship between ethical and emotional systems within an agent. Behind the debates lie ethical principles that are powerful but divergent. In some areas (e.g., data protection and research with human participants), explicit codes provide legal force. Elsewhere, they give rise to characteristic imperatives: to increase net positive affect, to avoid deception, to respect autonomy, to ensure that system's competence is understood, and to provide morally acceptable portraits of people. There are also widely discussed concerns with less clear connections either to moral philosophy or to the real abilities of the technology, but they still need to be addressed.

Key Words: emotion, affective computing, ethics, ethical codes, moral philosophy

Introduction

People who work in affective computing tend to have trained in disciplines allied to engineering and mathematics. Training in those areas is unlikely to have included courses on ethics. As a result, it can come as a shock to discover that ethical issues are very much part of the discipline that they have come into, and at several levels, not just one. At the most specific, when they collect data from human participants, they need to arrange an acceptable form of ethical approval. At the most general, they may find themselves pressed to answer high-profile claims that the whole enterprise of affective computing is ethically tainted. Particular applications, from artificial companions for the elderly to sex robots, pose various individual difficulties.

The aim of this chapter is to give people a grounding that lets them engage with that range of challenges in a rational way. There is no simple way to do that. The approach that the chapter takes is to provide some general conceptual background to

begin with and then to look at topics with a specific bearing on affective computing. Broadly speaking, it begins with the topics where the ethical concerns are most clearly defined and works toward those where the issues are hardest to articulate precisely. Particularly in the last group, the arguments are often about what people imagine a computer with emotions or emotion-related skills might be like rather than anything that can be built or realistically envisaged. This does not mean that those arguments can be ignored. In fact, they may be the most important for the future of the discipline.

People working in affective computing may well feel that the coverage overemphasizes particular parts of the discipline. That is essentially because a handbook chapter has to reflect the balance of the relevant literature. The literature says more about production than perception—at least partly because ethical theory has traditionally focused on evaluating actions, so its obvious application is to the actions that a system might take. However, the chapter does what it can to engage with less traditional issues that are important to the discipline, such as the way it portrays human beings.

Formal and Informal Foundations of Ethics

The discipline that discusses the foundations of ethics has traditionally been called moral philosophy. There is no universal agreement on the use of the terms *ethics* and *morality*, but it is reasonable to adopt the convention that morality includes ethics. In that sense, calling a judgment ethical implies that it is moral, but it also implies that it is grounded in reason rather than just a gut feeling for or against.

Nevertheless, the gut matters in ethics, and it is important for affective computing that it does. What we would call emotion was identified as the root of moral judgment by thinkers with a huge influence on the modern era, notably David Hume (1740) and Adam Smith (1759). For them, doing wrong is ultimately about producing situations that are unacceptable to our "moral sentiments." Later thinkers, notably Jeremy Bentham and John Stuart Mill, developed a very well known form of the idea: the "utilitarian" principle that our fundamental moral duty is to bring the greatest happiness to the greatest number (Driver, 2012). Whether or not one agrees with the arguments, they reflect a deep-seated intuition that emotion is at the core of what makes us moral beings. For that reason alone, nobody should be surprised that ethics cannot be kept out of affective computing.

Emotion-based theories contrast with two classical alternatives. One is associated with Kant (Wood, 1999). He argued that the bedrock of morality was exercising free will in accordance with intellectual principles rather than feelings. Specifically, we should act in accordance with principles that we could will all rational agents to follow. For those who accept that idea, affective computing has profound moral significance, because it raises the prospect of creating things that mimic human free will or impinge on it.

The last major alternative, famously advocated by Thomas Hobbes (1651), is that moral codes are contracts established for the purpose of maintaining a society that satisfies our basic desires. For Hobbes himself, the contract can and should be imposed by a strong authority. For others, it should emerge from shared values (Scanlon, 1998). People who set rules are quite likely to assume that Hobbes was broadly right.

These approaches are particularly important for affective computing, but many others are comparably important from a purely philosophical perspective. Examples include the revival of virtue ethics (MacIntyre, 1985), the argument that moral claims are simply errors (Mackie, 1977), sophisticated attempts to reconcile the major positions (Parfitt, 2011), and much more. The details are fascinating but probably not mandatory reading for people in affective computing.

Attempts to ground ethics in fundamental principles have two features that are important and troublesome for affective computing. First, many people regard one or more of the principles as self-evident and overwhelmingly important. For example, the concept of autonomous beings with free will seems self-evident, intellectually profound, and effectively sacrosanct to a great many people. Second, focusing on principles leads to disputes that no amount of rational argument will resolve, because what one party takes as a self-evident starting point seems opaque and counterintuitive to the other. Part of a sophisticated ethical stance is understanding that those difficulties are bound to arise when we try to argue from first principles.

Because that problem is well known, philosophers who work in practical ethics have developed systems that are closer to common sense and more likely to promote consensus. The approach was pioneered by W. D. Ross (1939). He aimed to identify a few basic principles that speak for or against a course of action. The best-known list consisted of *fidelity* (a duty to keep our promises); *reparation* (a duty to right a wrong we have done); *gratitude* (a duty to benefit those from whom we have accepted benefits); *nonmaleficence* (a duty not to harm others); and a duty to maximize the aggregate of good. Perhaps the most eminent philosopher to have written about ethics and affective computing, Peter Goldie (Döring, et al., 2011), directed the field to principlism, a related approach proposed by Beauchamp and Childress (2001). Their list includes Ross's last two items, nonmaleficence and benificence. The other items have a more Kantian flavor: they are autonomy (i.e., to promote rather than restrict people's ability to exercise free will) and equity (that is, not to treat people differently for no good reason).

An older, and even more compact summary is the Golden Rule: "Do as you would be done by." There are well-known problems with this (Blackburn, 2001)—it is famously not a good prescription for judges or masochists, and perhaps people who love programming should be added to the list. But there is a widespread sense that it is essentially sound, and it has been explicitly applied in fields allied to affective computing (Berdichevsky & Neuenschwander, 1999).

On the other hand, various documents called codes of ethics are essentially Hobbesian statements of what people in authority require of people under their authority. They often reflect views with very broad support, but sometimes they take highly contentious positions. For example, the British Engineering and Physical Research Council drew up "ethical rules for robotics."[1] These seem to stipulate that however closely robots' intelligence and emotions might approximate ours, the fact that they are manufactured requires them to be regarded as tools and perhaps to display bar codes declaring their status. To many, that seems quite the opposite of ethical.

The key point here is that following the dictates of one's own conscience and reason will not necessarily mean staying on the right side of the ethical codes that authorities establish. The two can and do diverge. Usually conforming is harmless. Deciding what to do when it seems genuinely wrong to conform is a notoriously difficult problem.

Public opinion raises similar issues. Quite possibly the biggest threat to affective computing is that the public may come to feel that it is ethically unacceptable. Nobody should doubt the importance of finding ways to counter the unease and certainly to avoid heightening it. The concerns to be countered, though, often seem to involve moral principles that are not traditionally central to moral philosophy.

The most obvious of the principles is that certain kinds of unnaturalness are bad. Since civilisation is based on unnaturalness, the concern obviously has to do with specific kinds of unnaturalness rather than unnaturalness in general. It may have to do with the way we think about things that are living or that behave at some level as if they were living; that would fit a line of argument developed by Foot (2001), which suggests that we have particularly strong intuitions about the way living things should or should not be. Be that as it may, there is clearly a widespread feeling that a computer which seems to have emotions is unnatural in a morally disturbing way.

A second principle is that there are parts of existence where it is morally wrong to venture. However people may rationalize it, the feeling is clearly akin to a religious one: The ground is sacrosanct, and treading there is sacrilege. We may or may not agree that emotion is an inner sanctum of humanity, but clearly a feeling of that kind comes into play when people judge how ethical or unethical the enterprise of affective computing is. Finding an effective answer to that reaction depends on understanding it.

A third principle, less deep but still to be reckoned with, is that certain kinds of frivolity are bad. Technology in particular should be concerned with real problems, like storing more information or solving problems faster. Making the user feel better is not a fitting use for technical skills and resources. The obvious name for that stance is *puritan*. The obvious response to it is probably that people are entitled to follow that principle in their own lives but not to impose it on others.

There are also values that academics are particularly likely to regard as having ethical force. The outstanding example is open access to information. That is reflected not only in attitudes to publication but also in the issue of open-source software. Both raise real conflicts with other parts of society.

It is entirely natural to wish that the research area were not beset with so many kinds of moral and ethical judgment, sophisticated or naïve. But since the issues are there, it is better to see them clearly than to stumble through them in the dark.

Formal Codes for Affective Computing
Ethics and Human Participants

The area where ethical guidelines are most formalized is human participation in research. This affects various roles that human participants play, such as providing material for databases, labeling it, and evaluating systems. Most of the activities are obviously harmless, but the fact that they are harmless still needs to be verified, and failure to do that can be disastrous. To complicate matters, the requirements vary with country, institution, and application. A chapter like this cannot cover all of the variants; the only safe rule is to check local regulations thoroughly before beginning research with human participants.

Concern about experiments with humans is enshrined in binding international agreements. For instance, the Charter of Fundamental Rights of the European Union[2] stipulates in Article 3 that the principle of free and informed consent must be respected. Strictly, it refers to medical and biological research, but *biological* is routinely understood in a broad sense. For research that is classified as medical, there is a worldwide convention, the Declaration of Helsinki.[3] For nonmedical research, the most highly developed codes are those that deal with psychological research. They have been used to govern experiments in affective computing (Sneddon et al., 2011), and it is useful to give more detail about one.

The American Psychological Association (APA) code of ethics[4] begins by setting out principles based broadly on Ross, Beauchamp, and Childress. They are followed up with detailed prescriptions for various aspects of the research process:

- Institutional approval
- Informed consent to research
- Informed consent for recording voices and images in research
- Client/patient, student, and subordinate research participants
- Dispensing with informed consent for research
- Offering inducements for research participation
- Deception in research
- Debriefing

The discussion of some of these issues is quite extensive, and it provides a useful starting point for anyone proposing to work with human participants.

Some systems are more restrictive than the APA code. For example, some ask for proof that the research will add to knowledge (if not, it should not be done). Medical protocols tend to be particularly exacting because they are designed to deal with areas where both risks and rewards are very high. It is always worth checking whether that level of scrutiny is needed.

In general, approval is obtained by completing a form that sets out issues to be considered and requires appropriate declarations on each. It is submitted to a research ethics committee. Specifications for the membership of the committee vary from place to place, but it is generally required to include "lay members," meaning (roughly) that they have no professional connection with the research area. Specialized knowledge about ethics is rarely expected.

From an institution's point of view, the research committee has a dual function: to prevent harm and to provide indemnity if harm is caused. Indemnity depends on agreement with the institution's insurers. Any group can constitute committees that carry out the first function, but they should be clear that the second is a different matter: if the experimenters are sued, the committee may simply end up sharing the bill.

Technological Codes

Information technology has general professional codes analogous to the APA code above. A good example is provided by the Association for Computing Machinery (ACM).[5] Like the APA code, it begins with relatively ethical standard principles, but it emphasizes specific issues of particular concern to information technology. The most salient of those is privacy of data. It states:

> Computing and communication technology enables the collection and exchange of personal information on a scale unprecedented in the history of civilization. Thus there is increased potential for violating the privacy of individuals and groups. It is the responsibility of professionals to maintain the privacy and integrity of data describing individuals.

Like the rights of participants, the status of personal data is an internationally recognised issue. Article 8 of the EU Charter of Fundamental Rights states that "Everyone has the right to the protection of personal data concerning him or her," and there is an ongoing process of articulating the implications of the principle. The results include legislation with strong implications for both the creation and the use of databases.[6] Data that individuate a person—which includes a great deal of material in affective databases—can be collected only "for specified, explicit and legitimate purposes," and must not be "further processed in a way incompatible with those purposes." It would seem that in a scientific context, the data may not be processed at all unless the subject of the data has unambiguously given his consent. There are very severe restrictions on the use of data revealing racial or ethnic origin, which both speech and photographs are likely to do.

These provisions are not static. For example, a recent EU report on Ethics of Information and Communication Technologies[7] describes strengthened legislation on data protection, including a reinforced "right to be forgotten" (people will be able to delete their data if there are no legitimate reasons for retaining it); and a requirement that consent for data to be processed will always have to be given explicitly rather than assumed. It also explicitly recognizes a range of other issues, including protection against cybercrime, restricting access for minors, and ensuring equality of access for groups who might be excluded. Some of these represent problems to be borne in mind, others quite possibly opportunities—for instance, removing affective barriers to computing may make a significant contribution to access (Cowie, 2012).

Although most of the report deals with well-trodden issues like confidentiality of data and equality of access, it picks out, largely in passing, a few concerns with more specific implications for affective computing—that the line between encountering reality and artificial surrogates may become blurred, and that vulnerable people may form undesirable attachments to artificial carers. The result is to bring those issues into a gray area between speculative discussion and binding codes. It means that, at the very least, they are unsafe to ignore.

A different technological perspective is reflected in a position paper mentioned earlier, produced by the UK Research Council for Engineering and Physical Science (EPSRC).[8] It is meant to govern research on robotics, but if one accepts the principles, it would be hard to doubt that they should apply to virtual agents as well as robots. Five main principles are proposed:

1. Robots should not be designed as weapons, except for national security reasons.

2. Robots should be designed and operated to comply with existing law, including privacy.

3. Robots are products: as with other products, they should be designed to be safe and secure.

4. Robots are manufactured artefacts: the illusion of emotions and intent should not be used to exploit vulnerable users.

5. It should be possible to find out who is responsible for any robot.

These principles have obvious links to Asimov's (1950) Laws of Robotics". Like Asimov, the authors are concerned with the risk of robots doing harm to humans, and they propose prohibiting it, even as a way of protecting valuable property (the robots themselves) from theft or vandalism; that is what lies behind point (3). Unlike Asimov, they oppose any blurring of the line between humans, who are responsible agents, and artefacts, however sophisticated. That makes "the illusion of emotions" a subject of concern. Because of their concern about potential dangers, they also question what should be available as open code.

The EPSRC paper is in an interesting category. It is not binding, but it gives an official status to concerns that are widely held and means that arguments to the contrary have to be carefully thought through. It also signals a point whose importance is hard to overstate. Formal codification is an ongoing process, and ignoring issues that have not yet been codified is a risky strategy.

Ethical Themes for Affective Computing

After the areas where there are quasilegal codes, there are several well-established ethical themes with direct connections to affective computing. This section picks out five. They are not wholly independent. That is not carelessness—the fact that ethical principles do overlap is well known and helps to make practical decision making simpler than one might fear.

Benificence

This section is about a point that is both simple and fundamental to any balanced discussion. Affective computing is a technology with unusually direct links to morally positive goals. Its most obvious function is to make technology better able to furnish people with positive experiences and/or less likely to impose negative ones. Thus it has a direct relationship to what one major ethical tradition, utilitarianism, regards as the fundamental moral imperative: maximizing net happiness. That general point is reflected in many specific efforts with morally positive goals. For examples, see Cowie (2012).

Once that is recognized, it is natural to separate two different types of objection to affective computing. On one side are concerns about unintended damage that might outweigh intended gains in net happiness—for instance, concerns about unintended effects on people involved in the research, or what the systems might do in the wrong hands. It is possible to engage with those. A different kind of difficulty arises when objectors deny that a shift toward positive affect has any moral value at all. In effect, they rule the natural positive out of court; what is left is very likely to appear negative. For example, it is hardly surprising if people who start from a Kantian emphasis on autonomy and rationality see many risks and few gains. Less obviously, the same is true of those who argue that the happiness we should maximize is not positive affect (*hedonia*) but a subtler sense that our life is worthwhile (*eudaimonia*) (e.g., Ryan, Huta, & Deci, 2008).

"Positive psychology," which also values positive affect, encounters similar problems (Csikszentmihalyi & Csikszentmihalyi, 2006). Both have to reckon with people who see no moral value in shifting the balance between positive and negative affect. There are more serious things that should be occupying us. Logic cannot compel people to change that stance. However, if it is the basis on which they judge, they should be pressed to be clear about it, because by no means everyone agrees.

Two final implications should be drawn out. First, one of the obvious roles of affective computing is remedial. It is to spare people distress that would otherwise be caused by interactions with affectively incompetent systems (Cowie, 2012; Scheutz, 2012). Second, if we believe that affective computing can increase the net happiness of humanity, our ethical duty would include countering misguided fears that might prevent that—and, of course, ensuring that we do not inflame the fears.

Deception

Deception is widely recognized as a key problem area (Bringsjord & Clark, 2012; Coeckelbergh, 2012; Cowie, 2012). It is not explicitly noted as an issue in most of the codes routinely invoked in ethics, but the implication that it is can be derived from the main codes. In terms of Ross's principles, it violates the duty of fidelity (to keep our promises). In terms of principlism, it infringes autonomy, because misinforming a person about the alternatives that are open prevents him or her from choosing rationally between them. The Golden Rule will appear shortly.

There are various more technical discussions of computing and deceptionIt is recognized as an issue in the ACM guidelines. The literature on persuasion includes well-known guidelines (Berdichevsky & Neuenschwander, 1999). There is also a more recent, high-profile literature on specifically emotional misdirection, usually in the context of artificial companions and carers. The sources take quite different approaches, reflecting deeper divisions in the ways that deception might come about.

It is useful to begin with the most general charge. It is said that the whole enterprise of affective computing is deceptive and cannot avoid being deceptive; therefore the whole enterprise is unethical. According to that argument, core parts of it rest on giving the impression that systems feel emotions when, in reality, they have no feelings of any sort (Coeckelbergh, 2012; Sparrow, 2002).

That kind of claim strays into questionable territory. It assumes that people normally treat emotion-related signals as declarations that some internal feeling state exists. That seems unlikely. Certainly people do not usually regard it as dishonest to give signs of a positive feeling that does not exist ("whistling in the dark"). Nor do they deplore artefacts that display signs of emotions which they do not have—paintings, movie images, dolls, and so on. Animals show signs that people are highly disposed to read as signaling emotion, but very few people are deeply concerned by the question of what feeling state, if any, goes with them. The point here is that whatever the concerns are, they need to be framed in a way that does not suggest we should be equally concerned about optimists, animals, dolls, and the *Mona Lisa*.

At the other extreme, it seems plain that systems should not be deliberately engineered to make people believe something that is actually false. Emotional competence certainly can enhance the ability to deceive, and for that reason it is natural to fear that if we start with the standard mechanical virtues of flawless logic, endless patience, and no conscience and add the ability to manipulate emotion, the result could be an almost irresistible persuader (Guerini & Stock, 2005). There would clearly be ethical objections if a system of that kind were used, for instance, to convince people that they should buy a financial service that was actually inappropriate.

A well-known discussion of "persuasive technologies" by Berdichevsky and Neuenschwander (1999) addresses that issue. It proposes a guideline based on the Golden Rule: "The creators of a persuasive technology should never seek to persuade anyone of something they themselves would not consent to be persuaded of." Various refinements of the approach have been proposed (e.g., Spahn, 2011), but it is clear that a principle of that general kind is ethically important.

The two concerns considered so far involve extremes—inevitable deception and deliberate deception. Between them is a difficult gray area. Two principles may help to separate legitimate worries from overstatement. First, people may not worry greatly about signs that do not truly reflect internal feeling states, but they do object if the signs mislead them about the way a system is likely to behave—particularly if the false impression affects their own choice of action. Second, signs of emotion are prone to create a particular kind of false impression, even when no outright deception occurs. The problem involves what has been called *pars pro toto* reasoning (Cowie, 2012). It occurs when a system shows some behaviors associated with an emotion and people infer that it has a complex of other characteristics that would be associated with that emotion in a human. In a sense, people who form that kind of impression are deceiving themselves; but it is such a characteristically human type of inference that the system designers can hardly disclaim responsibility.

The obvious illustration is where an agent acting as a teacher or a companion uses facial and vocal gestures that give an impression of caring. That may help the agent in its intended function, but it is a problem if the user drifts into assuming that it will show other kinds of caring behavior and relies on it for help that it cannot actually provide. Teacher and companion roles are mentioned because it is a problem that we might expect to be worst where users did not have full adult judgment.

There is no straightforward way to forestall that kind of problem. The obvious prescription is that users and/or their representatives should be involved in identifying possible misinterpretations at the design stage.

An important complication in this area is that it is not clear how far ethical responsibility goes back. In particular, what ethical responsibility attaches to a research team who designed a basic system with no intention to deceive but who did nothing to prevent it from being customized to deceive? The issue here is closely related to the "open source" clause in the EPSRC code that was mentioned in earlier sections. The code highlights the likely outcome: Both the law and the public would probably hold the basic research team responsible unless they had taken active steps to prevent foreseeable abuse.

Respect for Autonomy

A third widely recognised ethical theme which applies to affective computing is autonomy. Respect for autonomy is widely regarded as fundamental to a liberal society (e.g., Dworkin, 1988). That is partly because the implications that can be derived from the principle go much further than one might immediately realize. At least some of the implications clearly raise questions for affective technology.

Central to the implications is the notion of procedural independence. People have the potential for autonomy, but to exercise it they must have procedural independence—that is, freedom from factors that compromise or subvert their ability to achieve self-refection and decide rationally (Dworkin, 1988). The potential to infringe procedural independence is an issue in various ways.

One has already been mentioned in the discussion of deception. Deception violates two kinds of ethical principle: a duty of honesty in and of itself and a duty not to infringe autonomy. The reasoning is that giving people a misleading impression of the alternatives impairs their procedural independence and thereby their ability to make rational decisions.

That kind of impairment is not always a pressing issue, but when it is, deception is doubly unethical.

A second line of argument on autonomy has been developed by Baumann and Doring (2011). It turns on agents' ability to perceive emotion rather than to persuade. They argue that information about a person's emotional state has particular implications for procedural independence: If it becomes available, it can restrict their options in ways that they would not choose. Hence they propose two duties with respect to information about other people's emotional states:

> First, persons should respect other persons' control of access to information about their emotional states.
>
> Second, the fact that persons obtain or are entrusted with knowledge about emotional states of a person imposes special responsibilities upon them: They must not misuse the information and exploit the vulnerabilities of that person.

As a result, people need strong assurances about the use that will be made of any information that an artificial system obtains about their emotional states. The governing principle that they propose is that:

> Emotion-oriented systems should not undertake any actions that users—as autonomous persons—do not or cannot endorse.

— where the primary kind of action being considered is use of information about the person's emotional state. Clearly, this is a variant on concerns about access to information that were raised earlier. But as with deception, the concern may have a double force when the information in question is about emotions.

Issues in a third area are linked via the notion of respect. Respect for autonomy is at least often understood to mean that beings capable of autonomy have a unique status, which is owed respect, and their autonomy should not be threatened by undermining their self-respect. For that reason, communication that denies respect is ethically problematic. The implications are wide-reaching. One that is at least beginning to be explored is that agents should respect conventions of politeness (Brunet et al., 2012). On the standard account (Brown & Levinson, 1987), the function of politeness is to avoid threatening the other person's "face." Hence impolite communication does not simply violate conventions—it denies respect and threatens self-respect.

Affective computing is the technology best placed to develop polite communication. Most of the signals that are used to express emotion—smiles, nods, and postures as well as selected forms of verbal expression—have a key role in politeness, and the point is to affect people's feelings in particular ways (or to avoid affecting them). The ethics are not straightforward. Some forms of politeness may lead to misunderstandings (Bonnefon et al., 2011), so there can be tension between truthfulness and according respect. Nevertheless, it seems right to insist that there are good ethical reasons to explore ways of incorporating some functions of politeness into human-computer interactions.

Certifying Competence

The ACM code cited above includes a responsibility to "give comprehensive and thorough evaluations of computer systems and their impacts, including analysis of possible risks." One of the ethical problems that arise with affective computing is that it is extremely difficult to discharge that responsibility. It is well known that evaluation of affective systems is problematic (e.g., Schroeder et al., 2012). The problem is not avoidable because the computer systems' function is intrinsically bound up with human systems that we understand only very partially. It is usually impossible to guarantee analyses of risk, partly because the human systems are very complicated and partly because they are very incompletely understood. Added to those is an understandable reluctance to proclaim the limitations of a product that represents an enormous investment of effort and intelligence. Nevertheless, failure to proclaim them is a real ethical problem.

The most sustained discussions of the issue in the context of "semi-intelligent information filters" (Cowie, 2012; Goldie et al., 2011). These are supposed to detect practically important emotion-related states and to pass their conclusions on for action of some sort. The danger is that they will have limitations that are poorly understood by those who deploy them and, as a result, people will be subjected to actions that they do not deserve or will not receive responses that they ought to. The problem is not new. The classical example involves "lie detectors." Despite widespread belief in their powers, they were actually much more likely to stigmatize the innocent than pinpoint the guilty (National Research Council, 2003). That experience could easily be repeated in areas such as surveillance, monitoring employees, detecting distress in phone calls, and so on. There are overwhelming reasons, both practical and ethical, to avoid that.

The problem is approached from a different angle by Sloman (2010). He stresses the obligation to analyze fully what a function entails before we claim that a system can carry it out. His context is a discussion of artificial helpers, and he provides a daunting overview of the abilities that a system would need to be a competent helper. However, the principle generalizes. Before we think of claiming that a system is empathetic (Janssen, 2012) let alone loving, we need analyses of what those functions entail.: Only then are we in a position to assess what kind of correspondence that there is between what the system does, and what people normally understand by terms like 'empathetic', 'loving', and so on.

Portraying Humans

As noted earlier, the way ethical principles are usually formulated makes it natural to focus on what systems do. However, a different type of ethical issue arises too often to ignore. Broadly speaking, it involves the way affective computing portrays human beings. Its portrayals raise ethical issues because of the intimate connection between emotion and morality also noted earlier in the chapter. The issue arises at two main levels.

The more concrete level stems from the fact that in everyday language, descriptions of emotion are rarely morally neutral. Hence to use them is to pass a kind of moral judgment, and it is not obvious when a machine has the right to pass that kind of judgment. Cowie (2005) notes an extreme case. To say that a person is sulking is to pass a moral judgment, and it is hard to imagine people accepting that a machine had the right to do that. A subtler case involves a machine recording that a person is angry but not what made her angry. This means that the output provides no way of making the key moral judgment about anger, which is whether it is justified. If the default assumption is (as seems likely) that anger is not justified, then a person who felt that his or her anger was justified might have grounds to take exception.

A subtler issue involves presenting phenomena that are morally entitled to certain kinds of human response—typically empathic—in a way that disguises that kind of significance. For example, there is considerable interest in systems that detect pain and distress (e.g., Lucey et al., 2009; Roberts, 2010). Natural methods of detection involve responding to facial expressions and attributes of speech that evoke empathic as well as diagnostic responses. The diagnosis may be better if the situation is portrayed by a line on a graph showing levels of pain or distress, but eliminating the empathic elements is not a trivial matter.

The issues here are quite intricate. It might be argued, by analogy with the laws of libel, that there is no cause for concern unless the descriptions are used in ways that harm the person described. However, it is also intuitive to say that people have an obligation to recognize that they are simply not entitled to pass certain kinds of judgment even if they keep it private. We might expect the same to hold for a machine if indeed it is entitled to pass any kind of moral judgment. The main point is simple, though. People who deal in morally sensitive concepts have an obligation to recognize the moral issues that the concepts raise.

Moving to the more abstract level, one of the oldest debates in philosophy is how we should value parts of our makeup other than pure intellect. For the stoics, the right way to live (and therefore the morally proper goal) was to achieve *apatheia,* where emotion was completely subordinated to intellect. Augustine retorted that those who are "not stirred or excited by any emotions at all...lose every shred of humanity" (p. 566). The sketch of ethical traditions at the beginning of this chapter shows that the tension continues.

Affective computing cannot separate itself from that debate because it affects our understanding of the systems underlying human emotion—particularly how crude or sophisticated they are. A good deal of research argues that when we try to match what emotion-related processes achieve, what we find is that they are vastly more impressive than the unaided intellect usually recognizes (Cowie, 2009). That favors Augustine. However, on the other side, there is literature suggesting that emotions are nothing more than heuristics which can be incorporated in a toy dog (Aibo is said to have "real emotions and instincts"[9]) or a set of numbers that rise under certain eliciting conditions and decay in a certain temporal pattern (Bryson & Tanguy, 2010). The difference is ethically important because the weight we should attach to emotional reactions is, and has been for millennia, a central question in ethics.

A related but distinct issue arises for those who believe in the intrinsic value of life (see, for example, Link, 2013). From that viewpoint, it is morally disturbing to propose that there is any meaningful correspondence between a manifestly lifeless system and something as central to life as emotion. It is asserting that one of the things people value most deeply is, in reality, much like something that they do not value at all.

As before, the issues are intricate, but they point to a simple obligation. The way affective computing portrays emotion has far-reaching implications for the way people understand themselves. It may in the long run help to resolve ancient questions. In the meantime, people who work in the area have a moral obligation to recognize how sensitive their pronouncements are.

Application-Specific Concerns

The themes that have been sketched so far were chosen partly because they subsume most of the ethical issues in a wide range of application areas. Applications that seem to be reasonably well covered include games, advertising, presenting a corporate image, instruction, and nonmedical coaching or training. However, that leaves several areas which raise more specific issues.

AFFECTIVE SYSTEMS AS COMPANIONS

There is heated controversy over the use of affective systems as "companions"—most notably as part of a caring role for the elderly but also for children (Sharkey, 2008; Wilks, 2010). Previous sections have already covered concerns that are directly related to the contribution of affective computing, notably in the context of deception and certifying competence. However, if affective computing is involved, it also has to register ethical concerns involving the whole enterprise. At a general level are concerns that "the seductions of the robotic" may lead people "to sidestep encounters with friends and family" (Turkle, 2010, p. 7), or that "the robotic" allows friends and family to sidestep their responsibilities. Others are more technical, such as Newell's (2010) observation that providers owe users a duty to find out what they actually want. There is an ethical obligation on people who venture into the area to be informed about issues like these.

AFFECTIVE SYSTEMS IN MEDICINE

Affective computing has a growing range of applications related to medicine. Functions include counseling (Marsella et al., 2000), psychological therapy (Kang et al., 2012), and aids to diagnosis (Ashraf et al., 2009; Trevino et al., 2011). The outstanding issue in medical applications is the potential for extreme consequences when a therapy goes wrong, well reflected in the title of the standard text on medical ethics, *Causing Death and Saving Lives* (Glover, 1977). This is reflected in the particular thoroughness of ethical approval procedures in medical contexts, which has already been pointed out. Glover's book is an excellent introduction for anyone considering work in the area.

MILITARY

Affective computing does not immediately suggest military applications, but in fact some of the longest-established work in the area is concerned with detecting stress in combat situations (e.g., Vloeberghs et al., 2000). The EPSRC report cited earlier rejects the development of robots designed "to be used as weapons with deadly or other offensive capability" except for national security, but many would argue against any development of killing machines—literally—that might escape trustworthy control (Sharkey, 2008). Other issues involve concern that terrorists might acquire potentially deadly technologies (again, see the EPSRC report): that conflicts with the the ethic of open publication. Again, the main point is that people considering research with military connections should properly weigh the issues.

SEX ROBOTS

Providing for the satisfaction of sexual fantasies is one of the most potentially lucrative applications of affective computing. Widespread moral codes regard this as a thoroughly unethical activity. However, a recent paper on the subject (Sullins, 2012) concludes that "the attainment of erotic wisdom is an ethically sound goal" (p. 398) provided that the system respects limits on the manipulation of human psychology. There are few clearer examples of the point that there are ethical differences that pure logic will not resolve.

SURVEILLANCE

Some ethical positions imply that surveillance is almost always wrong because it infringes autonomy. For others, it is likely to promote happiness more often than distress and therefore it is seen as profoundly moral. As with military applications and sex robots, this is an issue that logic will not settle.

It should be noted that at this level, different cultures differ quite markedly—for example, there are very different tolerances for surveillance or the use of robots in traditionally human roles. Although that is widely accepted, systematic research on the topic is still in its early stages.[10]

The Enforcement of Ethical Principles and Concerns

The discussion so far has focused on what should and should not happen. This section considers how compliance is enforced and how that impacts the research process. Because different countries and cultures have different systems, what is said here can only be a starting point for someone working in a particular setting. However, nobody should forget that some constraints cut across local systems. An institution may allow research to go ahead without ethical scrutiny, only for the research team to discover that a journal will not publish their work because there is no ethical documentation.

It makes sense to begin with the effort to fund research. Funding bodies have very diverse procedures, but the process of deciding whether to fund a project tends to involve several levels of test. The European Union's Framework 7 (FP7) program can be taken as an example.

The program's rules underline the importance of ethics. They state that "any proposal which contravenes fundamental ethical principles...shall not be selected and may be excluded from the evaluation, selection and award procedures at any time."[11] As a first stage, applicants are routinely asked to complete a checklist of descriptions that are associated with well-known problems. The FP7 list includes the following items, which are potentially relevant to affective computing:

Informed Consent
• Does the proposal involve children?
• Does the proposal involve patients or persons not able to give consent?
• Does the proposal involve adult healthy volunteers?
• Does the proposal involve Human Genetic Material?
• Does the proposal involve Human biological samples?
• Does the proposal involve Human data collection?

Privacy
• Does the proposal involve processing of genetic information or personal data (e.g., health, sexual lifestyle, ethnicity, political opinion, religious or philosophical conviction)
• Does the proposal involve tracking the location or observation of people?

Dual Use
• Research having direct military application
• Research having the potential for terrorist abuse

It is noticeable that the list covers only issues that are well established and apply to a wide range of research areas. It does not touch on most of the issues that have been discussed up to this point. However, it is only the first step. The checklist needs to be followed by text explaining how the research will handle issues arising from the list, and any others. Checklist and text are considered in the evaluation process, and the last of five sections in the evaluators' report asks whether the proposal raises "ethical issues that need further attention." If it does, a specialist ethical review may be called for.

Specialist ethical reviews, and to a lesser extent panels, are informed by expert groups—in the case of FP7, the European Group on Ethics in Science and New Technologies.[12] It produced the report on Ethics of Information and Communication Technologies cited earlier. This system means that issues can become important in review panels' deliberations very quickly.

The EU is by no means isolated in that approach. For example, at the time of writing, the UK's EPSRC is sponsoring the development of a framework for ethics in Information and Computing Technology (ICT) based on "a comprehensive baseline study of current issues, challenges and responses to them as perceived by ICT researchers."[13] It is the norm for funding bodies to regard ethical use of technology as a moving target, and reasonably so.

Institutional scrutiny is considered early on in the chapter. The main point to be made here is a contrast. Whereas funding bodies will typically consider the broad outline of a proposal, local bodies may be very exercised by details like the exact wording of a consent form. Addressing details may take several iterations, and that may be a real problem if the committee meets only half a dozen times a year.

Once research has been done, another set of ethical filters applies at publication. The journal *PLoS ONE* is a useful example.[14] Its guidelines specify that if research has used human subjects, the method section must cover the following:

• The approving institutional review board or equivalent committee(s)
• How informed consent was obtained
• If humans were categorized, how that was done
• If potentially identifying material is published, explicit consent from the individual(s) concerned

For observational or field studies, there must be ethics statements that specify the permits and approvals obtained for the work, including the authority that approved the study. In addition, "outmoded terms and potentially stigmatizing labels should be changed to more current, acceptable terminology." Papers that fail these tests are returned without review.

Beyond formal sanctions, it is striking how often media reports focus on perceived ethical problems rather than technical achievements. For example, it was a surprise when a report following a recent interview on the recognition of natural speech concluded:

> Unfortunately, if computers do ever get to the point where they can understand our words and how we say them, it might not be a good thing. There is a hypothesised crisis [the "uncanny valley"] where interactions between humans and robots reach a level of realism that is uncomfortable and disconcerting.... So perhaps the question should be less about when we will be able to create computers that can draw on all the experiences and knowledge amassed over a lifetime when having a conversation, and more on whether we should be heading down this route at all.

Negative presentations in the media are not sanctions in themselves, but the risk that they will translate into sanctions is all too real. They shape public opinion, and public opinion sways funding bodies, particularly when the issue is perceived to be ethical: No politician wants to be held responsible for funding Dr. Frankenstein. Public opinion has made government funding for research on genetically modified crops an extremely delicate issue (UK Parliamentary Office of Science & Technology, 2012) and virtually ended some kinds of research with animals. Avoiding the same fate is not a trivial matter.

Public Intuitions and Duties to Explain

The discussion so far has emphasized links between ongoing research and well-established ethical principles. In general, though, the issues that preoccupy the public are different. They are usually more to do with gut feeling than with arguments based either on ethical principles or on knowledge of affective computing. However, as the first section above notes, the gut matters in ethics. It is ethically suspect as well as risky to persist with activities that genuinely perturb the public. The general response that this section proposes is, however, not to abandon the activities. It is to accept an ethical duty to ensure that the public can form rational judgments.

The Ethics of Unquantifiable Risk

An area where there is some clarity involves risk. The problem, as pointed out by Goldie et al. (2011), is that the risks involved are profoundly unquantifiable. Certainly the outcomes that people fear are deeply disturbing. On the other hand, there is no convincing case for thinking that they are likely. But yet again, they cannot be ruled out either.

One issue of that kind has already been mentioned. It is that surrogate worlds may become so engaging that people lose the will, and perhaps the ability, to relate to the real one. The EU, for example, regards that as a substantial issue. The ethically sound reply would seem to be that it does make sense to monitor the issue but also to make it clear that there is no obvious reason to expect effects that are either particularly pernicious or particularly difficult to control.

Even more disturbing is the fear that "mainds" will outstrip humanity and—at best—subordinate it[15]. Affective computing has a special place in that nightmare because it raises the prospect of machines that can decide, not necessarily rationally, what they like and dislike. If that were a realistic possibility, then people ought to worry about it. The ethical issue here would seem to be helping nonexperts to gauge the probability. If people's fears are unnecessary, then those who know the reality have an ethical obligation to avoid inflaming it and, if possible, to reduce it by exposing the limits of the machines that can actually be built or envisaged.

The Ethical Status of an Agent

Concepts like "autonomy" and "free will" loom large in ethics (particularly Kant's) and also in the public mind. In both cases, what they mean is not simply that an agent can operate without being told what to do at every choice point. It is that the choice is fundamentally its own rather than a product of various (probably ill defined) background influences. For Kant in particular, an agent cannot make an ethical choice unless it has that kind of freedom to begin with.

One of the recurring concerns about affective computing is that to give systems true emotions would be to give them that kind of autonomy, and to give them true autonomy is to court disaster. The EPSRC report, which has been cited repeatedly, illustrates various concerns of that kind. Part of it is that autonomy should not be taken out of human hands; part is that machines are not actually capable of it; part is that giving them autonomy would distance the machines' human makers from

responsibility for their actions; part of it is that machines with that kind of autonomy might turn on their human makers.

Concerns like that brings into play one of the oldest ideas in philosophy (expressed in Plato's image of the charioteer): that systems capable of initiating action, of which emotional systems are a prime example, need to be under rational control. The interplay between rational control and emotion-driven "action tendencies" (Frijda, 1987) is a central theme in ethics, and there are contrasting views of the way it could or should play out in artificial systems.

Perhaps the simplest view is that put forward by Beavers (2009). For him, the reason/emotion tension is a human phenomenon, which should not be imported into artificial agents. Their decision making can and should be wholly rational—which, on his Kantian view, would mean that it would not be moral at all. If so, morality has no place in artificial systems. In response, Guarini (2012) has argued that, practically, it is likely that conflicts like humans' will arise. If so, artificial emotion and artificial ethics must go hand in hand. Influential models suggest an even tighter connection. It has long been recognized that moral judgments are part and parcel of at least some emotions—for example, righteous anger (Plato's example) and remorse. Recently there has been growing interest in the connections between morality and emotions that seem at first sight purely biological, notably disgust (Schnall et al., 2008; Erskine et al., 2011). If so, attempts to model emotion apart from morality are misguided. More radical still is the proposal that empathy, which is primarily affective, not rational, lies at the root of moral behavior toward others (Baron-Cohen, 2012). It does not follow automatically that systems that lack humanlike emotions cannot behave ethically toward human beings, but it is certainly an issue to ponder.

Intellectually, these issues are fascinating. However, it bears emphasis that they belong in the realms of speculation, not practice, because the systems that we can currently build have, by human standards, very few courses of action to choose from. So long as we build systems to do only a few things and specify when they should do which, it is hard to dispute the EPSRC conclusion that attributing ethical responsibility to them simply clouds the issue: Responsibility lies firmly with the builder.

Mysterious Forebodings

It cannot be proved, but it is a fair guess that a great many ethical arguments draw sustenance from reactions with at least echoes of the supernatural. There are two obvious kinds of reaction in that category.

One is revulsion at things that approach naturalness but miss it in critical ways. The effect is usually described using Mori's (1970) phrase the "uncanny valley," suggesting a fall in acceptability that sets in when things that are not natural creatures become too similar to them. There is a strong tendency to attach ethical significance to the uncanny valley, as the press report cited above illustrates: It interprets the effect as a reason to question whether the research should be done.

The effect is not as inevitable as Mori's description suggests (MacDorman, 2006). Nevertheless, the horror industry testifies to the strength of human reaction to some things that are humanlike but not human. Clearly that kind of effect raises practical issues—systems that people find profoundly disturbing will fail because people will not use them. It would also raise ethical issues if people were forced to interact with systems having that effect on them; that might happen if, for instance, the systems were operating in a hospital or care environment.

It is another matter, though, to move from disconcerting experiences with a system to the conclusion that it, and the enterprise that produced it, were somehow evil. Since ethics presupposes rationality, from an ethical point of view, the appropriate response would presumably be that that was superstition and should be resisted.

Similar in some senses, contrasting in others, is the sense that there is ground where humans should not tread. Some things are too mysterious to tamper with, and if we do tamper, the consequences may be wildly unpredictable. The concept of artificial minds is certainly surrounded by that kind of thinking. For instance, in a recent science fiction novel, true artificial intelligence is brought into being accidentally when a schoolgirl uploads data on her pet rat's brain (Brin, 2012). What unfolds then depends more on the rat than on the humans. Ideas about emotion have a similar quality—it is natural to feel that once we coax the glowing fluid into the circuitry, we have released forces beyond our control.

If it were reasonable to believe that emotion was like that, then it would be ethical to oppose affective computing on the grounds that it was profoundly dangerous. However, the belief is not reasonable, and the ethical course is surely to explain to people who are troubled by that kind of image why it is not reasonable.

Conclusion

This chapter has covered a wide range of issues. The nature of the area makes that inevitable. Perhaps surprisingly, though, it converges on a reasonably short list of ethical obligations that anyone who worked in affective computing should respect.

• They should understand the premises on which ethical judgments are likely to be based, and the fact that others may rationally hold ethical premises different from their own.

• They should abide by the ethically motivated codes that govern studies with human beings and data privacy.

• They should uphold the ethical value of making interactions involving humans and machines more likely to generate positive affect and less likely to generate negative affect.

• They should seek to ensure that the systems they build will do nothing to others that they would not want to be subjected to themselves and nothing that users would object to if they understood what was happening.

• In particular, they should ensure that their systems do not deceive people or infringe their autonomy in ways that violate that principle.

• They should ensure that they have a clear understanding of the capabilities and limitations of their systems, grounded in an understanding of the corresponding human capabilities.

• Their communications with nonexperts should help them to form realistic assessments, both of the systems' abilities and of the risks that they might pose.

• They should be sensitive to the moral implications attached to terms that they use and models that they propose.

• Where the fields in which they work raise other ethical issues, they should become familiar with them.

It would be completely against the spirit of this chapter to expect instant agreement on that kind of list. However, it seems reasonable to offer it as a point of reference.

Notes

1. http://www.epsrc.ac.uk/ourportfolio/themes/engineering/activities/Pages/principlesofrobotics.aspx
2. http://eur-lex.europa.eu/LexUriServ/LexUriServ.do?uri=OJ:C:2010:083:0389:0403:en:PDF
3. http://www.wma.net/en/30publications/10policies/b3/
4. http://www.apa.org/topics/ethics/index.aspx
5. www.acm.org./constitution/code.html

6. http://eur-lex.europa.eu/LexUriServ/LexUriServ.do?uri=CE
  LEX:31995L0046:en:NOT
7. http://ec.europa.eu/bepa/european-group-ethics/docs/publi
  cations/ict_final_22_february-adopted.pdf
8. http://www.epsrc.ac.uk/ourportfolio/themes/engineering/
  activities/Pages/principlesofrobotics.aspx
9. http://www.robotbooks.com/sony_aibo.htm, downloaded
  28.2.2013
10. http://gow.epsrc.ac.uk/NGBOViewGrant.aspx?GrantRef=
  EP/G069808/1
11. ftp://ftp.cordis.europa.eu/pub/fp7/docs/guidelines-annex5ict.
  pdf
12. http://ec.europa.eu/bepa/european-group-ethics/index_en.
  htm
13. http://gow.epsrc.ac.uk/Search.aspx?search=ethics
14. http://www.plosone.org/static/guidelines.action#human
15. "Mainds" is a term used by the science fiction writer David
  Brin to describe minds whose intelligence is artificial rather
  than natural.

References

Ashraf, A. B., Lucey, S., Cohn, J. F., Chen, T., Ambadar, Z., Prkachin, K. M., & Solomon, P. E. (2009). The painful face—Pain expression recognition using active appearance models. *Image and Vision Computing, 27*(12), 1788–1796.

Asimov, I (1950). *I robot.* New York: Doubleday.

Augustine. (1984). *City of god* (H. Bettenson, Trans.). London: Penguin.

Baron-Cohen, S. (2012). *Zero degrees of empathy: A new theory of human cruelty and kindness.* London: Penguin.

Baumann, H., & Döring, S. (2011). Emotion-oriented systems and the autonomy of persons. In P. Petta, C. Pelachaud and R. Cowie (Eds.), *Emotion-oriented systems: The Humaine handbook* (pp. 735–752). Berlin: Springer.

Beauchamp, T. L. & Childress, J. F. (2001). *Principles of biomedical ethics,* 5th ed. New York, NY: Oxford University Press.

Beavers, A. (2009). Between angels and animals: The question of robot ethics, or is Kantian moral agency desirable? *Proceedings of the Association for Practical and Professional Ethics, 18th Annual Meeting.* Available at: http://faculty.evansville.edu/tb2/PDFs/Robot%20Ethics%20-%20APPE.pdf

Berdichevsky, D., & Neuenschwander, E. (1999). Toward an ethics of persuasive technology. *Communications of the ACM, 42*(5), 51–58.

Blackburn, S. (2001). *Ethics: A very short introduction.* Oxford, UK: Oxford University Press.

Bonnefon, J. F., Feeney, A., & De Neys, W. (2011). The risk of polite misunderstandings. *Current Directions in Psychological Science, 20*(5), 321–324.

Brin, D. (2012). *Existence.* London: Orbit Books.

Bringsjord, S., & Clark, M. H. (2012). Red-pill robots only, please. *IEEE Transactions on Affective Computing 3,* 394–397

Brown, P., & Levinson, S. C. (1987). *Politeness: Some universals in language usage.* Cambridge, UK: Cambridge University Press.

Brunet, P. M., Cowie, R., Donnan, H., & Douglas-Cowie, E. (2012). Politeness and social signals. *Cognitive Processing 13,* S447–S453.

Bryson, J. J., & Tanguy, E. (2010). Simplifying the design of human-like behaviour: Emotions as durative dynamic state for action selection. *International Journal of Synthetic Emotions, 1*(1), 30–50.

Coeckelbergh, M. (2102). Are emotional robots deceptive? *IEEE Transactions on Affective Computing 3,* 388–393.

Cowie, R. (2005). What are people doing when they assign everyday emotion terms? *Psychological Inquiry, 16*(1), 11–48.

Cowie, R. (2009). Perceiving emotion: Towards a realistic understanding of the task. *Philosophical Transactions of the Royal Society B: Biological Sciences, 364*(1535), 3515–3525.

Cowie, R. (2012). The good our field can hope to do, the harm it should avoid. *IEEE Transactions on Affective Computing 3,* 410–423.

Csikszentmihalyi, M., & Csikszentmihalyi, I. S. (Eds.). (2006). *A life worth living: Contributions to positive psychology.* New York, NY: Oxford University Press.

Döring, S., Goldie, P., & McGuinness, S. (2011). Principalism: A method for the ethics of emotion-oriented machines. In P. Petta, C. Pelachaud, & R. Cowie (Eds.), *Emotion-oriented systems: The Humaine handbook* (pp. 713–724). Berlin: Springer.

Driver, J. (2012). *Consequentialism.* Abingdon, UK: Routledge.

Dworkin, G. (1988). *The theory and practice of autonomy.* Cambridge, MA: Cambridge University Press.

Erskine, K. J., Kacinik, N. A., & Prinz, J. J. (2011). A bad taste in the mouth: Gustatory disgust influences moral judgment. *Psychological Science, 22*(3), 295–299.

Foot, P. (2001). *Natural goodness.* Oxford, UK: Oxford University Press.

Frijda, N. H. (1987). *The emotions* Cambridge, UK: Cambridge University Press.

Glover, J. (1977). *Causing death and saving lives.* London: Pelican Books.

Goldie, P., Döring, S., & Cowie, R. (2011). The ethical distinctiveness of emotion-oriented technology: Four long-term issues. In P. Petta, C. Pelachaud, & R. Cowie (Eds.), *Emotion-oriented systems: The Humaine handbook* (pp. 725–733). Berlin: Springer.

Guerini, M., & Stock, O. (2005). Toward ethical persuasive agents. In *Proceedings of the International Joint Conference of Artificial Intelligence Workshop on Computational Models of Natural Argument* Edinburgh: IJCAI.

Guarini, M. (2012). Conative dimensions of machine ethics: A defense of duty. *IEEE Transactions on Affective Computing, 3,* 434–442

Hobbes, T. (1996). *Leviathan* (J. C. A. Gaskin, Ed.). Oxford, UK: Oxford World Classics (Original work published 1651).

Hume, D. (2007). *A treatise of human nature.*(D. F. Norton & M. J. Norton Eds.). Oxford: Clarendon Press (Original work published 1740).

Janssen, J. H. (2012). A three-component framework for empathic technologies to augment human interaction. *Journal on Multimodal User Interfaces, 5,* 143–161.

Kang, S. H., Gratch, J., Sidner, C., Artstein, R., Huang, L., & Morency, L. P. (2012). Towards building a virtual counselor: Modeling nonverbal behavior during intimate self-disclosure. In *Proceedings of the 11th International Conference on Autonomous Agents and Multiagent Systems,* Valencia: AAMAS (Vol. 1, pp. 63–70).

Lau, H. (2012). The rise and fall of voice. Institute of Physics. Available at: http://www.physics.org/featuredetail.asp?id=76

Link. H. J. (2013). Playing god and the intrinsic value of life: Moral problems for synthetic biology? *Science and Engineering Ethics 19*(2), pp. 435–448.

Lucey, P., Cohn, J., Lucey, S., Matthews, I., Sridharan, S., & Prkachin, K. M. (2009). Automatically detecting pain using facial actions. In *Proceedings of Affective Computing and Intelligent Interaction 2009* Amsterdam: IEEE (pp.1–8).

MacDorman, K. F. (2006). Subjective ratings of robot video clips for human likeness, familiarity, and eeriness: An exploration of the uncanny valley. In *ICCS/CogSci-2006 Long Symposium: Toward Social Mechanisms of Android Science* Vancouver: Cognitive Science Society (pp. 26–29).

MacIntyre, A. (1985). *After virtue*, 2nd ed. London: Duckworth.

Mackie, J. L. (1977). *Ethics: Inventing right and wrong* London: Penguin.

Marsella, S., Johnson, W. L., & LaBore, C. (2003). Interactive pedagogical drama for health interventions. *Conference on Artificial Intelligence in Education, Sydney, Australia*. Available at: http://alelo.co.uk/files/AIED03-interactive_pedagogical.pdf

Mori, M. (1970). The uncanny valley. *Energy, 7*(4), 33–35.

National Research Council Committee to Review the Scientific Evidence on the Polygraph. (2003). *The polygraph and lie detection*. Available at: http://www.nap.edu/openbook.php?record_id=10420 downloaded 28.2.2013

Newell, A. (2010). Artificial companions in society: Consulting the users. In Y. Wilks (Ed.), *Close engagements with artificial companions* (pp. 173–178). Philadelphia: John Benjamins.

Parfitt, D. (2011). *On what matters*. Oxford, UK: Oxford University Press.

Roberts, L. (2010). Real and acted responses of distress: An auditory & acoustic analysis of extreme stress & emotion. *ExLing*, 149–152.

Ross, W. D. (1939). *Foundations of ethics*. Oxford, UK: Oxford University Press,

Ryan, R. M., Huta, V., & Deci, E. L. (2008). Living well: A self-determination theory perspective on eudaimonia. *Journal of Happiness Studies, 9*(1), 139–170.

Scanlon, T. M. (1998). *What we owe to each other*. Cambridge, MA: Harvard University Press.

Scheutz (2012). The affect dilemma for artificial agents: Should we develop affective artificial agents? *IEEE Transactions on Affective Computing, 3*, 424–433.

Schnall, S., Haidt, J., Clore, G. L., & Jordan, A. H. (2008). Disgust as embodied moral judgment. *Personality and Social Psychology Bulletin, 34*(8), 1096–1109.

Schroeder, M., Bevacqua, E., Cowie, R., Eyben, F., Gunes, H., Heylen, D. & Wollmer, M. (2012). Building autonomous sensitive artificial listeners. *IEEE Transactions on Affective Computing, 3*(2), 165–183.

Sharkey, N. (2008). The ethical frontiers of robotics. *Science, 322*(5909), 1800–1801.

Sloman, A. (2010). Requirements for artificial companions: It's harder than you think. In Y. Wilks (Ed.), *Close engagements with artificial companions* (pp 179–200). Philadelphia: John Benjamins.

Smith, A. (1759). *The theory of moral sentiments*. Printed for A. Millar in the Strand and A. Kincaid and J. Bell in Edinburgh.

Sneddon, I., Goldie, P. & Petta, P. (2011). Ethics in emotion-oriented systems: The challenges for an ethics committee. In P. Petta, C. Pelachaud and R. Cowie (Eds.), *Emotion-Oriented Systems: The Humaine Handbook* (pp. 753–767). Berlin: Springer.

Spahn, A. (2011). And lead us (not) into persuasion…? Persuasive technology and the ethics of communication. *Science and Engineering Ethics* (Published online first May 5, 2011), doi: 10.1007/s11948-011-9278-y

Sparrow, R. (2002). The march of the robot dogs. *Ethics and information Technology, 4*(4), 305–318.

Sullins, J. (2012). Robots, love and sex: The ethics of building a love machine. *IEEE Transactions on Affective Computing 3*, 398–409

Trevino, A. C., Quatieri, T. F., & Malyska, N. (2011). Phonologically-based biomarkers for major depressive disorder. *EURASIP Journal on Advances in Signal Processing*, (1), 1–18.

Turkle, S. (2010) In good company? On the threshold of robotic companions. In Y. Wilks (Ed.), *Close engagements with artificial companions* (pp. 3–10). Philadelphia: John Benjamins.

UK Parliamentary Office of Science & Technology. (2012). GM in agricultural development. Postnote Number 412.

Vloeberghs, C., Verlinde, P., Swail, C., Steeneken, H., & South, A. (2000). *The impact of speech under "stress" on military speech technology*. NATO Research and Technology Organization Technical Report ADA377422.

Wood, A. (1999). *Kant's ethical thought*. Cambridge, UK: Cambridge University Press.

CHAPTER
25

Research and Development Tools in Affective Computing

M. Sazzad Hussain, Sidney K. D'Mello, *and* Rafael A. Calvo

Abstract

There are a wide variety of software tools that automate various aspects of affective computing research. Researchers can increase the productivity and reproducibility of their work by reusing appropriate tools. This chapter aims to identify and describe the common tools in affective computing research. Eight hundred affective computing researchers were surveyed in order to obtain information related to the software tools used in their research. The survey collected information on programming languages and tools for data annotation, signal analysis, pattern recognition for affect classification, affect expression, and data collection. The responses of the 66 individuals who completed the survey highlight the most common tools used in affective computing research.

Key Words: affective computing, software tools, survey

Introduction

Affective computing researchers often collect large amounts of data (e.g., mouse/keyboard actions, videos, physiological signals) while a user interacts with a computer. The data collection itself can be a challenging task, as described in chapter 23 in this handbook. Complex algorithms must then be applied for processing and analyzing the data in order to make meaningful inferences (e.g., affect detection and modeling [Calvo & D'Mello, 2010]). Chapter 26 describes some of the issues involved at this stage. Often these algorithms require sophisticated software tools that researchers must either implement from the ground up or reuse if the proper tools are available. Irrespective of the stage of an affective computing project, be it data collection (Afzal & Robinson, 2011; Jameson, 2009), analysis (Fernandez & Picard, 1998; Healey & Picard, 1998), or adaptive system implementation (D'Mello, Graesser, & Picard, 2007; Jameson, 2009), the decisions regarding which software tools

to use can have a major impact on the success of the project. Indeed, researchers can increase their productivity and improve the reproducibility of their work by reusing appropriate software tools. This chapter aims to provide an overview of the popular software tools used in affective computing research. Our hope is that this overview will help affective computing researchers identify and reuse existing tools in order to increase productivity by avoiding the task of "reinventing the wheel" when solutions already exist.

A variety of tools can be used to address general or specific problems in affective computing. There are general tools (e.g., MATLAB) that can be used in a variety of situations such as data collection, signal processing, statistical analysis, and machine learning. Despite the versatility of these general tools, they do not offer plug-and-play solutions. They require customization, and tailoring them for a particular application requires effort and expertise, thus increasing the likelihood of errors. Then there

349

are application-specific tools (e.g., *Gtrace, OpenEar*) that are built for specific purposes. Some of these tools are used for data collection, whereas others are used for data processing, analysis, and visualization. There are tools that provide machine learning frameworks for the classification of affective states (e.g., *Weka, RapidMiner*) and tools that generate affective expressions. Various programming platforms (e.g., Java, Net) underlie these software tools, with some platforms being more common in affective computing research. Hence choosing the appropriate platform on which to build application-level tools is important when it comes to integrating with third-party tools.

In many cases, a tool can be used for more than one specific purpose. In other cases, several tools can be integrated to serve one purpose. Once the popular tools for each category are identified and their affordances analyzed, affective computing researchers may use these tools to suit their needs. Providing such a taxonomy of common tools is the major goal of this chapter. Unfortunately listing and describing all of the available tools is a challenging task that extends beyond the scope of this chapter. To circumvent this problem, we surveyed affective computing researchers to identity the most popular tools used in their work. This chapter discusses the demographics of the survey respondents and the popular tools developed and used by this community. These tools can be classified into the following main categories:

- *Data Collection*: Tools used for experimental data collection
- *Data Annotation*: Tools for annotating data and obtaining affect labels
- *Signal Analysis*: Tools for signal processing, feature extraction, and data visualization
- *Affect Classification*: General machine learning tools along with tools specifically developed for affect recognition
- *Affect Expression*: Tools for generating affective facial expressions, speech, and postures in embodied agents

Survey of Tools for Affective Computing

The survey collected information about the country, position, and discipline of affective computing researchers and the software tools they used. Invitations to participate in the survey were sent to 800 individuals who had published a paper in the 2007, 2009, and 2011 *Affective Computing and Intelligent Interaction* (ACII) conference series and to contributors to this handbook. A total of 66 responses (8.25% response rate) were obtained.

Figure 25.1 provides descriptions of the demographics of respondents. The respondents were from 20 countries, with a majority from the United States and Europe. Most were academics (e.g., professors, lecturers), research students, and research assistants.

The majority (85%) of the respondents were from engineering fields, including computer science, information technology, and electrical engineering. Researchers from other areas—such as cognitive science, psychology, learning science, art, and the humanities (12%)—also reported using affective computing research tools. Furthermore, as Figure 25.2 indicates, the respondents were quite open to sharing data and tools but varied on the particulars of their sharing policies. Specifically, a substantial percentage of researchers freely distribute their data (44%) and tools (50%), whereas a similar percentage (41% and 32% for data and tools, respectively) only share with collaborators. A very small percentage of tools and data are commercially distributed.

Software Tools in Affective Computing

We begin by discussing the popular programming languages and software development platforms. This is particularly important because the programming platforms underlie tool development and the right choice either facilitates or hinders code reuse. In addition, this section considers software tools that are used for affect annotation, signal analysis, affect classification, affect expression, and affective data collection. For the software tools, the survey inquired about the *frequency of use* ("occasional user," "frequent user," or "never use") and *expertise of user* ("occasional developer" or "frequent developer"). The *frequency of use* reflect researchers who use the tools without any customization, whereas *expertise of user* includes researchers who engage in minor or major customization of the tools. Respondents had the option of responding to more than one tool (*OpenEar, AuBT, In-house*, etc.) within a category (e.g., *signal processing and analysis*). In this chapter, the popularity of a tool is reported by calculating the percentage of respondents who have indicated either using or customizing the tool. For example, 21% of the respondents reported using *OpenEar*, which included 18% who use it without any customization and 3% who customize it. The remaining 79% of the respondents never reported using *OpenEar*.

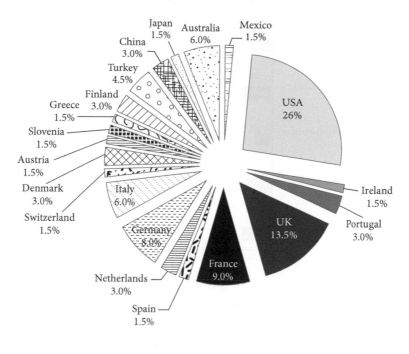

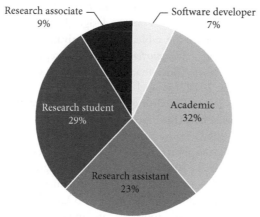

Fig. 25.1 Geographical and occupational demographics of respondents.

Programming Languages and Software Platforms

Figure 25.3 lists the most popular programming platforms based on the *frequency of usage*. MATLAB was found to be the most frequently used computing environment, followed by Java, Python, and C/C++/C#. MATLAB is a commercial platform and high-level programming language that is mainly used for numerical computation. It supports a variety of toolboxes for advanced data analyses in niche domains. Octave is mostly compatible with MATLAB and a good free alternative, although it is not used as frequently as MATLAB.

Open-source platforms and programming environments such as Perl (www.perl.org), R (www.r-project.org), and Qt (qt.digia.com) have also been reported. Perl is a high-level programming language, suitable for web programming. R is a programming language mostly suitable for statistical data analysis and data mining. Qt is a framework supporting C++ libraries for developing software applications and user interfaces. Cython (cython.org), Common Lisp, PHP, Max/MSP (cycling74.com), and MissionLab (www.cc.gatech.edu/ai/robot-lab/research/MissionLab) were used rather infrequently.

Labeling and Data Annotation

One of the most substantial problems encountered by affective computing researchers is data

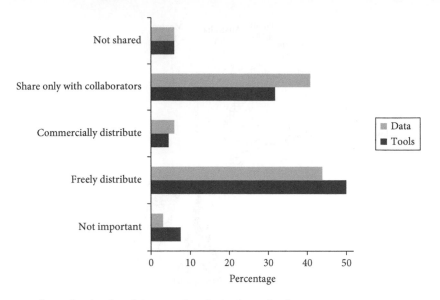

Fig. 25.2 Percentage of researchers based on their approach to sharing data and tools.

annotation (Picard, 2003). Table 25.1 gives the names, brief descriptions, and popularity of some of the tools for labeling affective data.

In addition to the tools depicted in the table, some researchers reported using *Wavesurfer* (Sjölander & Beskow, 2000), *Praat* (Boersma, 2002), and *Speechalyzer* (Burkhardt, 2012) for labeling data, although these are tools for audio editing and analyzing speech. EDM Workbench (Rodrigo, Baker, McLaren, Jayme, & Dy, 2012) is used for educational data mining but also supports data labeling. *Cowlog* (Hänninen & Pastell, 2009) and *ChronoViz* (Fouse, Weibel, Hutchins, & Hollan, 2011) are video-based tools that were reported to be used for labeling. *ELAN* (tla.mpi.nl/tools/tla-tools/elan) is a specialized tool used for annotating audio

and video contents. *Whissell's Dictionary of Affect in Language* (Whissell, 1989) is a web-based tool designed to quantify the pleasantness (i.e., valence) and activation (i.e., arousal) of emotional words. It has been reported to be useful, especially for integration with other tools (e.g., affect expression).

Signal Processing and Analysis

Raw data—such as videos, speech, physiological signal etc.—collected during affective computing studies require processing for subsequent analyses. Signal processing may involve sampling, noise reduction, compression, and feature extraction (Oppenheim & Schafer, 1975). The features are important for manual inspection as well as automatic affect detection using machine learning

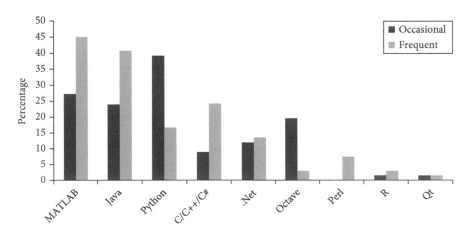

Fig. 25.3 Most popular programming platforms.

Table 25.1 Popular Tools for Data Labeling and Annotation

Tool	Description	Popularity
Geneva Emo Wheel	Self-reporting tool based on the Component Process Model (Scherer, 2005). A visual instrument with scales for measuring emotions and can be implemented in software applications.	21%
Feeltrace	For tracing emotional states in real-time on activation (i.e., arousal) and evaluation (i.e., valence) dimensions (Cowie et al., 2000).	20%
Gtrace	Extension of Feeltrace for creating traces from videos and displaying the emotional changes of a person. Available at: sites.google.com/site/roddycowie/work-resources	11%
TraceTools	Tool consisting a set of seven programs with tracing functionalities as follows: (1) if emotion present or not, (2) if emotion acted or not, (3) if emotion masked or not, (4) intensity of emotion, (5) intensity of arousal, (6) intensity of dominance, and (7) valence. Available at: emotion-research.net/download/ECatPack.zip	6%
ANVIL	Free software package for video annotation (Kipp, 2001). Allows users to define the coding scheme and supports multilayer annotation.	5%
SAM	Self-assessment manikin, a pictorial instrument for rating valence, arousal, and dominance (Bradley & Lang, 1994). This can be implemented in software applications.	5%
In house	Own built in house.	67%

techniques (Calvo & D'Mello, 2010). The most popular signal processing tools along with descriptions are provided in Table 25.2, although, most researchers prefer to implement signal processing tools in house.

There are some additional tools that were not represented in the survey but could be useful, such as *Sphinx* (cmusphinx.sourceforge.net), *openBliSSART* (Schuller, Lehmann, Weninger, Eyben, & Rigoll, 2009), *EmoVoice* (Vogt, André, & Bee, 2008), and *NLTK* (Bird, 2006) for audio and speech analysis. Both *EEGLab* (Delorme & Makeig, 2004) and *ELAN* (Aguera, Jerbi, Caclin, & Bertrand, 2011) are suitable for processing EEG, MEG, and other electrophysiological data. Affectiva's *Q Software* (www.affectiva.com) is used with the Affectiva Q sensor, and *Emotive Logger* (www.emotiv.com) is used with the Emotiv EEG system. *Tobii Studio* (www.tobii.com) is used for eye tracking–related analysis, and *CLM-Z* (Baltrusaitis, Robinson, & Morency, 2012) tracks facial features for different poses. Tools like *eMotion* (www.visual-recognition.nl) and *Fuzzy rules used to synthesize intermediate facial expressions* (Raouzaiou, Tsapatsoulis, Karpouzis, & Kollias, 2002) are used for emotion recognition, facial expression, and movement analysis. *EyesWeb* (www.infomus.org/eyesweb_ita.php) and *FUBI* (Kistler, Endrass, Damian, Dang, & André, 2012) are designed for real-time multimodal systems.

Data Mining and Affect Classification

The tools for data mining and machine learning can be divided into two categories; (1) generic tools used for statistical analysis and classification and (2) tools built specifically for affect classification. Many of the tools (e.g., *AuBT, openEar, eMotion*, etc.) mentioned in the previous section include classifiers along with their signal processing functionalities.

Table 25.3 lists the most popular statistical and data mining tools used for statistical analysis, pattern recognition, and classification.

Some additional generic tools for data mining and classification that could be useful for affective computing are briefly described in Table 25.4. These tools were reported by some of the respondents.

Some of the researchers have reported using *Statistical EmoText/Semantic EmoText*, which are tools for sensing affect from texts (Osherenko & André, 2009). *Geneva Affect Label Coder* is another such tool that detects affective states from words in natural languages (Scherer, 2005).

Affect Expression

Affect expression technologies have the ability to express a variety of affective states with embodied agents based on some conditions (Park, Ryu, Sohn, & Cho, 2007). Software tools for affect expression include software that generates

Table 25.2 Popular Tools for Signal Processing, Analysis, and Feature Extraction

Tool	Description	Popularity
Praat	Tool for analyzing speech and acoustic signals (Boersma, 2002). Open source and extendable with C/C++.	30%
Real-time eye gaze and head pose estimation	Software system in C/C++ that utilizes a webcam to estimate the user's eye gaze and head position (Asteriadis, Tzouveli, Karpouzis, & Kollias, 2009). Useful for analyzing attentional orientation.	24%
OpenEar	Open source tool in C++ used for extracting audio features (Eyben, Wollmer, & Schuller, 2009). Also provides some classification functionalities.	21%
Hand gesture analysis tool	Tool in MATLAB for tracking hand movements by identifying the location of hand and face from image sequences (Bevacqua et al., 2006).	17%
AuBT	Toolbox in MATLAB for physiological data analysis (Wagner, Kim, & Andre, 2005). Provides feature extraction from physiological signals and some machine learning functions.	11%
Kinect SDK	Development kit for building applications for Microsoft Kinect. Supports C++, C# and Visual Basic.Net. Available at: www.microsoft.com/en-us/kinectforwindows/	5%
OpenCV	Open-source library intended for real-time computer vision. Available at: opencv.org	3%
openSmile	Free tool in C++ for extracting audio features related to music and speech in real time (Eyben, Wöllmer, & Schuller, 2010).	3%
Wavesurfer	Free tool used for audio (speech and sound) editing and analysis (Sjölander & Beskow, 2000).	2%
In house	Own built in house.	59%

affect through synthesis, animations, characters, androids, etc.

The survey reflected a variety of affect expression tools, with *MARY* (Schröder & Trouvain, 2003) and *Greta* (perso.telecom-paristech.fr/~pelachau/Greta) being the most popular (18% respectively). *MARY* is an expressive text-to-speech system in Java and *Greta* is an expressive text-to-embodied agent tool in C++. Both of the tools are freely available as open-source software. Tools like *Festival, VHML, SmartBody, FaceFX, Xface, Horde3D*, and *Haptek* were reported to be useful by some researchers (Table 25.5). As usual, many researchers (30%) prefer to use and customize in-house systems for affect expression.

Besides the tools for affect expression, some generic frameworks such as ROS (Robot Operating System) by Willow Garage (www.willowgarage.com) and ICT Virtual Human Toolkit (confluence.ict.usc.edu/display/VHTK/Home) are useful for creating interactive systems. ROS is open source and provides useful tools for developing robot applications. Virtual Human Toolkit provides libraries, tools, and modules for creating virtual human characters.

Even though tools related to cognitive architectures were not represented in this survey, they could be useful in affective computing research. A few examples include SOAR (sitemaker.umich.edu/soar) and ACT-R (act-r.psy.cmu.edu). SOAR makes use of cognitive modeling and artificial intelligence, which allow the development of systems with intelligent behavior. ACT-R is a framework used for simulations to understand human cognition and also to represent applications such as cognitive tutors.

Data Collection

The survey did not include software tools for affective data collection, but some researchers reported some useful tools for running experiments and collecting data. *Superlab* (www.superlab.com) is a software tool for building experiments, stimulus presentation, and collecting data. The framework *Social Signal Interpretation (SSI)* (Wagner, Lingenfelser, Bee, & André, 2011) includes tools for data recording and real-time human behavior

Table 25.3 Popular Generic Pattern Recognition and Data Mining Tools

Tool	Description	Popularity
Weka	Free tool in Java for data mining (Hall et al., 2009). Includes a variety of machine learning algorithms for data preprocessing, feature selection, classification, clustering, etc.	55%
SPSS	Tool by IBM used for predictive analytics, statistical data analysis, and some data mining. Available at: www-01.ibm.com/software/analytics/spss	52%
PRTools	Free toolbox in MATLAB for pattern recognition (Duin et al., 2007). Includes machine learning algorithms similar to Weka.	42%
MATLABArsenal	Open-source wrapper for several machine learning packages such as Weka, NETLAB, SVMLight, mySVM, libSVM (Yan, 2006).	17%
R	Programming platform for statistical data analysis and graphing. Available at: www.r-project.org	8%
libSVM SVM light	Free libraries and implementation of support vector machines (Chang & Lin, 2011; Joachims). libSVM supports interfacing with a variety of programming languages. SVM light is implemented in C.	6%
HTK	Free toolkit for implementing hidden Markov models (HMMs) and supports interfacing with C. Popular in speech-recognition and related research (Young et al., 2002).	3%
SAS	System for statistical data analysis and data mining. Available at: www.sas.com	3%
RapidMiner	Open-source software for data mining. Provides APIs in Java and supports Weka integration. Available at: www.rapidminer.com	3%
In house	Own built in house.	77%

Table 25.4 Additional Pattern Recognition and Data Mining Tools

Tool	Description
SciPy	Open-source tool in Python for numerical and scientific computing (Jones, Oliphant, & Peterson, 2001).
RNNLIB, GMTK, JULIUS	Open-source tools applied to speech recognition. RNNLIB, based on recurrent neural networks, is available at: rnnlib.wikinet.org/wiki/Main_Page GMTK, for building graphical models, is available at: melodi.ee.washington.edu/~bilmes/gmtk JULIUS, based on n-gram and HMMs, is available at: julius.sourceforge.jp/en_index.php
ORACLE Data Miner	A data mining and analysis tool that can make use of ORACLE databases (Tamayo et al., 2005).
Liblinear	Open-source library inspired by libSVM for implementing logistic regression and linear support vector machines (Ho & Lin, 2012). Mostly dedicated to large-scale linear classification.
Orange	Free toolbox in Python but also supports visual programming and C++ for data mining. Available at: (orange.biolab.si
EDE	Toolbox for decoder comparison; for example, to compare classification labels from a machine with human labelers (Steidl, Levit, Batliner, Nöth, & Niemann, 2005).
DMML Feature Selection	Open-source feature selection package and Weka wrapper in MATLAB. Available at: featureselection.asu.edu/software.php

Table 25.5 Useful Tools for Affect Expression

Tool	Description
Festival	Free software in C++ for speech synthesis (Black, Taylor, & Caley). Provides a framework and APIs for implementing text to speech systems.
VHML	Markup language in XML called virtual human markup language or VHML (Marriott). Supports facial and body animations, gesture, speech synthesis, dialog-based interactions, etc., which are intended for virtual agents and related applications.
SmartBody	Open-source platform in C++ for character animation (Thiebaux, Marsella, Marshall, & Kallmann, 2008). Generates human-like expressions and animations in real time through behavioral markup language (BML).
FaceFX	Software to generate realistic facial animations. Suitable for game developers for adding expressions to animating characters. Available at: www.facefx.com
Xface	An open-source toolkit in C++/OpenGL to create animating agents in 3D (Balci, Not, Zancanaro, & Pianesi, 2007). Provides libraries and support for integrating third-party applications.
Horde3D	Mainly an open source tool in C++ for 3D rendering. Provides API and support for other programming languages. Available at: www.horde3d.org
Haptek	The PeoplePutty program from Haptek creates 3D interactive characters based on human pictures and speech. Accessories (such as hats, glasses etc.) can be added to the virtual character as extensions. Available at: www.haptek.com
HapFACS	Open-source tool for generating 3D facial expression (Amini, Yasavur, & Lisetti, 2012). Utilizes the facial action coding system (FACS) and provides API in C# for creating FACS-based expressions.
FACSGen	Another tool based on FACS for generating realistic facial expressions in 3D (Roesch et al., 2011). It utilizes FaceGen to produce facial identities. FaceGen is available at: facegen.com
Ontology of Body Expressions	Provides a structure to classify various gestures such as "raise hand" (for drawing attention), "oh my God" (expressed by both hands over head), "bored" (expressed by one hand under chin), "clapping" etc. (Garcia-Rojas et al., 2006). Uses Whissel's wheel activation-evaluation space (Whissell, 1989) to represent the emotions.
FAtiMA	An agent architecture that can represent behavior through appraisal, personality, planning, reasoning and emotions (Dias, Mascarenhas, & Paiva, 2011).

analysis. Tools such as Qualtrics (www.qualtrics.com) and SurveyMonkey (www.surveymonkey.com) are useful for conducting online surveys and collecting data.

Summary

This chapter, based on a survey of researchers in affective computing, discussed many of the software tools used in this area. Some third-party tools are more popular than the others, but most researchers prefer to create the tools in house and distribute them freely. However, in many cases the in-house tools are customizations and integrations of one or many of the third-party tools. Many of the researchers reported that they use or develop application software by combining some of the tools discussed in this chapter. For example, a researcher using MATLAB can build an application that integrates data acquisition by communicating with commercial sensors (e.g., BIOPAC for physiology) through an API (Calvo, Hussain, Aghaei Pour, & Alzoubi, 2011). The application could make use of media (stimuli) such as images (IAPS), audios (IADS), words (ANEW), and texts (ANET) for emotion induction (csea.phhp.ufl.edu/Media.html). The application could integrate *AuBT* to process the physiological signals and to extract features. Wrappers like the *DMML Feature Selection* package and *MATLABArsenal* can be used for affect classification.

In summary, this chapter aimed to provide information about popular software tools that may aid affective computing researchers in addressing specific problems or may help to identify the appropriate tools for in-house application development. In addition to describing several of the popular tools, the survey also revealed that affective computing researchers prefer to build a lot of tools in house and share resources freely with collaborators and the community at large. This code reuse will give birth to new, more powerful tools that can be distributed within the affective computing community.

Acknowledgments

M. Sazzad Hussain was supported by Australia Awards. Sidney D'Mello was supported by the National Science Foundation (NSF) (ITR 0325428, HCC 0834847, DRL 1235958). Any opinions, findings and conclusions, or recommendations expressed in this paper are those of the authors and do not necessarily reflect the views of the NSF.

References

Afzal, S., & Robinson, P. (2011). Natural affect data: Collection and annotation. In R. A. Calvo & S. K. D'Mello (Eds.), *New Perspectives on Affect and Learning Technologies*, (Vol. 3, pp. 55–70): Springer: New York.

Aguera, P. E., Jerbi, K., Caclin, A., & Bertrand, O. (2011). ELAN: A software package for analysis and visualization of MEG, EEG, and LFP signals. *Computational Intelligence and Neuroscience, 5*, 1–11.

Amini, R., Yasavur, U., & Lisetti, C. L. (2012, September 21). *HapFACS 1.0: Software/API for generating FACS-based facial expressions.* Paper presented at the ACM 3rd International Symposium on Facial Analysis and Animation (FAA'12), Vienna, Austria.

Asteriadis, S., Tzouveli, P., Karpouzis, K., & Kollias, S. (2009). Estimation of behavioral user state based on eye gaze and head pose—Application in an e-learning environment. *Multimedia Tools and Applications, 41*(3), 469–493.

Balci, K., Not, E., Zancanaro, M., & Pianesi, F. C. (2007, September 23–28). *Xface open source project and SMIL-agent scripting language for creating and animating embodied conversational agents.* Paper presented at the 15th International Conference on Multimedia, Augsburg, Bavaria, Germany.

Baltrusaitis, T., Robinson, P., & Morency, L. C. (2012, June 16–21). *3D constrained local model for rigid and non-rigid facial tracking.* Paper presented at the IEEE Conference on Computer Vision and Pattern Recognition (CVPR), Providence, RI, USA.

Bevacqua, E., Raouzaiou, A., Peters, C., Caridakis, G., Karpouzis, K., Pelachaud, C., & Mancini, M. (2006, June 19–21). *Multimodal sensing, interpretation and copying of movements by a virtual agent.* Paper presented at the Perception and Interactive Technologies, Kloster Irsee, Germany.

Bird, S. C. (2006). *NLTK: The natural language toolkit.* Paper presented at the COLING/ACL on Interactive Presentation Sessions, Sydney, Australia.

Black, A., Taylor, P., & Caley, R. The Festival speech synthesis system from www.cstr.ed.ac.uk/projects/festival

Boersma, P. (2002). Praat, a system for doing phonetics by computer. *Glot International, 5*(9/10), 341–345.

Bradley, M. M., & Lang, P. J. (1994). Measuring emotion: The self-assessment manikin and the semantic differential. *Journal of Behavior Therapy and Experimental Psychiatry, 25*(1), 49–59.

Burkhardt, F. C. (2012, May 23–25). *Fast labeling and transcription with the speechalyzer toolkit.* Paper presented at the LREC (Language Resources Evaluation Conference), Istanbul, Turkey.

Calvo, R. A., & D'Mello, S. (2010). Affect detection: An interdisciplinary review of models, methods, and their applications. *IEEE Transactions on Affective Computing, 1*(1), 18–37.

Calvo, R. A., Hussain, M. S., Aghaei Pour, P., & Alzoubi, O. (2011, October 9–12). *Siento: An experimental platform for behavior and psychophysiology in HCI.* Paper presented at the International Conference on Affective Computing and Intelligent Interaction (ACII2011), Memphis, TN, USA.

Chang, C. C., & Lin, C. J. (2011). LIBSVM: A library for support vector machines. *ACM Transactions on Intelligent Systems and Technology (TIST), 2*(3), 1–27.

Cowie, R., Douglas-Cowie, E., Savvidou, S., McMahon, E., Sawey, M., & Schröder, M. (2000, September 5–7). *FEELTRACE: An instrument for recording perceived emotion in real time.* Paper presented at the ISCA Tutorial and Research Workshop (ITRW) on Speech and Emotion, Newcastle, Northern Ireland, UK.

D'Mello, S., Graesser, A., & Picard, R. W. (2007). Toward an affect-sensitive AutoTutor. *IEEE Intelligent Systems, 22*(4), 53–61.

Delorme, A., & Makeig, S. (2004). EEGLAB: An open source toolbox for analysis of single-trial EEG dynamics including independent component analysis. *Journal of Neuroscience Methods, 134*(1), 9–21.

Dias, J., Mascarenhas, S., & Paiva, A. (2011). Fatima modular: Towards an agent architecture with a generic appraisal framework In *The Workshop on Standards for Emotion Modeling*, Leiden, Netherlands.

Duin, R. P. W. C., Juszczak, P., Paclik, P., Pekalska, E., de Ridder, D., Tax, D. M. J., & Verzakov, S. (2007). *PRTools4.1, A Matlab toolbox for pattern recognition.* The Netherlands: Delft University of Technology.

Eyben, F., Wollmer, M., & Schuller, B. C. (2009, Sept 10–12). *OpenEAR—Introducing the Munich open-source emotion and affect recognition toolkit.* Paper presented at the 3rd International Conference on Affective Computing and Intelligent Interaction and Workshops, Munich, Germany.

Eyben, F., Wöllmer, M., & Schuller, B. C. (2010, October 25–29). *Opensmile: The Munich versatile and fast open-source audio feature extractor.* Paper presented at the International Conference on Multimedia, Florence, Italy.

Fernandez, R., & Picard, R. W. (1998, May 12–15). *Signal processing for recognition of human frustration.* Paper presented at the IEEE International Conference on Acoustics, Speech and Signal Processing, Seattle, Washington, USA.

Fouse, A., Weibel, N., Hutchins, E., & Hollan, J. D. C. (2011, May 7–12). *Chronoviz: A system for supporting navigation of time-coded data.* Paper presented at the Annual Conference extended abstracts on Human Factors in Computing Systems (Part 1), Vancouver, BC, Canada.

Garcia-Rojas, A., Vexo, F., Thalmann, D., Raouzaiou, A., Karpouzis, K., & Kollias, S. (2006, June17). *Emotional body expression parameters in virtual human ontology.* Paper presented at the 1st International Workshop on Shapes and Semantics, Matsushima, Japan.

Hall, M., Frank, E., Holmes, G., Pfahringer, B., Reutemann, P., & Witten, I. H. (2009). The WEKA data mining software: An update. *ACM SIGKDD Explorations Newsletter, 11*(1), 10–18.

Hänninen, L., & Pastell, M. (2009). CowLog: Open-source software for coding behaviors from digital video. *Behavior Research Methods, 41*(2), 472–476.

Healey, J., & Picard, R. (1998, May 12–15). *Digital processing of affective signals*. Paper presented at the IEEE International Conference on Acoustics, Speech and Signal Processing, Seattle, Washington, USA.

Ho, C. H., & Lin, C. J. (2012). Large-scale linear support vector regression. *Journal of Machine Learning Research, 13,* 3323–3348.

Jameson, A. (2009). Adaptive interfaces and agents. In A. J. Julie & S. Andrew (Eds.), *The Human-Computer Interaction Handbook* (pp. 305-330): L. Erlbaum Associates Inc.

Joachims, T. Svmlight: Support vector machine. Available at: svmlight.joachims.org

Jones, E., Oliphant, T., & Peterson, P. (2001). SciPy: Open source scientific tools for Python. Available at: www.scipy.org

Kipp, M. (2001, September 3–7). Anvil—A generic annotation tool for multimodal dialogue. *Paper presented at The 7th European Conference on Speech Communication and Technology*, Aalborg, Denmark.

Kistler, F., Endrass, B., Damian, I., Dang, C. T., & André, E. (2012). Natural interaction with culturally adaptive virtual characters. *Journal on Multimodal User Interfaces, 6*(1–2), 39–46.

Marriott, A. Virtual Human Markup Language (VHML), from www.vhml.org

Oppenheim, A. V., & Schafer, R. W. (1975). *Digital signal processing*. Englewood Cliffs, NJ: Prentice Hall.

Osherenko, A., & André, E. (2009, September 10–12). Differentiated semantic analysis in lexical affect sensing. Paper presented at *The 3rd International Conference on Affective Computing and Intelligent Interaction and Workshops*. Amsterdam, The Netherlands.

Park, C., Ryu, J., Sohn, J., & Cho, H. (2007, June 20–23). *An emotion expression system for the emotional robot*. Paper presented at the IEEE International Symposium on Consumer Electronics, Dallas, TX, USA.

Picard, R. W. (2003). Affective computing: challenges. *International Journal of Human-Computer Studies, 59*(1–2), 55–64.

Raouzaiou, A., Tsapatsoulis, N., Karpouzis, K., & Kollias, S. (2002). Parameterized facial expression synthesis based on MPEG-4. *EURASIP Journal on Applied Signal Processing, 2002*(1), 1021–1038.

Rodrigo, M. M. T., Baker, R. S. J. d., McLaren, B. M., Jayme, A., & Dy, T. T. (2012, June 19–21). *Development of a workbench to address the educational data mining bottleneck*. Paper presented at the 5th International Conference on Educational Data Mining, Chania, Greece.

Roesch, E. B., Tamarit, L., Reveret, L., Grandjean, D., Sander, D., & Scherer, K. R. (2011). FACSGen: A tool to synthesize emotional facial expressions through systematic manipulation of facial action units. *Journal of Nonverbal Behavior, 35*(1), 1–16.

Scherer, K. R. (2005). What are emotions? And how can they be measured? *Social Science Information, 44*(4), 695–729.

Schröder, M., & Trouvain, J. (2003). The German text-to-speech synthesis system MARY: A tool for research, development and teaching. *International Journal of Speech Technology, 6*(4), 365–377.

Schuller, B., Lehmann, A., Weninger, F., Eyben, F., & Rigoll, G. C. (2009, March 23–26). *Blind enhancement of the rhythmic and harmonic sections by NMF: Does it help?* Paper presented at the International Conference on Acoustics (NAG/DAGA 2009), Rotterdam, The Netherlands.

Sjölander, K., & Beskow, J. (2000, Oct 16–20). *Wavesurfer—an open source speech tool*. Paper presented at the 6th International Conference of Spoken Language Processing (ICSLP), Beijing China.

Steidl, S., Levit, M., Batliner, A., Nöth, E., & Niemann, H. C. P. I. (2005, March 19–23). *Of all things the measure is man: Automatic classification of emotions and inter-labeler consistency*. Paper presented at the IEEE Conference on Acoustics, Speech, and Signal Processing (ICASSP'05), Philadelphia, PA.

Tamayo, P., Berger, C., Campos, M., Yarmus, J., Milenova, B., Mozes, A.,. . . Thomas, S. (2005). Oracle data mining. In O. Maimon & L. Rokach (Eds.), *Data mining and knowledge discovery handbook* (pp. 1315–1329): Springer US.

Thiebaux, M., Marsella, S., Marshall, A. N., & Kallmann, M. C. (2008, May 12–16). Smartbody: Behavior realization for embodied conversational agents. In *The 7th international joint conference on autonomous agents and multiagent systems*. Estoril, Portugal.

Vogt, T., André, E., & Bee, N. (2008, June 16–18). *EmoVoice—A framework for online recognition of emotions from voice*. Paper presented at the 4th IEEE Tutorial and Research Workshop on Perception and Interactive Technologies for Speech-based Systems, Kloster Irsee, Germany.

Wagner, J., Kim, J., & Andre, E. (2005, July 6). *From physiological signals to emotions: Implementing and comparing selected methods for feature extraction and classification*. Paper presented at the IEEE International Conference on Multimedia and Expo (ICME 2005), Amsterdam, The Netherlands.

Wagner, J., Lingenfelser, F., Bee, N., & André, E. (2011). Social signal interpretation (SSI). *KI—Künstliche Intelligenz, 25*(3), 251–256.

Whissell, C. (1989). The dictionary of affect in language. *Emotion: Theory, Research, and Experience, 4*(113–131).

Yan, R. (2006). MATLABArsenal: A Matlab package for classification algorithms. Available at: www.informedia.cs.cmu.edu/yanrong/MATLABArsenal/MATLABArsenal.htm

Young, S., Evermann, G., Kershaw, D., Moore, G., Odell, J., Ollason, D.,. . . Woodland, P. (2002). *The HTK book* (Vol. 3). Cambridge, UK: Cambridge University Engineering Department.

Emotion Data Collection and Its Implications for Affective Computing

Shazia Afzal *and* Peter Robinson

Abstract

Affective Computing has matured into an exciting and promising research discipline; several applications already show its immense potential in realizing the next generation of intelligent, intuitive, user-friendly interfaces. However, the nature of affective phenomena and their reliable measurement continue to pose fundamental problems. This chapter identifies the aims and potential challenges of affective computing and—in light of observations drawn from naturalistic data collection, emotion annotation and its analysis—highlights the need to understand the nature and expression of emotions in the context of technology use and proposes alternative ways of exploring emotional communication in human-computer interaction.

Key Words: affective computing, naturalistic data, emotion annotation

Affective Computing and Its Applications

The latest scientific findings indicate that emotions influence the very mechanisms of rational thinking and have a direct bearing on critical cognitive processes. Consequently, whether it is Don Norman reasoning about how emotional appeal lies at the heart of why we like or dislike everyday objects or Marvin Minsky arguing that the future of artificial intelligence (AI) lies in unpacking human mental states, it is believed that the next generation of computing interfaces will have to incorporate aspects of social intelligence in order to be intuitive, intelligent, and more user-friendly. Rosalind Picard set out a formal framework for studying affective phenomena, including the background of human emotions, requirements for emotionally intelligent computers, applications of the technology, as well as moral and social questions that arise from it in her influential book *Affective Computing* (Picard, 1997). It set the foundation for a new research and

technological domain aiming to equip computers with the ability to sense and understand human social signals through nonverbal behavior.

Affective Computing aims to represent, detect, and analyze nonverbal behavior in an attempt to model affective phenomena in human-computer interaction (HCI). Affect sensitive HCI is relevant in numerous application areas, such as learning technologies, security and surveillance, health care, interactive gaming and entertainment, sales and advertising, smart homes, remote collaboration, social monitoring, automated behavior research, and many others.

Beginning with a discussion of the problem space, this chapter briefly outlines the state of art in affective computing and the increasing inclination toward the use of naturalistic data. Drawing on our research data and the subsequent analyses, the major impediments in the collection and annotation of emotion data are highlighted and new directions for fruitful realization of affect-sensitive HCI are proposed.

Aims and Potential Challenges

The transition from our intuitive understanding of affect perception to formalizing it in a grammar for computational models presents a number of challenging issues. These are briefly introduced below. A more detailed and thorough discussion appears in several key publications, such as Peter and Herbon (2006); Cowie, Douglas-Cowie, and Cox (2005); Porayska-Pomsta and Pain (2004); Pantic (2003); Cowie et al. (2001); and Picard (1997), to name a few.

Definitional Issues

The study of emotion has an extensive and diverse literature ranging widely in perspectives—evolutionary, behaviorist, componential, socio-cultural, and neuroscientific approaches. An apt indicator of the terminological confusion itself is the compilation of 92 emotion definitions and 9 statements by Kleinginna and Kleinginna way back in 1981. This complexity in the general understanding of what emotion means is a major impediment to researchers investigating affective user interfaces (Porayska-Pomsta & Pain, 2004).

It has been recommended that researchers adopt a working definition of emotion in order to plan, communicate, and identify the scope of a project (Larsen & Fredrickson, 1999). By assuming such a working definition, one can construct a framework to ask experimental questions, design methodologies, and interpret results without getting embroiled in a psychological debate over how emotion is defined. The model definition proposed by Kleinginna and Kleinginna (1981), following their extensive review, is relevant for such a purpose and is reproduced here:

> Emotion is a complex set of interactions amongst subjective and objective factors, mediated by neural/hormonal systems, which can (a) give rise to affective experiences such as feelings of arousal, pleasure/displeasure; (b) generate cognitive processes such as emotionally relevant perceptual effects, appraisals, labeling processes; (c) activate widespread physiological adjustments to the arousing conditions; and (d) lead to behavior that is often, but not always, expressive, goal-directed, and adaptive.
>
> *(Kleinginna & Kleinginna, 1981, p. 355)*

This quotation captures two important and consensual aspects of emotion: (1) as a reaction to events deemed relevant to the needs, goals, or concerns of an individual and (2) as an experience encompassing physiological, affective, behavioral, and cognitive components (Brave & Nass, 2002).

Descriptive Issues

Descriptive issues are derived from the choice of conceptualizing affective content within an experimental framework and can be broadly classified along three main representational schemes: categorical, continuous, and appraisal-based (Cowie, Douglas-Cowie, & Cox, 2005).

Categorical schemes conform to the everyday use of language terms for verbalizing emotional experiences and are naturally suited for their descriptive ease and familiarity. There is an enormous variety of emotion words ranging from the six basic emotions—happiness, sadness, fear, anger, disgust, and surprise (Ekman & Freisen, 1971)—to more elaborate lexical taxonomies that allow the representation of more complex affect states beyond the prototypical ones (Baron-Cohen, Golan, Wheelwright, & Hill, 2004). However, the range of possible descriptors together with issues about their cross-cultural compatibility and meaning can be problematic (Peter & Herbon, 2006; Wierzbicka, 2003). The expression and triggering of emotions with text is described in the chapter by Strapparava and Mihalcea, this volume.

An alternative to categorical description is based on the dimensional view of emotions whereby an affect state is represented as a point in a space of two or more dimensions defined by psychological concepts. One of the most popular models is Russell's Circumplex Model of Affect (Russell, 1980), which posits that emotions conform to a circular or radix arrangement with the coordinates of this circular space defined along two orthogonal dimensions of arousal (activation) and valence (pleasantness). The primary advantage of dimensional models is that they make it easy to chart an emotional experience without requiring the explicit articulation of a specific emotion. However, collapsing an emotional state to dimensional constructs inevitably leads to a loss of discriminative information and makes some emotions like fear, anger, and disgust indistinguishable.

Appraisal-based schemes like Scherer's Component Process Model (2005) and Ortony, Clore, & Collins's (1988) Cognitive Theory of Emotion, provide a powerful predictive framework by specifying emotions as valenced reactions to critical events/objects arising out of an appraisal or evaluation of a given situation. Although appraisal-based methods enable a cause-effect reasoning of emotions and are attractive as an operational model, only a few affect recognition systems have adopted this method owing to the level of detail required as well as their reliance on subjective appraisal accounts. On the other hand, although the measurement issue between categorical and dimensional views has been a subject of discussion for over a hundred years (Darwin, 1872; Izard, 1993; Larsen & Fredrickson, 1999; Lazarus, 1991), both have been adopted with considerable success in numerous affect recognition systems.

In all, the choice of a description strategy is an important one that effectively determines the design and functionality of an affect-sensitive system. Defining a representational scheme implies characterizing the construct to be measured and therefore the output of the system itself.

Methodological Issues

The methodological issues in automatic affect inference arise from the sensitivity of emotion to the form and type of measurement method and are related to the validity, accuracy, timing, and context of emotion assessment (Larsen & Fredrickson, 1999). Since emotions are dynamic processes that unfold over time, measures obtained with minimum latency or, better still, concurrently during the emotional experience, albeit based on a small interval of earlier observations, maximize the chances of validity and accuracy. In order to ensure ecological validity of a measurement technique, the relevant contextual factors also need to be taken into account. Moreover, establishing the reliability of emotion assessment often requires the use of trained experts, which can be costly and time-consuming. The recent emphasis on the use of naturalistic databases as against the posed/acted ones for the real-world application of affective systems reflects all these concerns.

In general, identifying an emotional episode in an ongoing interaction is a complex task that is intricately related to the representation scheme used, type and level of emotion measurement, and the empirical agenda.

Technical Issues

Emotions are multidimensional constructs manifested across the visual, auditory, and physiological channels, often at varying time scales. As such, the robust tracking of behavioral signals associated with changes across these modalities is an active problem in computer vision research. For example, issues related to pose, scale, resolution, lighting, and occlusions are still relevant in the analysis of visual input (see Cohn's chapter, this volume, for details). Challenging factors to be considered include the independence of a technique from users' physiognomies, gender, age, and ethnicity; sensitivity to temporal dynamics; fusion of information from multiple channels; and context-sensitive interpretation (Pantic & Rothkrantz, 2003). A further concern is the training and validation of automatic affect analyzers across the diverse experimental conditions, databases, and annotation protocols used. While it is generally agreed that a reliable assessment of affect state requires concurrent use of multiple channels, the suitability of a modality or combination of several depends on the application requirements, types of emotions to be detected, technical feasibility, ethical concerns, and real-time requirements (Hudlicka, 2003).

State of the Art

Even though the semantics and manifestation of affective phenomena have been extensively studied across the disciplines of psychology, cognitive science, computer vision, physiology, behavioral psychology, and so on, it still remains a challenging task to develop reliable affect recognition technologies. Expression and measurement of affect, and specifically its interpretation, is person-, time-, and context-dependent. Sensory data are ambiguous and incomplete, as there are no clear criteria to map observations onto specific affect states. Lack of such ground truths makes the validation of developed techniques difficult and, worse still, application-specific. Consequently we do not know whether one system that achieves higher classification accuracy than another is actually better in practice (Pantic & Rothkrantz, 2003). Affect modeling in real time is thus a challenging task, given the complexity of emotions, their personal and subjective nature, the variability of their expression across and even within individuals, and frequently the lack of sufficient differentiation among associated visible and measurable signals (Hudlicka, 2003).

However, despite the difficulties, a whole body of research is persevering to give computers at least as much ability as humans have to recognize and interpret affective phenomena, thus enabling them to carry out intelligent behavior and dialogue with others. Advances in the field of affective computing have opened the possibility of envisioning integrated architectures by allowing for the formal representation, detection, and analysis of affective phenomena. The interested reader is referred to Calvo and D'Mello (2010) and Zeng et al. (2009) for a survey of general affect recognition methods using various modalities. In general, most affect recognition systems currently support a limited number of emotional states, ignore context while performing inference, rely on posed data that do not generalize to naturalistic data, and in most cases disregard the influence of culture and personality in the experience and expression of emotion.

Acted Versus Naturalistic Data

It is essential to have representative data in order to carry out realistic analysis, develop appropriate methods, and eventually perform validation of inferences. Therefore for viable applications of affect-sensitive technology, the use of naturalistic over posed data is being increasingly emphasized. Existing databases are often oriented to prototypical representations of a few basic emotional expressions, being mostly posed or recorded in scripted situations. Such extreme expressions of affect occur rarely if at all in HCI contexts. The applicability of such data therefore becomes severely limited because of its observed deviation from real-life situations (Batliner et al., 2003; Cowie, Douglas-Cowie, & Cox, 2005) and consequently its definite relevance as representative data. The findings of Hoque, McDuff, and Picard (2012), for example, highlight the differences between natural versus acted expressions of frustration and delight wherein, contrary to acted instances, the natural occurrences of frustration are accompanied by *smiling* in 90% of cases. There is actual evidence that naturalistic head and facial expressions of affect differ in configuration and dynamics from posed/acted ones and are, in fact, mediated by separate neural pathways (Cohn & Schmidt, 2004; Pantic & Patras, 2006). Ekman and Rosenberg (1997) identifies at least six characteristics that distinguish spontaneous from posed facial actions: morphology, symmetry, duration, speed of onset, coordination of apexes, and ballistic trajectory.

Ideally, then, a database should depict naturalism, limited or no experimental control, and be contextually relevant. Since existing databases mostly include deliberately expressed emotions and are recorded in contexts that differ from their eventual application, their relevance to naturalistic application scenarios is debatable conceptually and as found practically (Batliner, et al., 2003; Cowie, Douglas-Cowie, & Cox, 2005; Ekman & Rosenberg, 1997). Consequently, for developing applications that are generalizable to real-life situations, there is now an increasing shift from easier-to-obtain posed data to more realistic naturally occurring data in the target scenarios.

Naturalism is, however, at odds with the signal-processing quality required for efficient and robust analysis by computers (Cowie, Douglas-Cowie, & Cox, 2005). Importantly, handling the complexity associated with naturalistic data is a significant problem. Nonverbal behavior is rich, ambiguous, and hard to validate, making naturalistic data collection and labeling a tedious, expensive, and time-consuming exercise. In addition, the lack of a consistent model of affect makes the abstraction of observed behavior into appropriate labeling constructs very arbitrary. But to ensure ecological validity and assist in a more meaningful interpretation, it is necessary to study affect patterns as they occur naturally in context. The eventual purpose is to abstract this behavior in terms of features that can enable automatic prediction and reliable computational modeling of affect states.

Working with Naturalistic Data

Emotion and expressivity have contextual significance, so that if we adopt an application-oriented view, reliance on reusable general databases is perhaps of limited value. For affect recognition technology to operate reliably in target applications, we need context-specific corpora to serve not only as repositories of sample data but also, importantly, to shape our understanding of the problem itself. Our research presents one such attempt to capture naturalistic emotional data in a learning scenario. Two computer-based learning tasks, a card game and a tutorial, were used to collect samples of emotional behavior in an unconstrained setting. The data obtained went through three levels of annotation—one by the subjects immediately after the experiment and two by multiple external raters. Based on previous studies that highlight the importance of affective diagnoses in learning, a domain-relevant set of six affect groups was chosen using Baron-Cohen's (Baron-Cohen, Golan, Wheelwright, & Hill, 2004) lexical emotions taxonomy. The choice was validated during the annotation process and the proportion of final labeled instances showed the predominance of *confusion* followed by *surprised, interested, happy, bored,* and *annoyed.*

The annotation process revealed that it is indeed very difficult to derive clearly labeled samples from naturalistic data. We found that the main problems in annotation stem from the dynamic nature of emotions, the ambiguity in categorization, and the high subjectivity of emotion perception. This was evident from the low accuracy of emotion judgment as measured in terms of inter-rater reliability scores. Details of the data collection and annotation framework appear in Afzal and Robinson (2011), where significant findings relating to limitations in the use of self-report, technical and inferential complexity in the segmentation of video data, ambiguity in emotion categorization, and gender differences in affect perception are discussed.

Revisiting the Data

The data drawn upon in our research was aggregated to train an automatic facial affect recognizer. However, the process of designing and carrying out the data collection exercise and subsequent analysis produced more questions than answers. Conceptual and methodological issues, for example, kept recurring in different forms. It was difficult to identify the appropriate affect descriptors, and even though a domain-relevant set of categories was identified, their inclusiveness and perceived meaning remained questionable. The intricate relationship between the recording context and the resultant behavior posed questions with regard to ecological validity. Yet the conflict between the recording setup and the eventual video quality suitable for video processing made for some compromises, like shifting to a usability lab. The choice of the experimental environment also required careful consideration in order to minimize any potential confounds in the assessment and interpretation of emotional expressions.

After the video data were collected, their segmentation and annotation highlighted the complexity and variance in emotion judgment across a range of human raters. During self-annotation, participants' reflection and meaning making seemed to conflict with the required emotional account. Their surprise, amusement, or boredom in watching their videos affected their ability to judge. While this subjective interpretation is a known shortcoming of self-report (Larsen & Fredrickson, 1999), its use as a ground truth for training a classifier remains difficult.

Consequently, it was difficult to identify the emotional episodes from the continuous video records and extremely challenging to demarcate more specific boundaries into expressions indicative of different affect states. Not surprisingly, then, the interrater reliabilities were low, indicating the lack of consensus in emotion judgment between the human judges themselves. So even though a number of classification methods were explored with good success, a more fundamental problem was being concealed amid the focus on objective measures of recognition accuracy and error rates.

Such inconsistencies and practical issues as we encountered during the research prompted us to reflect on the practicality of incorporating automatic affect inference, as currently understood, in the target application. With the help of an ethnographer, an exploratory approach was taken to reexamine the data using video analysis. The objective was to develop a more qualitative understanding of emotion expression in this setting and reflect upon the role of emotions in human-machine interaction. The outcome was a reevaluation of the importance of context in human expressivity and the rethinking of assumptions inherent in the methods and goals of affective computing.

Qualitative Analysis

The nature of the task performed and situational reactions emerged as the dominant factors affecting the expression and display of emotions (Afzal, Morrison, & Robinson, 2009). Consistently across the participant group, sharp and frequent changes of expression were observed during the card game as compared with the tutorial task, wherein faces became slack and expression changes were infrequent, sustained, and slow. It appears, then, that the type of activity with a machine has a substantial impact on the nature and expressivity of an individual with deeper levels of concentration and engagement associated with subdued manifestations of affect. Moreover, the reactions of participants to three triggers/events presented during the card game highlighted the distinction between felt emotions versus situational reactions and, therefore, the difficulty of interpreting a behavioral cue in terms of users' internal mental processes, attitudes, and experiences.

In general, the technical challenge of acquiring relevant information from naturalistic displays together with the complexity of interpreting it amid factors of personality, attitude, and situations shows that spontaneous emotion recognition from user behavior may not be so practical. On the one hand, concentration and interest seem to reduce expressivity, causing technical difficulties; on the other hand, the distinction between felt emotions and situational reactions creates design issues. Interpretation of the higher-level affect state from observable signs requires, in effect, that we equip computers with the knowledge, experience, observations, and learning that we as humans acquire over our lifetimes.

Perhaps a more pragmatic solution could be to actively involve the user and shift the onus of interpretation from the computer to the user. As Ward and Marsden (2004) highlight, it is the intentional affect that is easier to recognize and, in fact, more important than the reactive affect in human-human interaction. Affect, they emphasize, has an intentional communicative function and is used to negotiate meaning in our interactions. This echoes Fridlund's (1994) functionalist view of emotions as being strategic acts that serve to control social interactions. In other words, facial expressions of emotion can be seen as social messages dependent on motive and context and therefore profoundly influenced by the nature and trajectory of ongoing social interactions. Consequently, in terms of incorporating nonverbal information in technology, Fridlund suggests "that it may be better to consider facial expressions to be declarations whose referents are external than as eruptions whose referents are internal" (Fridlund, p. 3).

For a more meaningful adaptation and interaction, then, an alternative approach of intentional affective interaction could be suggested where users—understanding the consequences of their nonverbal behavior—make an active effort to be understood. On the one hand, this is likely to encourage more expressivity in users, making emotion detection easier and perhaps more robust. On the other hand, it eases the design problem of not knowing if and how a facial expression should be interpreted, as the user will purposefully and proactively engage in the communication.

Such a system would also conform to the accepted ethical stance that users remain aware and in control of what information is being used by the computer and how it is used (Picard & Klein, 2002). Transparency about the machine's role and functionality is, in fact, one of the fundamental principles of Human Centered Design (Norman, 1988). The study by Axelrod and Hone (2005), for example, shows how user expectation and intentionality has a significant bearing on observable emotional behavior. However, apart from the obvious concerns of associated fatigue and distraction from the task at hand, the design of an intentional affect-responsive interface may involve more complex issues.

Since social context plays a significant role in the use of nonverbal expressions during interaction, awareness of the machine's passivity and lack of social and interpersonal context will affect the nature of user's expressivity and behavior. So far as the behavior is concerned, our data corroborates the "Computers as Social Actors" (Nass, Steuer, & Tauber, 1994) paradigm, which asserts that people mindlessly apply social rules in their interaction with computers. But as Nass and Moon (2000) emphasize, it has yet to be determined which characteristics of the interaction brings out this behavior in users and how similar it is to that obtained in a human-human setting. So while we know that people ascribe persona and social behavior to devices, we do not know the exact nature of this behavior. More research in this direction would be rewarding in order to clarify the design and implementation of realistic affective computing applications.

Reflections on the Way Forward

Nonverbal behavior outside controlled experimental conditions is subtle and varies significantly across individuals and contexts. Our analyses and experience while working with natural data have only questioned the robustness and the feasibility of the standard approach. The notion of developing automatic emotion recognition systems followed by appropriate intervention strategies—as if they were disparate stages—is based on a reductionist conceptualization of affect as a measurable and discrete entity independent of the interaction it actually emerges from and continually influences.

The computational modeling of "context" illustrates a similar representational problem invoking Dourish's (2004) proposition of reconsidering it as an interactional and situated problem instead. Asserting this stance, Boehner et al. argue against the general practice of using the information processing model of emotion in affective computing whereby emotion is construed as an internal, individual, and private phenomenon that can be delineated and formalized using well-defined constructs (Boehner, DePaula, Dourish, & Sengers, 2007; Sengers, Boehner, Mateas, & Gay, 2008). The interaction model of emotion thus provides a theoretical framework for exploring the emergent nature of affect and probing creative ways of modeling affect while explicitly accounting for intentionality.

Different Perspectives

At this stage the discussion can be extended to reflect on the differences in methodologies adopted in affective computing and how these influence the way emotion-sensitive systems are conceived to function. To analyze this, consider two seemingly conflicting approaches—namely, the design approach versus the engineering approach, which embody a difference in perspective in that a distinction can be drawn in terms of the approach being used as well as the evaluation strategy employed.

The engineering approach seeks to formalize affect in terms of precise computational models or rules. It presupposes a well-defined problem and seeks to find an optimal solution focusing on the right combination of features to give the right level of recognition accuracy. With the underlying focus on representation—be it categorical, dimensional, or appraisal-based—the definition of emotion is assumed to be universal, standardized, and therefore portable across contexts. The complex task of emotion perception is thus reduced to determining a mapping between patterns observed in one or more of the nonverbal channels to the affect construct(s) set out to be relevant for a system. Affect intelligence is then built in sets of algorithms using pattern recognition and machine learning techniques on datasets, mostly posed/acted, that conform to the required representational stance.

Embedded within this notion is the underlying concept of emotion as an absolute and unchanging entity that has its own meaning, which is separate across people and interaction contexts. Boehner et al. (2005) call this the information-processing model of emotion, in which affect is considered to be a kind of information that can be transmitted in a loss-free manner between computational systems and users. Emotion is abstracted in terms of units of information and plugged into an underlying system architecture as yet another component or module. This separation of emotion from its overall context results in an impoverished representation and is unlikely to be of any practical benefit in real-world applications. By codifying rich emotional behavior into arbitrary categorizations, the engineering approach implicitly tries to fit the problem of affect inference into a preconceived framework based on assumptions that may not even hold true in human-machine interactions. Consequently this account fails to incorporate the social and cultural context that is necessary to give emotional behavior its true meaning.

From a computational perspective, there is no clear consensus regarding the notion of context and what it means, what it includes, and what role it plays in HCI (Dourish, 2004). In affective computing, the term has been used in an equally uncertain manner to refer to everything outside of the behavioral pattern being studied; and therefore includes an infinite number of personal, cultural, historical, environmental, and situational factors. So while there is acknowledgment of the significance of context in the interpretation of emotion, the task of dealing with it practically has been sidelined by reductionist attempts to optimize the sensing and measurement technology first. The use of experimentally controlled posed or acted data, which are technically easier to deal with, has traditionally served to justify precisely this purpose. Now, when the field seems to have reached a saturation point in terms of performance evaluated through recognition accuracies, the issue can no longer be avoided. The fact that the developed techniques have not generalized to real-world settings has rightly shifted the focus from posed/acted data to naturalistic data.

However, it is in dealing with naturalistic emotional data that one actually understands the limitations of the engineering stance in arriving at an appropriate conceptualization of affect. Our research has, for example, uncovered the problems associated with affect measurement and interpretation and has discussed the subtlety and ambiguity of emotions and their co-occurrence as well as individual differences in their expression, regulation, and perception. Issues related to the nature of affective interventions and their reliability, the emergent ethical issues, and the influence on subsequent user emotional behavior have further been highlighted.

Despite these concerns, the engineering stance continues to dominate the field, and efforts to build standardized datasets, evaluation metrics, and emotion representation languages continue. While it may be argued that computers, as information systems, need to treat emotions as information at some level of abstraction, it may be more productive to determine the right form and level of abstraction by considering alternative and, importantly, interdisciplinary approaches that draw on both technology design methods as well as social and cultural analysis (Sengers, 2005). Arguing for a convergence of multiple investigative paradigms in affective computing, Muller (2004) cautions that lack of knowledge about part-whole relationships of components of user experience becomes particularly important with regard to affective aspects of user experience. He proposes taking insights from ethnographic observation and analysis and experimenting with them conceptually in design explorations. He further suggests engaging with actual/potential users to explore the diversity of their concepts and attitudes about relating emotionally with computers. The knowledge acquired through these experiences may then inform ideas for subsequent formal hypothesis testing.

Such an interdisciplinary approach is endorsed by Sengers (2005) in highlighting the futility of trying to engineer experiences, and it has been instantiated in several projects through the concept of technology probes. Technology probes are simple, flexible, and adaptable technologies serving the social science goal of collecting information about the use and users of the technology in a real-world setting, the engineering goal of field testing the technology, and the design goal of inspiring users and researchers to think of about new technologies to support their needs and desires (Hutchinson, et al., 2003). Examples of practical deployment include eMoto (Sundstrom, Stahl, & Hook, 2007) and the "Affective Diary" (Stahl et al. 2009), which make use of technology probes in a user-centered design process followed by exploratory end-user studies in an attempt to define, refine, and explore the boundaries between user and system roles in the communication of emotion.

In affective computing, design-based approaches thus symbolize a shift in purpose from modeling affect to supporting the interpretation of affect instead. They are based on the notion that emotion is not only mediated by social and cultural situations but also used to enact and sustain those settings. In other words, emotions are shaped not only by their expression but also by their reception. This forms the basis of adopting an interactional approach to emotion as an alternative to the information-processing one (Boehner et al., 2007). The interactional approach discounts the objective view of emotions and embraces its ambiguity and subjectivity by actively involving users in meaning making. Strategies for evaluation are then informed from phenomenological approaches and interpretive inquiry using personal accounts and reflection probes, among other methods, to elucidate the usage of technology and its relationship to practice (Sengers et al. 2008; Sengers & Gaver, 2006). Evaluation thus shifts from optimizing quantitative criteria, like recognition accuracy or probability, to assessing the design goals of how a system is received in practice. In engineering affect, we run the risk of imposing a definition and form that might alter the way affective communication ordinarily takes place. In contrast, the design-oriented stance relies on a more holistic study of technology use to account for affect in all its complexity and offers a reasonable alternative whereby to explore the concept of emotionality in computer systems. The field of affective computing can hugely benefit from comprehensive accounts of design-based studies, ideally longitudinal, to guide engineering efforts toward more practical and user-friendly emotion technologies.

Alternative Conceptualization

Even though emotional communication is an important aspect of our everyday social interactions, it seems that our ability to verbalize or articulate emotion perception in words is extremely impoverished and highly dependent on active vocabulary. This was consistently observed during the annotation process during which raters could identify "something" but found it quite difficult to express it explicitly in words. This highlighted the difficulty of formalizing emotional experience into discrete categories. The categorization approach also presented the difficulty of identifying precise boundaries of expressions to map onto distinct affect states.

Keeping these constraints in view, perhaps a more pragmatic approach would be to map behavioral signals onto broader learning-related concepts signifying conducive or obtrusive behavior along with an intensity component. This would mean adopting a dimensional approach to model emotions with the dimensions assuming a domain-relevant character. Making the measured construct a little more abstract can facilitate a more flexible judgment procedure while also reducing the scope of terminological confusion and any cross-cultural incompatibilities. The broad categorization of emotions on the lines of activating/deactivating (Pekrun, et al., 2002) or of pertinent behavior as on/off task (Baker, 2007; Kapoor & Picard, 2005) are relevant examples of such conceptualizations. Hussein, Monkaresi, and Calvo (2012), in fact, provide empirical evidence indicating the classification power of the dimensional over the categorical approach.

Such a representation would not only eliminate the need to accurately identify boundaries of emotional episodes but also facilitate labeling in a continuous manner as part of the ongoing interaction. Akin to what Cowie (2009) describes as "trace-like representations," this would enable capturing of a time-varying record of perceived emotional content or overall affective quality. One could, for example, visualize a labeling session wherein a coder, debriefed about noticing a behavior of interest, say level of engagement, watches the whole interaction video and is supposed to click a single button whenever he or she perceives anything significant. The density of such markings across multiple coders, preferably prescreened for their nonverbal decoding ability, would then highlight areas of relevant changes to focus on. The coder would no longer be burdened with assigning a specific category to a portion of video that, in most cases, is stripped out of context. The efficacy of such a judgment strategy is also supported by experimental findings on the suitability of a dimensional decoding strategy in the case of partial or ambiguous emotional expressions (Mendolia, 2007), as are likely to occur in naturalistic data.

Compromise on Functionalities: Separation of Measurement and Meaning

Explicitly assigning emotional meaning onto nonverbal signs is hard even for human raters, especially when they are provided with limited context information. Emotional judgments are extremely subjective and ambiguous and therefore difficult to formalize in rules and procedures. Factors like gender, culture, mood, emotional intelligence—and even disorders like autism—affect emotion judgments (Chakrabarti & Baron-Cohen, 2006; Elfenbein, Marsh, & Ambady, 2002; Jack, Blais, Scheepers, Schyns, & Caldara, 2009). People who are more empathetic, for example, would interpret nonverbal signs differently than those who are not and may not even be consistent about their judgments when in a different state of mind. The actual formulation of rules for computers to be able to do this is going to be difficult.

A compromise can be reached by pursuing two parallel methodological approaches focusing on (1) the measurement of behavioral signals by the computers and (2) the interpretation of these signals by actively involving the user or users. This would conform to Sengers and Gaver's (2006) design proposition—of "downplaying the system's authority" in dealing with an interpretively flexible concept like emotional interaction. This distinction can reduce the complexity of emotion judgment in human-computer interaction by aligning functionality with respective abilities—computers with continuous objective measurement and user(s) with meaning making and high-level interpretation.

As discussed in the previous section, a potential way to proceed in terms of measurement is to recover a more global-level picture of the affective quality by tracking unusual/interesting patterns from the continuously monitored behavioral signs. Further research could then pursue the task of finding associations between the relevant affect construct(s) and the selected feature descriptors. Efforts toward real-time automatic FACS coding in spontaneous and naturally evoked data (Bartlett et al., 2006; Valstar, Gunes, & Pantic, 2007), for example, can be instrumental in carrying out objective measurement of visual signs for real-world applications.

Having preprocessed the behavioral cues in terms of relevant constructs, the challenge then is to make use of this information in an effective manner. This is where shifting the onus of interpretation, as well as action, onto the user can help override the complexity of letting a computer do the same. By presenting the measured emotional behavior in creative visualizations, the user can be actively involved in meaning attribution, personal discovery, and reflection (Leahu, Schwenk, & Sengers, 2008). Affect modeling would thereby assume a more personal and subjective character, allowing the possibility of reflecting on individual emotional experiences. In the perceived application context, this would in fact serve as a form of feedback, prompting learners to revisit or consider interesting episodes during their interaction and possibly reinforcing learning in the process. The affective diary, for example—which represents affective body memorabilia in abstract visual representations using shapes and colors—is inspiring in this regard (Stahl, et al., 2009). A similar example is that of Emotional Flowers (Bernhaupt, Boldt, Mirlacher, Wilfinger, & Tscheligi, 2007), which deploys an ambient display to represent the emotional states of game participants; it uses flowers that shrink or grow depending on the emotions measured through facial expressions.

In summary, one can achieve a realistic notion of recognizing emotionally salient events by balancing a lower-level understanding of behavioral signals with the human ability to make sense of this information and interpret it in a personally meaningful way. When and how during the interaction this information should be provided would depend on the design of the specific application environment.

Exploring Intentionality

Affective computing envisages truly effective human-machine interactions as being affect-sensitive. Yet the field is both motivated and influenced by an understanding of emotion in an environment of person to person, which differs from its eventual application of person to machine. In light of the inconsistencies of expressivity observed in our data—the important influence of task type on the expression of emotion and the distinction between felt emotion and situational response—intentional affective interaction with a machine was proposed as a promising solution. The use of technology probes (Hutchinson, et al., 2003) along the lines of Gaver et al.'s (1999) cultural probes can be helpful in pursuing this idea for a more inclusive design approach. Technology probes deploy provocative artifacts in real-use contexts to stimulate design ideas and to elucidate user experience in an open-ended manner. This would allow for a shift from the psychological and subjective definition of emotions to a more phenomenological and shared one.

Using Eye Tracking During Labeling

An interesting avenue of future research is to incorporate eye tracking during the labeling process in order to identify the regions of interest as well to help understand how humans perceive emotions from visual clues. When used in a continuous emotion judgment task, the fixation times and traces of the focused regions can give vital clues for defining appropriate features as well as providing estimates of the temporal window of evidence required for segmentation. The utility of such an approach was demonstrated by the results of Jack et al. (2009), who used eye tracking during an emotional labeling task to uncover significant cultural differences in the decoding of even the so-called universal facial expressions of emotion.

Summary and Conclusions

Affective computing builds on the premise that adapting applications based on the emotional state of users leads to compelling and effective interaction with machines. This has often been interpreted to produce scenarios of use, such as the following: If a computer tutorial senses frustration, then it can adapt the content that the user receives to mollify that negative emotion, much as a human teacher would do. Such scenarios however, have an implicit assumption that people "interact" with machines just as they do with humans—that is, it is assumed that users follow the same protocols of emotional behavior. It is expected that nonverbal behavior associated with an emotional state will be similar to that observed in human-human interaction and that users will accept the same type of adaptive intelligence from a machine as from a person.

Furthermore, our inability to describe and achieve consensus on emotional behavior, as well as the individual differences in encoding/decoding nonverbal behavior, makes it is unlikely that computers will be able to perform the high-level interpretation necessary for emotion inference, at least in the foreseeable future. Nevertheless, there is substantial motivation to pursue this aim, and our proposition is that the most pragmatic way this can be achieved is to think beyond function approximation of specific patterns

of behavioral signals to actively engaging the user in meaning making. As Picard and Klein observe, "Just because humans are the best example we know, when it comes to emotional interaction it does not mean that we have to duplicate their emotional abilities in machines, which may not even be possible" (Picard & Klein, 2002, p. 154).

We need to understand the nature and expression of emotion in the context of technology use, and this may mean exploring alternative ways of what is perhaps a qualitatively different form of emotion expression and communication. In the beginning of the chapter the main issues in affective computing research were categorized along conceptual, methodological, technical, and ethical constraints. The conclusions and proposed directions for future work address each of these issues to advance the problem definition to a more practical redefinition.

Acknowledgments

This research was supported by the Gates Cambridge Trust and the Cambridge Overseas Research Studentship.

References

Afzal, S., Morrison, C., & Robinson, P. (2009). Intentional affect: An alternative notion of affective interaction with a machine. *23rd British HCI Group Annual Conference on People and Computers: Celebrating People and Technology* (pp. 370–374). Cambridge, UK: British Computer Society

Afzal, S., & Robinson, P. (2011), Natural affect data—Collection and annotation, In R. A. Calvo & S. D'Mello (Eds.), *New perspective on affect and learning technologies.* New York, NY: Springer.

Axelrod, L., & Hone, K. (2005). Uncharted passions: User displays of positive affect with an adaptive affective system. *Affective computing and intelligent interaction* (ACII) (pp. 890–897). New York, NY: Springer Verlag.

Baker, R. S. (2007). *Modeling and understanding students' off-task behaviour in intelligent tutoring systems* SIGCHI Conference on Human Factors in Computing Systems (CHI 2007) (pp. 1059–1068). New York, NY: Association for Computing Machinery.

Baron-Cohen, S., Golan, O., Wheelwright, S., & Hill, J. (2004). *Mind reading: The interactive guide to emotions.* London: Jessica Kingsley.

Bartlett, M. S., Littlewort, G., Frank, M., Lainscsek, C., Fasel, I., & Movellan, J. (2006). Fully automatic facial action recognition in spontaneous behavior. *7th International Conference on Automatic Face and Gesture Recognition* (FGR 2006), (pp. 223–230). Southampton, UK: IEEE.

Batliner, A., Fischer, K., Huber, R., Spilker, J., & Noth, E. (2003). How to find trouble in communication. *Speech Communication, 40* (1–2), 117–143.

Bernhaupt, R., Boldt, A., Mirlacher, T., Wilfinger, D., & Tscheligi, M. (2007). Using emotion in games: Emotional flowers. *International Conference on Advances in Computer*

Entertainment Technology (p. 48). New York, NY: Association for Computing Machinery.

Boehner, K., DePaula, R., Dourish, P., & Sengers, P. (2005). Affect: From information to interaction. *4th Decennial Conference on Critical Computing: Between Sense and Sensibility* (p. 68). New York, NY: Association for Computing Machinery.

Boehner, K., DePaula, R., Dourish, P., & Sengers, P. (2007). How emotion is made and measured. *International Journal of Human-Computer Studies, 65*, 275–291.

Brave, S., & Nass, C. (2002). Emotion in human-computer interaction. In J. Jacko, & A. Sears (Eds.), *Handbook of human-computer interaction* (pp. 251–271). Hillsdale, NJ: Lawrence Erlbaum Associates.

Calvo, R. A., & D'Mello, S. (2010). Affect detection: An interdisciplinary review of models, methods, and their applications. *IEEE Transactions in Affective Computing, 1*(1), 18–37.

Chakrabarti, B., & Baron-Cohen, S. (2006). Empathizing: Neurocognitive developmental mechanisms and individual differences. *Understanding Emotions, 156*, 403–417.

Cohn, J. F., & Schmidt, K. L. (2004). The timing of facial motion in posed and spontaneous smiles. *Wavelets, Multiresolution and Information Processing, 2*, 1–12.

Cowie, R. (2009). Perceiving emotion: Towards a realistic understanding of the task. *Philosophical Transactions of the Royal Society B: Biological Sciences, 364* (1535), 3515.

Cowie, R., Douglas-Cowie, E., & Cox, C. (2005). Beyond emotion archetypes: Databases for emotion modelling using neural networks. *Neural Networks, 18*, 371–388.

Cowie, R., Douglas-Cowie, E., Tsapatsoulis, N., Votsis, G., Kollias, S., Fellenz, W., Taylor, J. G. (2001). Emotion recognition in human-computer interaction. *IEEE Signal Processing Magazine, 18* (1), 32–80.

Darwin, C. (1872). *The expression of the emotions in man and animals*. London: Murray.

Dourish, P. (2004). What we talk about when we talk about context. *Personal and Ubiquitous Computing, 8*, 19–30.

Ekman, P., & Freisen, W. V. (1971). Constants across cultures in the face and emotion. *Journal of Personality and Social Psychology, 17*, 124–129.

Ekman, P., & Rosenberg, E. L. (1997). What the face reveals: Basic and applied studies of spontaneous expression using facial action coding system (FACS). New York, NY: Oxford University Press.

Elfenbein, H. A., Marsh, A. A., & Ambady, N. (2002). Emotional intelligence and the recognition of emotion from facial expressions. In L. F. Barrett, & P. Salovey (Eds.), *The wisdom of feelings: Processes underlying emotional intelligence* (pp. 37–59). New York, NY: Guilford Press.

Fridlund, A. J. (1994). *Human facial expression: An evolutionary view*. San Diego, CA: Academic Press.

Gaver, W., Dunne, T., & Pacenti, E. (1999). Cultural probes. *Interactions, 6* (1), 21–29.

Hoque, M. E., McDuff, D. J., & Picard, R. W. (2012). Exploring temporal patterns in classifying frustrated and delighted smiles. *IEEE Transactions on Affective Computing*, (99), 1–13

Hudlicka, E. (2003). To feel or not to feel: The role of affect in human-computer interaction. *International Journal of Human-Computer Studies, 59*, 1–32.

Hutchinson, H., Westerlund, B., Bederson, B., Druin, A., Beaudouin-Lafon, M., Evans, H.,...Sundblad, Y. (2003). Technology probes: Inspiring design for and with families. *SIGCHI Conference on Human Factors in Computing Systems*

(pp. 17–24). New York, NY: Association for Computing Machinery.

Hussein, M. S., Monkaresi, H., & Calvo, R. A. (2012). Categorical vs. dimensional representations in multimodal affect detection during learning. In S. A. Cerri, W. J. Clancey, G. Papadourakis, & K. Panourgia (Eds.), *Intelligent tutoring systems* (pp. 78–83). Chania, Greece: Springer Verlag.

Izard, C. E. (1993). Four systems for emotion activation: Cognitive and noncognitive processes. *Psychological Review, 100*, 68–90.

Jack, R. E., Blais, C., Scheepers, C., Schyns, P. G., & Caldara, R. (2009). Cultural confusions show that facial expressions are not universal. *Current Biology, 19* (18), 1543–1548.

Kapoor, A., & Picard, R. W. (2005). Multimodal Affect Recognition in Learning Environments. *13th Annual ACM International Conference on Multimedia* (pp. 677-682). New York, NY: Association for Computing Machinery.

Kleininna, P. R., & Kleininna, A. M. (1981). A Categorized list of emotion definitions, with suggestions for a consensual definition. *Motivation and Emotion, 5* (4), 345–379.

Larsen, R. J., & Fredrickson, B. L. (1999). Measurement issues in emotion research. In: Kahneman D, Diener E, Schwarz N, editors. *Well-being: The foundations of hedonic psychology* (pp. 40–60). New York: Russell Sage Foundation.

Lazarus, R. S. (1991). *Emotion and adaptation*. New York, NY: Oxford University Press.

Leahu, L., Schwenk, S., & Sengers, P. (2008). Subjective objectivity: Negotiating emotional meaning. In *Designing interactive systems (DIS)* (pp. 425–434). Cape Town, South Africa: Association for Computing Machinery.

Mendolia, M. (2007). Explicit use of categorical and dimensional strategies to decode facial expressions of emotion. *Journal of Nonverbal Behaviour, 31*, 57–75.

Muller, M. (2004). Multiple paradigms in affective computing. *Interacting with Computers, 16* (4), 759–768.

Nass, C., & Moon, Y. (2000). Machines and mindlessness: Social responses to computers. *Journal of Social Issues, 56* (1), 81–103.

Nass, C., Steuer, J., & Tauber, E. R. (1994). Computers are social actors. *SIGCHI Conference on Human Factors in Computing Systems: Celebrating Interdependence (CHI)* (pp. 72–78). New York, NY: Association for Computing Machinery.

Norman, D. A. (1988). *The psychology of everyday things*. New York: Basic Books.

Ortony, A., Clore, G. L., & Collins, A. (1998). *The cognitive structure of emotions*. Cambridge, UK: Cambridge University Press.

Pantic, M. (2009). Machine analysis of facial behaviour: Naturalistic & dynamic behaviour. *Philosophical Transactions of the Royal Society B: Biological Sciences, 364* (1535), 3505.

Pantic, M., & Patras, I. (2006). Dynamics of facial expression: Recognition of facial actions and their temporal segments from face profile image sequences. *IEEE Transactions on Systems, Man, and Cybernetics, 36* (2), 433–449.

Pantic, M., & Rothkrantz, L. J. (2003). Toward an affect-sensitive multimodal human-computer interaction. *Proceedings of the IEEE, 91* (9), 1370–1390.

Pekrun, R., Goetz, T., Titz, W., & Perry, R. P. (2002). Academic emotions in students' self-regulated learning and achievement: A program of qualitative and quantitative research. *Educational Psychologist, 37*, 91–105.

Peter, C., & Herbon, A. (2006). Emotion representation and physiology assignments in digital systems. *Interacting with Computers, 18*, 139–170.

Picard, R. W. (1997). *Affective computing*. Cambridge, MA: MIT Press.

Picard, R. W., & Klein, J. (2002). Computers that recognise and respond to user emotion: Theoretical and practical implications. *Interacting with Computers, 14*, 141–169.

Porayska-Pomsta, K., & Pain, H. (2004). Exploring methodologies for building socially and emotionally intelligent learning environments. *Workshop on Social and Emotional Intelligence in Learning Environments (SEILE), Intelligent Tutoring Systems*. Maceio, Brazil: Springer-Verlag.

Russell, J. A. (1980). A circumplex model of affect. *Journal of Personality and Social Psychology, 39*, 1161–1178.

Scherer, K. L. (2005). What are emotions? And how can they be measured? *Social Science Information, 44* (4).

Sengers, P. (2005). The engineering of experience. *Funology*, 19–29.

Sengers, P., & Gaver, B. (2006). Staying open to interpretation: Engaging multiple meanings in design and evaluation. *Proceedings of the 6th conference on Designing Interactive systems* (pp. 108–118). New York, NY: Association for Computing Machinery.

Sengers, P., Boehner, K., Mateas, M., & Gay, G. (2008). The disenchantment of affect. *Personal and Ubiquitous Computing, 12* (5), 347–358.

Stahl, A., Hook, K., Svensson, M., Taylor, A. S., & Combetto, M. (2009). Experiencing the affective diary. *Personal and Ubiquitous Computing, 13* (5), 365–378.

Sundstrom, P., Stahl, A., & Hook, K. (2007). In situ informants exploring an emotional mobile messaging system in their everyday practice. *International Journal of Human-Computer Studies, 65* (4), 388–403.

Valstar, M. F., Gunes, H., & Pantic, M. (2007). How to distinguish posed from spontaneous smiles using geometric features. *ACM International Conference on Multimodal Interfaces* (pp. 38–45). New York, NY: Association for Computing Machinery.

Ward, R. D., & Marsden, P. H. (2004). Affective computing: Problems, reactions and intentions. *Interacting with Computers, 16*, 707–713.

Wierzbicka, A. (2003). *Cross-cultural pragmatics: The semantics of human interaction*. Berlin: Mouton de Gruyter.

Zeng, Z., Pantic, M., Roisman, G. I., & Huang, T. S. (2009). A survey of affect recognition methods: audio, visual, and spontaneous expressions. *IEEE Transactions on Pattern Analysis & Machine Intelligence, 31* (1), 39–58.

Affect Elicitation for Affective Computing

Jacqueline M. Kory *and* Sidney K. D'Mello

Abstract

The ability to reliably and ethically elicit affective states in the laboratory is critical in studying and developing systems that can detect, interpret, and adapt to human affect. Many methods for eliciting emotions have been developed. In general, they involve presenting a stimulus to evoke a response from one or more emotion response systems. The nature of the stimulus varies widely. Passive methods include the presentation of emotional images, film clips, and music. Active methods can involve social or dyadic interactions with other people or behavioral manipulation in which an individual is instructed to adopt facial expressions, postures, or other emotionally relevant behaviors. This chapter discusses exemplar methods of each type, discusses advantages and disadvantages of each method, and briefly summarizes some additional methods.

Key Words: affect elicitation, emotional images, emotional film clips, emotional music, backward masking, behavior manipulation, social interaction, dyadic interaction

Introduction

One important goal of affective computing (AC) is to develop computational systems that can recognize and respond to the affective states of the user, thus enabling machines to interact with humans in what is hoped to be a more effective, naturalistic fashion (Picard, 1997). The success of affect-sensitive interfaces depends on their accuracy at detecting or recognizing users' affective states. Affect detectors typically rely on supervised classification techniques to develop models that associate particular behaviors (such as physiological measures and facial features) with emotion labels or dimensions. These detectors need large data sets for model development and validation. As such, it is critical to obtain reliable datasets of emotional expressions collected from a wide range of individuals. These data fall in three primary categories: (1) acted or posed expressions obtained by asking individuals, often actors, to portray emotions; (2) induced expressions, in which

emotional responses are elicited via some stimulus; and (3) naturalistic displays of emotion. Acted data are easy to collect, but an important concern is of the data's ecological validity. For example, when told to act frustrated, individuals do not smile, but during natural experiences of frustration, the majority of individuals *do* smile (Hoque & Picard, 2011). Naturalistic data, on the other hand, are certainly ecologically valid but notoriously difficult to collect. The middle road, in which specific emotions are elicited, may be a good compromise for AC researchers and this has been used to great effect already (see, e.g., Bailenson et al., 2008; Khalali & Moradi, 2009; Koelstra et al., 2011; Leon, Clarke, Callaghan, & Sepulveda, 2007; Monkaresi, Hussain, & Calvo, 2012; Soleymani, Pantic, & Pun, 2012). This chapter focuses on method to elicit particular affective states with an emphasis on methods that have been previously used or have considerable potential for use in AC research.

Emotions arise in response to many different stimuli, so a number of diverse strategies for eliciting emotions have been developed. These vary on a range of dimensions, including sensory modality, reliability, intensity of response, temporal length of response, and ecological validity. The most common emotion elicitation methods can be divided into two main categories: (1) passive or perception-based and (2) active or expression-based. In passive methods, individuals observe stimuli—such as film clips, images, or music—that are designed to evoke particular feelings and moods. In active methods, individuals are instructed to perform particular behaviors that might naturally evoke different emotions, such as posing facial muscles, adopting body postures, or interacting with other people. This chapter discusses exemplar methods from each of these categories in Passive Methods (p. 372) and Active Methods (p. 376). Other Methods (p. 379) presents a summary of some less common but still potentially useful methods. Many of the methods and some of the examples discussed in this chapter have been culled from the *Handbook of Emotion Elicitation and Assessment* (2007), and a wealth of additional information can be found in this handbook and in the references for this chapter.

Passive Methods
Emotional Images

In this method, images that evoke particular affective states are presented to an individual, one image at a time. For example, an image of a mutilated person might be presented to elicit disgust, while an image of a family might be used to elicit happiness. The images should have the capability to consistently evoke a particular level of a single affective state in the viewer (e.g., mild pleasure, strong disgust). The presentation method is standardized such that all individuals have the same viewing experience. For example, the images could each be presented for 10 seconds on a computer screen that is a fixed distance from where the individual is sitting, with a constant screen resolution, screen brightness, and image size (Monkaresi, Hussain, & Calvo, 2012). The images themselves can be selected on the basis of which emotions should be elicited from a database of standardized images. One of the most prominent databases of this kind is the International Affective Picture System (IAPS), which includes over a thousand images depicting people, objects, and events that have been standardized on the basis of pleasure and arousal (Bradley & Lang, 2007; Lang, Bradley, & Cuthbert, 2005). Another more recently developed database

is the Geneva Affective Picture Database (GAPED) (Dan-Glauser & Scherer, 2011).

Several researchers have used the IAPS to elicit emotions for use in training affect detection systems. For example, Khalili and Moradi (2009) focused on eliciting calm, positively excited, and negatively excited emotions. They selected 70 to 150 pictures for each emotion, which were shown to individuals in sets of five pictures, with each picture shown for 2.5 seconds. A self-reporting phase followed each set. They used these data to train unimodal and multimodal emotion detectors using EEG and peripheral physiological signals. Leon et al. (2007) and Monkaresi et al. (2012) followed similar protocols but collected self-reports after every IAPS image instead of after sets of images.

Using images to elicit emotions is advantageous for several reasons. First, images are noninvasive. They share features with actual physical objects and thus are generally good cues for eliciting the same emotions as the objects they represent (Bradley & Lang, 2007). In addition, because images are static cues, some of the difficulties in working with longer, dynamic stimuli are avoided (such as movement, narrative development, and complicated context). Nearly all aspects of the stimuli can be controlled or manipulated, including image size, duration of presentation, brightness, luminosity, spatial frequency, and color. Images are easily accessible via the databases listed above. It is relatively simple to set up a computer to display them, or, alternatively, one need not even use a computer to show the images.

However, the strength of emotions elicited via static images tends to be lower than when they are elicited via film or in anticipation of real events (discussed below). Emotional reactions to images tend to be short and transient, being present during and shortly after viewing and decaying rapidly thereafter. Physiological reactions to viewing unpleasant photos tend to be low, likely because pictures are only symbolic of people, objects, and events—they are not those real stimuli. As such, images may not be the best choice when a strong emotional reaction is desired. This lessened emotional response, does, however, alleviate concerns about causing participants undue stress when they are viewing particularly unpleasant photos. Bradley and Lang (2007) also suggest that there is no clear one-to-one relation between image content and discrete emotions because the background knowledge and life experience each person has when reacting to or appraising any given image ultimately determines his or her emotional reaction. However, researchers such as Asensio et al. (2010) have used this fact to their advantage, studying how individuals with cocaine addictions react differently to pleasant, unpleasant, and neutral IAPS images as compared with individuals without an addiction. Another concern is that the individual's mood and the experimental conditions, beyond reaction and habituation times, are generally not accounted for. As such, images might be more useful for inducing dimensional affect (e.g., positive, neutral, negative) rather than discrete affect (e.g., anger, surprise). That said, other research has indicated that IAPS images generally do, in fact, elicit one discrete emotion more than others (Mikels, Fredrickson, Larkin, Lindberg, Maglio, & Reuter-Lornez, 2005). Finally, utilizing images to elicit emotions may be useful for acquiring data from reactive modalities such as facial expressions, physiological signals (e.g., heart rate and skin conductance), and neural signals (e.g., functional near-infrared spectroscopy (fNIRS) or EEG data). However, because of the stationary visual nature of image presentation, images may not be as suitable for obtaining data from productive modalities, such as acoustic-prosodic cues, text or discourse, or gestures.

Emotional Film Clips

Short films can be presented to elicit target emotions (Rottenberg, Ray, & Gross, 2007). For comparison purposes, a neutral baseline film is generally shown prior to the presentation of each emotional film clip. For example, Soleymani et al. (2012) showed participants a series of 20 film clips to elicit emotions ranging from calm, aroused, pleasant, unpleasant, and neutral emotions. In each trial, a 15-second neutral clip was shown, then a 1- to 2-minute emotional clip, followed by a self-assessment phase. Video, sound, eye gaze, EEG, and various physiological signals were collected. Soleymani et al. (2012) used the eye gaze and EEG data to train and validate unimodal and multimodal affect classifiers. Instead of using short clips, Bailenson et al. (2008) recorded physiological data and video while individuals viewed a single 9-minute clip that contained amusing, neutral, and sad sections. There was no self-report of affect phase. Instead, trained coders rated the videos of individuals' facial expressions. The data was used to build various affect classifiers.

In presenting films as in presenting images, the physical situation should be standardized. For example, Rottenberg et al. (2007) suggest showing the films on a 20-inch monitor about 5 feet from the participant. Then, for each target emotion, one or two short clips that are 1 to 3 minutes in length and that are as homogenous as possible should be shown. All the film clips used should be matched on relevant dimensions so that when multiple emotion film conditions are compared, researchers can infer that any effects seen are due to the emotions, not differences in the films. Relevant matching characteristics include the length of the clip, its intensity, complexity, core themes, presence and number of humans, color, brightness, picture motion, and theoretically important dimensions such as activation level (see Rottenberg et al., 2007; also see Detenber, Simons, & Bennet, 1998). However, it is rarely possible to match films on every dimension.

Rottenberg et al. (2007) presented a list of film clip recommendations for eliciting seven different emotions (amusement, anger, disgust, fear, neutral, sadness, and surprise), with self-reported emotions for each clip and instructions for obtaining each clip. A larger database of emotion-eliciting films is discussed by Schaefer, Nils, Sanchez, and Philippot (2010), with many film clips available online (http://www.ipsp.ucl.ac.be/recherche/FilmStim/). For example, an abstract visual display from a screensaver can work well as a baseline/neutral film (Gross & Levenson, 1995). Another good baseline is a pleasant/low contentment clip depicting nature scenery, animals, and uplifting music, such as a segment from the nature film *Alaska's Wild Denali* (Hardesty, 1997). Clips depicting death scenes from the movies *The Champ* (Lovell & Zeffirelli, 1979) and *The Lion King* (Hahn, Allers, & Minkoff, 1994) can be used to elicit sadness, while clips from comedies such as *When Harry Met Sally* (Reiner, Scheinman, Stolt, & Nicolaides, 1989) and *Bill Cosby, Himself* (Cosby, 1996) can elicit amusement.

Films are advantageous because they capture attention well. They can elicit higher intensity emotions and more complex emotional states than images (Rottenberg et al., 2007). As such, they may be a good choice for studying the magnitude of emotional responses. Film clips may also be useful for studying emotion latency, rise time, duration, and offset because—unlike still images—they are dynamic stimuli, occurring as a sequence of images and sound through time.

It should be noted that the ecological validity of emotion displayed in film clips is in question. On one hand, the affectively charged situations depicted in films appear to be real. However, as Rottenberg et al. (2007) discuss, emotional responses to films require the willing suspension of disbelief. Films, like still images, are a step removed from reality. Participants may react emotionally in spite of *or* because of this as a result. An additional problem is that individuals may have previously seen the films from which the clips are taken. A film clip may not have as much impact if an individual has seen the whole film, or it may have a much stronger impact, since the individual knows the whole context of the clip. Finally, as could be seen in the examples above, film clips are useful for collecting facial expressions, physiological signals, and neural signals. However, like images, they are less ideal for collecting gestures or verbal behavior.

Music and Ideation

Music has generally been used to induce moods in psychological research. A mood can be defined as an enduring affective state that may not directed toward a specific object or event—that is, it is an underlying feeling versus an emotional episode, such as fear or surprise, that is directed at an object or event, such as a snake or a surprise party (Russell, 2003; Watson, 2000). However, Russell (2003) notes that the duration and stability of a mood is not well defined. Music, like moods, is also less object- or event-focused, unlike films or images. When music is combined with a secondary mood-induction technique, robust results can be obtained, such as a higher rate of successfully induced moods, stronger induced moods, and moods that are stable over time and across tasks (Eich, Ng, Macaulay, Percy, & Grebneva, 2007; Vastfjall, 2002).

In one study, Kim, Bang, and Kim (2004) used a combination of background music, a narrated story, and lighting color changes to elicit sadness, anger, stress, and surprise. For example, sadness might be elicited by using slower music, a sad story, and blue light, while the use of music with a faster tempo and red light might elicit anger. Each participant was presented with the four scenarios, with each followed by a self-report. Kim et al. (2004) collected physiological data, which they used to develop affect classifiers. Koelstra et al. (2011) showed music videos to participants to collect similar data.

Eich et al. (2007) describe a technique that combines music with contemplation/ideation and an idiographic approach (abbreviated MCI). Individuals listen to selections of cheerful or melancholy music while contemplating happy or depressing thoughts. Only after an individual is known to be sufficiently in the target mood state (via periodic self-reports) do further experimental procedures occur. Unlike some other music and

ideation procedures, the MCI technique ensures that all individuals reach the same predetermined level of the target mood, although the length of the mood-induction period will likely vary for each individual (see Vastfjall, 2002, for a comprehensive review of musical mood induction procedures; see Westermann, Spies, Stahl, & Hesse, 1996, for a review of other mood induction procedures). Eich et al. (2007) note that about 80% of the participants in their studies were able to develop the desired mood (very pleasant or very unpleasant) and that the mood elicited tended to be reasonably strong, stable, sincere, and reproducible.

The musical pieces used by Eich and colleagues (Eich et al., 2007; Eich & Metcalfe, 1989; Ryan & Eich, 2000) in the MCI were originally selected based on educated guesses. They are all classical compositions ranging in duration from 2 to 6 minutes. A full list is presented in Eich et al. (2007). The happy music includes several livelier pieces such as Vivaldi's *Four Seasons:* Spring I Allegro and Spring III Allegro, Mozart's *Eine Kleine Nachtmusik:* Allegro, and Tchaikovsky's *The Nutcracker:* Waltz of the Flowers. The sad music samples a wider set of composers, including Albinoni's Adagio in G Minor, Chopin's Prelude #4 in E Minor, and an excerpt from Stravinsky's *Firebird:* Lullaby. Eich et al. (2007) also point out several ways to improve music selection. For example, researchers could draw on the knowledge of musicology experts about which elements of music are key to inducing particular emotions. More care could be taken to match styles and genres of the music used. Self-chosen music is also an option, since some people may associate particular songs with the moods that are to be induced, and these songs may work better for the induction (e.g., see Carter, Wilson, Laweson, & Bulik, 1995; Vuoskoski & Eerola, 2012).

One disadvantage of using the MCI is that it takes time—on average, Eich et al. (2007) found that it takes individuals 15 to 20 minutes to reach an adequate level of pleasure or displeasure. However, it is conceivable that an individual's affective state could be changed in a shorter time. Songs are often 3 to 4 minutes in length, and musicians attempt to draw the listener through one or more states during the song. A second concern is that individuals are often explicitly told that the researchers are trying to get them into a positive or negative mood. This means that the individuals will possibly merely act in a manner consistent with their beliefs about moods rather than feeling the intended mood. To allay these concerns, Eich et al. (2007) recommend collecting self-reports from individuals about how genuine they think their moods are. Previously, individuals have generally reported that they do think their moods are genuine (Eich & Metcalfe, 1989; Ryan & Eich, 2000).

Music seems to be most useful for collecting reactive emotional expressions, such as physiological and neural signals. Because of its passive nature—the participant must sit still and listen to the music—it may not lend itself as well to data collection from other modalities.

Backward Masking and the Dissociation Paradigm

The previous three methods attempt to elicit emotion through the presentation of particular kinds of stimuli (such as films or music). This next method, however, studies a different kind of emotional response altogether: unconscious emotions. It has been argued that in emotional processing, stimuli are evaluated or appraised by both conscious and unconscious mechanisms (Berridge & Winkielman, 2003; Kihlstrom, 1999; LeDoux, 1996; Öhman, 1986; Wiens & Öhman, 2007). The presence of unconscious emotion can be inferred from changes in emotional experience, behavior, and psychophysiology if either (1) the stimulus was manipulated so that conscious awareness of the stimulus was prevented, such that any emotional response would be due to unconscious rather than conscious mechanisms, or (2) individuals display signs of emotional processing without reporting changes in their (conscious) emotional experience.

Backward masking in the *dissociation paradigm* is the most common method for manipulating the stimulus to elicit unconscious emotions (Wiens & Öhman, 2007). Conscious awareness of a visual stimulus is blocked in two steps: (1) the stimulus (also called the target) is shown very briefly, as for 15 to 60 milliseconds, then (2) a second visual stimulus (also called the mask) is shown for a longer duration, such as 500 milliseconds. Individuals tend to report being consciously aware only of the mask. Other masking techniques include sandwich masking (mask-target-mask) and energy masking (the mask is a light flash). The dissociation paradigm is an experimental design in which awareness of the target must be eliminated in order to test whether this awareness is necessary for responding. If an individual is unaware of the target, then any response to the masked target is the result of unconscious processes rather than the direct involvement of conscious awareness of

the target. For this paradigm to succeed, it must be demonstrated that the participant actually *is* unaware of the target. Furthermore, it is assumed that awareness does play some causal role in determining a participant's responses and is not epiphenomenal to emotional processing. Wiens and Öhman (2007) discuss in detail how unawareness can be measured; also see Cheesman and Merikle, 1984; Merikle and Reingold, 1998; and Öhman and Wiens, (1994).

The main practical issue to consider is stimulus presentation. Masking a stimulus requires (1) a very fast change from the first visual display to the next and (2) a stable picture presentation time across trials to avoid confounds. Two commonly used displays are cathode-ray tube (CRT) monitors and thin-film transistor (TFT) or liquid-crystal display (LCD) screens. Using these, however, limits the minimum stimulus display time owing to screen refresh rates. Wiens and Öhman (2007) recommend placing a mechanical shutter in front of a data projector that does not rewrite the screen after each refresh cycle (i.e., those based on TFT or LCD technology), thus allowing greater accuracy of presentation durations as well as millisecond-level control.

The method described here has been used successfully several times in the affective sciences but rarely by AC researchers. In a classic study, Öhman and Soares (1994) studied unconscious fear processing via a forced-choice classification task. On each trial, participants were shown a masked picture of a spider, snake, flower, or mushroom and had to indicate which of these four items the picture showed. Skin conductance and emotional ratings were recorded to index emotional processing. Öhman and Soares (1994) found that participants who were spider-phobic showed greater skin conductance responses to spiders but not snakes, while participants who were snake-phobic responded to snakes but not spiders. Neutral participants did not respond to either. This suggested that fear could be present without a person being consciously aware of the feared stimulus.

In another study, Winkielman, Berridge, and Wilbarger (2005) showed masked emotional faces to participants who were either thirsty or not thirsty. The participants then had to rate their mood and were allowed to consume a fruity drink. Winkielman et al. (2005) found that the consumption behavior of the thirsty participants changed in relation to the emotion of the face they had seen, although no mood differences were reported across these participants. Again, this seems to indicate that an emotional response can occur even without an effect on conscious emotional experience.

Although this method has not seen much if any use in AC research, it is still a potentially important technique if the goal is to train models to detect subtle unconscious emotional responses. A related method that has seen use places the visual stimulus in the background rather than masking it entirely or, as described in Emotional Images (p. 372), placing it in the foreground. Hussain, Calvo, and Chen (2013) placed images behind math tasks in order to study the interactions between emotion and cognitive load.

Active Methods
Behavioral Manipulation

Emotional episodes can generally include three components: (1) an eliciting event or stimulus, (2) an emotional feeling (for conscious emotions), and (3) emotional behaviors, such as facial expressions, physiological responses, and physical actions. The passive methods discussed so far have focused on (1)—that is, these methods vary the stimuli an individual encounters in order to evoke different emotions in that individual. The active methods we discuss next focus instead on (3), wherein individuals are instructed to adopt particular behaviors or expressions in order to change the emotions they experience. The first of these involves behavioral manipulation.

In this method, individuals are instructed to adopt particular muscular configurations or behavioral patterns that have been associated with emotional experiences, such as contracting or relaxing facial muscles or exaggerating natural emotional expressions (Ekman & Davidson, 1993; Laird, 1974; Levenson & Ekman, 2002). This, as Ekman (2007) argues, will generate the same kinds of automatic nervous system (ANS) activity patterns as are generated by emotional experiences. Ekman and colleagues developed a well-known method for eliciting emotion through the manipulation of facial expressions called the directed facial action task (Ekman, 2007; Ekman & Davidson, 1993; Levenson & Ekman, 2002). In this task, individuals are given general instructions about how to voluntarily move their facial muscles in particular ways in order to produce emotional responses. They are *not* told to pose a particular emotion. One example of this method in AC research can be found in Vural et al. (2007), who used a database of directed facial actions to develop a facial expression classifier.

In other muscle-by-muscle manipulations, researchers have tried to disguise the instructions given to participants in order to see whether muscle movement alone is sufficient to elicit emotion. For example, Zajonc, Murphy, and Inglehart (1989) had English-speaking participants pronounce various sounds as a way of inducing facial expressions. Strack, Martin, and Stepper (1988) recruited participants for a study purportedly about teaching writing to handicapped people. The participants were instructed to hold a pencil in their mouths with either their lips tightly clamped (as in a smile) or with their lips drawn back (as in an expression of disgust). After performing several writing exercises with the pencils in their mouths, participants rated the funniness of cartoons. Strack et al. (1988) found that participants who held the pencil in a smile-like expression rated the cartoons as funnier than those who had a disgust-like expression.

Another strategy is to modify existing emotional expressions, rather than attempting to create them (see Laird & Strout, 2007, for detailed discussion of this methodology). For example, Lanzetta, Cartwright-Smith, and Kleck (1976) asked participants to either inhibit or intensify their expressive reactions to a series of uncomfortable electric shocks. Lanzetta et al. (1976) recorded skin conductance as well as self-reports. When they were exaggerating their reactions, participants had higher skin conductance and reported that the shocks were more painful. Vice versa, when participants inhibited their reactions, they reported the shocks as being less painful and had lower skin conductance. In an earlier study by Bandler, Madaras, and Bem (1968), participants were instructed to place their hands on plate to receive an electric shock. One group was instructed to leave their hands on the plate; the other group was instructed to jerk their hands away quickly. Although the first group endured a longer duration of shock, the second described the shocks as more painful because of the jerk-away action. This highlights how performing emotional actions can affect the experienced emotion. Indeed, Duclos and Laird (2001) have suggested that one effective way of eliciting anger through behavior is to ask individuals to act angry.

Posture can be manipulated in much the same way as facial expressions, using muscle-by-muscle or exaggeration/minimization instructions (Duclos, Laird, Schneider, Sexter, Stern, & Van Lighten, 1989; Flack, Laird, & Cavallaro, 1999). Other behavioral manipulations that have been successful, though with generally weaker results than those mentioned above, include manipulations of breathing (Philippot, Chapelle, & Blairy, 2002), eye gaze patterns (Schnall et al 2000; Williams & Kleinke, 1993), and tone of voice (Hatfield et al., 1995; Siegman & Boyle, 1993) (see Laird & Strout, 2007, for some further discussion). Combinations of methods, such as expressions and postures (e.g., Flack et al., 1999), can produce more intense effects.

If one knows the physical behaviors associated with the target emotions, behavioral manipulation techniques can be fairly precise in eliciting the target, since behaviors are often distinct. The effects are moderately strong, though the strength of elicited emotional response often still falls short of natural or other induced methods (for example, from films). The effects vary across individuals as well. Some people report being relatively unaffected by posing facial expressions of happiness or anger, while others are dramatically affected. Laird and Strout (2007) point out that researchers using other methods, such as the passive methods described above, have not explored these individual differences as much and thus very likely encounter similar variations. Behavioral manipulations also have the advantage of not containing other cognitive material (as a film might), not containing verbal interaction (unless a verbal behavioral manipulation is being used), not taking too much time, and not involving very elaborate methodologies (Laird & Strout, 2007).

However, there are concerns about ecological validity—is eliciting emotions just from physical behaviors tantamount to inducing the emotions out of their context? Can one really say that emotions elicited through behavioral manipulations are more "pure" (as Laird & Strout, 2007 do) if emotions outside the laboratory occur in the complicated and messy context of the real world? Similar criticisms can be applied to most lab-based elicitation methods. In addition, most behavioral manipulations require the researcher to already have an understanding of which behaviors to perform or how to move one's muscles in ways to induce the target emotion. Although facial expressions linked to Ekman's six "basic" emotions have been identified (Ekman, 2007), relatively less research has looked at distinct facial expressions or behaviors related to, for example, more complex affective states like frustration, confusion, and engagement. This limits the range of possible target emotions that can be elicited with these methods. Furthermore, the poses or actions required can be difficult or complicated for individuals to perform and not all individuals may be able to perform them.

Behavioral manipulations may be most useful for collecting reactive expressions, such as physiological and neural signals, since the productive aspects of the emotional expression are tightly controlled.

Social Psychological Methods and Social Interaction

In this method, which comes from social psychology, researchers try to create realistic social scenarios that elicit emotions in a more naturalistic context (Harmon-Jones, Amodio, & Zinner; 2007). Manipulations tend to be high-impact. Deception is generally needed to keep participants unaware of variable manipulations. For example, to elicit high anxiety, participants in a study may be told that they will be given a series of electric shocks (e.g., Schachter, 1959). To induce anger, a participant may be given insulting evaluations or feedback from a fake "second participant" in the study (e.g., Harmon-Jones & Sigelman, 2001).

Not many examples using social psychological methods are found in the AC literature. There are however some notable exceptions. The SEMAINE database recorded interactions between users and four emotionally stereotyped characters in order to study social signals in conversations between humans and artificial intelligent agents as well as to collect data for training such agents (McKeown, Valstar, Cowie, Pantic, & Schroder, 2012). The characters were designed to draw users into their emotional states—happy, angry, sensible, and depressive. They were played either by a human operator who pretended to be an artificial agent or an autonomous but more limited artificial agent. The database has been used to develop multimodal affect classifiers (e.g., Wöllmer, Kaiser, Eyben, & Schuller, 2012). Kim (2007) had individuals play a structured quiz game with a virtual character in which a hidden person guided the course of the quiz in order to elicit certain emotions. Although this comes closer to the kind of social interaction that Harmon-Jones et al. (2007) discuss, it again is not a high-impact manipulation.

Harmon-Jones et al. (2007) laid out five critical steps for setting up social psychology studies with deception. (1) Construct a cover story as rationale for the experiment to distract participants from the experiment's true purpose. (2) Determine what the experimenter's behavior will be, such that it will be consistent over the data collection period and across participants. (3) Design a manipulation of the independent variable that minimizes participant awareness of the manipulation while ensuring that they respond just as they would if they encountered the stimulus outside the lab.

Make the experimenters blind to the condition when possible. (4) For the dependent variable, measure emotional responses with a behavioral, physiological, or self-report method. (5) Conduct a postexperimental interview to check for clarity of instructions, suspicion about the experiment's true goals, and to debrief the participant about purpose of experiment.

The cover story will vary with the emotion elicited. For example, to elicit joy and sadness, researchers have used social-comparison manipulations. Participants perform a task that is described as easy or difficult, such as solving a set of analogies, in order to induce an initial worry or stress state (e.g., Forgas, Bower, & Moylan, 1990). Then participants are given feedback on how they performed on the task relative to others. Positive feedback, such as being told that they are above average, leads to increased joy, while negative feedback leads to increased sadness.

Sympathy and guilt are two other complex emotions that can be elicited (Harmon-Jones et al., 2007). Sympathy scenarios generally involve perspective taking. For example, the participant may be asked to listen to a radio broadcast about a child diagnosed with cancer and then asked to imagine how the child and his or her family may feel (Harmon-Jones, Peterson, & Vaughn, 2003). Guilt requires more deception to elicit and has been successfully elicited using a false physiological feedback procedure (e.g., Monteith, Ashburn-Nardo, Voils, & Czopp, 2002). Participants who were not prejudiced were told that physiological arousal increases when a person is viewing negative images. Participants were then shown a series of images of people of different races, with each image followed by the supposed physiological measurements taken during its viewing. In reality, the measurements were faked such that participants were manipulated into thinking that they had prejudiced reactions to seeing people of other races, thus eliciting guilt.

The biggest advantage of using social psychological methods is that the emotions elicited through cover stories and social contexts are more realistic and similar to emotions occurring in the real world. Some emotions that are more difficult to elicit with other methods, such as anger and guilt, can be elicited with social psychological methods (Harmon-Jones et al., 2007). In addition, Harmon-Jones et al. (2007) suggest that issues present in other methodologies, such as responses that are merely due to demand characteristics, may be circumvented through social psychological methods.

However, more realistic scenarios also tend to allow a wider variability in responding, which can make it harder to elicit the specific discrete emotion one may want to study.

Social interaction thus seems best suited for collecting productive expressions of emotion, including body movements, gestures, acoustic-prosodic cues, and discourse or language. Facial expressions, if cameras are positioned appropriately, can be collected. With mobile equipment, physiological signals can be recorded. Neural signals, however, tend to require participants to be seated and stationary, which would be difficult in a social scenario.

Dyadic Interaction

In this method, a dyad is brought into the lab rather than an individual. The dyad is then instructed to engage in an unrehearsed, minimally structured conversation (Roberts, Tsai, & Cohen, 2007). Dyads can be romantic couples (e.g., Cohan & Bradbury, 1997; Gonzaga, Keltner, Londahl, & Smith, 2001; Tsai & Levenson 1997), siblings (e.g., Shortt & Gottman, 1997), or children and caregivers (e.g., Messinger et al., this volume; Weis & Lovejoy, 2002; Reppeti & Wood, 1997). Sometimes, an unfamiliar dyad is brought in, such as ethnically similar or dissimilar pairs, in order to study other aspects of interpersonal relations (e.g., Littleford, Wright, & Sayoc-Parial, 2005). Like social psychological methods, dyadic interactions have not been used nearly as much as other emotion elicitation methods in AC. One example is a corpus of human-human interactions collected by Zara, Maffiolo, Martin, and Devillers (2007) to aid in the design of affective interactive systems. Pairs of strangers played an emotional adaptation of the game Taboo, in which one player has to guess a word that the other player describes through speech and gesture but without using any of five forbidden words.

Dyadic interactions draw on the social context of emotion to elicit a wide range of spontaneous and realistic emotions and follow their natural temporal course while still remaining in a controlled situation. Therefore it has high ecological validity, perhaps higher than any other elicitation methods. Emotions often occur in social contexts and have social functions. Because the dyad regularly interacts outside the lab or is a pair of strangers, there is not the same worry as in other social interaction methods that reactions will be less natural due to the laboratory context. Emotions are dynamic, and this kind of scenario allows one to study their time course. A range of emotional responses can be elicited by varying (1) the kind of conversation the dyad can have and (2) individual factors that change the intensity of emotion displays. For example, Coan, Gottmann, Babcock, and Jacobson (1997) asked couples to discuss disagreements in their relationship in order to elicit intense negative emotion. Similarly, discussions of enjoyable topics can be used to elicit positive emotion (Roberts et al., 2007). The interaction is usually synchronous, but does not have to be—one recent study elicited emotions through an asynchronous dyadic interaction wherein one individual provided written feedback on another individual's essay (Calvo, personal communication, May 27, 2013).

However, the minimal structure of this method allows room for participant noncompliance and experimenter error. There can be great variability in emotional responding, and the facilitator for the task may establish different rapport with each dyad or otherwise act differently, which could influence emotional responses. Therefore this method may not be as well suited for eliciting precise, discrete emotions as it is for eliciting natural emotions over time. Because tasks are often 2 to 4 hours in length, significant resources are required (Roberts et al., 2007). In addition, the dyadic interaction provides only a snapshot sampling of emotion. Researchers lack the history of the dyad's relationship and have limited knowledge of why each member of the dyad responds to the other in the ways they do. That said, for some relationships (e.g., teacher-student or parent-child), some assumptions about the relationship can be made (e.g., power dynamics).

Dyadic interactions seem to be useful for the collection of much the same data as social interactions—gestures, body movements, verbal behavior, facial expressions, and physiological data.

Other Methods

This chapter has provided an introduction to the wide range of emotion elicitation methods available. We selected several of the most promising and popular methods to discuss, but there are many more. For example, individuals can perform a writing task, such as the autobiographical memory task (Dunn & Schweitzer, 2005; Myers & Tingley, 2001), in which they are prompted to recall and write about an emotional event. Stevenson and James (2008) have proposed an International Affective Digitized Sounds (IADS) database of affective auditory stimuli. Other researchers have instructed individuals to read and internalize positively or negatively valenced self-referential statements (Seibert & Ellis, 1991; Velten, 1968), used stimulus-reinforcement association learning to elicit emotions (Rolls, 2007) or have hypnotized individuals to make them think emotionally provocative thoughts (Friswell & McConkey, 1989). Emotional functioning can also be studied in neurologically impaired patients via lesion studies, brain imaging studies, and neural activation studies (for a review, see Levenson, 2007).

Conclusions

Many methods exist for eliciting emotions. Passive methods tend to be less ecologically valid and elicit less naturalistic emotions. They can, however, be easier to implement. In addition, most aspects of the stimuli—such as the color, size, and duration of presentation for an image—can be controlled with passive methods. Emotions elicited through passive methods vary in intensity and complexity, from less intense via images to more intense films or music. Active methods have a similar range of intensity and complexity: behavior manipulations are very precise but may not produce very strong responses, while social and dyadic interactions can elicit strong naturalistic emotions but are more imprecise. Active methods tend to have higher ecological validity and can elicit complex emotions, such as anger and guilt, that may be hard to achieve via other methods but may also have a wider variability in responses.

The stimuli used in contemporary emotion elicitation methods can be temporally short, such as images, or stretched through time, such as films or social interactions. As such, care must be taken when selecting methods for collecting participants' emotional responses to serve as manipulation checks that the intended emotion was in fact induced. Rottenberg et al. (2007) note that self-report questionnaires, which are often administered immediately following the stimuli, have two main problems. First, delays between the activation of an emotion and the assessment of the emotion can introduce measurement error. Second, collecting only retrospective emotion ratings has very low temporal resolution. To get finer-grained measurements, Rottenberg et al. (2007) suggest using a continuous measure of emotion experience, such as a rating dial method (validated by Levenson & Gottman 1983; also see Gottman & Levenson, 1985), recording video of expressive behavior during stimuli presentation, or recording central and peripheral physiological responses during stimuli presentation. The selection of appropriate ways of measuring emotion is just as crucial as the choice of method of emotion elicitation itself. Another concern is to ensure that an emotion elicitation method does not inadvertently induce nonintended emotions in addition to the intended emotion. For example, a method to induce *fear*, such as a clip of a traffic accident, might also induce *sadness* if a child is seriously injured. In fact, preventing the induction of untended emotions or mixed emotions is one of the most serious challenges facing most emotion elicitation methods.

Finally, as mentioned in the Introduction, emotion elicitation is only one of several methods for collecting emotional data for AC research. Where ecological validity is concerned, there is a clear hierarchy: recording natural emotional expressions is best, acted data less so, and elicited emotion varying in the middle. Training data have an important influence on affect classification. In a recent meta-analysis of 30 multimodal affect classifiers, the performance improvements of the multimodal classifiers over the best unimodal classifiers was three times higher (12.1% improvement) when trained on acted data as opposed to natural or elicited data (4.39% improvement) (D'Mello & Kory, 2012). The classifiers trained on natural or elicited data may better reflect current affect detection capabilities, since the ultimate goal of AC is to build interfaces that sense and respond to naturalistic expressions of emotion in the real world. Indeed, it seems prudent to use data that reflect, as closely as possible, the situations and emotional expressions that these interfaces will encounter—that is, naturalistic data. Owing to the difficulties of collecting completely natural affective data, in this chapter we surveyed what could be considered a good middle road for AC researchers: methods for emotion elicitation.

Acknowledgments

This research was supported by the National Science Foundation (NSF) (ITR 0325428, HCC 0834847, DRL 1235958, and NSF Graduate Research Fellowship under 1122374). Any opinions, findings and conclusions, or recommendations expressed in this paper are those of the authors and do not necessarily reflect the views of the NSF.

References

Asensio, S., Romero, M. J., Palau, C., Sanchez, A., Senabre, I., Morales, J. L.,...Romero, F. J. (2010). Altered neural response of the appetitive emotional system in cocaine addiction: an fMRI Study. *Addiction Biology*, *15*(4), 504–516.

Bailenson, J. N., Pontikakis, E. D., Mauss, I. B., Gross, J. J., Jabon, M. E., Hutcherson, C. A.,...John, O. (2008). Real-time classification of evoked emotions using facial feature tracking and physiological responses. *International Journal of Human-Computer Studies*, *66*(5), 303–317.

Bandler, R. J., Madaras, G. R., & Bem, D. J. (1968). Self observation as a source of pain perception. *Journal of Personality and Social Psychology*, *9*, 205–209.

Berridge, K. C., & Winkielman, P. (2003). What is an unconscious emotion: The case for unconscious "liking." *Cognition & Emotion*, *17*, 181–211.

Bradley, M. M., & Lang, P. J. (2007). The International Affective Picture System (IAPS) in the study of emotion and attention. In J. A. Coan & J. J. B. Allen (Eds.), *Handbook of Emotion Elicitation and Assessment* (pp. 29–46). New York, NY: Oxford University Press.

Carter, F. A., Wilson, J. S., Lawson, R. H., & Bulik, C. M. (1995). Mood induction procedure: Importance of individualizing music. *Behaviour Change*, *12*, 159–161.

Cheesman, J., & Merikle, P. M. (1986). Distinguishing conscious from unconscious perceptual processes. *Canadian Journal of Psychology*, *40*, 343–367.

Coan, J., & Allen, J. J. B. (Eds.) (2007). *Handbook of emotion elicitation and assessment*. New York, NY: Oxford University Press.

Coan, J., Gottman, J. M., Babcock, J., & Jacobson, N. (1997). Battering and the male rejection of influence from women. *Aggressive Behavior*, *23*(5), 375–388.

Cohan, C. L., & Bradbury, T. N. (1997). Negative life events, marital interaction, and the longitudinal course of newlywed marriage. *Journal of Personality and Social Psychology*, *73*(1), 114–128.

Cosby, W. (Producer/Director). (1996). *Bill Cosby, himself* [Motion picture]. United States: Twentieth Century Fox.

D'Mello, S., & Graesser, A. C. (2010). Multimodal semi-automated affect detection from conversational cues, gross body language, and facial features. *User Modeling and User-Adapted Interaction*. *20*(2), 147–187.

D'Mello, S. K., & Kory, J. (2012). Consistent but modest: A meta-analysis on unimodal and multimodal affect detection accuracies from 30 studies. In L. P. Morency, D. Bohus, & H. Aghajan (Eds.), *Proceedings of the 14th ACM International Conference on Multimodal Interaction*, (pp. 31–38). New York, NY: Association for Computing Machinery.

Dan-Glauser, E. S., & Scherer, K. R. (2011). The Geneva affective picture database (GAPED): A new 730-picture database focusing on valence and normative significance. *Behavior Research Methods*, *43*(2), 468–477.

Detenber, B. H., Simons, R. F., & Bennet, G. G. (1998). Roll 'em! The effects of picture motion on emotion responses. *Journal of Broadcasting and Electronic Media*, *21*, 112–126.

Duclos, S. E., & Laird, J. D. (2001). The deliberate control of emotional experience through control of expressions. *Cognition and Emotion*, *15*, 27–56.

Duclos, S. E., Laird, J. D., Schneider, E., Sexter, M, Stern, L., & Van Lighten, O. (1989). Emotion-specific effects of facial expressions and postures on emotional experience. *Journal of Personality and Social Psychology*, *57*, 100–108.

Dunn, J. R., & Schweitzer, M. E. (2005). Feeling and believing: The influence of emotion on trust. *Journal of Personality and Social Psychology*, *88*(5), 736–748.

Eich, E., & Metcalfe, J. (1989). Mood dependent memory for internal versus external events. *Journal of Experimental Psychology: Learning, Memory, and Cognition*, *15*, 443–455.

Eich, E., Ng, J. T. W., Macaulay, D., Percy, A., & Grebneva, I. (2007). Combining music with thought to change mood. In

J. A. Coan & J. J. B. Allen (Eds.), *Handbook of emotion elicitation and assessment* (pp. 124–136). New York, NY: Oxford University Press.

Ekman, P. (2007). The directed facial action task: Emotion responses without appraisal. In J. A. Coan & J. J. B. Allen (Eds.), *Handbook of emotion elicitation and assessment* (pp. 47–53). New York, NY: Oxford University Press.

Ekman, P., & Davidson, R. J. (1993). Voluntary smiling changes region brain activity. *Psychological Science, 4*, 342–345.

Flack, W. F., Laird, J. D., & Cavallaro, L. A. (1999). Additive effects of facial expressions and postures on emotional feelings. *European Journal of Social Psychology, 29*, 203–217.

Forgas, J. P., Bower, G. H., & Moylan, S. J. (1990). Praise or blame? Affective influences on attributions for achievement. *Journal of Personality and Social Psychology, 59*(4), 809–819.

Friswell, R., & McConkey, K. M. (1989). Hypnotically induced mood. *Cognition & Emotion, 3*(1), 1–26.

Gonzaga, G. C., Keltner, D., Londahl, D. A., & Smith, M. D. (2001). Love and the commitment problem in romantic relations and friendship. *Journal of Personality and Social Psychology, 81*(2), 247–262.

Gottman, J. M., & Levenson, R. W. (1985). A valid procedure for obtaining self-report of affect in marital interaction. *Journal of Consulting and Clinical Psychology, 53*, 151–160.

Gross, J. J., & Levenson, R. W. (1995). Emotion elicitation using films. *Cognition & Emotion, 9*(1), 87–108.

Hahn, D. (Producer), Allers, R., & Minkoff, R. (Directors). (1994). *The lion king* [Motion picture]. Burbank, CA: Walt Disney Pictures.

Hardesty, T. (Producer). *Alaska's Wild Denali: Summer in Denali National Park* [Motion picture]. Anchorage, AK: Alaska Video Postcards.

Harmon-Jones, E., Amodio, D. M., & Zinner, L. R. (2007). Social psychological methods of emotion elicitation. In J. A. Coan & J. J. B. Allen (Eds.), *Handbook of emotion elicitation and assessment* (pp. 91–105). New York, NY: Oxford University Press.

Harmon-Jones, E., & Sigelman, J. (2001). State anger and prefrontal brain activity: Evidence that insult-related relative left prefrontal activation is associated with experienced anger and aggression. *Journal of Personality and Social Psychology, 80*, 797, 803.

Harmon-Jones, E., Peterson, H., & Vaughn, K. (2003). The dissonance-inducing effects of an inconsistency between experienced empathy and knowledge of past failures to help: Support for the action-based model of dissonance. *Basic and Applied Social Psychology, 25*, 69–78.

Hatfield, E., Hsee, C. K., Costello, J., Weisman, M. S., & Denney, C. (1995). The impact of vocal feedback on emotional experience and expression. *Journal of Social Behavior and Personality, 10*(2), 293–312.

Hoque, M., & Picard, R. W. (March, 2011). Acted vs. natural frustration and delight: Many people smile in natural frustration. In *Automatic face & gesture recognition and workshops (FG 2011)*, 2011 IEEE International Conference (pp. 354–359). New York: Institute of Electrical and Electronics Engineers.

Hussain, S., Calvo, R. A., Chen, F. (2013). Automatic cognitive load detection from face, physiology, task performance and fusion during affective interference. *Interacting with Computers*, first published online June 6, 2013.

Kihlstrom, J F. (1999). The psychological unconscious. In L. A. Pervin & O. P. John (Eds.), *Handbook of personality: Theory and research* (2nd ed., pp. 424–442). New York: Guilford Press.

Kim, J. (2007). Bimodal emotion recognition using speech and physiological changes. In M. Grimm and K. Kroschel (Eds.), *Robust speech recognition and understanding* (pp. 265–280), Vienna, Austria: I-Tech.

Kim, K. H., Bang, S. W., & Kim, S. R. (2004). Emotion recognition system using short-term monitoring of physiological signals. *Medical and biological engineering and computing, 42*(3), 419–427.

Khalali, Z., and Moradi, M. (2009). Emotion recognition system using brain and peripheral signals: Using correlation dimension to improve the results of EEG. In *Proceedings of the International Joint Conference on Neural Networks* (pp. 1571–1575). New York: Institute of Electrical and Electronics Engineers.

Koelstra, S., Muhl, C., Soleymani, M., Lee, J. S., Yazdani, A., Ebrahimi, T.,...Patras, I. (2012). DEAP: A database for emotion analysis using physiological signals. *IEE Transactions on Affective Computing, 3*(1), 18–31.

Laird, J. D. (1974). Self-attribution of emotion: The effects of expressive behavior on the quality of emotional experience. *Journal of Personality and Social Psychology, 33*, 475–486.

Laird, J. D., & Strout, S. (2007). Emotional behaviors as emotional stimuli. In J. A. Coan & J. J. B. Allen (Eds.), *Handbook of emotion elicitation and assessment* (pp. 54–64). New York, NY: Oxford University Press.

Lang, P. J., Bradley, M. M., & Cuthbert, B. N. (2005). *International Affective Picture System (IAPS): Affective ratings of pictures and instruction manual*. Technical report no. A-6. Gainesville, FL: University of Florida.

Lanzetta, J. T., Cartwright-Smith, J., & Kleck, R. E. (1976). Effects of nonverbal dissimulation on emotional experience and autonomic arousal. *Journal of Personality and Social Psychology, 33*, 354–370.

LeDoux, J. (1996). *The emotional brain: The mysterious underpinnings of emotional life*. New York: Simon & Schuster.

Leon, E., Clarke, G., Callaghan, V., & Sepulveda, F. (2007). A user-independent real-time emotion recognition system for software agents in domestic environments. *Engineering Applications of Artificial Intelligence, 20*(3), 337–345.

Levenson, R. W. (2007). Emotion elicitation with neurological patients. In J. A. Coan & J. J. B. Allen (Eds.), *Handbook of emotion elicitation and assessment* (pp. 158–168). New York, NY: Oxford University Press.

Levenson, R. W., & Ekman, P. (2002). Difficulty does not account for emotion-specific heart rate changes in the directed facial action task. *Psychophysiology, 39*, 397–405.

Levenson, R. W., & Gottman, J. M. (1983). Marital interaction: Physiological linkage and affective exchange. *Journal of Personality and Social Psychology, 45*, 587–597.

Littleford, L. N., Wright, M., & Sayoc-Parial, M. (2005). White students' intergroup anxiety during same-race and interracial interactions: A multimethod approach. *Basic and Applied Social Psychology, 27*(1), 85–94.

Lovell, D. (Producer), & Zeffirelli, F. (Director). (1979). *The champ* [Motion picture]. Beverly Hills, CA: MGM/Pathe Home Video.

McKeown, G., Valstar, M., Cowie, R., Pantic, M. & Schroder, M. 2012. The SEMAINE database: Annotated multimodal records of emotionally coloured conversations between a person and a limited agent. *IEEE Transactions on Affective Computing, 3*, 5–17.

Merikle, P. M., & Reingold, E. M. (1998). On demonstrating unconscious perception: Comment on Draine and Greenwald (1998). *Journal of Experimental Psychology: General, 127*, 304–310.

Mikels, J. A., Fredrickson, B. L., Larkin, G. R., Lindberg, C. M., Maglio, S. M., & Reuter-Lorenz, P. A. (2005). Emotional category data on images from the International Affective Picture System. *Behavior Research Methods, 37*(4), 626–630.

Monkaresi, H., Hussain, M. S., & Calvo, R. A. (2012). Classification of affects using head movement, skin color features, and physiological signals. In *Proceedings of the IEEE International Conference on Systems, Man, and Cybernetics* (pp. 2664–2669). New York: Institute of Electrical and Electronics Engineers.

Monteith, M. J., Ashburn-Nardo, L., Voils, C. I., & Czopp, A. M. (2002). Putting the brakes on prejudice: On the development and operation of cues for control. *Journal of Personality and Social Psychology, 83*, 1029–1050.

Myers, D. & Tingley, D. (2011). *The influence of emotion on trust.* (Unpublished PhD thesis.) Princeton, NJ: Princeton University.

Öhman, A. (1986). Face the beast and fear the face: Animal and social fears as prototypes for evolutionary analyses of emotion. *Psychophysiology, 23*, 123–145.

Öhman, A., & Soares, J. J. F. (1994). "Unconscious anxiety": Phobic responses to masked stimuli. *Journal of Abnormal Psychology, 103*, 231–240.

Philippot, P., Chapelle, G., & Blairy, S. (2002). Respiratory feedback in the generation of emotion. *Cognition & Emotion, 16*(5), 605–627.

Picard, R. (1997). *Affective computing.* Cambridge, MA: MIT Press.

Reiner, R. (Producer/Director), Scheinman, A., Stolt, J., & Nicolaides, S. (Producers). (1989). *When Harry met Sally* [Motion picture]. Hollywood, CA: New Line Home Video.

Reppeti, R. L., & Wood, J. (1997). Effects of daily stress at work on mothers' interactions with preschoolers. *Journal of Family Psychology, 11*(1), 90–108.

Roberts, N. A., Tsai, J. L., & Coan, J. A. (2007). Emotion elicitation using dyadic interaction tasks. In J. A. Coan & J. J. B. Allen (Eds.), *Handbook of emotion elicitation and assessment* (pp.106–123). New York, NY: Oxford University Press.

Rolls, E. T. (2007). Emotion elicitation by primary reinforcers and following stimulus-reinforcement association learning. In J. A. Coan & J. J. B. Allen (Eds.), *Handbook of emotion elicitation and assessment* (pp. 137–157). New York, NY: Oxford University Press.

Rottenberg, J., Ray, R. D., & Gross, J. J. (2007). Emotion elicitation using films. In J. A. Coan & J. J. B. Allen (Eds.), *Handbook of emotion elicitation and assessment* (pp. 9–28). New York, NY: Oxford University Press.

Russell, J. (2003) Core affect and the psychological construction of emotion. *Psychological Review, 110*, 145–172.

Ryan, L., & Eich, E. (2000). Mood dependence and implicit memory. In E. Tulving (Ed.), *Memory, consciousness, and the brain* (pp. 91–105). Philadelphia: Psychology Press.

Schaefer, A., Nils, F., Sanchez, X., & Philippot, P. (2010). Assessing the effectiveness of a large database of emotion-eliciting films: A new tool for emotion researchers. *Cognition and Emotion, 24*(7), 1153–1172.

Schnall, S., Laird, J. D., Campbell, L., Swang, H., Silverman, S., & Sullivan, D. (2000). *More than meets the eye: Avoiding gaze makes you feel guilty.* Paper presented at the annual meeting of the Society for Personality and Social Psychology, Nashville, TN.

Shortt, J. W., & Gottman, J. M. (1997). Closeness in young adult sibling relationships: Affective and physiological processes. *Social Development, 6*(2), 142–164.

Seibert, P. S., & Ellis, H. C. (1991). A convenient self-referencing mood induction procedure. *Bulletin of the Psychonomic Society, 29*(2), 121–124.

Siegman, A. W., & Boyle, S. (1993). Voices of fear and anxiety and sadness and depression: The effects of speech rate and loudness on fear and anxiety and sadness and depression. *Journal of Abnormal Psychology, 102*, 430–437.

Soleymani, M., Pantic, M. & Pun, T.(2012). Multi-modal emotion recognition in response to videos. *IEEE Transactions on Affective Computing, 3*(2), 211–233.

Stevenson, R. A., Mikels, J. A., & James, T. W. (2007). Characterization of the affective norms for English words by discrete emotional categories. *Behavior Research Methods, 39*(4), 1020–1024.

Strack, F., Martin, L. L., & Stepper, S. (1988). Inhibiting and facilitating conditions of facial expressions: A non-obtrusive test of the facial feedback hypothesis. *Journal of Personality and Social Psychology, 54*, 768–776.

Tsai, J. L., & Levenson, R. W. (1997). Cultural influences on emotional responding: Chinese American and European American dating couples during interpersonal conflict. *Journal of Cross-Cultural Psychology, 28*(5), 600–625.

Vastfjall, D. (2001/2002). Emotion induction through music: A review of the musical mood induction procedure. *Musicae Scientiae* (Special Issue), 173–211.

Velten, E. (1968). A laboratory task for induction of mood states. *Behavior Research and Therapy, 6*(4), 473–482.

Vuoskoski, J. K., Eerola, T. (2012). Can sad music really make you sad? Indirect measures of affective states induced by music and autobiographical memories. *Psychology of Aesthetics, Creativity, and the Arts, 6*(3), 204.

Vural, E., Cetin, M., Ercil, A., Littlewort, G., Bartlett, M., & Movellan, J. (2007). Drowsy driver detection through facial movement analysis. *Human–Computer Interaction*, 6–18.

Watson, D. (2000). *Mood and temperament.* New York, NY: Guilford Press.

Weis, R., & Lovejoy, M. C. (2002). Information processing in everyday life: Emotion-congruent bias in mothers' reports of parent-child interactions. *Journal of Personality and Social Psychology, 83*(1), 216–230.

Westermann, R., Spies, K., Stahl, G., & Hesse, F. W. (1996). Relative effectiveness and validity of mood induction procedures: A meta-analysis. *European Journal of Social Psychology, 26*(4), 557–580.

Wiens, S., & Öhman, A. (2007). Probing unconscious emotional processes: On becoming a successful masketeer. In J. A. Coan & J. J. B. Allen (Eds.), *Handbook of emotion elicitation and assessment* (pp. 65–90). New York, NY: Oxford University Press.

Williams, G. P., & Kleinke, C. L. (1993). Effect of mutual gaze and touch on attraction, mood and cardiovascular reactivity. *Journal of Research in Personality, 27*, 170–183.

Winkielman, P., Berridge, K. C., & Wilbarger, J. L. (2005). Unconscious affective reactions to masked happy versus angry faces influence consumption behavior and judgments of value. *Personality and Social Psychology Bulletin, 31*, 121–135.

Wöllmer, M., Kaiser, M., Eyben, F., & Schuller, B. (2012). LSTM-modeling of continuous emotions in an audiovisual affect recognition framework. *Image and Vision Computing, 31*(2), 153–163.

Zajonc, R. B., Murphy, S. T., & Inglehart, M. (1989). Feeling and facial efference: Implications of the vascular theory of emotion. *Psychological Review, 96*, 395–416.

Zara, A., Maffiolo, V., Martin, J., & Devillers, L. (2007). Collection and annotation of a corpus of human-human multimodal interactions: Emotion and others anthropomorphic characteristics. *Affective Computing and Intelligent Interaction*, 464–475.

Crowdsourcing Techniques for Affective Computing

Robert R. Morris *and* Daniel McDuff

Abstract

In this chapter, we provide an overview of crowdsourcing, outlining common crowdsourcing platforms and best practices for the field as a whole. We illustrate how these practices have been applied to affective computing, surveying recent research in crowdsourced affective data and crowd-powered affective applications. We also discuss the ethical implications of crowdsourcing, especially as it pertains to affective computing domains. Finally, we look at the future of crowdsourcing and discuss how new developments in the field might benefit affective computing.

Key Words: affective computing, crowdsourcing, affective data, emotion regulation

Introduction

Crowdsourcing is a model of labor production that outsources work to large, loosely defined groups of people. In the past few years, crowdsourcing has proliferated widely throughout the fields of computer science and human-computer interaction, as exemplified by the dramatic increase in Association for Computing Machinery (ACM) citations for the term *crowdsourcing* (336 citations were reported in 2011, as compared with only 4 in 2007). Despite being a relatively nascent discipline, crowdsourcing already has numerous high-profile success stories to its name. For instance, in just 10 days, crowdworkers playing the *Fold-It* game managed to decipher the crystal structure of M-PMV—a feat of biochemistry that had previously eluded scientists for well over a decade (Khatib et al., 2011). M-PMV is a retrovirus that causes AIDS in chimps and monkeys; uncovering its protein structure could lead to the development of new antiretroviral drugs.

The ESP Game is another example of a wildly successful crowdsourcing endeavor. Remarkably, in just a few months of deployment, individuals playing the *The ESP Game* helped collect over 10 million image labels for the web (von Ahn, 2006). In neither *The ESP Game* nor *FoldIt* were participants paid for their contributions.

Crowdsourcing techniques have a lot to offer the field of affective computing. Human expression of emotion is complex, multimodal, and nuanced. To design computer algorithms that accurately detect emotional expressions, large amounts of labeled data need to be collected under conditions that reflect those seen in real life. Collection and labeling using traditional lab-based methods can be inefficient and sometimes impractical. By engaging a large workforce to collect, contribute, and label emotional expressions (often via the Internet), the time and expense required to create databases for training expression recognition systems can be greatly reduced.

Furthermore, crowdsourcing offers exciting new ways to power emotionally intelligent affective computing applications. Technologies that provide personalized and contextualized affective feedback require significant advances in natural language processing and commonsense reasoning. To sidestep this problem, crowds can be recruited on demand to support artificial intelligence, providing human computation when automated methods alone are insufficient. In this chapter, we describe how crowdsourcing techniques can be applied to these and other research challenges within the field of affective computing.

Crowdsourcing Overview
What Is Crowdsourcing?

The term *crowdsourcing* was first coined by Jeff Howe in a June 2006 article for *Wired* magazine. Following Howe's original conception of the term, we define crowdsourcing as a method for recruiting and organizing ad hoc labor using an open call for participation (Howe, 2006). Crucial to this definition is the notion of an extremely fluid workforce, one that is devoid of the managerial and contractual directives inherent to other, more traditional labor models, such as "outsourcing." The crowd has the freedom to do what it pleases, when it pleases, and it is often up to designers to find clever ways to recruit and retain this kind of ad hoc workforce.

Conversely, unlike the crowd itself, the entity requesting crowdsourced work is rarely fluid or loosely defined. Indeed, the request for work usually comes from a distinct organization or individual (known as the "requester" in crowdsourcing parlance). This distinguishes crowdsourcing from other, more decentralized labor structures, such as commons-based peer production.

While crowdsourcing can take many forms, three dominant platforms have emerged over the past decade: (1) games with a purpose, (2) microtask markets, and (3) open innovation contests. These platforms are also among the most relevant for affective computing research, so we will take a moment to describe how they work.

Games with a Purpose

Games with a purpose (GWAPs) are games played online, ostensibly for fun, but the output of the gameplay is used to solve real-world problems. Perhaps the first and best-known GWAP is the ESP game—an online social game that has helped to create millions of image labels for the web (von Ahn, 2006). While image labeling is ordinarily quite tedious, the ESP game uses social dynamics and game mechanics to make the experience fun and engaging. Image labels generated from the game are used as metadata for online images, improving image search and web accessibility for the individuals with visual impairments.

Other GWAPS have since been created to generate everything from simple image annotations to incredibly complex protein structures. GWAPs can be applied to many different problems, and they can be extremely powerful when done correctly. However, game design is challenging, and it is not always possible to magically alchemize tedious or frustrating work into highly engaging gameplay. Also, GWAPs may require advertisements or marketing to attract sufficient numbers of players. Sometimes it can be easier to simply pay the crowd to complete the work. In cases such as these, microtask markets can be an attractive option.

Microtask Markets

Microtask markets are systems in which workers complete short jobs in exchange for monetary compensation. Workers are not obligated to work beyond the tasks they elect to complete, and employers are given the freedom to propose any price for completing the jobs they want done. To date, the largest and most popular microtask market is Amazon's Mechanical Turk service (MTurk). MTurk hosts hundreds of thousands of tasks, ranging from image labeling to text transcription to spam filtering.

MTurk is an attractive resource because task completion is very fast and it has its own application programming interface (API,) allowing employers to coordinate tasks programmatically. The cost of labor is also very low—in 2010, the median wage on MTurk was only $1.38 per hour (Horton & Chilton, 2010). Unfortunately MTurk's speed, low cost, and programmability are offset by its poor quality control. The system does not employ reliable reputation systems and it is very easy for workers to do the bare minimum or even cheat and still get paid. As of this writing, it is still fairly easy for workers to artificially boost their performance rankings on MTurk.

To use MTurk effectively, researchers need to carefully consider how they recruit workers, manage quality, and design their tasks. For tasks that require English language fluency (such as sentiment analysis), it is often necessary to restrict enrollment to individuals from English-speaking countries. Using MTurk's built-in location filters can be a useful first step, but the data should also be pruned post hoc by assessing Internet Protocol (IP) addresses.

Task design also influences performance on MTurk (Kittur et al., 2008). Researchers should strive to make task instructions clear and provide examples of how to complete the task appropriately. "Gold standard" questions (i.e., questions with known answers) should also be placed within tasks to help investigators identify problematic data submitted by careless or cheating workers. Another popular technique is to ask workers to pass qualification tests before offering them a chance to work on actual paying tasks. This technique slows down the recruitment process and reduces the pool of available workers, but it can help to improve results dramatically.

Finally, for longer and more complex tasks, researchers might consider using other employment markets, such as oDesk, which tend to attract more specialized workers than those found on MTurk.

Open Innovation Contests

In addition to microtask markets, open innovation contests provide yet another platform for conducting crowdsourced work. Unlike markets, in which compensation is given for all work, open innovation contests compensate only top performers. Challenges are posted online, either through companywide initiatives—such as Nokia's Ideas Project, Dell's Idea Storm, and OpenIDEO—or through innovation hubs like Innocentive. Because these contests are crowdsourced and open, companies get the opportunity to glean insights from thousands of people from many different backgrounds and disciplines.

The benefits from open innovation contests are not restricted to industry; academic research teams can use this approach to crowdsource interesting ideas and technologies that might not otherwise be considered by members of their own fields. In 2011 members of the affective computing community hosted the Facial Expression Recognition Analysis (FERA) challenge—a contest designed to see which research group could best detect facial expressions using automated methods. The FERA challenge was not crowdsourced in the traditional sense (the call for participation was not "open" and was primarily directed toward members of the affective computing community), but future iterations could aim for a larger, more diverse contestant pool. Indeed, Lakhani and Wolf (2005) find that most solutions on Innocentive—an open innovation hub—came from workers just outside the relevant discipline of the problem (i.e., a biology problem was more likely to be solved by a physicist, than a biologist). Individuals from adjacent disciplines may have sufficient training to understand the problem space,

but they also have an outsider's perspective, which helps them to approach the issue from a radically new direction. An open innovation approach can attract fresh sets of eyes to difficult affective computing problems and possibly lead to exciting breakthroughs in the field.

Motivations for Participation

While many affective computing tasks can be crowdsourced using existing platforms such as those described in the preceding sections, many situations require researchers to construct crowdsourcing applications of their own. In considering new crowdsourcing systems for affective computing, perhaps the most important design questions pertain to incentive structures. Since crowdsourcing systems are typically open to anyone and do not rely on contractual relationships, people are not bound to participate. Instead, they must feel somehow compelled to participate, so the factors that make a given system compelling might also be those that make it succeed or fail. There are many ways to attract crowdworkers, but researchers such as Malone et al. (2009) describe three overarching motivations that govern most or all crowdsourcing platforms: money, love, and glory.

Money

The dominant incentive mechanism on microtask markets is money. Different markets have different norms for remuneration rates, but higher pay generally gets more workers to do more work more quickly (Mason & Watts, 2009). In some cases, money can be the only motivator that will work. When the work is tedious and unpleasant (such as transcribing pages and pages of handwritten documents), crowdworkers are unlikely to participate unless fair monetary compensation is guaranteed. Money is not necessarily the best way to ensure quality, however. Researchers studying MTurk have found that higher rates of pay do not necessarily lead to higher-quality work (Mason & Watts, 2009; Rogstadius et al., 2011).

Love

Of course money is not always required to fuel crowdsourcing endeavors. If workers simply love the task itself, they will contribute their time for free. Some people love tasks that challenge them and encourage them to think creatively. Software developers cite the creative challenges of coding as the primary reason they contribute to free and open-source software projects (Lakhani & Wolf,

2005). Others enjoy tasks that offer them a chance to exercise skills and talents that they do not get to use in their ordinary working lives (Howe, 2009).

Others may be driven by idealism. They may contribute simply because they support the overall goals of the project. In the NASA Clickworkers project, for example, researchers needed thousands of individuals to help label and classify craters on mars. At the outset, the project designers could not be sure that people would contribute without being paid. However, because people were genuinely excited by the scientific goals of the project, they were willing to work without pay, even though the task itself was somewhat repetitive.

Novelty can also be a powerful motivator. The chance to interact with new technology may be enough to encourage participation. For instance, participants may be willing to interact with affect recognition software simply because the technology is new and exciting and fun to experience at first hand. Affective computing researchers might consider using this as an angle to attract users to test out new designs or participate in research studies.

Glory

Finally, some crowdworkers are driven to compete for the recognition of their peers. Many programmers flock to coding contests for precisely this reason. Respect from one's peers can be a powerful motivator, and many systems incorporate leaderboards and other reputation signals to encourage participants to compete among their peers. Competition can also make a crowdsourcing task more gamelike and social and can help enhance worker motivation.

Crowding Out

More often than not, many of the aforementioned motivational structures are combined together into one crowdsourcing system. For instance, the *Fold-It* game combines the intrinsically rewarding properties of video games with the lofty ideals of solving some of biochemistry's most challenging problems (Cooper et al., 2010). The game also allows players to compete for high scores, offering reputational incentives.

However, it is not always the case that extra incentive mechanisms are a good thing. Motivation does not increase monotonically with the number of incentive structures, and some motivations may in fact "crowd out" others (Benkler, 2007; Deci, 1971; Frey & Jegen, 2001). Most notably, extrinsic

rewards, such as money, can overshadow a task's intrinsic rewards, causing people to put forth just enough effort to be paid. In some cases, additional incentive structures may have the opposite of their intended effect and may actually reduce motivation overall. In designing incentive structures for crowdsourcing applications, care should be taken to make sure that different motivations do not conflict with one another.

Quality-Control Techniques

Most of today's crowdsourcing systems are extraordinarily meritocratic. *Innocentive, the ESP Game, Threadless*, and countless others are built on an open call, such that anyone—regardless of educational, geographical, or occupational background—can sign up and contribute. Huge crowds, comprising people with diverse backgrounds, can often yield incredible results if managed successfully. But managing crowds successfully is not a trivial problem. The benefits of crowds can also be their drawback; while their size and diversity can bring new, innovative ideas, they can also bring about great variance in quality.

There are essentially two categories of quality management in crowdsourcing systems: input management and output management. On the input side, steps can be taken to ensure that, as information is collected, it is pruned for quality. On the output side, crowd contributions can be filtered such that only the best and most relevant material rises to the top.

Quality Control: Input Management
GRANULARITY

In his seminal paper "Coase's Penguin, or, Linux and the Nature of the Firm," Yochai Benkler outlines several components that underlie successful crowd-based systems (Benkler, 2002). Among them is the notion of "granularity"—a way to decompose complex tasks down into simple, digestible components. Benkler also describes how tasks should be heterogeneously grained in order to accommodate different motivations among the participants. Many people have limited spare cycles and can devote only a little bit of time to crowd-based systems. Others may have more time, and they may be more incentivized to work for longer hours. *Wikipedia*, while not a crowdsourcing system in the traditional sense, provides a nice illustration of heterogeneous granularity: The site offers the option to simply tweak one word as well as the option to write an entire article from start to finish.

ITERATION

Quality can sometimes be improved when workers are allowed to build on existing work. *Wikipedia* for instance, uses the Wiki structure to let contributors build on the contributions of others. Also, in the crowdsourced Matlab programming challenge, participants constantly build upon one another's codes throughout the contest. Rather than have everyone work in isolation until the contest is over, the event is structured so that participants can build upon the ideas of their peers throughout the contest.

With toolkits like *Turkit*, MTurk tasks can be coordinated via an iterative structure. In some cases, this approach can cause dramatic improvements in quality. For instance, Little et al. showed that when MTurk workers iteratively improved the description of an image, the final result was preferred over other methods 9 of 11 times (Little, Chilton, Goldman, & Miller, 2009).

While iterative approaches can improve quality in some cases, they are not without their perils. Iterative conditions can sometimes lead to information cascades, wherein people follow the actions of others simply because they believe that those that came before them were well informed (Bikhchandani, Hirshleifer, & Welch, 1992). In cases such as these, crowdsourcing tasks should be parallelized instead.

NORMS

In addition to the methods described so far, social norms can also affect the quality of contributions coming into crowdsourcing systems. Crowdsourcing news aggregator sites like *Slashdot* maintain norms in order to manage the quality of incoming news links. For sites such as these, there is a norm that governs the types of articles that should be submitted. In some cases, norms are made explicit, in writing, while in others they are implicit. Recently the website Pinterest sent all new users an email explicitly reminding them to "be respectful, be authentic, and to cite all sources." Norms such as these can be a simple yet powerful way to sculpt contributions from the crowd. Also, crowdsourcing researchers and employers should take care to understand the norms of different platforms. MTurk, for instance, does not prevent employers from posting incredibly long tasks. However, the norms of the site revolve around small microtasks, and extremely long tasks are sometimes eyed with suspicion. For instance, Soleymani and Larson found that many MTurk workers were worried about accepting a job that involved 125 video annotations (Soleymani & Larson, 2010). Workers may not want to sign up for an incredibly long task if they are not certain that they will be paid for their time.

REPUTATION

In many crowd-based systems, the potential for free riding is considerable. In Amazon's Mechanical Turk service, for example, workers can get away with producing low-quality work largely because the punishments are low. Reputation structures, such as those found on eBay.com, reduce the prevalence of free riders, thereby increasing the quality of the overall system. Indeed, studies of human cooperation show that when interactions have consequences that extend out into the future, defection and free riding drop dramatically (Axelrod, 2006). Individuals are more apt to cooperate when their interactions are recorded. These same principles can be applied to crowdsourcing systems for affective computing.

QUALITY CONTROL: OUTPUT MANAGEMENT

It is not always possible to manage the quality of information that comes into crowdsourcing systems. While many of the approaches described above can improve the quality of content coming into the system, additional filtering may still be needed.

STATISTICAL TECHNIQUES

When crowds are asked to make quantitative estimations, the group average can sometimes yield a more accurate result than any one person's estimation. This "wisdom of crowds" effect was first described by Francis Galton in the early twentieth century and has since been replicated in countless other studies (Surowiecki, 2005). Thus, in some crowdsourcing domains, quality can be ensured through simple statistical techniques (in some cases, depending on the distribution of the responses, one may be able to average the opinions of the crowd to get the best answer). Unfortunately not all crowd-based systems collect quantifiable information that can be neatly processed by simple parametric statistical techniques. In many cases the information going into a crowd-based system is subjective and qualitative and not directly amenable to statistical manipulation. Often the crowd is needed to rank contributions before statistics can be used. For instance, consider a case where crowds are recruited to contribute textual descriptions of affective images or movies. It may be hard to rank these descriptions or know which are the most relevant unless yet another set of crowdworkers is hired to curate them.

CROWD VOTING

Crowds can generate massive amounts of information, and sometimes it takes the power of a crowd to sift through it all. Interestingly, just as we can use the crowd to gather information, we can also use the crowd to rate information for relevance and value (Benkler, 2007; Howe, 2009; Malone, Laubacher, & Dellarocas, 2009). This approach can be employed passively, such that the crowd does not even know that its behaviors are being used to rank information (e.g., Google's PageRank or Amazon's collaborative filtering algorithms). Or it can be employed actively, such that the crowd is explicitly tasked to make objective ratings of crowd contributions—for example, the verify step in Soylent's "find, fix verify" algorithm (see Bernstein et al., 2010).

Crowdsourcing Affective Data
Data Collection

As with many domains of artificial intelligence, the performance of affective computing systems is dependent on the quality and quantity of training examples that are available. Crowdsourcing offers new ways to efficiently collect large amounts of affective data. However, there are a number of challenges in collecting data in relatively uncontrolled settings. In this section we discuss the potential for data collection via the crowd, along with the pitfalls and technological limitations of such a procedure.

We consider two forms of data collection: (1) using crowdworkers to generate original affective data, perhaps in response to a stimuli or by acting, and (2) using crowdworkers to source existing examples of affective data. Data can be in the form of text, audio, and/or visual material.

The widespread availability of webcams and video platforms such as YouTube has facilitated the collection of large amounts of rich image and video data. For instance, Taylor et al. (2011) and Spiro (2012) describe ways to use webcams to crowdsource posed data for training gesture-recognition systems. McDuff et al. (2012) present the first corpus of videos of naturalistic and spontaneous facial responses collected over the web. In this research, participants were asked to view a media clip in their web browser while their facial expressions were recorded using a webcam. Over five thousand video responses were collected in little over a month and none of the participants were paid.

Collecting naturalistic affective responses via the web raises some interesting issues. Opt-in participation is particularly important in cases where images from webcams are captured and stored. Another issue relates to data quality. High-bandwidth data—such as real-time videos—may be limited in resolution and frame rate, which can present challenges for data analysis and feature detection.

In addition to generating affective data, crowds can help curate and collect affective data. Naturalistic affective data can be mined from various online repositories of videos, most notably YouTube.com. For instance, Morency, Mihalcea, and Doshi (2011) created a corpus of 47 videos from YouTube for multimodal sentiment analysis. While their corpus was handpicked by the researchers themselves, future efforts could delegate crowdworkers to help collect and curate even larger corpora of videos. Websites such as YouTube contain a plethora of videos showcasing naturalistic affective expressions and reactions. Finding these videos is a challenge in itself, however, and sifting through them all often requires the combined efforts of a large crowd of people.

Collecting Labels

Ground-truth labels are a fundamental component of datasets. One of the most popular uses of crowdsourcing in affective computing is in collecting ground-truth labels of affective data. VidL was the first example of a distributed video-labeling tool specifically designed for labeling affective data (Ekhardt & Picard, 2009). Games with a purpose (GWAPs) have also enabled the efficient collection of labels. For instance, Riek, O'Connor, and Robinson (2011) present *Guess What?*—a GWAP with the intention of labeling affective video data of social situations. Soleymani and Larson (2010) sourced boredom annotations for a corpus of affective responses to videos. In this case the agreement between workers was low (Cohen's kappa = 0.01 for boredom labels and 0.07 for emotion word labels), which highlights the subjective nature of many of these tasks. Labeling motion tracks for training gesture-recognition systems is another example of a crowdsourcing application that could help provide useful datasets for training affective computing systems (Spiro et al. 2010). Sign-language recognition is a particular area in which this may prove useful.

So far we have mostly considered nonverbal affective data. However, crowdsourcing has also been used to label emotional speech and text. Tarasov et al. propose ways to crowdsource emotional speech assets (2010). Sentiment labels for text have been successfully crowdsourced (Hsueh et al. 2009), and Mohammad and Turney (2011) created a word-emotion lexicon using crowdsourced labels. GWAPs have been used for similar purposes (Pearl & Steyvers, 2010). Music can powerfully evoke affect and is frequently used as an affective stimulus. Several examples of crowdsourced emotion labeling for music have been presented (Kim et al., 2008; Morton et al., 2010; Speck et al., 2011; Turnbull et al., 2007).

Evaluating Labeler Agreement

There are certain nuances to labeling affective data, not least the fact that in many cases there is no objective ground truth. Rather, labels are often subjective judgments about perceived affective phenomena. Also, there is often inconsistency between multiple labelers. A number of methods have been proposed for evaluating agreement between multiple labelers. Cohen's kappa, κ, is the most commonly used statistic, although there is some disagreement over what thresholds indicate good, weak, or bad agreement (Tarasov, 2010). As a guide $\kappa > .6$ might be considered good. However, in a number of cases labels that have. $6 > \kappa > .3$ have been used even if this does not reflect strong agreement. Typically, greater numbers of labelers will increase the reliability of labels as random errors should begin to cancel out (Harrigan, 2005; Soleymani & Larson, 2010). In addition, techniques have been developed to identify good annotators over bad annotators and to identify biases that might exist in annotations (e.g., Tarasov, 2010).

As with most other crowdsourcing tasks, participants for affect-labeling tasks can be recruited using microtask markets (such as MTurk). However, social networking sites (such as Facebook) provide another efficient method of recruitment. Depending on the platform, be it a GWAP or a more explicit, for-hire labeling job, participants may be volunteers or paid workers.

Crowdsourcing labels for affective data raise many interesting questions about how to design crowdsourcing tasks. The optimal trade-off between expertise, number and diversity of labelers, time available, and cost is likely to be dependent on whether data are naturalistic or posed, of multiple or single modalities, and whether labeling requires training (e.g., facial action coding certification). For affect labeling in particular, designers need to consider whether labels will vary with different demographics (e.g., people from different cultural backgrounds). These differences, if undetected, could lead to unexplained heterogeneity in the labels.

Crowd-Powered Affective Applications

Recently researchers studying human-computer interaction have begun to explore user interfaces that utilize both automatic and human-powered processes. These "crowd-powered systems," as they are sometimes called, recruit human intelligence as needed when automatic processes alone are insufficient. Crowd-powered applications have been developed to help people see (Bigham et al., 2010), edit Word documents (Bernstein et al., 2010), plan itineraries (Zhang et al., 2012), and even operate remote-controlled robots (Lasecki et al., 2011). In this context, crowds are not simply used to train algorithms. Rather, they are recruited on demand, in response to the unique needs of the end user, and they comprise a large part of the application's computational power. This approach is still quite novel, and it has yet to be used widely by researchers in the affective computing community. That said, as of this writing, there are at least two affective computing applications that explore these on-demand, crowd-computing techniques.

Crowd-Powered Emotion Regulation

Morris and Picard (2012) describe ways to use crowd-powered techniques to power emotion regulatory technologies. Specifically, they outline ways to crowdsource elements of cognitive-based therapies, including cognitive reappraisal and cognitive restructuring, to help individuals regulate distressing emotions. In their design, crowds are recruited to help individuals reappraise and restructure emotion-eliciting thoughts and situations. Users submit short, one- to two- sentence descriptions of something causing them stress or untoward anxiety. These descriptions are sent to workers on MTurk, each of whom reframes the text in different ways. Some apply cognitive restructuring and examine the user's text for possible cognitive distortions (e.g., all-or-nothing thinking, overgeneralization). Others are asked to apply cognitive reappraisal—a technique that involves changing the meaning of a thought or situation to alter emotional experience (Gross & John, 2003). In all cases, crowdworkers are trained on demand and are given short one- to two- minute tutorials prior to completing the work. The crowd's work is coordinated programmatically, and a crowd-voting stage is implemented to help make sure that only the best responses are returned to the user. The basic design of the system utilizes a "wisdom of crowds" approach, wherein the unique perspectives of many workers is used to generate novel and intriguing reappraisals that might not ordinarily be considered by a small set of skilled experts. Finally, there is also an empathy component, wherein crowdworkers are taught to apply person-centered support to help the user know that he or she has been understood.

Analyses of the design revealed that, with minimal training, crowdworkers were able to classify cognitive distortions with 89% accuracy. The authors also tested the quality of the responses generated by their system. They found that responses with reappraisals were rated significantly higher than those generated by an open-response structure in which workers were simply asked to help the user feel better and contributions were not coordinated or filtered algorithmically.

Unfortunately this application has yet to be thoroughly tested in long-term user studies, and it remains unclear how it will be received by real end users. To be useful in real-world deployments, the system must be able to respond quickly and the quality of the responses will have to be high.

Crowd-Powered Social Stories

In addition to emotion regulation, crowd-powered design principles have also been applied to support individuals with autism spectrum disorder (ASD). To manage anxiety when faced with new situations, individuals diagnosed with ASD often rehearse a behavioral repertoire using social stories—scripted routines that outline the steps involved in a given task or interaction (such as getting tickets at a movie theater). However, despite advances in commonsense reasoning, it is still impossible for purely computational processes to generate context-appropriate social stories for many different situations. Moreover, authoring social stories for individuals with autism can be complex, and it can be very time-consuming for any one person to exhaustively list the sequence of events needed to navigate a given social situation. It can be especially difficult to generate all the contingencies that must be considered in case a problem arises. To deal with this difficulty, Boujarwah et al. (2012) describe ways to crowdsource the creation of models for social stories for individuals with ASD. Specifically, crowdworkers are asked to brainstorm and classify steps involved in completing a particular task (such as "eating lunch"). Crowdworkers are

then asked to brainstorm obstacles that an individual might encounter and ways to get around these obstacles. The general approach described by this work could potentially be applied to any individual facing a challenging new situation. In the future, the approaches described by Morris and Picard and Boujarwah et al. might be combined to help individuals navigate both the practical and emotional hurdles involved with stressful situations.

Ethical Considerations

Crowdsourcing is still an evolving field and many of the ethical implications it raises have yet to be resolved. As of this writing, MTurk does not impose minimum wage restrictions. Employers are free to offer any form of compensation, no matter how menial. While few people in the United States rely on MTurk as a primary source of income, many individuals in India consider their wages crucial for daily subsistence (Ipeirotis, 2010). In the future, greater oversight should be placed on wages to make sure that crowdsourcing work does not evolve into a digital sweatshop, as some researchers fear (Fort, Adda, & Cohen, 2011). Moreover, more work should be done to help crowdworkers develop new, meaningful skills that generalize to other work domains. All too often, crowdworkers are given tedious, rote tasks that contribute little in the way of new, marketable job skills.

Worker anonymity is another issue that can be particularly troublesome for crowdsourcing researchers, particularly those conducting affective computing studies. In most crowdsourcing systems, worker identities are kept hidden and it can be hard to know where they are from or how old they really are. Tasks that involve stress induction or exposure to challenging media (e.g., the International Affective Picture System [IAPs]) may be inappropriate for young persons, yet researchers may find it difficult or impossible to impose age restrictions on crowdsourcing platforms such as MTurk. While MTurk requires users to be over 18 years of age, it is not clear how well this policy is enforced. An adult could easily register as a worker and then hand over the account to a child.

Another potential problem relates to liability issues. This is particularly important for assistive devices that rely on crowdsourced work, such as those described in our previous section on crowd-powered affective applications. If members of the crowd mislead the user or provide malicious feedback, it will be unclear who is responsible. Should liability reside with the workers in the system or the designers of the system?

Finally, some have also considered how crowdsourcing design, by its very nature, can lead to malicious and dangerous applications. When work is parceled into tiny bits, it can be hard for crowdworkers to know whether their work, as a whole, is contributing to something virtuous or vicious. For instance, a despotic regime could easily crowdsource its efforts to identify dissidents in a large crowd of people. The regime's actual intent could, in a sense, be laundered by decomposing the overarching goal into small, nondescript microtasks.

The Future of Crowdsourcing

In general terms, crowdsourcing is simply a method of recruiting and organizing labor; its basic framework has been around for many years if not decades. Yet in recent years the practice has evolved considerably and proliferated rapidly. Advances in communication technologies, combined with new crowdsourcing platforms and techniques, have led to exciting new innovations for the field. And while the practice is still undergoing significant growing pains, particularly with regard to its ethical quandaries, it is likely to expand in the coming years. In this section, as we speculate on how the future of crowdsourcing will affect affective computing, we focus on three emerging trends in the field of crowdsourcing: (1) real-time crowdsourcing, (2) skilled crowdsourcing, and (3) offline crowdsourcing.

Real-Time Crowdsourcing

In most crowdsourcing situations, there exists a large gap between the time work is requested and the time work is completed. For microtasks that require mere seconds to complete, this latency is largely an effect of the time it takes to recruit and train new workers, not the time it takes to do the actual work. To solve this problem, Bernstein et al. (2011) describe ways to place crowdworkers on retainer, so that workers are already recruited and trained by the time requests for work arrive in the system. In their model, workers get paid small amounts to wait for tasks and are told to respond as soon as they are notified (a javascript alert and audio chime is used to notify workers that a new job is ready to be completed). Using this design, many workers can be recruited synchronously at a moment's notice, creating a sort of "flash mob" of workers. For affective computing technologies that require on-demand crowdsourcing, real-time crowdsourcing methods such as these will reduce latency dramatically and pave the way for new types of interactive systems. Currently, most interactive affective technologies

(e.g., social robots, emotional support systems) rely on automated algorithms and artificial intelligence. In the future, these technologies may be augmented by real-time crowdsourcing techniques, drawing on human intelligence when needed.

Skilled Crowdsourcing

For many affective computing applications, skilled workers are needed to label complex data or power sophisticated interactive systems. While some crowdsourcing platforms offer ways to train workers, it can be difficult to retain these trained workers for future tasks. In the future, crowdsourcing platforms will hopefully offer ways to target skilled workers, either by retaining and tracking those who have performed well in the past or by finding new workers who have the desired skills. GWAPs offer intriguing ways to find skilled workers by allocating jobs only to players who have completed certain levels in a game. While this model has been explored somewhat in systems like *Fold-It*, more work can certainly be done to clarify how best to allocate work based on a player's achievement in a game or instructional program.

Offline Crowdsourcing

For the most part, crowdsourced work is situated online. That said, new services like taskrabbit.com and gigwalk.com are applying the crowdsourcing model to real-world tasks, such as moving furniture or conducting in-store audits. As more crowdsourcing platforms move offline, affective computing researchers can begin to take advantage of real-world data collection. Many individuals are already wearing biosensors as part of the quantified health movement. Given the proper incentives, some of these individuals might be willing to share subsets of their data in order to help researchers develop more powerful affect-detection systems. For instance, if enough people are wearing biosensors and are willing to upload their data, intriguing new datasets of real-world affective experiences can be crowdsourced. Just as twitter has helped researchers understand contagions and flu outbreaks, crowdsourced biosensor data might help us understand complex emotional and psychophysiological patterns across large groups of people. For instance, researchers could get a better understanding as to how groups of people react to traffic jams or other urban inconveniences. Such data might help guide new infrastructure and might be used to build new emotional support systems that intervene in extremely context-specific ways.

Conclusion

Although crowdsourcing is still relatively new, it already has the potential to dramatically accelerate affective computing research. Large datasets are crucial for improving the performance of affect-recognition systems. Access to large groups of workers via crowdsourcing can make data collection and labeling much more efficient. Also, the augmentation of computer systems with human intelligence can engender exciting new applications, such as emotionally intelligent assistive devices.

It is hard to predict how crowdsourcing will evolve in the coming years. Perhaps the best way for affective computing researchers to secure a future that benefits them is to create it themselves. Designing systems with effective and sustainable motivation strategies, creating methods for validating and verifying data collected, and solving ethical issues associated with large-scale and distributed labor are the main areas that need to be addressed in the near future.

References

Axelrod, R. (2006). *The evolution of cooperation*, rev. ed. New York, NY: Basic Books.

Benkler, Y. (2002). Coase's penguin, or Linux and the nature of the firm. *Yale Law Journal, 112*, 369–446.

Benkler, Y. (2007). *The wealth of networks: How social production transforms markets and freedom*. New Haven, CT: Yale University Press.

Bernstein, M. S., Brandt, J., Miller, R. C., & Karger, D. R. (2011). Crowds in two seconds: Enabling realtime crowd-powered interfaces. *Proceedings of the 24th Annual ACM Symposium on User Interface Software and Technology*, UIST '11 (pp. 33–42). New York, NY: Association for Computing Machinery.

Bernstein, M. S., Little, G., Miller, R. C., Hartmann, B., Ackerman, M. S., Karger, D. R....Panovich, K. (2010). Soylent. *Proceedings of the 23nd Annual ACM Symposium on User Interface Software and Technology—UIST '10* (p. 313). New York, NY: Association for Computing Machinery.

Bigham, J. P., Jayant, C., Ji, H., Little, G., Miller, A., Miller, R....Yeh, T. (2010). VizWiz. *Proceedings of the 23nd Annual ACM Symposium on User Interface Software and Technology—UIST '10* (p. 333). New York, NY: Association for Computing Machinery.

Bikhchandani, S., Hirshleifer, D., & Welch, I. (1992). A theory of fads, fashion, custom, and cultural change in informational cascades. *Journal of Political Economy, 100*(5), 992–1026.

Boujarwah, F., Abowd, G., & Arriaga, R. (2012). Socially computed scripts to support social problem solving skills. *Proceedings of the 2012 ACM Annual Conference on Human Factors in Computing Systems*, CHI '12 (pp. 1987–1996). New York, NY: Association for Computing Machinery.

Cooper, S., Khatib, F., Treuille, A., Barbero, J., Lee, J., Beenen, M....Players, F. (2010). Predicting protein structures with a multiplayer online game. *Nature, 466*(7307), 756–760.

Deci, E. L. (1971). Effects of externally mediated rewards on intrinsic motivation. *Journal of Personality and Social Psychology, 18*, 105–115.

Fort, K., Adda, G., & Cohen, K. B. (2011). Amazon Mechanical Turk: Gold mine or coal mine? *Computational Linguistics, 37*(2), 413–420.

Frey, B. S., & Jegen, R. (2001). Motivation crowding theory. *Journal of Economic Surveys, 15*(5), 589–611.

Gross, J. J., &John, O. P. (2003). Individual differences in two emotion regulation processes: implications for affect, relationships, and well-being. *Journal of Personality and Social Psychology, 85*(2), 348–362.

Harrigan, J., Rosenthal, R., & Scherer, K. (2005). *New handbook of methods in nonverbal behavior research*. New York, NY: Oxford University Press.

Horton, J. J., & Chilton, L. B. (2010). The labor economics of paid crowdsourcing. *Proceedings of the 11th ACM Conference on Electronic Commerce*. Available at: http://ssrn.com/abstract=1596874

Howe, J. (2006, June). The rise of crowdsourcing. *Wired, 14*(6).

Howe, J. (2009). *Crowdsourcing: Why the power of the crowd is driving the future of business* (unedited ed.). New York, NY: Crown Publishing Group.

Hsueh, P. Y., Melville, P., & Sindhwani, V. (2009). Data quality from crowdsourcing: A study of annotation selection criteria. *Proceedings of the NAACL HLT 2009 Workshop on Active Learning for Natural Language Processing* (pp. 27–35). Stroudsburg, PA: Association for Computational Linguistics.

Ipeirotis, P. G. (2010). Demographics of Mechanical Turk. New York, NY: New York University Working Paper.

Khatib, F., DiMaio, F., Group, F. C., Group, F. V. C., Cooper, S., Kazmierczyk, M....Baker, D. (2011). Crystal structure of a monomeric retroviral protease solved by protein folding game players. *Nature Structural & Molecular Biology, 18*(10), 1175–1177.

Kim, Y. E., Schmidt, E., & Emelle, L. (2008). Moodswings: A collaborative game for music mood label collection. *Proceedings of the International Symposium on Music Information Retrieval* (pp. 231–236). Philadelphia, PA: International Conference on Music Information Retrieval.

Kittur, A., Chi, E. H., & Suh, B. (2008). Crowdsourcing user studies with Mechanical Turk. *Proceeding of the Twenty-Sixth Annual SIGCHI Conference on Human factors in Computing Systems*, CHI '08 (pp. 453–456). New York, NY: Association for Computing Machinery.

Lakhani, K. R., & Wolf, R. G. (2005). Why hackers do what they do: Understanding motivation and effort in free/open source software projects. In J. Feller, S. Fitzgerald, S. Hissam, & K. Lakhani (Eds.), *Perspective on Free and Open Source Software*. Cambridge, MA: MIT Press.

Lakhani, K. R., Jeppesen, L. B., Lohse, P. A., & Panetta. J. A. (2006). *The value of openness in scientific problem solving*. Cambridge, MA: Harvard Business School Working Paper No. 07-050

Lasecki, W. S., Murray, K. I., White, S., Miller, R. C., & Bigham, J. P. (2011). Real-time crowd control of existing interfaces. *Proceedings of the 24th Annual ACM Symposium on User Interface Software and Technology*, UIST '11 (pp. 23–32). New York, NY: Association for Computing Machinery.

Little, G., Chilton, L. B., Goldman, M., & Miller, R. C. (2009). TurKit: tools for iterative tasks on Mechanical Turk. *Proceedings of the ACM SIGKDD Workshop on Human Computation*, HCOMP '09 (pp. 29–30). New York, NY: Association for Computing Machinery.

Malone, T. (2009). *Harnessing crowds: Mapping the genome of collective intelligence*. Cambridge, MA: MIT Sloan Research.

Mason, W., & Watts, D. J. (2009). Financial incentives and the "performance of crowds." *Proceedings of the ACM SIGKDD Workshop on Human Computation—HCOMP '09* (p. 77). Presented at the ACM SIGKDD Workshop, Paris, France.

McDuff, D. J., Kaliouby, R. E., & Picard, R. W. (2012). Crowdsourcing facial responses to online videos. *IEEE Transactions on Affective Computing, 3*(4), 456–468

Mohammad, S. M., & Turney, P. D. (2011). Crowdsourcing: A word–emotion association lexicon. *Computational Intelligence, 59*(000), 1–24.

Morency, L. P., Mihalcea, R., & Doshi, P. (2011). Towards multimodal sentiment analysis: Harvesting opinions from the web. *Proceedings of the 13th International Conference on Multimodal Interfaces* (pp. 169–176). New York, NY: Association for Computing Machinery.

Morris, R. R., & Picard, R. (2012). Crowdsourcing collective emotional intelligence. *Collective Intelligence*, Cambridge, MA. Available at: http://arxiv.org/abs/1204.3481

Morton, B. G., Speck, J. A., Schmidt, E. M., & Kim, Y. E. (2010). Improving music emotion labeling using human computation. *Proceedings of the ACM SIGKDD Workshop on Human Computation* (pp. 45–48). New York, NY: Association for Computing Machinery.

Pearl, L., & Steyvers, M. (2010). Identifying emotions, intentions, and attitudes in text using a game with a purpose. *Proceedings of the NAACL HLT 2010 Workshop on Computational Approaches to Analysis and Generation of Emotion in Text* (pp. 71–79). Stroudsburg, PA: Association for Computational Linguistics.

Riek, L. D., O'Connor, M. F., & Robinson, P. (2011). Guess what? A Game for affective annotation of video using crowd sourcing. In S. D'Mello, A. Graesser, B. Schuller, & J.-C. Martin (Eds.), *Affective computing and intelligent interaction* (Vol. 6974, pp. 277–285). Berlin and Heidelberg: Springer Berlin Heidelberg. Available at: http://www.springerlink.com/content/a40471253r44t616/

Rogstadius, J., Kostakos, V., AniketKittur, Smus, B., Laredo, J., & Vukovic, M. (2011). An assessment of intrinsic and extrinsic motivation in crowdsourcing markets. *ICWSM11*. Presented at the Association for the Advancement of Artificial Intelligence (AAAI), Barcelona, Spain.

Soleymani, M., & Larson, M. (2010). Crowdsourcing for affective annotation of video: Development of a viewer-reported boredom corpus. *Proceedings of the ACM SIGIR 2010 workshop on crowdsourcing for search evaluation (CSE 2010)* (pp. 4–8). New York, NY: Association for Computing Machinery.

Speck, J. A., Schmidt, E. M., Morton, B. G., & Kim, Y. E. (2011). A comparative study of collaborative vs. traditional musical mood annotation. *Proceedings of the International Symposium on Music Information Retrieval* (pp. 549–554). Philadelphia, PA: International Conference on Music Information Retrieval.

Spiro, I. (2012). Motion chain: a webcam game for crowdsourcing gesture collection. *Proceedings of the 2012 ACM Annual Conference Extended Abstracts on Human Factors in Computing Systems Extended Abstracts* (pp. 1345–1350). Available at: http://dl.acm.org/citation.cfm?id=2212452

Spiro, I., Taylor, G., Williams, G., & Bregler, C. (2010). Hands by hand: Crowd-sourced motion tracking for gesture annotation. *Computer Vision and Pattern Recognition Workshops (CVPRW), 2010 IEEE Computer Society Conference on Computer Vision and Pattern Recognition* (pp. 17–24). Available at: http://ieeexplore.ieee.org/xpls/abs_all.jsp?arnumber=5543191

Surowiecki, J. (2005). *The Wisdom of Crowds*. New York, NY: Doubleday/Anchor.

Tarasov, A., Cullen, C., Delany, S. (2010). Using crowdsourcing for labeling emotional speech assets. *W3c Workshop on Emotion ML* (pp. 1–5). Available at: http://www.w3.org/2010/10/emotionml/papers/tarasov.pdf

Taylor, G. W., Spiro, I., Bregler, C., & Fergus, R. (2011). Learning invariance through imitation. *Computer Vision and Pattern Recognition (CVPR), 2011 IEEE Conference on Computer Vision and Pattern Recognition* (pp. 2729–2736). New York, NY: Institute of Electrical and Electronics Engineers.

Turnbull, D., Liu, R., Barrington, L., & Lanckriet, G. (2007). A game-based approach for collecting semantic annotations of music. *8th International Conference on Music Information Retrieval (ISMIR)*. Philadelphia, PA: International Conference on Music Information Retrieval.

von Ahn, L. (2006). Games with a purpose. *Computer, 39*(6), 92–94.

Zhang, H., Law, E., Miller, R., Gajos, K., Parkes, D., & Horvitz, E. (2012). Human computation tasks with global constraints. *Proceedings of the 2012 ACM Annual Conference on Human Factors in Computing Systems*, CHI '12 (pp. 217–226). New York, NY: Association for Computing Machinery.

Emotion Markup Language

Marc Schröder, Paolo Baggia, Felix Burkhardt, Catherine Pelachaud, Christian Peter, *and* Enrico Zovato

Abstract

There is no single agreed-upon description of emotions or related terms in the emotion research literature. A generally useful emotion markup language should, therefore, provide a rich set of descriptive mechanisms. EmotionML has been developed at the World Wide Web Consortium by members of the affective computing community with very diverse backgrounds. It provides representations of affective states that aim to satisfy the needs of the majority of emotion researchers and application developers alike. Emotions can be represented in terms of categories, dimensions, appraisals, and action tendencies, with a single <emotion> element containing one or more of such descriptors. As it is not possible to standardize a closed set of emotion terms nor desirable to leave the choice of labels completely undefined, EmotionML provides an "emotion vocabulary" mechanism to flexibly select descriptors. This chapter describes selected aspects of EmotionML 1.0 and the procedure and thinking behind its development.

Key Words: emotion, annotation, representation, markup, multimodality

Introduction

EmotionML, the emotion markup language, is a format for representing emotions for use in technological systems. It is obvious that computerized systems, to the extent that they can recognize, simulate, or otherwise process emotion-related information, need a representation format. If several components are to work collaboratively on the information, the format must be well defined. In order to reach the best possible interoperability, a standard representation format should be used (for a detailed description, see Schröder et al., 2012).

This chapter describes the work on defining and standardizing EmotionML, a long-running collaborative effort of members of the affective computing community with various emotion-related backgrounds.

The types of technology in which an emotion markup language might be used are very diverse. The 39 individual use cases collected by the emotion incubator group (Schröder et al., 2007) include such diverse topics as the annotation of the emotional connotation in words and sentences, in pictures, or in audio recordings; the description of the emotional state of participants in a multiparty conversation as it changes over time; emotion detection by various means (for example, for social robots); the use of computer games to induce emotions in the player; the reasoning about the emotional consequences of events; and the generation of emotional expressivity in synthetic faces and voices. The group structured the individual use case descriptions into three main types of use:

Use case 1: manual annotation of emotions in data

Use case 2: automatic detection of emotions

Use case 3: generation of emotion-related system behavior

This way of structuring the use cases seemed appropriate because the requirements arising from all the exemplars of a given use case are relatively similar. For example, the type of detail that humans tend to annotate (use case 1) is orders of magnitude more fine-grained than what machines can detect (use case 2). Both of these have a natural notion of confidence (i.e., of certainty that the annotation is correct). On the other hand, this notion makes little sense in the context of synthesizing system behavior (use case 3).

A standardized markup language in general is very useful as an exchange format for processors (i.e., consumers as well as producers of emotional content) of a specific technology. By using a common language, the development of an infrastructure of emotion-processing modules becomes possible. The concluding section of this chapter introduces some applications that already use EmotionML as exchange format.

Previous Work

The representation of emotions and related states has been part of several activities. In the area of labeling schemes, maybe the most thorough attempt to propose an encompassing labeling scheme for emotion-related phenomena has been the work on the HUMAINE database (Douglas-Cowie et al., 2007). The relevant concepts were identified and made available as a set of configuration files for the video annotation tool Anvil (Kipp, 2001). A formal representation format was not proposed in this work. However, members of the team working on the HUMAINE database were active in the first emotion incubator group and made sure that the concepts identified as relevant were present in the discussion on use cases and requirements.

Markup languages including emotion-related information were defined mainly in the context of research systems generating emotion-related behavior of embodied conversational agents (ECAs). The expressive richness is usually limited to a small set of emotion categories, possibly an intensity dimension, and in some cases a three-dimensional continuous representation of activation-evaluation-power space (cf. Schröder et al., 2011b).

For example, the virtual human markup language (VHML) (Gustavsson et al., 2001) was created in order to control the behavior of animated characters (virtual agents) in addition to markup for facial animation, speech synthesis, dialogue management, etc. The specification also contains a section for representing emotions. The actual representations are very simple: A set of nine emotions is encoded directly as XML elements. For example:

```
<afraid intensity="40">
Do I have to go to the dentist?
</afraid>
```

The affective presentation markup language (APML) (de Carolis et al., 2004) provides an attribute "affect" to encode an emotion category for an utterance (a "performative") or for a part of it:

```
<performative affect="afraid">
Do I have to go to the dentist?
</performative>
```

The rich representation language (RRL) (van Deemter et al., 2008) uses an element "emotion," embedded in a dialogue act, to represent the emotion. The emotion category and its intensity can be expressed, as well as the three emotion dimensions "activation," "evaluation," and "power." In addition, there is a conceptual distinction between feeling and expressing an emotion:

```
<dialogueAct>
...
<emotion>
<emotionExpressed type="afraid" intensity="0.3"
activation="0.3" evaluation="-0.6" power="-0.3"/>
</emotion>
<sentence>
<text>Do I have to go to the dentist?</text>...
</sentence>
</dialogueAct>
```

All these languages include the representation of an emotional state as one aspect in a complex representation oriented toward the generation of behavior for an ECA. None of the representations aim for reusability in different contexts, and none reach a representational power coming anywhere near the complexity considered to be necessary in emotion research (see e.g., Cowie et al., 2010).

An interesting contribution to the domain of computerized processing and representation of emotion-related concepts is a layered model of affect (ALMA), provided by Gebhard (2005). The model encompasses the concepts of emotion (short-term affect), mood (medium-term affect), and personality (long-term affect). Following the Ortony, Clore, and Collins (OCC) model (Ortony et al., 1988), ALMA uses appraisal mechanisms to trigger emotions from events, objects, and actions in the world. Emotions have an intensity varying over time. Each individual emotion influences mood as a longer-term affective state. ALMA uses an XML-based markup language named AffectML in two places: to represent the antecedents to emotion (i.e., the appraisals leading to emotions) and to represent the impact that emotions and moods have on a virtual agent's behavior.

The following snippet of markup shows how AffectML is used to describe a given character's affective predispositions (i.e., its propensity to react emotionally to different kinds of events) (from Gebhard, 2005):

```
<CharacterAffect name="Valerie" monitored="true"
docu="Valerie ">
<Personality open="0.4" con="0.8" extra="0.6"
agree="0.3" neur="0.4"/>
<Appraisal>
<Basic>
<GoodEvent desirability="0.7"/>
...
</Basic>
<SelfAct type="Calm">
<GoodActSelf agency="self"
praiseworthiness="0.5"/>
</SelfAct>
<DirectAct type="Attack" performer="Sven">
<BadEvent desirability="–0.5"/>
<BadActOther agency="other"
praiseworthiness="-0.3"/>
</DirectAct>
<SelfEmotion emotion="ReproachDisplay">
<BadEvent desirability="–0.3"/>
</SelfEmotion>
...
```

The current affective state of a character, to be expressed in the character's behavior, is represented in AffectML as follows (from Gebhard, 2005):

```
<AffectOutput>
<CharacterAffect name="Sven">
<DominantEmotion name="Disliking"
value="0.46"/>
<Mood moodword="Exuberant" intensity="slightly"
p="0.35" a="0.39" d="0.34"/>
<Personality open="0.3" con="–0.6" extra="0.7"
agree="0.4" neu="–0.1"/>
</CharacterAffect>
...
</AffectOutput>
```

The focus in ALMA has been on providing a working implementation of a particular model of affect based on OCC appraisals and emotions (Ortony et al., 1988), mood represented using Mehrabian's pleasure-arousal-dominance (PAD) space (Mehrabian, 1996), and personality described using the five-factor model (McCrae & John, 1992). Mappings are used to relate the different models to one another. The AffectML language used for representing the various aspects of the model's data in the system is not described in detail; its focus has not been on generic reuse or interoperability but on encoding the concepts relevant to this specific model. In recent work (Kipp et al., 2010), the output of ALMA has been represented using EmotionML.

The emotion annotation and representation language (EARL) (Schröder et al., 2006, 2011b) was introduced as an attempt to address reusability and to provide a representation approaching what is considered scientifically necessary. It can represent emotions alternatively in terms of categories, dimensions, or appraisals; the intensity of the state can be indicated; several kinds of regulation are previewed (e.g., the simulation, suppression, or amplified expression of an emotional state); and complex emotions can be represented, as in situations of regulation or when more than one emotion is present. For example:

```
<emotion category="afraid" intensity="0.4"
suppress="0.6"
activation="0.3" evaluation="–0.6" power="–0.3">
Do I have to go to the dentist?
</emotion>
```

The following sections show how the ideas embedded in EARL were broadened and made more generic and flexibly usable in the development of the EmotionML specification. The resulting syntax of EmotionML (see Scientific Descriptions of Emotion, p. 401) has changed quite substantially from the original EARL ideas; nevertheless, the motivating ideas have largely stayed the same.

Requirements for EmotionML

The emotion incubator group extracted requirements from the different use cases in an iterative process. First, each of the three use cases produced a separate set of requirements. These sets were then combined and aligned. The alignment process yielded an interesting exercise of aligning vocabulary: for example, the expressive behavior related to an emotion would be called "input" in use case 2 (emotion detection), but it would be considered to be "output" in use case 3 (synthesis).

The process of aligning requirements and concepts yielded consensus terms (e.g., *observable behavior* instead of *input* and *output*) and agreement to avoid ambiguous or context-specific terms such as *input* and *output*. Other terms were easier to align: The term *confidence* from use case 1 (manual annotation) was considered to be identical in its intended meaning with the term *probability* from use case 2; the consensus term in this case was *confidence*, since it was felt to be the more generally applicable term.

The following principles were agreed upon and used in order to align and consolidate the sets of requirements (Schröder et al., 2007):

1. The emotion language should not try to represent sensor data, facial expressions, environmental data, etc., but define a way of interfacing with external representations of such data.

2. The use of system-centric vocabulary such as *input* and *output* should be avoided. Instead, concept names should be chosen by following the phenomena observed, such as *experiencer, trigger* or *observable behavior.*

The process was also useful in establishing the intended boundaries of the EmotionML according to principle (1) above. With the broad range of targeted use cases, describing the respective domain concepts or modality-specific expressions was clearly unrealistic.

The emphasis of the emotion incubator group was on coverage, in the sense of including as broad a list of requirements as seemed reasonable. The group's final report (Schröder et al., 2007) included a list of 22 requirements structured into five sections: (1) information about the emotion properties, (2) metainformation about the individual emotion annotations, (3) links to the rest of the world, (4) information about a number of global metadata, and (5) ontologies.

After collecting this broad and encompassing list, the EmotionML incubator group focused on extracting a manageable subset by means of a collaborative prioritization process involving the research community at large.

Syntax

Based on the requirements, a syntax for EmotionML (Schröder et al., 2012) was produced in a sequence of steps. The following snippet exemplifies the principles of the EmotionML syntax.

```
<sentence id="sent1">
Do I have to go to the dentist?
</sentence>
```

```
<emotion xmlns="http://www.w3.org/2009/10/
emotionml"
category-set="http://www.w3.org/TR/emotion-voc/
xml#everyday-categories">
<category name="afraid" value="0.4"/>
<reference role="expressedBy" uri="#sent1"/>
</emotion>
```

The following properties can be observed.

• The emotion annotation is self-contained within an "<emotion>" element.
• All emotion elements belong to a specific name space.
• It is explicit in the example that emotion is represented in terms of categories.
• It is explicit from which category set the category label is chosen.
• The link to the annotated material is realized via a reference using a URI (Uniform Resource Identifier, a string of characters used to identify a name of a web resource), and the reference has an explicit role.

In the following subsections, we discuss the properties of the EmotionML syntax in more detail.

Design Principles: Self-Contained Emotion Annotation

EmotionML is conceived as a plug-in language with the aim of being usable in many different contexts. Therefore proper encapsulation is essential. All information concerning an individual emotion annotation is contained within a single "<emotion>" element. All emotion markup belongs to a unique XML namespace. EmotionML differs from many other markup languages in the sense that it does not enclose the annotated material. In order to link the emotion markup with the annotated material, either the reference mechanism in EmotionML or another mechanism external to EmotionML can be used; that is, for a video annotation system, the link to the individual videos might be given by the "reference" element, or each video could have assigned an own EmotionML document.

Structurally, EmotionML uses element and attribute names to indicate the type of information being represented; attribute values provide the actual information. The use of attribute values (e.g., "<category name='joy'/>") was preferred over enclosed text (e.g., "<category>joy</category>"), so that adding EmotionML to an XML node does not change that node's text content.

A top-level element "<emotionml>" enables the creation of stand-alone EmotionML documents, essentially grouping a number of emotion annotations together but also providing document-level mechanisms for annotating global metadata and for defining emotion vocabularies (see below). It is thus possible to use EmotionML both as a stand-alone markup and as a plug-in annotation in different contexts.

Representations of Emotion

Emotions can be represented in terms of four types of descriptions taken from the scientific literature (see Vocabularies for EmotionML, p. 401): "<category>," "<dimension>," "<appraisal>," and "<action-tendency>". An "<emotion>" element can contain one or more of these descriptors; each descriptor must have a "name" attribute and can have a "value" attribute indicating the intensity of the respective descriptor. For "<dimension>," the "value" attribute is mandatory, since a dimensional emotion description is always a position on one or more scales; for the other descriptions, it is possible to omit the "value" to only make a binary statement about the presence of a given category, appraisal, or action tendency.

The following example illustrates a number of possible uses of the core emotion representations:

```
<category name="affectionate"/>
<category name="amused" value="0.7"/>
<dimension name="valence" value="0.9"/>
<appraisal name="agent-self"/>
<appraisal name="urgency" value="0.2"/>
<action-tendency name="approach"/>
<action-tendency name="dominating" value="0.8"/>
```

Mechanism for Referring to an Emotion Vocabulary

Since there is no single agreed vocabulary for each of the four types of emotion descriptions (see Issues for Future Work, p. 403), EmotionML provides a mandatory mechanism for identifying the vocabulary used in a given "<emotion>." The mechanism consists in attributes of "<emotion>" named "category-set," "dimension-set," etc., indicating which vocabulary of descriptors for annotating categories, dimensions, etc., are used in that emotion annotation. These attributes contain a URI pointing to an XML representation of a vocabulary definition (see Issues for Future Work, p. 403). In order to verify that an emotion annotation is valid, an EmotionML processor must retrieve the vocabulary definition and check that every "name" of a corresponding descriptor is part of that vocabulary (see also Conclusion, p. 403).

For example, the following annotation uses Mehrabian's PAD model (Mehrabian, 1996) for representing a position in three-dimensional space:

```
<emotion dimension-set="http://www.w3.org/TR/
emotion-voc/xml#pad-dimensions">
<dimension name="arousal" value="0.3"/>
<!-- lower-than-average arousal -->
<dimension name="pleasure" value="0.9"/>
<!-- very high positive valence -->
<dimension name="dominance" value="0.8"/>
<!-- relatively high potency -->
</emotion>
```

Metainformation

Several types of metainformation can be represented in EmotionML.

First, each emotion descriptor (such as "<category>") can have a "confidence" attribute to indicate the expected reliability of this piece of the annotation. This can reflect the confidence of a human annotator or the probability computed by a machine classifier. If several descriptors are used jointly within an "<emotion>," each descriptor has its own "confidence" attribute. For example, it is possible to have high confidence in, say, the arousal dimension but be uncertain about the pleasure dimension:

```
<emotion dimension-set="http://www.w3.org/TR/
emotion-voc/xml#pad-dimensions">
<dimension name="arousal" value="0.7"
confidence="0.9"/>
<dimension name="pleasure" value="0.6"
confidence="0.3"/>
</emotion>
```

Each "<emotion>" can have an "expressed through" attribute providing a list of modalities through which the emotion is expressed. Given the open-ended application domains for EmotionML, it is naturally difficult to provide a complete list of relevant modalities. The solution provided in EmotionML is to propose a list of human-centric modalities, such as "gaze," "face," "voice," etc., and to allow arbitrary additional values. The following example represents a case where an emotion is recognized from or is to be generated in face and voice:

```
<emotion category-set="http://www.w3.org/TR/
emotion-voc/xml#everyday-categories"
expressed-through="face voice">
<category name="satisfaction"/>
</emotion>
```

For arbitrary additional metadata, EmotionML provides an "<info>" element that can contain arbitrary XML structures. The "<info>" element can occur as a child of "<emotion>" to provide local metadata (i.e., additional information about the specific emotion annotation); it can also occur in stand-alone EmotionML documents as a child of the root node "<emotionml>" to provide global metadata (i.e., information that is constant for all emotion annotations in the document. This can include information about sensor settings, annotator identities, situational contexts, etc). How to represent this information below "<info>" is up to the user.

References to the "Rest of the World"

Emotion annotation is always about something. There is a subject "experiencing" (or simulating) the emotion. This can be a human, a virtual agent, a robot, etc. There is observable behavior expressing the emotion, such as facial expressions, gestures, or vocal effects. With suitable measurement tools, this can also include physiological changes such as sweating or a change in heart rate or blood pressure. Emotions are often caused or triggered by an identifiable entity, such as a person, an object, an event, etc. More precisely, the appraisals leading to the emotion are triggered by that entity. And finally, emotions, or more precisely the emotion-related action tendencies, may be directed toward an entity, such as a person or an object.

EmotionML considers all of these external entities to be out of scope of the language itself; however, it provides a generic mechanism for referring to such entities. Each "<emotion>" can use one or more "<reference>" elements to point to arbitrary URIs. A "<reference>" has a "role" attribute, which can have one of the following four values: "expressedBy" (default), "experiencedBy," "triggeredBy," and "targetedAt." Using this mechanism, it is possible to point to arbitrary entities filling the above-mentioned four roles; all that is required is that these entities be identified by a URI.

Time

Time is relevant to EmotionML in the sense that it is necessary to represent the time during which an emotion annotation is applicable. In this sense, temporal specification complements the above-mentioned reference mechanism.

The representation of time is an astonishingly complex issue. A number of different mechanisms are required to cover the range of possible use cases.

First, it may be necessary to link to a time span in media, such as video or audio recordings. For this purpose, the "<reference role='expressedBy'>" mechanism can use a so-called media fragment URI (Troncy et al., 2010) to point to a time span within the media. In the following example, the emotion is expressed from seconds 3 to 7 in the video "party.avi":

```
<emotion category-set="http://www.w3.org/TR/
emotion-voc/xml#big6">
<category name="happiness"/>
<reference uri="party.avi#t=3,7"/>
</emotion>
```

Second, time may be represented on an absolute or relative scale. EmotionML follows EMMA (Johnston et al., 2009) in representing time in these cases. Absolute time is represented in milliseconds, since January 1, 1970, using the attributes "start" and "end." A combination of the "start" and "duration" attributes can also be used to represent time intervals. For example:

```
<emotion category-set="http://www.w3.org/TR/
emotion-voc/xml#big6"
start="1268647331" end="1268647831">
<category name="joy"/>
</emotion>
or, equivalently,
<emotion category-set="http://www.w3.org/TR/
emotion-voc/xml#big6"
start="1268647331" duration="500">
<category name="joy"/>
</emotion>
```

Absolute times are useful for applications such as affective diaries, which record emotions throughout the day and whose purpose it is to link emotions back to the situations in which they were encountered.

Other applications require relative time; for example, time since the start of a session. Here the mechanism borrowed from EMMA is the combination of "time-ref-uri" and "offset-to-start." The former provides a reference to the entity defining the meaning of time 0; the latter is time in milliseconds since that moment. In case the entity pointed to by "time-ref-uri" is itself a time span, it is possible to indicate using "time-ref-anchor-point" whether the start or the end of that time span is supposed to be the reference for the relative time. The following example represents an emotion observed from seconds 3 to 7 of the session identified by the URI "#my_session_id:"

```
<emotion category-set="http://www.w3.org/TR/
emotion-voc/xml#big6"
```

```
time-ref-uri="#my_session_id" offset-to-start="2000"
duration="5000">
<category name="surprise"/>
</emotion>
```

Representing Continuous Values and Dynamic Changes

As mentioned above, the emotion descriptors "<category>," "<dimension>," "<appraisal>," and "<action-tendency>" can have a "value" attribute to indicate the position on a scale corresponding to the respective descriptor. In the case of a dimension, the value indicates the position on that dimension, which is mandatory information for dimensions; in the case of categories, appraisals, and action tendencies, the value can be optionally used to indicate the extent to which the respective item is present.

In all cases, the "value" attribute contains a floating-point number between 0 and 1. The two end points of that scale represent the most extreme possible values; for example, the lowest and highest possible positions on a dimension or the complete absence of an emotion category versus the most intense possible state of that category.

The "value" attribute thus provides a fine-grained control of the position on a scale, which is constant throughout the temporal scope of the individual "<emotion>" annotation. It is also possible to represent changes over time of these scale values using the "<trace>" element, which can be a child of any "<category>," "<dimension>," "<appraisal>," or "<action-tendency>" element. The following example illustrates the use of a trace to represent an episode of fear during which intensity is rising, first gradually, then quickly to a very high value. Values are taken at a sampling frequency of 10 Hz (i.e., one value every 100 milliseconds).

```
<emotion category-set="http://www.w3.org/TR/
emotion-voc/xml#big6">
<category name="fear">
<trace freq="10Hz" samples="0.1 0.1 0.15 0.2 0.2
0.25 0.25
0.25 0.3 0.3 0.35 0.5 0.7 0.8 0.85 0.85"/>
</category>
</emotion>
```

Scientific Descriptions of Emotion

In the scientific literature on emotion research, there is no single agreed-upon description of emotions (Scherer, 2000). Moreover, Cowie (2010) suggests that most of the research focuses on the so-called emergent emotions—short-lived, intense response patterns triggered by clearly identifiable events—whereas the more relevant concept for technology, according to Cowie, is the notion of relevant "emotion-related" states, which include "mood," "stance toward object/situation," "altered states of arousal," "interpersonal bonds," "altered states of control," "emergent emotion," and "interpersonal states."

So far it appears important for an emotion markup language to be able to represent the most relevant aspects of emotions in the broader sense, including the emotion-related conditions. Given the lack of agreement in the literature on the most relevant aspects of emotion, the need to provide a relatively rich set of descriptive devices is inevitable.

Despite the diversity of approaches, however, there seems to be reasonable agreement in the scientific literature on a number of "components" or "facets" that play an important role in relation to emergent emotion and, to some extent, also for the other emotion-related states (Scherer, 2005). An emotion-eliciting event is appraised as somehow relevant for the individual, who "causes" or "triggers" the emotion. The experiencer has a subjective experience of the emotion; this may be accompanied by bodily symptoms and expressive behavior in a number of modalities. Finally, the emotion may also induce in the experiencer a tendency to act in a particular way; such an action tendency may be directed toward an object or target of some sort.

Within EmotionML specifications, the descriptions in terms of categories and dimensions provides a global account of all five components of the emotion. Appraisals are represented explicitly and are complemented by references to the "triggers" of emotion being appraised. Similarly, action tendencies are represented explicitly, and it is possible to refer to the "targets" toward which they are directed. Physiology and expressions are not represented in EmotionML itself but use a mechanism to refer to "observable behavior." Feelings are covered by the more global representations of categories and dimensions.

In conclusion, it can be said that the mechanisms in EmotionML are able to capture the main elements of what scientific theory considers important of emotion.

Vocabularies for EmotionML

Scientific Descriptions of Emotion (p. 401) has shown the key concepts from scientific emotion research that are taken into account in EmotionML. Four types of descriptions are available: categories, dimensions, appraisals, and action tendencies. Depending on the tradition of emotion research and on the use case, it may be appropriate to use any single one of these representations; alternatively, it may also make sense to use combinations of descriptions to characterize more fully the various aspects of an emotional state that are observed: how an appraisal of triggers caused the emotion; how it can be characterized using a global description in terms of a category and/or a set of dimensions; and the potential actions the individual may be executing as a result. Thus EmotionML is a powerful representational device.

This description glosses over one important detail, however. Whereas emotion researchers may agree to some extent on the types of facets that play a role in the emotion process (such as appraisals, feeling, expression, etc.), there is no general consensus on the descriptive vocabularies that should be used. Which set of emotion categories is considered appropriate varies dramatically between the different traditions; even within a tradition such as the Darwinian tradition of emotion research, there is no agreed set of emotion categories that should be considered as the most important ones (see, e.g., Cowie & Cornelius, 2003). Similarly, dimensional accounts of emotion do not agree on either the number or the names that should be given to the different dimensions.

It is thus neither possible to standardize a closed set of emotion terms nor desirable to leave the choice of labels completely undefined and up to the user. For this reason, the notion of an "emotion vocabulary" is introduced in EmotionML: Any specific emotion annotation must be specific about the vocabulary that is being used in that annotation. This makes it possible to define in a clear way the terms that make sense in a given research tradition or application field. Computer systems that want to interoperate need to settle on the emotion vocabularies to use; whether a given piece of EmotionML markup can be meaningfully interpreted by an EmotionML engine can be determined. In this way we have made it possible to define new vocabulary while still being able to refer to the most common and agreed-upon vocabularies.

The following vocabularies are defined. For categorical descriptions, the "big six" basic emotion vocabulary by Ekman (1972), an everyday emotion vocabulary by Cowie et al. (1999), and three sets of categories that lend themselves to mappings to appraisals, dimensions, and action tendencies: the OCC categories from Ortony et al. (1988), the categories used by Fontaine et al. (2007), and the categories from the work by Frijda (1986). Three-dimensional vocabularies are provided, PAD vocabulary by Mehrabian (1996), the four-dimensional vocabulary proposed by Fontaine et al. (2007), and a vocabulary providing a single "intensity" dimension for such use cases as want to represent solely the intensity of an emotion without any statement regarding the nature of that emotion. For appraisal, three vocabularies are proposed: the OCC appraisals from Ortony et al. (1988), the stimulus evaluation checks by Scherer (1984, 1999), and the EMA (EMotion and Adaptation, a computational process model) appraisals by Gratch and Marsella (2004). Finally, for action tendencies, only a single vocabulary is currently listed, namely that proposed by Frijda (1986).

While these vocabularies should provide users with a solid basis, it is likely that additional vocabularies or clarifications about the current vocabularies will be requested. The specification (Schröder et al., 2012) includes a mechanism for defining these emotion vocabularies. It consists of a "<vocabulary>" element containing a number of "<item>" elements. A vocabulary has a "type" attribute, indicating whether it is a vocabulary for representing categories, dimensions, appraisals, or action tendencies. A vocabulary item has a "name" attribute. Both the entire vocabulary and each individual item can have an "<info>" child to provide arbitrary metadata.

A separate W3C working draft (Schröder et al., 2011a) complements the specification to provide EmotionML with a set of emotion vocabularies taken from the scientific literature. When the user considers them suitable, these vocabularies rather than arbitrary other vocabularies should be used in order to promote interoperability. Whenever users have a need for a different vocabulary, however, they can simply define their own custom vocabulary and use it in the same way as the vocabularies listed in the "vocabularies" document. This makes it possible to add any vocabularies from scientific research that are missing from the predefined set as well as application-specific vocabularies. This approach promotes interoperability where this is considered meaningful by the users but leaves users the freedom to use the most suitable representations for their application.

In selecting emotion vocabularies, the group has applied the following criteria: The primary guiding principle has been to select vocabularies that are either commonly used in technological contexts, or represent current emotion models from the scientific literature. A further criterion is related to the difficulty to define mappings between categories, dimensions, appraisals, and action tendencies. For this reason, the above-mentioned groups of vocabularies were included, for which some of these mappings are likely to be definable in the future.

Owing to the rather informal nature of a non–recommendation-track working draft, it is rather easy to provide future versions of the document that provide the additional information required.

Issues for Future Work

The EmotionML 1.0 specification appears to be successful at resolving the majority of the requirements that arise from use cases. This was confirmed from the side of users as well as by psychological experts in emotion research at the W3C EmotionML workshop (http://www.w3.org/2010/10/emotionml/cfp.html).

Another interesting potential application area for EmotionML is user modeling (Rich, 1979). Generic user modeling systems attempt to collect general as well as domain-specific information about a human user in order to enable a computer system to adapt to the user's needs (Kobsa, 2001). One generic but highly relevant aspect of the user's properties is his or her emotional state.

EmotionML is of potential relevance for user modeling on several levels. The reference mechanism defined in EmotionML makes it explicit that it can be relevant to know who experiences the emotion, how it is expressed, which object or event has triggered it, and toward which entity any actions resulting from the emotion may be targeted. In addition to the emotion itself, it may be useful to make explicit the appraisals that are formed on the basis of events in the world. Affective reasoning components such as those by Gebhard (2005) and Gratch and Marsella (2004) can be used to derive the user's presumed emotion from those appraisals. Thus the user model could implement to some extent the emotional aspect of the computer's "theory of mind" (Baron-Cohen et al., 1999) of the user.

In extending user modeling toward the modeling of social relationships (Eagle & Pentland, 2006), EmotionML could potentially be used to represent one person's perception of another person's emotional expression. Here it becomes very important to distinguish the encoding from the decoding aspects of emotional expression (Cowie &

Cornelius, 2003; Scherer, 2000). If a user model includes a representation of emotion perception in this way, affective reasoning models could be extended to include appraisals of that behavior in context. Furthermore, emotional contagion models (Hatfield et al., 1994) could be implemented to capture, for example, mimicry and imitation effects.

Once EmotionML 1.0 has reached its full maturity, the above-mentioned directions can be developed in future versions of EmotionML or in complementary specifications that are more appropriate for the respective use cases.

Conclusion

The present chapter has presented an account of the thinking behind and the definition of the emotion markup language EmotionML.

We reported on the use cases and the resulting requirements as identified by two incubator groups at the W3C and then described the key properties of the EmotionML syntax as defined in the "Last Call Working Draft" version of the specification. We have compared the specification to scientific descriptions of emotion, concluding that the key concepts can be represented in EmotionML. Referring to the lack of agreement in the community regarding concrete vocabularies of emotion descriptors, we have motivated and described the mechanism in EmotionML to choose a suitable emotion vocabulary. Finally, we have discussed the issue of validating EmotionML and pointed out issues for future work.

EmotionML is currently going towards W3C recommendation status and has received several implementation reports required by the standardization process. The current implementation were delivered by: DFKI, Deutsche Telekom, Queens University of Belfast, Oak Ridge National Laboratory, University of Chemnitz, Sail, University of Freiburg, and other might be produced in the near future. They deal with a variety of emotion-related issues, some of which are listed here:

• The Speechalyzer of Deutsche Telekom Laboratories is used to train speech-based emotion classification systems.
• The Mary Synthesizer by DFKI is able to generate affective speech output.
• The Nviso system is used to analyze emotional expressions in videos of consumers dealing with a webpage.
• Systems like the emotional video analysis system of the Queen's University Belfast or the

emotional 20-question project of the University of Southern California are used for research.

References

Baron-Cohen, S., Ring, H. A., Wheelwright, S., Bullmore, E. T., Brammer, M. J., Simmons, A., & Williams, S. C. R. (1999). Social intelligence in the normal and autistic brain: An fMRI study. *European Journal of Neuroscience*, 11(6): 1891–1898.

Cowie, R. (2010). Describing the forms of emotional colouring that pervade everyday life. In P. Goldie (Ed.), *The Oxford handbook of philosophy of emotion* (pp. 63–94). Oxford, UK: Oxford University Press. doi:10.1093/oxfordhb/9780199235018.003.0004.

Cowie, R., & Cornelius, R. R. (2003). Describing the emotional states that are expressed in speech. *Speech Communication*, 40(1-2):5–32.

Cowie, R., Douglas-Cowie, E., Appolloni, B., Taylor, J., Romano, A., & Fellenz, W. (1999). What a neural net needs to know about emotion words. In N. Mastorakis (Ed.), *Computational intelligence and applications* (pp. 109–114). World Scientific & Engineering Society Press, Athens, Greece.

de Carolis, B., Pelachaud, C., Poggi, I., & Steedman, M. (2004). APML, a markup language for believable behavior generation. In H. Prendinger, & M. Ishizuka (eds.), *Life-like characters* (pp. 65–85). New York: Springer.

Douglas-Cowie, E., Cowie, R., Sneddon, I., Cox, C., Lowry, O., McRorie, M., . . . Karpouzis, K. (2007). The HUMAINE database: Addressing the collection and annotation of naturalistic and induced emotional data. In *Proceedings on affective computing and intelligent interaction* (pp. 488–500). Available at: http://dx.doi.org/10.1007/978-3-540-74889-2_43

Eagle, N., & Pentland, A. (2006). Reality mining: Sensing complex social systems. *Personal and Ubiquitous Computing*, 10(4), 255–268. Available at: http://dx.doi.org/10.1007/s00779-005-0046-3

Ekman, P. (1972). Universals and cultural differences in facial expressions of emotion. In J. Cole (Ed.), *Nebraska symposium on motivation* (Vol. 19, pp. 207–282). Omaha: University of Nebraska Press. Available at: http://www.paulekman.com/wp-content/uploads/2009/02/Universals-And-Cultural-Differences-In-Facial-Expressions-Of.pdf

Fontaine, J. R., Scherer, K. R., Roesch, E. B., & Ellsworth, P. C. (2007). The world of emotions is not two-dimensional. *Psychological Science*, 18(12):1050–1057. doi:10.1111/j.1467-9280.2007.02024.x

Frijda, N. H. (1986). *The emotions*. Cambridge, UK: Cambridge University Press.

Gebhard, P. (2005). ALMA—A layered model of affect. In *Proceedings of the fourth international joint conference on autonomous agents and multiagent systems* (AAMAS-05). Utrecht University, Utrecht, The Netherlands.

Gratch, J., & Marsella, S. (2004). A domain-independent framework for modeling emotion. *Cognitive Systems Research*, 5(4):269–306.

Gustavsson, C., Beard, S., Strindlund, L., Huynh, Q., Wiknertz, E., Marriot, A., & Stallo, J. (2001). VHML specification working draft v0.3. Available at: http://www.vhml.org/downloads/VHML/vhml.pdf

Hatfield, E., Cacioppo, J. T., and Rapson, R. L. (1994). *Emotional contagion*. Cambridge, UK: Cambridge University Press.

Johnston, M., Baggia, P., Burnett, D. C., Carter, J., Dahl, D. A., McCobb, G., & Raggett, D. (2009). *EMMA: Extensible multimodal annotation markup language. W3C Recommendation, World Wide Web Consortium*. Available at: http://www.w3.org/TR/emma/

Kipp, M. (2001). Anvil—A generic annotation tool for multimodal dialogue. In *Proceedings of Eurospeech* (pp. 1367–1370), Paul Dalsgaard, Center for Personkommunikation, Aalborg University.

Kipp, M., Heloir, A., Schröder, M., & Gebhard, P. (2010). Realizing multimodal behavior. In *Proceedings of intelligent virtual agents* (pp. 57–63).

Kobsa, A. (2001). Generic user modeling systems. *User Modeling and User-Adapted Interaction*, 11(1), 49–63, Springer.

McCrae, R. R., & John, O. P. (1992). An introduction to the five-factor model and its applications. *Journal of Personality*, 60, 175–215.

Mehrabian, A. (1996). Pleasure-arousal-dominance: A general framework for describing and measuring individual differences in temperament. *Current Psychology*, 14(4), 261–292. Available at: http://dx.doi.org/10.1007/BF02686918

Ortony, A., Clore, G. L., & Collins, A. (1988). *The cognitive structure of emotion*. Cambridge, UK: Cambridge University Press.

Rich, E. (1979). User modeling via stereotypes. *Cognitive Science*, 3(4), 329–354. Available at: http://www.sciencedirect.com/science/article/B6W48-4FWF9GC-9/2/f924f793eb153d455893e8d39982ef45

Scherer, K. R. (1984). On the nature and function of emotion: A component process approach. In K. R. Scherer, & P. Ekman (Eds.), *Approaches to emotion* (pp. 293–317). Hillsdale, NJ: Erlbaum.

Scherer, K. R. (1999). Appraisal theory. In T. Dalgleish & M. J. Power (Eds.), *Handbook of cognition & emotion* (pp. 637–663). Hoboken, NJ: Wiley.

Scherer, K. R. (2000). Psychological models of emotion. In J. C. Borod (Ed.), *The neuropsychology of emotion* (pp. 137—162). New York: Oxford University Press.

Scherer, K. R. (2005). What are emotions? and how can they be measured? *Social Science Information*, 44(4), 695–729. doi:10.1177/0539018405058216

Schröder, M., Baggia, P., Burkhardt, F., Pelachaud, C., Peter, C., & Zovato, E. (2012). *Emotion markup language (EmotionML) 1.0. W3C candidate recommendation, World Wide Web Consortium*. Available at: http://www.w3.org/TR/emotionml/

Schröder, M., Pelachaud, C., Ashimura, K., Baggia, P., Burkhardt, F., Oltramari, A., . . . Zovato, E. (2011a). *Vocabularies for EmotionML. W3C working draft, World Wide Web Consortium*. Available at: http://www.w3.org/TR/2011/WD-emotion-voc-20110407/

Schröder, M., Pirker, H., & Lamolle, M. (2006). First suggestions for an emotion annotation and representation language. In *Proceedings of LREC'06 workshop on corpora for research on emotion and affect* (pp. 88–92)., European Language Resources Association, Paris, France

Schröder, M., Pirker, H., Lamolle, M., Burkhardt, F., Peter, C., & Zovato, E. (2011b). Representing emotions and related states in technological systems. In P. Petta, R. Cowie, & C. Pelachaud (Eds.), *Emotion-oriented systems—The Humaine handbook* (pp. 367–386). New York: Springer.

Schröder, M., Zovato, E., Pirker, H., Peter, C., & Burkhardt, F. (2007). *W3C emotion incubator group final report.*

W3C incubator group report, World Wide Web Consortium. Available at: http://www.w3.org/2005/Incubator/emotion/XGR-emotion-20070710

Troncy, R., Mannens, E., Pfeiffer, S., & van Deursen, D. (2010). *Media fragments URI 1.0. W3C last call working draft, World Wide Web Consortium.* Available at: http://www.w3.org/TR/1998/REC-xml-19980210/

van Deemter, K., Krenn, B., Piwek, P., Klesen, M., Schröder, M., & Baumann, S. (2008). Fully Generated Scripted Dialogue for Embodied Agents. *Artificial Intelligence, 172*(10), 1219–1244.

Machine Learning for Affective Computing: Challenges and Opportunities

Ashish Kapoor

Abstract

The ability to recognize affect is one of the fundamental requirements in building a computerized affectively intelligent system. Although the ideas from traditional machine learning constitute the core of an affect recognition methodology, there are significant additional considerations that must be observed. These considerations include aspects of data collection and annotation, feature selection, algorithm design, and system evaluation. This chapter aims to highlight such deviations and provide an overview of how some of the current research has attempted to solve these problems.

Key Words: affect recognition, machine learning, active learning, feature selection

One of the critical functions of any affect-sensitive system is the ability to recognize affect. Without such capability, the system would be oblivious to the cognitive and mental states of the users with whom it is interacting or providing service to. In this chapter, we specifically focus on the task of recognizing affective states from sensor data. Although traditional models of supervised classification aim to learn a decision boundary given a set of observations, many scenarios in affective user modeling far exceed this simplistic model. For example, in many affect recognition scenarios, the researchers have very little labeled training data. They usually have much data (e.g., video), but most of it is unlabeled because labeling is tedious, costly, and error-prone. Similarly, in many affective computing scenarios, bits of information from multiple sensors are processed to recover the variable of interest, and one of the most crucial things is to identify which information bits are important for the purpose of classification. In this chapter, we specifically focus on some of these real-world issues in affective computing. We highlight many of these problems in the

context of recent research and discuss how some of these systems attempt to alleviate these issues. The structure of the chapter is organized as follows: first, we provide a short background on characteristics of classification tasks that are encountered in the realm of affect recognition. Next, we discuss the tough problem of acquiring labeled data and explain it in the context of several real-world applications. We conclude the chapter with a discussion on feature selection and future directions.

The Machine Learning Pipeline

Classification is a key task in many domains, including user modeling, affective computing, and machine perception. Consider, for example, the task of building a predictive model that aims to predict frustration in users. Figure 30.1 describes its architecture, in which nonverbal behaviors are sensed through a camera (Kapoor & Picard, 2002), a pressure-sensing chair (Mota & Picard, 2003), a pressure mouse (Reynolds, 2001), and a device that measures skin conductance (Strauss et al., 2005).

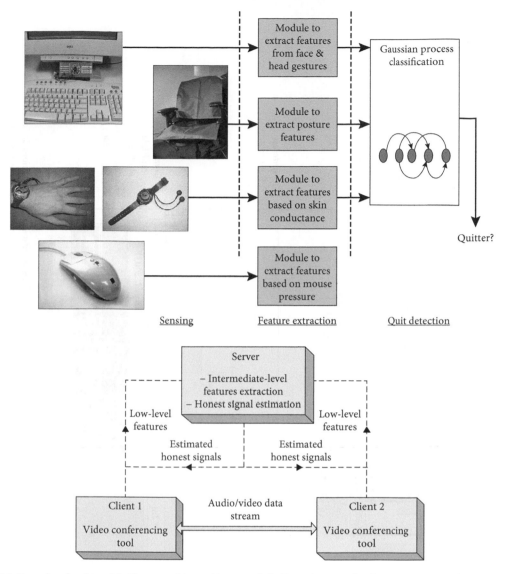

Sensing   Feature extraction   Quit detection

Fig. 30.1 Examples of multimodal affect recognition architectures. Left: The architecture for detecting quitters in learning environments (Kapoor, Burleson, & Picard, 2007). Right: The client-server architecture of the honest signals system (Byun et al., 2011) that has two participants in a video conference setting.

Figure 30.2 describes another application (Byun et al., 2011), one in which the system augments a video conference and provides insight to conversational patterns. Such affective and cognitive insights can be invaluable to the users of the video conference system in actively steering the conversation to be more productive.

At first, it might appear that these two applications are very different. They differ in terms of engineering architecture and number of active participants, as well as in how actively the affect data are acted on. The first example consists of many different sensors: the camera is equipped with

infrared (IR) LEDs for structured lighting to help in real-time tracking of pupils and in extracting other features from the face. Similarly, the data sensed through the chair are used to extract information about postures. In the second example, information is simply sensed via a webcam and a microphone. Also in the first example, the inferred affective state is provided to a software agent who in turn takes an appropriate action. By contrast, in the second example, the inferred conversational cues are simply presented to the user in graphical user interface (the subjects might choose to take an action or ignore those cues). Both systems, however, have many

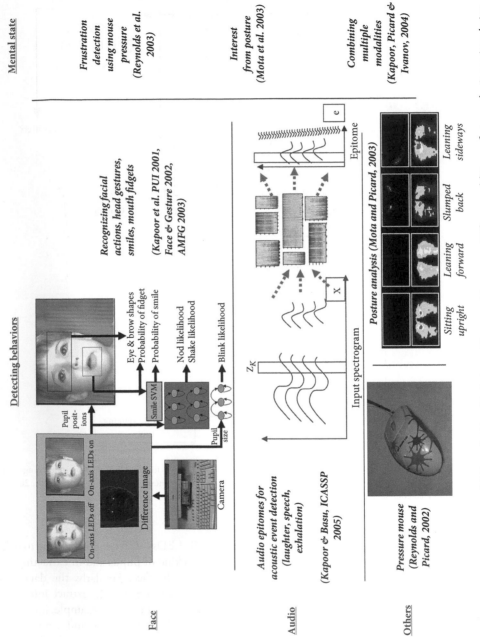

Fig. 30.2 A high-level depiction of different building blocks in an affect recognition system. Different modalities are first sensed using various devices. The feature extraction step itself can be rather involved (and as complex as a supervised learning task). These extracted features are then used to detect appropriate affective states.

similarities, and, from the perspective of affect recognition, their architecture is virtually identical.

Note that one of the main goals of a pattern recognition/machine learning system is to associate a class label with different observations, where the labels correspond to affective states such as frustration (as in the first application) or any conversational cues (as in the second application). All the information that is sensed through any of devices needs to be processed, and features are extracted before applying the predictive model. One additional thing to note is that the feature extractors themselves can be classifiers that are trained separately. For example, a separate classification system can be used to identify facial muscle movement and in turn be used as a feature extractor in the full affect-recognition pipeline. Other examples of extracted features include processing of global positioning system (GPS) data, the status of a cellular phone, pedometer readings, and the like in order to identify activities such as driving to the office, sitting, or walking home. Figure 30.2 summarizes the basic framework of an affect recognition system: there can be multiple sensors and channels (e.g. face, posture, video, audio, etc.) that are first preprocessed to extract features. The feature extractions themselves can be fairly complicated modules and might contain multiple classifiers within themselves. Finally, association to an affect label can be performed once the features are extracted and the appropriate machine learning system is trained. All of these classification systems need labeled data to be trained, and in the next section we discuss several ways of collecting tagged data in the context of affective computing.

Affect Databases and Annotation

One of the most crucial aspects of training a machine learning system is availability of labeled training data. There are many challenges in collecting labels for the purpose of building predictive models for affect recognition. In this section, we highlight some of these challenges and how many research efforts have overcome these problems.

Obtaining Labels via Human Judges

Much of the earlier work in affective computing has focused on either obtaining annotations via human judges (Ekman & Friesen, 1978; Mota & Picard, 2003; Picard, Vyzas, & Healey, 2001) or by asking participants to deliberately act and provide data for a requested set of labels. Research in facial expression/action analysis (Ekman & Friesen,

1978; Kapoor & Picard, 2002) has a history of using human coders to obtain labeled data. For example, in (Kapoor & Picard, 2002), videos of different subjects that were recorded by cameras were coded by a trained facial action coding system (FACS; Ekman & Friesen, 1978) expert. Similarly, the Cohn-Kanade database, which is a comprehensive facial action database, was collected and coded by a team of researchers and consists of adults performing a series of facial expressions in front of a camera. Another example is from Mota and Picard (2003), in which they use multiple human judges to obtain annotated data for analysis of interest among children immersed in a learning environment. It is unlikely that children in the age range of 8–11 years reliably articulate their feelings; consequently, using human judges is one of the better means to obtain annotations in that setting. Note that for these methods to be successful it is imperative that clear guidelines for coding are provided to the judges. In the realm of affective computing, such absolute and concrete guidelines are hard to formulate, and judges often use their subjective interpretation. In such cases, multiple judges should be used and researchers should verify intercoder reliability using statistical tools. Note that this method of obtaining annotations using human judges is a frequently used technique in other fields including psychology, human–computer interaction (HCI), computer vision, speech processing, and more.

Obtaining Ground Truth Labels via Self-Report

Self-report has been one of the most popular tools for gathering labeled data in the realms of affective computing and HCI. One particular instantiation of self-report was considered in the task of constructing models that can predict the cost of interrupting computer users. Horvitz et al. (Horvitz, Apacible, & Koch, 2004) have proposed BusyBody, a system that tackles the task of predicting interruptability of users with a Bayesian network. BusyBody contains an event infrastructure that logs desktop activities including such activities as typing, mouse movements, windows in focus, recent sequences of applications and window titles, and high-level statistics about the rates of switching among applications and windows. The system also considers several kinds of contextual variables, including the time of day and day of week, the name of the computer being used, the presence and properties of meetings drawn from an electronic calendar, and wireless signals. The BusyBody system employs experience sampling to construct personalized models for real-time predictions of the expected cost of interruption. When BusyBody is in a training mode, the system intermittently probes users with a pop-up query requesting an assessment of their current or recent interruptability. The initial version of the system probed users at random times, constrained to an overall rate set by users. Figure 30.3 shows a request by BusyBody for input, which in turn prompts the users to self-report about their state of interruptability. Responses to probes about interruptability are stored, along with the sensed evidence. The evidence then serves as training data, and a Bayesian structure search is employed to build predictive models to provide predictions about the cost of interruption from the stream of sensed data.

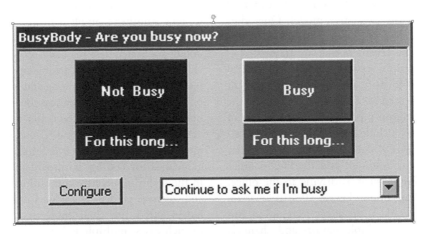

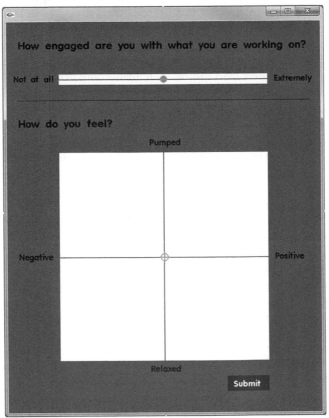

Fig. 30.3 Examples of self-report interfaces. Left: BusyBody probe for user feedback (Horvitz, Apacible, & Koch, 2004). The probe inquires about whether the user is highly noninterruptible versus in another state. Right: Another example of self-report interface, which was used in AffectAura application (McDuff, Karlson, Kapoor, Roseway, & Czerwinski, 2012).

Another example of successful use of self-report system is AffectAura (McDuff, Karlson, Kapoor, Roseway, & Czerwinski, 2012). AffectAura is an emotional prosthetic that allows users to reflect on their emotional states over time. A multimodal sensor set-up is used for continuous logging of audio, visual, physiological, and contextual data. A classification system then operates to predict affective dimensions, including valence, arousal, and engagement. To obtain affect labels for training, the participants reported their valence, arousal, and engagement levels at regular intervals during the day. In this phase, labels consisted of numerical values between −1 and +1 for the three dimensions of valence, arousal, and engagement, collected using the custom tool shown in Figure 30.3.

One of the big drawbacks of a self-report system is active user engagement. This active engagement often has the potential to disrupt the user and consequently can affect the affective state of the user. Another important consideration is that self-report assumes that the subjects are aware of their internal cognitive and affective state. Such an assumption is very hard to verify and, in certain cases, almost impossible to assert. For example, Kapoor et al. (Kapoor, Burleson, & Picard, 2007) have described an affective learning companion that interacts with children. In such cases, it is perhaps better to not assume that the child would be able to provide correct self-report labels consistently or effortlessly. In such cases, it is better to bypass collection of self-reported labels by performing in-stream supervision, in which tagging occurs in the course of normal activity.

One example of in-stream supervision happens in the Lookout system (Horvitz, 1999) for calendaring and scheduling, in which a probabilistic user model is used in real time to infer a user's intention to perform scheduling based on the content of email messages at the user's focus of attention. To build a case library, the system watches users working with email and assigns labels of a scheduling intention by noticing if calendaring actions occur within some time horizon of the reading of email at the focus of the user's attention. Another example is the Priorities system (Horvitz, Jacobs, & Hovel, 1999), which uses machine learning to assign incoming email messages a measure of urgency. Here, a set of policies is used to label messages with urgency values and is made available for training as draft case libraries. For example, messages that are deleted without being read are labeled as nonurgent.

Kapoor et al. (Kapoor, Burleson, & Picard, 2007) have tackled the case of an affect learning companion by using similar in-stream supervision. Specifically, children interact with an animated agent that presents two buttons that the children can press by saying, "While you are doing this activity there are two buttons in the upper right hand corner that you can click on if you need help, or if you are frustrated. Click on a disk to start, whenever you want. I'll just watch and help if I can." The learning task presented to the children involves recursion, and after several minutes of repeated attempts to make progress, many participants lose their motivation and are ready to end this experience. As they get to this stage, they may click on one of the buttons. When they click on one of the two buttons, the system automatically determines if the learner is "frustrated" or is just seeking help.

Unfortunately, many applications may not be amenable to in-stream supervision because labels for hidden states are not available and often cannot be easily mapped to users' actions. In such cases, the construction of predictive user models depends on manual training sessions (either judges or self-reports). Such manual labeling can be tedious, and active information acquisition is a technique that can help triage labeling resources.

Active Informative Acquisition

Active information acquisition (Kapoor, Horvitz, & Basu, 2007) is a machine learning technique that aims to guide labeling efforts. The key motivation behind development of these techniques was the growing availability of large datasets but scarce availability of labels or tags. Given the cost of labeling previously unlabeled cases and the cost of misclassification—which may be different for different classes—the key idea is to quantify the expected gain in expected value associated with seeking information on an unlabeled data point. This expected gain, which corresponds to the value of information provided by labeling, is the guiding principle for the active learning framework.

Active learning is primarily employed in a pool-based setting: there is a pool of data, most of which is not labeled. As an example, Kapoor et al. (Kapoor, Horvitz, & Basu, 2007) describe a problem scenario in which they have access to several thousand voice messages stored on a server and wish to build a classification system that could automatically classify voicemail messages into different categories. Unfortunately, performing

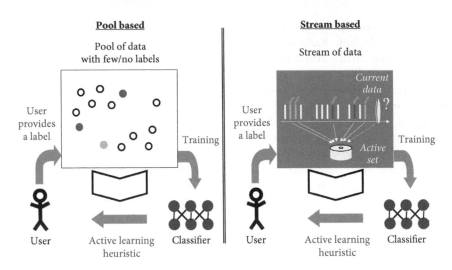

Pool based

Pool of data
with few/no labels

User
provides
a label

Training

User

Active learning
heuristic

Classifier

Stream based

Stream of data

*Current
data*

?

*Active
set*

User
provides
a label

Training

User

Active learning
heuristic

Classifier

Fig. 30.4 The active learning (selective sampling) framework for pool-based (left) and stream-based (right) recognition tasks.

supervised learning with the dataset would require the manual effort of listening to voice messages and applying labels. The solution they propose is active learning, in which they use value-of-information to triage human tagging efforts. Figure 30.4 describes pool-based active learning setting. The scheme consists of an interactive loop in which first a prediction system is trained on existing labeled data, and then it reasons about best unlabeled data to present to the user for tagging. This loops repeats until either all the data are labeled or the labeling budget is exhausted.

Most work to date on active learning assumes a pool-based setting in which the sets of labeled and unlabeled data are provided and the algorithm selects cases from the pool to query. However, stream-based learning resonates more deeply with the goals of an autonomous affect-sensitive system that also learns and adapts throughout its life cycle. Figure 30.4 describes the stream-based setting in which the learner sees a series of unlabeled data points and continues to make decisions about whether to query for missing labels. In distinction to pool-based scenarios, learners in stream-based settings may not have complete information about the underlying data distribution. Furthermore, in many dynamic environments, data observed in the past can become outdated due to unmodeled changes in the world. This is a relatively new area, and few efforts (Kapoor & Horvitz, 2007; Kapoor & Horvitz, 2008a; 2008b) have pursued the challenge of developing systems with the ability to adapt continuously to their environment over the course of their lifetimes. The core component

in these systems is to keep learning by continuing to use the current predictive model to make decisions about if and when to probe users for feedback and by considering the long-term value associated with such feedback.

Feature Extraction for Affect Recognition

Once the training data are collected, features relevant for discrimination should be extracted. Feature extraction itself is a fairly complex topic and in the context of affective computing is often nontrivial due to the multimodal nature of the problem. Here, we briefly mention some of the important issues that arise in the context of affective computing. Readers should refer to machine learning texts for a deeper and more thorough analysis of feature selection.

The performance of affect recognition depends highly on the features that are extracted from the data. The key idea is that features by themselves or together with other groups of features should be informative about the classification task. Finding the right set of all these parameters can be a challenge. Many discriminative models often use cross-validation. Cross-validation is a technique in which some validation data from the training set is left out, and models are trained using the rest of the data. These models differ in the sets of features being used to train a classifier. Eventually, all of these models are trained and evaluated on the validation set. The model that achieves highest accuracy thus informs about the important features. Note that there are many variants of this strategy, and it is not possible to describe them all here.

Many of these existing feature selection strategies can be prohibitively expensive for real-world problems. Furthermore, an additional challenge in affective computing is the lack of large quantities of training data. When we have few labeled data points, then many of the cross-validation strategies work poorly due to the sample size.

One of the most effective ways to deal with the feature selection problem is to utilize researchers' insight into the affect recognition problem. For example, it has been known for several decades now that electrodermal activity (EDA) correlates very well with a subject's arousal level. Consequently, filters can be hand-designed to match researcher's belief about EDA response to arousal (Picard et al., 2001). Such hand-designed features can provide a great deal of discriminatory information about the task at hand.

Although hand-designed features are appealing due to their ease of implementation, they often are not easy to scale. For example, a multimodal affect recognition system (Kapoor, Burleson, & Picard, 2007; Kapoor, Ahn & Picard 2005; Kapoor & Picard, 2005; Kapoor, Picard, & Ivanov, 2004; Kapoor, Qi, Ahn & Picard 2005) might have

several signals, and it might be virtually impossible for a researcher to handcraft individual features. Additionally, there might be statistical relationships across two or more channels that would be very beneficial for discrimination but almost impossible to be handcrafted. Consequently, there is a need for fully automated feature selection strategies that can learn important features using a small amount of data.

Automatic relevance detection (ARD; Qi, Minka, Picard, & Ghahramani, 2004) is one such technique that allows feature selection under a Bayesian paradigm. The key idea in ARD is to assume that, a priori, all features are equally likely, but as more and more data are observed, only a few of those features would be relevant to the task. That sparse set of features is determined using hierarchical Bayesian modeling. Figure 30.5 highlights results of an ARD procedure when applied on multimodal data collected for the task of building a frustration predictor (Kapoor, Burleson, & Picard, 2007).

From the boxplot, we can see that the fidgets, velocity of the head, and the ratio of the postures are the three most discriminative features. However, there are a lot of outliers for the fidgets, which

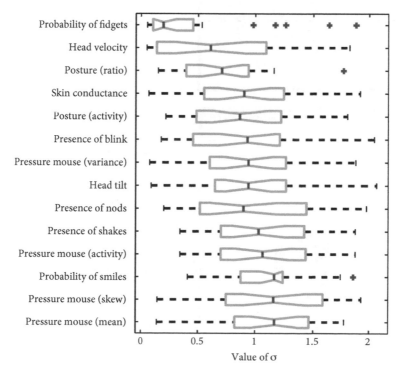

Fig. 30.5 Finding the most discriminative features for detecting frustrated students (Kapoor, Burleson, & Picard, 2007). The MATLAB boxplot of the kernel parameters optimized during the 24 leave-one-out runs. The lines in the middle of the box represent the median, the bounding box represents quartile values, the whiskers show the extent of the values, and the + represent the statistical outliers. A low value corresponds to high discriminative power of the feature.

implies that the fidgets can be unreliable possibly due to sensor failure and individual differences. Note that all the parameters span a range of values, suggesting that despite some statistical trends the discriminative power of a feature might depend on each individual learner. Thus, it might be beneficial for the Learning Companion to discover the patterns in user behavior rather than follow some pre-programmed rules. Readers should refer to Kapoor, Burleson, and Picard (2007) for details of the relevance determination procedure.

Machine Learning: An Affective Computing Perspective

Whereas at the core of an affect recognition system lies a machine learning system, there are significant additional considerations from the perspective of affective computing. One of the most important aspects is how to measure the effectiveness of an affect recognition system. Although almost all machine learning systems focus on maximizing recognition accuracy, there are many examples in affective computing where such myopic optimization of a single number is useless. For example, in the honest signals system (Byun et al., 2011; see Figure 30.6), the user sees a high-level summary of his conversational behaviors, and the inferred signals play a passive role (as opposed to being a causal variable for the system to take an action).

It is up to the user to observe these and consider modifying his conversational behavior. Consequently, the inference system can still provide

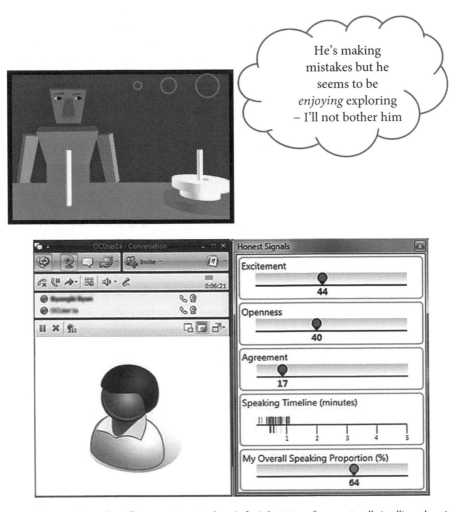

Fig. 30.6 Some applications that utilize affect recognition pipeline. Left: A depiction of an emotionally intelligent learning companion (Kapoor, Burleson, & Picard, 2007) that is sensitive to the affective aspects of learning. Right: The honest signals (Byun et al., 2011) graphical user interface showing conversation feedback that could be useful for teleconference participants. The right subpanel shows the signal levels, speaking timeline, and proportion.

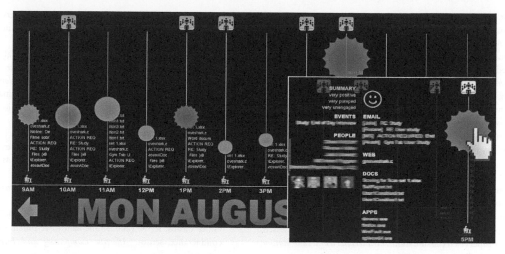

Fig. 30.7 The AffectAura interface. Detailed exploration of an hour (5 PM) enabled by hovering over the bubble.

useful insights to the user even if it is not correct all the time. Instead, here, it might be better to focus on engineering a system that works flawlessly in terms of execution performances (e.g., minimum latency in inference, real-time performance, etc.).

Similarly, AffectAura system (McDuff et al.; see Figure 30.7) is used as a tool for retrospective analysis. Consequently, it is not critical for this system to provide real-time feedback. However, the utility of the system can be maximized if the classification system could produce moderately good results. Note that we still do not require a fully correct inference because this application still does not take actions based on the affective state of the users.

Affective Learning Companion (Kapoor, Burleson, & Picard, 2007; Kapoor, Mota, & Picard, 2001; see Figure 30.6), on the other hand, seeks to provide feedback and take actions in real time based on the affective system of the user. In this case, it is fairly important to get the recognition right. One thing that still differs from the traditional machine learning system is that different affective states might have different utility: for example, incorrectly assuming that a learner is frustrated and providing an intervention is far more expensive than incorrectly assuming that the learner is doing all right and needs no intervention. Similar *cost-asymmetry* also occurs in discriminating urgent voice messages (Kapoor, Horvitz, & Basu, 2007) from nonurgent ones. Although traditional machine learning has been oblivious to such cost-asymmetry, applications in affective computing need to actively address this issue. As the number of functional affective computing applications grows quickly, we'll see newer problems, newer scenarios, and consequently newer

techniques, both in the field of machine learning and in affective computing, that will tackle the challenges.

Acknowledgments

Most of the author's research mentioned in the chapter was done in close collaboration with many researchers, including Eric Horvitz, Rosalind Picard, Mary Czerwinski, Phil Chou, Selene Mota, Sumit Basu, and Winslow Burleson.

References

Byun, B., Awasthi, A., Chou, P. A., Kapoor, A., Lee, B., & Czerwinski, M. (2011). Honest signals in video conferencing. *International Conference on Multimedia and Exposition.*

Ekman, P., & Friesen, W. V. (1978). *The facial action coding system: A technique for measurement of facial movement.* Consulting Psychologists Press.

Horvitz, E. (1999). Principles of mixed-initiative user interfaces. *Conference on Human Factors in Computing Systems.*

Horvitz, E., Apacible, J., & Koch, P. (2004). BusyBody: Creating and fielding personalized models of the cost of interruption. *Conference on Computer Supported Cooperative Work.*

Horvitz, E., Jacobs, A., & Hovel, D. (1999). Attention-sensitive alerting. *Uncertainty in Artificial Intelligence.*

Kapoor, A., & Horvitz, E. (2007). Principles of lifelong learning for predictive user modeling. *User Modeling.*

Kapoor, A., & Horvitz, E. (2008a). Experience sampling for building predictive user models: A comparative study. *Conference on Human Factors in Computing Systems.*

Kapoor, A., & Horvitz, E. (2008b). On discarding, caching, and recalling samples in active learning. *Uncertainty in Artificial Intelligence.*

Kapoor, A., & Picard, R. W. (2002). Real-time, fully automatic upper facial feature tracking. *Automatic Face and Gesture Recognition.*

Kapoor, A., & Picard, R. W. (2005). Multimodal affect recognition in learning environments. *ACM Conference on Multimedia.*

Kapoor, A., Ahn, H., & Picard, R. W. (2005). Mixture of Gaussian processes to combine multiple modalities. *Workshop on Multiple Classifier Systems.*

Kapoor, A., Burleson, W., & Picard, R. W. (2007). Automatic prediction of frustration. *International Journal of Human Computer Studies.*

Kapoor, A., Horvitz, E., & Basu, S. (2007). Selective supervision: Guiding supervised learning with decision-theoretic active learning. *International Joint Conference on Artificial Intelligence.*

Kapoor, A., Mota, S., & Picard, R. W. (2001). Towards a learning companion that recognizes affect. *AAAI Fall Symposium.*

Kapoor, A., Picard, R. W., & Ivanov, Y. (2004). Probabilistic combination of multiple modalities to detect interest. *International Conference on Pattern Recognition.*

Kapoor, A., Qi, A., Ahn, H., & Picard, R. W. (2005). Hyperparameter and kernel learning for graph based semi-supervised classification. *Advances in Neural Information Processing Systems.*

McDuff, D., Karlson, A., Kapoor, A., Roseway, A., & Czerwinski, M. (2012). AffectAura: An intelligent system for emotional memory.

Mota, S., & Picard, R. W. (2003). Automated posture analysis for detecting learner's interest level. *Workshop on Computer Vision and Pattern Recognition for Human-Computer Interaction.*

Picard, R. W., Vyzas, E., & Healey, J. (2001). Toward machine emotional intelligence: Analysis of affective physiological state. *Pattern Analysis and Machine Intelligence.*

Qi, A., Minka, T. P., Picard, R. W., & Ghahramani, Z. (2004). Predictive automatic relevance determination by expectation propagation. *International Conference on Machine Learning.*

Reynolds, C. (2001). *The sensing and measurement of frustration with computers.* Master's thesis. MIT.

Strauss, M., Reynolds, C., Hughes, S., Park, K., McDarby, G., & Picard, R. W. (2005). The handwave Bluetooth skin conductance sensor. *Affective Computing and Intelligent Interaction.*

Applications of Affective Computing

Feeling, Thinking, and Computing with Affect-Aware Learning Technologies

Sidney K. D'Mello *and* Art C. Graesser

Abstract

This chapter discusses some of the exciting research in the nascent field of affect-aware learning technologies (AALTs)—educational technologies that compute affect in addition to cognition, metacognition, and motivation. We begin by positioning AALTs in the complex ecology comprising diverse phenomena and technologies in the cognitive, affective, learning, and computing sciences. This is followed by an overview of the major findings of a recent meta-analysis aimed at identifying a subset of learning-centered affective states that generalize across students, learning technologies, learning tasks, and experimental methodologies. We then turn our attention to the two major types of AALTs: reactive systems that respond to affect once it occurs and proactive systems that aim to induce or impede certain affective states. Affective AutoTutor, GazeTutor, and UNC-ITSpoke are presented as examples of reactive AALTs, while *Crystal Island* and ConfusionTutor are included as examples of proactive AALTs. Some of the open issues in the area of AALTs are discussed. These include scalability for real-world contexts, "good-enough" classification accuracy, and levels of analysis for affective responding. The chapter concludes by outlining two broad avenues of research for the field.

Key Words: affect-aware learning technology, proactive systems, reactive systems, Affective AutoTutor, GazeTutor, UNC-ITSpoke, *Crystal Island*, ConfusionTutor

Introduction

About 15 years ago, the idea of an "affect-aware learning technology," or the fusion of "affect" and "learning," was a misnomer at best and was considered to be as odd a pairing as *affect* and *computing*. "What on earth does affect have to do with learning?" would have been a pertinent question at that time because learning, characterized as the acquisition of knowledge and the construction of meaning, was considered to be in the exclusive realm of cognition. Affect, at best, was considered to play a negligible role in learning. At worst, it was considered to be harmful to learning, as documented by the approximately 1,000 studies on test anxiety that have emerged over the last few decades (Zeidner, 2007).

Much has changed over the last decade, of course. Just as we know that affect and computing have a natural symbiosis that is played out in the field of affect computing, so do affect and learning. This recent emphasis on affect in the learning sciences is paralleled by a similar renaissance in the cognitive sciences, where it is now widely believed that affect and cognition are inextricably coupled and that affect is both served by and services cognition (Clore & Huntsinger, 2007; Mandler, 1999; Ortony et al., 1988; Schwarz, 2012).

It is easy to make a case for the relevance of affect to cognition in general and learning in particular. Affect performs *signaling functions* (Schwarz, 2012) by pointing out problems with knowledge (confusion), problems with motivation (boredom), concerns with impending performance (anxiety), and challenges that cannot be easily surpassed (frustration). It performs *evaluative functions* by appraising events in terms of their value, goal relevance, and goal congruence (Izard, 2010). Affect also performs *modulation functions* by constraining or expanding cognitive focus, as is the case when negative emotions engender narrow, bottom-up, and focused modes of processing (constrained focus) (Barth & Funke, 2010; Schwarz, 2012) compared with positive emotions that facilitate broader, top-down, generative processing (expanded focus) (Fredrickson & Branigan, 2005; Isen, 2008). Indeed, affect pervades cognition, as evident by its effects on memory, problem solving, decision making, and other facets of cognition (see Clore & Huntsinger, 2007, for a review). As such, affect, along with motivation and cognition, has finally claimed its rightful place as a core component of learning (Snow et al., 1996).

The last 15 years has also witnessed a wider-scale adoption of *advanced learning technologies* (ALTs) that serve educational goals (Koedinger et al., 1997; Woolf, 2009). Quite different from the computer-based training systems (CBTs) of the '70s and '80s, twenty-first-century ALTs are an order of magnitude more sophisticated in how they interact with students, how they model student knowledge, how they implement macro- and microadaptive strategies to dynamically tailor the instruction to individual students, and how they support motivation, metacognition, and self-regulated learning. Some broad categories of these ALTs include intelligent tutoring systems (VanLehn, 2011; Woolf, 2009), educational games (Dickey, 2005; Gee, 2003), and simulations, animations, multimedia, and hypermedia environments (Ainsworth, 2008; Johnson et al., 2000; Mayer, 2005).

ALTSs have come a long way toward modeling students' knowledge levels and cognitive states. However, the inextricable link between affect and learning suggests that next-generation ALTs should be more than mere cognitive machines. They should be affective processors as well. In line with this, the last decade has witnessed the emergence of a few ALTs that incorporate some form of affective modeling in addition to the traditional cognitive modeling performed by these systems (Conati & Maclaren, 2009; D'Mello et al., 2010, 2012; Forbes-Riley & Litman, 2011b; Sabourin et al., 2011; Woolf et al., 2009). We refer to these systems as *affect-aware advanced learning technologies* (AALTs). Although AALTs can take on several forms in terms of focus and scope, for the purpose of simplicity, we broadly

categorize them as (1) systems that either induce or impede particular affective states (proactive systems) and (2) systems that respond to specific affective states as they arise (reactive systems).

The purpose of this chapter is to discuss some of the core themes, advances, and open issues in the emerging field of AALTs. We set the stage by positioning AALTs within the complex landscape of affect, learning, and technology. Next, we briefly review the results of a recent meta-analysis aimed at uncovering the affective states that occur during learning with technology. The next two sections provide examples of reactive and proactive AALTS, respectively. Important challenges and open issues in this field are discussed, followed by some broad avenues of research that are ripe for exploration.

Finding a Niche for AALTs Within Affect, Learning, and Technology

Positioning AALTs within the landscape of affect, learning, and technology is no simple task. Figure 31.1 provides a simplified organization of the constructs, systems, and research in the relevant fields of the affective, cognitive, learning, and computing science as one attempt to find a niche for AALTs in this complex landscape.

At the first level, one encounters different forms of learning: shallow, complex, and procedural. *Shallow learning* consists of basic encoding of information into memory, such as memorizing a list of words or a definition of a concept. *Procedural learning*, sometimes called implicit learning, concerns the acquisition of perceptual-motor (e.g., playing a musical instrument) and cognitive (e.g., mathematical operations) skills through repeated and/or deliberate practice (Ericsson et al., 1993). Finally, *complex learning* (also known as deep or conceptual learning) involves comprehending conceptual information, such as a mathematical proof, a legal document, or a difficult physics principle, or acquiring a complex skill, such as learning computer programming or argumentative writing. Complex learning can be distinguished from shallow and procedural learning in that it requires more complex cognitive processes, such as inference generation, problem solving, conceptual comparisons, and explanation generation in addition to more basic cognitive processes (memory encoding, attentional orientation, rehearsal, tuning of perceptual-motor systems).

Affect plays a role in all three types of learning activities. It influences shallow learning activities by biasing memory encoding and retrieval as documented by the mood-congruent memory encoding

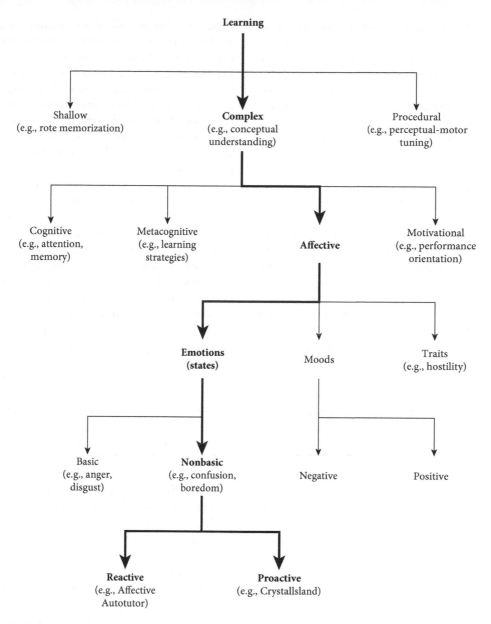

Fig. 31.1 Niche for AALTs in ecology of learning, affect, and technology.

(e.g., happy people are more likely to remember happy words than sad words) and retrieval (e.g., happy words are more likely to be retrieved when a person is in a happy mood rather than a sad mood) effects (Blaney, 1986; Bower, 1981). Affective arousal has also been shown to play a facilitative role in some procedural learning tasks (Steidl et al., 2011). However, in our view, affect is most influential in complex learning activities, which require considerable concentration, effortful problem solving, and conceptual meaning making, all activities that inevitably give rise to a range of complex affective reactions. For example, cognitive processes

that underlie complex learning tasks (e.g., reading Shakespeare or learning about dynamic programming) are accompanied by affective processes such as confusion, frustration, irritation, anger, and sometimes rage when the learner makes mistakes, struggles with troublesome impasses, and experiences failure. On the other hand, positive affective states—such as flow, delight, excitement, and eureka—are experienced when tasks are completed, challenges are conquered, insights are unveiled, and major discoveries are made.

In addition to affect, complex learning requires thinking and reasoning (cognition), thinking about thinking (metacognition), and motivation (Snow et al., 1996). Although affective processes interact with cognitive, motivational, and metacognitive processes in meaningful and interesting ways, our lens is currently on affect, knowing fully well that affect must ultimately be studied within the context of these other processes.

Affect is quite a general term that encompasses multiple systems at multiple levels and at multiple time scales (Izard, 2010). One possible organization involves distinguishing between affective traits, background moods, and affective states (Rosenberg, 1998). Affective traits are relatively stable, mostly unconscious, and predispose the individual toward particular affective experiences. They operate by lowering the threshold for experiencing certain emotions (i.e., hostile people have a lower threshold for experiencing anger but not necessarily other negative emotions). Moods also perform a threshold reduction function on emotion activation but are considered to be more transitory and have a background influence on consciousness. In contrast to affective traits and moods, affective states (or emotions) are brief, intense, reactions that occupy the forefront of consciousness, have significant physiological and behavioral manifestations, and rapidly prepare the bodily systems for action. The present emphasis is on affective states, which also have variable durations when analyzed at a finer-grained time scale (D'Mello & Graesser, 2011). States, such as engagement and boredom, can last for tens of seconds to a few minutes, while others (e.g., delight, surprise) are more ephemeral. Nevertheless, affective states are more transitory than moods, which can last for several hours to days (Rosenberg, 1998; Watson & Clark, 1994).

Researchers in the affective sciences have proposed a number of taxonomies to categorize the affective states that occur in everyday experiences (Ekman, 1992; Ortony et al., 1988; Plutchik, 2001). Broadly, the emotions can be divided into *basic* and *nonbasic* emotions. According to Ekman (1992), basic emotions are considered to be (1) universal, (2) innate, and (3) cross-cultural. They (4) have unique elicitation contexts; (5) have distinguishable neural, physiological, and behavioral correlations; (6) show coherence among different response systems; (7) have a quick onset and brief duration; and (8) occur automatically. Emotions such as anger, surprise, happiness, disgust, sadness, and fear typically make the list of basic emotions (Ekman, 1992). Affective states such as boredom, confusion, frustration, engagement, and curiosity share some but not all of the features commonly attributed to basic emotions. Consequently these emotions are labeled as *nonbasic* states. The term *affective states* is used broadly in this chapter to include both bona fide emotions (e.g., anger) and cognitive-affective blends such as engagement and confusion. As discussed in the next section, nonbasic affective states appear to be more relevant during interactions with ALTs, so most AALTs focus on modeling these nonbasic states.

AALTs that model nonbasic affect can adopt many forms based on the strategies used for intelligent handling of learner affect. One simple categorization broadly distinguishes between *proactive* and *reactive* systems. At the most basic level, proactive systems aspire to increase the likelihood that the learner will experience affective states deemed beneficial to learning (e.g., interest, curiosity, engagement) while simultaneously decreasing the likelihood of states believed to negatively influence the process and product of learning (e.g., boredom, frustration). Reactive systems make no notable a priori attempt to upregulate or downregulate positive and negative affect, respectively. Instead, they simply detect and respond to affective states as they arise. Reactive systems typically focus on identifying and responding to negative affective states such as frustration and boredom.

Which Affective States Are Relevant to Learning with Technology?

An AALT can never model learner affect if it does not know which affective states to model. Hence there is the foundational question of identifying the affective states that learners experience during interactions with ALTs. D'Mello (2013) recently completed a meta-analysis of 24 studies that have systematically tracked the affective states that naturally occur during interactions with learning technologies. The results of this analysis are summarized in this section.

A total of 1,740 students in middle school, high school, and college students as well as adults from the United States, Canada, the United Kingdom, Philippines, and Australia were represented in the 24 studies. On average, each student spent 45 minutes interacting with a learning technology, so the total aggregate training time was approximately 76,000 minutes. There was considerable variance in learning contexts, topics, and technologies. Learning contexts included classroom (i.e., computer lab in a school), research lab, and online studies. Learning topics (subject domains) included algebra, analytical reasoning, argumentative writing, chemistry, computer literacy, ecology, genetics, geography, graphing, logic puzzles, microbiology, prealgebra, and social studies. Learning technologies included intelligent tutoring systems, serious games and simulations environments, virtual labs, and interfaces for problem solving, reading comprehension, and essay writing. In all, a total of 17 affective states—consisting of achievement, epistemic, and topic emotions, and encompassing both basic and nonbasic emotions—were tracked with a number of methodologies. These methods included online self-reports, emote-aloud protocols, online observations, and retrospective coding of video after a learning session by the students themselves or by peers, observers, or trained judges.

The analyses focused on the magnitude and significance of affect incidence across studies (formally quantified with weighted mean effect sizes—see D'Mello, 2013). Engagement/flow was the most frequent state, while contempt, anger, disgust, sadness, anxiety, delight, fear, and surprise were relatively infrequent. There was considerable between-study variability in the occurrence of boredom, confusion, curiosity, happiness, and frustration. However, these states, particularly boredom and confusion, were more likely to occur than the eight infrequent states listed above. The meta-analysis also revealed that the incidence of the affective states was moderated by the source of the affect judgments (self versus observers) and the authenticity of the learning context (classroom versus laboratory).

The take-home message was that engagement/flow, boredom, confusion, curiosity, happiness, and frustration were the major affective states exhibited by learners in these 24 studies. These five states are good candidates for modeling in AALTs. Furthermore, with the exception of happiness, the basic emotions had a relatively minor role to play. This is not entirely surprising, as there is inadequate theoretical justification to expect notable levels of some of the basic emotions, such as disgust and fear, during short one-on-one learning sessions with computers.

Reactive Affect-Aware Learning Technologies

Reactive AALTs focus on automatically *detecting* student affect and *responding* to the sensed affect in order to upregulate positive affective states (e.g., curiosity, engagement) and downregulate negative affective states (e.g., frustration). Fully automated affect detection can use predictive models that infer student affect by analyzing the context of the interaction and other relevant cues (Baker et al., 2012; Conati & Maclaren, 2009; Sabourin et al., 2011) and/or diagnostic models that sense affect from communicative channels like facial features, speech, postures, gestures, central and peripheral physiology, and textual responses (Calvo & D'Mello, 2010; Chaouachi & Frasson, 2010; Pour et al., 2010). Once the learner's affective state is detected with reasonable accuracy, a reactive AALT must dynamically alter its pedagogical strategies in response to the detected state. An AALT has a number of paths to pursue once it has detected learner affect. It could do nothing if the learner is engaged and is on a positive learning trajectory. Hints and just-in-time explanations can be provided when confusion or frustration is detected. The system could provide choice, encourage breaks, or adjust levels of challenge when it detects that a student is bored. Some of the implemented responses to student affect include affect mirroring (Burleson & Picard, 2007), empathetic responses (Woolf et al., 2010), and a combination of politeness, empathy, and encouragement (D'Mello et al., 2010).

The ideal affect-detection and affect-response strategies are ultimately tied to aspects of the global and local situational context. The global context refers to stable, nonmalleable factors such as the specific ALT, domain, student, and interaction context. The local context pertains to unstable factors that can be manipulated to regulate student affect. These include the current topic or question, system messages, system feedback, etc. In this section, we briefly discuss three systems as examples of contemporary reactive AALTs. These include the Affective AutoTutor, GazeTutor, and UNC-ITSpoke.

Affective AutoTutor: Responding to Boredom, Confusion, and Frustration

The Affective Tutor was perhaps the first reactive AALT and was developed from 2004 to 2010. AutoTutor is a conversational intelligent tutoring system that helps students develop mastery of difficult topics in Newtonian physics, computer literacy, and scientific reasoning by holding a mixed-initiative dialogue in natural language (Graesser et al., 2005, 2012). AutoTutor has a set of fuzzy production rules that are sensitive to the cognitive but not to the affective states of the learner. The Affective AutoTutor augments these rules with the ability to map dynamic assessments of learners' affective and cognitive states with tutor actions to address the presence of boredom, confusion, and frustration

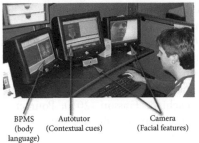

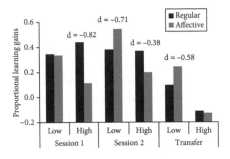

BPMS
(body
language)

Autotutor
(Contextual cues)

Camera
(Facial features)

Sensing affect from posture, facial features, and dialog

(b) Affect modeling

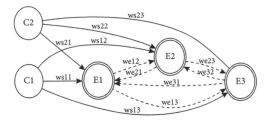

Decision-level fusion with spreading activation network

(c) Learning gains

Affective autotutor helps learning

(d) Affect responses

Tutor displaying skepticism when learner is hedging

Fig. 31.2 Stages in the design and validation of the Affective AutoTutor.

(D'Mello et al., 2008b, 2010; D'Mello & Graesser, 2012b).

The Affective AutoTutor automatically detects boredom, confusion, frustration, and neutral by monitoring conversational cues and other discourse features (predictive modeling) along with gross body language and facial features (diagnostic modeling—as in Figure 31.2A) (D'Mello & Graesser, 2010, 2012b). Each channel independently provides its own evaluation of the learner's affective state. These individual diagnoses are combined with a decision-level fusion algorithm that selects a single affective state and a confidence value of the detection (Figure 31.2B). The algorithm relies on a voting rule enhanced by a few simple heuristics.

The Affective AutoTutor's production rules address the presence of boredom, confusion, and frustration by incorporating perspectives from a number of psychological theories, including attribution theory (Weiner, 1986), cognitive disequilibrium during learning (Piaget, 1952), politeness (Brown & Levinson, 1987), and empathy (Lepper & Chabay, 1988), along with the recommendations of two tutoring experts. The tutor responds with empathetic, encouraging, and

motivational dialogue moves and emotional displays. For example, the tutor might respond to mild boredom with, "This stuff can be kind of dull sometimes, so I'm gonna try and help you get through it. Let's go." A response to confusion would include attributing the source of confusion to the material: "Some of this *material* can be confusing. Just keep going and I am sure you'll get it." These affective responses are accompanied by an appropriate emotional facial expression and emotionally modulated speech (Figure 31.2C).

We tested the effectiveness of the Affective Tutor in improving learning over the nonaffective AutoTutor in a controlled experiment where 84 learners completed two 30-minute training sessions with either tutor (D'Mello et al., 2010). The results indicated that the Affective Tutor helped learning for low-domain knowledge learners during the second 30-minute learning session. The Affective Tutor was less effective at promoting learning for high-domain knowledge learners during the first 30-minute session. Importantly, learning gains increased from Session 1 to Session 2 with the Affective Tutor, whereas they plateaued with the nonaffective AutoTutor (Figure 31.2D).

(a) Screen shot of interface

(b) Gaze before and after intervention

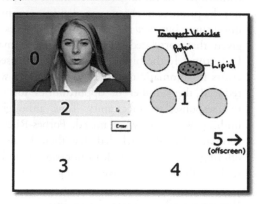

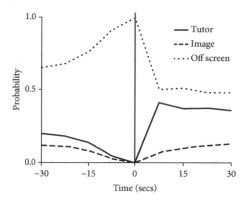

Fig. 31.3 Gaze-Tutor interface and gaze-reorienting results.

Learners who interacted with the Affective Tutor also demonstrated better performance on subsequent transfer tests. A follow-up analysis into learners' perceptions of both tutors indicated that their perceptions of how closely the computer tutors resembled human tutors increased across learning sessions, was related to the quality of tutor feedback, and was a powerful predictor of learning (D'Mello & Graesser, 2012a). Interestingly, the positive change in perceptions was greater for the Affective Tutor.

GazeTutor: Responding to Boredom and Disengagement

It is generally acknowledged that engagement is an important requirement for learning. Attention to task-related thoughts at the expense of task-irrelevant thoughts is one critical precursor of engagement in a learning activity. Therefore developing interventions that monitor periods of waning attention and attempt to encourage more productive use of *attentional resources* might be one promising way to increase engagement and promote learning.

We tested this claim with a multimedia interface consisting of an animated conversational agent that provided explanations on biology concepts with synthesized speech that was synchronized with annotated images (Figure 31.3A) (D'Mello et al., 2012). The system used a Tobii T60 eye tracker in order to identify when learners were not attending to the important parts of the interface (i.e., the tutor or image). The interface did not directly track off-task thought; it simply assumed that learners were disengaged when their gaze was not on the tutor or image for at least 5 consecutive seconds.

It attempted to reengage learners with statements directing them to reorient their attention toward the animated pedagogical agent or the image (e.g., "Please pay attention").

We evaluated the efficacy of the gaze-reactive tutor in promoting learning, motivation, and engagement in an experiment where 48 learners were tutored on four biology topics: two with the gaze-reactive component enabled (experimental condition) and two with the gaze-reactive component disabled (control condition). Learners completed a posttest on all four topics after interacting with the system. The results indicated that the gaze-sensitive intervention was successful in dynamically reorienting learners' attention patterns to the important areas of the interface (Figure 31.3B). Prior to the intervention, the probability that students would be looking away from the screen steadily increased, while there was a corresponding decrease in focus on the tutor and the image. A reverse pattern was discovered after students received an intervention message; off-screen gaze behaviors rapidly decreased while focus on the tutor steadily increased. Importantly, posttest scores for deep reasoning questions were higher when learners interacted with the gaze-sensitive interface compared with its nonreactive counterpart. Interestingly, individual differences in scholastic aptitude moderated the impact of gaze reactivity on learning gains. Gaze reactivity was associated with a small improvement in overall learning for learners with average aptitude, but learning gains were substantially higher for learners with high aptitude and somewhat lower for their low-aptitude counterparts.

In summary, the results of this preliminary study suggest that gaze-sensitive statements can reorient attention and thereby improve comprehension and learning. Future enhancements of the system include replacing the expensive eye tracker with web cameras, more fine-grained modeling of disengagement behaviors, a larger repertoire of context-specific gaze-reactive dialogues, and incorporating individual differences in selecting appropriate gaze-sensitive responses.

UNC-ITSpoke

Forbes-Riley and Litman have developed an AALT called UNC-ITSPOKE to examine whether automatic responses to learner uncertainty could improve learning outcomes (Forbes-Riley & Litman, 2007, 2009, 2011b). Uncertainty is a state similar to confusion and plays an important role on the process and products of learning. ITSPOKE is a speech-enabled ALT that teaches learners about various physics topics with spoken dialogues that are automatically recognized with the Sphinx 2 Speech Recognizer (Litman et al., 2006). UNC-ITSPOKE extends the basic functionality of ITSPOKE with the ability to automatically detect and respond to learners' certainty/uncertainty in addition to correctness/incorrectness. Uncertainty detection is performed by extracting and analyzing the acoustic-prosodic features in the learners' spoken responses in conjunction with lexical features and dialogue-based features (similar to contextual cues in Affective AutoTutor).

It is beyond the scope of this chapter to delve deeply into the adaptive strategies to resolve uncertainty except to point out that this involved launching explanation-based subdialogues when the student is correct in his or her response but uncertain about the response. This was taken to signal an impasse (see the next section for more details) because the students was unsure about the state of his or her knowledge despite being correct. The efficacy of the adaptive condition was first verified in a pilot "Wizard-of-Oz" study where an unseen human (the wizard) performed all of the difficult natural language processing tasks (speech recognition, response understanding, and uncertainty annotation) (Forbes-Riley & Litman, 2010).

In a recent study, Forbes-Riley and Litman (2011b) compared learning outcomes between learners who received adaptive responses to uncertainty (adaptive condition), random responses to uncertainty (random condition), or no responses (control condition). The adaptive condition achieved slightly (but not significantly) higher learning outcomes than the random and control

conditions. The findings revealed that it was perhaps not the presence or absence of adaptive responses to uncertainty but *how many* adaptive responses were given that correlated with learning performance. Unfortunately the biggest challenge was caused by errors in automatic uncertainty annotation, which reduced the number of opportunities for adaptive responses to uncertainty. Thus, although the findings were somewhat mixed, Forbes-Riley and Litman (2011b) concluded that there is merit in offering adaptive feedback to uncertainty and that such feedback can improve learning outcomes.

Proactive Affect-Aware Learning Technologies

In contrast to reactive AALTs that primarily act once particular affective states have been detected, proactive AALTs have inherent strategies that are specifically designed to engender particular affective responses. One common approach is to implement some of the competitive and motivational features of games in educational environments (Halpern et al., 2012; Jackson et al., 2012). These educational games are hypothesized to be the ideal learning environments capable of turning work into play by minimizing boredom, optimizing engagement/flow, presenting challenges that reside within the optimal zone of proximal development, preventing persistent frustration, and engineering delight and pleasant surprises (Lepper & Henderlong, 2000; Ritterfeld et al., 2009). One system, discussed in this chapter, is called *Crystal Island* (Rowe et al., 2009) and is an educational game that aims to promote positive affect by carefully embedding the learning content in a game that supports a narrative context, realism, and immersion (Dede, 2009; Spires et al., 2011).

Taking a very different approach, the second proactive AALT we describe intentionally *confuses* learners in an attempt to promote deeper modes of inquiry (D'Mello et al., 2014). Although this may sound somewhat odd at face value, it is important to note that confusion itself has a rather counterintuitive relationship with learning in that it is positively correlated with learning in some ALTs (Craig et al., 2004; D'Mello & Graesser, 2011; Graesser et al., 2007). This suggests that there might be some merits to strategically inducing confusion at key moments in a learning session.

Crystal Island

Designing educational games can be quite challenging, because game designers must balance a trade-off between game environments that are engaging but tangential to learning and environments that promote deep learning but fail to foster engagement (Johnson & Mayer, 2010). This balance is nicely achieved in *Crystal Island* (Rowe et al., 2009; Spires et al., 2011), an immersive educational game that capitalizes on the principle of narrativity. This principle posits that learners may benefit most from educational games that weave a narrative theme into the context of the learning environment. Ostensibly immersive narratives motivate learners to initiate and persist in game play and to remain engaged in the learning activity, which might contribute to increased learning.

In *Crystal Island*, the learner takes on the role of a protagonist named Alex, who arrives on the island. Alex discovers that members of a research team are falling ill; and is charged with identifying the source of their infectious disease. Alex proceeds with the investigation by visiting various areas of the island (dining hall, lab, infirminary, dorm), interviewing other islanders, and manipulating objects in the world. Through the generation of questions and hypotheses as well as the collection and analysis of data, learners take gradual steps toward diagnosing the cause of the disease.

Evidence from learners' interactions with *Crystal Island* indicate that it is highly engaging and motivating and can improve learning outcomes (McQuiggan et al., 2008). There is also some evidence to suggest that *Crystal Island* meets one of its intended goals of increasing positive affect, at least when compared to more traditional ALTs like intelligent tutoring systems (Lester et al., 2011). For example, Sabourin et al. (2011) conducted a study in which 450 middle-school students interacted with *Crystal Island* for 55 minutes. Students self-reported one of seven affective states (anxious, bored, confused, curious, excited, focused, and frustrated) at 5-minute intervals during the learning session. Positive affective states such as focused, curious, and excited were found to be more frequent (55%) than negative affective states like confused, frustrated, anxious, and bored (46%). Importantly, recent findings suggest that engagement and learning in the context of *Crystal Island* share a positive relationship, so this system helps both learning and engagement (Rowe et al., 2010).

ConfusionTutor—Inducing Confusion via Trialogues with Animated Agents

Although most would consider confusion to be a negative affective state, both in terms of its subjective experience (i.e., most people do not like being confused) and its assumed impact on learning (i.e., intuition suggests that confusion is harmful to learning), there is some correlational evidence suggesting a positive relationship between confusion and learning gains (Craig et al., 2004; D'Mello & Graesser, 2011; Graesser et al., 2007). The question is whether there is a causal relationship between confusion and learning. To test this question, we developed a proactive AALT (ConfusionTutor) that experimentally induced confusion and measured the consequences of the induced confusion and learning (D'Mello et al., 2014).

This research was conducted in the context of *trialogues* (conversations between three agents) very similar to those developed in a serious game called *Operation ARA* (Halpern et al., 2012). ARA teaches scientific research methods and critical thinking skills through a series of game modules, including those with two or more animated pedagogical agents. In the trialogues, a three-way conversation transpired between the human student, a tutor agent, and a student agent. The tutor-agent was an expert on scientific inquiry, whereas the student agent was a peer of the human learner. A series of research case studies with experiments that had a crucial design flaw with respect to proper scientific methodology was presented by the tutor agent. For example, one case study described an experiment that tested a new pill that purportedly helps people lose weight, but there was no control group. The goal of the human learner was to identify the flaws and express them in natural language, while the tutor agent helps scaffold this goal by guiding the human learner and the peer student agent.

ConfusionTutor attempted to induce confusion by manipulating whether or not the tutor agent and the student agent contradicted each other during the trialogue. This was accomplished by expressing points that were incorrect and asking the human learners to intervene by deciding which opinion had more scientific merit and providing explanations for their justifications. The tutor agent expressed a correct assertion and the student agent agreed with the tutor in the *true-true* control condition. In the *true-false* condition, the tutor expressed a correct assertion but the student agent disagreed by expressing an incorrect assertion. In the *false-true* condition, it was the student agent who provided the correct assertion and the tutor agent who disagreed. In the *false-false* condition, the tutor agent provided an incorrect assertion and the student agent agreed, so both agents were incorrect in this condition. It should be noted that all misleading information was corrected over the course of the learning session and there was no evidence to suggest that the contradictions themselves had a negative impact on learning (see below).

Confusion was operationally defined as occurring if both (1) the human learners manifested uncertainty/incorrectness in their decisions when asked by the agents (e.g., long pauses, changing decisions), (2) the learner reported being confused when probed, and (3) there were visible displays of confusion on video recordings of the learner's face. The data always satisfied criterion (1) and sometimes satisfied criterion (2). Preliminary analyses have indicated that it also satisfies criterion (3), although we are only beginning to analyze the facial videos.

Interestingly, there was evidence that the induced confusion caused more learning at deeper levels of mastery, as reflected in a delayed test on scientific reasoning. The results indicated that contradictions in the experimental conditions produced higher performance on multiple-choice questions that tapped deeper levels of comprehension than performance in the no-contradiction true-true condition, but *only if learners were confused* by the contradictions. Similarly, learners who were confused by the contradictions were more likely to correctly identify flaws in subsequent case studies that differed from the case studies discussed in the trialogues on surface-level features (near transfer) or both surface and structural features (far transfer). These data suggest there may be a causal relationship between confusion and deep learning, with confusion playing moderating role on the effect of the contradictions on learning.

Open Issues

In this section, we discuss some of the critical issues, challenges, and open problems in the field of AALTs. In the interest of brevity, we focus on three core problems, knowing fully well that there are several more issues that warrant further research and development.

Sensors, Sensorless, or Sensor-Lite? Issues of Scalability

Many schools in developed nations have a computer lab that can be used for data collection and system deployment. However, it is unlikely that any school has a computer lab that is specially equipped with affective sensors (e.g., physiological sensors, eye trackers, and posture sensors), because several sensors require customized, nonportable, expensive hardware and software. Hence, scalability concerns become paramount when one wants to take a program of research on AALTs into the real world. Some of these issues are expected to be mitigated as sensor technologies develop to the point that nonintrusive wireless sensors can be deployed at little cost in authentic educational contexts. This is a future that is likely but not guaranteed to occur, so it might be worthwhile to consider alternate solutions.

One possible solution is to take the sensors to the classroom, an approach that was pioneered by Arroyo et al. (2009). In this study, approximately 70 students were monitored for 4 to 5 days with four affect sensors (a pressure-sensitive mouse, pressure-sensitive mats for a chair, a video camera, and a bracelet to sense skin conductance) while they completed their normal classroom activities with a mathematics ALT. This *sensor approach* is certainly a viable approach for short-term studies in school contexts, but is unlikely to be sustainable in the longer term. The state of the art in affect detection using sensors is described in several chapters in this volume (see Finding a Niche for AALTs Within Affect, Learning, and Technology p. 420 on Affect Detection).

In contrast to the sensor approach, some researchers have taken a *sensorless* approach, in which affective states are detected by monitoring interaction patterns (e.g., clicks, responses) and other contextual cues from the ALT (e.g., type of feedback being provided, difficulty of problem). No sensors are used in this approach. We first demonstrated the possibility of this approach in a 2006 study (D'Mello et al., 2006) and subsequently expanded its capabilities in a 2008 study (D'Mello et al., 2008a). These studies were conducted in a laboratory setting because of the nature of our research questions. However, Baker and colleagues have since conducted an impressive program of research that focuses on developing sensorless affect detectors in real-world environments (see chapter by Baker and Ocumpaugh, this volume). Some of the more recent attempts have focused on tracking engagement during writing activities (Bixler & D'Mello, 2013; Liu et al., 2013). Although this sensorless approach certainly is a viable solution to the scalability problem, there is the question of quantifying the extent to which affect detection accuracies are affected by the lack of sensors.

This approach is a *sensor-lite* approach. It involves including scalable sensors when feasible (cameras and microphones) and replacing nonscalable sensors with scalable proxies, "soft sensors," or "virtual sensors." Cameras seem to be ideal for this purpose, as web cams are already integrated in most laptops and can be purchased at low cost if needed. For example, we have successfully applied motion tracking techniques to video data, thereby effectively replacing a cost-prohibitive posture sensor with simple web cams (D'Mello, Dale, & Graesser, 2012). Some initial work also suggests that cameras can be used to monitor heart rate (Poh et al., 2010) and eye gaze (Sewell & Komogortsev, 2010). Hence, in our view, camera-based proxy sensing coupled with interactional and contextual features appears to be the most promising way to solve the scalability problem.

How Good Is Good Enough? Issues of Detection Accuracy

A reactive AALT obviously needs to detect learner affect before it can respond adaptively. The detection of naturalistic affective experiences in noncontrolled settings has come a long way in the last decade, as evidenced by recent surveys (Calvo & D'Mello, 2010; Zeng et al., 2009) and several chapters on affect detection in this volume. Although numerous advances have been made, the field is still grappling with persistent problems. There is the previously discussed problem of intrusive, expensive, and noisy sensors that are largely unscalable. There are the technical challenges associated with detecting latent psychological constructs (i.e., affect) from weak signals embedded in noisy channels. There are difficulties associated with collecting adequate and realistic training data for machine learning models. There are the challenges of incorporating top-down models of context and appraisals with bottom-up body- and physiologically based sensing. There is the lack of clarity of the affective phenomenon being modeled (e.g., moods versus emotions, categorical versus dimensional representations). Finally, there are issues pertaining to generalizability across contexts, time, individual differences, and cultural differences.

In general, affect detection is an extremely difficult problem, and it is unlikely that *perfect* affect detectors that generalize to new individuals and interactional contexts and that can operate under messy real-world conditions can ever be developed. One can spend a long time waiting for perfect or almost perfect affect detection accuracies before closing the loop by developing affect-aware interventions. In our view, a moderate degree of recognition accuracy is sufficient provided that the affect-aware interventions are fail-soft in that they do no harm if delivered incorrectly. Possible fail-soft interventions include never directly acknowledging a learners' affective state, adjusting parameters of the task that are beyond the radar of the learners (e.g., decreasing problem difficulty), and providing cognitive scaffolds in the form of hints and explanations. The severity of the interventions can also be calibrated to the system's confidence in detection accuracy.

How Adaptive Is Adaptive Enough? Issues of Levels of Analysis

Assuming that an AALT can detect a learner's affective state with moderate accuracy, the next pertinent question pertains to how to adaptively respond to that state. This is where there is perhaps the most significant paucity of guiding theory and empirical research. We have discussed some of the strategies that have been implemented in our discussion of reactive AALTs, but these only scratch the surface of possible affect-sensitive responses. Although there are several critical issues that must be considered in designing an affective response strategy, here we focus on one such issue, namely *levels of analysis*.

The expression "levels of analysis" pertains to the specificity by which an affective state needs to be modeled for a meaningful affect-sensitive response. Current approaches primarily model affect in two ways. Some model arousal and valence independently, jointly, and in conjunction with other relevant dimensions. Others take a categorical view and model discrete affective states, sometimes with their intensity. It is easy to see that simply modeling just the presence of an affective state (either dimensionally or categorically) is unlikely to suffice. Take, for example, the case of boredom. According to the control-value theory of achievement emotions, subjective appraisals of control and value of a learning activity are the critical predictors of boredom (Pekrun, 2010). Subjective control pertains to the perceived influence that a learner has over the activity, while subjective value represents the perceived value of the outcomes of the activity. Boredom is expected to be heightened when learners perceive low value in the outcome of the activity, whereas learners are more engaged when the perceived value is high (Pekrun et al., 2010). The situation is more complex for perceived control because there appears to be a curvilinear relationship between perceived control and boredom. Boredom is frequent when control is too high (i.e., skill outweighs challenges) (Csikszentmihalyi, 1990) but also when control is too low (challenges outweigh skill) (Pekrun et al., 2010). This counterintuitive finding can be interpreted from emerging theoretical perspectives positing that boredom is not unitary; there are multiple types of boredom that occur in different situations and impact performance in unique ways (Acee et al., 2010; Forbes-Riley & Litman, 2011a; Vodanovich et al., 2005). Similar arguments can be made for several other affective states. This suggests that affective response strategies must be differentially sensitive to different types of affect, which requires modeling of the immediate situational context surrounding the experience of an affective state in addition to detecting the affect state itself.

Some Suggested Broad Steps Forward

This chapter surveyed some of the burgeoning research in the field of affect-aware learning technologies. Although affect has claimed its rightful place as a critical component to learning, there is still much more to be done. In the remainder of this chapter, we highlight two possible avenues of work, with an emphasis on more big-picture advances of this field.

First, there is the pressing need for the development and advancement of a science of nonbasic emotions. Researchers in the field of affective sciences are currently engaged in a vigorous debate with respect to the existence of basic emotions and the value of a crisp basic versus nonbasic distinction (Lench et al., 2013; Lindquist et al., 2013). Despite the outcome of this debate, if there ever will be an outcome, it is quite clear that much of the emotion research has still emphasized the basic emotions at the expense of overlooking other nonbasic emotions (Rozin & Cohen, 2003). This is particularly unfortunate for the field of AALTs, because available data indicate that the basic emotions are mostly muted during interactions with ALTs. Instead, it is the nonbasic affective states—such as confusion, frustration, and boredom—that play a more critical role during interactions with technology. Unfortunately we know very little about these nonbasic states, and they are of little interest to the mainstream affect sciences community. For example, efforts to promote interest in studying confusion in the affective sciences (Rozin & Cohen, 2003) were met by prompt resistance from some in the affective science community (Ellsworth, 2003; Hess, 2003; Keltner & Shiota, 2003). The success

of the field of AALTs relies on a strong foundation of theory and empirical data, so there is a pressing need for a science of nonbasic affect (D'Mello & Calvo, 2013).

Second, there is a need to extend the scope of our theories, experiments, and models to be sensitive to the situational contexts in which learning unfolds. This is because the affect–cognition technology relationship does not exist in a vacuum but is situated in a complex ecology with multiple layers of influences and interactions. At the individual level, motivation and metacognition interact with affect and cognition in any meaningful learning context. For example, a learner with mastery-oriented motivational tendencies (Daniels et al., 2009), who is an academic risk taker (Clifford, 1988; Meyer & Turner, 2006) and who has a high degree of conscientiousness, persistence, or grit (Duckworth et al., 2007) would be able to handle difficult tasks, failure, and the resultant negative emotions more readily than one who is performance-oriented, a cautious learner, and easily gives up. Beyond the processes that unfold within the mind of an individual learner, learning itself is situated in an external learning context involving a learner completing a learning task with a learning technology. Different affective profiles are expected to emerge as a function of what the learner brings to the task and what the task and technology afford the learner. For example, a learning environment designed to teach problem-solving strategies for an upcoming high-stakes standardized test is expected to induce a different affective profile than *Crystal Island* or AutoTutor. The social environment in which the learner, learning technology, and learning task are situated is also expected to influence learners' affect. For example, social emotions like pride and jealousy are likely to be experienced more profoundly in group learning or other socially relevant learning contexts, while they are somewhat more muted during one-on-one human-computer learning interactions.

This discussion has only sketched out some of the influences that are likely to influence a learner's affective states. There are numerous other factors that play a role, so there is much more theory development and empirical testing that needs to be done. Indeed, a program of research aimed at uncovering the factors that influence affect so as to inform the design of affect-aware technologies can be sustainable and rewarding for several decades.

Acknowledgments

This research was supported by the National Science Foundation (NSF) (ITR 0325428, HCC 0834847, DRL 1235958). Any opinions, findings and conclusions, or recommendations expressed in this paper are those of the authors and do not necessarily reflect the views of the NSF.

References

Acee, T. W., Kim, H., Kim, H. J., Kim, J. I., Chu, H. N. R., Kim, M.,... Wicker, F. W. (2010). Academic boredom in under-and over-challenging situations. *Contemporary Educational Psychology, 35*(1), 17–27.

Ainsworth, S. (2008). How do animations influence learning? In D. Robinson & G. Schraw (Eds.), *Recent innovations in educational technology that facilitate student learning* (pp. 37–67). Information Age Publishing.

Arroyo, I., Woolf, B., Cooper, D., Burleson, W., Muldner, K., & Christopherson, R. (2009). Emotion sensors go to school. In V. Dimitrova, R. Mizoguchi, B. Du Boulay, & A. Graesser (Eds.), *Proceedings of the 14th international conference on artificial intelligence in education* (pp. 17–24). Amsterdam: IOS Press.

Baker, R. S. J., Kalka, J., Aleven, V., Rossi, L., Gowda, S. M., Wagner, A. Z.,... Ocumpaugh, J. (2012). Towards sensor-free affect detection in cognitive tutor algebra. In K. Yacef, O. Zaïane, H. Hershkovitz, M. Yudelson, & J. Stamper (Eds.), *Proceedings of the 5th international conference on educational data mining* (pp. 126–133). International Educational Data Mining Society.

Barth, C. M., & Funke, J. (2010). Negative affective environments improve complex solving performance. *Cognition and Emotion, 24*(7), 1259–1268. doi: 10.1080/02699930903223766

Bixler, R., & D'Mello, S. (2013). Detecting engagement and boredom during writing with keystroke analysis, task appraisals, and stable traits *Proceedings of the 2013 international conference on intelligent user interfaces (IUI 2013)* (pp. 225–234). New York: Association for Computing Machinery.

Blaney, P. H. (1986). Affect and memory: A review. *Psychological Bulletin, 99*(2), 229.

Bower, G. (1981). Mood and memory. *American Psychologist, 36*, 129–148.

Brown, P., & Levinson, S. (1987). *Politeness: Some universals in language usage.* Cambridge, UK: Cambridge University Press.

Burleson, W., & Picard, R. (2007). Evidence for gender specific approaches to the development of emotionally intelligent learning companions. *IEEE Intelligent Systems, 22*(4), 62–69.

Calvo, R. A., & D'Mello, S. K. (2010). Affect detection: An interdisciplinary review of models, methods, and their applications. *IEEE Transactions on Affective Computing, 1*(1), 18–37. doi: 10.1109/T-AFFC.2010.1

Chaouachi, M., & Frasson, C. (2010). Exploring the relationship between learners EEG mental engagement and affect. In J. Kay & V. Aleven (Eds.), *Proceedings of 10th international conference on intelligent tutoring systems* (pp. 291–293). Berlin and Heidelberg: Springer.

Clifford, M. (1988). Failure tolerance and academic risk-taking in ten- to twelve-year-old students. *British Journal of Educational Psychology, 58*(15–27). doi: 10.1111/j.2044-8279.1988.tb00875.x

Clore, G. L., & Huntsinger, J. R. (2007). How emotions inform judgment and regulate thought. *Trends in Cognitive Sciences, 11*(9), 393–399. doi: 10.1016/j.tics.2007.08.005

Conati, C., & Maclaren, H. (2009). Empirically building and evaluating a probabilistic model of user affect. *User Modeling and User-Adapted Interaction, 19*(3), 267–303.

Craig, S., Graesser, A., Sullins, J., & Gholson, B. (2004). Affect and learning: An exploratory look into the role of affect in learning. *Journal of Educational Media, 29*, 241–250. doi: 10.1080/1358165042000283101

Csikszentmihalyi, M. (1990). *Flow: The psychology of optimal experience.* New York: Harper & Row.

D'Mello, S. (2013). A selective meta-analysis on the relative incidence of discrete affective states during learning with technology. *Journal of Educational Psychology. 105*(4), 1082–1099.

D'Mello, S., & Calvo, R. (2013). Beyond the basic emotions: What should affective computing compute? In S. Brewster, S. Bødker, & W. Mackay (Eds.). *Extended Abstracts of the ACM SIGCHI conference on human factors in computing systems (CHI 2013)* (pp. 2287–2294). New York: Association for Computing Machinery.

D'Mello, S., Craig, S., Sullins, J., & Graesser, A. (2006). Predicting affective states expressed through an emote-aloud procedure from AutoTutor's mixed-initiative dialogue. *International Journal of Artificial Intelligence In Education, 16*(1), 3–28.

D'Mello, S., Craig, S., Witherspoon, A., McDaniel, B., & Graesser, A. (2008a). Automatic detection of learner's affect from conversational cues. *User Modeling and User-Adapted Interaction, 18*(1–2), 45–80.

D'Mello, S. K., Dale, R. A., & Graesser, A. C. (2012). Disequilibrium in the Mind, Disharmony in the Body, *Cognition & Emotion, 26*(2), 362–374.

D'Mello, S., & Graesser, A. (2010). Multimodal semi-automated affect detection from conversational cues, gross body language, and facial features. *User Modeling and User-Adapted Interaction, 20*(2), 147–187.

D'Mello, S., & Graesser, A. (2012a). Malleability of students' perceptions of an affect-sensitive tutor and its influence on learning. In G. Youngblood & P. Mccarthy (Eds.), *Proceedings of 25th Florida artificial intelligence research society conference* (pp. 432–437). Menlo Park, CA: AAAI Press.

D'Mello, S. K., & Graesser, A. C. (2012b). AutoTutor and Affective AutoTutor: Learning by Talking with Cognitively and Emotionally Intelligent Computers that Talk Back, *ACM Transactions on Interactive Intelligent Systems, 2*(4), 23:2–23:39.

D'Mello, S., Jackson, G., Craig, S., Morgan, B., Chipman, P., White, H.,... Graesser, A. (2008b). *AutoTutor detects and responds to learners affective and cognitive states.* Paper presented at the Proceedings of the workshop on emotional and cognitive issues in ITS held in conjunction with the ninth international conference on intelligent tutoring systems, Montreal, Canada.

D'Mello, S., Lehman, B., Sullins, J., Daigle, R., Combs, R., Vogt, K.,... Graesser, A. (2010). A time for emoting: When affect-sensitivity is and isn't effective at promoting deep learning. In J. Kay & V. Aleven (Eds.), *Proceedings of the 10th international conference on intelligent tutoring systems* (pp. 245–254). Berlin and Heidelberg: Springer.

D'Mello, S., Lehman, S., Pekrun, R., & Graesser, A. (2014). Confusion can be beneficial for learning. *Learning and Instruction. 29*(1), 153–170.

D'Mello, S., Olney, A., Williams, C., & Hays, P. (2012). Gaze tutor: A gaze-reactive intelligent tutoring system. *International Journal of human-computer studies, 70*(5), 377–398.

D'Mello, S. K., & Graesser, A. C. (2012). AutoTutor and Affective AutoTutor: Learning by talking with cognitively and emotionally intelligent computers that talk back. *ACM transactions on interactive intelligent systems, 2*(4), 23:2–23:39.

D'Mello, S., & Graesser, A. (2011). The half-life of cognitive-affective states during complex learning. *Cognition & Emotion, 25*(7), 1299–1308.

Daniels, L. M., Pekrun, R., Stupnisky, R. H., Haynes, T. L., Perry, R. P., & Newall, N. E. (2009). A longitudinal analysis of achievement goals: From affective antecedents to emotional effects and achievement outcomes. *Journal of Educational Psychology, 101*(4), 948–963. doi: 10.1037/a0016096

Dede, C. (2009). Immersive interfaces for engagement and learning. *Science, 323*(5910), 66–69.

Dickey, M. D. (2005). Engaging by design: How engagement strategies in popular computer and video games can inform instructional design. *Educational Technology Research and Development, 53*, 67–93.

Duckworth, A. L., Peterson, C., Matthews, M. D., & Kelly, D. R. (2007). Grit: Perseverance and passion for long-term goals. *Journal of Personality and Social Psychology, 92*(6), 1087.

Ekman, P. (1992). An argument for basic emotions. *Cognition & Emotion, 6*(3–4), 169–200.

Ellsworth, P. C. (2003). Confusion, concentration, and other emotions of interest: Commentary on Rozin & Cohen (2003). *2003, 3*(1), 81–85.

Ericsson, K. A., Krampe, R. T., & Tesch-Römer, C. (1993). The role of deliberate practice in the acquisition of expert performance. *Psychological Review, 100*(3), 363.

Forbes-Riley, K., & Litman, D. (2007). *Investigating Human Tutor Responses to Student Uncertainty for Adaptive System Development*. Paper presented at the Proceedings of the 2nd international conference on affective computing and intelligent interaction, Lisbon, Portugal.

Forbes-Riley, K., & Litman, D. (2009). Adapting to student uncertainty improves tutoring dialogues. In V. Dimitrova, R. Mizoguchi & B. Du Boulay (Eds.), *Proceedings of the 14th international conference on artificial intelligence in education* (pp. 33–40). Amsterdam: IOS Press.

Forbes-Riley, K., & Litman, D. (2010). Designing and evaluating a wizarded uncertainty-adaptive spoken dialogue tutoring system. *Computer Speech and Language, 25*(1), 105–126. doi: http://dx.doi.org/10.1016/j.csl.2009.12.002

Forbes-Riley, K., & Litman, D. (2011a). When does disengagement correlate with learning in spoken dialog computer tutoring? In S. Bull & G. Biswas (Eds.), *Proceedings of the 15th international conference on artificial intelligence in education* (pp. 81–89). Berlin and Heidelberg: Springer.

Forbes-Riley, K., & Litman, D. J. (2011b). Benefits and challenges of real-time uncertainty detection and adaptation in a spoken dialogue computer tutor. *Speech Communication, 53*(9–10), 1115–1136. doi: 10.1016/j.specom.2011.02.006

Fredrickson, B., & Branigan, C. (2005). Positive emotions broaden the scope of attention and thought-action repertoires. *Cognition & Emotion, 19*(3), 313–332. doi: 10.1080/02699930441000238

Gee, J. P. (2003). *What video games have to teach us about learning and literacy*. New York: Palgrave Macmillan.

Graesser, A., Chipman, P., Haynes, B., & Olney, A. (2005). AutoTutor: An intelligent tutoring system with mixed-initiative dialogue. *IEEE Transactions on Education, 48*(4), 612–618. doi: 10.1109/TE.2005.856149

Graesser, A., Chipman, P., King, B., McDaniel, B., & D'Mello, S. (2007). Emotions and learning with AutoTutor. In R. Luckin, K. Koedinger & J. Greer (Eds.), *Proceedings of the 13th international conference on artificial intelligence in education* (pp. 569–571). Amsterdam: IOS Press.

Graesser, A. C., D'Mello, S. K., X., Hu., Cai, Z., Olney, A., & Morgan, B. (2012). AutoTutor. In P. McCarthy & C. Boonthum-Denecke (Eds.), *Applied natural language processing: Identification, investigation, and resolution* (pp. 169–187). Hershey, PA: IGI Global.

Halpern, D. F., Millis, K., Graesser, A., Butler, H., Forsyth, C., & Cai, Z. (2012). Operation ARA: A computerized learning game that teaches critical thinking and scientific reasoning. *Thinking Skills and Creativity, 7*(93–100).

Hess, U. (2003). Now you see it, now you don't—The confusing case of confusion as an emotion: Commentary on Rozin & Cohen (2003). *Emotion, 3*(1), 76–80.

Isen, A. (2008). Some ways in which positive affect influences decision making and problem solving. In M. Lewis, J. Haviland-Jones, & L. Barrett (Eds.), *Handbook of emotions*, 3rd ed. (pp. 548–573). New York: Guilford.

Izard, C. (2010). The many meanings/aspects of emotion: Definitions, functions, activation, and regulation. *Emotion Review, 2*(4), 363–370. doi: 10.1177/1754073910374661

Jackson, G. T., Dempsey, K. B., & McNamara, D. S. (2012). Game-based practice in reading strategy tutoring system: Showdown in iSTART-ME. In H. Reinders (Ed.), *Computer games* (pp. 115–138). Bristol, UK: Multilingual Matters.

Johnson, C. I., & Mayer, R. E. (2010). Applying the self-explanation principle to multimedia learning in a computer-based game-like environment. *Computers in Human behavior, 26*(6), 1246–1252.

Johnson, W., Rickel, J., & Lester, J. (2000). Animated pedagogical agents: Face-to-face interaction in interactive learning environments. *International Journal of Artificial Intelligence in Education, 11*, 47–78.

Keltner, D., & Shiota, M. (2003). New displays and new emotions: A commentary on Rozin and Cohen (2003). *Emotion, 3*, 86–91. doi: 10.1037/1528-3542.3.1.86

Koedinger, K., Anderson, J., Hadley, W., & Mark, M. (1997). Intelligent tutoring goes to school in the big city. *International Journal of Artificial Intelligence in Education, 8*, 30–43.

Lench, H. C., Bench, S. W., & Flores, S. A. (2013). Searching for evidence, not a war: Reply to Lindquist, Siegel, Quigley, & Barrett (2013). *Psychological Bulletin, 113*(1), 264–268.

Lepper, M., & Chabay, R. (1988). Socializing the intelligent tutor: Bringing empathy to computer tutors. In H. Mandl & A. Lesgold (Eds.), *Learning issues for intelligent tutoring systems* (pp. 242–257). Hillsdale, NJ: Erlbaum.

Lepper, M. R., & Henderlong, J. (2000). Turning" play" into" work" and" work" into" play": 25 years of research on intrinsic versus extrinsic motivation. In C. Sansone & J. M. Harackiewicz (Eds.), *Intrinsic and extrinsic motivation: The search for optimal motivation and performance* (pp. 257–307). San Diego, CA: Academic Press.

Lester, J. C., McQuiggan, S. W., & Sabourin, J. L. (2011). Affect recognition and expression in narrative-centered learning environments. In R. Calvo & S. D'Mello (Eds.), *New perspectives on affect and learning technologies* (pp. 85–96). New York: Springer.

Lindquist, K. A., Siegel, E. H., Quigley, K. S., & Barrett, L. F. (2013). The hundred-year emotion war: Are emotions natural kinds or psychological constructions? Comment on Lench, Flores, & Bench (2011). *Psychological Bulletin, 139*(1), 264–268.

Litman, D., Rose, C., Forbes-Riley, K., VanLehn, K., Bhembe, D., & Silliman, S. (2006). Spoken versus typed human and computer dialogue tutoring. *International Journal of Artificial Intelligence In Education, 16*(2), 145–170.

Liu, M., Calvo, R., & Pardo, A. (2013). Tracer: A tool to measure and visualize student engagement in writing activities. *Proceedings of the13th IEEE international conference on advanced learning technologies* (pp. 421–425). Washington, DC: IEEE.

Mandler, G. (1999). Emotion. In B. M. Bly & D. E. Rumelhart (Eds.), *Cognitive science. Handbook of perception and cognition* (2nd ed., pp. 367–382). San Diego, CA: Academic Press.

Mayer, R. (Ed.). (2005). *The Cambridge handbook of multimedia learning.* New York: Cambridge University Press.

McQuiggan, S., Mott, B., & Lester, J. (2008). Modeling self-efficacy in intelligent tutoring systems: An inductive approach. [Article]. *User Modeling and User-Adapted Interaction, 18*(1–2), 81–123. doi: 10.1007/s11257-007-9040-y

Meyer, D., & Turner, J. (2006). Re-conceptualizing emotion and motivation to learn in classroom contexts. *Educational Psychology Review, 18*(4), 377–390. doi: 10.1007/s10648-006-9032-1

Ortony, A., Clore, G., & Collins, A. (1988). *The cognitive structure of emotions.* New York: Cambridge University Press.

Pekrun, R. (2010). Academic emotions. In T. Urdan (Ed.), *APA educational psychology handbook* (Vol. 2). Washington, DC: American Psychological Association.

Pekrun, R., Goetz, T., Daniels, L., Stupnisky, R. H., & Perry, R. (2010). Boredom in achievement settings: Exploring control-value antecedents and performance outcomes of a neglected emotion. *Journal of Educational Psychology, 102*(3), 531–549. doi: 10.1037/a0019243

Piaget, J. (1952). *The origins of intelligence.* New York: International University Press.

Plutchik, R. (2001). The nature of emotions. *American Scientist, 89*(4), 344–350.

Poh, M. Z., McDuff, D. J., & Picard, R. W. (2010). Non-contact, automated cardiac pulse measurements using video imaging and blind source separation. *Optics Express, 18*(10), 10762–10774.

Pour, P. A., Hussein, S., AlZoubi, O., D'Mello, S., & Calvo, R. (2010). The impact of system feedback on learners' affective and physiological states. In J. Kay & V. Aleven (Eds.), *Proceedings of 10th international conference on intelligent tutoring systems* (pp. 264–273). Berlin and Heidelberg: Springer.

Ritterfeld, U., Cody, M., & Vorderer, P. (Eds.). (2009). *Serious games: Mechanisms and effects.* New York and London: Routledge.

Rosenberg, E. (1998). Levels of analysis and the organization of affect. *Review of General Psychology, 2*(3), 247–270. doi: 10.1037//1089-2680.2.3.247

Rowe, J., Mott, B., McQuiggan, S., Robison, J., Lee, S., & Lester, J. (2009). *Crystal island: A narrative-centered learning environment for eighth grade microbiology.* Paper presented at the workshop on intelligent educational games at the 14th international conference on artificial intelligence in education, Brighton, UK.

Rowe, J., Shores, L., Mott, B., & Lester, J. (2010). Integrating learning and engagement in narrative-centered learning environments. In J. Kay & V. Aleven (Eds.), *Proceedings of the 10th international conference on intelligent tutoring systems* (pp. 166–177). Berlin and Heidelberg: Springer.

Rozin, P., & Cohen, A. (2003). High frequency of facial expressions corresponding to confusion, concentration, and worry in an analysis of maturally occurring facial expressions of Americans. *Emotion, 3*, 68–75.

Sabourin, J., Mott, B., & Lester, J. (2011). Modeling learner affect with theoretically grounded dynamic bayesian networks In S. D'Mello, A. Graesser, B. Schuller, & J. Martin (Eds.), *Proceedings of the fourth international conference on affective computing and intelligent interaction* (pp. 286–295). Berlin and Heidelberg: Springer.

Schwarz, N. (2012). Feelings-as-information theory. In P. Van Lange, A. Kruglanski & T. Higgins (Eds.), *Handbook of theories of social psychology* (pp. 289–308). Thousand Oaks, CA: Sage.

Sewell, W., & Komogortsev, O. (2010). *Real-time eye gaze tracking with an unmodified commodity webcam employing a neural network.* Paper presented at the Proceedings of the 2012 ACM annual conference on human factors in computing systems, Austin, TX.

Snow, R. E., Corno, L., & Jackson, D. (1996). Individual differences in affective and conative functions. In D. Berliner & R. Caldee (Eds.), *Handbook of educational psychology* (pp. 243–310). New York: Macmillan.

Spires, H. A., Rowe, J. P., Mott, B. W., & Lester, J. C. (2011). Problem solving and game-based learning: Effects of middle grade students' hypothesis testing strategies on learning outcomes. *Journal of Educational Computing Research, 44*(4), 453–472.

Steidl, S., Razik, F., & Anderson, A. K. (2011). Emotion enhanced retention of cognitive skill learning. *Emotion, 11*(1), 12.

VanLehn, K. (2011). The relative effectiveness of human tutoring, intelligent tutoring systems, and other tutoring systems. *Educational Psychologist, 46*(4), 197–221.

Vodanovich, S. J., Wallace, J. C., & Kass, S. J. (2005). A confirmatory approach to the factor structure of the Boredom Proneness Scale: Evidence for a two-factor short form. *Journal of Personality Assessment, 85*(3), 295–303.

Watson, D., & Clark, L. A. (1994). Emotions, moods, traits, and temperaments: Conceptual distinctions and empirical findings. In P. Ekman & J. Davidson (Eds.), *The nature of emotion: Fundamental questions* (pp. 89–93). New York: Oxford University Press.

Weiner, B. (1986). *An attributional theory of motivation and emotion.* New York: Springer.

Woolf, B. (2009). *Building intelligent interactive tutors.* Burlington, MA: Morgan Kaufmann Publishers.

Woolf, B., Arroyo, I., Muldner, K., Burleson, W., Cooper, D., Dolan, R., & Christopherson, R. (2010). The effect of motivational learning companions on low achieving students and students with disabilities In J. Kay & V. Aleven (Eds.), *Proceedings of the 10th international conference on intelligent tutoring systems* (pp. 327–337). Berlin and Heidelberg: Springer.

Woolf, B., Burleson, W., Arroyo, I., Dragon, T., Cooper, D., & Picard, R. (2009). Affect-aware tutors: Recognizing and responding to student affect. *International Journal of Learning Technology, 4*(3/4), 129–163.

Zeidner, M. (2007). Test anxiety in educational contexts: Concepts, findings, and future directions. In P. Schutz & R. Pekrun (Eds.), *Emotions in Education* (pp. 165–184). San Diego, CA: Academic Press.

Zeng, Z., Pantic, M., Roisman, G., & Huang, T. (2009). A survey of affect recognition methods: Audio, visual, and spontaneous expressions. *IEEE Transactions on Pattern Analysis and Machine Intelligence, 31*(1), 39–58.

Enhancing Informal Learning Experiences with Affect-Aware Technologies

H. Chad Lane

Abstract

Institutions of informal learning often seek to influence interest, attitudes, and feelings about the topics they address. The quality of visitor experiences depend on many factors, including the content of the exhibits, the ability of exhibits to promote sustained engagement, and the nature of the conversations visitors have with each other and staff. This chapter discusses the role of emotions during informal learning experiences and how affect-aware technologies could be used to enhance cognitive and affective outcomes. Four potential application areas are presented: (1) automation of evaluation tasks for informal learning, (2) sparking visitors' interest and magnifying the attracting power of exhibits, (3) deepening engagement during learning activities, and (4) promoting productive conversational behaviors in groups as well as single visitors (with virtual agents). Key challenges ahead include the development of robust detection algorithms, addressing privacy concerns, tracking visitors beyond single exhibits, and integrating heterogeneous sources of information into useful estimates of visitors' knowledge, emotions, and goals.

Key Words: informal learning, engagement, affect-aware technologies, evaluation

Introduction

It is now widely acknowledged that learning is an emotional process. In schools or workplace training programs, those emotions often emerge in pursuit of goals put in place by some outside authority, such as a teacher or certification program. Further, attainment of such goals is usually dependent on performance on tests or other quantifiable measures of competence. In a way, students are almost "captive" to these goals, both in the sense that they are assigned and in whether they are achieved. In the language of motivation, learners are set up to pursue *extrinsic rewards*, which position learning as a means to the end of receiving a good grade or earning a piece of paper declaring achievement. Most research on the role of emotions in learning occurs in formal contexts like these, where emotions are emergent and the unspoken goal of the educator (or software) is to "minimize the pain" associated with learning.

Of course learning does not occur only in formal settings and the motivations for learning vary greatly. In reality, we learn continuously throughout our lives: It is estimated that through the age of 17, we spend only 18.5% of our waking hours in school (Bell, Lewenstein, Shouse, & Feder, 2009, pp. 28–29). Although time spent in formal learning environments drops dramatically after this, the idea that learning is somehow reserved for schools is outdated. Indeed, studies on brain plasticity and cognitive aging confirm that it is beneficial and even pleasurable to engage in intellectual activities throughout life, gain new skills, and pursue continuous personal growth (Greenwood, 2007; Hultsch, Hertzog, Small, & Dixon, 1999).

Modern theories of learning are beginning to incorporate these more nuanced perspectives. One such characterization brings together

(1) "implicit" processes in the brain (normally outside of our conscious awareness), (2) formal learning experiences, and (3) informal learning experiences (Bransford et al., 2006). Furthermore, thinking and learning are no longer assumed be solely cognitive activities. Deep links have been uncovered between emotions and cognition, reasoning, and decision making in general (Blanchette & Richards, 2009), so it is unsurprising that emotions have also been shown to play key roles in both the acquisition of new knowledge and in people's ability to manage their own learning (Calvo & D'Mello, 2011).

This chapter considers the role that emotions play in informal learning environments such as museums, science centers, and zoos. These institutions of learning are *designed* to promote understanding, conversation, and positive attitudes about their content. Importantly, *choice* plays a key role in all phases of the experience: visitors decide *what* to see, *when* to engage, and *how* long to stay.[1] Emotions play a key role in each of these decisions, so the best activities tend to take emotional factors into consideration. Because of these choices, learners tend to have more opportunities for self-directed learning than they are used to in formal settings. This means if an experience is not judged to be of value or sufficiently interesting, learners will simply disengage or seek other activities. There are no inherent consequences for this choice, as there are in formal learning situations (e.g., a poor grade). Thus creating and maintaining learner *engagement* is fundamental to the success of designed learning spaces. The purpose of this chapter is to explore the application of user sensing and affect-aware technologies to promote engagement and, more generally, increase the power of designed learning spaces to achieve their goals. Of course, to do this well it is important to understand the role of emotions in informal learning, how it differs from other learning contexts, and how this understanding can be leveraged in principled ways.

The Emotional and Social Contexts of Informal Learning

Visitors who walk into museums, science centers, and zoos[2] are instantly thrust into a position of choice. They have to first decide *how* to navigate—should they be spontaneous and impulsive? Or should they get a map and systematically work through the space? Once on their way, more decisions await: when to stop, how long to stay in one

place, and when to engage in conversations. On top of all of this, the decisions are usually negotiated with friends and family, who may or may not share common preferences. Of course these decisions are not necessarily consciously deliberated, and part of the charm of informal learning is precisely this prominent positioning of choice (Falk & Dierking, 2002). In this section, we discuss the context of these choices by briefly describing the motivations for museum visits, what is involved in "free choice" learning, and typical desired outcomes for informal science learning.

Why Do People Go to Museums?

Falk and Dierking (2000) posit that humans are fundamentally seekers and makers of meaning. They refer to a "knowledge-thirsty public" and point out that in 1970, only 1 in 10 Americans visited museums regularly, while in 2000, that number increased to between 5 or 6 (p. 2). To understand the cognitive and emotional processes involved in informal learning activities, it is first important to know why people choose to pursue them. To answer this question, Moussouri conducted a large-scale study of museum visitors, asking them for the reasons behind their visit (1997). Perhaps unsurprisingly, visitors gave a wide range of responses:

• Many cited educational and entertainment goals, such as a desire to learn or have an enjoyable day.
• Many referred to social desires, such as to be with friends, children, and family.
• Some suggested that it was because of the "place"—to be the kind of person who goes to museums.
• Finally, some gave practical reasons (e.g., "it was raining that day" or "the location was convenient").

Other researchers have suggested that social motivations seem to be the primary force behind the decision to visit a museum. Perry (2012) summarizes by saying "for the most part, museum visits seem to be driven by a social agenda" and qualifies by adding that learning is "a highly valued characteristic of museum settings." The observation that museum experiences are simultaneously social and educational is critical for the design of effective learning experiences. Tensions need not exist between these goals: It is best to view the shared goals of learning (by visitors to the museum) as a vehicle for enabling the achievement of social goals.

Free-Choice Learning

Free-choice learning is a broad term that positions the learner firmly in the center of his or her own educational choices. Falk and Dierking (2002) suggest that free-choice learning by definition "involves a strong measure of choice—choice over what, why, where, when, and how we will learn." They go on to describe it as "self-directed, voluntary, and guided by individual needs and interests" (Falk & Dierking, 2002, p. 9). In its full sense, free choice describes learning decisions made throughout life, such as how to use the Internet, which books to read, what television shows to watch, what to visit when vacationing, and so on.

The power of free-choice learning is that it leads to *intrinsically motivated* activities. These are activities that people find inherently interesting or beneficial and that they engage in for no reason other than the activity itself (Deci & Ryan, 1985). *Extrinsic motivation*, on the other hand, requires an external source of the motivation to engage, such as a grade or financial reward. Whether or not an activity is deemed intrinsically motivating is entirely determined by the person doing the activity, but the provision of choice, as well as the context of a learner having made a choice, has been found to dramatically increase intrinsic motivation as well as learning (Cordova & Lepper, 1996).

An overarching goal for informal learning institutions, therefore, is to provide experiences that have value in and of themselves—visitors should *choose* to engage in learning activities because they find them inherently satisfying. The emotions a visitor experiences during learning have a profound impact on whether or not such satisfaction is achieved. Clearly free-choice learning is a concept that is ubiquitous in our lives and reflects the affordances of modern technologies such as easy Internet access and the widespread use of mobile technologies. While the focus of this chapter is on designed spaces for informal learning, it is nonetheless valuable to consider this broader context and speculate that positive experiences in designed spaces might translate to more general habits associated with lifelong learning.

Desired Outcomes of Informal Science Education

What should people take away from a visit to a museum? How do we want the experience to change them? While formal learning environments typically focus on knowledge gains as the most important outcome, informal learning often seeks broader impacts. The National Science Foundation (NSF) in the United States, for example, requires funded projects to apply a framework for evaluating informal science education technologies that incorporates affective dimensions as well as knowledge (Friedman, 2008). Specifically, NSF proposes five categories: *awareness, knowledge or understanding; engagement or interest; attitude, behavior,* and *skills* (Table 32.1).

Projects are required to articulate the desired impacts of a program, such as an exhibit or after-school activity, and align them with these categories. For example, an exhibit on the respiratory system may have the knowledge/understanding goal to teach visitors that oxygen is absorbed by the lungs while carbon dioxide is expelled by them. In addition, it might seek a behavioral impact to reduce the occurrence of smoking in the life of a visitor. Museums and science centers also often seek to provide "sparks" for young learners—to inspire them to pursue careers in science, technology, engineering, and math (STEM). For NSF, a long-term mission is to increase the number of college students who pursue STEM degrees as well as the number of people entering the workforce with competency in STEM-related skills (National Research Council, 2011).

Of course, changing attitudes or behavior is an extremely tall order, especially for museum exhibitions. The typical "holding time" for an exhibit is exceedingly brief by formal learning standards: Visitors are generally expected to spend less than 4 minutes at an exhibit (Falk & Dierking, 2000).[3] Complicating things even further, a phenomenon known as "museum fatigue" settles in after about 30 minutes of deep engagement with exhibits (Davey, 2005; Falk, Koran, Dierking, & Dreblow, 1985). Visitors are said to "cruise" after this initial—and very precious—period of engagement, severely reducing further opportunities to produce any long-term impacts.

So the windows of opportunity are brief, and informal learning spaces need to be carefully designed to achieve their goals. Ultimately, solving societal problems such as interest in STEM and changing attitudes about important topics, for example, transcends any single exhibition or informal learning opportunity. Although the burden is not assumed to be entirely on informal learning, it is widely regarded as a critical part of solving national challenges related to education. What is most important for the purposes of this chapter is the observation that when designed informal

Table 32.1 NSF Impact Categories for Informal Science Education

Impact Category	Description
Awareness, knowledge, or understanding	What a participant in an informal science learning activity consciously knows, whether it is during, immediately after, or long after the experience.
Engagement or interest	How an experience affects a participant in terms of excitement for a topic or involvement in the activity or a related activity.
Attitude	Captures long-term changes in THE perspective of a participant as he or she relates to a topic, group of people, theories, or careers. Projects may strive to help participants formulate attitudes (where none existed) or adjust existing attitudes.
Behavior	Encompasses the choices and actions of participants over time and often relates to everyday activities. Many projects that focus on behavior focus on environmental or health concerns.
Skills	Focuses on the procedural aspects of knowledge, such as engaging in scientific inquiry, problem solving, or acting creatively.

Source: Friedman, 2008, pp. 21–24.

experiences seek to influence a visitor's attitude or behavior, affective concerns gain a heightened level of importance.

Designing and Building Engaging Informal Learning Exhibits

Like any instructional design activity, it is important to design informal learning experiences, such as those available at museums, based on sound principles of learning and engagement. This section briefly summarizes the context of museum learning and discusses what it means to be engaged in a learning activity.

A Simple Model of Learning in Designed Spaces

Informal learning educators have embraced the notion that visitors to museums are not to be treated as "receivers" of knowledge but rather as active and engaged learners who construct their own knowledge. A substantial amount of research has been devoted to developing models of informal learning as well as identifying design principles that promote this constructivist view of learning (Falk & Dierking, 2000; Perry, 2012). For example, an established approach for reducing early disengagement from an interactive exhibit is to design for *immediate apprehendability*. This principle states that exhibits should use simple interfaces, leverage familiar ideas and controls, and give immediate feedback that allows visitors to self-monitor and observe changes (Allen, 2007). Deterring frustration, especially when it is due to a lack of usability,

is essential as a visitor is making a judgment about the exhibit's potential value.

As mentioned earlier, visitors are confronted with choices throughout their informal learning experience in a museum. To frame the discussion below, we consider a simplified model of a typical visit to a museum. The model includes three basic phases:

1. *Arrival*: The moment a visitor enters (or reenters) a space that has multiple learning choices available. This can be a specialized area of a museum (e.g., that focuses on a specific discipline or topic) or the entire space.

2. *Navigation*: When the visitor walks around the space (either impulsively or systematically), evaluating the potential value of exhibits and making "stop" decisions. A stop is likely the result of an underlying curiosity or some other "hook."

3. *Experience*: After a visitor has decided to engage an exhibit, the visitor is in the driver's seat to have the intended learning experience. Typically, designers hope that visitors stay engaged long enough to achieve the intended outcome and feel satisfied. It is considered a lost opportunity if the visitor leaves abruptly.

Upon deciding to disengage from a specific exhibit, the visitor loops back to make the choice about what to do next. This outer loop can end for any number reasons, such as having explored the full space, boredom, or social pressures to leave.

Missing from this very simplified model are the social elements of the experience, but they are

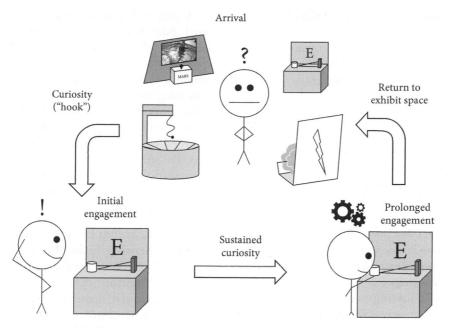

Arrival

Curiosity
("hook")

Return to
exhibit space

!

Initial
engagement

Sustained
curiosity

Prolonged
engagement

Fig. 32.1 A simple model of unguided navigation behavior in museums. The visitor identifies Exhibit E, navigates to it, engages with it, and then returns to the space to decide on his or her next activity.

critical. For example, a decision to stop is often due to someone else in a party stopping or asking to stop. Furthermore, exhibits are rarely designed for a single visitor (despite the situation shown in Figure 32.1)—it is precisely the social interactions that are often responsible for much of the learning that occurs (Leinhardt & Knutson, 2004). User-sensing and affect-aware technologies have the potential to dramatically improve the quality of these conversations. We return to this notion later.

What Does It Mean to Be Engaged?

The idea of being engaged in or achieving engagement can apply on a number of levels. Broadly, it can be used to indicate interest or simply a desire to know more about a topic. In terms of outcomes, the NSF states that impacts in the engagement category should seek to "capture the excitement and involvement of participants in a topic, area, or aspect of STEM" (Friedman, 2008, p. 22). An example of an indicator of an engagement outcome is whether or not a visitor pursues additional information related to his or her experience at a later time. Another window into understanding visitor engagement is to analyze visitors' timing and movement patterns, especially between variable layouts and designs for the same content (Yalowitz & Bronnenkant, 2009). Although these are certainly important indicators, for the purposes of this chapter, we drill down into

the more moment-to-moment aspects of engagement. Although increasing holding time is not universally ideal, we adopt the goal of maximizing the educational quality of the several minutes of time available during a single exhibit visit. If that also translates into extending the stay time, it is difficult to view this as a bad outcome for an individual or small group, at least.

Engagement in an activity can be unpacked in a number of ways depending on the nature, context, and goals of the activity. In a multidisciplinary review of empirical studies about the concept, O'Brien and Toms (2008) propose that engagement consists of four distinct stages: (1) the point of engagement, (2) sustained engagement, (3) disengagement, and (4) reengagement. With respect to learning, education researchers often draw a distinction between three different categories of engagement, although the specific meanings vary between communities and are not widely agreed upon[4] (Christenson, Reschly, & Wylie, 2012; Fredricks, Blumenfeld, & Paris, 2004):

1. *Behavioral*: Deep and meaningful involvement in learning activities, such as persistence, concentration, question asking, and making contributions
2. *Emotional*: Marked by learners' "affective reactions to the activity, such as interest, boredom,

happiness, sadness, and anxiety" (Fredricks et al., 2004, p. 63).

3. *Cognitive:* Deliberate use of cognitive resources, such as memory and reasoning skills (e.g., problem solving); also includes use of self-regulated learning strategies

It is worth noting that other researchers have articulated more precise categories that account for additional factors such as motivation and social behaviors (Pekrun & Linnenbrink-Garcia, 2012). Related to these, the notion of *conversational engagement* refers to the depth and quality of interactions between visitors and museum staff (Leinhardt & Knutson, 2004). For informal learning contexts, the general aim is to promote on-topic conversations that suggest the coconstruction of knowledge and enjoyment of the experience.

An elaborate investigation into engagement was conducted in the early 2000s at the Exploratorium in San Francisco. The resulting model, known as active prolonged engagement (APE), sought to balance the needs of providing visitor-driven, open-ended experiences with the goal of conveying knowledge and understanding about STEM topics (Humphrey, Gutwill, & Exploratorium APE Team, 2005). They sought to position visitors as participants rather than recipients, for them to ask and answer their own questions, and to stay actively engaged for longer periods of time. Although holding time is not widely agreed upon as a conclusive measure of engagement, studies conducted by the APE team found it to be correlated with other measures of learning (p. 9). Based on hundreds of hours of recordings of visitors and interview data as well as a wide variety of different designs, the team found that people would leave APE exhibits because of external factors (such as others in their group wanting to go) rather than thinking that they had reached the "end."

Thus APE exhibits that were mostly *open ended*, with no obvious stopping point, were the most effective. In a related finding, the provision of a variety of actions at every point—rather than an experience "on rails"—led to deeper engagement. Giving the visitor primary control over an informal learning experience is a key part of the APE formula. APE principles also encompass groups and social interactions. Exhibits that offered multiple interaction stations that allowed several visitors to use an exhibit simultaneously, perhaps to pursue a common objective, produced higher levels of conversational engagement and interaction.

A great deal of design knowledge has accumulated about how to design effective and engaging exhibits. Visits to museums have steadily increased over the last several decades; therefore research must continue to focus on efficacy and design. In the remaining sections, we outline one possible contributor to this goal by discussing the possibility of *adaptive* exhibits: those that can sense and change based on what it is detected or known about visitors. The idea of personalized education is a widely recognized grand challenge (Woolf, 2010), and there are many reasons to include informal learning in the conversation.

Adaptive Learning Environments and User Sensing Technologies

According to Shute and Zapata-Rivera, "Adaptive educational systems monitor important learner characteristics and make appropriate adjustments to the instructional milieu to support and enhance learning" (2012, p. 7). The assumption is that not all learners are the same and that learning experiences should be designed with learners' needs and progress in mind. Shute and Zapata-Rivera propose a four-phase model (p. 9):

1. *Capture:* Gather input about the learner, whether it be cognitive (about problems being solved, for example) or physical (such as from user sensing).

2. *Analyze:* Infer estimates of the learner's knowledge, emotions, motivations, and so on. This step involves the maintenance of a learner model.

3. *Select:* Choose information that is best for a learner given the system's current estimate of his or her knowledge, emotions, etc.

4. *Present:* Convey the selected content to the learner using available and appropriate technologies.

Although much of the work on adaptive educational systems has focused on the goals of formal learning, there is promise to generalize and extend these approaches to informal contexts. Hardware and software approaches now exists to reliably identify human forms, track movement, and classify emotional states (see Part 2 of this handbook). For example, the depth-sensing Kinect camera, built by PrimeSense and marketed by Microsoft, changed the nature of home video consoles by allowing video game players to use their own bodies as controllers. Newer generations of the camera will have enhanced capabilities for face recognition, eye tracking, and even estimating heart rate.

User sensing technologies most suitable for use in museums are those that can be used unobtrusively and that impose no requirements on the part of visitors. Privacy concerns are nontrivial and the use of such technologies presents significant societal challenges for us all. It may very well be that museums choose to not adopt such technologies based on these concerns (although they have been around for decades in the form of security cameras). In this discussion, however, we focus on affective dimensions that are detectable by technologies such as vision (e.g., cameras), sound (e.g., microphones), location tracking (e.g., GPS, radio-frequency identification [RFID]), and built-in physiological sensors (e.g., pressure grips, posture detectors). Although museums are often noisy and active environments, we assume that enough meaningful detection of emotions would still be possible. More importantly, if exhibits were able to *adaptively* present information based on estimates of the visitor's emotions or, even better, adjust the complexity or behavior of an exhibit's function, it is likely that more visitors would have engaging and powerful experiences.

The application of adaptive learning technologies for designed spaces is a relatively recent development. For example, if someone's "visiting style" can be inferred, it is possible to present information in more digestible ways for him or her (Antoniou & Lepouras, 2010). The next step is to seek to automate these learner modeling tasks and adaptation approaches. Our first example application area in the next section focuses on using only the inputs of user sensing hardware (for evaluation purposes), but the following three sections explore the idea of exhibits that adapt, predict, and seek to create more meaningful informal learning experiences for visitors.

Some Opportunities to Enhance Informal Learning

Although many museums have embraced advanced learning technologies, especially to increase the overall level of interactivity of their exhibits, only a few projects have sought to directly personalize learning experiences based on visitor behaviors. Researchers in Germany, for example, showed that adaptive presentation of information on a mobile device (used to track the location of visitors) led to increased awareness of learning goals and produced corresponding gains in knowledge (Mayr, Zahn, & Hesse, 2007). Similarly, researchers at the Exploratorium in San Francisco used RFID tracking technology to provide personalized content via the web (for viewing later) based on visitor exhibit visiting patterns (Hsi & Fait, 2005). These examples provide an important foundation for the idea of adaptive exhibits. So how might affect-aware technologies help solve the same kinds of informal learning challenges? How could exhibits enhance engagement when visitors' emotional states can be inferred? This section explores several possible uses of affect-detection technologies for informal learning that, quite plausibly, could be implemented with today's hardware and automatic classification techniques.

Application Area 1: Automating Evaluations

The first and most straightforward use of user- and affect-sensing technologies involves the automation of activities normally performed by evaluators. For example, to capture holding times, evaluators normally stand off to the side and manually record arrival and departure times for individuals and groups at an exhibit as well as a great deal of behavioral information like buttons pressed, signs read, and so on. It is relatively straightforward to use depth-sensing cameras to automate the detection of the arrival and departure of visitors, their number, and general demographic information (e.g., child, young teen, adult). A number of researchers have explored the use of video recordings to automatically supply such data (Ross & Lukas, 2005). With a live connection, this information could even be made available on a real-time basis for essentially all museum visitors and all exhibits equipped with a camera.

More interestingly, though, recent advances in affect detection could provide a far more detailed, real-time analysis of visitor behaviors. For example, head-tracking algorithms are now robust enough to reliably identify behaviors like nodding, smiling, and change of gaze (Morency, Sidner, Lee, & Darrell, 2005), which could all be mapped into outcome categories. Nodding and smiling, for example, would indicate agreement, understanding, and generally positive emotions. On the other hand, frustration, frowning, and head shaking would suggest the opposite (at least in the United States). Such data would help evaluators to track the general impact of exhibits over time and across categories, and it would not require a human to be present during any phase of the data collection. For the day-to-day operation of a museum, a sudden change in the emotions associated with an exhibit might suggest that something had gone wrong (e.g., a component missing or broken). It is important to note that even if the sensing technology failed from time to time because of changes in lighting or occlusion, for example, the large amount of available and accurate data would still likely have some use.

It is easy to imagine other uses for evaluation using the other available technologies. Microphones could be used to detect conversations, even if the words could not be fully recognized. Detecting *meaningful* conversations would be a taller order but perhaps still not out of the question by identifying keywords related to the exhibit and other words related to process, cause-effect, and other sense-making clue words (i.e., deep natural language understanding would not be needed to detect explanatory evidence in conversations). Of course, emotional cues would also be detectable from speech patterns, such as frustration, anger, or excitement. When combined with visual cues, the models could be made more precise. Beyond speech and vision, if an exhibit used buttons, joysticks, or chairs, they could be equipped with pressure sensors that could inform evaluators about how "rough" people were being or how engaged they might be based on their physical position and posture (D'Mello & Graesser, 2009).

Clearly there are weaknesses with the automated detection of visitor behaviors and emotions, but the technologies and approaches are robust enough to begin to ease the burden of evaluation for evaluation professionals (which is substantial). Further, there are many shared goals for evaluators and systems that track engagement, as we will see in application area 3: sustained engagement.

Application Area 2: Sparking Interest and Acquiring the Visitor's Attention

As the visitor approaches an exhibit, the first few seconds are critical as to whether he or she decides to invest some time and engage more deeply. As mentioned, design principles, such as immediate apprehendability (Allen, 2007) and the provision of simple and direct instructions (Perry, 2012) can make a substantial difference during this *initial engagement* (see Figure 32.1). Visitors make rapid judgments of the potential value of exhibits—they quickly assess the look, usability, and content of exhibits to decide whether they should invest more effort. The incoming state and properties of the visitor (or visitors) likely play a big role in predicting the choice to engage or not (Falk et al., 1985).

The key research question, then, is: How might the initial presentation of content or appearance of the exhibit be adapted based on initial assessments of detected visitors' emotional (or other) states?

The *select* phase of an adaptive system is responsible for prescribing initial instruction (Shute & Zapata-Rivera, 2012). Of course that decision can draw from any number of dimensions resolved during the brief *capture* and *analyze* phases. For example, if the exhibit addresses a topic of less inherent interest to a particular visitor, there is likely a lower threshold for disengagement. In this case, it may make sense to present a narrative or emotionally compelling example in an effort to appeal to the visitor's emotions and stir up interest. Alternatively, the exhibit could provide a quick hook in the form of a surprising scientific fact or demonstration. The number of possibilities are obviously constrained by the exhibit itself, but a simple computer monitor could provide a wide range of possibilities, such as short videos, different texts and images, or even a helpful pedagogical agent to activate social obligations. On the other hand, for visitors who display high initial interest or curiosity (e.g., smiling, leaning forward, or concentrating), the system may be able to assume that this person will have more patience and be motivated to engage. Such visitors may be anxious to dive into the details more quickly and thus there may be less need to deliver motivation-inducing content. These are hypotheses that would need to be investigated, of course, and affect-detection technologies could play a key role in conducting such studies to see whether adaptive changes do increase the number of visitors who choose to engage, for how long, and to what end.

Application Area 3: Sustaining Engagement

As discussed earlier, engagement is a rich concept that involves behavior, emotions, and cognition. Attempts to strengthen engagement benefit by addressing all three categories as well as the interactions between them. Although the application of good design principles can promote engagement (Humphrey et al., 2005; Perry, 2012), it is not at all clear that a ceiling has been reached in terms of the depth and quality of engagement possible in informal learning environments. In fact, sustained engagement is often associated with highly pleasurable and engulfing experiences sometimes referred to as *flow* states that carefully balance challenge with skill level (Csíkszentmihályi, 1991). A variety of measures have been proposed and validated for assessing and tracking flow, including some that distinguish between different flavors and properties of flow experiences (Martin & Jackson, 2008). Despite the controversy surrounding formal definitions of flow, notions of *task absorption* and engagement share important similarities that may provide theoretical guidance on how to leverage user-sensing technologies for adaptive informal learning experiences.

Unfortunately it is unclear whether flow is always desirable in learning contexts. For example, several studies have demonstrated the value of confusion during learning (D'Mello et al., 2010), which is not normally considered a pleasurable state. Reaching a confused state implies that some learning has occurred—it is a normal developmental stage on the way to deep understanding. The risk with confusion, of course, is that it may persist for too long and devolve into frustration, a key trigger for disengagement. James Gee, using a different sense of the word, has described good games as being "pleasantly frustrating" because they can motivate players to seek to learn more than the bare minimum needed for success (Gee, 2003). As a final example of why flow may not always be the ideal construct for learning, when experts are engaged in deliberate practice, they have been found to purposely avoid flow states in order to perfect their skills and maintain growth (Ericsson & Ward, 2007). In this case, it is a matter of experts not wanting to "get too comfortable" and desiring to understand and correct their weaknesses.

In terms of adapting an exhibit to promote sustained engagement, the availability of a monitor or speakers would make it possible to deliver appropriate help messages to a visitor or group of visitors with the goal of promoting their involvement. If feasible, an exhibit could also be equipped with an intelligent tutoring system to monitor user actions and provide guidance at appropriate times via a pedagogical agent (Lane, Noren, Auerbach, Birch, & Swartout, 2011). In the case of confusion, there may be a limited window of time in which to support resolution of the confusion and prevent disengagement, so it is critical to ensure that issued challenges are at the right level of difficulty. This could even be influenced by estimated ages of visitors based on height or other detectable physical traits. If the experiences are virtual, it may even be possible to adjust the corresponding simulations on the fly to further increase or decrease difficulty as needed (Lane & Johnson, 2009).

Returning again to museum fatigue, although generally believed to have a detrimental impact on visitors' choices, learning, and experience (Davey, 2005), significant open questions remain regarding its causes and effects and the best strategies for amelioration (Bitgood, 2009). If museum fatigue is detected, it may be beneficial to proactively adjust the level of challenge and depth of content to increase the chances of at least limited forms of engagement. In other words, assuming that cognitive processing is a contributor to museum fatigue, it would suggest that a fatigued visitor approaching a new exhibit might be less willing or even unable to accept complex content.

Application Area 4: Promoting Productive Conversations

Conversations between museum visitors and with staff play a critical role during visits to museums (Leinhardt & Knutson, 2004). As mentioned, the quality of these conversations often predicts how much learning occurs and whether affective outcomes are achieved (see Perry, 2012, for an extended discussion of the social nature of learning in designed spaces). How might an adaptive exhibit adjust its presentation to promote such conversations?

Conversational behaviors of groups can vary dramatically based on the makeup of the group, such as age and relationships. Extensive studies of group behaviors at exhibits have uncovered some expected and unexpected results (McManus, 1987, 1988). For example, singletons tend to read signage to a high degree, whereas groups with children spent most of their time in conversations and not reading except for occasional glances to support conversational goals. Groups of adults, interestingly, tended not to engage in exhibits as deeply, whereas couples had lower levels of conversation and read more extensively. McManus's findings are interesting in suggesting that the makeup of a group is a reliable predictor of the way its members will use an exhibit. Thus if a vision system could classify a group as it approached and used monitors to present information accordingly, the system could adaptively present the same information in different ways. For example, a group with children could provide with shorter nuggets of information that might be useful to the adults as the interacted with the children. If the exhibit were able also to track actions being taken, this information could easily be aligned with the group's activities (e.g., by providing explanations at appropriate times during the interaction).

Moving beyond these basic categories, modern sensing technologies are also able to recognize nonverbal cues for understanding, such as head-nodding behaviors (Morency et al., 2005). Combining these inputs with detected speech (regardless of understanding) could enable even richer models of conversations occurring at exhibits. In essence, exhibits could be aware of (1) if visitors are talking about the desired content and (2) the general tone and attitude of the conversational participants. An exhibit that could classify the conversations taking place along these lines could adjust its operation, such as providing information on lower screens specifically tailored for younger visitors. If completely off-topic conversations were detected (which could likely be inferred by combinations of gaze and speech patterns), the exhibit could seek to gain the attention of the visitors by presenting a surprise, adjusting lighting, or making attention-grabbing sounds. Of course, if the exhibit were inhabited by a pedagogical agent, this agent could attempt to draw the group in through humor or intrigue. The social affordances of an agent could also lead to interesting modes of reflection on the experience and possibly adjusting behavior based on conversations judged as negative or positive. A generally negative conversation might lead to an interaction on how to improve the exhibit, or a positive one could focus on what was best and why. The idea of a "self-modifying" exhibit based on large datasets could quickly open up the techniques of educational data mining to informal learning.

Challenges and Future Research

Although the last decade has seen tremendous progress in user-sensing technologies, there are still many fundamental problems that need to be addressed. Most importantly, many informal learning institutions are loud and busy environments that pose significant challenges for speech, vision, and affect detection in general. As the field progresses, these environments represent intriguing opportunities to test the robustness and fault tolerance of new algorithms. The primary goal of adaptive educational systems is to be responsive to individual differences between learners; therefore improvements in affect detection technologies will lead to an improved ability to adapt. The vision to build "adaptive museums" represents a new set of challenges for user modeling, intelligent learning environments, and informal education research.

The key to adaptive systems lies in their ability to model learners as accurately and appropriately as possible. This is extraordinarily difficult in a museum setting: Visitors come with different agendas and widely different backgrounds; they are often members of groups and have very brief learning experiences. Physically tracking individual learners around a museum is possible with RFID or GPS technologies, but it is not easy to make accurate inferences about their learning, interests, or emotions from these data alone. Thus a key challenge lies in interpreting multiple, heterogeneous sources of inputs into a reasonable model that can feed an adaptive system. The task of mapping these often very different clues into estimates of visitors' emotions, thinking, and goals presents brand new directions for informal learning research.

Of course visitors do not enter museums as blank slates. Having some understanding of the backgrounds or incoming knowledge of visitors points to the need for lifelong and sharable learner models (Kay, 2008). Thus a visitor attending a museum would need to proactively share his or her learner model (only the relevant parts) so that personalized information could be provided, either via a mobile device or actually at the exhibits themselves. Of course privacy must be respected, so museums would need to provide for visitors who are neither willing to be identified nor to share their information with the traditional "one-size-fits-all" approach historically used. On the other hand, museums very often have membership arrangements with local visitors, and such existing relationships may engender higher levels of trust. Exhibits could recognize return visits and provide them with adapted experiences that reflect prior exposure to the topics.

Ultimately the success of a designed informal learning space depends on the quality of the experiences that visitors have. In this chapter we have argued that emotions play a big role in the decisions visitors make and that affect-aware technologies can be used to enhance these experiences. Although we have focused on the very specific challenge of designing interactive exhibits—and promoted the use of digital technologies to increase the level of possible adaptivity—there is a much larger view of informal learning to address. "Free-choice" learning involves choices made throughout life. A visit to a museum, science center, or zoo is an educator's opportunity to highlight the joys of learning and the value of self-improvement. We want visitors to not only gain a little knowledge and maybe change their behaviors but also to leave as better decision makers. In the pursuit of more deeply engaging experiences, sometimes the goal of "entertaining" visitors, rather than educating them, can threaten learning (Shortland, 1987). But in the end, learning, changing, and feeling go hand in hand. Therefore it makes sense to always design with these aims in mind and to leverage the full capabilities of modern technology to achieve society's educational goals.

Notes

1. Although many informal learning institutions support formal learning goals, such as offering field trips and special lectures for groups of students, the most common category of use is that of a small group, like a family, visiting during open hours and self-navigating their way through the space. This use case is the focus of this chapter.
2. We refer only to "museums" from here on but note that the implication is to include all open, designed informal learning spaces.
3. Holding times vary dramatically, of course, based on the nature of the exhibition as well as a long list of contextual variables, such as the social situation, motivation for being in the museum, and so on. The take-away message is that informal science educators who design for unguided, free exploration (the most common form of visit) think in terms of seconds and minutes rather than tens of minutes or hours.
4. Because of the goals of the chapter, these definitions focus again on the fine-grained aspects of engagement and draw from the cognitive psychological perspective. In other academic circles, behavioral engagement has also been characterized as a willingness to follow rules, for example.

References

Allen, S. (2007). Exhibit design in science museums: Dealing with a constructivist dilemma. In J. Falk, L. Dierking & S. Foutz (Eds.), *In principle, in practice: Museums as learning institutions* (pp. 43–56). Lanham, MD: AltaMira Press.

Antoniou, A., & Lepouras, G. (2010). Modeling visitors' profiles: A study to investigate adaptation aspects for museum learning technologies. *Journal on Computing and Cultural Heritage*, 3(2), 1–19. doi: 10.1145/1841317.1841322

Bell, P., Lewenstein, B., Shouse, A., & Feder, M. (Eds.). (2009). *Learning science in informal environments: People, places, and pursuits*. Washington, DC: National Academy Press.

Bitgood, S. (2009). Museum fatigue: A critical review. *Visitor Studies*, 12(2), 93–111. doi: 10.1080/10645570903203406

Blanchette, I., & Richards, A. (2009). The influence of affect on higher level cognition: A review of research on interpretation, judgement, decision making and reasoning. *Cognition & Emotion*, 24(4), 561–595. doi: 10.1080/02699930903132496

Bransford, J. D., Barron, B., Pea, R. D., Meltzoff, A., Kuhl, P., Bell, P., ... Sabelli, N. H. (2006). Foundations and opportunities for an interdisciplinary science of learning. In R. K. Sawyer (Ed.), *The Cambridge handbook of the learning sciences* (pp. 19–34). New York: Cambridge University Press.

Calvo, R. A., & D'Mello, S. (2011). *New perspectives on affect and learning technologies*. New York and London: Springer.

Christenson, S., Reschly, A. L., & Wylie, C. (2012). *Handbook of research on student engagement*. New York: Springer.

Cordova, D. I., & Lepper, M. R. (1996). Intrinsic motivation and the process of learning: beneficial effects of contextualization, personalization, and choice. *Journal of Educational Psychology*, 88(4), 715–730.

Csíkszentmihályi, M. (1991). *Flow the psychology of optimal experience*. New York: HarperPerennial.

D'Mello, S. K., & Graesser, A. C. (2009). Automatic detection of learner's affect from gross body language. *Applied Artificial Intelligence*, 23(2), 123–150. doi: http://dx.doi.org/10.1080/08839510802631745

D'Mello, S., Lehman, B., Sullins, J., Daigle, R., Combs, R., Vogt, K., ... Graesser, A. (2010). A time for emoting: When affect-sensitivity is and isn't effective at promoting deep learning. In V. Aleven, J. Kay & J. Mostow (Eds.), *Intelligent tutoring systems* (Vol. 6094, pp. 245–254): Berlin and Heidelberg: Springer.

Davey, G. (2005). What is museum fatigue? *Visitor Studies Today*, 8(3), 17–21.

Deci, E. L., & Ryan, R. M. (1985). *Intrinsic motivation and self-determination in human behavior*. New York: Plenum.

Ericsson, K. A., & Ward, P. (2007). Capturing the naturally occurring superior performance of experts in the laboratory: Toward a science of expert and exceptional performance. *Current Directions in Psychological Science*, 16(6), 346–350. doi: 10.1111/j.1467-8721.2007.00533.x

Falk, J. H., & Dierking, L. D. (2000). *Learning from museums: Visitor experiences and the making of meaning*. Walnut Creek, CA: AltaMira Press.

Falk, J. H., & Dierking, L. D. (2002). *Lessons without limit: How free-choice learning is transforming education*. Walnut Creek, CA: AltaMira Press.

Falk, J. H., Koran, J. J., Dierking, L. D., & Dreblow, L. (1985). Predicting visitor behavior. *Curator: The Museum Journal*, 28(4), 249–258. doi: 10.1111/j.2151-6952.1985.tb01753.x

Fredricks, J. A., Blumenfeld, P. C., & Paris, A. H. (2004). School engagement: Potential of the concept, state of the evidence. *Review of Educational Research*, 74(1), 59–109. doi: 10.3102/00346543074001059

Friedman, A. J. (Ed.). (2008). *Framework for evaluating impacts of informal science education projects*. Arlington, VA: National Science Foundation.

Gee, J. P. (2003). *What video games have to teach us about learning and literacy*. New York: Palgrave MacMillan.

Greenwood, P. M. (2007). Functional plasticity in cognitive aging: Review and hypothesis. *Neuropsychology*, 21(6), 657–673. doi: 10.1037/0894-4105.21.6.657

Hsi, S., & Fait, H. (2005). RFID enhances visitors' museum experience at the Exploratorium. *Communications of the ACM*, 48(9), 60–65. doi: 10.1145/1081992.1082021

Hultsch, D. F., Hertzog, C., Small, B. J., & Dixon, R. A. (1999). Use it or lose it: Engaged lifestyle as a buffer of cognitive decline in aging? *Psychology and Aging*, 14(2), 245–263. doi: 10.1037/0882-7974.14.2.245

Humphrey, T., Gutwill, J. P., & Exploratorium APE Team. (2005). *Fostering active prolonged engagement*. Walnut Creek, CA: Left Coast Press.

Kay, J. (2008). Lifelong learner modeling for lifelong personalized pervasive learning. *IEEE Transactions on Learning Technologies*, 1(4), 215–228.

Lane, H. C., & Johnson, W. L. (2009). Intelligent tutoring and pedagogical experience manipulation in virtual learning environments. In D. Schmorrow, J. Cone & D. Nicholson (Eds.), *The handbook of virtual environments for training and education: VE components and training technologies* (Vol. 2, pp. 393–406). Westport, CT: Praeger Security International.

Lane, H. C., Noren, D., Auerbach, D., Birch, M., & Swartout, W. (2011). Intelligent tutoring goes to the museum in the big city: A pedagogical agent for informal science education. In G. Biswas & S. Bull (Eds.), *Artificial intelligence in education* (Vol. *6738*, pp. 155–162). Berlin and Heidelberg: Springer.

Leinhardt, G., & Knutson, K. (2004). *Listening in on museum conversations*. Walnut Creek, CA: AltaMira Press.

Martin, A., & Jackson, S. (2008). Brief approaches to assessing task absorption and enhanced subjective experience: Examining "short" and "core" flow in diverse performance domains. *Motivation and Emotion*, 32(3), 141–157. doi: 10.1007/s11031-008-9094-0

Mayr, E., Zahn, C., & Hesse, F. W. (2007). *Supporting information processing in museums with adaptive technology*. Paper presented at the Proceedings of the 29th Annual Cognitive Science Society. Nashville, TN.

McManus, P. M. (1987). It's the company you keep…: The social determination of learning—related behaviour in a science museum. *International Journal of Museum Management and Curatorship*, 6(3), 263–270. doi: 10.1080/09647778709515076

McManus, P. M. (1988). Good companions: More on the social determination of learning-related behaviour in a science museum. *International Journal of Museum Management and Curatorship*, 7(1), 37–44. doi: 10.1080/09647778809515102

Morency, L.-P., Sidner, C., Lee, C., & Darrell, T. (2005). *Contextual recognition of head gestures*. Paper presented at the Proceedings of the 7th international conference on Multimodal interfaces, Toronto, Italy.

Moussouri, T. (1997). Family agendas and family learning in hands-on museums. Doctoral dissertation. Leicester, UK: University of Leicester.

National Research Council. (2011). *Successful K-12 STEM Education: Identifying effective approaches in science, technology, engineering, and mathematics*. Washington, DC: The National Academies Press.

O'Brien, H. L., & Toms, E. G. (2008). What is user engagement? A conceptual framework for defining user engagement with technology. *Journal of the American Society for Information Science and Technology*, 59(6), 938–955. doi: 10.1002/asi.20801

Pekrun, R., & Linnenbrink-Garcia, L. (2012). Academic emotions and student engagement. In S. L. Christenson, A. L. Reschly & C. Wylie (Eds.), *Handbook of research on student engagement* (pp. 259–282). New York: Springer.

Perry, D. L. (2012). *What makes learning fun? Principles for the design of intrinsically motivating museum exhibits*. Lanham, MD: AltaMira Press.

Ross, S. R., & Lukas, K. E. (2005). Zoo visitor behavior at an African Ape exhibit. *Visitor Studies Today*, 8(1), 4–12.

Shortland, M. (1987). No business like show business. *Nature*, 328, 213–214.

Shute, V., & Zapata-Rivera, D. (2012). Adaptive educational systems. In P. Durlach & A. Lesgold (Eds.), *Adaptive technologies for training and education*. New York: Cambridge University Press.

Woolf, B. P. (2010). *A roadmap for education technology*. Washington, DC: National Science Foundation (NSF), Computing Community Consortium (CCC), & Computing Research Association (CRA).

Yalowitz, S. S., & Bronnenkant, K. (2009). Timing and tracking: Unlocking visitor behavior. *Visitor Studies*, 12(1), 47–64. doi: 10.1080/10645570902769134

Affect-Aware Reflective Writing Studios

Rafael A. Calvo

Abstract

Writing involves complex affective and cognitive processes highly influenced by the environments wherein we write, which are undergoing critical change. Today writing is typically performed using digital devices connected to the Internet, enabling writers to interact with content and with other people in new ways. This increased interconnectedness offers new opportunities as well as challenges. This chapter proposes a new type of tool, Reflective Writing Studios (RWS), which can be used to study writing phenomena in an encompassing way, taking into account the writer's physical and social surroundings and his or her emotions, mental states, and cognitive processes. The chapter introduces the architecture for an affect-aware multimodal interaction system, its components, and their evaluation. Two types of data are used: structured information about the activity and multimodal sensor data from the writer and the environment. This framework opens new avenues for research in terms of multimodal data collection and interpretation.

Key Words: writing, cognitive technologies, affective computing, ubiquitous computing, reflection

Introduction

Writing skills are required to varying degrees in all professional disciplines, not only as a method of communication but also as a catalyst for higher cognitive functions such as analysis and synthesis (Emig, 1977). Teaching writing is notoriously challenging, and the development of writing skills in learners at any level has been acknowledged as one of the biggest challenges in education (*The Neglected "R": The Need for a Writing Revolution*, 2003). The challenges are now compounded by the disruptive changes produced by ubiquitous new technologies. The Internet has become an external memory, changing the ways we remember the facts needed for writing (Sparrow, Liu, & Wegner, 2011); social networking changes the way we work, feel, and relate to others (as shown by a myriad of studies, some of which are described in this volume), and technologies designed to grab our attention (e.g.,

mobile phones) are embedded in the environments that surround us (Vertegaal, 2003). Although writing has rarely been done in complete isolation, new technologies are now interjected into all its underlying processes: cognitive, affective, and behavioral.

New tools and theories that help us understand the effect of these digital environments and help writers to cope with them are gaining urgency. Even before these new developments appeared, researchers acknowledged that writing environments had not helped to improve writing skills or learning (Pea & Kurland, 1987), instead focusing on improving productivity and presentation. This limitation was first raised soon after word processors became widely available (Pea & Kurland, 1987) and still applies.

These tools would use data about the writer and her or his environment. Current methods used to collect data about writing processes include methods to help understand behavior [screen capture, eye tracking, keystroke logging (Bixler & D'Mello, 2013; Wengelin et al., 2009)], qualitative methods, field and ethnographical studies that help understand the cultural and environmental conditions, natural language processing, and think-aloud protocols that help to elucidate, among other things, the subjective experience of writers. So far, analyzing the data collected through these methods requires a researcher's time and expertise, and this means that individual writers do not generally see, and benefit from, the outcome of such analysis.

The data can then be used to scaffold the writer's reflection about the process. Writers make a myriad of complex decisions regarding the composing activity (e.g., topic and argument), the reading, the environment and tools, the timing, and so forth. We argue that current sensing and affective computing techniques can be used gather empirical evidence for new writing theories and automated feedback that go beyond the document's quality features. Learning about these many issues requires reflection—particularly reflection in action (Schön, 1983)—as a transformative element. The literature on reflection is used as a framework for our proposal on how to build systems that help novice writers develop their skills. The human-computer interaction (HCI) community has used sensor data to create tools that support reflection—for example, in "personal informatics" (Sas & Dix, 2009). We aim to develop these ideas further and to contribute to the design of novel writing support tools.

Our research on RWS takes into account behavioral and emotional expressions. As often found in descriptions of learning interactions, such as the dialogues between a coach and student described by Schön (1983), the behavioral and emotional expressions of subjects are key to understanding the writing and reflection phenomena. For example, Schön (1983) describes how the learner may express "surprise" at something the coach says or mention the perceived approval or disapproval in the coach's voice. These emotional variables are being increasingly studied in the literature. Computer-based approaches to the detection of emotions and behavioral information are progressing rapidly (Calvo & D'Mello, 2010), specifically in the context of learning interactions (Calvo & D'Mello, 2011).

In Theoretical Perspectives (p. 448), we briefly discuss how different perspectives come together to inform the idea of RWS. These include (1) the cognitive process model of Flower and Hayes (1981); (2) the information processing model of Gailbraith (Torrance & Galbraith, 2006), (3) theories that focus on the social aspects or on the materiality of writing (Haas, 1995); and (4) the reflection and modeling processes of Schön and those who study the affective/emotional aspects of writing. In Theoretical Perspectives (p. 448) we also discuss a series of questions that a writer can reflect on. These include conceptions and motivation, the process and outcomes of the activity, the environment, mental states, and ancillary activities that arise during the activity. In System Design (p. 451) we describe the system architecture of our RWS and review four projects that form the key components of the system. The first one, iWrite, focuses on managing the writing activity (deadlines, topic and genre, group members—if collaborative), integrating tools for peer and tutor feedback, and providing disciplinary specific tutorials for the support of writing in different genres. This component covers the formal structure of the activity (i.e., what the tutor had planned). The second component represents an ongoing effort to build systems that collect extensive information about the computer-human interaction taking place while the user is writing. This component covers what actually happens during the activity and the aspects that the instructional design did not consider—for example, when the writer engages in extracurricular activities such as reading email. The third component is the engine that fuses the information sources from the above two. The fourth component provides the user interface with questions that scaffold the reflection and interactive visualizations generated from the data analyzed. In Discussion and Conclusions (p. 455) we discuss the results and forthcoming challenges.

Theoretical Perspectives

We ground our research program in the extensive literature at the intersection of writing research, psychology, and human-computer interaction. The theoretical models used to understand writing processes and the technologies that afford functionalities suggested by these models may be useful to researchers in other application domains, but comprehensive descriptions of these theories are beyond the scope of this chapter. We recommend, for example, the *Handbook of Writing Research* (MacArthur, Graham, & Fitzgerald, 2006) and the *Sage Handbook of Writing Development* (Beard & Riley, 2009). The most widely used models of writing since the 1980s are probably the cognitive models of writing (e.g., Flower & Hayes, 1981), which inform the design of functionalities found in today's word-processing tools, such as tools for writing outlines, an online thesaurus, and spell checkers. Debates about the human information processing limits and dual task interference have driven research into attentive computing. Socially situated models of writing were proposed to address the cognitive model's emphasis on the solitary author (Cooper, 1986). These models led some HCI researchers to develop social awareness tools (Dourish & Bellotti, 1992). Others have focused on the physical aspects of writing, such as the actual places and situations where writing takes place (Haas, 1995). HCI and ubiquitous computing researchers also use sensors to study the embodiment of cognition and how behavioral (Dourish, 2004) and physiological (Sharma, Pavlovic, & Huang, 1998) information can be used to improve computer interactions.

Grounded in a cross section of these theoretical frameworks, we have worked on supporting aspects of writing and issues that writers could reflect on, together with specific functionalities that RWS provide. Some of these elements arise before the writing activity has even begun and are driven by the literature on relational student learning (Marton & Booth, 1997) and motivation:

1. What is the purpose of this activity? (*Conceptions*)
2. How much effort do I need to invest? How likely am I to succeed? (*Metacognition and Motivation*)

Other questions are more closely related to the cognitive model and relate directly to the process and the outcomes of writing:

3. Have I addressed the requirements of the assignment? Covered the topics? Addressed the quality measures by which I will be assessed? (*Outcomes*)
4. How will I or did I complete the assignment? Should I Google this term? (*Process*)

A third group of questions refers to the context of the cognitive activities, the environment, and ancillary activities that surround the writing:

5. Should I work at home or in the café? Should I turn down the music? Should I turn off IM? (*Environment*)
6. Am I tired? Bored? Did I enjoy this task? (*Affective states*)
7. Should I take a break and read my email or look at Facebook? (*Ancillary activities*)

Conceptions

Relational student learning research (Marton & Booth, 1997) has shown how students' conceptions of a task influence what they do and what they learn. This body of research has provided particularly strong evidence that the way students think about a task and the few qualitatively distinct strategies they adopt are closely related to their levels of achievement (Calvo & Ellis, 2010). Studies (e.g., Calvo & Ellis, 2010) have shown that writers have a few (two to four) qualitatively different conceptions of writing (e.g., surface versus deep learning), and that these variations affect their learning outcomes. These views are also similar to those in other studies that explore the conceptions of writing among college students (Hounsell, 1997; Lavelle, 1993). What is of particular importance about this literature is that, at a certain level, the computer interfaces do not have to be particularly intelligent to help writers. Because since conceptions are so important, writing systems can be augmented to include content emphasizing the purpose (e.g., learning) and the value of both writing and feedback (Calvo & Ellis, 2010). This is of particular importance when writing is not an acknowledged core skill (e.g., in the engineering disciplines), so that students might have widely varying conceptions about its purpose.

Motivation

There is extensive psychological research on the sociocultural influences on motivation and learning; there are also comprehensive surveys of the literature (e.g., McInerney & Van Etten, 2004). Some of these models of motivation have been extensively evaluated. One example is Keller's (1987a) ARCS model, which assumes that an individual will be motivated (i.e., engaged) with an activity in proportion to how much *value* can apparently be gained from it and in terms of the perceived likelihood of being successful (the *expectancy* component). The model defines four dimensions of motivation: attention, relevance, confidence, and satisfaction (ARCS).

Although the literature provides a number of models like ARCS for understanding the major influences on the motivation to learn, the understanding that students have of their own motivation, or the effect of reflecting on this, has not been as frequently studied. Of relevance to the discussion here is that these metamotivational drivers may be more relevant than the motivation itself. As an example of how motivational drivers can be used by reflective writers, this chapter considers the first condition of the ARCS model. Sustaining students' attention during an activity is a key concern for instructional designers. According to the ARCS model, novice writers would benefit by reflecting on how certain external events—for example, external stimuli (e.g., environmental noise)—affect their attention. This can be achieved using the types of sensing devices and software discussed in the next section.

Outcomes

Once the writing task is completed, writers need metacognitive skills to assess the quality of the final product. Students should reflect and deepen their understanding of how well their writing fulfils expectations.

The Glosser system, discussed in more detail further on, provides several tools for helping writers identify the topics they have covered—for example through concept maps (Villalon & Calvo, 2011)—and to tell whether those topics form a coherent argument (O'Rourke & Calvo, 2009b). These visual and text representations are complemented with trigger questions such as: *Could the ideas in the essay be organized in a clearer way? Does the composition address the topics requested?*

Process

Reflection on questions such as "How will or did I complete the assignment?" can help develop metacognitive understanding on the process followed. Log files can be analyzed to produce process models (Van der Aalst, Weijters, & Maruster, 2004), an approach that is increasingly popular in educational data mining (Baker & Yacef, 2009; Romero & Ventura, 2007). In the context of teaching writing, this type of feedback is being provided in the WriteProc project (Southavilay, Yacef, & Calvo, 2010), described in more detail further on. Most writing activities are assessed on the basis of the product (i.e., the student's submission) rather than the process. It should then not be a surprise that students focus mainly on the document they must submit. Their time on task and their reflection would not likely be on the process they followed.

When a writer reflects on the process by which he or she got to certain point or achieved certain outcomes, the reflection can help to identify the important cognitive (e.g., in-depth understanding of the topic), affective (e.g., engagement) and behavioral (e.g., longer writing sessions) patterns. Feedback does not generally promote process-oriented reflection either. In the classroom, students and instructors are accustomed to receiving feedback on the assignment that was submitted but not often on what the student did in order to get to that outcome. For example, if a team working on a proposal for an innovative product does not engage in

a brainstorming session and focuses on the first idea that came to a team member's mind, the outcome might not be as innovative or the learning experience as valuable.

Increased focus on the process can have other benefits. For example, since plagiarism, a common problem in writing assignments, is a means to an end (i.e., to skip the process that requires effort), one could argue that the focus on outcomes is a main factor that drives students to plagiarize. If the focus were more on the process, inappropriate behaviors could be reduced.

Most automated feedback tools and all those that focus on summative assessment analyze only the writing product. To provide technical feedback on the process of writing is possible only when the document's history is stored and mined. Writing processes can be studied to improve the effectiveness of an individual or team. Fortunately there are modern-day writing tools (e.g., Google Docs) that record the revision history in a way we can use in feedback systems.

Surroundings: Physical and Social

Ede and Lundsford (1992) showed that 85 percent of the documents produced in offices and universities had at least two authors. This line of research has raised awareness of the impact of social environment on writing activities. Most of this progress has come from the computer-supported collaborative work area, which provides new forms of social awareness and collaboration tools. Interestingly, despite the importance of learning to write as part of a group, students tend to dislike these activities or consider them to require more effort than they are worth (Aditomo, Calvo, & Reimann, 2011).

The systems we and other affective computing researchers are developing combine sensor data about the social and physical context in which an activity happens. The HCI community is increasingly interested in building tools for reflecting on data collected through sensors and self-reports (Li, Forlizzi, & Dey, 2010), but as far as we know none have involved writing.

Emotions and Mental States

Among learning technologies there has been a surge of research on affect (Calvo & D'Mello, 2011). Until now, the focus of most research had been on issues such as test anxiety (Pekrun, Goetz, Titz, & Perry, 2002; Schutz & Pekrun, 2007), but new affective computing and sensor technologies make possible computer models that can detect affect automatically. They require self (by the subject) or expert reports to be collected, arguably for each subject, and used to train supervised models. These models then "recognize" the mental state from facial expressions, physiology, posture, or other expressive and behavioral channels, some no more invasive than a webcam. Visualizations of such states—for example, a view of mental states across the time line—can provide significant avenues for reflection.

Ancillary Activities: Distractions and Breaks

Writing activities often require many hours of work. Writers must stage their work in phases, between which rest and other activities occur. These activities will influence the way in which we approach the writing task and its outcomes. If we do not rest when we are tired, we cannot be productive; but if the rest time is used for other cognitive activities, it may not have the desired effect. On the other hand, if rest becomes procrastination, these interruptions might not be fruitful either.

System Design

Our RWS is made up of the four components shown in Figure 33.1. Each component and its evaluation is described in the following subsections. Each of the components maps onto a set of requirements:

1. Structured information about the activity (e.g., deadlines and genre) are provided by a writing activity management system such as iWrite (Calvo, O'Rourke, Jones, Yacef, & Reimann, 2011), described further on. This component also manages structured content that learners can use for modeling (e.g., sample documents) and the system can use to infer the topics automatically. The information is generally provided by the instructor.

2. The system also needs to collect contextual information—including information not specified by the instructor—about the user and the environment using sensors and ubiquitous computing methods not included in the original specification by the instructor. In our system this is to be performed by WebEmo (Aghaei Pour, & Calvo, 2011), a browser extension that records multimodal information (e.g., from a webcam) together with the actual content written.

3. Machine learning techniques are used to process and integrate the multimodal signals coming from the sensors and the structured information from the activities (in our implementation, this is provided by the Siento module).

4. The aim of the RWS is to provide feedback to writers. This is done through a framework that uses the processed data to provide automated or human feedback and scaffold reflection. In our writing environment this would be an extension of the current Glosser project.

Writing Activity Management System

In order to provide meaningful feedback, RWS require knowledge about the context of the activity. Our iWrite (Calvo et al., 2011) writing activity management system uses genre, deadlines, and the nature of the activity (e.g., individual versus

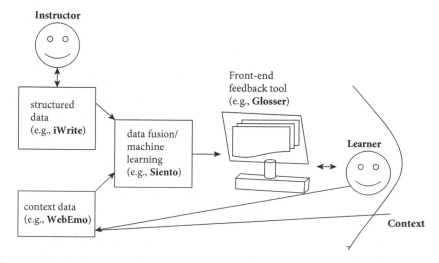

Fig. 33.1 Reflective Writing Studio components.

collaborative) to customize feedback. iWrite is a web-based application that supports individual and collaborative writing. For students, it is the main point of access to the writing activity, collaboration, and instructor-provided resources. It also allows researchers and instructors to learn more about the student writing activities, particularly about features of individual and group writing activities that correlate with quality outcomes. It leverages mainstream writing tools (e.g., Google Docs) within which students do the actual writing and facilitates the provision of human (peer and tutor) and automated feedback. iWrite is currently used to support the teaching of academic writing at the Faculty of Engineering and IT at the University of Sydney to around 600 undergraduate and postgraduate students each semester.

The instructional feedback provided aims to advance the students' conceptual understanding beyond surface features of writing and grammar to greater awareness of the writing process and textual practices.

The system provides these innovative elements:

• Features to manage writing activities in large cohorts, particularly the management and allocation of groups, peer reviewing, and assessment.
• Combines synchronous and asynchronous modes of collaborative writing.
• Use of computer-based process discovery methods to provide additional information on the team process. The combination of these methods with text mining is particularly novel and will allow feedback about the team processes based not only on events but also on their semantic significance.

The system uses Google Docs revision management and application programming interfaces (APIs) to record detailed information on the process of writing. In a recent study (Calvo et al., 2011) involving 491 students who completed 642 individual and collaborative writing assignments, 102,538 revisions representing over 51,000 minutes of students writing work were recorded (revisions are saved only when a change is made). The revisions of a document are used to identify different "activities" (e.g., editing, outlining) that students engage in at different stages of the writing process (Southavilay et al., 2010). These activities are used to produce visualizations that show writers what they have done and aid reflection

about which sequence of activities leads to better outcomes.

The revision data also allows for inferences and reflection on time-management issues. Analysis of the data (Calvo et al., 2011) suggested that:

• Students with low grades engage in more revisions (individually and as a group) compared with those with medium grades.
• Students with low and medium grades engaged in fewer writing sessions compared with students with high grades.
• Students with low and medium grades engaged in fewer writing days compared with students with high grades.

Students who obtained high grades were in teams that engaged more frequently in sustained writing sessions. In contrast, shorter burst of document revisions were associated with lower grades. These results seem to agree with those documented by Torrance and Galbraith (2006).

We are planning an integration of iWrite with two learning management systems (Moodle and Blackboard) to collect information about prior experiences of the student. This will be used to provide a user model to generate better feedback.

Recording Platform

Reading, writing, and collaborative activities are generally computer-based. The writer can engage in the prewriting activities (e.g., research on the topic to write about), collaborate with peers and tutors, and do the writing itself, all on a browser connected to the Internet. Given the central role of the browser, we used a platform called WebEmo (Aghaei Pour & Calvo, 2011) to manage the collection of environmental information while a person reads and writes.

The tool consists of several components, as shown in Figure 33.2. The client-side component works as an extension in Google's Chrome browser and does not require any code in the web page to be altered. Through integration with other systems, it currently records physiological signals such as the electrocardiographic (heart), electromyographic (facial), and respiration patterns. It also records video of the user currently from a webcam and using the openCV library. The actual recording is left to third-party software managed by an acquisition system controller, allowing the framework to be extended to include other modalities. All data collected from each sensor (different physiological modalities and

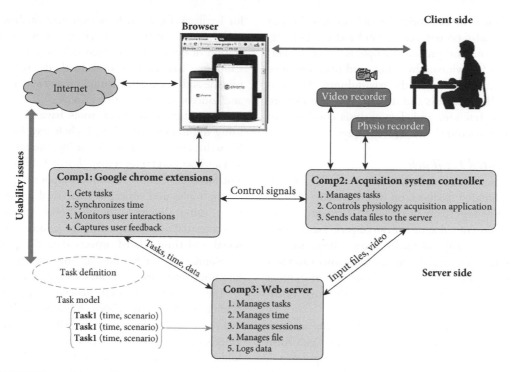

Fig. 33.2 WebEmo architecture for recording users' video, physiology, and web interaction data.

camera recording) are stored locally and uploaded to the processing server at the end of the session. Video recording can be done with any webcam or with a range camera such as Microsoft Kinect. For physiological recording, WebEmo integrates in-house and commercial systems. We generally use the BIOPAC MP150 system with AcqKnowledge software to capture data. Biopac's Matlab API can also be used for real-time data acquisition. The Biopac system can be used to record a variety of physiological signals (electrocardiography, galvanic skin response, electromyography, electroencephalography, etc).

When self-reports of the affective impact of a page or activity need to be recorded, the framework can intervene with psychometric questionnaires such as the Self-Assessment Mannequin (Lang, Greenwald, Bradley, & Hamm, 1993).

Some studies, those that examine writing in complex realistic settings, would require all of the user's activities to be recorded (perceptions might be affected by what happened immediately before or after the task). For example, a student writing an activity on Google Docs would visit Wikipedia for information on a particular topic, so that in testing such a system the interaction on both websites would have to be recorded. A challenge for the system is that the user can be interacting with different websites running on different browser tabs.

Data Fusion and Processing

The systems described here can be used to collect vast amounts of multimodal information on what writers do, think, and feel as well as on the environment that surrounds them. These data are complex, highly dimensional, and dynamic, a situation increasingly common in ubiquitous computing scenarios. Researchers in different fields are trying to make sense of such data.

In the area of emotion detection, affective computing techniques (Calvo & D'Mello, 2010) are being used. These methods examine data recorded from different modalities (sensory features) to train computational models to recognize patterns that correlate with what people report as emotional states. Facial expressions, speech, and metalinguistic information were among the earliest types of data to be analyzed; currently behavior, posture, breathing, and physiology are all commonly used in affective computing. Many researchers believe that computers that aim at a detection accuracy similar to that of humans should also use multimodal approaches (Sharma et al., 1998).

We have built Siento, a system to record and process multimodal signals and predict affective states. This tool has been used in several affective computing studies combining physiological signals with facial expressions. The system allows for dimensional or categorical models of emotions as well as self-reported versus third-party reporting; it can record and process multiple types of modalities including video, physiology, and text. This type of system can improve the repeatability of experiments. The system is also used for data acquisition, feature extraction, and data analysis consisting of applying machine learning techniques.

Automated Feedback

Glosser is a web-based framework for providing automated feedback on writing (Calvo & Ellis, 2010; Villalón, Kearney, Calvo, & Reimann, 2008). Any version of a document can be processed to produce a wide range of feedback on collaborative or individual writing activities spanning visual and text modalities. Feedback can be on surface or content features, on the writing product (the final document), or on the process.

For each activity one or more forms of feedback can be selected by the instructor. Each form of feedback, such as the one shown in Figure 33.3, is made up of (1) a set of guiding questions aimed at scaffolding reflection on particular aspects of the writing; (2) a "gloss," a visual or text-based representation of automatically generated feedback specific to the student's composition; and (3) guiding text explaining on how to use the gloss to reflect on the questions. The architecture incorporates features

for feedback forms such as argument quality, textual features (such as coherence), automatic generation of questions, and feedback on the process. Computer-based text analysis methods are used to provide additional information on text surface-level and concept-level to writing groups.

A number of feedback tools have been built using the framework. These include two for helping writers reflect on flow: one using interactive text and another employing a map (Calvo & Ellis, 2010; Villalón et al., 2008). Three tools support reflection on the topics and concepts: two visual representations using different computational approaches and a textual one. One tool is for reflecting on the social and time related aspects (i.e., the process) (O'Rourke & Calvo, 2009a) and one generates questions automatically (Liu, Calvo, & Rus, 2010).

The automatic question generation techniques (Liu et al., 2010; Liu, Calvo, Aditomo, & Pizzato, 2012) are used to help students reflect on different aspects of their literature reviews. The system scaffolds students' reflection on their academic writing with content-related trigger questions automatically generated (using Natural Language Processing - NLP techniques) from citations. A taxonomy of different types of citations relevant to literature review papers (Liu et al., 2010) is used (with categories for opinion, result, aim of study, system, method, and application). For example, if a student (citer)

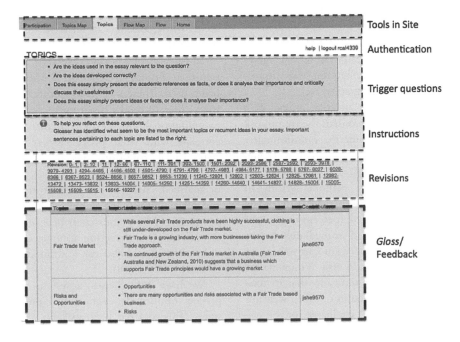

Fig. 33.3 Glosser feedback.

cites the following opinion in his review: "Cannon (1927) challenged this view mentioning that physiological changes were not sufficient to discriminate emotions," the system can generate the following trigger questions that help the writer reflect on the relevance to the project at hand: *Why did Cannon challenge this view mentioning that physiological changes were not sufficient to discriminate emotions? How is this relevant to your project?*

The system was evaluated in a study with 57 participants (33 PhD student writers and 24 supervisors), where each PhD student submitted a research proposal to iWrite, our writing management system. Each proposal was read by a peer and the PhD supervisor, both of whom provided feedback in the form of reflection questions. The peer and supervisor questions were compared to the automatic questions and also to a set of generic questions. A total of 615 questions were generated based on the 33 literature review papers. Each student was then asked to rate the quality of questions received on measures of "acceptability" (whether it is grammatically correct, not vague, and makes sense according to the context) and "usefulness" (whether it is helpful to trigger reflection). These ratings were used to evaluate the system's performance and to analyze human expert generated questions. We compared automatically generated questions with human-generated and generic questions on these dimensions using a Bystander Turing test, and the top questions (selected using an automated ranking system) were reported to be as useful as those generated by peers and supervisors (after removing questions with surface errors).

The computational techniques (e.g., latent semantic analysis) used in Glosser are similar to those in automatic essay assessment systems. Criterion (by ETS Technologies), MyAccess (by Vantage Learning) and WriteToLearn by Pearson Knowledge Technologies are all commercial products that are increasingly used in classrooms. These programs sometimes provide an editing tool with grammar, spelling, and low-level mechanical feedback. Some of them can also be integrated with university systems using APIs. Some provide resources such as thesaurus and graphic features, many of which would be available in tools such as MS Word. Glosser is distinct in several ways, including that it is the only tool that provides support for collaborative writing activities and the only one that can analyze (and provide feedback on) the writing processes.

With regard to process, recent work, such as our Writeproc system (Southavilay et al., 2010),

a component of Glosser, shows that the writing processes can be analyzed by detecting writing "activities." WriteProc uses a taxonomy of writing activities proposed by Lowry, Curtis, and Lowry (2004). We plan to study how such information can help students reflect on their own processes. If the results of these observations can be generalized to other learning situations, students may benefit from the realization of how important it is to work on an assignment for dedicated stretches of time. This is a key outcome of learning time management skills.

We have also evaluated how students' conceptions of automated feedback—such as Glosser—affect the way they use it and what the quality of the learning outcomes is in terms of the grades obtained (Calvo & Ellis, 2010).

Discussion and Conclusions

Each of the four components of our RWS has been evaluated in the studies described earlier. The integration of these software/hardware components poses a significant engineering challenge, so an evaluation of its impact on learning is still some time away. As a way of discussing some of these challenges, I provide an account of how I personally used the system. In a recent session, I wrote a blog post during a one-hour session. The Kinect camera recorded my facial expressions, voice, and environmental situation. The writing tool (used by iWrite) was Google Docs, which keeps a history of the document (a very simplified version of keystroke logging). Finally, WebEmo recorded my interactions with the browser. The purpose of the blog post was to summarize a research project I was learning about. During the session, a phone call interrupted my work and I had to stop when someone came in the room. I was following a think-aloud protocol so that my speech could be automatically transcribed using a speech recognition system and key events in the writing process could be identified. Speech recognition systems are not absolutely accurate but produce a stream of words that can be used by text-mining algorithms. The same happens with facial expression recognition. About twenty behavioural events were identified in the video by an annotator. These included affective states, such as surprise and engagement, that we have detected automatically, as well as typing and "habits" (e.g., playing with my ear). My posture was used to detect when a phone call and a visitor interrupted my work. My research (e.g., reading web pages about the project) and writing strategies (e.g., copy and paste of certain details) were all recorded. All this

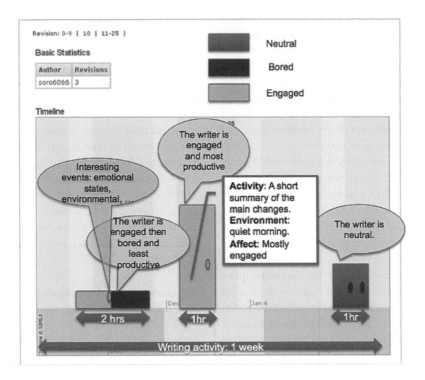

Fig. 33.4 Reflective time line.

information can be used as evidence in writing research studies and to generate visualizations (integrated into Glosser) that support reflection.

Figure 33.4 shows a time line of significant events, such as the ones above, to help a writer reflect on positive and negative aspects across multiple sessions. The height of the bars represents a measure of productivity, such as the number of text revisions, additions, or deletions over each time period, and the width is the amount of time averaged over thirty-minute or one-hour blocks. The color of the bars represents the most common automatically detected mental state, and the square dialog box (which appears on a rollover) provides a description of the block. This description summarizes the structured information coming from iWrite with process data. Small markers can appear on the time line (e.g., in the first block), highlighting specific meaningful events (e.g., a phone call, which may have produced distraction). The curved bubbles provide explanatory material to support new users of the interface.

There are two sets of challenges for RWS. First are the technical issues of building a reliable, accurate, and scalable platform. The second is to produce visualizations and feedback that summarize the massive amount of data being collected in a way

that is meaningful to the researcher and/or reflective user.

Automated feedback systems have focused on the writing product rather than the process—for example, those based on automated essay scoring. It is not yet clear that students benefit from seeing how their writing products measure up against certain scales, but the results are still useful to inform educational design decisions. We speculate that the relationship of such systems to student learning would be stronger if systems focused on process factors such as decisions on topic and argument, supporting reading activities, the selection of environment and tools, the timing, and so forth. The pervasiveness of computing devices as well as the easy access to supporting material and social interaction add many factors that have not previously been included in the study of writing phenomena, thus potentially influencing the way we think, feel, and write.

As a consequence, this chapter argues that the writer's affect and his or her environment must also be taken into account in designing systems that support writing. With rare exceptions, this has not been the case. Researchers have not taken this inclusive approach partly because such a complex system is difficult to study using traditional methods. It is not possible to control for all possible variables occurring in the mind, body, and world around the writer.

The RWS described here offers an example of an affective computing application aimed at supporting novice writers through data-driven functionalities that scaffold their reflection. The functionalities described can help novice writers reflect on those situations when they enjoyed their work and were productive in writing, answer questions such as *why* they engaged in the activity, *how* they went about it, *what* the outcomes were (so they can be improved on), and *who* did what (in working in a team). This chapter first reviewed the literature coming from different pedagogical traditions, including cognitive, social, situated, and embodied cognition perspectives; it argued for approaches that take into account a wider set of variables. It then argued that new enabling technologies such as affective and ubiquitous computing allow researchers to develop new type of interfaces that can support new forms of reflective feedback.

We have described the different components of the system and their evaluations: the writing activity management system manages activities where writers use Google Docs and stores structured data about the activity. Since most of the writing and the ancillary reading activities happen on the browser, the recording platform was built as an extension of Google Chrome and integrates the webcam (with video and sound), screen recording and other sensing devices. The data collected by the extension and its devices are then merged and mined. We have summarized the evaluations of these components. The final component is the user interface used to provide feedback to the student. We are building this as an extension to Glosser, an open-source feedback framework, which we have already described and evaluated elsewhere. A time-line visualization has been proposed but not yet evaluated to represent the data provided to writers.

Owing to the significant amount of information that RWS collects, such as data about the writing process, it is important that writers avoid becoming distracted or feel overwhelmed by it. It is also important that they do not see it as surveillance of their activities. They must feel in control of their data. An approach we have used for tackling this challenge is to make anonymous all process data shown to instructors. With this setup, students can get feedback at any stage of their writing process but know that instructors access only the final product (as occurs traditionally).

Acknowledgments

Assignment Manager was funded by a University of Sydney TIES grant. Glosser was funded by Australia Research Council DP0665064, AQG and WriteProc were funded by DP0986873, and a Google Research Award.

References

Aditomo, A., Calvo, R. A., & Reimann, P. (2011). Collaborative writing: Too much of a good thing? Exploring engineering students' perceptions using the Repertory Grid. *Computer supported collaborative learning—CSCL*. Hong Kong: University of Hong Kong.

Aghaei Pour, P., & Calvo, R. A. (2011). Towards automatic measurements of web usability using affective computing techniques. *Affective computing and intelligent interaction* ACII 2011 Part I, LNCS 6974, pp. 447–456. Memphis, TN: Springer LNCS.

Baker, R., & Yacef, K. (2009). The state of educational data mining in 2009: A review and future visions. *Journal of Educational Data Mining*, *1*(1), 3–17.

Beard, R., & Riley, J. (2009). *The SAGE handbook of writing development*. London, UK: Sage.

Bixler, R., & D'Mello, S. (2013). Detecting boredom and engagement during writing with keystroke analysis, task appraisals, and stable traits. *Proceedings of the 2013 international conference on Intelligent user interfaces* (pp. 225–234). New York: Association for Computing Machinery.

Calvo, R. A., & D'Mello, S. K. (2010). Affect detection: An interdisciplinary review of models, methods, and their applications. *IEEE Transactions on Affective Computing*, *1*(1), 18–37. doi: 10.1109/T-AFFC.2010.1

Calvo, R. A., & D'Mello, S. K. (2011). *New perspectives on affect and learning technologies* (p. 284). New York: Springer.

Calvo, R. A., & Ellis, R. A. (2010). Student conceptions of tutor and automated feedback in professional writing. *Journal of Engineering Education*, *99*(4), 427–438.

Calvo, R. A., O'Rourke, S. T., Jones, J., Yacef, K., & Reimann, P. (2011). Collaborative writing support tools on the cloud. *IEEE Transactions on Learning Technologies*, *4*(1), 88–97. doi: 10.1109/TLT.2010.43

Cooper, M. (1986). The ecology of writing. *College English*, *48*, 364–375.

Dourish, P. (2004). *Where the action is: The foundations of embodied interaction*. Cambridge, MA: MIT Press.

Dourish, P., & Bellotti, V. (1992). Awareness and coordination in shared workspaces. *Proceedings of the 1992 ACM conference on Computer-supported cooperative work* (pp. 107–114). New York: Association for Computing Machinery.

Ede, L. S., & Lunsford, A. A. (1992). *Singular texts/plural authors: Perspectives on collaborative writing*. Carbondale: Southern Illinois Univ Press.

Emig, J. (1977). Writing as a mode of learning. *College Composition and Communication*, *28*, 122–128.

Flower, L., & Hayes, J. R. (1981). A cognitive process theory of writing. *College Composition and Communication*, *32*(4), 365–387.

Haas, C. (1995). *Writing technology: Studies on the materiality of literacy*. Mahwah NJ: Erlbaum.

Hounsell, D. 1997. "Contrasting conceptions of essay writing". In The experience of learning, (2nd edn), Edited by: Marton,

F., Hounsell, D. and Entwistle, N. (Chapter 7, pp. 106–125). Edinburgh: Scottish Academic Press.

Keller, J. M. (1987a). The systematic process of motivational design. *Performance+ Instruction, 26*(9–10), 1–8.

Lang, P. J., Greenwald, M., Bradley, M. M., & Hamm, A. O. (1993). Looking at pictures: Evaluative, facial, visceral, and behavioral responses. *Psychophysiology, 30*(3), 261–274.

Lavelle, E. (1993). Development and validation of an inventory to assess processes in college composition. *British Journal of Educational Psychology, 63*(3), 489–499.

Li, I., Forlizzi, J., & Dey, A. (2010). Know thyself: Monitoring and reflecting on facets of one's life. *Proceedings of the 28th of the international conference extended abstracts on Human factors in computing systems* (pp. 4489–4492). New York: Association for Computing Machinery.

Liu, M., Calvo, R. A., & Rus, V. (2010). automatic question generation for literature review writing support. In V. Aleven, J. Kay, & J. Mostow (Eds.), *Intelligent tutoring systems* (Vol. 6094, pp. 45–54). Berlin & Heidelberg: Springer Berlin Heidelberg. doi: 10.1007/978-3-642-13388-6

Liu, M., Calvo, R., Aditomo, A., & Pizzato, L. A. (2012). Using Wikipedia and conceptual graph structures to generate questions for academic writing support. *IEEE Transactions on Learning Technologies, 5*(3), 251–263.

Lowry, P. B., Curtis, A., & Lowry, M. R. (2004). Building a taxonomy and nomenclature of collaborative writing to improve interdisciplinary research and practice. *Journal of Business Communication, 41*(1), 66.

MacArthur, C. A., Graham, S., & Fitzgerald, J. (Eds.). (2006). *Handbook of writing research.* New York: Guilford Press.

Marton, F., & Booth, S. (1997). *Learning and Awareness.* Mahwah, NJ: Erlbaum.

McInerney, D. M., & Van Etten, S. (Eds.). (2004). *Big Theories Revisited* (p. 367). Grenwich, CT: Information Age Publications.

O'Rourke, S., & Calvo, R. (2009a). Semantic visualisations for academic writing support. *14th conference on artificial intelligence in education* (pp. 173–180). Brighton, UK: IOS Press.

O'Rourke, S. T., & Calvo, R. A. (2009b). Analysing semantic flow in academic writing. In V. Dimitrova, R. Mizoguchi, B. du Boulay, & A. Graesser (Eds.), *Artificial intelligence in education—AIED* (pp. 173–180). Brighton, UK. doi: 10.3233/978-1-60750-028-5-173

Pea, R. D., & Kurland, D. M. (1987). Cognitive technologies for writing. *Review of Research in Education, 14*, 277–326.

Pekrun, R., Goetz, T., Titz, W., & Perry, R. P. (2002). Academic emotions in students' self-regulated learning and achievement: A program of qualitative and quantitative research. *Emotions in Education: A Special Issue of Educational Psychologist, 37*(2), 91–105.

Romero, C., & Ventura, S. (2007). Educational data mining: A survey from 1995 to 2005. *Expert Systems with Applications, 33*, 135–146.

Sas, C., & Dix, A. (2009). Designing for reflection on experience. *Proceedings of the 27th international conference extended abstracts on Human factors in computing systems* (pp. 4741–4744). New York: Association for Computing Machinery.

Schön, D. (1983). *The reflective practitioner.* London: Temple Smith.

Schutz, P. A., & Pekrun, R. (2007). *Emotion in education.* Academic Press.

Sharma, R., Pavlovic, V. I., & Huang, T. S. (1998). Toward multimodal human-computer interface. *Proceedings of the IEEE, 86*(5), 853–869.

Southavilay, V., Yacef, K., & Calvo, R. A. (2010). Process mining to support students' collaborative writing. In A. Merceron, P. Pavlik, & R. Baker (Eds.), *Third international conference on educational data mining (EDM2010).* Pittsburgh, PA.

Sparrow, B., Liu, J., & Wegner, D. M. (2011). Google effects on memory: Cognitive consequences of having information at our fingertips. *Science, 333*(6043), 776.

The neglected "R": The need for a writing revolution. (2003). New York: College Entrance Examination Board—National Commission on Writing in American Schools and Colleges.

Torrance, M., & Galbraith, D. (2006). The processing demands of writing. In C. MacArthur, S. Graham, & J. Fitzgerlad (Eds.), *Handbook of writing research* (pp. 67–82). New York: Guilford Press.

Van der Aalst, W., Weijters, T., & Maruster, L. (2004). Workflow mining: Discovering process models from event logs. *IEEE Transactions on Knowledge and Data Engineering, 16*(9), 1128–1142.

Vertegaal, R. (2003). Attentive user interfaces. *Communications of the ACM, 46*(3), 30–33.

Villalon, J., & Calvo, R. A. (2011). Concept maps as cognitive visualizations of writing assignments. *Journal of Educational Technology and Society, 14*(3), 16–27.

Villalón, J., Kearney, P., Calvo, R. A., & Reimann, P. (2008). Glosser: Enhanced feedback for student writing tasks. *2008 eighth IEEE international conference on advanced learning technologies* (pp. 454–458). New York: IEEE. doi: 10.1109/ICALT.2008.78

Wengelin, A., Torrance, M., Holmqvist, K., Simpson, S., Galbraith, D., Johansson, V., & Johansson, R. (2009). Combined eyetracking and keystroke-logging methods for studying cognitive processes in text production. *Behavior Research Methods, 41*(2), 337–351.

Emotion in Games

Georgios N. Yannakakis *and* Ana Paiva

Abstract

Emotion has been investigated from various perspectives and across several domains within human-computer interaction (HCI) including intelligent tutoring systems, interactive web applications, social media, and human-robot interaction. One of the most promising and also challenging applications of affective computing research is within computer games. This chapter focuses on the study of emotion in the computer games domain, reviews seminal work at the crossroads of game technology, game design, and affective computing, and details the key phases for efficient affect-based interaction in games.

Key Words: computer games, game technology, game design, affect-based interaction

Introduction

People choose to play games as a "voluntary attempt to overcome unnecessary obstacles" (Suits, 2005), as play is among the main motivators for learning, mental and physical development, and an essential element of evolution (Deci & Ryan, 2000). Arguably players seek games for enjoyment and for emotional experiences; they pursue in-game challenges that—when achieved—do not necessarily result in immediate, tangible rewards. What is fascinating is that players willingly engage in an experience that is likely to involve even negative emotions such as frustration and fear (Salen & Zimmerman, 2003). So while games can be utilized as an arena for eliciting, evaluating, expressing, and even synthesizing emotions, we argue that one of the primary aims of the study of emotion in games is the understanding of players' emotions and how they are linked with their experience. Indeed, by the nature of what constitutes a game, one cannot dissociate games from emotions. Emotions are not only the trigger for the positive game experiences but also one of the main targets for game design.

For this purpose, this chapter focuses on emotions that can be detected, modeled from, and expressed in games with human players.

Computer games are dynamic media that embed rich forms of user interactivity. Collectively, such human-computer interaction (HCI) attributes allow for high levels of player incorporation (Calleja, 2011) and yield dynamic and complex emotion manifestations. The potential that games have to influence players is mainly due to their ability of placing the player in a continuous mode of interaction (loop) with the game, which develops complex cognitive, affective, and behavioral responses. Undoubtedly the study of emotion in games not only advances our knowledge about human emotions but also contributes to the design of better HCI. Moreover, affect-based game interaction can drive players in particular emotional patterns, which, in turn, can enhance game-based training and educational activities (McQuiggan & Lester, 2009; McQuiggan, Robison, & Lester, 2010; Yannakakis et al., 2010b). Arguably, as this chapter shows, games offer the best and most meaningful domain of affective interaction for the realization of the *affective loop*, which defines a system that is able to successfully elicit, detect, and respond to the emotions of its user (Sundstrom, 2005).

Every game features a *user* (i.e., *player*)—or a number of users—that control an avatar or a group of miniature entities in a virtual/simulated environment (Calleja, 2011). The interaction between the player and the game context (i.e., the game state containing all pieces of game content) is of key importance for affective computing (AC) research and modern game development, as it breeds emotional stimuli and yields emotional manifestations to the player. Those manifestations, however, cannot trivially be captured by standard methods in AC research. Given the particularities of emotion research in games, we both discuss what games can offer to emotion research and what emotion research can bring to game design and game technology research.

What Games Can Do for Emotion Research

As mentioned earlier, games can offer contextual building blocks (i.e., game content) that can elicit a broad spectrum of emotional responses and emotional patterns. Games—as a medium—have unique properties that make this possible, as they incorporate rich forms of interaction with the player within a virtual world, provide a direct placement of a player onto an avatar and a player detachment from reality, and finally allow for direct control of the context presented to the player. For these unique features, games can be used (and have been used quite extensively) by emotion researchers as handy and off-the-shelf emotion elicitors.

More importantly, games can offer the most meaningful realization of the *affective loop* (Sundstrom, 2005). As games are by definition both *entertaining* (whether used for pure satisfaction, training, or education) and *interactive* activities that are played within *fantasy* worlds; any limitations of affective interaction (such as justifiability of affective-based game decisions) are absorbed. Games are designed to offer affective experiences influenced by player feedback and players are willing to go through, for example, frustrating, anxious, and fearful episodes of play to experience involvement and powerful emotional gaming. To that end, a user under gaming conditions—more than any other form of HCI—is generally open to affective-based alterations of the interaction, and this influences his or her emotional state.

What Can Emotion Research Do for Games?

The use of AC research and development in games is beneficial for the design of better games for various reasons. First, emotions can drive the design process of most game genres. Game designers usually explore and test a palette of mechanics and game dynamics that yield emotional states and emotional state sequences they want to put the player through. Emotional states such as engagement, fear and stress, frustration, and anticipation but also cognitive states such as challenge define critical aspects of the design of player experience, which is dependent on the genre, the narrative, and the objectives of the game. Second, the holy grail of game design, that is *player experience*, can be improved and tailored to each player but also augmented via richer and more affective-based interaction. As the following section shows and in the discussion of this chapter, emotion-driven game adaptation primarily targets the personalization of the playing experience. Third, as a direct consequence of better and faster design, the whole game-development process is boosted and improved. Fourth, games that incorporate rich emotion-based interaction, which is further tailored to the needs of the player, can enhance learning in training or educational (game-based learning) settings, as indicated by numerous studies in the literature (McQuiggan & Lester, 2009; McQuiggan, Robison, & Lester, 2010; Yannakakis et al., 2010b).

Research on emotion in games is nowadays becoming increasingly important in research and development departments of top-class (i.e., AAA) and indie game developers (Yannakakis, 2012). More specifically, there are several commercial-standard games that incorporate emotion as a core (or peripheral) part of gameplay, including the arousal-driven appearance of nonplayer characters (NPCs) in *Left 4 Dead* 2 (Valve Corporation, 2009), the fearful combat skills of the opponent NPCs in *F.E.A.R.* (Monolith, 2005), the avatars' emotion expression in the *Sims* series (Maxis, 2000) and *Black and White* (Lionhead Studios, 2001), the emotional play-through for characters in *Psychonauts* (Double Fine Productions, 2005), the emotional responses of game characters in *Prom Week* (McCoy et al., 2010) and *Façade* (Mateas & Stern, 2003), the emotion-driven narrative-building system in *Storybricks* (Namaste Entertainment, 2012), the personality-based adaptation in *Silent Hill: Shattered Memories* (Konami, 2010), the affect-based cinematographic representation of multiple cameras in *Heavy Rain* (Quantic Dream, 2010), the aesthetically pleasing locations of *World of Warcraft* (Blizzard Entertainment, 2004) and affect-centered game narratives such as the one of *Final Fantasy VII* (Square Product, 1997).

Ultimately all of the above-mentioned intelligible benefits from the coupling of games and emotion research can be revealed as long as phases of the affective loop (or the affective loop as whole) are successfully realized within a game.

The Affective Loop in Games

Within games, emotions are elicited via stimuli offered during the interaction. Emotions can then be detected and modeled, assessing the responses of the player to the corresponding game stimuli. Such detection can then affect the game responses that may involve emotions expressed in several ways via game-adjustable elements such as game content and nonplayer characters; finally, controllable game elements can be adapted dynamically to cater for the current emotional state of the player and the specific game context. The affective loop (Sundstrom, 2005) applied to games can be viewed as comprising three sequential key phases organized in a closed loop (Figure 34.1):

1. The player expresses her emotions through the interaction with a game.
2. The game then detects the emotional reactions of the player and interprets those reactions according to the context of the game.
3. Based on that interpretation, the game makes adjustments that can be achieved via emotional modeling and the expression of NPCs or via affect-driven content generation adapting the game to the player. This, in turn, affects the player (both her mind and body), making her respond through

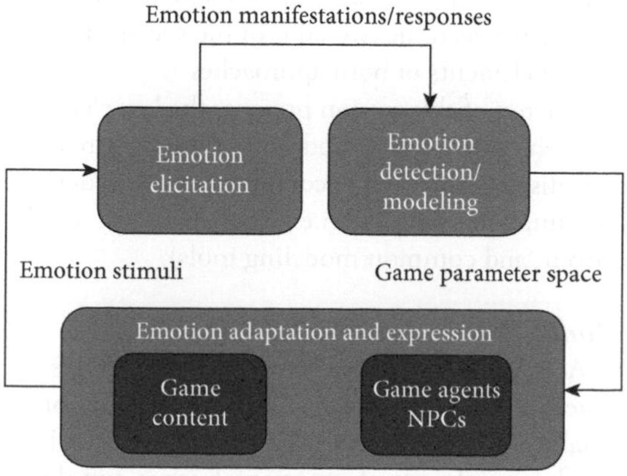

Fig. 34.1 Realization of the affective loop in games.

game actions and emotional reactions (step 1 again).

The remaining three sections of this chapter discuss the three affective loop phases in detail under the games domain. The chapter ends with a discussion on the open questions and the future of research on emotion in games.

Games as Emotion Elicitors

Emotion elicitation in games can be achieved primarily through interaction with particular game elements (such as game characters and the rest of the game content). While social interaction—shared involvement (Calleja, 2011)—may have a clear impact on a player's emotional state, it cannot be directly controlled via an affective loop mechanism and thereby is not included in the list of emotional stimuli considered in this chapter. On that basis, we may define *two* key clusters of possible emotion elicitors in games:

1. *Game content*: Beyond any narrative or player-agent interaction there is game content that can influence the emotional state of the player. *Game content* refers to the game environment (i.e., spatial involvement according to Calleja, 2011) but also refers to fundamental game-design building blocks, such as game mechanics (i.e., ludic involvement, according to Calleja, 2011), story plot points, and reward systems. Beyond the game environment itself—such as a game level/ map (Hullett & Whitehead, 2010; Togelius et al., 2010)—game content includes audiovisual settings such as lighting (Seif, Vasilakos, & Zupko, 2009), saturation, and music (Eladhari, Nieuwdorp, & Fridenfalk, 2006); (Plans & Morelli, 2012); virtual camera profiles (Picardi, Burelli, & Yannakakis, 2011; Yannakakis et al., 2010a); and game rules (Togelius & Schmidhuber, 2008). All these types of content can be adjusted to affect the playing experience and influence player emotions.

The environment is linked to stories and narratives as a form of their representation, and it is also linked to NPCs (if existent in the game), as it forms their context, living habitats and surroundings. In a broader sense, both agents and narratives can be viewed as game content that can be parameterized and altered (Yannakakis & Togelius, 2011). Stories play an essential part in creating the ambience, style, climax, and feelings of a game; whether games can tell stories (Juul, 2001) or games are instead a form of narrative (Aarseth, 2004) is still, however, an open research question in game studies. Players seek the moment-to-moment experiences they build in a game and the climax and relief moments created by prescripted story elements. Some games, such as *World of Warcraft* (Blizzard Entertainment, 2004), take advantage of the story components and, in particular, cut scenes to raise the climax and lead the player to particular emotional states. Other systems, as in the area of interactive storytelling, use the story as an evolving and adaptive mechanism that in itself varies according to the actions of the players and adjusts the story to different players and actions, offering variant emotional experiences (see, for example, the work of Roberts et al., 2009, among others). Further, by breaking the game narrative into subareas of game content (and perhaps according to the different plot phases), we can find core game content elements such as the game's plot line (Giannatos, Nelson, Cheong, & Yannakakis, 2012; Riedl, 2012), but also the ways in which this story/plot is represented in the game environment.

In summary, all game content surrounding NPCs (whether those are existent in the game or not)—including game mechanics, rules, story nodes, and reward systems—may have an effect on the experience of the player (Yannakakis & Togelius, 2011).

2. *Game non-player characters*: Complex, social and emotional nonplayer characters (NPCs) can be used as triggers of desired emotions for the player. The main goal of these characters is to be believable (Hingston, 2009) in such a way that players establish relations with them, thus leading to particular emotional reactions when something good or bad happens in the game. To achieve that, agents may embed computational models of cognition, behavior, and emotion and attempt to react in a believable and humanlike fashion to human player actions. Typical agent architectures rely on particular theories of emotion, such as the OCC theory of Ortony, Clore, and Collins (1988) or Lazarus theory (Lazarus, 1994) as the basis for their emotional processing and simulation. One of these architectures, called FAtiMA (Dias & Paiva, 2005), is based on OCC and extends the typical the belief-desire-intention (BDI) (Georgeff, Pell, Pollack, Tambe, & Wooldridge, 1999) model with emotional processing capabilities. A noninclusive list of games that make use of emotion-driven NPCs includes the kittens in *Kinectimals* (MS Game Studios, 2010), the complex social agents in *FearNot!* (Paiva et al., 2004), the emotional

opponents in the iterative prisoner's dilemma (De Melo, Zheng, & Gratch, 2009), and the agents of *Prom Week* (McCoy et al., 2010).

Emotion Detection and Modeling in Games

The detection and modeling of emotion in games is primarily the study and use of artificial and computational intelligence (AI and CI) techniques for the construction of computational models of the emotions of players. Emotion detection and emotion modeling bring an AI umbrella to the multidisciplinary intersection of the fields of user (player) modeling, affective computing, experimental psychology, and HCI. Emotion detection in games is an area that has given rise to the most research studies thus far, leaving, however, large unexplored spaces.

One can detect the emotion of either a human player or a nonplayer game character. While the challenges faced in the latter case are substantial, the issues raised from emotion detection on human players define a far more complex and important problem for the realization of the affective loop in games. In clustering the available approaches for emotion modeling, we are faced with either *model-based* or *model-free* approaches (Yannakakis & Togelius, 2011) as well as potential hybrids between them. The space between a completely model-based and a completely model-free approach can be viewed as a continuum along which any emotion modeling approach might be placed. While a completely model-based approach relies solely on a theoretical framework that maps a player's responses to affect, a completely model-free approach assumes there is an unknown function between modalities of user input and affect that a machine learner (or a statistical model) may discover but without assuming anything about the structure of this function. Relative to these extremes, all approaches may be viewed as hybrids between the two ends of the spectrum, containing elements of both approaches.

The rest of this section presents the key elements of both model-based and model-free approaches and discusses the core components of a derived computational model (i.e., model input, model output, and common modeling tools).

Model-Based (Top-Down) Approaches

According to a model-based (Yannakakis & Togelius, 2011) approach, a model of emotion is usually built on a theoretical framework or is entirely based on a theory of emotion. Such a top-down approach to emotion detection and modeling refers to emotional models derived from emotion theories such as cognitive appraisal theory (Frijda, 1986) or the emotional dimensions of arousal and valence (Feldman, 1995) and Russell's circumplex model of affect (Russell, 1980), in which emotional manifestations are mapped directly to specific emotional states (e.g. the increased heart rate of a player corresponds to high arousal and therefore to player excitement). Examples within the field of game studies include the theoretical model of incorporation (Calleja, 2011), proposed as an approach to capture player immersion in games composed of six types of player involvement: affective, kinesthetic, spatial, shared, ludic, and narrative. Seminal work in psychology-based approaches to player emotion includes the concepts of *challenge, curiosity,* and *fantasy* of Malone (1980), which collectively contribute to high entertainment, and the theory of *flow* (Csikszentmihalyi, 1990) incorporated in games (Sweetser & Wyeth, 2005). Koster's (2005) theory of "fun," the notion of the "magic circle" in games (Salen & Zimmerman, 2003), and the four-fun-factor model of Lazzaro (2004) constitute popular views that place players' emotions at the center of players' experience. Model-based approaches can also be inspired by a general theoretical framework of behavioral analysis and/or cognitive modeling, such as usability theory (Isbister & Schaffer, 2008), the belief-desire-intention (BDI) model, the cognitive theory of Ortony, Clore, and Collins (1988), Skinner's model (1938), and Scherer's theory (1993).

Even though the literature of theories on emotion is rich, one needs to be cautious with the application of such theories to games (and game players), as the majority have not been derived from or tested on ergodic (i.e., interactive) media such as games. Calleja (2011), for instance, reflects on the inappropriateness of the concepts of "flow," "fun," and "magic circle" (among others) for games. Finally, while ad hoc designed emotion models can be an extremely powerful and expressive way of representing emotions, these models need to be cross-validated empirically, which is a rare practice in AC research.

Model-Free (Bottom-Up) Approaches

Model-free approaches comprise the construction of an unknown mapping (model) between (player) input and an emotional state representation. Player data and annotated affective states are collected and used to derive the model. Classification, regression, and preference learning techniques adopted from machine learning or statistical approaches are commonly used for the construction of the computational model. This approach is very common, for instance, for facial expression and head pose recognition, since subjects are asked to annotate facial (or head pose) images of users with particular affective states (see Shaker, Asteriadis, Yannakakis, & Karpouzis, 2011, among others) in a crowdsourcing fashion. A bottom-up approach is also common in studies of psychophysiology in games (see Tognetti, Garbarino, Bonarini, & Mateucci, 2010; Yannakakis et al., 2010a; and others).

The model-free approach to emotion modeling offers the tremendous advantages of data-driven (and even large-scale crowdsourced) model building, but it is also limited by the quantity and quality of the data gathered.

The Model's Input

The model's input can be of three main types: (1) anything a human player (or an agent) is doing in a game environment gathered from *gameplay* data (i.e., behavioral data); (2) *objective* data collected as bodily responses to game stimuli such as physiology and body movements; and (3) the *game context* that includes any player-agent interactions but also any type of game content viewed, played through, and/or created. The three input types are detailed in the remainder of this section.

GAMEPLAY (BEHAVIORAL) INPUT

The main assumption behind the use of behavioral (gameplay-based) player input is that player actions and real-time preferences are linked to player experience, as games may affect the player's cognitive processing patterns and cognitive focus. On the same basis, cognitive processes may influence emotions; one may infer the player's emotional state by analyzing patterns of the interaction and associating user emotions with context variables (Conati, 2002; Gratch & Marsella, 2005). Any element derived from the interaction between the player and the game forms the basis for gameplay-based emotion detection and modeling. This includes detailed attributes from the player's behavior (i.e., *game metrics*) derived from responses to system elements (i.e., nonplayer characters, game levels, or embodied conversational agents). Game metrics are statistical spatiotemporal features of game interaction (Drachen, Thurau, Togelius, Yannakakis, & Bauckhage, 2013). Such data is usually mapped to levels of cognitive states such as attention, challenge, and engagement (Conati, 2002; Shaker, Asteriadis,

Yannakakis, & Karpouzis, 2011). In addition, both general measures (such as performance and time spent on a task) and game-specific measures (such as the weapons selected in a shooter game) are relevant.

OBJECTIVE INPUT

Games can elicit player emotional responses that, in turn, may affect changes in the player's physiology; reflect on the player's facial expression, posture, and speech; and alter the player's attention and focus level. Monitoring such bodily alterations may help to recognize and synthesize the emotional responses of the player. The *objective* approach to emotion modeling (i.e., the second type of model input) incorporates access to multiple modalities of player input.

Within objective emotion modeling, a number of real-time recordings of the player may be investigated. There are several studies that explore the interplay between physiology and gameplay by investigating the impact of different gameplay stimuli to dissimilar physiological signals. Such signals are usually obtained by electrocardiography (ECG) (Yannakakis et al., 2010a), photoplethysmography (Tognetti, Garbarino, Bonarini, & Mateucci, 2010; Yannakakis et al., 2010a), galvanic skin response (GSR) (Mandryk & Inkpen, 2004), respiration (Tognetti, Garbarino, Bonarini, & Mateucci, 2010), electroencephalography (EEG) (Nijholt, 2009), and electromyography (EMG).

In addition to physiology, one may track the player's bodily expressions (motion tracking) at different levels of detail and infer the real-time affective responses from the gameplay stimuli. The core assumption of such input modalities is that particular bodily expressions are linked to basic emotions and cognitive processes. Motion tracking may include body posture (Savva, Scarinzi, & Bianchi-Berthouze, 2012) and head pose (Shaker, Asteriadis, Yannakakis, & Karpouzis, 2011) as well as gaze (Asteriadis, Karpouzis, & Kollias, 2008) and facial expression (Pantic & Caridakis, 2011).

GAME CONTEXT INPUT

In addition to gameplay and objective data, the context of the game is a necessary input for emotion modeling. *Game context* refers to the real-time parameterized state of the game. Without the game context input, affective player models run the risk of inferring erroneous affective states for the player. For example, an increase in GSR can be linked to a set of dissimilar high-arousal affective states such as *frustration* and *excitement*; thus the cause of the GSR increase (e.g., a player's death or the level completion) needs to be fused within the GSR signal and embedded in the model.

The Model's Output

The model's output is usually a set of particular affective states (i.e., classes), a scalar (or a vector of numbers) that maps to an emotion such as the emotional dimensions of arousal and valence, or the relative strength of an emotion (i.e., rank or preference). The output of the model is provided through an annotation process that can be driven either by first-person reports (self-reports) or reports expressed indirectly by experts or external observers (Yannakakis & Togelius, 2011).

The most direct way to annotate an emotion is to ask the players themselves about their playing experience and build a model based on these annotations. Subjective emotion annotation can be based on either player's free-response during play or on forced data retrieved through questionnaires. Alternatively, experts or external observers may annotate the playing experience in a similar fashion. Third-person emotion annotation entails the identification of particular affective states (given in various types of representation, as shown below) by user experience and game design experts. The annotation is usually based on the triangulation of multiple modalities of player and game input such as the player's head pose, in-game behavior, and game context (Shaker, Asteriadis, Yannakakis, & Karpouzis, 2011).

Annotations (either forced self-reports or third-person) can be classified as *rating (scalar)*, *class,* and *preference*. In *rating*, annotators are asked to answer questionnaire items given in a rating/scaling form—for example, in Mandryk and Inkpen (2004)—such as the affective aspects of the Game Experience Questionnaire (Poels & IJsselsteijn, 2008), which labels affective states with a scalar value (or a vector of values). In a *class*-based format, subjects are asked to pick an affective state from a particular representation, which could vary from a simple boolean question ("Was that game level frustrating or not? Is this a sad facial expression?") to an affective state selection from, for example, the Geneva Emotion Wheel (Scherer, 2005). Finally, subjects are able to provide answers in a *preference* format, in which they are asked to compare an affective experience in two or more variants/sessions of the game (e.g., Yannakakis, 2009, among others). They may be asked "Was that level more engaging that this level? Which facial expression looks happier?" A recent comparative study has exposed the limitations of rating approaches over ranking questionnaire schemes (e.g., pairwise preference), which include increased order of play and inconsistency effects (Yannakakis & Hallam, 2011).

Modeling Tools

The tools for constructing models of emotion rely on the modeling approach followed: model-based or model-free. For the model-based approach, components of the model and any parameters that describe them are constructed in an ad-hoc manner and sometimes tested for validity on a trial-and-error basis. No machine learning or sophisticated computational tools are required for model-based approaches, even though one could envisage the optimization of the parameter space to yield more accurate models; that, however, would require empirical studies, which brings the approach closer to a model-free perspective.

Model-free tools for creating models of emotion, on the other hand, are dependent on the type of model output available. If data recorded includes either a *scalar* representation of affect (e.g., via ratings) or *classes* of annotated labels of affective states, any of a large number of machine learning (regression and classification) algorithms can be used to build affective models. Available methods include artificial neural networks, Bayesian networks, decision trees, support vector machines, and standard linear regression. Alternatively, if affect is annotated in a *preference* (i.e., ranked) format, standard supervised learning techniques are inapplicable, as the problem becomes one of preference learning (Yannakakis, 2009). Neuroevolutionary preference learning (Yannakakis, 2009) and rank-based support vector machines (Joachims, 2002) but also simpler methods such as linear discriminant analysis (Tognetti, Garbarino, Bonarini, & Mateucci, 2010) are some of the available approaches for learning preferences. Finally, unsupervised methods such as self-organizing maps, neural gas, and sequence mining (Martinez & Yannakakis, 2011) can be used to identify clusters within the model's input space and profile players accordingly. Empirical studies suggest that the model accuracy is improved when such clusters are fed as complementary input to the model (Martinez, Hullett, & Yannakakis, 2010).

Emotional Adaptation and Expression in Games

Emotions are fundamental for players to deeply engage with games. Players' responses in a game are affected by their emotional states. If, in turn, these states could be used to affect the way the game responds, the player-game interaction could be augmented and enriched by magnitudes, realizing *affective loop*–enabled games. Games may evolve and adapt to the player in many different ways and convey emotions through a variety of techniques and effects. In this section we discuss emotion adaptation and emotion expression, placing them in the context of the affective loop discussed earlier. The adaptation module of the affective loop should be able to provide satisfactory answers to at least some of the following questions: Which stimulus (or playful experience) should be presented next? When should it be presented? Which game elements should be adjusted and how?

Arguably we can achieve meaningful adaptation in games because players are prepared for personalized experiences more than in any other form of HCI. The players' relationship to game adaptation is dependent on their playing style, experience, personality, etc., and the form of adaptation (e.g., implicitly or explicitly) needs to comply with the players' needs. So in creating and designing emotional games, one needs to consider all the processes involved, starting with the game design process itself. Further, while emotion models can be used to inform game designers in a mixed-initiative design fashion (see Liapis et al., 2012, and Smith et al., 2011, among others), we argue that a semi- or fully automated approach to emotion-driven game design can ultimately lead to an improved playing experience. But as the game design entails the definition of many aspects of a game, one fundamental question to ask in referring to emotional game adaptation is: What game elements can one adjust? In other words, what does emotional adaptation entail? A high-level observation of available game elements derives two key classes of adaptable game features: game agents (and NPCs) and game content (see Figure 34.1). Both of these can be manipulated to convey emotional responses and adaptation in a manner that leads the player to become more emotionally involved with the game.

Adapting and Expressing Emotion Through Agents and NPCs

One of the two main ways by which emotions can be manifested in games is through their game characters (see Figure 34.1). Characters in a game need to act, and their actions should be determined by emotional reactions to events occurring in the game. This can be achieved in a completely scripted manner or through an automatic, autonomous approach by using emotional agent architectures (Gratch & Marsella, 2004) underlying cognitive models to generate the behavior of the characters. Such architectures are usually model-based, as they seek inspiration from psychological or physiological models of humans and other species and embed features that allow them to go beyond purely "rational" behavior. Emotional agent architectures naturally include a way to capture emotions or other affective states, such as moods or even personality (Doce, Dias, Prada, & Paiva, 2010). These affective states often have symbolic representations or can be the resulting pattern of behavior arising from a variety of different processes embedded in the agent. Examples of these architectures are EMA (Gratch & Marsella, 2004) and FAtiMA, used for research on serious games in the areas of social and emotional training (Aylett et al., 2009; Lim, Dias, Aylett, & Paiva, 2012; Paiva et al., 2004), ALMA (Gebhard, 2005), or the MindModule (Eladhari & Mateas, 2008) for player characters. Further, these characters may portray social roles and have different personalities leading the users to raise expectations concerning the characters' actions, and as such triggering emotional reactions by the players when those expectations are not met. A game character that plays an ally or a mentor (see (Isbister, 2006) will lead to certain emotional reactions when, for example, the character deceives the player. The personality of a game character can be established by the nature and strength of the emotions that the character portrays in different situations and its tendency to act in a certain manner. For example, an extrovert character will use more speech acts and more expressive actions than an introvert character. These features of personality may be achieved by the appropriate parameterization of the agents (see Doce, Dias, Prada, & Paiva, 2010).

Characters should not only trigger emotional states as a response to a given situation but also need to express emotions in a way that conveys their "internal" emotional state. Thus emotions guide not only the decision making of the characters but also the expressions they portray, which again can be generated in an automatic manner. Expressions of different emotional states—such as, for example, fear, surprise, sadness, or happiness—may blend handcrafted animations to express both strong and subtle emotions with procedural animation techniques to achieve real-time behavior-animated characters (Perlin & Goldberg, 1996).

Characters provide a rich medium to express emotions, trigger emotions, and adapt to the emotions of players. Further, these emotional manifestations can be augmented via adaptive narrative and camera profiles (Picardi, Burelli, & Yannakakis, 2011), allowing for the emphasis on particular emotional states or features and combining this with game content adaptation (see Figure 34.1). We should, however, stress the research-oriented nature of these early systems, acknowledging that autonomous emotional NPCs are still in the realm of a few exploratory research projects. However, we believe that by addressing this challenge, this area will become one of the major pillars of AI in games (Yannakakis, 2012).

Adapting and Expressing Emotion Through Game Content

Yet games may or may *not* include agents. Games, however, definitely include a form of virtual environment where agents "live" (if existent) and the interaction is taking place. There are a number of elements (i.e., game content) from the game world that an adaptive process can alter in order to drive the player to particular affective patterns. As mentioned already, game content may include every aspect of the game design, such as game rules (Togelius & Schmidhuber, 2008), reward systems, lighting (De Melo & Paiva, 2007), camera profiles (Yannakakis et al., 2010a), maps (Togelius et al., 2010), levels, tracks (Togelius, Yannakakis, Stanley, & Browne, 2011), story plot points (Riedl, 2012), and music (Eladhari, Nieuwdorp, & Fridenfalk, 2006). Even behavioral patterns of NPCs, such as their navigation meshes, their parameterized action space, and their animations can be viewed as content.

The adaptive process in this case is referred to as *procedural content generation* (PCG) which is the generation of game content via the use of algorithmic means. According to the taxonomy presented in Togelius, Yannakakis, Stanley, and Browne (2011), game content can be *necessary* (e.g., game rules) or *optional* (e.g., trees in a level or flying birds on the background). Further, PCG can be either *offline* or *online*, *random* or based on a *parameterized space*, *stochastic* or *deterministic*, and finally it can be either *constructive* (i.e., content is generated once) or *generate-and-test* (i.e., content is generated and tested). The experience-driven PCG framework (Yannakakis & Togelius, 2011) views game content as an indirect building block of player affect and proposes adaptive mechanisms for synthesizing personalized game experiences.

Integration in the Affective Loop: When and How to Adapt

Once sufficient amounts of appropriate game stimuli (which include the actions of the game characters and stimuli in the environment) have been presented to the player, aspects of the playing experience can be detected and modeled. For the affective loop to close effectively, the game logic needs to adapt to the current state of the game-player interaction. Whether agent behavior or parameterized game content is at issue, a mapping is required that links a user's affective state to the game context. That mapping is available, as it is essentially the outcome of the emotion modeling phase. Any search algorithm (varying from local and global search to exhaustive search) is applicable for searching in the parameterized search space and finding particular game states (context) that are appropriate for a particular affective state of a specific player. For example, one can envisage the optimization of agent behavior attributes for maximizing engagement, frustration, or empathy toward a player (Leite et al., 2010). As another example, the study of Shaker et al. (2010) presents the application of exhaustive search for generating *Super Mario Bros* (Nintendo, 1985) levels that are maximally frustrating, engaging, or challenging for any player. In that study, parameterized game levels are linked to in-game player behavior attributes and a set of affective states are inferred from crowdsourced player reports. The *model-free* affective model is built via evolving neural networks that learn the crowdsourced pairwise preferences (i.e., neuroevolutionary preference learning).

A critical question once an adaptation mechanism is designed is how often particular attributes should be adjusted. The frequency can vary from simple predetermined or dynamic time windows (Yannakakis & Hallam, 2009), but adaptation can also be activated every time a new level (Shaker, Yannakakis, & Togelius, 2010) or a new game (Yannakakis & Hallam, 2007) starts, or even after a set of critical player actions, as in *Façade* (Mateas & Stern, 2003). The time window of adaptation is heavily dependent on the game under examination and the desires of the game designer. Regardless of the time window adopted, adaptation needs to be interwoven well with design if is to be successful.

One approach for assessing the appropriate time window for game adaptation is to test the validity of the emotion models in different time windows and then make a compromise between adaptation frequency and model performance (Yannakakis &

Hallam, 2009). As models are expected to yield lower accuracies the more deviant they are from the interaction time window they were built on, one needs to evaluate their accuracy with respect to different time windows. A good compromise between accuracy and performance would yield sensible decisions about the length of the adaptation time windows. In general, those can be either static across all gameplay or dynamic (dependent on, for example, different levels).

Evaluating Adaptation

Affective game adaptation can lead to personalized experiences for the player. A key research question, however, is: How do we appropriately evaluate the efficacy of the adaptation mechanism? While several different methods from human factors research are available, all seem to converge to control-based experiments where games are usually evaluated *with* and *without* the adaptation module (e.g., see Yannakakis & Hallam, 2009, among others). The outcome of such an experimental protocol usually allows concluding whether adaptation seems to have an impact on the player's engagement (or any other relevant emotional state). The efficacy of adaptation can be indirectly measured from standard usability metrics (such as response time) or more directly from the output of the emotional model itself (i.e., testing to see whether adaptation yields higher values for the model's output). In addition, one may perform a user survey that asks players to evaluate the adaptation experience (e.g., see Yannakakis & Hallam, 2009).

The Road Ahead

In this final section we list a number of promising research directions for the area of emotion in games that, we believe, will contribute to the advancement of the field in the near future.

• *Mixed-initiative experience design*: The mixed-initiative (i.e., human-machine) approach to co-creativity is becoming increasingly important for game design. Innovative projects such as *Sentient Sketchbook* (Liapis, Yannakakis, & Togelius, 2013), *Sketchaworld* (Smelik, 2011), and *Tanagra* (Smith, Whitehead, & Mateas, 2011) have focused on aspects of level design. However, the potential of emotion-driven mixed-initiative design has not been investigated in depth as yet. We believe that co-creative environments that are affected by emotion, intention, and preference models (of players and/or designers) may enhance creative thinking in game design (Liapis et al, 2013a).

• *Emotion in the game development pipeline*: The impact of emotion in game development can be evident in all phases of game production. Future research needs to focus on establishing protocols for the integration of emotion research in the pipeline of game production. Placing emotion research as the driving force of game production can ultimately lead to better game design, more efficient development, more reliable testing, and richer quality assurance.

• *Links to adjacent fields of study*: The study of emotion in games as represented by the AC community can only benefit from stronger links to and collaborations with adjacent research fields, which include the areas of game studies, game design, user and user experience research, and experimental psychology. In that way, advances in a field can inform relevant research areas for the better understanding of player emotion and its particularities.

• *Content creation is automated*: The use of procedural content generation techniques for the design of better games has reached a peak of interest in commercial and indie game development which is showcased by successful (almost entirely procedurally generated) games such as *Minecraft* (Mojang, 2011) and *Love* (Eskil Steenberg, 2010). Future games are, in general, expected to contain less manual and more user- or procedurally generated content, as the cost of content creation and the content creation bottleneck are key challenges for commercial game production. As the number of games that are partially or fully automatically generated grows, the challenge of detecting and monitoring emotion in never-ending open worlds of infinite replayability value increases substantially. The automation of content creation, however, offers a unique opportunity toward realizing affect-driven content generation in games (Yannakakis & Togelius, 2011).

• *Multimodal game interaction*: Several modalities of player input are still implausible within commercial game development. For instance, existing techniques for physiological recording require the contact of body parts (e.g., head or fingertips) to the sensors, making physiological signals such as EEG, respiration, and skin conductance rather impractical and highly intrusive. Modalities such as facial expression and speech could be technically plausible in games, even though most of the vision-based affect-detection systems currently available cannot operate in real time (Zeng, Pantic, Roisman, & Huang, 2009). On a positive note, recent advances in sensor technology have resulted in low-cost unobtrusive biofeedback devices appropriate for gaming applications (such as the Emotiv[1] EEG system and Empatica[2] bracelet). In addition, top game developers have recently started to experiment with multiple modalities of player input (e.g., physiological and behavioral patterns) for the personalization of experience of popular AAA games such as *Left 4 Dead* (Ambinder, 2011; Valve, 2008). Finally, recent technological advances in gaming peripherals, such as the PrimeSense[3] camera, showcase a promising future for multimodal natural interaction in games.

• *General emotions across games*: After sufficient research has been put into the study of emotion in different game genres, methods for recognizing emotional manifestations across game genres would be required. Such methods could focus on the inference of generic emotions linked to reward systems and game mechanics across game genres.

• *Game data mining*: Massive sets of player metrical data (metrics) are currently available and analyzed, thus empowering the design of future games (Drachen, Thurau, Togelius, Yannakakis, & Bauckhage, 2013). While such data usually contain behavioral aspects of playing experience, data mining and data analysis research will need to focus on inferring the relationship between detailed player metrics and cognitive and affective maps of experience. Making sense of massive game datasets is among the largest challenges from both an analysis and an algorithmic perspective.

Acknowledgments

The authors would like to thank Mirjam P. Eladhari for insightful discussions. This work was supported in part by the FP7 ICT project SIREN (project no: 258453).

Notes

1. http://emotiv.com
2. http://www.emoticalab.com
3. http://www.primesense.com

References

Aarseth, E. (2004). Genre trouble. In N. Wardrip-Fruin (Ed.) *First person: New media as story, performance, and game*. Cambridge, MA: MIT Press.

Ambinder, M. (2011). Biofeedback in gameplay: How valve measures physiology to enhance gaming experience. In *Game Developers Conference*, San Francisco, California, US.

Asteriadis, S., Karpouzis, K., & Kollias, S. D. (2008). A neuro-fuzzy approach to user attention recognition. In *Proceedings of ICANN* (pp. 927–936), Prague, Czech Republic, Springer.

Aylett, R., Vannini, N., Andre, E., Paiva, A., Enz, S., & Hall, L. (2009). But that was in another country: Agents and intercultural empathy. In *Proceedings of the 8th international conference on autonomous agents and multiagent systems - Volume 1 (AAMAS' 09)*, Vol. 1. (pp. 329–336), Richland, SC. International Foundation for Autonomous Agents and Multiagent Systems

Calleja, G. (2011). *In-game: From immersion to incorporation.* Cambridge, MA: MIT Press.

Conati, C. (2002). Probabilistic assessment of user's emotions in educational games. *Journal of Applied Artificial Intelligence, Special Issue on Merging Cognition and Affect in HCI*, 16, 555–575.

Csikszentmihalyi, M. (1990). *Flow: The psychology of optimal experience.* New York: HarperCollins.

de Melo, C., & Paiva, A. (2007). Expression of emotions in virtual humans using lights, shadows, composition and filters. In *Proceedings of Affective Computing and Intelligent Interaction* (pp. 546–557), Lisbon, Portugal. Springer.

de Melo, C., Zheng, L., & Gratch, J. (2009). Expression of moral emotions in cooperating agents. In *Proceedings of the 9th international conference on Intelligent Virtual Agents* (pp. 301–307). Springer Berlin Heidelberg.

Deci, E. L., & Ryan, R. M. (2000). The "what" and "why" of goal pursuits: Human needs and the self-determination of behavior. *Psychological Inquiry*, 11, 227–268.

Dias, J., & Paiva, A. (2005). Feeling and reasoning: A computational model for emotional characters. In *Progress in artificial intelligence* (pp. 127–140). Springer Berlin Heidelberg.

Doce, T., Dias, J., Prada, R., & Paiva, A. (2010). Creating individual agents through personality traits. In *Proceedings of the International Conference on Intelligent Virtual Agents* (pp. 257–264). Springer Berlin Heidelberg.

Drachen, A., Thurau, C., Togelius, J., Yannakakis, G., & Bauckhage, C. (2013). Game data mining. In M. Seif El-Nasr, A. Drachen, A. Canossa, (Eds.) *Game Analytics* (pp. 205-253). Springer London.

Ekman, P., & Friesen, W. (1978). *Facial action coding system: A technique for the measurement of facial Movement.* Palo Alto, CA: Consulting Psychologists Press.

Eladhari, M., & Mateas, M. (2008). Semi-autonomous avatars in World of Minds: A case study of AI-based game design. In *Proceedings of the 2008 International Conference on Advances in Computer Entertainment Technology* (pp. 201–208). ACM.

Eladhari, M., Nieuwdorp, R., & Fridenfalk, M. (2006). The soundtrack of your mind: Mind music-adaptive audio for game characters. In *Proceedings of the 2006 ACM SIGCHI international conference on Advances in computer entertainment technology* (p. 54). ACM.

Feldman, L. (1995). Valence focus and arousal focus: Individual differences in the structure of affective experience. *Journal of Personality and Social Psychology*(69), 53–166.

Frijda, N. (1986). *The emotions.* New York: Cambridge University Press.

Gebhard, P. (2005, July). ALMA: a layered model of affect. In *Proceedings of the fourth international joint conference on Autonomous agents and multiagent systems* (pp. 29–36). ACM.

Georgeff, M., Pell, B., Pollack, M., Tambe, M., & Wooldridge, M. (1999). The belief-desire-intention model of agency. In *Intelligent Agents V: Agents Theories, Architectures, and Languages* (pp. 1–10). Springer Berlin Heidelberg.

Giannatos, S., Nelson, M., Cheong, Y., & Yannakakis, G. N. (2012). Generating narrative action schemas for suspense. In *Proceedings of the 5th workshop on intelligent narrative technologies, AIIDE.* Stanford, Palo Alto, California, US. AAAI.

Gratch, J., & Marsella, S. (2004). A domain-independent framework for modeling emotion. *Cognitive Systems Research*, 5(4), 269–306.

Gratch, J., & Marsella, S. (2005). Evaluating a computational model of emotion. *Autonomous Agents and Multi-Agent Systems*, 11(1), 23–43.

Hingston, P. (2009). A turing test for computer game bots. *IEEE Transactions on Computational Intelligence and AI in Games*, 1(3), 169–186.

Hullett, K., & Whitehead, J. (2010). Design patterns in FPS levels. In *Proceedings of the fifth international conference on the foundations of digital games* (pp. 78–85). Monterey, California, USA. ACM

Isbister, K. (2006). *Better game characters by design: A psychological approach.* Taylor & Francis US.

Isbister, K., & Schaffer, N. (2008). *Game usability: Advancing the player experience.* Taylor & Francis US.

Joachims, T. (2002). Optimizing search engines using click-through data. In *Proceedings of the eighth ACM SIGKDD international conference on Knowledge discovery and data mining* (pp. 133-142). ACM.

Juul, J. (2001). Games telling stories? A brief note on games and narratives. *Game Studies*, I(1).

Koster, R. (2005). *A theory of fun for game design.* Paraglyph Press.

Lazarus, R. (1994). *Emotion and adaptation.* New York: Oxford University Press.

Lazzaro, N. (2004). Why we play games: Four keys to more emotion without story. In *Game Developers Conference*. San Franscisco, US.

Leite, I., Mascarenhas, S., Pereira, A., Martinho, C., Prada, R., & Paiva, A. (2010). Why can't we be friends? An empathic game companion for long-term interaction. In *Proceedings of Intelligent Virtual Agents* (pp. 315–321). Springer Berlin Heidelberg.

Liapis, A., Yannakakis, G. N., & Togelius, J. (2012). Adapting models of visual aesthetics for personalized content creation. *IEEE Transactions on Computational Intelligence and AI in Games, Special Issue on Computational Aesthetics in Games*, IV(3), 213–228.

Liapis, A., Yannakakis, G. N., & Togelius, J. (2013). Sentient sketchbook: Computer-aided game level authoring. In *Proceedings of ACM conference on foundations of digital games* (pp. 213–220). Chania, Crete, Greece.

Liapis, A., Yannakakis, G. N., & Togelius, J. (2013a). Designer Modeling for Personalized Game Content Creation Tools. In *Ninth Artificial Intelligence and Interactive Digital Entertainment Conference*. Boston, MA, US.

Lim, M. Y., Dias, J., Aylett, R., & Paiva, A. (2012). Creating adaptive affective autonomous NPCs. *Autonomous Agents and Multi-Agent Systems*, 24(2), 287–311.

Malone, T. W. (1980). What makes things fun to learn? heuristics for designing instructional computer games. In *Proceedings of the 3rd ACM SIGSMALL symposium and the first SIGPC symposium on small systems* (pp. 162–169).

Mandryk, R., & Inkpen, K. (2004). Physiological indicators for the evaluation of co-located collaborative play. In *Proceedings of the 2004 ACM conference on Computer supported cooperative work* (pp. 102–111). ACM.

Martinez, H. P., & Yannakakis, G. N. (2011). Mining Multimodal Sequential Patterns: A Case Study on Affect Detection. In *Proceedings of the 13th international conference on multimodal interfaces* (pp. 3–10). ACM.

Martinez, H. P., Hullett, K., & Yannakakis, G. N. (2010). Extending neuro-evolutionary preference learning through player modeling. In *Proceedings of the 2010 IEEE conference on computational intelligence and games* (pp. 313–320). Copenhagen, Denmark. IEEE.

Mateas, M., & Stern, A. (2003). Façade: An experiment in building a fully-realized interactive drama. In *Game developers conference, game design track*. San Francisco, CA, US.

McCoy, J., Treanor, M., Samuel, B., Tearse, B., Mateas, M., & Wardrip-Fruin, N. (2010). Comme il faut 2: A fully realized model for socially-oriented gameplay. In *INT3 '10: proceedings of the intelligent narrative technologies III workshop* (pp. 1–8). Palo Alto, CA. AAAI Press.

McQuiggan, S., & Lester, J. (2009). Modeling affect expression and recognition in an interactive learning environment. *International Journal of Learning Technology*, 4(3), 216–233.

McQuiggan, S., Robison, J., & Lester, J. (2010). Affective transitions in narrative-centered learning environments. *Educational Technology & Society*, 1(13), 40–53.

Nijholt, A. (2009). BCI for games: A state of the art survey. In *Proceedings of entertainment computing—ICEC* (pp. 225–228). Paris, France. Springer.

Ortony, A., Clore, G., & Collins, A. (1988). *The cognitive structure of emotions*. Cambridge, UK: Cambridge University Press.

Paiva, A., Dias, J., Sobral, S., Aylett, R., Sobreperez, S., Woods, S., Zoll, C., & Hall, L. E. (2004). Caring for agents and agents that care: Building empathic relations with synthetic agents. In *Proceedings of the Third International Joint Conference on Autonomous Agents and Multiagent Systems-Volume 1* (pp. 194–201). IEEE Computer Society.

Pantic, M., & Caridakis, G. (2011). Image and video processing for affective applications. In *Emotion-oriented systems: The Humaine handbook* (pp. 101–117). Berlin and Heidelberg: Springer.

Perlin, K., & Goldberg, A. (1996). Improv: A system for scripting interactive actors in virtual worlds. *Proceedings of the 23rd annual conference on computer graphics and interactive techniques* (pp. 205–216). New Orleans, LA, USA. ACM

Picardi, A., Burelli, P., & Yannakakis, G. N. (2011). Modelling virtual camera behaviour through player gaze. In *Proceedings of the 6th international conference on foundations of digital games* (pp. 107–114). Chania, Crete, Greece.

Plans, D., & Morelli, D. (2012). Experience-driven procedural music generation for games. *IEEE Transactions on Computational Intelligence and AI in Games 4*, *IV*(3), 192–198.

Poels, K., & IJsselsteijn, W. (2008). Development and validation of the game experience questionnaire. In *FUGA workshop mini-symposium*

Riedl, M. O. (2012). Interactive narrative: A novel application of artificial intelligence for computer games. In *Proceedings of the 26th AAAI conference on artificial intelligence*. Toronto, Ontario, Canada.

Roberts, D. L., Narayanan, H., & Isbell, C. L. (2009). Learning to Influence Emotional Responses for Interactive Storytelling. In *AAAI Spring Symposium: Intelligent Narrative Technologies II* (pp. 95–102).

Russell, J. A. (1980). A circumplex model of affect. *Journal of Personality and Social Psychology*, 39(6), 1161–1178.

Salen, K., & Zimmerman, E. (2003). *Rules of play: Game design fundamentals*. Cambridge, MA: MIT Press.

Savva, N., Scarinzi, A., & Bianchi-Berthouze, N. (2012). Continuous recognition of player's affective body expression as dynamic quality of aesthetic experience. *IEEE Transactions on CI and AI in Games, Special Issue on Computational Creativity*, *IV*(3) 199–212.

Scherer, K. R. (1993). Studying the emotion-antecedent appraisal process: An expert system approach. *Cognition and Emotion*, 7, 325–355.

Scherer, K. R. (2005). What are emotions? And how can they be measured? *Social Science Information*, 4(44), 693–727.

Seif El-Nasr, M., Vasilakos, A., Rao, C., & Zupko, J. (2009). Dynamic intelligent lighting for directing visual attention in interactive 3D scenes. *IEEE Transactions on Computational Intelligence and AI in Games*, I(2),145–153.

Shaker, N., Asteriadis, S., Yannakakis, G. N., & Karpouzis, K. (2011). A game-based corpus for analysing the interplay between game context and player experience. In *Proceedings of the 2011 affective computing and intelligent interaction conference; Emotion in games workshop*. Memphis, TN, US.

Shaker, N., Yannakakis, G. N., & Togelius, J. (2010). Towards automatic personalized content generation for platform games. In *AAAI conference on artificial intelligence and interactive digital entertainment (AIIDE)*. Palo Alto, CA, US. AAAI Press

Skinner, B. F. (1938). *The behavior of organisms: An experimental analysis*. Cambridge, KA: B. F. Skinner Foundation.

Smelik, R. M. (2011). *A declarative approach to procedural generation of virtual worlds*. Ph.D. thesis. Delft, The Netherlands: Delft University of Technology.

Smith, G., Whitehead, J., & Mateas, M. (2011). Tanagra: Reactive planning and constraint solving for mixed-initiative level design. *IEEE Transactions on Computational Intelligence and AI in Games*, III(3), 201–215.

Suits, B. (2005). *The grasshopper: Games, life and utopia*. Broadview Press.

Sundstrom, P. (2005). *Exploring the affective loop*. Stockholm: Stockholm University.

Sweetser, P., & Wyeth, P. (2005). Game flow: A model for evaluating player enjoyment in games. *ACM Computers in Entertainment*, 3(3). 3–3.

Togelius, J., & Schmidhuber, J. (2008). An experiment in automatic game design. In *Proceedings of the IEEE symposium on computational intelligence and games (CIG)* (pp. 111–118). Perth, Australia. IEEE Press.

Togelius, J., Preuss, M., Beume, N., Wessing, S., Hagelback, J., & Yannakakis, G. N. (2010). Multiobjective exploration of the starcraft map space. In *2010 IEEE conference on computational intelligence and games (CIG)* (pp. 265–272). Copenhagen, Denmark. IEEE Press

Togelius, J., Yannakakis, G. N., Stanley, K. O., & Browne, C. (2011). Search-based procedural content generation: a taxonomy and survey. *IEEE Transactions on Computational Intelligence and AI in Games, Special Issue on Procedural Content Generation*, III(3), 172–186.

Tognetti, S., Garbarino, M., Bonarini, A., & Mateucci, M. (2010). Modeling enjoyment preference from physiological responses in a car racing game. In *Proceedings of the IEEE conference on computational intelligence and games* (pp. 321–328). Copenhagen, Denmark. IEEE Press

Yannakakis, G. N. (2009). Preference learning for affective modeling. In *Proceedings of international confernece on affective computing and intelligent interaction* (pp. 126–131). Amsterdam, The Netherlands. IEEE.

Yannakakis, G. N. (2012). Game AI revisited. In *ACM computing frontiers conference* (pp. 285–292). Cagliari, Italy. ACM

Yannakakis, G. N., & Hallam, J. (2009, June). Real-time game adaptation for optimizing player satisfaction. *IEEE Transactions on Computational Intelligence and AI in Games,* 1(2), 121–133.

Yannakakis, G. N., & Hallam, J. (2011). Rating vs. preference: A comparative study of self-reporting. In *Proceedings of Affective Computing and Intelligent Interaction,* pp. 437–446. Memphis, TN, US. Springer.

Yannakakis, G. N., & Togelius, J. (2011). Experience-driven procedural content generation. *IEEE Transactions on Affective Computing,* 2(3), 147–161.

Yannakakis, G. N., Martinez, H. P., & Jhala, A. (2010a). Towards affective camera control in games. *User Modeling and User-Adapted Interaction,* 4(20), 313–340.

Yannakakis, G. N., Togelius, J., Khaled, R., Jhala, A., Karpouzis, K., Paiva, A., & Vasalou, A. (2010b). Siren: Towards adaptive serious games for teaching conflict resolution. In *Proceedings of the 4th European conference on games based learning.* 412–417. Copenhagen, Denmark.

Zeng, Z., Pantic, M., Roisman, G., & Huang, T. (2009). A survey of affect recognition methods: Audio, visual, and spontaneous expressions. *IEEE Transactions on Pattern Analysis and Machine Intelligence,* I(31), 39–58.

Autonomous Closed-Loop Biofeedback: An Introduction and a Melodious Application

Egon L. van den Broek, Joris H. Janssen, *and* Joyce H. D. M. Westerink

Abstract

This chapter defines the core concepts surrounding biofeedback and denotes their relations. Subsequently, a closed-loop human-machine architecture is introduced in which a biofeedback protocol is executed. This architecture is brought from theory to practice via a personalized affective music player (AMP). Regression and kernel density estimation are applied to model the physiological changes elicited by music. The AMP was validated via a real-world evaluation over the course of several weeks. Results show that our autonomous closed-loop biofeedback system can cope with noisy situations and handle large interindividual differences in the music domain. The AMP augments music listening, where its techniques enable autonomous affect guidance. Our approach provides valuable insights for affective computing and autonomous closed-loop biofeedback systems in general.

Key Words: autonomous, closed-loop model, biofeedback, affect, music, personalized, physiological changes, validation

Biofeedback has been proposed as a technique to improve health and performance by measuring an individual's physiological activity and thus supporting him or her in changing it (Moss & Gunkelman, 2002). Throughout its existence, biofeedback has been criticized almost continuously (Moss & Gunkelman, 2002). Nevertheless, affective computing has shown that biofeedback can work quite effectively. In line with this, this chapter provides a solid foundation for biofeedback in the domain of affective computing, followed by a discussion of a study that brings this theory to real-world practice.

In the first part of this chapter the core concepts surrounding biofeedback are defined and their relations denoted. Subsequently, the closed-loop human-machine architecture—in which the biofeedback protocol is executed—is introduced. In the second part, we present our autonomous closed-loop biofeedback system, a personalized affective music player (AMP), and its real-world validation. We end this chapter with a summative discussion.

Description of an Autonomous Closed-Loop Biofeedback System
Biosignals, Biofeedback, and Affect

Physiological signals, or biosignals, can be conceptualized as bioelectrical signals recorded on the surface of the body[1]. The bioelectrical signals are related to ionic transport, which arises as a result of the electrochemical activity of cells in specialized tissue (e.g., the nervous system), so-called autonomic responses. This leads to changes in the electrical currents produced by the sum of electrical potential differences across the tissue. This process is the same regardless of where in the body the cells are located (e.g., the heart, muscles, skin, or brain) (Sörnmo & Laguna, 2005). Therefore biosignals reflect a person's physiological activity (see also Chapters 7 and 14), among other things. Note that the latter definition also includes both nonelectrical biosignals, which comprise signals with a magnetic, mechanical, optical, acoustic, chemical, and thermal origin (Kaniusas, 2012).

On May 18, 2008, the Association for Applied Psychophysiology and Biofeedback (AAPB), the Biofeedback Certification International Alliance (BCIA), and the International Society for Neurofeedback and Research (ISNR)[2] jointly agreed on a standard definition of biofeedback, as noted below:

> Biofeedback is a process that enables an individual to learn how to change physiological activity for the purposes of improving health and performance. Precise instruments measure physiological activity such as brainwaves, heart function, breathing, muscle activity, and skin temperature. These instruments rapidly and accurately "feed back" information to the user. The presentation of this information—*often in conjunction with changes in thinking, emotions, and behavior*—supports desired physiological changes. Over time, these changes can endure without continued use of an instrument.

This was one of the results of a joint task force initiated by the AAPB and the ISNR in 2001 (Moss & Gunkelman, 2002). The definitions of both biosignals and biofeedback provide the premises for this chapter. To also understand the criticism biofeedback has been subjected to, we need to go back in time, to the invention of biofeedback, and place the work on biofeedback into historical perspective.

The origin of biofeedback takes us back to 1932, the year in which Johannes Heinrich Schultz published a book on a relaxation technique he called autogenic training. In 2003, the twentieth edition of this book was published, which marks its continuing influence (Schultz, 2003). However, Schultz did not provide direct biofeedback, since his technique relies on introspection, and no signals are fed back to the user. It took more than 25 years until biofeedback, as defined here, was reported by Mandler, Mandler, and Uviller (1958). They defined it as "the relationship between autonomic response and the subject's reported perception of such response-induced stimulation" (Mandler et al., 1958, p. 367) and denoted it as autonomic feedback. The latest boost of criticism and a response to it dates from around the turn of the century. Among many issues of criticism, the lack of proven efficacy, the absence of standards, and the fuzzy relation between biosignals and psychological constructs were noted (Moss & Gunkelman, 2002).

The work of Mandler et al. (1958) was conducted more than half a century ago, in the early years of computing machinery. At that time, computers were invented for highly trained operators to help them do massive numbers of calculations. However, much has changed since then. Today we are in touch with various types of computers throughout our normal daily lives, including our smartphones (Agrawal, 2011). Computation is on track to become even smaller and more pervasive. Not only computing machinery but also biomedical apparatus is miniaturized (Ouwerkerk, Pasveer, & Langereis, 2008). Consequently biosignals (or physiological signals; see also Healey, this volume) still receive increasing interest as an interface between users and their computing devices. It is envisioned that computers will become a window to the world as a whole, to our social life, and even to ourselves (Bons, Van den Broek, Herpers, Scheepers, Rommelse, & Buitelaar, 2013; Janssen, Bailenson, IJsselsteijn, & Westerink, 2010; Van den Broek, 2010).

Computers are slowly becoming dressed, huggable, and tangible (cf. Van den Broek, 2010, and see Mühl et al., Paiva et al., and Arkin & Moshkina, all this volume). Affective concepts such as mood, stress, and emotions, which were originally the playing field of philosophers, sociologists, and psychologists (Izard et al., 2010), have already become entangled in computers (and in computer science) as well (Giakoumis et al., 2012). This handbook illustrates this fusion par excellence. It has become much easier for us than before to accept emotions as being omnipresent (Konijn, 2013), biosignals as relevant reflections of our lives (cf. Janssen, Bailenson, IJsselsteijn, & Westerink, 2010), and biofeedback as a means to alter them. Additionally, biofeedback standards can emerge more easily with the help of information and communications technology. And while the embedding of biofeedback into psychological constructs remains unclear, the first efficacy evaluations of biofeedback have started to show its usefulness (Gruzelier, Egner, & Vernon, 2006). Thus two of the traditional criticisms of biofeedback are on the verge of being tackled. In the next section, we provide a concise overview of our working model: an autonomous closed-loop biofeedback model.

The Closed-Loop Autonomous Biofeedback Model[3]

To enable autonomous biofeedback, a closed-loop model, incorporating both measurement and feedback components, must be adopted. Such a model can involve human intervention but does not necessarily do so. Consequently closed-loop biofeedback systems can be positioned in the large market of consumer electronics. For over a century, closed-loop models have been known in science and engineering, in particular in control theory and electronics (Neamen, 2010). Closed-loop models can be defined as control systems with an active feedback loop. This loop allows the control unit to dynamically compensate for deviations in the system. The output of the system is fed back through a sensor measurement to a control unit, which takes the error between a reference and the output to change the inputs to the system under control.

Biofeedback systems belong to a special class of closed-loop models: that is, closed loops that take a human into the loop (see also Figure 35.1). Although the descriptions of biofeedback systems target various areas, these descriptions are essentially the same. In essence, biofeedback systems can be described by three basic steps:

1. *Sensing*: Data collection starts at the sensors, where a raw signal that contains an indication of a person's psychological state is generated. Relevant signals can include both overt and covert bodily signals, such as facial camera recordings (see Cohn & De la Torre, this volume; and Zeng, Pantic, Roisman, & Huang, 2009), movements (see Bianchi-Berthouze and Kleinsmith, this volume; and Giakoumis et al., 2012), speech samples (see Jeremy Lee et al., this volume; Van den Broek, Van der Sluis, & Dijkstra, 2013; and Zeng, Pantic, Roisman, & Huang, 2009), and biosignals (see Healey and Mühl et al., this volume; and Kim & André, 2008).

2. *Signal processing and pattern recognition*: Exploiting signal features that contain information on the psychological state; for example, the statistical moments of biosignals (e.g., electrodermal activity [EDA], electromyography [EMG], and electrocardiography [ECG]) can be calculated to serve as a measure of arousal (Giakoumis et al., 2012; Van den Broek & Westerink, 2009). For more information on this step, we refer to Kapoor's chapter, this volume, and to Van den Broek, Nijholt, and Westerink (2010).

3. *Influencing and feedback*: Given the obtained psychological state of the user, a decision is

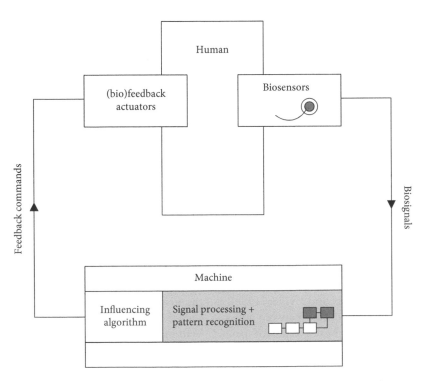

Fig. 35.1 The (general) biofeedback closed-loop model. For details on the model's signal processing and pattern recognition component, see Van den Broek, Nijholt, and Westerink, 2010.

made as to what feedback to provide to the user. Part 3 of this handbook provides seven chapters on how affect can be generated, which can be a form of feedback; however, other types of (nonaffective) feedback can be provided as well. The feedback is provided by a set of actuators that can communicate directly with the body, either physically (Hatzfeld, Kern, & Werthschützky, 2010) or chemically (Mielle et al., 2010). Alternatively, actuators can communicate indirectly and influence our environment as we sense it either consciously or unconsciously; for instance, a song can be played (Van der Zwaag, Dijksterhuis, de Waard, Mulder, Westerink, & Brookhuis, 2012) or lighting can be activated (Bialoskorski, Westerink, Van den Broek, 2009, 2010) to create a certain ambiance.

Note that the loop always closes with a new measurement of the sensors that is again evaluated as to whether or not the intended effect has indeed been reached. If the intended effect has been reached, the system will perform no further adjustments but will continue to monitor its user.

In the next section, music is introduced as a feedback actuator. For several other examples of feedback actuators, we refer the reader to Part 5 of this handbook: Applications of Affective Computing.

Application of an Autonomous Closed-Loop Biofeedback System: The Affective Music Player[4]

Over the last 20 years, new technologies have digitalized our music listening experience. In today's world, we have ubiquitous access to large amounts of music. We listen to music while traveling, while working, and while reading a book. Par excellence, music can tap into the listener's emotional state. Music can energize people, relax them, or make them happier. If a music player had such qualities, it could tune itself in to a user's mood, fitting the selected music to the user's current or desired emotional state. As we show in the remainder of the chapter, this can be realized. However, first let us concisely describe how we define emotions and mood and how they relate to affect.

The term *affect* is often used to describe both processes related to emotions and processes related to mood (Russell, 2003, chapter 4); however, it is important to untangle these two. We define emotions as relatively short-lasting hedonic reactions to specific stimuli in the (internal or external) environment (Van den Broek et al., 2011, 2013). They

result in physiological and behavioral changes so as to deal with the sudden change in the environment. In contrast, moods (1) are long-lasting and change gradually, (2) are not object-related, and (3) are often experienced without awareness of their origin (Frijda, 1986; Izard et al., 2010; Rosenberg, 1998). Moods can also be accompanied by physiological changes but do not result in direct action tendencies (Beedie, Terry, & Lane, 2005). Instead, they influence behavior indirectly (Gendolla & Krüsken, 2002). Moods are often operationalized in terms of valence and energy or arousal (Matthews, Jones, & Chamberlain, 1990; Thayer, 1989). Note that mood also influences cognitive performance (Gendolla & Krüsken, 2002), health and well-being (Van den Broek & Westerink, 2012), creativity, improved decision-making processes, and enhances social relationships (Baas, Dreu, & Nijstad, 2008). For our music player, we are not specifically interested in influencing short-lived emotional changes but in more gradual changes in the listener's mood.

The affective power of music was already utilized by Picard (1997). She showed that an affective music player (AMP) is not only a promising application in itself but also a useful carrier application to explore strategies for affective computing. One such prominent strategy is personalization, as the field of affective computing has already experienced how large individual differences can be (Zeng et al., 2009), which is no different for music preferences (Kim & André, 2008; Van den Broek, Janssen, Healey, & Van der Zwaag, 2010; Van der Zwaag, Westerink, & Van den Broek, 2011). Throughout the last decade, several AMPs have been proposed (e.g., Healey, Picard, & Dabek, 1998; Janssen, Van den Broek, & Westerink, 2012; Oliver & Kregor-Stickles, 2006; Picard, 1997). However, little thorough real-world testing over longer periods of time has been conducted. No matter how well founded and integrated a system may be in theory, the complexities of human affect and physiological responses make it necessary to rigorously test a proposed system in the real world (Aviezer, Trope, & Todorov, 2012; Van den Broek, Janssen, & Westerink, 2009). We attempt to do this in three consecutive phases: (1) we gather data from different users over different days during their regular working activities; (2) we use these data to train our user models; and (3) we use these trained personalized models to make music selections and see whether or not these music selections elicit the desired affective state or states.

Sensing and Signal Processing

Three male volunteers (aged 22, 26, and 27) participated and rated 400 randomly selected songs from their own music library on a 5-point valence scale expressing how they expected the songs would make them feel. From the ratings, nine positive songs, nine negative songs, and nine neutral songs were randomly selected. This resulted in 27 songs per participant for which physiological and mood data were gathered. For details on the acquisition design, we refer to Janssen, Van den Broek, and Westerink (2012).

The data-gathering sessions were conducted during regular working activities in the office, including writing and data analysis. The volunteers who participated were at their own desks in a room that they shared with multiple colleagues. Hence, the data gathered contained various types of noise (e.g., caused by physical movements, joking colleagues, and disrupting emails). A very small skin temperature sensor (Figure 35.2) was connected to a NeXus-10 apparatus of Mind Media to measure skin temperature. The NeXuS-10 was connected to a computer, using a wireless Bluetooth data connection. Consequently the participants were free to walk around while participating in this research.

Each song was listened to nine times over nine different sessions. In each session, every song was played exactly once. For each session, we used a different trigram-balanced order (similar to Wagenaar, 1969) based on the feeling ratings (positive/neutral/negative). A trigram-balanced order is completely counterbalanced and, additionally, the type of the two items preceding the third item is also counterbalanced. So for each feeling (positive/neutral/negative), all nine sequences of two feelings preceded every feeling once in an order. For details on the specific design, we refer to Janssen, Van den Broek, and Westerink (2012). The participants decided when to run a session. The complete data gathering took about a month per participant.

The data was preprocessed by calculating the change in the signal after each song and by standardizing that change relative to the current session. These relative changes were used in the user models described later on. To be able to calculate the skin temperature changes, a number of preprocessing steps were performed. For every song k in every session n, the mean skin temperature of the last minute of the song, denoted by x_{kn}, was extracted. This mean was standardized over the session using

$$Z_{kn} = \frac{x_{kn} - \mu_n}{\sigma_n}, \qquad (1)$$

where μ_n is the mean σ_n and the standard deviation over all songs of session n. This has proved to be a successful method for standardizing physiological signals (Boucsein, 1992). Next, delta scores Δz_{kn}

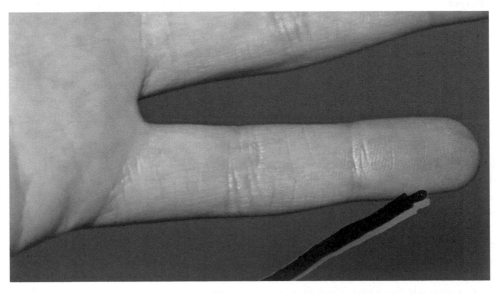

Fig. 35.2 The skin temperature sensor that was attached to the NeXuS-10 wearable recording device. The sensor was attached with medical adhesive tape to the nondominant hand's proximal phalanx. Note that the utter tip of the cable is the sensor itself. The sensor's very small size makes it possible to integrate it in small wearables such as a watch, a necklace, gloves, and even earrings (e.g., see Ouwerkerk, Pasveer, & Langereis, 2008).

that indicated the effect of song k in session n on the physiology were computed by using

$$\Delta z_{kn} = z_{kn} - z_{(k-1)n}, \qquad (2)$$

with $k \geq 2$.

These delta scores describe the skin temperature change during a song and were used as input for our user models.

Pattern Recognition, Influencing, and Feedback

The AMP was personalized using the preprocessed gathered data, as described next. The user models consisted of a probability distribution for each song for each user over the change scores in the physiological signals, as explained in the previous paragraphs. These probability distributions could subsequently be used to predict the effect of a certain song. To get to these distributions. several steps were taken.

First, we corrected for the law of initial values (LIV) (Wilder, 1967; Geenen & Vijver, 1993). The LIV states that a future change in physiological activity depends on the current state; for instance, when heart rate is very high, it is more likely to decrease when no external force is applied to keep it high. We operationalize the LIV using a delta score Δz_{kn} of a stimulus that depends on the prestimulus level $\Delta z_{(k-1)n}$. The delta score tends to decrease when the prestimulus level is high, whereas it tends to increase when the prestimulus level is low. Conveniently, a regression line can be used to model this relation:

$$y(z) = w_1 z - w_0, \qquad (3)$$

where w_0 and w_1 are the parameters of the regression line and $y(z)_0$ is the predicted change based on the prestimulus value z. The parameters w_0 and w_1 were approximated using all data for each participant. Next, the corrected delta scores $\Delta' z_{kn}$ were computed as follows:

$$\Delta'_{kn} = \Delta z_{kn} - y(z_{(k-1)n}). \qquad (4)$$

Next, a probabilistic model of the corrected delta scores for each song was needed. We used a pdf (probability density function) over $\Delta' z$ to describe the physiological change that accompanied a song. Since the pdfs are unknown and only a limited number of observations of $\Delta' z$ is available, we used Kernel Density Estimates (KDEs) to estimate the pdfs. For every song k, the KDE contains a radial kernel function $k(\Delta' z | \Delta' z_{kn}, n_k)$, with precision n_k,

around all of the song's N_k measured points $\Delta' z_{kn}$. The KDE averages over these N_k kernels:

$$p_k(\Delta' z) = \sum_{n=1}^{N_k} K(\Delta' z \mid \Delta' z_{kn}, n_k)/N_k, \qquad (5)$$

which yields the pdf $p_k(\Delta' z)$ over $\Delta' z$ for song k (see Figure 35.3). To calculate h, we adopted:

$$n_k = 1.06\sqrt{N_k} \min\left(\sigma k, \frac{R_k}{1.34}\right), \qquad (6)$$

where R_k is the interquartile range and σk is the standard deviation of the song k's corrected delta scores $\Delta' z_{kn}$. A radial Gaussian kernel was used with mean $\Delta' z_{kn}$ and standard deviation n_k because of its analytical properties and its ability to provide a smooth distribution (Heinz & Seeger, 2008):

$$k(\Delta' z \mid \Delta' z_{km}, n_k)$$
$$= \exp\left(\frac{(\Delta' z - \Delta' z_{kn})^2}{2n_k^2}\right)/n_k \sqrt{2\pi}. \qquad (7)$$

Music can be selected using the probabilities calculated from the KDEs. The physiological signal can be directed to either one of the extreme values or its neutral range (Figure 35.3). However, sometimes, the desired affective state is not reached at either one of the extremes of a physiological measure. For instance, in trying to focus on a task, music that is too relaxing will lower the working spirit, whereas music that is too arousing might distract the listener from the task (Van den Broek, 2012; Van der Zwaag et al., 2011). In those cases, the physiological models should also allow direction toward a specific point instead of directing to either the low or high extremes. To do this, the necessary change to Δz get to that specific point must first be calculated. Subsequently, a song that is most likely to induce such a physiological state must be selected. If this music is available, the KDEs do allow selection of the song with the highest probability in a specific interval.

Validation

As an ultimate test for our personalized AMP, we submitted our participants to a 2-week real-world trial, using the same setup as during the data gathering. The same three participants participated in four sessions of music listening; each session comprised 18 songs. To be able to assess μn and σn for session standardization (see also Equation 1), every session started with eight neutral songs defined as the songs

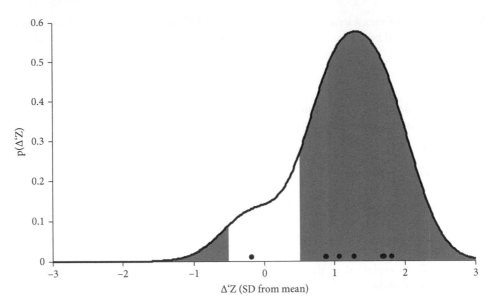

Fig. 35.3 The KDE of one song, where the black dots depict measured changes in skin temperature (ST) for this song. The three areas under the curve indicate respectively the probability of a decrease (left), stable (center), and increase (right) in skin temperature during this song. Hence, this KDE shows that it is likely that the skin temperature will increase during this song.

with the highest probabilities for Δz to be in the $\langle 0.5, 0.5 \rangle$ range. Then two conditions followed: one that aimed to increase skin temperature level and one that aimed to decrease it (Baumgartner, Esslen, & Jäncke, 2006; McFarland & Kennison 1989; Rimm-Kaufman & Kagan, 1996). For both of these conditions, we selected a block of five songs from the trained personalized models, as described in the previous section. For each participant, two blocks of five songs were selected; one with the highest increasing probability and one with the highest decreasing probability. This was realized by integrating the pdf (Equation 5) over $\Delta z \in [0.5, \infty\rangle$ and $\Delta z \in \langle -\infty, 0.5]$, respectively, and selecting the songs with the highest probabilities in each interval. The order of the two conditions was counterbalanced over the four sessions. The sessions were conducted on different days but again during regular working activities. The mean skin temperature of the last minute of each song was selected and standardized over all songs in the session, using Equation 1. The complete validation phase took about 2 weeks per participant. In the case of one participant, one session contained measurement errors due to a loose sensor and hence was excluded from further analysis.

Changes in participants' skin temperature were examined by running repeated-measures ANOVAs with session being the level of analysis on skin temperature for each individual participant, with song

number and direction as respectively within- and between-block factors. For the first participant, a main effect of direction was found ($F(1, 4) = 13.7$, $P < .021$, $eta^2 = .77$), where skin temperature was higher in the increasing direction ($M = 0.45$) than in the decreasing direction ($M = -0.31$). For the second participant, only an interaction effect of song number and direction was found ($F(5, 30) = 4.74$, $P < .003$, $eta^2 = .44$). A t-test showed that skin temperature declined in the decreasing direction ($t(6) = 3.64$, $P < .011$, $d = 2.97$ sigma) but remained stable in the increasing direction. For the third participant, three sessions also showed that skin temperature increased in the increasing direction, but an inverted pattern was found for the fourth session, which resulted in the overall absence of the expected effects.

An additional extensive user study that validated the concept of the AMP is reported by Van der Zwaag, Janssen, and Westerink (2013). This study extended the work described in this chapter in several ways. First, Van der Zwaag and colleagues (2013) focused on EDA as a biosignal to direct arousal with music. Furthermore, the validation was extended to eight participants, and each session lasted for 30 minutes instead of 20. As such, this study extends the work described in this chapter (e.g., including multiple biosignals and testing over longer periods). Both subjective ratings and skin conductance showed the pattern as expected based on the target condition. To clarify, in conditions where skin conductance was directed upward, it ended up being the highest, with subjective ratings also being the highest in energy. The values for the condition in which the skin conductance was directed downward ended up being the lowest (in both skin conductance and arousal self-report); the values for the neutral condition were in between. By using more participants and longer induction periods, the study further validates the concept of the affective music player in practice. The authors conclude that music can indeed be used to reliably direct mood toward a desired state.

Discussion

This chapter proposed autonomous closed-loop biofeedback as a design principle for affective computing. In the first half of the chapter, the two main aspects underlying this design principle were introduced—namely, biofeedback and closed-loop systems. In the second half of the chapter, theory was brought to (real-world) practice with the design and evaluation of such a system, a personalized AMP. We close the chapter with a discussion and reflect on the design principle introduced.

The biofeedback principle, as discussed at the start of this chapter, is not new and has also already been applied in the field of affective computing. However, in the field of affective computing, in most cases, the notion of biofeedback has not been made explicit. Consequently standardization on biofeedback is problematic and the same principles are reinvented over and over. With this chapter, we do not claim to bring something new to bear; however, we intend to make a start toward developing design principles for biofeedback-based affective computing. For the biofeedback component of many affective computing technologies, this chapter hopefully provides a start to what will result in some common ground on the application of biofeedback for affective computing.

The design principles have been brought into practice with the development of an AMP. It uses individual probabilistic models that deal with both differences in its users and environmental noise. Additionally, we have employed the law of initial values (LIV) in a closed-loop system. Finally, instead of measuring short-term emotions, we studied longer-term effects of moods. The development and validation of the AMP comprised three steps: (1) physiological responses during real-world music listening were gathered; (2) the AMP was personalized (cf. Kim & André, 2008); and (3) the

system was validated in the real world, using skin temperature (McFarland & Kennison, 1989; Rimm-Kaufman & Kagan, 1996).

The validation of the AMP and hence of the design principles in general was successful. The songs selected to reduce skin temperature did indeed do so, although a delay was present before these effects reached significance. However, this time period is in line with controlled experiments that use music to induce mood (Gendolla & Krüsken, 2002). Moreover, these results were found not only over all data but also for each individual participant. This is important, as we aimed to develop individual models instead of a generic population model (cf. Kim & André, 2008).

A first limitation of our work is the fact that we used only skin temperature as a physiological measure (McFarland & Kennison, 1989; Rimm-Kaufman & Kagan, 1996), where multiple physiological measures would have been possible (Calvo & D'Mello, 2010). The use of more physiological measures might significantly improve the performance of the system as well as the resolution of mood states the system can model. Fortunately our model can be extended to deal with multiple physiological measures using multidimensional KDEs (Scott & Sain, 2005), which enables the generation of a model of the effects of multiple physiological signals in one pdf.

A second limitation of our system is its cold-start problem; that is, new users have to listen to each song a few times before accurate predictions can be made. To overcome this problem, various approaches can be explored. First, a population model can be generated using aggregates of other users' physiological responses to songs. Such a population model can serve as an a priori distribution that is updated with KDEs each time the user listens to the song. Second, after a user model has been constructed for one song, this user model can be used as an a priori model for similar songs (Sotiropoulos, Lampropoulos, & Tsihrintzis, 2008). Third and finally, a priori models can also be founded on personality and music preference, which determine affective responses up to a significant extent (Van der Zwaag et al., 2011; Van der Zwaag, Janssen, & Westerink, 2013).

The AMP distinguished two contrasting moods: very positive and very negative. As such we have only explored the dimension valence of the mood construct and did not control on its other dimensions, such as tension and energy (Matthews et al., 1990; Thayer, 1989). More research on the

AMP presented here can be found in Janssen and colleagues (2012) and Van der Zwaag et al. (2013). Additional follow-up research should explore whether or not these dimensions can be assessed using similar methods.

Although there are still issues to be resolved with future research, we did successfully introduce an autonomous closed-loop biofeedback model for affective computing and developed and validated a carrier application for it. This application, the AMP, was tested in the real world; hence, the autonomous closed-loop biofeedback model for affective computing showed its value not only in theory but also in practice, and a high level of ecological validity was realized. This remains important, as the use of biofeedback in the uncontrolled real world remains challenging. Nevertheless, the application of our biofeedback model was found to be robust against real-world noise. As we stated in the Introduction, the autonomous closed-loop biofeedback model can be of great value when developing affective technology.

This chapter deviates from the majority of research in affective computing in that it assessed mood instead of emotions, which seems advisable in many real-world applications. Further, the use of biosignals has once more been shown to be both important, given their relation to psychological constructs; it has also proved feasible, with apparatus rapidly becoming miniaturized and wireless and with extended battery life. We used the biosignal skin temperature, which is not done very often; however, literature provided strong indications that it is related to valence (McFarland & Kennison, 1989; Rimm-Kaufman & Kagan, 1996). In addition, the LIV (Wilder, 1967) was applied to correct our measured values for prestimulus levels. This approach reduced the amount of noise the model had to deal with and consequently improved its performance. Last, affective responses are very personal, so user-specific models should be employed. Par excellence, autonomous closed-loop biofeedback models have been shown to serve this aim.

While this chapter illustrated the principle of autonomous closed-loop biofeedback models for affective computing by means of a specific carrier application, the AMP, various other applications can benefit from a similar approach. First, consider an in-car system that detects a driver's stress and responds appropriately (Healey & Picard, 2005; Van der Zwaag, Dijksterhuis, de Waard, Mulder, Westerink, & Brookhuis, 2012). This idea stems from the birth of affective computing, where it was explored in the late 1990s (Healey & Picard,

1998; Healey & Picard, 2005). Such a system could use physiological signals to continually measure stress levels. Hence it could benefit from employing the LIV to correct the measured physiology. Furthermore, the autonomous closed-loop biofeedback approach could be used to model how users respond to different adaptations the system makes to reduce driver stress. Second, consider an application that communicates its user's emotions (Bialoskorski, Westerink, Van den Broek, 2009, 2010; Janssen, Bailenson, IJsselsteijn, & Westerink, 2010). As such, it could augment our communication channels when biofeedback is received by another person than the one who transmitted it. In particular, such an application could be of interest if people do not know each other that well or are not physically located close to each other, as is also done in media entertainment (Konijn, 2013). Third and last, our autonomous closed-loop biofeedback approach could also be interesting for applications outside the area of affective computing. For instance, the domain of mental health care could benefit from autonomous closed-loop biofeedback models (Bons et al., 2013; Van den Broek, Van der Sluis, & Dijkstra, 2013; Van den Broek & Westerink, 2012). Bons et al. (2013) provide a set of diagnostic tools, including both eye tracking and biosignals, to unveil differences in the three dimensions of empathy between adolescents with conduct disorders and those with autism syndrome disorder. Van den Broek and colleagues (2013) explored the value of such models in a clinical setting for patients suffering from posttraumatic stress disorder. Van den Broek and Westerink (2012) discuss the use of autonomous closed-loop biofeedback models for mental health care in general and for stress reduction in particular.

To conclude, the autonomous closed-loop biofeedback model presented in this chapter is relevant not only for affective computing but also for other fields. It holds the promise of bridging affective computing's gap from theory to practice. To verify whether or not these models can live up to this promise, a carrier application was developed and tested in the real world. We stress the need for such evaluations to cope with the drawbacks and challenges of every day, which is required to develop demonstrators into end products. In turn, such an approach can help science to find its way to technology and hence to meaningful innovation.

Acknowledgments

We gratefully acknowledge Marjolein D. van der Zwaag, Tim Tijs, Kathryn Segovia, and Maurits

Kaptein for their helpful comments and vivid discussions on an earlier draft of this chapter. We also thank Sidney D'Mello for his detailed review and constructive comments on an earlier version of this chapter. Thanks to these comments and suggestions, we have been able to revise this chapter substantially. Finally, we gratefully acknowledge Lynn Packwood for her careful proofreading.

Notes

1. For more information, an extended version of this section can be consulted, which is published as Van den Broek and Westerink (2012). Available at: http://eprints.ewi.utwente.nl/21516/
2. For more information, see http://www.aapb.org/, http://www.bcia.org/, and http://www.isnr.org/
3. For more information, an extended version of this section can be consulted, which is published as a part of Chapter 1 of Van den Broek, (September 16, 2011). *Affective Signal Processing (ASP): Unraveling the mystery of emotions.* Ph.D. thesis, University of Twente, The Netherlands. This publication is *open access* and is available at: http://dx.doi.org/10.3990/1.9789036532433
4. For more information, an extended version of this section can be consulted, which is published as Janssen, Van den Broek, and Westerink (2012). This publication is *open access* and is available at: http://dx.doi.org/10.1007/s11257-011-9107-7

References

Agrawal, D. P. (2011). Designing wireless sensor networks: From theory to applications. *Central European Journal of Computer Science, 1*(1), 2–18.

Aviezer, H., Trope, Y., & Todorov, A. (2012). Body cues, not facial expressions, discriminate between intense positive and negative emotions. *Science, 338*(6111), 1225–1229.

Baas, M., Dreu, C. K. W. de, & Nijstad, B. A. (2008). A meta-analysis of 25 years of mood—creativity research: Hedonic tone, activation, or regulatory focus? *Psychological Bulletin, 134*(6), 779–806.

Baumgartner, T., Esslen, M., & Jäncke, L. (2006). From emotion perception to emotion experience: emotions evoked by pictures and classical music. *International Journal of Psychophysiology, 60*(1), 34–43.

Beedie, C. J., Terry, P. C., & Lane, A. M. (2005). Distinctions between emotion and mood. *Cognition & Emotion, 19*(6), 847–878.

Bialoskorski, L. S. S., Westerink, J. H. D. M., & Van den Broek, E. L. (2009). Mood Swings: Design and evaluation of affective interactive art. *New Review of Hypermedia and Multimedia, 15*(2), 1–19.

Bialoskorski, L. S. S., Westerink, J. H. D. M., & Van den Broek, E. L. (2010). Experiencing affective interactive art. *International Journal of Arts and Technology, 3*(4), 341–356.

Bons, D., Van den Broek, E. L., Herpers, P., Scheepers, F., Rommelse, N., & Buitelaar J. K. (2013). Motor, emotional, and cognitive empathy in children and adolescents with autism spectrum disorder and conduct disorder. *Journal of Abnormal Child Psychology, 41*(3), 425–443.

Boucsein, W. (1992). *Electrodermal activity.* New York: Plenum Press.

Calvo, R. A., & D'Mello, S. (2010). Affect detection: An interdisciplinary review of models, methods, and their applications. *IEEE Transactions on Affective Computing, 1*(1), 18–37.

Frijda, N. H. (1986). *The emotions.* Cambridge, UK: Cambridge University Press.

Geenen, R., & Van de Vijver, F. J. R. (1993). A simple test of the law of initial values. *Psychophysiology, 30*(5), 525–530.

Gendolla, G. H. E., & Krüsken, J. (2002). Mood state, task demand, and effort-related cardiovascular response. *Cognition & Emotion, 16*(5), 577–603.

Giakoumis, D., Drosou, A., Cipress, P., Tzovaras, D., Hassapis, G., Gaggioli, A., and Riva, G. (2012). Using activity-related behavioural features towards more effective automatic stress detection. *Plos One, 7*(9), e43571.

Gruzelier, J., Egner, T., & Vernon, D. (2006). Validating the efficacy of neurofeedback for optimising performance. In C. Neuper & W. Klimesch (Eds.), *Event-related dynamics of brain oscillations: Section VI. Brain-computer interfaces and neurofeedback* (Vol. 159, pp. 421–431). Amsterdam, the Netherlands: Elsevier.

Hatzfeld, C., Kern, T. A., & Werthschützky, R. (2010). Design and evaluation of a measuring system for human force perception parameters. *Sensors and Actuators A: Physical, 162*(2), 202–209.

Healey, J. A., & Picard, R. W. (2005). Detecting stress during real-world driving tasks using physiological sensors. *IEEE Transactions on Intelligent Transportation Systems, 6*(2), 156–166.

Healey, J. A., Picard, R. W., & Dabek, F. (1998). A new affect-perceiving interface and its application to personalized music selection. In M. Turk (Ed.), *Proceedings of the 1998 Workshop on Perceptual User Interfaces (PUI).* Available at: http://www.acm.org/icmi/1998/Papers/Healey.pdf.

Heinz, C., & Seeger, B. (2008). Cluster kernels: Resource-aware kernel density estimators over streaming data. *IEEE Transactions on Knowledge and Data Engineering, 20*(7), 880–893.

Izard, C. E. (2010). The many meanings/aspects of emotion: Emotion definitions, functions, activation, and regulation. *Emotion Review, 2*(4), 363–370.

Janssen, J. H., Bailenson, J. N., IJsselsteijn, W. A., & Westerink, J. H. D. M. (2010). Intimate heartbeats: Opportunities for affective communication technology. *IEEE Transaction on Affective Computing, 1*(2), 72–80.

Janssen, J. H., Van den Broek, E. L., & Westerink, J. D. H. M. (2012). Tune in to your emotions: A robust personalized affective music player. *User Modeling and User-Adapted Interaction, 22*(3), 255–279.

Kaniusas, E. (2012). *Biomedical signals and sensors I: Linking physiological phenomena and biosignals.* Berlin and Heidelberg: Springer.

Kim, J., & André, E. (2008). Emotion recognition based on physiological changes in music listening. *IEEE Transactions on Pattern Analysis and Machine Intelligence, 30*(12), 2067–2083.

Konijn, E. A. (2013). The role of emotion in media use and effects. In K. E. Dill (Ed.), *The Oxford handbook of media psychology* (pp. 186–211). New York: Oxford University Press, Inc.

Mandler, G., Mandler, J. M., & Uviller, E. T. (1958). Autonomic feedback: The perception of autonomic activity. *Journal of Abnormal and Social Psychology, 56*(3), 367–373.

Matthews, G., Jones, D. M., & Chamberlain, A. G. (1990). Refining the measurement of mood: The UWIST mood adjective checklist. *The British Journal of Psychology, 81*(1), 17–42.

McFarland, R. A., & Kennison, R. (1989). Asymmetry in the relationship between finger temperature changes and emotional state in males. *Biofeedback and Self-Regulation, 14*(4), 281–290.

Mielle, P., Tarrega, A., Sémon, E., Maratray, J., Gorria, P., Liodenot, J. J.,..., Salles, C. (2010). From human to artificial mouth, from basics to results. *Sensors and Actuators B: Chemical*, *146*(2), 440–445.

Moss, D., & Gunkelman, J. (2002). Task force report on methodology and empirically supported treatments: Introduction. *Applied Psychophysiology and Biofeedback*, *27*(4), 271–272.

Neamen, D. A. (2010). *Microelectronics: Circuit analysis and design*, 4th ed. New York: McGraw-Hill.

Oliver, N., & Kregor-Stickles, L. (2006). PAPA: Physiology and purpose-aware automatic playlist generation. In K. Lemström, A. Tindale, & R. Dannenberg (Eds.), In *Proceedings of the 7th international conference on music information retrieval* (pp. 250–253). Victoria, BC, Canada: ISMIR—The International Society for Music Information Retrieval.

Ouwerkerk, M., Pasveer, F., & Langereis, G. (2008). Unobtrusive sensing of psychophysiological parameters: Some examples of non-invasive sensing technologies. In J. H. D. M. Westerink, M. Ouwerkerk, T. Overbeek, W. F. Pasveer, & B. de Ruyter (Eds.), *Probing experience: From assessment of user emotions and behaviour to development of products* (Vol. 8, pp. 163–193). Dordrecht, The Netherlands: Springer.

Picard, R. W. (1997). *Affective computing*. Boston: MIT Press.

Rimm-Kaufman, S. E., & Kagan, J. (1996). The psychological significance of changes in skin temperature. *Motivation and Emotion*, *20*(1), 237–244.

Rosenberg, E. (1998). Levels of analysis and the organization of affect. *Review of General Psychology*, *2*(3), 247–270.

Russell, J. A. (2003). Core affect and the psychological construction of emotion. *Psychological Review*, *110*(1), 145–172.

Schultz, I. H. (2003). *Das autogene Training: Konzentrative Selbstentspannung—Versuch einer klinisch-praktischen Darstellung*, 20th ed. Stuttgart: Georg Thieme Verlag.

Scott, D. W., & Sain, S. R. (2005). Multidimensional density estimation. In C. R. Rao, E. J. Wegman, & J. L. Solka (Eds.), *Handbook of statistics: Data mining and data visualization* (Vol. 24, pp. 229–261). Amsterdam, the Netherlands: North-Holland.

Sörnmo, L., & Laguna, P. (2005). *Bioelectrical signal processing in cardiac and neurological applications*. Burlington, MA: Elsevier.

Sotiropoulos, D. N., Lampropoulos, A. S., & Tsihrintzis, G. A. (2008). MUSIPER: A system for modeling music similarity perception based on objective feature subset selection. *User Modeling and User-Adapted Interaction*, *18*(4), 315–348.

Thayer, R. E. (1989). *The biopsychology of mood and arousal*. New York: Oxford University Press.

Van den Broek, E. L. (2010). Robot nannies: Future or fiction? *Interaction Studies*, *11*(2), 274–282.

Van den Broek, E. L. (2012, August 28–31). On making engagement tangible. In A. J. Spink, F. Grieco, O. E. Krips, L. W. S. Loijens, L. P. J. J. Noldus, & P. H. Zimmerman (Eds.), *Proceedings of measuring behavior 2012: 8th international conference on methods and techniques in behavioral research* (pp. 90–93). Wageningen, the Netherlands: Noldus Information Technology bv.

Van den Broek, E. L. (2013). Ubiquitous emotion-aware computing. *Personal and Ubiquitous Computing*, *17*(1), 53–67.

Van den Broek, E. L., Janssen, J. H., Healey, J. A., & Van der Zwaag, M. D. (2010). Prerequisites for affective signal processing (ASP)—Part II. In A. Fred, J. Filipe, & H. Gamboa (Eds.), *Biosignals 2010: proceedings of the international conference on bio-inspired systems and signal processing* (pp. 188–193). Setubal, Portugal: INSTICC/ SciTePress.

Van den Broek, E. L., Janssen, J. H., & Westerink, J. H. D. M. (2009, 10–12 September). Guidelines for affective signal processing (ASP): From lab to life. In J. Cohn, A. Nijholt, & M. Pantic (Eds.), *Proceedings of the IEEE 3rd international conference on affective computing and intelligent interaction, ACII* (Vol. 1, pp. 704–709). Amsterdam: IEEE Press.

Van den Broek, E. L., Janssen, J. H., Westerink, J. H. D. M., & Healey, J. A. (2009). Prerequisites for affective signal processing (ASP). In P. Encarnação & A. Veloso (Eds.), *Biosignals 2009: Proceedings of the international conference on bio-inspired systems and signal processing* (pp. 426–433). Setubal, Portugal: INSTICC/ SciTePress.

Van den Broek, E. L., Lisý, V., Janssen, J. H., Westerink, J. H. D. M., Schut, M. H., & Tuinenbreijer, K. (2010). Affective man-machine interface: Unveiling human emotions through biosignals. In A. Fred, J. Filipe, & H. Gamboa (Eds.), *Biomedical engineering systems and technologies: BIOSTEC2009 selected revised papers* (Vol. 52, pp. 21–47). Berlin and Heidelberg: Springer.

Van den Broek, E. L., Nijholt, A., & Westerink, J. H. D. M. (2010, August 24–27). Unveiling affective signals. In E. Barakova, B. de Ruyter, & A. Spink (Eds.), *ACM Proceedings of measuring behavior 2010: Selected papers from the 7th international conference on methods and techniques in behavioral research* (p. a6). New York: ACM.

Van den Broek, E. L., Van der Sluis, F., & Dijkstra, T. (2011). Telling the story and re-living the past: How speech analysis can reveal emotions in post-traumatic stress disorder (PTSD) patients (pp. 153–180). In J. H. D. M. Westerink, M. Krans, & M. Ouwerkerk (Eds.), *Sensing emotions: The impact of context on experience measurements*. Vol. 10 of the Philips Research Book Series. Dordrecht, the Netherlands: Springer.

Van den Broek, E. L., Van der Sluis, F., & Dijkstra, T. (2013). Cross-validation of bimodal health-related stress assessment. *Personal and Ubiquitous Computing*, *17*(2), 215–227.

Van den Broek, E. L. & Westerink, J. H. D. M. (2012, February 01–04). Biofeedback systems for stress reduction: Towards a bright future for a revitalized field. In E. Conchon, C. Correia, A. Fred, & H. Gamboa (Eds.), *Proceedings of health Inf 2012: International conference on health informatics* (pp. 499–504). Setubal, Portugal: INSTICC/ SciTePress.

Van der Zwaag, M. D., Dijksterhuis, C., de Waard, D., Mulder, B. L. J. M., Westerink, J. H. D. M., & Brookhuis, K. A. (2012). The influence of music on mood and performance while driving. *Ergonomics*, *55*(1), 12–22.

Van der Zwaag, M. D., Janssen, J. H., & Westerink, J. H. D. M. (2013). Directing physiology and mood through music: Validation of an affective music player. *IEEE Transactions on Affective Computing*, *4*(1), 57–68.

Van der Zwaag, M. D., Westerink, J. H. D. M., & Van den Broek, E. L. (2011). Emotional and psychophysiological responses to tempo, mode, and percussiveness. *Musicae Scientiae*, *15*(2), 250–269.

Wagenaar, W. A. (1969). Note on the construction of digram-balanced Latin squares. *Psychological Bulletin*, *72*(6), 384–386.

Wilder, J. F. (1967). *Stimulus and response: The law of initial value*. Bristol, UK: John Wright.

Zeng, Z., Pantic, M., Roisman, G. I., and Huang, T. S. (2009). A survey of affect recognition methods: Audio, visual, and spontaneous expressions. *IEEE Transactions on Pattern Analysis and Machine Intelligence*, *31*(1), 39–58.

Affect in Human-Robot Interaction

Ronald C. Arkin *and* Lilia Moshkina

Abstract

More and more, robots are expected to interact with humans in a social, easily understandable manner, which presupposes effective use of robot affect. This chapter provides a brief overview of research advances into this important aspect of human-robot interaction. In particular, we focus on the benefit provided for a human interacting with a robot using mechanisms for increasing the bandwidth in communication, including nonverbal methods to create a more effective and stronger relationship between artifact and person. This is illustrated in the context of a range of robot architectural exemplars.

Key Words: human-robot interaction, affective robotics, robot behavior, robot emotions, robot architectures

Introduction and Motivation

Humans possess an amazing ability to attribute life and affect to inanimate objects (Melson et al., 2009; Reeves & Nass, 1996). Robots take this to the next level, even beyond that of virtual characters, owing to their embodiment and situatedness. They offer people the opportunity to bond with them by maintaining a physical presence in their world, in some ways comparable to other beings, such as fellow humans and pets.

This raises a broad range of questions in terms of the role of affect in human-robot interaction (HRI), which is discussed in this chapter:

• What is the role of affect for a robot and in what ways can it add value and risk to human-robot relationships? Can robots be companions, friends, and even intimates to people?

• Is it necessary for a robot to actually experience emotion in order to convey its internal state to a person? Is emotion important in enhancing HRI, and if so, when and where?

• What approaches, theories, representations, and experimental methods inform affective HRI research?

Roles of Emotion in Robotics

There are at least two different roles for emotion in robotic systems. The first, which is only briefly discussed here, is to serve an adaptive function that increases the probability of correct behavior, some of which may relate to survival of an agent (human or robotic) in its environment. The second is for the benefit of the human interacting with a robot by providing a means and mechanism for increasing the bandwidth in communication, using nonverbal methods to create a more effective and stronger relationship between artifact and person.

ADAPTIVE BEHAVIOR FOR SURVIVAL

Moravec (1988) notes that humans may even perceive emotions in robots even without deliberately modeling them: For example, if a robot backs away from a staircase, it might be interpreted as a fear of falling by a person observing. Braitenberg (1984), using a series of *Gedanken* (thought) experiments, also demonstrates that vehicles can exhibit love, fear, and aggression attributed to them solely by virtue of human observation. These perceived emotions are likely to attune the robot more closely to its environment and thus enhance its survivability, but they are not geared expressly for HRI. People have a natural propensity to anthropomorphize artifacts (Reeves & Nass 1996) even if their designer had not deliberately intended to make this happen.

HUMAN-ROBOT INTERACTION

Many other researchers, some of which are discussed in more detail below, have chosen to deliberately embed explicit models of affect into robots with the express purpose of enhancing the relationship between the human and robot and in some cases of fostering a strong attachment by a person to the artifact. The underlying goal here is to produce a robotic platform that can be a friend or even a lifelong companion to a human (Arkin et al., 2003) and in some cases could even approach the possibility of intimate human-robot relations (Levy, 2008).

Definitions in Context

Definitions of nebulous affective terms such as *emotions* can be debated ad infinitum (Arkin, 2005). This volume undoubtedly addresses that in other chapters. We should note, however, that we take a solipsist stance, which is that robots do not need to experience affective phenomena in the same way as humans do, or even at all, in order for them to be perceived as possessing them. So no claim is made that the robot actually experiences emotions but rather that the goal of affective HRI is to *convey the perception* to a person that it does. While this may be unsatisfying to a philosopher, it is a pragmatic solution to the roboticist, where affect lies in the eye of the beholder.

A Few Short Exemplars

In order to carry out this illusion, many psychological models of human affect have been explored. Two examples that have had commercial success are described below.

AIBO

Aibo (Figure 36.1a) was a robotic dog marketed by Sony Corp. from 1999 to 2006; hundreds of thousands of units were sold. Intended to serve as a long-term companion and friend, it incorporated

an instinct-emotional model, which ranged from an initial simplistic variable-based version to considerably more complex forms in some of its variants (Arkin et al., 2003). An expanded version of this model was later incorporated into Sony's QRIO humanoid robot as well.

PARO

Paro, on the other hand, is a therapeutic robot for the elderly; it is also commercially available (Figure 36.1b). It has been evaluated in terms of physiological, psychological, and social benefits to the human with whom it interacts (Shibata, 2012). Paro yields its benefits by eliciting emotional responses in its users through direct physical interaction and appears not to rely on a sophisticated internal emotional model.

Affective Robotics

Research in affective HRI has come a long way since the early forays of Moravec (1988), Tolman (Endo & Arkin 2001), Grey Walter (Holland, 2003), and others, both in terms of breadth and depth. The following subsections discuss a number of representative recent examples showcasing a wide variety of approaches to robot affect.

Affective Models and Architectures

Several roboticists take a systematic approach of incorporating affective models into robotic architectures. Two such systems are described below: the TAME framework, which stands for traits, attitudes, moods, and emotions (Moshkina 2011; Moshkina et al., 2011) and the DIARC architecture, which stands for distributed integrated affect cognition and reflection (Scheutz et al., 2007). Although these two systems differ in a number of important aspects, they both emphasize including affect as an integral part of a robotic architecture and have been designed with the goal of facilitating overall HRI.

TAME: TRAITS, ATTITUDES, MOODS, EMOTIONS

The TAME framework comprises four psychologically inspired interrelated affective phenomena that provides mechanisms for affect generation, affective behavior modification, and affect expression. TAME is platform-independent and can work with a variety of robot architectures, although it is particularly well suited for the behavior-based paradigm (Arkin, 1998). Given relevant perceptual input—such as the categories of visible objects and distances to them (stimuli and their strengths) as

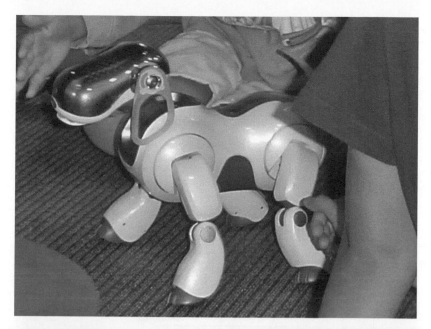

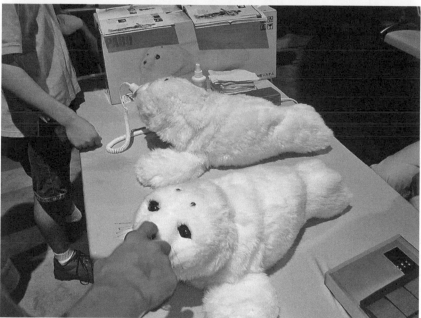

Fig. 36.1 (a) AIBO (on the left) and (b) Paro (on the right).
Source: Wikimedia Commons.

well as some internal state information (e.g., battery level) and environmental conditions (e.g., light and noise levels)—the TAME system produces situation-appropriate affect intensities, which in turn modify currently active task behaviors through parameter-adjustment. (Figure 36.2 presents a conceptual overview.)

The affective components comprising the framework provide a comprehensive, time-varying base for a robot and differ with respect to duration (from almost instantaneous to lifelong) and object specificity (from very specific to diffuse and global). Emotions and moods constitute a robot's dynamically changing, transient affective state (object-specific and short-term for emotions, and diffuse and prolonged for moods). Moods provide an affective background, or "emotional color," and can vary cyclically, whereas emotions can be viewed

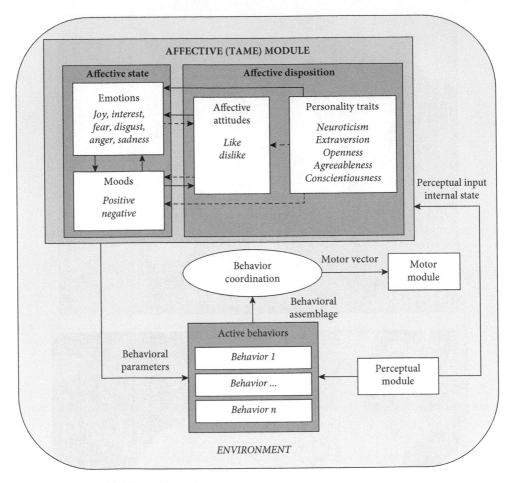

Fig. 36.2 Conceptual view of the TAME framework.

Source: Adapted from Moshkina, 2011.

as "phasic perturbations on this background activity" (Davidson, 1994). In contrast, personality traits and attitudes are more or less time-invariant and define general dispositions to behave and process information in certain ways. Like emotions, affective attitudes (sentiments) are object-specific; however, unlike emotions, they refer to ways of seeing and treating an object rather than to momentary responses, thus guiding behavior toward desirable goals and away from aversive objects. Finally, *personality* refers to enduring individual differences in behavior and information processing of a more general, object-independent kind and serves as an adaptation mechanism to specialized tasks and environments.

The TAME framework was implemented as an independent software module and integrated within MissionLab, a multiagent mission specification and execution robotic software toolset

(MacKenzie et al., 1997[1]) based on AuRA, a hybrid reactive-deliberative robotic architecture (Arkin & Balch, 1997). Aspects of the resulting system were tested on Aldebaran Robotics' Nao biped humanoid platform in two human-robot experiments with over 70 participants. In one of these studies, the impact of Negative Mood and the emotion of fear was assessed in a mock-up search-and-rescue scenario, where the participants found the robot expressing affect more compelling, sincere, convincing, and "conscious" than its nonaffective counterpart. Another study showed that different robotic personalities are better suited for different tasks: An extraverted robot was found to be more welcoming and fun for a task as a museum robot guide, where an engaging and gregarious demeanor was expected; whereas an introverted robot was rated as more appropriate for a problem-solving task requiring concentration (Moshkina, 2011).

DIARC ARCHITECTURE

Unlike system-independent TAME, DIARC is an example of a novel robotic architecture incorporating general affect throughout its functional components. The architecture integrates cognitive capabilities (e.g., natural language understanding and action planning) and lower-level activities (such as perceptual processing, feature detection and tracking, etc.) In this system, positive and negative affect (not differentiated into separate phenomena) plays a vital role in goal and task selection by changing utilities of actions currently under consideration for selection; this is based on a short-term history of failures that produce increases in negative affect and successes that produce increases in positive affect (Scheutz & Schermerhorn, 2009). This mechanism serves as a kind of affective memory, allowing a robot to take into account past information without perfect knowledge of prior probabilities—a mechanism that is possibly also used by humans in their decision making.

In addition to affective goal action selection, which takes place in every functional component of the architecture, DIARC also provides means for affect recognition, appraisal, and affective expression generation. DIARC has been used extensively as a test bed for research in HRI, including a number of experiments involving human subjects and AAAI robot competitions. In one experiment (Scheutz, Schermerhorn, & Kramer, 2006), subjects and robots were paired in the context of a hypothetical space exploration scenario where they had to work together to achieve a common goal. The results showed that when the robot and its human teammate were physically colocated, the robot's expression of anxiety over its lowering battery level (via voice) led to a performance advantage.

Socially Interactive Affective Robots

The two aforementioned affective robotic systems fall under the general umbrella of socially interactive robots, defined in Fong, Nourbakhsh, and Dautenhahn (2003) as "robots for which social interaction plays a key role." A wide variety of other affective robotic systems also follow this research paradigm, focusing on affect as a key human social characteristic.

ROBOT EMOTIONS

Emotion has been by far the most frequent affective phenomenon modeled in robots, although in some cases the distinction between emotion per se and other related phenomena has been blurred.

The research in this category varies in terms of emotion generation mechanisms, modes of emotional expression, and underlying psychological and/or engineering approaches. Because of its practical applicability, facial emotional expressiveness has received a lot of attention, ranging from realistic robot heads to schematic faces to imaginary animals. Hanson Robotics' android head EINSTEIN (Wu et al., 2009) is a good example of more or less realistic facial expressivity; the system is capable of learning and producing a large number of facial expressions based on Ekman's Facial Action Coding System (FACS) (Ekman & Friesen, 1978). Another system using FACS for displaying emotional expressions, though not as physically complex, is the expressive robotic head EDDIE (Sosnowski et al., 2006), capable of displaying affect based on the circumplex model of emotion (Posner, Russell, & Peterson, 2005). A highly stylized socially interactive robot head, ERWIN (Murray et al., 2009), expresses five basic emotions generated through the modulation of hormone-like parameters based on the context of current interactions. Farther down on the less realistic axis, an imaginary animal-like huggable robot, Probo (Goris et al., 2009), designed specifically for children, also produces emotional expressions based on the circumplex model of affect.

Although facial emotional display is the primary cue for emotion recognition in humans, not all physical platforms allow for this capability, lacking either facial motors or heads altogether. A number of researchers have addressed this challenge by designing for nonfacial emotional expressivity. For example, Robovie-mini R2 and Robovie M (Nakagawa et al., 2009) are equipped with a method to control affective nuances by mapping dimensions of valence and arousal onto velocity and extensiveness of motion and body posture. In Park et al. (2010), expressions of Fear and Joy, as well as Introversion and Extraversion, were achieved on a biped humanoid robot called Nao (Aldebaran Robotics) through a combination of body posture and characteristic kinesics that were successfully recognized in an online survey. For an extensive survey of nonfacial nonverbal affective robot expressions, the reader is directed to Bethel and Murphy (2008).

BEYOND EMOTIONS: MULTIPLE AFFECTIVE PHENOMENA IN ROBOTS

A small subset of affective robotic systems differentiates between emotion and other affective phenomena, making the resulting affective capabilities richer and more compelling. Owing to space limitations, apart from the aforementioned TAME, only four of these systems are showcased here.

Roboceptionist—A Combination of Emotions, Moods, and Attitudes

This affective system (Kirby et al., 2010) was implemented on a virtual robot face placed on a rotating monitor at a receptionist's desk. It was used to interact with people on a daily basis for a prolonged time and incorporated a generative model of affect consisting of emotions, moods, and attitudes. The affect is expressed through animated facial expressions and a priori composed narrative rather than body language or mobility. The categorical emotions modeled in the system are joy, sadness, disgust, and anger and are generated in response to interaction with people and displayed immediately after an eliciting event. The robot's moods are primarily caused by its personal history and "live" events. Values for moods are assigned to the story line by dramatic writers and are influenced by the emotions the robot experienced during the day. Finally, attitudes are represented as a long-term mood associated with a particular person or thing, where each person who visits the robot may cause various emotional responses, which, through mood modulation, influence the "opinion" of this person. In addition, familiarity with the person influences the robot's attitude toward that person.

A number of experiments have been conducted testing the components of this affect model. An online emotion recognition survey showed that people were able to detect differences between the robot's emotional expressions and to differentiate between their intensities. Another study examined the influence of the robot's mood on people's interaction during a longer-term (9 weeks, during which the robot was typically operating 8 hours a day, 5 days a week). During "low traffic" weeks, people interacted with the robot in positive mood for a shorter period of time than with the robot in neutral mood; in contrast, during "high traffic" weeks, where there were significantly more visitors, the robot in neutral mood elicited the least amount of interaction. This model is psychologically inspired to a certain extent but relies heavily on input from the designers who write the robot's "life story."

Waseda Eye No. 4—A Combination of Emotions, Moods, and Personality

The latest incarnation of the robot Waseda Eye No.4 Refined combines emotions, moods, and personality (Miwa et al., 2001, 2004). The overall goal of the system is to achieve smooth and effective communication for a humanoid robot. The Eemotion space is defined along three dimensions: activation, pleasantness, and certainty. Emotions are represented as second-order differential equations based on laws of motion and are influenced by three emotion coefficient matrices: Emotional Inertia, Emotional Viscosity, and Emotional Elasticity. The stimuli for emotion generation are extensive and include visual (e.g., target is near), tactile (pushed, stroked, etc.), auditory (loud sound), temperature, and olfactory (alcohol, smoke, etc.) stimuli. The personality of the robot consists of Sensing and Expression Personalities. The Sensing sensing Personality personality provides a mapping from sensory input to emotion generation; it also influences emotion duration and decay via the emotion coefficient matrices. The Expression expression Personality personality determines a particular emotional expression (Miwa et al., 2001). Finally, mood is represented along pleasantness and activation axes. The mood pleasantness component is an integral of the emotion vector; its activation component is based on an internal clock (Miwa et al., 2004). The resulting emotional expression is not limited to the face but also includes neck, waist, and arms; the speed of the motion is also varied depending on the emotion.

Although many elements of this system are not psychologically or biologically founded, it provides a few interesting mechanisms, such as modeling the influence of personality on emotion via a variety of coefficient matrices and using internal-clock activation component in moods. No extensive HRI studies have been conducted to date to evaluate this system.

Combining Emotions and Moods on iCat

Leite and colleagues (2008) implemented emotional reactions and moods on the Philips iCat robot within the context of a chess game. Emotional reactions were modeled as an "emotivector"—an anticipatory system that generates an affective signal resulting from a mismatch between the expected and sensed values of the sensor to which it is coupled. Mood is expressed as a less intense affective state, where positive values are associated with good scores in the game and negative ones are related to bad scores. Moods are filtered over time and are explicit when emotional reactions are not occurring. In two HRI experiments, it was found that the emotional behavior of the robot helped users to have a better perception of the game (Leite et al., 2008). Additionally, a later study (Castellano et al., 2009) suggested that when the iCat displayed facial expressions during a game of chess, the level of user engagement toward the robot increased.

Combining Emotions and Motivational Drives in Kismet

The robotic creature Kismet (Breazeal, 2003) is one of the earliest and most influential affective robotic systems. It is modeled after an infant and is capable of protosocial responses, providing an untrained user with a natural and intuitive means of communication. Kismet's motivation system consists of drives (motivations) and emotions, where emotions are a result of its affective state. The affective space is defined along three dimensions: arousal, valence, and stance; each emotion is computed as a combination of contributions from drives, behaviors, and percepts. The motivation system plays a role in the behavior selection process and attention selection process as well as providing activation for facial emotional expressions and speech.

Affect for Enhancing Robotic Behavior

The affective robotic systems up to this point have all had a common goal for the inclusion of affect—that is, to facilitate HRI. However, this review would be remiss if it ignored efforts that did not have HRI as their primary focus, where the general projected improvements in performance due to the addition of affect may well prove useful in making potential interaction with humans more robust.

With a focus on improving the robot's behavior through decision making, learning, or action selection, a number of researchers have used the fuzzy logic approach to emotion generation. In the emotional system for decision making in mobile robots developed by El-Nasr et al., (2000), the emotional states have no definite boundaries and are represented by fuzzy sets with intensities of low, medium, and high. Their values are generated according to fuzzy logic inference rules and the OCC model of Ortony, Clore, and Collins (1988); they are based on goals and expectations where, at different intensities, the same emotion can trigger different actions. In another fuzzy logic–based system (Hashimoto, Hamada, & Akazawa, 2003), fuzzy cognitive maps (FCMs) are used to represent the generation and effects of emotional states.

FCMs allow a robot to learn associations between stimuli and emotional states as well as between emotions and tasks. Finally, (Yu & Xu, 2004) present an emotional system consisting of four fuzzy emotions (sad, lonely, disgust, and fear) and four sensory inputs (energy, friendship, cleanness, and brightness). Emotions are based on both sensor input and current emotional history and can influence behavior selection by increasing/decreasing corresponding action-selection weights.

Murphy and colleagues (2002) describe the use of emotions to control a group of robots working on interdependent tasks by dynamically adapting current behaviors to the context or changing the set of active behaviors altogether. The emotion model is based on Scherer's multilevel process theory of emotions (Leventhal & Scherer, 1987). The emotional state generator (a finite state machine) accepts measures of task progress as input; then emotion influences the task selection of the behavioral state generator. The use of emotions led to the following advantage: They help to break cyclic dependency problems without centralized planning and with minimal communication.

Another control architecture for autonomous mobile robots that incorporates biologically inspired artificial emotions was implemented by Lee-Johnson and Carnegie (2007). The five emotions modeled in the system are fear, sadness, anger, surprise, and happiness. They are characterized by certain elicitation/response patterns (e.g., fear is invoked if the robot is damaged and anger if progress toward a goal is obstructed). Once elicited, emotions modulate a robot's planning and control parameters, providing bias toward certain drives without overtly controlling the behavior (e.g., anger helps achieve the current goal even at the expense of secondary considerations). This model was implemented on a simulated version of MARVIN, a custom-built mobile robot, and was shown to have certain advantages in a navigation task, such as fewer collisions and greater exploration coverage.

Methods and Metrics—Measures of Success in Affective HRI

One of the major challenges facing affective HRI is effective testing and evaluation. In the task- or function-oriented areas of HRI (such as collaborative endeavors between people and robots, or learning by imitation), the measurement of a robot's performance is more or less straightforward. In the case of affective robots, however, it is often not the robot's performance per se that needs to be evaluated but rather the social responses that the robot evokes in the people with whom it interacts. These could be reflected in their subjective impressions (measured through self-assessments), behavioral responses and expressions (obtained through observation), certain physiological responses, or in objective differences in human task performance due to the presence of robot affect.

Self-Assessments

These are subjective evaluations used to uncover people's perceptions of and attitudes toward their interactions with robots. In the HRI community, these methods of evaluation commonly include Likert-style questionnaires designed for evaluating the specific goals of a particular study (often applied in an ad hoc manner in this new field [Bartneck et al., 2009]); reusable semantic differential scales or other psychometric scales for measuring certain concepts relevant to HRI (also designed specifically for use in HRI); and established psychological and sociological measures borrowed from corresponding research communities.

EXISTING PSYCHOMETRIC TESTS

These methods have the advantage of having been tested and validated on a large number of subjects; however, only a few of them have been tested to date with regard to affective robots. Two such measurement scales, particularly suitable for the affective HRI domain, are (1) a brief version of Goldberg's unipolar "big-five" markers (which provides personality trait assessment) (Saucier, 1994) and (2) the positive affect/negative affect schedule (which measures current mood state) (Watson et al., 1998). These two instruments have been used successfully for assessing both subjects' and robots' personality and mood states in a number of HRI experiments conducted as part of TAME evaluations. The reader is referred to Moshkina (2011) for further details on their use and recommendations for their application in HRI.

HRI-SPECIFIC TOOLS

Social robotics is a very young field and only a few reusable self-assessment tests are currently in existence. One of the most widely used is the Negative Attitudes toward Robots Scale (NARS) developed and tested by Nomura and Kanda (2003) and Nomura et al. (2008). NARS measures general negative attitudes towards robots via three subscales: situations and interactions with robots, social influence of robots, and emotions and interaction with robots, with each subscale item given as a Likert-style question.

Bartneck et al. (2009) present an overview of other scales that have been successfully used in HRI experiments and have acceptable internal reliability. These scales (most of them translated by the authors into semantic differential scales from Likert scales) measure impressions of robots in terms of the concepts of anthropomorphism, animacy, likeability, perceived intelligence, and perceived safety.

Finally, two recent HRI studies (Moshkina 2011, 2012) presented seven alternative semantic differential scales for measuring concepts of relevance to affective HRI. These 5-item scales assess the following concepts with acceptable internal consistency reliability (Cronbach's alpha for each 0.7 or higher): persuasiveness, naturalness, understandability, appropriateness, welcome, appeal, unobtrusiveness, and ease. These scales were specifically designed with the goal of facilitating reuse and replicability in future HRI experimentation.

Although self-assessments are among the most commonly used methods of evaluation in HRI studies and allow querying people's perceptions of their interaction directly, they suffer from a lack of objectivity. They can be notoriously unreliable, as they reflect a large amount of individual differences and make the replication of results and comparisons between different studies rather difficult.

Behavioral and Psychophysiological Measures

Behavioral measures are observational and refer to an analysis of participants' micro and macro behaviors and speech utterances during interaction. In this case, the human-robot interactions are recorded; the human behaviors to watch for are carefully selected and accurately described and then are extracted from the video either automatically or by independent human coders (cf. Cohn's chapter in this volume). Although not specifically within the affective domain, Dautenhahn et al. (2002) and Dautenhahn and Werry (2002) successfully used a combination of quantitative and qualitative behavioral techniques in HRI experiments. The quantitative approach was based on an analysis of microbehaviors presented as well-identifiable, low-level, action-oriented categories; the examples of such categories include touch, eye gaze and eye contact, handling (picking up, pushing), approach, and moving away. The qualitative approach was based on conversation analysis (Psathas 1995), which provides a systematic analysis of everyday and institutional talk in interaction. Although these methods avoid some of the biases inherent in self-assessments, the differences in individual behavioral styles, possible interpretation bias, and the amount of time required for workload can be cited as weaknesses in using these behavioral measures.

Another way to avoid participant subjectivity is to measure certain physiological responses (such as heart rate, skin conductance, and temperature) before, during, and after the interaction; such responses can be correlated with a subject's emotional state and arousal level (cf. Healey's chapter in this volume). The primary advantage of this method is that participants usually cannot manipulate the responses of their autonomic nervous systems; therefore the results obtained by this means are free from self-report bias. Perhaps the main disadvantage of this method is the limitation as to what can be measured; for example, participants cannot distinguish anger from joy but rather report the overall level of arousal. This method works well when, for example, the level of human anxiety must be determined (Kulic & Croft, 2006; Rani et al., 2004), and has been used especially for affect recognition, but it would have to be supplemented by other measures to obtain cross-validation and additional information.

Task Performance

Finally, human task-performance metrics provide a fair amount of objectivity, as they allow for the quantification of benefits that a particular robot type, behavior, or algorithm might have. This is accomplished through such variables as accuracy, performance success, task completion time, error rate, resource usage, and others, depending on a particular task and scenario. One example of employing a task performance metric to evaluate the effectiveness of robot affect is presented in (Scheutz et al., 2006). In their study, changes in task performance as a result of a robot's expression of anxiety during an exploration scenario were measured. In particular, as the robot's anxiety increased (expressed by changes in the robot's speech rate and pitch), the human participants were alerted to the impending deadline and worked more efficiently.

Another HRI study examined the effect of robot expressions of negative affect (mood) and fear on human subjects' compliance with a robot's request to evacuate a potentially dangerous area (Moshkina, 2012). This study, set as a mock-up

search-and-rescue scenario, showed that the participants responded to the request earlier and moved faster and further in response to the affective robot when compared to one without affect. Although task performance metrics provide objective and easily quantifiable results, their use in affective HRI is far from trivial. The biggest challenge lies in predicting which types of tasks would directly or indirectly benefit from affective robotic behaviors and how people would respond to a robot's expressed affective state.

Each type of evaluation has its associated pros and cons, and we join Bethel and Murphy (2010) in advocating the inclusion of more than a single method of evaluation to obtain comprehensive understanding and convergent validity in assessments of affective HRI.

Ethical Questions and Future Directions

The ethical issues confronting roboticists relate to questions such as: What if we succeed? What if we are able to create robotic artifacts that interact more effectively with humans than other humans do? Could we engineer out the difficulties in relationships that people often encounter with each other through the use of affective models (among other techniques)?

Philosophers and social scientists (e.g., Sparrow, 2002; Turkle, 2011) have written about the potential dangers of highly interactive robots in human lives, broaching a broad range of issues including the following:

• The introduction of a deliberate misapprehension of the world in the aged. Is there not a fundamental right to perceive the world as it really is? (That is, the robots are not alive, even if they appear to be to a human observer.)
• The abrogation of responsibility among humans by relegating the role of a human caregiver to a robot, and the resulting impact on those being cared for and the caregiver alike.
• The deterioration of the fabric of society and human relationships in general by potentially creating artifacts that are more appealing to interact with than fellow humans.

There are no obvious answers to these questions at this time, and considerable discussion and precaution is wise as robots move into ubiquity in our lives, perhaps during our lifetimes.

Nonetheless the frontier remains to be explored. There are interesting models and a new understanding arising from deeper insights in neuroscience and the role that emotions play (Gazzaniga, 2005). The role of mirror neurons (Arbib, 2012) may show new ways to elicit emotional responses in both humans and robots. Understanding secondary emotions, such as those governing moral judgment, may lead to robots that can even outperform humans in ethical respects (Arkin & Ulam, 2005). The list goes on and on. It is an exciting time for the young field of HRI, and affect will play a central role in its progression.

Note

1. MissionLab is freely available for research and development and can be found at http://www.cc.gatech.edu/ai/robot-lab/research/MissionLab/

References

Arbib, M. (2012). *How the brain got language: The mirror system hypothesis*. New York: Oxford University Press.

Arkin, R. (1998). *Behavior-based robotics*. Cambridge, MA: MIT Press.

Arkin, R., & Balch, T. (1997). AuRA: Principles and practice in review. *Journal of Experimental and Theoretical Artificial Intelligence, 9*(2), 175–189.

Arkin, R., Fujita, M., Takagi, T., & Hasegawa, R. (2003). An ethological and emotional basis for human-robot interaction. *Robotics and Autonomous Systems, 42*(3–4).

Arkin, R. C. (2005). Moving up the food chain: motivation and emotion in behavior-based robots. In J. Fellous & M. Arbib (Eds.), *Who needs emotions: The brain meets the robot* (pp. 245–271). New York: Oxford University Press.

Arkin, R. C., & Ulam, P. (2009). An ethical adaptor: Behavioral modification derived from moral emotions. In *IEEE international symposium on computational intelligence in robotics and automation* (pp. 381–387).

Bartneck C., Kulic, D., Croft E., & Zoghbi S. (2009). Measurement instruments for the anthropomorphism, animacy, likeability, perceived intelligence, and perceived safety of robots. *International Journal of Social Robotics, 1,* 71–81.

Bethel, C. L., & Murphy, R. R. (2008). Survey of non-facial/non-verbal affective expressions for appearance-constrained robots. In *IEEE Transactions on Systems, Man, and Cybernetics, Part C—Applications and Reviews, 38*(1), 83–92.

Bethel, C. L., & Murphy, R. R. (2010). Review of human studies methods in hri and recommendations. *International Journal of Social Robotics, 2,* 347–359.

Braitenberg, V. (1984). *Vehicles: Experiments in synthetic psychology*. Cambridge, MA: MIT Press.

Breazeal, C. (2003). Emotion and sociable humanoid robots. *International Journal of Human-Computer Studies, 59,* 119–155.

Castellano, G., Leite, I., Pereira, A., Martinho, C., Paiva, A., & McOwan, P. W. (2009). It's All in the Game: Towards an Affect Sensitive and Context Aware Game Companion. *Proceedings of the International Conference on Affective Computing and Intelligent Interaction.* IEEE Press (pp. 1–8)

Dautenhahn, K., & Werry, I. (2002). A quantitative technique for analysing robot-human interactions. In *International conference on intelligent robots and systems* (pp. 1132–1138 vol.2)., IEEE Press.

Dautenhahn, K., Werry, I., Rae, J., Dickerson, P., Stribling, P., & Ogden, B. (2002). Robotic playmates: Analysing interactive competencies of children with autism playing with a mobile robot. In K. Dautenhahn, A. H. Bond, L. Canamero, & B. Edmonds (Eds.), *Socially intelligent agents* (pp. 117–124). Dordrecht, the Netherlands: Kluwer Academic Publishers.

Davidson, R. J. (1994). On emotion, mood and related affective constructs. In P. Ekman & R. J. Davidson (Eds.), *Nature of emotion: Fundamental questions* (pp. 51–56). New York: Oxford University Press.

Ekman, P., & Friesen, W. V. (1978). *Facial action coding system.* Palo Alto, CA: Consulting Psychologist Press.

El-Nasr, M. S., Yen, J., & Ioerger, T. (2000). FLAME—A fuzzy logic adaptive model of emotions. *Journal of Autonomous Agents and Multi-Agent Systems, 3*(3), 219–257.

Endo, Y. & Arkin, R. C. (2001). Implementing Tolman's schematic sowbug: Behavior-based robotics in the 1930s. In *IEEE international conference on robotics and automation* (pp. 477–484, vol.1). IEEE Press.

Fong, T., Nourbakhsh, I., & Dautenhahn, K. (2003). A survey of socially interactive robots. *Robotics and Autonomous Systems, 42,* 143–166.

Gazzaniga, M. S. (2005). *The ethical brain.* New York: Dana Press.

Goris, K., Saldien, J., & Lefeber D. (2009). Probo, a testbed for human robot interaction. In *ACM/IEEE international conference on human-robot interaction* (pp. 253–254).

Hashimoto, T., Hamada, T., & Akazawa, T. (2003). Proposal of emotion-driven control model for robot-assisted activity. In *IEEE international symposium on computational intelligence in robotics and automation* (pp. 125–129, vol. 1). IEEE Press.

Holland, O. (2003). The first biologically inspired robots. *Robotica, 21*(4), 351–363.

Kirby, R., Forlizzi, J., & Simmons, R. (2010). Affective social robots. *Robotics and Autonomous Systems, 58,* 322–332.

Kulic, D., & Croft, E. (2006). Physiological and subjective responses to articulated robot motion. *Robotica, 15*(1), 13–27.

Lee-Johnson, C. P., & Carnegie, D. A. (2007). Emotion-based parameter modulation for a hierarchical mobile robot planning and control architecture. In *IEEE international conference on intelligent robots and systems* (pp. 2839–2844). IEEE Press.

Leite, I., Pereira, A., Martinho, C., & Paiva, A. (2008). Are emotional robots more fun to play with? In *IEEE international symposium on robot and human interactive communication (RO-MAN* (pp. 77–82). IEEE Press

Leventhal, H., & Scherer, K. (1987). The relationship of emotion to cognition: A functional approach to a semantic controversy. *Cognition and Emotion, 1,* 3–28.

Levy, D. (2008). *Love and sex with robots: The evolution of human-robot relationships.* New York: Harper Perennial.

MacKenzie, D. C., Arkin, R. C., & Cameron, J. M. (1997). Multiagent mission specification and execution. *Autonomous Robots, 4*(1), 29–52.

Manual for MissionLab Version 7.0. Georgia Tech Mobile Robot Laboratory, 2007. Available at: http://www.cc.gatech.edu/ai/robot-lab/research/MissionLab/

Melson, G. F., Kahn, P. H. Jr., Beck A., & Friedman, B. (2009). Robotic pets in human lives: Implications for the human-animal bond and for human relationships with personified technologies. *Journal of Social Issues, 65,* 545–567.

Miwa, H., Etoh, K., Matsumoto, M., Zecca, M. Takanobu, H., Rocella, S.,...Takanishi, A. (2004). Effective emotional expressions with emotion expression humanoid robot WE-4RII. In *IEEE international conference on intelligent robots and systems* (pp. 2203–2208, vol. 3). IEEE Press.

Miwa, H., Takanishi, A., & Takanobu, H. (2001). Experimental study on robot personality for humanoid head robot. In *IEEE international conference on intelligent robots and systems* (pp. 1183–1188, vol. 2). IEEE Press.

Moravec, H. (1988). *Mind children: The future of robot and human intelligence*. Cambridge, MA: Harvard University Press.

Moshkina, L. (2011). An integrative framework of time-varying affective robotic behavior. Ph.D. dissertation. Georgia Institute of Technology, Atlanta, GA.

Moshkina, L. (2012). Improving request compliance through robot affect. In *AAAI conference on artificial intelligence* (pp. 2031 –2037

Moshkina, L., Park, S., Arkin, R. C., Lee, J., & Jung, H. (2011). TAME: Time varying affective response for humanoid robots. *International Journal of Social Robotics, 3*(3), 207–221.

Murphy, R. M., Lisetti, C., Tardif, R., Irish, L., & Gage, A. (2002). Emotion-based control of cooperating heterogeneous mobile robots. *IEEE Transactions on Robotics and Automation, 18*(5), 744–757.

Murray, J. C., Canamero, L. & Hiolle, A. (2009). Towards a model of emotion expression in an interactive robot head. In *IEEE international symposium on robot and human interactive communication (RO-MAN)* (pp. 627–632). IEEE Press.

Nakagawa, K. S., Ishiguro, H., Akimoto, T. & Hagita, N. (2009). Motion modification method to control affective nuances for robots. In *IEEE international conference on intelligent robots and systems* (pp. 5003–5008). IEEE Press.

Nomura, T., & Kanda, T. (2003). On proposing the concept of robot anxiety and considering measurement of it. In *IEEE international workshop on robot and human interactive communication (RO-MAN)* (pp. 373–378).

Nomura, T., Kanda, T., Suzuki, T., & Kato, K. (2008). Prediction of human behavior in human-robot interaction using psychological scales for anxiety and negative attitudes towards robots. *IEEE Transactions on Robotics, 24*(2), 442–451.

Ortony, A., Clore, G. L., & Collins, A. (1988). *The cognitive structure of emotions*. Cambridge, UK: Cambridge University Press.

Park, S., Moshkina, L., & Arkin, R. C. (2010). Recognizing nonverbal affective behavior in humanoid robots. In *IEEE international conference on intelligent autonomous systems*.

Posner, J., Russell, J., & Peterson, B. (2005). The circumplex model of affect: An integrative approach to affective neuroscience, cognitive development, and psychopathology. *Development and Psychopathology, 17*(3), 715–734.

Psathas, G. (1995). *Conversation analysis*. Thousand Oaks, CA: Sage.

Rani, P., Sarkar, N., Smith, C. A., & Kirby, L. D. (2004). Anxiety detecting robotic system—Towards implicit human-robot collaboration. *Robotica, 22*(1), 85–95.

Reeves, B., & Nass, C. (1996). *The media equation: How people treat computers, television, and new media like real people and places*. Cambridge, UK: Cambridge University Press.

Saucier, G. (1994). Mini-markers: A brief version of Goldberg's unipolar big-five markers. *Journal of Personality Assessment, 63*(3), 506–516.

Scheutz, M., & Schermerhorn, P. (2009). Affective goal and task selection for social robots. In J. Vallverdu & D. Casacuberta (Eds.), *Handbook of research on synthetic emotions and sociable robotics: New applications in affective computing and artificial intelligence* (pp. 74–87). IGI Global, Hershey, PA.

Scheutz, M., Schermerhorn, P., & Kramer, J. (2006). The utility of affect expression in natural language interactions in joint human-robot tasks. In *ACM international conference on human-robot interaction* (pp. 226–233). ACM, New York, NY.

Scheutz, M., Schermerhorn, P., Kramer, J., & Anderson, D. (2007). First steps toward natural human-like HRI. *Autonomous Robots, 22*(4), 411–423.

Shibata, T., Life innovation with therapeutic robot, Paro. Available at: http://www.bbvaopenmind.com/article/en/60/life-innovation-with-therapeutic-robot-paro/ (Accessed August 2012.)

Sosnowski, S., Bittermann, A., Kuhnlenz, K., & Buss, M. (2006). Design and evaluation of emotion-display EDDIE. In *IEEE international conference on intelligent robots and systems* (pp. 3113–3118). IEEE Press.

Sparrow, R. (2002). The march of the robot dogs. *Ethics and Information Technology, 4*(4), 305–318.

Turkle, S. (2011). *Alone together: Why we expect more from technology and less from each other*. New York: Basic Books.

Watson, D., Clark, L. A., & Tellegen, A. (1998). Development and validation of brief measures of positive and negative affect: The PANAS scales. *Journal of Personality and Social Psychology, 56*(6), 1063–1070.

Wu, T., Butko, N. J., Ruvulo, P., Bartlett, M. S., & Movellan, J. R. (2009). Learning to Make Facial Expressions. In *IEEE international conference on development and learning* (pp. 1–6). IEEE Press, Piscataway, NJ.

Yu, C., & Xu, L. (2004). An emotion-based approach to decision-making and self learning in autonomous robot control. In *5th world congress on intelligent control and automation* (pp. 2386–2390, vol. 3). IEEE Press.

Virtual Reality and Collaboration

Jakki O. Bailey *and* Jeremy N. Bailenson

Abstract

Collaboration is an integral part of human interaction and human-computer interaction. Collaborative virtual environments (CVEs) unite multiple users from remote locations in a common virtual space. CVEs utilizing immersive virtual environment technology (IVET) create sensory and socially rich experiences, allowing users to express affect via verbal and nonverbal behaviors. Embodiment is important in expressing emotion, and people interact in CVEs through avatars, or digital representations of their identities. The users' behaviors are tracked to inform computer system responses and provide insight into the users' current state. CVEs can enhance collaboration by creating a sense of presence in the virtual world, and the technology can alter social behaviors (e.g., eye gaze) to differ in the virtual world from how they are enacted in the physical world. Although IVET has many benefits, it raises important ethical concerns. As affective computing technology develops, CVEs will become more commonplace, changing organizations, institutions, and industries.

Key Words: virtual reality, collaboration, collaborative virtual environments, embodiment, presence, nonverbal behaviors

Virtual Reality and Collaboration

Collaboration is an essential part of the human experience. As a species, working together with others has allowed for our survival against animal predation, improvement in nutritional opportunities, and the development of social support. To achieve a successful collaboration, group members may need to effectively maximize cooperation, requiring them to distinguish friend from foe. The expression and reading of emotions allow people to communicate their intentions and desires. Many scholars view emotional responses (both verbal and nonverbal) as an evolutionary inheritance that has facilitated survival (Lang, Greenwald, Bradley, & Hamm, 1993; Wirth & Schramm, 2005).

Today collaborative interaction still remains an important part of life and has expanded beyond face-to-face interactions to virtual worlds. Many businesses exist solely online, with coworkers from around the globe contributing to group projects on shared digital documents. Friends organize events using social networking websites. Multiuser online games host elaborate virtual raids consisting of fanciful creatures like trolls and elves. These are a few of the multiple application areas for virtual collaboration. However, these examples often neglect to incorporate two important elements of communication: nonverbal behavior and real-time feedback. A student learning remotely may need smiling approval from a teacher for motivation (Lepper & Woolverton, 2002). Negotiations may go awry without eye contact to promote trust. Virtual reality (VR) has the ability to alleviate some of these limitations by capturing behaviors and expressions and sharing that information with others (both humans and computers). The immersive capabilities and effects of VR resonate with Picard's (2003) critical aspects of affective computing: "recognizing, expressing, modeling, communicating, and responding to emotion" (p. 56) and "adapting to you, vs. treating you like some fictionalized idealized user" (p. 58).

Major Aims and Goals

This chapter provides an overview of the history and general technological components of collaborative virtual environments. Methodological and conceptual issues and the unique affordances and challenges of immersive virtual reality technology are highlighted. Finally, some ethical questions related to the use of virtual reality to capture and express emotions/behaviors are proposed, as well as some possible future applications.

Ivan Sutherland created what many consider to be the first virtual world; he has been considered the father of computer graphics (Lanier, 2001; Sutherland, 1968). He created a virtual reality headset, called a head-mounted display (HMD), which visually placed users in a stereoscopic three-dimensional environment. In the mid- to late-1980s, Jaron Lanier first coined the term *virtual reality*. He expanded on Sutherland's idea by imagining a technology that placed multiple users in a virtual world using an HMD. Many researchers have since explored the use of VR technology to adequately express speech, emotion, and nonverbal behavior (see Lanier, 2001, for a discussion of the development of VR technology).

Environments in virtual reality can represent both actual and imagined locations. In general, a virtual environment (VE) is any digital space that tracks users' movements and renders or digitally updates the world to reflect those motions in real time. For example, a home console device like the Microsoft Kinect tracks a player's body movements with over 20 degrees of freedom, and his or her character can be rendered to move according to these tracked movements (e.g., a video game character jumping over a hurdle when the user jumps). As the player moves, a tracking device detects the movement and the rendering technology updates the world to reflect that movement, providing the user with sensory feedback. Tracking devices can determine where a person is at any given moment in the VE and the direction in which he or she moves. Gross body movements are located as translations (X, Y, and Z directions in a Cartesian plane) and orientation (pitch, roll, and yaw). Technology like the Microsoft Kinect, an affordable commercial gaming product, can track several points on the body without physical tracking devices (though within a limited range of space and at a relatively low frame rate).

Tracking and rendering behaviors generate a rich dataset on each individual user. Such tracked and collected data can be used to better inform affective computing systems. For example, machine learning could be utilized to infer the user's emotional states at various time points during virtual interactions. These data can then be used to inform the system as to when and how to provide appropriate responses to the user.

Collaborative Virtual Environments

A collaborative virtual environment (CVE) is a virtual reality technology that supports multiple users simultaneously in a shared VE. CVEs combine the fields of virtual reality and computer-supported cooperative work (e.g., Benford, Greenhalgh, Rodden, & Pycock, 2001). The three broad goals of CVEs are (1) to bring together pairs or groups of people regardless of distance for collaboration; (2) to use objects and/or environments not easily accessible in the physical world; and (3) to provide the key elements of collaborative work into a virtual space (flexible and multiple viewpoints, shared context, awareness of others, and clear communication) (Churchill & Snowdon, 1998).

Virtual environments can be broadly categorized as either using immersive or nonimmersive technology. Immersive technology can provide a surrounding and vivid experience that shuts out the sensory information of the physical world (Biocca, 1997; Fox, Arena, & Bailenson, 2009; Slater & Wilbur, 1997). An example of a nonimmersive VE is an online role-playing game on a desktop computer in which only a keyboard and mouse are used. Here the user may be distracted by the sensory information of the outside world as he or she navigates through the VE. Immersive virtual environment technology (IVET) provides sensory feedback on a variety of levels such as visual, haptic, auditory, and olfactory. An HMD is a type of immersive display. It provides users with a three-dimensional (3D) first-person point of view of the virtual world; some such devices offer a wide field of view, which provides users with peripheral vision. Immersive experiences can also occur without the use of an HMD. A Cave Automatic Virtual Environment (CAVE) is another type of IVET in which the walls, ceiling and/or floor of a specially designed room project images of the virtual world (Cruz-Neira, Sandin,

DeFanti, Kenyon, & Hart, 1992). It is not necessary for all the surfaces to project an image for the room to be considered a CAVE. Images can be displayed, for example, on a projection screen or 3D television screens (see Cruz-Neira, Sandin, DeFanti, Kenyon, & Hart, 1992, for details on CAVE development). Special eyewear can be used to create 3D views, but new displays are utilizing autostereoscopic technology to create a glasses-free 3D experience.

The remainder of this chapter focuses on IVET and collaboration, as IVET provides several levels of sensory feedback as well as many possibilities for acting out and experiencing nonverbal behaviors (which are critical to communicate affective cues). Furthermore, IVET can induce psychological and physiological responses in VR similar to those in the physical world. For example, users' heart rates accelerate when they are standing at the edge of a virtual pit (Meehan, Insko, Whitton, & Brooks Jr., 2002), and children have been shown to confuse memories of their virtual experiences with experiences that occurred in the physical world (Segovia & Bailenson, 2009).

Methodological Considerations and Research Challenges

As mentioned previously, shared context, awareness of others, clear communication, and multiple viewpoints are important elements of collaboration. It can be argued that to create an effective CVE, users must feel part of the virtual experience, connect with other users in the virtual space, and have the ability to express emotion. In investigating CVEs, areas that researchers need to consider are presence, embodiment, and the transformation of behaviors using computer algorithms. For example, education research indicates that actual experience (virtual or real) improves learning (Barab, Thomas, Dodge, Carteaux, & Tuzun, 2005) and that nonverbal behaviors via computer-animated faces can evoke a wide range of emotions in people (Gratch et al., 2002).

Presence

In general, *presence* is the subjective psychological experience of "being there" or being in the virtual environment (Lombard & Ditton, 1997; Loomis, 1992; Nowak & Biocca, 2003; Steuer, 1992). It is important to note that *presence* refers to a psychological experience and is not tied to a specific technology. In other words, it is a subjective response and can vary across individuals given

similar technological configurations. How people experience presence in some instances can be related to individual differences such as the degree to which a person is imaginative (Heeter, 2003; Lombard & Ditton, 1997; O'Hare, 2003; Wirth et al., 2007), and thus may require more or less sensory feedback to feel as if he or she were part of the virtual world. For example, a study using virtual reality showed that participants who were more creative and/or had a high capacity to be immersed in a VE felt a greater sense of presence as compared with others who were low in these qualities (Sas & O'Hare, 2003).

According to Lee (2004), virtual objects can feel like actual objects in either sensory or nonsensory ways. Media such as books are nonsensory—they don't necessarily replace senses with computer-generated stimuli but are able to involve the user psychologically in the story or action. Steuer (1992) points out that describing VR in terms of the human experience (as opposed to technologically) is to describe presence.

In general, presence can be conceptually viewed as a way to determine how involved and connected a person is with a mediated experience. Those who experience high presence tend to react to virtual experiences as if they were real (Blascovich & Bailenson, 2011). A successful virtual collaboration requires that all parties involved share a common context even if they fail to share the same physical location; understanding the idea of presence may provide researchers with a better understanding of users' natural responses to mediated interactions in VEs. There are three subtypes of presence that are commonly measured in CVEs: physical presence, social presence, and self-presence.

Physical presence, sometimes referred to as spatial or environmental presence, is the perceptual experience of physical objects in the virtual world (both the VE itself and the objects within it) as being real. Physical presence is typically experienced through visual and audio technology but can also be stimulated through haptic and olfactory devices (although the technology for the latter is currently less developed). Human beings are social creatures even in virtual spaces, and *social presence* measures the psychological state in which virtual social actors are experienced as actual social actors. It is the feeling of connection a person feels with others. Lee (2004) writes that:

> Just as people pay special attention to other humans more than any other physical objects, technology users pay great attention to technology-generated

stimuli manifesting humanness both in physical (e.g., voice, face, anthropomorphic shape, etc.) and psychological (e.g., personality, reciprocity, interactivity, social roles, understanding language, etc.) ways. (p. 39)

The combination of social presence and behavioral realism in immersive virtual environments can allow for actors to socially influence one another (Blascovich et al., 2002). According to Blascovich and colleagues' (2002) psychological framework in virtual environments, social influence is described as the way people influence others and themselves attitudinally and behaviorally. Behavioral realism is defined as the extent to which virtual objects and humans behave as they would in the physical world. It is a continuous dimension that runs from low to high. Photographic realism is only one aspect of behavioral realism and is often not necessary. For example, readers can find themselves feeling connected to characters in a newspaper comic strip even though these characters are not photographically realistic. For social presence to occur, behaviors in the virtual world must be similar to those that would occur in the physical world. Blascovich and colleagues (2002) contend that as social presence increases, so does the belief that the virtual human present represents a real person in the physical world in real time. Under this model, if social presence is high, behavioral realism need not be necessary for social influence to occur. If social presence is low (e.g., if one believes one is interacting with a computer), then behavioral realism will need to be high for social influence to occur. Finally, the effects of social influence are absent when both social presence and behavioral realism are low

Co-presence is similar to social presence and the terms are often used interchangeably. However, some scholars have refined the notion of co-presence to indicate feeling that others are present in the virtual space regardless of how connected the user feels to them (Lee, 2004). Research has implicated a positive association between feelings of co-presence and overall presence (Gerhard, Moore, & Hobbs, 2004; Slater, Sadagic, Usoh, & Schroeder, 2000).

Self-presence is the extent that a person identifies with how he or she is digitally represented in the VE, or the level at which the virtual self is experienced as the actual self. Biocca (1997) defines self-presence as how a virtual environment impacts one's perception of one's body, physiological states, emotional states, traits, and identity.

Researchers from various disciplines have created numerous measures of presence. Currently the most common tool is the self-report questionnaire. There has been a recent shift toward utilizing behavioral and physiological measurements (Bailenson et al., 2004; Slater, 2004). However, a lack of a universal and specific conceptual definition of presence (though many have attempted to create one) exists; therefore many terms are used to describe in essence the same underlying idea (e.g., *telepresence, mediated presence, virtual presence*, as pointed out by Lee, 2004). Consequently, much like emotion, presence has proven to be a difficult construct to consistently measure and compare across studies.

Embodiment

Collaboration involves the nuances of social interactions such as shared context, proximity, nonverbal behaviors, gaze, awareness of others, and clear communication (Churchill & Snowdon, 1998). As such, embodiment in virtual spaces is crucial in allowing for affective realism in collaboration. Virtual bodies facilitate interhuman communication by allowing users to identify their own bodies and recognize the bodies of others (Biocca, 1997; Gerhard, Moore, & Hobbs, 2004). One view could be that virtual bodies provide a focus for the conversation and any interactions. Embodiment in VR allows for a digital equivalent to face-to-face communication with individuals or multiple people. According to Benford, Bowers, Fahlén, and Snowdon (1995):

> Our bodies provide immediate and continuous information about our presence, activity, attention, availability, mood, status, location, identity, capabilities, and many other factors (p. 242)....Thus, an embodiment can be likened to a "marionette" with active autonomous behaviors together with a series of strings which the user is continuously "pulling" as smoothly as possible. (p. 243)

A digital embodiment or representation that is controlled by a person is called an *avatar*. Often avatars take a human or anthropomorphic form. However, the form an avatar takes is limited only by the imagination of the designer and/or the capabilities of the technology to render its appearance or behaviors. Through IVET, users can take on multiple perspectives by customizing their avatar's appearance and behavior. For example, a marine biologist may choose to navigate through a virtual ocean by embodying an octopus. Avatar appearance affects people in both the virtual and physical worlds.

Labeling it the Proteus effect, a study by Yee and Bailenson (2007) illustrated how an avatar's appearance impacts people's behaviors. Study participants were each assigned an avatar that was previously scored as unattractive, neutral, or attractive by a different set of participants. While embodying their new avatars, they completed a task in which they looked at their digital representation in a mirror. Afterward they interacted with a confederate avatar in a CVE who was blind to condition (the IVET allowed the confederate to view the participant as what was rated through pretesting as a neutral level of attractiveness). Results demonstrated that participants assigned to the unattractive avatar adopted the affective cues related to appearance; they kept a greater distance from the confederate and disclosed less information as compared with those inhabiting attractive avatars. In a follow-up study, virtual height was manipulated such that participants were either taller than, the same height as, or shorter than the confederate. The participant and the confederate engaged in a negotiation task in VR with the goal of agreeing on a monetary split between the two of them. Those with taller avatars made significantly more offers in their favor as compared with those in the short condition. Furthermore, those in the shorter condition were twice as likely to accept an unfair split in the final round of negotiation compared with both the normal and taller conditions. These results indicate that people conform to their avatar's appearance and the expectations associated with that (i.e., attractiveness relates to friendliness and height to confidence).

In contrast to an avatar, a digital representation driven by computer algorithms is called an *agent*. According to Nass and Reeves (1996), people treat media technology as social actors. Participants have treated agents as social actors even after knowing they are interacting with a computer (e.g., Gerhard, Moore, & Hobbs, 2004; Gratch et al., 2002). In particular, when agents possess morphology and behaviors that are similar to those of humans, users expect them to behave as humans and respond to the agents as if they were real people (Biocca, 1997; Gratch et al., 2002).

The model of social influence in virtual environments can also be applied to agent behaviors. Agents express situational and socially appropriate verbal and nonverbal responses to create the appearance of "intelligence." A study by Garau, Slater, Pertaup, and Razzaque (2005) investigated how people in VR responded to visually identical virtual agents that differed in behavioral responsiveness.

Participants entered a virtual reading room in which the agents were either static, moving randomly, responsive to the participant (i.e., when approached the agent would change body posture and engage in gaze behavior), or responsive with speech (gibberish language, but meaning was conveyed through tone). Participants reported attributing a significantly higher sense of social presence to the virtual characters that were responsive (without speech) as compared with the other conditions. However, social presence appears to be highest when users believe that they are interacting with another human. In alignment with Garau and colleague's study results, research by Lim and Reeves (2010) demonstrated that participants become physiologically more aroused when they believe they are interacting with an avatar as opposed to an agent regardless of the actual behavior of the virtual human. The results of these two studies suggest that users' responses to others in a virtual environment are an interaction between the behavior of the agent or avatar and the users' perception of the agent or avatar.

What would collaboration involving both avatars and agents look like? Leveraging the data collected through tracking technology (as previously mentioned), computer algorithms (embodied as agents) might be able to read nuanced cues from actual human interactants and then intervene with the appropriate affective and semantic responses. CVE researchers have proposed that virtual environments should incorporate an avatar/agent hybrid (Bailenson, 2006; Gerhard, Moore, & Hobbs, 2004). For example, psychology literature has demonstrated that subtle mimicry or mirroring of another person's nonverbal behaviors can influence social interactions (often referred to as the "chameleon effect") (Chartrand & Bargh, 1999). Using IVET, collected user tracking data can be played back through an agent's behaviors. For example, when participants in VR interacted with an agent that mimicked their head movements, they found the mimicking agent more persuasive and rated it as more positive than a nonmimicking agent (Bailenson & Yee, 2005). An additional application would be to customize an avatar's behavior to become automated during specific times or scenarios: when the user is present, the avatar operates under his or her control, and when the person is absent (perhaps to attend to tasks in the physical world), computer algorithms take control over the virtual interactions. This idea of utilizing agent technology as part of avatar actions is part of a research paradigm called transformed social interactions

(TSIs), which is described in greater detail below (see Bailenson, 2006, for a theoretical description).

Transformed Social Interactions

Transformed social interactions (TSIs) involves the decoupling of an avatar's appearance or behavior from the actual person. It is a form of self-presentation management, controlling the identity and nonverbal behavior of the user through the deliberate use of computer algorithms. The three dimensions of TSIs are self-representation, sensory abilities, and situational context (Bailenson, Yee, Blascovich, & Guadagno, 2008). Through self-representation, users can present different version of themselves to different people simultaneously, which can impact the type of interactions and emotional responses people have with each other in virtual environments by manipulating nonverbal behaviors that communicate emotion. CVE technology can project different affective states to multiple people simultaneously; for example, a supervisor can express frustration to one set of employees while nodding in approval to another group of workers. TSIs have the ability to separate automatic physical responses of emotion such as sweating or shaking from how they are expressed in the CVE. As such, TSIs tailor a collaborative experience to individual needs and preferences. Much of the affordances of TSIs can be illustrated in a virtual classroom setting. For example, some students may learn information better from a smiling face while others might excel by watching a teacher with a stoic expression (Bailenson, 2006). In CVEs, all students would see different versions of a real-time teacher tailored to their affective needs.

Sensory abilities in TSIs can be thought of as "invisible consultants" who provide sensory feedback that is only visible to certain users (Bailenson, 2006). For example, a study by Bailenson, Yee, Blascovich, Beall, Lundblad, and Jin (2008) used augmented gaze in an immersive virtual environment to improve teaching behaviors. While the teacher was giving a lesson, the opacity level of each student was directly related to the amount of time the teacher spent looking at him or her. The longer the student stayed out of the teacher's gaze, the more translucent she or he became, thereby cuing the teacher to change his or her field of view. Results showed that teachers with the augmented perception of the classroom ignored students less than those without the change.

Finally, situational context provides spatial or temporal alterations. During a discussion or speech among a large crowd, with TSIs each person can have the perspective of sitting directly in front of the speaker. A recent study indicated that students who had the perception of being at the front of the classroom were more persuaded by the speaker and had more positive impressions of the speaker compared with those located in the back of the room (McCall, Bunyan, Bailenson, Blascovich, & Beall, 2009). In addition, TSIs provide the opportunity for users to engage in a type of rewind or fast forward technique during a real time interaction in an effort to increase comprehension (Bailenson, Yee, Blascovich, & Guadagno, 2008).

TSIs afford a unique opportunity to manage and elicit emotional responses. With tracked movements and behaviors, users in a CVE have the potential for personalized experiences. Computer systems have the potential to monitor behavior and provide feedback at the appropriate time. Another important ability of TSIs in CVEs is that users are granted a high level of interactivity. If the experience becomes frustrating or overwhelming, the user can pause or play back what he or she needs without disturbing other people in the same environment, similar to pausing and resuming live cable television.

Technological Challenges

The major challenges that affect CVE work typically revolve around the technology. For example, there is a trade-off between realism or fidelity in the virtual world and rendering speed. If there is too much detail, it may take a perceptible amount of time for a computer to process and update the world accordingly, creating a lag in the user's point of view. A participant can experience "simulator sickness" or feelings of nausea and disorientation due to lag during rendering. In addition, it is difficult to track all of the human body's degrees of freedom precisely. However, programmers can typically use smoothing algorithms to generate a relatively accurate estimation of the movement (e.g., using measurements captured from other related parts of the body). Researchers must also consider which limbs, if any, will be tracked and rendered and how that will impact the rate that the world is rendered.

Although the use of an HMD provides a highly sensory and engaging experience, the bulky equipment hinders capturing nuanced facial expressions, particularly involuntary expressions such as surprise or shock (there is, however, facial tracking software commonly available for nonimmersive virtual environments). Currently, tracking and rendering can determine the general direction in which a user is looking. Specific eye gaze in CVE is difficult to effectively measure because eye trackers typically restrict the users from moving around in physical space.

Finally, given how many different software and hardware configurations of CVEs exist in academia, industry, and other organizations, a major difficulty will be integrating various systems and capabilities into a universal software package. A specific software program may not be able to run scripts created in a different program. In addition, scalability (the ability to house a large number of users in one VE) may be difficult to achieve if systems differ in significant ways.

Ethical Considerations

CVEs and IVET are able to provide a number of advantages through their interactive, sensory, and tracking capabilities. However, these capabilities raise ethical questions. Appearance can easily be manipulated such that the identity of an avatar may not match the user. A photorealistic 3D model used to create an avatar can be generated with just two digital photographs (Bailenson, Beall, Blascovich, & Rex, 2004). Misleading others by misrepresenting oneself violates the trust necessary for cooperative collaboration. As mentioned previously, nonverbal behaviors can be altered using TSIs. Algorithms can mimic nearly any nonverbal behavior (including mirroring others' behaviors), thus potentially generating misleading or stolen emotional responses. Finally, the technology itself (particularly IVET) collects large amounts of data at a continuous rate, which data can then be digitally stored. The stored traces of behaviors in virtual environments are called "digital footprints" and can act as personal identifiers (see "Digital Footprints" chapter in Blascovich & Bailenson, 2011, for more detail). Behaviors and actions recorded in the past can easily be played back again at a different times in different contexts, thus violating a person's privacy and autonomy.

Future Directions and Conclusion

Virtual reality technology can act as a social actor to simulate unique experiences for users and serve as a tool to enhance human-to-human interaction and human-to-computer interaction. CVEs have great potential to improve the quality of virtual collaboration. They can respond and update quickly according to the user's needs while simultaneously interacting with multiple individuals. Through virtual embodiment, CVEs allow users to express themselves both verbally and nonverbally. IVET can create an immersive experience integrating sensory feedback. The use of computer algorithms can customize virtual interactions to each user's viewpoint and experience, combining human and computer actions. CVEs can grant individuals various perspectives and alter social interactions such as empathy (Yee & Bailenson, 2006). With these affordances come serious ethical issues regarding trust, privacy, and autonomy, raising the question of what can and should be tracked digitally. As research has demonstrated that virtual reality can impact real-world behaviors, how those elements are manipulated must be carefully considered.

With the development of cost-effective technology, virtual environments can be better integrated into daily life. There will be increased opportunities for embodied experiences, and virtual environments will be easier to alter by nonexperts (e.g., those outside of academia or industry). The technology will likely become less intrusive—for example, with the use of smaller devices like portable displays in glasses. In addition, the control of avatars will be more automatic and map closer to actual behaviors. This is already seen in current technology (e.g., in the use of touch screens, or video game play without a physical controller). There will be improved realism of virtual environments, objects, and people, and changes in industries and institutions are likely to follow. The meaning of a "live" concert or travel may change and become more linked to virtual environments. Music fans could experience an intimate performance taking place a continent away without leaving the comfort of their homes. Finally, the agent-avatar hybrid will most likely become an integral part of VR and affective computing. Development and research could address creating more appropriately responsive and interactive agents.

Computers can respond to the needs of humans by performing critical actions through communicating messages, managing individual levels of emotional expression, and manipulating extensive amounts of data for larges audiences. By bringing together various individuals from remote locations and incorporating nonverbal behaviors, technology like virtual reality can be used to further the human desire and necessity for effective collaboration.

References

Bailenson, J. N. (2006). Transformed social interaction in collaborative virtual environments. In P. Messaris & L. Humphreys

(Eds.), *Digital media: Transformations in human communication* (pp. 255–264). New York, NY: Peter Lang.

Bailenson, J. N., Aharoni, E., Beall, A. C., Guadagno, R. E., Dimov, A., & Blascovich, J. (2004). Comparing behavioral and self-report measures of embodied agents' social presence in immersive virtual environments. *Proceedings of the 7th Annual International Workshop on Presence* (pp. 216–223). Available at: http://www.temple.edu/ispr/prev_conferences/proceedings/2004/Bailsenson,%20Aharoni,%20Beall,%20Guadagno,%20Dimov,%20Blascovich.pdf

Bailenson, J. N., Beall, A. C., Blascovich, J., & Rex, C. (2004). Examining virtual busts: Are photogrammetrically generated head models effective for person identification? *Presence: Teleoperators & virtual environments, 13*(4), 416–427.

Bailenson, J. N. & Yee, N. (2005). Digital chameleons: Automatic assimilation of nonverbal gestures in immersive virtual environments. *Psychological Science, 16*(10), 814–819.

Bailenson, J. N., Yee, N., Blascovich, J., Beall, A. C., Lundblad, N., & Jin, M. (2008). The use of immersive virtual reality in the learning sciences: Digital transformations of teachers, students, and social context. *The Journal of the Learning Sciences, 17*, 102–141.

Bailenson, J. N., Yee, N., Blascovich, J., & Guadagno, R. E. (2008). Transformed social interaction in mediated interpersonal communication. In E. A. Konijn, S. Utz, M. Tanis, & S. B. Barnes (Eds.), *Mediated interpersonal communication* (pp. 77–99). Mahwah, NJ: Lawrence Erlbaum.

Benford, S., Greenhalgh, C., Rodden, T., & Pycock, J. (2001). Collaborative virtual environments. *Communications of the ACM, 44*(7), 79–85.

Biocca, F. (1997) The cyborg's dilemma: Embodiment in virtual environments (1997). *Humanizing the information age: Proceedings of the 2nd International Conference on Cognitive Technology* (pp. 12–26). doi: 10.1109/CT.1997.617676.

Blascovich, J. & Bailenson, J. (2011). *Infinite reality: Avatars, eternal life, new worlds, and the dawn of the virtual revolution.* New York, NY: HarperCollins.

Blascovich, J., Loomis, J., Beall, A. C., Swinth, K. R., Hoyt, C. L., & Bailenson, J. N. (2002). Immersive virtual reality technology as a methodological tool for social psychology. *Psychology Inquiry: An International Journal for the Advancement of Psychological Theory, 13*(2), 103–124.

Benford, S. Bowers, J., Fahlén, L. E., Greehalgh, C., & Snowdan, D. (1995). User embodiment in collaborative virtual environments. *Proceedings from CHI '95: Conference on Human Factors in Computing Systems.* New York, NY: Association for Computing Machinery.

Chartrand, T. L. & Bargh, J. A. (1999). The chameleon effect: The perception-behavior link and social interaction. *Journal of Personality and Social Psychology, 76*(6), 893–910.

Churchill, E. F., & Snowdon, D. (1998). Collaborative virtual environments: An introductory review of issues and systems. *Virtual Reality, 3*, 3–15.

Cruz-Neira, C., Sandin, D. J., DeFanti, T. A., Kenyon, R. V., & Hart, J. C. (1992). The CAVE: Audio visual experience automatic virtual environment. *Communications of the ACM, 35*(6), 64–72. doi:10.1145/129888.129892.

Fox, J., Arena, D., & Bailenson, J. N. (2009). Virtual reality: A survival guide for the social scientist. *Journal of Media Psychology, 21*(3), 95–113.

Garau, M., Slater, M., Pertaub, D.-P., Razzaque, S. (2005). The responses of people to virtual humans in an immersive virtual environment. *Presence: Teleoperators & Virtual Environments, 14*(1), 104–116.

Gerhard, M., Moore, D., & Hobbs, D. (2004). Embodiment and copresence in collaborative interfaces. *International Journal of Human-Computer Studies, 61*, 453–480.

Gratch, J., Rickel, J., André, E., Cassell, J., Petajan, E., & Badler, N. (2002). Creating interactive virtual humans: Some assembly required. *IEE Intelligent Systems*, 54–63.

Heeter, C. (2003). Reflections on presence by a virtual person. *Presence: Teleoperators & Virtual Environments, 12*(4), 335–345.

Lanier, J. (2001). Three-dimensional tele-immersion may eventually bring the world to your desk. *Scientific American, 284*(4), 66–75.

Lang, P. J., Greenwald, M. K., Bradley, M. M., & Hamm, A. O. (1993). Looking at pictures: Affective, facial, visceral, and behavioral reactions. *Psychophysiology, 30*, 261–273.

Lee, K. M. (2004). Presence, explicated. *Communication Theory, 14*, 27–50.

Lepper, M., & Woolverton, M. (2002). The wisdom of practice: Lessons learned from the study of highly effective tutors. In J. Aronson (Ed.), *Improving academic achievement: Impact of psychological factors on education* (pp. 135–158). Orlando, FL: Academic Press.

Lim, S., & Reeves, B. (2010). Computer agents versus avatars: Responses to interactive game characters controlled by a computer or other player. *International Journal of Human-Computer Studies, 68*, 57–68.

Lombard, M., & Ditton, T. (1997). At the heart of it all: The concept of presence. *Journal of Computer-mediated Communication, 3*(2). doi: 10.1111/j.1083–6101.1997.tb00072.x. Available at: http://onlinelibrary.wiley.com/doi/10.1111/j.1083-6101.1997.tb00072.x/

Loomis, J. M. (1992). Distal attribution and presence. *Presence: Teleoperators and Virtual Environments, 1*(1), 113–119.

McCall, C., Bunyan, D. P., Bailenson, J. N., Blascovich, J., & Beall, A. C. (2009). Leveraging collaborative virtual environment technology for inter-population research on persuasion in a classroom setting. *Presence: Teleoperators & Virtual Environments, 18*(5), 361–369.

Meehan, M., Insko, B., Whitton, M., & Brooks, F. P. Jr. (2002). Physiological measures of presence in stressful virtual environments. *SIGGRAPH '02: Proceedings of the 29th Annual Conference on Computer Graphics and Interactive Techniques* (pp. 645–653). New York, NY: Association for Computing Machinery. doi: 10.1145/566654.566630.

Nass, C., & Reeves, B. (1996). *The media equation: How people treat computers, television, and new media like real people and places.* New York, NY: Cambridge University Press.

Nowak, K. L., & Biocca, F. (2003). The effect of agency and anthropomorphism on users' sense of telepresence, copresence, and social presence in virtual environments. *Presence: Teleoperators and Virtual Environments, 12*, 481–494.

Picard, R. W. (2003). Affective computing: Challenges. *International Journal of Human-Computer Studies*, 55–64.

Sas, C., & O'Hare, G. M. P. (2003). Presence equation: An investigation into cognitive factors underlying presence. *Presence: Teleoperators and Virtual Environment, 12*(5), 523–537.

Segovia, K. Y. & Bailenson, J. N. (2009). Virtually true: Children's acquisition of false memories in virtual reality. *Media Psychology, 12*, 371–393.

Slater, M. (2004). How colorful was your day? Why questionnaires cannot assess presence in virtual environments. *Presence: Teleoperators & Virtual Environments, 13*(4), 484–493.

Slater, M., & Wilbur, S. (1997). A framework for immersive virtual environments (FIVE): Speculations on the role of presence in virtual environments. *Presence: Teleoperators and Virtual Environments, 6*, 603–616.

Slater, M., Sadagic, A., Usoh, M., & Schroeder, R. (2000). Small-group behavior in a virtual and real environment: A comparative study. *Presence: Teleoperators & Virtual Environments, 9*(1), 37–51.

Steuer, J. (1992). Defining virtual reality: Dimensions determining telepresence. *Journal of Communication, 42*(4), 73–93.

Sutherland, I. E. (1968). A head-mounted three dimensional display. *AFIPS '68: Proceedings of the Fall Joint Computer Conference, Part I* (pp. 757–764). New York, NY: Association for Computing Machinery. doi: 10.1145/1476589.1476686.

Wirth, W., Hartman, T., Bocking, S., Vorderer, P., Klimmt, C., Schramm, H.,…Jancke, P. (2007). A process model of the formation of spatial presence experiences. *Media Psychology, 9*(3), 493–525.

Wirth, W., & Schramm, H. (2005). Media emotions. *Communication Research Trends, 24*(3).

Yee, N., & Bailenson, J. N. (2006). Walk a mile in digital shoes: The impact of embodied perspective-taking on the reduction of negative stereotyping in immersive virtual environments. *Proceedings of PRESENCE 2006: The 9th Annual International Workshop on Presence.* Available at: http://vhil.stanford.edu/pubs/2006/yee-digital-shoes.pdf

Yee, N., & Bailenson, J. N. (2007). The Proteus effect: The effect of transformed self-representation on behavior. *Human Communication Research, 33*, 271–290.

Unobtrusive Deception Detection

Aaron Elkins, Stefanos Zafeiriou, Maja Pantic, *and* Judee Burgoon

Abstract

In response to national security needs and the limitations of human deception detection—along with advances in sensor and computing technology—research into automated deception detection has increased in recent years. In order to interpret when behavioral and physiological cues reveal deception, these technologies rely on psychological and communication theories of deception. Despite the need, the technology for detecting deception that is available to law enforcement or border guards is very limited. Deception theories suggest that liars are likely to exhibit both strategic and nonstrategic behavior. In order to develop algorithms and technology to detect and classify deception, such behaviors and physiological cues must be measured remotely. These measurements can be categorized by their theoretical causes when a person is lying; they include arousal, negative affect, cognitive effort, behavioral control, memory processes, and strategic activity. One major challenge to deception detection is accounting for the variability introduced by human interviewers. Future research should focus more on behavior over the entire interaction, thus fusing multiple behavioral indicators.

Key Words: deception, nonverbal behavior, physiological cues, automated deception detection, strategic and nonstrategic behavior, theoretical

Introduction

We could conjure a myriad of personal reasons why someone might try to deceive us. It is in the context of national security and law enforcement that failing to identify deception can have the most devastating consequences. Most officers or border guards at a congested border entry point in the United States or European Union have less than 20 seconds to make an initial credibility assessment of passengers. This rapid credibility assessment is further confounded by their divided attention to their physical environment, monitoring of behavior, and operation of technology. Despite high confidence in their ability to detect deception, the accuracy of even these experts tends to be near chance levels (Bond & DePaulo, 2006). In response to these challenges and in view of advances in sensor and

computing technology, research into automated deception detection has increased in recent years.

Deception is defined as the intentional transmission of a message intended to foster false beliefs or perceptions in the recipient (Knapp & Comadena, 1979). This definition implies that deception is a communicative act between at least two parties (i.e., sender and receiver) and that the deceptive message can take many forms, such as equivocation (omission or ambiguous messages), white lies, hedging, exaggerations, or bluffing. This implication is critical in investigating and researching affective computing applications for unobtrusively detecting deception.

Liars do not exhibit universal behavior or physiological signals in all situations. Deception is often inappropriately reduced to either simply telling the truth or lying. There are many strategies for lying, situations where lying occurs, varying consequences and power dynamics among subjects and interviewers, and different interviewing styles employed to detect liars. All of these factors contribute to the types of behaviors and physiological responses exhibited and measurable for automated classification by computers.

The goal of this chapter is to provide an introduction to deception, its detection, the methods for computationally modeling its behavioral indicators, and the potential applications of deception detection technologies. The next section of this chapter introduces the existing theories that explain and predict the behaviors exhibited during interviews with deceptive and truthful people. The reader should come away from this section appreciating that deception is a complex act and that the behavioral indicators are contingent on many situational and person-dependent factors that must be accounted for in attempting to classify deception.

Despite the prevalence of deception in daily life and social interactions (e.g., white lies), people are poor judges of deception. The third section highlights the importance and need for deception detection technologies to aid human decision makers and augment traditional tools such as the polygraph. The polygraph remains one of the only technological tools available to professional deception detectors. However, it has limited applicability (e.g., it requires a lengthy examination period and trained examiners) and calls for the physical attachment of sensors.

The fourth section of this chapter reviews the mechanisms that cause differences in behavior between liars and truth tellers. From these mechanisms, section five reviews the corresponding behaviors, when taken in light of deception theory, that are suitable for measurement and inclusion into a computational model of deceptive behavior. In addition to describing the behaviors, this section also introduces some of the recent research into their automated analysis and use for deception detection. The chapter concludes with a discussion of other potential applications for deception detection technology and future research directions.

Theories of Deception

Using computers to detect deception has great potential to improve and automate the detection of liars. There is no universal set of indicators for deception. Each deception interaction introduces its own situational contingencies, which can dramatically modify the interpretation of observed behaviors. Psychological and communication theories of deception inform the interpretation of behavioral and physiological cues. These theories, summarized next, must be incorporated into the computational modeling of deceptive or truthful behavior for reliable classification.

Leakage Hypothesis

In a seminal work, Ekman and Friesen (1969) hypothesized that liars would experience involuntary physiological reactions driven by increased arousal, negative affect, and discomfort, which would "leak out" in their nonverbal behavior cues, particularly in the hands, legs, and feet. For example, nervous people may unintentionally tap their feet or touch their faces to relieve internal tension—behaviors called adaptors, which are meant to address physical or psychological discomfort.

Just as important as the observed leakage cues are the omitted ones. Liars are predicted to neglect natural gesturing and facial expressions that should accompany messages, rendering their message conveyance to appear unnatural. The nonverbal behaviors most susceptible to leakage are the behaviors over which liars have the least control. In western culture, people have the greatest awareness and control of their facial expressions. This makes less controllable gestures in the hands and legs as particularly diagnostic for leaked cues of deception.

Four-Factor Theory

The four-factor theory extended the leakage hypothesis to further explain the causes for the observed behaviors (Zuckerman, DePaulo, & Rosenthal, 1981). It postulates four potential causes of leakage cues: (1) arousal, (2) negative affect. (3) cognitive effort, and (4) behavioral control. For example, if the stakes or consequences are high should a liar be caught, he or she may experience fear (emotion), which increases arousal and in turn affects behavior, such as causing an increase in vocal pitch and intensity (Juslin & Scherer, 2005; Nunamaker, Derrick, Elkins, Burgoon, & Patton, 2011).

As hypothesized by Ekman and Friesen (1969), the four-factor theory explains dissimulated nonverbal cues omitted during deceptive verbal messages as a result of excessive awareness and control of behavior that would normally occur naturally and automatically. Finally, the theory introduces an increased focus on the cognitive and memory influences on behavior. For unrehearsed deception, it should be more difficult to lie and maintain plausibility than when one is simply telling the truth.

Information Manipulation Theory

Information manipulation theory reflects the strategic element of deception in how the interaction dictates the message crafted by liars (McCornack, 1992). Specifically, liars capitalize on the tacit assumption that communication partners speak truthfully, relevantly, completely, and in an easily understood manner. For example, a liar may reduce the quantity of relevant information in his or her message so as to obfuscate the deceptive content. A liar might omit relevant details of a story and focus disproportionately on tangential conversation topics to avoid direction deception. Within this theory, liars can be considered uncooperative speaking partners who use verbal strategies that violate conversational assumptions.

Self-Presentational Perspective

Long a staple in the nonverbal communication literature (Burgoon & Saine, 1978), self-presentation is the regulation of behavior for the purpose of creating an impression on others (Jones & Pittman, 1982). All people are concerned with how they present themselves regardless of truth (e.g., competent, intelligent, kind), but deception can be considered a type of self-presentation where liars regulate their behaviors to present themselves falsely to others. DePaulo (1992) and Miller and Stiff (1993) applied this perspective to deceptive communication, contending that liars first form an intention to lie and then regulate their nonverbal behavior—making their subsequent behaviors conscious and deliberate. Next, liars must translate their intentions to actual nonverbal behaviors meant to present themselves as truthful or honest. Liars may lack the ability, motivation, emotion, confidence, or ability to recreate spontaneous expressiveness or manage their behavior consciously. From this perspective, liars are predicted to embrace their self-presentations unconvincingly and to exhibit unnatural deliberateness in their actions (DePaulo et al., 2003). Based on these predictions, liars should appear more tense and less pleasant or compelling than someone speaking sincerely. Nonverbal indicators of these states include forced smiles, increased vocal pitch, rigid motions, and lack of engagement or holding-back movements.

DePaulo and Kirkendol (1989) introduced the moderating influence of motivation on deceptive nonverbal behavior. They predicted that an increase in motivation will cause a redoubling of self-regulation—already inherent in self-presentation—that inhibits nonverbal behavior and increases leakage cues (DePaulo et al., 2003). Burgoon and Floyd (2000) found that motivation can actually improve both verbal and nonverbal behavior irrespective of deception. Motivation is an important moderator of deceptive behavior, but there are individual and situational differences in how it affects verbal and nonverbal behavior.

Interpersonal Deception Theory

To account for the complex interplay between liars and the deceived, Buller and Burgoon (1996) introduced interpersonal deception theory (IDT). Rather than focusing only on the liar during deceptive communication, it expanded and conceptualized deception as a strategic interaction between a sender and receiver. Liars must simultaneously manage information, their behavior, and appearance during the interaction. Moreover, liars will use different strategies depending on their skill, relationship with the interaction partner, preparation, motivation, and time.

Liars are predicted to act both strategically (purposefully) and nonstrategically (involuntarily) in response to the interaction. An important element of IDT is the dynamics of behavior over the course of the interaction (time). A deceiver's behavior early in the interaction likely will differ later in response—both strategically and nonstrategically—to the feedback from the speaking partner. For example, deceivers might attempt to reduce the quality and quantity of message details to obfuscate what they are saying. If liars sense that they have aroused suspicion in the speaking partner, they might shift strategies to increase their believability. Because deceivers are vigilant, cognitively taxed, and focused on their own behavior, nonstrategic behaviors (e.g., leakage cues) are predicted to be exhibited, but IDT predicts that deceivers will make efforts to repair these performance impairments so that, over time, their verbal and nonverbal behavior comes to resemble that of truth tellers.

Deception Detection by Humans

People, whether unaided or trained, detect deception at near chance levels. A meta-analysis of over 206 deception studies that required participants to judge the honesty of liars or truth tellers

(Bond & DePaulo, 2006) showed that on average, judges of liars during deception experiments performed slightly above chance, with 54% accuracy in detection overall; they classified 47% of lies as deceptive and 61% of truths as truthful. Unless they are vigilant or suspicious, people maintain a truth bias and accept the truth of what they hear (i.e., deceivers go undetected). The converse is also true; a lie bias is often observed in law enforcement, where deception is assumed (i.e., truthful individuals are falsely accused). Regardless of lie or truth bias, the overall accuracy of detection still remains at near chance. It is argued that one reason for this inaccuracy is that people tend to rely on stereotypical and incorrect indicators of deception, such as lack of eye contact or fidgeting (Hartwig & Bond, 2011; The Global Deception Research Team, 2006; Vrij, Davies, & Bull, 2008). Hartwig and Bond (2011) conducted a meta-analysis which found that judges of deception, despite their overall inaccuracy, perceived deception indicators accurately. Hartwig and Bond argue that judges of deception have an implicit sensitivity to reliable deception cues. Only when asked to explicitly describe their decision criteria do people fall back on stereotypical cues.

Another reason offered for inaccuracy is that deceptive behavioral cues may not occur often or strongly enough to be noticed during interactions (DePaulo et al., 2003; Hartwig & Bond, 2011). This is further complicated in view of IDT's prediction that behaviors indicating deception change over the course of the interaction and in response to the situational demands. Thus deception indicators are ephemeral and replaced by behaviors that evoke credibility.

Regardless of the reason, people may profit from technological aids in identifying the correct behavioral cues and thus detecting deception. Notwithstanding this ever-present need, current technologies for detecting deception that are available to law enforcement or border guards are very limited. The polygraph examination, which was primarily developed between 1895 and 1945 (Inbau, 1948; Reid, 1947; Skolnick, 1960), remains the most widespread deception detection technology.

Because (1) the polygraph requires attaching multiple physiological instruments (blood pressure cuff, respiratory rate pneumograph, and galvanic skin resistance galvanometer) to the interviewee. (2) the protocol for administering the polygraph examination requires a lengthy (3- to 5-hour) multiphase interview to obtain reliability, and (3) these interviews are often preceded by background investigations giving polygraph examiners additional information to use in interpreting and guiding an interview, the polygraph is unsuitable for rapid screening environments such as an airport or border. The latter call for unobtrusive and automated deception detection technology. Consequently other tools must be developed, preferably ones that are theoretically driven and can detect the same classes of indicators that reliably discriminate truthful from deceptive communication. The next section reviews the causal mechanisms that are believed to produce reliable indicators of truth or deception.

Causal Mechanisms

The various theories of deception indicators and deception point to an array of strategic and non-strategic behaviors that are both valid and reliable discriminators of truth from deception. In order to develop algorithms and technology to detect and classify deception, these behaviors and physiological cues must be measured remotely. Next, the theorized causes of observable deceptive behavior are reviewed in turn.

Arousal

The most commonly associated class of indicators of deceit involves arousal. Engaging in deceit is theorized to be distressing, causing liars to experience increased arousal such that the sympathetic nervous system excites the body in response to an imminent fight-or-flight event or potential threat monitoring evoked by the security motivation system (Woody & Szechtman, 2011). It is these cardiorespiratory and galvanic skin responses that are captured by the polygraph and are the impetus for most of the commercial products that have been billed as lie detection systems.

Previous research has revealed that liars often exhibit one of two types of response patterns: either a generalized activation response or greater tension. Negatively valenced arousal can be revealed through greater pupillary dilation or instability; postural shifting; fidgeting; random trunk and limb movements; hand adaptor gestures such as touching the face, neck, or head with the hand; or lip adaptors such as biting, licking, or puckering the lips. Tension, on the other hand, can manifest itself through frozen and rigid postures, lack of gestures, or a tightening of the muscles of the vocal folds, which causes them to vibrate faster and produce a higher pitch (fundamental frequency) when a person is speaking (Titze & Martin, 1998).

Although arousal is the most commonly acknowledged overt manifestation of deceit, the relationship between deception and arousal is not deterministic. First, deceit does not inevitably trigger arousal. White lies, lies told for the benefit of the target, lies that are sanctioned by a given culture or community or by an experimenter or authority, as well as omissions, exaggerations, and evasions, and the like may not cause the perpetrator of deceit to experience physiological changes. Second, internal experiences do not necessarily translate into external, observable cues. People are capable of masking, minimizing, and replacing distress and arousal signals with outward displays that are socially appropriate and do not reveal their true internal state (Ekman, 1992; Fridlund, 1991). Third, a variety of factors other than deceit can cause arousal. Truth tellers, for example, may show signs of arousal if accused of wrongdoing or if questioned by authority. People may blush because they are embarrassed, even though they are not being deceptive. If both liars and truth tellers exhibit signs of arousal, such signs cannot be used to identify truth. Fourth, different people may exhibit arousal in different ways. For example, one person may swivel in a chair, whereas another may "freeze" into a fixed posture with virtually no movement. Put differently, arousal can take many different forms (Burgoon, Kelley, Newton, & Keeley-Dyreson, 1989). Finally, the indicators of arousal may be feeble and transitory (DePaulo et al., 2003; Hartwig & Bond, 2011), thus eluding detection because humans or instruments lack the sensitivity to capture them or because detection efforts are ill timed (Hamel, Burgoon, Humpherys, & Moffitt, 2007). For all these reasons, there is a lack of one-to-one correspondence between truth and arousal indicators, which undermines the diagnostic value of such indicators.

Affect

Ekman and Friesen (1969) initially posited that deceivers might show positive or negative emotions: negative emotions if they feared being detected or felt guilt about lying, positive emotions if they experienced "duping delight," or enjoyment at having fooled others. However, writings about deception have most often claimed that deceivers will experience and express negative affect, such as guilt or fear.

Nonverbally, in addition to expectations that such emotions will be displayed through the face in either full-fledged emotional displays or in fleeting microexpressions (Ekman, 2003), some research has suggested that positive emotion is evident through felt smiles as opposed to feigned ones (Ekman et al., 1990). The voice is also said to convey positive or negative affect both in the form of specific emotional states and in general degrees of pleasantness or unpleasantness. Fearful people often speak louder and at a faster tempo (Juslin & Laukka, 2003; Juslin & Scherer, 2005).

In addition to nonverbal displays, affective states may be revealed through verbal content and linguistic style. For example, the words *love* and *nice* connote more positive emotion than *hurt* or *ugly* when used in speech or text (Francis & Pennebaker, 1993; Newman, Pennebaker, Berry, & Richards, 2003; Tausczik & Pennebaker, 2010). Although deceivers have been said to use more affectively negative language than truth tellers, some results have shown them to use more affective language—both positive and negative—than truth tellers but only under certain circumstances (Burgoon & Qin, 2006; Burgoon, Hamel, & Qin, 2012).

Cognitive Effort

Because of self-regulation and increased strategic interaction requirements, deception is predicted to be more cognitively demanding then telling the truth (Buller & Burgoon, 1996; DePaulo et al., 2003). This prediction was borne out by a substantial meta-analysis by Sporer and Schwandt (2006), who found that when a liar lacks preparation or rehearsal, the enhanced burden on his or her working memory increases cues due to cognitive effort. When they are cognitively taxed, people often speak more haltingly (e.g., "um," "uh," speech errors), take longer to respond to questions, cease gesturing, and avert their gaze. Eyeblinks occur spontaneously every few seconds, but only a fraction of these blinks are required for ocular lubrication. Eyeblinks signal disengagement from the external stimulus (e.g., no longer watching speaking partner) so that mental resources can be reallocated to facilitate cognitive behavior (Irwin & Thomas, 2010; Nakano, Kato, Morito, Itoi, & Kitazawa, 2012) A longer pause before the onset of an eyeblink indicates attention to external stimuli and minimization of the loss of visual information (Fukuda, 2001; Shultz, Klin, & Jones, 2011).

Behavioral Control

Deception is often associated with a lack of movement. Deceivers, in an effort to control telltale signs of their deceit, may overcompensate by unnaturally overcontrolling their behaviors. Their excessive control can result in wooden postures, inexpressive faces and gestures, and elevated vocal pitch. However, if such control is not extreme, it can instead look like a composed, poised demeanor (Burgoon & Floyd, 2000; Twyman, Elkins, & Burgoon, 2011). Thus efforts to measure tension and postural rigidity may require identifying a threshold beyond which the level of inactivity becomes unnatural.

Memory

The role of memory in deceptive communication concerns the ability to access real versus imagined memories and the taxation that deceit imposes upon working memory. In their revision of the original four-factor theory and Vrij's (1999) perspective on cognitive effort, Sporer and Schwandt (2007) recast cognitive effort behavioral changes as being caused by accessing working memory. In the case of complex lies, working memory is taxed by the effort to come up with plausible stories and alibis. Liars must not only simultaneously plan what they are saying and avoid contradicting themselves or on facts known to the listener but must also observe the listener's reactions, monitor their own behavior, and control their behavior. These multiple demands force them to think hard and to do such things as look away or delay responding as they construct answers—behaviors that may give them away (Mann, Vrij, & Bull, 2002).

Computational Modeling and Classifying Deception

Based on deception theory and the predicted causes of verbal, nonverbal, and physiological behavioral differences between liars and truth tellers, computational models can be developed to classify deception. This section details current sensor-based methods for automatically detecting deception.

The Polygraph

One of the first methods for the automatic extraction of deception-related cues was the polygraph. Because of the subject's elevated arousal when being deceptive, it can monitor uncontrolled changes in heart rate, blood pressure, respiration, and electrodermal response. Contact sensors are placed on the subject during an examination. The resulting signals are then heuristically analyzed by experts (Ben-Shakhar & Bar-Hillel, 1986; Elaad, 1998; Honts, Raskin, & Kircher, 1987; Kleinmuntz &

Szucko, 1984; Saxe, Dougherty, & Cross, 1985; Stern, 2002; Yankee, 1965).

The polygraph process comes with various disadvantages. The subject's comfort is affected by the attached sensors, and this can influence physiological measurements (Yankee, 1965). The person examined must be cooperative and in close proximity to the device. The analysis of the polygraph is performed manually, based the subjective perceptions of the examiner and the scoring of the exam. Despite the existence of automated scoring systems built into modern polygraph systems, most examiners base their decisions on their own scoring of the exam.

Having conducted a set of laboratory tests, Vrij et al. (2008) suggested that the polygraph is about 82% accurate at identifying deceivers. The National Academy of Sciences (National Research Council, 2002), concluded that such experimental numbers are often overestimates of actual results. It is argued that laboratory examinations are conducted with complete control over threats to internal validity, unrepresentative subjects, unrealistic and uniform ground truth; moreover, it is said that experimental polygraph exams occur immediately after the investigated issue, which is uncommon in the real world.

Vocalics

Vocalics comprise a family of techniques that analyze the voice during deceptive speech to measure changes in arousal and cognition (Cestaro, 1995; Cestaro & Dollins, 1994; Janniro & Cestaro, 1996). Vocal stress analysis (VSA) is a commercial application of vocalics marketed to law enforcement for deception detection (Cestaro, 1995). Many independent tests on various VSA applications have failed to yield detection rates that are better than chance (Harnsberger & Hollien, 2009). Recently new attempts were made to reinitiate research and investigate the validity of vocal analysis for deception detection (Elkins, Burgoon, & Nunamaker, 2012a). Previous research on commercial vocal analysis software has focused on validating their built-in classifications of truth or falsehood. An analysis of the commercial software's calculated vocal measurements (rather than the falsehood or truth classification) revealed sensitivity to both deception and arousal during deception experiments (Elkins, 2010; Elkins & Burgoon, 2010). While commercial vocal analysis software is beginning to yield promising results for deception detection in the field, its contribution to research is limited because of the software's proprietary nature and ambiguously calculated vocal measurements. For example, the LVA 6.50 (Nemesysco, 2009) contains variables simply named SOS and AVJ, which are documented to measure fear and thinking level respectively. These variables have demonstrated sensitivity to experimentally induced deception; but although the results may support the validity of the software, they contribute little to our understanding of deceptive vocal behavior.

Research with standard acoustic measures—using freely available software tools such as Praat (Boersma, 2002) or openSMILE (Eyben, Wöllmer, & Schuller, 2010)—has found that liars speak with greater and more varied vocal pitch (Apple, Streeter, & Krauss, 1979; DePaulo et al., 2003; Zuckerman et al., 1981), shorter durations (Rockwell, Buller, & Burgoon, 1997; Vrij et al., 2008), and less fluency; it was also found that they reply with greater response latencies (DePaulo, Stone, & Lassiter, 1985; deTurck & Miller, 2006; Rockwell et al., 1997; Sporer & Schwandt, 2006).

Linguistics

Considerable research has been conducted to develop automatic linguistic analysis of text for extracting deceptive cues (Burgoon, Blair, Tiantian, & Nunamaker, 2003; Fuller & Biros, 2013; Hancock, Curry, Goorha, & Woodworth, 2004; Newman, Pennebaker, Berry, & Richards, 2003; Toma & Hancock, 2012; Zhou et al., 2003). There are many different lines of research. The main two revolve around (1) synchronous communication (Burgoon et al., 2003; Hancock et al., 2004; Newman et al., 2003; Toma & Hancock, 2012), where the lie has to be told on the spot (for example, during interviews or online chat) and (2) asynchronous scenarios (Fuller & Biros, 2013; Zhou et al., 2003), where the lie can be carefully prepared beforehand (for example, a deceitful court statement).

In a constant topic setting (Newman et al., 2003), as compared with truth tellers, liars' responses demonstrated lower cognitive complexity (more concrete verbs and less evaluative and judging language), used fewer self-references, and used more negative emotion words. In dyadic communication (Hancock et al., 2004), liars used more words overall, increased references to others, and more sense-based descriptions (e.g., seeing, touching). Burgoon et al. investigated linguistic deception during a mock theft scenario (2003), where an interview was conducted using face to face communication, text chat, or audio conferencing. Deceivers' messages were briefer (i.e., lower on quantity of language), less complex in their choice of vocabulary and sentence structure, and lacked specificity or expressiveness in their text-based chats.

In asynchronous scenarios (Zhou et al., 2003), detailed lies can be produced with many complexities. This is more evident in high-stakes asynchronous deception. Zhou and Zhang surveyed cues for each of these scenarios (2008).

Using automated text analysis and validated emotion dictionaries, previous research has revealed 21 linguistic cues and their corresponding categories that discriminate between deceptive verbal messages (Newman et al., 2003; Zhou et al., 2003; Zhou, Burgoon, Nunamaker, & Twitchell, 2004). Linguistic cues can be extracted from deceptive verbal messages using automated linguistic analysis software such as structured programming for linguistic cue extraction (SPLICE) (Moffitt, 2010), which incorporates the "Dictionary of Affect in Language" (DAL) (Whissell, 1989), and the "Linguistic Inquiry and Word Count" (LIWC) (Francis & Pennebaker, 1993).

Oculesics

Eye behavior and blinks can be very useful cues in deceit detection (Bhaskaran, 2011; Fukuda, 2001; Minkov, Zafeiriou, & Pantic, 2012; Nwogua, Frank, & Govindaraju, 2010). Bhaskaran (2011) proposed an online person-specific learning approach for learning the typical eye behavior in baseline questions (no deception); this model was later tested on the critical questions (deception) in order to spot differences (i.e., deceitful behavior). Eyeblink dynamics, such as blink duration and rate (frequency), were used as cues for spotting deceit in the controversial TV show *Moment of Truth* (Minkov et al., 2012). Pupillary characteristics, such as pupil dilations, are cues of arousal or stress. Deception impacts pupillary response and leads to pupil dilation (Dionisio, Granholm, Hillix, & Perrine, 2001; Lubow & Fein, 1996).

When presented with a visual stimulus, deceivers possessing guilty knowledge fixate on lie-relevant images and increase their pupillary dilation. Elkins, Derrick, and Gariup (2012c) conducted an experiment where some participants lied about their identity (imposters) and presented a legitimate visa document during a simulated border screening. During the screening interview, participants were shown their own documents. Liars fixated on the incorrect fields (e.g., date of birth) of their documents two times longer than truth tellers. Research investigating cognitively induced eye-gaze activity (e.g., looking left when lying) has been limited and based only on unsupported predictions from neurolinguistic programming (Wiseman et al., 2012).

Body Posture, Gesture, and Kinesics

Multiple methods have been proposed for deriving indicators of deception from body posture (Burgoon et al., 2009; Lu, Tsechpenakis, Metaxas, Jensen, & Kruse, 2005; Meservy et al., 2005; Meservy, Jensen, Kruse, Burgoon, & Nunamaker, 2008). These methods focus on deriving cues by tracking the location of the head and hands (Burgoon et al., 2009; Lu et al., 2005; Meservy et al., 2005, 2008). Gesture analysis, posture, and kinesics-based features were extracted from the video using a method called "blob analysis" (i.e., head and hands were represented as blobs). The blobs of the head and hands were tracked and segmented from the video. Features include average and variance of the head position and angle, the average and variance of the positions of the head and hands, and the average distance between the hands. Burgoon et al. (2009) developed behavioral profiles that automatically detected agitation (e.g., frequent face touching and hand-to-hand touching), excessive control (e.g., infrequent gesturing and rigid movement), and relaxed behavior (neither overcontrolled nor agitated) from video. These observed behavioral states taken in the context of an interaction can be caused by deception.

Facial Behavior

Current work in facial expression–based deception detection seeks to identify either insincere emotional expressions (e.g., fake smiles) or leaked true expressions of emotion (Hurley & Frank, 2011; Porter, Brinke, Baker, & Wallace, 2011); taken in context, these contradict a truthful person's expected emotion. In addition to emotion, facial expressions can also provide indicators of deception-induced behavioral control (Michael, Dilsizian, Metaxas, & Burgoon, 2010).

Current work in automated facial expression recognition involves first identifying the face from each frame of a video (Viola & Jones, 2004) and then applying facial point tracking methods such as active shape modeling (ASM) (Cootes, Taylor, Cooper, & Graham, 1995) or active appearance modeling (AAM) (Cootes, Edwards, & Taylor, 2001; Tzimiropoulos, Alabort-i-medina, Zafeiriou, & Pantic, 2012). Once facial points are tracked, methods can be applied to detect expressions from the temporal dynamics and activation of facial muscle action units (Pantic & Patras, 2006; Valstar & Pantic, 2006).

Cardiorespiratory Indicators

Pulse rate, blood pressure and respiration rate can be reliable indicators of emotional stress. Emotional stress can vary between truth tellers and liars (Cutrow, Parks, Lucas, & Thomas, 1972; Kurohara, Terai, Takeuchi, & Umezawa, 2001). Differences in cardiovascular measures such as increased pulse rate have been identified during deceptive communication (Cutrow et al., 1972). Furthermore, studies have shown that individuals tend to inhibit breathing when faced with the kind of stress commonly found during deceptive situations (Kurohara et al., 2001). In contrast to a plethysmograph (heart rate sensor used in the polygraph) cardiorespiratory measurements can be collected in a noncontact manner using a laser doppler vibrometer (LDV) and computer vision. The LDV uses a laser to measure carotid artery pulsations on the neck, which are then processed to calculate cardiorespiratory measurements such as heart rate and blood pressure.

Fusion

Derrick et al. conducted a study on deception detection using a mock crime experimental paradigm that included the fusion of multiple behavioral sensors (Derrick, Elkins, Burgoon, Nunamaker, & Zeng, 2010). They found that deceivers increased their heart rate (measured using LDV) in anticipation to a lie-relevant stimulus and then decreased their heart rate after experiencing the stimulus. Building a deception classifier using LDV alone resulted in a 77% true-positive rate but a 42% false-positive rate. Human judges of deception during the same experiment had an accuracy of 71.2% overall. When the LDV and human judgments were fused into a single classification, the true-positive rate increased to 90%, with only a 2.8% increase in false positives.

Fusion pools multiple sensors to increase the reliability and validity of deception judgments by measuring multiple causal mechanisms and behavioral modalities. This improves detection accuracy because there is high variance between people on the behaviors they express when lying. In some people, the voice is strongly affected (e.g., increased vocal pitch); others my increase their postural rigidity. While the ability to control some of their behaviors varies from one person to another, no one can control them all; fusion decreases the likelihood of missing important behavioral cues and improves reliability and convergent validity.

Current Applications of Deception Detection
Border Control and Automated Screening

One major challenge to deception detection is accounting for the variability introduced by human interviewers. Every interviewer has his or her own style (e.g., aggressive, friendly, neutral), asks questions inconsistently, and gets tired. The behavior and approach of the interviewer strongly influence the behavior and reactions of the interviewee. For example, if the interviewer is angry, the interviewee will be affected by this and display reciprocal anger or even distress. Perhaps, after a lunch break, the interviewer will be fresh and in better spirits and return to a more friendly interaction. Any deception detection system that relies on consistent behavioral cues will have to account for the variability and diverse range of behavior in the human interviewer.

To address this challenge, Nunamaker et al. (Elkins, Derrick, & Gariup, 2012c; Elkins & Derrick, 2013; Elkins, Sun, Zafeiriou, & Pantic, 2013; Nunamaker Jr. et al., 2011) developed an Embodied Conversational Agent (ECA) based deception detection system called AVATAR. AVATAR was developed to optimize internal validity by controlling question delivery, dynamically branching based on interrogation protocols such as Behavioral Analysis Interview (Horvath, Blair, & Buckley, 2008), to improve the reliability of behavioral cue interpretation. The ECA system uses multiple integrated behavioral sensors (e.g., microphone, camera, eye tracker) to monitor verbal and nonverbal behavior during the interview. The sensor streams are fused and submitted to a robust classification engine that does not rely on any single indicator or modality of deceptive behavior (Elkins, Derrick, Burgoon, & Nunamaker Jr, 2012b).

Because the AVATAR consistently administers interviews (unlike human judges), it does not contribute additional behavioral variance into the deception classification. The ECA within the AVATAR can also take on any demeanor (e.g., friendly, stern) or embodiment (e.g., male, female) that will elicit the most diagnostic behavior. The AVATAR conducts an interview protocol designed to exaggerate the differences in predicted behavior between liars and truth tellers. For example, Elkins, Derrick, and Gariup (2012c) conducted an experiment where participants were interviewed in a mock screening scenario by the AVATAR. Some of the participants were assigned to the imposter group and lied to the AVATAR about their identities. Using eye behavior and voice, the AVATAR was able to identify pseudo-imposters with over 94% accuracy. In contrast with traditional deception research, studies conducted with AVATAR are very specific and unique to the scenario deployed. There are no expectations that the eye behavior or voice exhibited by liars should generalize outside of the imposter context in which it has been tested.

Other Applications

While the initial applications for automated verbal and nonverbal behavior analysis are for deception detection, the underlying detection of emotion, cognition, arousal, and causal factors is relevant to many HCI scenarios. For example, Elkins and Derrick (2013) propose the voice for the measurement of trust by new employees and team members to facilitate management and collaboration. Any scenario where one could benefit from real-time feedback of a speaking partner can could be a potential application—hospital patient triage and treatment, clinical therapy, insurance fraud detection, law enforcement interviewing, assisted communication for the disabled, and richer interactions and interfacing with computers.

Future Research

Future research should focus more on behavior over the entire interaction. While some of the deception predictions using behavioral measurements perform better than chance, there is still much variability overall that remains unaccounted for. Interpersonal deception theory (IDT) predicts that deceptive behavior is dynamic and varies as a function of sender, receiver, time, deception, suspicion, motivation, and social skills. However, most deception experiments and even the polygraph exam focus on behavior difference scores over a set of questions. It is clear that this design ignores all of the important contextual and temporal information, such as the interaction between the behavior of speaking partners (e.g., synchrony, mimicry). Additionally, most deception research to date has focused on individual indicators or modalities of deception. Just as when we appraise the behavior of a speaking partner—relying on the voice, facial expressions, body posture, or language—we will need to provide computers with at least as much information as we process in evaluating or classifying deception. To accomplish this, future research, in modeling emotion and deception, must fuse and analyze multiple behavioral and physiological sensors.

References

Apple, W., Streeter, L. A., & Krauss, R. M. (1979). Effects of pitch and speech rate on personal attributions. *Journal of Personality and Social Psychology, 37*(5), 715–727. doi:10.1037/0022–3514.37.5.715

Ben-Shakhar, G., & Bar-Hillel, M. (1986). Trial by polygraph: Scientific and juridical issues in lie detection. *Behavioral Sciences & the Law, 4*(4), 459–479. Retrieved from http://onlinelibrary.wiley.com/doi/10.1002/bsl.2370040408/abstract

Bhaskaran, N. (2011). Lie to Me: Deceit detection via online behavioral learning. *Automatic Face & Gesture Recognition,* 24–29. Retrieved from http://ieeexplore.ieee.org/xpls/abs_all.jsp?arnumber=5771407

Boersma, P. (2002). Praat, a system for doing phonetics by computer. *Glot international, 5*(9/10), 341–345.

Bond, C. F., & DePaulo, B. M. (2006). Accuracy of deception judgments. *Personality and Social Psychology Review, 10*(3), 214.

Buller, D. B., & Burgoon, J. K. (1996). Interpersonal Deception Theory. *Communication Theory, 6*(3), 203–242. doi:10.1111/j.1468-2885.1996.tb00127.x

Burgoon, J., & Floyd, K. (2000). Testing for the motivation impairment effect during deceptive and truthful interaction. *Western Journal of Communication, 64*(3), 243–267. Available at: http://www.tandfonline.com/doi/abs/10.1080/10570310009374675

Burgoon, J. K., Hamel, L., & Qin, T. (2012). Predicting veracity from linguistic indicators. In *Proceedings of the 2012 European Intelligence and Security Informatics Conference* (pp. 323–328). IEEE.

Burgoon, J. K., Blair, J., Tiantian, Q., & Nunamaker, J. F. (2003). Detecting deception through linguistic analysis. In *Proceedings of the 1st NSF/NIJ conference on intelligence and security informatics.* (pp. 91–101). Springer-Verlag: Berlin. Available at: http://link.springer.com/chapter/10.1007/3-540-44853-5_7

Burgoon, J. K., Kelley, D. L., Newton, D. A., & Keeley-Dyreson, M. P. (1989). The nature of arousal and nonverbal indices. *Human Communication Research, 16*(2), 217–255.

Burgoon, J. K., & Qin, T. (2006). The dynamic nature of deceptive verbal communication. *Journal of Language and Social Psychology, 26,* 76–96.

Burgoon, J. K., & Saine, T. J. (1978). *The unspoken dialogue.* Boston: Houghton-Mifflin.

Burgoon, J. K., Twitchell, D. P., Jensen, M. L., Meservy, T. O., Adkins, M., Kruse, J.,…Younger, R. E. (2009). Detecting concealment of intent in transportation screening: A proof of concept. *Intelligent Transportation Systems, IEEE Transactions on Intelligent Transportation Systems, 10*(1), 103–112.

Cestaro, V. (1995). A comparison between decision accuracy rates obtained using the polygraph instrument and the computer voice stress analyzer (CVSA) in the absence of jeopardy. *Polygraph, 25*(2), 117–127. Available at: http://oai.dtic.mil/oai/oai?verb=getRecord&metadataPrefix=html&identifier=ADA300334

Cestaro, V., & Dollins, A. (1994). An analysis of voice responses for the detection of deception. *Polygraph, 25*(1), 15–342.

Available at: http://oai.dtic.mil/oai/oai?verb=getRecord&metadataPrefix=html&identifier=ADA298417

Cootes, T., Edwards, G., & Taylor, C. (2001). Active appearance models. *IEEE Transactions on Pattern Analysis and Machine Intelligence, 23*(6), 681–685. Available at: http://ieeexplore.ieee.org/xpls/abs_all.jsp?arnumber=927467

Cootes, T., Taylor, C., Cooper, D., & Graham, J. (1995). Active shape models-their training and application. *Computer Vision and Image Understanding, 61*(1), 38–59. Available at: http://www.sciencedirect.com/science/article/pii/S1077314285710041

Cutrow, R., Parks, A., Lucas, N., & Thomas, K. (1972). The objective use of multiple physiological indices in the detection of deception. *Psychophysiology. 9*(6), 578–588. Available at: http://onlinelibrary.wiley.com/doi/10.1111/j.1469–8986.1972.tb00767.x/abstract

DePaulo, B. M. (1992). Nonverbal behavior and self-presentation. *Psychological Bulletin, 111*(2), 203–243. Available at: http://www.ncbi.nlm.nih.gov/pubmed/1557474

DePaulo, B. M., & Kirkendol, S. E. (1989). The motivational impairment effect in the communication of deception. In J.Yuille (Ed.), *Credibility Assessment* (p. 1996). Deurne, Belgium: Kluwer.

DePaulo, B. M., Lindsay, J. J., Malone, B. E., Muhlenbruck, L., Charlton, K., & Cooper, H. (2003). Cues to deception. *Psychological Bulletin, 129*(1), 74–118. doi:10.1037/0033-2909.129.1.74

DePaulo, B. M., Stone, J. I., & Lassiter, G. D. (1985). In B. R. Schenkler (Ed.), Deceiving and detecting deceit. *The self and social life* (pp. 323–370), New York: McGraw-Hill.

Derrick, D. C., Elkins, A. C., Burgoon, J. K., Nunamaker, J. F. Jr., & Zeng, D. D. (2010). Border security credibility assessments via heterogeneous sensor fusion. *IEEE Intelligent Systems, 25*(May/June), 41–49. Available at: http://www.computer.org/portal/web/csdl/doi/10.1109/MIS.2010.79

deTurck, M., & Miller, G. (2006). Deception and arousal. *Human Communication Research, 12,* 181–201.

Dionisio, D., Granholm, E., Hillix, W. A., & Perrine, W. F. (2001). Differentiation of deception using pupillary responses as an index of cognitive processing. *Psychophysiology, 38*(2), 205–211. Available at: http://onlinelibrary.wiley.com/doi/10.1111/1469–8986.3820205/full

Ekman, P. (1992). *Telling lies: Clues to deceit in the marketplace, politics, and marriage.* New York: Norton.

Ekman, P. (2003). Darwin, deception and facial expression. *Annals of the New York Academy of Sciences,* (1000), 205–221.

Ekman, P., Davidson, R. J., & Friesen, W. V. (1990). The Duchenne smile: Emotional expression and brain physiology II. *Journal of Personality and Social Psychology, 58*(2), 342–353.

Ekman, P., & Friesen, W. V. (1969). Nonverbal leakage and clues to deception. *Psychiatry, 32*(1), 88–106.

Elaad, E. (1998). The challenge of the concealed knowledge polygraph test. *Expert Evidence, 6,* 161–187. Available at: http://link.springer.com/article/10.1023/A:1008855511254

Elkins, A. C. (2010). Evaluating the credibility assessment capability of vocal analysis software. In Proceedings of the Credibility Assessment and Information Quality in Government and Business Symposium at Forty-third annual Hawaii international conference on system sciences (pp. 41–47). http://www.hicss.hawaii.edu/reports.htm

Elkins, A. C., & Burgoon, J. K. (2010). Validating vocal analysis software to assess credibility in interpersonal interaction: A multilevel factor analytic approach. In J.Priem (Chair), Session at *National Communication Association 96th Annual Convention,* San Francisco, California.

Elkins, A. C., Burgoon, J. K., & Nunamaker, J. F. (2012a). Vocal analysis software for security screening: Validity and deception detection potential. *Homeland Security Affairs, 8.*

Elkins, A. C., & Derrick, D. C. (2013). The sound of trust: Voice as a measurement of trust during interactions with embodied conversational agents. *Group Decision and Negotiation, 22*(5), 897–913.

Elkins, A. C., Derrick, D. C., Burgoon, J. K., & Nunamaker, J. F. Jr. (2012b). Predicting users' perceived trust in embodied conversational agents using vocal dynamics. In *Forty-fifth annual Hawaii international conference on system sciences,* (pp. 579–588), Computer Society Press.

Elkins, A. C., Derrick, D. C., & Gariup, M. (2012c). The voice and eye gaze behavior of an imposter: automated interviewing and detection for rapid screening at the border. In *Proceedings of the Workshop on Computational Approaches to Deception Detection at the 13th Conference of the European chapter of the association for computational linguistics* (pp. 49–54). Stroudsburg, PA: Association for Computational Linguistics.

Elkins, A. C., Sun, Y., Zafeiriou, S., & Pantic, M. (2013). The face of an imposter: Computer vision for deception detection. In Proceedings of the Rapid Screening Technologies, Deception Detection and Credibility Assessment Symposium at Forty-sixth annual Hawaii international conference on system sciences (pp. 106–110). http://www.hicss.hawaii.edu/reports.htm

Eyben, F., Wöllmer, M., & Schuller, B. (2010). Opensmile: The Munich versatile and fast open-source audio feature extractor (pp. 1459–1462). Available at: http://portal.acm.org/citation.cfm?id=1874246

Francis, M. E., & Pennebaker, J. W. (1993). *LIWC: Linguistic inquiry and word count.* Dallas: Southern Methodist University.

Fridlund, A. J. (1991). Evolution and facial action in reflex, social motive, and paralanguage. *Biological Psychology, 32*(1), 3–100.

Fukuda, K. (2001). Eye blinks: New indices for the detection of deception. *International Journal of Psychophysiology, 40*(3), 239–245. Available at: http://www.sciencedirect.com/science/article/B6T3M-42DP0HD-9/2/42558dccec4cd2e4c1c959566fc35c41

Fuller, C., & Biros, D. (2013). An examination and validation of linguistic constructs for studying high-stakes deception. *Group Decision and Negotiation, 22*(1), 1–18. Available at: http://link.springer.com/article/10.1007/s10726-012-9300-z

Hamel, L., Burgoon, J. K., Humpherys, S., & Moffitt, K. (2007). The "when" of deception detection. In M. L.Johnson (Chair), Session at *National Communication Association 93rd Annual Convention,* Chicago, IL.

Hancock, J. T., Curry, L. E., Goorha, S., & Woodworth, M. T. (2004). Lies in conversation: An examination of deception using automated linguistic analysis. An examination of deception using automated linguistic analysis. *Annual conference of the cognitive science society* (Vol. 26, pp. 534–540), Mahwah, New Jersey: Lawrence Erlbaum Associations, Inc.

Harnsberger, J., & Hollien, H. (2009). Stress and deception in speech: evaluating layered voice analysis. *Journal of Forensic Sciences, 54*(3), 642–50. doi:10.1111/j.1556-4029.2009.01026.x

Hartwig, M., & Bond, C. F. (2011). Why do lie-catchers fail? A lens model meta-analysis of human lie judgments. *Psychological bulletin, 137*(4), 643–59. doi:10.1037/a0023589

Honts, C. R., Raskin, D. C., & Kircher, J. C. (1987). Effects of physical countermeasures and their electromyographic detection during polygraph tests for deception. *Journal of Psychophysiology, 1,* 241–247.

Horvath, F., Blair, J., & Buckley, J. P. (2008). The behavioural analysis interview: Clarifying the practice, theory and understanding of its use and effectiveness. *International Journal of Police Science and Management, 10*(1), 101–118. doi:10.1350/ijpsm.2008.10.1.68

Hurley, C. M., & Frank, M. G. (2011). Executing facial control during deception situations. *Journal of Nonverbal Behavior, 35*(2), 1–13. doi:10.1007/s10919-010-0102-1

Inbau, F. E. (1948). *Lie detection and criminal interrogation.* Baltimore, MD: Williams & Wilkins.

Irwin, D. E., & Thomas, L. E. (2010). Eyeblinks and cognition. *Tutorials in visual cognition* (pp. 121–141), New York, NY: Psychology Press.

Janniro, M., & Cestaro, V. (1996). Effectiveness of detection of deception examinations using the computer voice stress analyzer (pp. 28–34). Available at: http://oai.dtic.mil/oai/oai?verb=getRecord&metadataPrefix=html&identifier=ADA318986

Jones, E., & Pittman, T. S. (1982). Toward a general theory of strategic self-presentation. In J.Suls (Ed.), *Psychological perspectives on the self* (pp. 231–262). Hillsdale, NJ: Erlbaum.

Juslin, P. N., & Laukka, P. (2003). Communication of emotions in vocal expression and music performance: Different channels, same code? *Psychological Bulletin, 129*(5), 770–814.

Juslin, P., & Scherer, K. R. (2005). Vocal expression of affect. *The new handbook of methods in nonverbal behavior research* (pp. 65–135). New York: Oxford University Press. Available at: http://scholar.google.com/scholar?hl=en&btnG=Search&q=intitle:Vocal+expression+of+affect#0

Kleinmuntz, B., & Szucko, J. (1984). Lie detection in ancient and modern times: A call for contemporary scientific study. *The American Psychologist, 39*(7), 766. Available at: http://cat.inist.fr/?aModele=afficheN&cpsidt=8921762

Knapp, M. L., & Comadena, M. E. (1979). Telling it like it isn't: A review of theory and research on deceptive communications. *Human Communication Research, 5*(3), 270–285.

Kurohara, A., Terai, K., Takeuchi, H., & Umezawa, A. (2001). Respiratory changes during detection of deception: Mechanisms underlying inhibitory breathing in response to critical questions. *Japanese Journal of Physiological Psychology and Psychophysiology, 19*(2), 75–85. Available at: http://sciencelinks.jp/j-east/article/200205/000020020501A1025296.php

Lu, S., Tsechpenakis, G., Metaxas, D., Jensen, M., & Kruse, J. (2005). Blob analysis of the head and hands: A method for deception detection. In *Thirty-eighth annual Hawaii international conference on system sciences.* Available at: http://ieeexplore.ieee.org/xpls/abs_all.jsp?arnumber=1385269

Lubow, R., & Fein, O. (1996). Pupillary size in response to a visual guilty knowledge test: New technique for the detection of deception. *Journal of Experimental Psychology: Applied, 2*(2), 164–177. Available at: http://psycnet.apa.org/?fa=main.doiLanding&doi=10.1037/1076-898X.2.2.164

Mann, S., Vrij, A., & Bull, R. (2002). Suspects, lies, and videotape: An analysis of authentic high-stake liars. *Law and Human Behavior, 26*(3), 365–376.

McCornack, S. (1992). Information manipulation theory. *Communications Monographs*, *59*(March). Available at: http://www.tandfonline.com/doi/abs/10.1080/03637759209376245

Meservy, T., Jensen, M., Burgoon, J. K., Nunamaker, J. F., Twitchell, D. P., Tschpenakis, G., & Metaxas, D. (2005). Deception detection through automatic, unobtrusive analysis of nonverbal behavior. *Intelligent Systems, IEEE*, *20*(5), 35–43. Available at: http://ieeexplore.ieee.org/xpls/abs_all.jsp?arnumber=1511998

Meservy, T., Jensen, M., Kruse, W., Burgoon, J. K., & Nunamaker, J. F. (2008). Automatic extraction of deceptive behavioral cues from video. *Terrorism Informatics*. Available at: http://link.springer.com/chapter/10.1007/978-0-387-71613-8_23

Michael, N., Dilsizian, M., Metaxas, D., & Burgoon, J. K. (2010). Motion profiles for deception detection using visual cues. *Computer Vision–ECCV*, 462–475. Available at: http://link.springer.com/chapter/10.1007/978-3-642-15567-3_34

Miller, G. R., & Stiff, J. B. (1993). *Deceptive communication*. Thousand Oaks, CA: Sage.

Minkov, K., Zafeiriou, S., & Pantic, M. (2012). A comparison of different features for automatic eye blinking detection with an application to analysis of deceptive behavior. In *Proceedings of the 5th international symposium on communications, control and signal processing* (pp. 1–4). Rome, Italy: Communications Control and Signal Processing (ISCCSP). Retrieved from http://ieeexplore.ieee.org/xpls/abs_all.jsp?arnumber=6217806

Moffitt, K. (2010). Structured programming for linguistic cue extraction. Available at: http://splice.cmi.arizona.edu

National Research Council (2002). *The polygraph and lie detection: Report of the National Research Council Committee to review the scientific evidence on the polygraph*, Washington, DC: The National Academies Press.

Nakano, T., Kato, M., Morito, Y., Itoi, S., & Kitazawa, S. (2012). Blink-related momentary activation of the default mode network while viewing videos. *Proceedings of the National Academy of Sciences*, 3–7. doi:10.1073/pnas.1214804110

Nemesysco. (2009). Layered voice analysis (LVA) technology white paper introduction. Available at: http://www.lva650.com/

Newman, M., Pennebaker, J., Berry, D., & Richards, J. (2003). Lying words: Predicting deception from linguistic styles. *Personality and Social Psychology Bulletin*, *29*(5), 665–675. Available at: http://psp.sagepub.com/content/29/5/665.short

Nunamaker, J. F., Derrick, D. C., Elkins, A. C., Burgoon, J. K., & Patton, M. (2011). A system model for human interactions with intelligent, embodied conversational agents. *Journal of Management Information Systems*.

Nunamaker, J. F. Jr, Derrick, D. C., Elkins, A. C., Burgoon, J. K., Patton, M. W., & Nunamaker, J. F. (2011). Embodied conversational agent-based kiosk for automated interviewing. *Journal of Management Information Systems*, *28*(1), 17–48. doi:10.2753/MIS0742-1222280102

Nwogua, I., Frank, M., & Govindaraju, V. (2010). An automated process for deceit detection. In *Proceedings SPIE 7667, Biometric Technology for Human Identification VII* (Vol. 7667). Available at: http://proceedings.spiedigitallibrary.org/data/Conferences/SPIEP/8052/76670R_1.pdf

Pantic, M., & Patras, I. (2006). Dynamics of facial expression: Recognition of facial actions and their temporal segments from face profile image sequences. *IEEE Transactions on Systems, Man and Cybernetics—Part B*, *36*(2), 433–449.

Porter, S., Brinke, L., Baker, A., & Wallace, B. (2011). Would I lie to you?"Leakage" in deceptive facial expressions relates to psychopathy and emotional intelligence. *Personality and Individual Differences*, *2*(51), 133–137.

Reid, J. E. (1947). A revised questioning technique in lie-detection tests. *Journal of Criminal Law and Criminology (1931–1951)*, 542–547. Available at: http://www.jstor.org/stable/1138979

Rockwell, P., Buller, D., & Burgoon, J. (1997). The voice of deceit: Refining and expanding vocal cues to deception. *Communication Research Reports*, *14*(4), 451–459 Available at: http://www.tandfonline.com/doi/full/10.1080/08824099709388688

Saxe, L., Dougherty, D., & Cross, T. (1985). The validity of polygraph testing: Scientific analysis and public controversy. *American Psychologist*, *40*, 355–366. Available at: http://www.ncjrs.gov/App/abstractdb/AbstractDBDetails.aspx?id=97661

Shultz, S., Klin, A., & Jones, W. (2011). Inhibition of eye blinking reveals subjective perceptions of stimulus salience. In *Proceedings of the National Academy of Sciences of the United States of America*, *108*(52), 21270–21275. doi:10.1073/pnas.1109304108

Skolnick, J. H. (1960). Scientific Theory and scientific evidence: An analysis of lie-detection. *The Yale Law Journal*, *70*, 694. Available at: http://heinonlinebackup.com/hol-cgi-bin/get_pdf.cgi?handle=hein.journals/ylr70&section=53

Sporer, S. L., & Schwandt, B. (2006). Paraverbal indicators of deception: a meta-analytic synthesis. *Applied Cognitive Psychology*, *20*(4), 421–446. doi:10.1002/acp.1190

Sporer, S., & Schwandt, B. (2007). Moderators of nonverbal indicators of deception: A meta-analytic synthesis. *Psychology, Public Policy, and Law*, *13*(1), 1–34. Available at: https://litigation-essentials.lexisnexis.com/webcd/app?action=DocumentDisplay&crawlid=1&doctype=cite&docid=13+Psych.+Pub.+Pol.+and+L.+1&srctype=smi&srcid=3B15&key=118b051dc965e49db51b1fd4db1de66c

Tausczik, Y. R., & Pennebaker, J. W. (2010). The psychological meaning of words: LIWC and computerized text analysis methods. *Journal of Language and Social Psychology*, *29*, 24.

The Global Deception Research Team. (2006). A world of lies. *Journal of Cross-Cultural Psychology*, *37*(1), 60–74. doi:10.1177/0022022105282295

Titze, I. R., & Martin, D. W. (1998). Principles of voice production. *Acoustical Society of America Journal*, *104*, 1148.

Toma, C., & Hancock, J. (2012). What lies beneath: The linguistic traces of deception in online dating profiles. *Journal of Communication*, *62*(1), 78–97. Available at: http://onlinelibrary.wiley.com/doi/10.1111/j.1460-2466.2011.01619.x/full

Twyman, N., Elkins, A. C., & Burgoon, J. K. (2011). A Rigidity Detection System for the Guilty Knowledge Test In Proceedings of the Credibility Assessment and Information Quality in Government and Business Symposium at Forty-fourth annual Hawaii international conference on system sciences.

Tzimiropoulos, G., Alabort-i-medina, J., Zafeiriou, S., & Pantic, M. (2012). Generic active appearance models revisited. In *11th Asian conference on computer vision* (pp. 650–663) Berlin: Springer Berlin Heidelberg.

Valstar, M., & Pantic, M. (2006). Fully automatic facial action unit detection and temporal analysis. In *Conference on* computer vision and pattern recognition workshop (p. 149). IEEE. doi:10.1109/CVPRW.2006.85

Viola, P., & Jones, M. J. (2004). Robust real-time face detection. *International Journal of Computer Vision, 57*(2), 137–154.

Vrij, A, Davies, G., & Bull, R. (2008). *Detecting lies and deceit: Pitfalls and opportunities.* West Sussex, UK: Wiley-Interscience.

Vrij, A., & Heaven, S. (1999). Vocal and verbal indicators of deception as a function of lie complexity. *Psychology, Crime & Law, 5*(3), 203–215. doi:10.1080/10683169908401767

Vrij, A., Mann, S., Fisher, R., Leal, S., Milne, R., & Bull, R. (2008). Increasing cognitive load to facilitate lie detection: The benefit of recalling an event in reverse order. *Law and Human Behavior, 32*, 253–265.

Whissell, C. M. (1989). The dictionary of affect in language. In RobertPlutchik and HenryKellerman (Ed.), *Emotion: Theory, Research, and Experience* (pp. 113–131). New York: Academic Press.

Wiseman, R., Watt, C., Ten Brinke, L., Porter, S., Couper, S.-L., & Rankin, C. (2012). The eyes don't have it: Lie detection and neuro-linguistic programming. *PloS one, 7*(7), e40259. doi:10.1371/journal.pone.0040259

Woody, E. Z., & Szechtman, H. (2011). Adaptation to potential threat: The evolution, neurobiology, and psychopathology of the security motivation system. *Neuroscience and biobehavioral reviews, 35*(4), 1019–1033. doi:10.1016/j.neubiorev.2010.08.003

Yankee, W. (1965). An investigation of sphygmomanometer discomfort thresholds in polygraph examinations. *Police, 9*(6), 12.

Zhou, L., Burgoon, J. K., Nunamaker, J. F., & Twitchell, D. (2004). Automating Linguistics-Based Cues for Detecting Deception in Text-Based Asynchronous Computer-Mediated Communications. *Group Decision and Negotiation, 13*(1), 81–106. doi:10.1023/B:GRUP.0000011944.62889.6f

Zhou, L., Twitchell, D. P., Qin, T., Burgoon, J. K., Nunamaker, J. F (2003). An exploratory study into deception detection in text-based computer-mediated communication. In *Thirty-sixth annual Hawaii international conference on system sciences* (Vol. 51, p. 10). IEEE. Available at:http://ieeexplore.ieee.org/xpls/abs_all.jsp?arnumber=1173793

Zhou, L., & Zhang, D. (2008). Following linguistic footprints: Automatic deception detection in online communication. In *Communications of the ACM*. Available at: http://dl.acm.org/citation.cfm?id=1389972

Zuckerman, M., DePaulo, B. M., & Rosenthal, R. (1981). Verbal and nonverbal communication of deception. *Advances in experimental social psychology* (pp. 1–59). New York: Academic Press.

Affective Computing, Emotional Development, and Autism

Daniel S. Messinger, Leticia Lobo Duvivier, Zachary E. Warren, Mohammad Mahoor,
Jason Baker, Anne Warlaumont, *and* Paul Ruvolo

Abstract

Affective computing can illuminate early emotional dynamics and provide tools for intervention in disordered emotional functioning. This chapter reviews affective computing approaches to understanding emotional communication in typically developing children and children with an autism spectrum disorder (ASD). It covers the application of automated measurement of the dynamics of emotional expression and discusses advances in the modeling of infant and parent interactions based on insights from time-series analysis, machine learning, and recurrence theory. The authors discuss progress in the automated measurement of vocalization in infants and children and new methods for the efficient measurement of sympathetic activation and its application in children with ASD. They conclude by presenting translational applications of affective computing to children with ASD, including the use of embodied conversational agents (ECAs) to understand and influence the affective dynamics of learning, and the use of robots to improve the social and emotional functioning of children with ASD.

Key Words: children, automated measurement, infant–parent interaction, autism spectrum disorder, high-risk siblings, modeling, embodied conversational agent, robotics

Introduction
Affective Computing and Child Development

Children's development is a fertile application of affective computing. The nonverbal emotional communication of children and infants may be less impacted by social display rules than the communication of older individuals, thus offering a rich environment for the automated detection and modeling of emotion. Substantively, early dyadic interaction between infants and parents offers a model for understanding the underpinnings of nonverbal communication throughout the lifespan. These interactions, for example, may lay the basis for the development of turn-taking and mutual smiling that are fundamental to later nonverbal communication (Messinger, Ruvolo, Ekas, & Fogel, 2010). At the same time, the child's development affects

the adult he or she will become. Interventions based in affective computing that help children develop optimally have the potential to benefit society in the long term. Throughout, whenever appropriate, we discuss how the reviewed studies of detection and modeling of emotions have contributed to our understanding of emotional development in children with ASD.

Affective Computing and the Development of Autism Spectrum Disorders

Disordered development can provide insights into typical development. This chapter discusses the detection and modeling of emotion—and the application of interventions grounded in affective computing—in children with autism spectrum disorders (ASDs) and their high-risk siblings. Autism spectrum disorders are pervasive disorders of social communication and impact a broad range of non-verbal (as well as verbal) interactive skills (American Psychiatric Association, 2000). Because the symptoms of these developmental disorders emerge before 3 years of age, ASDs provide a window into early disturbances of nonverbal social interaction. In addition, the younger siblings of children with an ASD—high-risk siblings—can offer a prospective view of the development of ASDs and related symptoms. Approximately one-fifth of these ASD siblings will develop an ASD and another fifth will exhibit ASD-related symptoms by 3 years of age that are below the threshold for a clinical diagnosis (Boelte & Poustka, 2003; Bolton, Pickles, Murphy, & Rutter, 1998; Constantino et al., 2006; Messinger et al., 2013; Murphy et al., 2000; Ozonoff et al., 2011; Szatmari et al., 2000; Wassink, Brzustowicz, Bartlett, & Szatmari., 2004). Automated measurement and modeling often focuses on high-risk siblings to provide objective data on the development of ASD-related symptoms.

Chapter Overview

In a developmental context, affective computing involves the use of computer software to detect behavioral signs of emotions and model emotional functioning and communication and the construction of software and hardware agents that interact with children. The chapter begins with a review of automated measurement of facial action and the application of those measures to better understand early emotion expression. Emotional communication is complex, and the chapter then reviews time-series and machine-learning approaches to modeling emotional communication in early interaction, which includes comparisons between typically developing children and children with ASDs. Next, we review automated approaches to emotion detection—and to the identification of ASDs—from children's vocalizations, and we discuss efforts to model the vocal signal using graph-based and time-series approaches. The final measurement section reviews new approaches to the collection of electrophysiological data (electrodermal activation [EDA]), focusing on efforts in children with ASD. Finally, we review translational applications of affective computing in two areas that have shown promise in helping children with ASD develop skills in the areas of emotional development and social communication: embodied conversational agents (ECAs) and robotics. The chapter ends with a critical discussion of accomplishments and opportunities for advancement in affective computing efforts with children.

Automated Measurement of Emotional Behavior

Automated Facial Measurement

The face is central to the communication of emotion from infancy through old age. However, manual measurement of facial expression is laborious and resource-intensive (Cohn & Kanade, 2007). As a consequence, much more is known about the perception of facial expressions than of the production of facial expressions. Software-based automated measurement offers the possibility of efficient, objective portraits of facial expression and emotion communication. Here, we describe a methodological framework for the automated measurement of facial expression in infants and their parents during early interaction.

A growing body of research on infant–parent interaction uses automated measurement based on the facial action coding system (FACS) (Ekman & Friesen, 1992; Ekman, Friesen, & Hager, 2002) and its application to infants (BabyFACS) (Oster, 2006). FACS is a comprehensive manual system for recording anatomically based appearance changes in the form of facial action units (AUs; Lucey, Ashraf, & Cohn, 2007). To better understand the dynamics of expression and emotional communication, the strength of key AUs is measured using an intensity metric that specifies whether a facial action its present and, if present, its strength from minimal to maximal using FACS criteria (Mahoor et al., 2008). Objective measurement of facial expression intensity allows for time-series modeling of interactive influence.

A commonly used automated measurement pipeline combines active appearance and shape models (AASMs) and support vector machines (SVMs) (Messinger et al., 2012). Active appearance and shape models are used to detect and track facial movement (see Figure 39.1). The shape component of the AASM unites the two-dimensional representations of the movement of 66 vertices (Baker, Matthews, & Schneider, 2004; Cohn & Kanade, 2007). Mouth opening can be measured as the vertical distance between the upper and lower lips in the shape component of the AASM. The appearance component of the AASM contains the grayscale values for each pixel contained in the modeled face. Appearance is the grayscale texture within the region defined by the mesh. In the research reported here, nonlinear manifold learning (Belkin & Niyogi, 2003) was used to reduce the dimensionality of the appearance and shape data to produce a set of variables that are used to train SVMs. Support vector machines are machine learning classifiers that were used to determine whether the AU in question was present and, if present, its intensity level. To make this assignment, a one-against-one classification strategy was used (each intensity level was pitted against each of the others) (Chang & Lin, 2001; Mahoor et al., 2008).

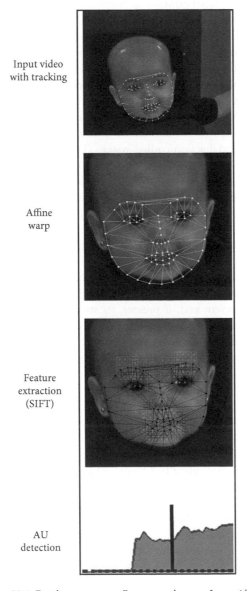

Input video with tracking

Affine warp

Feature extraction (SIFT)

AU detection

Fig. 39.1 Facial measurement. From top to bottom: Input video with overlaid shape model, affine warp to control for orientation and size, extracted features, and action unit (AU) detection with respect to support vector machine threshold and ground truth (manual facial action coding system [FACS] coding).

Emotion Measurement via Continuous Ratings

Here, we describe a method for collecting continuous ratings of emotion constructs in time that can be modeled in their own right and used to validate automated measurements of emotional behavior. In the automated facial expression measurement, expert manual measurement of facial actions' levels of cross-system (automated vs. manual) reliability are typically comparable to standard interobserver (manual vs. manual) reliability. However, intersystem agreement speaks to the validity of the automated measurements but not to the emotional meaning of the underlying behaviors. One approach to validating automated measurements of the face as indices of emotion intensity are continuous ratings made by third-party observers (http://measurement.psy.miami.edu/).

Continuous emotion measurement is similar to the affect rating dial in which participants in an emotional experience can provide a continuous report on their *own* affective state (Gottman & Levenson, 1985; Levenson & Gottman, 1983; Ruef & Levenson, 2007). In the research described here, however, continuous ratings were made by observes who moved a joystick to indicate the affective valence they perceived in an interacting infant or parent. The ratings of multiple independent observers were united into a mean index of perceived emotional valence (Waldinger, Schulz, Hauser, Allen, & Crowell, 2004). Continuous nonexpert ratings have strong face validity because they reflect a precise, easily interpretable description of a construct such as positive ("joy, happiness, and pleasure") or negative emotion ("anger, sadness, and distress").

Applying Automated and Other Measurement to Early Emotion Expression
THE CASE OF SMILING

Automated measurement of the intensity of smiling has yielded insights into early positive emotion. Although infant smiles occur frequently in social interactions and appear to index positive emotion, adult smiles occur in a range of contexts, not all of which are associated with positive emotion. This has led some investigators to propose that a particular type of smiling, Duchenne smiling, is uniquely associated with the expression of positive emotion whereas other smiles do not reflect positive emotion (Ekman & Friesen, 1982). In Duchenne smiling, the smiling action around the mouth— produced by zygomaticus major (AU12)—is complemented by eye constriction produced by the muscles around the eyes, the orbicularis oculi and pars orbitalis (AU6). Anatomically, however, smiling and eye constriction are not yes/no occurrences but reflect a continuum of muscular activation (Williams, Warick, Dyson, & Bannister et al., 1989). Automated measurement of the intensity of these two actions could indicate whether there is a continuum of Duchenne smiling.

A CONTINUUM OF DUCHENNE SMILING

Automated measurement of the intensity of smiling and eye constriction indicated that smiling was a continuous signal (Messinger, Mahoor, Chow, & Cohn, 2009; Messinger, Mattson, Mahoor, & Cohn, 2012). Infant smile strength and eye constriction intensities were highly correlated and were moderately associated with degree of mouth opening. Mouth opening is another continuous signal that frequently occurs with smiling, where it may index states of high positive arousal such as laughing. Mothers exhibited similar associations between smiling and eye constriction intensity, whereas links to mouth opening were less strong. In essence, there did not seem to be different "types" of smiling—for example, Duchenne and non-Duchenne—during infant–mother interactions (Messinger, Cassel, Acosta, Ambadar, & Cohn, 2008). Rather, associations between smiling and eye constrictions revealed by automated measurement made it more appropriate to ask a quantitative question: "How much Duchenne smiling is being displayed?" or, even more simply, "How much smiling is present?"

A GRAMMAR OF EARLY FACIAL EXPRESSION

Automated measurements of facial expressions and continuous ratings of affect have yielded insights into similarities between early positive and negative emotion. Infants exhibit a tremendous range of affective expression, from intense smiles to intense cry-face expressions. The cry-face expression—and not expressions of discrete negative emotion such as sadness and anger—is the preeminent index of negative emotion in the infant.

Since Darwin and Duchenne de Boulogne, investigators have asked how individual facial actions combine to convey emotional meaning (Darwin, 1872/1998; Duchenne, 1990/1862; Frank, Ekman, & Friesen, 1993). Darwin, in particular, suggested that a given facial action—to wit, eye constriction—might be associated not only with intense positive affect but with intense negative affect as well. Ratings of still photographs suggested that eye

constriction and mouth opening index the intensity of both positive and negative infant facial expressions (Bolzani-Dinehart et al., 2005). However, automated measurements—complemented by continuous ratings of emotion—were required to determine whether this association was present in dynamically unfolding, real-time behavior.

Messinger et al. (2012) used automated measurements of infants and parents in the face-to-face/still-face (FFSF) procedure to examine these associations. When infants smiled—as noted earlier—the intensity of the smile, the intensity of eye constriction, and the degree of mouth opening were all associated. In parallel fashion, when infants engaged in cry-face expressions, the intensity of eye constriction and the degree of mouth opening were also associated (see Figure 39.2A). That is, automated measurement revealed similar signatures of facial intensity in both positive and negative expressions. In both smile and cry-face expressions, degree of eye constriction intensity and mouth opening predicted the absolute intensity of continuously rated emotional valence (see Figure 39.2B). That is, pairing automated measurement and continuous ratings indicated a parsimony in the expression of early negative and positive emotion that was first suggested by Darwin. Automated measurement and continuous emotional ratings can be used to understand not only emotional expression but—through modeling of interaction—emotional communication.

Modeling Emotional Communication

Here, we review windowed cross-correlations, advances in time-series modeling, and machine learning approaches to modeling dyadic emotional communication. Fundamental questions in infant–parent communication concern the influence of each partner on the other. Previous research indicates that the degree to which parents match the affective states of their infants predicts subsequent self-control, internalization of social norms, and cognitive performance (Feldman & Greenbaum, 1997; Feldman, Greenbaum, & Yirmiya, 1999; Feldman, Greenbaum, Yirmiya, & Mayes, 1996; Kochanska, 2002; Kochanska, Forman, & Coy, 1999; Kochanska & Murray, 2000). Yet it is not clear that the degree to which one partner responds to the other—or the degree to which both partners are synchronous with one another—is stable over the course of several minutes. Both automated measurement and continuous emotion rating have been used to ascertain the temporal stability of measures of interactive responsivity.

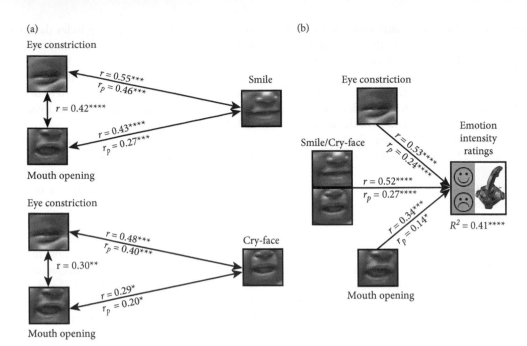

(a)

Eye constriction

$r = 0.55***$
$r_p = 0.46***$

$r = 0.42****$

$r = 0.43****$
$r_p = 0.27***$

Mouth opening

Smile

Eye constriction

$r = 0.48***$
$r_p = 0.40***$

$r = 0.30**$

$r = 0.29*$
$r_p = 0.20*$

Cry-face

Mouth opening

(b)

Eye constriction

Smile/Cry-face

$r = 0.53****$
$r_p = 0.24****$

$r = 0.52****$
$r_p = 0.27****$

$r = 0.34***$
$r_p = 0.14*$

Emotion intensity ratings

$R^2 = 0.41****$

Mouth opening

Fig. 39.2 (A) The intensity of eye constriction and mouth opening are associated with the intensity of both infant smiles and cry-face expressions. Overall (r) and partial correlations (r_p) between the intensity of smiles, eye constriction, and mouth opening and between the intensity of cry-faces, eye constriction, and mouth opening. Frames of video in which neither smiles nor cry-faces occurred (zero values) were randomly divided between the smile and cry-face correlation sets to maintain independence. (B) Eye constriction and mouth opening intensity predict affective valence (emotion intensity) ratings during both smile and cry-face expressions. R2, r, and r_p from regressing affective valence ratings on the intensity of smile/cry-faces, eye constriction, and mouth opening. All statistics represent mean values across infants. p values reflect two-tailed, one-sample t tests of those values: * $p < .05$. ** $p < .01$. ***_$p < .001$. **** $p < .0001$.

WINDOWED CROSS-CORRELATIONS AND TIME-VARYING CHANGES IN INTERACTION

Automated measurement of Duchenne smiling intensity illustrated apparent variability in interactive synchrony in two infant–mother dyads engaged in face-to-face play (Messinger et al., 2009). Differences in interaction existed between the two dyads and in the microstructure of interaction within these segments (see Figure 39.3). At the dyad level, there were differences in tempo, with one dyad's interactions being faster paced than the other's. Within dyads, the microstructure of coordination was examined using windowed cross-correlations of sliding 3-second epochs of interaction (Boker, Rotondo, Xu, & King, 2002). The midline of the rectangular plot in Figure 39.3 indicates the changing levels of zero-order correlation of Duchenne smiling intensity over time. The varying associations produced by windowed cross-correlations of automated measurement indicate continuous changes in the degree of dyadic synchrony over the course of interaction. This changing pattern suggests that disruptions and repairs of emotional synchrony—a potential predictor of

social resiliency—are a common feature of infant–mother interactions (Schore, 1994; Tronick & Cohn, 1989).

TIME-SERIES MODELS CHARACTERIZING DYNAMIC CHANGES IN THE STRENGTH OF INTERACTION

Descriptions of temporal changes in synchrony are not a statistical demonstration of time-varying changes in interaction dynamics. To address this issue, statistical modeling of time-varying changes in interactive influence was carried out using nonexpert ratings of affective valence (Chow, Haltigan, & Messinger, 2010). Infants and parents were observed in the FFSF procedure in order to present infants with the stressor of parental nonresponsivity. In the FFSF, a naturalistic face-to-face interaction is disrupted by the still-face, in which the parent is asked not to initiate or respond to the infant, and ends with a 3-minute reunion in which the parent re-engages with the infant (Adamson & Frick, 2003; Bendersky & Lewis, 1998; Cohn, Campbell, & Ross, 1991; Delgado, Messinger, & Yale., 2002; Matias & Cohn, 1993; Tronick,

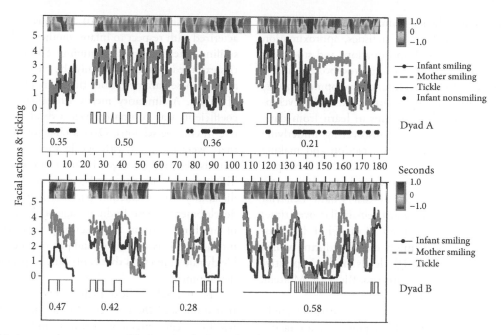

Fig. 39.3 Automated measurements of the intensity of infant and mother smiling activity plotted over successive seconds of interaction. This is Duchenne smiling activity, the mean of smile strength and eye constriction intensity. Correlations between infant and mother smiling activity are displayed below each segment of interaction. Above each segment of interaction is a plot of the windowed cross-correlations between infant and mother smiling activity. As seen in the color bar to the right of the plots, high positive correlations are deep red, null correlations are pale green, and high negative correlations are deep blue. The horizontal midline of these plots indicates the zero-order correlation between infant and mother smiling activity. The correlations are calculated for successive 3-second segments of interaction. The plots also indicate the associations of one partner's current smiling activity with the subsequent activity of the other partner. Area above the midline indicates the correlation of current infant activity with subsequent mother smiling activity. Area beneath the midline indicates the reverse. Reprinted from *Infancy*.

Als, Adamson, Wise, & Brazelton, 1978; Yale, Messinger, & Cobo-Lewis, 2003).

A stochastic regression approach applied in the context of a time-series analysis allowed the investigators to test whether interactive influence itself changed dynamically over time. These analyses address the longstanding problem of nonstationarity in time-series by modeling changes in interactive influence (Boker et al., 2002; Newtson, 1993). During face-to-face interaction, and particularly during the reunion episode following the still-face perturbation, the strength of interactive influence varied with time. The finding of changes in the dynamics of interaction suggests new avenues of research in statistical modeling of dyadic interaction. Applications include not only infant–parent interaction, but dyadic interchanges involving children, adults, and, potentially, software agents and robots.

MODELING DYNAMICS AMONG ASD SIBLINGS

Bivariate time-series models with random effects have been used to document ASD-related differences in temporal processes (Chow et al., 2010). These time-series models incorporated siblings at high risk

for an ASD in order to address potential deficits in emotional expressivity and reciprocal social interaction among these ASD siblings (Baker, Haltigan, Brewster, Jaccard, & Messinger, 2010; Cassel et al., 2007; Constantino et al., 2003; Yirmiya et al., 2006). No risk-related differences in interactive influence were apparent, but differences in self-regulation emerged (Chow et al., 2010). Infant siblings of children with ASDs (ASD-sibs) exhibited higher levels of self-regulation—indexed by lower values of autoregression variance parameters—than comparison infants. This tendency of ASD-sibs to exhibit less variability in their self-regulatory dynamics than comparable control siblings (COMP-sibs) was evident during the still-face and reunion, suggesting that ASD-sibs were less emotionally perturbed by the still-face than were other infants (Chow et al., 2010).

Machine Learning Approaches to Modeling Dyadic Interaction

Machine learning approaches can be used not only to measure emotional signals but to model emotional communication and social interaction more broadly. Machine learning draws on algorithms and theory from a wide range of disciplines including Bayesian statistics, approximation algorithms, numerical optimization, and stochastic optimal control, providing a rich toolbox applicable to the study of interaction and development. At its core, machine learning is concerned with developing computational algorithms to learn from data. Of particular relevance is discovering underlying structural relationships in interaction and making predictions about the development of these patterns. Using entropy as a dependent measure, for example, researchers found that infant behavior was most predictable (most self-similar over time) during the still-face episode of the FFSF but least predictable in the reunion episode, during which infants may exhibit high levels of both positive and negative affect (Montirosso, Riccardi, Molteni, Borgatti, & Reni, 2010).

Researchers have used machine learning methods to characterize the development of interactive behavior between mothers and infants both at the level of weekly sessions and at the level of specific interactive contexts in a longitudinal dataset covering the first 6 months of life (Messinger et al., 2010). The researchers first asked whether weekly sessions of infant–mother face-to-face interaction become more similar to each other—and so more predictable to each partner—over developmental

time (Messinger et al., 2010). Sessions were characterized with respect to infant, mother, and dyadic smiling states (e.g., mutual smiling). Similarity metrics explored included not only the mean and variance of these parameters but the entire distribution of values. A similarity metric (the Bhattacharyya coefficient) was computed over a dyad's consecutive interactive sessions. Over a range of measures, there were increases with age in the similarity of models describing consecutive interactions sessions. This suggests that the consistency—and thus predictability—of interaction patterns increases with development. These findings suggest the potential of machine learning for describing how repeated interactions between infant and parent produce stable dyadic differences that contribute to personality development.

The researchers next focused on those factors that influenced the predictability of infant smiling within specific interactive contexts and asked how that predictability changed with development (see Figure 39.4). That is, they predicted the timing of the infant's next social action based on the current state of the interaction. To do so, they built a model predicting when the infant would initiate or terminate a smile given the current state of the dyad (whether the infant and the mother were each currently smiling and which of the partners had smiled

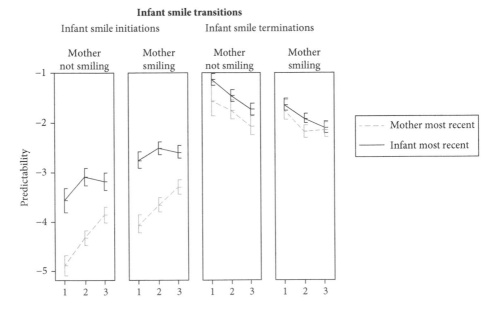

Fig. 39.4 Predictability (reverse-signed entropy) of infant smiling actions in multiple contexts. Each panel describes the predictability of a given infant action in a given context (e.g., infant smile initiation while mother is not smiling in the hand panel of the top left graph) both when the infant acted most recently (infant last) and when the mother acted most recently (mother last). Predictability is described with respect to infant age categories: 4–10 weeks (1–2.5 months), 11–17 weeks (2.5–4 months), and 18–24 weeks (4.5–6 months). Figure component reprinted from *Neural Networks*.

or stopped smiling most recently) and the infant's age. The researchers assessed predictability by measuring the entropy of the probability distribution of the time until the infant's next action. Entropy is the inverse of predictability, such that more entropic distributions are more difficult to predict.

Infant smile initiations become more predictable (less entropic) with development, whereas infant smile terminations become less predictable with age. That is, infant smiling became a more stable state with development. Both infant smile initiations and terminations were more predictable if the infant—rather than the mother—had last changed his or her smiling state. Overall, then, infants were most predictable when their last action had created the dyadic conditions in which they were acting. Thus, parents who smile to elicit an infant smile may, paradoxically, lessen the predictability of that smile occurring. The results point to the potential of machine learning approaches to produce insights into real-time emotional communication and development, a theme that we next explore with respect to infant vocalizations.

Automated Measurement of Emotion in Vocalizations

The majority of work on the automated detection of infant emotion from vocalizations has focused on infant cries, whereas the detection of other emotional characteristics of child vocalizations is less frequent. Infant crying is a ubiquitous signal of distress that develops into a more variegated expression of negative emotion in the first year of life (Gustafson & Green, 1991). Researchers have distinguished among the communicative functions of infant cries and other vocalizations (Fuller, 1991; Petroni, Malowany, Johnston, & Stevens, 1995). Petroni et al. classified cries as pain/distress cries or other using a neural network approach, whereas Fuller (1991) classified cries as pain-induced, hunger-related, or fussy using discriminant function analysis. A robotics group used low-level auditory features to achieve both cry detection (Ruvolo & Movellan, 2008) and the classification of both crying and playing/singing from ambient sound in a preschool environment (Ruvolo, Fasel, & Movellan, 2008). More generally, researchers have used partial least squares regression to classify child sounds according to child mood and energy level (Yuditskaya, 2010) and achieved some success using a least squares minimum distance classifier to distinguish between infant vocalizations that mothers' interpreted as more emotional and

more communicative (Papaeliou, Minadakis, & Cavouras, 2002). Overall, automated identification and characterization of cries is a more mature area of research than is classification of other features of child emotional vocalizations.

AUTOMATED MEASUREMENT OF VOCALIZATIONS AND ASD

There is evidence for differences between the vocalization of children with ASD, their high-risk siblings, and the vocalizations of low-risk, typically developing infants (Paul, Fuerst, Ramsay, Chawarska, & Klin, 2011; Sheinkopf, Iverson, Rinaldi, & Lester, 2012; Sheinkopf, Mundy, Oller, & Steffens, 2000). The cries of infant high-risk ASD siblings tend to have a higher fundamental frequency than those of other children, and it appears that siblings who will go on to an ASD diagnosis have among the highest pitched cries. Although automated vocalization research typically uses samples of relatively short duration, the LENA system identifies child and adult speech characteristics during day-long naturalistic audio recordings. Oller et al. (2010) used LENA to distinguish among typically developing children, children with an ASD, and children with a non-ASD developmental delay based on acoustic features of their vocalizations (Oller, Yale, & Delgado, 1997). The LENA system includes a cry and a laugh detector, although only the reliability of detection of speech-related child vocalizations versus non–speech-related vocalizations (including cries, laughter, and vegetative sounds) has been established (Xu, Yapanel, & Gray, 2009). It remains to be seen whether automated detection of emotional features of vocalization—or more general acoustic features of vocalizations—could be used for the prospective classification of ASD. As in facial measurement, audio measurements have also led to new advances in the modeling of emotional signals in the audio domain.

DEVELOPMENTAL PREDICTIONS FROM MODELED VOCALIZATION

In a seminal longitudinal study, researchers Jaffe, Beebe, Feldstein, Crown, and Jasnow (2001) implemented automated measurement of the timing of infant and adult vocalizations during infant–parent and infant–stranger interactions at 4 months of age (Feldstein et al., 1993). Time-series analyses of interactive patterns indicated that the quantity of infant vocal interruptions was predicted by the immediately previous quantity of previous mother interruptions, a demonstration of what the researchers term *coordinated interpersonal timing*. Overall, higher levels of coordinated interpersonal timing at 4 months were associated with a predilection toward disorganized attachment at 12 months, whereas secure attachment was associated with mid-range pattern levels of interactive influence timing. The results point to curvilinear patterns in development, which suggests the importance of nonlinear modeling in understanding vocal interaction.

Modeling Vocal Interactions with Cross-Recurrence Quantification Analysis

Cross-recurrence quantification analysis (CRQA) and recurrence quantification analysis (RQA) are promising visual approaches to the analysis of interactions. The analyses document patterns within time-series data that either recur within a single time series (RQA) or are coordinated across two separate time series (CRQA). Recurrence quantification analysis is a recurrence plot in which a single time-series is represented in a 2-D plot, with time increasing along both the x-axis and y-axis. In most approaches, a pixel is filled in when the value of the time-series at the x-axis time point matches (or comes within some threshold of similarity to) the value of the time-series at the y-axis time point. Other pixels are not filled in. Diagonal lines in the recurrence plot indicate recurring sequences of values in the time-series (Webber & Zbilut, 2005). Cross-recurrence quantification analysis begins with a cross-recurrence plot that compares the values of two time-series—such as those produced by two conversation partners—with one time-series being represented along the x-axis and one time-series being represented along the y-axis. The cross-recurrence allows for the creation of a diagonal cross-recurrence profile, which shows the degree of coordination between the two time-series at each of a range of lags (Dale, Warlaumont, & Richardson, 2011).

Although researchers have used RQA and CRQA to analyze heart rate coordination among groups of individuals (Konvalinka et al., 2011), these approaches are typically applied to the analysis of dyadic communication—often in the vocal modality—and have been used to characterize the interactions of children with an ASD. Focusing on mother and infant gaze data during a reunion episode of a still-face procedure, researchers derived a "trapping time" metric from the lengths of vertical lines in an RQA plot that indexed the flexibility of gaze interactions between child and mother (de Graag, Cox, Hasselman, Jansen, &

de Weerth, 2012). Cross-recurrence quantification analysis can also be applied to mother–infant acoustic coordination, such as pitch coordination (Buder, Warlaumont, Oller, & Chorna, 2010). Warlaumont, Oller, Dale, Richards, Gilkerson, and Xu (2010) found that there was less vocal interaction between children with ASD and adults (reflected in the height of the diagonal cross recurrence profile) and that, in cross-recurrence plots across a variety of lags (Warlaumont et al., 2010), the ratio of child leading to adult following was smaller in dyads including a child with ASD. Taken together, this literature suggests that RQA and CRQA can be usefully applied to the study of emotional and behavioral coordination dynamics between children and caregivers and, in some cases, can reveal differences between typically developing children and children with ASD.

Electrodermal Activity, Measurement, and Applications to ASD

In addition to facial and vocal signals, physiological indices of arousal are key to understanding emotional dynamics in both typically children and children with developmental disorders such as autism. Electrodermal activity is measured by skin conductance and can serve as an index of sympathetic nervous system arousal. As such, it can provide a reasonable physiologic index of children's emotional responses and regulation, providing information on baseline arousal (tonic EDA), reactions to events (phasic EDA), and subsequent return to baseline (recovery or habituation) (Benedek & Kaernbach, 2010; Rogers & Ozonoff, 2005). In non-ASD samples, there is evidence that higher EDA may be linked to more internalizing problems in children, whereas lower EDA may convey risk for externalizing behaviors (El-Sheikh & Erath, 2011). Complicating associations between EDA and child outcomes, however, is evidence that it is involved with and predicted by interactive effects involving various biological (e.g., the long allele of the 5-HTTLPR serotonin genetic variant) and environmental factors (e.g., harsh parenting; El-Sheikh, Keiley, Erath, & Dyer, 2013; Erath, El-Sheikh, Hinnant, & Cummings, 2011; Gilissen, Bakermans-Kranenburg, Ijzendoorn, & Linting, 2008).

ELECTRODERMAL ACTIVATION IN CHILDREN WITH ASD

The measurement of EDA can provide information regarding the form and correlates of individual differences in children with ASD. Recent trends emphasize the need to understand heterogeneity in ASD from a social-cognitive perspective (Mundy, Henderson, Inge, & Coman, 2007), and the same is true for emotion and its regulation (Mazefsky, Pelphrey, & Dahl, 2012). Mazefsky and colleagues have argued cogently for the benefits of integrating traditional autism emotion research with emotion regulation frameworks more widely applied to normative populations. Such an integration would require that EDA patterns be tied to children's behavioral responses, emotional expressions, regulation "strategies," broader functioning, and/or to other internal and external correlates (Cole, Martin, & Dennis, 2004).

As an index of sympathetic nervous system arousal, EDA has been of longstanding interest to ASD researchers examining sensory dysfunction in these children. Despite the increased presence of sensory-related behaviors in ASD, the extant literature on sensory dysfunction has not supported propositions that children with ASD exhibit atypical general arousal or hyperarousal reactions, with the little evidence for group differences suggesting reduced reactivity to certain stimuli (Rogers & Ozonoff, 2005). In reaction, researchers have proposed that group differences in

EDA may be obscured by the presence of distinct subgroups of children with ASD who exhibit patterns of either high or very low arousal (Hirstein, Iversen, & Ramachandran, 2001; Schoen, Miller, Brett-Green, & Hepburn, 2008).

Traditional electrodermal measurement tends to be more difficult for children than for adults due to difficulties with the application and tolerance of the sensors (Fowles & Fowles, 2007). Moreover, children with ASD may have difficulties with comprehension, high sensory discomfort, and behavioral noncompliance that represent challenges to the feasibility of traditional EDA measurement. A recent development is wireless wearable wrist sensors that approximate the size and appearance of a watch (Poh et al., 2012; Poh, Swenson, & Picard, 2010) and can be worn continuously during naturalistic laboratory tasks, thus facilitating the integration of EDA data with behavioral observations of emotion. A pilot study, for example, is currently being conducted of children with ASD in which the wrist sensors are used to track arousal across a series of naturalistic and structured parent–child and child-alone laboratory tasks (Baker, Fenning, Howland, & Murakami, 2014). In selected EDA data tasks for two early participants (see Figure 39.5), one child

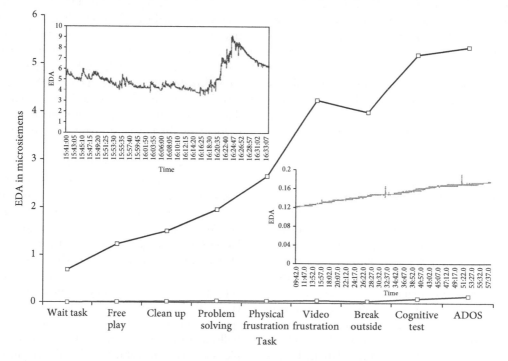

Fig. 39.5 Electrodermal activity (EDA) measurements for two children. The large plot visualizes EDA across laboratory tasks, whereas specific measurements for each child within the Autism Diagnostic Observation Schedule (ADOS) task are inset. Of note, the phasic peak in EDA for the child in the blue inset occurred when the examiner asked the child about uncomfortable emotions and problematic peer interactions.

appears to be exhibiting more typical EDA levels whereas the profile of the other child appears more consistent with the underaroused group discussed in the literature (Hirstein et al., 2001). More generally, the potential for extended use of such sensors would allow for measurement of EDA in children with ASD during completely natural daily activities in the home, school, and community. Continuously collected acquisition of EDA measurements in naturalistic settings has the potential to spur new research initiatives that parallel similar initiatives in vocalization research sparked by continuous recording of vocalization data through the LENA system.

Translational Applications of Affective Computing to Children with ASD

In addition to advances in emotion recognition and modeling, affective computing approaches can also be used to model a system's "emotional response" to a user and to express emotion via embodied conversational agents or robots (Graesser & D'Mello, 2011; Picard, 1997). Children with ASD have special challenges in the areas of social communication, social interaction, and stereotyped behaviors. From an affective perspective, children with ASD often have difficulty recognizing emotions in others and sharing enjoyment, interests, or accomplishments, as well as in interpreting facial cues to decode emotion expression. Many children with ASD also display a preference for sameness and routines, indicating that the uniform, predictable interactions offered by translational applications such as embodied conversational agents and robotics may also be particularly beneficial for these children. This section reviews recent studies on translational applications to facilitate the socioemotional development of children (including children with ASD) through the use of agents and robots.

Embodied Conversational Agents

Embodied conversational agents are software-based automata with varying degrees of autonomy that can be used to assist children in emotional or other tasks. Agents are represented with a human audiovisual form whose appearance ranges from cartoon-like to photographic. Typically, developing children appear to communicate as much with an embodied conversational agent as with a human psychologist using the same script (Black, Flores, Mower, Narayanan, & Williams., 2010), make similar nonverbal gestures with both, and smile more often and fidget less when interacting with an agent than with a psychologist (Mower, Black, Flores,

Williams, & Narayan, 2011). Agents have primarily been geared toward improving the academic performance of intelligent tutoring systems (ITS) within typically developing children domains (Graesser, Chipman, Haynes, & Olney, 2005; Lane, Noren, Auerbach, Birch, & Swartout, 2011) and tend to focus on cognitive aspects of learning, to the neglect of emotional dimensions of learning.

Recent decades have seen increased recognition of the interplay between emotions and learning and of the centrality of the role of emotions to learning (Cicchetti & Sroufe, 1976; Graesser & D'Mello, 2011; Kort, Reilly, & Picard, 2001). Findings from the growing literature on emotions and computing suggest that a broader array of emotions are relevant to learning than those mentioned in discrete theories of emotion, and learners often report negative emotions such as frustration, confusion, and boredom, some of which facilitate, rather than hinder, deep learning (Graesser & D'Mello, 2011). Partially as a result, many ITSs are increasingly incorporating affect-based agents (e.g., Mao & Li, 2010) in a range of tutoring systems, including more traditional academic applications (e.g., Arroyo, Woolf, Royer, & Tai, 2009). An example is Affective Auto-Tutor, arguably the first fully automated, affect-aware dialogue-based ITS for computer literacy (D'Mello & Graesser, 2013). This affective tutoring system was designed to detect students' emotions and use this information to guide response selection to help children regulate their emotions during learning (D'Mello & Graesser, 2012). The tutor led to better learning outcomes than its non–affect-aware equivalent counterpart, particularly for novice students with low domain knowledge.

Agent-based intervention systems can also directly target emotional responsiveness by eliciting empathy to help the learner practice experiencing and expressing different target emotional states. *FearNot!* (Fun with Empathic Agents to Achieve Novel Outcomes in Teaching) is a prime example of an agent-based system used to elicit emotion and teach typically developing children regulation and coping skills related to bullying prevention (Paiva et al., 2004). *FearNot!* taught different coping strategies to children using three affect-based agents: a bully, a victim, and a narrator. Children, for example, acted as an invisible friend to the victim agent. They watch the victim agent interact with the bully, have a private conversation with the victim agent about what happened—where they offer coping strategies that the agent might accept or refuse—and then watch the outcome of the agent's chosen coping strategy. *FearNot!* agents were autonomous, with a complex architecture guiding their behavioral decisions, including a model of the world representing the agent's own emotions as well as those of others (based on agent appraisals). Agents had a parameter-based personality including role-based (e.g., victim or bully) thresholds for experiencing different emotions, speed of decay for different emotions, and a function for recalculating the intensity of equivalent emotions. Agents also had an action selection module, which included unplanned action tendencies based on the agent's role and personality (e.g., in the victim role, the agent would cry if bullied, but did not know it would cry). The efficacy of these empathy-eliciting agents was examined empirically with 52 children aged 8–12 and appeared successful: 86% of children felt empathy for an agent (usually the victim), and 72% felt angry (usually with the bully). *FearNot!* offers a prime example of a future direction for using agents to target important core emotional skills for children that might also be applied to children with ASD (Paiva et al., 2004).

AGENTS AND CHILDREN WITH ASD

As with typically developing children, embodied conversational agents can facilitate academic learning among children with ASD (Bosseler & Massaro, 2003). Increased learning in systems that incorporate an embodied agent (an animated face) versus disembodied voice-based teaching, for example, have been found in children with ASD (Massaro & Bosseler, 2006). Agents also have the potential to help children with ASD learn to recognize emotions in others and in themselves. Rachel is an example of pedagogical emotional coach that collects multimodal data from children with ASD as they engage in emotion recognition and emotion storytelling tasks using a "person-in-the-loop" paradigm in which children interact with the agent and the system is guided in real time by a therapist, unbeknownst to the child (Mower et al., 2011). Support vector machine classification indicated that children's speech patterns were not distinguishable between parent and Rachel, suggesting that Rachel is able to elicit ecologically valid interactions from children with ASD in the context of emotional learning.

Despite these promising efforts, there is substantial untapped potential in the use of embodied conversational agent applications for children with ASD. To facilitate self-recognition and expression of emotion, systems might detect facial expressions and physiological signals in children with ASD and prompt them to report on their emotional experiences by matching their emotional experience to sample emotional faces. Alternately, posing facial expressions could be integrated into playing an ongoing game (see Cockburn et al., 2008). In summary, the main untapped potential in the use of agents to help children with ASD arguably rests with matching emerging technological potential to the core social deficits of children with these disorders.

Robots and Autism

An increase in the presence of social robots around children appears likely (Movellan, Eckhardt, Virnes, & Rodriguez, 2009; Tanaka, Cicourel, & Movellan, 2007), although the potential developmental effects of interactions with these robots are only beginning to receive attention in the psychological literature (Kahn, Gary, & Shen, 2013). Several research groups have studied the response of children with ASD to both humanoid robots and nonhumanoid toy-like robots in the hope that these systems will be useful for understanding affective, communicative, and social differences seen in individuals with ASD and to utilize robotic systems to develop novel interventions and enhance existing treatments for children with ASD (see Diehl, Schmitt, Villano, & Crowell, 2012).

Many individuals with ASD show a preference for robot-like characteristics over nonrobotic toys (Dautenhahn & Werry, 2004; Robins, Dautenhahn, Boekhorst, & Billard, 2005) and, in some circumstances, respond faster when cued by robotic movement than by human movement (Bird, Leighton, Press, & Heyes, 2007; Pierno, Mari, Lusher, & Castiello, 2008). Although these findings concern school-aged children and adults, the preference for very young children with ASD to orient to nonsocial contingencies rather than biological motion suggests that downward extension of this preference may be particularly promising (Annaz et al., (2012) Klin, Lin, Gorrindo, Ramsay, & Jones, 2009). Furthermore, a number of studies have indicated the advantages of robotic systems over animated computer characters for skill learning and optimal engagement, likely due to the capability of robotic systems to utilize physical motion in a manner not possible in screen technologies (Bainbridge, Hart, Kim, & Scassellati, 2011; Leyzberg, Spaulding, Toneva, & Scassellati, 2012).

Despite this hypothesized advantage, there have been relatively few systematic and adequately controlled applications of robotic technology investigating the impact of directed intervention and feedback approaches (Duquette, Michaud, & Mercier, 2008; Feil-Seifer & Matarić, 2009; Goodrich, Colton, Brinton, & Fujiki, 2011; Kim et al., 2012). Kim and colleagues (2012) demonstrated that children with ASD spoke more to an adult confederate when asked by a robot than when asked by another adult or by a computer. Duquette and colleagues (2008) found that children paired with a robot had greater increases in shared attention than did those paired with a human. Goodrich and colleagues reported (2011) that a low-dose robot-assisted ASD exposure with a humanoid robot yielded enhanced positive child–human interactions immediately afterward. Feil-Seifer and Mataric (2009) showed that when a robot acted contingently during an interaction with a child with ASD, it had a positive effect on that child's social interaction. Although these approaches have demonstrated the potential and value of robots for more directed intervention, the majority of robotic systems studied to date have been unable to perform autonomous closed-loop interaction. As such, these platforms have limited applicability to intervention settings necessitating extended and meaningful adaptive interactions.

By contrast, examples of adaptive robotic interaction with children with ASD include proximity-based closed-loop robotic interaction (Feil-Seifer & Mataric, 2011), haptic interaction (Amirabdollahian, Robins, Dautenhahn, & Ji, 2011), and adaptive game interactions based on affective cues inferred from physiological signals (Liu, Conn, Sarkar, & Stone, 2008). Although these systems are capable of adaptive interaction, the paradigms explored were focused on simple task and game performance and had little direct relevance to the core deficits of ASD. Recent work has explicitly focused on realizing co-robotic interaction architecture capable of measuring behavior and adapting performance in a way that addresses fundamental early attentional and affective impairments of ASD (i.e., joint attention skills). Mazzei et al. (2011) used a combination of hardware, wearable devices, and software algorithms to measure the affective states (e.g., eye gaze attention, facial expressions, vital signals, skin temperature, and EDA signals) of children with ASD, and these were used for controlling the robot reactions and responses. Bekele and colleagues (Bekele, et al., 2013a; Bekele et al., 2013b) studied the development and application of a humanoid robotic system capable of intelligently administering joint attention prompts and

adaptively responding based on within-system measurements of gaze and attention. Preschool children with ASD directed their gaze more frequently toward the humanoid-robot administrator, were frequently capable of accurately responding to robot-administered joint attention prompts, and also looked away from target stimuli at rates comparable to typically developing peers. This suggests that robotic systems endowed with enhancements for successfully pushing toward correct orientation to target might be capable of taking advantage of baseline enhancements in nonsocial attention preference in order to meaningfully enhance skills related to coordinated attention.

For effective ASD intervention, innovative therapeutic approaches using robot systems should have the ability to perceive the environment and users' behaviors, states, and activities. Increasingly, researchers are attempting to detect and flexibly respond to individually derived, socially, and disorder-relevant behavioral cues within intelligent adaptive robotic paradigms for children with ASD. Systems capable of such adaptation may ultimately be utilized to promote meaningful change related to the complex and important social communication impairments of the disorder itself. However, questions regarding generalization of skills remain for the expanding field of robotic applications for ASD. Although many are hopeful that sophisticated clinical applications of adaptive robotic technologies may demonstrate meaningful improvements for young children with ASD, it is important to note that it is both unrealistic and unlikely that such technology will constitute a sufficient intervention paradigm addressing all areas of impairment for all individuals with the disorder. However, if systems are able to discern measurable and modifiable aspects of adaptive robotic intervention with meaningful effects on skills important to neurodevelopment, the field may realize transformative robotic technologies with pragmatic real-world application of import.

Conclusion and Discussion of Alternate Approaches
Overview
Children potentially offer a relatively simple model for the application of software-based tools for the automated measurement and modeling of emotional behaviors. At the same time, the affective computing tools implemented in software- and hardware-based nonhuman agents have the potential to help children—both with and without

serious developmental and clinical conditions such as ASD—confront social and emotional problems that may impact their development. Here, we present a critical summary of key issues in the detection and modeling of emotional behaviors in and the implementation of autonomous software and hardware agents designed to help children.

Facial Expressions

The automated detection of infant and parent facial expressions—paired with continuous ratings of emotional valence—has yielded insights into the continuous flow of emotion expression during interaction and suggested parallels between infant positive and negative emotion expression (Messinger et al., 2009; Messinger et al., 2012). To date, however, this research has been conducted with relatively small sample sizes, and the efficiency promised by automated facial measurement has not been clearly realized. It is also of note that although substantial research has been conducted on the detection of emotion signals in infants younger than 1 year of age, there is relatively little research on facial expressions of emotion in older children. Developments that may begin to correct this imbalance include plans for the release of (1) a large database of annotated audio and video measurements of children between 1 and 2 years of age (Rehg et al., 2013); (2) a multilaboratory repository of audio-visual data on older children collected in multiple laboratory settings via the Databrary project (http://databrary.org/); and (3) the availability of publicly available databases containing child behavior, such as YouTube.

Vocalizations and Electrodermal Activation

The automated detection of cry-vocalizations—a key signal of infant negative emotion—is relatively robust. However, automated differentiation between cries on the basis of apparent communicative intent and the classification of emotional signals other than cries appears to be a more difficult challenge. However, the advent of systems for day-long recording of ambient audio in naturalistic settings and their automated analysis suggests the tremendous potential of affective computing to understand naturalistic behavior in context. Likewise, continuous measurement of EDA in extended and naturalistic conditions offers substantial potential for understanding the time course of arousal in response to naturalistic stressors among typically developing children and children with ASD.

Multimodal Fusion

In the research reviewed, visual and vocal (audio) signals of emotion were measured separately. Recently, however, Rehg and colleagues fused video-based (e.g., smile and gaze-at-examiner detection) and audio-based measurements (e.g., number and fundamental frequency of child speech segments) to index child engagement (Rehg et al., 2013). Although such efforts are rare, the importance of fusing multimedia measurements—including physiological as well as visual and audio sensors—cannot be underestimated. Such fusion offers the possibility of a better understanding of the emergence of emotional states from the interplay of their behavioral and physiological constituents (Calvo, 2010), as well as a better understanding of children's emotional interaction and development.

Modeling Advances

Although not commonly used in the analysis of automated measurements, there have been widespread advances in the modeling of complex communicative systems that are important to affective computing researchers. Time-series approaches can now be used to assess the communicative influence of one partner on another (e.g., parent to infant influence) across dyads (Beebe et al., 2007). Additional progress in time-series modeling has led to the quantification of time-varying changes in communicative influence and group-based differences in self-regulation (autocorrelation) (Chow et al., 2010). At the same time, innovative approaches based in recurrence quantification analysis and machine learning approaches that quantify entropy (the predictability of a given action during communication) are gaining prominence.

What Modeling Approach Is Most Appropriate?

Generally, time-series approaches are appropriate when a continuous signal such as the intensity of a facial action is being modeled. The modeling of discrete emotional signals (e.g., the presence of a smile) is well-suited to recurrence quantification analysis and entropy-based approaches. Descriptive approaches to modeling, such as windowed cross-correlations, offer an intuitive description of emotional communication dynamics whereas approaches based in time-series analyses offer the ability to conduct inferential testing of hypotheses. Despite these rules of thumb, however, there is not yet consensus on which modeling approach is most appropriate to understanding a given expressive or communicative system. Projected future growth in automated measurement (e.g., via Kinect) and the need to understand and control how software- and hardware-based agents interact suggests that modeling may become a more central aspect of affective computing initiatives with children in the future.

Modeling to Detect Interaction

In the research reviewed, behavior was measured and then modeled to detect and understand interaction. Rehg and colleagues have demonstrated an alternate approach that involves directly detecting interaction structures and defined as quasi-periodic spatiotemporal patterns (Prabhakar, Oh, Wang, Abowd, & Rehg, 2010; Prabhakar & Rehg, 2012; Rehg, 2011). Sequencing video into a string of visual words, they detected patterns in naturalistic YouTube videos and used supervised learning to identify instances of adult–child interaction directly from those videos. This approach highlights the potential importance of modeling—broadly construed—in the measurement of interaction.

Modeling to Simulate Development

The modeling approaches reviewed are concerned with characterizing communicative systems. Additional models that simulate interaction and development have been implemented by Deák and collaborators (Deák, Fasel, & Movellan, 2001; Fasel, Deák, Triesch, & Movellan, 2002; Jasso, Triesch, & Gedeon, 2008; Lewis, Gedeon, & Triesch, 2010; Triesch, Teuscher, Deák, & Carlson, 2006). Using a bottom-up perspective, these researchers posit a set of infant perceptual preferences, the ability to learn spatiotemporal contingencies, and a relatively structured environment that is based on the researchers' coding of observed infant–parent play with toys. By assigning variable reward values to gazes at the parent's face and toys, the researchers shed light on the basic abilities required for more complex developmental processes. Modeled processes include following a parent's gaze (responding to joint attention) and turning toward a parent's face when confronted with an unknown object and responding to the parent's positive or negative emotional expression (social referencing). This approach highlights the potential of modeling to contribute to an understanding of how development occurs in both typical and atypical (e.g., ASD) cases.

Software Agents

Initial "person-in-the-loop" systems for children with ASD have targeted emotional competencies (e.g., Rachel; Mower et al., 2011). More advanced, agent-based systems intended for typically developing children detect and respond to learner's emotions in real time in teaching an academic content area (e.g., Affective Auto-Tutor; D'Mello & Graesser, 2012). Ideally, future applications for children with and without ASD would synthesize these features. These applications could address core emotional functioning, including both the identification and the expression of emotion in dynamic (e.g., dyadic) contexts as targets, while using detection and user-modeling approaches to detect emotions such as boredom, confusion, and frustration. Such a synthetic approach could provide automated, emotion-based feedback to children with ASD—as is being done to some degree with typically developing children—during ongoing interactions.

Robots

In comparison with embodied conversational agents, relatively more research has been conducted in which hardware-based agents—robots—have been used to interact and intervene with children with ASD (Diehl et al., 2012). Children tend to respond positively to robots, and they offer potential for facilitating emotional development in children with ASD. As with conversational agents, the greatest area for future development is likely to be the development of autonomous closed-loop systems that apply to social-emotional targets of core importance to children with ASD. In addition, the extent to which social-emotional skills acquired and developed via conversational agents and robots are generalized to social interaction with other children and adults is not clear. Finally, the degree to which agent-based interventions can supplement more established clinical interventions in real-world settings has yet to be addressed.

Ethics and Outcomes in a Changing World

In addition to scientific concerns, a recent review suggests that the projected increase in autonomous agents such as robots presents complex ethical issues (Kahn et al., 2013). Children are likely to interact with technologically "smart" entities such as social robots as play partners but have ultimate control over these partners. That is, the reciprocity inherent in social relationships with another child does not exist with robots which, ultimately, can be turned off. Although children may benefit from many aspects of these interactions, there is concern that they may generalize their likely objectification of the robots to their interactions with other children (Kahn et al., 2013). Finally, parental-sensitive responsivity is a robust predictor of optimal outcomes (Belsky & Fearon, 2002; NICHD-ECCRN, 2001). It is of some concern, then, that little is known about the emotional impact of parent-, child-, and infant-held personal digital assistants on children's outcomes. If the potential of affective computing is to be used for children's benefit, the ethical, moral, and developmental impact of both academic and commercial affective computing tools require continued investigation.

Acknowledgments

The first author's contribution to this chapter was supported by grants from the National Institutes of Health (R01HD047417 & R01GM105004), the National Science Foundation (DLS 1052736), Autism Speaks, and the Marino Autism Research Institute. The authors thank the families who generously participated in the research described.

References

Adamson, L. B., & Frick, J. E. (2003). The still face: A history of a shared experimental paradigm. *Infancy, 4*(4), 451-474.

American Psychiatric Association (APA). (2000). *Diagnostic and statistical manual of mental disorders (DSM-IV-TR) Fourth Edition (Text Revision)*. Washington, DC: American Psychiatric Association.

Amirabdollahian, F., Robins, B., Dautenhahn, K., & Ji, Z. (2011). Investigating tactile event recognition in child-robot interaction for use in autism therapy. *Conference Proceedings of IEEE Engineering in Medicine & Biology Society, 2011*, 5347–5351. doi: 10.1109/iembs.2011.6091323

Annaz, D., Campbell, R., Coleman, M., Milne, E., & Swettenham, J. (2012). Young children with autism do not preferentially attend to biological motion. *Journal of Autism and Developmental Disorders*. doi: 10.1007/s10803-011-1256-3

Arroyo, I., Woolf, B. P., Royer, J. M., & Tai, M. (2009). Affective Gendered Learning Companions. *14th International conference on Artificial Intelligence and Education (AIED 2009)* V. Dimitrova and R. Mizoguchi (eds), IOS Press..

Bainbridge, W. A., Hart, J. W., Kim, E. S., & Scassellati, B. (2011). The benefits of interactions with physically present robots over video-displayed agents. *International Journal of Social Robotics, 3*(1), 41–52.

Baker, J. K., Fenning, R. M., Howland, M., & Murakami, C. (2014). I second that emotion: Concordance and synchrony in physiological arousal between children with ASD and their parents. In A. Esbensen (Chair), *Expanding research on family environment: How, who, and when to measure*. Symposium presented at the 47th Annual Gatlinburg Conference on Intellectual and Developmental Disabilities. Chicago, IL.

Baker, J. K., Haltigan, J. D., Brewster, R., Jaccard, J., & Messinger, D. (2010). Non-expert ratings of infant and parent emotion: Concordance with expert coding and relevance to early autism risk. *International Journal of Behavioral Development, 34*(1), 88–95. doi: 10.1177/0165025409350365

Baker, S., Matthews, I., & Schneider, J., (2004). Automatic construction of active appearance models as an image coding problem. *IEEE Transactions on Pattern Analysis and Machine Intelligence, 26*(10), 1380-1384.

Beebe, B., Jaffe, J., Buck, K., Chen, H., Cohen, P., Blatt, S.,...Andrews, H. (2007). Six-week postpartum maternal self-criticism and dependency and 4-month mother-infant self- and interactive contingencies. *Developmental Psychology, 43*(6), 1360–1376.

Bekele, E., Swanson, A., Davidson, J., Sarkar, N., & Warren, Z. (2013a). Pilot Clinical Application of an Adaptive Robotic System for Young Children with Autism. *Autism: International Journal of Research and Practice*, DOI: 10.1177/1362361313479454. PMID: 24104517, 2013.

Bekele, E. T., Lahiri, U., Swanson, A. R., Crittendon, J. A., Warren, Z. E., & Sarkar, N. (2013b). A step towards developing Adaptive Robot-Mediated Intervention Architecture (ARIA) for children with autism. *Neural Systems and Rehabilitation Engineering, IEEE Transactions, 21*(2), 289–299. doi: 10.1109/TNSRE.2012.2230188

Belkin, M., & Niyogi, P. (2003). Laplacian Eigenmaps for dimensionality reduction and data representation. *Neural Computation Archive, 15*(6), 1373–1396.

Belsky, J., & Fearon, R. M. P. (2002). Early attachment security, subsequent maternal sensitivity, and later child development: Does continuity in development depend upon continuity of caregiving? *Attachment & Human Development, 4*(3), 361–387. doi: 10.1080/14616730210167267

Bendersky, M., & Lewis., M. (1998). Arousal modulation in cocaine-exposed infants. *Developmental Psychology, 34*(3), 555-564.

Benedek, M., & Kaernbach, C. (2010). Decomposition of skin conductance data by means of nonnegative deconvolution. *Psychophysiology, 47*(4), 647–658.

Bird, G., Leighton, J., Press, C., & Heyes, C. (2007). Intact automatic imitation of human and robot actions in autism spectrum disorders. *Proceedings of the Royal Society B: Biological Sciences, 274*(1628), 3027–3031. doi: 10.1098/rspb.2007.1019

Black, M. P., Flores, E., Mower, E., Narayanan, S. S., & Williams, M. (2010). *Comparison of child-human and child-computer interactions for children with ASD*. Paper presented at the International meeting for autism research (IMFAR), Philadelphia, PA.

Boelte, S., & Poustka, F. (2003). The recognition of facial affect in autistic and schizophrenic subjects and their first-degree relatives. *Psychological Medicine, 33*(5), 907–915.

Boker, S. M., Rotondo, J. L., Xu, M., & King, K. (2002). Windowed cross-correlation and peak picking for the analysis of variability in the association between behavioral time series. *Psychological Methods, 7*(3), 338–355.

Bolton, P., Pickles, A., Murphy, M., & Rutter, M. (1998). Autism, affective and other psychiatric disorders: Patterns of familial aggregation. *Psychological Medicine, 28*(Mar), 385–395.

Bolzani-Dinehart, L., Messinger, D. S., Acosta, S., Cassel, T., Ambadar, Z., & Cohn, J. (2005). Adult perceptions of positive and negative infant emotional expressions. *Infancy, 8*(3), 279–303.

Bosseler, A., & Massaro, D. W. (2003). Development and evaluation of a computer-animated tutor for vocabulary and language learning in children with autism. *Journal of Autism and Developmental Disorders, 33*(6), 653–672.

Buder, E. H., Warlaumont, A. S., Oller, D. K., & Chorna, L. B. (2010). Dynamic indicators of mother-infant prosodic and illocutionary coordination. In the Proceedings of Speech Prosody 2010.

Calvo, R. A. (2010). Latent and emergent models in affective computing. *Emotion Review*, 2(3), 288–289. doi: 10.1177/1754073910368735

Cassel, T. D., Messinger, D. S., Ibanez, L. V., Haltigan, J. D., Acosta, S. I., & Buchaman, A. C. (2007). Early social and emotional communication in the infant siblings of children with autism spectrum disorders: An examination of the broad phenotype. *Journal of Autism and Developmental Disorders*, 37, 122–132.

Chang, C.-C., & Lin, C.-J., (2001). *LIBSVM: A library for support vector machines*, 2001. Software available at http://www.csie.ntu.edu.tw/~cjlin/libsvm.

Chow, S., Haltigan, J. D., & Messinger, D. S. (2010). Dynamic infant-parent affect coupling during the Face-to-Face/Still-Face. *Emotion*, 10, 101–114.

Cicchetti, D., & Sroufe, L. A. (1976). The relationship between affective and cognitive development in Down's syndrome infants. *Child Development*, 47(4), 920–929.

Cockburn, J., Bartlett, M., Tanaka, J. Movellan, J., & Schultz, R. (2008). SmileMaze: A tutoring system in real-time facial expression perception and production in children with Autism Spectrum Disorder, Proceedings from the IEEE International Conference on Automatic Face & Gesture Recognition (peer-reviewed conference proceeding), 978-986..

Cohn, J., Campbell, S. B., & Ross, S. (1991). Infant response in the still-face paradigm at 6 months predicts avoidant and secure attachment at 12 months. *Development and Psychopathology*, 3(4), 367-376.

Cohn, J., & Kanade, T. (2007). Automated facial image analysis for measurement of emotion expression. In J. A.Coan & J. B. Allen (Eds.), *The handbook of emotion elicitation and assessment* (pp. 222–238). New York: Oxford.

Cole, P. M., Martin, S. E., & Dennis, T. A. (2004). Emotion regulation as a scientific construct: methodological challenges and directions for child development research. *Child Development*, 75(2), 317-333. doi:10.1111/j.1467-8624.2004.00673.x

Constantino,DavisTodd,Schindler,Gross,Brophy,S.L.,...Reich, W. (2003). Validation of a brief quantitative measure of autistic traits: Comparison of the Social Responsiveness Scale with the Autism Diagnostic Interview-Revised. *Journal-of-Autism-and-Developmental-Disorders*, 33(4), 427–433.

Constantino, J., Lajonchere, C., Lutz, M., Gray, T., Abbacchi, A., McKenna, K.,...Todd, R. (2006). Autistic social impairment in the siblings of children with pervasive developmental disorders. *American Journal of Psychiatry*, 163(2), 294–296.

D'Mello, S. K. & Graesser, A. C. (2012). Malleability of Students' Perceptions of an Affect-Sensitive Tutor and its Influence on Learning. *In G. Youngblood & P. McCarthy (Eds.)* Proceedings of 25th Florida Artificial Intelligence Research Society Conference (pp. 432-437). Menlo Park, CA: AAAI Press.

D'Mello, S. K., & Graesser, A. (2013). AutoTutor and affective AutoTutor: Learning by talking with cognitively and emotionally intelligent computers that talk back. *ACM Transactions in Interactive. Intelligence System*, 2(4), 1–39. doi: 10.1145/2395123.2395128

Dale, R., Warlaumont, A. S., & Richardson, D. C. (2011). Nominal cross recurrence as a generalized lag sequential analysis for behavioral streams. *International Journal of Bifurcation and Chaos*, 21(4), 1153–1161. doi: 10.1142/s0218127411028970

Darwin, C. (1872/1998). *The expression of the emotions in man and animals* (3rd edition). New York: Oxford University.

Dautenhahn, K., & Werry, I. (2004). Towards interactive robots in autism therapy: Background, motivation and challenges. *Pragmatics & Cognition*, 12(1), 1–35. doi: 10.1075/pc.12.1.03dau

de Graag, J. A., Cox, R. F. A., Hasselman, F., Jansen, J., & de Weerth, C. (2012). Functioning within a relationship: Mother–infant synchrony and infant sleep. *Infant Behavior and Development*, 35(2), 252–263. doi: 10.1016/j.infbeh.2011.12.006

Deák, G. O., Fasel, I., & Movellan, J. (2001). The emergence of shared attention: Using robots to test developmental theories. *Proceedings 1st International Workshop on Epigenetic Robotics: Lund University Cognitive Studies*, 85, 95–104.

Delgado, C. E. F., Messinger, D. S., & Yale, M. E. (2002). Infant responses to direction of parental gaze: A comparison of two still-face conditions. *Infant Behavior & Development*, 25(3), 311-318.

Diehl, J. J., Schmitt, L. M., Villano, M., & Crowell, C. R. (2012). The clinical use of robots for individuals with autism spectrum disorders: A critical review. *Research in Autism Spectrum Disorders*, 6(1), 249–262.

Duchenne, G. B. (1990/1862). *The mechanism of human facial expression* (R. A. Cuthbertson, Trans.). New York: Cambridge University Press.

Duquette, A., Michaud, F., & Mercier, H. (2008). Exploring the use of a mobile robot as an imitation agent with children with low-functioning autism. *Autonomic Robots*, 24(2), 147–157. doi: 10.1007/s10514-007-9056-5

Ekman, P., & Friesen, W. (1992). Changes in FACS Scoring (Instruction Manual). San Francisco, CA: Human Interaction Lab.

Ekman, P., Friesen, W. V., & Hager, J. C. (2002). Facial Action Coding System Investigator's Guide. Salt Lake City, UT, A Human Face.

Ekman, P., & Friesen, W. V. (1982). Felt, false, and miserable smiles. *Journal of Nonverbal Behavior*, 6(4), 238–252.

El-Sheikh, M., & Erath, S. A. (2011). Family conflict, autonomic nervous system functioning, and child adaptation: State of the science and future directions. *Development and Psychopathology*, 23(2), 703-721. doi:10.1017/S0954579411000034

El-Sheikh, M., Keiley, M., Erath, S., & Dyer, W. J. (2013). Marital conflict and growth in children's internalizing symptoms: The role of autonomic nervous system activity. *Developmental Psychology*, 49(1), 92–108. doi: 10.1037/a0027703

Erath, S. A., El-Sheikh, M., Hinnant, J. B., & Cummings, E. M. (2011). Skin conductance level reactivity moderates the association between harsh parenting and growth in child externalizing behavior. *Developmental Psychology*, 47(3), 693–706. doi: 10.1037/a0021909

Fasel, I., Deák, G. O., Triesch, J., & Movellan, J. (2002). Combining embodied models and empirical research for understanding the development of shared attention. Paper presented at the Development and Learning, 2002.

Proceedings. The 2nd International Conference on Development and Learning, 2, 21–27

Feil-Seifer, D., & Mataric, M. (2011). *Automated detection and classification of positive vs. negative robot interactions with children with autism using distance-based features.* Paper presented at the Proceedings of the 6th international conference on Human-robot interaction, Lausanne, Switzerland.

Feil-Seifer, D., & Matarić, M. (2009). Toward socially assistive robotics for augmenting interventions for children with autism spectrum disorders. In O. Khatib, V. Kumar, & G. Pappas (Eds.), *Experimental robotics* (vol. 54, pp. 201–210). Berlin Heidelberg: Springer.

Feldman, R., & Greenbaum, C. W. (1997). Affect regulation and synchrony in mother-infant play as precursors to the development of symbolic competence. *Infant Mental Health Journal, 18*(1), 4–23.

Feldman, R., Greenbaum, C. W., & Yirmiya, N. (1999). Mother-infant affect synchrony as an antecedent of the emergence of self-control. *Developmental Psychology, 35*(1), 223–231.

Feldman, R., Greenbaum, C. W., Yirmiya, N., & Mayes, L. C. (1996). Relations between cyclicity and regulation in mother-infant interaction at 3 and 9 months and cognition at 2 years. *Journal of Applied Developmental Psychology, 17*(3), 347–365. doi: http://www.sciencedirect.com/science/article/pii/S0193397396900313

Feldstein, S., Jaffe, J., Beebe, B., Crown, C. L., Jasnow, L., Fox, H., & Gordon, S. (1993). Coordinated interpersonal timing in adult-infant vocal interactions: A cross-site replication. *Infant Behavior & Development, 16*, 455–470.

Fowles, D. (2008) The Measurement of Electrodermal Activity in Children. *In Louis A. Schmidt & Sidney J. Segalowitz, Developmental Psychophysiology: Theory, systems, and method,s* (pp. 286-316). New York: Cambridge University Press.

Frank, M. G., Ekman, P., & Friesen, W. V. (1993). Behavioral markers and the recognizability of the smile of enjoyment. *Journal of Personality and Social Psychology, 64*(1), 83–93.

Fuller, B. F. (1991). Acoustic discrimination of three types of infant cries. *Nursing Research, 40*(3), 156–160.

Gilissen, R., Bakermans-Kranenburg, M. J., Ijzendoorn, M. H. v., & Linting, M. (2008). Electrodermal reactivity during the Trier Social Stress Test for Children: Interaction between the serotonin transporter polymorphism and children's attachment representation. *Developmental Psychobiology, 50*(6), 615–625. doi: 10.1002/dev.20314

Goodrich, M. A., Colton, M. A., Brinton, B., & Fujiki, M. (2011). *A case for low-dose robotics in autism therapy.* Paper presented at the Proceedings of the 6th international conference on Human-robot interaction, Lausanne, Switzerland.

Gottman, J., & Levenson, R. W. (1985). A valid measure for obtaining self-report of affect. *Journal of Consulting and Clinical Psychology, 53*, 151–160.

Graesser, A., Chipman, P., Haynes, B. C., & Olney, A. (2005). AutoTutor: An intelligent tutoring system with mixed-initiative dialogue. *IEEE Transactions on Education, 48*(4), 612–618. doi: Citeulike-article-id:9781567; doi: 10.1109/TE.2005.856149

Graesser, A., & D'Mello, S. K. (2011). Theoretical perspectives on affect and deep learning. In R. A. Calvo & S. K. D'Mello (Eds.), *New perspectives on affect and learning technologies* (vol. 3, pp. 11–21). New York: Springer.

Gustafson, G. E., & Green, J. A. (1991). Developmental coordination of cry sounds with visual regard and gestures. *Infant Behavior & Development, 14*(1), 51–57. doi: 10.1016/0163-6383(91)90054-V

Hirstein, W., Iversen, P., & Ramachandran, V. S. (2001). Autonomic responses of autistic children to people and objects. *Proceedings of the Royal Society: B Biological Sciences, 268*(1479), 1883–1888.

Jaffe, J., Beebe, B., Feldstein, S., Crown, C. L., & Jasnow, M. D. (2001). Rhythms of dialogue in infancy: Coordinated timing in development. *Monographs of the Society for Research in Child Development, 66*(2), vi-131.

Jasso, H., Triesch, J., & Gedeon, D. (2008, 9–12 Aug. 2008). *A reinforcement learning model of social referencing.* Paper presented at the Development and Learning, 2008. ICDL 2008. 7th IEEE International Conference on.

Kahn, P. H., Gary, H. E., & Shen, S. (2013). Children's social relationships with current and near-future robots. *Child Development Perspectives, 7*(1), 32–37. doi: 10.1111/cdep.12011

Kim, E. S., Berkovits, L. D., Bernier, E. P., Leyzberg, D., Shic, F., Paul, R., & Scassellati, B. (2012). Social robots as embedded reinforcers of social behavior in children with autism. *Journal of Autism and Developmental Disorders.* doi: 10.1007/s10803-012-1645-2

Klin, A., Lin, D. J., Gorrindo, P., Ramsay, G., & Jones, W. (2009). Two-year-olds with autism orient to non-social contingencies rather than biological motion. *Nature, 459*(7244), 257–261. doi: 10.1038/nature07868

Kochanska, G. (2002). Mutually responsive orientation between mothers and their young children: A context for the early development of conscience. *Current Directions in Psychological Science, 11*(6), 191–195.

Kochanska, G., Forman, D. R., & Coy, K. C. (1999). Implications of the mother-child relationship in infancy socialization in the second year of life. *Infant Behavior & Development, 22*(2), 249–265.

Kochanska, G., & Murray, K. T. (2000). Mother-child mutually responsive orientation and conscience development: From toddler to early school age. *Child Development, 71*(2), 417–431.

Konvalinka, I., Xygalatas, D., Bulbulia, J., Schjodt, U., Jegindo, E. M., Wallot, S., . . . Roepstorff, A. (2011). Synchronized arousal between performers and related spectators in a fire-walking ritual. *Proceedings of the National Academy of Sciences, 108*(20), 8514–8519. doi: 10.1073/pnas.1016955108

Kort, B., Reilly, R., & Picard, R. W. (2001). *An affective model of interplay between emotions and learning: Reengineering educational pedagogy—Building a learning companion.* Paper presented at the International Conference on Advanced Learning Technologies, Madison, USA.

Lane, H. C., Noren, D., Auerbach, D., Birch, M., & Swartout, W. (2011). *Intelligent tutoring goes to the museum in the big city: A pedagogical agent for informal science education.* Paper presented at the Proceedings of the 15th international conference on Artificial intelligence in education, Auckland, New Zealand.

Levenson, R. W., & Gottman, J. M. (1983). Marital interaction: Physiological linkage and affective exchange. *Journal of Personality & Social Psychology, 45*, 587–597.

Lewis, J. M., Gedeon, D., & Triesch, J. (2010). *Building a model of infant social interaction.* Paper presented at the Proceedings of the 32nd Annual Conference of the Cognitive Science Society, Austin, TX.

Leyzberg, S., Spaulding, M. Toneva, B., & Scassellati, B. (2012). *The physical presence of a robot tutor increases cognitive learning gains.* Paper presented at the Proceedings of the 34th Annual Conference of the Cognitive Science Society (cogSci 2012), 1882-1887. Austin, TX|Saporro, Japan: Cognitive Science Society. Austin, TX|Saporro, Japan, August 1-4

Liu, C., Conn, K., Sarkar, N., & Stone, W. (2008). Online affect detection and robot behavior adaptation for intervention of children with autism. *IEEE Transactions on Robotics, 24*(4), 883-896. doi: 10.1109/tro.2008.2001362

Lucey, S., Ashraf, A. B., & Cohn, J. (2007). Investigating spontaneous facial action recognition through AAM representations of the face. In K. Kurihara (Ed.), *Face recognition.* Mammendorf, Germany: Pro Literatur Verlag.

Mahoor, M. H., Messinger, D. S., Ibanez, L., Kimijima M., Wang, Y., Cadavid, S., & Cohn, J. F. (2008). *Studying facial expressions using manifold learning and support vector machines.* Paper presented at the IEEE 7th International Conference on Development and Learning, Monterey, CA.

Mao, X., & Li, Z. (2010). Agent based affective tutoring systems: A pilot study. *Computers and Education, 55*(1), 202–208. doi: 10.1016/j.compedu.2010.01.005

Massaro, D. W., & Bosseler, A. (2006). Read my lips: The importance of the face in a computer-animated tutor for vocabulary learning by children with autism. *Autism, 10*(5), 495–510. doi: 10.1177/1362361306066599

Matias, R., & Cohn, J. F. (1993). Are MAX-specified infant facial expression during the face-to-face interaction consistent with differential emotions theory? *Developmental Psychology, 29*(3), 524-531.

Mazefsky, C. A., Pelphrey, K. A., & Dahl, R. E. (2012). The need for a broader approach to emotion regulation research in autism. *Child Development Perspectives, 6*(1), 92–97. doi: 10.1111/j.1750-8606.2011.00229.x

Mazzei, D., Lazzeri, N., Billeci, L., Igliozzi, R., Mancini, A., Ahluwalia, A.,…De Rossi, D. (2011). Development and evaluation of a social robot platform for therapy in autism. *Conference Proceedings of IEEE Engineering in Medicine & Biology Society, 2011,* 4515–4518. doi: 10.1109/iembs.2011.6091119

Messinger, D., Cassel, T., Acosta, S., Ambadar, Z., & Cohn, J. (2008). Infant smiling dynamics and perceived positive emotion. *Journal of Nonverbal Behavior, 32,* 133–155.

Messinger, D., Mahoor, M., Chow, S., & Cohn, J. F. (2009). Automated measurement of facial expression in infant-mother interaction: A pilot study. *Infancy, 14,* 285–305. NIHMS99269.

Messinger, D., Mahoor, M., Chow, S., Haltigan, J. D., Cadavid, S., & Cohn, J. F. (2014). Early Emotional Communication: Novel Approaches to Interaction. *Social emotions in nature and artifact: Emotions in human and human-computer interaction.* J. Gratch and S. Marsella, Oxford University Press, USA. 14: 162-180.

Messinger, D., Ruvolo, P., Ekas, N., & Fogel, A. (2010). Applying machine learning to infant interaction: The development is in the details. *Neural Networks, 23*(10), 1004–1016.

Messinger, D., Young, G. S., Ozonoff, S., Dobkins, K., Carter, A., Zwaigenbaum, L.,…Sigman, M. (2013). Beyond autism: A baby siblings research consortium study of high-risk children at three years of age. *Journal of the American Academy of Child and Adolescent Psychiatry, 52*(3), 300–308 e301. doi: 10.1016/j.jaac.2012.12.011

Messinger, D. S., Mattson, W. I., Mahoor, M. H., & Cohn, J. F. (2012). The eyes have it: making positive expressions more positive and negative expressions more negative. *Emotion. 12*(3): 430-436.

Montirosso, R., Riccardi, B., Molteni, E., Borgatti, R., & Reni, G. (2010). Infant's emotional variability associated to interactive stressful situation: A novel analysis approach with Sample Entropy and Lempel–Ziv Complexity. *Infant Behavior and Development, 33*(3), 346–356. doi: http://dx.doi.org/10.1016/j.infbeh.2010.04.007

Movellan, J. R., Eckhardt, M., Virnes, M., & Rodriguez, A. (2009). Sociable robot improves toddler vocabulary skills. *In Proceedings of the 4th ACM/IEEE International Conference on Human-Robot Interaction* (HRI 2009) (pp. 307-308, http://dx.doi.org/10.1145/1514095.1514189). La Jolla, CA, USA: ACM/IEEE.

Mower, E., Black, M. P., Flores, E., Williams, M., & Narayanan, S. (2011). *Rachel: Design of an emotionally targeted interactive agent for children with autism.* Paper presented at the Proceedings of the 2011 IEEE International Conference on Multimedia and Expo (ICME) Barcelona, Spain.

Mundy, P. C., Henderson, H. A., Inge, A. P., & Coman, D. C. (2007). The modifier model of autism and social development in higher functioning children with autism. *Research & Practice for Persons with Severe Disabilities, 32*(2), 1–16.

Murphy, M., Bolton, P. F., Pickles, A., Fombonne, E., Piven, J., & Rutter, M. (2000). Personality traits of the relatives of autistic probands. *Psychological Medicine, 30*(6), 1411–1424.

Newtson, D. (1993). The dynamics of action and interaction. A dynamic systems approach to development: Applications. Anonymous. Cambridge, MA, MIT Press: 241-264.

NICHD-ECCRN. (2001). Child-care and family predictors of preschool attachment and stability from infancy. *Developmental Psychology, 37*(6), 847–862.

Oller, D. K., Niyogi, P., Gray, S., Richards, J. A., Gilkerson, J., Xu, D.,…Warren, S. F. (2010). Automated vocal analysis of naturalistic recordings from children with autism, language delay, and typical development. *Proceedings of the National Academy of Sciences of the United States of America, 107*(30), 13354–13359. doi:10.1073/pnas.1003882107

Oller, D. K., Yale, M. E., & Delgado, R. E. (1997). *Development of coordination across modalities of communication: Coding and analysis tools.* Paper presented at the Biennial Meeting of the Society for Research in Child Development, Washington, D. C.

Oster, H. (2006). *Baby FACS: Facial Action Coding System for infants and young children.* Unpublished monograph and coding manual. New York University.

Ozonoff, S., Young, G. S., Carter, A., Messinger, D., Yirmiya, N., Zwaigenbaum, L.,…Stone, W. L. (2011). Recurrence risk for autism spectrum disorders: A Baby Siblings Research Consortium study. *Pediatrics, 128*(3), 15.

Paiva, A., Dias, J., Sobral, D., Aylett, R., Sobreperez, P., Woods, S.,…Hall, L. (2004). *Caring for agents and agents that care: Building empathic relations with synthetic agents.* Paper presented at the Proceedings of the Third International Joint Conference on Autonomous Agents and Multiagent Systems—Volume 1, New York.

Papaeliou, C., Minadakis, G., & Cavouras, D. (2002). Acoustic patterns of infant vocalizations expressing emotions and communicative functions. *Journal of Speech Language and*

Hearing Research, 45(2), 311–317. doi: 10.1044/1092-4388(2002/024)

Paul, R., Fuerst, Y., Ramsay, G., Chawarska, K., & Klin, A. (2011). Out of the mouths of babes: Vocal production in infant siblings of children with ASD. *Journal of Child Psychology and Psychiatry*, 52(5), 588–598. doi: 10.1111/j.1469-7610.2010.02332.x

Petroni, M., Malowany, A. S., Johnston, C. C., & Stevens, B. J. (1995). Classification of infant cry vocalizations using artificial neural networks (ANNs). *1995 International Conference on Acoustics, Speech, and Signal Processing (ICASSP-95)*, 5, 3475–3478. doi: 10.1109/ICASSP.1995.479734

Picard, R. (1997). *Affective computing*. Cambridge: MIT Press.

Pierno, A. C., Mari, M., Lusher, D., & Castiello, U. (2008). Robotic movement elicits visuomotor priming in children with autism. *Neuropsychologia*, 46(2), 448–454. doi: 10.1016/j.neuropsychologia.2007.08.020

Poh, M.-Z., Loddenkemper, T., Reinsberger, C., Swenson, N. C., Goyal, S., Sabtala, M. C.,...Picard, R. W. (2012). Convulsive seizure detection using a wrist-worn electrodermal activity and accelerometry biosensor. *Epilepsia*, 53(5), e93–e97. doi: 10.1111/j.1528-1167.2012.03444.x

Poh, M. Z., Swenson, N. C., & Picard, R. W. (2010). A wearable sensor for unobtrusive, long-term assessment of electrodermal activity. *IEEE Transactions Biomedical Engineering*, 57(5), 1243–1252. doi: 10.1109/tbme.2009.2038487

Prabhakar, K., Oh, S., Wang, P., Abowd, G. D., & Rehg, J. M. (2010). *Temporal causality for the analysis of visual events*. Paper presented at the IEEE Conference on Computer Vision and Pattern Recognition (CVPR), pp. 1967-1974., Barcelona, Spain

Prabhakar, K., & Rehg, J. (2012). Categorizing turn-taking interactions. In A. Fitzgibbon, S. Lazebnik, P. Perona, Y. Sato, & C. Schmid (Eds.), *Computer vision—ECCV 2012* (vol. 7576, pp. 383–396). Berlin/Heidelberg: Springer.

Rehg, J. M. (2011). *Behavior imaging: Using computer vision to study autism*. Paper presented at the MVA.IAPR Conference on Machine Vision Applications, June 13-15, 2011, Nara, Japan.

Rehg, J. M., Abowd, G. D., Rozga, A., Romero, M., Clements, M. A., Sclaroff, S.,...Ye, Z. (2013). *Decoding children's social behavior*. Paper presented at the IEEE Conference on Computer Vision and Pattern Recognition (CVPR), Portland, OR.

Robins, B., Dautenhahn, K., Boekhorst, T., & Billard, A. (2005). Robotic assistants in therapy and education of children with autism: Can a small humanoid robot help encourage social interaction skills? *Universal Access in the Information Society*, 4(2), 105–120. doi: 10.1007/s10209-005-0116-3

Rogers, S. J., & Ozonoff, S. (2005). Annotation: What do we know about sensory dysfunction in autism? A critical review of the empirical evidence. *Journal of Child Psychology and Psychiatry*, 46(12), 1255–1268. doi: 10.1111/j.1469-7610.2005.01431.x

Ruef, A., & Levenson, R. (2007). Studying the time course of affective episodes using the affect rating dial. In J. A. Coan & J. J. B. Allen (Eds.), *The handbook of emotion elicitation and assessment*.

Ruvolo, P., Fasel, I., & Movellan, J. (2008). Auditory mood detection for social and educational robots. *IEEE International Conference on Robotics and Automation*, 2008, 3551–3556. doi: 10.1109/ROBOT.2008.4543754

Ruvolo, P., & Movellan, J. (2008). Automatic cry detection in early childhood education settings. *7th International Conference on Development and Learning (ICDL 2008)*, 204–208. doi: 10.1109/DEVLRN.2008.4640830

Schoen, S. A., Miller, L., Brett-Green, B., & Hepburn, S. L. (2008). Psychophysiology of children with autism spectrum disorder. *Research in Autism Spectrum Disorders*, 2(3), 417–429. doi: 10.1016/j.rasd.2007.09.002

Schore, A. N. (1994). *Affect regulation & the origin of self: The neurobiology of emotional development*. Hillsdale, NJ: Erlbaum.

Sheinkopf, S. J., Iverson, J. M., Rinaldi, M. L., & Lester, B. M. (2012). Atypical cry acoustics in 6-month-old infants at risk for autism spectrum disorder. *Autism Research*, 5(5), 331–339. doi: 10.1002/aur.1244

Sheinkopf, S. J., Mundy, P., Oller, D. K., & Steffens, M. (2000). Vocal atypicalities of preverbal autistic children. *Journal of Autism and Developmental Disorders*, 30(4), 345–354.

Szatmari, P., MacLean, J. E., Jones, M. B., Bryson, S. E., Zwaigenbaum, L., Bartolucci, G.,...Tuff, L. (2000). The familial aggregation of the lesser variant in biological and nonbiological relatives of PDD probands: A family history study. *Journal of Child Psychology and Psychiatry*, 41(5), 579–586.

Tanaka, F., Cicourel, A., & Movellan, J. R. (2007). Socialization between toddlers and robots at an early childhood education center. *Proceedings of the National Academy of Sciences*, 104(46), 17954–17958. doi: 10.1073/pnas.0707769104

Triesch, J., Teuscher, C., Deák, G. O., & Carlson, E. (2006). Gaze following: Why (not) learn it? *Developmental Science*, 9(2), 125–147.

Tronick, E. Z., Als, H., Adamson, L., Wise, S., Brazelton, B. (1978). The infant's response to entrapment between contradictory messages in face-to-face interation. *American Academy of Child Psychiatry*, 17(1), 1-13.

Tronick, E. Z., & Cohn, J. F. (1989). Infant-mother face-to-face interaction: Age and gender differences in coordination and the occurrence of miscoordination. *Child Development*, 60(1), 85–92.

Waldinger, R. J., Schulz, M. S., Hauser, S. T., Allen, J. P., & Crowell, J. A. (2004). Reading others' emotions: The role of intuitive judgments in predicting marital satisfaction, quality, and stability. *Journal of Family Psychology*, 18, 58–71.

Warlaumont, A. S., Oller, D. K., Dale, R., Richards, J. A., Gilkerson, J., & Xu, D. (2010). Vocal interaction dynamics of children with and without autism. In S. Ohlsson & R. Catrambone (Eds.), *Proceedings of the 32nd Annual Conference of the Cognitive Science Society*. Austin, TX: Cognitive Science Society, 121-126.

Wassink, T. H., Brzustowicz, L. M., Bartlett, C. W., & Szatmari, P. (2004). The search for autism disease genes. *Mental Retardation and Developmental Disabilities Research Reviews*, 10(4), 272–283.

Webber, C. L., Jr., & Zbilut, J. P. (2005). Recurrence quantification analysis of nonlinear dynamical systems. In M. A. Riley & G. Van Orden (Eds.), *Tutorials in contemporary nonlinear methods for the behavioral sciences* (pp. 26–94).

Williams, P. L., Warick, R., Dyson, M., & Bannister, L. H. (1989). *Gray's anatomy*. Edinburgh: Churchill Livingstone.

Xu, D., Yapanel, U., & Gray, S. (2009). *Reliability of the LENA (TM) language environment analysis system in young children's natural home environment* (No. LTF-05-2). Boulder, CO: LENA Foundation. Retrieved from http://www.lenafoundation.org/TechReport.aspx/Reliability/LTR-05-2

Yale, M. E., Messinger, D. S., Cobo-Lewis, A. B. (2003). The temporal coordination of early infant communication. *Developmental Psychology, 39*(5), 815-824.

Yirmiya, N., Gamliel, I., Pilowsky, T., Feldman, R., Baron-Cohen, S., & Sigman, M. (2006). The development of siblings of children with autism at 4 and 14 months: Social engagement, communication, and cognition. *Journal of Child Psychology and Psychiatry, 47*(5), 511–523. doi: 10.1111/j.1 469-7610.2005.01528.x

Yuditskaya, S. (2010). *Automatic vocal recognition of a child's perceived emotional state within the Speechome corpus.* Massachusetts Institute of Technology. Retrieved from http://dspace.mit.edu/handle/1721.1/62086

Relational Agents in Health Applications: Leveraging Affective Computing to Promote Healing and Wellness

Timothy W. Bickmore

Abstract

Computer agents can emulate the best practices of human healthcare providers in automated health education and health behavior change systems designed to promote healthy behavior such as diet, exercise, medication adherence, and self-care management. By simulating face-to-face counseling with a healthcare provider who is attuned to patients' affective state, and simulating empathy and other emotions in turn, patient–agent rapport, trust, and therapeutic alliance can be established. These qualities of working relationships are known to be significant determiners of health outcomes in human–human counseling. This chapter surveys research in building such agents and clinical trials of their efficacy.

Key Words: relational agents, therapeutic alliance, health behavior change

Introduction

In the helping professions—including healthcare, counseling, and psychotherapy— the quality of the working relationship between a patient and his or her provider is known to be a significant determiner of patient satisfaction, retention in long-term interventions, adherence to the provider's recommendations, and ultimate health outcomes. Affective communication—including recognizing negative emotional states in patients and demonstrating empathy—is key to developing these relationships. As we develop automated health education and health behavior change systems, it is essential that they be imbued with these same capabilities to maximize their effectiveness.

Definition of Relational Agents

Relational agents are computational artifacts designed to build and maintain long-term, social-emotional relationships with users. In order to do this, they must be programmed with detailed knowledge of the behavior that people use to build

and maintain personal relationships and how this behavior changes over time as relationships develop, along with an explicit model of the user–agent relationship, methods for updating the model (relational assessment), and an action planning mechanism that takes current and desired relationship into account and deploys relational behaviors as needed to move the relationship in the desired direction (Bickmore & Picard, 2005).

Examples of behaviors that are strategically used to develop personal relationships include prosocial behaviors (e.g., telling a joke, initiating interaction), ritual behaviors (such as greetings and farewells), meta-relational communication (talking about the relationship), and assurances (explicit statements about commitment to the relationship) (Dainton & Stafford, 1993; Dindia, 1994; Gilbertson, Dindia, & Allen, 1998; Stafford & Canary, 1991). Other behaviors are used to maintain relationships once established; for example, continuity behaviors that are enacted before, during, and after an absence to bridge the gap in the relationship caused by the absence (Gilbertson et al., 1998), including telling one's partner what will be done during the time apart, affirmations, and farewells. Nonverbal relational behaviors include immediacy behaviors to demonstrate positive interpersonal attitude, including close conversational distance, direct body and facial orientation, forward lean, increased and direct gaze, smiling, pleasant facial expressions and facial animation in general, nodding, frequent gesturing, and postural openness (Argyle, 1988; Richmond & McCroskey, 1995). More recent longitudinal and cross-sectional studies of dyadic conversational behavior have further identified verbal and nonverbal correlates of relationship, including fewer explicit acknowledgments when giving or receiving information and less nonverbal behavior related to coordination (head nods and mutual gaze during acknowledgments) (Cassell, Gill, & Tepper, 2007; Schulman & Bickmore, 2011; 2012; Tickle-Degnen & Rosenthal, 1990).

Although most of the relational agents developed to date are purely software agents using embodied conversational agent interfaces (including most of the examples in this chapter), they can also be non-humanoid, or embodied in various physical forms, from robots, to pets, to jewelry, clothing, hand-helds, and other interactive devices. For example, Autom is a robotic weight loss coach that maintains a simple state-based model of its relationship with users and uses explicit relationship-building behaviors in its interactions with them (Kidd, 2008).

Motivation for Relational Agents in Health Counseling

In addition to their ability to establish ideal working relationships with users, there are several other reasons why relational agents may be particularly effective as automated health counselors. Given their use of verbal and nonverbal conversational behavior, these agents have been shown to be particularly effective for reaching individuals with low computer literacy (Bickmore et al., 2010; Bickmore, Pfeifer, & Jack, 2009). By presenting these users with an interface that is not only familiar to them—namely, face-to-face conversation—but one that also draws them into the interaction in a social manner, disadvantaged users who have little or no computer experience have been found to have no problems interacting with relational agents, and they express very high levels of satisfaction with these systems (Bickmore, Caruso, Clough-Gorr, & Heeren, 2005).

Relational agents may also be particularly effective at explaining written medical instructions—such as clinical trial informed consent documents and hospital discharge instructions—to patients who have difficulty reading and following these instructions: an ability known as *health literacy*. Approximately 36% of American adults have inadequate health literacy, and these individuals have been shown to have significantly more severe health problems across a number of conditions and measures. Relational agents have been developed that emulate the verbal and nonverbal behavior of providers using best practices to explain written medical instructions to patients (Bickmore, Pfeifer, & Yin, 2008). Studies have found that individuals with low health literacy express even higher levels of satisfaction with relational agents than do users with high levels of health literacy, and studies have also found that these users also prefer receiving these explanations from an agent rather than from their health providers (Bickmore, et al., 2009). Because these disadvantaged individuals are in particular need of health interventions, relational agents have the potential to provide significant impact for those in our society who are most in need.

The Role of Affect

Affect plays a crucial role in all human relationships, including professional–client relationships in healthcare. In personal relationships in general, emotions (e.g., love, joy) and behaviors that help manage emotions (e.g., empathy) are among the most important things that partners provide each other. Many kinds of relationship stereotypes, such as passionate love, are even defined in terms of the emotions felt by one partner toward the other (Brehm, 1992). According to Goleman, being able to manage emotions in someone else is key to the art of handling relationships (Goleman, 1995), and the ability to provide emotional support is also frequently mentioned as one of the requisite characteristics of a good friend or intimate partner (Cole & Bradac, 1996; Gill, Christensen, & Fincham, 1999; Goldsmith, McDermoot, & Alexander, 2000; McGuire, 1994).

Emotional communication between partners is a crucial ingredient in most relationships. Relationship quality is often defined in terms of the quality of emotional communication between partners (Berscheid & Reis, 1998). Empathy— the process of attending to, understanding, and responding to another person's expressions of emotion—is a prerequisite for providing emotional support which, in turn, provides the foundation for relationship-enhancing behaviors, including accommodation, social support, intimacy, and effective communication and problem solving (Berscheid & Reis, 1998; Okun, 1997).

Emotions also play an important role in the negotiation process of relationship building and maintenance. The negotiation of relationships is usually conducted in a tacit, off-record manner, with the proposals and uptakes or rejections handled in an indirect manner to save face (Goffman, 1967). Uptakes and rejections, in particular, are often achieved through positively and negatively valenced emotional displays (e.g., happiness display for uptake; disgust, contempt, or anger displays for rejection).

Not only is affect an important aspect of personal relationships, relationships play a central role in the emotional life of people. According to Lazarus "most emotions involve two people who are experiencing either a transient or stable interpersonal relationship of significance" (Lazarus, 1994), and Bowlby contends that most intense emotions arise when people are forming, maintaining, disrupting, terminating, or renewing close relational ties with others (Bowlby, 1979). Many emotions, such as jealousy or passionate love, can only occur within a relationship, whereas other emotions, such as loneliness, occur because of problems with or lack of a desired social relationship. As we develop relational agents that move from a professional role to that of a personal companion or intimate partner (Vardoulakis, Ring, Barry, Sidner, & Bickmore, 2012), predicting and managing the emotional impact of the user–agent relationship on users will become increasingly important.

Affect in Health Provider–Patient Relationships

In addition to being important in personal relationships, emotional support provisions are also crucially important in most health professions. For example, in physician–patient interactions, physician empathy for a patient plays a significant role in prescription compliance, and a physician's lack of empathy for a patient is the single most frequent source of complaints (Frankel, 1995). Buller and Street found that physicians who are more expressive, particularly of positive emotion, are more "satisfying" to their patients; that inconsistent or confused emotional expressions by the physician lead to more negative evaluations of them; and that expression of negative affect by physicians (anger

and anxiety) are associated with higher compliance and better patient health (Buller & Street, 1992).

Therapeutic Alliance

There is a strong correlation between the quality of professional–client relationships and outcomes across a wide range of healthcare professions but particularly in psychotherapy. The dimension of the provider–patient relationship that is credited with the significant influence on outcome—the *therapeutic alliance*—is based on the trust and belief that the therapist and patient have in each other as team members in achieving a desired outcome and has been hypothesized to be the single common factor underlying the therapeutic benefit of psychotherapies ranging from behavioral and cognitive therapies to psychodynamic therapy (Gelso & Hayes, 1998).

The therapeutic alliance construct has three subcomponents: a goal component, reflecting the degree to which the therapist and client agree on the goals of the therapy; a task component, reflecting the degree to which the therapist and client agree on the therapeutic tasks to be performed; and a bond component, reflecting the trusting, empathetic relationship between the client and therapist (Gelso & Hayes, 1998; Horvath & Greenberg, 1989).

Trust, rapport, and empathy (reflected in the bond dimension of the alliance) are frequently mentioned in the literature on helping to be prerequisites for successful therapy of any kind. According to Okun (1997), there are two stages to the helping process, with the first stage focused on building rapport and trust between the helper and helpee, in which the helper supports self-disclosure to uncover and explore as much information and as many feelings as possible before moving on to the second stage of strategy planning, implementation, and evaluation (Okun, 1997). In the literature on the therapeutic alliance, the relational factor that is most often mentioned as crucial in forming and maintaining the alliance is the patient's perception of the therapist's empathy for him or her (Gelso & Hayes, 1998).

Empathetic language in psychotherapy involves seeing the world through the client's eyes, with statements such as "It is awful" or "How awful it is" (Havens, 1986). Simple empathetic statements include paraverbals (from backchannel feedback to crying out), adjectives of empathy (e.g., "awful," "wonderful"), accented adjectives ("How awful!"), and translations ("It is terrifying" "Isn't it terrifying?"). Empathetic statements can also be more complex, such as "No wonder you were frightened!"

In addition to being a significant predictor of outcomes in psychotherapy—across a wide range of treatment disciplines and mental health conditions (Horvath & Symonds, 1991)—the therapeutic alliance has also been shown to be a significant predictor of outcomes in many other areas of healthcare, including physical therapy (Ferreira et al., 2012), chronic disease management (Attale et al., 2010), and post-acute brain injury rehabilitation (Evans, Sherer, Nakase-Richardson, Mani, & Irby, 2008).

Therapeutic Alliance with Relational Agents

Several agents have been designed to explicitly establish trust, rapport, and therapeutic alliance with users to improve task outcomes. For example, Laura—a virtual exercise counselor agent—used a wide range of verbal and nonverbal relational behavior in her interactions with users, including social chat (off-task talk), demonstration of common ground and history with the user, empathetic communication, agreeing with the user, humor, meta-relational communication, and talking about past and future interactions. In a 30-day longitudinal study involving 101 users, the relational agent demonstrated significantly improved therapeutic alliance relationships with users compared to the same agent with these relational behaviors removed (Bickmore & Picard, 2005).

In a more recent experiment, a relational museum tour guide agent named Tinker used empathy, self-disclosure, reference to common ground, shared values and beliefs, humor, and expressions of liking of the user and desire to continue interacting with the user to build trust and rapport with museum visitors. In a study involving 1,607 museum visitors randomized to the relational agent or the agent with relational behavior removed, those in the relational group rated the exhibit significantly higher on satisfaction, spent more time at the exhibit, and learned significantly more (via a knowledge test) compared to visitors who interacted with the nonrelational agent (Bickmore, Pfeifer, & Schulman, 2011).

Gratch et al. demonstrated that an embodied conversational agent that provides natural verbal and nonverbal backchannel (listener) behaviors established rapport with users. In one study involving 30 participants, those who interacted with the rapport agent were significantly more engaged—as evidenced by the amount of time they spent talking to it—compared to users who interacted with the agent displaying random feedback behavior (Gratch, 2006). Other studies demonstrated that users self-disclosed more intimate information to this rapport agent compared to disclosures made to other people (Kang & Gratch, 2010).

Multimodal Display of Affect by Relational Agents

Given the importance of empathetic feedback and immediacy behavior in personal relationships in general and therapeutic alliance relationships in particular, relational agents need to be able to effectively communicate these and other nonverbal affective cues. Although there is a significant amount of research in the verbal and nonverbal display of affect by embodied conversational agents and social robots (see Section 3 of this book), this section focuses on findings within the context of automated health counseling applications.

One study evaluated various representations for a virtual agent in a personal digital assistant (PDA)-based health counseling system. Four representations were compared: text-based dialogue only (TEXT), a static image of the agent with text-based dialogue (IMAGE), an animated character with text balloons (ANIM), and the animated character with audio (FULL). Study participants conducted a 5-minute conversation with each version (counterbalanced order and pairings with four different agent designs). Each conversation consisted of relational dialogue and health counseling content. Results indicated that the ANIM and FULL versions resulted in significantly higher therapeutic alliance scores relative to the other two conditions, indicating the importance of having an animated representation of a health counseling agent in establishing the alliance (Bickmore & Mauer, 2006).

A second series of studies explored the use of physical touch in health counseling conversations with a relational agent, motivated by the frequent use of comforting touch by nurses. The touch was delivered by an air bladder sewn into a glove worn by users that could be inflated in synchrony with other behaviors by an embodied conversational agent. A prestudy investigated the differential impact of facial display, speech prosody, and touch on perceptions of the affective valence of a message delivered by the agent. Three facial displays, three prosodic configurations, and three touch patterns were selected to span the affect valence dimension for each channel. Users rated the valence of all combinations of cues, with results indicating that agent facial display dominated user assessments of affect. A second study explored the impact of touch when used in empathetic messages by the agent. Results indicated that touch increased the impact of empathy on therapeutic alliance ratings, but only for users who were comfortable with being touched by strangers; for other users, touch had a negative impact (Bickmore, Fernando, Ring, & Schulman, 2010).

Detecting and Reacting to User Emotion

In most of the healthcare relational agents described in this section, the agent identifies user affective states that warrant empathetic feedback through dialogue, either by explicitly asking (e.g., "How are you?") or by inferring it from other user responses (e.g., "I'm not taking my medicine because it makes me feel sick"). Ideally, relational agents should be able to automatically detect users' emotional states from a variety of verbal and nonverbal cues, using many of the techniques described in Section 2 of this volume. Such automated identification would enable an agent to respond in a more timely manner whenever a significant patient emotional state arises, without having to constantly ask the patient how he or she is doing.

However, as Klein observed, it is very crucial that detected emotions be confirmed with the user before the agent acts on them, for example, by providing empathetic feedback (Klein, Moon, & Picard, 2002). To confirm this, a study was conducted that compared an agent delivering empathetically accurate comforting in response to restricted user input (via forced choice description of their emotional state) to an agent that provided much less empathically accurate feedback in response to users who could freely describe their emotional state. Results indicated that empathic accuracy by the agent was more important than user expressivity in impacting emotional state (measured by PANAS scores; Watson, Clark, & Tellegen, 1988) and satisfaction with the agent (Bickmore & Schulman, 2007).

Another important use of affect sensing in healthcare is in automated diagnosis of health conditions. Several researchers have now identified approaches for identifying depression based on speech prosody and other behavioral cues (Cohn, 2010; Dickerson, Gorlin, & Stankovic, 2011; Sung, Marci, & Pentland, 2005), and commercial products are available for automatically detecting depressive symptoms over the phone.

Longitudinal Aspects

Because the vast majority of research in affective computing focuses on emotions—transient affective states that last only a few seconds—most research studies are performed in brief, single-contact, laboratory sessions. However, more durative constructs must be considered and studied when affective computing is applied to healthcare. Many health conditions last days to years (or the rest of a patient's life, for chronic conditions such as diabetes or hypertension), health behavior change interventions such as smoking cessation typically span many months, and some health conditions are defined by abnormalities in long-term affect, such as depression.

One of the key challenges in developing automated health behavior change and chronic disease management systems is maintaining user engagement over the months or years required. Relational agents represent a particularly compelling medium to use for these interventions because they can use the same behaviors that people use to maintain long-term relationships with each other. Several studies have investigated specific techniques that relational agents can use to maintain long-term engagement. In one study, the repetitiveness of an agent was manipulated so that users either interacted with a virtual exercise coach that looked the same and used the same language every day or with a variable coach that delivered the same intervention (same semantic content) but using language and visual appearance that was superficially changed daily. In a 141-day longitudinal study with 24 participants, users who were randomized to the variable coach conducted significantly more conversations and expressed a significantly higher desire to continue working with the coach compared to the nonvariable group. In a second study, one version of the exercise coach agent told personal stories about its childhood ("backstories"), and this was compared to an equivalent agent that told the same stories but in the third-person, as if the stories were about one of other users of the system. In a 37-day longitudinal study with 26 participants, those who interacted with the backstory agent conducted significantly more conversations compared to the other group, demonstrating that users are more engaged with agents that present themselves as humans (Bickmore, Schulman, & Yin, 2010).

Ring et al. conducted a series of longitudinal studies of users interacting with a relational exercise coach agent in order to understand the construct of user mood in this context and how it could be leveraged in health counseling applications. Mood is an affective state that differs from emotion in that it lasts significantly longer and is generally less intense and less specific (Larsen, 2000). One study demonstrated that human judges who observed videotaped user interactions with agents could reliably rate mood on arousal and valence scales. An analysis of within-conversation, between-conversation, and between-user variances in arousal and valence ratings demonstrated that mood (assumed to change between conversations but not within conversations) did account for a significant portion of the variance observed. A third study demonstrated that different health behavior change counseling techniques should be used depending on user mood: for users in a positively valenced mood, counseling agents do better if they directly request that users perform a healthy behavior ("Would you take a walk before our next session?"), whereas if users are in a negative mood, agents are more effective if they ask users in a more polite manner ("I was wondering if you'd mind doing me a favor and take a walk...") (Ring, Bickmore, & Schulman, 2012).

Examples

This section briefly reviews some of the relational agents that have been developed for health counseling applications.

Relational Agents in the Hospital Environment

The hospital experience can be disempowering, disorienting, and lonely. Patients are deprived of sleep and exposed to constant noise, frequent interruptions, an unfamiliar environment filled with changing staff, and are often given medications with psychoactive side effects. These conditions often lead to discomfort and anxiety and can induce delirium (especially in older adults), a neuropsychiatric condition in patients that results in significant cognitive and perceptual problems. In addition, because patients are usually alone in their rooms until a medical intervention is required, they often are bored and starved for personal attention.

To address these issues, a computerized hospital companion agent was developed to support a patient throughout his or her hospital stay. The Hospital Buddy appears on a touch screen computer attached to an articulated arm at the bedside (Figure 40.1). The agent chats with patients about their hospital experience, provides empathetic feedback and emotional support, and engages in a range of topics that have medical and entertainment functions. In a pilot test with three hospital patients who had the Buddy in their rooms for 24 hours each, patients reported high levels of acceptance of and satisfaction with the agent and indicated that the agent helped address their loneliness (Bickmore, Bukhari, Vardoulakis, Paasche-Orlow, & Shanahan, 2012).

A virtual discharge nurse agent has also been developed that counsels hospital patients just before they leave the hospital about their postdischarge

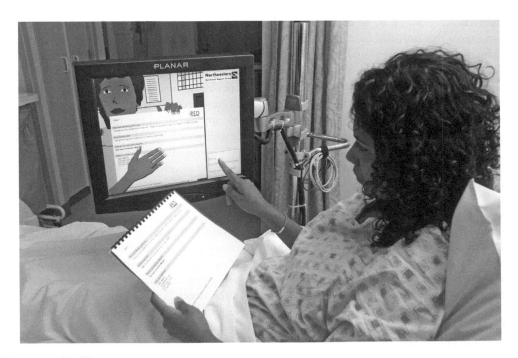

Fig. 40.1 Hospital Buddy.

self-care procedures. This agent talks to patients for 30 minutes (on average) about their discharge medications, follow-up appointments, and pending lab tests, in addition to exhibiting relational behavior including social chat, empathetic displays, humor, and meta-relational talk. In a pilot test, 19 hospitalized participants were randomized to discuss their discharge instructions with the relational virtual nurse or a version of the nurse that only conducted task talk about the discharge. Participants who interacted with the relational agent felt the virtual nurse cared significantly more about them and felt that the information she provided was significantly more useful compared to those who interacted with the task-only nurse, even though the information content was the same in the two groups. When asked if they would have rather received the discharge instructions from their doctors or nurses in the hospital, 74% of all participants said they preferred receiving it from the agent because they felt she provided information in a more friendly and less pressured manner (Bickmore et al., 2009).

Toward the Virtual Doula

Healthcare applications in which extreme patient affective states arise—such as in pain management,

palliative care, or psychotherapy—represent a particularly impactful space for affective agents to operate in. A compelling example of such an agent is a virtual doula that could assist with childbirth. A doula is a nonmedical labor coach, whose responsibilities include the provision of information and emotional support, in addition to real-time coaching in pain management. A relational agent, particularly one that could respond to a mother's voice (volume and pitch) with advice, soothing words, and physical touch (via haptics) could be an effective stand-in for mothers who cannot afford doulas and do not have birth partners. The use of doulas is associated with improved maternal and fetal health, and the continual presence of a doula during labor and delivery reduces the use of analgesics, forceps delivery, cesarean delivery, and duration of labor time (Scott, Berkowitz, & Klaus, 1999, p. 180).

A relational agent that promotes breastfeeding and provides breastfeeding instruction to women in labor, delivery, and maternity rooms in a hospital has been developed and represents an initial step toward the virtual doula (Figure 40.2).

Although most women in the United States are motivated to start breastfeeding, only 15% of US infants are actually breastfed exclusively for

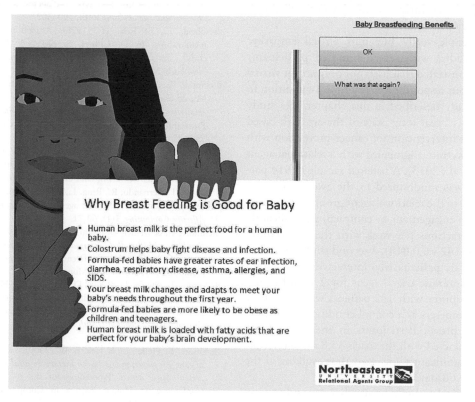

Fig. 40.2 Breastfeeding Promotion Agent.

6 months, per the recommendations of the U.S. Centers for Disease Control (CDC) and many professional organizations. The virtual lactation consultant interacts with a woman in her third trimester in a 30-minute session in her obstetrician's office to motivate her to breastfeed. Once the woman arrives in the hospital for delivery, the agent is wheeled into her room to provide further motivation, "breastfeeding 101" instruction, and support. In a pilot study involving 15 women who were expecting their first child randomized to the virtual lactation consultant or standard care, those in the agent group had higher intentions to exclusively breastfeed for 6 months and greater breastfeeding self-efficacy compared to the control group (Edwards, Bickmore, Jenkins, & Foley, 2012)

Conclusion

Conversational agents designed as automated health counselors can be effective at providing information and health behavior change counseling to patients across a variety of settings to address a number of health conditions. Giving these agents the ability to provide emotional support and empathy to patients, in addition to other relational competencies, increases patients' trust in the agents and their recommendations, leading to greater retention in longitudinal interventions, greater adherence, and better outcomes.

Do people really buy into virtual empathy? Several studies with several hundred participants have demonstrated that users not only accept virtual empathy but respond positively to it. In addition to those already described in this chapter, one study compared a year-long state-of-the-art web-based behavioral intervention for cancer prevention with the same website augmented with a relational agent (Velicer et al., 2013). A national sample of 914 participants was randomized to the two conditions, with those in the relational agent group demonstrating higher engagement by completing significantly more interactions per week with the intervention system (0.142 vs. 0.048). A second study compared 131 geriatric patients who interacted daily with a relational exercise coach agent for 2 months on a home computer with 132 patients who were only given pedometers as a control condition (Bickmore et al., in press). Participants in the intervention group interacted with the coach 35.8 times on average and significantly increased their walking at the end of the 60-day intervention.

Is it ethical to build agents that pretend to care, understand, and empathize when, in fact, they have no emotions of their own? As observed by Turkle, people seem quite comfortable with computational artifacts that only appear to have emotions (Turkle, 1995), and, as confirmed by most patients in the studies described in this chapter, the ends seem to justify the means. As one user put it:

> She's a computer character. I don't know if she cared about me. I don't know if she feels. She's a character and has a role, but I don't know if she has feelings. But, it worked for me and I'm happy.
> *(Bickmore & Picard, 2005)*

Acknowledgments

Many students and clinical and behavioral science collaborators have contributed to this work, including Daniel Schulman, Laura Pfeifer Vardoulakis, Langxuan Yin, Lazlo Ring, and Roger Edwards at Northeastern University, and Michael Paasche-Orlow, Brian Jack, and Chris Shanahan at Boston Medical Center.

References

Argyle, M. (1988). *Bodily communication*. New York: Methuen & Co. Ltd.

Attale, C., Lemogne, C., Sola-Gazagnes, A., Guedeney, N., Slama, G., Horvath, A., et al. (2010). Therapeutic alliance and glycaemic control in type 1 diabetes: a pilot study. *Diabetes and Metabolism*, 36(6), 499–502.

Berscheid, E., & Reis, H. (1998). Attraction and close relationships. In D. Gilbert, S. Fiske, & G. Lindzey (Eds.), *The handbook of social psychology* (pp. 193–281). New York: McGraw-Hill.

Bickmore, T., Bukhari, L., Vardoulakis, L., Paasche-Orlow, M., & Shanahan, C. (2012). *Hospital buddy: A persistent emotional support companion agent for hospital patients*. Proceedings of the Intelligent Virtual Agents conference, Santa Cruz, CA..

Bickmore, T., Caruso, L., Clough-Gorr, K., & Heeren, T. (2005). "It's just like you talk to a friend"—Relational agents for older adults. *Interacting with Computers*, 17(6), 711–735.

Bickmore, T., Fernando, R., Ring, L., & Schulman, D. (2010). Empathic touch by relational agents. *IEEE Transactions on Affective Computing*, 1(1), 60-71.

Bickmore, T., & Mauer, D. (2006). *Modalities for building relationships with handheld computer agents*. Paper presented at the ACM SIGCHI Conference on Human Factors in Computing Systems (CHI), Montreal.

Bickmore, T., Pfeifer, L., Byron, D., Forsythe, S., Henault, L., Jack, B., et al. (2010). Usability of conversational agents by patients with inadequate health literacy: Evidence from two clinical trials. *Journal of Health Communication* 15(Suppl 2), 197–210.

Bickmore, T., Pfeifer, L., & Jack, B. W. (2009). *Taking the time to care: Empowering low health literacy hospital patients with virtual nurse agents*. Proceedings of the ACM SIGCHI Conference on Human Factors in Computing Systems (CHI), Boston, MA.

Bickmore, T., Pfeifer, L., & Yin, L. (2008). The role of gesture in document explanation by embodied conversational agents. *International Journal of Semantic Computing*, 2(1), 47–70.

Bickmore, T., Pfeifer, L., Schulman, D. (2011). *Relational agents improve engagement and learning in science museum visitors.* Paper presented at the Intelligent Virtual Agents conference (IVA), Reykjavic, Iceland.

Bickmore, T., & Picard, R. (2005). Establishing and maintaining long-term human-computer relationships. *ACM Transactions on Computer Human Interaction*, 12(2), 293–327.

Bickmore, T., & Schulman, D. (2007). *Practical approaches to comforting users with relational agents.* Proceedings of the ACM SIGCHI Conference on Human Factors in Computing Systems (CHI), San Jose, CA.

Bickmore, T., Schulman, D., & Yin, L. (2010). Maintaining engagement in long-term interventions with relational agents. *International Journal of Applied Artificial Intelligence*, 24(6), 648–666.

Bickmore, T., Silliman, R., Nelson, K., Cheng, D., Winter, M., Henaulat, L., et al. (2013). A randomized controlled trial of an automated exercise coach for older adults. *Journal of the American Geriatrics Society*, 61, 1676–1683

Bowlby, J. (1979). *The making and breaking of affectional bonds.* London: Tavistock.

Brehm, S. (1992). *Intimate Relationships.* New York: McGraw-Hill.

Buller, D., & Street, R. (1992). Physician-patient relationships. In R. Feldman (Ed.), *Application of nonverbal behavioral theories and research* (pp. 119–141). Hillsdale, NJ: Lawrence Erlbaum.

Cassell, J., Gill, A., & Tepper, P. (2007). *Coordination in conversation and rapport.* Paper presented at the ACL Workshop on Embodied Natural Language, Prague, CZ.

Cohn, J. (2010). *Social signal processing in depression.* Proceedings of the 2nd international workshop on Social signal processing (SSPW), Florence, Italy.

Cole, T., & Bradac, J. (1996). A lay theory of relational satisfaction with best friends. *Journal of Social and Personal Relationships*, 13(1), 57–83.

Dainton, M., & Stafford, L. (1993). Routine maintenance behaviors: A comparison of relationships type, partner similarity and sex differences. *Journal of Social and Personal Relationships*, 10, 255–271.

Dickerson, R., Gorlin, E., & Stankovic, J. (2011). *Empath: A continuous remote emotional health monitoring system for depressive illness.* Proceedings of the 2nd Conference on Wireless Health, La Jolla, CA.

Dindia, K. (1994). A multiphasic view of relationship maintenance strategies. In D. Canary & L. Stafford (Eds.), *Communication and relational maintenance* (pp. 91–112). New York: Academic Press.

Edwards, R., Bickmore, T., Jenkins, L., & Foley, M. (2012). *Pilot study of the use of a computer agent to provide information and support to breastfeeding mothers.* Paper presented at the American Public Health Association Annual Meeting, San Francisco, CA.

Evans, C., Sherer, M., Nakase-Richardson, R., Mani, T., & Irby, J. (2008). Evaluation of an interdisciplinary team intervention to improve therapeutic alliance in post-acute brain injury rehabilitation. *Journal of Head Trauma Rehabilitation*, 23(5), 329–338.

Ferreira, P., Ferreira, M., Maher, C., Refshauge, K., Latimer, J., & Adams, R. (2012). The therapeutic alliance between clinicians and patients predicts outcome in chronic low back pain. *Physical Therapy*, 93(4), 470–478

Frankel, R. (1995). Emotion and the physician-patient relationship. *Motivation and Emotion*, 19(3), 163–173.

Gelso, C., & Hayes, J. (1998). *The psychotherapy relationship: Theory, research and practice.* New York: John Wiley and Sons.

Gilbertson, J., Dindia, K., & Allen, M. (1998). Relational continuity constructional units and the maintenance of relationships. *Journal of Social and Personal Relationships*, 15(6), 774–790.

Gill, D., Christensen, A., & Fincham, F. (1999). Predicting marital satisfaction from behavior: Do all roads really lead to Rome? *Personal Relationships*, 6, 369–387.

Goffman, I. (1982). *Interaction ritual: Essays on face-to-face behavior.* New York: Pantheon.

Goldsmith, D., McDermoot, V., & Alexander, S. (2000). Helpful, supportive and sensitive: Measuring the evaluation of enacted social support in personal relationships. *Journal of Social and Personal Relationships*, 17(3), 369–391.

Goleman, D. (1995). *Emotional intelligence.* New York: Bantam Books.

Gratch, J., Okhmatovskaia, A., Lamothe, F., Marsella, S., Morales, M., van der Werf, R., & Morency, L.-P. (2006). Virtual rapport. *LNCS (LNAI)*, 4133, 14–27.

Havens, L. (1986). *Making contact: Uses of language in psychotherapy.* Cambridge, MA: Harvard University Press.

Horvath, A., & Greenberg, L. (1989). Development and validation of the working alliance inventory. *Journal of Counseling Psychology*, 36(2), 223–233.

Horvath, A., & Symonds, B. (1991). Relation between working alliance and outcome in psychotherapy: A meta-analysis. *Journal of Counseling Psychology*, 38(2), 139–149.

Kang, S., & Gratch, J. (2010). *The effect of avatar realism of virtual humans on self-disclosure in anonymous social interactions.* Proceedings of the ACM SIGCHI Conference on Human Factors in Computing Systems (CHI), Atlanta, GA,.

Kidd, C. D. (2008). *Designing long-term human-robot interaction and application to weight loss.* MIT, Cambridge, MA.

Klcin, J., Moon, Y., & Picard, R. (2002). This computer responds to user frustration: Theory, design, results, and implications. *Interacting with Computers*, 14, 119–140.

Larsen, R. (2000). Toward a science of mood regulation. *Psychological Inquiry*, 11(3), 129–141.

Lazarus, R. (1994). Appraisal: The long and the short of it. In P. Ekman & R. J. Davidson (Eds.), *The nature of emotion: Fundamental questions* (pp. 208–215). New York: Oxford University Press.

McGuire, A. (1994). Helping behaviors in the natural environment: Dimensions and correlates of helping. *Personality and Social Psychology Bulletin*, 20(1), 45–56.

Okun, B. F. (1997). *Effective helping: Interviewing and counseling techniques* (5th ed.). Pacific Grove, CA: Brooks/Cole Publishing.

Richmond, V., & McCroskey, J. (1995). Immediacy. In *Nonverbal behavior in interpersonal relations* (pp. 195–217). Boston: Allyn & Bacon.

Ring, L., Bickmore, T., & Schulman, D. (2012). *Longitudinal affective computing: Virtual agents that respond to user mood.* Proceedings of the Intelligent Virtual Agents conference (IVA), Santa Cruz, CA.

Schulman, D., & Bickmore, T. (2011). *Posture, relationship, and discourse structure: Models of nonverbal behavior for long-term interaction.* Proceedings of the Intelligent Virtual Agents conference (IVA), Reykjavik, Iceland.

Schulman, D., & Bickmore, T. (2012). *Changes in verbal and nonverbal conversational behavior in long-term interaction.* Proceedings of the ACM International Conference on Multimodal Interaction (ICMI), Santa Monica, CA.

Scott, K., Berkowitz, G., & Klaus, M. (1999). A comparison of intermittent and continuous support during labor: A meta-analysis. *American Journal of Obstetrics and Gynecology, 180,* 1054–1059.

Stafford, L., & Canary, D. (1991). Maintenance strategies and romantic relationship type, gender and relational characteristics. *Journal of Social and Personal Relationships, 8,* 217–242.

Sung, M., Marci, C., & Pentland, A. (2005). *Technical report 595: Objective physiological and behavioral measures for identifying and tracking depression state in clinically depressed patients.* Cambridge, MA: MIT Media Laboratory, Human Dynamics Group.

Tickle-Degnen, L., & Rosenthal, R. (1990). The nature of rapport and its nonverbal correlates. *Psychological Inquiry, 1*(4), 285–293.

Turkle, S. (1995). *Life on the screen: Identity in the age of the Internet.* Englewood Cliffs, NJ: Simon & Schuster.

Vardoulakis, L., Ring, L., Barry, B., Sidner, C., & Bickmore, T. (2012). *Designing relational agents as long term social companions for older adults.* Proceedings of the Intelligent Virtual Agents conference (IVA), Santa Cruz, CA.

Velicer, W., Reading, C., Blissmer, B., Meier, K., Babbin, S., Paiva, A., et al. (2013). *Using relational agents in tailored interventions for multiple risk factors: Preliminary 12 month results.* Paper presented at the Society of Behavioral Medicine 2013 Annual Meeting, San Francisco, CA.

Watson, D., Clark, L., & Tellegen, A. (1988). Development and validation of brief measures of positive and negative affect: The PANAS scales. *Journal of Personality and Social Psychology, 54,* 1063–1070.

Cyberpsychology and Affective Computing

Giuseppe Riva, Rafael A. Calvo, *and* Christine Lisetti

Abstract

Cyberpsychology is a recent branch of psychology whose main research objects are the processes of change induced by new technologies. Some of these processes are related to and involve a variety of affective processes. The discipline's overlaps with affective computing and human–computer interaction in general are significant, yet its psychological origins suggest that the research communities have somewhat different focuses. This chapter reviews their histories and discusses the similarities and differences that are currently found in the different bodies of literature. The authors focus in particular on how technologies can be used to help people change behavior in both clinical situations (cybertherapy) and in personal development (positive technology/computing and smart health).

Key Words: cyberpsychology, cybertherapy, positive technology, smart health

Introduction

Clinical psychology has been traditionally based on face-to-face interactions that involve verbal and nonverbal language, without any technological mediation. However, emerging technologies—the Internet, mobile devices, virtual reality (VR), and the like—are modifying these traditional settings (Castelnuovo, Gaggioli, Mantovani, & Riva, 2003; Preziosa, Grassi, Gaggioli, & Riva, 2009; Riva & Mantovani, 2012). As the availability of these technologies expands the ways in which treatment can be provided, psychologists are expected to incorporate these innovations into their practice and research (Barak, 2008). Cyberpsychology is a recent branch of psychology that is trying to support this process. In particular, it aims at the understanding, forecasting, and induction of the different processes of change related to the use of new technologies.

Within this broad focus, cyberpsychology has two faces. On one side, cyberpsychology tries to understand how technologies can be used to induce clinical change (cybertherapy). On the other side, cyberpsychology focuses on the possible use of technology for improving personal development and well-being (positive technology/computing and smart health).

Both aspects of cyberpsychology are related to and involve a variety of affective processes. The discipline's overlap with affective computing and human–computer interaction (HCI) in general are significant, yet its psychological origins mean that the research communities have somewhat different focuses. Affective computing started as an engineering discipline, driven by a motivation to engineer new technologies that could better understand humans and be more effective for humans. Cyberpsychology originated in psychology and has been driven by the quest to help humans deal with their digital environments and use these environments to promote well-being. The object of study in cyberpsychology, as it is for many HCI researchers, is the change introduced by the technology and not the technology itself. In this chapter, we review these histories and discuss how affective computing can (or could in the future) assist cyberpsychology in terms of both treating existing mental diseases (e.g., anxiety disorders, depression, mood disorders, personality disorders) and in terms of preventive approaches to nurture health and well-being (e.g., promoting healthy lifestyles, behavior change interventions). Many mental diseases are directly related to a variety of affective processes: emotional experience (e.g., sadness, stress), mood disorders (e.g., bipolar), depression (hopelessness, helplessness), and personality (e.g., borderline). Similarly, preventively nurturing health and well-being often involves making life changes (e.g., toward health-promoting lifestyles), which in themselves are often associated with a variety of fluctuating affective states (e.g., hopefulness of being healthy, frustration of not managing to stay away from fatty foods, discouragement of postponing to join the gym indefinitely, joy of having lost 2 pounds in a week, pride in having implemented a major lifestyle change).

Affective computing—whose main focus is to develop technologies to sense, recognize, understand, and simulate affective processes—can therefore make important contributions to the enhancement of existing cybertherapies and positive technologies, as well as to the design and development of novel ones.

Cybertherapy and Affective Computing
What Is Cybertherapy?

Cybertherapy is the branch of psychology that uses new technology to induce clinical change. Historically e-therapy—the use of the Internet and related media for clinical care—has been the first area of cyberpsychology to have an impact on psychological treatments (Manhal-Baugus, 2001). It is generally agreed that innovative e-therapy approaches are an opportunity for earlier and better care for the most common mental health problems (Christensen & Hickie, 2010). The successful models of e-therapy services include different levels of interactivity and support:

• *Content-centric systems that offer prevention, self-help, and self-care to users.* Multiple charities and government-funded projects offer support that follows this approach.
• *Consumer-assisted support,* in which the level of peer interaction is offered online through volunteers with lived experience of a mental disorder

• *Virtual clinics and general practice,* in which a professional offers early interventions and treatment through the Internet
• *Blended approaches,* in which a range of services, such as Internet and face-to-face, are integrated to offer prevention and care

These e-therapy approaches allow the patient to engage in treatment without having to accommodate to office appointments, often reducing the social anxiety of face-to-face treatment (Mair & Whitten, 2000). Internet-based therapies have shown to be economically sound by being effective at a low cost (Kadda, 2010). They also have the potential to reach people in isolated places, where mental health is often a problem (Hordern, Georgiou, Whetton, & Prgomet, 2011).

Furthermore, Internet-based applications allow for the use of interactive monitoring systems that give the therapist instant access to clinical data during therapy and gives the individual patient the possibility of monitoring his or her progress. This is in line with the "know thyself" motto of recent HCI research (Li, Forlizzi, & Dey, 2010), which posits that reflecting on personal data, such as our exercise patterns, can help us lead more healthy lifestyles.

A great number of studies have shown significant results in Internet-aided psychotherapy applied to both individual therapy (Andersson, 2009; Bergstrom et al., 2010) and self-help support (Andersson et al., 2005; Carlbring, Ekselius, & Andersson, 2003). Journals such as *CyberPsychology, Behavior and Social Networking, IEEE Transactions on Biomedical Engineering, Journal of Cybertherapy and Rehabilitation, Journal of Medical Internet Research, Telemedicine and e-health* are dedicated to reporting progress in this field. However, cybertherapy also involves two emerging technologies: VR and mobile devices.

The characteristics of VR therapy, the use of VR for clinical care, include a high level of control of the interaction with the tool and the enriched experience provided to the patient (Riva, 2005; 2009). Typically in VR, the patient learns to cope with problematic situations related to his or her problem. For this reason, the most common application of VR in this area is the treatment of anxiety disorders and phobias, such as fear of heights, fear of flying, and fear of public speaking (Emmelkamp, 2005; Wiederhold & Rizzo, 2005). Emerging applications of VR in psychotherapy include eating disorders and obesity (Ferrer-Garcia & Gutierrez-Maldonado,

2012; Riva et al., 2006; Riva, Manzoni, Villani, Gaggioli, & Molinari, 2008), posttraumatic stress disorder (Reger & Gahm, 2008), addictions (Bordnick et al., 2008), sexual disorders (Optale, 2003), and pain management (Hoffman, 2004).

M-health—the use of mobile devices such as smartphones and tablets for clinical care—is also an emerging area of cybertherapy (Istepanian, Jovanov, & Zhang, 2004). The wide availability and acceptance of mobile devices—significantly higher than PCs—make them the perfect tools to bridge the gap between inpatient and outpatient treatment (Preziosa et al., 2009). On one side, mobile devices offer a nonintrusive way to monitor patients in their real-life contexts (Gaggioli, Cipresso et al., 2012), thereby affording the therapist the possibility of optimizing the patient's treatment (Gaggioli, Pioggia et al., 2012; Kauer et al., 2012). On the other side, advanced multimedia capabilities of these devices give developers the ability to create interactive applications that allow the patients to autonomously experience clinical support (Cipresso et al., 2012).

Affective Computing in Cybertherapy

Affective computing offers new interaction opportunities for the different modalities of e-therapy just described (Luneski, Konstantinidis, & Bamidis, 2010), specifically in the field of anxiety and stress management (Parsons & Rizzo, 2008; Riva, Grassi, Villani, Gaggioli, & Preziosa, 2007; Villani et al., 2012; Villani, Lucchetta, Preziosa, & Riva, 2009). Moreover, affect detection, from verbal or nonverbal expressions, can be used to adapt the interaction with an avatar or other Internet-based systems (Yang & Bhanu, 2012). Many of these techniques have or could be used in e-therapy conditions. Affect generation techniques such as those discussed by [see section on Affect Generation in this volume] are being used to make more expressive avatars. In the next paragraphs, we list some examples of the use of affective computing in cybertherapy.

AFFECTIVE COMPUTING AND EMOTIONAL WRITING

Many e-therapy approaches use writing activities as an essential element for reflection. This is based on research that suggests that writing about thoughts and feelings of past upsetting experiences is beneficial to some individuals. One of the leading researchers in this field has been J. W. Pennebaker (1997) who developed a short-term (3–5 sessions) writing therapy involving participants writing

for 15–20 minutes about traumatic or emotional experiences.

A recent meta-analysis of 146 research trials (Frattaroli, 2006) using various unstructured emotion writing methods concluded that the impact of this type of writing approach may have some benefits for some individuals, but the overall effect size was very small (r-effect size = 0.075).

One alternative method to unstructured writing is to structure how participants write during the writing task. Writing instructions could be manipulated to increase the likelihood that participants write in a way that is suggested to be therapeutic (e.g., write about something that you are thinking or worrying about too much, about something that you feel is affecting your life in an unhealthy way, etc.) and therefore increase the likelihood that they obtain benefits from the task.

A number of emotion writing studies have manipulated the writing condition in such a manner (King, 2001; King & Miner, 2000) but could not demonstrate causal links between hypothesized theoretical processes and outcomes. Difficulties have been due to the absence of clear operational definitions of the processes within the writing sessions and therefore poorly targeted assessment of expected changes according to these processes of change. For example, King and Miner (2000) found writing about positive benefits from past upsetting experiences was beneficial to health and suggested this may have been due to enhanced self-regulation skills and a sense of self-efficacy. The study did not, however, measure changes in self-regulation or self-efficacy and could not confirm the proposed mechanisms of action. One final area to be studied is how affective computing techniques can be used to detect emotions in text (Calvo & Kim 2012).

AFFECTIVE COMPUTING AND VIRTUAL REALITY

In general, the most common application of VR in cybertherapy is in the treatment of anxiety disorders and phobias (Emmelkamp, 2005; Wiederhold & Rizzo, 2005). Indeed, VR exposure therapy (VRE) has been proposed as a new medium for exposure therapy (Riva, 2005) that is safer, less embarrassing, and less costly than reproducing real-world situations. The rationale is simple: in VR, the patient is intentionally confronted with the feared stimuli while allowing the anxiety to attenuate. Avoiding a dreaded situation reinforces a phobia, and each successive exposure to it reduces the anxiety through the processes of habituation and extinction. In fact, VR can be described as an *advanced imaginal system*: an experiential form of imagery that is as effective as reality in inducing emotional responses (Vincelli, Molinari, & Riva, 2001). As underlined by Baños, Botella, and Perpiña, the VR experience can help the course of therapy (Baños, Botella, & Perpiña, 1999) through "its capability of reducing the distinction between the computer's reality and the conventional reality." In fact, "VR can be used for experiencing different identities and . . . even other forms of self, as well" (p. 289). The possibility of structuring a large amount of realistic or imaginary stimuli and, simultaneously, of monitoring the possible responses generated by the user of the technology offers a considerable increase in the likelihood of therapeutic effectiveness as compared to traditional procedures (Riva & Davide, 2001).

A more detailed discussion related to the use of affective computing methodologies in VR has been discussed in Bickmore's chapter in this volume.

AFFECTIVE COMPUTING AND MOBILE DEVICES

Mobile phone usage has already been harnessed in health care generally, but in the past few years applications of this technology are also being explored in the mental health field. In general, the most common mobile feature used in mental health is text messaging, both to help patients to express themselves and to support them in real-life settings (Preziosa et al., 2009). However, an emerging group of researchers have tried to test the effectiveness of multimedia mobile phones applied to emotion induction. Preziosa and colleagues (Preziosa, Villani, Grassi, & Riva, 2006; Riva, Grassi, et al., 2007; Riva, Preziosa, Grassi, & Villani, 2006) tested the efficacy of a mobile protocol for helping students manage exam stress in controlled studies by comparing it with other media (DVD, mobile without video, mobile with video, CD). The trial showed a better efficacy of video mobile narratives experienced on mobile phones in reducing the level of exam stress and in helping the student to relax. This result was recently replicated with a larger sample (Grassi, Gaggioli, & Riva, 2011). In a different study, Grassi and colleagues (Grassi, Gaggioli, & Riva, 2009) tested the ability of mobile narratives (narrated video) supported by multimedia mobile phones to enhance positive emotions and reduce work anxiety in a sample of commuters. Here again, the use of a mobile narrative was significantly better than other media in

decreasing anxiety levels and increasing relaxation levels. A similar approach was also used for reducing anxiety before outpatient surgery (Mosso et al., 2009) and for improving stress management in a sample of nurses working with cancer patients (Villani et al., 2012; Villani et al., 2013). All these mobile protocols share a similar approach: first, they use the multimedia capabilities of mobile phones to train the user to the use of easy relaxation techniques (e.g., breathing control); second, they use the *stress inoculation training* paradigm (e.g., exposure to stressful situations) to help the user gain confidence in his or her ability to cope with anxiety and fear stemming from the situation.

Several research groups are also experimenting with mobile, noninvasive data collection solutions for the automatic detection of affective states. For example, Gaggioli et al. developed PsychLog (http://sourceforge.net/projects/psychlog/) a free, open source mobile psycho-physiological data collection platform that allows gathering self-reported psychological information and electrocardiogram (ECG) data (Gaggioli, Cipresso et al., 2012). These signals are sensed and wirelessly transmitted to the mobile phone and gathered by a computing module that stores and processes the signals for the extraction of heart rate variability (HRV). Heart rate variability is considered a useful psycho-physiological measure because it reflects the natural variability of heart rate in response to affective and cognitive states. Heart rate variability indexes have been used to characterize a number of psychological illnesses, including major depression and panic disorders (Kimhy et al., 2010). Using PsychLog, ECG data can be correlated with user's self-reported feelings and activities. In this way, it is possible to investigate the relationship between behavioral, psychological, and physiological variables, as well as to monitor their dynamic fluctuations over time.

Affective Computing for Positive Technology

Psychologists began to recognize that the discipline's focus on helping people with mental health problems, the diagnostic-treatment model, left many outside their scope. Early in the past decade, psychologists such as Seligman and Csikszentmihalyi proposed increasing the attention giving to developing well-being (Seligman & Csikszentmihalyi, 2000). *Positive psychology*, as they called it, was to study what makes people happier, in the broadest sense. Since then, the positive psychology field has flourished. In his book *Authentic*

Happiness Seligman talked about the "three pillars" of a good life (Seligman, 2002):

- *the pleasant life*: achieved through the presence of positive emotions;
- *the engaged life*: achieved through engagement in satisfying activities and utilization of one's strengths and talents;
- *the meaningful life*: achieved through serving a purpose larger than oneself.

Notwithstanding its fast growth, some have underlined that positive psychology has relevant methodological limitations related to the focus and length of most studies (McNulty & Fincham, 2012). To address this issue, Riva recently suggested that positive psychology may be the science of personal experience (Riva, 2012*a*) in that its aim should be understanding how it is possible to manipulate the quality of personal experience with the goals of increasing wellness and generating strengths and resilience in individuals, organizations, and society.

In this view, positive functioning is a combination of three types of well-being (Keyes & Lopez, 2002)—high emotional well-being, high psychological well-being, and high social well-being—that are achieved through the manipulation of three characteristics of our personal experience—affective quality, engagement/actualization, and connectedness.

Riva and colleagues (Riva, 2012*b*; Riva, Banos, Botella, Wiederhold, & Gaggioli, 2012) also suggested that it is possible to combine the objectives of positive psychology with enhancements in information and communication technologies (ICTs) in a move toward a new paradigm: *positive technology*.

The main objective of this new paradigm is to use technology to manipulate and enhance features of our personal experience for increasing wellness and generating strength and resilience in individuals, organizations, and society (Wiederhold & Riva, 2012). In the proposed framework (see Figure 41.1), positive technologies are classified according to their effects on the pertinent features of personal experience (Botella et al., 2012):

- *Hedonic* technologies are used to induce positive and pleasant experiences.
- *Eudaemonic* technologies are used to support individuals in reaching engaging and self-actualizing experiences.
- *Social/Interpersonal* technologies are used to support and improve social integration and/or connectedness between individuals, groups, and organizations.

Affective computing can contribute to systems at all these levels. The first dimension of positive technology is concerned with how to use technology to foster positive emotional states. At this level, affective computing can exploit the link between user experience and emotions (Norman, 2004). According to the model of emotions developed by James Russell (Russell, 2003; 2005), it is possible to modify the affective quality of an experience through the manipulation of "core affect." Simply put, a positive emotion is achieved by increasing the valence (positive) and arousal (high) of core affect (affect regulation) and by getting the user to attribute this change to the contents (affective quality) of the proposed technological experience (object).

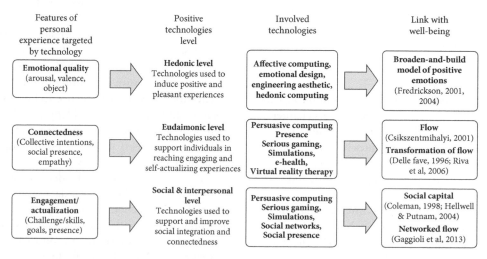

Fig. 41.1 Riva Cyberpsychology Applications. Positive technology levels.

The second dimension requires exploring systems that can engage us more with what we do, for example during learning interactions. This has been a growing research focus of the artificial intelligence in education community (Calvo & D'Mello, 2012). For example, different authors (Calvo & D'Mello, 2011) have investigated the occurrence of engagement, together with confusion, delight, and other emotions in the context of learning environments. Engagement, confusion, frustration, boredom, curiosity, and happiness are the most commonly occurring affective states observed across a range of technologies (D'Mello, in press). Dimensional representations can also be used to model affect during learning (Hussain, AlZoubi, Calvo, & D'Mello, 2011). In one study, a fully automated, affect-sensitive, intelligent tutoring system for computer literacy—*Affective AutoTutor*—(Graesser et al., 2008) was developed (see D'Mello & Graesser, this volume). The Affective AutoTutor can promote engagement by automatically detecting students' boredom, confusion, and frustration through gross body movements, facial features, and contextual cues. The affective states detected by the system are used to adapt the computer tutor's responses. A pedagogical agent (i.e., avatar) synthesizes affect via its verbal responses and nonverbal facial expressions and speech intonation.

It is less clear how affective computing or HCI can be used to support the eudaemonic level. A possible strategy comes from Rogers (2006), who called for a shift from "proactive computing" to "proactive people," in which "technologies are designed not to do things for people but to engage them more actively in what they currently do" (p. 406). Following this path, Calvo and Peters (2012) have speculated on features that would support such systems, particularly informed by the psychological literature. These include:

- *Intrapersonal skills*, particularly *introspection, reflection*, and *self-criticism*.
- *Interpersonal skills*, including *social intelligence, empathy*, and *compassion* (see Bickmore's chapter [this volume] for a discussion of how these are particularly important attributes in healthcare).
- *Change and uncertainty* features that remind us how things change, are impermanent, and uncertain.
- *Balance* of intrapersonal, interpersonal, and extrapersonal interests over the short and long term has been identified as a key developmental achievement (Sternberg, 2001).

- *Relativism,* an understanding of the multiple perspectives that can be taken with regards to common life events.
- *Mindfulness,* the conscious attention to the present moment (or task), is of increasing interest in HCI (Sengers, 2011).
- *Reflective insight*, mainly ways to develop *reflection, emotion-regulation,* and *dialectical thinking.*
- *Social consciousness*, to promote the selfless motivation to help others and take action toward improving the human condition.

The theory of flow, developed by positive psychology pioneer Mihaly Csikszentmihalyi (1990), provides a theoretical framework for addressing this challenge. Flow, or optimal experience, is a positive and complex state of consciousness that is present when individuals act with total involvement in a task. The basic feature of this experience is the perceived balance between high environmental opportunities for action (challenges) and adequate personal resources in facing them (skills). Additional characteristics are intrinsic motivation, deep concentration, clear rules in and unambiguous feedback from the task at hand, loss of self-consciousness, control of one's actions and environment, and positive affect.

Ghani and Deshpande (1994) identified three factors that influence the occurrence of flow in HCI: perceived control, fitness of task (i.e., the difference between challenges and skills), and cognitive spontaneity ("playfulness").

The final level of positive technology—the social and interpersonal one—is concerned with the use of technologies to support and improve the connectedness among individuals, groups, and organizations. Here, affective computing may be used to understand how to use technology to create a mutual sense of awareness. Following this vision, Morris (2005) recently described how social networking and pervasive computing technologies can be effectively used to help reduce feelings of social isolation and depression in elderly individuals. In their approach, sensor data measuring phone calls and visits were used to derive public displays of social interactions with relatives and friends, which they introduced into selected elders' homes. These ambient displays, which reflect data on remote and face-to-face interaction gathered by wireless sensor networks, were intended to raise awareness of social connectedness as a dynamic and controllable aspect of well-being. According to findings, this strategy was effective in reducing the feeling of social isolation in elderly users.

Affective Technologies for Smart Health

Recent epidemics of behavioral-related health issues, such as excessive alcohol, tobacco, or drug use, overeating, and lack of exercise, place people at risk of serious health problems. In 2013, the World Health Organization reported that worldwide obesity has more than doubled since 1980. It found that 1.5 billion adults were overweight, of which 500 million were obese, and 43 million children under the age of 5 were overweight. In the United States alone, obesity afflicts 33.8% of adults, 17% (or 12.5 million) of US children and teens, and obesity has tripled in one generation (WHO, 2013). As well, excessive alcohol use is the third leading preventable cause of death in the United States (79,000 deaths annually) and is responsible for a wide range of health and social problems (e.g., risky sexual behavior, domestic violence). Alcoholism is estimated to affect 10–20% of US males and 5–10% of US females at some time in their lifetimes. Similar risks exist with other forms of substance abuse.

Medicine and healthcare have therefore started to move toward finding ways of preventively promoting wellness rather than solely treating already established illness. Health promotion interventions aimed at helping people to change their behavior toward healthier lifestyles are being deployed, but the epidemic nature of these problems calls for drastic measures to rapidly increase access to effective behavior change interventions for diverse populations. It is economically impossible for medical and healthcare professionals to provide appropriate medical care and health education for millions of people in need (and the numbers are growing). Interventions must involve the use of automation to provide help to people in need. Smart health and well-being technologies that leverage the latest technological advances (e.g., sensors and sensors networks, actuators, robots, and virtual assistants) to build intelligent care (e.g., smart homes for independent living, wearable prosthetics, life-style modification coaching) are therefore being researched and developed at increasing speed (Pavel, 2012). One important aspect of smart health and well-being that affective computing is particularly relevant to deals with patient-centric approaches, whether home- or mobile-based, to empower people *before* they get sick (as well patients) to become active informed participants about preserving or

regaining their own health (Pavel, 2012). As mentioned earlier, preventively nurturing health and well-being often involves making life change (e.g., toward health-promoting lifestyles), which itself is often associated with a variety of fluctuating affective states. Affective computing with its main focus on developing technologies to sense, recognize, understand, and simulate affective processes such as emotions, attitudes, personality, and motivation, can therefore make important contributions to novel smart health and well-being approaches because emotion is a major motivating factor in decision making.

For example, computer vision researchers are developing techniques to automatically detect depression from video of the patients' face (Ellgring, 2008). In one such study, McIntyre et al. (2009) used *active appearance models* to track local shape and texture features in the face and then a Multiboost classifier to build the automated detection model.

Smart Health Behavior Change Interventions

Although multiple approaches to smart health and well-being involve sensing and monitoring the patient's physiological signals related to their health (e.g., ECG, BVP, GSR) in real-life settings using mobile technologies, communicating them (in real time if needed) to their physicians, and storing them for individual's self-monitoring, other approaches involve computer-based interventions (CBIs) for behavior change and are delivered via the internet in the privacy and comfort of one's home. There are multiple advantages to CBIs for behavior change (see Bewick et al., 2008; Hester, Squires, & Delaney, 2005; Krebs, Prochaska, & Rossi, 2010; Lustria, Cortese, Noar, & Glueckauf, 2009 for useful reviews). In particular, research has already shown that computer-based assessment and feedback systems can:

• *Increase accessibility and cost-effectiveness and decrease barriers to access:* Research shows that as few as one or two motivational interviewing sessions often yield greater change than no counseling at all (Miller & Rollnick, 2002), and yet these short interventions are often unavailable. Furthermore, even though follow-up sessions have been shown to increase positive outcome, they are unfortunately not always offered in medical and public health settings due to a lack of human resources. On the other hand, there is some evidence that people will accept computer-based assessment and feedback programs (Lustria et al., 2009), which can be as effective as interventions delivered by a person (Hester et al., 2005). Computer-based interventions can easily be reproduced and delivered over the Internet, on mobile devices, or in community-based waiting rooms.

• *Increase confidentiality and sensitive information divulgence:* Patients who engage in behaviors that can put them at risk (e.g., excessive drinking, unsafe sex, overeating) tend to report more information to a computer interviewer than to a human (Servan-Schreiber, 1986). The knowledge that a computer does not have an intrinsic value system to judge the patient favors the divulgence of sensitive information. Provided with sensitive information that a human would not have access to, CBIs can address issues that would otherwise be ignored.

• *Tailor information:* Tailored communication, intended to reach one specific person's needs versus generic communication (e.g., a brochure) leads to better patient outcomes and is derived from individual assessment (see for reviews Krebs et al., 2010; Noar, Benac, & Harris, 2007). Computer-based interventions can assess and create a user model to deliver tailored information and dynamically update the user profile over multiple adaptive sessions (Yasavur, Amini, & Lisetti, 2012). The user model can be produced using affective computing models that can be used to target an intervention when certain emotions are detected.

• *Diminish variability:* There is wide variability (from 25% to 100%) in different counselors' rates of improvement among their patients (Miller & Rollnick, 2002). In medical or public health settings, for example, personnel well trained in delivering motivational interventions are not always available. When trained personnel are not available, a good CBI can alleviate variability, thus providing more people with motivating experiences.

• *Avoid righting reflex:* One of the traps many counselors experience when they try to help people is the righting reflex or the tendency to set things right, employing direct advocacy for the advantages of change and thereby acting out patients' ambivalence toward changing (increasing resistance rather than simple awareness of discrepancy). This behavior is common within the traditional biomedical model of counseling, in which the counselor acts as an expert by providing advice

or extrinsic motivation. Successful counselors are those who can inhibit their righting reflex (Miller & Rollnick, 2002). Although we strive to enable computers to be more human-like, computer-based systems inherently do not have such drives to overdo helping and therefore can be at an advantage with respect to the righting reflex.

• *Demonstrate infinite patience:* Another trap for counselors is to try to move a patient toward change more quickly than he or she is ready for. Respecting the various stages of change (Prochaska & Velicer, 1997) and the patient's pace toward change can be challenging for therapists. However, computers have infinite patience.

Other Smart Health Behavior Change Interventions

Personal informatics and quantified self are yet another form of intervention, commonly associated with a new motto "Know thyself" (through behavioral data that we store on the cloud). The basic tenet of this research (Li et al., 2010) is that by reflecting on our past we can improve the way we lead our lives. For example, if we are shown evidence that we are not getting enough exercise or are eating too much, we are more likely to change our behaviors accordingly.

This has prompted the definition of ecological momentary assessment methods (EMA) that use technology to analyze and record behavior in naturalistic settings. An advantage of EMA over conventional psychological assessment includes the ability to assess the temporal relationship between variables, high ecological validity, and recording of highly detailed information on subjective experience (Barrett & Barrett, 2001). In the past, EMA-based studies have been mainly done via paper-and-pencil measures. Today, smart phones allow researchers to develop EMA tools that take advantage of the latest advances in computational recognition and sensing technologies to automatically detect critical (e.g., stressful) events that can trigger data collection (Gaggioli & Riva, 2013).

One such tool is MyExperience (http://myexperience.sourceforge.net/), a mobile platform that allows the combination of sensing and self-report to collect both quantitative and qualitative data on user experience and activity. The platform supports 50 built-in smartphone sensors, which include GPS, GSM-based motion sensors, and device usage information. Sensed events can be used to trigger custom actions such as sending SMS messages to the researcher and/or presenting in situ self-report surveys.

Morris and colleagues (Morris et al., 2010) used this platform to develop a mobile application that combines experience sampling of mood with exercises of emotional awareness and self-regulation inspired by cognitive behavioral therapy. Participants were prompted via their mobile phones to report their moods several times a day on a Mood Map and a series of single-dimension mood scales. Using the prototype, participants could also activate different mobile therapy contents as needed.

Consolvo and colleagues have developed guidelines (Consolvo, Everitt, Smith, & Landay, 2006) to encourage physical activity: give proper credit; provide history, current status, and performance measures; support social influence (i.e., use social pressures and support); and consider practical constraints. These guidelines are becoming a common principle in the design of commercial "motivational" products in sports.

One of the underlying theories for these designs is that of *cognitive dissonance* (Festinger, 1957) which describes the psychological discomfort (dissonance) felt by a person when his or her behavior is at odds with his or her attitudes or values. These researchers argue that when the person is motivated (and has the option) to eliminate this internal conflict, behavior change can be achieved.

For example, Lane and colleagues developed BeWell (https://www.bewellapp.org/) a real-time, continuous sensing application that allows monitoring of different user activities (sleep, physical activity, social interaction) and provides feedback that should promote healthier lifestyle decisions (Lane et al., 2011). A similar application, YourWellness, supports older adults in monitoring their emotional well-being, as well as other parameters of well-being they consider important to their overall health (Doyle, O'Mullane, McGee, & Knapp, 2012). It can also check if some action or behavior change is required on the part of the older person. Other mobile well-being applications help users to monitor and manage stress levels. Gaggioli and colleagues (Gaggioli, Pioggia et al., 2012) describe a mobile system designed to automatically detect psychological stress events during daily activities from heart rate and activity data collected with a wearable ECG platform coupled to a smartphone. Detected stress levels are provided to the user in the form of graphs displayed on the mobile phone application; apart from these instantaneous values, the user can check the history of stress-level variations during the monitoring period.

Conclusion

In this chapter, we reviewed how cyberpsychology and cybertherapy are combining with affective computing to offer new ways of delivering therapies for mental health, positive psychology, and behavior change toward health well-being. Sensors, multimodal user interfaces, mobile technologies, intelligent virtual characters, user modeling, and natural language processing are all smart technologies that need to be coupled with progress in psychology, healthcare, and medicine to promote health and well-being anytime, anywhere, and for everyone.

References

Andersson, G. (2009). Using the Internet to provide cognitive behaviour therapy. *Behaviour Research and Therapy, 47*(3), 175–180.

Andersson, G., Bergstrom, J., Hollandare, F., Carlbring, P., Kaldo, V., & Ekselius, L. (2005). Internet-based self-help for depression: Randomised controlled trial. [Randomized Controlled Trial Research Support, Non-U.S. Gov't]. *The British Journal of Psychiatry, 187*, 456–461. doi: 10.1192/bjp.187.5.456

Aylett, R., Vala, M., Sequeira, P., & Paiva, A. (2007). FearNot! An emergent narrative approach to virtual dramas for anti-bullying education. *Lecture Notes in Computer Science, 4871*, 202–205.

Baños, R. M., Botella, C., & Perpiña, C. (1999). Virtual reality and psychopathology. *CyberPsychology & Behavior, 2*(4), 283–292.

Barak, A. (Ed.). (2008). *Psychological aspects of cyberspace: Theory, research, applications.* Cambridge, UK: Cambridge University Press.

Barrett, L. F., & Barrett, D. J. (2001). An introduction to computerized experience sampling in psychology. *Social Science Computer Review, 19*(2), 175–185.

Bergstrom, J., Andersson, G., Ljotsson, B., Ruck, C., Andreewitch, S., Karlsson, A.,...Lindefors, N. (2010). Internet-versus group-administered cognitive behaviour therapy for panic disorder in a psychiatric setting: A randomised trial. *BMC Psychiatry, 10*, 54. doi: 10.1186/1471-244X-10-54

Bewick, B. M., Trusler, K., Barkham, M., Hill, A. J., Cahill, J., & Mulhern, B. (2008). The effectiveness of web-based interventions designed to decrease alcohol consumption–a systematic review. *Preventive Medicine, 47*(1), 17–26.

Bordnick, P. S., Traylor, A., Copp, H. L., Graap, K. M., Carter, B., Ferrer, M., & Walton, A. P. (2008). Assessing reactivity to virtual reality alcohol based cues. *Addictive Behavior, 33*(6), 743–756.

Botella, C., Riva, G., Gaggioli, A., Wiederhold, B. K., Alcaniz, M., & Banos, R. M. (2012). The present and future of positive technologies. [Research Support, Non-U.S. Gov't]. *Cyberpsychology, Behavior and Social Networking, 15*(2), 78–84. doi: 10.1089/cyber.2011.0140

Calvo, R. A., & D'Mello, S. (2012). Frontiers of affect-aware learning technologies. *IEEE Intelligent Systems.* Submitted for publication.

Calvo, R. A., & D'Mello, S. K. (Eds.). (2011). *New perspectives on affect and learning technologies.* New York: Springer.

Calvo, R. A., & Kim, S. (2012). Emotions in text: Dimensional and categorical models. *Computational Intelligence,.*

Calvo, R. A., & Peters, D. (2014). Positive computing: Technology for wellbeing and human potential. *ACM Interactions, 19*(2), 28–31.

Carlbring, P., Ekselius, L., & Andersson, G. (2003). Treatment of panic disorder via the Internet: A randomized trial of CBT vs. applied relaxation. *Journal of Behavior Therapy and Experimental Psychiatry, 34*(2), 129–140.

Castelnuovo, G., Gaggioli, A., Mantovani, F., & Riva, G. (2003). New and old tools in psychotherapy: The use of technology for the integration of traditional clinical treatments. *Psychotherapy: Theory, Research, Practice and Training, 40*(1–2), 33–44.

Christensen, H., & Hickie, I. B. (2010). E-mental health: A new era in delivery of mental health services. *The Medical journal of Australia, 192*(11 Suppl.), S2–S3.

Cipresso, P., Gaggioli, A., Serino, S., Raspelli, S., Vigna, C., Pallavicini, F., & Riva, G. (2012). Inter-Reality in the Evaluation and Treatment of Psychological Stress Disorders: The INTERSTRESS project. *Studies in Health Technology and Informatics, 181*, 8–11.

Consolvo, S., Everitt, K., Smith, I., & Landay, J. A. (2006). *Design requirements for technologies that encourage physical activity.* Paper presented at the SIGCHI conference on Human Factors in computing systems.

Csikszentmihalyi, M. (1990). *Flow: The psychology of optimal experience.* New York: HarperCollins.

D'Mello, S. K. (2013). A selective meta-analysis on the relative incidence of discrete affective states during learning with technology. *Journal of Educational Psychology. 105*(4), 1082-1099.

Doyle, J., O'Mullane, B., McGee, S., & Knapp, R. B. (2012). *YourWellness: Designing an application to support positive emotional wellbeing in older adults.* Paper presented at the Proceedings of the 26th Annual BCS Interaction Specialist Group Conference on People and Computers, Birmingham, United Kingdom.

Ellgring, H. (2008). *Nonverbal communication in depression.* Cambridge, UK.: Cambridge University Press.

Emmelkamp, P. M. (2005). Technological innovations in clinical assessment and psychotherapy. *Psychotherapy & Psychosomatics, 74*(6), 336–343.

Ferrer-Garcia, M., & Gutierrez-Maldonado, J. (2012). The use of virtual reality in the study, assessment, and treatment of body image in eating disorders and nonclinical samples: A review of the literature. *Body Image, 9*(1), 1–11.

Festinger, L. (1957). *A theory of cognitive dissonance.* Evanston, IL: Row & Peterson.

Frattaroli, J. (2006). Experimental disclosure and its moderators: A meta-analysis. *Psychological Bulletin, 132*(6), 823–865. doi: 10.1037/0033–2909.132.6.823

Gaggioli, A., Cipresso, P., Serino, S., Pioggia, G., Tartarisco, G., Baldus, G.,...Riva, G. (2012). An open source mobile platform for psychophysiological self tracking. *Studies in Health Technology and Informatics, 173*, 136–138.

Gaggioli, A., Pioggia, G., Tartarisco, G., Baldus, G., Ferro, M., Cipresso, P.,...Riva, G. (2012). A system for automatic detection of momentary stress in naturalistic settings. *Studies in Health Technology and Informatics, 181*, 182–186.

Gaggioli, A., & Riva, G. (2013). From mobile mental health to mobile wellbeing: Opportunities and challenges. *Studies in Health Technology and Informatics, 184*, 356–362.

Ghani, J. A., & Deshpande, S. P. (1994). Task characteristics and the experience of optimal flow in human-computer interaction. *The Journal of Psychology, 128*(4), 381–391.

Graesser, A. C., D'Mello, S. K., Craig, S. D., Witherspoon, A., Sullins, J., McDaniel, B., & Gholson, B. (2008). The relationship between affective states and dialog patterns during interactions with AutoTutor. *Journal of Interactive Learning Research, 19*(2), 293–312.

Grassi, A., Gaggioli, A., & Riva, G. (2009). The Green Valley: The use of mobile narratives for reducing stress in commuters. *CyberPsychology & Behavior, 12*(2), 1–7.

Grassi, A., Gaggioli, A., & Riva, G. (2011). New technologies to manage exam anxiety. [Randomized Controlled Trial]. *Studies in Health Technology and Informatics, 167*, 57–62.

Hester, R. K., Squires, D. D., & Delaney, H. D. (2005). The drinker's check-up: 12-month outcomes of a controlled clinical trial of a stand-alone software program for problem drinkers. *Journal of Substance Abuse Treatment, 28*(2), 159–169.

Hoffman, H. G. (2004). Virtual-reality therapy: Patients can get relief from pain or overcome their phobias by immersing themselves in computer-generated worlds. *Scientific American. 291* (2), 58-65.

Hordern, A., Georgiou, A., Whetton, S., & Prgomet, M. (2011). Consumer e-health: An overview of research evidence and implications for future policy. [Review]. *The HIM Journal, 40*(2), 6–14.

Hussain, M. S., AlZoubi, O., Calvo, R. A., & D'Mello, S. K. (2011). *Affect detection from multichannel physiology during learning sessions with AutoTutor.* Paper presented at the 15th International Conference on Artificial Intelligence in Education, Auckland, New Zealand.

Istepanian, R., Jovanov, E., & Zhang, Y. T. (2004). Introduction to the special section on M-Health: Beyond seamless mobility and global wireless health-care connectivity. [Editorial]. *IEEE transactions on information technology in biomedicine, 8*(4), 405–414.

Kadda, A. (2010). Social utility of personalised e-health services: The study of home-based healthcare. [Review]. *International Journal of Electronic Healthcare, 5*(4), 403–413.

Kauer, S. D., Reid, S. C., Crooke, A. H., Khor, A., Hearps, S. J., Jorm, A. F.,...Patton, G. (2012). Self-monitoring using mobile phones in the early stages of adolescent depression: Randomized controlled trial. [Research Support, Non-U.S. Gov't]. *Journal of Medical Internet Research, 14*(3), e67. doi: 10.2196/jmir.1858

Keyes, C. L. M., & Lopez, S. J. (2002). Toward a science of mental health: Positive directions in diagnosis and interventions. In C. R. Snyder & S. J. Lopez (Eds.), *Handbook of positive psychology* (pp. 45–59). New York: Oxford University Press.

Kimhy, D., Delespaul, P., Ahn, H., Cai, S., Shikhman, M., Lieberman, J. A.,...Sloan, R. P. (2010). Concurrent measurement of "real-world" stress and arousal in individuals with psychosis: Assessing the feasibility and validity of a novel methodology. *Schizophrenia bulletin, 36*(6), 1131–1139. doi: 10.1093/schbul/sbp028

King, L. A. (2001). The health benefits of writing about life goals. *Personality and Social Psychology Bulletin, 27*(798–807).

King, L. A., & Miner, K. N. (2000). Writing about the perceived benefits of traumatic events: Implications for physical health. *Personality and Social Psychology Bulletin, 26*, 220–230.

Krebs, P., Prochaska, J. O., & Rossi, J. S. (2010). A meta-analysis of computer-tailored interventions for health behavior change. *Preventive medicine, 51*(3–4), 214–221.

Lane, N. D., Choudhury, T., Campbell, A., Mohammod, M., Lin, M., Yang, X.,...Berke, E. (2011). *BeWell: A smartphone application to monitor, model and promote wellbeing.* Paper presented at the Pervasive Health *11*, Dublin, Ireland.

Li, I., Forlizzi, J., & Dey, A. (2010). *Know thyself: Monitoring and reflecting on facets of one's life.* Paper presented at the CHI 2010: 28th International conference on Human Factors in Computing Systems, Atlanta, GA.

Luneski, A., Konstantinidis, E., & Bamidis, P. D. (2010). Affective medicine. A review of affective computing efforts in medical informatics. [Review]. *Methods of Information in Medicine, 49*(3), 207–218. doi: 10.3414/ME0617

Lustria, M. L., Cortese, J., Noar, S. M., & Glueckauf, R. L. (2009). Computer-tailored health interventions delivered over the Web: Review and analysis of key components. *Patient Education and Counseling, 74*(2), 156–173,.

Mair, F., & Whitten, P. (2000). Systematic review of studies of patient satisfaction with telemedicine. *British Medical Journal, 320*(7248), 1517–1520.

Manhal-Baugus, M. (2001). E-therapy: Practical, ethical, and legal issues. *Cyberpsychology & Behavior: The Impact of the Internet, Multimedia and Virtual Reality on Behavior and Society, 4*(5), 551–563.

McNulty, J. K., & Fincham, F. D. (2012). Beyond positive psychology? Toward a contextual view of psychological processes and well-being. *American Psychologist, 67*(2), 101–110.

Mcintyre, G., Goecke, R. Hyett, M., Green, M., & Breakspear, M. (2009). An approach for automatically measuring facial activity in depressed subjects. In *Affective computing and intelligent interaction (ACII)* (pp. 1–8). IEEE.

Miller, W. R., & Rollnick, S. (1991). *Motivational interviewing: Preparing people to change addictive behavior.* New York: Guilford Press.

Morris, M. E. (2005). Social networks as health feedback displays. *IEEE Internet Computing, 9*, 29–37.

Morris, M. E., Kathawala, Q., Leen, T. K., Gorenstein, E. E., Guilak, F., Labhard, M., & Deleeuw, W. (2010). Mobile therapy: Case study evaluations of a cell phone application for emotional self-awareness. *Journal of Medical Internet Research, 12*(2), e10. doi: 10.2196/jmir.1371

Mosso, J. L., Gorini, A., De La Cerda, G., Obrador, T., Almazan, A., Mosso, D., … Riva, G. (2009). Virtual reality on mobile phones to reduce anxiety in outpatient surgery. [Randomized Controlled Trial]. *Studies in Health Technology and Informatics, 142*, 195–200.

Noar, S., Benac, C., & Harris, M. (2007). Does tailoring matter? Meta-analytic review of tailored print health behavior change interventions. *Psychological bulletin, 133*(4), 673.

Norman, D. A. (2004). *Emotional design: Why we love (or hate) everyday things.* New York: Basic Books.

Optale, G. (2003). Male sexual dysfunctions and multimedia immersion therapy. *CyberPsychology & Behavior, 6*(3), 289–294.

Parsons, T. D., & Rizzo, A. A. (2008). Affective outcomes of virtual reality exposure therapy for anxiety and specific phobias: A meta-analysis. *Journal of Behavior Therapy and Experimental Psychiatry, 39*(3), 250–261.

Pavel, M. (2012). Smart health and well-being. *NSF 12–512 CISE IIS Webinar,* January 11.

Pennebaker, J. W. (1997). *Opening up: The healing power of expressing emotions.* New York: Guilford Press.

Preziosa, A., Grassi, A., Gaggioli, A., & Riva, G. (2009). Therapeutic applications of the mobile phone. *British Journal of Guidance & Counselling, 37*(3), 313–325. doi: 10.1080/03069880902957031

Preziosa, A., Villani, D., Grassi, A., & Riva, G. (2006). Managing exam stress: The use of mobile phones for enhancing emotion regulation. *Cyberpsychology & Behavior, 9*(6), 710–711.

Prochaska, J. O., & Velicer, W. F. (1997). The transtheoretical model of health behavior change. *American Journal of Health Promotion, 12*(1), 38–48.

Reger, G. M., & Gahm, G. A. (2008). Virtual reality exposure therapy for active duty soldiers. *Journal of Clinical Psychology, 64*(8), 940–946.

Riva, G. (2005). Virtual reality in psychotherapy: Review. *CyberPsychology & Behavior, 8*(3), 220–230; discussion 231–240.

Riva, G. (2009). Virtual reality: An experiential tool for clinical psychology. *British Journal of Guidance & Counselling, 37*(3), 337–345. doi: 10.1080/03069880902957056

Riva, G. (2012a). Personal experience in positive psychology may offer a new focus for a growing discipline. *American Psychologist, 67*(7), 574–575.

Riva, G. (2012b). What is positive technology and its impact on cyberpsychology. *Studies in Health Technology and Informatics, 181*, 37–41.

Riva, G., Bacchetta, M., Cesa, G., Conti, S., Castelnuovo, G., Mantovani, F., & Molinari, E. (2006). Is severe obesity a form of addiction? Rationale, clinical approach, and controlled clinical trial. *CyberPsychology and Behavior, 9*(4), 457–479.

Riva, G., Banos, R. M., Botella, C., Wiederhold, B. K., & Gaggioli, A. (2012). Positive technology: Using interactive technologies to promote positive functioning. *Cyberpsychology, behavior and social networking, 15*(2), 69–77. doi: 10.1089/cyber.2011.0139

Riva, G., & Davide, F. (Eds.). (2001). *Communications through virtual technologies: Identity, community and technology in the communication age.* Amsterdam: Ios Press. Retrieved from http://www.emergingcommunication.com/volume1.html

Riva, G., Grassi, A., Villani, D., Gaggioli, A., & Preziosa, A. (2007). Managing exam stress using UMTS phones: The advantage of portable audio/video support. *Studies in Health Technology and Informatics, 125*, 406–408.

Riva, G., & Mantovani, F. (2012). Being there: Understanding the feeling of presence in a synthetic environment and its potential for clinical change. In C. Eichenberg (Ed.), *Virtual reality in psychological, medical and pedagogical applications* (pp. 3–34). New York: InTech. Retrieved from http://www.intechopen.com/books/virtual-reality-in-psychological-medical-and-pedagogical-applications/being-there-understanding-the-feeling-of-presence-in-a-synthetic-environment-and-its-potential-for-c).

Riva, G., Mantovani, F., Capideville, C. S., Preziosa, A., Morganti, F., Villani, D., … Alcaniz, M. (2007). Affective interactions using virtual reality: The link between presence and emotions. *Cyberpsychology and Behavior, 10*(1), 45–56.

Riva, G., Manzoni, M., Villani, D., Gaggioli, A., & Molinari, E. (2008). Why you really eat? Virtual reality in the treatment of obese emotional eaters. *Studies in Health Technology and Informatics, 132*, 417–419.

Riva, G., Preziosa, A., Grassi, A., & Villani, D. (2006). Stress management using UMTS cellular phones: A controlled trial. *Studies in Health Technology and Informatics, 119*, 461–463.

Rogers, Y. (2006). Moving on from Weiser's vision of calm computing: Engaging UbiComp experiences. In P. Dourish & A. Friday (Eds.), *Ubicomp 2006 proceedings* (pp. 404–421). New York: Springer-Verlag.

Russell, J. A. (2003). Core affect and the psychological construction of emotion. *Psychological Review, 110*(1), 145–172.

Russell, J. A. (2005). Emotion in human consciousness is built on core affect. *Journal of Consciousness Studies, 12*, 26–42.

Seligman, M. E. P. (2002). Authentic happiness: Using the new positive psychology to realize your potential for lasting fulfillment. New York: Free Press.

Seligman, M. E. P., & Csikszentmihalyi, M. (2000). Positive psychology. *American Psychologist, 55*, 5–14.

Sengers, P. (2011). What I learned on change islands: Reflections on IT and pace of life. *ACM Interactions, 18*(2), 40–48.

Servan-Schreiber, D. (1986). Artificial intelligence and psychiatry. *Journal of Nervous and Mental Disease, 174*, 191–202.

Sternberg, R. (2001). Why schools should teach for wisdom: The balance theory of wisdom in educational settings. *Educational Psychologist, 36*(4), 227–245.

Villani, D., Grassi, A., Cognetta, C., Cipresso, P., Toniolo, D., & Riva, G. (2012). The effects of a mobile stress management protocol on nurses working with cancer patients: A preliminary controlled study. *Studies in Health Technology and Informatics, 173*, 524–528.

Villani, D., Grassi, A., Cognetta, C., Toniolo, D., Cipresso, P., & Riva, G. (2013). Self-help stress management training through mobile phones: An experience with oncology nurses. *Psychological Services, 10*(3):315-322.

Villani, D., Lucchetta, M., Preziosa, A., & Riva, G. (2009). The role of affective media features on the affective response: A virtual reality study. *e-Minds: International Journal on Human Computer Interaction, 1*(5), 35–55.

Vincelli, F., Molinari, E., & Riva, G. (2001). Virtual reality as clinical tool: Immersion and three-dimensionality in the relationship between patient and therapist. *Studies in Health Technology and Informatics, 81*, 551–553.

Wiederhold, B. K., & Riva, G. (2012). Positive technology supports shift to preventive, integrative health. *Cyberpsychology, Behavior and Social Networking, 15*(2), 67–68. doi: 10.1089/cyber.2011.1533

Wiederhold, B. K., & Rizzo, A. (2005). Virtual reality and applied psychophysiology. *Applied Psychophysiology and Biofeedback, 30*(3), 183–185.

Yang, S., & Bhanu, B. (2012). Understanding discrete facial expressions in video using an emotion avatar image. *IEEE Transactions on Systems, Man, and Cybernetics, Part B: Cybernetics.* doi: 10.1109/TSMCB.2012.2192269

Yasavur, U., Amini, R., & Lisetti, C. (2012). User modeling for pervasive alcohol intervention systems. In *Proceedings of the 6th ACM Conference on Recommender Systems (RecSys'12) Workshop on Recommendation Technologies for Lifestyle Change.*

WHO. (2013). Obesity and overweight - Fact sheet N°311. Geneva: World Health Organization.

GLOSSARY

Action units (AUs)—visible results from the contraction or relaxation of one or more muscles, used also to describe higher-level concepts in the Facial Action Coding System (Ekman et al., 2002; Petta et al., 2011). (Cited by Ochs, Niewiadomski, & Pelachaud—Chapter 18)

Active learning— a form of data preselection by the machine for human labeling to reduce manual labeling efforts by "cherry picking." (Schuller—Chapter 23)

Affect detector—a model that can infer student affect in real time. (Baker & Ocumpaugh—Chapter 16)

Affect elicitation—methods used to evoke (or induce) affective responses in individuals. These methods generally involve presenting a stimulus or immersing the subject in a situation to evoke a response from one or more emotion response systems. The nature of the stimulus varies and could include the presentation of images, film, or music; facial expressions or postures; and social or dyadic interactions, among others. (Kory & D'Mello—Chapter 27)

Affect-aware learning technology—an intelligent learning technology that considers a learner's affective and cognitive states in its pedagogical decision making. (D'Mello & Graesser—Chapter 31)

Affective AutoTutor—a natural language intelligent tutoring system that automatically senses and responds to a learner's confusion, boredom, and frustration by monitoring facial features, body movements, and conversational cues. (D'Mello & Graesser—Chapter 31)

Affective body expressions—static postures and/or body movements. In the context of their chapter, the authors specifically refer to postures and motions performed or recognized in the context of an affective state or affective dimension. Body expressions may involve the entire body or only part of it, such as affective gait or affective actions such as knocking. (Bianchi-Berthouze & Kleinsmith—Chapter 11)

Affective brain-computer interfaces (aBCIs)—devices that allow the detection of the affective state of their users based on the neurophysiological activity associated with such states. (Mühl, Heylen & Nijholt—Chapter 15)

Affective dimensions—dimensions focused on how the world is experienced. Dimensional theorists consider affective states as existing in a continuous, multidimensional space, with the dimensions being bipolar and independent. The primary affective dimensions investigated are valence (levels ranging from pleasure to displeasure), arousal (levels of alertness ranging from calm to excited) dominance/potency (levels of control over an event) (Mehrabian, 1996), and action tendency (the action that one is ready to make in response to the event) (Frijda, 1986). (Cited by Bianchi-Berthouze & Kleinsmith—Chapter 11)

Agent—a digital representation in a virtual environment controlled by computer algorithms. (Bailey & Bailenson—Chapter 37)

Appraisal—process whereby people perceive or interpret the evaluative significance of an emotional object or event, typically as an antecedent to reacting emotionally. (Parkinson—Chapter 6)

Approach and withdrawal motivations—fundamental motivational states on which emotional reactions are based. The approach system controls appetitive and other goal directed behaviors, while the withdrawal system facilitates behavior that removes the individual from sources of aversive stimulation. The left prefrontal cortex plays a key role in approach motivation (including positive affect, social engagement, and anger) while the right prefrontal cortex (e.g., fear) plays a key role in withdrawal. (Kemp, Krygier, & Harmon-Jones—Chapter 4)

Autism spectrum disorder (ASD)—a pervasive developmental disorder characterized by disordered social communication (the absence or miscoordination of social gazes, facial expressions, gestures, and vocalizations) and clinically salient repetitive behaviors (or unusual interests) that are present by three years of age. (Messinger et al.—Chapter 39)

Automated measurement—the use of machine learning to map image data to behavioral codes (annotations). (Messinger et al.—Chapter 39)

Autonomous—functioning independently without explicit control from the outside. (Broek, Janssen, & Westerink—Chapter 35)

Avatar—a digital representation in a virtual environment controlled by human actions. (Bailey & Bailenson—Chapter 37)

Backward masking—a method used to block conscious awareness of a visual stimulus. The target stimulus is shown to an individual very briefly (e.g., 15 to 60 milliseconds), followed immediately by a "mask" stimulus shown for a longer time (e.g., 500 milliseconds). Individuals report being consciously aware of only the mask. (Kory & D'Mello—Chapter 27)

Behavior manipulation—a method in which individuals are instructed to adopt particular behaviors—such as body postures or facial expressions—in order to induce particular affective states. (Kory & D'Mello—Chapter 27)

Behavior Markup Language—representation language comprising all those representations that are necessary for the realization of behavior. It includes directives for the realization of textual and prosodic information, facial display, gestures and postures, eye gaze, and, very importantly, directives for the temporal synchronization of behaviors (Petta et al., 2011). (Cited by Ochs, Niewiadomski, & Pelachaud——Chapter 18)

Biofeedback—the use of measurements of physiological functions in order to control them. (Broek, Janssen, & Westerink—Chapter 35)

Brain-computer interfaces (BCIs)—mechanisms that allow for the control of devices and applications based on the neurophysiological activity of a user, thereby bypassing muscular pathways. (Mühl, Heylen, & Nijholt—Chapter 15)

Closed-loop model—control systems with an active feedback loop. (Broek, Janssen, & Westerink—Chapter 35)

Collaborative virtual environment (CVE)—a virtual environment that supports multiple users from remote locations in a common virtual space. (Bailey & Bailenson—Chapter 37)

Confusion Tutor—a learning environment that aims to promote deeper comprehension by strategically induces confusion in the minds of learners. (D'Mello & Graesser—Chapter 31)

Contextual features—features hypothesized or discovered to play key roles of relevance in interpreting unfolding events and states beyond an isolated occurrence, taking into account the context of interaction (e.g., task, user preferences, presence of other people, behavior of the interactants, etc.). The consideration of context is necessary in cases where the meaning of a feature of interest cannot be determined or disambiguated in isolation (i.e., without reference to other features). (Castellano, Gunes, Peters, & Schuller—Chapter 17)

Crystal Island—a learning technology that embeds the learning content in a narrative-centered game supporting narrativity, realism, and immersion. (D'Mello & Graesser—Chapter 31)

Cultural dichotomies—Scales used to characterize different cultures by their position between two poles. Examples of culture dichotomies include power distance, identity, gender, uncertainty avoidance, long-term orientation, and context. (Andre—Chapter 22)

Cyberpsychology—a new branch of psychology that aims at the understanding, forecasting, and induction of the different processes of change related to the use of new technologies. (Riva, Calvo, & Lisetti—Chapter 41)

Cybertherapy—the branch of cyberpsychology that tries to understand how technologies can be used to induce clinical change. (Riva, Calvo, & Lisetti—Chapter 41)

Discrete emotions— instances of unique and separate states (e.g., anger or happiness). Many discrete emotion theorists also consider a number of emotions as *basic* or *primary*, yet there is no consensus on either the number of categories or which emotions are considered basic (Ortony & Turner, 1990). (Cited by Bianchi-Berthouze & Kleinsmith—Chapter 11)

Display rule—cultural norm about when, where, and with whom it is appropriate to express or not express a particular emotion on the face. (Parkinson—Chapter 6)

Dyadic interaction—a social interaction specifically between two individuals (see *Social Interaction*). One affect elicitation method focuses on bringing pairs of individuals together to engage in an unrehearsed, minimally structured conversation in order to evoke affective states in a more naturalistic context. (Kory & D'Mello—Chapter 27)

Educational data mining—the research area that uses data mining methods to model and understand learners and learning. Closely related to learning analytics. (Baker & Ocumpaugh——Chapter 16)

Electroencephalography (EEG)—a portable neuroimaging method for the temporally high-resolution recording of variations in electrophysiological brain activity from the scalp. (Mühl, Heylen, & Nijholt—Chapter 15)

Embodied conversational agent (ECA)—a humanlike conversational character able to engage with the user in multimodal communication. The usual modalities include speech, facial expression, eye gaze, head movement, body posture, and hand-arm gesture (Petta et al., 2011). (Cited by Ochs, Niewiadomski, & Pelachaud—Chapter 18) (Messinger et al.—Chapter 39)

Emotion—a term used colloquially to reflect a wide range of affective responses (feelings, mood, disposition, etc.). In emotion theory, emotions are generally perceived as short-term affective responses and often perceived as both "basic" versus "social/moral/higher-order" emotions, where the first category is more often tied to primary physiological responses. (Healey—Chapter 14).

Often defined also as a multicomponent response to a significant stimulus characterized by brain and bodily arousal and a subjective feeling state that elicits a tendency toward motivated action. Note, however, that there may be instances of emotion in which significant stimuli (e.g., emotions without obvious causes), subjective feeling states (e.g., unconscious emotions), and motivated action (e.g., sadness) are not necessary. (Kemp, Krygier, & Harmon-Jones—Chapter 4)

Emotion contagion—process whereby an individual (automatically) "catches" the emotional state of another individual, often thought to be mediated by mimicry of expressive movements or generation of complementary motor codes. (Parkinson—Chapter 6)

Emotion object—what an emotion is about. The (intentional) "object" may be an imagined or anticipated event rather than a physical thing. (Parkinson—Chapter 6)

Emotion regulation—the process of actively modifying the causes, content, or consequences of emotion. (Parkinson—Chapter 6)

Emotion theories—while there are many different theories of emotion, a significant proportion of affective computing research focuses on discrete emotions and/or affective dimensions. (Bianchi-Berthouze and Kleinsmith—Chapter 11)

Emotional film clips—short movie segments, usually including both images and sound, that have been selected and evaluated for their potential to evoke affective states in the viewer. (Kory and D'Mello—Chapter 27)

Emotional images—digital images or photographs that have been carefully selected and evaluated for their potential to evoke affective states in the viewer. (Kory & D'Mello—Chapter 27)

Emotional music—a recorded musical piece that has been selected and evaluated for its ability to evoke affective states in the listener. (Kory & D'Mello—Chapter 27)

Empathy—the feeling of being affected by other people's emotions because you care about those people or see things from their perspective. (Parkinson—Chapter 6)

Evaluator—a term used synonymously with *annotator, labeler*, and *rater* in this section for the person who attaches labels to affective data. (Schuller—Chapter 23)

Event-related potentials (ERPs)—a stereotyped electrophysiological response to a specific stimulus or event that is estimated by averaging the recorded EEG traces recorded immediately after several occurrences of the same event. (Mühl, Heylen, & Nijholt—Chapter 15)

Facial action coding system—a categorization system for facial behaviors based on the underlying musculature. Facial behaviors are coded in terms of action units involved in a change in appearance as well as duration, intensity, and asymmetry (Petta et al., 2011). (Cited by Ochs, Niewiadomski, & Pelachaud—Chapter 18)

Feature representation and selection—descriptions of the way features are represented to a machine-learning algorithm. Usually, this is done with a vector or time series of vectors. The selection of features deals with reaching a more compact representation—usually by excluding features of lower relevance. This is commonly done either by a suited measure such as correlation or information gain or with the classifier in the loop. In addition, a search function that leads to a local optimum rather than a global one is needed mainly for efficiency reasons. (Castellano, Gunes, Peters, & Schuller—Chapter 17)

Features—attributes of a data record used as predictors in a data mining analysis. (Baker & Ocumpaugh—Chapter 16)

Functional magnetic resonance imaging (fMRI)—a neuroimaging method for the spatial high-resolution recording of brain activity by detecting associated changes in blood flow. (Mühl, Heylen, & Nijholt—Chapter 15)

Functional near-infrared spectroscopy (fNIRS)—a portable neuroimaging method for the recording of brain activity by detecting associated changes in blood flow via magnetic impulses. (Mühl, Heylen, & Nijholt—Chapter 15)

Galvanic skin response—also commonly referred to as electrodermal activity (EDR), or skin conductance, this is a commonly used physiological metric that determines a person's sweat levels by measuring the conductance of the skin. The skin is normally an insulator, but sweat is ionic and conducts electricity, so that when a person starts sweating, skin conductivity increases. This phenomenon is most often measured by placing two electrodes on two adjacent fingers and measuring the voltage in response to a small injection current that runs between the two electrodes across the skin of the palm of the hand, where many of the most emotionally reactive sweat glands are found. (Healey—Chapter 14)

GazeTutor—a learning environment that senses and responds to patterns of disengagement by monitoring eye gaze. (D'Mello & Graesser—Chapter 31)

Gold standard—represents the compromise made to get as close as possible to the ground truth if the phenomenon cannot be easily measured. For affective data, this may be difficult to reach, and several evaluators (see below) are often used to get closer to the ground truth. (Schuller—Chapter 23)

Ground truth—the affective label assigned to an affective expression. This ground truth affective state or dimension level may be predetermined by the researcher or assigned by expert or nonexpert observers (i.e., people who judge the affective state or level of affective dimension by viewing or listening to the affective expression). (Bianchi-Berthouze & Kleinsmith—Chapter 11)

Heart rate variability—a term used to describe how successive heart beats differ from one another (e.g., how the lengths of the intervals between successive heart beats vary). The term *heart rate variability* is used to describe a number of metrics, some of which are calculated in the time domain and others in the frequency domain. (Healey—Chapter 14)

High-risk sibling—the younger brother or sister of a child with an autism spectrum disorder (ASD). Typically studied before three years of age, these siblings are themselves at risk both for an ASD and ASD-related symptoms that do not meet criteria for an ASD diagnosis. (Messinger et al.—Chapter 39)

Immersive virtual environment technology (IVET)—technology that immerses users in a sensory rich virtual environment (e.g., onethat provides visual, haptic, and olfactory feedback). (Bailey & Bailenson—Chapter 37)

Infant-parent interaction—the exchange of communicative signals between infants (typically twelve months of age and under) and parents in whom the behavior of infant

or parent (or both) influences the behavior of the other partner; also referred to as emotional communication. (Messinger et al.—Chapter 39)

Intelligent Tutoring System—An online learning system that provides interactive activities and adapts in real time to differences in student learning, behavior, affect, or other individual differences. (Baker & Ocumpaugh—Chapter 16)

Interaction log—a detailed historical record of behavior enacted within a computerized learning system by one or more students. It typically includes data on the student actions, the system responses, and any semantic interpretation of student behavior that is feasible at run time. By definition, interaction logs do not include data from behavioral and physiological sensors. (Baker & Ocumpaugh—Chapter 16)

Interpersonal emotion transfer—phenomenon of one person's emotion inducing a corresponding emotion in someone else (operating by a range of processes). (Parkinson—Chapter 6)

Lexicon—a list of correspondences between signals and meanings. (Poggi, Pelachaud, & de Rosis, 2000). (Cited by Ochs, Niewiadomski, & Pelachaud—Chapter 18)

Magnetoencephalography (MEG)—a neuroimaging method for the temporally high-resolved recording of variations in electric brain activity by detecting associated changes in the magnetic fields. (Mühl, Heylen & Nijholt—Chapter 15)

Mimicry—making movements whose characteristics correspond to the characteristics of observed movements being made by other people. (Parkinson—Chapter 6)

Mirror neuron—nerve cell (or group of cells) that fires both when a movement is observed in someone else and when the same movement is enacted by self. (Parkinson—Chapter 6)

Modality fusion—An approach to combine data at different levels, from multiple homogenous or heterogeneous streams, to predict the final label or class. (Castellano, Gunes, Peters, & Schuller—Chapter 17)

Modeling—quantitative characterization of relationships between the components of complex expressive or communicative systems. (Messinger et al.—Chapter 39)

Mood—a relatively long-lasting emotional state. (Broek, Janssen, & Westerink—Chapter 35)

Multimodal—more than a single modality is present. In affective databases, typically such modalities include audio, video, physiological, and textual data. Different views exist on what is multimodal, or rather multi*stream*: For example, speech contains acoustic and usually verbal content as well. Strictly speaking, the modality is speech, but often the combination of these two streams—acoustic and textual content—is already considered multimodal. (Schuller—Chapter 23)

Multimodal affect recognition—a process that performs automatic affect recognition by using several input modalities, such as behavioral (e.g., face, gesture, posture, speech prosody, etc.,), physiological (e.g., electrodermal activity, etc.), and contextual (e.g., task, user preferences, etc.) data. (Castellano, Gunes, Peters, & Schuller—Chapter 17)

Music—(the product of) an art form deploying sound, silence, rhythm, melody, etc. (Broek, Janssen, & Westerink—Chapter 35)

Natural kinds—fundamental processes in the brain that exists across species and human cultures; a phenomenon that is discovered, not created, by the human mind. In this regard the basic emotions are characterized as "natural kinds," hardwired into the brain and associated with distinctive patterns of neural activation. Note that different conceptualizations of the basic emotions have been proposed (e.g., Ekman versus Panksepp). (Kemp, Krygier, & Harmon-Jones—Chapter 4)

Nonverbal behavior— behavior corresponding to "facial expressions, body language, social touching, vocal acoustics, and interpersonal distance" (Ambady & Weisbuch, 2010). Nonverbal behavior may convey several kinds of information—for instance, on one's emotions or attitude. *Nonverbal communication* "refers to the sending or the receiving of thoughts and feeling via nonverbal behavior" (Ambady & Weisbuch, 2010). (Cited by Ochs, Niewiadomski, & Pelachaud—Chapter 18)

Overfitting—a model is said to be overfitted when it so closely matches the data it was trained on that it cannot generalize to new data, such as data from new students or different populations. Overfitting typically occurs as a result of using an overly flexible or complex model for the data set size and the actual strength of the relationship(s) being modeled. An assessment of model goodness that is less vulnerable to overfit can be obtained through the use of appropriate cross-validation, with student-level cross-validation considered particularly useful in educational domains. (Baker & Ocumpaugh—Chapter 16)

Personalization—the process of accommodating the differences between individuals. (Broek, Janssen, & Westerink—Chapter 35)

Physical presence—the perceptual experience that measures how real the virtual environment and the objects within it feel. (Bailey & Bailenson—Chapter 37)

Physiological—in general, physiology is a branch of biology that deals with the functions of activities of life. With respect to affective computing, physiological affect in general refers to responses that come from the body, more especially those associated with the autonomic nervous systems. Although brain activity is in essence physiological, the field of neurophysiology provides a more specific view of brain function and the term *physiological* is usually used to refer to other types of bodily responses. (Healey—Chapter 14)

Positive computing—the design and development of technology to support well-being and human potential (Riva, Calvo, & Lisetti—Chapter 41)

Positive technology—the branch of cyberpsychology that uses technology to manipulate and enhance the features of our personal experience for increasing wellness and generating strength and resilience in individuals, organizations, and society. (Riva, Calvo, & Lisetti—Chapter 41)

Positron emission tomography (PET)—a neuroimaging method for the spatial high-resolution recording of brain activity by detecting associated changes in blood flow via radioactive tracers. (Mühl, Heylen, & Nijholt—Chapter 15)

Presence—the subjective psychological experience of being in a virtual environment. (Bailey & Bailenson—Chapter 37)

Proactive systems—an affect-aware learning technology that aims to induce or impede certain affective states. (D'Mello, Graesser—Chapter 31)

Psychological constructionism—this view considers emotions as a construct resulting from more basic building blocks like core dimensions like approach-withdrawal or valence-arousal. The debate over whether emotions are "natural kinds" versus a "psychological construction" has been likened to the Hundred Years' War between England and France (Lindquist, Siegel, Quigley, & Barrett, 2013). (Cited by Kemp, Krygier, & Harmon-Jones—Chapter 4)

Psychophysiology—the field that studies the impact of psychological states on the physiological system and vice versa. (Broek, Janssen, & Westerink—Chapter 35)

Reactive systems—an affect-aware learning technology that senses and responds to affective states. (D'Mello & Graesser—Chapter 31)

Reappraisal—the process whereby the perceived emotional meaning of an event is modified. May be actively used as a means of emotion regulation. (Parkinson—Chapter 6)

Resource—a term used here as a synonym for *corpus* or *database*. (Schuller—Chapter 23)

Robot—a hardware-based agent with sufficient autonomy to interact with children—for example, to assist with emotion or other learning tasks. (Messinger et al.—Chapter 39)

Self presence—the extent to which a person identifies with how he or she is digitally represented in the virtual environment or the level in which the virtual self is experienced as the actual self. (Bailey & Bailenson—Chapter 37)

Sensing—using a physical instrument to detect a physical stimulus. In affective computing, sensing is used to capture information that can be used by a computer to incorporate into algorithms, for example to sense skin conductance, a GSR sensor is used and to sense heart rate a heart rate sensor (such a an electrocardiogram –ECG) is used. (Healey—Chapter 14)

Signals— a time varying response that communicates information about phenomena. In the context of physiological affective computing, a signal is usually a two-dimensional time-voltage signal, measured from some part of the body. For example, a skin conductance signal conveys information about how a person's sweat level changes over time and a heart rate signal conveys information about how a person's heart rate changes over time. (Healey—Chapter 14)

Smart health—a new branch of medicine that uses the latest technological advances (e.g., sensors and sensors networks, actuators, robots and virtual assistants) to build intelligent care (e.g., smart homes for independent living, wearable prosthetics, lifestyle modification coaching). (Riva, Calvo, & Lisetti—Chapter 41)

Social appraisal—process whereby another person's perceived emotion, expression, or behavior modifies one's appraisal of an emotion object. (Parkinson—Chapter 6)

Social attitudes—positive or negative evaluation of a person or a group of people. Social attitudes include cognitive elements like beliefs, opinions, and social emotions. (Pantic & Vinciarelli—Chapter 7)

Social emotions—emotions such as admiration, envy, and compassion that can be felt only toward another person (Pantic & Vinciarelli—Chapter 7)

Social evaluations—social evaluations relate to assessing whether and how much the characteristics of a person comply with our standards of beauty, intelligence, strength, justice, altruism, etc. (Pantic & Vinciarelli—Chapter 7)

Social interaction—a relationship between two or more individuals, fleeting or enduring, in which an individual's actions and behavior are responsive to the actions and behavior of the other or others. In one affect elicitation method, researchers try to create realistic social interaction scenarios that might evoke emotions in a more naturalistic context. (Kory & D'Mello—Chapter 27)

Social interactions are events in which actually or virtually present agents exchange an array of *social actions* (i.e., communicative and informative signals performed by one agent in relation to one or more other agents). (Pantic & Vinciarelli—Chapter 7)

Social presence—the psychological state that measures the extent that other virtual social actors are experienced as actual social actors. (Bailey & Bailenson—Chapter 37)

Social relations—a social relation is a relation between two (or more) persons in which these persons have related goals. (Pantic & Vinciarelli—Chapter 7)

Social signals—communicative or informative signals which provide information about social facts (social interactions, social emotions, social evaluations, social attitudes and social relations) (Pantic & Vinciarelli—Chapter 7)

Stereotypical expression—according to many theorists, there are universal facial expression patterns linked to the six basic emotions (joy, disgust, anger, surprise, sadness, and fear) as defined by Paul Ekman (Ekman and Friesen, 1975). (Cited by Ochs, Niewiadomski, & Pelachaud—Chapter 18)

Suppression—consequence-focused emotion regulation that reduces visible expression. (Parkinson—Chapter 6)

Transformed social interaction (TSI)—decoupling of an avatar's appearance or behavior from the actual person through the use of computer algorithms. (Bailey & Bailenson—Chapter 37)

UNC-ITSpoke—a speech-enabled intelligent tutoring system that automatically senses and responds to a learner's uncertainty and response accuracy. (D'Mello & Graesser—Chapter 31)

Validation—confirming that a product or service meets specifications. (Broek, Janssen, & Westerink—Chapter 35)

Weakly supervised learning—subsumes different types of machine learning where full supervision is not given. Usually, this means that data without labels are used by the machine to autonomously adapt or (even entirely) train itself by semisupervised or unsupervised learning. (Schuller—Chapter 23)

INDEX

Note: Figures are indicated by an f; tables by a t, and footnotes by an n.

affect classification tools, 350, 353

affect classifiers, 373, 374

affect-consequent model, 62

affect correlates, 227

affect-derivation model, 62

affect descriptors, 363

affect detection
  algorithms, 6
  alternate approach, 233
  as an extremely difficult problem, 429
  facial expression-based, 3
  fully automated using predictive models, 423
  physiologically based, 4
  Section 2 focusing on, 2
  system, robots requiring, 296
  from text, 196–201
  from verbal or nonverbal expressions, 549

affect-detection and affect-response strategies, ideal, 423

affect detectors, 234, 242, 371, 559

affect dimensions, representing social emotions, 88

affect elicitation, 371–380, 559

affect/emotion modeling, developing an overall theory for, 99

affect expression, 353–356
  tools, 350, 356t

affect generation, 2, 4–5

affect incidence, across studies, 423

affect induction
  approaches, 227
  limitations of, 224
  procedures, 224
  protocols, 227, 228

affect intelligence, building sets of algorithms, 365

affect intensities, situation-appropriate, 483, 484f

affect-intensity model, 62

affective agents, modeling of realistic, 75

affective arousal, 421

Affective AutoTutor, 423–425, 424f, 526, 552, 559

affective biases, modeling on cognition, 100

affective biofeedback systems, 7

affective body expressions, 559
  automatic recognition of, 151–165
  identifying clusters of, 160
  perception of, 153–156

affective brain-computer interfaces (aBCIs), 217, 222–227, 559
  approaches, 224
  different approaches, 225–227
  main challenges for reliable, 229
  motivation behind, 217–218
  multitude of possible applications for, 227
  neurotechnological challenges, 228–229
  parts of, 222–225

research, 222
studies, 223
systems, 224

affective communication, 537

affective computations, 54

affective computing (AC)
  applications, 6–8, 359, 384
  assisting cyberpsychology, 548
  biofeedback in the domain of, 472
  child development and, 516
  community, 2
  contributing to systems at all levels of positive technology, 551
  defined, 13
  developing systems recognizing and responding to the affective states of the user, 371
  development of autism spectrum disorders and, 516–517
  differences in methodologies adopted, 364–366
  disparate terminology used in, 8
  emotion psychology and, 34
  as ethically unacceptable, 336
  giving talks on, 17
  history and theory, 2–3
  introduction to, 1–8
  making contributions to health and well-being approaches, 553
  methodologies, 5–6
  multidisciplinary field, 1
  opportunities for different modalities of e-therapy, 549
  portraying human beings, 341
  powerful and deeply important area of research, 19
  promise of, 11–20
  roles of, 339
  supporting health and well-being, 7–8
  systems, 81, 495
  tools, 528–529
  trying to integrate all the disciplines, 222
  types of objection to, 338
  whole enterprise as deceptive, 339

Affective Computing (Picard), 2, 359

Affective Computing and Intelligent Interaction conference, 8

affective concepts, entangled in computers, 473

affective content, conceptualizing, 360

affective crowdsourcing, 6

affective data, collecting, 5, 389

affective databases, building, 6

affective diary, 366, 367

affective dimensions, 411, 441, 559

affective disorders, modeling, 102–103

affective events, response to, 227

affective experiences, 48, 460

affective expressions, 152, 350, 519

affective expressive behavior, 95

affective gestures, studying, 212

affective interactive systems, 378

affective learning companion, 411, 415

affective lexicons, 185, 191, 192t

affective loop
  describing, 5
  establishing, 251–252, 296
  expression of emotion in, 299
  in games, 461
  integration in, 467
  realization of, 460

affective loop-enabled games, realizing, 465

affective models, incorporating into robotic architectures, 484–487

affective music player (AMP)
  distinguished two contrasting moods, 479
  exploring strategies for affective computing, 475
  personalized using the preprocessed gathered data, 477
  validation of, 477–479

affective NLP. *See* natural language processing (NLP)

affective norms for English words (ANEW), 186, 186t

affective phenomena, 94, 99

affective predispositions, 397

affective processes, 421, 422

affective profiles, 430

affective rating system, 186

affective reasoning components, 403

affective representation model, 6

affective responses, 424, 424f

affective response strategies, 430

affective robotics, 484–489

affective robots, new opportunities for, 305

affective science, 22

affective self-induction techniques, 226

affective signals, 214

affective space, 489

affective states, 455
  automatic detection of, 550
  automatic recognition of spontaneous, nonprototypical, 247
  capturing in an emergent manner, 298
  of children with ASD, controlling robot reactions and responses, 528
  comparing to the neutral state, 236
  comparison of contrasting, 237
  computational models of, 102
  detecting, 428
  emerging at specific instants of the interaction, 248
  incidence moderated by the source of the affect judgements, 423
  labels corresponding to, 409
  model predicting, 236
  more transitory than moods, 422
  occuring during interactions with learning technologies, 422
  rapidly prepare the bodily systems for action, 422

animation
early film depictions of, 114
principles, for expressing emotions in
robots, 299–300
Anna on IKEA, emotional behavior
of, 310
annotated corpus of human or virtual
faces, analysis of, 264
annotating (coding) data, with appropriate emotion labels, 175
annotation(s)
of affect, 248
classification of, 464
controlling for errors, 188
of the corpus attributing labels to
expressions, 264
formalisms, 288–289
guidelines for, 188
performing, 189
process, 362
saving labor, 328–330
speech recordings, 293
annotators, 324, 390
anonymity, 78
ANS. See autonomic nervous system
(ANS)
anterior cingulate, 39
anterior cingulate cortex (ACC), 41
anterior insula, 42
anthropomorphic agents, 100, 310–311
anthropomorphic designs, popular publications favoring, 113
anthropomorphizing artifacts, 484
anticipatory system, generating an affective signal, 298
ANVIL, 353t
Anvil software, 176, 396
anxiety
associated with decreased HRV, 45
robot's expression of, 487, 491
anxiety disorders
modeling alternative mechanisms
underlying, 103
treatment of, 548, 549–550
apatheia, achieving, 342
APE exhibits, leaving because of external
factors, 440
apex phase, of face and body expressions
stream, 251
apocalypticism, sense of, 112
appearance, 145, 500
appearance component, of the AASM,
517
appearance features, extracting, 136
applications
of AC, 2
adapting the behavior of, 226
for affective body expression recognition, 161–162
reflecting the current affective state, 224
application scenarios, influencing choice
of the window length, 249
application-specific tools, 350

applicative scenarios, for affective analysis, 185
appraisal(s), 559
depending on other people's apparent
reactions and orientations, 70
dimensions of, 25
by Gratch and Marsella, 402
as a means to influence behavior, 59
modeled as the cause of emotion, 59
processing constraints underlying, 57
represented explicitly, 401
resulting from an attraction to or
repulsion from objects, 298
as a special kind of value judgments,
34n2
of a state of affairs, 25
three vocabularies proposed, 402
used in a broad sense, 34n4
appraisal approach, 263
appraisal-based agent architecture, 102
appraisal-based schemes, Scherer's
Component Process Model,
360–361
appraisal-based theories, of emotion, 97
appraisal-derivation model, 61–62, 61f
appraisal dimensions, 55, 97
appraisal mechanisms, triggering emotions, 396
appraisal models, 54–64
family history of, 60f
appraisal theories, 178, 261, 275, 288
affinity for computational scientists of
emotion, 59
agent architecture, and cognitive
models, 101–102
challenges and future directions,
63–64
connection between emotion and
symbolic reasoning processes, 55–59
drawing connections with other areas
of automated reasoning, 64
impacting individual and social
behavior, 57
improved, 26
Lazarus,' 101
modeled within the affective computing community, 97
representing emotions in computer
systems, 2–3
traditional, 69
appraisal theorists, 55, 56, 56t
appraisal variables, 55, 56t, 62, 275
assigning specific values to, 97
from componential theories, 102
defined by Scherer, 102
evaluation of the event through, 263
representing the resulting emotion,
101
approach and withdrawal motivations,
43, 559
approach-related emotions, 48
approval, obtaining, 337
arbitrary speech synthesis, 287

ARCS model, 449
ARD (automatic relevance detection),
413, 413f
Aristotle, physiological view of emotions, 204–205
Arkin, Ronald, 7
arm movement, 279, 280t
AR model, 60f, 62
Arnold, Magda B., 24, 48, 55, 298
Arnold-Lazarus theory, 24–25
arousal, 97, 247, 250, 360
liars experiencing increased, 506
people exhibiting in different ways,
507
reporting overall level of, 491
taking many different forms, 507
arousal-based model, of dyadic
human-robot attachment interactions, 102
"arousal" dimension, acoustic modification rules for, 288
arrival, at a museum, 438
articulators
at anatomical level, 277
tangential speed of critical, 174
articulatory data, collecting, 172
articulatory kinematics, interplay
between voice source and, 173, 174f
articulatory mechanisms, of expressive
speech, 172
articulatory models, 290
articulatory speed dimension, 174f
artifacts, 210, 228, 491
artificial agents, 33, 89, 95
artificial bodies, animation of, 114
artificial entities, portrayed in the
media, 3
artificial helpers, discussion of, 341
artificial intelligence (AI), 54, 94, 288
artificial life, 113, 114
artificial person, 121
artificial sciences, 60
artificial-sounding systems, preferred in
certain conditions, 290
artificial women, marked by their sexuality, 120
art performances, context of, 162
ASD. See autism spectrum disorder
(ASD)
Asimov, Isaac, 116, 117, 118, 127n5
ASM (active shape modeling), 510
aspects, of objects, 98
Association for Applied
Psychophysiology and Biofeedback
(AAPB), 473
Association for Computing Machinery
(ACM), 19, 337
associative learning experiences, 23
assurances, 537
Astounding Science Fiction, 118
asynchronous deception, high-stakes,
509
asynchronous HMMs, 250

cultural dichotomies, 560
cultural differences, 316, 317
cultural models, linking emotions to, 311–312
cultural norms and values, determining emotions experienced, 309
cultural probes, 367
cultural schema theory, combining appraisal theory with, 315
cultures
    automated recognition of emotions across, 312–313
    data-driven computational models of, 314–315
    defined using five scales, 311
    differences in perceiving emotion from whole-body postures, 153
culture-specific agents, creating emotional expressions for, 315
culture-specific appraisal and coping mechanisms, modeling, 310
culture-specific emotional displays, generating, 310
culture-specific virtual characters and robots, emotional responses to, 317–318
curse of dimensionality, 224
CVEs. See collaborative virtual environments (CVEs)
cybernetic entities, 118
cybernetic organism, 119–120
cyberpsychology, 547–555, 560
cybertherapy, 103, 548–550, 560
cyborg(s), 118
    criticism, 112
    humanlike bodies of fictional, 119–120
    as a theoretical entity, 111
cyperpunk works, 112
Cython, 351
Cytowic, Richard, 14

D

Damasio, Antonio, 15, 99
dance choreographers, 276, 278
dance sequences, recognizing basic emotions from, 157
Darwin, Charles, 4, 95, 205, 273, 519
data
    pool of, 411
    recording or reusing, 325
    revising, 363
data annotation, 189–190, 350, 352
database(s), 137–138
    building an affective, 6
    of emotional examples, 287
    usage of very large, for nonuniform unit selection, 293
data-based approaches, 290–291
database for emotion analysis using physiological signals (DEAP), 331
database specific biases, multiple sources of, 144
Databrary project, 529

data collection, 247–248, 324–327, 354, 356, 389
data collection tools, 350
data-driven approach, 318
data-driven computational models, of cultural behavior, 314–315
data fusion and processing, 453–454
data labeling and annotation, popular tools for, 353t
data mining, 353, 468
data quality, of webcam videos, 389
data reduction/selection, 136
datasets
    of news headlines, 189
    in orders of magnitude larger needed to achieve optimal AFA, 144
The Day the Earth Stood Still, 116
deceit detection, useful cues in, 509
deceivers, 507
deception, 339–340
    algorithms and technology used to detect and classify, 7
    attributing to the performer, 279
    classifier, 510
    defined, 503
    future research, 511–512
    needed to keep participants unaware of variable manipulations, 377
    people tending to rely on stereotypical and incorrect indicators of, 506
    predicted to be more cognitively demanding, 507
    theories of, 504–505
    violating two kinds of ethical principle, 340
deception detection, 140
    current applications of, 511
    by humans, 505–506
    unobtrusive, 503–512
deception-induced behavioral control, providing indicators of, 510
deception interactions, introducing situational contingencies, 504
deceptive communication, 78, 510
deceptive facial expressions, 269
deceptive message, forms of, 503
deceptive nonverbal behavior, 505
deceptive verbal messages, 504
decision-level fusion algorithm, 424, 424f
decision-making algorithms, 100
decision-making mechanisms, 99
decision to stop, 439
decision tree, for classifying emotion-evoking situations, 57
Declaration of Helsinki, on research classified as medical, 336
decoding, 274
    emotions, 80
    facial expressions, 269
decreased HRV, 45
deictic gesture, transforming, 281
deictic gestures, 277
De la Torre, Fernando, 3

deliberate deception, 339
delirium, 542
del Rey, Lester, 120
delta activity, 220
dematerialization, tendency toward, 122
Demon Seed, 119
deployment, target rate for, 162
depression
    approaches for identifying, 541
    associated with decreased HRV, 45
    detecting from video of patients' faces, 553
    discriminating between people suffering from and people not suffering from, 161
    functions of, 140
    glabellar botulinum toxin treatment associated with, 39
    indicators of disorder severity, 139
    nonpharmacological treatment for, 40
    vocal prosody highly related to severity of symptoms, 145
depression-type words, culture sharing similar lexicons for, 153
depressive tendency, artificial people displaying, 125
depth cameras, 145
de Rosis, Fiorella, 18
Descarte's Error, 15
descriptions, using combinations of, 402
description strategy, for an affect-sensitive system, 361
descriptive approaches, to modeling, 529
design approach, versus engineering approach, 364
design-based approaches, in affective computing, 366
designed spaces, 438–439, 441
design principles, for biofeedback-based affective computing, 479
desires, treatment of conflicting in Blade Runner, 120
detection paradigms, integration with other, 238–239
detector building system, additive, 235
detectors, 30
    cross-validated at the student level, 237
    integrating sensor and interaction data found in analysis of Prime Climb, 239
    predicting confusion, 235
developed techniques, 365
development partitions, 326, 327
devices, ascribing persona and social behavior to, 364
diagnostic models, sensing affect from communicative channels, 423
dialogue feature, incorporated from interaction logs, 239
DIARC architecture (distributed integrated affect cognition and reflection), 484, 487

functions of, 27–28
as fundamental processes, 42
generally accepted theory of, 22
having different interpersonal effects, 74
hierarchy classifying 22 different types, 98
how models define, 62
in human interactions, 125
inducing nonintended, 379
influencing motivation partly through the hedonistic route, 28
influencing rational thinking, 359
as inner sanctum of humanity, 336
intentional object of, 25
interacting deeply in the brain with perception, 14
in interpersonal life, 68–81
involving a continuous cycle of appraisal, response, and reappraisal, 64
knowledge-based classification of, 191–192
linking to cultural models, 311–312
machine for measuring, 13
managing in someone else, 538
modeled explicitly, 298
model of, 551
modulating a robot's planning and control parameters, 489
as multidimensional constructs, 361
nature of, 28–30
neural structures and processes underlying, 24
neurobiological basis of, 2
neurophysiological basis of, 32–33
neuroscientific perspectives of, 38–50
not associated with specific facial expressions, 42
not indispensable for generation of adaptive actions, 28
nuances not reflected in physiological signals, 205
objective measures analyzing the effects of, 269
with objective physical signals, 13
OCC dividing into three broad classes, 57
occurring in human-human communication, 309
one of the main targets for game design, 459
oriented to other people's emotional orientations, 74
overall adaptive, 27
phenomenal character of, 23
physiological sensing of, 204–214
physiology and, 204–206
playing major roles in perception and in many other aspects of intelligence, 14
presenting themselves to the subject, 24–25

presupposing beliefs and desires, 25
presupposing cognitions of their objects, 25
as "primary" or "basic," 96
psychological perspectives on, 2, 21–34
recent surge of interest in, 22
recorded using actors/actresses as subjects, 172
reflected verbally, 184
relationship with cognition, 55
remaining ill-defined, 42
representations of, 399
represented by four types of data, 6
represented in terms of categories, 398
representing, 488
representing a way to model different responses, 297–298
resulting from affective state, 489
for a robot, 485–486, 487
role in relationship building and maintenance, 539
roles for, in robotic system, 483
salient exemplars of conscious mental states, 21
sample headlines and manual annotations, 190t
scientific descriptions of, 401
serving distancing or avoidant interpersonal functions, 74
shaped by expression and by reception, 366
sharing the same expression, 96
signaling what matters, 14
similarities with sensations, 23
in social life, 68–71
specificity of, 47–49
starting to look vital for solving difficult engineering problems, 14
strength of elicited via static images, 372
study of, 2
viewed as being about something, 62
vital in forming memory and attention and in rational decision making, 14
for which no facial signals exist, 96
in which stimulus is not necessary, 39
for writing, 450–451
eMotion, 353
"<emotion>" element, 398, 399
emotion adaptation, in robots, 302–305
emotional 20-question project, of the University of Southern California, 404
emotional actions, affecting experienced emotion, 376
emotional adaptation and expression in games, 465–467
emotional agent architectures, 466
emotional architectures for robots, inspiration for, 298

emotional arousal, collecting data related to, 11
emotional behaviors, 376
    approaches to creating culture-specific variants, 318
    highly variable, 310
    inability to describe and achieve consensus on, 368
    influenced by other factors, 318
    measuring the effects of a virtual character's, 269
    notion of, 286
    of Pakistani and Dutch children playing card games together, 317
    in a particular social situation, 313
    resulting from culture-specific norms and values, 315
emotional brain, 39–42
emotional categories, 187, 188t
emotional circuitry, 44–45
emotional communications
    aligning and realigning orientations, 78
    as a crucial ingredient in most relationships, 538
    modeling, 519–521
emotional components, sequence of, 64
emotional contagion models, 403
emotional cues, 164, 442
emotional dimensions, of arousal and valence, 463
emotional display rules, conflicts resulting from, 318
emotional displays, 270, 312
emotional engagement, 81, 439–440
emotional episodes, 361, 376
emotional exchanges, between people from different cultures, 309
emotional experiences
    as conscious evaluations, 34n7
    difficulty of formalizing discrete categories, 366
    generated simultaneously with expression, 32
    having "warmth," 22
emotional expressions
    culture-specific differences in, 309
    distinguishing encoding from decoding, 403
    modifying existing, 376
    obtaining reliable datasets of, 371
    in robots, 299–302
    of a single subject, 88
emotional expressivity, presenting an asymmetry in, 279
emotional facial expressions
    in interaction, 267–270
    synthesis from annotated human faces, 264
emotional feedback exchange, between two subjects, 88
emotional feelings, 23, 29, 376
emotional film clips, 560

EmotionML, 326
  emotion markup language, 395
  markup language for AC, 6
  referring to external entities, 400
  relevance for user modeling, 403
  requirements for, 397–398
  self-contained emotion annotation, 398–399
  syntax for, 398–401
  vocabularies for, 401–403
EmotionML 1.0 specification, issues for future work, 403
emotion model, choice of the most appropriate, 325
emotion modeling, 288, 462
emotion modules, 30, 31, 33
emotion object, 74, 560
emotion pairs, getting confused, 293
emotion perception, 43, 366
emotion processing, simplified model of, 47, 47f
emotion profile, representation of emotion as, 176
emotion psychology
  affective computing and, 33–34
  five questions of, 22
Emotion Recognition, in the Wild Challenge and Workshop (EmotiW 2013), 138
emotion regulation, 69, 560
emotion-related issues, variety of, 403
"emotion-related" states, relevant, 401
emotion research, 95
emotions and feelings, Damasio's theory of, 101
emotion signals, integrated system capable of decoding, 80
emotion signature proper, characterized by emotion-specific responses, 48
emotion speech processing, using, 288
emotion synthesizer, quality of, 288
emotion system
  evolutionary core of, 30–32
  involving when you make a decision, 19
  origins of, 22
emotion theories, 560
  central influence on the study of emotionally expressive behavior, 275
  tool for confronting imprecision, 54
emotion transmission, divided into sequential processes of encoding and decoding, 79
emotion triggers, 102
emotion vocabulary
  introduced in EmotionML, 402
  mechanism for referring to, 399
emotion writing studies, manipulating the writing condition, 549
"emotivector," 488
Emotiv EEG system, 468
Emotive Logger, 353

emotive tendencies, in the design of affective systems, 125
eMoto, 366
EmoTV corpus, exploiting film clips, 330
EmoVoice, 353
empathetic accuracy, by the agent, 541
empathetic language, in psychotherapy, 539
empathic behavior, 303, 304
empathic emotion transfer, 71
empathic intervention, 254
empathic model, based on perspective taking, 303–304
empathic responses, types of, 304
empathy, 70–71, 424, 560
  adjectives of, 539
  between adolescents, 480
  affecting human attitudes toward robots, 303
  attempt at, 69
  defined, 302
  distinguishing from related processes, 71
  one of the major determinants of pro-social actions, 303
  prerequisite for providing emotional support, 538–539
  process of, 303
  as a research topic, 303
  at the root of moral behavior toward others, 345
  seeming to enhance interaction, 268
"empathy-arousing" mechanism, 303
empathy component, crowdworkers taught to apply person-center support, 391
empathy-eliciting agents, efficacy of, 527
empathy profile questionnaires, 157
Empatica bracelet, 468
emphatic responses, to another person's emotion expression, 71
empirical evidence, for informational effects, 27
empirical foundation, data-driven computational models of cultural behavior, 314
eMuu, 301, 301f
EMYS robot, 300, 301
encoding, 274
  emotions, 79–80
  individual differences in, 277–278
encoding-decoding cycles, integrating, 80–81
encoding-decoding distinction, making, 274
encoding dictionary, between a contextual feature and visual gestures, 249
encoding nonverbal expressions, obtaining realistic, 274
endogenous input, 225
end-user license agreement, 326–327
energy masking, 375
engaged life, 551

engagement
  achieving, 439–440
  augmenting, 297
  defined, 297
  as an important requirement for learning, 425
  occurrence of in the context of learning environments, 552
  stages of, 439
  sustaining, 442–443
  tracking during writing activities, 428
engagement/flow, as most frequent state, 423
engagement outcome, indicator of, 439
engineering applications, potential, 171
engineering approach, formalizing affect, 365
engineering stance, continuing to dominate the field, 365
eNTERFACE corpus, targeting, 330
entertaining, games as, 460
entropy, 522, 523, 529
environment
  of a game, 461
  speech affected by, 176
  in virtual reality, 495
  for writing, 449
environmental conditions, posing challenges for vision-based systems, 152–153
epinephrine, 205, 206
epistemic function, of emotions, 27
EPSRC EP/L00416X/1 Digital Personhood project, 255
equity, 335
ergodic interactive media, such as games, 463
ERPs (event-related potentials), 219–220
error potentials, detection of, 226
error-related negativity (ERN), 226
ERWIN socially interactive robot head, 487
The ESP Game, 6, 384, 385
e-therapy, 548
ethical filters, applying at publication, 344
ethical issues
  addressing, 5–6
  in affective computing, 334–346
  confronting roboticists, 491–492
  of crowdsourcing, 391–392
  regarding trust, privacy, and autonomy, 500
ethical principles and concerns, enforcement of, 343–344
ethical themes, for affective computing, 338–343
ethics
  considering, for affect data collection, 324–325
  formal and informal foundations of, 335–336
ethnographic observation and analysis, 365

distinguishing spontaneous from posed, 362

learning, 145

facial action unit recognition system, example, 135f

facial and multimodal expression, automated analyses of, 139

facial animation, weaknesses of procedural approaches to, 264

facial animation parameters (FAPs), 262

facial attractiveness, automatic estimations of, 88

facial behavior, 269, 510

facial displays, oriented to specific recipients, 69

facial emotional expressiveness, received a lot of attention, 487

facial expression(s), 100

  agreed upon standard, 276

  automated detection of infant and parent, 529

  avoiding interferences from, 278

  of cartoon figures, 316

  conveying a large number of meanings, 261

  correlating with events, 261

  creation of a lexicon of virtual characters, 262–267

  cross-cultural studies of, 31

  dictionary of, 262

  ECAs capable of generating a gamut of, 4

  of emotion in older children, 529

  encoding person identity, 145

  humans expressing emotions via, 3

  majority of research on nonverbal affect recognition, 151

  manipulation of, 376

  most extensively studied, 273

  muscular activity of, 101

  pattern of appraisal variables eliciting, 56

  perception along the 3D space PAD, 265

  range of, 133

  regulating face-to-face interactions, 131

  research on, 42

  as social messages dependent on motive and context, 364

  stimuli, 70

  study on the cross-cultural recognition of, 312

  systems, 134

  taxonomies based on observer-based schemes, 145

  theoretical-based lexicon of, 262–263

facial expression-based deception detection, 510

facial expression classifier, developing a, 376

facial expression recognition, 101, 455

Facial Expression Recognition Analysis (FERA) challenge, 386

facial features, tracking a dense set of, 135

facial feedback, reduction not diminishing emotional experience, 29

facial geometry, changing markedly over the course of development, 145

facial landmarks, representing, 136

facial measurement, 518f

facial motion, midlevel representation of, 136

facial movements, stimulus set containing a wide range of possible, 79

facial muscles

  effects of electrically stimulating, 132

  EMG used on to study facial expression, 212

  voluntary contraction of, 38–39

facial performance, passing the Turing test, 266

facial point tracking methods, applying, 510

facial rendering and animation, algorithm to produce, 266

facial stimuli, computer-generated, 79

FACS. *See* facial action coding system (FACS)

FACS coders, varying markedly in their expertise, 137

FACS coding, manually annotating facial expressions using, 264

FACSGen, 356t

FACS model, ground truth based on, 156

factual appraisals, postulating additional, as well as partly different, 26

factual belief, appraisals referring to, 25

factual cognition, 25

fail-soft interventions, 429

fake smiles, leaked true expressions of emotion, 510

false-false condition, 427

false positive and false negatives, obtaining, 243

false-true condition, 427

Far Eastern cultures, categorizing facial expressions differently, 75

Fast, Cheap & Out of Control, 113f

Fast-FACS, 144

FAtiMA model, 60f, 63, 356t, 466

  agent mind architecture, 315

  extending the typical the belief-desire-intention (BDI), 462

  open-source computational model, 268

FAU AIBO database, 178

fear

  adrenaline hypothesis of, 48

  associated with activation in the amygdala, 43

  caused by certain thoughts, 24

  emotion-specific features of, 48

  evaluating body posture for, 152

  experiencing, 25

  feeling generated, 23

  present without a person being consciously aware, 375

robot expressions, 491

F.E.A.R., 460

fear conditioning, 44, 98

feared stimuli, patient intentionally confronted with, 549

fear elicitation, noncognitive, 27

fearful and sad movements, 279

fearful people, speaking louder and at a faster tempo, 507

fear-inducing stimuli, differential responses to, 48

fear module, 30

FearNot! (Fun with Empathic Agents to Achieve Novel Outcomes in Teaching), 462, 526–527

fear processing, unconscious, 375

fear regulation, at the heart of many psychopathologic conditions, 99

fear response, responses characteristic of the, 44

feature engineering, 242, 244

feature extraction, 136, 248–249, 412–414

feature extractors, as classifiers trained separately, 409

feature-level fusion, obtaining, 251

feature representation, 248–249, 250, 255, 560–561

features, 561

feature selection, 175, 242, 249

feedback

  generally promoting process-oriented reflection, 450

  provided by a set of actuators, 475

  providing to writers, 451

  on writing, 454

feedback vocalizations, 291, 292

feeling, 42, 119

feeling theory, James opting for radical version of, 23

Feeltrace, 179, 248, 353t

Fellous, Jean-Marc, 18

females, faster in recognizing affect from body posture, 154

feminine cultures, 311

FERA 2011 Facial Expression Recognition Challenge, 138

FERA GEMEP corpus, consisting of emotion portrayals from only 10 actors, 144

Festival, 354, 356t

fiction, intertwined with reality, 111

fictional entities, 110

fictional intelligent machines, 110

fictional media, 124

fictional robots, 111, 126

fictional tradition, tracing, 114

fidelity, 335, 339

field coding, 240

field observations, 240

field observer, 240

field testing, 366

fight-or-flight responses, 48, 205, 299

film clips, eliciting target emotions, 373–374
film robots, beloved, 116–117
films, capturing attention well, 373
Final Fantasy VII, 461
"find, fix verify" algorithm, verify step in Soylent's, 389
fine-grained evaluations, 190
finger behavior, 163
finger dotting, 163
first-person reports (self-reports), 464
five-factor model, personality described using, 397
FLAME model, 60f, 62
flaming, phenomenon of, 77
FLASH/EMYS, 301f
"flash mob," of workers, 392
fleeting (micromomentary) expressions, capturing, 76
Fleiss' kappa, 327
Fletcher, Rich, 20
flow
    desirable in learning contexts, 443
    theory of, 463, 552
flow states, 442
fluidity, 281
fMRI. *See* functional magnetic resonance imaging (fMRI)
focus modes, defined, 282
Fold-It game, 384, 387
Forbidden Planet, 116
forced smiles, 49
force-feedback joystick, 163
forces, releasing beyond our control, 346
Ford, Harrison, 121
Fore tribesman, Ekman experiments on isolated, 42
formal codes, for affective computing, 336–338
formal learning environments, time spent in, 435
form features, 164
form-from-motion features, 164
form information, instrumental in the recognition of biological motion, 154
form level, describing form of the movement, 277
forms, of feedback, 454
4D (3D * time) AU-coded database, of facial behavior, 138
four-dimensional vocabulary, proposed by Fontaine, 402
four-factor theory, 504–505, 508
four-fun-factor model, of Lazzaro, 463
frame-based classification, 250
frame-level emotion assessment, 253
frame rate, of the audio stream, 251
frameworks, representing movement, 276
Frankenstein (film), 114, 115f, 116f
Frankenstein or The ModernPrometheus, 114
free-choice learning, 437, 444
free riding, potential for, 388

free will, exercising in accordance with intellectual principles, 335
frequency-domain correlates, 220–222
frequency ranges, of conventional broad frequency bands, 220
Frijda, 59
frontal alpha asymmetries, 221
frontomedial theta, 221
frontoparietal brain regions, activation within, 48
frustrated students, features for detecting, 413f
frustration
    confusion devolving into, 443
    distinguishing it from students' neutral states, 236
    measuring that a product reduces, 12
    method to generate, 264
    platform for detecting, 237
    prompting robots to adjust collaborative task strategy, 101
    smiling during natural experiences of, 371
    in a text replay, 242f
FTF interaction, with liars, 76
FUBI, 353
fully continuous annotation, choosing, 325
fully continuous emotion assessment, particular challenges of, 253
functionality, aligning respective abilities, 367
functional level, distinguishing between emblems, illustrators, and manipulators gestures, 277
functional magnetic resonance imaging (fMRI), 33, 39, 43, 218, 561
functional markup language (FML), 300
functional motions, versus expressive motions, 300
functional near-infrared spectroscopy (fNIRS), 218, 373, 561
functionals, 248
functions, of emotions, 27–28
funding bodies, regarding ethical use of technology as a moving target, 344
fusion, 510–511
fuzzy logic approach, to emotion generation, 489
Fuzzy rules used to synthesize intermediate facial expressions, 353
Fysneck, Hans, 205

G

Gabor filter responses, 88
Gabor wavelets or magnitudes, 136
Gage, Phineas, 46
Galatea 2.2 (novel), 119
Galen of Pergamum, theory of humours, 55
Galton, Francis, 388
galvanic skin response (GSR), 210, 212, 331, 464, 561

game(s)
    affective loop in, 461
    as being pleasantly frustrating, 443
    commercial-standard, incorporating emotion as a core part of gameplay, 460
    emotion detection and modeling in, 462–465
    emotion elicitation in, 461–462
    emotion in, 459–468
    general emotions across, 468
    offering contextual building blocks, 460
    people choosing to play, 459
    realization of the affective loop, 461f
game adaptation, player's relationship to, 465
game agents (and NPCs), 465
game-based learning system, for mathematics, 236
game-based scenario, appraisal module implemented for, 263
game content, 465
    adapting and expressing emotion through, 466
    described, 461
    influencing the emotional state of the player, 461–462
    surrounding NPCs, 462
game context, 460, 463, 464
game data mining, 468
game design, as challenging, 385
game-design building blocks, fundamental, 461
game development pipeline, emotion in, 468
Game Experience Questionnaire, affective aspects of, 464
game logic, adapting, 467
game metrics, 463
game narratives, affect-centered, 461
game non-player characters (NPC), 462
gameplay (behavioral) input, 463–464
game rules, 461
game scenario, automatic affect recognition in, 249
games with a purpose (GWAPs), 385, 389
gaming, emotion transfer in, 142
gaming experiences, AC improving, 7
gamma rhythm, 222
GATE model, 102
Gaussian mixture model (GMM), 179
Gaussian tree-augmented naive Bayes classifiers, 137
gaze direction, toward objects, 74
gaze-reactive tutor, evaluating the efficacy of, 425
Gaze Tutor, 425f, 561
Gee, James, 443
gelotophiles, 154
GEMEP corpus, 155, 277
gender
    of the users, 269

quality assessment, 327–328
quality control techniques, 387–389
quality of movement, 280–281
Qualtrics, 356
quantity, of data, 324
quasi-periodic spartiotemporal patterns, 530
quasistationary, emotion as, 329
questionnaire methods, conducted in multiple fashions, 241

R

R, 351, 352f, 355t
R2-D2, 110, 111f, 123
Rabiner, Larry, 17
Rachel, eliciting ecologically valid interactions from children with ASD, 527
"radically cognitive" theory, of the nature of emotions, 34n7
raised eyebrows movement, wrinkles for, 267f
raising, 200
random partitioning, as a somewhat suboptimal choice, 326
rank-based support vector machines, 465
RapidMiner, 355t
rapport, 72, 103
rapport agent, interacting with, 540
rapport and trust, building between helper and helpee, 539
raters, 324
rater-weighted gold standard, reaching, 327
rating, annotations, 464
rating dial method, 379
rational control, interplay with emotion-driven "action tendencies," 345
rationality, emotional guidance helping, 99
raw data, collected during affective computing studies, 352
reaction patterns, becoming modified, 23
reaction program, 30
reactions to events (phasic EDA), providing information on, 524
reactive AALTs, 423
reactive emotional expressions, music most useful for collecting, 375
reactive expressions, behavioral manipulations most useful for collecting, 377
reactive reasoning, complexity underlying, 63
reactive systems, 7, 420, 422, 562
readability, of a robot's actions, 300
reading between the lines, effort of, 77
reality mining, 86
real settings, more studies in, 305
Real Steel, 126
real-time automatic FACS coding, 367
real-time crowdsourcing, 392

real-time eye gaze and head pose estimation, 354t
real-time feedback, 494
(real time) magnetic resonance imaging (MRI), 172
realtime recognition, feasibility for instructional technology, 143
real-world HCI and HRI, 246, 247
real-world problems, output gameplay used to solve, 385
reappraisal, 69, 562
reason/emotion tension, as human phenomenon, 345
reasoning and action selection mechanism, 296
receptionist's desk, virtual robot face played on a rotating monitor, 488
reciprocity, 530
recognition accuracy, 429
recognition system, 248
recognition tasks, 164
RECOLA multimodal corpus, 331
recorded facial expressions, reproduced on synthetic models, 266
"the recording epoch," 209
recording platform, 452–453, 453f
recordings, made for speech synthesis, 293
rectangular matrix, finding correlations among rows and columns, 191
recurrence quantification analysis (RQA), 524, 529
reengagement, 439
"<reference>" elements, pointing to arbitrary URIs, 400
referential structure, of the affective lexicon, 185
reflectance PPG reading, of a blood volume pulse signal, 208, 208f
reflection, as a transformative element, 448
reflective insight, 552
reflective time line, 456, 456f
reflective writing studios, 447–457
    functionalities provided by, 449
    sets of challenges for, 456
    system design, 451–455, 451f
registration, of images, 135–136
regulatory role, of the central autonomic network, 47
reinforced learning, 329
Reinforcement Learning (RL) algorithm, learning types of supportive behaviors, 304
Reisenzein, Rainer, 2, 58–59
relational agents
    affect-aware, 8
    definition of, 537–538
    developed for health counseling applications, 542–544
    effective as automated health counselors, 538

in health applications, 537–544
maintaining long-term engagements, 541
moving from a professional role to that of a personal companion or intimate partner, 539
multimodal display of affect by, 540–541
promoting breastfeeding, 543–544, 543f
responding to a mother's voice, 543
therapeutic alliance with, 540
relational construct, emotions as, 59
relation alignment, 68, 73–74
relationships
    central role in the emotional life of people, 539
    discussing disagreements in, 379
    quality of emotional communication, 538
relative time, mechanism borrowed from EMMA, 400–401
relativism, 552
relaxation techniques, 550
release of data, 324, 326–327
reliability
    of emotion assessment, 361
    of measurement, 134
    measuring, 327
remote communication, speed and range of, 76
reparation, 335
repetition, 281
Replicants, 120–121
representation, underlying focus on, 365
representational schemes, for affective computing, 360
representative data, for realistic analysis, 362
REPTree algorithm, 238
reputation, 14–16, 388
requester, in crowdsourcing parlance, 385
requests, encoding posture and gesture, 278
resampled data, models validated on, 236
resampled distribution, validating on, 243
research, effort to fund, 343
research and development tools, in affective computing, 349–357
research committee, dual function of, 337
research directions, for the area of emotion in games, 467–468
research fields, adjacent, 468
research projects, publicizing robot prototypes and robotic toys, 113
resource, 562
respect, for autonomy, 340
respiration, 206, 213
respondents, demographics of, 350, 351f
responsiblity, abrogation of, among humans, 491

smoothing algorithms, 499
Soar cognitive architecture, 18
SOAR-Emote model, 101
SOAR theory, 101, 354
social actions, 87, 164
social appraisal, 69, 70, 73, 562
social attitudes, 562
　automatic assessment of, 88–89
　defined, 87
　machine synthesis of, 90
social awareness tools, HCI researchers
　developing, 449
social categories, identification in terms
　of, 74
social cognition, implications of
　appraisal theory on, 57
social-comparison manipulations, 378
social consciousness, 552
social contacts, between individuals, 86
social context
　affecting emotion expression, 69
　importance of, 268
　playing a significant role in use of
　nonverbal expressions, 364
social cues, people responding to com-
　puters displaying, 103
social emotions, 87, 562
　likely to be experienced more pro-
　foundly in group learnings, 430
　machine analysis of, 88
　machine synthesis of, 89
　underdeveloped in many appraisal
　theories, 64
social engagement, 45
social environment, impact on writing
　activities, 450
social evaluations, 87, 88, 89–90, 562
social facts, interpreting detected social
　signals in terms of, 87
social force model, 89
social identifications, 75
social identities, 74, 75
social influence, 497, 498
social intelligence, in men and
　machines, 84–85
social interactions, 87, 562–563
　best suited for collecting productive
　expressions of emotion, 378
　having a clear impact on a player's
　emotional state, 461
　machine analysis of, 87–88
　machine synthesis of, 89
　relevance of appraisal theory, 64
　responsible for much of the learning
　that occurs, 439
　technology-oriented events and publi-
　cations revolving around, 85, 85f
social interpersonal technologies, 551
socialized cultural display rules, 69
social life, emotions in, 68–71
socially assistive robots, 302
socially interactive affective robots,
　487–489

socially supportive behaviors, 303
social motivations, behind the decision
　to visit a museum, 436
social network analysis approaches, 86
social networking sites, 390
social norms, 57, 388
social perception abilities, 246
social presence, 496–497, 563
　attributing to virtual characters, 498
　augmenting in the long term, 297
　lack of cues reducing, 77
　maximizing, 76
　when high, behavioral realism not
　necessary for social influence, 497
social psychological point of view, social
　signals, 86
social psychology, 84, 377
social referencing, in toddlers, 70
social referencing studies, mothers
　directing their gaze to the object of
　evaluation, 74
social relations, 87, 89, 90, 563
social relationships, modeling of, 403
social resiliency, 520
social responses, 490
social robot Kismet, 102
social robots
　emotion modeling for, 296–305
　increase in the presence of around
　children, 527
　research addressing empathy in, 303
social scenarios, eliciting emotions, 377
social settings, people smiling more
　in, 69
Social Signal Interpretation (SSI), 354,
　356
social signal processing (SSP), 84–90
　components of, 87
　definition and context, 85–86
　described, 84–85
　field of, 3
social signals, 563
　definition of, 85, 86–87
　machine analysis of, 87–89
　machine synthesis of, 89–90
　underlying manifestation of various
　social facts, 88
social simulation, populated by artificial
　agents, 34
social situation, roles observable in every, 89
social skills, requiring embodied agents
　and robots to be endowed with,
　246
social status, more important to Japanese
　than it is to Americans, 153
social stories, 391
social talk, engaging in, 103
social withdrawal, associated with per-
　ception of threat, 45
sociotechnical systems, design of, 86
soft level, decision-level fusion at, 251
soft sensors, 428
soft skills, humans naturally use, 252

software agents
　with natural language processing
　capabilities, 5
　"person-in-the-loop" systems, for chil-
　dren with ASD, 530
software-based automated measurement,
　of facial expression, 517
software/hardware components, posing
　a significant engineering challenge,
　455–457
software tools
　in affective computing, 350–356
　for affective data collection, 354
　reusing appropriate, 349
somatic marker hypothesis, 45, 46
somatic markers, 99
songs, 199, 200
sound and light, augmenting expressiv-
　ity, 302
source activities, 171
source filter model-based synthesis, 294
source filter theory, 171
source of bias, protection against, 134
source signal waveforms, for different
　phonation types, 292f
space, surrounding a phenomenon, 249
spamming, drawback of potential, 188
sparks, for young learners, 437
sparse-instances-based strategy, 328
spatial extent, 281, 313
spatial or environmental presence, 496
spatial positioning, 87
spatio-temporal features, detecting
　engagement, 161
spatiotemporal motor primitives,
　extracting and validating, 155
speaker-hearer interactions, 293
speaker normalization, 176
"speaking styles," synthesizer to express
　different, 288
Spearman's rank correlation coefficient,
　327
specialist ethical reviews, informed by
　expert groups, 344
specific emotions, decoded from a static
　posture, 278, 279t
spectral characteristics, measures, 175
spectral description, 248
spectral features, 287, 289
spectrograms, of emotions, 289, 290f
speech
　in affective computing, 170–180
　generating understandable and
　natural-sounding, 286
　hallmark of human-human commu-
　nication, 3
　produced by the vocal organs, 4
Speechalyzer, for labeling data, 352
Speechalyzer of Deutsche Telekom, 403
speech processing community, 88
speech production, 171–173
speech recognition systems, 455
speech signal

synthetic emotions, creating in robots, 297–299

system architecture, of reflective writing studios, 448

systematic models, for mapping body expressions, 156

"system modeling" approaches, in contrast to "signal modeling," 290

T

TABASCO model, 60f

tablet computers, allowing use of facial data, 239

Taboo, 378

Tactical Language System, 315

tactile behavior, types of, 163

tagged data, collecting, 409

tailored communication, 554

taller avatars, 498

TAME framework (traits, attitudes, moods, and emotions), 484–486, 486f

Tan, Tienu, 18

Tanagra, 467

Tao, Jianhua, 18

target dimensions, producing continuous values for, 250

task, total involvement in, 552

task absorption, notions of, 443

task component, 539

task definition, for emotion classification of news headlines, 189

task design, on MTurk, 385–386

task-irrelevant regions, 221

task-oriented dialogue, avoiding, 252

task-performance metrics, providing a fair amount of objectivity, 491

taskrabbit.com, 392

taxonomies
  of classes of emotions, 98
  proposed to categorize affective states, 422

technical issues, building a reliable, accurate, and scalable platform, 456

technological codes, 337–338

technologies
  creating a mutual sense of awareness, 552
  interjected into all of writing's underlying processes, 447
  manipulating and enhancing features of personal experience, 551
  measuring frustration caused by, 12
  modifying traditional settings, 547
  popular writing about future, 112
  sense of frustration with, 123

technology-oriented events, with social in the title, 85f

technology probes, 366, 367–368

telemedicine robot, projecting signals on the ground, 302

telephone, investigations of communicating by, 77

telepresence. *See* presence

temperament, as a mixture of humors, 205

temporal coordination, 140

temporal extent, 281

temporal gamma rhythms, 222

temporal modeling, 137

temporal relationship, 554

temporal specification, 400

temporal unification, 329

temporal unit of analysis. *See* unit of analysis

tension, manifestations of, 506

tension-relaxation feelings, 29

The Terminator (film), 120

term similarity, estimated from a large-scale corpus, 191

terrorists, acquiring potentially deadly technologies, 343

test anxiety, 419, 450

testing and evaluation, of affective HRI, 489–491

test partitions, 326

test-retest unreliability, 137

text, automatic recognition of affect in, 185

text analysis methods, computer-based, 454

text-based communication, becoming hyperpersonal, 77

text-based dialogue only (TEXT), 540

text-based physics tutor, 234

text categorization approaches, 189

text classifiers, using naive Bayes, 197

text messaging, 78, 550

"text replays" of data, labeling, 241

texts
  affect detection in, 184–201
  annotating with emotions, 187–190
  low social costs associated with, 78
  recognizing emotions in, 190–196

text-to-speech synthesizer, converting text into speech, 287

texture-based methods, using bump mapping for wrinkles, 266

tf-idf weighting schema, 191

thalamus, information from going directly to the amygdala, 98

theater performances, expressed through body expressions and speech during, 162

theoretical models, used to understand writing processes and technologies, 448–451

theories
  defining emotions and emotion processes differently, 274
  of emotion, 22, 95–99

theory of "fun," Koster's, 463

theory of mind, 303, 403

therapeutic alliance, 539–540

therapeutic robot, for the elderly, 484, 485f

thermal cameras, imaging the face, 140

THESPIAN model, 60f, 61, 315

theta activity, in cognitive processes, 220–221

thin-film transistor (TFT) screens, 375

"thinking characters," 300

thirsty participants, consumption behavior, 375

Thomas, Frank, 299

threat, shifting responses, 48

3D control device, participants navigating in a PAD space, 263

3D hand tracking, using a Kinect sensor, 153

3D pose, inferring, 135

3D views, eyewear creating, 496

three-dimensional (3D) first-person point of view, of the virtual world, 495

three-dimensional (3D) space of emotional state, 262–263

three-dimensional transformations, 135

three-dimensional vocabularies, 402

"Three Laws of Robotics," 118

"three pillars," of a good life, 551

time, relevant to EmotionML, 400–401

time-domain analysis techniques, limited for affective BCIs, 220

time-domain correlates, 219–220

time lines
  of significant events, 456, 456f
  tracing a prehistory for modern robotics, 112

time-management issues, 452

time-series approaches, 529

time-series models, 520–521

time span, linking in media, 400

time stamps or markers, aligned, allowing for later synchronization, 325

time-varying skin conductance response, 211, 211f

time window
  of adaptation, 467
  for the heart-rate series, 209

Tinker, relational museum tour guide agent, 540

Tin Man, from L. Frank Baum's Oz stories, 115

Tobii Studio, used for eye tracking-related analysis, 353

Tobii T60 eye tracker, 425

toddlers, social referencing in, 70

tokenizer, 192

top-down approach, attributing an emotion label to each facial expression, 264

top performers, compensating, 386

touch
  affective, 162–163
  increasing impact of empathy, 541

touch-based game devices, naturalistic touch behavior in, 163

touch behavior, 162, 163

"<trace>" element, 401

trace-like representations, 366

Printed in the USA/Agawam, MA
December 17, 2020

766748.005